Household Words

Compiled by Anne Lohrli

University of Toronto Press

Household Words

A Weekly Journal
1850-1859
Conducted by
Charles Dickens

TABLE OF CONTENTS
LIST OF CONTRIBUTORS AND
THEIR CONTRIBUTIONS
based on
THE *Household Words* OFFICE BOOK
in
THE MORRIS L. PARRISH COLLECTION OF
VICTORIAN NOVELISTS
PRINCETON UNIVERSITY LIBRARY

Printed in Canada
Toronto and Buffalo
ISBN 0-8020-1912-9
LC 71-185722

CONTENTS

ACKNOWLEDGMENTS

Basic to the compilation of this book is the *Household Words* Office Book, in the Morris L. Parrish Collection of Victorian Novelists, Princeton University Library. I wish to thank Princeton University Library for the permission given me to base my work on the Office Book as, also, for permission to reproduce, as Plate 2 in this book, the first page of the Office Book. I wish, in particular, to thank Mr. Alexander D. Wainwright, Assistant Librarian for Acquisitions, for his careful examination of Office Book notations difficult to decipher and for recording for me what seem to be the intended readings, in answer to my questions concerning the readings; and for sending me the information stated on page 35 concerning the front end-paper of the Office Book. I wish to thank the editors of the *Princeton University Library Chronicle* for permission to make use of the material contained in the article "*Household Words* and Its 'Office Book,' " published in the *Library Chronicle*. The material, somewhat revised, forms the basis of the section of the Introduction titled "The *Household Words* Office Book."

While the Office Book was in the possession of Mr. John Lehmann, London, Mr. Lehmann very kindly gave me permission to refer to and to quote from the Book. I wish to express my thanks to Mr. Lehmann for this permission.

Mr. Christopher C. Dickens has very kindly given me permission to refer to and to quote from unpublished letters of Charles Dickens and of Charles Dickens, Jr. I wish to express to Mr. Dickens my appreciation of this courtesy.

Transcripts of certain unpublished letters to which I refer are in the collection of the editors of the Pilgrim Edition of *The Letters of Charles Dickens*. I wish to thank the editors for most kindly permitting me to consult their files of letters in my search for clues as to the identity of *Household Words* contributors. The letters referred to will appear in forthcoming volumes of the Pilgrim Edition.

Unpublished materials in the Henry E. Huntington Library to which I refer and from which I quote are the following: manuscript letters, HM 18034–18380; typescript letters, HM 27634; the *All the Year Round* Letter-Book, HM 17507. I wish to thank Mr. Robert O. Dougan, Librarian, and Mr. Herbert C. Schulz, Curator of Manuscripts, for permission to read this unpublished material and for permission to refer to and to quote from it.

Other manuscript or typescript material that I have been given permission to read, to refer to, or to quote from is the following: a letter from Dickens, January 3, 1850, to W. C. Bennett, MS in the possession (in 1965) of the Times Bookshop, London; a letter from Dickens to Thomasina Ross, January 29, 1850, MS in the Miriam Lutcher Stark Library, the University of Texas; a note by Margaret Emily Gaskell appended to a letter written by Mrs. Gaskell [September 25, 1852], MS in the Yale University Library; MS poems by George Meredith in an interleaved copy of his *Poems* [1851] in the Henry W. and Albert A. Berg Collection, the New York Public Library; excerpt from a letter from John Forster to Mrs. Gaskell, January 20, 1853, typescript in the Brotherton Collection, the Library of the University of Leeds.

Most of the research for this book was done at the Huntington Library, the Library of Congress, and the British Museum. I wish to thank the librarians, directors, and keepers of these libraries for permission to consult their collections. Some research was done also at other libraries and institutions, among them, in the United States, the Newberry Library, Chicago; the Library of the University of Chicago; the Library of the University of California, Los Angeles; the Zimmerman Library, the University of New Mexico; and, in London, the Guildhall Library, the India Office Library, the Polish Research Centre, the Public Record Office, and the Wellcome Historical Medical Library. I wish to thank the librarians and directors for permission to consult their collections.

Librarians of numerous libraries have been most helpful in answering in detail the biographical and bibliographical questions that I have asked of them by letter and in person. For this kind help I wish to thank Mr. Sergius Yakobson, Chief of the Slavic and Central European Division, and Miss Montgomery McCrary, Research Assistant, of the Library of Congress; Mr. George J. Maciuszko of the Cleveland Public Library, Cleveland, Ohio; Mr. David J. Hampton of the Library of the Pioneer Museum, Stockton, California; Mr. A. P. Burton, Assistant Keeper of the Library, Victoria and Albert Museum; Mrs. M. L. Danilewicz and Mr. K. Zdziechowski of the Polish Library, London; Mr. Donovan Dawe, Principal Keeper, and Mr. Godfrey Thompson, Librarian, of the Guildhall Library, London; Mr. R. J. Fulford of the Department of Printed Books, the British Museum; Mr. M. J. Pearce of the India Office Library, Commonwealth Relations Office, London; Mr. John Bebbington, City Librarian and Information Officer, the Central Library, Sheffield; Mr. M. J. Harkin, Language and Literature Librarian, the Central Library, Manchester; Mr. David I. Masson, Sub-Librarian, the Library of the University of Leeds; Mr. R. F. M. Immelman, University Librarian, the University of Cape Town; Mr. T. A. Kealy, Principal Librarian, the State Library of Victoria, Melbourne; Mrs. Marjorie Hancock and Miss Suzanne Mourot, Deputy Librarians, the Mitchell Library, Sydney; Mrs. H. Blakeley, Reference Librarian, the Alexander Turnbull Library, Wellington. I wish also to thank Miss Margery Paterson, Assistant Registrar, McGill University, Montreal; Mr. John R. Rodman, Registrar, Tusculum College, Tennessee; and Dr. Erwin Schmidt, Universitätsarchiv, Justus Liebig-Universität, Giessen, for information sent to me.

I wish to thank the librarians and directors of the following libraries, societies, and other institutions for information sent to me from official records, directories, registers, and other documents and books in their collections: the National Archives and Records Service, Washington, D.C.; the National Library of Medicine, Bethesda, Maryland; the Harvard University Library; the New York Public Library; the Historical Society of Pennsylvania, Philadelphia; the Armstrong Browning Library, Baylor University, Waco, Texas; the Library of the University of Texas; these institutions in California: the California Historical Society, San Francisco; the Public Library, Stockton; the Board of Supervisors, Alpine County; the Linden Cemetery Association, Linden; these institutions in England and Scotland: the Library of the King's Beam House, H.M. Customs and Excise, London; the Public Record Office, London; the Royal Society of Medicine, London; the University of London Library; the County Record Office, Bedford; the Bristol Public Library; the Central Library, Stockport; the City Library, Salisbury; the Society of Antiquaries of Scotland, Edinburgh; these libraries in Ireland: the City Library, Cork, and the National Library of Ireland, Dublin; and these libraries and institutions elsewhere: the Bibliotheek en Leeszalen der Gemeente, Rotterdam; the Archives du Pas-de-Calais, Arras; the Bibliothèque Nationale, Paris; the Deutsche Staatsbibliothek, Berlin; the Library of the Karl-Marx-Universität, Leipzig; the Staatsbibliothek, Marburg; the Universitetsbiblioteket, Copenhagen.

Other assistance I am pleased to acknowledge: that of Mr. John Lehmann for suggesting the possible identity of the *Household Words* contributor Mrs. Lehmann; that of Professor Beatrice Corrigan of the University of Toronto for suggesting the identity of the contributor recorded as "Mrs. Gaskell's friend"; that of Mr. Simon Nowell-Smith, Oxford, for calling to my attention the two anonymous volumes of verse published by the contributor Harris. Correspondence with Miss Isobel C. M. Healing, London, has given me valuable information on the contributor Knighton, and correspondence with Mr. John Geoffrey Sharps, Scarborough, has made possible the identification of the contributor Mrs. Holland. I wish to express my thanks to these correspondents. In addition, and in particular, I wish to thank Professor and Mrs. Walter E. Houghton for their kind assistance – for their letting me, while the first volume of *The Wellesley Index to Victorian Periodicals* was in preparation, consult their list of contributors' names; for their helpful answers to questions that I have asked them concerning periodical writers; and for their encouraging interest in my work from its outset.

To Mr. Anthony C. Laude, Cambridge, I am grateful for obtaining for me certain books that I was otherwise unable to obtain. To Miss Eileen R. Quelch,

Canterbury, I gratefully record my thanks for her unfailing patience and conscientiousness in answering my questions concerning books and documents in the British Museum and elsewhere.

The librarians of the Thomas C. Donnelly Library, New Mexico Highlands University, have been most helpful in obtaining for me books and other materials, and have extended to me other courtesies. I wish to express to them my thanks. Professor Jean Johnson of the Department of Modern Foreign Languages, New Mexico Highlands University, I wish to thank for her help in various linguistic matters; Professor Thomas Oliver Mallory of the Department of English, for his answering the many questions that I have asked of him and for reading parts of the Introduction to this book.

A.L.

Las Vegas, New Mexico
October 1971

Introduction

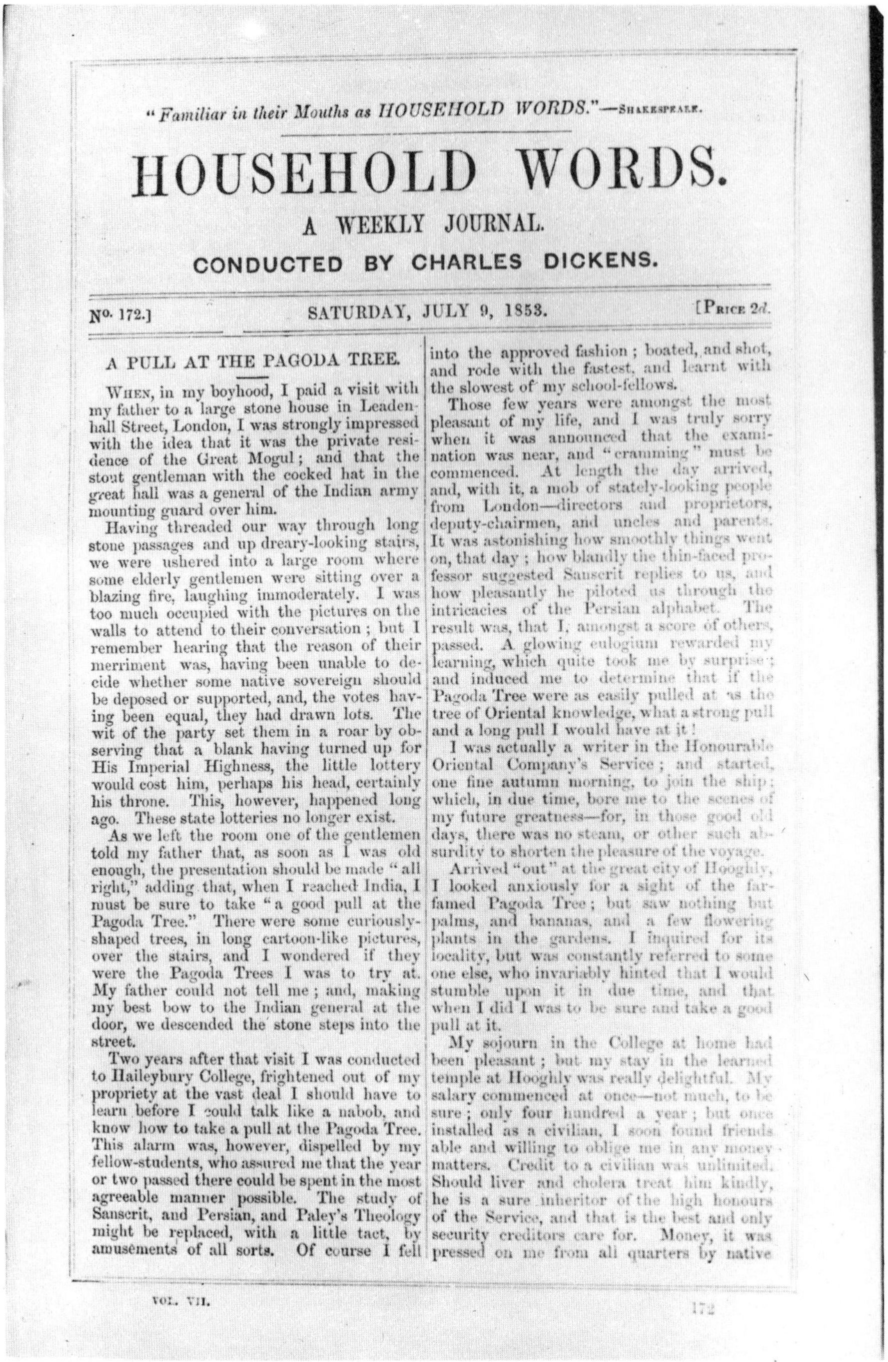

"*Familiar in their Mouths as HOUSEHOLD WORDS.*"—SHAKESPEARE.

HOUSEHOLD WORDS.

A WEEKLY JOURNAL.

CONDUCTED BY CHARLES DICKENS.

No. 172.] SATURDAY, JULY 9, 1853. [PRICE 2*d*.

A PULL AT THE PAGODA TREE.

WHEN, in my boyhood, I paid a visit with my father to a large stone house in Leadenhall Street, London, I was strongly impressed with the idea that it was the private residence of the Great Mogul; and that the stout gentleman with the cocked hat in the great hall was a general of the Indian army mounting guard over him.

Having threaded our way through long stone passages and up dreary-looking stairs, we were ushered into a large room where some elderly gentlemen were sitting over a blazing fire, laughing immoderately. I was too much occupied with the pictures on the walls to attend to their conversation; but I remember hearing that the reason of their merriment was, having been unable to decide whether some native sovereign should be deposed or supported, and, the votes having been equal, they had drawn lots. The wit of the party set them in a roar by observing that a blank having turned up for His Imperial Highness, the little lottery would cost him, perhaps his head, certainly his throne. This, however, happened long ago. These state lotteries no longer exist.

As we left the room one of the gentlemen told my father that, as soon as I was old enough, the presentation should be made "all right," adding that, when I reached India, I must be sure to take "a good pull at the Pagoda Tree." There were some curiously-shaped trees, in long cartoon-like pictures, over the stairs, and I wondered if they were the Pagoda Trees I was to try at. My father could not tell me; and, making my best bow to the Indian general at the door, we descended the stone steps into the street.

Two years after that visit I was conducted to Haileybury College, frightened out of my propriety at the vast deal I should have to learn before I could talk like a nabob, and know how to take a pull at the Pagoda Tree. This alarm was, however, dispelled by my fellow-students, who assured me that the year or two passed there could be spent in the most agreeable manner possible. The study of Sanscrit, and Persian, and Paley's Theology might be replaced, with a little tact, by amusements of all sorts. Of course I fell into the approved fashion; boated, and shot, and rode with the fastest, and learnt with the slowest of my school-fellows.

Those few years were amongst the most pleasant of my life, and I was truly sorry when it was announced that the examination was near, and "cramming" must be commenced. At length the day arrived, and, with it, a mob of stately-looking people from London—directors and proprietors, deputy-chairmen, and uncles and parents. It was astonishing how smoothly things went on, that day; how blandly the thin-faced professor suggested Sanscrit replies to us, and how pleasantly he piloted us through the intricacies of the Persian alphabet. The result was, that I, amongst a score of others, passed. A glowing eulogium rewarded my learning, which quite took me by surprise; and induced me to determine that if the Pagoda Tree were as easily pulled at as the tree of Oriental knowledge, what a strong pull and a long pull I would have at it!

I was actually a writer in the Honourable Oriental Company's Service; and started, one fine autumn morning, to join the ship; which, in due time, bore me to the scenes of my future greatness—for, in those good old days, there was no steam, or other such absurdity to shorten the pleasure of the voyage.

Arrived "out" at the great city of Hooghly, I looked anxiously for a sight of the far-famed Pagoda Tree; but saw nothing but palms, and bananas, and a few flowering plants in the gardens. I inquired for its locality, but was constantly referred to some one else, who invariably hinted that I would stumble upon it in due time, and that when I did I was to be sure and take a good pull at it.

My sojourn in the College at home had been pleasant; but my stay in the learned temple at Hooghly was really delightful. My salary commenced at once—not much, to be sure; only four hundred a year; but once installed as a civilian, I soon found friends able and willing to oblige me in any money matters. Credit to a civilian was unlimited. Should liver and cholera treat him kindly, he is a sure inheritor of the high honours of the Service, and that is the best and only security creditors care for. Money, it was pressed on me from all quarters by native

VOL. VII. 172

Plate 1 First page of *Household Words* No. 172, with one of John Capper's articles as lead item

HOUSEHOLD WORDS – THE PERIODICAL

Household Words was the fulfilment of Dickens's long-cherished wish to conduct a journal in which he could speak personally to the large circle of readers whom his novels had drawn to him.

To John Forster, on September 24, 1849, he wrote: "The old notion of the Periodical, which has been agitating itself in my mind for so long, I really think is at last gradually growing into form. ... "[1] During the following months, Dickens abandoned or changed certain of the ideas that he had at first entertained for the periodical, but toward the end of the year his plans were so well decided on that he announced the appearance, in March next, of the first number of his "WEEKLY MISCELLANY Of General Literature."[2] Deciding on a title for the miscellany took some time. Dickens thought of and rejected many titles before he made what seemed to him a happy choice – "a very pretty name" – "Household Words."

Household Words was to be issued from the editorial office, 16 Wellington Street North, Strand, London; Bradbury & Evans, holders of one-fourth share in the enterprise, were to be printers and publishers; William Henry Wills was to be subeditor.

In the early months of 1850, Dickens was soliciting manuscripts from potential contributors, obtaining papers from his literary friends, "getting a great mass of matter together, from a variety of sources,"[3] and conferring with Wills on subjects to be dealt with in *Household Words* and on matters of layout and arrangement.[4] Already letters of inquiry began to arrive from writers eager to have their con-

1 Unless otherwise stated, quotations from Dickens's letters after 1841 are from *The Letters of Charles Dickens*, ed. Walter Dexter, 1938, cited as Nonesuch *Letters*. Quotations from letters from 1820 to 1841 are from Vols. I and II of the Pilgrim Edition of *The Letters of Charles Dickens*, ed. Madeline House and Graham Storey, 1965–69, cited as Pilgrim *Letters*. Since the completed Pilgrim Edition will supersede the Nonesuch Edition, reference to dated letters is by date only, not by volume and page.

2 Harry Stone, ed., *Charles Dickens' Uncollected Writings from Household Words*, Plate 5, reproduces a handbill, dated Dec. 27, 1849, announcing the forthcoming miscellany.

3 Dickens to Mary Howitt, in C. R. Woodring, *Victorian Samplers*, p. 152.

4 See Philip Collins, "W. H. Wills' Plans for *Household Words*," *Victorian Periodicals Newsletter*, No. 8 (April 1970), pp. 33–46.

tributions appear in the new periodical – letters heralding the "whole sacks"[5] of manuscripts that were to be submitted to *Household Words* during the nine years of its existence.

The first number of *Household Words* appeared under date of Saturday, March 30, 1850.[6] Dickens had entered on the strenuous editorial work that he was to continue to the end of his life.

Household Words was a twopenny miscellany of "Instruction and Entertainment,"[7] a family journal for a middle-class audience, intended, in part, to replace with wholesome fare the "villainous" periodical literature of crime and sensation that formed the literary diet of a portion of the reading public. It was to be the mouthpiece of its "Conductor," the embodiment of his "Household tenderness," his optimism, his humour, his indignation against social wrong. Such principles as it had were the opinions that Dickens held. These were to be reflected in the contributed material, most of which (like most of Dickens's own writings in the periodical) appeared without author's name.

Certain advertisements for *Household Words* stated that the periodical, in addition to providing "Instruction and Entertainment," was designed also "to help in the discussion of the most important social questions of the time."[8] This oblique suggestion Dickens made specific in his letters to potential contributors: "the general mind and purpose" of *Household Words* was "the raising up of those that are down, and the general improvement of our social condition"; "all social evils" Dickens was particularly anxious to have dealt with.[9]

The contents of *Household Words* thus fall roughly into the three categories indicated – material of social import, informational articles, and material for entertainment.

Articles on the raising up of those that are down, articles warring against social evils and abuses, occupied an important place in *Household Words* pages. *Household Words* espoused the cause of the poor and the working classes. It pictured the plight of the shelterless poor in London; it dealt with slum children and their inevitable path to criminality unless moral and industrial training were provided for them. It crusaded against illiteracy; it advocated a national system of public education and free elementary and industrial schools for the poor. It pictured the squalid dwellings of the poor and the working classes and crusaded for adequate

5 Percy Fitzgerald, *Memories of Charles Dickens*, p. 4.

6 *Household Words* numbers bore a Saturday date but appeared on the preceding Wednesday. In the following footnotes, the periodical title is abbreviated to *H.W.*

7 Or of "Entertainment and Instruction." In some announcements and advertisements the two words appeared in reverse order.

8 This purpose was stated in the handbill referred to above (fn. 2); it was stated in advertisements in periodicals, as in the *Examiner*, the *Athenaeum*, the *Ladies' Companion*. In some advertisements the wording varied somewhat. One advertisement in the *Ladies' Companion*, for instance, read "to help in the Advancement of the most Important Social Questions of the Time."

9 To Elizabeth Gaskell, Jan. 31, 1850; to Mary Howitt, in Woodring, *Victorian Samplers*, p. 152.

housing. In matters of sanitation and health, which affected all classes, *Household Words* dealt with impure water supply, inadequate drainage, fetid sewers, polluted rivers, foul-smelling city graveyards. *Household Words* urged the removal of the cattle market from Smithfield. It denounced the hideousness of ostentatious funerals. It advocated the suppression of preventible accidents in factories, collieries, and ships by making criminally responsible for the accidents those persons who could have prevented them but failed to do so. It argued the right of workers to organize into unions. It described life in the forecastle and urged improvement in the living and working conditions of seamen. It described the shameless lack of privacy for soldiers' wives in barracks and demanded an end to conditions that turned modest women into sluts. It criticized the army system of officer promotion by purchase of commission. It denounced favouritism and nepotism as the basis of selection and advancement of men in the Indian civil service and in the diplomatic corps. It demanded the reform of laws that made persons "martyrs of chancery," that made a married woman "a legal fiction," that resulted in injustices under law administration. It denounced the over-leniency of law to debtors and malefactors; it denounced prison administrations that provided better for criminals than the labouring poor could provide for themselves. It exposed the misappropriation of charity funds, the scandalously lax custodianship of wills in cathedral registries, and the grossly inadequate arrangements for the housing of public records. It enumerated the labyrinthine steps involved in the obtaining of a patent, and pointed out the inadequacy of the patent, when finally obtained, to protect the rights of the holder. Among glaring abuses further afield that *Household Words* dealt with were the practices of the Hudson's Bay Company and the East India Company – the first, with its monopolistic obstruction to progress, its decimation of the aborigines; the second, with its corrupt administration, its connivance at mistreatment – even torture – of the ryots. Finally, *Household Words* pointed to culpability in high places – Government apathy in dealing with needed domestic legislation; Government incompetence, mismanagement, and irresponsibility, as in its conduct of the Crimean War.

None of the abuses decried in *Household Words*, none of the reforms advocated, none of the conditions criticized, were first brought to public attention by *Household Words*; but the popular – "readable" – discussion of these matters in Dickens's widely read periodical brought them attention that their sober presentation in specialized journals and in upper-class journals did not give them.

Informational articles on a wide variety of subjects were designed to provide *Household Words* readers with instruction, as also with entertainment. There were numerous articles on natural history, articles on science for the layman – medicine, physiology, physics, astronomy, geology. There were articles on the natural resources, industries, and manufactories of the British Isles; articles on inventions, trade, commerce, business; descriptions of cities, towns, and localities;

accounts of institutions and landmarks – Bethlehem Hospital, Greenwich Observatory, the South Kensington Museum, Billingsgate market, Lloyd's, Tattersall's. Numerous articles dealt with foreign countries. Some were historical accounts; others were descriptions of social life, customs, people, institutions, and political conditions. Of these, most were based on a writer's actual residence abroad or on his travels and experiences. Most numerous were the articles on France, though a series was devoted to Russia, a series to Holland, and a considerable number to Spain and Italy. Many concerned the Near East. Of British colonies, India served most frequently as the subject of articles. Information on conditions in Australia, both before and after the gold-rush, appeared mainly in articles written by emigrants – permanent or temporary, and in emigrants' letters that found their way to the editorial office.

Household Words contained articles on food, drink, and cookery; on public houses and sporting matters; on superstitions and mythological monsters, and on subjects of mildly antiquarian interest. There were occasional accounts of murders and murder trials, historical and contemporary. There was an account of Swedenborgianism and one of Mormonism. There were articles on philology and language. Occasional articles dealt with the arts – with music and musicians; with the theatre, drama, and dramatists; with art, art collections, and artists. Articles on literature and writers were more numerous. There were, for instance, discussions of fairy tales, songs, and ballads; a recounting of the story of *Beowulf* and of *Havelok the Dane*; an account of the Cid, the relation of an episode from the Prose Edda, a shortened version of *Reineke Fuchs*. Character books, conduct books, and a fifteenth-century herbal were the subjects of other articles. Tom D'Urfey, Robert Dodsley, and Elijah Fenton were resurrected as forgotten curiosa; Ebenezer Elliott, Wordsworth, and Margaret Fuller, as recently deceased, were each made the subject of an article.

Household Words did not review books, nor did it discuss books as literary works. It described or related their content in part or whole; it summarized and paraphrased, and quoted selections; sometimes it "gossiped" about a book. Its most frequent recommendation of a book was that it was "interesting," sometimes that it was "good" or "useful" or "profitable." Contemporary books thus dealt with were mainly biographies, books of travel, and accounts of foreign countries. Of English books, the only noteworthy one was Carlyle's *History of Friedrich II*; of foreign works, the only ones by writers of any lasting reputation were Pushkin's *The Captain's Daughter* and Turgenev's *A Sportsman's Sketches*.

Aside from musicians, artists, and authors, persons discussed in biographical articles were a heterogeneous lot. They included "Old Parr," Admiral Blake, Alexander Danilovich Menshikov, the imposter William Fuller, the poisoner Madame Ursinus, the financier Stephen Girard, Giovanni Belzoni; and, among more recent figures, the engineer George Stephenson, Lieutenant Thomas Waghorn, the French philanthropist Edmé Champion, and the English philanthropist Thomas Wright.[10] An article on Sarawak related the career of Rajah Brooke.

Topical matters dealt with in *Household Words* ranged from domestic interests to matters of wider concern: the arrival of a hippopotamus at the Zoological Gardens, Layard's sending to England the Bull of Nineveh, James Wyld's "Great Globe" in Leicester Square, the laying of the Dover-Calais telegraph cable, the Great Exhibition, a Birmingham poultry show, the exhibit of an ant bear in Bloomsbury, the removal of the Crystal Palace to Sydenham, the search for Sir John Franklin and his crews, the shooting of an eagle in Windsor Forest, the Covent Garden Theatre fire, a rhododendron display in Chelsea, the finding adrift of an infant corpse, the launching of the *Great Eastern*, the Burns centennial celebrations. In a miscellany designed for popular instruction and entertainment, detailed consideration of matters of national and international policy had obviously no place. England's involvement in Persia, in China, in one of the Kaffir wars was referred to, but received no extended discussion. The Crimean War and the Indian Mutiny were strongly reflected in *Household Words* pages, but were not dealt with in any reasoned or analytical manner.

For entertainment, *Household Words* provided – in addition to many of the articles – short stories, novels, and verse; and, at Christmas time, there were "extra" numbers with stories and poems to be read by the Christmas fire. Not all stories or poems, of course, were purely for entertainment; some were didactic and edifying in purpose. What seemed a story might be an object lesson on the foolishness of not buying insurance; what seemed a poem, rhymed sanitation propaganda.

In content – except for greater diversity of subjects discussed – Dickens's periodical did not differ from other miscellanies; in purpose, it did not differ from other social-minded journals. *Douglas Jerrold's Shilling Magazine*, for instance, was intended to be a vehicle of "instruction, amusement, and utility," devoted "to a consideration of the social wants and rightful claims of the PEOPLE";[11] *Eliza Cook's Journal* was to blend "instruction and amusement" and "to advance the broad interests of Humanity."[12] The individuality that Dickens sought to give his periodical lay, first, in its personal attitude, and, second, in its handling of non-fiction prose.

The personal attitude, the intimacy between *Household Words* and its readers, Dickens dwelt on in his introductory address. "We aspire," he wrote, "to live

10 *D.N.B.* cites as source material on Wright the *H.W.* article on him ("An Unpaid Servant of the State"); it cites as source material on John Cutler, Hugh C. Goldsmith, Thomas Edmondson, Joseph Train, and William Reid, respectively, the *H.W.* articles "Pope's Sir John Cutler," "The 'Logging' Stone," "The English Passport System," "Joseph Train," and "The Good Governor."

11 I, iii, prefatory comment, dated June 1845, citing prospectus.

12 Eliza Cook to Mrs. Gaskell, in R. D. Waller, ed., "Letters Addressed to Mrs. Gaskell," *Bulletin of the John Rylands Library*, XIX (Jan. 1935), 147.

in the Household affections, and to be numbered among the Household thoughts, of our readers." *Household Words* was to be its readers' friend and comrade in happiness and in sorrow, their fireside companion.

Carrying out this personal relationship were the many familiar essays, the informal "chats" and "talks," the "gossips"[13] (the writer of "Cities in Plain Clothes"[14] asked his readers' patience "while I babble" on a subject). Reader and writer were conversationally bracketed together as having like interests and attitudes: "philosophers like you, gentle reader,[15] and myself" ("What Sand Is"); "do you or I, reader, affect the perusal of that portentous broad-sheet" ("Houses to Let"); "You and I can remember" ("A Cup of Coffee"); "looking at 'Bell's Life' as you and I do" ("The Sporting World"). Readers were personally addressed, questioned, appealed to: "You are not to suppose, gentle reader" ("Jack Alive in London"); "you may be sure, reader" ("The Sister-Ship"); "My gentle readers will now perceive" ("Truffles"); "What think you, reader" ("Graves and Epitaphs"); "Are you grimacing, reader?" ("Butter"); "Have you any distinct idea of Spitalfields, dear reader?" "Will you come to Spitalfields?" ("Spitalfields"); "No, my good friends, not so" ("My Man. A Sum"); "and, reader, smile if you will" ("The Crusade of the Needle"); "Dear readers, ... pause a little" ("Getting Up a Pantomime"); "Sometimes, oh reader of mine" ("Houses to Let"); "A true story, friends and children, that will do our hearts good as we gather round the fire" ("Frozen Up in Siberia").

Comparatively little was done to establish "Mr. Conductor" as a person to whom readers would supposedly address communications, though a few items, on serious or pretendedly serious matters of public concern, attempted this.[16] Some offered Mr. Conductor advice and information, or asked his advice and help; some endorsed his stand on a matter or took him to task; some aired grievances. Mr. Christopher Shrimble took up his pen to communicate his opinions to Mr. Conductor ("Topography and Temperance"); Mr. Thomas Bovington wrote to ask Mr. Conductor "a few questions" ("From Mr. Thomas Bovington"). A highly respectable old lady, expounding her own "household words" for Mr. Conductor's benefit, opened her letter with a compliment: "Gracious, Mr. Con-

13 Henry Morley reprinted a selection of his *H.W.* contributions under the title *Gossip*.

14 For location of items, see Title Index, included in this volume.

15 The "gentle reader" appeared in *H.W.* despite Dickens's dislike of the phrase. See his letter, Feb. 28, 1853, to correspondent unknown. See also the *H.W.* article titled "H.W."

16 By actual readers, of course, numerous letters were directed to *H.W.* (see explanation of "Chips," July 6, 1850; also "Sabbath Pariahs"). Some readers endorsed a stand that *H.W.* had taken; some sent information to supplement what had appeared in an article; some corrected misstatements in articles; some appealed to *H.W.* to publicize a matter. Among the last mentioned group was a Government clerk, who stated the case for monthly, rather than quarterly, payment of clerks' salaries and "earnestly" asked *H.W.*'s "interference" to procure this "great good" ("Monthly Salaries"); another was an army officer who asked that the scarcity of reading material available to soldiers serving in India be brought to public attention ("Books for the Indian Army"). In their letters, readers sometimes referred to *H.W.* as Dickens's "valuable" or "renowned" journal.

ductor ... what a nice new journal you have got!" ("Letter from a Highly Respectably Old Lady"). Miss Marie Crumpet entreated Mr. Conductor to let her "appeal through [his] pages to an awe-stricken universe" on behalf of herself and her papa and mama ("Starvation of an Alderman"); another young lady, in an appeal hardly to be resisted, wrote: "Dear Mr. Conductor, please, dear, help me, and I will never use anything but 'Household Words' for curl-paper, to the last moments of my existence" ("What Is Not Clear about the Crystal Palace").

Dickens's policy on the handling of non-fiction prose was that such material be treated in some distinctive manner – not in literal, matter-of-fact, "encyclopaedical"[17] fashion. Factual, informative, instructional, didactic material was to be presented in a "fanciful," "imaginative," "picturesque," "quaint" way. Discussion of even "the driest subjects," as John Hollingshead wrote, was to be invested with "some degree of fancy and imagination."[18] Writing was to be "lively"; dullness was "hideous," as was heaviness.

As one means to this end, writers resorted to such devices as personification, fantasy, vision, fable, fairy tale, imaginary travels, contrived conversations, and the use of fictitious characters to serve as mouthpieces of information and opinion.

Another means to this end was, basically, exaggeration and distortion. "A mere natural, unaffected account of any transaction, it was felt, was out of place," wrote Percy Fitzgerald. "Everything, even trivial, had to be made more comic than it really was."[19] – Or more heinous, more undue, more wrong. As a reviewer in the *Press* wrote, in describing *Household Words'* manner of handling material of social import, "isolated blemishes in the social system are magnified through the hazy medium of exaggerated phrases to the dimensions of the entire system, and casual exceptions are converted into a universal rule and practice."[20] In large part, this exaggeration and distortion had its origin in writers' attempts to imitate Dickens's style – their copying, as Fitzgerald said, of its "forms and 'turns' and blemishes."[21]

Other distinctive characteristics of *Household Words'* treatment of non-fiction prose were the provocative introductory paragraphs and the "tricky," "smart" titles[22] (often puns), intended to lure a reader into what might be an article of serious import. *Household Words* readers were to be "instructively amused,"[23] or – indirectly, unwittingly – instructed.

17 Concerning the assignment of articles, John Hollingshead recorded Dickens as saying "more than once": "Let Hollingshead do it. ... He's the most ignorant man on the staff, but he'll cram up the facts, and won't give us an encyclopaedical article" (*My Lifetime*, I, 190).

18 "Preface," *Under Bow Bells*.

19 *Memories of Charles Dickens*, p. 170.

20 Oct. 22, 1859: review of Hollingshead, *Under Bow Bells*.

21 *Memoirs of an Author*, II, 156.

22 Hollingshead, *My Lifetime*, I, 104: "We were always very tricky with our *Household Words* titles, and many of them, very smart in themselves, served the purpose of raising curiosity in the mind of the reader, and concealing the subject which the writer was embroidering."

23 The phrase appears in the *H.W.* article "A Call upon Sophy."

Wills felt that this manner of handling material was successful. "It is universally acknowledged," he wrote to Dickens, "that subjects of an uninviting nature are treated – as a rule – in *Household Words* in a more playful, ingenious and readable manner than similar subjects have been hitherto presented in other weekly periodicals. ..."[24]

Actually, the results were at times distressing, in the inappropriateness and unsuitability of devices used, in the crudity and callousness displayed.

The explanation of elementary facts of physics through the facetious conversation of a bright lad and his dull-witted uncle ("The Chemistry of a Candle," "The Mysteries of a Tea-Kettle") was tedious. The presentation of geographical and other information by means of the reader's voyaging on "Our Phantom Ship" was childish ("Mercy upon us! There's a young crocodile flying. ... there's your reptile, the Iguanodon. ... Don't fear. You are not a vegetable; he will not eat you"). The heavily playful monologue of an old gentleman was an ill-chosen vehicle for advice on the treatment of catarrh and an account of its attendant mucous discharges ("An Ugly Nursling"). The mention in figurative language of the death of English sons and fathers in the Crimea was indecent: "the lance of a Cossack can give employment to Mr. Mattock, the mortuary sculptor, and Mr. Jay, the mourning furnisher, and Mr. Resurgam, the herald painter" ("The Girl I Left behind Me"). Crudity and insensitivity characterized various attempts at concreteness and humour: "he spends more time in picking pimples on his face, than in anything else" ("Twelve Miles from the Royal Exchange"); "Who cuts his corns? He is always going up and down the pavements, and must have corns of a prodigious size" ("The Best Authority"). Pretended indignation at the reappearance of the same artists' models in one painting after another found expression in the suggestion that the young man who posed for legs be confined in Greenwich Hospital "and that his legs be there immediately amputated (under chloroform), and decently buried within the precincts of the building" ("An Idea of Mine").

Not all articles, to be sure, attempted the fanciful and the picturesque. Some were as ordinary in presentation as in content. Nor were all characterized by exaggeration, over-writing. Some were clear, straightforward accounts and discussions. Nevertheless, the personal attitude and the frequent "playful, ingenious" handling of subjects combined to give a distinctive tone to *Household Words,* a tone best described by Mrs. Gaskell's coinage "Dickensy."[25] Mrs. Gaskell used the term in other than a complimentary sense.

One result of the attempt to make *Household Words* lively reading, the attempt to avoid heaviness, was a superficiality in the handling of many subjects and, in

24 Oct. 17, 1851, in R. C. Lehmann, ed., *Charles Dickens As Editor*, p. 74.

25 To C. E. Norton, *Letters of Mrs Gaskell*, ed. J. A. V. Chapple and Arthur Pollard, Letter No. 418.

some derivative articles, a kind of dishonesty. Reflecting with something of dissatisfaction on certain ill-informed papers of his that had appeared in *Household Words*, Hollingshead remarked: "It was less my fault than Charles Dickens's. He wanted 'readable' papers."[26] Articles based on books at times stated as fact what appeared in the source as qualified statement. In *The Dovecote and the Aviary*, for instance, E. S. Dixon had written, concerning certain kingfishers of the interior of Australia: "Mr. Gould believes that water is not essential to their existence, and that they seldom or never drink. ..."; in the *Household Words* discussion of Dixon's book this information appeared as the statement: "there are kingfishers in Australia which never see water at all, and never drink it" ("A Flight with the Birds"). In his scholarly edition of Ralegh's *Discovery of the Empire of Guiana*, Schomburgk had written that Diego de Ordaz "is considered to have been" the first European who ascended the Orinoco to any distance; the *Household Words* article based on Schomburgk's book disregarded the qualifying phrase: Diego de Ordaz "was" the first European who attempted to explore the river ("A Golden Legend"). Many derivative articles owed much more to their source than was acknowledged; some half dozen made no acknowledgment whatever of their source.[27] "Japanese Social Life," for instance, gave no indication that the information recorded was taken entirely from Andrew Steinmetz's *Japan and Her People*, in paraphrase and verbatim citation. "A New Idea of an Old Slave-Captain" did not mention Hugh Crow's *Memoirs*, on which the entire article was based. "A Russian Singing-Match" appeared without explanation that it was a chapter of Turgenev's *A Sportsman's Sketches*. That Dickens did not think reprehensible such unacknowledged appropriation of material is evident from his comment concerning "Hermit Island"; his objection to the article was that it looked "like a wretched translation from a wretched original"[28] – not that the "original" was unacknowledged.

In addition to being lively and "readable," *Household Words* articles, Dickens insisted, were to be accurate in information recorded and, in information and opinion, consistent with one another.

"Nothing can be so damaging to Household Words as carelessness about facts," Dickens wrote to Wills (March 18, 1853). "It is as hideous as dullness." Contributed articles on specialized subjects Dickens at times instructed Wills to have checked for accuracy by persons competent in the field. Misstatements that did appear in *Household Words*, when brought to the attention of the editorial office

26 *My Lifetime*, I, 190.

27 In contrast, some articles scrupulously stated the publication on which they were based, including at times publisher and date. The article "Mother Shipton" recorded even the Brit. Mus. shelf-mark of one of the pamphlets from which material was cited.

28 To Wills, March 10, 1853. Cf. also Dickens's instruction to Wills, Aug. 7, 1853, concerning another item: "Ask Miss Costello what it is translated from, and whether it is literally translated. If otherwise (of which there is very little hope) I think it might be well altered for the Xmas No."

by readers or when discovered by writers themselves, were conscientiously corrected. "Brimstone," for example, recorded a reader's correction of the statement in a preceding article that "We have no sulphur deposits in this country." "Workers in Kent Street" listed certain matters misrepresented in "Turpin's Corner" on which "we are glad to be set right." "Houses in Flats" explained, concerning certain charges made in a preceding article, that "we have since found" a portion of them "to be untrue"; accordingly, the article unsaid "all that we have said, so far as it weighs upon the individual referred to." "The Stereoscope" corrected the misstatement in "Photography" that pyrogallic acid was the agent used to fix a picture on a metallic plate. "Millionnaires and Measures" instructed the reader to substitute in a preceding article the word "multiples" for "divisions," "in correction of a blunder."

Errors of fact in at least two articles, however, remained unretracted: in "The Last Crusader," the identification of Louis IX, "Saint Louis" ("the Last Crusader" of the article), as "Louis the Twelfth"; and, in "Over the Water," the identification of the American physician and scientist John Jeffries as "the English Doctor" "James Jefferies."

In a periodical in which items were unsigned, Dickens, of necessity, laid stress on consistency between what appeared in one article and what appeared in another. Informative articles were not to be contradictory in statement; articles dealing with matters of policy or principle were not to blow "hot and cold" on the same subject; nor were they, obviously, to advocate ideas and opinions at variance with those that Dickens himself was "known to hold."[29] For all that the reader knew to the contrary, almost any article might be Dickens's own writing. As Dickens's mouthpiece, *Household Words* was a periodical in which ideas and opinions were advanced, not one in which opposing points of view were debated. When an article accepted for publication did express opinions that ran counter to Dickens's, that fact was stated. "In a Military Prison," which contained some such ideas on prison discipline, was prefaced by the editorial comment: "We do not adopt [the writer's] opinions, but we give him the opportunity of expressing them." So, also, in publishing a "communication from Dr. Rae," *Household Words* gave John Rae the opportunity to defend his conclusion that the survivors of the Franklin expedition had resorted to cannibalism; *Household Words'* position, emphatically stated, was that Rae's conclusion was ill founded and unjustified.

The circumstances under which Rae's article appeared in *Household Words* involved, of course, the statement of Rae's authorship. *Household Words'* policy, however, was anonymity. With the exception of some of Dickens's own writings, of Mrs. Gaskell's *North and South*, and of Wilkie Collins's *The Dead Secret*,

29 Dickens to Wills, Sept. 25, 1854; March 10, 1853.

materials appeared without formal statement of authorship.[30] Occasionally, when some knowledge about a writer was necessary for readers' better understanding of one of his contributions, such information was supplied in editorial comment or explanation, though without revealing the writer's name. Otto von Wenckstern, for instance, was identified as "a German gentleman of education" who had left his country because of "hopeless poverty, occasioned by political persecution"; George Laval Chesterton, as "the governor of a metropolitan prison"; Anna Mary Howitt, as a young lady studying painting, in company with a female friend, in Munich – the two young ladies leading there lives of "perfect propriety and security." Articles consisting of extracts from emigrants' letters were usually accompanied by editorial comment giving some information about the writers. In the absence of such information, as in travel articles, writers themselves at times had to establish at least the fact that they were authors or authoresses. In "Notes from Norway" appeared the explanation: "(be it known, I am a lady)."

In occasional articles, a writer masquerading under an assumed personality referred in passing to the protection that anonymous publication gave him or to the freedom of comment that it afforded. "As my name is not appended to this paper, and therefore I can hardly be suspected by the public of egotism," wrote a supposed barrister (Dickens himself), "I will remark that I have always had a pretty turn for humour" ("Legal and Equitable Jokes"). "Under shelter ... of an anonymous publication," the friend of a railway director ventured to make a few comments on railway management that he would not make to the director personally ("My Model Director").

Unsigned articles permitted what would in signed articles have been objectionable practice – a writer's commendatory reference to his own work. In an article based on his enlarged edition of John S. Rarey's booklet on horse taming, Samuel Sidney referred to that edition as "a full and clear account" of the Rarey system ("Amateur Horse-Training"). Richard Owen mentioned "two beautiful plates" that were to appear "in the forthcoming number of Owen's History of British Fossil Reptiles" ("A Leaf from the Oldest of Books"). William Howitt quoted almost three columns from what the well-informed "Mr. Howitt" had written in his *Year-Book of the Country* ("Epping Forest"). Four of Richard H. Horne's articles

30 *A Child's History of England* was stated in *H.W.* advertisements for the book publication of the *History* to be by Dickens, but appeared in the text without his name; *Hard Times* was announced as by Dickens and appeared in the text with his name; the item "Personal" bore Dickens's name as signature. *North and South* was announced as by the author of *Mary Barton* and appeared in the text with the same authorship ascription. *The Dead Secret* was announced as by Collins, but appeared in the text without authorship ascription. Circumstances connected with the publication of the item by Francis Bergh, that by John and William Gaunt, that by Robert Arbuthnot, and that by William Rogers involved the statement of these writers' names in the *H.W.* text. See, in Part Two, identification note on each of these writers.

mentioned or quoted from Horne's own writings.[31] Dickens, in various of his articles, referred to characters in his novels and to his *American Notes.*

There was, of course, no attempt to keep authorship a secret. Readers who wrote to ask who had written an item that particularly pleased them were given the information. Mrs. Cowden Clarke, for instance, learned from Dickens that Edmund Ollier was author of "The Host's Story" in the 1852 Christmas number; Mrs. Gaskell was informed by Wills that Henry Morley had written "Brother Mieth and His Brothers."

Readers often guessed – and often guessed rightly – who had written one or another item. Howitt detected William Allingham's authorship of "The Irish 'Stationers' ";[32] Crabb Robinson decided that "The Sickness and Health of the People of Bleaburn" was "evidently by H. Martineau";[33] Tom Taylor thought that he saw Mrs. Gaskell's hand in the "sweet story" "Lizzie Leigh";[34] Thackeray recognized one of Allingham's poems by its "Tennysonian cadence."[35] And Allingham wrote to Leigh Hunt: "I did not fail to catch your sparkles of poetry amid the utilitarianism of *Household Words,* like Polycrates's ring in the boiled codfish."[36] According to H. B. Forman, Horne's authorship of "The Great Peace-Maker" was general knowledge in literary circles at the time that the poem appeared; all of George Sala's friends knew "Colonel Quagg's Conversion" to be Sala's writing. Among manufacturers and millowners, the news soon "got abroad" that Harriet Martineau wrote for *Household Words* articles on manufacturing processes.[37] By the general public, however, articles and stories not by Dickens were often taken to be his writing. The "best productions" of Mr. Dickens's "young men," wrote Hollingshead, were "always credited" to Dickens – indeed, "all the good things in *Household Words*" were so credited.[38] Sala made the same comment. When an attractive article appeared in a number, he wrote, "people used to say that 'Dickens was at his best that week,' whereas in many cases in that particular number he had not written a single line except the weekly instalment of the 'Child's History'. ..."[39]

About a fourth of *Household Words* was the writing of Dickens and members of his staff – Wills, Horne, Morley, Wilkie Collins;[40] the remainder of the ma-

31 The complimentary phrase – a "charming book" – applied to Horne's *The Poor Artist* is probably Dickens's insertion. See, in Part Two, identification note on Horne. Not every reference to himself or to his writings that appears in items assigned to a contributor can be taken as the contributor's self-reference. Some such references were obviously editorial insertions or additions. In "News of Natal," assigned to Samuel Sidney, the mention of Sidney as "author of the 'Emigrant's Guide' " is obviously an editorial comment; Sidney wrote no work specifically so titled.

32 H. Allingham and E. Baumer Williams, eds., *Letters to William Allingham,* p. 205.

33 *On Books and Their Writers,* II, 704.

34 Waller, ed., "Letters Addressed to Mrs. Gaskell," *Bulletin of the John Rylands Library,* XIX (Jan. 1935), 116.

35 *Letters to William Allingham,* p. 279.

36 *Letters to William Allingham,* p. 15.

37 Martineau, *Autobiography,* II, 69.

38 *My Lifetime,* I, 96, 166.

39 *Things I Have Seen,* I, 80.

40 This calculation includes what Horne wrote not only while he was a staff member, but also what he wrote before and after he was on the staff; it includes what Morley and

terial was written by journalists and authors who became established as regular contributors, and by occasional contributors. From submitted contributions, Dickens and Wills selected what they considered suitable for the periodical, the material being revised as necessary to bring it into accord with what Dickens desired as concerned readability, accuracy, and consistency.[41]

Editorial revision was extensive – and drastic. Dickens sometimes rewrote articles and stories almost entirely. He condensed material, made it more compact; he cut lines, passages, and whole segments; he interpolated material and revised transitions; he altered phraseology. In stories, he at times "touched" an ending to make it less unpleasant for readers; in articles he modified statements that he considered too sweeping or that contradicted his views. He re-titled contributions. In the editorial office, staff members – Wills and Morley in particular – revised contributed material in accordance with their concept of how it should be revised, or in pursuance of Dickens's instructions. Items were cut to make them fit into the allotted space. Technical references "that the public don't understand, and don't in the least care for"[42] were deleted. Diction was altered; spelling and punctuation were "looked to." Verse, as well as prose, was "bettered."

The "public" that constituted the *Household Words* readership was mainly the middle class. In his "Preliminary Word," however, Dickens envisioned this readership as all-inclusive: people of both sexes, "of all ages and conditions," "the well-to-do" and "the poor," "children and old people." In a letter rejecting certain submitted papers as unsuited to *Household Words*, Dickens stated that it was "the constant endeavour ... to adapt every paper to the reception of a number of classes and various orders of mind at once."[43] Actually, material published in *Household Words* was material of general interest, and reader adaptation was attempted mainly in the broad sense of popularizing such material for a mass audience.

The poor, in the sense of the "humbler orders," the "lower classes," were not addressed in *Household Words*. They were discussed, their lives and hardships described, and their cause championed. The working class, taken to include workers who made a fair living as well as what were termed "the industrious poor," was at times directly addressed, and articles were published on subjects of special interest to readers of this class, as also on matters of their immediate practical concern, as on emigration. At the same time, readers of higher station were appealed to to concern themselves with the welfare of those below them. Persons "interested in improving the condition of the poor" were urged, for instance, to

Collins wrote not only while they were staff members, but also what they wrote before they were on the staff.

41 Writings of staff members were also revised; Wills's were revised only by Dickens.

42 Dickens's comment to Wills, March 10, 1853, concerning a paper that was to be revised.

43 To Charles Mayne Young, July 21, 1852. The rejected papers had been submitted by Young on behalf of a woman writer.

encourage window gardening among "the lower classes" ("Back Street Conservatories"); the "Ladies of England" were entreated to help with their sympathy "the labouring man who seeks to right himself, and asks, for himself and for those still poorer than he is, power to inhabit decent homes" ("Conversion of a Heathen Court").

Children were occasionally addressed in *Household Words*, as in "To My Young Friends" and "Garden-Games." The periodical published non-fiction material that children could read and understand, as also childish stories. Two submitted stories, however, Dickens rejected on the specific ground that they were "children's stories" and therefore "quite out of the road of a publication addressing so large an audience as this of ours does."[44] Actually, *Household Words* was for children only in the sense that Dickens stated in a letter to H. G. Adams (Feb. 19, 1866) – that "a good miscellany for grown people, should have much in it of interest to growing people." The incongruous appearance in *Household Words* of *A Child's History of England* can be accounted for only on the basis that readers in general – as Percy Fitzgerald remarked – were interested in learning the opinion of Dickens "on any subject whatever."[45] Dickens was not unaware of this interest.

Reader adaptation indicated the avoidance in *Household Words* of what might be offensive to the middle class,[46] of what might give rise to painful apprehensions, and of what was objectionable as family reading. Dickens rejected stories dealing with hereditary insanity, on the ground that the subject would awaken fear and despair in the "numerous families in which there is such a taint."[47] He deleted from Sala's "The Key of the Street" what might shock "young and lady readers."[48] Wills, in "The Great Penal Experiments," quoted a Government report only in part, "by reason of some of the passages being too revolting for reproduction in these pages."

In the matter of language, *Household Words* was liberal enough to print in its pages an occasional "God dam." Some contributors, however, pretended great concern for propriety. "Hell," "trousers," and other words were in some articles coyly avoided or self-consciously used: "Reader, were you ever in – I have difficulty in expressing the word. Four little letters would serve my turn; but I dare

44 To Charles Mayne Young, July 21, 1852.

45 *Memories of Charles Dickens*, p. 135.

46 Dickens to Wills, Sept. 24, 1858: "... I particularly wish you to look well to Wilkie's [Wilkie Collins's] article about the Wigan schoolmaster, and not to leave anything in it that may be sweeping, and unnecessarily offensive to the middle class." There was, of course, in conformity with the time, no attempt to avoid what might be "unnecessarily offensive" to other separate groups of possible readers. The Irish were generally depicted as superstitious and dirty. Typical comments on Jews described them as having "that clever, sensual, crafty countenance, which contains the epitome of the whole Hebrew history" ("Passing Faces") or as being "at times unpleasantly economical of soap" ("Going Circuit at the Antipodes"). One article, however, did contain a pleasant description of the Jewish women in the shops of the dirty, rickety Jewish fruit market in London: "The handsome nut-brown, dark-haired daughters of Israel, jewelled and ribboned, and smiling, seen dimly amidst the shadows of those murky spots, appear like breathing pictures of a master hand" ("Oranges and Lemons").

47 To Wills, Feb. 8, 1853; July 22, 1855.

48 Sala, *Things I Have Seen*, I, 68.

not – this being above all for Household eyes – write them down" ("The Golden Calf"); "Who the ——— I won't write the word in full – ever spelt book with an e at the end of it" ("Your Life or Your Likeness"); " 'I'll pull yer ear-rings, I will, ye blessed limb o' mischief ...,' growled the mother – only the word was not 'blessed,' but as opposite in meaning as the reader pleases to imagine" ("Shadows of the Golden Image"); " 'Ugh!' cried the other ..., 'we shall be smelt' (she used a stronger word) 'we shall be smelt to death' " ("A Train of Accidents"). Mention, as landmarks in life, of a boy's first trousers and of the first time of a man's getting drunk was circumspectly approached: "the first – well, there is no harm in it! – the first pair of trousers"; "persons of the male sex who may remember ... the first time they ever got – elevated" ("First Fruits").

"Writing down" to readers, held Dickens, was "as great a mistake as can be made." "... don't think," he insisted to Wills (Oct. 12, 1852), "that it is necessary to write *down* to any part of our audience." Certain of the devices by means of which informational and other material was presented in *Household Words*, as also the manner in which books were dealt with, certainly seem today a "writing down" to any reader of moderate intelligence; but, of course, Dickens envisioned his readers as "of all ages and conditions," and such handling of material was part of his attempt to make *Household Words* popular reading. Aside from this approach, there was no "writing down" to "our audience."

An occasional article admitted that some readers might be ignorant on one matter or another: "there may possibly be some among our readers," stated one article, who would profit by having pointed out to them the absurdity of astrological predictions; but readers in general were taken to be aware of such absurdity ("Francis Moore, Physician"). Many articles addressed readers as a travelled, educated audience, conversant with books and writers. Some articles took for granted readers' knowledge of the French language;[49] one suggested that "many of our readers may have read" in the original *Goethe's Correspondence with a Child* ("Adventures of a Translation"). "I suppose," began another article, "that most readers of Household Words have dipped at times into the pages of the 'Prose Edda' " ("The London Tavern"); "most of our readers" were taken to know that Mr. Carlyle had been for some time hard at work on the biography of Frederick II ("Apprenticeship of Frederick the Great"). Articles – even on quite non-literary subjects – were studded with literary references, obviously considered not inappropriate to the *Household Words* audience. "Lobsters," for instance, and "Madame Busque's" (an account of a Paris eating-house) cited Dante on remembrance of happy days in time of sorrow; "Coco-Eaters" quoted two lines from George Herbert; "Beef, Mutton, and Bread" brought in reference to Jeanie Deans; and

49 Cf. Leigh Hunt to Macvey Napier, Aug. 4, 1842: For an article that he was writing for the *Edin. Rev.*, Hunt asked permission to give French extracts in English, with only an occasional quotation in French, in view of the readers "in these progress-of-knowledge times" who understood no language but their own (*Correspondence of Leigh Hunt*, II, 30).

"To My Young Friends" philosophized: "we come – as Herr Teufelsdröck says – nobody knows whence."

Even more indicative of the acquaintance with literature, specifically with English classics and contemporary writings, that readers were assumed to have were the many echoes and parodies of quotations and the literary allusions woven into the text of articles – literary material that would, obviously, be pleasing or amusing to the reader only on his recognition of its source. Such recognition was assumed. The following are random examples: "This quiet old 'Dreadnought,' whose fighting days are all over – *sans* guns, *sans* shot, *sans* shells, *sans* everything – did fight at Trafalgar" ("The 'Dreadnought' "); "and so the linked sweetness is drawn out through all the voyage" ("Back at Trinity"); "the acute genealogist may raise many a mortal to the skies from which vulgar custom has brought angels down" ("Family Names"); "for, if to its lot some floral errors fall, look in its face, and you'll forget them all" ("Roses"); "To teach the young idea how to cook" ("For the Benefit of the Cooks"); "Full many a fruit of purest juice serene the dark unfathom'd woods of Gallia bear; full many a mushroom springs to rot unseen, and wastes its ketchup on the desert air" ("Wet Garden Walks"); "My little Dutchwoman hath a face fair and fat ...; fresh, as though newly come from an English hayfield, yet without Molly Seagrim's blowzabel hue" ("Down among the Dutchmen"); "who knows but that every one of those eccentric appellations here recorded are, by this time (like Uncle Toby's oath), blotted out for ever" ("American Changes of Names"); "The clock tower, contrived a double or say 'treble debt to pay' " ("The Metropolitan Cattle Market"); "In the time of Kublai Khan, and the Abyssinian maid playing on a dulcimer" ("The Eastern Kingdom"); "Mon Dieu! the very cook is fast asleep,/And all that bullock's heart is baking still!" ("Too Weak for the Place"); "and, after years of absence, I have lately been revisiting my Yarrow" ("In Presence of the Sword"); "So we set forward accordingly – our way lying 'all among the bearded barley' – like the road to 'many-towered Camelot' " ("A Visit to Robinson Crusoe"); "I can conceive how Colonel Rawdon managed to live upon 'nothing a year;' but how my friend private Tourlourou and his comrades contrive to drink Bourdeaux, to smoke the Indian weed, and to play piquet ... upon a surplus income of a halfpenny a-day is beyond my ken" ("French Soldiers in Camp").

Household Words had a decidedly literary flavour.

There was no fixed plan for the composition of a *Household Words* number, except that it should contain diversity of material and that the most important item should of course occupy lead position. Typical numbers contained material in each of the three areas of *Household Words* interest – social concern, instruction and information, and entertainment. Poems, for edification and for pleasure, appeared more frequently in earlier volumes than in later ones. The first volume contained more than forty poems; the second, thirty-nine. Vol. XVI contained only ten.[50] There was no specific policy as to what was to appear as lead item, though this was frequently an article of social import. The first instalment of a long prose item, as on travel, for instance, at times occupied lead position, as did the first instalment of a story or a novel.[51] All instalments of *The Lazy Tour of Two Idle Apprentices* and of *Hard Times* appeared in lead position.

Household Words numbers, normally of twenty-four pages,[52] contained an average of six to seven items. Dickens disliked having many short pieces in a number, holding that they made it look "patchy."[53] Beginning with the fifteenth number, various miscellaneous prose items, some less than a half column in length, but some as long as four columns, were grouped together under the heading "Chips."[54] Comments sent in by readers often appeared under this heading. Aside from this, there were no departments in *Household Words*, though there were four series of items that appeared, at irregular intervals, under a common main title – "Illustrations of Cheapness," "Our Phantom Ship," "Shadows," and "The Roving Englishman."

Advertisements and announcements published in *Household Words* followed the last item in a number. They concerned the two supplementary publications (the *Household Narrative of Current Events* and the *Household Words Almanac*), the availability of *Household Words* in monthly parts and in bound volumes, the extra Christmas numbers, forthcoming serials, the publication in book form of three *Household Words* serials (*A Child's History of England*, *Hard Times*, and *The Dead Secret*), and Dickens's public readings.

In format, *Household Words* was not attractive, its double-columned pages being closely printed and without illustrations.[55] Editorially, the periodical was a respectable publication, though there were, naturally, throughout the nineteen volumes, various editorial infelicities and inconsistencies. The "Contents" prefaced to each volume was not always complete or accurate. Cross-references to articles (in text and footnote) were not always accurate. Occasional running titles differed from article titles (as "The Irish Use of the Globe" / "The Irish Use of the Globes"; "Acorn-Coffee" / "Corn-Coffee"; "Colonel Grunpeck and Mr. Parkinson" / "Colonel Grumpeck and Mr. Parkinson"); in one instance two instalments

50 Dickens to Wills, Oct. 2, 1858: "Pray, pray, *pray*, don't have Poems unless they are good. We are immeasurably better without them. ..." Dickens at times decided against poems that Wills had selected for insertion.

51 The first instalment of *North and South* and of *The Dead Secret*, the two longest novels published in *H.W.*, did not, however, appear in lead position.

52 Nineteen numbers contained only twenty pages.

53 To Wills, Sept. 25, 1855.

54 In early volumes, single items also appeared under this heading. Beginning with Vol. X, however, single items usually carried the heading "Chip." Occasional prose items published under individual titles were shorter than some of those placed under the "Chips" ("Chip") heading.

55 Writers discussing illustrated books at times expressed regret that their articles could not be accompanied by illustrations: "More Alchemy," "Bird History," "A Hint from Siam."

of an article differed in title ("The Old and New Squatter" / "The Old and New Squatters"). In some items, numbers were written as figures; in others, they were spelled out as words. The latter seemed to be the preferred editorial practice. It resulted, in the article "Beltane," for instance, in the cumbersome mention of "the Gentleman's Magazine for seventeen hundred and eighty-three, seventeen hundred and eighty-four, and seventeen hundred and eighty-eight." The practice also made into textual errors what might otherwise have passed as typographical errors, as in the comment: "in the Gentleman's Magazine of February, eighteen hundred and sixty-five, we read" ("A Wonderful Wild Beast"). There was little consistency in spelling ("gaol" and "jail" were both used, as were "colour" and "color," "waggon" and "wagon," "chesnut" and "chestnut," "Kaffir," "Kafir," and "Caffre," etc.), and umlauts were erratic, the author of *Faust* appearing at times as "Goëthe."

Material was, in general, printed with fair accuracy, the "villainously read" proofs that at times roused Dickens's wrath being reasonably well corrected in the editorial office before copies were struck off. Errors in names of persons, however, resulting obviously from the printers' inability to read copy, often escaped the proof-reader, as, for instance, "Samuel Smuthy" for Samuel Smatty ("Weird Wisdom"), "Romien" for François Auguste Romieu ("Mr. Bendigo Buster on Our National Defences against Education"), "Andebert" for Jean-Baptiste Audebert ("The Tresses of the Day Star"), "Otto von Bahr" for Otto von Behr ("Germans in Texas"), "Hassel" and "Hassell" for Arthur Hill Hassall ("Several Heads of Hair"), "Dean French" for Richard Chenevix Trench ("Saxon-English"), "Gottfried Heller" for Gottfried Keller ("Cat's Grease"). The same occurred with geographical names, as "Toufet" for Foufet ("Abd-el-Kader on Horseback"), "Tunkeria" for Tankaria ("India Pickle"), "Ceno de Pasco" for Cerro de Pasco ("The Topmost City of the Earth"). Of these, the last mentioned was probably the only one that might have distressed readers.

Occasional uncorrected mistranscriptions made sentences into nonsense, as in "the natural unborn desire of man" for "inborn desire" ("Running Away"); "calling out 'Ruke!' ('Order!')" for "calling out 'Ruhe!' " ("A Taste of Austrian Jails"), "Girard Cottage" for "Girard College" ("Stephen Girard"), or the reference to a quotation from Lamb as by "dear Eliza" instead of by "dear Elia" ("Going A-maying"). Other uncorrected mistranscriptions changed the entire meaning of a sentence, as in "burning billets of oak wood in a chamber" for "in a chauffer" ("Lighthouses and Light-Boats"); a fish recommences "its more immediate rudimental duties" for "more immediate nidimental duties" ("Tittlebat Tactics"); "the dreadful trade of sapphire gathering" for "samphire gathering" ("Another Tight Little Island"). Reference to Sidney Smith's *The Mother Country: or, The Spade, the Wastes, and the Eldest Son* cited the subtitle as "the Spade, the Wastes, and the Eldest Sow" ("The Spade"). Occasionally a mistranscription or a typographical error was corrected in a "chip." The "chip" "Ballinglen," for instance, corrected the mistranscription "Ballinglew" that had appeared in "The Spade in Ireland"; "The Salt in the Sea" corrected in "Minerals That We Eat" "a typographical error so glaring that it almost corrects itself."

Material that appeared in *Household Words* was to be previously unpublished material. His tentative plan of using "selected" material Dickens abandoned after the first number.[56] Dickens took pains to detect among submitted contributions what might be plagiarized or what might have been already published. Despite editorial vigilance, however, an occasional item was admitted that had been published elsewhere.[57]

The stated rate of payment for prose contributions was a guinea for a two-column page.[58] The rate for verse was not stated, but payments recorded for verse were often at twice the rate for prose, though they varied considerably. Contributions to Christmas numbers were paid for at a higher rate than were those to regular numbers. It was Wills, however, who handled routine payments, and he was not disposed to be wasteful of *Household Words* moneys. Of the some ninety contributed prose items in Vol. I for which he recorded payment, more than eighty he paid for at less than the stated rate, in amounts varying from pence to pounds. Fractions of columns and even whole columns were omitted in the payment calculation; guineas emerged as pounds.[59] For the occasional articles that had to be entirely rewritten, there was justification for the underpayment; but for most there was none. Payments recorded for items contributed to later volumes were more fairly in accord with the stated rate.

Dickens made it a rule, he stated, "to pay for everything that is inserted in Household Words."[60] He insisted on paying for the contributions of his friend Bryan Waller Procter, who "would not be paid" for his first one, and for the verses of William C. Macready's daughter, evidently intended to be gratuitous. He seems, however, to have exempted an occasional friend – Thomas Noon Talfourd, for

56 The only item in *H.W.* that is actually "selected" material is "Metal in Sea-Water," taken from the *Athenaeum*; it appeared in the original issue only of *H.W.* No. 1 (see below, p. 46. The two "fillers" "Good Verses of a Bad Poet" and "Curious Epitaph," both in Vol. I, were, however, in the nature of "selected" material. The policy of using only original material did not, of course, rule out occasional articles the text of which consisted almost entirely of material quoted from a published work, as "A London Parish" and "The New Colonists of Norfolk Island."

57 At least two of J. C. Prince's poems had been published in other periodicals before they appeared in *H.W.* Some of the material that Mrs. Gaskell contributed to *H.W.* was a reworked and expanded form of two of her contributions that had appeared in another periodical. Approximately half of Mrs. Howitt's "The Poetry of Finland" was taken practically verbatim from the Howitts' *Literature and Romance of Northern Europe.*

58 Hollingshead considered this rate "ample, but not sentimentally liberal." He recorded, however, that *Good Words* paid him for one of his papers (rejected by *H.W.*) "double the Dickens's scale" (*My Lifetime*, I, 97).

59 Dickens's payment instructions to Wills occasionally hint at Wills's tendency to pare payments. Of Sala, for instance, Dickens wrote, Aug. 7, 1854: "Don't run him too close in the money way. I can't bear the thought of making anything like a hard bargain with him." For a paper that Dickens expected Charles Whitehead to send to the editorial office, Dickens suggested payment "with a turn of the scale" in Whitehead's favour (Dec. 30, 1855).

60 To W. C. Macready, Aug. 8, 1856.

instance – from the rule of obligatory payment. Exceptions to the payment rule were, of course, the readers' letters motivated by *Household Words* items and published in whole or part in "chips," though an occasional such letter was paid for. Payment was at times made to persons who suggested the idea for a paper or provided other assistance, as for "A Suburban Romance," "To Clergymen in Difficulties," and "Bill-Sticking." Occasionally Dickens instructed Wills to pay an established contributor for an article that was to "stand over" or not to be used at all.

Dickens's friends who recorded their opinion of *Household Words* were extravagant in its praise. Percy Fitzgerald exhausted the list of commendatory adjectives in his attempt to do justice to the periodical. Edmund Yates thought the early volumes "perfect models of what a magazine intended for general reading should be."[61] Forster's *Examiner* (October 5, 1850) pronounced the first volume of Mr. Dickens's "delightful" *Household Words* one of the most agreeable and instructive collections of miscellaneous reading ever published. Landor declared that the "pure pleasure" and "useful knowledge" imparted by *Household Words* exceeded that imparted by any other publication "since the invention of letters."[62] Leigh Hunt wrote of the periodical as Dickens's "new-found music of our spheres" to the sound of which, he hoped, the world might "haste to days of harmony."[63]

Even the *Press*, severely critical of the style of later volumes of *Household Words*, described the first volume – with its "charming succession of tales and essays," its "mixture of pathos, humour, and admirably graphic description" – as "one of the most delightful books in the language."[64]

Not all readers, of course, liked Dickens's periodical. Morley, having seen the first (and possibly the second) number, decided: "I don't care very much for *Household Words*"; he much doubted whether Dickens was "the right man to edit a journal of literary mark."[65] Crabb Robinson, looking over two early numbers and finding only one article that pleased him, recorded his agreement with William Bodham Donne's opinion "that Dickens's management of a periodical is bad." In later numbers, however, Robinson did find articles much to his liking.[66] *Lives of the Illustrious*, 1852, stated that the content of *Household Words* was "good" on the whole, "though of not so solid a character" as that of *Chambers's Journal*.[67] *Household Words'* crusades in various areas of reform aroused the antagonism of certain groups. Millowners denounced the articles on preventible factory accidents, one of which they described as "trash" and "poison" ("Death's Cyphering-Book"). Harriet Martineau, in connection with the same articles, de-

61 *Recollections and Experiences*, p. 146.

62 Note accompanying "A Modern Greek Idyl," *Athenaeum*, April 22, 1854.

63 "To Charles Dickens," *Poetical Works of Leigh Hunt*, ed. H. S. Milford, p. 252.

64 Nov. 12, 1859: review of Vol. I of *A.Y.R.*

65 Henry Shaen Solly, *The Life of Henry Morley*, p. 149.

66 *On Books and Their Writers*, II, 696, 704, 722.

67 II, 295: article on Dickens.

plored Dickens's irresponsibility in his setting up *Household Words* "as an avowed agency of ... social reform," lacking, as he did, a knowledge of basic principles of political philosophy.[68] At least one "Reverend Gentleman" described as "false and calumnious" the *Household Words* articles on the state of documents in cathedral registries.[69] Dickens's attitude toward prison chaplains, as expressed in *Household Words*, turned at least some of those clergymen against the periodical. Henry Mayhew found that *Household Words* was not among the reading materials provided for convicts in the Woolwich Hulks. "The chaplain objects," he was told, "to it being in the library."[70]

Objective criticism of *Household Words*, however, concerned not its content, but its style. The *Press* pointed out the over-writing, the distortion, that characterized typical *Household Words* articles. It commented on the writing of the young imitators of Dickens who adopted, in their treatment of the most dissimilar subjects, "the peculiar sentiment, the peculiar humour, or the peculiar word-painting, as the case might be, of their celebrated teacher," and remarked: "A mannerism which a single great genius finds it difficult to sustain at its highest level was certain to become ere long unbearable in the hands of his professed imitators." The *Press* saw a "monotony of tone" in the later volumes, "a falling off" from the standard of the earlier volumes; it considered it "a rather fortunate thing for Mr. Dickens that *Household Words* should have terminated while its reputation remained comparatively unimpaired, and the beginnings only of its degeneracy were as yet visible."[71] Even Percy Fitzgerald, enthusiastic admirer that he was of *Household Words*, admitted that the "strained and exaggerated sham 'Dickensese'" that appeared in its pages must have had "the result of wearying and disgusting" readers.[72]

With the uncritical public, however, *Household Words* was extremely popular. It had a sale of some forty thousand copies a week[73] and became, as Dickens hoped it would, "a good property," yielding "a good round profit."[74] Dickens brought the periodical to an end, in 1859, only because of his altercation with his pub-

68 *The Factory Controversy*, p. 36.

69 William Downing Bruce, *An Account of the Present Deplorable State of the Ecclesiastical Courts of Record*, pp. 34–35.

70 Henry Mayhew and John Binny, *The Criminal Prisons of London and Scenes of Prison Life*, p. 219. "Small-Beer Chronicles," *A.Y.R.*, Dec. 6, 1862, stated that Dickens's comments on prison chaplains resulted in his being "severely mauled at the hands of certain Reverend Ordinaries."

71 Nov. 12, 1859: review of Vol. I of *A.Y.R.* See also, Oct. 22, 1859: review of Hollingshead, *Under Bow Bells*; Dec. 10, 1859: review of W. M. Thomas, *When the Snow Falls*.

72 *Memoirs of an Author*, II, 156.

73 Basing his calculations on the figures given in the *Dickensian*, XLVI, 197–203, Edgar Johnson (*Charles Dickens*, II, 946) states that *H.W.* "during its very best years" sold "perhaps some forty thousand copies a week." *Men of the Time*, 1852 (p. 120), stated that *H.W.* readers were understood to number "somewhere about sixty thousand per week." Percy Fitzgerald (*Memories of Charles Dickens*, p. 135) recorded that "nearly one hundred thousand copies of the first number" were sold. The Christmas number "Wreck of the Golden Mary," he stated, reached "the unprecedented sale of a hundred thousand copies" ("Two English Essayists," *Afternoon Lectures on Literature and Art*, p. 95).

74 To Miss Burdett-Coutts, April 12, 1850; to the Rev. James White, July 13, 1850.

lishers, and then only to establish a second periodical – *All the Year Round* – on the same plan as the first.

THE *HOUSEHOLD WORDS* CONTRIBUTORS

The large interest of *Household Words* lies in its connection with Dickens – his own writings in the periodical, his concept of the role of editor, his work as editor. Large interest lies, too, in the contents themselves, which reflect nine years of mid-century Victorian England – its attitude and its concerns, the literary taste of its middle-class readers. A third interest lies in the contributors to the periodical – the some three hundred ninety writers[75] – and non-writers – who were eager or willing to have their contributions appear anonymously under the aegis of Dickens.

Taken as a whole, the *Household Words* contributors were a diverse group. They included an occasional poet and novelist whose works are still acclaimed – and persons so obscure that their names appear in no biographical compilation. They included writers old and young – from veteran survivors of the Romantic Age to writers who lived well into the twentieth century. They included people of all social classes – from the factory worker to the gentleman, from the self-taught to the master of arts and the honorary doctor of laws. They included men of various professions – barristers and divines, medical men and naturalists, soldiers and sailors. They included people from most parts of the British Isles and from various parts of the Empire – India, Ceylon, Australasia, as well as an occasional foreigner – American, German, Belgian, Italian, Polish, Hungarian. They included, incidentally, some ninety women contributors, *Household Words* not having the reputation assigned by Mary Russell Mitford to *Fraser's* and *Blackwood's* – that they were hardly such periodicals "as a lady likes to write for."[76] Appropriately for a family journal, contributorship to *Household Words* became in some families a common activity, so that the names of husband and wife, for instance, mother and daughter, father and son, brother and sister appear in the contributor list.

Of the some three hundred ninety contributors, the majority wrote for *House-*

75 The number cannot be precisely stated: Contributors listed in the Office Book as "Earle" and "Erle," as "Osborn" and "Osborne," etc., may be one person or two. A contributor listed for one item as another contributor's "friend" may or may not be a writer listed under his own name for another item (Henrietta Jenkin appears under the "friend" designation and also under her name). The writers of at least ten unassigned prose items seem clearly to be individual persons, rather than writers listed by name as contributors of other items. The unassigned poems may or may not be by writers listed by name as contributors of other items (the unassigned "The Sower" is by a writer listed for other items; the unassigned "Hiram Power's Greek Slave" is by a writer not listed for other items).

76 Letter to Mrs. Frances Trollope, 1832, cited in T. A. Trollope, *What I Remember*, p. 496. Despite her comment, Miss Mitford did contribute to *Blackwood's*, 1826–27. Until 1850, however, the periodical had few women contributors.

hold Words only occasionally. Throughout the nine years of its existence, however, *Household Words* came to have an established corps of contributors – the "regulars," as they were called – who wrote a substantial amount in the periodical. Including staff members (except Dickens), these writers numbered thirty-five. The group did not remain constant; some of the writers contributed during only two or three years; others, during the entire nine. The writers varied greatly in the number of their contributions; some wrote as few as twenty items; some, more than a hundred; and one – Morley – more than three hundred. The writers varied in their literary background, some being well-established periodical contributors and authors of books; others, mere beginners as journalists or verse writers. The thirty-five became connected with *Household Words* in various ways.

Dickens's staff consisted of William Henry Wills as subeditor, with Richard H. Horne, Henry Morley, and Wilkie Collins as his assistants during various years. Wills, two years older than Dickens, was a journalist by profession. He had been some years assistant editor of *Chambers's Journal*; he had been engaged by Dickens on the staff of the *Daily News* and had continued as staff member after Dickens's resignation as editor. Wills wrote some fifty full-length articles and stories for *Household Words* and somewhat fewer short items. Horne, as staff member and as contributor, was connected with *Household Words* during the first four years of its publication. Nine years older than Dickens, he had been contributing to periodicals for more than twenty years, had been for a year editor of the *Monthly Repository*, and had been engaged by Dickens as reporter for the *Daily News*. He had published various prose works and had achieved some reputation as author of poetic dramas and of the epic *Orion*. Horne contributed to *Household Words* some seventy-five items, prose and verse. Morley, ten years Dickens's junior, began to contribute to *Household Words* in 1850 at Dickens's request; in the following year he became a staff member; he remained on the staff throughout the life of the periodical. Morley had, by 1850, published two books of poems and tales and some tracts and periodical articles on health and sanitation. He wrote more in *Household Words* than did any other writer. Collins, twelve years younger than Dickens, began to contribute to *Household Words* in April 1852, by which date he had published four books. He became a staff member in 1856 and remained on the staff to the end of the periodical's publication. Collins contributed to *Household Words* more than fifty items, one of them being *The Dead Secret*, reprinted in book form in two volumes.

Of the established group of writers, some who were unconnected with the staff received from Dickens, some weeks before the first number of *Household Words* appeared, a personal invitation to become contributors. Among these was Mrs. Gaskell, who in 1848 had aroused a storm of controversy by her first novel, *Mary Barton*. Mrs. Gaskell contributed to *Household Words* from the first number to the 1858 Christmas number, one of her contributions being *North and South*, reprinted in book form in two volumes. Other writers personally invited by

Dickens to become contributors were Charles Knight, the Rev. James White, and Harriet Martineau. All were older than Dickens; all were, of course, established writers of some reputation. Knight had begun work as reporter in the year that Dickens was born; as author, editor, and publisher, he had since that time been bringing out compilations and books designed to appeal to a mass reading public. During 1850–52, he contributed twenty items to *Household Words* (counting as individual items those that appeared under a common main title). White, a good friend of Dickens, had been for more than twenty years a contributor to *Blackwood's*; he was author of some miscellaneous volumes of prose and verse, and of several historical plays of some merit. From 1852 to 1859, White contributed some forty items to *Household Words.* Miss Martineau, long a celebrity, agreed to become a contributor despite the opinion of her relatives and friends that the connection with Dickens's periodical was "*infra dig*": "... Mr. Dickens himself being a contributor," she commented, "disposed of the objection abundantly."[77] Miss Martineau wrote more than forty items for *Household Words,* but remained a contributor for only five years.

Not all writers whom Dickens invited to contribute, however, accepted the invitation. Tom Taylor wrote nothing for *Household Words* despite the assurance of Dickens that he would be "very sincerely gratified" by whatever Taylor might contribute (to Taylor, March 4, 1850). Douglas Jerrold refused to contribute because of Dickens's policy of anonymous publication.

Grenville Murray became a *Household Words* contributor, in 1850, at Wills's suggestion to him that Dickens would have no objection to publishing in the periodical any sketches of foreign manners that Murray might pick up on the Continent. Murray had published little by that time. To *Household Words,* during a period of six years, he contributed some eighty items (counting as individual items those that appeared under a common main title). Samuel Sidney, co-author (with his brother) of *Sidney's Australian Hand-book* and editor of *Sidney's Emigrant's Journal*, was asked in 1850 to write for *Household Words* on emigration, a subject that Dickens wanted discussed. Sidney contributed some sixty articles and stories, continuing his connection with *Household Words* to October 1858.

Among the *Household Words* "regulars" were four journalists (aside from Wills and Horne) who had been associated with Dickens on the *Daily News*: Dudley Costello, Frederick Knight Hunt, Sidney Laman Blanchard, and William Blanchard Jerrold. Their writing for Dickens's new periodical was a logical continuation of their having written for the earlier one. Costello, who had been engaged as foreign editor of the *Daily News,* had long been established as a journalist by the time that *Household Words* began, and had by that date published a book of travels. He contributed some forty items to *Household Words,* writing for the periodical during every year of its publication. Hunt, who had been engaged as provincial editor of the *Daily News,* became editor of that paper in

77 *Autobiography,* II, 91.

1851. He had previously established two periodicals of his own. He contributed, during 1850–51, twenty items to *Household Words*. The two young journalists Blanchard and Jerrold had both been reporters for the *Daily News*. Blanchard had had, aside from that work as reporter, little writing experience by the time that he began to write for *Household Words* in 1851. He contributed twenty items to the periodical during a period of five years. Jerrold had had considerable experience in journalism by the date that *Household Words* began and had published two books. He wrote some fifty items for the periodical, from the first to the last year of its publication, but did not contribute during every year.

Blanchard was the son of Dickens's friend Laman Blanchard; Jerrold, of Dickens's friend Douglas Jerrold. But friendship played no part in the acceptance of the contributions of the two young writers, or – with rare exception[78] – of contributions of other writers. What was accepted for publication in *Household Words* was accepted for what was considered its merit and its suitability for the periodical. In a letter to Wills, July 27, 1851, Dickens wrote, concerning a Mr. Keys: "Pray explain to him ... that whatever goes into the Journal goes in for its own sake, and not through any interest of any sort. ..."

Adelaide Procter, however, thinking that friendship might play a part in the acceptance of contributions, tactfully submitted hers under a pseudonym. Only after he had been publishing Miss Procter's poems for almost two years did Dickens discover that "Miss Berwick" was the daughter of his friend Bryan Waller Procter. Miss Procter contributed some seventy poems to *Household Words*, from 1853 to the end of the periodical's publication; they were, except for some verses contributed to the *Book of Beauty*, her first published poems. Unlike Miss Procter, George Sala, in submitting to *Household Words* his first contribution, did not keep his acquaintance with Dickens a secret. Rather, he accompanied the manuscript by a letter in which he reminded Dickens "that he had known me when I was a boy." Sala's paper was accepted, however, not on the basis of the acquaintance, but on its merits, and Sala became a regular contributor to *Household Words*. During six years he wrote more than one hundred forty items for the periodical, one of them of book length. Before becoming a *Household Words* contributor, Sala had been for some months editor of a halfpenny weekly and had published some ephemeral pieces.

At least two of the established group of writers owed their *Household Words* connection to the kind offices of a friend connected with the periodical – George Meredith to Horne, Percy Fitzgerald to John Forster. Meredith was an unpublished writer at the time that his verses began to appear in *Household Words* in 1850. He contributed some twenty items, mainly verse, but ceased to write for the periodical after 1856. (He was, incidentally, annoyed when the immature verses were identified, some fifty years later, as his writing.) Fitzgerald, the youngest of the established group of contributors, had been writing for "trifling magazines," he

78 See, in Part Two, identification note on Townshend, also on Chorley.

stated, before he became connected with *Household Words* in 1856. He contributed forty-one items, one of them in twelve instalments.

Fitzgerald wrote of Dickens's "collecting together" his "band" of *Household Words* contributors.[79] Some writers who became established contributors were, as stated above, specifically asked to write for the periodical; some who became only occasional contributors were also asked. Most contributors, however, acquainted or unacquainted with Dickens, undoubtedly sent their papers to his periodical as they did to any other miscellany – *Bentley's, Chambers's, Ainsworth's, Sharpe's* – on the chance of acceptance, and thereafter continued or discontinued their contributorship as pleased them. This statement applies to most – probably to all – of the established contributors still to be mentioned.

Among these were the Rev. Edmund Saul Dixon, George Dodd, and Henry G. Wreford, all somewhat older than Dickens. Dixon, by the time that he began to write for *Household Words,* had published a sermon and two ornithological works, as also periodical articles. From 1852 to the end of *Household Words'* publication, he contributed to the periodical more than one hundred forty items. Dodd, for many years associated with Charles Knight's cyclopaedias and other publications, had published three books by the time that he began to write for *Household Words* in 1852. He continued his connection with the periodical through August 1857, contributing some sixty items. Wreford, author of a book on Rome and, from about 1840, newspaper correspondent from Rome and from Naples, contributed twenty items to *Household Words* during 1850–58.

Among other writers who became established *Household Words* contributors were two colonial journalists – John Capper and John Lang. Both were somewhat younger than Dickens. Capper, for many years connected with the press in Ceylon and India, wrote for *Household Words* about sixty items during a period of seven years. Lang, newspaper proprietor and editor in India, had contributed to *Fraser's Magazine* a novel that was being serialized in 1853, the year in which he began to contribute to *Household Words.* He continued his connection with the periodical to the end of its publication, contributing twenty-three items, one of them in twelve instalments.

Three writers who became established *Household Words* contributors, among those still to be mentioned, had been connected with the staff of another journal before they began to write for *Household Words.* James Hannay had been for about two years on the staff of the *Morning Chronicle.* He had also been co-founder and co-editor of a short-lived comic weekly, and had published five books. During 1850–55, he contributed to *Household Words* twenty-three items. Eliza Lynn (later Mrs. Linton) had been for two years on the staff of the *Morning Chronicle.* Before becoming a *Household Words* contributor in 1853, she had published three novels. She wrote for *Household Words* to the last year of its publication, contributing more than sixty items. Walter Thornbury had been for some years on the staff of the *Athenaeum.* By 1857, when he began to contribute

79 *Memories of Charles Dickens,* p. 292.

to *Household Words*, he had published five books of prose and verse. To *Household Words* he contributed twenty-seven items.

Of other *Household Words* "regulars," some had considerable writing to their credit at the time that they began to contribute to *Household Words*; others, very little. Bayle St. John, of a "writing family," like the Trollopes, had published four books, as well as many periodical articles, by 1851, the date that he began to write for *Household Words*. He contributed forty (or forty-one) items, the last appearing in 1859. James Payn, who had brought out two volumes of poems while a Cambridge undergraduate, had at that time also begun to submit contributions to periodicals – among them, to *Household Words*. For *Household Words* he wrote, during a period of six years, more than sixty items. Harriet Parr published her first novel in 1854, the year in which she began to write for *Household Words*. She wrote for the periodical to the last year of its publication, contributing some thirty items, prose and verse. Edmund Ollier had been a periodical contributor for some years before *Household Words* began. Before the first number appeared, he had written to Dickens to ask about a connection with the periodical; he had been informed, of course, that Dickens could offer him no regular engagement, but that plans called for the use of good occasional contributions. Ollier wrote for *Household Words* almost fifty items, prose and verse, his last contribution appearing in the 1859 New Year's number. William Allingham had not yet published a volume of poems when he became a contributor to *Household Words*. One of his twenty contributions – a poem – appeared in the first number of the periodical. He did not contribute after 1857. William Moy Thomas, who had been for some years private secretary to Charles Wentworth Dilke of the *Athenaeum*, had published no books by the time that he began to contribute to *Household Words* in 1851. During a period of eight years, he wrote for the periodical more than thirty items. John Hollingshead, who began to write for *Household Words* in 1857, was motivated to become a contributor by the example of Thomas. "Like my friend, Moy Thomas," he wrote concerning his first contribution, "I threw myself boldly at *Household Words* and Charles Dickens, with a little sketch of City life. ..."[80] The sketch was accepted, as were some fifty items that Hollingshead thereafter sent to *Household Words*, the last one appearing in the final number of the periodical. Before beginning to write for *Household Words*, Hollingshead had written a farce and a few articles for the *Press* and had been for about a year a contributor to the *Train*.

Completing the list of the thirty-five writers that constituted *Household Words'* established corps were Robertson and Harper. Robertson, probably the John Robertson associated with John Stuart Mill in the editorship of the *London and Westminster Review*, began to write for *Household Words* in 1855 and continued his connection with the periodical to the last year of its publication. He contributed twenty-nine articles. Harper, not identified, contributed almost thirty poems during 1850–53.

80 *My Lifetime*, I, 94.

The established corps of contributors were competent writers. The contributors of verse wrote for the most part acceptable verses, though some of their contributions deserve higher praise than this; others illustrate Miss Mitford's observation that Dickens did "not know good verse from bad."[81] The contributors of fiction included, in Mrs. Gaskell, Collins, Miss Lynn, and Miss Parr, four of the popular novelists of the day (though Miss Lynn and Miss Parr were represented in *Household Words* by stories, rather than by novels). Payn, not yet emerged as a novelist, contributed amusing stories and sketches; Thomas contributed stories of some distinction and charm. Fitzgerald's contributions included murder and mystery stories. Two of White's stories were distinctive in their curious blending of fact and fiction. St. John's legends were pleasantly told.

Of the established group of writers who contributed mainly non-fiction prose, some wrote on subjects on which they were well informed by reason of their background, as Capper on Ceylon and India, Lang on India, Wreford on Italy. Some wrote on subjects related to their experience and professional training: Costello had been in the army, Hannay in the navy; Hunt and Morley were both licensed medical men; Morley, in addition, had been a schoolmaster, and became, in 1857, a King's College lecturer in English language and literature. On subjects of their special knowledge, these writers, and others of comparable background or experience, wrote with some authority.

Some of the contributors who wrote mainly non-fiction prose, however, were miscellaneous writers and journalists of no specialized experience or professional training. They could, and did, turn their hand to any subject. Some had, as Sala said of Blanchard, "drifted" into journalism. Hollingshead, for one, considered his having written a farce, earned a few guineas from the *Press*, and served an "apprenticeship" on the *Train* "sufficient to justify me in becoming an author and journalist."[82] The lack of experience and knowledge was, of course, no hindrance to the writers. Their familiar essays, semi-autobiographical articles, observations on men and manners and places, required no specialized knowledge. And their informational articles were intended to be popular, not technical or academic, discussions.

The established corps of contributors were well suited to carrying out Dickens's purpose of providing entertainment and instruction for his middle-class audience; they were hardly what Percy Fitzgerald called Dickens's contributors as a whole – "a brilliant array of writers."[83] By its very nature, a "cheap weekly journal of general literature" did not attract thinkers or great writers as contributors.

The list of the some three hundred fifty-five occasional contributors to *Household Words* is of interest for the names of popular writers that it includes, as also for

81 Letter to H. H. Milman, cited in Dawson's Book Shop *Catalogue 323*.

82 *My Lifetime*, I, 93–94.

83 *Recreations of a Literary Man*, pp. 37–38. Sala used the same adjective, referring to Dickens's contributors as a "brilliant staff of authors" (*Charles Dickens*, p. 87).

the names of some eminent professional men – and of obscure and unidentified writers. Of this group, almost two hundred are represented in *Household Words* by but one item each; the remainder, by from two items to nineteen (inclusive).

Like the established corps of contributors, the occasional contributors included writers whom Dickens invited to write for his periodical: William and Mary Howitt, Geraldine Jewsbury, Percival Leigh, John Delaware Lewis. The Howitts accepted the invitation willingly; Miss Jewsbury casually informed Dickens that she would write something for his periodical when she had time.

Some of his close friends among the occasional contributors – Bulwer-Lytton, Thomas Noon Talfourd, Chauncy Hare Townshend, for instance – Dickens may have asked in person for whatever stray pieces they might let him have for his periodical; and from some of these writers he apparently accepted as a gift the contributions so intended.

John Forster, as occasional contributor, occupied a position distinct from that of other contributors. In consideration of the one-eighth share that he held in *Household Words*, he was to contribute without payment occasional literary articles. Forster terminated this arrangement in 1854, having to that date written six items for *Household Words* (his total contributions), one of them a correction of his "blunder" – as Dickens called it – in a preceding item.

Among occasional contributors were other of Dickens's friends – some of old standing, some of new: Leigh Hunt, Walter Savage Landor, Bryan Waller Procter, Mark Lemon, Henry Chorley, Peter Cunningham, Albert Smith, William Howard Russell, Marguerite Power, Mary Boyle, John Westland Marston, Charles Kent, Edmund Yates. Among them were also the children of some of his old friends – the son and daughter of Thomas Hood, a son of William Johnson Fox, a daughter of William C. Macready. The widow of Sydney Smith contributed one item to *Household Words*. George Hogarth, Dickens's father-in-law, contributed four items, all but one of them to the first volume; Charles Allston Collins, later Dickens's son-in-law, contributed a few items to the later volumes.

Some of the occasional contributors had had association with Dickens on other periodicals. Charles Whitehead and William Jerdan had contributed to *Bentley's Miscellany* under Dickens's editorship. William Weir, Eyre Evans Crowe, and Joseph Archer Crowe had been engaged by Dickens on the *Daily News*.

At least two writers who became occasional contributors – Thomasina Ross and William Cox Bennett – wrote to Dickens before the first number of *Household Words* appeared to ask about writing for his forthcoming periodical. The majority of the occasional contributors, however, probably sent in their manuscripts unheralded. So, too, probably, did the numerous would-be writers who did not become contributors – occasional or otherwise. The *Household Words* article titled by the initials of Dickens's periodical – "H.W." – told of the legion of "Voluntary Correspondents" who sent to the editorial office their verses and stories and articles – the vast majority of which it was impossible to use.

Poets, among occasional contributors, ranged from the eminent to the obscure. At the head of the list was Landor, represented by one dramatic piece; next, Robert Stephen Hawker, by one poem and two prose items; Elizabeth Barrett Browning, by a sonnet (though obviously not contributed directly by her); Leigh Hunt, by contributions in both verse and prose. Among popular poets of the day whose popularity has waned were Procter, Talfourd, Edwin Arnold, Coventry Patmore, Mary Howitt, and Dora Greenwell. The once widely read William Cox Bennett appeared among the verse contributors, as did John Critchley Prince, the "factory bard," and Thomas Miller, the "basket-maker poet." Writers whose names are associated with the annuals sent an occasional verse contribution: Caroline Norton, Alaric Alexander Watts, Thomas Kibble Hervey and his wife. Theodosia Trollope, praised by Landor in her youth as a more gifted poet than Elizabeth Barrett, was represented by one poem; Mary Jane Tomkins, who in her day "had some reputation as a writer of poems," by seven. Of the some sixty other occasional contributors whose verses (sometimes also their prose writings) appeared in *Household Words*, about half cannot be identified or cannot be positively identified.

Writers of fiction represented among the occasional contributors included Charles Whitehead, Henry Spicer, Thomas Wilkinson Speight, and the women novelists whose writings were popular at the circulating libraries – Julia Kavanagh, Geraldine Jewsbury, Catherine Crowe, Georgiana Marion Craik, Dinah Maria Mulock, Emily Jolly, Henrietta Jenkin, Amelia Edwards. John Westland Marston, known as a dramatist, rather than as a story writer, contributed five stories and sketches to *Household Words*. One of Hans Christian Andersen's stories appeared in its pages, though it was obviously not contributed by its author.

Writers outside the field of letters who sent to *Household Words* articles related to their profession or to their professional experience occupy a place of some importance, in view of the many *Household Words* articles on all manner of subjects that were written by journalists and miscellaneous writers who had no special qualification for discussing the subjects that they dealt with. Robert Hunt, for instance, keeper of Mining Records for almost forty years, contributed the article "Gold in Great Britain"; Richard Owen, Thomas Satchell, William Sweetland Dallas, and Francis T. Buckland wrote occasionally on natural history; Matthew Davenport Hill and John Oswald Head sent articles connected with their field of specialization in law; the medical men Christopher Wharton Mann, William Overend Priestley, Thomas Stone, Dr. Oliver (probably Richard Oliver) contributed articles connected with their profession. Malcolm R. L. Meason's articles on the army were based on his more than ten years' military experience. William Charles Milne's articles on Chinese ways and customs had their origin in his long residence as missionary in China.

Fugitive items on subjects unrelated to the profession in which a contributor was or became prominent are of much interest. The mathematician Augustus De Morgan, for instance, sent to *Household Words* a brief memorandum concerning the signatures of the poet Edmund Waller. Frederick Law Olmsted, already known as a writer, but later important also for his work as landscape architect, contributed an article on a forthcoming American presidential election. Thomas Spencer Wells, later appointed surgeon to the Queen's Household, told of an excursion to the plains of Troy. Gustav Bergenroth, later distinguished as a historical scholar, contributed an account of his experiences among adventurers and desperadoes in California – his first published composition in English.

Some "remarkable descriptions in this Journal," stated the article "H.W.," "have come to us from wholly unaccustomed writers, who have faithfully and in thorough earnest put down what they have undergone or seen." Bergenroth was – at least in English – one of these "unaccustomed writers." So, too, in English, was Otto von Corvin, whose articles on his experiences in revolutionary Germany were revised in the editorial office to conform to English idiom. Samuel Rinder was an unaccustomed writer at the time that he sent to *Household Words* his description of the guano diggings on the islands off the coast of Peru. George Henry Snow's account of his experiences as apprentice on a South Seas whaler may well have been Snow's first and only published writing; so, too, may Lieutenant Hugh Elliot's account of his being seized by a tigress on a shooting expedition in India. Other contributors who, as far as can be ascertained, had published nothing before their articles were accepted by *Household Words* were Private William Douglas, who described life in the military prison where he was serving time; Andrew Mitchell, who recounted his adventures in Canada and in south Africa; and Mrs. Charles B. Hillier, who told of her life in Siam. The old sailor Frances Bergh, whose autobiography appeared in *Household Words*, "related," rather than wrote, the story of his fifty years of sea-faring life in war and peace. His pages are at times reminiscent of Defoe and Smollett.

Household Words' practice, during its early years, of publishing letters from emigrants resulted in a few persons' becoming contributors *malgré eux*, their letters, written to relatives and friends in England, reaching the editorial office through one means or another. One of these letter-writers was Francis Gwynne, pioneer squatter in Australia, who told of the raids of the blacks on the cattle stations held by him and his brothers. Another was a young emigrant, unidentified, who wrote of his work at a copper mine in South Australia. An emigrant named Mulock recorded his success as a farmer in the Geelong district. C. B. Harrold and his sister, working-class people from Leicestershire, wrote of their making a good livelihood during the gold-rush days in California – "a money-making place for any who will work." Letters from a Northumbrian named Harvey, many years a cattle rancher in the Argentine, appeared in *Household Words* under the title "Life in an Estancia." Finally, a letter – not to a relative or friend, but to the Conductor of *Household Words* – places the name of John Pascoe Fawkner, pioneer settler in Australia, the "Romulus" of Melbourne, in the list of *Household Words* writers.

Of the some three hundred fifty-five occasional contributors, more than one hundred are marked in the present contributor list (Part Two) as not identified; for a few additional contributors, identification is little more than a tentative suggestion.

The interest of these unidentified names lies in their very obscurity. They confirm, first of all, the statement of Dickens and his co-workers that all contributions were – if not carefully read – at least critically glanced at, and that their acceptance or rejection was based on their suitability for the periodical, not on the author's name attached to the manuscript. In the anonymous publication of material, all distinction of authorship vanished. The story or sketch of the unknown writer held equal place with that of the writer of reputation – indeed, with that of Dickens himself. The obscure names testify, also, to the appeal of Dickens's periodical – an appeal inherent in the very ordinariness of some of its content. In the humble verses, the uninspired account of a dull journey, the tiresome relation of trivial happenings that appeared in some of its pages, the commonplace reader saw so true a reflection of his own interests that the periodical seemed the destined place of publication for his own attempts at authorship.

Whether occasional contributors or regular, writers set store by their writings that had been found acceptable for publication in Dickens's journal. More than seventy-five writers reprinted their contributions, in whole or part, from Mary Eliza Rogers – her one poem, to Sala – some hundred of his prose writings. In all, more than nine hundred contributed items, ranging from a quatrain to a two-volume novel, were held worthy by their contributors to appear between the covers of a book.

THE *HOUSEHOLD WORDS* OFFICE BOOK

The basis for the authorship ascription recorded in the present Table of Contents to *Household Words* is the *Household Words* Office Book, in the Morris L. Parrish Collection of Victorian Novelists, Princeton University Library.

The Office Book bears on its cover no indication of its content, but to the free half of the front end-paper, recto, is pasted the notation:

> This Office Book of Household Words belonged to William Henry Wills who was Charles Dickens's sub editor. It covers every issue of Household Words. Mr. Wills entered in this book the names of all the contributors with the titles of their articles and the amounts paid for them.

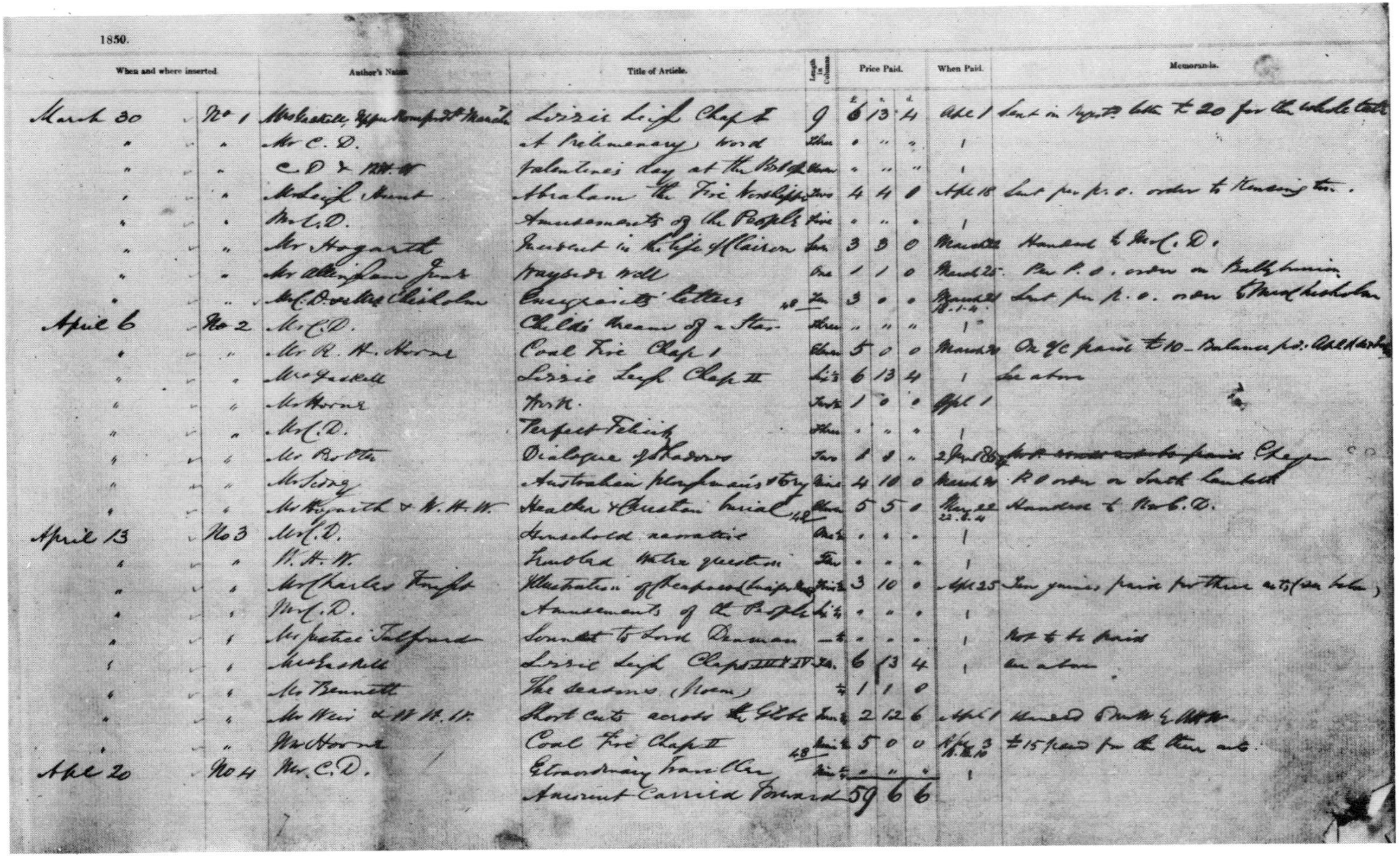

1850.

When and where inserted		Author's Name	Title of Article	Length in Columns	Price Paid £	s.	d.	When Paid	Memoranda
March 30	No 1	Mrs Gaskell, Upper Rumford St Manchester	Lizzie Leigh Chap I	9	6	13	4	Apl 1	Sent in [illegible] letter £20 for the whole tale
"	"	Mr C.D.	A Preliminary word	three	"	"	"	1	
"	"	C.D. & W.H.W.	Valentine's day at the Workhouse	[illegible]	"	"	"	1	
"	"	Mr Leigh Hunt	Abraham the Fire Worshipper	two	4	4	0	Apl 18	Sent per p.o. order to Kensington.
"	"	Mr C.D.	Amusements of the People	five	"	"	"	1	
"	"	Mr Hogarth	Incident in the Life of Mlle Clairon	two	3	3	0	March 28	Handed to Mr C.D.
"	"	Mr Allingham Junr	Wayside well	one	1	1	0	March 25	Per P.O. order on Ballyshannon
"	"	Mr C.D. & Mrs Chisholm	Emigrants' letters	two	3	0	0	[illegible]	Sent per p.o. order to Mrs Chisholm
April 6	No 2	Mr C.D.	Child's dream of a Star	three	"	"	"	1	
"	"	Mr R.H. Horne	Coal Fire Chap I	three	5	0	0	March 30	On a/c paid £10 – Balance pd. [illegible]
"	"	Mrs Gaskell	Lizzie Leigh Chap II	[illegible]	6	13	4	1	See above
"	"	Mr Horne	Work.	two	1	0	0	Apl 1	
"	"	Mr C.D.	Perfect Felicity	three	"	"	"	1	
"	"	Mr Potter	Dialogue of Shadows	two	1	1	"	2 June 1850	[illegible] Cheque
"	"	Mr Sidney	Australian Ploughman's story	nine	4	10	0	March 30	P.O. order on South Lambeth
"	"	Mr Hogarth & W.H.W.	Heathen & Christian burial	eleven	5	5	0	May 22	Handed to Mr C.D.
April 13	No 3	Mr C.D.	Household narrative	[illegible]	"	"	"	1	
"	"	W.H.W.	Troubled water question	ten	"	"	"	1	
"	"	Mr Charles Knight	Illustrations of cheapness ([illegible])	[illegible]	3	10	0	Apl 25	Ten guineas paid for three acts (see below)
"	"	Mr C.D.	Amusements of the People	[illegible]	"	"	"	1	
"	"	Mr Justice Talfourd	Sonnet to Lord Denman	—	"	"	"	1	Not to be paid
"	"	Mrs Gaskell	Lizzie Leigh Chaps III & IV	[illegible]	6	13	4	1	See above.
"	"	Mr Bennett	The seasons (Poem)	¼	1	1	0		
"	"	Mr Weir & W.H.W.	Short Cuts across the Globe	[illegible]	2	12	6	Apl 1	Handed to Mr W & W.H.W.
"	"	Mr Horne	Coal Fire Chap II	[illegible]	5	0	0	[illegible]	£15 paid for the three acts.
Apl 20	No 4	Mr C.D.	Extraordinary traveller	[illegible]	"	"	"	1	
			Amount Carried Forward		59	6	6		

Plate 2 First page of the *Household Words* Office Book. Reproduced by permission of the Morris L. Parrish Collection of Victorian Novelists, Princeton University Library

This notation substitutes for an earlier one pasted in the Office Book and then removed. The earlier notation is cited by B. W. Matz, who used the Office Book (then in the possession of R. C. Lehmann) for the identification of Dickens's *Household Words* writings that he included in the National Edition of Dickens's *Works*, 1906–1908. In his "Introduction" to the volume titled *Miscellaneous Papers* in that edition, Matz stated, concerning the Office Book: "In order that no doubt may exist as to the genuineness of this book we quote the certificate of its authenticity which is pasted in the front cover ...":

Westbrook Hall
Horsham,
Surrey.

1*st* Feby., 1903.

This book belonged to Mr. Wills and was left to me by his widow, my Aunt Janet.

I now present it to my nephew Rudolph Lehmann as a memento of Mr. and Mrs. Wills, who loved him as a child.

(Signed)
Eliza Priestley.

(Matz's words "front cover" should read "front end-paper." There is no evidence that anything was ever pasted to the inside of the front cover of the Office Book. But when held up to the light, the front end-paper shows thin spots in the section where the present note is pasted. The thin spots indicate that something pasted to the page has been pulled away.)

The history of the Office Book is, thus, as follows: After Wills's death in 1880, it became the possession of his widow, Janet Chambers Wills, who survived her husband by twelve years. Mrs. Wills left the book to her niece Eliza Chambers Priestley; Lady Priestley presented it in 1903 to her nephew Rudolph Chambers Lehmann; from him it passed into the possession of his son, John Lehmann, Esq., London. In 1961 it became the property of Princeton University Library.

The Office Book is a bulky, oblong ledger (26½ x 42 cm.) bound in black cloth over boards with brown leather corners and spine. The pages of the ledger are ruled for seven headings: "When and where inserted," "Author's Name," "Title of Article," "Length in Columns," "Price Paid," "When Paid," "Memoranda" (see Plate 2). The printed date 1850 appears above the horizontal rule in the upper left-hand corner on each page. The title "Household Words" is not printed or written on the pages. The ledger shows evidence of its almost daily handling for more than nine years in the *Household Words* editorial office. The leather corners are worn; the front cover is partially broken from the binding.

The Office Book covers every number of *Household Words*, the entries for all but three of the numbers being in Wills's handwriting.[84] The early pages of the book are crowded with entries, no space being left between those for one number and those for another. In later pages, blank lines separate the entries for the various numbers.

The Office Book is a carefully kept record; but it is, of course, a working record, with, inevitably, certain mis-recordings and omissions. Four numbers are misdated.[85] The entries for No. 264 are begun, then marked out because of error and written (still not correctly) below. Entries for two numbers, No. 365 in part and No. 385 in entirety, are recorded for the wrong week of publication, then marked out and written in their proper place. The entries for No. 417 are twice recorded, once in the proper place and again two numbers later, the second listing being marked out.

The notations recorded in the various columns are as indicated by the column headings. Entries in the memoranda-column concern mainly the manner and disposition of payment for items (see below) and the revision of items. Such notations are more frequent in early pages than in later ones. Wills evidently began his record with the intention that it should include all information concerning items published, but later found such detailed notation unnecessary. The column headed "Length in Columns" is not filled in for all entries. The lengths recorded for items generally approximate the length of items as they were printed. Some length notations are so blotted or overwritten as to be almost or entirely indecipherable.

The Office Book payment record is not entirely complete. For Mrs. Gaskell's *North and South* and for Sala's *A Journey Due North* the payment is not recorded. For some twenty other items that are actual writings of contributors and intended to be paid for,[86] the payment is not recorded. Some of these ("Degree Day at Cambridge," for instance, and "Locking Up the Tower of London") are by unnamed contributors, but all are not. One is by William Jerdan,[87] one by Marguerite Power, and one by John Hollingshead. Payments made or credited to Dickens for his *Household Words* writings are not recorded. Under the terms of the agreement under which *Household Words* was set up, Dickens was to receive payment for such writings.

Payment notations recorded in error appear for occasional items by Horne, Morley, and Collins written during the time that these writers were staff mem-

84 In Nos. 252, 253, and 254, authors' names and the titles of items, as also the length notations, are in another hand.

85 Nos. 54, 260, 261, 383. For Nos. 260 and 261, notations signed "B. W. Matz" indicate the error and its correction.

86 Not intended to be paid for, because not considered actual contributions, were readers' letters, published in *H.W.*, which merely corrected or qualified a statement in a *H.W.* article, stated information in addition to that given in an article, or asked *H.W.* to give publicity to a matter. T. N. Talfourd's contributions were evidently intended not to be paid for. The first is marked "Not to be paid"; payment for none is recorded.

87 In a letter to Jerdan, Dickens recorded sending him Wills's cheque in payment for the item for which the Office Book records no payment; the letter does not state the amount of the cheque.

bers, during which time their writings were considered as paid for in their staff salary; also recorded in error is the payment notation for an item by Sala contributed during the time that he was being paid on a basis other than that of payment for individual items. All but three of these notations are marked out.[88]

For a few early numbers of *Household Words*, the Office Book records the total amount paid for contributed items in each number; on the first and the second page of the Office Book, the amounts paid for contributed items are totalled at the foot of the payment-column. For items consisting of several instalments, the Office Book frequently records the total payment for the item, usually with payment notations also for the individual instalments (these notations being intended, obviously, for calculation of the total amount paid for contributed items in any one number). For an occasional item, there is a discrepancy between the total payment recorded and the sum of the payment notations for individual instalments. In payment notations for items of joint authorship by non-staff members, the amount allotted to each writer is usually, though not always, recorded. Some payment notations are so blotted or overwritten as to be almost indecipherable.

Office Book entries frequently state the manner in which payment for items was made, as by cash, cheque, post-office order, draft. Some entries state the contributor's address to which payment was sent; some state other disposition of payment. Amounts due to Grenville Murray, for instance, are at times recorded as deposited to Murray's account at Coutts's; payment for some of Charles Knight's contributions, as taken to Knight's Fleet Street office. Payments sent or handed to a person other than the contributor are so recorded. A post-office order for each of Matthew Davenport Hill's contributions, for instance, is recorded as sent to Miss Hill; payment for one of Dora Greenwell's poems, as "Handed to Mrs. Tom Taylor"; payment for a contribution by Florence Wilson (then in St. Petersburg), as "Handed to Mrs. Wills to send to Miss F.W." Payment for some of Louisa Costello's contributions is recorded as made by cheque to her brother Dudley. A frequent payment notation is "Enclosed & fetched," meaning, apparently, that payment was enclosed in an envelope and handed to the contributor at the editorial office. Many payments are marked "Advanced."

The order in which items are listed in the Office Book was meant to be the order in which they were to appear in *Household Words*. In twenty numbers, however, the Office Book order differs slightly from the *Household Words* order. (The most obvious of the differences is the entry for Dickens's "A Preliminary Word," which in the Office Book follows, rather than precedes, the entry for Mrs. Gaskell's "Lizzie Leigh.") For one number, in addition, the Office Book lists an item twice, first in the position in which it appeared in *Household Words*, then again at the end of the listing.

88 The three not marked out record payment for items by Morley. One of the payments recorded (that for "Forty Famous Arm-Chairs") is marked "Cheque" with date of payment. This entire payment notation may be in error; or the payment may be an exception to the regular payment arrangement.

Titles of items as recorded in the Office Book do not always accord with titles as they appeared in *Household Words*. Some entries, obviously, Wills wrote in haste. Occasional words in titles he misspelled. Long titles he at times abbreviated; some he jotted down, apparently, as he recollected them at the moment, sometimes at variance with what was obviously the proper wording that appeared in *Household Words*. "The Tomb in Ghent," for instance, stands in the Office Book as "The Tombs of Ghent"; "A Small Monkish Relic" as "A Small Monkish Legend." Occasional titles Wills may have altered from the form in which he had originally recorded them in the Office Book, as "A Smock-Frock Parliament," which appears in the Office Book as "Smock Frocks in Parliament."

Fifteen items published in *Household Words* the Office Book does not list. Some of them (in Vol. I) are "fillers"; some are poems; some are "chips"; some are full-length articles. Among the omitted items are Leigh Hunt's quatrain "Dream within Dream" and Hollingshead's "How I Fell among Monsters."

Authors' names are variously recorded in the Office Book. Some are, in some entries, given in full (Florence Wilson, for instance, Edmund Ollier, Peter Cunningham); for some, the surname is, in some entries, accompanied by some part of the given name or by initial or initials; most frequently, however, only the surname is given. Wills's name is recorded by initials only, as is that of an occasional other author; Dickens's name is almost always so recorded. Some authors are listed by the pseudonym under which they contributed; Murray, on occasion, is listed by the initials of the pseudonym that he acquired as *Household Words* contributor. An author's name is sometimes accompanied by an address (as Mrs. Crowe, Edinburgh; Dr. Russell, Maynooth).

Not all authors' names are correctly written. One of Matthew Davenport Hill's articles, for instance, is listed as by "D. M. Hill"; one of Bryan Waller Procter's poems, as by "W. B. Procter." Sidney Blanchard's name appears in its correct spelling, but also with the spelling "Blanshard"; Andrew Wynter appears also as "Winter"; John Lang, also as "Laing." Hollingshead's name is rarely written correctly.

For some fifteen items, a contributor's name is entered as author, then erased or marked out, and substituted by another (in one entry, not substituted by another). "The Shadow of the Hand," for instance, is assigned to Miss Procter, the name being corrected to read "Miss Macready"; "A Daisy on a Grave" is assigned to Mrs. MacIntosh, then reassigned correctly to Mrs. Broderip.

At least five misassignments, however, stand uncorrected: Robert McCormick's "Christmas in the Frozen Regions" to "Dr. Cormack"; William Knighton's "The Buried City of Ceylon" to "Kingston"; Miss Procter's "The Two Interpreters" to Prince and her "Patient and Faithful" to Yates; Sophia De Morgan's "A Plea for Playgrounds" to Mrs. Howitt. A sixth misassignment is Jennett Humphreys's "Walker" to "J.R."; in this entry, the contributor's name, written in another hand than Wills's, appears after the recorded initials.

As stated above, the Office Book does not list every item published in *Household Words*; likewise, it does not record the author of every item that it lists. For some items it gives non-specific or partial authorship; for some it gives none. Non-specific or partial authorship notation accompanies twenty-one items. The non-specific ascriptions are the notations "Correspondent," "Chance correspondent," "Communicated," and "Anonymous." Partial indication of authorship – or, actually, of revision – occurs in such entries as " ——— & Mr. Horne," "——— & Morley." Such partial authorship indication appears also with occasional items of non-specific ascription, as "Correspondent & W.H.W."[89] In addition, four contributors are listed by the designation "friend": "Mrs. Gaskell's friend," for instance, is credited with the story "Coralie"; "Miss Lynn's friend," with three poems.

For thirty-six items, however, neither the above-mentioned authorship-designations nor any other are recorded in the Office Book author-column.

Two of these omissions of author's name result from errors in recording – the repetition of the title in the author-column. Five omissions occur in the instances in which the Office Book records, instead of the author of an item, only the name of the person responsible for directing it to the editorial office. The poem "The Outcast Lady," for instance, is indicated merely as "per Mrs. Gaskell"; "Life in the Burra Mines of South Australia" (a letter from an emigrant), as "per R. Bell." In the remaining twenty-nine entries the author-column is simply left blank,[90] except that, for one item, is entered the beginning of an authorship ascription ("Mrs. ——— ") and for another is entered, then marked out, an author's name.

Among the entries for which a blank occurs in the author-column are "The Sower" by Henry Morley, "Leaves from Lima" by Clements R. Markham, and "A Small Monkish Relic" by Francis T. Buckland. These titles stand, respectively, next below the entry for an item by Wills, one by William Moy Thomas, and one by Arnold Ruge. Clearly, therefore, the blank in the author-column does not have the value of ditto marks; that is, it does not mean that the item by which it occurs is by the author of the item listed immediately above.

The unwarranted assumption that this was so has led to the misattribution of some *Household Words* items. Matz, in the National Edition of Dickens's *Works*, attributed to Dickens Mrs. Browning's sonnet "Hiram Power's [*sic*] Greek Slave" and the verse "Aspire!" (authorship not ascertained). Neither item is assigned in the Office Book; each stands next below the entry for an item by Dickens. C. K. Shorter, in the World's Classics Edition of Mrs. Gaskell's *Novels and Tales* (Vol. x, 1915), attributed to Mrs. Gaskell the verse "A Christmas Carol" (authorship not

89 Howitt, however, had no part in the writing of "A Colonial Patriot," assigned to "Correspondent & Howitt." See, in Part Two, identification note on Fawkner.

90 For the entry of one of the items ("Summer in Rome") there appears, in the memoranda-column, the notation that payment for the item was sent to J. Kenyon. Kenyon was not the author of the item.

ascertained). The item is unassigned in the Office Book; it stands next below the entry for an item by Mrs. Gaskell.[91]

Of the some three thousand items listed in the Office Book, more than two hundred – mainly articles, but also some stories and poems – are accompanied by more than one name in the author-column. In most of these entries, the name of an outside contributor (occasionally two outside contributors) stands with that of a member (occasionally two members) of the *Household Words* staff. In some entries stand the names of two staff members; in one, the names of three. In addition, in a few entries stand the names of two writers neither of whom was connected with the editorial office. The staff member listed most frequently in the entries is Wills; next, Morley, then Dickens; occasionally, in the early pages, Horne.

The joint names have various significances. For an occasional article – "A Bundle of Emigrants' Letters," for instance, or "The Poor Brothers of the Charterhouse" – they mean no more than that the person whose name appears jointly with that of the staff member provided the information for the article. For some items the joint names mean joint composition of an item or the writing by two authors of individual sections of an item. Examples are "One Man in a Dockyard," assigned in the Office Book to Dickens and Horne, and "The Lazy Tour of Two Idle Apprentices," assigned to Dickens and Wilkie Collins. The first was the result of a visit to Chatham by Dickens and Horne, made for the purpose of viewing the dockyard as the basis of a descriptive article; in a letter to Wills, July 30, 1851, Dickens had outlined his plan for the article. The second had its genesis in Dickens's asking Collins (August 29, 1857) to suggest a tour or other expedition on which "we could write something together."

More frequently, however, the joint names mean not co-authorship of items, but editorial revision and rewriting of items. This applies to items written by staff members, which were revised or rewritten by other staff members – Dickens

91 In "Some Unknown Poems of George Meredith," *T.P.'s Weekly*, Feb. 17, 1911, Matz stated that while going through the Office Book to find items previously unidentified as Dickens's writing, he "also discovered half a dozen stories by Mrs. Gaskell," which discovery he "put at the service of Messrs. Smith, Elder and Co., and made it possible for the stories to be included in their Knutsford edition of Mrs. Gaskell's works." The Knutsford Edition (1906) contains three *H.W.* articles (not stories) by Mrs. Gaskell which she had not herself reprinted, but for her authorship of which there is evidence outside the Office Book. (See, in Part Two, identification note on Mrs. Gaskell.) The World's Classics Edition of Mrs. Gaskell's works contains, in addition to the three *H.W.* prose items that Mrs. Gaskell had not reprinted, three *H.W.* verse items: "Bran," "The Scholar's Story," and "A Christmas Carol." Shorter stated that the basis of his attribution to Mrs. Gaskell of "some [*H.W.*] poems not before gathered into volume form" was the Office Book, then in the possession of R. C. Lehmann, which Shorter either consulted himself or had consulted for him. In Vol. x of the World's Classics Edition, he wrote: "I am indebted to the courtesy of Mr. R. C. Lehmann for being able to identify these contributions of Mrs. Gaskell to *Household Words*." (For explanation of Shorter's misattribution to Mrs. Gaskell of "Bran" and "The Scholar's Story," see, in Part Two, identification note on William Gaskell.)

or Wills (or both), and to items written by outside contributors, which were revised or rewritten by staff members.

Examples of articles written by staff members which were revised or rewritten by other staff members are Morley's "Soldiers' Wives" and "The Stereoscope" and Wilkie Collins's "Doctor Dulcamara, M.P." The joint names recorded for these items in the Office Book accord with Dickens's instructions to Wills concerning the articles. Of "Soldiers' Wives," Dickens wrote to Wills (August 22, 1851) that the introductory part "must be entirely re-written." Wills must have done so; he assigned the article to himself and to Morley. "The Stereoscope" Dickens criticized to Wills (August 5, 1853) as "dreadfully literal." Wills must have attempted to make it less literal; he assigned it to Morley and to himself. "Doctor Dulcamara," Dickens wrote to Wills (November 10, 1858), was not to go to press "without my seeing it." Dickens must have revised the article or added material to it; Wills assigned it to Collins and Dickens.

Among items written by outside contributors which were revised or rewritten by staff members are certain articles by Murray and by Wreford for which Morley's name is jointly listed in the Office Book. The joint names accord with the account of Morley's editorial duties as recorded in *The Life of Henry Morley* – his "turn[ing] into an article," for instance, material sent in by Murray ("a gentleman at Vienna") and his "recasting" material sent in by Wreford (material "from Naples") to make it "suitable for the journal."[92]

For occasional items, Wills indicated revision or rewriting not by the record of joint names in the author-column, but by a notation in the memoranda-column. "Spy Police," for instance, assigned in the Office Book to Wreford alone, is marked "Cut down from three times the quantity by W.H.W."; "Troops and Jobs in Malta," assigned to Wenckstern alone, is marked "The result of a great pile of MS."

Not all items that were revised or rewritten, however, are accompanied in the Office Book by joint names or by notation of revision. Allingham's "The Lady Alice" must have undergone some alteration in the editorial office; at least, Allingham complained of its editorial mutilation. Yet the Office Book records for the poem neither joint name nor memorandum of revision. Dickens, as his letters to Wills indicate, made changes in Sala's "The Key of the Street," "The Foreign Invasion," and other papers (Sala himself mentioned the alteration of some of his papers by Dickens); yet the Office Book lists only one of Sala's contributions – "First Fruits" – as by "Sala & C.D." Mrs. Marsh's "The Spendthrift's Daughter" Dickens practically rewrote; yet the Office Book does not list Dickens's name jointly with that of Mrs. Marsh. Various other entries might be cited to indicate that Wills's recording, or not recording, of the reviser's name was frequently arbitrary. Also, of course, Wills could have had no predetermined or absolute standard for the amount of revision that he thought warranted his writing the

92 Solly, *The Life of Henry Morley*, p. 196.

reviser's name jointly with that of the author. For an occasional item he was of two minds as to whether or not to record the reviser's name. "How I Went to Sea" stands in the Office Book as by "Sala & C.D.," the "& C.D." being marked out; "A Lift in a Cart" stands as by "Mr. Duthie & Morley," the "& Morley" being marked out.

In itself, the record of the joint names does not, of course, indicate the nature or the extent of revision. Only for a few items so assigned is there a notation stating that the item was "altered," "partly rewritten," or "rewritten." One such item, "A Day in a Pauper Palace," assigned to Taylor and Wills, is accompanied by the notation "Rewritten almost entirely by W.H.W. & abridged one half."

The usual order in which joint names stand in the author-column is what would seem to be the normal order, that is, the author first, the reviser second. The significance of deviation from this order, if it has significance, can only be guessed at. Of Thomasina Ross's three articles that he revised, Wills assigned two to Miss Ross and himself, the other to himself and Miss Ross. Of three articles by William Weir that he revised, Wills again recorded two as by Weir and himself, the other as by himself and Weir. The reversal of names may perhaps indicate that Wills's revision was extensive.

In recording joint names of which Dickens's was one, Wills likewise placed Dickens's name (actually, his initials) first for certain articles that Dickens merely revised. Examples are Morley's "The Wind and the Rain" and Murray's "On Her Majesty's Service." Again, the order of names may indicate that Wills considered Dickens's revision extensive; or it may merely indicate that he attached some prestige to position No. 1 among the writers listed in the author-column and that he for that reason allotted that position to Dickens. The latter suggestion seems supported by Wills's Office Book recording of his own articles written in collaboration with Dickens or revised by Dickens. Of the fifteen such articles that he reprinted as his writing (with acknowledgment to Dickens for their "brightest tints"), twelve he had assigned in the Office Book not to "W.H.W. & C.D.," but to "C.D. & W.H.W." (or to "Mr. C.D. & W.H.W."). The yielding of first place to Dickens here seems a gesture of courtesy or respect.

In a letter to Miss Ross, January 21, 1850, Dickens explained that the plan of *Household Words* made it impossible to attach authors' names to their contributions. However, he added, "I don't anticipate any objection to their [i.e., the names'] appearing in the Index to the volume." Dickens evidently made the suggestion without serious intention of carrying it into effect. No index with contributors' names was ever published to any volume of *Household Words.*

In the absence of a published index, confusion has resulted concerning the authorship of *Household Words* items, the extent of various writers' contributions, and, indeed, whether or not certain writers actually were contributors.

Confusion on the last of these matters resulted, in part, from the fact that Dickens began publication of *All the Year Round*, the successor to *Household Words*, before he terminated *Household Words*. For five weeks (April 30-May 28, 1859) the two periodicals appeared simultaneously.

Writers who contributed to both periodicals stated, at times, that an item that they had contributed to the first had appeared in the second, or vice versa. Percy Fitzgerald, for instance, listed "Down among the Dutchmen," his only extended contribution to *Household Words*, as one of his contributions to *All the Year Round*.[93] Dickens himself was at times confused as to who had written for the first periodical and who for the second. In a letter of December 25, 1868, he referred to the type of subjects that he had "invariably offered" to J. C. Parkinson during "my editorship both of Household Words and All the Year Round." Parkinson was not a contributor to *Household Words*.

Similarly, compilers of anthologies and biographical works, as well as commentators on Dickens, have confused the contributors to the two periodicals or have designated as frequent contributors to *Household Words* writers of but three or four items – or of none. Miles's *The Poets and the Poetry of the Century*, for instance, records William James Linton's "Grenville's Last Fight" as appearing in *Household Words*, whereas the poem actually appeared in *All the Year Round*. The *Dictionary of National Biography* records Amelia Edwards as doing, in her early literary career, "a good deal of work for 'Household Words' and 'All the Year Round,' usually providing the ghost story for Dickens's Christmas numbers." Miss Edwards's only contribution to *Household Words* was a story published in one of the regular numbers. J. W. T. Ley stated that Edmund Yates was "a frequent contributor" to *Household Words*;[94] Yates contributed four items. Percy Fitzgerald wrote that "Owen Meredith" "used to furnish contributions ... in prose and verse" to both of Dickens's periodicals;[95] Owen Meredith contributed to *All the Year Round*, not to *Household Words*. Commentators who recorded Thomas Adolphus Trollope as a *Household Words* contributor had Trollope's own statement as the basis for their assertion. "I was for several years a frequent contributor to *Household Words*," wrote Trollope, "my contributions for the most part consisting of what I considered tid-bits from the byways of Italian history, which the persevering plough of my reading turned up from time to time."[96] Trollope's tid-bits of Italian history appeared in *All the Year Round*.

The only trustworthy record of *Household Words* contributors, of course, is that kept by Wills in the *Office Book*; and, in that nine-year record, even the methodical and careful Wills made an occasional mis-recording.

93 *Memoirs of an Author*, Vol. II, "Bibliography."

94 *The Dickens Circle*, p. 298. Ley based his statement on the comment by Yates (*Recollections and Experiences*, pp. 197–98) that he made his first appearance in *H.W.* in 1856 and became thereafter "a frequent contributor."

95 *Memories of Charles Dickens*, p. 278.

96 *What I Remember*, p. 357.

BIBLIOGRAPHICAL NOTE

REGULAR AND EXTRA NUMBERS

Household Words consisted of 479 "regular" numbers and eight "extra" Christmas numbers. Regular numbers were understood to contain twenty-four pages each; that is, the thirty-six-page extra numbers were announced as "containing the amount of One Regular Number and a Half." Nineteen regular numbers, however, contained only twenty pages. The price of regular numbers was twopence. The numbers bore a Saturday date but appeared on the preceding Wednesday. The number for January 1, 1859, was announced as "A New Year's Number," but was not so designated on the masthead of the number.

The 1851 extra Christmas number contained twenty-four pages. All following extra Christmas numbers contained thirty-six. The price of the 1851 extra Christmas number was twopence; that of the following extra Christmas numbers, threepence. Some extra Christmas numbers appeared early in December; one (according to the announced publication date), as late as December 19. The 1851 extra Christmas number was titled simply "Extra Number for Christmas"; all following extra Christmas numbers were individually titled (see Table, p. 513). The extra Christmas number for each year was usually bound in the current *Household Words* volume.

ISSUANCE

Household Words was issued in weekly numbers, in "Monthly Parts," and in volume form.

The weekly numbers were issued without wrappers.

The monthly parts, price ninepence, containing four or five weekly numbers, were issued with wrappers. The wrapper of one of the 1857 monthly parts, in the Brotherton Collection, University of Leeds Library, is blue.

The nineteen bound volumes of *Household Words* each contained from twenty-four to twenty-six weekly numbers, thus extending over approximately a half year of publication. The half-yearly volume was normally available within a week or two weeks after the publication of the last weekly number included in it, though Vol. I, which ended with the number of September 21, 1850, was announced as to be published on September 20. The volumes were described in *Household Words* advertisement as "Bound in cloth," "neatly Bound in Cloth," or as bound in "cloth boards," price five shillings sixpence. Of the sets of these volumes in contemporary binding that I have seen, some are bound in brown cloth, some in greyish black, some in drab green; some are bound in marbled paper boards, with leather corners and spine.

In addition to the nineteen individually bound volumes, double-volumes were made available "for greater convenience, and cheapness of binding." The first such volumes, brought out in February 1855, consisted of the ten volumes thus far published "bound in Five Double instead of Ten Single Volumes." They were described in *Household Words* advertisements as "five handsome volumes, with a general index to the whole"; they were also referred to as the "Library Edition." In eighteen advertisements the price of the set of Vols. I-X, bound in the five double-volumes, was stated to be £2.10.0; in two advertisements the price was stated to be £2.12.6. The double-volume set that I have seen is bound in marbled paper boards, with leather corners and spine. The words "Library Edition" do not appear on the title page.

VARIANT READINGS IN COPIES

The printed text of *Household Words* numbers was reproduced on stereotyped plates, copies in addition to those originally issued being printed from the plates as demand warranted. The non-textual material set below the double rule that encloses the text (that is, the publisher-printer imprint and the notation of volume and number) seems in some copies to have been a part of the stereotyped plate; in other copies, not.

The publisher-printer imprint, appearing below the double rule at the end of every number and usually reading "Published at the Office, No. 16, Wellington Street North, Strand. Printed by BRADBURY & EVANS, Whitefriars, London," differs, in some printings of the same number, in its position on the page and in punctuation. In some printings of No. 19, mention of Bradbury & Evans is substituted by the notation "Published every Saturday" and a statement of the price and the issuance in monthly parts. In No. 384, where the usual publisher-printer imprint is substituted by "London: Published at the Office, No. 16, Wellington Street North, Strand. New York: DIX & EDWARDS," "London" is, in some printings, followed by a colon; in other printings, not.

The notation of volume and number that appears below the double rule at the foot of the first page of every regular number differs, in some printings of the same number, in its position on the page, in punctuation (presence or absence of periods), and occasionally in the notation itself. In one printing of No. 25, for instance, the notation reads VOL. I.; in another printing, merely VOL. In one printing of No. 388, the notation reads (correctly) VOL. XVI.; in another printing it reads (incorrectly) VOL. XV (no period).

Writing to an angry reader who wanted himself disassociated from an item that had appeared in *Household Words*, Dickens stated: "... it is quite out of the question that the text of the article can be altered in future copies (for it is printed and stereotyped and done with). ..."[97] All copies of any one number of *Household Words* printed by Bradbury & Evans should therefore be identical. A comparison of several copies of the same number indicates that this is so (except as noted below); that is, changes were not made in "future copies" to correct, for example, typographical errors and errors in use of apostrophes. All copies that I have seen contain, for instance, the comma and period at the end of the subtitle "An Adventure in the Bush" (I, 141, col. 1), the reading "ercently" for "recently" (I, 341, col. 2), "may he seen" for "may be seen" (XII, 452, col. 1), "dailed peopled" for "daily peopled" (XVI, 301, col. 1); and "childrens' cause" (XI, 582, col. 1), "childrens' books" (XIV, 291, col. 2).

A change was made, however, in the advertisement (for bound Vol. XVIII) that appears at the end of No. 452. One printing reads "Containing from No. 430 ..."; another reads "Containing from No. 480. ..."

The change made in an article in the first number of *Household Words* was so extensive that it makes of subsequently printed copies a second issue. In the original issue of the number, "A Bundle of Emigrants' Letters" ends at the top of the second column on page 24, the remaining space in the column being taken up by two paragraphs that serve as "fillers" – "Milking in Australia," from an unpublished work, and "Metal in Sea-Water," from the *Athenaeum*. In the reissue, the text of "A Bundle of Emigrants' Letters" that appears in the first column is in part changed, and the article is lengthened to occupy the entire space of the second column (see Plates 3 and 4). (In the original issue, the publisher-printer imprint appears above the double rule that encloses the text; in the reissue, it appears below the double rule, as in other numbers.) This is the only variant in text that I have found in *Household Words*.

The deletion of the *Athenaeum* paragraph, and, at the same time, of the excerpt from the unpublished work, obviously resulted from the decision not to use "selected" material in *Household Words*. Dickens had at first thought of using such material.

INDEXES

Preceding the text in each bound volume of *Household Words* appear two pages marked "Contents." "Contents" is not a table of contents, but an index, listing alphabetically the items contained in the volume, almost always by title, and, for many items, also by content words or phrases or by variations of the title words. For some items there are ten or more such entries; some are arbitrary; some are uninformative. For the article "Economic Botany" appear eighteen content phrases, some of them referring to products only briefly mentioned in the article. For "A

97 To Holman Hunt, in Diana Holman-Hunt, *My Grandfather, His Wives and Loves*, p. 193.

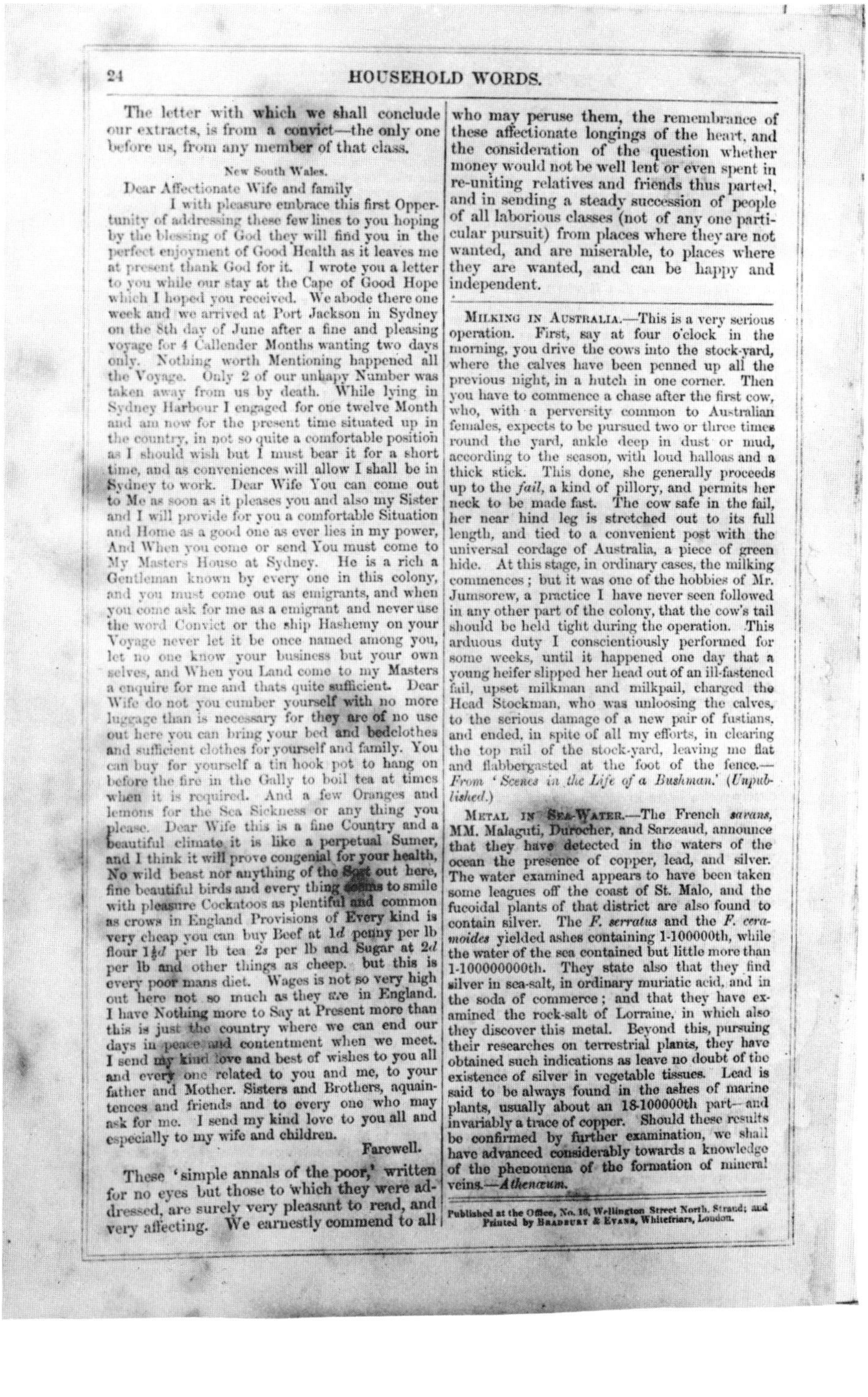

24 HOUSEHOLD WORDS.

The letter with which we shall conclude our extracts, is from a convict—the only one before us, from any member of that class.

New South Wales.

Dear Affectionate Wife and family

I with pleasure embrace this first Oppertunity of addressing these few lines to you hoping by the blessing of God they will find you in the perfect enjoyment of Good Health as it leaves me at present thank God for it. I wrote you a letter to you while our stay at the Cape of Good Hope which I hoped you received. We abode there one week and we arrived at Port Jackson in Sydney on the 8th day of June after a fine and pleasing voyage for 4 Callender Months wanting two days only. Nothing worth Mentioning happened all the Voyage. Only 2 of our unhapy Number was taken away from us by death. While lying in Sydney Harbour I engaged for one twelve Month and am now for the present time situated up in the country, in not so quite a comfortable position as I should wish but I must bear it for a short time, and as conveniences will allow I shall be in Sydney to work. Dear Wife You can come out to Me as soon as it pleases you and also my Sister and I will provide for you a comfortable Situation and Home as a good one as ever lies in my power, And When you come or send You must come to My Masters House at Sydney. He is a rich a Gentleman known by every one in this colony, and you must come out as emigrants, and when you come ask for me as a emigrant and never use the word Convict or the ship Hashemy on your Voyage never let it be once named among you, let no one know your business but your own selves, and When you Land come to my Masters a enquire for me and thats quite sufficient. Dear Wife do not you cumber yourself with no more luggage than is necessary for they are of no use out here you can bring your bed and bedclothes and sufficient clothes for yourself and family. You can buy for yourself a tin hook pot to hang on before the fire in the Gally to boil tea at times when it is required. And a few Oranges and lemons for the Sea Sickness or any thing you please. Dear Wife this is a fine Country and a beautiful climate it is like a perpetual Sumer, and I think it will prove congenial for your health, No wild beast nor anything of the Sort out here, fine beautiful birds and every thing seems to smile with pleasure Cockatoos as plentiful and common as crows in England Provisions of Every kind is very cheap you can buy Beef at 1*d* penny per lb flour 1½*d* per lb tea 2*s* per lb and Sugar at 2*d* per lb and other things as cheep. but this is every poor mans diet. Wages is not so very high out here not so much as they are in England. I have Nothing more to Say at Present more than this is just the country where we can end our days in peace and contentment when we meet. I send my kind love and best of wishes to you all and every one related to you and me, to your father and Mother. Sisters and Brothers, aquaintences and friends and to every one who may ask for me. I send my kind love to you all and especially to my wife and children.

Farewell.

These 'simple annals of the poor,' written for no eyes but those to which they were addressed, are surely very pleasant to read, and very affecting. We earnestly commend to all who may peruse them, the remembrance of these affectionate longings of the heart, and the consideration of the question whether money would not be well lent or even spent in re-uniting relatives and friends thus parted, and in sending a steady succession of people of all laborious classes (not of any one particular pursuit) from places where they are not wanted, and are miserable, to places where they are wanted, and can be happy and independent.

MILKING IN AUSTRALIA.—This is a very serious operation. First, say at four o'clock in the morning, you drive the cows into the stock-yard, where the calves have been penned up all the previous night, in a hutch in one corner. Then you have to commence a chase after the first cow, who, with a perversity common to Australian females, expects to be pursued two or three times round the yard, ankle deep in dust or mud, according to the season, with loud halloas and a thick stick. This done, she generally proceeds up to the *fail*, a kind of pillory, and permits her neck to be made fast. The cow safe in the fail, her near hind leg is stretched out to its full length, and tied to a convenient post with the universal cordage of Australia, a piece of green hide. At this stage, in ordinary cases, the milking commences; but it was one of the hobbies of Mr. Jumsorew, a practice I have never seen followed in any other part of the colony, that the cow's tail should be held tight during the operation. This arduous duty I conscientiously performed for some weeks, until it happened one day that a young heifer slipped her head out of an ill-fastened fail, upset milkman and milkpail, charged the Head Stockman, who was unloosing the calves, to the serious damage of a new pair of fustians, and ended, in spite of all my efforts, in clearing the top rail of the stock-yard, leaving me flat and flabbergasted at the foot of the fence.—*From 'Scenes in the Life of a Bushman.' (Unpublished.)*

METAL IN SEA-WATER.—The French *savans*, MM. Malaguti, Durocher, and Sarzeaud, announce that they have detected in the waters of the ocean the presence of copper, lead, and silver. The water examined appears to have been taken some leagues off the coast of St. Malo, and the fucoidal plants of that district are also found to contain silver. The *F. serratus* and the *F. ceramoides* yielded ashes containing 1-100000th, while the water of the sea contained but little more than 1-100000000th. They state also that they find silver in sea-salt, in ordinary muriatic acid, and in the soda of commerce; and that they have examined the rock-salt of Lorraine, in which also they discover this metal. Beyond this, pursuing their researches on terrestrial plants, they have obtained such indications as leave no doubt of the existence of silver in vegetable tissues. Lead is said to be always found in the ashes of marine plants, usually about an 18-100000th part—and invariably a trace of copper. Should these results be confirmed by further examination, we shall have advanced considerably towards a knowledge of the phenomena of the formation of mineral veins.—*Athenæum.*

Published at the Office, No. 16, Wellington Street North, Strand; and Printed by BRADBURY & EVANS, Whitefriars, London.

Plate 3 Last page of *Household Words* No. 1, original issue

The letter with which we shall conclude our extracts, is from a convict—the only one before us, from any member of that class.

New South Wales.

Dear Affectionate Wife and family

We arrived at Port Jackson in Sydney on the 8th day of June after a fine and pleasing voyage for 4 Callender Months wanting two days only. Nothing worth Mentioning happened all the Voyage. Only 2 of our unhapy Number was taken away from us by death. While lying in Sydney Harbour I engaged for one twelve Month and am now for the present time situated up in the country, in not so quite a comfortable position as I should wish but I must bear it for a short time, and as conveniences will allow I shall be in Sydney to work. Dear Wife You can come out to Me as soon as it pleases you and also my Sister and I will provide for you a comfortable Situation and Home as a good one as ever lies in my power, And When you come or send You must come to My Masters House at Sydney. He is a rich a Gentleman known by every one in this colony, and you must come out as emigrants, and when you come ask for me as a emigrant and never use the word Convict or the ship Hashemy on your Voyage never let it be once named among you let no one know your business but your own selves, and When you Land come to my Masters a enquire for me and thats quite sufficient. Dear Wife do not you cumber yourself with no more luggage than is necessary for they are of no use out here you can bring your bed and bedclothes and sufficient clothes for yourself and family. You can buy for yourself a tin hook pot to hang on before the fire in the Gally to boil tea at times when it is required. And a few Oranges and lemons for the Sea Sickness or anything you please. Dear Wife this is a fine Country and a beautiful climate it is like a perpetual Sumer and I think it will prove congenial for your health, No wild beast or anything of the Sort out here, fine beautiful birds and everything seems to smile with pleasure Cockatoos as plentiful and common as crows in England Provisions of Every kind is very cheap you can buy Beef at 1*d* penny per lb flour 1½*d* per lb tea 2*s* per pound and Sugar 2*d* per lb and other things as cheep. but this is every poor mans diet. Wages is not so very high out here not so much as they are in England. I have Nothing more to Say at Present more than this is just the country where we can end our days in peace and contentment when we meet. I send my kind love and best of wishes to you all and every one related to you and me, to your father and Mother. Sisters and Brothers, acquaintences and friends and to every one who may ask for me. I send my kind love to you all and especially to my wife and children.

Farewell.

Placed, as the writers of these letters are, in a position to judge of the advantages and drawbacks of the new world upon which they have entered; they ask, in inviting their relatives to join them, the trial of no mere experiment: the hopes and fears, the doubts and anxieties, which beset the head of an emigrant party in journeying to an untried region, are mitigated, or, in a great measure, smoothed away. Each of the families which Mrs. Chisholm's system proposes to aid in emigrating, has already their pioneer at work for them to obviate at least one principal source of failure in the prospects of emigrants;—ignorance of the local and social circumstances of the new sphere. In the letters we have just read, every sort of information which is useful to the out-goer is given to him, precisely in a way which enables him best to understand it. When arguments only moderately feasible are advanced, or prospects no more than partially encouraging are held out in the simple language, and from the affectionate hopefulness of kith and kin—a hopefulness justified by experience of the country—they are irresistible, even when they appeal to mere self-interest; but when such inducements are warmed and intensified by the yearnings of natural affection and the pangs of exile; when a husband writes a longing invitation to his wife; a father craves, in his own homely language, to be united to his children; when a brother asks a brother, or a sister, to join him in the land where "all who will work may eat;" the desires of the invited to hasten to the land of promise are strengthened and redoubled. When, therefore, indigence forbids the faintest encouragement of the hope that such relatives will ever be able to transport themselves to the adopted land of those they love, their disappointment and distress amount to despair.

For the interest, then, of this country, as well as for the interest of our colonies, it is well to encourage the emigration of exactly the class of persons whom Mrs. Chisholm proposes to assist;—those who have already relations in the more distant colonies. The best persons to settle in a new colony are those whose morals are subject to the check of family responsibilities. Nothing can be more unwise than the preference which colonial employers show for single men, without what they are pleased to term "encumbrances." A wife and children are precisely the encumbrances which, in a new country, chain a man to hard work and to probity. They also tend to confine him to his place of service, if it be a good one, and prevent him from making rash and fruitless changes.

But, apart from these considerations, the simple "annals of the poor," from which we have quoted—written for no eyes but those to which they were addressed—are surely very pleasant to read, and very affecting. We earnestly commend to all who may peruse them, the remembrance of these affectionate longings of the heart, and the consideration of the question whether money would not be well lent or even spent in re-uniting relatives and friends thus parted, and in sending a steady succession of people of all laborious classes (not of any one particular pursuit) from places where they are not wanted, and are miserable, to places where they are wanted, and can be happy and independent.

Published at the Office, No. 16, Wellington Street North, Strand. Printed by Bradbury & Evans, Whitefriars, London

Plate 4 Last page of *Household Words* No. 1, reissue

Small Monkish Relic" appear three phrases, none of which makes clear what the article deals with. An article recounting the story of *Beowulf* is listed under its title ("A Primitive Old Epic") and under two content phrases, but the word "Beowulf" does not appear in "Contents." An article on Angelica Kauffmann is listed under its title ("Poor Angelica") and under "Angelica Kauffmann," but not under "Kauffmann." An article based on Richard Burton's *First Footsteps in East Africa* is listed under the article-title ("The Orsons of East Africa") and under four content phrases, but not under "Burton." Florence Nightingale's name does not appear in the "Contents" of Vol. XVII, though an article in that volume ("The Nurse in Leading Strings") is based largely on a pamphlet written by her.

In "Contents," verse is listed separately from prose. In the eight volumes that contain extra Christmas numbers, the title of the Christmas number or the content of the number (or both) is stated at the end of the regular "Contents." There are some inaccuracies in "Contents" in the wording of titles of items, as also in page numbers.

Household Words advertisements on the availability of the first ten volumes of the periodical in five double-volumes stated that the double-volume set included "a general index to the whole," the index being available also separately. The double-volume set that I have seen does not have for the first ten volumes "a general index to the whole."

SUPPLEMENTARY PUBLICATIONS

Two supplementary publications were issued in conjunction with, though separately from, *Household Words* – the *Household Narrative of Current Events*[98] and the *Household Words Almanac*, both printed by Bradbury & Evans.

The *Narrative* was a twenty-four-page pamphlet (sixteen-page pamphlet for December numbers), published monthly, price twopence. A brief article by Dickens in *Household Words*, April 13, 1850, announced the advent of the *Narrative*, and the first published number appeared at the end of that month. Numbers for January, February, and March were brought out later in that year to make complete the record for 1850. The last number published was that for December 1855. The *Narrative* was available also in yearly volumes, price three shillings.

The *Narrative* was what its title indicated. The first volume was described in *Household Words* advertisements as "a complete and carefully-digested ANNUAL REGISTER of Public Occurrences, in every part of the Globe, during the year 1850." The *Narrative* was issued as an unstamped publication. The question as to whether

98 Announcements in *H.W.* stated that the *Narrative* was "issued with the Magazines," "issued regularly with the Magazines," or "published with the Magazines." This meant that the *Narrative* appeared at the same time as did the "Monthly Part" of *H.W.*, not that it was a part of "the Magazines." The *Narrative* had to be purchased separately from *H.W.*

it was a newspaper, and therefore subject to the stamp duty, was brought before the Court of Exchequer. Pending the Court's decision, the *Narrative* continued to be published. The decision, announced in *Household Words*, January 24, 1852, was that the *Narrative* did not come within the provisions of the Stamp Act. Announcements in *Household Words*, in November and December 1855, of the discontinuance of the *Narrative* gave no reason for the discontinuance.

The *Household Words Almanac* was a twenty-eight-page pamphlet, price fourpence. A brief article by Dickens in *Household Words*, November 24, 1855, announced the publication of the *Almanac* for the coming year and described its contents. An announcement in the preceding number stated that that *Almanac* would be published November 22, "Almanack Day." The only other number of the almanac published was that for the year 1857. The *Almanac* was, as stated, issued separately from *Household Words*. However, in some copies of *Household Words* Vol. XIII, a copy of the 1856 *Almanac* was bound with the periodical contents; in some copies of Vol. XIV, a copy of the 1857 *Almanac* was so bound.

Neither the *Narrative* nor the *Almanac* is dealt with in the present compilation.

REPRINTING OF SELECTIONS FROM *Household Words*

The extensive reprinting of selections from *Household Words* was in the *Collection of British Authors*, Tauchnitz Edition, Leipzig. Thirty-six volumes of the *Collection*, 1851–56, titled *Household Words. Conducted by Charles Dickens*, reprinted almost the entire contents of the first twelve volumes of the periodical, and part of the thirteenth volume. Eleven volumes in the *Collection*, 1856–59, titled *Novels and Tales Reprinted from Household Words*, reprinted mainly fiction, but also some historical and other accounts, from the last seven volumes of the periodical.

A few volumes of selections were published in the United States. In 1852 George P. Putman brought out, in Putnam's Library for the People, four such volumes. The preface to the first, *Home and Social Philosophy: or, Chapters on Every-Day Topics*, explained that the books were to be "a classified reprint" of *Household Words*, each volume to contain material on a related subject. *Home and Social Philosophy* contained "essays which relate to domestic and social economy, familiar illustrations of natural philosophy, and kindred topics." A second series of selections, *The World Here and There: or, Notes of Travellers*, was to consist of "travellers' narratives and geographical notes." A third series, *Home Narratives*, was to include "the best of the stories and imaginative sketches" that appeared in *Household Words*. "It is thus intended," stated the preface, "to make a complete reprint of Dickens's admirable work from the commencement, and to continue the series, omitting the articles which are of temporary or local interest." The Putnam series seems not to have been continued after 1852. Of the books published, *Home and Social Philosophy* (two separate series) contained thirty-five selections; *The World Here and There* contained sixteen. Of *Home Narratives* I have not seen a copy. *The World Here and There* and *Home Narratives*, listed in Roorbach, *Bibliotheca Americana*, as published by Bunce & Brother, 1854, may be a reissue of the *Household Words* selections contained in the Putnam volumes, or they may be other selections. I have not seen a copy of either book.

In 1854 the publisher John E. Beardsley, Auburn and Buffalo (New York state), brought out *Choice Stories from Dickens' Household Words*. Dickens's periodical, stated the prefatory "Publishers' Notice," had had a smaller circulation in the United States than its merits entitled it to, "in consequence of its being issued in such form as to make it troublesome to preserve the numbers, and have them bound." Many *Household Words* papers, too, stated the notice, were of local and somewhat temporary interest, which scarcely touched the popular mind of American readers. "It is believed, therefore, that judicious selections from [*Household Words*], embracing some of its best stories, in which the hand of the master is readily discerned, will be welcomed with delight in many a home in which the name of DICKENS has become as 'familiar as household words.' " The book contained ten selections, none of them by "the hand of the master." The prefatory notice stated that *Choice Stories* was intended to be the first in a series of stories selected from *Household Words*. I have found no reference to the publication of further volumes in the series.

Pearl-Fishing. Choice Stories, from Dickens' Household Words, first series, brought out in 1854 by Alden, Beardsley & Co., Auburn, was identical with *Choice Stories*, except for the title page.

Fortune Wildred, the Foundling. Also, Lizzie Leigh, and The Miner's Daughters. By Charles Dickens, brought out by the New York publishers De Witt & Davenport, n.d., was a pirated edition of three *Household Words* stories – one by Georgiana Craik, one by Mrs. Gaskell, and one by Howitt. The book was published probably soon after Miss Craik's story appeared (in November 1852) in *Household Words*.

In 1859 the Philadelphia publishers T. B. Peterson and Brothers published a selection of Dickens's *Household Words* essays and stories, under the title *Dickens' Short Stories. Containing Thirty-one Stories Never Before Published in This Country*. The book contained no items that Dickens had not included in *Reprinted Pieces*, 1858.

In addition to collections of *Household Words* items, individual items were reprinted, in whole or part, by such periodicals as *Harper's New Monthly Magazine*, Littell's *Living Age*, the *Eclectic Magazine*, and the *International Magazine*; selections from *Household Words* items were reprinted in the *Athenaeum*, the *Times*, the *Examiner*, and other periodicals.

REISSUES AND REPRINTINGS OF *Household Words*

The nineteen volumes of *Household Words* were reissued in monthly parts, also in half-crown volumes, 1868–73, by the London publishers Ward, Lock, & Tyler. The publication was announced in the *Publishers' Circular*, 1868, as "a reissue"; it was, however, not an exact reissue. Samuel O. Beeton, in charge of the publication, stated that though the reissue was "printed from the original stereotyped plates" of *Household Words*, the agreement was that "all mere announcements and advertisements" that had appeared therein "should be omitted"[99] – to be substituted, obviously, by other material. One item omitted in the reissue was the brief article "The Household Narrative," which was substituted (without indication of the substitution) by a poem by Thomas Bailey Aldrich.[100]

Among American publishers who reissued or reprinted some parts of *Household Words* were George P. Putnam; Angell, Engel & Hewitt; McElrath & Lord and McElrath & Barker (same firm but with change of partner); Dix & Edwards; and John Jansen & Co. W. E. Buckler states that the history of reprinting *Household Words* in the United States "is almost absolutely dark."[101]

REVIVAL OF *Household Words*

In 1881 Charles Dickens, Jr., resuscitated *Household Words* – or, rather, the title – – in a "householdy" magazine that made no pretence at being like the original *Household Words*. He edited it for some ten years. Later *Household Words* served for a time as the official organ of the Dickens Fellowship. Only the original *Household Words*, 1850–59, is dealt with in the present compilation.

99 Letter, *Athenaeum*, Oct. 17, 1868, p. 498.

100 See G. J. L. Gomme, "T. B. Aldrich and 'Household Words,'" *Papers of the Bibliographical Society of America*, XLII (First Quarter, 1948), 70–72. I have not seen the Ward, Lock, & Tyler reissue. The copy listed in the *Brit. Mus. Cat.* is reported destroyed by bombing.

101 "'Household Words' in America," *Papers of the Bibliographical Society of America*, XLV (Second Quarter, 1951), 160.

PART ONE

Household Words Table of Contents

EXPLANATORY NOTE

The information given for each item is in the following order: (1) title, (2) category or subject notation, (3) page[s] on which item appears, (4) length, (5) payment, (6) Office Book authorship ascription, (7) confirmed, ascertained, or accepted authorship.

Title: Titles of items are given in full. The period at the end of a title in the *H.W.* text is not retained. Chapter titles in items of fiction are not recorded. Chapter or section titles in most non-fiction items are not recorded. Those recorded are separated from the main title by a colon. In the four series of items appearing under a common main title ("Illustrations of Cheapness," "Our Phantom Ship," "Shadows," and "The Roving Englishman") with subtitles for the individual items, subtitles are recorded. They are separated from the main title by a colon (except in the occasional instances in which the phrase that in most items is punctuated as a subtitle appears as part of the main title).

The heading "Chip" or "Chips" is recorded in the singular when it stands as heading for one "chip"; in the plural when it stands as heading for more than one (*H.W.* usage is inconsistent in this matter).

Category, subject: In general, the category of writing to which an item belongs or the subject with which it deals is stated only when the title does not make the category or subject clear (though all verse items, irrespective of title, are marked "verse"). Occasional subject notations are gratuitous; they are included on the supposition that the reader may not have at hand the necessary reference books. Narrative items related for the story interest are marked "novel," "story" (four or fewer instalments), "legend," etc. Narrative items in which the narrative serves largely as a vehicle for criticism, instruction, etc., are marked with a subject notation. For some items, the choice between category and subject marking is arbitrary.

For an item based on a book or on a periodical article (occasionally on two books or two articles) in the way of discussion, summary, selection or excerpt from, etc., the source is usually indicated. (Some sources I have been unable to identify.) For an item based on several books, the subject, rather than the source, is indicated if such indication is necessary. For items based on statistical compilations, Government and other reports, etc., the subject rather than the source is usually indicated if such indication is necessary.

Length: The length of an item is recorded as given in the Office Book, since it is on that length that payment was based. For items for which the Office Book gives no length, as also for items not listed in the Office Book, the length is supplied from the *H.W.* text (without notation of the fact). Length notations that are so blotted or overwritten as to be almost indecipherable are recorded as what seems to be the reading; for notations that are entirely indecipherable, the length of items is recorded from the *H.W.* text (without notation of the fact). A discrepancy of ¾ col. or more between the Office Book length notation and the text-length of an item is indicated by the notation "should read ... "; lesser discrepancies are not marked.

Lead items: The length supplied for a lead item includes the space occupied by the masthead (approximately half of the Office Book length notations for lead items include the space occupied by the masthead). Length correction for a lead item is given only when the Office Book notation, either with or without allowance for the space occupied by the masthead, differs ¾ col. or more from the text-length. The correction given includes the space occupied by the masthead.

End items: For the end item in a number in which the last page is left partially blank or is occupied in part by advertisements or announcements, the length supplied is the text-length. The length correction given is the text-length.

Payment: Unless otherwise stated, all payments recorded are from the Office Book. Blotted or overwritten notations are recorded as what seems to be the reading.

All payments given in the Office Book are recorded, but not all payment notations: For items consisting of several instalments marked in one or more of the entries with a payment notation for the entire item, the total payment is recorded with the entry for the first instalment; repetitions of the payment notation are not recorded. For items consisting of several instalments marked in one or more of the entries with a payment notation for the entire item and marked also with payment notations for individual instalments, only the total payment is recorded (with the entry for the first instalment). If, for such items, there is a discrepancy between the total payment notation and the sum of the individual payment notations, the discrepancy is noted.

For items assigned jointly to an outside contributor (or two outside contributors) and to a staff member (or two staff members), the payment recorded is to the outside contributor (or contributors). (This is the arrangement in the Office Book, so stated for occasional items so assigned; e.g., for "The French Workman," assigned to Duthie and Morley, payment is marked "To Duthie.") For joint-authorship items by outside contributors, the sum allotted to each writer is recorded (if this allotment is given), not the total payment. If the allotment is not given, the total payment is recorded.

Payment notations that are in error (i.e., notations of payment to Morley during the time that he was a staff member: see Introduction, pp. 36–37, and fn. 88) are recorded without comment, as are payments for improbable amounts.

Not recorded are the Office Book memoranda on the manner in which payment was made (as by cash, cheque, post-office order, draft), by whom it was made, etc. (These matters, if they are of significance in the identification or possible identification of a contributor, are mentioned in the identification note on the contributor.) Not recorded is the Office Book payment notation "Advanced," since this has no connection (or no connection that can be established) with the amount of a payment.

Authorship ascription: In the first ascription position are recorded the single or joint names (or other designations) of contributors as they appear in the Office Book. (Ascriptions are transcribed as written in the Office Book; misspellings of names and errors in initials and titles are not marked *sic.*) Names and initials not clearly written in the Office Book are recorded as what seems to be the reading, and questioned.

The recording is made uniform in the following indifferent matters: Superscript letters that appear in some abbreviations and contractions (M^{rs}, Honble, etc.) are lowered, except when the superior position must be retained for clarity (Alex^{r}, Chris^{er}). Periods are placed after abbreviations and initials regardless of whether or not they appear in the Office Book entry. A comma is placed after each name (or other designation) in a series, regardless of what mark, if any, appears in the Office Book entry. The "&" or "and" linking joint names (or other designations) is uniformly recorded as "&".

Not recorded in this ascription position are the Office Book memoranda on revision, which occasionally indicate that an item assigned to a single writer was as much revised as were certain items for which joint names are recorded. (This matter, as concerns any individual contributor, is mentioned in the identification note on the contributor.)

The address of a contributor (or the address to which payment for an item was sent) as given in the Office Book is recorded only when it serves to distinguish contributors of the same name. The Office Book notation "per ... " is recorded only when it serves to distinguish contributors of the same name or when it appears with an unassigned item the authorship of which has not been ascertained (or not positively ascertained).

A rule indicates that the Office Book gives no author for an item, or only partial authorship.

In the second ascription position is recorded, for an identified contributor, his complete (or reasonably complete) name; for a contributor of probable identification, his name marked "prob."; for an unidentified contributor listed in the Office Book by a designation other than "Correspondent" or "Anonymous" and appearing only once, the designation given in the Office Book; for such a contributor appearing more than once, what seems the most nearly complete and correct designation. (Occasional entries require a slightly different form of recording.) For unidentified (or not positively identified) men contributors designated in the Office Book as "Dr.," the title is retained in the second ascription position; the title "Mr." is not retained. For unidentified women contributors designated as "Miss" or "Mrs.," the title is retained.

Names and initials of unidentified contributors not written clearly in the Office Book are recorded in the second ascription position as in the first.

A rule in the second ascription position indicates that the authorship (or complete authorship) of an item has not been ascertained. For the two prose "fillers" "Metal in Sea-Water" and "Curious Epitaph" that appear in Vol. I, as also for the lines from Blackmore and from Southey in the same volume, the rule actually means that the name of the person who inserted the items is not known.

Office Book ascriptions found to be incorrect are corrected in the second ascription position; the basis of the reassignment is stated in the identification note on the contributor whose item is misassigned. For items for which the Office Book ascription seems to be incorrect but cannot be proved to be so, the contributor's name given in the Office Book is recorded in the second ascription position without indication that the ascription may be in error. The probable misassignment is discussed in the identification note on one of the two contributors concerned, and referred to in the identification note on the other.

Some fifteen items, most of them consisting of letters or extracts from letters, the Office Book assigns not to the actual writer, but to the contributor who supplied the item to the editorial office or to the staff member who inserted it in *H.W.* Some of the items appear with editorial comment; some, without. For these (except when the actual authorship has been ascertained) the contributor's or staff member's name given in the Office Book is recorded in the second ascription position; the explanatory phrase accompanying each item makes it clear that the contributor or staff member whose name appears in that position is not the actual writer (or the sole writer) of the item.

In the matter of assigning an item to single or joint authorship in the second ascription position, the Office Book assignment is followed for all items but four ("A Colonial Patriot," assigned in the second ascription position to single authorship; "A Woman's Experience in California," "Ballinglen," and "A London Parish," assigned to joint authorship. See explanation in identification note on Fawkner, Harrold, Lady Grey, and W. Rogers). Not assigned to joint authorship are the items assigned in the Office Book to single authorship, but indicated by Dickens's letters – occasionally by letters or other writings of staff members or contributors – to have been cut or added to, slightly or extensively altered, or otherwise edited by Dickens or by members of his staff. (This matter, as it concerns any individual contributor, is mentioned in the identification note on the contributor.)

Extra Christmas numbers: At the head of the table of contents for each extra Christmas number are recorded the announced date of publication and the running date (if these dates are given) and the volume in which the number is stated to be bound (if this information is given). To make it possible for the reader to locate the tables of contents without knowing the specific date on which the numbers were published, the tables are placed in the Dec. 25 position of the year of publication. (This arrangement places the table of contents for the 1857 Christmas number among the tables of contents of Vol. XVII and that of the 1858 Christmas number among the tables of contents of Vol. XIX, rather than among the tables of contents of the volumes in which the two numbers are stated to be bound.)

Listed as the tables of contents for the extra Christmas numbers are the actual items that constitute a number. Not included in the tables of contents are the passages in the framework numbers* that introduce a story (prose or verse) or that serve as concluding comment or as transition from one story to a following, since these passages, whether or not set off typographically from the item that they precede or follow, do not of themselves constitute separate items. (The passages are mentioned in footnotes.)

Unless otherwise indicated by title or by subject notation, prose items in the extra Christmas numbers are understood to be stories; the category notation "story" is not given, since the context of the items makes the category clear.

*Four of the extra Christmas numbers are actual framework numbers. Two – "A Round of Stories by the Christmas Fire" and "Another Round of Stories by the Christmas Fire" – are framework numbers in the sense indicated by the title, the setting and audience that constitute the framework being referred to in comments in some of the stories.

VOLUME I March 30 – September 21, 1850

March 30, 1850. No. 1, pp. 1–24

A Preliminary Word, 1–2. 3 cols. *Mr. C.D.* / **Charles Dickens**

Lizzie Leigh [story], chap. i, 2–6. 9 cols. £20.0.0 for the 3 instalments. *Mrs. Gaskell* / **Elizabeth Gaskell**

Valentine's Day at the Post-Office [post-office routine and procedure], 6–12. 11 cols. *C.D. & W.H.W.* / **Charles Dickens & W. H. Wills**

Abraham and the Fire-Worshipper. A Dramatic Parable [verse], 12–13. 2 cols. £4.4.0. *Mr. Leigh Hunt* / **Leigh Hunt**

The Amusements of the People [cheap theatrical entertainment] [i], 13–15. 5 cols. *Mr. C.D.* / **Charles Dickens**

An Incident in the Life of Mad^{lle} Clairon [from letter appended to *Mémoires d'Hippolyte Clairon*], 15–19. 7 cols. £3.3.0. *Mr. Hogarth* / **George Hogarth**

The Wayside Well [verse], 19. 1 col. £1.1.0. *Mr. Allingham, Junr.* / **William Allingham**

A Bundle of Emigrants' Letters [from Australia], 19–24. 10 cols. £3.0.0. *Mr. C.D. & Mrs. Chisholm* / **Charles Dickens & Caroline Chisholm**

Milking in Australia [from unpub. "Scenes in the Life of a Bushman"], 24. ½ col. *Item not in Office Book* / **Samuel Sidney & John Sidney**

Metal in Sea-Water [from "Scientific Gossip," *Athenaeum*, Jan. 19, 1850], 24. ½ col. *Item not in Office Book* / ———

April 6, 1850. No. 2, pp. 25–48

A Child's Dream of a Star, 25–26. 3 cols. *Mr. C.D.* / **Charles Dickens**

The True Story of a Coal Fire [origin of coal; coal mining, etc.], chap. i, 26–31. 11 cols. £15.0.0 for the 3 instalments. *Mr. R. H. Horne* / **Richard H. Horne**

Lizzie Leigh, chap. ii, 32–35. 6½ cols. *Mrs. Gaskell* / **Elizabeth Gaskell**

Work! An Anecdote, 35–36. 2½ cols. £1.0.0. *Mr. Horne* / **Richard H. Horne**

Good Verses of a Bad Poet [4 lines from Sir Richard Blackmore, with 3-line comment], 36. ⅛ col. *Item not in Office Book* / ———

Perfect Felicity. In a Bird's-Eye View [vested interests, prison discipline, etc.], 36–38. 3 cols. *Mr. C.D.* / **Charles Dickens**

A Dialogue of Shadows [verse], 38. 2 cols. £1.1.0. *Mr. Procter* / **Bryan Waller Procter**

An Australian Ploughman's Story [story], 39–43. 9 cols. £4.10.0. *Mr. Sidney* / **Samuel Sidney**

Heathen and Christian Burial, 43–48. 11 cols. £5.5.0. *Mr. Hogarth & W.H.W.* / **George Hogarth & W. H. Wills**

April 13, 1850. No. 3, pp. 49–72

The Household Narrative [announcement of], 49. 1½ cols. *Mr. C.D.* / **Charles Dickens**

The Troubled Water Question [London water supply], 49–54. 10 cols. *W.H.W.* / **W. H. Wills**

Illustrations of Cheapness [i]: The Lucifer Match, 54–57. 5½ cols. £3.10.0. *Mr. Charles Knight* / **Charles Knight**

The Amusements of the People [ii], 57–60. 6¼ cols. *Mr. C.D.* / **Charles Dickens**

Sonnet to Lord Denman. Retiring from the Chief Justiceship of England [verse], 60. ¼ col. *Mr. Justice Talfourd* / **Thomas Noon Talfourd**

Lizzie Leigh, chaps. iii–iv, 60–65. 10 cols. *Mrs. Gaskell* / **Elizabeth Gaskell**

The Seasons [verse], 65. ¼ col. £1.1.0. *Mr. Bennett* / **William Cox Bennett**

Short Cuts across the Globe [i] [need for a Panama canal], 65–68. 4¾ cols. £2.12.6. *Mr. Weir & W.H.W.* / **William Weir & W. H. Wills**

The True Story of a Coal Fire, chap. ii, 68–72. 9½ cols. *Mr. Horne* / **Richard H. Horne**

April 20, 1850. No. 4, pp. 73–96

Some Account of an Extraordinary Traveller [dioramas, panoramas], 73–77. 9¼ cols. *Mr. C.D.* / **Charles Dickens**

Loaded Dice [story], 77–82. 10 cols. £5.0.0. *Mrs. Crowe* / **Catherine Crowe**

Dream within Dream; or, Evil Minimised [verse], 82. ⅛ col. *Item not in Office Book* / **Leigh Hunt**

The Schoolmaster at Home and Abroad [in large part from Joseph Kay, *The Social Condition and Education of the People in England and Europe*, 1850], 82–84. 3½ cols. *W.H.W.* / **W. H. Wills**

The Lady Alice [verse], 84. 1 col. £1.1.0. *Mr. Allingham, Junr.* / **William Allingham**

Illustrations of Cheapness [ii]: A Globe, 84–87. 6 cols. £3.10.0. *Mr. Chas. Knight* / **Charles Knight**

The Ghost of the Late Mr. James Barber. A Yarn Ashore [story], 87–90. 6 cols. *W.H.W.* / **W. H. Wills**

The True Story of a Coal Fire, chap. iii, 90–96. 10¾ cols. *Mr. Horne* / **Richard H. Horne**

Supposing! [i] [needed reforms], 96. 1½ cols. *Mr. C.D.* / **Charles Dickens**

April 27, 1850. No. 5, pp. 97–120

Pet Prisoners [Pentonville Prison], 97–103. 12½ cols. *Mr. C.D.* / **Charles Dickens**

A Tale of the Good Old Times [barbarous conditions of the past], 103–106. 7 cols. £4.0.0. *Mr. Percival Leigh* / **Percival Leigh**

Baptismal Rituals, 106–108. 3¾ cols. *W.H.W.* / **W. H. Wills**

Arctic Heroes. A Fragment of Naval History [verse], 108–109. 2 cols. £3.3.0. *Mr. Horne* / **Richard H. Horne**

A Coroner's Inquest, 109–113. 7¼ cols. *W.H.W.* / **W. H. Wills**

Francis Jeffrey, 113–18. 11 cols. *Mr. J.F.* / **John Forster**

The Young Jew of Tunis [a fanatic guilty of attempted murder], 118–20. 4½ cols. £2.2.0. *Miss Jewsbury* / **Geraldine Endsor Jewsbury**

May 4, 1850. No. 6, pp. 121–44

The Heart of Mid-London [Smithfield cattle market], 121–25. 9½ cols. *Mr. C.D. & W.H.W.* / **Charles Dickens & W. H. Wills**

The Miner's Daughters. – A Tale of the Peak [story], chap. i, 125–30. 10 cols. £12.0.0 for the 3 instalments. *Mr. William Howitt* / **William Howitt**

New Life and Old Learning [antiquated course of study at Oxford], 130–32. 4 cols. *Mr. J.F.* / **John Forster**

The Railway Station [verse], 132–33. 1 col. £1.11.6. *Miss Dora Greenwell* / **Dora Greenwell**

The Brown Hat [tolerance of differences], 133–35. 4 cols. £2.0.0. *Mr. Chorley* / **Henry Fothergill Chorley**

Alchemy and Gunpowder, 135–39. 7½ cols. £4.0.0. *Mr. Dudley Costello* / **Dudley Costello**

"A Good Plain Cook" [Englishwomen's ignorance of cookery], 139–41. 4 cols. *W.H.W.* / **W. H. Wills**

Two-Handed Dick the Stockman. An Adventure in the Bush [story], 141–44. 8 cols. £6.0.0. "Of this sum £10/ is for Australian Ploughman in No. 2." *Mr. Samuel Sidney* / **Samuel Sidney**

May 11, 1850. No. 7, pp. 145–68

The Fire Brigade of London, 145–51. 13 cols. £6.10.0. *Mr. Horne* / **Richard H. Horne**

Poetry in the Bye-Ways [imitative verse vs. true folk poetry], 151–53. 4 cols. £2.0.0. *Mr. Chorley* / **Henry Fothergill Chorley**

The Miner's Daughters. – A Tale of the Peak, chap. ii, 153–56. 5½ cols. *Mr. W. Howitt* / **William Howitt**

The Uses of Sorrow [verse], 156. ½ col. £0.10.6. *"Sophy Traddles"* / apparently **Miss Norris**

From the Raven in the Happy Family [i] [reprehensible human traits and acts], 156–58. 3¾ cols. *Mr. C.D.* / **Charles Dickens**

Illustrations of Cheapness [iii]: Eggs, 158–61. 5½ cols. £3.10.0. *Mr. Charles Knight* / **Charles Knight**

Music in Humble Life [work of John P. Hullah], 161–64. 6 cols. £3.0.0. *Mr. Hogarth & W.H.W.* / **George Hogarth & W. H. Wills**

A Paris Newspaper [*Le Constitutionnel*], 164–67. 5½ cols. £2.10.0. *Mr. Joseph Crowe* / **Joseph Archer Crowe**

Lines by Robert Southey [verse, "From an Unpublished Autograph"], 167. ¼ col. *Item not in Office Book* / ———

Short Cuts across the Globe [ii]: The Isthmus of Suez, 167–68. 3½ cols. £2.0.0. *Mr. Weir & W.H.W.* / **William Weir & W. H. Wills**

Curious Epitaph, 168. ¼ col. *Item not in Office Book* / ———

May 18, 1850. No. 8, pp. 169–92

The Begging-Letter Writer, 169–72. 6½ cols. *Mr. C.D.* / **Charles Dickens**

The Great Cat and Dog Question [allegory], 172–75. 7 cols. £3.3.0. *Mr. Meadows Taylor* / **Philip Meadows Taylor**

A Card from Mr. Booley [concerning "Extraordinary Traveller," April 20], 175–76. ½ col. *Mr. C.D.* / **Charles Dickens**

Law at a Low Price [County Courts], 176–80. 9 cols. £4.14.6. *Mr. W. T. Haly & W.H.W* / **William Taylor Haly & W. H. Wills**

Swedish Folk-Songs: Fair Carin [verse], 180. 1 col. £1.1.0. *Mrs. W Howitt* / **Mary Howitt**

A Visit to the Arctic Discovery Ships, 180–82. 3½ cols. £2.0.0. *Mr. F. K. Hunt* / **Frederick Knight Hunt**

The Miner's Daughters. – A Tale of the Peak, chap. iii, 182–86. 9 cols.; should read 7½. *Mr. W. Howitt* / **William Howitt**

Letter from a Highly Respectable Old Lady [sanitation, health], 186–87. 2¼ cols. £1.1.0. *Mr. H. Morley* / **Henry Morley**

A Sample of the Old School. By an Old Boy, 187–92. 10¼ cols. £5.0.0. *Mr. Percival Leigh* / **Percival Leigh**

May 25, 1850. No. 9, pp. 193–216

The Sickness and Health of the People of Bleaburn [Mary Pickard Ware's work for sanitation in Yorkshire village, fictionized account], chaps i–ii, 193–99. 12½ cols.; should read 13¼. £20.0.0 for the 4 instalments. *Miss Martineau* / **Harriet Martineau**

Spring-Time in the Court [verse], 199. ¾ col. £1.1.0. *Mr. Mark Lemon* / **Mark Lemon**

The Planet-Watchers of Greenwich [the Observatory], 200–204. 9 cols. £5.0.0. *Mr. F. K. Hunt* / **Frederick Knight Hunt**

Swedish Folk-Songs: The Dove on the Lily [verse], 204. ¾ col. £0.10.6. *Mrs. Howitt* / **Mary Howitt**

A Walk in a Workhouse [visit to London workhouse], 204–207. 5 cols.; should read 6. *Mr. C.D.* / **Charles Dickens**

The "Irish Difficulty" Solved by Con McNale [individual initiative and enterprise vs. Govt. schemes], 207–210. 5½ cols. £2.10.0. *Mr. Browne,* Boulogne / **Browne**

William Wordsworth, 210–13. 7 cols. £3.3.0. *Mr. Weir* / **William Weir**

Father and Son [story], 213–16. 6 cols. £3.0.0. *Miss Hoare* / **Mrs. Hoare**

June 1, 1850. No. 10, pp. 217–40

A Popular Delusion [Billingsgate market], 217–21. 10 cols. *Mr. C.D. & W.H.W.* / **Charles Dickens & W. H. Wills**

Greenwich Weather-Wisdom [meteorological observations], 222–25. 7 cols. £3.10.0. ——— / **Frederick Knight Hunt**

My Wonderful Adventures in Skitzland [fantasy], 225–29. 8 cols. £4.0.0. *Mr. Morley* / **Henry Morley**

Birth Song. Song of Death [verse], 229–30. 1¼ cols. £1.1.0. *Mrs. W. Howitt* / **Mary Howitt**

The Sickness and Health of the People of Bleaburn, chaps. iii–v, 230–38. 16½ cols. *Miss Martineau* / **Harriet Martineau**

The Son of Sorrow. A Fable from the Swedish [verse], 238. ½ col. £0.10.6. *See No. 7* / apparently **Miss Norris**

The Appetite for News [newspapers and newspaper readers], 238–40. 4½ cols. *W.H.W.* / **W. H. Wills**

June 8, 1850. No. 11, pp. 241–64

From the Raven in the Happy Family [ii] [ostentatious funerals], 241–42. 4 cols. *Mr. C.D.* / **Charles Dickens**

How We Went Fishing in Canada, 243–45. 6 cols. £3.0.0. *Mr. Alex Mackay* / **Alexander Mackay**

A Wish [verse], 245. ¼ col. Payment included with item below. *Mr. Horne* / **Richard H. Horne**

The Black Diamonds of England [coal], 246–50. 9¼ cols. £4.4.0 for this and above item. "Done before Mr. H's engtm May 18" (i.e., before Horne's engagement as staff member). *Mr. Horne* / **Richard H. Horne**

The Great Penal Experiments [Pentonville and other English prisons], 250–53. 5 cols. *W.H.W.* / **W. H. Wills**

The Orphan's Voyage Home [verse], 253. 1 col. £0.10.6. *Mr. Horne & Miss Earle* / **Richard H. Horne & Miss Earle**

Illustrations of Cheapness [iv]: Tea, 253–56. 6 cols. £3.0.0. *Mr. C. Knight* / **Charles Knight**

The Sickness and Health of the People of Bleaburn, chaps. vi–vii, 256–61. 10½ cols. *Miss Martineau* / **Harriet Martineau**

Young Russia [Vladimir A. Sollogub, *The Tarantas,* 1850], 261–64. 6 cols. *W.H.W.* / **W. H. Wills**

June 15, 1850. No. 12, pp. 265–88

Old Lamps for New Ones [Pre-Raphaelite paintings], 265–67. 5¼ cols. *Mr. C.D.* / **Charles Dickens**

Savings' Bank Defalcations, 267–70. 5½ cols. £2.2.0. *Mr. Haly & W.H.W.* / **William Taylor Haly & W. H. Wills**

The Summer Sabbath [verse], 270. ¼ col. £0.10.6. *Calder Campbell* / **Robert Calder Campbell**

Newspaper Antecedents [in part from F. K. Hunt, *The Fourth Estate,* 1850], 270–74. 7¼ cols. *W.H.W.* / **W. H. Wills**

The Royal Rotten Row Commission [Govt. red tape], 274–76. 4¾ cols. £2.2.0. *Mr. Haly & W.H.W.* / **William Taylor Haly & W. H. Wills**

A Village Tale [verse], 276–77. 1¼ cols. £1.1.0. *Bennet* / **William Cox Bennett**

The Fire Annihilator, 277–82. 11¾ cols. *R. H. Horne* / **Richard H. Horne**

The Sickness and Health of the People of Bleaburn, chaps. viii–ix, 283–88. 10 cols. *Miss Martineau* / **Harriet Martineau**

The Revenge of Æsop. Imitated from Phædrus [verse], 288. ¼ col. *Sir Bulwer Lytton* / **Edward George Bulwer-Lytton**

The Golden Fagots. A Child's Tale, 288. 1½ cols. £0.15.0. *Mr. Morley* / **Henry Morley**

June 22, 1850. No. 13, pp. 289–312

The Sunday Screw [Sunday closing of post offices], 289–92. 7¼ cols. *Mr. C.D.* / **Charles Dickens**

The Young Advocate [story], 292–97. 9 cols. £4.0.0. *Mrs. Crowe* / **Catherine Crowe**

Earth's Harvests [verse], 297. ½ col. ——— / ———

"The Devil's Acre" [Ragged Dormitory and industrial schools in squalid London district], 297–301. 8 cols. £4.0.0. *Mr. Alexander Mackay* / **Alexander Mackay**

"Press On." A Rivulet's Song [verse], 301. ¾ col. *Mr. ——— & Mr. Horne* / **Mr. ——— & Richard H. Horne**

Address from an Undertaker to the Trade. (Strictly Private and Confidential), 301–304. 5 cols. £2.2.0. *Mr. P. Leigh* / **Percival Leigh**

The Two Sacks. Imitated from Phædrus [verse], 304. ¼ col. ——— / prob. **Edward George Bulwer-Lytton**

The Modern "Officer's" Progress [army life], i, 304–307. 5½ cols. £12.0.0 for the 3 instalments. *Mr. Dudley Costello* / **Dudley Costello**

Pictures of Life in Australia, 307–310. 6¼ cols. £1.11.6. *Mrs. Chisholm & R.H.H.* / **Caroline Chisholm & Richard H. Horne**

Ebenezer Elliott, 310–12. 4 cols.; should read 5½. £1.11.6. *Mr. Thomas Old* / **Thomas Old**

June 29, 1850. No. 14, pp. 313–36

The Golden City [San Francisco: in part from Bayard Taylor, *Eldorado*, 1850], 313–17. 9 cols. *W.H.W.* / **W. H. Wills**

The Modern "Officer's" Progress, ii, 317–20. 6½ cols. *Dudley Costello* / **Dudley Costello**

The Belgian Lace-Makers [Johann Georg Kohl, *Reisen in den Niederlanden*, 1850], 320–23. 4½ cols. £1.11.6. *Miss Ross & W.H.W.* / **Thomasina Ross & W. H. Wills**

The Power of Mercy [story], 323–25. 4¼ cols. £1.11.6. *Earle* [preceded by indecipherable word, overwritten by capital letter: perh. "H"?] *& W.H.W.* / **Miss Earle & W. H. Wills**

Flowers [verse], 325. ¾ col. £1.1.0. *Mr. Procter* / **Bryan Waller Procter**

The Cattle-Road to Ruin [London slaughter-houses], 325–30. 10 cols. *Mr. Horne* / **Richard H. Horne**

Class Opinions. A Fable, 330. ½ col. £0.10.0. *Mr. Morley* / **Henry Morley**

The Registrar-General on "Life" in London [mortality statistics], 330–33. 6¼ cols. £2.11.6. *Mr. F. K. Hunt* / **Frederick Knight Hunt**

Bed, 333–36. 6¼ cols. £2.11.6. *Mr. R. H. Patterson* / **Robert Hogarth Patterson**

July 6, 1850. No. 15, pp. 337–60

The Old Lady in Threadneedle Street [Bank of England], 337–42. 10¼ cols. *C.D. & W.H.W.* / **Charles Dickens & W. H. Wills**

The Serf of Pobereze [a Polish prima donna], 342–50. 15½ cols. £5.5.0. *Mad. Sczszpanowska & W.H.W.* / **Mme. Szczepanowska & W. H. Wills**

A Stroll by Starlight [verse], 350. 1½ cols. £1.1.0. *Mr. Morley & R.H.H.* / **Henry Morley & Richard H. Horne**

Chips:
- [explanation of], 350–51. ½ col. *Mr. C.D.* / **Charles Dickens**
- Destruction of Parish Registers [in the main from William Downing Bruce, ... *On the Condition and Unsafe State of Ancient Parochial Registers*, 1850], 351. 2 cols. *W.H.W.* / **W. H. Wills**
- From Mr. T. Oldcastle concerning the Coal Exchange [apparently reader's reply to comments about him in "Black Diamonds," June 8], 352. 1 col. *Mr. Horne* / prob. **Thomas Oldcastle**
- New Shoes [from French trans. of Jacob von Stählin-Storcksburg, *Originalanekdoten von Peter dem Grossen*, 1785], 352. 1 col. £0.10.0. *Miss Le France* / **Miss Le France**

The Modern "Officer's" Progress, iii, 353–56. 7 cols. *Mr. Dudley Costello* / **Dudley Costello**

How to Spend a Summer Holiday [John Forbes, *A Physician's Holiday*, 1850 ed.], 356–58. 6½ cols.; should read 4¾. £2.0.0. *Mr. F. K. Hunt* / **Frederick Knight Hunt**

Christopher Shrimble on the "Decline of England" [A. A. Ledru-Rollin, *The Decline of England*, 1850], 358–60. 4 cols. *W.H.W.* / **W. H. Wills**

July 13, 1850. No. 16, pp. 361–84

A Day in a Pauper Palace [institution for pauper children, Swinton], 361–64. 7¾ cols. £3.3.0. *Mr. Taylor*, Manchester, *& W.H.W.* / **Taylor & W. H. Wills**

How We Went Hunting in Canada, 364–68. 6½ cols. £2.11.6. *Mr. Alexr Mackay* / **Alexander Mackay**

The Modern Science of Thief-Taking [London detective police], 368–72. 8 cols. *W.H.W.* / **W. H. Wills**

The Ballad of Richard Burnell [verse], 372–74. 5 cols. £3.3.0. *Mrs. W. Howitt* / **Mary Howitt**

A Few Facts about Matrimony [from Registrar-General's Reports], 374–77. 6 cols. £2.10.0. *Mr. F. K. Hunt* / **Frederick Knight Hunt**

Chips:
- From Mr. Thomas Bovington [re-location of Smithfield market], 377. ½ col. *W.H.W.* / **W. H. Wills**
- The Old Churchyard Tree. A Prose Poem, 377–78. 1½ cols. £0.10.0 ——— *& Mr. Horne* / ——— **& Richard H. Horne**
- Sabbath Pariahs [Sunday closing of post offices], 378–79. 1¼ cols. *W.H.W.* / **W. H. Wills**

Dust; or Ugliness Redeemed [a dust-heap and "cinder-sifters"], 379–84. 11½ cols. *Mr. Horne* / **Richard H. Horne**

July 20, 1850. No. 17, pp. 385–408

The Ghost of Art [an artists' model], 385–87. 6 cols. *Mr. C.D.* / **Charles Dickens**

The Wonders of 1851 [designs for Great Exhibition structure], 388–92. 8½ cols. *Mr. Horne* / **Richard H. Horne**

"I Would Not Have Thee Young Again" [verse], 392. ¼ col. £0.10.6. *Mr. Mark Lemon* / **Mark Lemon**

Little Mary. A Tale of the Black Year [story], 392–96. 7¾ cols. £2.12.6. *Miss Hoare* / **Mrs. Hoare**

A Great Man Departed [verse], 396. ¾ col. *Mr. Horne* / **Richard H. Horne**

The Adventures of the Public Records [unsuitable repositories for Records], 396–99. 6¼ cols. £2.2.0. *Mr. Charles Cole & W.H.W.* / **Charles Augustus Cole & W. H. Wills**

A Mightier Hunter Than Nimrod [R. G. Gordon-Cumming, *Five Years of a Hunter's Life in ... South Africa*, 1850], 399–402. 6¼ cols. *W.H.W.* / **W. H. Wills**

Chips:
- A Marriage in St. Petersburg, 402–403. 2¼ cols. £0.15.0. *Miss Florence Wilson* / **Florence Wilson**
- A New Joint-Stock Pandemonium Company [French], 403–404. 1 col. *W.H.W.* / **W. H. Wills**

Youth and Summer, 404–407. 5¾ cols. £2.12.6. *Mr. Paterson* / **Robert Hogarth Patterson**

The Power of Small Beginnings [Westminster Ragged Dormitory], 407–408. 3¾ cols. *W.H.W.* / **W. H. Wills**

July 27, 1850. No. 18, pp. 409–432

A Detective Police Party [interview with Scotland Yard police] [i], 409–414. 10¼ cols. *Mr. C.D.* / **Charles Dickens**

"Swinging the Ship." A Visit to the Compass Observatory, 414–18. 9¼ cols.; should read 8½. £3.3.0. *Mr. F. K. Hunt* / **Frederick Knight Hunt**

An Exploring Adventure [in Australia], 418–20. 5 cols. £2.2.0. *Mr. S. Sidney* / **Samuel Sidney**

The Birth of Morning [verse], 420. ½ col. £0.10.6. *Mr. Henry Morley* / **Henry Morley**

An Excellent Opportunity [story], 421–26. 11 cols. £4.4.0. *Miss Julia Kavannah & W.H.W.* / **Julia Kavanagh & W. H. Wills**

Review of a Popular Publication. In the Searching Style [bank-notes], 426–31. 10¾ cols. *W.H.W.* / **W. H. Wills**

Innocence and Crime. An Anecdote [pickpockets], 431–32. 2¼ cols. *Mr. Horne & ———* / **Richard H. Horne & ———**

August 3, 1850. No. 19, pp. 433–56

The Last of a Long Line [story], chap. i, 433–39. 13¼ cols. £10.10.0 for the 2 instalments. *Mr. W. Howitt* / **William Howitt**

The Chemistry of a Candle [based on Faraday's notes for lectures at Royal Institution], 439–44. 9 cols.; should read 10. £4.4.0. *Mr. P. Leigh* / **Percival Leigh**

An Old Haunt [verse], 444–45. 1 col. £1.1.0. *Mr. Lawson* / **E. Lawson**

The Hippopotamus [at Zoological Gardens], 445–49. 8¼ cols. *Mr. Horne* / **Richard H. Horne**

Chips:
- Railway Comfort, 449–50. 2¼ cols. £0.15.0. *W.H.W. & Mr. Murray* / **W. H. Wills & Grenville Murray**
- Improving a Bull [emigration], 450–51. 3½ cols. £1.10.0. *W.H.W. & Mr. Morley* / **W. H. Wills & Henry Morley**
- Lungs for London [proposed park for Finsbury], 451–52. 1¾ cols. *W.H.W.* / **W. H. Wills**

The Love of Nature [verse], 452. ½ col. £0.10.6. *Mr. Morley* / **Henry Morley**

The Preservation of Life from Shipwreck, 452–54. 4¼ cols. £1.1.0. *W.H.W. & Mr. Shillinglaw* / **W. H. Wills &** prob. **John Joseph Shillinglaw**

Winged Telegraphs [Johann Georg Kohl, *Reisen in den Niederlanden*, 1850], 454–56. 4¼ cols. £1.1.0. *W.H.W. & Miss Ross* / **W. H. Wills & Thomasina Ross**

August 10, 1850. No. 20, pp. 457–80

A Detective Police Party [ii], 457–60. 6½ cols. *Mr. C.D.* / **Charles Dickens**

Health by Act of Parliament, 460–63. 7½ cols. *W.H.W.* / **W. H. Wills**

What There Is in the Roof of the College of Surgeons [storerooms, laboratories], 464–67. 7¾ cols. £3.3.0. *Mr. F. K. Hunt* / **Frederick Knight Hunt**

Chip:
- Nice White Veal [slaughter-house torture], 467–68. ¾ col. £0.10.6. *W.H.W. & J. D. Parry* / **W. H. Wills & John Docwra Parry**

"All Things in the World Must Change" [verse], 468. ½ col. £1.1.0. *Mark Lemon* / **Mark Lemon**

The Last of a Long Line, chap. ii, 468–75. 13½ cols. *W. Howitt* / **William Howitt**

Two Letters from Australia, 475–80. 10¼ cols. £3.3.0. *Mr. Gywnne & W.H.W.* / **Francis Gwynne & W. H. Wills**

Supposing [ii] [charges on the public purse], 480. ¾ col. *Mr. C.D.* / **Charles Dickens**

August 17, 1850. No. 21, pp. 481–504

The Railway Wonders of Last Year, 481–82. 3¾ cols. *W.H.W.* / **W. H. Wills**

The Water-Drops. A Fairy Tale [water pollution], 482–89. 13½ cols. £5.5.0. *H. Morley* / **Henry Morley**

A Christian Brotherhood [organization of lay teachers, France: in the main from Hugh S. Tremenheere, *Report of the Commissioner Appointed ... to Inquire ... into the State of the Population in the Mining Districts*, 1850, Parliamentary Paper], 489–92. 6¼ cols. *W.H.W.* / **W. H. Wills**

An Every-Day Hero [verse], 492–94. 3 cols. £2.10.0. *Mrs. W. Howitt* / **Mary Howitt**

The Life and Labours of Lieutenant Waghorn, 494–501. 15 cols. *Horne* / **Richard H. Horne**

Chips:
- The Knocking-up Business [waking factory workers], 501–502. 1¼ cols. £0.10.6. *C. Strange* / **Charles Strange**
- Statistics of Factory Supervision, 502. 1 col. *W.H.W.* / **W. H. Wills**

Comic Leaves from the Statute Book [laws restricting trade and industry], 502–504. 4¼ cols. £1.1.0. *W.H.W. & Weir* / **W. H. Wills & William Weir**

August 24, 1850. No. 22, pp. 505–528

From the Raven in the Happy Family [iii] [human stupidity, conceit, etc.], 505–507. 5 cols. *C.D.* / **Charles Dickens**

A Shilling's Worth of Science [exhibit at Royal Polytechnic Institution], 507–510. 6½ cols. £2.12.6. *Dr. T. Stone* / **Thomas Stone**

The Gentleman Beggar. An Attorney's Story [story], 510–14. 8 cols. £3.15.0. *S. Sidney* / **Samuel Sidney**

Chips:
- Family Colonisation Loan Society, 514–15. 2¼ cols. £0.15.0 *S. Sidney* / **Samuel Sidney**
- The Strangers' Leaf for 1851 [proposed publishing of names of Exhibition visitors], 515–17. 3 cols. £0.15.0. *E. Murray & W.H.W.* / **Grenville Murray & W. H. Wills**
- No Hospital for Incurables, 517. ¾ col. *W.H.W.* / **W. H. Wills**

Sorrows and Joys [verse], 517–18. ¾ col. £1.1.0. *Meredith & Horne* / **George Meredith & Richard H. Horne**

The Home of Woodruffe the Gardener [story], chaps. i–iii, 518–24. 12¼ cols. £18.0.0 for the 3 instalments. *Miss Martineau* / **Harriet Martineau**

Topography and Temperance. From Mr. Christopher Shrimble [signboards of public houses], 524–25. 2¼ cols. *W.H.W.* / **W. H. Wills**

The Late American President [Zachary Taylor], 525–28. 7¾ cols. £2.10.0. *F. K. Hunt* / **Frederick Knight Hunt**

August 31, 1850. No. 23, pp. 529–52

A Paper-Mill, 529–31. 5 cols. *Mr. C.D. & Mark Lemon* / **Charles Dickens & Mark Lemon**

Cheerful Arithmetic [England's commercial prosperity], 531–34. 5 cols. *W.H.W.* / **W. H. Wills**

An Emigrant Afloat [autobiog.], 534–39. 11 cols. £4.10.0. *Mr. Alex Mackie* / **Alexander Mackay**

The Sister's Farewell [verse], 539–40. ¾ col. £0.15.0. *Miss Browne & Horne* / **Miss Browne & Richard H. Horne**

The Home of Woodruffe the Gardener, chaps. iv–vi, 540–47. 14 cols. *Miss Martineau* / **Harriet Martineau**

Lines to a Dead Linnet. By a Solitary Student [verse], 547. ¾ col. *Mr. Horne* / **Richard H. Horne**

The Good Governor [of Bermuda: Sir William Reid], 547–49. 4 cols. £2.0.0. *Mr. S. Sidney* / **Samuel Sidney**

London Pauper Children [pauper school, Norwood], 549–52. 7 cols. £3.0.0. *Mr. Hunt (F. K.)* / **Frederick Knight Hunt**

September 7, 1850. No. 24, pp. 553–76

Illustrations of Cheapness [v]: The Steel Pen, 553–55. 5½ cols. £2.12.6. *Mr. Charles Knight* / **Charles Knight**

Two Chapters on Bank Note Forgeries, chap. i, 555–60. 9¾ cols. *W.H.W.* / **W. H. Wills**

The Two Guides of the Child [wrong and right way of teaching], 560–61. 2¼ cols. £1.1.0. *Morley* / **Henry Morley**

Chips:
- Easy Spelling and Hard Reading [letter from illiterate emigrant], 561–62. 2½ cols. £0.10.6. *Miss Cox & W.H.W.* / **Miss Cox & W. H. Wills**
- A Very Old Soldier [Johann Georg Kohl, *Reisen in den Niederlanden*, 1850], 562–64. 3¼ cols. £1.1.0. *Miss Ross & W.H.W.* / **Thomasina Ross & W. H. Wills**

The Household Jewels [verse], 564–65. 1½ cols. £1.1.0. *Mr. Prince* / **John Critchley Prince**

The Laboratory in the Chest [respiratory process], 565–69. 8 cols.; should read 8¾. £3.3.0. *P. Leigh* / **Percival Leigh**

The Home of Woodruffe the Gardener, chaps. vii–viii, 569–74. 10¼ cols. *Miss Martineau* / **Harriet Martineau**

The Singer [verse], 574–75. 1½ cols. £1.1.0. *Miss Greenwell* / **Dora Greenwell**

A Little Place in Norfolk [training school for pauper children], 575–76. 2¼ cols.; should read 3¼. *W.H.W.* / **W. H. Wills**

September 14, 1850. No. 25, pp. 577–600

Three "Detective" Anecdotes [related by Scotland Yard police], 577–80. 7¼ cols. *C.D.* / **Charles Dickens**

"Evil Is Wrought by Want of Thought" [story], 580–87. 13½ cols. £5.0.0. *Coventry Patmore* / **Coventry Patmore**

Chip:
- Torture in the Way of Business [by poulterers and butchers], 587–88. 1½ cols. *W.H.W.* / **W. H. Wills**

A Cottage Memory [verse], 588. 1¼ cols. £1.1.0. *Allingham* / **William Allingham**

"Cape" Sketches [Cape of Good Hope] [i], 588–91. 6 cols. £2.5.0. *Mr. Cole* / **Alfred Whaley Cole**

Chemical Contradictions, 591–94. 5 cols. £2.2.0. *Dr. Stone* / **Thomas Stone**

An Irish Peculiarity [the "wild Irish"], 594–96. 4 cols. £1.1.0. *Mrs. Hoare* / **Mrs. Hoare**

Where Dwell the Dead? [verse], 596. ½ col. £0.10.6. *Mrs. Shale St. George* / **Frances George**

Fate Days [superstitions], 596–98. 4 cols. £1.11.6. *W. B. Jerrold* / **William Blanchard Jerrold**

A Letter about Small Beginnings [letter from reader: Ragged Schools and Dormitories; correction of statement in "Small Beginnings," July 20], 598–600. 4¾ cols. *W.H.W.* / **W. H. Wills**

September 21, 1850. No. 26, pp. 601–620

Foreigners' Portraits of Englishmen, 601–604. 6½ cols. £1.1.0. *C.D., W.H.W., & Eustace Murray* / **Charles Dickens, W. H. Wills, & Grenville Murray**

The Steam Plough, 604–607. 6 cols. *Horne* / **Richard H. Horne**

A Sacred Grove [verse], 607. ½ col. *Horne* / **Richard H. Horne**

"Cape" Sketches [ii], 607–610. 6 cols. £3.0.0. *Alfred Cole* / **Alfred Whaley Cole**

"Battle with Life!" [verse], 611. ½ col. ——— / ———

Spy Police [in Kingdom of Naples], 611–14. 6 cols. £3.0.0. *H. Wreford* / **Henry G. Wreford**

Chips:
- The Individuality of Locomotives, 614. ¾ col. *C.D.* / **Charles Dickens**
- The Oldest Inhabitant of the Place de Grêve [woman who remembers Robespierre], 614–15. 1¾ cols. *Horne* / **Richard H. Horne**

Two Chapters on Bank Note Forgeries, chap. ii, 615–20. 11 cols. *W.H.W. & C.D.* / **W. H. Wills & Charles Dickens**

VOLUME II September 28, 1850 – March 22, 1851

September 28, 1850. No. 27, pp. 1–24

The Doom of English Wills [custodianship of documents in cathedral registries] [Cathedral Number One], 1–4. 6½ cols. *C.D. & W.H.W.* / **Charles Dickens & W. H. Wills**

Gentle Words [verse], 4. ¼ col. £0.10.6. *Mark Lemon* / **Mark Lemon**

Zoological Sessions. (Exclusive) [hippopotamus at Zoological Gardens], 4–10. 13 cols. *R.H.H.* / **Richard H. Horne**

The Subscription List [charity subscriptions], 10–12. 3 cols. £1.0.0. *W. B. Jerrold & W.H.W.* / **William Blanchard Jerrold & W. H. Wills**

The Emigrant's Bird [verse], 12. ½ col. £0.10.6. *Mark Lemon* / **Mark Lemon**

The Warilows of Welland; or, The Modern Prodigal [story], 12–19. 13 cols. £6.6.0. *Mr. William Howitt* / **William Howitt**

Genius and Liberty, 19–22. 5 cols.; should read 6½. £2.0.0. *H. Pattison* / **Robert Hogarth Patterson**

Atlantic Waves [scientific observations of William Scoresby, F.R.S.], 22–24. 5 cols. £2.0.0. *W. B. Jerrold* / **William Blanchard Jerrold**

October 5, 1850. No. 28, pp. 25–48

The Doom of English Wills: Cathedral Number Two, 25–29. 8 cols. *C.D. & W.H.W.* / **Charles Dickens & W. H. Wills**

The Irish "Stationers" [Catholic penitential pilgrimage], 29–33. 8½ cols. £4.0.0. *W. Allingham* / **William Allingham**

German Advertisements, 33–35. 5½ cols. £1.0.0 to Murray; £0.10.6 to Walker. *W.H.W., E. C. Murray, & Mr. Walker* / **W. H. Wills, Grenville Murray, &** prob. **Thomas Walker**

A Lay of London Streets [verse], 36. 1 col. £1.1.0. *E. Ollier* / **Edmund Ollier**

The Methusaleh Pill [quack remedies], 36–38. 4½ cols. £2.0.0. *W. B. Jerrold* / **William Blanchard Jerrold**

Mr. Van Ploos on Penmanship, 38–42. 9½ cols. *Horne* / **Richard H. Horne**

Gossip about Brussels [Johann Georg Kohl, *Reisen in den Niederlanden*, 1850], 42–45. 4¾ cols. £1.5.0. *Miss Ross* / **Thomasina Ross**

"Good Intentions." A Story of the African Blockade, 45–47. 4 cols. £1.5.0. *A. Cole* / **Alfred Whaley Cole**

Hints on Emergencies [John Flint South, *Household Surgery; or, Hints on Emergencies*, prob. 1850 ed.], 47–48. 3½ cols. £1.1.0. *W.H.W. & Dr. Stone* / **W. H. Wills & Thomas Stone**

October 12, 1850. No. 29, pp. 49–72

The "Good" Hippopotamus [absurd justifications for erecting statues], 49–51. 5 cols. *C.D.* / **Charles Dickens**

The Irish Use of the Globe, in One Lesson [land ownership as inducement to industry], 51–56. 9 cols. £4.14.6. *Morley* / **Henry Morley**

Adventures of a Translation [Elisabeth von Arnim's *Goethes Briefwechsel mit einem Kinde*], 56–58. 5 cols. £1.11.6. *Miss Prince Smith* / prob. **Mrs. Prince Smith**

How We Went Whaling off the Cape of Good Hope, 58–59. 3 cols. £1.1.0. *A. Cole* / **Alfred Whaley Cole**

A Lament for the Fairies [verse], 59–60. 1 col. £2.12.6. *A. A. Watts* / **Alaric Alexander Watts**

Gunpowder and Chalk [demolition of cliff to form sea-wall], 60–65. 10½ cols. *Horne* / **Richard H. Horne**

A Lesson for Future Life [verse], 65. ½ col. £0.10.6. ——— / ———

Spiders' Silk, 65–67. 3¼ cols. £1.10.0. *W. B. Jerrold* / **William Blanchard Jerrold**

Father Gabriel; or, The Fortunes of a Farmer [in Australia], 67–71. 7¾ cols. £3.3.0. *S. Sidney* / **Samuel Sidney**

A German Picture of the Scotch [on stage], 71–72. 2¾ cols. £1.11.6. *E. Murray* / **Grenville Murray**

October 19, 1850. No. 30, pp. 73–96

A Poor Man's Tale of a Patent [based on proof-sheets of a report by Henry Cole, later pub. by Society of Arts in *Rights of Inventors*, 1850], 73–75. 5¼ cols. *Mr. C.D.* / **Charles Dickens**

The New Zealand Zauberflöte [account of Maori chief], chap. i, 75–81. 11½ cols.; should read 12½. *Horne* / **Richard H. Horne**

The Penny Saved; a Blue-Book Catechism [restrictions on opportunity of working men to invest savings], 81–84. 4½ cols. £2.12.6. *Morley* / **Henry Morley**

A Guernsey Tradition [verse], 84–85. 2¼ cols.; should read 3¼. £2.2.0. *Mrs. Bradburn* / **Mrs. Bradburn**

Father Gabriel's Story [continuation of "Father Gabriel," Oct. 12], 85–90. 9¼ cols. £4.4.0. *Sidney* / **Samuel Sidney**

The Modern Robbers of the Rhine [inn-keepers, casino managers, etc.], 90–93. 7¼ cols. £3.0.0 *F. K. Hunt* / **Frederick Knight Hunt**

Chips:
- An Anecdote of the Irish Poor Law, 94. 1¼ cols. £0.10.6. *P. Dowdall* / **P. Dowdall**
- The Treasures of the Deep [whales], 94–95. ½ col. £0.5.0. *A. Cole* / **Alfred Whaley Cole**

The Monster Promenade Concerts [street music], 95–96. 4 cols. *W.H.W.* / **W. H. Wills**

October 26, 1850. No. 31, pp. 97–120

Lively Turtle [political conservatism], 97–99. 5½ cols. *C.D.* / **Charles Dickens**

Hiram Power's Greek Slave [verse], 99. ¼ col. ——— / **Elizabeth Barrett Browning**

The Duties of Witnesses and Jurymen, 100–104. 9½ cols. £3.13.6. *D. M. Hill* / **Matthew Davenport Hill**

Two Adventures at Sea, 104–108. 7 cols. £3.0.0. *S. Sidney* / **Samuel Sidney**

The Two Trees [verse], 108. 1 col. £1.0.0. *Prince* / **John Critchley Prince**

Protected Cradles [day-nurseries for working mothers' infants], 108–112. 7¼ cols. £2.10.0. *W. B. Jerrold* / **William Blanchard Jerrold**

A Memory [verse], 112. ½ col. £0.10.6. ——— / ———

The New Zealand Zauberflöte, chap. ii, 112–17. 10¼ cols.; should read 9½. *R. H. Horne* / **Richard H. Horne**

"Give Wisely!" An Anecdote, 117–18. 2 cols. £1.0.0. *Mrs. Hoare* / **Mrs. Hoare**

"Cape" Sketches [iii], 118–20. 5½ cols. £2.2.0. *A. Cole* / **Alfred Whaley Cole**

November 2, 1850. No. 32, pp. 121–44

Gottfried Kinkel; a Life in Three Pictures, 121–25. 8½ cols. *R. H. Horne* / **Richard H. Horne**

The Doom of English Wills: Cathedral Number Three, 125–28. 7 cols. *W.H.W.* / **W. H. Wills**

The Sower [verse], 128. ¼ col. ——— / **Henry Morley**

The New Zealand Zauberflöte, chap. iii, 128–32. 7¼ cols.; should read 8. *R. H. Horne* / **Richard H. Horne**

The Golden Age [verse], 132–33. 1 col. £1.1.0. *Coventry Patmore* / **Coventry Patmore**

Bits of Life in Munich [i], 133–37. 9 cols. £3.10.0. *Miss Howitt* / **Anna Mary Howitt**

A Great Day for the Doctors [commencement of new term in medical schools], 137–39. 4 cols. £1.10.0. *F. K. Hunt* / **Frederick Knight Hunt**

The Ghost That Appeared to Mrs. Wharton [a human intruder], 139–43. 7 cols.; should read 7¾. £3.3.0. *Miss Martineau* / **Harriet Martineau**

Chip:
- A Voice from a "Quiet" Street [street music], 143–44. 3 cols. £2.0.0. *Mr. Delaware Lewis* / **John Delaware Lewis**

November 9, 1850. No. 33, pp. 145–68

The Cow with the Iron Tail [based in part on Henry Hodson Rugg, *Observations on London Milk, Showing Its Unhealthy Character, and Poisonous Adulterations*, n.d.], 145–51. 12½ cols. *R. H. Horne* / **Richard H. Horne**

A Lunatic Asylum in Palermo [trans. from Italian source], 151–55. 9 cols. £3.0.0. *Miss Ross* / **Thomasina Ross**

Poison Sold Here! [nonrestricted sale of arsenic], 155–57. 2¾ cols. *W.H.W.* / **W. H. Wills**

The Two Blackbirds [verse], 157. 1 col. £1.1.0. *Mr. Meredith & R.H.H.* / **George Meredith & Richard H. Horne**

The "Freshman's" Progress [at University], 157–63. 11½ cols. £5.5.0. *Mr. Delaware Lewis* / **John Delaware Lewis**

Chips:
- "Sloped for Texas" [incident in Arkansas gaming-house], 163–64. 2 cols. £0.15.0. *Whitelock* / **Whitelock**
- Rio de Janeiro and Its Feather-Flowers ["from the manuscript journal of a traveller"], 164–65. 2 cols. £0.15.0. *S. Sidney* / **Samuel Sidney**

"Cape" Sketches [iv], 165–67. 3¾ cols.; should read 4½. £1.10.0. *A. Cole* / **Alfred Whaley Cole**

Why People Let Lodgings, 167–68. 2¾ cols. £1.1.0. *W. B. Jerrold* / **William Blanchard Jerrold**

November 16, 1850. No. 34, pp. 169–92

Views of the Country [England's social progress], 169–72. 6½ cols. £3.13.6. *Mr. Morley* / **Henry Morley**

What a London Curate Can Do If He Tries, 172–76. 9¼ cols. £3.13.6. *F. K. Hunt* / **Frederick Knight Hunt**

The Mysteries of a Tea-Kettle [based on Faraday's lectures at Royal Institution], 176–81. 10 cols. £4.4.0. *Percival Leigh* / **Percival Leigh**

Wayconnell Tower [verse], 181. ¾ col. £1.1.0. *W. Allingham* / **William Allingham**

The Well of Pen-Morfa [story], chap. i, 182–86. 9 cols. £5.5.0. *Mrs. Gaskell* / **Elizabeth Gaskell**

Chips:
- Lieutenant Waghorn and His Widow [correction of statements in "Lieutenant Waghorn," Aug. 17], 186–87. 1¼ cols. *W.H.W.* / **W. H. Wills**
- "Household Words" and English Wills [concerning "Doom of English Wills," Oct. 5], 187. ¾ col. *W.H.W.* / **W. H. Wills**
- Letters of Introduction to Sydney [an emigrant's account of Sydney life], 187–88. 2½ cols. £1.1.0. *S. Sidney* / **Samuel Sidney**

Crotchets of a Playgoer, 188–90. 4 cols. £2.2.0. *H. Heraud* / **John Abraham Heraud**

Life in an Estancia [in the Argentine], part i, 190–92. 4¾ cols. £5.5.0 for the 3 instalments. *Mr. Harvey per C. Knight* / **Harvey**

November 23, 1850. No. 35, pp. 193–216

A Crisis in the Affairs of Mr. John Bull. As Related by Mrs. Bull to the Children ["papal aggression"], 193–96. 6 cols. *Mr. C.D.* / **Charles Dickens**

The Jolly Burglars [story], 196–203. 14 cols. *H. Horne* / **Richard H. Horne**

The Doom of English Wills: Cathedral Number Four, 203–205. 4¼ cols. *W.H.W.* / **W. H. Wills**

The Dumb Child [verse], 205. 1¼ cols. £1.11.6. *Eliza Griffiths* / **Miss Eliza Griffiths**

The Well of Pen-Morfa, chap. ii, 205–210. 8½ cols. £5.5.0. *Mrs. Gaskell* / **Elizabeth Gaskell**

Chip:
– The Sunday Question in the Last Century [from Andrew Burnaby, "Observations on the State of Boston," *Universal Magazine,* March 1775], 210. 1 col. *W.H.W.* / **W. H. Wills**

Life in an Estancia, part ii, 210–14. 5 cols.; should read 7. *Mr. Harvey per Mr. Knight* / **Harvey**

Rats! [based on pamphlet], 214–16. 8 cols.; should read 5½. £2.12.6. *F. K. Hunt* / **Frederick Knight Hunt**

November 30, 1850. No. 36, pp. 217–40

Mr. Booley's View of the Last Lord Mayor's Show [sanitary reform], 217–19. 5½ cols. *Mr. C.D.* / **Charles Dickens**

University Omission and Commission, 219–25. 12 cols. £6.0.0. *Mr. Delaware Lewis* / **John Delaware Lewis**

Food for the Factory [cotton for English mills], 225–29. 6½ cols. £2.12.6. *W. B. Jerrold* / **William Blanchard Jerrold**

Human Brotherhood [verse], 229. ¼ col. £0.10.6. *Mr. Harper* / **Harper**

The King of the Hearth [fantasy], 229–33. 8¼ cols. £5.0.0. *Mr. Morley* / **Henry Morley**

Life in an Estancia, part iii, 233–35. 3¼ cols. *Mr. Harvey per Mr. Knight* / **Harvey**

A Visit to the Registrar-General, 235–40. 12 cols. £6.0.0. *Mr. F. K. Hunt* / **Frederick Knight Hunt**

December 7, 1850. No. 37, pp. 241–64

Wings of Wire [the telegraph], 241–45. 9½ cols. £4.0.0. *F. K. Hunt* / **Frederick Knight Hunt**

A Coal Miner's Evidence [on colliery explosions], 245–50. 9½ cols. *R. H. Horne* / **Richard H. Horne**

The Martyrs of Chancery [i], 250–52. 4¾ cols. £2.2.0. *A. Cole* / **Alfred Whaley Cole**

The Outcast Lady [verse], 252. ½ col. £0.10.6. ——— *per Mrs. Gaskell* / ———

A Cape Coast Cargo [on American slaver], 252–57. 8½ cols. £3.3.0. *Mr. Franklyn Fox & W.H.W.* / **Franklin Fox & W. H. Wills**

The Sea-Side Churchyard [lives lost at sea], 257–62. 11 cols. £4.4.0. *W. Howitt* / **William Howitt**

The Youth and the Sage [verse], 262. ⅛ col. *R. H. Horne* / **Richard H. Horne**

The Devonshire Dorado [natural resources of Dartmoor], 262–64. 4¾ cols. £2.0.0. *Sidney Smith & W.H.W.* / **Sidney Smith & W. H. Wills**

December 14, 1850. No. 38, pp. 265–88

A December Vision [responsibility for righting social wrongs], 265–67. 4 cols. *C.D.* / **Charles Dickens**

A Suburban Romance [story], 267–71. 9½ cols. £0.10.6 to Mrs. Hoare for idea suggested by her. *W.H.W.* / **W. H. Wills**

Back Street Conservatories [in part from N. B. Ward, *On the Growth of Plants in Closely Glazed Cases*, 1842], 271–75. 7 cols. £2.2.0. *Mr. Ward & W.H.W.* / **Nathaniel Bagshaw Ward & W. H. Wills**

Chips:
- "Streetography" [London street names], 275–76. 1¾ cols. *W.H.W.* / **W. H. Wills**
- Land Ho! – Port Jackson [an arrival's impression of Sydney: from "his travelling note-bote" – i.e., "note-book"], 276–77. 2 cols. £1.0.0. *Sidney* / **Samuel Sidney**
- Death in the Teapot [deleterious substances in tea], 277. 1 col. £0.10.6. *Strange & W.H.W.* / **Charles Strange & W. H. Wills**

City Graves [verse], 277. ¾ col. £1.1.0. *Delaware Lewis* / **John Delaware Lewis**

The Hunterian Museum, 277–82. 8½ cols. £4.0.0. *F. K. Hunt* / **Frederick Knight Hunt**

The Wealth of the Woods [forests of New Brunswick, Canada], 282–84. 5 cols. £1.11.6. *W. B. Jerrold* / **William Blanchard Jerrold**

The Magic Crystal [divining crystals; *Zadkiel's Almanac*], 284–88. 8¼ cols. £1.1.0 to Wilson; £3.13.6 to Costello. *T. H. Wilson, D. Costello, & W.H.W.* / **T. H. Wilson, Dudley Costello, & W. H. Wills**

December 21, 1850. No. 39, pp. 289–312. Above periodical title is heading: The Christmas Number.

A Christmas Tree, 289–95. 13¾ cols. *Mr. C.D.* / **Charles Dickens**

Christmas in Lodgings, 295–98. 5¾ cols. £2.12.6. *W. B. Jerrold & W.H.W.* / **William Blanchard Jerrold & W. H. Wills**

Christmas in the Navy, 298–300. 4 cols. £2.12.6. *J. Hannay* / **James Hannay**

A Christmas Pudding [free trade, protection, monopoly], 300–304. 7 cols. £3.10.0. *Charles Knight* / **Charles Knight**

Christmas among the London Poor and Sick, 304–305. 2¼ cols. £1.1.0. *F. K.* [2nd initial unclear] *Hunt* / **Frederick Knight Hunt**

Christmas in India, 305–306. 2 cols.; should read 3. £1.11.6. *J. Stoqueler* / **Joachim Heyward Siddons**

Christmas in the Frozen Regions, 306–309. 4¼ cols. £1.11.6. *Dr. Cormack & C.D.* / **Robert McCormick & Charles Dickens**

Christmas Day in the Bush, 309–310. 3¾ cols. £1.10.0. *S. Sidney* / **Samuel Sidney**

Household Christmas Carols [verse], 310–12. 4 cols. *R. H. Horne* / **Richard H. Horne**

December 28, 1850. No. 40, pp. 313–36

Mr. Bendigo Buster on Our National Defences against Education [Prussian school system: from Joseph Kay, *The Social Condition and Education of the People in England and Europe*, 1850], 313–19. 12½ cols. £5.5.0. *Mr. C.D. & Mr. Morley* / **Charles Dickens & Henry Morley**

Railway Waifs and Strays [lost articles and luggage], 319–22. 6 cols. £1.1.0. *W.H.W. & Chris^er Hill* / **W. H. Wills & Christopher Hill**

Chips:
- The Baron of Beef and the Marquis of Wellington [anecdote concerning Wellington], 322–23. 1¼ cols. *R. H. Horne* / **Richard H. Horne**
- Death in the Bread-Basket [deleterious substances in bread], 323. 1 col. £0.10.0. *W.H.W. & Strange* / **W. H. Wills & Charles Strange**
- A Remedy for Colliery Explosions [letter from reader], 323–25. 3 cols. *Item not in Office Book* / ———

New Year's Eve [verse], 325. ¾ col. £1.1.0. *Mr. Meredith* / **George Meredith**

The Heart of John Middleton [story], 325–34. 18¼ cols. £10.0.0. *Mrs. Gaskell* / **Elizabeth Gaskell**

The Chords of Love [verse], 334–35. ¼ col. £1.1.0. *Mr. Harper* / **Harper**

The Death of a Goblin [story], 335–36. 3¾ cols. £1.11.6. *H. Morley* / **Henry Morley**

January 4, 1851. No. 41, pp. 337–60

The Last Words of the Old Year [needed reforms], 337–39. 5½ cols. *Mr. C.D.* / **Charles Dickens**

Mrs. Ranford's New Year's Dinner [story], 339–48. 16 cols.; should read 17. £7.7.0. *Mr. Howitt* / **William Howitt**

The Burial of the Old Year [verse], 348. 1½ cols. £1.11.6. *Miss Siddons* / **Miss Siddons**

The Irish California [extraction of chemical products from peat], 348–53. 7¾ cols.; should read 8¾. £4.0.0. *Mr. Percival Leigh* / **Percival Leigh**

A New Phase of Bee-Life, 353–55. 4½ cols.; should read 3½. £1.11.6. *Mr. Tom Satchell* / **Thomas Satchell**

The Queen's Tobacco-Pipe [incineration of damaged imports], 355–58. 6 cols. £2.0.0. *Mr. Howitt* / **William Howitt**

Bits of Life in Munich [ii], 358–59. 2½ cols. £1.10.0. *Miss Howitt* / **Anna Mary Howitt**

A Metaphysical Mystery [story], 359–60. 3½ cols. £1.11.6. *Mr. Hannay* / **James Hannay**

January 11, 1851. No. 42, pp. 361–84

Railway Strikes, 361–64. 6 cols. *Mr. C.D.* / **Charles Dickens**

The Other Garret [story], 364–69. 11½ cols. £4.4.0. *Mr. Thomas* / **William Moy Thomas**

Efforts of a Gentleman in Search of Despair ["the Doleful School" of versifiers], 369–72. 6½ cols. £2.10.0. *W. B. Jerrold* / **William Blanchard Jerrold**

A Winter Sermon [verse], 372–73. ½ col. £0.15.0. *Harper* / **Harper**

Lighthouses and Light-Boats [in large part from Alan Stevenson, *A Rudimentary Treatise on ... Lighthouses*, 1850], 373–79. 13½ cols. *R. H. Horne* / **Richard H. Horne**

The Coral Fishery in the Mediterranean, 379–83. 6½ cols. £2.15.0. *Wreford* / **Henry G. Wreford**

The Story of Fine-Ear [prisoner's companionship with a rat], 383–84. 4 cols. £1.1.0. *Mrs. Hoare* / **Mrs. Hoare**

January 18, 1851. No. 43, pp. 385–408

The Private History of the Palace of Glass [origin and development of Joseph Paxton's design], 385–91. 12 cols. *W.H.W.* / **W. H. Wills**

The Modern Soldier's Progress [army life], part i, 391–95. 9 cols. £4.4.0. *Dudley Costello* / **Dudley Costello**

Bits of Life in Munich [iii], 395–97. 5 cols. £2.2.0. *Miss Howitt* / **Anna Mary Howitt**

Thomas Harlowe [verse], 397–400. 5 cols. £2.12.6. *Mrs. Howitt* / **Mary Howitt**

Our Phantom Ship: Negro Land, 400–407. 15 cols. £6.6.0. *Morley* / **Henry Morley**

The Law [instance of prolonged litigation on trifling matter: from "an esteemed correspondent," a lawyer], 407–408. 2 cols. £1.1.0. *C. Knight* / **Charles Knight**

January 25, 1851. No. 44, pp. 409–432

A Child's History of England [compiled in large part from Thomas Keightley, *The History of England*, and from George L. Craik and Charles MacFarlane, *The Pictorial History of England*], chap. i, 409–412. 8 cols. *C.D.* / **Charles Dickens**

Aspire! [verse], 412–13. ½ col. ——— / ———

Physiology of Intemperance, 413–17. 9 cols. £3.13.6. *Dr. Stone* / **Thomas Stone**

Life in a Saladero [slaughter-house in the Argentine], 417–20. 5 cols. *Dr. Von Corning & W.H.W.* / **Dr. Von Corning & W. H. Wills**

The Church Poor-Box [verse], 420. 1¼ cols. *R.H. Horne* / **Richard H. Horne**

A Biography of a Bad Shilling [counterfeit coinage], 420–26. 10½ cols. £3.13.6. *Blanshard* / **Sidney Laman Blanchard**

Chips:
- Death in the Sugar Plum [poison in sweetmeats], 426–27. 2 cols. *W.H.W.* / **W. H. Wills**
- The True Remedy for Colliery Explosions, 427. 1 col. *S.R.* / **S.R.**

The Modern Soldier's Progress, part ii, 427–31. 7 cols. £3.12.0. *Dudley Costello* / **Dudley Costello**

"Judge Not!" [account of Stanislaw Staszic], 431–32. 3½ cols. £1.1.0. *Mrs. Hoare* / **Mrs. Hoare**

February 1, 1851. No. 45, pp. 433–56

Plate Glass, 433–37. 9¾ cols. *C.D. & W.H.W.* / **Charles Dickens & W. H. Wills**

A Guild Clerk's Tale [story], 437–44. 14 cols. £5.5.0. *Thomas* / **William Moy Thomas**

Mercy [verse], 444–45. 1 col. £1.1.0. *Prince* / **John Critchley Prince**

Father Thames [polluted water], 445–50. 9½ cols. *Horne* / **Richard H. Horne**

Chip:
- A Woman's Experience in California, 450–51. 2 cols. *W.H.W.* / **W. H. Wills, C. B. Harrold, & Harrold's sister**

The Modern Soldier's Progress, part iii, 451–55. 8 cols. £4.4.0. *Dudley Costello* / **Dudley Costello**

Peace and War [verse], 455. ¾ col. £0.10.6. *W. B. Jerrold* / **William Blanchard Jerrold**

How to Be Idolised [episode concerning a Frenchman and a Malagasy: from "a French author"], 455–56. 3 cols. £1.0.0. *Mrs. Hoare* / **Mrs. Hoare**

February 8, 1851. No. 46, pp. 457–80

Twenty-four Hours in a London Hospital, 457–65. 16 cols. £7.0.0. *F. K. Hunt* / **Frederick Knight Hunt**

A Confident Prediction [story], 465–68. 7 cols. £3.0.0. *Miss Ellis* / **Miss Ellis**

The Nineveh Bull [history of the statue], 468–69. 3 cols. £1.1.0. *W. H. Stone* / **W. H. Stone**

Wealthy and Wise [verse], 469–70. ½ col. £1.0.0. *Morley* / **Henry Morley**

Sleep, 470–75. 11 cols. £4.4.0. *Dr. Stone* / **Thomas Stone**

Chips:
- The Invited Invasion [visitors to Great Exhibition], 475–77. 3 cols. *W.H.W.* / **W. H. Wills**
- The Ace of Spades [John Sillett, *A New Practical System of Fork and Spade Husbandry*, 1850 ed.], 477–78. 3½ cols. £1.1.0. *Sidney Smith* / **Sidney Smith**

The Forest Temple [verse], 479. ¾ col. £1.0.0. *Mr. E. Lawson* / **E. Lawson**

Pleb-Biddlecumb Education [a rural Mutual Improvement society], 479–80. 3 cols. £1.1.0. *Hannay* / **James Hannay**

February 15, 1851. No. 47, pp. 481–504

Red Tape, 481–84. 7 cols. *Mr. C.D.* / **Charles Dickens**

The Broken Chain [verse], 484. ¼ col. £0.10.6. *Miss Greenwell* / **Dora Greenwell**

Two Scenes in the Life of John Bodger [story], 484–91. 14 cols. £6.6.0. *Sidney* / **Samuel Sidney**

Chips:
- Degree Day at Cambridge, 491–92. 1¼ cols. ——— / ———
- A Welsh Wedding, 492–93. 2 cols. £0.10.6. *Mrs. Wyley* / **Mrs. Wyley**

Saint Valentine [verse], 493. 1¼ cols. £1.1.0. *Miss Rogers* / **Mary Eliza Rogers**

The Martyrs of Chancery, ii, 493–96. 6 cols. £2.2.0. *W.H.W. & A. Cole* / **W. H. Wills & Alfred Whaley Cole**

A Prison Anecdote, 496–98. 3 cols. £1.1.0. *Chesterton* / **George Laval Chesterton**

The Chemistry of a Pint of Beer, 498–502. 7¾ cols.; should read 8½. £4.0.0. *P. Leigh* / **Percival Leigh**

A Salt Growl [Admiralty mismanagement], 502–504. 5 cols. £2.0.0. *J. Hannay* / **James Hannay**

February 22, 1851. No. 48, pp. 505–528

"Births. Mrs. Meek, of a Son" [treatment of infants], 505–507. 4 cols. *C.D.* / **Charles Dickens**

The Tyrant of Minnigissengen [adapted from a novelette by Alphonse Karr], 507–513. 12 cols. £2.10.0. *W.H.W. & J. Knox* / **W. H. Wills & James Knox**

The Builder's House, and the Bricklayer's Garden. By an Eye-Witness and Sufferer [shoddy construction], 513–16. 7 cols. *R. H. Horne* / **Richard H. Horne**

A Christian Paynim. A Legend [verse], 516. ¾ col. £1.1.0. *Evelyn* / **Evelyn**

Our Phantom Ship: Central America, 516–22. 10¼ cols. £4.10.0. *H. Morley* / **Henry Morley**

The Queen's Bazaar [customs house sale], 522–24. 5 cols. £2.2.0. *W. B. Jerrold* / **William Blanchard Jerrold**

Likeness in Difference [verse], 524. ¼ col. £0.10.6. *Miss Greenwell* / **Dora Greenwell**

A Child's History of England, chap. ii, 524–28. 8¼ cols. *C.D.* / **Charles Dickens**

March 1, 1851. No. 49, pp. 529–52

Ten Minutes with Her Majesty [opening of Parliament], 529–32. 7¼ cols. *W.H.W* / **W. H. Wills**

A Dark Suspicion [sailor wrongfully suspected of theft], 532–35. 6¼ cols. £2.12.6. *Franklyn Fox* / **Franklin Fox**

Bits of Life in Munich [iv], 535–40. 8¼ cols. £3.3.0. *Miss Howitt* / **Anna Mary Howitt**

The Waste of War [verse], 540. ¾ col. £1.10.0. *Mr. Prince* / **John Critchley Prince**

The Crocodile Battery [killing crocodiles, India], 540–43. 7 cols. £2.10.0. *Mr. Peppé* / **Peppé**

Chips:
- A Royal Speech by James the First [*Report of a Speech ... , 20 June 1616. Taken at the Time by Edward Wakeman*, 1848], 543–45. 4 cols. *W.H.W.* / **W. H. Wills**
- National-Debt Doctors [in part "from a correspondent"], 545–46. 1¾ cols. *W.H.W.* / **W. H. Wills**

A Cinnamon Garden [in Ceylon], 546–48. 4 cols. £1.10.0. *Mr. Capper* / **John Capper**

The Story of Giovanni Belzoni [in part from Belzoni, *Narrative of the ... Recent Discoveries ... in Egypt and Nubia*, first pub. 1820], 548–52. 9 cols. £1.5.0. *W.H.W. & Mrs. Hoare* / **W. H. Wills & Mrs. Hoare**

March 8, 1851. No. 50, pp. 553–76

A Monument of French Folly [well-managed cattle market and abattoir], 553–58. 10¼ cols. *Mr. C.D.* / **Charles Dickens**

My Mahogany Friend [story], 558–62. 8¾ cols. £3.3.0. *The Honble Miss Boyle & C.D.* / **Mary Louisa Boyle & Charles Dickens**

A Suburban Connemara [squalid London district], 562–65. 6¾ cols. £3.13.6. *T. M. Thomas* / **T. M. Thomas**

A World at Peace [verse], 565–66. ½ col. £1.1.0. *Harper* / **Harper**

Dreams, 566–72. 13 cols. £5.15.6. *Dr. Stone* / **Thomas Stone**

The Congress of Nations [verse], 572. ½ col. £0.10.6. *Meredith* / **George Meredith**

Chip:
- The Smithfield Model of the Model Smithfield [cattle market], 572–73. 1 col. *Ossian Macpherson* / **Ossian Macpherson**

A Plea for British Reptiles, 573–76. 7¼ cols. £3.13.6. *Morley* / **Henry Morley**

March 15, 1851. No. 51, pp. 577–600

The Female School of Design in the Capital of the World, 577–81. 9½ cols. *R.H.H.* / **Richard H. Horne**

Darling Dorel [Valentin Gierth's account of Dorothea Sibylla, Duchess of Brieg], 581–85. 7¾ cols. £3.3.0. *Lady Duff Gordon & W.H.W.* / **Lucie Duff-Gordon & W. H. Wills**

The Cocoa-Nut Palm, 585–89. 8 cols. £2.12.6. *J. Capper* / **John Capper**

The Smithfield Bull to His Cousin of Nineveh [verse], 589–90. 1½ cols. *R.H.H.* / **Richard H. Horne**

Indian Railroads and British Commerce [based on John Chapman, *The Cotton and Commerce of India*, 1851], 590–95. 9¼ cols. £3.15.0. *S. Sidney* / **Samuel Sidney**

Chips:
- The Spade [advantage of spade husbandry], 595–97. 4¼ cols. £1.0.0. *Sidney Smith & W.H.W.* / **Sidney Smith & W. H. Wills**
- The Short Cut to California [obstructed by red tape], 597–98. 1½ cols. £0.10.6. *H. Morley & W.H.W.* / **Henry Morley & W. H. Wills**

A Specimen of Russian Justice [innocent Frenchwoman sent to Siberia], 598–600. 5½ cols. £1.11.6. *J. Jackowski & W.H.W.* / **Ignacy Jackowski & W. H. Wills**

March 22, 1851. No. 52, pp. 601–620

Bill-Sticking, 601–606. 10½ cols. £1.0.0 to (name unclear) "the Bill Sticker." *Mr. C.D.* / **Charles Dickens**

"To Clergymen in Difficulties" [clergyman in hands of swindlers], 606–612. 12 cols. £2.2.0 to man (name unclear) "who furnished the idea." *W.H.W.* / **W. H. Wills**

The Mother's Test [verse], 612. 1 col. £1.1.0. *Miss Tomkins* / **Mary Jane Tomkins**

The Sailors' Home [Sailors' Homes], 612–15. 6 cols. £3.3.0. *Hannay* / **James Hannay**

A Time for All Things [England's achievements and non-achievements], 615–17. 4¼ cols. *R.H.H.* / **Richard H. Horne**

The Modern Haroun-al-Raschid [an Algerian sheik], 617–20. 6 cols. £2.15.0. *Mrs. Hoare* / **Mrs. Hoare**

VOLUME III March 29 – September 20, 1851

March 29, 1851. No. 53, pp. 1–24

Alice and the Angel [story], 1–9. 17¼ cols. £9.0.0. *Mr. Thomas* / **William Moy Thomas**

Bits of Life in Munich [v], 9–13. 8 cols. £3.15.0. *Miss Howitt* / **Anna Mary Howitt**

A Vagrant's Deathbed [verse], 13. ½ col. £1.1.0. *Mr. Harpur* / **Harper**

The Rational Doctor [nature and treatment of disease], 13–18. 9 cols. £4.4.0. *Leigh* / **Percival Leigh**

Chip:
- Lives and Cargoes [salvage of, in shipwrecks], 18–19. 3 cols. *R.H.H.* / **Richard H. Horne**

A Child's History of England, chap. iii, 19–24. 10 cols. *C.D.* / **Charles Dickens**

April 5, 1851. No. 54, pp. 25–48

Spitalfields, 25–30. 11 cols. *C.D. & W.H.W.* / **Charles Dickens & W. H. Wills**

The Cape and the Kaffirs. A History, 30–35. 10½ cols. £4.15.0. *Morley* / **Henry Morley**

A Voice from the Factory [verse], 35–36. 1 col. £1.11.6. *Prince* / **John Critchley Prince**

The Blue-Jacket Agitation [merchant marine legislation], 36–41. 10 cols. £5.0.0. *J. Hannay* / **James Hannay**

Chips:
- Small Beginnings [boys reformed by industrial school, now successful emigrants], 41–42. 1½ cols. *W.H.W. & C.D.* / **W. H. Wills & Charles Dickens**
- Domestic Servants in Austria, 42–43. 2¼ cols. £1.1.0. *Murray* / **Grenville Murray**

Bits of Life in Munich [vi], 43–46. 6 cols. £3.0.0. *Miss Howitt* / **Anna Mary Howitt**

A Spider in Disguise, 46–48. 5½ cols. £2.12.6. *Satchell* / **Thomas Satchell**

April 12, 1851. No. 55, pp. 49–72

The Great Coffee Question, 49–53. 8 cols. £4.10.0. *J. Hannay* / **James Hannay**

The Marsh Fog and the Sea Breeze [story], chap. i, 53–58. 11 cols. £5.5.0. *Miss Martineau* / **Harriet Martineau**

Mr. Bubs on Planetary Disturbances [orbit of Mars], 58–60. 4¼ cols. £2.0.0. *C. T. Hudson* / **Charles Thomas Hudson**

The Grave of Faction [verse], 60–61. ½ col. £1.1.0. *Harper* / **Harper**

Common-Sense on Wheels [cabs and cab drivers], 61–66. 10 cols. £1.1.0. *C.D., W.H.W., & Murray* / **Charles Dickens, W. H. Wills, & Grenville Murray**

Our Phantom Ship among the Ice, 66–72. 13 cols. £6.6.0. *Morley* / **Henry Morley**

The Two Roads [admonition to the young], 72. 1 col. £0.10.0. *Mrs. Hoare* / **Mrs. Hoare**

April 19, 1851. No. 56, pp. 73–96

Three May-Days in London, i: The May-Pole in Cornhill. (1517) ["Evil May-Day"], 73–75. 5½ cols. £3.3.0. *Charles Knight* / **Charles Knight**

My Pearl-Fishing Expedition [Ceylon], 75–80. 10 cols. £4.10.0. *Capper* / **John Capper**

Free Public Libraries, 80–83. 4½ cols. £2.2.0. *Morley & Lynn* / **Henry Morley & Lynn**

News of Natal [letter to Samuel Sidney from Oxford graduate in south Africa], 83–85. 4 cols. £1.11.6. *Sidney* / **Samuel Sidney**

Infancy and Age [verse], 85. ½ col. £0.10.6. *Meredith* / **George Meredith**

London Sparrows [juvenile pickpockets], 85–88. 5½ cols.; should read 6½. *R.H.H.* / **Richard H. Horne**

The Marsh Fog and the Sea Breeze, chap. ii, 88–94. 13 cols. £5.5.0. *Miss Martineau* / **Harriet Martineau**

A Mysterious City [on Yucatan peninsula], 94–96. 4¼ cols. *W.H.W.* / **W. H. Wills**

April 26, 1851. No. 57, pp. 97–120

The Metropolitan Protectives [London police], 97–105. 17 cols. *C.D. & W.H.W.* / **Charles Dickens & W. H. Wills**

Three May-Days in London, ii: May Fair. (1701), 105–109. 6½ cols. £3.3.0. *C. Knight* / **Charles Knight**

Geraldine [verse], 109. ½ col. £1.0.0. *Prince* / **John Critchley Prince**

Coffee Planting in Ceylon, 109–114. 9½ cols. £4.0.0. *Capper* / **John Capper**

Chips:
- The Spade in Ireland [experimental farm in Ballinglen], 114–15. 3¾ cols. £1.10.0. *Sidney Smith* / **Sidney Smith**
- A Breton Wedding, 115–17. 3¾ cols. £1.1.0. *Mrs. Martin* / **Mrs. Martin**

The Palace of Flowers [Kew Gardens], 117–120. 6¼ cols. £3.3.0. *Hannay* / **James Hannay**

May 3, 1851. No. 58, pp. 121–44

Three May-Days in London, iii: The May Palace. (1851) [the Crystal Palace], 121–24. 7 cols. £3.3.0. *Charles Knight* / **Charles Knight**

The Last of the Sea-Kings [Charles Johnson, *A General History of the Pyrates*, 18-cent. compilation], 124–30. 11¼ cols. £6.10.0. *Morley* / **Henry Morley**

Chips:
- The British Museum a Century Ago, 130–31. 2 cols. £1.1.0. *W. B. Jerrold* / **William Blanchard Jerrold**
- The Great Southern Reflector [telescope], 131–32. 1½ cols. £0.15.0. *Morley* / **Henry Morley**

The Blast of War [verse], 132. ½ col. £1.1.0. *Harper* / **Harper**

Somnambulism, 132–38. 12½ cols. £5.5.0. *Dr. Stone* / **Thomas Stone**

A New Plea for a New Food [maize], 138–40. 3½ cols. £1.10.0. *Miss Martineau* / **Harriet Martineau**

A Child's History of England, chap. iv, 140–44. 9 cols. *C.D.* / **Charles Dickens**

May 10, 1851. No. 59, pp. 145–68

The Guild of Literature and Art, 145–47. 4½ cols. *C.D.* / **Charles Dickens**

Cain in the Fields [rural crime], 147–51. 9 cols. *R.H.H. & C.D.* / **Richard H. Horne & Charles Dickens**

Some Account of Chloroform, 151–55. 8½ cols. £4.4.0. *P. Leigh* / **Percival Leigh**

Work Away! [verse], 155–56. 1¼ cols. £1.11.6. *Miss Dora Greenwell* / **Dora Greenwell**

Epping Forest [proposed enclosure of], 156–60. 8 cols. £3.13.6. *W. Howitt* / **William Howitt**

Chip:
- The Sailor at Home [Sailors' Homes], 160. ¾ col. £0.10.0. *W.H.W. & Mr. Byng* / **W. H. Wills & Byng**

Our Phantom Ship: Japan, 160–67. 13¼ cols. £6.0.0. *Morley* / **Henry Morley**

The Momentous Question [stating one's age on census questionnaire], 167–68. 2¾ cols. £1.11.6. *Lewis* / **John Delaware Lewis**

May 17, 1851. No. 60, pp. 169–92

The Finishing Schoolmaster [the hangman], 169–71. 4¼ cols. *C.D.* / **Charles Dickens**

The Successful Candidate. Committee-Room, with Closed Doors [electioneering tactics], 171–79. 15¾ cols. £7.0.0. *R. H. Horne* / **Richard H. Horne**

London Musical Clubs, 179–81. 3½ cols.; should read 4½. £1.11.6. *H. Cole* / **H. Cole**

The Legend of the Ladye's Cross [verse], 181–82. 2 cols. £1.11.6. *Miss Dutton* / **Miss Dutton**

A Short Trip into Bosnia, 182–87. 10¼ cols. £5.10.0. *Dr. Wenckstern* / **Otto von Wenckstern**

Chips:
- A Card [to *H.W.* verse contributors], 187. ¼ col. *W.H.W.* / **W. H. Wills**
- Mr. Bubb's Visit to the Moon [tide-generating force of moon], 187–88. 1¼ cols. £0.10.6. *Mr. Hughes* / **Hughes**
- True Anecdote of the Last Century [case of mistaken identity], 188–89. 1¾ cols. *Mrs. Sidney Smith & W.H.W.* / **Catharine Amelia Smith & W. H. Wills**
- Coolness among Thieves [prison episode], 189–90. 2¼ cols. £1.1.0. *Col. Chesterton* / **George Laval Chesterton**

A Ball at the Barriers [in outskirts of Paris], 190–92. 5 cols. £2.12.6. *Sidney Blanchard* / **Sidney Laman Blanchard**

May 24, 1851. No. 61, pp. 193–216

The Pen and the Pickaxe [sewerage and drainage of outlying London districts], 193–96. 6½ cols. "Included in [Horne's] former engagement" (i.e., as staff member). *R. H. Horne* / **Richard H. Horne**

The One Black Spot [story], 196–201. 9¾ cols. £5.0.0. *Addiscott & W.H.W.* / **Addiscott & W. H. Wills**

Cheap Pleasures. – A Gossip, 201–203. 5¼ cols. £1.11.6. *Murray & W.H.W.* / **Grenville Murray & W. H. Wills**

Chip:
- Acorn-Coffee, 203–204. ¾ col. £0.10.6. *W. B. Jerrold* / **William Blanchard Jerrold**

Time [verse], 204. ¼ col. £0.10.6. *Meredith & W.H.W.* / **George Meredith & W. H. Wills**

The World of Water, 204–209. 10½ cols. £5.5.0. *Morley* / **Henry Morley**

Bits of Life in Munich [vii], 209–211. 4 cols. £2.0.0. *Miss Howitt* / **Anna Mary Howitt**

The Story of a Sailor's Life [autobiog.], chap. i, 211–16. 11 cols. £15.0.0 for the 5 instalments. *Francis Bergh* / **Francis Bergh**

May 31, 1851. No. 62, pp. 217–40

The Wind and the Rain, 217–22. 10 cols. £4.10.0. *C.D. & Morley* / **Charles Dickens & Henry Morley**

The Story of a Sailor's Life, chap. ii, 222–28. 9½ cols.; should read 11¾. *Francis Berg* / **Francis Bergh**

Chips:
- Safety for Female Emigrants, 228. 1 col. *W.H.W.* / **W. H. Wills**
- Mr. Bubbs and the Moon [correction of error in "Mr. Bubb's Visit," May 17], 228. ¼ col. *W.H.W.* / **W. H. Wills**
- Profitable Investment of Toil – New Zealand [excerpt from emigrant's letter], 228–29. ¼ col. *Sidney* / **Samuel Sidney**

Precepts of Flowers [verse], 229. ½ col. £1.1.0. *W. B. Procter* / **Bryan Waller Procter**

Elephants. Wholesale and Retail [elephants in general; elephants at Zoological Gardens], 229–35. 12 cols. £5.0.0. *R. H. Horne* / **Richard H. Horne**

Painting the Lily [story], 235–38. 5¾ cols. £2.12.6. *Sidney Blanchard* / **Sidney Laman Blanchard**

A Child's History of England, chap. v, 238–40. 5¾ cols. *C.D.* / **Charles Dickens**

June 7, 1851. No. 63, pp. 241–64

Epsom [racing stable; Derby Day], 241–46. 11¾ cols. *W.H.W. & C.D.* / **W. H. Wills & Charles Dickens**

Disappearances [of persons], 246–50. 6¾ cols.; should read 7¾. £4.0.0. *Mrs. Gaskell* / **Elizabeth Gaskell**

Life in the Burra Mines of South Australia [emigrant's letter to Robert Bell], 250–52. 3 cols. £1.1.0. ——— *per R. Bell* / ———

Two Sonnets [with brief prose comment]: The Good Great Man [by Coleridge]; Answer, 252. ¾ col. £1.0.0. *R. H. Horne* / **Richard H. Horne**

A Peep at the "Peraharra" [Buddhist religious festival, Ceylon], 252–56. 7¼ cols. £3.0.0. *Capper* / **John Capper**

The Story of a Sailor's Life, chap. iii, 256–61. 10½ cols. *Francis Bergh* / **Francis Bergh**

Bits of Life in Munich [viii], 261–64. 5¾ cols.; should read 6¾. £2.12.6. *Miss Howitt* / **Anna Mary Howitt**

Supposing [iii] [disparity in treatment of prisoners], 264. ½ col. *C.D.* / **Charles Dickens**

June 14, 1851. No. 64, pp. 265–88

On Duty with Inspector Field [thieves' resorts and lodgings], 265–70. 11½ cols. *C.D.* / **Charles Dickens**

Madagascar: A History, 270–75. 9¾ cols. £4.4.0. *Morley* / **Henry Morley**

The Great Peace-Maker. A Sub-Marine Dialogue [verse], 275–77. 4¼ cols. £4.0.0. *Horne* / **Richard H. Horne**

Our Phantom Ship in Dock, 277–80. 6½ cols. £3.3.0. *Hannay* / **James Hannay**

The Story of a Sailor's Life, chap. iv, 280–86. 10¼ cols. *Francis Bergh* / **Francis Bergh**

Student Life in Paris, 286–88. 6 cols. £2.10.0. *Blanshard* / **Sidney Laman Blanchard**

June 21, 1851. No. 65, pp. 289–312

The Tresses of the Day Star [John Gould's exhibition of humming-birds], 289–91. 5 cols. £2.12.6. *Charles Knight & C.D.* / **Charles Knight & Charles Dickens**

A Real Sister of Charity [story], 291–98. 13½ cols. £6.0.0. *Miss Martineau* / **Harriet Martineau**

A Chapter of Models [a model Bavarian prison; a cathedral model], 298–301. 6 cols. £2.12.6. *Miss Howitt* / **Anna Mary Howitt**

Knowledge and Ignorance [verse], 301. ½ col. "10£ for six poems," i.e., this one, the 4 assigned to Harper in the 3 following nos., and prob. the unassigned "Smiles," July 19. *Harper* / **Harper**

Tahiti [Ida Pfeiffer, *Eine Frauenfahrt um die Welt*, 1850], 301–305. 8¼ cols. £3.10.0. *Miss Ross* / **Thomasina Ross**

Chips:
- A Disappearance [information from a reader concerning a person mentioned in "Disappearances," June 7], 305–306. ½ col. *W.H.W.* / **W. H. Wills**
- Complaint and Reply [identification of Coleridge poem cited in "Two Sonnets," June 7], 306. ⅛ col. *R. H. Horne* / **Richard H. Horne**

The Story of a Sailor's Life, chap. v, 306–310. 8½ cols. *Francis Bergh* / **Francis Bergh**

A Fuqueer's Curse [Indian fakirs], 310–12. 5 cols. £2.2.0. *Pepé* / **Peppé**

June 28, 1851. No. 66, pp. 313–36

A Few Conventionalities [stereotyped phrases, conventional actions], 313–15. 5 cols. *C.D.* / **Charles Dickens**

The Island in the River [story], part i, 315–21. 11¼ cols. £11.11.0 for the 3 instalments. *Thomas* / **William Moy Thomas**

A Pilgrimage to the Great Exhibition from Abroad, 321–24. 7¼ cols. £3.3.0. *W. Howitt* / **William Howitt**

The Brothers. A Tale of "Araby the Blest" [verse], 324–25. 1½ cols. £2.2.0. *Ollier* / **Edmund Ollier**

Our Phantom Ship: China, 325–31. 13 cols. £6.6.0. *Morley* / **Henry Morley**

The Warnings of the Past [verse], 331–32. ½ col. £1.10.0, included in the £10.0.0 recorded with item of June 21. *Harper* / **Harper**

Old Cairo and Its Mosque, 332–34. 4¼ cols. £1.11.6. *St. John* / **James Augustus St. John** or **Bayle St. John**

Chip:
- Gas Perfumery [substances derived from coal refuse], 334. ¾ col. *W.H.W.* / **W. H. Wills**

The History of a Rose [account of Louise de la Vallière, from Eugène de Mirecourt], 334–36. 4¼ cols. £1.5.0. *Mrs. Hoare* / **Mrs. Hoare**

July 5, 1851. No. 67, pp. 337–60

Mr. Bendigo Buster on the Model Cottages, 337–41. 9 cols. *Mr. Morley* / **Henry Morley**

The Island in the River, part ii, 341–48. 13 cols. *Thomas* / **William Moy Thomas**

The Song of the Sabre [verse], 348. ½ col. £1.10.0, included in the £10.0.0 recorded with item of June 21. *Harper* / **Harper**

The "Mouth" of China [Ida Pfeiffer, *Eine Frauenfahrt um die Welt*, 1850], 348–53. 10 cols. £4.0.0. *Miss Ross* / **Thomasina Ross**

Chips:
- Another Leaf from the Story of a Sailor's Life [correction of statement in "Sailor's Life," June 7], 353–54. 1½ cols. *W.H.W.* / **W. H. Wills**
- A Few Facts about Salt [tax on, in India], 354–55. 2 cols. £1.0.0. *Macpherson* / prob. **Ossian Macpherson**
- Excursion Trains, 355–56. 1¾ cols. £1.0.0. *Do.* / prob. **Ossian Macpherson**

The Claims of Labour [verse], 356. ½ col. £1.0.0, included in the £10.0.0 recorded with item of June 21. *Harper* / **Harper**

The Great Exhibition and the Little One [Great Britain contrasted with China], 356–60. 8½ cols. £3.13.6. *Horne & C.D.* / **Richard H. Horne & Charles Dickens**

July 12, 1851. No. 68, pp. 361–84

A Narrative of Extraordinary Suffering [railway travel, Bradshaw's railway guides], 361–63. 5½ cols. *C.D.* / **Charles Dickens**

The Island in the River, part iii, 363–70. 13 cols. *Thomas* / **William Moy Thomas**

The Globe in a Square [James Wyld's "Great Globe" in Leicester Square], 370–72. 5 cols. *Morley* / **Henry Morley**

The Use of Wealth [verse], 372. ½ col. Payment included in the £10.0.0 recorded with item of June 21. *Harper* / **Harper**

Lost in London [autobiog.], 372–78. 12 cols. £5.5.0. *Dr. Wencstern* / **Otto von Wenckstern**

South American Scraps [i]: La Plata, 378–81. 5 cols. £3.0.0. *Dr. Von Corning & Keys* / **Dr. Von Corning & Keys**

The Curates of Tittlebatington [Puseyism in a country parish], 381–84. 7 cols. £3.3.0. *Buckley* / **Theodore Buckley**

July 19, 1851. No. 69, pp. 385–408

In the Name of the Prophet – Smith! [Joseph Smith and Mormonism], 385–89. 8 cols. £4.10.0. *Hannay & W.H.W.* / **James Hannay & W. H. Wills**

The Highest House in Wathendale [story], 389–96. 14 cols. £7.17.6. *Miss Martineau* / **Harriet Martineau**

Chips:
- The Lighting of Eastern Seas [need for lighthouses: letter from reader], 396. ¾ col. *Morley* / **Henry Morley**
- The Tax on Excursion Trains [reader's qualification of statement in "Excursion Trains," July 5], 396. ¾ col. *W.H.W.* / **W. H. Wills**

Smiles [verse], 396–97. ½ col. Payment prob. included in the £10.0.0 recorded with Harper item of June 21. ——— / prob. **Harper**

A Visit to Robinson Crusoe [dining resort outside Paris], 397–400. 6 cols. £3.3.0. *Sidney Blanshard* / **Sidney Laman Blanchard**

What Is Not Clear about the Crystal Palace [disposition of], 400–402. 4 cols. *Morley* / **Henry Morley**

Shots in the Jungle [shooting excursion, Ceylon], 402–404. 4½ cols. £2.2.0. *Gore* / **Augustus Frederick Gore**

A Child's History of England, chap. vi, 404–408. 9 cols. *C.D.* / **Charles Dickens**

July 26, 1851. No. 70, pp. 409–432

The Great Bar in the Harbour of London [customs inspection], 409–414. 11 cols. *W.H.W.* / **W. H. Wills**

Edward Baines [*The Life of Edward Baines*, by his son, 1851], 414–19. 9¼ cols.; should read 10. £5.5.0. *Hannay & W.H.W.* / **James Hannay & W. H. Wills**

Chip:
- A Hint to Hatters, 419–21. 3 cols. *Morley* / **Henry Morley**

The Price of Time [verse], 421. ¼ col. £0.10.6. *Prince* / **John Critchley Prince**

Fish Dinners, 421–25. 7¾ cols. *Morley* / **Henry Morley**

South American Scraps [ii]: The Pampas Indians; An Adventure with a Lizard; The Sierra de St. Catherina, 425–30. 11 cols. £4.4.0. *Dr. Corning, Keys, & W.H.W.* / **Dr. Von Corning, Keys, & W. H. Wills**

A Word to Young Poets [verse], 430. ½ col. £0.10.6. *Horne* / **Richard H. Horne**

Shadows: The Shadow of Lucy Hutchinson [*The Memoirs of ... Colonel Hutchinson*, first pub. 1806], 430–32. 4¼ cols. £2.2.0. *Charles Knight* / **Charles Knight**

August 2, 1851. No. 71, pp. 433–56

Our Watering Place [Broadstairs], 433–36. 7½ cols. *C.D.* / **Charles Dickens**

A Penitent Confession [story], 436–45. 18 cols. £10.10.0. *Horne* / **Richard H. Horne**

Arcadia [verse], 445–46. 1½ cols. £1.1.0. *Do.* / **Richard H. Horne**

Foreign Airs and Native Places [air-controlled sanatoriums], 446–50. 7 cols. *Morley* / **Henry Morley**

Chips:
- Ballinglen [experimental farm in Ireland; and visit to, by Lady Grey], 450–51. 3¼ cols. *W.H.W.* / **W. H. Wills & Anna Sophia Grey**
- Chamouny, 451–52. 2¼ cols. £1.10.0. *Brockenden* / **William Brockedon**

The Jews in China, 452–56. 8 cols. £3.0.0. *Soutar, Keys, & Morley* / **Soutar, Keys, & Henry Morley**

August 9, 1851. No. 72, pp. 457–80

The History of a Certain Grammar-School [misappropriation of foundation-school funds: based on Robert Whiston case], 457–61. 9½ cols. £5.5.0. *Buckley* / **Theodore Buckley**

A Tale of the Forest of Dean [story], 461–64. 5½ cols. £1.1.0. *Wickenden & Morley* / **William S. Wickenden & Henry Morley**

Shadows: The Shadow of Margery Paston [*Paston Letters*, 1840–41 ed., pub. by Knight], 464–68. 7¾ cols. £3.13.6. *C. Knight* / **Charles Knight**

Winter Violets [verse], 468. ¾ col. £1.1.0. *Miss Tomkins & Horne* / **Mary Jane Tomkins & Richard H. Horne**

Science at Sea [seasickness prevention], 468–71. 4½ cols. £2.2.0. *B. Jerrold* / **William Blanchard Jerrold**

Chips:
- A "Ranch" in California, 471–72. 1¾ cols.; should read 2¾. £1.1.0. *Harrold & W.H.W.* / **C. B. Harrold's sister & W. H. Wills**
- Very Long Chalks [astronomical distances], 472–73. 2¾ cols. £1.10.0. *Hudson* / **Charles Thomas Hudson**

The Right One [story], 473–77. 7 cols. £2.2.0. *Miss Howitt* / **Anna Mary Howitt**

A Child's History of England, chaps. vii–viii, 477–80. 7¼ cols. *C.D.* / **Charles Dickens**

August 16, 1851. No. 73, pp. 481–504

Ice, 481–84. 7 cols. *Morley & W.H.W.* / **Henry Morley & W. H. Wills**

The Story of Reineke the Fox [condensed from Goethe, *Reineke Fuchs*], chaps. i–vi, 484–91. 15½ cols. *Morley* / **Henry Morley**

Never Despair [verse], 491–92. ½ col. £1.1.0. *Miss Blackwell & W.H.W.* / **Anna Blackwell & W. H. Wills**

Our Phantom Ship on an Antediluvian Cruise, 492–96. 8 cols. *Morley* / **Henry Morley**

The Bohemian Schoolmaster [writer's recollections of school-days], 496–501. 11 cols. £5.5.0. *Dr. Wenckestern* / **Otto von Wenckstern**

The Vicar of St. Carrabas [improvement of neglected parish], 501–504. 6¾ cols. £3.3.0. *Buckley* / **Theodore Buckley**

August 23, 1851. No. 74, pp. 505–528

Whole Hogs [fanatic advocacy of temperance, peace, vegetarianism], 505–507. 5½ cols. *Mr. C.D.* / **Charles Dickens**

The Dealer in Wisdom [legend], 507–511. 7½ cols. £3.3.0. *Bayle St. John* / **Bayle St. John**

The May Festival at Starnberg, 511–16. 8¼ cols. £3.10.0. *Miss Howitt* / **Anna Mary Howitt**

The Water-Elf [verse], 516. 1½ cols. £2.0.0. *Edmund Ollier* / **Edmund Ollier**

The "Dreadnought" [hospital ship], 516–19. 5 cols. £2.2.0. *Hannay* / **James Hannay**

The Catalogue's Account of Itself [catalogue of Great Exhibition], 519–23. 7½ cols. *Morley* / **Henry Morley**

Chip:
- A Bush Fire in Australia, 523–24. 2 cols. £1.1.0. *Mulock* / **Mulock**

The Story of Reineke the Fox, chaps. vii–xii, 524–27. 6½ cols. *Morley* / **Henry Morley**

Shadows: The Shadow of Peter Carewe [John Hooker, "The Lyffe of Sir Peter Carewe," *Archaeologia*, 1840], 527–28. 3½ cols. £2.0.0. *Charles Knight* / **Charles Knight**

August 30, 1851. No. 75, pp. 529–52

A Flight [trip from London to Paris], 529–33. 9 cols. *C.D.* / **Charles Dickens**

The Fortunes of the Reverend Caleb Ellison [story], 533–39. 11¾ cols. £6.0.0. *Miss Martineau* / **Harriet Martineau**

Change and the Changeless [verse], 539. ½ col. £1.1.0. *Harper* / **Harper**

A Day at Waterloo [the battlefield], 539–44. 12 cols.; should read 10¾. £6.0.0. *Howitt* / **William Howitt**

Lambs to Be Fed [Mary Carpenter, *Reformatory Schools*, 1851], 544–49. 9½ cols. £4.4.0. *Hannay* / **James Hannay**

The Dean of St. Vitus [an indolent ecclesiastic], 549–52. 7½ cols. £3.3.0. *Buckley* / **Theodore Buckley**

September 6, 1851. No. 76, pp. 553–76

One Man in a Dockyard [account of Chatham dockyard], 553–57. 9½ cols. £3.3.0. *C.D. & Horne* / **Charles Dickens & Richard H. Horne**

The Flying Artist [account of a German inventor], 557–61. 6½ cols. £2.10.0. *Bayle St. John* / **Bayle St. John**

Chips:
- Soldiers' Wives, 561–62. 3 cols. *W.H.W. & Morley* / **W. H. Wills & Henry Morley**
- Seals and Whales, 562–64. 4½ cols. £1.11.6. *Knox* / **James Knox**

Shadows: The Shadows of Ellen and Mary [verse], 564–65. 2 cols. £2.2.0. *Charles Knight* / **Charles Knight**

The Key of the Street [London streets at night], 565–72. 12½ cols. £5.0.0. *Sala* / **George A. Sala**

The Treatment of the Insane, 572–76. 9 cols. £2.12.6. ——— *per C.D.* / prob. **Richard Oliver**

Supposing [iv] [treatment of paupers vs. that of prisoners], 576. ½ col. *C.D.* / **Charles Dickens**

September 13, 1851. No. 77, pp. 577–600

A Gallop for Life [story], 577–81. 8½ cols. £4.4.0. *S. Sidney* / **Samuel Sidney**

The Labourer's Reading-Room, 581–85. 7¾ cols. *Morley* / **Henry Morley**

More French Revolutions [the spirit of republican Paris], 585–88. 6 cols. £2.12.6. *S. Blanshard & W.H.W.* / **Sidney Laman Blanchard & W. H. Wills**

Force and His Master [verse], 588–89. 1½ cols. £1.11.6. *Meredith* / **George Meredith**

The Work of the World [far-reaching results of scientific discoveries], 589–92. 7¾ cols. *Morley* / **Henry Morley**

Chips:
- Ruins with Silver Keys [public admission to historic sites], 592–94. 3½ cols. £1.10.0. *W. B. Jerrold* / **William Blanchard Jerrold**
- The Bush-Fire Extinguisher, 594–95. ½ col. *W.H.W. & correspondent* / **W. H. Wills & ———**
- The Latest Intelligence from the Irish California [chemical products obtainable from peat], 595. 1½ cols. £1.1.0. *P. Leigh* / **Percival Leigh**

Fishing for Herrings, 595–99. 6½ cols. £3.0.0. *Knox* / **James Knox**

The Constant Reader [the writer of "To the Editor" letters], 599–600. 3¼ cols. £1.1.0. *W. B. Jerrold* / **William Blanchard Jerrold**

September 20, 1851. No. 78, pp. 601–620

A Witch in the Nursery [nursery rhymes and stories], 601–609. 17¾ cols. £7.7.0. *R. H. Horne* / **Richard H. Horne**

Shadows: The Shadow of Ben Jonson's Mother [relationship of mother and son], 609–611. 3¼ cols. £1.5.0. *Charles Knight* / **Charles Knight**

Chip:
- A Lynch Trial in California, 611–12. 2¼ cols. £1.1.0. *Mr. Brooks per C. Buxton Esq.* / **Brooks**

The Last Words of Summer [verse], 612. ½ col. £0.15.0. *Harpur* / **Harper**

Light and Air [elementary physics], 612–16. 6½ cols. *Morley* / **Henry Morley**

A Child's History of England, chap. ix, 616–20. 9 cols. *C.D.* / **Charles Dickens**

VOLUME IV September 27, 1851 – March 13, 1852

September 27, 1851. No. 79, pp. 1–24

The Birth and Parentage of Letters [development of alphabet; writing materials], 1–6. 10½ cols. *Morley* / **Henry Morley**

Two Aspects of Ireland, i [poverty, injustice, bloodshed], 6–10. 8¾ cols. £4.4.0. *W. Howitt* / **William Howitt**

The French Flower Girl, 10–12. 4½ cols. £1.11.6. *Sidney Blanshard* / **Sidney Laman Blanchard**

Uncultured Gifts [verse], 12–13. ½ col. £1.1.0. *Harper* / **Harper**

Man Magnified [Arthur Hill Hassall, *The Microscopic Anatomy of the Human Body*, 1849], 13–15. 4¼ cols. £1.11.6. *F. K. Hunt* / **Frederick Knight Hunt**

Hampstead Heath, 15–18. 6 cols.; should read 7. £3.0.0. *Buckley* / **Theodore Buckley**

An Austrian State Trial, 18–22. 8 cols. £3.13.6. *Dr. Wenckstern* / **Otto von Wenckstern**

Budding Chathams [young men's debating clubs], 22–24. 4 cols. £1.11.6. *W. B. Jerrold* / **William Blanchard Jerrold**

October 4, 1851. No. 80, pp. 25–48

Shakspeare and Newgate [Samuel Phelps and Sadler's Wells], 25–27. 5 cols. *C.D. & Horne* / **Charles Dickens & Richard H. Horne**

Two Aspects of Ireland, ii [economic and agric. development], 27–32. 9 cols. £4.4.0. *W. Howitt* / **William Howitt**

Pottery and Porcelain [Joseph Marryat, ... *A History of Pottery and Porcelain*, 1850], 32–37. 11¼ cols. *Morley* / **Henry Morley**

The Gentleness of Death [verse], 37–38. ½ col. £1.1.0. *Meredith* / **George Meredith**

Bringing Out the Truth [the Law of Evidence Bill], 38–40. 4 cols. £2.0.0. *M. D. Hill* / **Matthew Davenport Hill**

A Glimpse of the Cairngorm Mountains, 40–45. 10½ cols. *Mr. Justice Talfourd* / **Thomas Noon Talfourd**

Chip:
– A Bird-Hunting Spider, 45–46. 3 cols.; should read 2¼. £1.10.0. *Satchell* / **Thomas Satchell**

The Tub School [narrow religionists], 46–48. 4½ cols. £2.2.0. *Loader* / **Loader,** perh. **Richard H. Horne**

October 11, 1851. No. 81, pp. 49–72

Our School [schoolboy reminiscences], 49–52. 6½ cols. *C.D.* / **Charles Dickens**

The Spendthrift's Daughter [story], chaps. i–ii, 52–56. 8 cols. £20.0.0 for the 4 instalments, but sum of payment notations for individual instalments = £14.0.0. *Mrs. Marsh* / prob. **Anne Marsh**

The Good Side of Combination [political economy], 56–60. 8 cols. *Morley* / **Henry Morley**

The Law of Mercy [verse], 60. ½ col. £1.1.0. *Harper* / **Harper**

The Foreign Invasion [visitors to Great Exhibition], 60–64. 9 cols. £4.4.0. *Sala* / **George A. Sala**

Chips:
- Eyes Made to Order [artificial eyes], 64–66. 2¾ cols. £1.5.0. *W. B. Jerrold* / **William Blanchard Jerrold**
- Adventures of a Diamond [Eduard Jerrmann, *Unpolitische Bilder aus St. Petersburg*, 1851], 66–67. 2¼ cols. £1.5.0. *Miss Ross* / **Thomasina Ross**

Malvern Water [visit to Malvern], 67–71. 6¼ cols.; should read 7¼. £4.4.0. *Miss Martineau* / **Harriet Martineau**

Thirty Days of Pleasure for Fifteen Francs [amusement project, Paris], 71–72. 4 cols. £1.11.6. *S. Blanshard* / **Sidney Laman Blanchard**

October 18, 1851. No. 82, pp. 73–96

The London Tavern, 73–77. 9 cols. £4.4.0. *Hannay & W.H.W.* / **James Hannay & W. H. Wills**

Gold, 77–82. 8½ cols. *Morley* / **Henry Morley**

Flower Shows in a Birmingham Hot-House [papier mâché and its uses], 82–85. 7½ cols. £3.13.6. *Miss Martineau* / **Harriet Martineau**

A Sultan's Warning [verse], 85–87. 2¼ cols. £2.2.0. *Edmund Ollier* / **Edmund Ollier**

The Spendthrift's Daughter, chaps. iii–iv, 87–92. 11 cols. *Mrs. Marsh* / prob. **Anne Marsh**

Chips:
- Superstitious Murder [in India: letter from officer in Madras], 92. ¾ col. £0.10.6. *Peter Cunningham* / **Peter Cunningham**
- Animal and Vegetable Disguises, 92–94. 2¼ cols. £1.5.0. *Satchell* / **Thomas Satchell**

A Musician in California [Henri Herz], 94–96. 6 cols. £2.12.6. *S. Blanshard* / **Sidney Laman Blanchard**

October 25, 1851. No. 83, pp. 97–120

Ballooning, 97–105. 16 cols. £8.0.0. *Horne* / **Richard H. Horne**

The Way I Made My Fortune [story], 105–107. 5¾ cols. £2.10.0. *Cramer* / **Cramer**

Indian Furlough Regulations, 107–109. 3 cols. *Morley* / **Henry Morley**

A Word from the Cannon's Mouth [verse], 109. 1 col. £1.1.0. *Meredith* / **George Meredith**

The Spendthrift's Daughter, chap. v, 109–113. 8 cols. *Mrs. Marsh* / prob. **Anne Marsh**

The Magic Troughs at Birmingham [electroplating], 113–17. 8 cols. £4.4.0. *Miss Martineau* / **Harriet Martineau**

A Child's History of England, chap. x, 117–20. 6¼ cols. *C.D.* / **Charles Dickens**

November 1, 1851. No. 84, pp. 121–44

Mr. Bull at Home in the Middle Ages [Thomas Hudson Turner, ... *Domestic Architecture in England*, 1851], 121–26. 10 cols. *Morley* / **Henry Morley**

Down Whitechapel Way, 126–31. 11¼ cols. £5.5.0. *Sala* / **George A. Sala**

Queen Zuleima [verse], 131–32. 1¼ cols. £1.5.0. *Meredith* / **George Meredith**

The Spendthrift's Daughter, chap. vi, 132–38. 12 cols. *Mrs. Marsh* / prob. **Anne Marsh**

The Wonders of Nails and Screws, 138–42. 7 cols. £3.3.0. *Miss Martineau* / **Harriet Martineau**

Wanted, an Organist! [church music], 142–44. 6 cols. £2.10.0. *Buckley* / **Theodore Buckley**

November 8, 1851. No. 85, pp. 145–68

Sucking Pigs [bloomerism; women with "a Mission"], 145–47. 5 cols. *C.D.* / **Charles Dickens**

The Garden of Nutmeg Trees [story], 147–52. 10 cols. £5.0.0. *Capper* / **John Capper**

Life and Luggage [salvage of, in shipwrecks], 152–56. 7½ cols. £2.15.0. *Horne* / **Richard H. Horne**

The Heart of England. (Suggested by Seeing a Venerable Oak in Warwickshire, Which Is Supposed to Occupy the Exact Centre of England) [verse], 156. 1 col. £1.11.6. *Dora Greenwell* / **Dora Greenwell**

Chips:
- A Zoological Problem [snake's swallowing a blanket], 156–57. 2 cols. £1.5.0. *Horne* / **Richard H. Horne**
- Tribunals of Commerce, 157–58. 1¾ cols. *Morley* / **Henry Morley**

Building and Freehold Land Societies, 158–64. 11 cols. *Morley* / **Henry Morley**

The First Time, and the Last Way, of Asking [a matrimonial bureau], 164–66. 4 cols. *Morley* / **Henry Morley**

An Arabian Night-mare [fantasy], 166–68. 5¾ cols. £2.12.6. ——— / ———

November 15, 1851. No. 86, pp. 169–92

A Free (and Easy) School [abuses practised in endowed grammar schools], 169–73. 9 cols. *Morley & C.D.* / **Henry Morley & Charles Dickens**

English Songs, 173–78. 9 cols. £4.10.0. *Hannay* / **James Hannay**

A Fashionable Forger [story], 178–82. 8¾ cols. £4.10.0. *Sidney* / **Samuel Sidney**

An Abiding Dream [verse], 182–83. 1¾ cols. £2.2.0. ——— / ———

Kendal Weavers and Weaving [carpet manufacture], 183–89. 13½ cols. £6.16.6. *Miss Martineau* / **Harriet Martineau**

Chip:
- Homœopathy [from John Epps, *Homœopathy and Its Principles Explained*, 1850], 189–90. ½ col. *C.D.* / **Charles Dickens**

The True Bohemians of Paris [unsuccessful writers, musicians, painters], 190–92. 5½ cols. £2.12.6. *S. Blanshard* / **Sidney Laman Blanchard**

November 22, 1851. No. 87, pp. 193–216

A Black Eagle in a Bad Way [Austria], 193–95. 5½ cols. £1.11.6. *Murray, Morley, & C.D.* / **Grenville Murray, Henry Morley, & Charles Dickens**

The Home of the Hundred Blind Men [story], 195–204. 17 cols. £8.10.0. *Thomas* / **William Moy Thomas**

Britain [verse], 204. ½ col. £0.15.0. *Meredith* / **George Meredith**

Our Parish Poor Box [unwise dispensation of charity-funds], 204–207. 6 cols. £3.3.0. *Buckley* / **Theodore Buckley**

Chips:
- A Golden Newspaper [Sydney *Morning Herald*], 207–208. 2¼ cols. £1.1.0. *Mr. Keene & W.H.W.* / **John Keene** or **James Keene & W. H. Wills**
- Wisdom in Words [language], 208–209. 1½ cols. *Morley* / **Henry Morley**

The Pasha's New Boat [paper mâché and its uses], 209–213. 7 cols. £3.13.6. *Horne* / **Richard H. Horne**

Sonnet. To Robert Browning; Suggested by a Sunset of Unusual Beauty [verse], 213. ¼ col. *Justice Talfourd* / **Thomas Noon Talfourd**

French Horse-Racing, 213–16. 7 cols. £3.13.6. *S. Blanshard* / **Sidney Laman Blanchard**

November 29, 1851. No. 88, pp. 217–40

Need Railway Travellers Be Smashed? [C. F. Whitworth's invention to prevent collisions], 217–21. 8½ cols. *Morley* / **Henry Morley**

A Roving Englishman: Benighted; Out Shooting [in Austria], 221–24. 6½ cols. £2.12.6. *Murray & Morley* / **Grenville Murray & Henry Morley**

The Bobbin-Mill at Ambleside, 224–28. 9 cols. £4.4.0. *Miss Martineau* / **Harriet Martineau**

Room in the World [verse], 228–29. ¼ col. £0.15.0. *Harper* / **Harper**

The Overland Mail Bag [Russia's designs on India: in large part from John W. Kaye, *History of the War in Afghanistan,* 1851], 229–34. 11 cols. £5.0.0. *R. Bell* / **Robert Bell**

Chips:
- Wonderful Swallows [objects that animals swallow], 234–35. 2½ cols. £1.1.0. *Horne* / **Richard H. Horne**
- Neapolitan State Prisoners, 235–37. 3 cols. £1.1.0. *Wreford & Morley* / **Henry G. Wreford & Henry Morley**

Sonnet. On Mr. Lough's Statute of "Lady Macbeth" [verse], 237. ¼ col. *Mr. Justice Talfourd* / **Thomas Noon Talfourd**

A Child's History of England, chap. xi, 237–40. 7¼ cols. *C.D.* / **Charles Dickens**

December 6, 1851. No. 89, pp. 241–64

My Uncle [pawnbrokers], 241–46. 10 cols. *W.H.W. & C.D.* / **W. H. Wills & Charles Dickens**

A Curious Page of Family History [concerning Yorkshire family, 18 cent.; told as though factual], 246–49. 7½ cols. £3.15.0. *Miss Jewsbury* / **Geraldine Endsor Jewsbury**

The Story of a Nation [Hungary], chap. i, 249–54. 8 cols. *Morley* / **Henry Morley**

Familiar Things [verse], 254. ½ col. £1.1.0. *Meredith* / **George Meredith**

Jack Alive in London [maritime London], 254–60. 12 cols. £6.0.0. *Sala* / **George A. Sala**

Chip:
- A Free (and Easy) School [disclaimer of having quoted from actual prospectus of school described in article of same title, Nov. 15], 260. ¼ col. *C.D.* / **Charles Dickens**

A Few Miracles [from Roger of Wendover, Bede, etc.], 260–64. 8½ cols. £4.0.0. *Buckley* / **Theodore Buckley**

December 13, 1851. No. 90, pp. 265–88

Our Society at Cranford [story], 265–74. 19 cols. £10.10.0. *Mrs. Gaskell* / **Elizabeth Gaskell**

The "Merchant Seaman's Fund," 274–77. 4½ cols. £2.0.0. *Hannay* / **James Hannay**

A Child's Prayer [verse], 277. ½ col. £0.10.6. ——— / ———

Household Crime [arsenic poisonings], 277–81. 7½ cols. £4.0.0. *Horne* / **Richard H. Horne**

The Story of a Nation, chap. ii, 281–85. 8½ cols. *Morley* / **Henry Morley**

Chip:
- Pork Insurance, 285–86. 2¼ cols. £1.1.0. *W. B. Jerrold* / **William Blanchard Jerrold**

A Beginning and an End [a christening and a funeral, Munich], 286–88. 5 cols. £2.10.0. *Miss Howitt* / **Anna Mary Howitt**

December 20, 1851. No. 91, pp. 289–312

Getting Up a Pantomime, 289–96. 14 cols. £6.6.0. *Sala* / **George A. Sala**

The Legend of the Weeping Chamber, 296–99. 6 cols. £3.0.0. *Bayle St. John* / **Bayle St. John**

A Roving Englishman: The Apple-Green Spencer [an innkeeper's daughter, Austria]; Gastein Baths, 299–301. 5 cols. £2.2.0. *Murray & Morley* / **Grenville Murray & Henry Morley**

The Glastonbury Thorn [verse], 301–302. ½ col. £0.10.6. *Meredith* / **George Meredith**

A Premier's Correspondents [letters to John Stuart Bute: MSS in Brit. Mus.], 302–305. 6¾ cols. £2.12.6. *A. Watts (Junr.)* / **Alaric Alfred Watts**

A Lesson of Hope [verse], 305. ½ col. £1.1.0. *Harper* / **Harper**

The Art of Catching Elephants, 305–310. 10 cols. £4.4.0. *Capper* / **John Capper**

A Christmas Piece, 310–12. 4 cols. *Morley* / **Henry Morley**

Christmas 1851. Extra Number for Christmas, pp. 1–24. Announced in advt., Dec. 20, as "Showing What Christmas Is to Everybody," "Now Ready." Contents of no. listed at end of "Contents" of Vol. IV.

What Christmas Is, As We Grow Older, 1–3. 4 cols. *C.D.* / **Charles Dickens**

What Christmas Is to a Bunch of People, 3–7. 9 cols. £4.4.0. *Horne* / **Richard H. Horne**

An Idyl for Christmas In-Doors [verse], 7–8. 2 cols. £4.4.0. *Ollier* / **Edmund Ollier**

What Christmas Is in Country Places, 8–11. 6¾ cols. £3.3.0. *Miss Martineau* / **Harriet Martineau**

What Christmas Is in the Company of John Doe [in gaol], 11–16. 8½ cols. £5.0.0. *Sala* / **George A. Sala**

The Orphan's Dream of Christmas [verse], 16–17. 2 cols. £2.2.0. *Miss Griffiths* / **Miss Eliza Griffiths**

What Christmas Is after a Long Absence, 17–20. 6¾ cols. £4.4.0. *Sidney* / **Samuel Sidney**

What Christmas Is If You Outgrow It, 20–23. 6¼ cols. £2.12.6. *Buckley* / **Theodore Buckley**

The Round Game of the Christmas Bowl [verse, with instructions in prose], 23–24. 2 cols. £3.3.0. *Horne* / **Richard H. Horne**

December 27, 1851. No. 92, pp. 313–36

Liberty, Equality, Fraternity, and Musketry [Paris after the Dec. coup d'état], 313–18. 11 cols. £5.10.0. *Sala* / **George A. Sala**

The Five Travellers [Englishmen crossing Isthmus of Panama], 318–21. 5 cols. £2.12.6. *Sidney* / **Samuel Sidney**

An Englishman's Castle [householders' grievances], 321–24. 6 cols. £3.3.0. *Thomas* / **William Moy Thomas**

The Voice of Cheer [verse], 324. ½ col. £0.10.6. *Harpur* / **Harper**

Little Red Working-Coat [work of Ragged School boys], 324–25. 2 cols. *Morley* / **Henry Morley**

The German Exile's New Year's Eve [autobiog.], 325–29. 8 cols. £4.4.0. *Wenckstern* / **Otto von Wenckstern**

The True Tom Tiddler's Ground [uses of peat-charcoal], 329–32. 5½ cols. *Morley* / **Henry Morley**

A Child's History of England, chap. xii, 332–36. 7¾ cols.; should read 9½. *C.D.* / **Charles Dickens**

January 3, 1852. No. 93, pp. 337–60

Pearls from the East [Hindu mythology], 337–41. 8½ cols. £4.4.0. *Mr. Loader per Horne* / **Loader**, perh. **Richard H. Horne**

What *I* Call Sensible Legislation [Scots statutes, 15–17 cent.], 341–44. 5½ cols. £2.10.0. *Knox & Morley* / **James Knox & Henry Morley**

Going Circuit at the Antipodes, 344–48. 9 cols. £4.4.0. *Mitchie & Morley* / **Archibald Michie & Henry Morley**

A Wassail for the New Year [verse], 348–49. 1½ cols. £2.10.0. *Meredith* / **George Meredith**

A Love Affair at Cranford [story], 349–57. 15¼ cols. £9.10.0. *Mrs. Gaskell* / **Elizabeth Gaskell**

Chips:
- "My Uncle" and "My Aunt" [pawnshops], 357. ¼ col. *Chance correspondent* / ———
- Anecdotes of Monkeys, 357–58. 2 cols. £1.1.0. *Satchell* / **Thomas Satchell**

The Roving Englishman: A Masked Ball [Vienna]; Advertisements [in Austrian newspapers], 358–60. 5 cols. £2.10.0. *Murray & Morley* / **Grenville Murray & Henry Morley**

January 10, 1852. No. 94, pp. 361–84

Irish Ballad Singers and Irish Street Ballads, 361–68. 14 cols. £5.5.0. *Allingham* / **William Allingham**

A Taste of Austrian Jails [autobiog.], 368–72. 8 cols. £3.13.6. *Duthie* / **William Duthie**

The Linnet-Hawker [verse], 372. ¾ col. £1.1.0. *Meredith* / **George Meredith**

A Dutch Family Picture [Ceylon], 372–76. 7¾ cols. £3.13.6. *Capper* / **John Capper**

Chip:
– Street-Cab Reform, 376. 1 col. *W.H.W.* / **W. H. Wills**

My First Place [story], 376–82. 12 cols. £6.6.0. *Miss Bakewell* / **Esther Bakewell**

The Great Convocation of Poultry [poultry show, Birmingham], 382–84. 4½ cols. £2.12.6. *The Revd. J. Dixon* / **Edmund Saul Dixon**

January 17, 1852. No. 95, pp. 385–408

A Curious Dance round a Curious Tree [St. Luke's Hospital for Lunatics], 385–89. 8½ cols. *C.D. & W.H.W.* / **Charles Dickens & W. H. Wills**

The Peasants of British India, 389–93. 8 cols. £3.10.0. *Capper* / **John Capper**

Three and Sixpence [misappropriation of foundation-school funds], 393–97. 7¾ cols. £3.13.6. *Buckley* / **Theodore Buckley**

The Source of Joy [verse], 397. ½ col. £1.1.0. *Harper* / **Harper**

Things Departed [customs, fashions, etc.], 397–401. 8¾ cols. £4.4.0. *Sala* / **George A. Sala**

How Charity Begins at Home, near Hamburg [Das Rauhe Haus, home for child delinquents], 401–403. 3¼ cols. *Morley* / **Henry Morley**

New Discoveries in Ghosts [estrasensory perception], 403–406. 6¾ cols. *Morley* / **Henry Morley**

The Roving Englishman: In Praise of Salad, 406–408. 4¼ cols. £1.11.6. *Murray & Morley* / **Grenville Murray & Henry Morley**

January 24, 1852. No. 96, pp. 409–432

A Rainy Day on "The Euphrates" [women emigrants bound for Australia], 409–415. 13½ cols. *Morley* / **Henry Morley**

The Miller and His Men [flour manufacture, bread making], 415–20. 9 cols. £4.15.0. *Miss Martineau* / **Harriet Martineau**

Forgive! [verse], 420. ¾ col. £1.0.0. *Harper* / **Harper**

An Ascent of Adam's Peak, 420–24. 8¾ cols. £4.0.0. *Knighton* / **William Knighton**

Chip:
– Penny Banks, 424–25. 1¾ cols. *Morley* / **Henry Morley**

Esther Hammond's Wedding-Day [story], 425–31. 11 cols. £4.10.0. *Mrs. Crowe* / **Catherine Crowe**

The Roving Englishman: A Brace of Blunders [on part of the writer], 431–32. 3½ cols. £2.0.0. *Murray & Morley* / **Grenville Murray & Henry Morley**

January 31, 1852. No. 97, pp. 433–56

Three Colonial Epochs [Australia], 433–38. 10½ cols. £5.15.6. *Sidney* / **Samuel Sidney**

The Pedigree of Puppets, 438–43. 10¼ cols. £4.10.0. *W.H.W. & Dudley Costello* / **W. H. Wills & Dudley Costello**

Chip:
– Fox-Hunting, 443–44. 2½ cols. £1.1.0. *Sidney* / **Samuel Sidney**

Fragment of a Poet's Life [verse], 444–45. 1¼ cols. £1.1.0. *Miss Griffith* / **Miss Eliza Griffiths**

Monsieur Gogo's [boys' boarding school, Paris], 445–49. 8½ cols. £5.0.0. *Sala* / **George A. Sala**

An Account of Some Treatment of Gold and Gems, 449–55. 11 cols. £6.6.0. *Miss Martineau* / **Harriet Martineau**

Paradise Lost [story], 455–56. 4 cols. £2.12.6. *Bayle St. John* / **Bayle St. John**

February 7, 1852. No. 98, pp. 457–80

Gunpowder, 457–65. 16½ cols. £8.8.0. *Horne* / **Richard H. Horne**

Lord Peter the Wild Woodsman; or, The Progress of Tape [Govt. inaction, red tape], 465–67. 5 cols. £2.2.0. *Horne* / **Richard H. Horne**

Lazzaroni Literature [govt. censorship, Naples], 467–69. 2¼ cols. £1.1.0. *Wreford* / **Henry G. Wreford**

Roll On! [verse], 469. ½ col. £1.1.0. *Harper* / **Harper**

Strings of Proverbs [i], 469–72. 5¾ cols. £2.10.0. *Horne* / **Richard H. Horne**

A New Way of Manufacturing Glory [museum of M. Robyns, Brussels], 472–76. 7¾ cols. £4.0.0. *Meredith* / **George Meredith**

A Child's History of England, chap. xiii, 476–80. 10 cols. *C.D.* / **Charles Dickens**

February 14, 1852. No. 99, pp. 481–504

City Spectres [bankrupt speculators, merchants, etc.], 481–85. 8½ cols. £4.14.6. *Sala* / **George A. Sala**

Rainbow Making [ribbon manufacture], 485–90. 11 cols. £5.5.0. *Miss Martineau* / **Harriet Martineau**

Continental Ways and Means [living on the Continent], 490–92. 3¾ cols. £1.11.6. *Lever* / **Charles James Lever**

Friendship's Valentine [verse], 492–93. 1½ cols. £1.10.6. *Miss Greenwell* / **Dora Greenwell**

The Little Sisters [charity institution, France], 493–94. 2¾ cols. *Morley* / **Henry Morley**

Picture Advertising in South America [newspaper advertisements], 494–98. 6½ cols. £3.10.0. *Dudley Costello* / **Dudley Costello**

The Duke's Agent [story], 498–502. 9 cols.; should read 9¾. £4.14.6. *W. Howitt* / **William Howitt**

Wonderful Toys [automata], 502–504. 4 cols. *W.H.W.* / **W. H. Wills**

February 21, 1852. No. 100, pp. 505–528

An Indian Wedding [Cingalese wedding], 505–510. 10 cols. £5.5.0. *Capper* / **John Capper**

The Queen's Head [postage stamps], 510–13. 5½ cols. £3.3.0. *Hannay & W.H.W.* / **James Hannay & W. H. Wills**

Chip:
– A Disappearance Cleared Up [facts of the Gaunt case, correcting misrepresentation in "Disappearances," June 7, 1851], 513–14. 2 cols. *Communicated* / **John Gaunt & William Gaunt**

The Roving Englishman: Concerning a Pair of Demons [incident told by Austrian guide], 514–17. 5¾ cols. £3.0.0. *Murray* / **Grenville Murray**

War [verse], 517. ½ col. £1.1.0. *Meredith & Horne* / **George Meredith & Richard H. Horne**

Travels in Cawdor Street [spurious antiques and paintings], 517–21. 8½ cols. £4.4.0. *Sala* / **George A. Sala**

Choice Secrets [Hans Jacob Wecker, ... *Secrets of Art & Nature*, 1661 ed.], 521–24. 6 cols. *Morley* / **Henry Morley**

Strings of Proverbs [ii], 524–26. 4 cols. £2.0.0. *Horne* / **Richard H. Horne**

Pipe-Clay and Clay Pipes, 526–28. 4½ cols. £2.12.6. *W. B. Jerrold* / **William Blanchard Jerrold**

February 28, 1852. No. 101, pp. 529–52

Better Ties Than Red Tape Ties [Caroline Chisholm's work for emigration], 529–34. 10½ cols. £5.15.6. *Sidney* / **Samuel Sidney**

A Forgotten Celebrity [Marie de Jars de Gournay], 534–38. 7¼ cols. £3.13.6. *Miss Jewsbury* / **Geraldine Endsor Jewsbury**

Strings of Proverbs [iii], 538–40. 4½ cols. £2.6.6. *R.H.H.* / **Richard H. Horne**

A Cry from the Dust! [verse], 540. ½ col. £1.1.0. ——— *per R.H.H.* / ———

Needles, 540–46. 11 cols. £6.0.0. *Miss Martineau* / **Harriet Martineau**

Gable College [a progressive, well-managed school], 546–50. 8¾ cols. £5.0.0. *Buckley* / **Theodore Buckley**

Sentimental Journalism [French newspapers], 550–52. 4½ cols. £2.2.0. *Thomas* / **William Moy Thomas**

March 6, 1852. No. 102, pp. 553–76

An Unpaid Servant of the State [Thomas Wright, prison philanthropist], 553–55. 5 cols. *Morley* / **Henry Morley**

Time and the Hour [manufacture of watches], 555–59. 8 cols. £4.10.0. *Miss Martineau* / **Harriet Martineau**

A Genteel Establishment [story], 559–64. 8½ cols. £4.0.0. *Sidney Blanshard & W.H.W.* / **Sidney Laman Blanchard & W. H. Wills**

The Mighty Magician [verse], 564. ½ col. £1.1.0. *Harper* / **Harper**

Zoological Stories, 564–67. 7 cols.; should read 6. *Morley* / **Henry Morley**

Chips:
- A Visit to the Burra Burra Mines, 567–68. 2¾ cols. £1.10.6. *Mitchie* / **Archibald Michie**
- A Novelty in Railway Locomotion [atmospheric railway], 568–69. 2¼ cols. *Morley* / **Henry Morley**
- Sensitive People [correction of statement in "New Discoveries in Ghosts," Jan. 17], 569–70. ½ col. *Morley* / **Henry Morley**

A Child's History of England, chap. xiv, 570–76. 13½ cols. *C.D.* / **Charles Dickens**

March 13, 1852. No. 103, pp. 577–600

A Sleep to Startle Us [a Ragged School and Dormitory, London], 577–80. 7 cols. *C.D.* / **Charles Dickens**

Guns and Pistols, 580–85. 10 cols. £5.5.0. *Miss Martineau* / **Harriet Martineau**

From a Settler's Wife [life in Auckland], 585–88. 6 cols. £2.12.6. *Mrs. St. George & Morley* / **Frances George & Henry Morley**

The Use of Flowers [verse], 588. ½ col. £1.1.0. *Harper* / **Harper**

Memory at Cranford [story], 588–97. 16¾ cols. £9.0.0. *Mrs. Gaskell* / **Elizabeth Gaskell**

Chips:
- The Fine Arts in Australia [Marshall Claxton's painting *Christ Blessing the Little Children*], 597. 1 col. *C.D.* / **Charles Dickens**
- A Sea-Coroner [determining causes of shipwrecks], 597–98. ¾ col. *W.H.W.* / **W. H. Wills**

If This Should Meet His Eye – [Cornwall; search for choughs], 598–600. 5¾ cols. £2.12.6. *Dixon* / **Edmund Saul Dixon**

VOLUME V March 20 – September 11, 1852

March 20, 1852. No. 104, pp. 1–20

Post-Office Money-Orders, 1–5. 8 cols. *C.D. & W.H.W.* / **Charles Dickens & W. H. Wills**

Houses to Let, 5–11. 12¼ cols. £5.5.0. *Sala* / **George A. Sala**

The Camera-Obscura. A Sunday Morning Lecture [verse], 11–12. 1¾ cols. £3.10.0. *Horne* / **Richard H. Horne**

What Has Become of Winter?, 12–15. 6¼ cols. *Morley* / **Henry Morley**

Chip:
– Locking Up the Tower of London, 15–16. ¾ col. *Correspondent & W.H.W.* / ——— **& W. H. Wills**

Three Guns in Albania [shooting excursion], 16–19. 6½ cols. £2.2.0. *Hale* / **Hale**

Village Funerals in Naples, 19–20. 3¼ cols. £1.1.0. *Wreford* / **Henry G. Wreford**

March 27, 1852. No. 105, pp. 21–44

Floating Sentinels [buoys and light ships], 21–25. 8 cols. £4.4.0. *Horne* / **Richard H. Horne**

The Buried City of Ceylon [Anuradhapura], 25–27. 5 cols. £2.2.0. *Kingston & Morley* / **William Knighton & Henry Morley**

A True Account of an Apparition [story], 27–31. 8¾ cols. £4.14.6. *Thomas* / **William Moy Thomas**

King Dirt. A Song Adapted to a Slow Sanitary Movement [verse], 31–32. 1 col. £2.2.0. *Tiffin* / **Tiffin**

Birmingham Glass Works, 32–38. 13 cols. £6.6.0. *Miss Martineau* / **Harriet Martineau**

Chips:
– Nobility in Spain, 38–41. 5 cols. £2.12.6. *Murray* / **Grenville Murray**
– Our House [advantages of housing built as flats], 41–42. 2¾ cols. *Morley* / **Henry Morley**

How to Be an Evergreen [keeping abreast of the times], 42–44. 4¼ cols. £2.5.6. *Thomas* / **William Moy Thomas**

April 3, 1852. No. 106, pp. 45–68

Drooping Buds [Hospital for Sick Children, London], 45–48. 6½ cols. *C.D. & Morley* / **Charles Dickens & Henry Morley**

Northern Lights and – Shadows [Benjamin Thorpe, *Northern Mythology*, 1851–52], 48–51. 6¾ cols. *Morley* / **Henry Morley**

British Cotton ["cottonized" flax], 51–54. 6¼ cols. £2.12.6. *Capper* / **John Capper**

The Growth of Good [verse], 54–55. ¾ col. £1.11.6. ——— / **Elizabeth Holland**

Visiting at Cranford [story], 55–64. 17½ cols. £9.9.0. *Mrs. Gaskell* / **Elizabeth Gaskell**

Sledging, 64–66. 4¼ cols. £2.2.0. *Miss Howitt* / **Anna Mary Howitt**

A Tower of Strength [Tower of London], 66–68. 5½ cols. £3.13.6. *R. H. Horne* / **Richard H. Horne**

April 10, 1852. No. 107, pp. 69–92

The Great Invasion [growth of London], 69–73. 9 cols. £4.14.6. *Sala* / **George A. Sala**

Norfolk Island, 73–77. 7 cols. £3.0.0. *Irwin & Morley* / **Irwin & Henry Morley**

Saint George and the Dragon [St. George's Hospital], 77–80. 7 cols. £3.3.0. *Winter* / **Andrew Wynter**

An Emigrant's Glance Homeward [verse], 80. ¾ col. £1.1.0. *Mrs. St. George* / **Frances George**

Old Household Words [ancient medical remedies and charms: from Ayscough MSS], 80–83. 4¾ cols. £2.12.6. *Dudley Costello* / **Dudley Costello**

The Ghost-Raiser [story], 83–84. 4 cols.; should read 3¼. £1.11.6. *Mrs. Hoare* / **Mrs. Hoare**

The New School for Wives [evening school for women, Birmingham], 84–89. 8½ cols. £4.10.0. *Miss Martineau* / **Harriet Martineau**

A Child's History of England, chap. XV, 89–92. 8 cols. *C.D.* / **Charles Dickens**

April 17, 1852. No. 108, pp. 93–116

Old Clothes!, 93–98. 11½ cols. £6.0.0. *Sala* / **George A. Sala**

A Clouded Skye [economic plight of Skye], 98–101. 6¼ cols. *Morley* / **Henry Morley**

Town and Gown [relationship between], 101–104. 4¼ cols. £2.2.0. *Buckley & Morley* / **Theodore Buckley & Henry Morley**

From Gold to Gray [verse], 104. 1 col. £1.11.6. *Miss Griffiths* / **Miss Eliza Griffiths**

Chips:
- A Great Catch [reader's correction of statement in "If This Should Meet His Eye," March 13], 104. ¼ col. *W.H.W.* / **W. H. Wills**
- A Primitive People [the Transylvanians], 104–106. 2¼ cols. £1.5.0. *Murray* / **Grenville Murray**

What There Is in a Button [button manufacture], 106–112. 12¾ cols. £6.6.0. *Miss Martineau* / **Harriet Martineau**

My Aunt in Paris [govt. pawnshops], 112–16. 9 cols. £5.0.0. *Sidney Blanshard* / **Sidney Laman Blanchard**

April 24, 1852. No. 109, pp. 117–40

A Plated Article [pottery manufacture], 117–21. 8 cols. *C.D. & W.H.W.* / **Charles Dickens & W. H. Wills**

Margaret Fuller [*Memoirs*, 1852], 121–24. 6 cols. £2.12.6. *T. M. Thomas* / **T. M. Thomas**

More Dumb Friends [observations on animals], 124–27. 6¼ cols. £3.3.0. *R. H. Horne* / **Richard H. Horne**

A Sentiment in Stone [Cologne Cathedral], 127–28. 3 cols. £1.1.0. *J. A. Crowe & Morley* / **Joseph Archer Crowe & Henry Morley**

The Legend of the Miraculous Rose-Trees [verse], 128–29. 2 cols. £2.2.0. *Ollier* / **Edmund Ollier**

A Terribly Strange Bed [story], 129–37. 15 cols. £7.10.0. *Wilkie Collins* / **Wilkie Collins**

The Thirsty Boys of Bonn [university students], 137–38. 3¼ cols. £1.1.0. *J. A. Crowe & Morley* / **Joseph Archer Crowe & Henry Morley**

The Sister-Ship [the *Orinoco*], 138–40. 4 cols. £2.10.0. *J. Hannay* / **James Hannay**

May 1, 1852. No. 110, pp. 141–64

For India Direct [the *Bentinck* leaving Southampton], 141–45. 9¼ cols. *W.H.W.* / **W. H. Wills**

The Man from the West [account of a Libyan merchant], 145–49. 8½ cols. £3.13.6. *Bayle St. John* / **Bayle St. John**

Young France at the Easel [atelier of Paul Delaroche], 149–52. 4¼ cols. £2.0.0. *J. A. Crowe & Morley* / **Joseph Archer Crowe & Henry Morley**

The Tale Unfinished [verse], 152. ¾ col. £1.1.0. *Miss Griffith* / **Miss Eliza Griffiths**

One of the Evils of Match-Making ["phosphorus disease"], 152–55. 7 cols. *Morley* / **Henry Morley**

Chips:
- Official Emigration [under Govt. auspices], 155–56. 1¾ cols. *W.H.W.* / **W. H. Wills**
- A Melancholy Place [anachronistic official posts], 156–57. 1¼ cols. £1.1.0. *R. H. Horne* / **Richard H. Horne**

The Hunter and the Student [hunters' narratives vs. naturalists' writings], 157–62. 10½ cols. £4.14.6. *R. H. Horne* / **Richard H. Horne**

Smithfield Races, 162–64. 4½ cols. £2.0.0. *W. B. Jerrold* / **William Blanchard Jerrold**

May 8, 1852. No. 111, pp. 165–88

Open-Air Entertainments [a fair, an execution], 165–69. 8½ cols. £4.14.6. *Sala* / **George A. Sala**

My Little French Friend [a teacher], 169–71. 5 cols. £2.12.6. *Miss Costello* / **Louisa Stuart Costello**

The City of Sudden Death [Pompeii], 171–76. 9½ cols. £4.14.6. *Lewis* / **John Delaware Lewis**

A Recollection of Sir Martin Shee. On the Last Occasion of His Presiding at the Festival of the Royal Academy of Art [verse], 176. ¼ col. *Mr. Justice Talfourd* / **Thomas Noon Talfourd**

Stone Pictures [lithography], 176–81. 9¼ cols. £4.4.0. *Sala* / **George A. Sala**

Bombay, 181–86. 9½ cols. £5.5.0. *Napier* / **Napier**

Not Found Yet! [Cornwall; search for choughs], 186–88. 5¼ cols. £2.12.6. *Dixon* / **Edmund Saul Dixon**

May 15, 1852. No. 112, pp. 189–212

First Fruits [landmarks in life], 189–92. 7 cols. £4.0.0. *Sala & C.D.* / **George A. Sala & Charles Dickens**

Tubal-Cain [brass founding], 192–97. 9½ cols. £4.10.0. *Miss Martineau* / **Harriet Martineau**

A Tale of Mid-Air [story], 197–98. 2¼ cols. £1.5.0. *Mrs. Hoare* / **Mrs. Hoare**

The Harmonious Blacksmith [Gretna Green], 198–202. 7¼ cols. £3.13.6. *W. B. Jerrold* / **William Blanchard Jerrold**

The Great British Gum Secret [adhesive paste], 202–203. 3 cols. £1.5.0. *Sommerville* / **Sommerville**

Chip:
- Privileges of the French Nobility, 203–204. 2½ cols. £1.1.0. *D. Costello* / **Dudley Costello**

Still on the Wing [Cornwall; search for choughs], 204–207. 6 cols. £3.3.0. *Dixon* / **Edmund Saul Dixon**

A Child's History of England, chap. xvi, 207–212. 10 cols. *C.D.* / **Charles Dickens**

May 22, 1852. No. 113, pp. 213–36

The Harvest of Gold [Australia], 213–18. 11½ cols. £2.2.0 to Macpherson; £1.11.6 to Mulock. *Morley, Macpherson, & Mulock* / **Henry Morley, Ossian Macpherson**, prob., **& Mulock**

The Rights of French Women, 218–21. 6 cols. £3.3.0. *Dixon* / **Edmund Saul Dixon**

A Dish of Vegetables [geog. distribution of edible plants], 221–24. 4¼ cols. *Morley* / **Henry Morley**

Angel Eyes [verse], 224. 1 col. £2.2.0. *Louisa Hill* / **Louisa Hill**

Phases of "Public" Life [London public houses], chap. i, 224–30. 12½ cols. £6.10.0. *Sala* / **George A. Sala**

Notes from Norway [descr. and travel] [i], 230–35. 9 cols. £4.0.0. *Miss Williamson* / **Miss Williamson**

Up Vesuvius, 235–36. 3 cols. £1.11.6. *Dulton* / **Dulton**

May 29, 1852. No. 114, pp. 237–60

The Great Chowsempoor Bank [unsound banking practices, India], 237–40. 7 cols. £4.4.0. *Capper* / **John Capper**

Snails, 240–44. 7 cols. £4.4.0. *Horne* / **Richard H. Horne**

Departed Beggars [London beggars of the past], 244–46. 4 cols. £2.2.0. *Woods* / **Woods**

Submarine Geography [findings of U.S. Navy], 246–48. 5¾ cols. *Morley* / **Henry Morley**

The Fiery Trial. A Legend [verse], 248–50. 2½ cols. £4.14.6. *Miss Griffiths* / **Miss Eliza Griffiths**

Phases of "Public" Life, chap. ii, 250–55. 10 cols. £5.5.0. *Sala* / **George A. Sala**

Notes from Norway [ii], 255–58. 6 cols.; should read 7½. £3.3.0. *Miss Williamson* / **Miss Williamson**

Last Homes [French cemeteries], 258–60. 4 cols. £2.2.0. *Dixon* / **Edmund Saul Dixon**

June 5, 1852. No. 115, pp. 261–84

Volunteer Apostles [religious impostors], 261–66. 10 cols. £6.6.0. *W. Howitt* / **William Howitt**

The Wild-Flower of the Danube [Hungarian legend], 266–70. 9 cols. £4.14.6. *Mad. De Meley* / **Mme. De Mérey**

The Treatment of the Insane, 270–73. 5½ cols. £2.12.6. *Morley & Dr. Oliver* / **Henry Morley &** prob. **Richard Oliver**

The Wonders of Mincing Lane [wholesale auction of pharmaceutical products], 273–76. 5 cols. £3.0.0. *Capper* / **John Capper**

Among the Moors [Tangier], 276–79. 5 cols. £2.12.6. *Mrs. Grenville Murray* / **Mrs. Grenville Murray**

Chip:
– Change for a Sovereign [decrease in value of gold], 279–80. 3 cols. *Morley* / **Henry Morley**

Preservation in Destruction [Museo Borbonico, Naples], 280–84. 8¾ cols. £4.0.0. *Delaware Lewis* / **John Delaware Lewis**

June 12, 1852. No. 116, pp. 285–308

The Poor Brothers of the Charterhouse, 285–91. 12½ cols. £5.5.0. *Morley & Moncrieff* / **Henry Morley & William Thomas Moncrieff**

Too Much Blue [incident concerning Pierre Jean David], 291–93. 3¾ cols. £2.10.0. *Mrs. Hoare* / **Mrs. Hoare**

King Charles's Post-Bag [postal service, past and present], 293–95. 5¾ cols.; should read 5. £2.12.6. *W. B. Jerrold* / **William Blanchard Jerrold**

Chip:
– Twenty Shillings for a Napoleon [visit to St. Helena], 295–97. 3 cols. £1.5.0. *Dr. Ord.* [? or *O.W.*?] *Mackenzie* / **Dr. Ord.?** or **O.W.? Mackenzie**

Hope. An Epigram [verse], 297. ¼ col. ——— / ———

Swords and Ploughshares [political economy, Switzerland], 297–302. 9 cols.; should read 9¾. £5.5.0. *E. E. Crowe* / **Eyre Evans Crowe**

Hyde Park, 302–304. 5 cols. £2.12.6. *Wynter* / **Andrew Wynter**

A Child's History of England, chap. xvii, 304–308. 8½ cols. *C.D.* / **Charles Dickens**

June 19, 1852. No. 117, pp. 309–332

Going to the Dogs [an adventure in Australia], 309–312. 6 cols. £3.3.0. *Sidney* / **Samuel Sidney**

Dumbledowndeary [Erith, Kent], 312–17. 10 cols.; should read 10¾ £5.5.0. *Sala* / **George A. Sala**

The Schah's English Gardener [John Burton's work and experiences in Teheran], 317–21. 8½ cols. £4.4.0. *Mrs. Gaskell* / **Elizabeth Gaskell**

Bread of Life [verse], 321–22. ¾ col. £1.5.0. *Prince* / **John Critchley Prince**

The Widow of Sixteen [daughter-in-law of Buffon], 322–24. 5¼ cols. £3.3.0. *Miss Costello* / **Louisa Stuart Costello**

Chips:
- Highland Emigration [endorsement of purpose and plan of Society for Assisting Emigration from the Highlands and Islands of Scotland], 324–25. 1½ cols. *Morley* / **Henry Morley**
- Darkness in Devonshire [ignorance, superstition], 325–26. 1¼ cols. ——— *& Morley* / ——— **& Henry Morley**

Bold Admiral Blake [W. Hepworth Dixon, *Robert Blake*, 1852], 326–31. 9¾ cols. £5.5.0. *Hannay* / **James Hannay**

A Chinaman's Ball [in Singapore], 331–32. 4 cols. £2.2.0. *J. A. St. John* / **James Augustus St. John**

June 26, 1852. No. 118, pp. 333–56

Betting-Shops, 333–36. 7 cols. *C.D.* / **Charles Dickens**

Four Stories [Paris lodging-house and lodgers], 336–42. 12 cols. £6.6.0. *Sala* / **George A. Sala**

Quarter-Day, 342–45. 5½ cols. £3.0.0. *Buckley* / **Theodore Buckley**

The Lady and the Child [verse], 345–46. 1½ cols. £2.12.6. *Miss Griffith* / **Miss Eliza Griffiths**

Shadows: The Shadows of Philip Sidney and Fulke Greville [imagined boyhood conversation], 346–47. 3½ cols. £2.2.0. *Charles Knight* / **Charles Knight**

Law in the East [Ceylon], 347–52. 8 cols. £4.14.6. *Capper* / **John Capper**

What Is to Become of Us? [erosion of England's coastline], 352–56. 9¾ cols. £5.5.0. *Dixon* / **Edmund Saul Dixon**

July 3, 1852. No. 119, pp. 357–80

The Popular Poets of Fifty Years Ago [mainly Robert Bloomfield], 357–59. 5 cols. £2.12.6. *Charles Knight* / **Charles Knight**

The Three Sisters [story], chaps. i–ii, 359–64. 9 cols. £6.10.0. *Miss Craik* / **Georgiana Marion Craik**

Chip:
- What to Take to Australia, 364–66. 4 cols. £2.2.0. *Sidney* / **Samuel Sidney**

A Play in a Great Many Acts [vexations of obscure playwright with Théâtre Français], 366–68. 6 cols. £3.3.0. *Rev. J. White* / **the Rev. James White**

China with a Flaw in It [John F. Davis, *China, during the War and since the Peace*, 1852], 368–74. 10 cols. *Morley* / **Henry Morley**

Literary Mystifications [forgeries], 374–77. 7½ cols. £3.13.6. *S. Blanchard* / **Sidney Laman Blanchard**

The Schoolmasters of Broad-Bumble [examples of bad and good masters], 377–80. 6½ cols. £3.13.6. *Buckley* / **Theodore Buckley**

July 10, 1852. No. 120, pp. 381–404

A Flight with the Birds [Edmund Saul Dixon, *The Dovecote and the Aviary*, 1851], 381–84. 6½ cols. *Morley & W.H.W.* / **Henry Morley & W. H. Wills**

The Three Sisters, chaps. iii–iv, 384–88. 9 cols. £4.0.0. *Miss Craik* / **Georgiana Marion Craik**

Our Doubles [duality of human nature], 388–91. 6¼ cols. £3.13.6. *Sala* / **George A. Sala**

Chip:
- Climate of Australia [from Paul E. de Strzelecki, *Physical Description of New South Wales and Van Diemen's Land*, 1845], 391–92. 1 col. £1.1.0. *Sidney* / **Samuel Sidney**

The First-Born [verse], 392. ½ col. £1.1.0. *Meredith* / **George Meredith**

Shadows: The Shadow of Fanny Burney at Court [*Diary and Letters of Madame d'Arblay*, 1842–46], 392–96. 7½ cols. £4.0.0. *C. Knight* / **Charles Knight**

We, and Our Man Tom [a farmer's life in Australia], 396–98. 4 cols. £2.2.0. *Mulock* / **Mulock**

Animal Mechanics [why bones are filled with marrow], 398–400. 4 cols. £1.11.6. *Kelly* / **Kelly**

A Child's History of England, chaps. xviii–xix, 400–404. 10 cols. *C.D.* / **Charles Dickens**

July 17, 1852. No. 121, pp. 405–428

Off to the Diggings! [an emigrant ship], 405–410. 10½ cols. £5.10.0. *Capper* / **John Capper**

The German Workman, 410–15. 10 cols. £5.5.0. *Duthie* / **William Duthie**

Spanish Romance [the Cid, with trans. from Herder's *Der Cid*], 415–17. 4 cols.; should read 5¼. £3.0.0. *White* / **the Rev. James White**

Cities in Plain Clothes [realist's view of Constantinople, Venice, and other cities], 417–22. 10 cols. £5.5.0. *Sala* / **George A. Sala**

Chip:
- Mr. Bovington on the New Cattle-Market [proposed site of], 422–23. 1 col. *W.H.W.* / **W. H. Wills**

Constitutional Trials [food adulteration], 423–26. 6½ cols. *Morley* / **Henry Morley**

Round the Midsummer Fire [bonfires on St. John's eve, Ireland], 426–28. 4½ cols. £2.10.0. *Allingham* / **William Allingham**

July 24, 1852. No. 122, pp. 429–52

Little Blue Mantle [Edmé Champion, philanthropist], 429–31. 5 cols. £2.12.6. *Sala* / **George A. Sala**

The Forbidden Land [Evariste Régis Huc, *Travels in Tartary, Thibet, and China*, W. Hazlitt, trans., 1852], 431–36. 10 cols. £5.5.0. *Miss Martineau* / **Harriet Martineau**

"Who Murdered Downie?" [outcome of student prank, Marischal College, 18 cent.], 436–38. 3¼ cols. £2.2.0. *Knox* / **James Knox**

Chips:
- What Godfathers Have Done for Omnibuses [non-informative designations on omnibuses], 438–39. 1¼ cols. £1.0.0. *W. B. Jerrold* / **William Blanchard Jerrold**
- The Gossip of Lebanon [the Druses], 439–40. 2½ cols. £2.2.0. *Jones & Morley* / **Jones & Henry Morley**

A Household Word to My Cousin Helen [verse], 440. ¾ col. £1.11.6. *Hon. Mrs. Norton* / **Caroline Norton**

French Provincial News [newspapers], 440–44. 7¼ cols. £4.4.0. *Dixon* / **Edmund Saul Dixon**

Printed Forgeries, 444–50. 12½ cols. £4.14.6. *S. Blanchard* / **Sidney Laman Blanchard**

Shadows: Day and Night [ignominious last days of hist. personages], 450–52. 4½ cols. £2.10.0. *Sala* / **George A. Sala**

July 31, 1852. No. 123, pp. 453–76

Our Honorable Friend [M.P. "for Verbosity" – Disraeli (according to *Lives of the Illustrious*, II, 295)], 453–55. 5¼ cols. *C.D.* / **Charles Dickens**

Transported for Life [William Henry Barber, solicitor, transported to Norfolk Island, 1844: account "taken down from the lips of the narrator, whose sufferings are described"], part i, 455–64. 18 cols. £10.10.0. *Thomas* / **William Moy Thomas**

The Thinker and the Doer [verse], 464. ½ col. £1.1.0. *Harper* / **Harper**

Ten Minutes "Cross Country" [a walk not taken], 464–66. 3½ cols. £1.11.6. *Sala* / **George A. Sala**

The Flying Bridge [Paul Lacroix, *Quand j'étais jeune*, 1833], 466–71. 9¾ cols. £5.0.0. *Dixon* / **Edmund Saul Dixon**

All about Pigs, 471–74. 6¼ cols. £3.3.0. *Dodd* / **George Dodd**

A Page from a Sad Book [witchcraft examination, Salem, Mass., 1692], 474–76. 5 cols. £2.12.6. *Miss Jewsbury* / **Geraldine Endsor Jewsbury**

August 7, 1852. No. 124, pp. 477–500

The Farmer of Tiptree Hall [John Joseph Mechi], 477–82. 11 cols. *Morley* / **Henry Morley**

Transported for Life, part ii, 482–89. 13½ cols. £5.5.0. *Thomas* / **William Moy Thomas**

The Cities of Time [verse], 489. 1¼ cols. £2.2.0. *R. H. Horne* / **Richard H. Horne**

Dining with the Million [in France], 489–93. 7½ cols. £3.13.6. *Blanchard* / **Sidney Laman Blanchard**

Chip:
- Berrington's Knapsack [Govt. inaction on needed improvements], 493–94. 1¼ cols. *Morley* / **Henry Morley**

Wreck and Ruin [a boat wreck off Capri], 494–95. 3 cols. £1.11.6. *Wreford* / **Henry G. Wreford**

A Child's History of England, chaps. xx–xxi, 495–500. 10¼ cols. *C.D.* / **Charles Dickens**

August 14, 1852. No. 125, pp. 501–524

Tapping the Butts [story], chap. i, 501–506. 10½ cols. £5.5.0. *Rev. James White* / **the Rev. James White**

Monsters of Faith [religious festival, India], 506–508. 5 cols. £2.12.6. *Capper* / **John Capper**

Up a Court [London slum tenements], 508–512. 6 cols. £3.13.6. *Sala* / **George A. Sala**

The Rhyme of the Caliph [verse], 512–13. 2¼ cols. £2.12.6. *Ollier* / **Edmund Ollier**

Household Scenery [wallpaper], 513–19. 11¾ cols. £6.6.0. *Miss Martineau* / **Harriet Martineau**

Chips:
- An Equestrian Miracle [correct version of incident mentioned in "If This Should Meet His Eye," March 13], 519. 1¼ cols. *General Sir Robert Abruthnot* / **Robert Arbuthnot**
- Something New [first no. of *Universal Magazine*, 1747], 519–21. 4 cols. £1.11.6. *Miss Costello* / **Louisa Stuart Costello**
- Our Ruins ["restoration" of historic ruins], 521–22. 1½ cols. £1.0.0. *W. B. Jerrold* / **William Blanchard Jerrold**

The Roving Englishman: A Ramble to Rehburg, 522–24. 4¾ cols. £2.2.0. *E. C. Murray* / **Grenville Murray**

August 21, 1852. No. 126, pp. 525–48

The City Parliament [Corporation of the City of London], 525–30. 11 cols. *Morley* / **Henry Morley**

Tapping the Butts, chap. ii, 530–35. 10 cols. £5.5.0. *White* / **the Rev. James White**

Chip:
- Healthy Figures [mortality and other statistics, Geneva], 535–37. 4 cols. *Morley* / **Henry Morley**

News of an Old Place [Leadhills, Lanark], 537–42. 9¼ cols.; should read 10¼. £5.15.6. *Miss Martineau* / **Harriet Martineau**

Shadows: The Shadow of the Island of Madeira [discoverers of the island], 542–46. 7¼ cols. £4.4.0. *Charles Knight* / **Charles Knight**

A Great Idea [exhibiting the physically abnormal], 546–48. 5 cols. *Morley* / **Henry Morley**

August 28, 1852. No. 127, pp. 549–72

Our Vestry [Parliament in miniature], 549–52. 6 cols. *C.D.* / **Charles Dickens**

Shawls, 552–56. 8½ cols. £4.14.6. *Miss Martineau* / **Harriet Martineau**

The Garden of Flowers [a Ceylon village], 556–61. 10½ cols. £5.5.0. *Capper* / **John Capper**

The Path of Faith [verse], 561–62. ½ col. £1.1.0. *Harper* / **Harper**

A Cup of Coffee [history of coffee, coffee-houses, etc.], 562–66. 10 cols. £5.5.0. *Sala* / **George A. Sala**

Chip:
- Transportation for Life [concerning "Transported for Life," July 31, Aug. 7], 566–67. ¾ col. *W.H.W.* / **W. H. Wills**

Among the Moors. The Legend of the Castle, 567–70. 6¼ cols. £2.12.6. *Mrs. Murray* / **Mrs. Grenville Murray**

London Bridge in the Afternoon, 570–72. 5¼ cols. £3.0.0. *Hannay* / **James Hannay**

September 4, 1852. No. 128, pp. 573–96

A Handful of Foreign Money [history told in coins], 573–77. 8¼ cols. £4.4.0. *Sala* / **George A. Sala**

The Enemy [fresh air for health], 577–80. 5 cols.; should read 5¾. *Morley* / **Henry Morley**

Tom's Salad Days [a model curate], 580–82. 5¼ cols.; should read 4½. £2.2.0. *Buckley* / **Theodore Buckley**

Chips:
- The Cup and the Lip [anecdote concerning a Florentine], 582. 1 col. *Leigh Hunt* / **Leigh Hunt**
- Cornish Choughs Found at Last, 582–83. 1 col. *Correspondent* / **Charles Mass**

A Wholesome Policy [needed adjustment in insurance premiums], 583–85. 3 cols. *Morley* / **Henry Morley**

Kilspindie [verse], 585. 1¼ cols. £4.14.6. *Leigh Hunt* / **Leigh Hunt**

Underwriting [Lloyd's], 585–89. 7 cols.; should read 7¾. £3.13.6. *Capper* / **John Capper**

The Present Hollow Time [riveted sheet iron and its uses], 589–93. 6¾ cols. £3.3.0. *Dodd* / **George Dodd**

Down in a Silver Mine [in Saxony], 593–96. 7¾ cols. £3.13.6. *Duthie* / **William Duthie**

September 11, 1852. No. 129, pp. 597–616

Boys to Mend [Philanthropic Farm School, Surrey], 597–602. 11¾ cols. *Morley & C.D.* / **Henry Morley & Charles Dickens**

The Merry Men of Cairo [wags and jokers], 602–606. 6½ cols. £3.10.0. *Bayle St. John* / **Bayle St. John**

The Life of a Salmon, 606–610. 8 cols. £4.4.0. *Miss Martineau* / **Harriet Martineau**

Chip:
- The World's Fairest Rose [story], 610. 1 col. *Andersen* / **Hans Christian Andersen**

Walking-Sticks, 610–13. 4½ cols. £2.12.6. *Dodd* / **George Dodd**

A Child's History of England, chap. xxii, 613–16. 8 cols. *C.D.* / **Charles Dickens**

VOLUME VI September 18, 1852 – February 26, 1853

September 18, 1852. No. 130, pp. 1–24

North American Slavery [Casimir Leconte, "Les Noirs libres et les noirs esclaves," *Revue des deux mondes*, July 1852], 1–6. 10 cols. *Morley & C.D.* / **Henry Morley & Charles Dickens**

Shadows: The Shadow of a Dutch Painter [Pieter van Laer], 6–10. 8 cols. £4.4.0. *Sala* / **George A. Sala**

Chips:
- Hoary Abuses [from *Humphry Clinker*], 10–11. 3 cols. £1.11.6. *Murray* / **Grenville Murray**
- Our Own Temperature [based on papers read by John Davy, M.D., before Royal Society], 11–12. 1½ cols. *Morley* / **Henry Morley**

The Trumpets of Doolkarnein [verse], 12–13. 1¼ cols. Payment "Advanced," no sum recorded. *Leigh Hunt* / **Leigh Hunt**

Peatal Aggression [Irish peat bogs], 13–18. 10½ cols. £5.5.0. *Miss Martineau* / **Harriet Martineau**

More Work for the Ladies [work of Frenchwomen], 18–22. 7¾ cols. £3.13.6. *Dixon* / **Edmund Saul Dixon**

Little Mari's Betrothal. From the Danish, 22–24. 6 cols. £3.0.0. *Miss F. Rowan* / **Frederica Maclean Rowan**

September 25, 1852. No. 131, pp. 25–48

Cheerily, Cheerily! [emigrant-laden ships leaving Liverpool], 25–31. 13 cols. £6.16.6. *Sala* / **George A. Sala**

The English Passport System [printed railway tickets], 31–34. 6½ cols. £3.13.6. *Miss Martineau* / **Harriet Martineau**

Chips:
- Fairy Rings, 34–35. 2½ cols. *Morley* / **Henry Morley**
- A Cheap Dinner [in Germany], 35–36. 2½ cols. £1.11.6. *Murray* / **Grenville Murray**

Alice's Posies [verse], 36–37. 2 cols. £3.3.0. *Miss Tomkins* / **Mary Jane Tomkins**

Dead, or Alive? [story], 37–42. 9 cols. £5.0.0. *White* / **the Rev. James White**

The Guano Diggings [Islas de Chincha, Peru], 42–46. 8¾ cols. £3.13.6. *Render* / **Samuel Rinder**

The Roving Englishman: A Golden Wedding [in Germany], 46–48. 4½ cols. £2.8.6. *Murray* / **Grenville Murray**

October 2, 1852. No. 132, pp. 49–72

How I Went to Sea [a boyhood adventure], 49–55. 13 cols. £5.15.6. *Sala* / **George A. Sala**

The Gardens of Rye [Rye horticultural exhibition], 55–60. 10 cols. *Morley* / **Henry Morley**

The Tower of the Seine [verse], 60–61. 2 cols. £2.2.0. *Miss Griffiths* / **Miss Eliza Griffiths**

"Moving," 61–63. 3¾ cols. £2.2.0. *W. B Jerrold & W.H.W.* / **William Blanchard Jerrold & W. H. Wills**

The Theatres of Paris, 63–69. 11 cols. *Morley* / **Henry Morley**

Chips:
- A Tiger's Jaws [shooting expedition, India], 69. 1½ cols. ——— / **Hugh Hislop Elliot**
- Lloyd's List [correction of statement in "Underwriting," Sept. 4], 69–70. ¼ col. *Correspondent* / ———

Belgian Briskness [railway regulations], 70–72. 6 cols. £2.12.6. *Russell* / **William Howard Russell**

October 9, 1852. No. 133, pp. 73–96

Our Bore, 73–76. 7 cols. *C.D.* / **Charles Dickens**

Wholesale Diving [P. A. Payerne's diving bell], 76–81. 9½ cols. £5.0.0. *Dixon* / **Edmund Saul Dixon**

Sunday Morning, 81–84. 6 cols. £3.0.0. *Sala* / **George A. Sala**

Speed the Plough [verse], 84–85. 2¼ cols. £2.12.6. *Ollier* / **Edmund Ollier**

Blind Sight-Seeing [sight-seeing in company with blind man, at Loches], 85–90. 9 cols. £5.0.0. *Miss Costello* / **Louisa Stuart Costello**

Pic-nics in the Prairie [Edward R. Sullivan, *Rambles and Scrambles in North and South America,* 1852], 90–93. 7½ cols. *Morley* / **Henry Morley**

A Child's History of England, chap. xxiii, 93–96. 6 cols. *C.D.* / **Charles Dickens**

October 16, 1852. No. 134, pp. 97–120

Penny Wisdom [utilization of refuse and waste products], 97–101. 8½ cols. £4.14.6. *Dodd* / **George Dodd**

Phases of "Public" Life, chap. iii, 101–105. 8½ cols. £4.14.6. *Sala* / **George A. Sala**

Graves and Epitaphs, 105–109. 8½ cols. £4.4.0. *Hannay* / **James Hannay**

Hops, 109–115. 11¼ cols. £6.6.0. *Thomas* / **William Moy Thomas**

A Gun among the Grouse [shooting in Scotland], 115–18. 6 cols. £3.0.0. *Mrs. Murray* / **Mrs. Grenville Murray**

An Opium Factory [in India], 118–20. 4 cols. £2.2.0. *H. H. Maxwell* / **H. H. Maxwell**

October 23, 1852. No. 135, pp. 121–44

Triumphant Carriages [coach manufactory, Dublin], 121–25. 9¼ cols. £5.5.0. *Miss Martineau* / **Harriet Martineau**

The Topmost City of the Earth [Cerro de Pasco, Peru], 125–29. 7¼ cols. £3.10.0. *Render & Morley* / **Samuel Rinder & Henry Morley**

The Babbleton Book Club [benefit of reading, for lower class], 129–33. 6½ cols. £3.3.0. *Buckley* / **Theodore Buckley**

The Sporting World [*Bell's Life in London*], 133–39. 14 cols. £7.0.0. *Sala* / **George A. Sala**

What We Do with Our Letters [handling of letters in a Govt. office], 139–42. 6 cols. £2.12.6. *Peter Cunningham* / **Peter Cunningham**

The Roving Englishman: A German Joe Miller [extracts from a German almanac], 142–44. 4 cols. £2.2.0. *Murray* / **Grenville Murray**

October 30, 1852. No. 136, pp. 145–68

Lying Awake, 145–48. 6 cols. *C.D.* / **Charles Dickens**

Johan Falsen; from the Danish of Mr. Goldschmidt [Meïr A. Goldschmidt, "Onkel og hans Hus," *Fortællinger,* 1846], 148–55. 16 cols. £5.15.6. *Mrs. Howitt* / **Mary Howitt**

The Reason Why [the Trelawny ballad], 155–56. 1¼ cols. *J.F.* / **John Forster**

Hope with a Slate Anchor [slate quarries, Ireland], 156–61. 10 cols. £5.5.0. *Miss Martineau* / **Harriet Martineau**

Tricks upon Travellers [prejudices in eating], 161–65. 8 cols. £4.4.0. *Dixon* / **Edmund Saul Dixon**

A Child's History of England, chaps. xxiv–xxv, 165–68. 7¼ cols. *C.D.* / **Charles Dickens**

November 6, 1852. No. 137, pp. 169–92

The Irish Union [a workhouse], 169–75. 12 cols. £6.6.0. *Miss Martineau* / **Harriet Martineau**

A Guest for the Night [story], 175–81. 12½ cols. £6.16.6. *Thomas* / **William Moy Thomas**

School Friendship [verse], 181. 2 cols. £2.5.0. *Miss Griffiths* / **Miss Eliza Griffiths**

Milton's Golden Lane [squalid London district], 181–86. 8¼ cols. £3.13.6. *Thomas* / **William Moy Thomas**

Poisonous Serpents, 186–88. 6 cols. £3.3.0. *Professor Owen* / **Richard Owen**

Chip:
– The Crimes of Cotton [18-cent. opposition to cotton cloth], 188–89. 1¼ cols. *W.H.W.* / **W. H. Wills**

Yourself at Turin [descr. of people, shops, churches, etc.], 189–92. 6¾ cols. £3.13.6. *Russell* / **William Howard Russell**

November 13, 1852. No. 138, pp. 193–216

Discovery of a Treasure near Cheapside [gold refining], 193–97. 9 cols. *C.D. & Morley* / **Charles Dickens & Henry Morley**

Francis Moore, Physician [*Moore's Almanack*], 197–201. 7 cols. *Morley* / **Henry Morley**

Umbrellas, 201–204. 5¼ cols. £2.12.6. *Dodd* / **George Dodd**

A Child's First Letter [verse], 204. 1 col. £2.2.0. *Miss Griffiths* / **Miss Eliza Griffiths**

Day-Break, 204–208. 7 cols. £3.13.6. *Sala* / **George A. Sala**

Justice to Chicory, 208–210. 5½ cols. *Morley* / **Henry Morley**

Chip:
– An Oriental Firman [of the Shah of Persia], 210–11. 1 col. *W.H.W.* / **W. H. Wills**

The Roving Englishman: His Hints to Travellers, 211–14. 6½ cols. £3.3.0. *Murray* / **Grenville Murray**

The Famine Time [in Ireland], 214–16. 5 cols. £3.0.0. *Miss Martineau* / **Harriet Martineau**

November 20, 1852. No. 139, pp. 217–40

The Ghost of the Cock Lane Ghost [spirit rapping; a séance], 217–23. 12½ cols. *Morley* / **Henry Morley**

My Fortune [story], 223–29. 12½ cols. £5.15.6. *Miss Craik* / **Georgiana Marion Craik**

The Deeds of Wellington [verse], 229–31. 2½ cols. £2.12.6. *Bennett* / **William Cox Bennett**

The Roving Englishman: His Philosophy of Dining, 231–33. 5½ cols. £2.10.0. *Murray* / **Grenville Murray**

Chips:
– The Reason Why [correction of error in "Reason Why," Oct. 30], 233–34. 1¼ cols. *J.F.* / **John Forster**
– The "Logging" Stone [Lieut. Hugh C. Goldsmith's capsizing of], 234–35. 2¼ cols. *W.H.W.* / **W. H. Wills**

A Dip in the Nile [Bayle St. John, *Village Life in Egypt*, 1852], 235–39. 7¼ cols. *Morley* / **Henry Morley**

An Interview with the Madiai [imprisoned Italian man and wife], 239–40. 3¼ cols. £1.10.0. *Phipps (Ed.)* / **Edmund Phipps**

November 27, 1852. No. 140, pp. 241–64

Trading in Death [the Wellington state funeral], 241–45. 8 cols. *C.D.* / **Charles Dickens**

When I Served in the Militia [Prussian military system], 245–50. 11 cols. £5.15.6. *Dr. Wenkstern* / **Otto von Wenckstern**

The Great Yorkshire Llama [alpaca-cloth manufacture], 250–53. 5½ cols. £2.10.0. *Capper* / **John Capper**

Cogswell's [a coffee-house], 253–57. 9¼ cols. £4.14.6. *Thomas* / **William Moy Thomas**

Chips:
- Funerals in Paris, 257–60. 4¼ cols. *Morley & W.H.W.* / **Henry Morley & W. H. Wills**
- Tittlebat Tactics [sticklebacks], 260–61. 3¼ cols. £1.10.0. *Dallas* / **William Sweetland Dallas**

A Wedding in the Clouds [in Anacapri], 261–64. 6 cols. £2.10.0. *Wreford* / **Henry G. Wreford**

December 4, 1852. No. 141, pp. 265–88

A House Full of Horrors [Practical Art exhibition at Marlborough House], 265–70. 11½ cols. *Morley* / **Henry Morley**

Imperial Anecdotes [Josephine and Napoleon], 270–75. 9¾ cols. £5.0.0. *Miss Costello* / **Louisa Stuart Costello**

Chip:
- Another Lung for London [plan for model living and working community], 275–77. 2½ cols. *Morley* / **Henry Morley**

The Ghosts' Banquet [verse], 277–78. 3¾ cols. £3.3.0. *Ollier* / **Edmund Ollier**

Mechanics by Instinct [Samuel H. Berthoud's observations on animals], 278–81. 4½ cols. £1.10.0. *Mrs. Hoare* / **Mrs. Hoare**

Stop Thief! [story], 281–84. 7 cols. £3.10.0. *White* / **the Rev. James White**

A Child's History of England, chap. XXVI, 284–88. 8½ cols. *C.D.* / **Charles Dickens**

December 11, 1852. No. 142, pp. 289–312

A Foe under Foot [foul London sewers], 289–92. 6¼ cols. *Morley* / **Henry Morley**

Doctor Chillingworth's Prescription [story], 292–96. 8¼ cols. £5.0.0. *Thomas* / **William Moy Thomas**

Really a Temperance Question [wine importation], 296–300. 7¼ cols. £3.13.6. *Capper* / **John Capper**

Forty Famous Arm-Chairs [the French Academy], 300–306. 11¼ cols. £5.5.0. *Morley* / **Henry Morley**

The Crusade of the Needle [sewed-muslin industry], 306–309. 6 cols. £3.3.0. *Capper* / **John Capper**

The Roving Englishman: On Horseback, 309–312. 7 cols. £3.13.6. *Murray* / **Grenville Murray**

December 18, 1852. No. 143, pp. 313–36

Some Compliments of the Season [Christmas food and drink], 313–17. 8 cols. £2.2.0 to Thomas; £2.2.0 to Sala. *Thomas & Sala* / **William Moy Thomas & George A. Sala**

When the Mill Goes – [story], 317–24. 15½ cols. £7.0.0. *Dixon* / **Edmund Saul Dixon**

The Bush with the Bleeding Breast [verse], 324–25. ½ col. £1.1.0. *Hawker* / **Robert Stephen Hawker**

South American Christmas, 325–28. 7 cols. £2.12.6. *Render* / **Samuel Rinder**

A Pack of Cards [history and manufacture of], 328–33. 9½ cols. £4.4.0. *Dodd* / **George Dodd**

The Roving Englishman: With a Baron Much Interested in Him [life in Dresden], 333–36. 7¼ cols. £3.13.6. *Murray* / **Grenville Murray**

Christmas 1852. Extra Christmas Number: A Round of Stories by the Christmas Fire, pp. 1–36. Announced pub. date: Dec. 18. Stated on title page of Vol. VI as included in that vol.; contents of no. listed at end of "Contents" of that vol.

The Poor Relation's Story, 1–5. 9 cols. *C.D.* / **Charles Dickens**

The Child's Story, 5–7. 3¼ cols. *C.D.* / **Charles Dickens**

Somebody's Story, 7–11. 8¾ cols. £5.15.6. *Thomas* / **William Moy Thomas**

The Old Nurse's Story, 11–20. 17½ cols. £10.0.0. *Mrs. Gaskell* / **Elizabeth Gaskell**

The Host's Story [verse], 20–21. 3¼ cols. £5.5.0. *E. Ollier* / **Edmund Ollier**

The Grandfather's Story, 21–25. 7½ cols. £5.5.0. *White* / **the Rev. James White**

The Charwoman's Story, 25–27. 2½ cols. £1.10.0. *Dixon* / **Edmund Saul Dixon**

The Deaf Playmate's Story, 27–30. 7 cols. £5.5.0. *Miss Martineau* / **Harriet Martineau**

The Guest's Story, 30–33. 6½ cols. £4.10.0. *Sidney* / **Samuel Sidney**

The Mother's Story [verse], 33–36. 6 cols. £6.0.0. *Miss Griffiths* / **Miss Eliza Griffiths**

December 25, 1852. No. 144, pp. 337–60

Rational Schools [Birkbeck Schools], 337–42. 10 cols. *Morley & W.H.W.* / **Henry Morley & W. H. Wills**

The Golden Age of Hungary, 342–44. 4½ cols. £2.2.0. *Miss Birkbeck* / **Sándor Mednyánszky**

Butter, 344–50. 11¼ cols. £5.15.6. *Miss Martineau* / **Harriet Martineau**

Frozen Up in Siberia [Ewa Felińska, *Revelations of Siberia*, 1852], 350–56. 12 cols. *Morley* / **Henry Morley**

Chip:
– Christmas Customs in Norway, 356. ¾ col. ——— / prob. **Miss Williamson**

Time and the Hour [reflections on time and man], 356–58. 4¼ cols. £2.2.0. *Sala* / **George A. Sala**

The Roving Englishman: A Few More Hints [to travellers], 358–60. 4¼ cols. £2.12.6. *Murray* / **Grenville Murray**

January 1, 1853. No. 145, pp. 361–84

Where We Stopped Growing [childhood memories], 361–63. 5 cols. *C.D.* / **Charles Dickens**

French National Defences [sabots and sabot making], 363–68. 9¼ cols. £4.14.6. *Dixon* / **Edmund Saul Dixon**

My Friend Spanner [story], 368–71. 6½ cols. £3.13.6. *Sidney* / **Samuel Sidney**

The Masque of the New Year [verse], 371–73. 3 cols. £5.0.0. *Ollier* / **Edmund Ollier**

Justice to the Hyæna, 373–77. 8¾ cols. £4.14.6. *Professor Owen* / **Richard Owen**

The Golden Vale [strife between estate manager and tenant farmers, Ireland], 377–81. 8 cols. £4.0.0. *E. E. Crowe* / **Eyre Evans Crowe**

Chip:
– Municipal Lights [lanterns in Falaise], 381. 1 col. £1.1.0. *Dixon* / **Edmund Saul Dixon**

Pass-Words through All the Russias [gratuities and bribes], 381–84. 6 cols. £3.3.0. *Wenckstern* / **Otto von Wenckstern**

January 8, 1853. No. 146, pp. 385–408

My Man. A Sum [apportionment of hours in man's lifetime], 385–88. 7 cols. £3.13.6. *Sala* / **George A. Sala**

Silk from the Punjaub, 388–90. 4 cols. *Morley* / **Henry Morley**

The Great Cranford Panic [story], chap. i, 390–96. 13 cols. £13.13.0 for the 2 instalments. *Mrs. Gaskell* / **Elizabeth Gaskell**

The Dirty Old Man. A Lay of Leadenhall [verse], 396–97. 1¼ cols. £2.12.6. *Allingham* / **William Allingham**

Tit for Tat [duty on imports], 397–99. 4¾ cols. £2.10.0. *Dixon* / **Edmund Saul Dixon**

Black-Skin A-head! [whaling], 399–404. 8 cols. £3.0.0. *Rinder* / **Samuel Rinder**

A Child's History of England, chap. xxvii, 404–408. 10 cols. *C.D.* / **Charles Dickens**

January 15, 1853. No. 147, pp. 409–432

Scholastic [advertisements of private schools], 409–413. 8 cols. *Morley* / **Henry Morley**

The Great Cranford Panic, chap. ii, 413–20. 13½ cols. *Mrs. Gaskell* / **Elizabeth Gaskell**

Chip:
– The Ghost of the Cock Lane Ghost Wrong Again [denial of a false report], 420. ½ col. *C.D.* / **Charles Dickens**

Travel on Tramp in Germany [i]: Hamburgh to Lubeck, 420–22. 4 cols. £2.2.0. *Duthie & Morley* / **William Duthie & Henry Morley**

What Sand Is [Norfolk coast], 422–27. 10 cols. £5.0.0. *Dixon* / **Edmund Saul Dixon**

Information against a Poisoner [malaria], 427–30. 6¼ cols. *Morley* / **Henry Morley**

Playthings, 430–32. 4½ cols. *Morley* / **Henry Morley**

January 22, 1853. No. 148, pp. 433–56

The Club Surgeon [surgeon to working men's benefit society], 433–37. 9 cols. *Morley* / **Henry Morley**

Miss Harrington's Prediction [story], 437–45. 15¾ cols. £8.0.0. *Miss Lynn* / **Eliza Lynn**

Last Christmas Eve [verse], 445. 1 col. £1.1.0. *Prince* / **John Critchley Prince**

Cumberland Sheep-Shearers, 445–51. 11½ cols. £6.0.0. *Mrs. Gaskell* / **Elizabeth Gaskell**

Hobson's Choice [slum children], 451–53. 3¼ cols. £1.11.6. *W. B. Jerrold* / **William Blanchard Jerrold**

The Roving Englishman: Travelling Servants; Yachting, 453–56. 7½ cols. £3.15.0. *Murray* / **Grenville Murray**

January 29, 1853. No. 149, pp. 457–80

A Digger's Diary [partly fictionized] [i], 457–62. 10½ cols. £5.15.6. *R. H. Horne* / **Richard H. Horne**

Overland Tour to Bermondsey [leather market, tanneries, fellmongers' yards, etc.], 462–66. 7 cols. £3.13.6. *Dodd* / **George Dodd**

The Field of the Cloth of Flax [flax and linen], 466–69. 6 cols. £3.13.6. *Dixon* / **Edmund Saul Dixon**

The Leaf [verse], 469. ½ col. £1.1.0. *Mr. Keene* / **Keene**

The Captain's Prisoner [story], 469–74. 10½ cols. £5.5.0. *Sala* / **George A. Sala**

Madame Obé's Establishment [French domestic life], 474–78. 7½ cols. £4.14.6. *Miss Costello* / **Louisa Stuart Costello**

The Roving Englishman: Cares of State [life in a petty German kingdom], 478–80. 5¼ cols. £2.12.6. *Murray* / **Grenville Murray**

February 5, 1853. No. 150, pp. 481–504

Down with the Tide [Thames Police], 481–85. 8½ cols. *C.D.* / **Charles Dickens**

My Shadowy Passion [story], 485–92. 13 cols. £6.16.6. *Thomas* / **William Moy Thomas**

Old Echoes [verse], 492. ½ col. £1.1.0. *Miss Berwick* / **Adelaide Anne Procter**

Travel on Tramp in Germany [ii]: Lübeck to Berlin, 492–96. 8¼ cols. £3.13.6. *Duthie* / **William Duthie**

Chips:
- Clean Water and Dirty Water [sewage disposal, water supply], 496–97. 1½ cols. *W.H.W.* / **W. H. Wills**
- Look Before You Leap [bleak prospects in Australia for emigrants], 497–99. 3¾ cols. £0.10.6 to Horne; £1.1.0 to Hogarth. *Horne & Hogarth* / **Richard H. Horne & Hogarth, Jr.**

Wallotty Trot [cloth manufacture], 499–503. 9 cols. £4.14.6. *Dodd* / **George Dodd**

Barryhooraghan Post-Office [County Cork], 503–504. 3 cols. £1.1.0. *Mrs. Hoare* / **Mrs. Hoare**

February 12, 1853. No. 151, pp. 505–528

Proposals for Amusing Posterity [public honours; hereditary titles; the criminal law], 505–507. 4 cols. *C.D.* / **Charles Dickens**

Berthalde Reimer's Voice [story], 507–515. 16 cols. £6.16.6. *Miss Craik* / **Georgiana Marion Craik**

Chip:
- Doctor of Philosophy [selling of diplomas by German universities], 515. 1 col. *W.H.W.* / **W. H. Wills**

The Gauger's Pocket [smuggling on Cornish coast], 515–17. 4 cols. £2.2.0. *Hawker* / **Robert Stephen Hawker**

A Pill-Box, 517–21. 7½ cols. £3.3.0. *Dodd* / **George Dodd**

Crossing the Isthmus of Panama, 521–24. 8 cols. £3.3.0. *Markham* / **Clements Robert Markham**

A Child's History of England, chap. xxviii, 524–28. 8 cols. *C.D.* / **Charles Dickens**

February 19, 1853. No. 152, pp. 529–52

Sailors' Homes Afloat [forecastle life on English merchantmen], 529–33. 8 cols. £5.0.0. *Rinder & Morley* / **Samuel Rinder & Henry Morley**

Munchausen Modernised [Edmond Texier, *Lettres sur l'Angleterre*, 1851], 533–38. 11¾ cols. £5.15.6. *Blanchard* / **Sidney Laman Blanchard**

A Penny a Week [a penny savings society], 538–40. 4 cols. £2.2.0. *Capper* / **John Capper**

The Two Statues [verse], 540–41. 1 col. £2.2.0. *Miss Tomkins* / **Mary Jane Tomkins**

Wood, and How to Cut It, 541–45. 7¼ cols. £3.13.6. *Dodd* / **George Dodd**

A Digger's Diary [ii], 545–51. 12 cols. £6.6.0. *Horne* / **Richard H. Horne**

Wedding Bells [murder by a Thug, 1847], 551–52. 4 cols. £2.2.0. *Lang* / **John Lang**

February 26, 1853. No. 153, pp. 553–72

We Mariners of England [grievances of merchant seamen], 553–57. 8 cols. £3.0.0. *Rinder & Morley* / **Samuel Rinder & Henry Morley**

The Little Oak Wardrobe [story], 557–62. 10 cols. £5.0.0. *The Revd. J. White* / **the Rev. James White**

The Flowing of the Waters [verse], 562. 1¼ cols. £2.12.6. *Ollier* / **Edmund Ollier**

Wolf Nurses ["wolf children" in India], 562–63. 1¾ cols. £1.0.0. *Lang* / **John Lang**

Beet-Root Sugar, 563–69. 11¼ cols. £4.14.6. *Dixon* / **Edmund Saul Dixon**

Black Monday [schoolboy reminiscences], 569–72. 7½ cols. *Morley* / **Henry Morley**

VOLUME VII March 5 – August 27, 1853

March 5, 1853. No. 154, pp. 1–24

Seventy-eight Years Ago [*Journal and Letters of the Late Samuel Curwen*, 1842] [i], 1–6. 11 cols. *J.F.* / **John Forster**

Fisher's Ghost [a murder, New South Wales], 6–9. 6 cols. £3.3.0. *Lang* / **John Lang**

A Walk through a Mountain [Salzburg salt mine], 9–13. 7½ cols. £3.0.0. *Duthie & Morley* / **William Duthie & Henry Morley**

Friend Sorrow [verse], 13. ½ col. £1.0.0. *Miss Berwick* / **Adelaide Anne Procter**

The Last Crusader [Louis IX], 13–17. 7¼ cols. £3.13.6. *Sala* / **George A. Sala**

Diets of Gold and Silver [regulations concerning goldsmiths' manufactures], 17–20. 6½ cols. £3.3.0. *Dodd* / **George Dodd**

The Roving Englishman: Monsieur le Curé; Ma Sœur, the Governess, 20–22. 3 cols. £2.2.0. *Murray* / **Grenville Murray**

I Give and Bequeath [charity bequests], 22–24. 6 cols. £3.3.0. *W. B. Jerrold* / **William Blanchard Jerrold**

March 12, 1853. No. 155, pp. 25–48

Perfidious Patmos [foreign refugees in London], 25–29. 9 cols. £4.14.6. *Sala* / **George A. Sala**

India-Rubber, 29–33. 7 cols. £3.13.6. *Dodd* / **George Dodd**

The Whispering Tree [legend], 33–36. 7 cols. £3.13.6. *Bayle St. John* / **Bayle St. John**

Two Old Saints [visit to St. Riquier and Rue], 36–41. 10¼ cols. £5.5.0. *Miss Costello* / **Louisa Stuart Costello**

Snakes Magical and Mythological [in part from Ernst H. Meier, *Deutsche Sagen, Sitten und Gebräuche aus Schwaben*, 1852], 41–43. 3¾ cols. £2.2.0. *Oxenford* / **John Oxenford**

Self-Acting Railway Signals [invention of Jonathan Crowley], 43–45. 4 cols. *Morley* / **Henry Morley**

A Child's History of England, chap. xxix, 45–48. 6 cols. *C.D.* / **Charles Dickens**

March 19, 1853. No. 156, pp. 49–72

Received, a Blank Child [Foundling Hospital, London], 49–53. 9 cols. *C.D. & W.H.W.* / **Charles Dickens & W. H. Wills**

An Inundation in Bengal, 53–54. 2½ cols. £2.2.0. *J. Lang* / **John Lang**

Photography, 54–61. 13½ cols. *Morley & W.H.W.* / **Henry Morley & W. H. Wills**

The Ballad of the Gold-Digger [verse], 61–63. 2¾ cols. £2.10.0. *Ollier* / **Edmund Ollier**

Leicester Square, 63–67. 9 cols. £4.14.6. *Sala* / **George A. Sala**

The Roving Englishman: The Great Do [by rail and boat from Paris to Marseilles], 67–72. 11 cols. £5.15.6. *Murray* / **Grenville Murray**

March 26, 1853. No. 157, pp. 73–96

My Swan [a public house], 73–76. 8 cols.; should read 7¼. £4.4.0. *Sala* /**George A. Sala**

Saint Crispin [shoemaking], 76–80. 7 cols. £3.13.6. *Dodd* / **George Dodd**

The Deluge at Blissford [story], 80–84. 9 cols. £4.14.6. *White* / **the Rev. James White**

Lost and Found in the Gold Fields [advertisements in Australian newspapers], 84–88. 8 cols. £3.10.0. *Sidney* / **Samuel Sidney**

Hermit Island [La Galite, off north coast of Tunisia], 88–94. 11 cols. £5.10.0. *Dixon* / **Edmund Saul Dixon**

Starting a Paper in India, 94–96. 5¾ cols. £3.0.0. *Lang* / **John Lang**

April 2, 1853. No. 158, pp. 97–120

How to Kill Labourers [Settlement and Poor Removal laws], 97–102. 12½ cols.; should read 10½. *Morley* / **Henry Morley**

The Kingdom of Reconciled Impossibilities [dream world], 102–105. 6 cols. £3.13.6. *Sala* / **George A. Sala**

Gentlemen and Bullocks [a bullock drive, Australia], 105–107. 3¾ cols.; should read 4½. £2.12.6. *Horne* / **Richard H. Horne**

Chip:
– Fresh Air in Finsbury [proposed park], 107–108. ¾ col. *Morley* / **Henry Morley**

The Feast of Life [verse], 108. ½ col. £1.1.0. *Harper* / **Harper**

Stopped Payment, at Cranford [story], 108–115. 14½ cols. £8.0.0. *Mrs. Gaskell* / **Elizabeth Gaskell**

Colza Oil, 115–18. 6 cols. £3.3.0. *Dixon* / **Edmund Saul Dixon**

The Roving Englishman: After the Boars [in France], 118–20. 5 cols. £3.0.0. *Murray* / **Grenville Murray**

April 9, 1853. No. 159, pp. 121–44

Gentleman Cadet [Royal Military Academy, Woolwich], 121–25. 8 cols. £3.13.6. *J. Payne & Morley* / **James Payn & Henry Morley**

A Digger's Diary [iii], 125–29. 9 cols. £4.14.6. *Horne* / **Richard H. Horne**

Silken Chemistry [assaying of silk], 129–31. 3½ cols. £2.2.0. *Capper* / **John Capper**

Jane Markland. A Tale [verse], 131–34. 5 cols. £7.0.0. *White* / **the Rev. James White**

Six Years among Cannibals [sailor shipwrecked on one of Marquesas Islands], 134–38. 8 cols. £4.4.0. *Dr. Inman* / **Thomas Inman**

Receipt of Fern-Seed [Ernst H. Meier, *Deutsche Sagen, Sitten und Gebräuche aus Schwaben*, 1852], 138–39. 3¾ cols. £2.2.0. *Oxenford* / **John Oxenford**

A Child's History of England, chap. xxx, 139–44. 10¼ cols. *C.D.* / **Charles Dickens**

April 16, 1853. No. 160, pp. 145–68

H.W. [contributors to; printing of], 145–49. 9 cols. *C.D. & Morley* / **Charles Dickens & Henry Morley**

Gabriel's Marriage [story], chap. i, 149–57. 15¾ cols. £5.15.6. *Wilkie Collins* / **Wilkie Collins**

Dirge [verse], 157. ¾ col. £1.1.0. *Miss Erle* / **Miss Erle**

Seventy-eight Years Ago [ii], 157–63. 11½ cols. *J.F.* / **John Forster**

The Norfolk Gridiron [Great Yarmouth], 163–65. 3¾ cols.; should read 4¾. £2.2.0. *Dixon* / **Edmund Saul Dixon**

Aground up the Ganges, 165–68. 6¼ cols. £3.3.0. *Jonathan Webb* / **Jonathan Webb**

April 23, 1853. No. 161, pp. 169–92

Home for Homeless Women [Miss Burdett-Coutts's Urania Cottage], 169–75. 13 cols. *C.D.* / **Charles Dickens**

Red-Hot Bubble-Blowing [bottle manufacture], 175–79. 8½ cols. £4.4.0. *Dixon* / **Edmund Saul Dixon**

Chloroform, 179–81. 3 cols. *Morley* / **Henry Morley**

The Secret of the Stream [verse], 181. ¾ col. £1.11.6. *T. Hood, Junr.* / **Tom Hood**

Gabriel's Marriage, chap. ii, 181–90. 17¼ cols. £5.15.6. *Wilkie Collins* / **Wilkie Collins**

Abd-el-Kader on Horseback [from Melchior J. E. Daumas, *Les Chevaux du Sahara*, first pub. 1851], 190–92. 6½ cols.; should read 5¾. £3.3.0. *Dixon* / **Edmund Saul Dixon**

April 30, 1853. No. 162, pp. 193–216

Myself and My Family [story], 193–202. 19 cols. £10.0.0. *Thomas* / **William Moy Thomas**

Leaves from Lima [excursions near Lima, Peru], 202–205. 6 cols. £3.3.0. ——— / **Clements Robert Markham**

The Test of Time [verse], 205–206. 1¾ cols. £3.13.6. *Ollier* / **Edmund Ollier**

The Black Lad [ancient Lancashire custom], 206–208. 4½ cols. £2.12.6. *Miss Jewsbury* / **Geraldine Endsor Jewsbury**

Four-Legged Australians, 208–214. 12 cols. £6.6.0. *Rinder* / **Samuel Rinder**

The Ropemaker's Wife [Louise Labé], 214–16. 5½ cols. £3.0.0. *Miss Costello* / **Louisa Stuart Costello**

May 7, 1853. No. 163, pp. 217–40

The Spirit Business [excerpts from New York *Spiritual Telegraph*], 217–20. 7 cols. *C.D.* / **Charles Dickens**

Friends in Need, at Cranford [story], 220–27. 13 cols. £7.10.0. *Mrs. Gaskell* / **Elizabeth Gaskell**

Bavarian Poachers [Charles Boner, *Chamois Hunting in ... Bavaria*, 1853], 227–29. 4½ cols. *Morley* / **Henry Morley**

"And He Took a Child" [verse], 229. ¾ col. £1.11.6. *Miss Erle* / **Miss Erle**

Patent Wrongs [J. M. Heath and the patent law], 229–34. 9½ cols. *Morley* / **Henry Morley**

A Puff of Smoke [tobacco smoking], 234–35. 2¼ cols. *Morley* / **Henry Morley**

Powder Dick and His Train [public houses], 235–40. 11 cols. £5.15.6. *Sala* / **George A. Sala**

May 14, 1853. No. 164, pp. 241–64

In and Out of Jail [Frederic Hill, *Crime: Its Amount, Causes, and Remedies*, 1853], 241–45. 9 cols. *C. D., Morley, & W.H.W.* / **Charles Dickens, Henry Morley, & W. H. Wills**

Ten Years Old [autobiog.], 245–48. 6½ cols. *Morley* / **Henry Morley**

Domestic Pets, 248–53. 8¾ cols. £5.5.0. *Dixon* / **Edmund Saul Dixon**

Hush! [verse], 253. ½ col. £1.11.6. *Miss Berwick* / **Adelaide Anne Procter**

Legal Houses of Call [public houses], 253–57. 8½ cols. £4.14.6. *Sala* / **George A. Sala**

Summer in Rome, 257–61. 8 cols. £3.3.0. ——— / ———

A Child's History of England, chap. xxxi, 261–64. 7 cols. *C.D.* / **Charles Dickens**

May 21, 1853. No. 165, pp. 265–88

Our Last Parochial War [opposition to enforcement of Public Health Act], 265–70. 10 cols. *Morley* / **Henry Morley**

English Milords [French concept of], 270–73. 6¾ cols. £3.13.6. *Sala* / **George A. Sala**

Exploring Expedition to the Isle of Dogs, 273–77. 7½ cols. £4.0.0. *Dodd* / **George Dodd**

The Settlers [verse], 277. ¾ col. £1.11.6. *Miss Berwick* / **Adelaide Anne Procter**

A Happy Return to Cranford [story], 277–85. 15 cols. £8.8.0. *Mrs. Gaskell* / **Elizabeth Gaskell**

Chips:
- Twenty Guinea Diplomas [traffic in Ph.D. degrees], 285. 1 col. *W.H.W.* / **W. H. Wills**
- Diffusion of Knowledge among Cattle [letter from reader in Elbing], 285–86. 1 col. *Morley* / **Henry Morley**

The Life of Poor Jack [merchant ships and seamen], 286–88. 6 cols. *Morley* / **Henry Morley**

May 28, 1853. No. 166, pp. 289–312

Bookstalls, 289–93. 9¼ cols. £4.14.6. *Thomas* / **William Moy Thomas**

The First of Streams [the river Aa, France], 293–97. 7½ cols. £3.13.6. *Dixon* / **Edmund Saul Dixon**

Music Measure [mechanical musical instruments], 297–301. 8 cols. £3.13.6. *Dodd* / **George Dodd**

Griper Greg. A Capriccio [verse], 301–302. 1½ cols. £2.2.0. *Cooper* / **Thomas Cooper**

The Roving Englishman: Beautiful Naples, 302–305. 6½ cols. £3.5.0. *Murray* / **Grenville Murray**

Roger the Monk [*Roger of Wendover's Flowers of History*, 1849 ed.], 305–309. 8½ cols. £4.10.0. *Sala* / **George A. Sala**

A Shepherd's Autobiography [story], 309–312. 7 cols. £3.3.0. *Hough* / **Lewis Hough**

June 4, 1853. No. 167, pp. 313–36

Idiots, 313–17. 9 cols. *C.D. & W.H.W.* / **Charles Dickens & W. H. Wills**

The Borrowed Book [story], 317–24. 14 cols. £7.7.0. *Thomas* / **William Moy Thomas**

Choosing a Field-Flower [verse], 324. ¾ col. £1.5.0. *Allingham* / **William Allingham**

House-Tops, 324–29. 9 cols. £4.14.6. *Dodd* / **George Dodd**

Holiday Times [in France], 329–32. 7 cols. £3.13.6. *Dixon* / **Edmund Saul Dixon**

A Child's History of England, chap. xxxii, 332–36. 8 cols. *C.D.* / **Charles Dickens**

June 11, 1853. No. 168, pp. 337–60

The Noble Savage, 337–39. 5½ cols. *C.D.* / **Charles Dickens**

The Mahommedan Mother [account of an Indian woman, apparently factual], 339–46. 14¼ cols. £7.7.0. *Lang* / **John Lang**

A Bowl of Punch, 346–49. 4¾ cols. £2.12.6. *Cunningham* / **Peter Cunningham**

Eleusinia: Lines Suggested by the Bas-reliefs on the Portland Vase; the Figures of Which Are Supposed to Be Illustrative of the Eleusinian Mysteries [verse], 349. 1¼ cols. £3.0.0. *Ollier* / **Edmund Ollier**

A French Audience [at theatre], 349–52. 5 cols. £2.12.6. *Oxenford* / **John Oxenford**

Dolls, 352–56. 8½ cols. £4.14.6. *Dodd* / **George Dodd**

Chip:
- Magazines of Meat [meat preservation], 356–57. 1¾ cols. *Morley* / **Henry Morley**

Dunkerque Tower [Dunkerque and its environs], 357–60. 7 cols. £3.13.6. *Dixon* / **Edmund Saul Dixon**

June 18, 1853. No. 169, pp. 361–84

Canvass Town [living conditions in Melbourne], 361–67. 12 cols. £6.6.0. *Horne* / **Richard H. Horne**

A Century of Inventions [*The Century of Inventions of the Marquis of Worcester*, 1825 ed.], 367–70. 7¼ cols. £3.13.6. *Dodd* / **George Dodd**

Ben Close, of Baggenham [account of a poacher], 370–72. 4½ cols. £2.2.0. *White*, Doncaster, *& Morley* / **James White & Henry Morley**

The Lover and Birds [verse], 372–73. 1 col. £1.11.6. *Allingham* / **William Allingham**

The Roving Englishman: Diplomacy [British diplomatic corps], 373–75. 3¾ cols. £2.2.0. *Murray* / **Grenville Murray**

The Gwalior Janissaries [disbandment, by force of arms, of insubordinate troops], 375–76. 2 cols. £1.11.6. *W. H. Clarke* / **W. H. Clarke**

Arcadia [London arcades], 376–82. 13 cols. £6.16.6. *Sala* / **George A. Sala**

A Child's History of England, chap. xxxiii, 382–84. 5 cols. *C.D.* / **Charles Dickens**

June 25, 1853. No. 170, pp. 385–408

Cats' Mount [Trappist monastery, France], 385–90. 10 cols. £5.5.0. *Dixon* / **Edmund Saul Dixon**

A Reference to Character [Perry's Bankrupt and Insolvent Register Office], 390–94. 8 cols. £4.4.0. *Capper* / **John Capper**

Gentlemen in History, 394–96. 5¼ cols. £3.0.0. *W. B. Jerrold* / **William Blanchard Jerrold**

Express [verse], 396–97. ¾ col. £1.1.0. *W. Allingham* / **William Allingham**

Justice for "Natives" [maladministration of law, India], 397–402. 10¼ cols. £5.15.6. *Stocqueler* / **Joachim Heyward Siddons**

More Modern Munchausens [German and French observations on the English], 402–405. 6 cols. £2.12.6. *Blanchard* / **Sidney Laman Blanchard**

Shops, 405–408. 7½ cols. £3.13.6. *Sala* / **George A. Sala**

July 2, 1853. No. 171, pp. 409–432

Market Gardens, 409–414. 12 cols.; should read 11¼. £6.0.0. *Thomas* / **William Moy Thomas**

The Sensitive Mother [story], 414–19. 10¼ cols. £5.5.0. *Miss Lynn* / **Eliza Lynn**

A Golden Coppersmith [heroic deed of a Russian serf], 419–21. 3 cols. £1.11.6. *Florence Wilson* / **Florence Wilson**

School and Summer [verse], 421. 1½ cols. £2.12.6. *Miss Griffith* / **Miss Eliza Griffiths**

Books for the Blind [Report of Jury XVII, *Exhibition of the Works of Industry of All Nations, 1851, 1852*], 421–25. 6½ cols. £3.3.0. *Dodd* / **George Dodd**

Chip:
– Digging Sailors [successful enterprises of two sailors, Australia], 425–26. 2 cols. £1.1.0. *Horne* / **Richard H. Horne**

Country News [a provincial newspaper], 426–30. 8 cols. *Morley* / **Henry Morley**

Something to Drink [a public house], 430–32. 5¼ cols. £3.13.6. *Sala* / **George A. Sala**

July 9, 1853. No. 172, pp. 433–56

A Pull at the Pagoda Tree [a career in the East India Co.], 433–37. 8 cols. £4.4.0. *Capper & W.H.W.* / **John Capper & W. H. Wills**

Cause and Effect [anti-Jewish incident, Karlsruhe], 437–40. 6 cols. £2.12.6. *Duthie* / **William Duthie**

The Power-Loom [Mary Strickland, *A Memoir of ... Edmund Cartwright*, 1843], 440–45. 10¾ cols. *J.F.* / **John Forster**

The Wondrous Well [verse], 445. ½ col. £1.1.0. *Allingham* / **William Allingham**

Provisionally Registered [setting up a stock company], 445–48. 5¾ cols. £2.12.6. *W. B. Jerrold & W.H.W.* / **William Blanchard Jerrold & W. H. Wills**

Quails [slaughter of, in Capri], 448–50. 4½ cols. £2.2.0. ——— *& Morley* / **Henry G. Wreford & Henry Morley**

The River of Yesterday [Marquette's travels: from John Gilmary Shea, *Discovery and Exploration of the Mississippi Valley*, 1852], 450–54. 9 cols. *Morley* / **Henry Morley**

St. Vorax's Singing-Birds [inadequate schooling and moral training of choir boys], 454–56. 4 cols. £2.2.0. *Buckley & W.H.W.* / **Theodore Buckley & W. H. Wills**

July 16, 1853. No. 173, pp. 457–80

Apartments, Furnished [London lodgings], 457–63. 13½ cols. *Morley* / **Henry Morley**

Good Lac [lac factory, India], 463–66. 4¼ cols. £2.2.0. *H. H. Maxwell & Morley* / **H. H. Maxwell & Henry Morley**

Mahuot Cocquiel [hist. episode, 15-cent. France: in part from André Le Glay, "Notice sur les duels judiciaires," *Archives historiques*, 1829], 466–69. 7 cols. £3.13.6. *Dixon* / **Edmund Saul Dixon**

Windlass Song [verse], 469. ½ col. £1.1.0. *Allingham* / **William Allingham**

A Day after Battle Fair [excursion to Chobham military camp], 469–72. 6 cols. £3.3.0. *Sala* / **George A. Sala**

The Roving Englishman: A Canter with Polychronopulos [in Greece], 472–75. 4¼ cols. £2.12.6. *Murray* / **Grenville Murray**

Joseph Train [the antiquary], 475–77. 4½ cols. £2.12.6. *Hannay* / **James Hannay**

A Child's History of England, chap. xxxiv, 477–80. 7½ cols. *C.D.* / **Charles Dickens**

July 23, 1853. No. 174, pp. 481–504

A Haunted House [House of Commons], 481–83. 6 cols. *C.D.* / **Charles Dickens**

Over the Water [balloon Channel-crossing of J. P. Blanchard and John Jeffries, 1785], 483–88. 10 cols. £5.5.0. *Dixon* / **Edmund Saul Dixon**

Sir John Barleycorn at Home [beer brewing], 488–92. 6 cols. £3.3.0. *Sala* / **George A. Sala**

The Boy Mahomet [verse], 492. 1¼ cols. £2.12.6. *Ollier* / **Edmund Ollier**

In Presence of the Sword [cases tried in the Old Bailey], 492–98. 10¾ cols. *Morley* / **Henry Morley**

A Last Emotion [story], 498–99. 3½ cols. £2.0.0. *Dixon* / **Edmund Saul Dixon**

Fishing for Tunny, 499–503. 7 cols. £3.3.0. *Dr. Michelsen & Morley* / **Edward Henry Michelsen & Henry Morley**

The Legend of Bucharest, 503–504. 3¼ cols. £1.11.6. *Bayle St. John* / **Bayle St. John**

July 30, 1853. No. 175, pp. 505–528

Covent Garden Market, 505–511. 13¾ cols. £7.7.0. *Thomas* / **William Moy Thomas**

Chips:
- A Digger's Wedding [in Melbourne], 511–12. 1¼ cols. £1.5.0. *R. H. Horne* / **Richard H. Horne**
- Corporation Dreams [City taxes and tolls imposed on costermongers, etc], 512–13. 1½ cols. £1.1.0. *Horace Mayhew* / **Horace Mayhew**

A Literary Lady's Maid [*Mémoires de Madame de Staal*, 1755], 513–16. 5 cols. £2.12.6. *Miss Costello* / **Louisa Stuart Costello**

Listening Angels [verse], 516. ¾ col. £1.10.0. *Miss Berwick* / **Adelaide Anne Procter**

Honourable John [the East India Co.], 516–18. 4 cols. £2.2.0. *Capper* / **John Capper**

Marie's Fever [story], 518–26. 14¾ cols. £7.17.6. *Miss Lynn* / **Eliza Lynn**

A Child's History of England, chap. xxxv, 526–28. 5¾ cols. *C.D.* / **Charles Dickens**

August 6, 1853. No. 176, pp. 529–52

Flags to Furl [electioneering tactics], 529–33. 8¼ cols. £4.14.6. *Sala* / **George A. Sala**

Lounging through Kensington [literary and hist. associations of Kensington], 533–38. 11½ cols. £6.0.0. *Leigh Hunt* / **Leigh Hunt**

Garden-Games [for children], 538–41. 5 cols. £2.12.6. *Oxenford* / **John Oxenford**

Private Bridoon [Chobham military camp], 541–45. 9 cols. £4.14.6. *Costello* / **Dudley Costello**

Whip and Spur [history of], 545–48. 5 cols. £2.10.0. *Dodd & W.H.W.* / **George Dodd & W. H. Wills**

A Midsummer Night's Lodging [story], 548–52. 9½ cols. £5.0.0. *Dixon* / **Edmund Saul Dixon**

August 13, 1853. No. 177, pp. 553–76

Gone Astray [a childhood incident], 553–57. 9¾ cols. *C.D.* / **Charles Dickens**

Something Divine [story], 557–60. 4¼ cols. £2.10.0. *Bayle St. John* / **Bayle St. John**

Why Shave?, 560–63. 7½ cols. *Morley & W.H.W.* / **Henry Morley & W. H. Wills**

Lighten the Boat! [verse], 563–64. 1½ cols. £2.2.0. *King & W.H.W.* / **John William King & W. H. Wills**

The Mind of Brutes [Alphonse Toussenel, *L'Esprit des bêtes: ... mammifères de France,* 1853 ed.], 564–69. 11 cols. £5.15.6. *Dixon* / **Edmund Saul Dixon**

Down Whitechapel, Far Away [Liverpool], 569–73. 8 cols. £4.4.0. *Sala* / **George A. Sala**

Lilliput in London [two dwarfed children exhibited], 573–76. 6¾ cols. *Morley & W.H.W.* / **Henry Morley & W. H. Wills**

August 20, 1853. No. 178, pp. 577–600

Brother Bruin [Alphonse Toussenel, *L'Esprit des bêtes: ... mammifères de France,* 1853 ed.], 577–82. 11¼ cols. £5.15.6. *Dixon* / **Edmund Saul Dixon**

The Length of the Quays [Dublin], 582–86. 7½ cols. £4.0.0. *Sala* / **George A. Sala**

Little Bits [mosaics], 586–89. 6 cols. £3.0.0. *Dodd* / **George Dodd**

Grains of Gold [verse], 589. 1½ cols. £1.11.6. *T. Hood, Junr., & W.H.W.* / **Tom Hood & W. H. Wills**

Gore House, 589–93. 6¼ cols. £3.10.0. *Leigh Hunt* / **Leigh Hunt**

Licensed to Juggle [a street-performer in Paris], 593–94. 2¼ cols. £2.0.0. *Duthie* / **William Duthie**

What Mushrooms Cost, 594–97. 6½ cols. £3.13.6. *Dixon* / **Edmund Saul Dixon**

A Child's History of England, chap. xxxvi, 597–600. 6¾ cols. *C.D.* / **Charles Dickens**

August 27, 1853. No. 179, pp. 601–620

Want Places [female servants], 601–608. 14¼ cols. £7.5.0. *Sala* / **George A. Sala**

Sick Grapes [vine disease, Italy], 608–609. 3¼ cols. £1.11.6. *Wreford* / **Henry G. Wreford**

Sir Graelent. A Breton Legend [verse], 609–611. 2¾ cols. £2.2.0. *Ollier* / **Edmund Ollier**

Equine Analogies [Alphonse Toussenel, *L'Esprit des bêtes: ... mammifères de France,* 1853 ed.], 611–15. 9 cols. £4.14.6. *Dixon* / **Edmund Saul Dixon**

Quicksilver [mine in Almadén, Spain], 615–17. 3 cols. £1.11.6. *Shiel* / **Shiel**

An Irish Stew [Dublin], 617–20. 8 cols.; should read 7¼. £4.4.0. *Sala* / **George A. Sala**

VOLUME VIII September 3, 1853 – February 11, 1854

September 3, 1853. No. 180, pp. 1–24

Lodged in Newgate [autobiog.], 1–6. 11 cols. £5.15.6. *T. H. Wilson & Morley* / **T. H. Wilson & Henry Morley**

A Digger's Diary [iv], 6–11. 9 cols. £4.14.6. *R. H. Horne* / **Richard H. Horne**

Crowns in Lead [despoliation of St. Denis Abbey], 11–13. 4 cols. £2.2.0. *J. A. Crowe* / **Joseph Archer Crowe**

Echoes [verse], 13. ½ col. £0.15.0. *Miss Berwick* / **Adelaide Anne Procter**

Kensington, 13–17. 9 cols. £4.14.6. *Leigh Hunt* / **Leigh Hunt**

Number Forty-two [Colombo bazaar-keepers], 17–20. 5¾ cols. £3.3.0. *Capper* / **John Capper**

An Exploded Magazine [contents of a 1798 periodical], 20–24. 8½ cols. £4.4.0. *Sala* / **George A. Sala**

September 10, 1853. No. 181, pp. 25–48

Out for a Walk [pleasures of walking], 25–27. 5 cols. *Morley* / **Henry Morley**

A Dead Secret [story], 27–36. 18 cols. £9.9.0. *Sala* / **George A. Sala**

Pictures in the Fire [verse], 36–37. 1 col. £2.2.0. *Miss Berwick* / **Adelaide Anne Procter**

The Stereoscope, 37–42. 10½ cols. *Morley & W.H.W.* / **Henry Morley & W. H. Wills**

First Stage to Australia [Govt. emigration office and depots], 42–45. 5¼ cols. £2.15.0. *Capper & W.H.W.* / **John Capper & W. H. Wills**

A Brilliant Display of Fireworks [pyrotechnics], 45–48. 6½ cols.; should read 7½. £3.3.0. *Dodd* / **George Dodd**

September 17, 1853. No. 182, pp. 49–72

Convicts in the Gold Regions [penal stockades and hulks, Victoria], 49–54. 10 cols. £5.5.0. *R. H. Horne* / **Richard H. Horne**

The Merchant's Heart [legend], 54–57. 6¼ cols. £3.3.0. *Bayle St. John* / **Bayle St. John**

Nothing Like Leather, 57–60. 5½ cols. £2.15.0. *Dodd* / **George Dodd**

Life and Death [verse], 60. ½ col. £1.1.0. *Miss Berwick* / **Adelaide Anne Procter**

The Great Indian Bean-Stalk [corrupt native officials, India], 60–64. 8 cols. £4.4.0. *Capper* / **John Capper**

The Phalansterian Menagerie [Alphonse Toussenel, *L'Esprit des bêtes: ... mammifères de France*, 1853 ed.], 64–69. 10½ cols. £5.15.6. *Dixon* / **Edmund Saul Dixon**

A Child's History of England, chap. xxxvii, 69–72. 7 cols. *C.D.* / **Charles Dickens**

September 24, 1853. No. 183, pp. 73–96

Slang, 73–78. 10 cols. £5.5.0. *Sala* / **George A. Sala**

A Norman Story [story], 78–83. 10½ cols. £5.15.6. *Dixon* / **Edmund Saul Dixon**

Old Bones [found in England], 83–84. 2¾ cols. £1.11.6. *Buckland* / **Francis Trevelyan Buckland**

Moonrise [verse], 84. ½ col. £0.10.6. *Miss Berwick* / **Adelaide Anne Procter**

Moldo-Wallachia, 84–88. 8½ cols.; should read 7½. £4.14.6. *Bayle St. John* / **Bayle St. John**

Accommodation for Quidnuncs [penny reading-rooms, news-rooms], 88–91. 5¾ cols. £2.2.0. *Dodd & Morley* / **George Dodd & Henry Morley**

A Russian Stranger [malachite], 91–94. 5½ cols. £2.15.0. *Dodd* / **George Dodd**

Trust and No Trust [attitude toward life], 94–96. 5½ cols. *Morley* / **Henry Morley**

October 1, 1853. No. 184, pp. 97–120

Frauds on the Fairies [altering of fairy tales for propaganda purposes], 97–100. 6½ cols. *C.D.* / **Charles Dickens**

Tribunals of Commerce, 100–104. 7½ cols. £3.13.6. *Capper* / **John Capper**

Bucharest, 104–108. 9¾ cols. £4.14.6. *Bayle St. John* / **Bayle St. John**

Starlight in the Garden [verse], 108–109. 1½ cols. £2.12.6. *Edmund Ollier* / **Edmund Ollier**

The Great Saddleworth Exhibition [excursion to Yorkshire], 109–112. 5½ cols. £2.15.0. *Miss Jewsbury* / **Geraldine Endsor Jewsbury**

Dead Reckoning at the Morgue [the Morgue, Paris], 112–16. 6¾ cols. £3.13.6. *Dudley Costello* / **Dudley Costello**

A Child's History of England, chaps. xxxviii–xxxix, 116–20. 10 cols. *C.D.* / **Charles Dickens**

October 8, 1853. No. 185, pp. 121–44

Things That Cannot Be Done [leniency of law to malefactors], 121–23. 4½ cols. *C.D.* / **Charles Dickens**

Lanna Tixel [story], 123–28. 10 cols. *Morley* / **Henry Morley**

Air Maps [wind currents: based on work of M. F. Maury], 128–33. 9 cols. £4.14.6. *Capper* / **John Capper**

Gone! [verse], 133. ¾ col. £1.11.6. *Mrs. MacIntosh* / **Mrs. MacIntosh**

Bad Luck at Bendigo [at gold diggings], 133–39. 12 cols. £5.0.0. *Morley's brother & Morley* / **Joseph Morley & Henry Morley**

The Gipsy Slaves of Wallachia, 139–42. 5½ cols. £2.15.0. *Bayle St. John* / **Bayle St. John**

Mr. Gulliver's Entertainment [ridicule of "entertainments"], 142–44. 5 cols. *Morley* / **Henry Morley**

October 15, 1853. No. 186, pp. 145–68

African Zephyrs [French troops in Algeria], 145–50. 11¾ cols. £5.15.6. *Dixon* / **Edmund Saul Dixon**

A Splendid Match [story], 150–56. 11 cols. £5.15.6. *Miss Lynn* / **Eliza Lynn**

A Lament for the Summer [verse], 156. ½ col. £0.15.0. *Miss Berwick* / **Adelaide Anne Procter**

More Places Wanted [female servants], 156–62. 12 cols. £6.6.0. *Sala* / **George A. Sala**

A Brazilian in Bloomsbury [an ant bear], 162–65. 6 cols. *Morley* / **Henry Morley**

A Child's History of England, chap. xl, 165–68. 7 cols. *C.D.* / **Charles Dickens**

October 22, 1853. No. 187, pp. 169–92

The Modern Practice of Physic, 169–73. 9 cols. *Morley* / **Henry Morley**

The Eve of a Journey [story], 173–77. 8 cols. £4.14.6. *Dora Greenwell* / **Dora Greenwell**

Caught in a Typhoon [autobiog.], 177–79. 4½ cols. £2.5.0. *Irwin* / **Irwin**

Bran [verse], 179–81. 2¼ cols. £3.3.0. *Mr. Gaskell* / **William Gaskell**

A Great Screw [screw propeller], 181–84. 6½ cols. £3.13.6. *Capper* / **John Capper**

Chip:
- A Locust Hunt [in Capri], 184–85. 1½ cols. £1.11.6. ——— / **Henry G. Wreford**

Eternal Lamps [sepulchral lamps], 185–88. 6½ cols. £3.13.6. *Ollier* / **Edmund Ollier**

Old Settlers of Tennessee [James G. M. Ramsey, *The Annals of Tennessee*, 1853], 188–91. 6 cols. *Morley* / **Henry Morley**

North Country Courtesies [social life, 18 cent.], 191–92. 3 cols. £1.11.6. *Cunningham* / **Peter Cunningham**

October 29, 1853. No. 188, pp. 193–216

Fashion, 193–96. 6½ cols. £3.13.6. *Sala* / **George A. Sala**

Flower-Bells [naturalization of fuchsia in England], 196–99. 7 cols. £2.12.6. *Morley & Mrs. Hoare* / **Henry Morley & Mrs. Hoare**

The French Workman, 199–204. 8 cols.; should read 8¾. £3.13.6. *Duthie & Morley* / **William Duthie & Henry Morley**

Old London Bridge [verse], 204. 1½ cols. £2.12.6. *Miss Tomkins & W.H.W.* / **Mary Jane Tomkins & W. H. Wills**

The Roving Englishman at Constantinople, 204–207. 6 cols. £3.3.0. *Murray* / **Grenville Murray**

Chips:
- An Ashantee Palaver [British administration on Gold Coast], 207–209. 3 cols. £2.0.0. *W. H. Clarke* / **W. H. Clarke**
- Oxford Fossils [skeleton and other objects in Clarendon Museum], 209–210. 2¼ cols. £1.11.6. *Buckland* / **Francis Trevelyan Buckland**

A Child's History of England, chaps. xli–xlii, 210–16. 13 cols. *C.D.* / **Charles Dickens**

November 5, 1853. No. 189, pp. 217–40

Adeliza Castle [housing of the middle class], 217–20. 7 cols. *Morley* / **Henry Morley**

Always United [Abelard and Heloise], 220–25. 9 cols. £4.14.6. *Sala* / **George A. Sala**

The Northern Wizard [manufacture of industrial chemicals], 225–28. 6¾ cols. £3.10.0. *Capper* / **John Capper**

The Casket [verse], 228. ½ col. £1.1.0. *Harper* / **Harper**

A Wallachian Squire, 228–30. 4 cols. £2.2.0. *Bayle St. John* / **Bayle St. John**

Bouquets [artificial flower making], 230–33. 5½ cols. £2.15.0. *Dodd* / **George Dodd**

Among the Shallows [disparity in sentences for petty larcency], 233–35. 4¼ cols. £1.11.6. *Payne & Morley* / **James Payn & Henry Morley**

Only an Earthquake [trip in Albania], 235–38. 5¾ cols. £3.3.0. *W. L. Reynolds & Morley* / **W. L. Reynolds & Henry Morley**

Mine Inn [literary associations of inns], 238–40. 4½ cols. £2.12.6. *Sala* / **George A. Sala**

November 12, 1853. No. 190, pp. 241–64

Unspotted Snow [arctic navigators], 241–46. 11 cols. *Morley* / **Henry Morley**

Two Cousins [story], 246–52. 12¼ cols. £6.15.0. *Miss Lynn* / **Eliza Lynn**

The Deseret News [Mormon newspaper], 252–55. 6 cols. £3.3.0. *James Lowe* / **James Lowe**

Colour-Blindness [George Wilson, "On the Prevalence of Chromato-Pseudop sis," *Monthly Jour. of Medical Science*, Nov. 1853], 255–57. 3½ cols. £2.0.0. *Knox & W.H.W.* ; **James Knox & W. H. Wills**

Turks in Bulgaria, 257–59. 3½ cols. £1.15.0. *Bayle St. John* / **Bayle St. John**

A Child's History of England, chap. xliii, 259–64. 11 cols. *C.D.* / **Charles Dickens**

November 19, 1853. No. 191, pp. 265–88

Morton Hall [story], chap. i, 265–72. 14 cols. £16.16.0 for the 2 instalments. *Mrs. Gaskell* / **Elizabeth Gaskell**

The Camp at Helfaut [military camp, France], 272–76. 8 cols. £4.4.0. *Dixon* / **Edmund Saul Dixon**

Song for November [verse], 276. ½ col. £0.15.0. *Ollier* / **Edmund Ollier**

Kensington Church, 276–81. 11¼ cols. £6.0.0. *Leigh Hunt* / **Leigh Hunt**

Chips:
- Chinese Players [stage plays and gaming in George Town, Penang], 281–83. 2¼ cols. £1.1.0. *Dr. Michelsen* / **Edward Henry Michelsen**
- An Ancient Tariff [on imports, 1642], 283–84. 2¼ cols. £1.1.0. *J. R. Keene* / **J. R. Keene**

A Little Republic [a Saint-Simonist, Egypt], 284–86. 4 cols. £2.2.0. *Bayle St. John* / **Bayle St. John**

The House That Jack Built [transportable houses], 286–88. 5½ cols. £2.15.0. *Dodd* / **George Dodd**

November 26, 1853. No. 192, pp. 289–312

Little Children, 289–93. 8½ cols. £5.0.0. *Sala* / **George A. Sala**

Morton Hall, chap. ii, 293–302. 18 cols. *Mrs. Gaskell* / **Elizabeth Gaskell**

Now [verse], 302. ½ col. £1.1.0. *Miss Berwick* / **Adelaide Anne Procter**

A Sensible Town [Amiens], 302–305. 6½ cols. £5.5.0. *Dixon* / **Edmund Saul Dixon**

Chips:
- The Light of Other Days [smuggling on Cornish coast, 18 cent.], 305–306. 2 cols. £1.1.0. *Mr. Hawker* / **Robert Stephen Hawker**
- Sentimental Geography [Tasman's naming of places in Australasia], 306–307. 1¼ cols. £1.1.0. *Irwin* / **Irwin**

A Child's History of England, chap. xliv, 307–312. 10 cols.; should read 10¾. *C.D.* / **Charles Dickens**

December 3, 1853. No. 193, pp. 313–36

Fairyland in 'Fifty-four [the Crystal Palace at Sydenham], 313–17. 9 cols. £4.4.0. *W.H.W. & Sala* / **W. H. Wills & George A. Sala**

The Cradle and the Grave [gold-mining experiences, New South Wales], 317–25. 15 cols. £6.10.0. *Hogarth, Junr., & Morley* / **Hogarth, Jr., & Henry Morley**

The Bright Little Girl. Song to an Irish Tune [verse], 325. ½ col. £1.1.0. *Allingham* / **William Allingham**

Kensington Worthies, 325–30. 10 cols. £5.5.0. *Leigh Hunt* / **Leigh Hunt**

In the Dardanelles [excursion to plains of Troy], 330–33. 5½ cols. £3.3.0. *Wells* / **Thomas Spencer Wells**

Pot and Kettle Philosophy [cooking apparatuses], 333–36. 7 cols. £3.13.6. *Dodd* / **George Dodd**

December 10, 1853. No. 194, pp. 337–60

Near Christmas [fantasy], 337–39. 4¼ cols. *Morley* / **Henry Morley**

Mr. Wiseman in Print [a newspaper office], 339–43. 7½ cols. £4.4.0. *Miss Martineau* / **Harriet Martineau**

Protégés of the Czar [Bulgaria], 343–45. 5 cols. £2.12.6. *Bayle St. John* / **Bayle St. John**

Locked Out [the Preston lock-out], 345–48. 6½ cols. £3.13.6. *Lowe* / **James Lowe**

Miasma [verse], 348. ½ col. £1.1.0. *Cape* / **Cape**

Traits and Stories of the Huguenots, 348–54. 11¼ cols. £5.15.6. *Mrs. Gaskell* / **Elizabeth Gaskell**

Chip:
- The History of a Coal Cell, 354–55. 2½ cols. £1.11.6. *E. A. Hart* / **Ernest Abraham Hart**

The Roving Englishman; and the Prince de Vendome [a French adventurer], 355–60. 8¼ cols. £4.4.0. *Murray* / **Grenville Murray**

A Child's History of England, chap. xlv, 360. 1½ cols. *C.D.* / **Charles Dickens**

December 17, 1853. No. 195, pp. 361–84

My French Master [a French émigré], chap. i, 361–65. 8¾ cols. £10.10.0 for the 2 instalments. *Mrs. Gaskell* / **Elizabeth Gaskell**

By Dawk to Delhi, 365–70. 9½ cols.; should read 10¾. £5.5.0. *Clark*, Delhi / **Clark**

The Lady of the Fen [verse], 370–73. 5¼ cols. £4.4.0. *Ollier* / **Edmund Ollier**

Varna, 373–77. 7½ cols. £3.13.6. *Bayle St. John & W.H.W.* / **Bayle St. John & W. H. Wills**

Manchester Men at Their Books [Manchester Free Library], 377–79. 4 cols. *Morley* / **Henry Morley**

Blank Babies in Paris [a foundling hospital], 379–82. 7 cols. £4.4.0. *Costello* / **Dudley Costello**

"The Corner" [Tattersall's], 382–84. 5 cols. £2.12.6. *Sidney* / **Samuel Sidney**

December 24, 1853. No. 196, pp. 385–408

Beef, 385–88. 7 cols. *Morley* / **Henry Morley**

My French Master, chap. ii, 388–93. 10¾ cols. *Mrs. Gaskell* / **Elizabeth Gaskell**

The Roving Englishman: A Greek Feast [in Mytilene], 393–97. 6½ cols. £3.13.6. *Murray* / **Grenville Murray**

Holidays [verse], 397. ¾ col. £1.11.6. *Meredith* / **George Meredith**

Ghostly Pantomimes [18-cent. pantomimes], 397–400. 5½ cols. £2.12.6. *Ollier* / **Edmund Ollier**

The Harmonious Blacksmith [musical instruments], 400–403. 6 cols. £3.3.0. *Dodd* / **George Dodd**

Our Wine Merchant [based on advertising pamphlet], 403–406. 7 cols. £2.12.6. *Dudley Costello* / **Dudley Costello**

An Ugly Nursling [catarrh], 406–408. 4½ cols. *Morley* / **Henry Morley**

Christmas 1853. Extra Christmas Number: Another Round of Stories by the Christmas Fire, pp. 1–36. Announced pub. date: Dec. 19. Stated on title page of Vol. VIII as included in that vol.; contents of no. listed at end of "Contents" of that vol.

The Schoolboy's Story, 1–5. 8½ cols. *C.D.* / **Charles Dickens**

The Old Lady's Story, 5-9. 9 cols. £6.0.0. *Miss Lynn* / **Eliza Lynn**

Over the Way's Story, 9–17. 15¾ cols. £10.10.0. *Sala* / **George A. Sala**

The Angel's Story [verse], 17–19. 3 cols. £4.4.0. *Miss Berwick* / **Adelaide Anne Procter**

The Squire's Story, 19–25. 13 cols. £7.7.0. *Mrs. Gaskell* / **Elizabeth Gaskell**

Uncle George's Story, 25–29. 6¾ cols. £3.13.6. *Dixon & W.H.W.* / **Edmund Saul Dixon & W. H. Wills**

The Colonel's Story, 29–32. 7½ cols.; should read 6½. £5.0.0. *Sidney* / **Samuel Sidney**

The Scholar's Story* [verse], 32–34. 4½ cols. £4.4.0. *Mrs. Gaskell* / **William Gaskell**

Nobody's Story [the lot of the labouring poor], 34–36. 4½ cols. *C.D.* / **Charles Dickens**

*Introduced by two paragraphs linking the narrator with the framework and commenting on his story. The paragraphs are stated to be by Mrs. Gaskell. See, in Part Two, identification note on Mrs. Gaskell and that on William Gaskell.

December 31, 1853. No. 197, pp. 409–432

The Long Voyage [hist. voyages and the voyage of life], 409–412. 7½ cols. *C.D.* / **Charles Dickens**

Iron Incidents [London and North-Western Railway Co.], 412–15. 5¼ cols. £3.0.0. *Capper* / **John Capper**

The Roving Englishman: Greek Easter at Constantinople; A Defence of Fleas, 415–18. 5¼ cols. £2.12.6. *Murray* / **Grenville Murray**

New Year's Eve [verse], 418. 1½ cols. £3.3.0. *Ollier* / **Edmund Ollier**

Down among the Dead Men [story], 418–24. 11¼ cols. £6.6.0. *White* / **the Rev. James White**

Chip:
- Voices from the Deep [sailors' grievances: letters from readers], 424. 1½ cols. *Morley* / **Henry Morley**

Tucked Up [beds and sleep], 424–28. 6 cols. £2.12.6. *Cattermole* / **Richard Cattermole**

The Horse Guards Rampant [Lewis E. Nolan, *Cavalry; Its History and Tactics*, 1853], 428–31. 7 cols. *Morley* / **Henry Morley**

Amy, the Child [story from "an old German pocket-book"], 431–32. 3 cols. *Townsend* / **Townsend**

January 7, 1854. No. 198, pp. 433–56

On Her Majesty's Service [the diplomatic corps], 433–37. 9 cols. £5.0.0. *C.D. & Murray* / **Charles Dickens & Grenville Murray**

A Leaf from the Parish Register [story], 437–40. 6¼ cols. £3.13.6. *Thomas* / **William Moy Thomas**

The Steam Whistle in India [first railway, 1852], 440–42. 2½ cols. £1.11.6. *Arnold* / **William Delafield Arnold**

Off! Off! [the damning of plays], 442–45. 6¼ cols. £3.3.0. *Whitehead* / **Charles Whitehead**

The Bells [verse], 445–46. 1¼ cols. £3.3.0. *Mrs. MacIntosh* / **Mrs. MacIntosh**

Mighty Hunters [John Palliser, *Solitary Rambles ... of a Hunter in the Prairies*, 1853], 446–49. 7 cols. £3.13.6. *Sidney* / **Samuel Sidney**

The Stop the Way Company [Hudson's Bay Co.], 449–54. 10½ cols. £5.15.6. *Capper* / **John Capper**

Seasonable Gains [Christmas gifts], 454–56. 4½ cols. *Morley* / **Henry Morley**

January 14, 1854. No. 199, pp. 457–80

Case of Real Distress [fancy and imagination in utilitarian world], 457–60. 6¼ cols. £3.15.0. *Sala* / **George A. Sala**

The Sack of Chesnuts [story], 460–66. 12 cols. £6.6.0. *Miss Costello* / **Louisa Stuart Costello**

Slates, 466–69. 6 cols. £3.3.0. *Dodd* / **George Dodd**

One Spot of Green [verse], 469. ½ col. £1.1.0. *Procter* / **Bryan Waller Procter**

Completely Registered [setting up a stock company], 469–71. 4½ cols. £2.12.6. *W. B. Jerrold* / **William Blanchard Jerrold**

Regular Trappers [Hudson's Bay Co.], 471–76. 10½ cols. £5.5.0. *Capper* / **John Capper**

Chip:
- The Antecedents of Australia [first penal settlement], 476–77. 1 col. £0.15.0. *Irwin* / **Irwin**

Ignoble Conduct of a Nobleman [story], 477–80. 7½ cols. £4.4.0. *White* / **the Rev. James White**

January 21, 1854. No. 200, pp. 481–504

Fire and Snow [a winter trip, winter scene], 481–83. 5½ cols. *C.D.* / **Charles Dickens**

Lives of Plants, 483–86. 5½ cols. £3.0.0. *Hart* / **Ernest Abraham Hart**

Pharisees and Sinners [story], 486–91. 10¾ cols. £6.16.6. *Miss Lynn* / **Eliza Lynn**

The Goblins of the Marsh. A Masque [verse], 491–92. 1¾ cols. £2.2.0. *Ollier* / **Edmund Ollier**

Half-a-Dozen Leeches [odd facts about leeches], 492–95. 6 cols. £3.3.0. *Dodd* / **George Dodd**

A Border of the Black Sea [Bulgaria], 495–99. 8 cols. £4.4.0. *St. John* / **Bayle St. John**

School-Keeping, 499–504. 10½ cols. *Morley* / **Henry Morley**

January 28, 1854. No. 201, pp. 505–528

Science and Sophy [Louis Aimé Martin, *Lettres à Sophie sur la physique, la chimie et l'histoire naturelle*, 1847 ed.], 505–508. 7 cols. *Morley* / **Henry Morley**

The Blankshire Hounds [story], 508–512. 8¾ cols. £4.14.6. *Sidney* / **Samuel Sidney**

The Styrian Mecca [Mariazell], 512–16. 6¼ cols. *Morley* / **Henry Morley**

The Lady Hertha [verse], 516–17. 3¼ cols. £3.3.0. *Oxenford* / **John Oxenford**

Bulls and Bears [British Stock Exchange], 517–23. 11 cols. £5.15.6. *Capper* / **John Capper**

Chip:
– Her Majesty's Service Again [the diplomatic corps], 523–24. 2¾ cols. £1.11.6. *Murray* / **Grenville Murray**

Your Very Good Health [Southwood Smith, *Results of Sanitary Improvement*, 1854], 524–26. 4 cols.; should read 3¼. *Morley* / **Henry Morley**

Standing on Ceremony [Sir John Finett, *Finetti Philoxenis*, 1656], 526–28. 5 cols. £2.12.6. *White* / **the Rev. James White**

February 4, 1854. No. 202, pp. 529–52

Bottled Information [data obtained from notes in containers cast adrift at sea], 529–32. 8 cols. £4.4.0. *Dodd* / **George Dodd**

Chip:
– Ready Wit [a reader's reaction to "Ignoble Conduct," Jan. 14], 532–33. ½ col. *C.D.* / **Charles Dickens**

Frozen and Thawed [Karl August Wildenhahn, "Die Dorel," *Erzgebirgische Dorfgeschichten*, Vol. II, first pub. 1848 or 1850], 533–39. 12 cols. *Morley* / **Henry Morley**

Motley [verse], 539–40. 2¼ cols. £2.2.0. *Meredith* / **George Meredith**

The Complaint of the Old Magician [magic and fairylore], 540–46. 12¾ cols. *Sala* / **George A. Sala**

Too Late [story], 546–49. 4¼ cols. £1.11.6. *Mrs. Hawker* / **Charlotte Elizabeth Hawker**

Lancashire Witchcraft [cotton-cloth manufacture], 549–51. 5¼ cols. £2.12.6. *Capper* / **John Capper**

Anybody's Child [slum children], 551–52. 2½ cols. £1.5.0. *Jerrold (W. B.)* / **William Blanchard Jerrold**

February 11, 1854. No. 203, pp. 553–76

On Strike [the Preston strike], 553–59. 12 cols. *C.D.* / **Charles Dickens**

The Ghost of a Love Story [Breton legend], 559–61. 4½ cols. £2.12.6. *Miss Costello* / **Louisa Stuart Costello**

Modern Human Sacrifices [preventible shipwrecks], 561–64. 6 cols. *Morley* / **Henry Morley**

Wishing. A Nursery Song [verse], 564. ½ col. £1.1.0. *Allingham* / **William Allingham**

Why My Uncle Was a Bachelor [story], 564–70. 11½ cols. £4.14.6. *Miss Louisa King* / **Miss Louisa King**

Change of Air [climate], 570–72. 4½ cols. *Morley* / **Henry Morley**

Neapolitan Purity [corrupt public officials], 572–75. 5 cols. £2.12.6. *Wreford* / **Henry G. Wreford**

The Iron Seamstress [sewing-machine], 575–76. 4 cols. £2.2.0. *W. B. Jerrold* / **William Blanchard Jerrold**

VOLUME IX February 18 – August 12, 1854

February 18, 1854. No. 204, pp. 1–20

Birth of Plants, 1–4. 6 cols. £2.12.6. *Hart* / **Ernest Abraham Hart**

Founded on Fact [story], 4–8. 8¾ cols. £4.14.6. *Dixon* / **Edmund Saul Dixon**

The Prisoner [verse], 8. ¾ col. £1.10.0. *Cattermole* / **Richard Cattermole**

Holland House, chap. i, 8–15. 13¾ cols. £10.0.0 for the 2 instalments, but sum of payment notations for individual instalments = £10.10.0. *Leigh Hunt* / **Leigh Hunt**

Chip:
- The Albatross at Home [in Auckland Islands], 15–16. 1 col. £0.10.6. *Irwin* / **Irwin**

A Dish of Fish [natural history], 16–17. 3¾ cols. £2.2.0. *Buckland* / **Francis Trevelyan Buckland**

History in Wax [waxworks museum], 17–20. 6 cols. £2.10.0. *Costello* / **Dudley Costello**

February 25, 1854. No. 205, pp. 21–44

The Longest Night in a Life [story], 21–25. 8 cols. £4.4.0. *Mrs. Bell* / **Mrs. Bell**

Modern Greek Songs [Claude C. Fauriel, *Chants populaires de la Grèce moderne*, 1824–25], 25–32. 14½ cols. £7.7.0. *Mrs. Gaskell* / **Elizabeth Gaskell**

Jack and the Union Jack [seamen in British navy], 32–33. 3½ cols. *Morley* / **Henry Morley**

Died in India [verse], 33–34. ½ col. £1.1.0. *Miss Perrott* / **Miss Perrott**

A Lift in a Cart [travel in Europe], 34–37. 6 cols. £3.3.0. *Mr. Duthie* / **William Duthie**

Moiré Antique, 37–38. 3 cols. £1.11.6. *Dodd* / **George Dodd**

Holland House, chap. ii, 38–42. 7 cols. *Leigh Hunt* / **Leigh Hunt**

For the Benefit of the Cooks [French cooks' holiday], 42–44. 5¼ cols. £2.12.6. *W. B. Jerrold* / **William Blanchard Jerrold**

March 4, 1854. No. 206, pp. 45–68

The Secrets of the Gas [gaslight as an eye-witness], 45–48. 7 cols. *Sala* / **George A. Sala**

Breakfast with the Black Prince [Henri Christophe], 48–51. 6¼ cols. £3.13.6. *Smith, per Ollier, & Morley* / **Smith & Henry Morley**

The Blind Man's Wreath [account of blind man, stated to be fact], 51–56. 8½ cols. £3.13.6. *Mrs. George Gretton* / **A. L. V. Gretton**

Proserpina in the Shades [verse], 56. 2½ cols.; should read 1¾. £3.0.0. *Ed. Ollier* / **Edmund Ollier**

The Turk at Home, 56–61. 10 cols. £5.5.0. *W. B. Jerrold* / **William Blanchard Jerrold**

Several Heads of Hair [human hair, traffic in and use of], 61–65. 7 cols. £3.13.6. *Dodd & W.H.W.* / **George Dodd & W. H. Wills**

My Dream [story], 65–68. 7 cols. £3.13.6. *Miss Jewsbury* / **Geraldine Endsor Jewsbury**

March 11, 1854. No. 207, pp. 69–92

The Bottle of Hay [a publican on public houses], 69–75. 12 cols. *Sala* / **George A. Sala**

An Old Book of Geography [Peter Heylyn, *Mikrokosmos*, 1629 ed.], 75–79. 9 cols. £4.14.6. *Ollier* / **Edmund Ollier**

The Roving Englishman: Education in Turkey, 79–80. 2½ cols. £1.5.0. *Murray* / **Grenville Murray**

The Voice of the Wind [verse], 80–81. 1 col. £2.2.0. *Miss Berwick* / **Adelaide Anne Procter**

Miriam the Shadow [legend], 81–85. 9¾ cols. £5.0.0. *Bayle St. John* / **Bayle St. John**

Splitting Straws [uses of straw], 85–89. 6¾ cols. £3.13.6. *Dodd* / **George Dodd**

Mr. Speaker in the Chair [a session of House of Commons], 89–92. 8 cols. £4.4.0. *W. D. Arnold* / **William Delafield Arnold**

March 18, 1854. No. 208, pp. 93–116

Shadows of Dark Days [supernatural beings once believed in], 93–98. 10 cols. *Morley* / **Henry Morley**

Oil upon the Waves [theories concerning], 98–100. 4¼ cols. £2.2.0. *Dodd* / **George Dodd**

The Present Moment [reflections on life], 100–102. 4¾ cols. *Sala* / **George A. Sala**

The Roving Englishman: Captain Jorgey [an honest Greek seaman, duped], 102–104. 4 cols. £2.5.0. *Murray* / **Grenville Murray**

Home-Sickness [verse], 104–105. ¾ col. £2.2.0. *Miss Berwick* / **Adelaide Anne Procter**

Preventible Accidents, 105–106. 4 cols.; should read 3. *Morley* / **Henry Morley**

My Folly [story], 106–114. 14½ cols. £7.7.0. *Dixon* / **Edmund Saul Dixon**

Club Law [story], 114–16. 5¾ cols. £3.0.0. *White* / **the Rev. James White**

March 25, 1854. No. 209, pp. 117–40

The Late Mr. Justice Talfourd, 117–18. 2 cols. *C.D.* / **Charles Dickens**

A Russian Cauldron in Full Boil [Edward T. Turnerelli, *Russia on the Borders of Asia*, 1854], 118–23. 10½ cols. *Morley* / **Henry Morley**

Amber Witchery [amber], 123–26. 5½ cols. £2.12.6. *Dodd* / **George Dodd**

The Hermit of Damburgville [an executioner], 126–28. 5 cols. £2.12.6. *Miss Rankin* / **Miss Rankin**

The Robins [verse], 128–29. 1 col. £2.2.0. *Mrs. MacIntosh* / **Mrs. MacIntosh**

Plant Architecture [botany], 129–32. 6 cols. £3.3.0. *Hart* / **Ernest Abraham Hart**

The Roving Englishman: Greek Fire [excursions in Mytilene], 132–34. 4 cols. £2.2.0. *Murray* / **Grenville Murray**

Deaf Mutes, 134–38. 8½ cols. £4.14.6. *Miss Martineau* / **Harriet Martineau**

Deadly Lively [Montmartre cemetery], 138–40. 5 cols. £2.12.6. *W. B. Jerrold* / **William Blanchard Jerrold**

April 1, 1854. No. 210, pp. 141–64

Hard Times [novel], chaps. i–iii, 141–45. 9 cols. *Charles Dickens* / **Charles Dickens**

Oranges and Lemons, 145–50. 8½ cols. £4.14.6. *Capper* / **John Capper**

Sharpening the Scythe [story], 150–52. 5 cols. £2.12.6. *Payne* / **James Payn**

Our Coachman [verse], 152. ½ col. £1.1.0. *Allingham* / **William Allingham**

Where Are They? [people advertised for in "Personal" columns; petition and testimonial signers, etc.], 152–58. 11¼ cols. *Sala* / **George A. Sala**

Rights and Wrongs of Women, 158–61. 5½ cols. £2.12.6. *Miss Lynn* / **Eliza Lynn**

Chip:
- The Bottle at Sea [further instances of "Bottled Information"], 161. 1 col. *W.H.W.* / **W. H. Wills**

The Girl I Left behind Me [soldiers bound for Crimean War], 161–64. 6½ cols. *Sala* / **George A. Sala**

April 8, 1854. No. 211, pp. 165–88

Hard Times, chaps. iv–v, 165–70. 10¼ cols. *C.D.* / **Charles Dickens**

Goblin Life [old superstitions], 170–74. 9 cols. *Morley* / **Henry Morley**

A Call upon Sophy [Louis Aimé Martin, *Lettres à Sophie sur la physique, la chimie et l'histoire naturelle*, 1847 ed.], 174–76. 3¾ cols. *Morley* / **Henry Morley**

Sonnet in a Spring Grove [verse], 176. ¼ col. £0.10.6. *Allingham* / **William Allingham**

From California [descr. of a village], 176–78. 3 cols. £1.10.0. ——— / ———

Patchwork [marquetry, buhlwork, etc.], 178–81. 7 cols. £3.13.6. *Dodd* / **George Dodd**

Love and Self-Love [story], 181–85. 7½ cols. £3.13.6. *St. John* / **Bayle St. John**

Behind the Louvre [street-performers and hawkers], 185–88. 6 cols.; should read 6¾. £3.3.0. *W. B. Jerrold* / **William Blanchard Jerrold**

April 15, 1854. No. 212, pp. 189–212

Hard Times, chap. vi, 189–94. 10½ cols. *C.D.* / **Charles Dickens**

Out in the Desert [Libyan desert], 194–97. 5¼ cols. £2.15.0. *Bayle St. John* / **Bayle St. John**

Idiots Again, 197–200. 7¾ cols. £4.4.0. *Miss Martineau* / **Harriet Martineau**

Gradation [verse], 200–201. ¾ col. £1.11.6. ——— / ———

The Quiet Poor [in Bethnal Green], 201–206. 10¼ cols. *Morley* / **Henry Morley**

The Roving Englishman: Free Quarters [church-maintained travellers' home]; A Saint's Brother [a Greek funeral; a martyr], 206–209. 7 cols. £3.13.6. *Murray* / **Grenville Murray**

Legs, 209–212. 6 cols. *Sala* / **George A. Sala**

April 22, 1854. No. 213, pp. 213–36

Hard Times, chaps. vii–viii, 213–17. 9¾ cols. *Charles Dickens* / **Charles Dickens**

Wire-Drawing [manufacture and use of wire], 217–21. 7½ cols. £4.0.0. *Dodd* / **George Dodd**

Modern Ancients [the Bretons], 221–24. 5¼ cols. £2.12.6. *Miss Costello* / **Louisa Stuart Costello**

Ground in the Mill [factory accidents], 224–27. 5½ cols. *Morley* / **Henry Morley**

Missing, a Married Gentleman [from William King, *Political and Literary Anecdotes*, 1818], 227–28. 2¼ cols. £2.2.0. *Thomas* / **William Moy Thomas**

A Marvellous Journey with the Old Geographer [Peter Heylyn, *Mikrokosmos*, 1629 ed.], 228–33. 10½ cols. £5.15.6. *Ollier* / **Edmund Ollier**

A Syrian Legend, 233–36. 6½ cols. £3.3.0. *St. John* / **Bayle St. John**

April 29, 1854. No. 214, pp. 237–60

Hard Times, chaps. ix–x, 237–42. 10½ cols. *Charles Dickens* / **Charles Dickens**

Busy with the Photograph, 242–45. 7 cols. £4.14.6. *Dodd* / **George Dodd**

Paris with a Mask On [carnival], 245–48. 5¾ cols. £3.3.0. *Jerrold* / **William Blanchard Jerrold**

At Thy Peril [verse], 248–49. 1 col. £2.2.0. *Miss Tomkins* / **Mary Jane Tomkins**

A Canny Book [Newcastle jest books], 249–53. 9½ cols. *Sala* / **George A. Sala**

Chip:
- Primoguet [Breton sea captain], 253–54. 2 cols. £1.1.0. *Miss Costello* / **Louisa Stuart Costello**

The Roving Englishman: The Cadi; Britons in Turkey [in Mytilene], 254–57. 5¾ cols. £3.10.0. *Murray* / **Grenville Murray**

One of Our Legal Fictions [Caroline Norton, *English Laws for Women in the Nineteenth Century*, 1854], 257–60. 6½ cols. £3.13.6. *Miss Lynn* / **Eliza Lynn**

May 6, 1854. No. 215, pp. 261–84

Hard Times, chaps. xi–xii, 261–66. 10 cols. *C.D.* / **Charles Dickens**

Troops and Jobs in Malta, 266–68. 5¼ cols. £3.13.6. *Wenckstern* / **Otto von Wenckstern**

A Manchester Warehouse, 268–72. 7 cols. £3.13.6. *Lowe* / **James Lowe**

Words upon the Waters [verse], 272. ¾ col. £1.11.6. *Miss Berwick* / **Adelaide Anne Procter**

The Green Ring and the Gold Ring [story], 272–77. 10½ cols. £5.10.0. *Mrs. Bell* / **Mrs. Bell**

Last Moments of an English King [Charles II: MS source], 277–80. 6 cols. £2.12.6. *P. Cunningham* / **Peter Cunningham**

Doctor Pablo [Paul Proust de la Gironière, *Vingt années aux Philippines*, 1853], 280–84. 8½ cols. *Morley* / **Henry Morley**

May 13, 1854. No. 216, pp 285–308

Hard Times, chaps. xiii–xiv, 285–90. 10¼ cols. *C.D.* / **Charles Dickens**

The True Story of the Nuns of Minsk, 290–95. 10½ cols. £5.10.0. *Miss Lynn* / **Eliza Lynn**

The Art of Boreing [tunnelling], 295–97. 3½ cols.; should read 4¼. £3.0.0. *Dodd* / **George Dodd**

Treasures [verse], 297. ½ col. £1.11.6. *Miss Berwick* / **Adelaide Anne Procter**

Tattyboys Rents [in London], 297–304. 12½ cols. *Sala* / **George A. Sala**

Nature's Changes of Dress [botany], 304–306. 5½ cols. £3.3.0. *Hart* / **Ernest Abraham Hart**

My Cavass and I [British consular service], 306–308. 4 cols. £2.12.6. *Murray* / **Grenville Murray**

May 20, 1854. No. 217, pp. 309–332

Hard Times, chaps. xv–xvi, 309–314. 10½ cols. *C.D.* / **Charles Dickens**

The Cankered Rose of Tivoli [Alfred Michiels, "Biographie de Philippe Roos," appended to *L'Architecture et la peinture en Europe*, 1853], 314–17. 6 cols. *Morley* / **Henry Morley**

Three Graces of Christian Science [training of children devoid of the senses], 317–20. 7 cols. £3.13.6. *Miss Martineau* / **Harriet Martineau**

A True Knight [verse], 320–21. 1 col. £1.11.6. *Miss Berwick* / **Adelaide Anne Procter**

The Roving Englishman: A Greek Girl, 321–23. 3½ cols. £2.2.0. *Murray* / **Grenville Murray**

Company Manners [motivated by Victor Cousin's articles on Mme. de Sablé in *Revue des deux mondes*, 1854], 323–31. 16¾ cols. £8.18.6. *Mrs. Gaskell* / **Elizabeth Gaskell**

Broken Language [Gallic-English], 331–32. 3½ cols. £1.15.0. *W. B. Jerrold* / **William Blanchard Jerrold**

May 27, 1854. No. 218, pp. 333–56

Hard Times, chap. xvii, 333–38. 10½ cols. *C.D.* / **Charles Dickens**

John Dunton Was a Citizen [*The Life and Errors of John Dunton*, 1705], 338–44. 12 cols. £6.6.0. *Miss Laurence* / **Hannah Lawrance**

An Old Offender [verse], 344. ½ col. £1.1.0. *Procter* / **Bryan Waller Procter**

Brother Mieth and His Brothers [Moravian school, Germany], 344–49. 9¼ cols. *Morley* / **Henry Morley**

The Roving Englishman: Regular Turks, 349–52. 5¾ cols. £3.3.0. *Murray* / **Grenville Murray**

Revolvers, 352–56. 9¾ cols. £4.15.0. *Thomas* / **William Moy Thomas**

June 3, 1854. No. 219, pp. 357–80

Hard Times, chaps. xviii–xix, 357–62. 10½ cols. *C.D.* / **Charles Dickens**

The Roving Englishman: A Turkish Auctioneer, 362–64. 3½ cols. £2.2.0. *Murray* / **Grenville Murray**

Basque Blood [story], 364–68. 8¾ cols. £4.14.6. *Tyas* / **Tyas**

Invocation [verse], 368. ½ col. £1.1.0. *Ed. Arnold* / **Edwin Arnold**

Under Canvas [Austen Henry Layard in Mesopotamia], 368–73. 9¾ cols. £4.14.6. *Miss Lynn* / **Eliza Lynn**

Chip:
- Sensible News of a Sea-Snake, 373–74. 2 cols. £1.1.0. *Buckland* / **Francis Trevelyan Buckland**

Strollers at Dumbledowndeary [itinerant actors], 374–80. 13 cols. *Sala* / **George A. Sala**

June 10, 1854. No. 220, pp. 381–404

Hard Times, chaps. xx–xxi, 381–86. 11½ cols. *C.D.* / **Charles Dickens**

British Phenomena [Joseph Méry, *Les Nuits anglaises,* 1853], 386–90. 7½ cols. *Morley* / **Henry Morley**

Waste [unused products of Canada and India], 390–93. 5 cols. £2.12.6. *Capper* / **John Capper**

The Sailor. A Romaic Ballad [verse], 393. 1 col. £1.11.6. *Allingham* / **William Allingham**

The Little Flower [legend of Bulgarian outlaw], 393–98. 9 cols. £4.14.6. *Bayle St. John* / **Bayle St. John**

Chip:
- A Lesson in Multiplication [population increase], 398. 1½ cols. *Morley* / **Henry Morley**

Death's Doors [dwellings of the London poor], 398–402. 7½ cols. *Morley* / **Henry Morley**

The Roving Englishman: Greek Waters [mineral springs in Mytilene], 402–404. 4¼ cols. £2.15.0. *Murray* / **Grenville Murray**

June 17, 1854. No. 221, pp. 405–428

Hard Times, chap. xxii, 405–409. 11½ cols.; should read 9¾. *C.D.* / **Charles Dickens**

Man As a Monster [old superstitions], 409–414. 8 cols.; should read 9¼. *Morley* / **Henry Morley**

Turks under Arms [review of troops, Constantinople], 414–17. 6 cols. £2.12.6. *Fusco & Morley* / **Edoardo Nicolà Fusco & Henry Morley**

Miss Furbey [story], 417–21. 8 cols. £4.4.0. *Thomas* / **William Moy Thomas**

Blindness, 421–25. 8¼ cols. £4.10.0. *Miss Martineau* / **Harriet Martineau**

Doing Business in France [passports, money-changing], 425–28. 7 cols. £3.13.6. *Costello* / **Dudley Costello**

June 24, 1854. No. 222, pp. 429–52

Hard Times, chap. xxiii, 429–34. 10 cols. *C.D.* / **Charles Dickens**

French Domesticity, 434–38. 8½ cols. £4.4.0. *Miss Lynn* / **Eliza Lynn**

Done to a Jelly [gelatinous substances], 438–40. 5 cols. £2.12.6. *Dodd* / **George Dodd**

Exiled [verse], 440–41. ¾ col. £1.11.6. *Harris* / **Harris**

The Ruined Potter [story], 441–44. 6½ cols. £3.13.6. *Wood* / **Wood**

Turks at Sea [Adolphus Slade, *Records of Travels in Turkey, Greece, Etc.,* prob. 1854 ed.], 444–47. 6½ cols. £3.3.0. *W. B. Jerrold* / **William Blanchard Jerrold**

The War with Fever [William Hay, *Second Report ... on the Operation of the Common Lodging-Houses Act,* 1854, Parliamentary Paper], 447–49. 3 cols. *Morley* / **Henry Morley**

General and Mrs. Delormo [story], 449–52. 8 cols. £4.4.0. *White* / **the Rev. James White**

July 1, 1854. No. 223, pp. 453–76

Hard Times, chap. xxiv, 453–58. 10 cols. *C.D.* / **Charles Dickens**

The Learned Sailor [need for knowledge on part of seamen: based on works of M. F. Maury and Robert Methven], 458–62. 8 cols. *Morley* / **Henry Morley**

The Roving Englishman: The Pasha, 462–64. 5 cols. £2.12.6. *Murray* / **Grenville Murray**

Progress [verse], 464. ¼ col. £0.10.6. *Wood* / **Wood**

Smoke or No Smoke ["smoke nuisance," London], 464–66. 3¾ cols. ——— / ———

Tattyboys Renters [continuation of "Tattyboys Rents," May 13], 466–71. 9¼ cols. *Sala* / **George A. Sala**

Our Sister [Liverpool], 471–74. 5½ cols. £3.13.6. *Capper* / **John Capper**

The Incomplete Letter-Writer [illiterate letter-writers], 474–76. 6 cols. £3.13.6. *Costello* / **Dudley Costello**

July 8, 1854. No. 224, pp. 477–500

Hard Times, chaps. xxv–xxvi, 477–82. 10 cols. *C.D.* / **Charles Dickens**

Her Majesty's Consular Service, 482–87. 11½ cols. £5.15.6. *Murray* / **Grenville Murray**

Illusion [verse], 487–88. ¾ col. £1.5.0. *Miss Berwick* / **Adelaide Anne Procter**

Barbara's Nuptials [in Poland, 1759], 488-92. 9 cols. £4.14.6. *Madm. Schszepanowska* / **Mme. Szczepanowska**

A Good Brushing [brushes], 492–95. 6¾ cols. £3.3.0. *Dodd* / **George Dodd**

A Tour in Bohemia [upper-class English Bohemia], 495–500. 10 cols. *Sala* / **George A. Sala**

July 15, 1854. No. 225, pp. 501–524

Hard Times, chaps. xxvii–xxviii, 501–506. 10½ cols. *C.D.* / **Charles Dickens**

Sea Views [Philip H. Gosse, *The Aquarium*, 1854], 506–510. 7½ cols. *Morley* / **Henry Morley**

The Roving Englishman: Village Diplomatists; The Schoolmaster and His Lesson [Greeks under Turkish rule], 510–13. 6 cols. £3.3.0. *Murray* / **Grenville Murray**

Recollections [verse], 513. ¾ col. £1.11.6. *Miss Berwick* / **Adelaide Anne Procter**

The Last Howley of Killowen [story], 513–19. 11½ cols. £6.0.0. *Thomas* / **William Moy Thomas**

Rabbit-Skins [traffic in], 519–21. 5¼ cols. £3.0.0. *W. B. Jerrold* / **William Blanchard Jerrold**

Some Amenities of War [Crimean War], 521–24. 6 cols. *Sala* / **George A. Sala**

July 22, 1854. No. 226, pp. 525–48

Hard Times, chaps. xxix–xxx, 525–31. 12 cols. *C.D.* / **Charles Dickens**

Called to the Savage Bar [*Avantures du S*r*. C. Le Beau, ... ou voyage ... parmi les sauvages de l'Amérique Septentrionale*, 1738], 531–33. 4½ cols. £2.12.6. *Costello* / **Dudley Costello**

A Bundle of Crotchets [desiderata in inventions and engineering projects], 533–36. 7 cols. £3.10.0. *Dodd* / **George Dodd**

Shining Stars [verse], 536–37. ½ col. £1.1.0. *Miss Berwick* / **Adelaide Anne Procter**

Freedom, or Slavery? [Fugitive Slave Law], 537–42. 10 cols. £5.5.0. *Miss Martineau* / **Harriet Martineau**

The Roving Englishman: The Bin-Bashee [Turkish officer], 542–43. 3½ cols. £1.11.6. *Murray* / **Grenville Murray**

Left Behind [old buildings in London], 543–46. 5 cols. £2.12.6. *Ollier* / **Edmund Ollier**

The French Waiter, 546–48. 5½ cols. £2.15.0. *Jerrold* / **William Blanchard Jerrold**

July 29, 1854. No. 227, pp. 549–72

Hard Times, chaps. xxxi–xxxii, 549–56. 14 cols. *C.D.* / **Charles Dickens**

The Roving Englishman: Hadji Hassan [Turkish coffee-house owner], 556–58. 4 cols. £2.2.0. *Murray* / **Grenville Murray**

Herb Gardens, 558–60. 5¾ cols. £2.12.6. *Dodd* / **George Dodd**

Mary [verse], 560–61. 1 col. £1.11.6. *Harris* / **Harris**

The Musical World [London], 561–67. 11¾ cols. £6.6.0. *Sala* / **George A. Sala**

Lobsters, 567–69. 5 cols. £2.10.0. *Costello* / **Dudley Costello**

An Old Portrait from The Hague [*Lettres sur les Anglois et François*, 1747], 569–72. 6½ cols. £3.13.6. *W. B. Jerrold* / **William Blanchard Jerrold**

August 5, 1854. No. 228, pp. 573–96

Hard Times, chaps. xxxiii–xxxiv, 573–80. 14 cols. *C.D.* / **Charles Dickens**

Imitation [duplication processes in manufactures], 580–83. 5¾ cols. £2.12.6. *Dodd* / **George Dodd**

The Poetry of Finland [in part from William and Mary Howitt, *The Literature and Romance of Northern Europe*, 1852], 583–88. 10 cols. £5.5.0. *Mrs. Howitt* / **Mary Howitt**

The Faculty [medical men], 588–93. 11 cols. £5.15.6. *Sala* / **George A. Sala**

Heroes Afloat [writer's passage from Malta to Constantinople], 593–96. 6¾ cols. £3.3.0. *Wenckstern* / **Otto von Wenckstern**

August 12, 1854. No. 229, pp. 597–616

Hard Times, chaps. xxxv–xxxvii, 597–606. 18 cols. *C.D.* / **Charles Dickens**

The Roving Englishman: The Sea Captain and His Ship [the Turkish navy], 606–608. 4½ cols. £2.2.0 to Murray; £1.1.0 to Sala. *Murray & Sala* / **Grenville Murray & George A. Sala**

Mine Host [verse], 608. ¼ col. £1.1.0. *E. Arnold* / **Edwin Arnold**

Flying Coaches [coach travel, 17 and 18 cent.], 608–613. 10 cols. £5.0.0. *Miss Laurence* / **Hannah Lawrance**

Near the Pantheon [student life in Paris], 613–16. 7 cols. £3.13.6. *W. B. Jerrold* / **William Blanchard Jerrold**

VOLUME X August 19, 1854 – January 27, 1855

August 19, 1854. No. 230, pp. 1–24

A Little More Harmony [a morning concert], 1–5. 9 cols. £4.14.6. *Sala* / **George A. Sala**

Catch-Pennies [ingenious penny-articles], 5–6. 3 cols. £1.11.6. *Buckland* / **Francis Trevelyan Buckland**

Pastimes and Plays [games of old times; Richelieu's *Mirame*], 6–9. 5 cols. £2.12.6. *Miss Costello* / **Louisa Stuart Costello**

The Dodderham Worthy [a north-country auctioneer, broker], 9–12. 5¾ cols. £3.3.0. *Sala* / **George A. Sala**

The Withered King [verse], 12. 1¼ cols. £2.2.0. *Ollier* / **Edmund Ollier**

Faithful Margaret [story], 12–18. 11 cols. £5.15.6. *Miss Lynn* / **Eliza Lynn**

More Splendid Than a Badger [mythical zoology], 18–20. 4 cols. £2.12.6. *Oxenford* / **John Oxenford**

Back Ways to Fame [expedients of authors, lawyers, etc.], 20–24. 9 cols. *Morley* / **Henry Morley**

August 26, 1854. No. 231, pp. 25–48

Wild and Tame [story], 25–31. 12 cols. £6.6.0. *Miss Lynn* / **Eliza Lynn**

Wings and Toes [Alphonse Toussenel, *L'Esprit des bêtes. Le Monde des oiseaux,* part i, 1853], 31–37. 12 cols. £6.6.0. *Dixon* / **Edmund Saul Dixon**

Hidden Light [verse], 37. ¾ col. £1.11.6. *Miss Berwick & C.D.* / **Adelaide Anna Procter & Charles Dickens**

Music in Paving Stones [foreign musicians in London], 37–43. 12 cols. £6.6.0. *Sala* / **George A. Sala**

Going a Little Farther [novelties in manufactures], 43–46. 6½ cols. £3.13.6. *Dodd* / **George Dodd**

The Oriental Merchant [legend], 46–48. 5 cols. £2.12.6. *Bayle St. John* / **Bayle St. John**

September 2, 1854. No. 232, pp. 49–72

It Is Not Generally Known [Parliamentary irresponsibility; restriction on amusements of working class; etc.], 49–52. 6½ cols. *C.D.* / **Charles Dickens**

Cheshire Cheese, 52–56. 8¼ cols. £4.14.6. *Miss Martineau* / **Harriet Martineau**

Chip:
- Brute Sense, 56–57. 1½ cols. *Morley* / **Henry Morley**

Devil Worshippers [the Yezidis: in part from Austen Henry Layard, *Nineveh and Its Remains,* 1848–49], 57–61. 7 cols. £4.4.0. *Miss Lynn* / **Eliza Lynn**

North and South [novel], chaps. i–ii, 61–68. 14¾ cols. £210 (so stated in Nonesuch *Letters,* II, 619n) plus £50 (so implied in Dickens's letter to Mrs. Gaskell, Feb. 1, 1855) for the 22 instalments. *Mrs. Gaskell* / **Elizabeth Gaskell**

Twenty Miles [on observing while travelling], 68–72. 8¾ cols. £4.14.6. *Sala* / **George A. Sala**

September 9, 1854. No. 233, pp. 73–96

Sunday Out [Sundays of the working class], 73–77. 9½ cols. £4.15.0. *Sala* / **George A. Sala**

The Roving Englishman: A Greek Carnival [in Mytilene], 77–79. 4 cols. £2.2.0. *Murray* / **Grenville Murray**

Old Domestic Intelligence [the periodical *Domestick Intelligence*, 1679–80], 79–83. 7½ cols. £3.13.6. *Miss Laurence* / **Hannah Lawrance**

Chip:
- Justice Is Satisfied [bribe to Berlin constable], 83–84. 2½ cols. £2.2.0. *Sala* / **George A. Sala**

The True Voice [verse], 84–85. ¼ col. *Townshend* / **Chauncy Hare Townshend**

North and South, chaps. iii–iv, 85–92. 15¾ cols. *Mrs. Gaskell* / **Elizabeth Gaskell**

Cornish Stone, 92–96. 7¾ cols. £3.13.6. *Dodd* / **George Dodd**

September 16, 1854. No. 234, pp. 97–120

Faces [physiognomy], 97–101. 8 cols. £4.4.0. *Ollier* / **Edmund Ollier**

Doctor Pantologos [story], 101–106. 11¾ cols. £5.15.6. *Sala* / **George A. Sala**

The Poigné-Bandel Property [a stay in France], 106–109. 4¼ cols. £2.2.0. *Miss Costello* / **Louisa Stuart Costello**

North and South, chap. v, 109–113. 9¾ cols. *Mrs. Gaskell* / **Elizabeth Gaskell**

Beef, Mutton, and Bread [agric. show, Lincoln], 113–18. 9¼ cols. £4.14.6. *Sidney & W.H.W.* / **Samuel Sidney & W. H. Wills**

The Turks' Cellar [accounts of Turks' attacks on Austrian towns], 118–20. 4 cols. £2.2.0. *Duthie* / **William Duthie**

September 23, 1854. No. 235, pp. 121–44

Legal and Equitable Jokes [inequalities and injustices in law and law administration: from evidence of Graham Willmore, May 26, 1854, in Appendix to *First Report of the Commissioners Appointed to Inquire into the State of the County Courts* (appears in Parliamentary Paper, 1855)], 121–24. 6½ cols. *C.D.* / **Charles Dickens**

The Betrothed Children [legend], 124–29. 10 cols. £5.5.0. *Bayle St. John* / **Bayle St. John**

Pilchards [Cornish fisheries], 129–32. 7 cols. £3.13.6. *Dodd* / **George Dodd**

Remedy [verse], 132–33. ½ col. *Townshend* / **Chauncy Hare Townshend**

North and South, chaps. vi–vii, 133–38. 11 cols. *Mrs. Gaskell* / **Elizabeth Gaskell**

Chip:
- Colouring [Michel E. Chevreul, *The Principles of Harmony and Contrast of Colours*, 1854], 138–40. 4 cols. *Morley* / **Henry Morley**

Madame Grondet's [young ladies' school, Paris], 140–44. 8¾ cols. £4.14.6. *Miss Lee & Morley* / **Harriet Parr & Henry Morley**

September 30, 1854. No. 236, pp. 145–68

Sunday Tea-Gardens, 145–48. 6½ cols. £3.10.0. *Sala* / **George A. Sala**

Sick Body, Sick Brain [J. F. C. Hecker, *The Epidemics of the Middle Ages*, 1844 ed.], 148–51. 6¾ cols. *Morley* / **Henry Morley**

An Excursion Train, before Steam [from MS diary], 151–56. 10¼ cols. £5.5.0. *Miss Laurence* / **Hannah Lawrance**

What May Be Ours [verse], 156–57. ¾ col. £1.1.0. *Miss Fanny Farmer* / **Miss Fanny Farmer**

North and South, chaps. viii–ix, 157–62. 11 cols. *Mrs. Gaskell* / **Elizabeth Gaskell**

Notes from the Lebanon [Habeeb Risk Allah, *The Thistle and the Cedar of Lebanon*, first pub. 1853], 162–65. 6 cols.; should read 5¼. £3.3.0. *Bayle St. John* / **Bayle St. John**

Demetrius the Diver [Greek refugee in Marseilles], 165–68. 7¾ cols. £4.4.0. *Sala* / **George A. Sala**

October 7, 1854. No. 237, pp. 169–92

To Working Men [their obligation to insist on sanitary reforms], 169–70. 3½ cols. *C.D.* / **Charles Dickens**

The Ghost of Pit Pond [story], 170–76. 10½ cols. £5.10.0. *Costello* / **Dudley Costello**

Crabs, 176–81. 10 cols. £5.0.0. *Costello* / **Dudley Costello**

North and South, chaps. x–xi, 181–87. 13 cols. *Mrs. Gaskell* / **Elizabeth Gaskell**

Cornwall's Gift to Staffordshire [history of porcelain manufacture], 187–90. 6 cols. £3.3.0. *Dodd* / **George Dodd**

The Irish Letter-Writer [letters of "half-educated" Irishmen], 190–92. 4½ cols. £2.2.0. *Mrs. Hoare* / **Mrs. Hoare**

October 14, 1854. No. 238, pp. 193–216

Mars a la Mode [military attire], 193–96. 6 cols. £3.3.0. *Sala* / **George A. Sala**

Piping Days [London drainage, sewerage], 196–99. 6 cols. *Morley* / **Henry Morley**

The Compassionate Broker [continuation of "Dodderham Worthy," Aug. 19], 199–203. 8¼ cols. £4.4.0. *Sala* / **George A. Sala**

Francis Moore in China [Chinese almanacs], 203–204. 4 cols.; should read 3. £1.11.6. *Mylne* / **William Charles Milne**

Waiting [verse], 204–205. 1 col. £1.11.6. *Miss Berwick* / **Adelaide Anne Procter**

North and South, chaps. xii–xiii, 205–209. 9¾ cols. *Mrs. Gaskell* / **Elizabeth Gaskell**

Out in the Wilds [John R. Bartlett, *Personal Narrative of Explorations*, 1854], 209–213. 8 cols. *Morley* / **Henry Morley**

Conscript Sons [French army], 213–16. 6½ cols. £3.13.6. *Bayle St. John* / **Bayle St. John**

October 21, 1854. No. 239, pp. 217–40

Medical Practice among the Poor, 217–21. 9 cols. *Morley* / **Henry Morley**

Numbers of People [1851 census], 221–28. 13 cols.; should read 14¼. £6.16.6. *Sala* / **George A. Sala**

My Picture [verse], 228–29. 1 col. £1.11.6. *Miss Berwick* / **Adelaide Anne Procter**

North and South, chaps. xiv–xv, 229–37. 17 cols. *Mrs. Gaskell* / **Elizabeth Gaskell**

Holidays at Madame Grondet's [continuation of "Madame Grondet's," Sept. 23], 237–40. 7 cols. £3.13.6. *Miss Lee* / **Harriet Parr**

October 28, 1854. No. 240, pp. 241–64

How to Get Paper, 241–45. 8 cols. £4.4.0. *Miss Martineau* / **Harriet Martineau**

Shot through the Heart [Edmund Hoefer, "Das verlassene Haus," *Aus dem Volk*, 1852], 245–48. 7½ cols. *Morley* / **Henry Morley**

Old Clothes and New Clothes [fashions in men's apparel], 248–53. 8¾ cols. £4.14.6. *Sidney* / **Samuel Sidney**

North and South, chaps. xvi–xvii, 253–59. 12¼ cols. *Mrs. Gaskell* / **Elizabeth Gaskell**

An Imaginary Voyage [Friedrich von Raumer, "Eine Reise nach Südamerika," *Historisches Taschenbuch*, 1854], 259–62. 7 cols. £3.13.6. *Oxenford* / **John Oxenford**

The Game Season at Spürt [gaming], 262–64. 4¾ cols. £2.12.6. *Crowe (W.)* / **W. Crowe**

November 4, 1854. No. 241, pp. 265–88

Our French Watering-Place [Boulogne], 265–70. 11½ cols. *C.D.* / **Charles Dickens**

The Home Office, 270–75. 9 cols. £4.4.0. *Clark & Morley* / **Clark** or **Clarke & Henry Morley**

Chip:
- Henry the Ninth of England! [Henry Stuart, Cardinal York], 275–76. 2 cols. £1.1.0. *Day* / **Day**

The Moral of This Year [verse], 276–77. 1 col. £2.2.0. *Smales* / **Smales**

North and South, chaps. xviii–xix, 277–84. 15 cols. *Mrs. Gaskell* / **Elizabeth Gaskell**

On the Yorkshire Moors [an excursion], 284–87. 5¼ cols. £2.12.6. *Mrs. Holland* / prob. **Elizabeth Holland**

Mr. Whittlestick [H. C. Williston, *California Characters, and Mining Scenes and Sketches*, n.d.], 287–88. 4 cols. *Morley* / **Henry Morley**

November 11, 1854. No. 242, pp. 289–312

An Unsettled Neighbourhood [influence of railway], 289–92. 6 cols. *C.D.* / **Charles Dickens**

A Home Question [public health], 292–96. 8½ cols. *Morley* / **Henry Morley**

Mildred's Lovers [story], 296–300. 8½ cols. £4.14.6. *Miss Lynn* / **Eliza Lynn**

A Vision [verse], 300–301. 1 col. £1.11.6. *Miss Berwick* / **Adelaide Anne Procter**

North and South, chaps. xx–xxi, 301–307. 16 cols.; should read 13¾. *Mrs. Gaskell* / **Elizabeth Gaskell**

Jean Raisin [French vineyards and grapes], 307–312. 10½ cols. £5.15.6. *Dixon* / **Edmund Saul Dixon**

November 18, 1854. No. 243, pp. 313–36

Reflections of a Lord Mayor [obsolescence of his office], 313–15. 4½ cols. *C.D.* / **Charles Dickens**

Wild Legends [Ernst Adolf Willkomm, *Sagen und Mährchen aus der Oberlausitz*, first pub. 1843], 315–19. 10 cols.; should read 9¼. *Morley* / **Henry Morley**

Commission and Omission [London drainage, sewerage], 319–24. 10 cols. *Morley* / **Henry Morley**

Give [verse], 324–25. ¼ col. £0.10.6. *Miss Berwick* / **Adelaide Anne Procter**

North and South, chaps. xxii–xxiii, 325–33. 16¼ cols. *Mrs. Gaskell* / **Elizabeth Gaskell**

Chip:
- Our Russian Relations [trade with Russia], 333. 1 col. £0.10.6. *Capper* / **John Capper**

Bullfrog [impostion, pretence, sham], 333–36. 6¾ cols. £3.13.6. *Sala* / **George A. Sala**

November 25, 1854. No. 244, pp. 337–60

Mr. Bull's Somnambulist [Lord Aberdeen], 337–39. 5½ cols. *C.D.* / **Charles Dickens**

Field Service [military], 339–44. 8½ cols. £4.4.0. *Sharp* / **Sharp**

Chip:
- During Her Majesty's Pleasure [legislation concerning insane criminals], 344. 1 col. £0.10.6. *Capper* / **John Capper**

Rag Fair in Paris, 344–48. 9 cols. £5.5.0. *Costello* / **Dudley Costello**

Two Sonnets [verse], 348–49. ½ col. £1.1.0. *Osborne* / **Osborne**

North and South, chaps. xxiv–xxvi, 349–57. 16½ cols. *Mrs. Gaskell* / **Elizabeth Gaskell**

Play [gaming], 357–60. 6½ cols.; should read 7½. £4.4.0. *Sala* / **George A. Sala**

December 2, 1854. No. 245, pp. 361–84

The Lost Arctic Voyagers [of Franklin Expedition] [i], 361–65. 8½ cols. *C.D.* / **Charles Dickens**

Be Assured [insurance], 365–69. 8½ cols. £4.4.0. *Dodd* / **George Dodd**

The Roving Englishman: Dolma Bakjah [a Turkish palace]; A Turkish Bath, 369–73. 7 cols. £3.13.6. *Murray* / **Grenville Murray**

North and South, chaps. xxvii–xxviii, 373–82. 18¼ cols. *Mrs. Gaskell* / **Elizabeth Gaskell**

Paris upon Wheels [cabs, carriages, omnibuses, and drivers], 382–84. 5¼ cols. £2.15.0. *W. B. Jerrold* / **William Blanchard Jerrold**

December 9, 1854. No. 246, pp. 385–408

The Lost Arctic Voyagers [ii], 385–93. 16 cols. *C.D.* / **Charles Dickens**

Madame Busque's [an eating-house, Paris], 393–96. 6 cols. £3.3.0. *Sala* / **George A. Sala**

The Saucy Arethusa [officers and men of the battleship], 396–97. 2 cols. £1.1.0. *Murray* / **Grenville Murray**

North and South, chaps. xxix–xxx, 397–404. 14½ cols. *Mrs. Gaskell* / **Elizabeth Gaskell**

The Great Red Book [Kelly's *Post Office London Directory*], 404–408. 9¾ cols.; should read 9. £5.5.0. *Sala* / **George A. Sala**

December 16, 1854. No. 247, pp. 409–432

Conversion of a Heathen Court [renovation of squalid London tenements], 409–413. 8 cols. *Morley* / **Henry Morley**

The First Mentchikoff [Alexander Danilovich Menshikov], 413–20. 15 cols. £7.7.0. *Miss Costello* / **Louisa Stuart Costello**

The Wreck of 'The Arctic' [verse], 420–21. 1½ cols. £3.3.0. *T. K. Hervey* / **Thomas Kibble Hervey**

North and South, chaps. xxxi–xxxiii, 421–29. 16 cols. *Mrs. Gaskell* / **Elizabeth Gaskell**

Old Friends with New Faces [animals in Zoological Gardens], 429–31. 4 cols. £2.2.0. *Dudley Costello* / **Dudley Costello**

Army Interpreters, 431–32. 4 cols. £2.2.0. Murray / **Grenville Murray**

December 23, 1854. No. 248, pp. 433–56

The Lost Arctic Voyagers [iii] [Rae's reply to "Lost Arctic Voyagers," Dec. 2, Dec. 9], 433–37. 8 cols. *Dr. Rae & C.D.* / **John Rae & Charles Dickens**

The Golden Calf [stock company speculations], 437–41. 9 cols. £4.4.0. *Sala* / **George A. Sala**

An Old French Town [Meaux], 441–45. 6 cols. £3.3.0. *Miss Costello* / **Louisa Stuart Costello**

North and South, chaps. xxxiv–xxxv, 445–53. 16 cols. *Mrs. Gaskell* / **Elizabeth Gaskell**

Chip:
– Criminal Lunatics [reader's comment concerning "Her Majesty's Pleasure," Nov. 25], 453. ½ col. *W.H.W.* / **W. H. Wills**

A Scientific Figment [spontaneous generation], 453–56. 7 cols. £3.13.6. *E. Ollier* / **Edmund Ollier**

Christmas 1854. Extra Christmas Number: The Seven Poor Travellers, pp. 1–36. Announced pub. date: Dec. 14. Stated on title page of Vol. x as included in that vol.; title listed at end of "Contents" of that vol.

The First, 1–10. 20 cols. *C.D.* / **Charles Dickens**

The Second Poor Traveller,* 10–16. 12 cols.; should read 10½. £8.8.0. *Sala* / **George A. Sala**

The Third Poor Traveller [verse], 16–19. 6 cols. £8.8.0. *Miss Adelaide Procter (Mary Berwick)* / **Adelaide Anne Procter**

*In this and in the prose story of the fourth, fifth, and sixth traveller, introductory passages identifying the narrator and linking him with the framework are not set off typographically from the stories themselves. Stone, ed., *Charles Dickens' Uncollected Writings from Household Words*, states that Dickens probably wrote the introductory passage to the story of the second, fourth, and sixth traveller and may have written or modified the introductory passage to the story of the fifth traveller.

The Fourth Poor Traveller,† 19–26. 16 cols.; should read 14. £10.0.0. *Wilkie Collins* / **Wilkie Collins**

The Fifth Poor Traveller, 26–29. 7 cols. £5.5.0. *Sala* / **George A. Sala**

The Sixth Poor Traveller, 29–34. 10 cols. £7.7.0. *Miss Lynn* / **Eliza Lynn**

The Seventh Poor Traveller‡ [verse], 34–35. 3 cols. £5.5.0. *Miss Procter (Mary Berwick)* / **Adelaide Anne Procter**

The Road, 35–36. 2 cols. *C.D.* / **Charles Dickens**

†In reprinting the story as part of a framework narrative, Collins included some lines of the introductory passage.
‡Introduced by a paragraph identifying the narrator and linking him with the framework. The paragraph is probably by Dickens.

December 30, 1854. No. 249, pp. 457–80

Dr. Rae's Report [continuation of "Lost Arctic Voyagers," Dec. 23], 457–59. 4½ cols. *Dr. Rae* / **John Rae**

Colonel Quagg's Conversion [story], 459–65. 13 cols. £6.16.6. *Sala* / **George A. Sala**

Chip:
– The Christmas Cattle Show, 465–66. 2 cols. £1.1.0. *Sidney* / **Samuel Sidney**

Walter Hurst [verse], 466–69. 4½ cols. £5.5.0. *Ollier* / **Edmund Ollier**

North and South, chaps. xxxvi–xxxvii, 469–77. 16¾ cols. *Mrs. Gaskell* / **Elizabeth Gaskell**

The Roving Englishman: A Roadside Picture [Asia Minor]; Locusts [Mytilene], 477–80. 6 cols.; should read 7. £3.3.0. *Murray* / **Grenville Murray**

January 6, 1855. No. 250, pp. 481–504

Wheel within Wheel [trade relations between France and England], 481–83. 6 cols. £3.3.0. *Dixon* / **Edmund Saul Dixon**

Mark Hansel's Visitor [story], 483–88. 10 cols. £5.5.0. *Ollier* / **Edmund Ollier**

The Author of Gil Blas, 488–93. 8½ cols. £4.10.0. *Cattermole* / **Richard Cattermole**

North and South, chaps. xxxviii–xxxix, 493–501. 17½ cols. *Mrs. Gaskell* / **Elizabeth Gaskell**

A Mail-Packet Town [Southampton], 501–504. 6 cols. £3.3.0. *Capper* / **John Capper**

January 13, 1855. No. 251, pp. 505–528

The Rampshire Militia [training of], 505–511. 13 cols. £7.7.0. *Miss Martineau* / **Harriet Martineau**

Second-Hand Sovereigns [Napoleon relics in the Louvre], 511–16. 9¼ cols. £4.14.6. *Sala* / **George A. Sala**

The Two Spirits [verse], 516–17. 1½ cols. £2.12.6. *Miss Procter* / **Adelaide Anne Procter**

North and South, chaps. xl–xli, 517–27. 20 cols. *Mrs. Gaskell* / **Elizabeth Gaskell**

The Man of Ross [John Kyrle], 527–28. 4 cols. £2.2.0. *Peter Cunningham* / **Peter Cunningham**

January 20, 1855. No. 252, pp. 529–52

Doors, 529–33. 8¾ cols. £4.14.6. *Sala* / **George A. Sala**

At Home with the Russians [*The Englishwoman in Russia .... By a Lady, Ten Years Resident in That Country*, 1855], 533–38. 10½ cols. *Morley* / **Henry Morley**

Chip:
– Teasle, 538–40. 2½ cols. £1.5.0. *Starr* / **Starr**

North and South, chaps. xlii–xliv, 540–51. 22¾ cols. *Mrs. Gaskell* / **Elizabeth Gaskell**

The Fate of a Toast [Anne Long, the friend of Swift], 551–52. 3 cols. £1.11.6. *Cunningham* / **Peter Cunningham**

January 27, 1855. No. 253, pp. 553–72

Robertson, Artist in Ghosts [Etienne-Gaspard Robertson, *Mémoires*, 1831–33], 553–58. 11½ cols. *Morley* / **Henry Morley**

When London Was Little, 558–60. 4 cols. £2.2.0. *Capper* / **John Capper**

The Cradle Song of the Poor [verse], 560–61. 1 col. £1.11.6. *Miss Procter* / **Adelaide Anne Procter**

North and South, chaps. xlv–xlvii, 561–70. 19 cols. *Mrs. Gaskell* / **Elizabeth Gaskell**

The Roving Englishman at the Pera Theatre, 570–72. 4½ cols. £2.12.6. *Murray* / **Grenville Murray**

VOLUME XI February 3 – July 28, 1855

February 3, 1855. No. 254, pp. 1–24

That Other Public [public toleration of extortion and of irresponsible Govt.], 1–4. 6½ cols. *C. Dickens* / **Charles Dickens**

The Secret of the Well [legend], 4–10. 12 cols. £6.6.0. *Bayle St. John* / **Bayle St. John**

Vails to Servants, 10–12. 3¾ cols. £2.2.0. *Cunningham* / **Peter Cunningham**

The Lesson of the War [verse], 12. 1 col. £2.2.0. *Miss Procter* / **Adelaide Anne Procter**

Sir John Franklin and His Crews [copy of Rae's report, Sept. 1, 1854, to Hudson's Bay Co.], 12–20. 16 cols. £5.5.0. *Dr. Rae* / **John Rae**

Chip:
- Pulp [for paper making], 20–21. 1¼ cols. *Item not in Office Book* / ———

Obsolete Cookery [Robert May, *The Accomplisht Cook*, 1660], 21–24. 7¼ cols. £3.13.6. *Miss Lynn* / **Eliza Lynn**

February 10, 1855. No. 255, pp. 25–48

Gaslight Fairies [bit players in pantomimes], 25–28. 6½ cols. *C.D.* / **Charles Dickens**

The Hill of Gold [vineyards of Côte-d'Or], 28–36. 16¼ cols. £8.18.6. *Dixon* / **Edmund Saul Dixon**

Fifty-two, Wriothesley Place [a young ladies' school], 36–39. 6¼ cols. £3.3.0. *Miss Kay* / **Miss Kay**

Vampyres, 39–43. 8¾ cols. £4.4.0. *Edmund Ollier* / **Edmund Ollier**

Mr. Pope's Friend [Elijah Fenton], 43–48. 10 cols. £5.5.0. *Sala* / **George A. Sala**

Supposing [v] [mismanagement of commissariat in the Crimea], 48. ¼ col. *C.D.* / **Charles Dickens**

February 17, 1855. No. 256, pp. 49–72

Prince Bull. A Fairy Tale [the Aberdeen Ministry; mismanagement of commissariat in the Crimea], 49–51. 5 cols. *C.D.* / **Charles Dickens**

A Bottle of Champagne, 51–57. 13 cols. £6.16.6. *Dixon* / **Edmund Saul Dixon**

Banoolah [verse], 57–62. 9¼ cols. £7.7.0. *White* / **the Rev. James White**

The Black Sea Five Centuries Ago [*Voyages d'Ibn Batoutah*, Société Asiatique edition, Vol. II, 1854], 62–67. 9 cols. £4.14.6. *B. St. John* / **Bayle St. John**

Chip:
- Long Life of Locusts, 67. ¼ col. *Cardale* / **John Bate Cardale**

The Chinese Adam [Yin and Yang; creation of universe], 67–68. 2¼ cols. £1.10.0. *Mylne* / **William Charles Milne**

Père Panpan [a Frenchman and his family], 68–72. 9 cols. £4.14.6. *Duthie* / **William Duthie**

February 24, 1855. No. 257, pp. 73–96

Very Advisable [story], 73–76. 8 cols. £4.4.0. *White* / **the Rev. James White**

An Old Scholar [*Ephemerides Isaaci Casauboni,* 1850], 76–82. 11 cols. £5.15.6. *Hannay* / **James Hannay**

The Roving Englishman: Very Cold at Bucharest; The Theatre; The Terrible Officer [Austrian interdict of Wallachian festivities], 82–85. 6½ cols. £3.13.6. *Murray* / **Grenville Murray**

Before Sebastopol [verse], 85. ¾ col. £1.11.6. *Miss Tomkins* / **Mary Jane Tomkins**

Convicts, English and French, 85–88. 5¼ cols. £3.0.0. *Sala* / **George A. Sala**

Tinder from a Californian Fire [Francis S. Marryat, *Mountains and Molehills,* 1855], 88–93. 10 cols. *Morley* / **Henry Morley**

My Confession [story], 93–96. 6¾ cols. £3.13.6. *Miss Lynn* / **Eliza Lynn**

March 3, 1855. No. 258, pp. 97–120

Old Ladies, 97–101. 8½ cols. £4.14.6. *Sala* / **George A. Sala**

The Board of Trade, 101–105. 9¾ cols. £5.0.0. *Clarke* / **Clark** or **Clarke**

Two French Farmers [father and son], 105–108. 6½ cols. £3.13.6. *Browne*, Paris / **Browne** or **Brown**

Aspiration and Duty [verse], 108. ¼ col. ——— / ———

The Children of the Czar [Turgenev, *A Sportsman's Sketches,* 1854 French trans.], 108–114. 10½ cols. £5.5.0. *Dixon* / **Edmund Saul Dixon**

Ruined by Railways [story], 114–19. 9¾ cols. £6.16.6. *Sidney* / **Samuel Sidney**

Back from the Crimea [the sick and the wounded], 119–20. 4 cols. £2.2.0. *Payn* / **James Payn**

March 10, 1855. No. 259, pp. 121–44

Gone to the Dogs [wrecked lives, deteriorated property; the Govt. and its conduct of Crimean War], 121–24. 7 cols. *C.D.* / **Charles Dickens**

The Sister of the Spirits [legend], 124–29. 9½ cols. £4.14.6. *Bayle St. John* / **Bayle St. John**

Potichomania [decorated glassware], 129–32. 7 cols. £3.13.6. *Dodd* / **George Dodd**

Passing Clouds [verse], 132. ½ col. £2.2.0. *Miss Procter* / **Adelaide Anne Procter**

Chambers in the Temple [prison escape of Sir Sidney Smith], 132–40. 15¾ cols. £8.8.0. *Sala* / **George A. Sala**

Chips:
- Stealing a Calf's Skin [1787 letter of John Howard's], 140–41. 1½ cols. £1.1.0. *Cunningham* / **Peter Cunningham**
- A Few More Leeches [leech cultivation in France], 141. 1 col. £1.1.0. *Dodd* / **George Dodd**
- Prevention Better Than Cure [rural labourers' lack of reading materials], 141–42. ½ col. £0.10.6. *Capper* / **John Capper**

The Roving Englishman: From Constantinople to Varna, 142–44. 6 cols. £3.3.0. *Murray* / **Grenville Murray**

March 17, 1855. No. 260, pp. 145–68

A Yarn about Young Lions [Admiral Sir Edmund Lyons], 145–49. 9 cols. £4.14.6. *White* / **the Rev. James White**

The Royal Balloon [death of aeronauts J. F. Pilâtre de Rozier and P. A. Romain, 1785], 149–53. 8 cols. £4.4.0. *Dixon* / **Edmund Saul Dixon**

The Roving Englishman: From Varna to Balaklava, 153–57. 7¾ cols. £4.4.0. *Murray* / **Grenville Murray**

One by One [verse], 157. ½ col. £1.11.6. *Miss Procter* / **Adelaide Anne Procter**

Ralph the Naturalist [story], 157–62. 11 cols. £5.15.6. *Miss Lynn* / **Eliza Lynn**

Our Bedfordshire Farmer [a well-managed farm], 162–67. 9¾ cols. £5.5.0. *Sidney* / **Samuel Sidney**

Fatalism [Vuk Stefanović Karadžić, "Das Schicksal," *Volksmärchen der Serben*, 1854], 167–68. 3¾ cols. £2.2.0. *G. Lumlay* / prob. **George Lumley**

March 24, 1855. No. 261, pp. 169–92

Fast and Loose [Govt. mismanagement, irresponsibility], 169–70. 4 cols. *C.D.* / **Charles Dickens**

A Ghost Story [story], 170–81. 24 cols.; should read 22. £11.11.0. *Miss Mulock* / **Dinah Maria Mulock**

Spring Lights and Shadows [verse], 181–82. 1 col. £2.2.0. *Miller* / **Thomas Miller**

Houses in Flats, 182–86. 8½ cols. *Morley* / **Henry Morley**

Tom D'Urfey, 186–88. 4½ cols. £2.12.6. *P. Cunningham* / **Peter Cunningham**

When the Wind Blows [law of storms; its application to navigation], 188–91. 5¾ cols. £3.3.0. *Capper* / **John Capper**

The Roving Englishman: A Dinner in Camp [Balaklava], 191–92. 3 cols. £1.11.6. *Murray* / **Grenville Murray**

March 31, 1855. No. 262, pp. 193–216

Frost-Bitten Homes [the poor in Bethnal Green], 193–96. 7 cols. *Morley* / **Henry Morley**

A Set of Odd Fellows [mythical creatures], 196–202. 12 cols. £5.15.6. *Ollier* / **Edmund Ollier**

The Chinaman's Parson [the Sacred Edict], 202–204. 4¼ cols. £2.2.0. *Milne* / **William Charles Milne**

Honour [verse], 204. ½ col. £1.11.6. *Patmore* / **Coventry Patmore**

Bright Chanticleer [broadsides of Seven Dials], 204–209. 11 cols. £5.5.0. *Sala* / **George A. Sala**

A Very Little Town [sketch of village life], 209–213. 8 cols. £4.4.0. *Miss Lee* / **Harriet Parr**

Starvation of an Alderman [Arthur Hill Hassall, *Food and Its Adulterations*, 1855], 213–16. 6 cols. *Morley* / **Henry Morley**

April 7, 1855. No. 263, pp. 217–40

Sister Rose [story], chap. i, 217–25. 17 cols. £40.0.0 for the 4 instalments. *W. Collins* / **Wilkie Collins**

The Camel-Troop Contingent [military red tape, confusion], 225–26. 3 cols. £1.11.6. *Payn* / **James Payn**

The Unknown Grave [verse], 226–27. ½ col. £1.11.6. *Miss Procter* / **Adelaide Anne Procter**

More Children of the Czar [Turgenev, *A Sportsman's Sketches*, 1854 French trans.], 227–32. 10½ cols. £5.10.0. *Dixon* / **Edmund Saul Dixon**

Misprints, 232–38. 12 cols. £6.6.0. *D. Costello* / **Dudley Costello**

Birthdays, 238–40. 5 cols. £2.12.6. *Sala* / **George A. Sala**

April 14, 1855. No. 264,* pp. 241–64

Fencing with Humanity [factory owners and the Factory Act], 241–44. 6 cols. *Morley* / **Henry Morley**

Sister Rose, chaps. ii–iii, 244–51. 15½ cols. *Collins* / **Wilkie Collins**

Electric Light, 251–54. 4½ cols. *Dodd* (no ampersand) *Capper* / **George Dodd &** (or) **John Capper**

A False Genius [verse], 254. ¾ col. £1.11.6. *Miss Procter* / **Adelaide Anne Procter**

Colonel Grunpeck and Mr. Parkinson [Richard Parkinson, *A Tour in America*, 1805], 254–59. 10¼ cols. £5.10.0. *Sala* / **George A. Sala**

*Contents partially recorded in Office Book, then marked out because of error and recorded anew, still incorrectly. In cancelled listing, the names *Dodd Capper* (no ampersand) stand in author-column for "Electric Light"; in uncancelled listing, Miss Procter's name, through misalignment, stands in that position. The mis-recording results in absence of payment notation for "Electric Light."

The Chinese Postman [postal system], 259–61. 4 cols. £2.2.0. *Milne* / **William Charles Milne**

Passing Faces [Londoners], 261–64. 6½ cols. £3.10.0. *Miss Lynn* / **Eliza Lynn**

April 21, 1855. No. 265, pp. 265–88

The Thousand and One Humbugs [the Palmerston Ministry; Palmerston] [i], 265–67. 5¾ cols. *C. D.* / **Charles Dickens**

Sister Rose, chaps. iv–v, 267–78. 21 cols. *Wilkie Collins* / **Wilkie Collins**

The Flowers' Petition [verse], 278. ¾ col. £1.11.6. *Duthie* / **William Duthie**

The Soldier's Wife, 278–80. 3 cols. *Morley & W.H.W.* / **Henry Morley & W. H. Wills**

Gambling, 280–86. 14¾ cols.; should read 12¼. £7.0.0. *Sala* / **George A. Sala**

Nothing Like Russia-Leather [Turgenev, *A Sportsman's Sketches*, 1854 French trans.], 286–88. 4¼ cols. £2.12.6. *Dixon* / **Edmund Saul Dixon**

April 28, 1855. No. 266, pp. 289–312

The Thousand and One Humbugs [ii], 289–92. 6¾ cols. *C.D.* / **Charles Dickens**

Sister Rose, chaps. vi–vii, 292–303. 22 cols.; should read 23. *Wilkie Collins* / **Wilkie Collins**

Baby Beatrice [verse], 303–304. 1½ cols. £2.2.0. *Mrs. Trollope* / **Theodosia Trollope**

Physic A-field [*A Rich Storehouse or Treasurie for the Diseased*, 16-cent. treatise], 304–307. 5¼ cols. £2.2.0. *MacAdam* / **MacAdam**

The Roving Englishman: From Varna to Rustchuk, 307–308. 3 cols. £1.11.6. *Murray* / **Grenville Murray**

The Muse in Livery [Robert Dodsley], 308–312. 8½ cols. £4.0.0. *Peter Cunningham* / **Peter Cunningham**

May 5, 1855. No. 267, pp. 313–36

The Thousand and One Humbugs [iii], 313–16. 6½ cols. *C.D.* / **Charles Dickens**

Plagues of London [the Great Plague; also robbery, etc., in old times], 316–19. 6 cols. £3.10.0. *Browne* / **Browne** or **Brown**

God's Gifts [verse], 319. 1 col. £2.2.0. *Miss Procter* / **Adelaide Anne Procter**

Yadacé [Algerian game of forfeits], 319–23. 7½ cols. £3.13.6. *Sala* / **George A. Sala**

Trade, 323–26. 6¼ cols. £3.3.0. *Capper* / **John Capper**

Bread Cast on the Waters [story], 326–35. 18¾ cols. £10.0.0. *White* / **the Rev. James White**

The Roving Englishman: A Bulgarian Post-House, 335–36. 2¼ cols. £1.5.0. *Murray* / **Grenville Murray**

May 12, 1855. No. 268, pp. 337–60

Death's Cyphering-Book [factory owners and the Factory Act], 337–41. 9 cols. *Morley* / **Henry Morley**

Mother and Step-Mother [story], chaps. i–v, 341–48. 13 cols. £22.0.0 for the 3 instalments. *Miss King* / **Miss Louisa King**

Boots and Corns, 348–54. 12½ cols. £6.6.0. *Costello* / **Dudley Costello**

Embarkation [troops for foreign service], 354–56. 4 cols. £2.2.0. *Payn* / **James Payn**

An Old Picture of Justice [Oscar Honoré, *Histoires de la vie privée d'autrefois*, 1853], 356–60. 10 cols. *Morley* / **Henry Morley**

May 19, 1855. No. 269, pp. 361–84

Cognac, 361–67. 13¼ cols. £7.0.0. *E. S. Dixon* / **Edmund Saul Dixon**

Mother and Step-Mother, chaps. vi–viii, 367–76. 17¼ cols. *Miss King* / **Miss Louisa King**

A First Sorrow [verse], 376. ¾ col. £1.1.0. *Miss Procter* / **Adelaide Anne Procter**

Important Rubbish [slag], 376–79. 5 cols. £2.12.6. *Capper* / **John Capper**

Chips:
- A River Picture in Summer, 379. 1¾ cols. £1.1.0. *Blackborne* / **Blackborne**
- The Scale of Promotion [in East India Co.], 379–80. 1 col. £0.10.6. *Capper* / **John Capper**

What It Is to Have Forefathers [story], 380–84. 9¼ cols. £4.14.6. *White* / **the Rev. James White**

May 26, 1855. No. 270, pp. 385–408

The Toady Tree [Englishmen's truckling to titles], 385–87. 5 cols. *C.D.* / **Charles Dickens**

Mother and Step-Mother, chaps. ix–xiv, 387–98. 22 cols.; should read 22¾. *Miss King* / **Miss Louisa King**

Chip:
- Brimstone [reader's correction of statement in "Electric Light," April 14], 398–99. ¼ col. *W.H.W.* / **W. H. Wills**

Poultry Abroad [France], 399–402. 6 cols. £3.3.0. *Dixon* / **Edmund Saul Dixon**

The Story of a King [legend], 402–406. 8½ cols. £4.14.6. *B. St. John* / **Bayle St. John**

A Leviathan Indeed [the *Great Eastern* under construction], 406–408. 5 cols. £2.12.6. *Capper* / **John Capper**

June 2, 1855. No. 271, pp. 409–432

Mechanics in Uniform [Thomas W. J. Connolly, *The History of the Corps of Royal Sappers and Miners*, 1855], 409–414. 10 cols. *Morley* / **Henry Morley**

Poetry on the Railway [railway as subject for poets], 414–18. 9 cols. £4.14.6. *Sala* / **George A. Sala**

What My Landlord Believed [a foreigner's concept of Englishmen], 418–20. 4¼ cols. £2.12.6. *Duthie* / **William Duthie**

The Wind [verse], 420. ½ col. £1.11.6. *Miss Procter* / **Adelaide Anne Procter**

Australian Carriers [carters], 420–27. 13 cols. £6.16.6. *Rinder* / **Samuel Rinder**

The Roving Englishman: Rustchuk, 427–29. 3½ cols. £2.2.0. *Murray* / **Grenville Murray**

Doctor Dubois [story], 429–32. 8 cols. £4.4.0. *B. St. John* / **Bayle St. John**

June 9, 1855. No. 272, pp. 433–56

Cheap Patriotism [Govt. offices: clerks and reorganizers], 433–35. 5¾ cols. *C.D.* / **Charles Dickens**

Vesuvius in Eruption, 435–39. 6½ cols. £3.13.6. *Wreford* / **Henry G. Wreford**

Strictly Financial [James Emerson Tennent, *Wine, Its Use and Taxation*, 1855], 439–42. 6 cols. £2.12.6. *Capper* / **John Capper**

French Love, 442–46. 8¼ cols. £4.4.0. *Miss Lynn* / **Eliza Lynn**

Strive, Wait, and Pray [verse], 446. ½ col. £1.11.6. *Miss Procter* / **Adelaide Anne Procter**

India Pickle [economic misadministration, India], 446–53. 14½ cols. £7.10.0. *Capper* (no ampersand) *Sidney* / **John Capper &** (or) **Samuel Sidney**

Petition Extraordinary [the clergyman's disabilities], 453–56. 6¾ cols. £3.13.6. *White* / **the Rev. James White**

June 16, 1855. No. 273, pp. 457–80

Specimens of the Alchemists, chap. i, 457–65. 16 cols. £12.0.0 for the 2 instalments, but sum of payment notations for individual instalments = £12.12.0. *Miss Jewsbury* / **Geraldine Endsor Jewsbury**

The Roving Englishman: The Passage of the Danube, 465–68. 7½ cols. £3.13.6. *Murray* / **Grenville Murray**

The First Death [verse], 468–70. 3 cols. £3.3.0. *Ollier* / **Edmund Ollier**

A Very Little House [life in a small town], 470–74. 8 cols. £4.4.0. *Miss Lee* / **Harriet Parr**

Quite Revolutionary [trade restrictions, class barriers], 474–77. 7½ cols. £3.15.0. *Dixon* / **Edmund Saul Dixon**

By Rail to Parnassus [Leigh Hunt, *Stories in Verse*, 1855], 477–80. 6½ cols. *Morley* / **Henry Morley**

June 23, 1855. No. 274, pp. 481–504

Smuggled Relations [unacknowledged kin], 481–83. 5 cols. *C.D.* / **Charles Dickens**

French Soldiers in Camp [Honvault], 483–88. 10¼ cols. £2.2.0 to Sala; £3.3.0 to Dixon. *Sala & Dixon* / **George A. Sala & Edmund Saul Dixon**

Specimens of the Alchemists, chap. ii, 488–92. 8½ cols. *Miss Jewsbury* / **Geraldine Endsor Jewsbury**

Fiend-Fancy [characters in nursery tales and legends], 492–94. 3½ cols. £2.2.0. *Oxenford* / **John Oxenford**

Chips:
- Deadly Shafts [factory accidents], 494–95. 1¾ cols. *Morley* / **Henry Morley**
- The Right Man in the Right Place [letter of application for position of workhouse master], 495. ½ col. *Correspondent* / ———

Curiosities of London [motivated by John Timbs, *Curiosities of London*, 1855], 495–502. 12¾ cols. £6.6.0. *Sala* / **George A. Sala**

Under the Sea [diving bell], 502–504. 5½ cols. £2.12.6. *Payn* / **James Payn**

June 30, 1855. No. 275, pp. 505–528

A Dear Cup of Coffee [French merchant defrauding army], 505–509. 9 cols. £4.14.6. *Dixon* / **Edmund Saul Dixon**

The School of the Fairies [fairy tales], 509–513. 8 cols. *Morley* / **Henry Morley**

Latest Intelligence from Spirits [excerpts from *New England Spiritualist*, April 1855], 513–15. 5¼ cols.; should read 4½. *Morley* / **Henry Morley**

A Vision of Hours [verse], 515–16. 1 col. £1.11.6. *Miss Procter* / **Adelaide Anne Procter**

Cats and Dogs, 516–19. 7 cols. £4.0.0. *Sala* / **George A. Sala**

Back at Trinity [an old Cantab's visit], 519–22. 4¼ cols. £2.2.0. *Payn* / **James Payn**

Rice, 522–26. 8½ cols. £4.10.0. *Capper* / **John Capper**

Two Nephews [story], 526–28. 5½ cols. £2.12.6. *Lunn* / prob. **William Arthur Brown Lunn**

July 7, 1855. No. 276, pp. 529–52

The Yellow Mask [story], chaps. i–iii, 529–39. 20 cols. £33.0.0 for the 4 instalments, but sum of payment notations for individual instalments = £35.6.6. *Wilkie Collins* / **Wilkie Collins**

Whittington in Servia [Serbian version of nursery tale], 539–40. 3 cols. £1.11.6. *Oxenford* / **John Oxenford**

The Angel [verse], 540. ¾ col. £1.11.6. *Miss Procter* / **Adelaide Anne Procter**

More Alchemy [in part from Elias Ashmole, *Theatrum Chemicum Britannicum*, 1652], 540–43. 6½ cols. £3.13.6. *Miss Jewsbury* / **Geraldine Endsor Jewsbury**

The Audit Board, 543–46. 6 cols. £3.3.0. *Clarke & Morley* / **Clark** or **Clarke & Henry Morley**

The Old Boar's Head [Shakespeare references to], 546–50. 7 cols. £3.13.6. *Miller* / **Thomas Miller**

Routine [bureaucracy, social stratification, etc.], 550–52. 5½ cols. £3.0.0. *Gostick* / **Joseph Gostick**

July 14, 1855. No. 277, pp. 553–76

Mr. Philip Stubbes [Stubbes, *The Anatomie of Abuses*, 1585 ed.], 553–58. 10 cols. £5.5.0. *Sala* / **George A. Sala**

The Roving Englishman: From Giurgevo to Bucharest, 558–61. 6¾ cols. £3.13.6. *Murray* / **Grenville Murray**

A Dip in the Brine [Droitwich salt works], 561–65. 7¾ cols. £3.13.6. *Dodd* **George Dodd**

Time's Cure [verse], 565. ¼ col. £1.1.0. *Miss Procter* / **Adelaide Anne Procter**

The Yellow Mask, chaps. iv–vi, 565–73. 15¾ cols. *Wilkie Collins* / **Wilkie Collins**

Chip:
– Pensioners [employment for], 573. 1 col. £0.10.6. *W.H.W.* / **W. H. Wills**

Alexander the First [trans. from *Einiges über die letzten Lebenstage des Kaisers Alexander* (not identified)], 573–76. 6½ cols. £3.3.0. *White* / **the Rev. James White**

July 21, 1855. No. 278, pp. 577–600

Infant Gardens [Fröbel and the kindergarten], 577–82. 11 cols. *Morley* / **Henry Morley**

Unfortunate James Daley [David Collins, *An Account of the English Colony in New South Wales*, 1804 ed.], 582–84. 4½ cols.; should read 3½. £2.10.0. *Sala* / **George A. Sala**

Sardinian Forests and Fisheries [John Warre Tyndale, *The Island of Sardinia*, 1849], 584–87. 6½ cols. £3.13.6. *Sidney* / **Samuel Sidney**

The Yellow Mask, chaps. vii–ix, 587–98. 20 cols.; should read 20¾. *Wilkie Collins* / **Wilkie Collins**

A Legal Fiction [Caroline Norton, *A Letter to the Queen on Lord Chancellor Cranworth's Marriage and Divorce Bill*, 1855], 598–99. 4 cols. £2.2.0. *W.H.W.* / **W. H. Wills**

County Guy [militiaman's uniform], 559–600. 2 cols. £1.5.0. *Sala* / **George A. Sala**

July 28, 1855. No. 279, pp. 601–620

My Garden Walks [Flemish market gardens], 601–605. 8 cols. £4.4.0. *Dixon* / **Edmund Saul Dixon**

More Grist to the Mill [factory owners and the Factory Act], 605–606. 3 cols. *Morley* / **Henry Morley**

Cries from the Past [boyhood memories], 606–609. 6¼ cols. £3.5.0. *Sala* / **George A. Sala**

A Poet's Home [verse], 609. ¾ col. £1.11.6. *Blackmore* / **Blackmore**

The Yellow Mask, chaps. x–xii, 609–619. 19¾ cols. *Collins* / **Wilkie Collins**

Wigs, 619–20. 2½ cols. £1.5.0. *Brown* / **Browne** or **Brown**

VOLUME XII August 4, 1855 – January 12, 1856

August 4, 1855. No. 280, pp. 1–24

The Great Baby [Sunday closing of public houses], 1–4. 6¾ cols. *C.D.* / **Charles Dickens**

Two Days in Rio Janeiro, 4–11. 13½ cols. £6.16.6. *W. Howitt* / **William Howitt**

On the Downs [Berkshire], 11–13. 6 cols. £3.3.0. *Payn* / **James Payn**

The Masque of Life [verse], 13–14. 2 cols. £3.3.0. *Ollier* / **Edmund Ollier**

Robertson in Russia [Etienne-Gaspard Robertson, *Mémoires*, 1831–33], 14–18. 6 cols. *Morley* / **Henry Morley**

Mistress Hannah Woolley [Woolley (or Wolley), *The Gentlewomans Companion* and *The Queen-Like Closet*, 17-cent. books], 18–22. 9 cols. £4.14.6. *Miss Laurence* / **Hannah Lawrance**

To Hang or Not to Hang [Jean-François Lesnier, 1833–1858, murder suspect, found innocent], 22–24. 5 cols. £2.12.6. *Dixon* / **Edmund Saul Dixon**

August 11, 1855. No. 281, pp. 25–48

Our Commission [Govt. corruption, incompetence], 25–27. 6 cols. *C.D.* / **Charles Dickens**

The Little Chorister [story], 27–36. 17½ cols. £8.8.0. *Agnes Loudon* / **Agnes Loudon**

Judge Not [verse], 36. ½ col. £1.1.0. *Miss Procter* / **Adelaide Anne Procter**

Wrecks at Sea [Merchant Shipping Act], 36–39. 6 cols. *Morley* / **Henry Morley**

School-Girls [rules of a young ladies' school], 39–41. 4 cols. £2.2.0. *Payn* / **James Payn**

Brides for Sale [slavery in Egypt], 41–45. 7 cols. £3.13.6. *Bayle St. John* / **Bayle St. John**

Dreamers [story], 45–48. 7 cols. £3.13.6. *Marston* / **John Westland Marston**

August 18, 1855. No. 282, pp. 49–72

Parish Broils [story], 49–53. 9 cols. £4.14.6. *White* / **the Rev. James White**

Wet Garden Walks [canal gardens, St. Omer], 53–58. 9½ cols. £4.14.6. *Dixon* / **Edmund Saul Dixon**

Regulars and Irregulars [British and native cavalry, India], 58–60. 5 cols. £2.12.6. *Meason* / **Malcolm Ronald Laing Meason**

Comfort [verse], 60. ½ col. £1.11.6. *Procter (Miss)* / **Adelaide Anne Procter**

Coralie [story], 60–66. 11½ cols. £6.6.0. *Mrs. Gaskell's friend* / **Henrietta Camilla Jenkin**

The Papyrus, 66–68. 4 cols. £2.2.0. *Oxenford* / **John Oxenford**

Doctoring Begins at Home [François V. Raspail, *Manuel annuaire de la santé*], 68–72. 9 cols. £4.14.6. *Sala* / **George A. Sala**

August 25, 1855. No. 283, pp. 73–96

The Worthy Magistrate [Police Magistrate Thomas James Hall unfit for his office], 73. 1¾ cols. *C.D.* / **Charles Dickens**

An Accursed Race [the Cagots: from Francisque Michel, *Histoire des races maudites*, 1847], 73–80. 13 cols. £7.7.0. *Mrs. Gaskell* / **Elizabeth Gaskell**

The Child-Seer [Indian massacre, 1778, New York state], 80–85. 10¾ cols. £5.5.0. *Mrs. Jenkyn* / **Henrietta Camilla Jenkin**

Wild Court Tamed [renovation of squalid London tenements], 85–87. 4 cols. *Morley* / **Henry Morley**

Poor Angelica [Angelica Kauffmann], 87–93. 10½ cols. £6.6.0. *Sala* / **George A. Sala**

Something Like a Dramatic Author [Lope de Vega], 93–96. 7½ cols. £4.4.0. *Brough* / prob. **Robert Barnabas Brough**

September 1, 1855. No. 284, pp. 97–120

A Wife's Story [story], chap. i, 97–105. 16 cols. £24.5.0 for the 4 instalments. *Miss Jolley* / **Emily Jolly**

Flags [as naval signals], 105–107. 4½ cols. £2.10.0. *Dodd* / **George Dodd**

The Carver's College [art of carving at table], 107–108. 2½ cols. £1.5.0. *A. Watts, Junior* / **Alaric Alfred Watts**

The Invalid's Mother. To the Sun, at Lisbon [verse], 108–109. 1½ cols. £2.12.6. *The Honble Mrs. Norton* / **Caroline Norton**

The Roving Englishman: From Bucharest to Kraiova, 109–112. 6 cols. £3.3.0. *R.E.* / **Grenville Murray**

Old Scandinavian Heroes [Anders M. Strinnholm, *Svenska folkets historia*, Vol. II, 1836], 112–15. 6½ cols. £3.13.6. *Mrs. W. Howitt* / **Mary Howitt**

First under Fire [battle of Cerro Gordo, U.S. war with Mexico], 115–17. 3½ cols. £2.5.0. *Ballantine* / **George Ballentine**

Last Words with Philip Stubbes [Stubbes, *The Anatomie of Abuses*, 1585 ed.], 117–20. 8 cols. £3.15.0. *Sala* / **George A. Sala**

September 8, 1855. No. 285, pp. 121–44

Sydney Smith [Lady Holland, *A Memoir of the Reverend Sydney Smith. ... With a Selection from His Letters, Edited by Mrs. Austin*, 1855], 121–23. 4½ cols. £2.12.6. *White* / **the Rev. James White**

A Wife's Story, chaps. ii–iii, 123–30. 15 cols. *Miss Jolly* / **Emily Jolly**

Two Shillings per Horse-Power [factory owners and the Factory Act], 130–31. 2½ cols. *Morley* / **Henry Morley**

The Sardinians [John Warre Tyndale, *The Island of Sardinia*, 1849], 131–37. 11½ cols. £5.10.0. *Sidney* / **Samuel Sidney**

Music in Poor Neighbourhoods, 137–41. 7 cols. £3.13.6. *Dodd* / **George Dodd**

Chip:
- Coal Mining on the Ohio [account from English miner in the U.S.], 141. 1½ cols. £1.0.0. *Sidney* / **Samuel Sidney**

Weird Wisdom [a prophecy of Mother Shipton's; life of William Lilly], 141–44. 6 cols. £3.3.0. *Brown* / **Browne** or **Brown**

September 15, 1855. No. 286, pp. 145–68

A Very Tight Little Island [Heligoland], 145–49. 8 cols. £2.2.0 to Dixon; £2.2.0 to Mrs. Lehmann. *Dixon & Mrs. Lehmann* / **Edmund Saul Dixon &** prob. **Nina Lehmann**

A Wife's Story, chaps. iv–v, 149–55. 13½ cols. *Miss Jolly* / **Emily Jolly**

Turkish Poems on the War, 155–58. 5 cols. £2.12.6. *Dr. Athans* / **Dr. Athans**

Roses, 158–64. 12½ cols. £6.16.6. *Dixon* / **Edmund Saul Dixon**

Two Dinner Failures, 164–68. 9 cols. £4.14.6. *Sala* / **George A. Sala**

September 22, 1855. No. 287, pp. 169–92

The Buckler Squires [enlightened estate-management], 169–76. 14½ cols. £7.10.0. *Sidney* / **Samuel Sidney**

The Ursinus [the female poisoner], 176–80. 8¼ cols. £4.4.0. *Howitt* / **William Howitt**

Wishes [verse], 180. ¾ col. £1.11.6. *Miss Procter* / **Adelaide Anne Procter**

A Wife's Story, chaps. vi–vii, 180–86. 11 cols.; should read 12. *Miss Jolly* / **Emily Jolly**

Chip:
– What Shall a Railway-Clerk Have for Dinner? [company-owned eating-houses for employees], 186–87. 1½ cols. £1.5.0. *Buckley* / **Theodore Buckley**

Supernatural Zoology [*Ortus Sanitatis*, 15-cent. herbal], 187–90. 5 cols. *Morley* / **Henry Morley**

War and Washing [household economies], 190–92. 5¾ cols. £3.3.0. *White* / **the Rev. James White**

September 29, 1855. No. 288, pp. 193–216

Out of Town [Folkestone], 193–96. 6 cols. *C.D.* / **Charles Dickens**

Winifred's Vow [story], 196–201. 10¾ cols. £5.15.6. *Miss Lynn* / **Eliza Lynn**

The Light of Other Days [witchcraft], 201–203. 3 cols.; should read 4. £1.11.6. *Brown* / **Browne** or **Brown**

Ghost-Music [verse], 203–204. 2 cols. £3.3.0. *Ollier* / **Edmund Ollier**

Model Officials [Charles Richard, *Algérie. Scènes de mœurs arabes*, 1850], 204–209. 10¾ cols. £5.15.6. *Dixon* / **Edmund Saul Dixon**

Italian Village Doctors, 209–211. 4 cols. £2.2.0. *Wreford* / **Henry G. Wreford**

Instructive Comparisons [industrial schools], 211–14. 5½ cols. £2.2.0. *Morley & Miss Jewsbury* / **Henry Morley & Geraldine Endsor Jewsbury**

Holiday Quarters [a country cottage and its inmates], 214–16. 4½ cols. £2.10.0. *Murray* / **Grenville Murray**

October 6, 1855. No. 289, pp. 217–40

Sportsmanship in Earnest [Jules Gérard, *La Chasse au lion*, first pub. 1854], 217–23. 13 cols. £7.0.0. *Dixon* / **Edmund Saul Dixon**

Peter the Great in England, 223–28. 9 cols. £4.14.6. *Peter Cunningham* / **Peter Cunningham**

London Stones [geology], 228–29. 2½ cols. £1.11.6. *Blackwell* / **Blackwell**

A Dream [verse], 229. ½ col. £1.11.6. *Miss Procter* / **Adelaide Anne Procter**

Half a Life-Time Ago [story], chaps. i–ii, 229–37. 15¾ cols. £26.5.0 for the 3 instalments. *Mrs. Gaskell* / **Elizabeth Gaskell**

The Caitiff Postman [story], 237–38. 3 cols. £1.1.0. *Morley & Evans* / **Henry Morley & Evans**

Pierre Erard [life and work of the Erards], 238–40. 4¼ cols. £2.5.0. *Robinson* / prob. **John Robertson**

October 13, 1855. No. 290, pp. 241–64

A Dash through the Vines [from Paris to Bordeaux], 241–47. 12½ cols. £6.6.0. *Dixon* / **Edmund Saul Dixon**

Barbarous Torture [barbers and barbering], 247–49. 5 cols. £2.2.0. *Browne* / **Browne** or **Brown**

Yellowknights [children's theatricals], 249–52. 6¾ cols. £3.13.6. *Sala* / **George A. Sala**

The Present [verse], 252–53. ½ col. £1.11.6. *Miss Procter* / **Adelaide Anne Procter**

Half a Life-Time Ago, chap. iii, 253–57. 9 cols. *Mrs. Gaskell* / **Elizabeth Gaskell**

Bound for Brazil [the *Bella Donna* about to leave Southampton], 257–61. 6½ cols. £3.13.6. *Sidney* / **Samuel Sidney**

Sunday Music [band concerts in parks], 261–64. 8½ cols. £4.6.6. *Sala* / **George A. Sala**

October 20, 1855. No. 291, pp. 265–88

An Enemy's Charge [William H. Hale, *Intramural Burial ... Not Injurious to the Public Health*, 1855], 265–70. 11 cols. *Morley* / **Henry Morley**

An Excursion Train, 270–73. 5½ cols. £3.3.0. *Brough* / **Robert Barnabas Brough**

Another Tight Little Island [Sark], 273–76. 5 cols.; should read 7¼. £2.12.6. *Payn* / **James Payn**

Half a Life-Time Ago, chaps. iv–v, 276–82. 11 cols. *Mrs. Gaskell* / **Elizabeth Gaskell**

The Roving Englishman: From Kraiova to London, 282–84. 4 cols. £2.2.0. *Murray* / **Grenville Murray**

Truffles, 284–88. 10 cols. £5.5.0. *Dixon* / **Edmund Saul Dixon**

October 27, 1855. No. 292, pp. 289–312

The Beechgrove Family [story], 289–96. 14 cols. £7.7.0. *Sidney* / **Samuel Sidney**

Nostradamus, 296–98. 5 cols. £2.12.6. *White* / **the Rev. James White**

Tardy Justice [criminal case, France, 17 cent.], 298–301. 5½ cols. £3.0.0. *Miss Jewsbury* / **Geraldine Endsor Jewsbury**

A City Weed [verse], 301. ½ col. £1.1.0. *Duthie* / **William Duthie**

A Ladies' Warehouse [wholesale house for women's apparel], 301–305. 7¾ cols. £4.4.0. *Sidney* / **Samuel Sidney**

The Post-Mistress [of a country town], 305–309. 8¼ cols. £4.4.0. *Miss Parr* / **Harriet Parr**

The Roving Englishman in Belgium, 309–312. 6½ cols. £3.5.0. *Murray* / **Grenville Murray**

November 3, 1855. No. 293, pp. 313–36

A Slight Depreciation of the Currency [monetary gifts substituting for reformatory action], 313–15. 5 cols. *C.D.* / **Charles Dickens**

Sentiment and Action [story], chaps. i–ii, 315–21. 12 cols. £28.0.0 for the 4 instalments. *Miss Lynn* / **Eliza Lynn**

Coats and Trousers [woollen cloth industry], 321–25. 8½ cols. £4.10.0. *Sidney* / **Samuel Sidney**

The Regimental Market [purchase of commissions in British army], 325–28. 6 cols. £3.13.6. *Laing Meason* / **Malcolm Ronald Laing Meason**

The Porcupine Club [Jules Gérard, *La Chasse au lion*, first pub. 1854], 328–33. 9¾ cols. £5.5.0. *Dixon* / **Edmund Saul Dixon**

Twelve Miles from the Royal Exchange [a backward, reactionary village], 333–36. 7¾ cols. £3.17.6. *Thomas* / **William Moy Thomas**

November 10, 1855. No. 294, pp. 337–60

Hobbies, 337–39. 5½ cols. *Morley* / **Henry Morley**

Sentiment and Action, chaps. iii–iv, 339–47. 15 cols. *Miss Lynn* / **Eliza Lynn**

The Santals [tribe in India], 347–49. 4½ cols. £2.12.6. *Sidney Blanchard* / **Sidney Laman Blanchard**

Asleep [verse], 349. ¾ col. £1.11.6. *R*[?]. *Sketchley* / **R.? Sketchley**

Decimal Money, 349–56. 13½ cols. £7.17.6. *Dixon* / **Edmund Saul Dixon**

Lodgings, 356–60. 8¼ cols. £4.10.0. *Payn* / **James Payn**

November 17, 1855. No. 295, pp. 361–84

Paris Improved [buildings, streets, etc.], 361–65. 9½ cols. £4.14.6. *W.H.W.* / **W. H. Wills**

Decimal Measures, 365–70. 9¾ cols. £6.6.0 for this and following item. *Dixon* / **Edmund Saul Dixon**

Chip:
– My Garden Library, 370–71. 2 cols. Payment included with item above. *Dixon* / **Edmund Saul Dixon**

The Dark Side [verse], 371–72. ¾ col. £1.11.6. *Miss Procter* / **Adelaide Anne Procter**

Sentiment and Action, chaps. v–vi, 372–79. 13½ cols. *Miss Lynn* / **Eliza Lynn**

What a Man May Not Do in the Kingdom of Naples, 379–81. 5¼ cols. £3.3.0. *Wreford* / **Henry G. Wreford**

A Cousin in Need [incident concerning Frederick William I], 381–84. 6½ cols. £3.13.6. *Miss Godfrey* / **Miss Godfrey**

November 24, 1855. No. 296, pp. 385–408

Our Almanac [announcement of], 385. 1¼ cols. *C.D.* / **Charles Dickens**

Mind Your Manners [a French book of etiquette; and Melchior J. E. Daumas, *Mœurs et coutumes de l'Algérie*, 1853], 385–90. 10¼ cols. £5.5.0. *Dixon* / **Edmund Saul Dixon**

The Workmen of Europe [Frédéric Le Play, *Les Ouvriers européens*, 1855], 390–94. 8 cols. £4.10.0. *Miss Lynn* / **Eliza Lynn**

Chip:
- Wanted, Some General Information [ignorance of the educated], 394–96. 2½ cols. £1.11.6. *Payn* / **James Payn**

Work for Heaven [verse], 396. ½ col. *Townshend* / **Chauncy Hare Townshend**

Sentiment and Action, chap. vii, 396–402. 11 cols. *Miss Lynn* / **Eliza Lynn**

A Russian Singing-Match [Turgenev, *A Sportsman's Sketches*, 1854 French trans.], 402–405. 6½ cols. £3.3.0. *Dixon* / **Edmund Saul Dixon**

Out and Home Again [thoughts on travel], 405–408. 7¼ cols. £3.13.6. *Marston* / **John Westland Marston**

December 1, 1855. No. 297, pp. 409–432

Charter-House Charity, 409–414. 11½ cols. *Morley* / **Henry Morley**

Princess Ilse [German legend], 414–20. 10½ cols. £5.5.0. *Miss Smale* / **Miss Smale**

Literal Claims [Englishmen's pronunciation], 420–22. 5 cols. £3.0.0. *Dixon* / **Edmund Saul Dixon**

Much Ado about Nothing [story], 422–27. 9½ cols. £4.10.0. *Brown*, Paris / **Browne** or **Brown**

Pope's Sir John Cutler, 427–29. 4 cols. £2.2.0. *Peter Cunningham* / **Peter Cunningham**

Miss Davies [a philanthropic Welshwoman], 429–32. 7 cols. £3.10.0. *Payn* / **James Payn**

December 8, 1855. No. 298, pp. 433–56

The Old and New Squatter [in Australia] [i]: The Old Squatter, 433–41. 16¼ cols. £7.17.6. *W. Howitt* / **William Howitt**

The Railway Companion [incidents of travel], 441–44. 6 cols. £3.3.0. *Payn* / **James Payn**

Dew [verse], 444. ¾ col. £1.11.6. *Prince* / **John Critchley Prince**

The Metamorphosed Pagoda [Brighton], 444–50. 12¾ cols. £6.6.0. *Sala* / **George A. Sala**

Chip:
- The Community of Gault [in France], 450–51. 2 cols. £1.1.0. *Miss Lynn* / **Eliza Lynn**

The Crown of Ionia [Smyrna], 451–55. 7½ cols. £2.2.0 to Murray; £2.2.0 to Knight. *Murray & Knight* / **Grenville Murray & Knight**

Our Shakespeare [a drama-reading club], 455–56. 3 cols. £1.11.6. *Payn* / **James Payn**

December 15, 1855. No. 299, pp. 457–80

Hospitals, 457–61. 8½ cols. *Morley* / **Henry Morley**

Daisy Hope [story], 461–69. 15½ cols. £8.0.0. *White* / **the Rev. James White**

The Two Interpreters [verse], 469. 1 col. £2.2.0. *Prince* / **Adelaide Anne Procter**

The Golden Mean [reflections on human nature], 469–71. 4¼ cols. £2.10.0. *Marston* / **John Westland Marston**

The Old and New Squatters [ii]: The New Squatter, 471–78. 14¾ cols. £7.17.6. *W. Howitt* / **William Howitt**

A German Table d'Hôte, 478–80. 4¼ cols. £2.2.0. *Owen (Junr.)* / **William Owen**

December 22, 1855. No. 300, pp. 481–504

Disputed Identity [account of transported convict], 481–87. 15 cols.; should read 13¾. £7.17.6. *Miss Jewsbury* / **Geraldine Endsor Jewsbury**

Chip:
– Millionnaires and Measures [reply to reader concerning "Decimal Money," Nov. 10; and "Decimal Measures," Nov. 17], 487–89. 2¼ cols. £1.5.0. *Dixon* / **Edmund Saul Dixon**

An English Wife [verse], 489–90. 3 cols. £3.13.6. *Mrs.* ——— / **Mrs.** ———

The Cruise of the Tomtit [to Scilly Islands], 490–99. 18¼ cols. £10.0.0. *Wilkie Collins* / **Wilkie Collins**

Scrooby [Joseph Hunter, *Collections concerning the Church ... of Protestant Separatists Formed at Scrooby ... in the Time of King James I*, 1854], 499–502. 5½ cols. £2.12.6. *Brown* / **Browne** or **Brown**

The Roving Englishman: Down the Danube, 502–504. 5 cols. £2.12.6. *R.E.* / **Grenville Murray**

Christmas 1855. Extra Christmas Number: The Holly-Tree Inn, pp. 1–36. Announced pub. date and running date: Dec. 15. Stated on title page of Vol. XII as included in that vol.; title and contents of no. listed at end of "Contents" of that vol.

The Guest, 1–9. 17 cols. *C.D.* / **Charles Dickens**

The Ostler,* 9–18. 18¼ cols. £16.16.0. *Collins* / **Wilkie Collins**

The Boots, 18–22. 8½ cols. *C.D.* / **Charles Dickens**

The Landlord, 22–30. 14½ cols. £11.11.0. *W. Howitt* / **William Howitt**

The Barmaid† [verse], 30–31. 3 cols. £5.5.0. *Miss Procter* / **Adelaide Anne Procter**

The Poor Pensioner,‡ 31–35. 8¼ cols. £6.6.0. *Miss Parr* / **Harriet Parr**

The Bill, 35–36. 2½ cols. *C.D.* / **Charles Dickens**

*The opening passage and the concluding passage, linking the story to the framework, are set off typographically from the story itself. In reprinting the story as part of a framework narrative, Collins included parts of the opening passage and (with minor changes) all of the concluding passage. The Office Book gives no length notations for the items in this number; the 18¼ col. length supplied includes the length (1¾ cols.) of the opening passage and the concluding passage.

†Introduced by a paragraph linking the story to the framework. The paragraph is probably by Dickens. The 3-col. length supplied for this item includes the length (¼ col.) of the introductory paragraph.

‡Neither the opening nor the concluding paragraphs, which link the story to the framework, are set off typographically from the story itself. Stone, ed., *Charles Dickens' Uncollected Writings from Household Words*, states that the paragraphs are probably by Dickens. Miss Parr reprinted the entire "Poor Pensioner" item.

December 29, 1855. No. 301, pp. 505–528

Travellers' Contrivances [for survival in uninhabited or uncivilized lands], 505–511. 12¾ cols. £6.16.6. *Sidney* / **Samuel Sidney**

Christmas in Southern Italy, 511–13. 5½ cols. £2.12.6. *Wreford* / **Henry G. Wreford**

Blobbs of Wadham [story], 513–15. 3 cols. £1.11.6. *Payn* / **James Payn**

The Tomb in Ghent [verse], 515–17. 4 cols. £4.4.0. *Miss Procter* / **Adelaide Anne Procter**

The Road in India [travel by dawk], 517–21. 7¾ cols. £3.13.6. *Sidney Blanchard* / **Sidney Laman Blanchard**

Colours and Eyes [George Wilson, *Researches on Colour-Blindness*, 1855], 521–24. 5½ cols.; should read 6¾. *Morley* / **Henry Morley**

Dr. Graves of Warwick Street [murder of, 18 cent.], 524–28. 8¾ cols. £4.14.6. *Thomas* / **William Moy Thomas**

January 5, 1856. No. 302, pp. 529–52

The Sisters [story], 529–38. 19 cols. £11.11.0. *Miss Emily Jolly* / **Emily Jolly**

Chip:
– Smuggling Notes [evasion of customs duty], 538–39. 2 cols. £1.5.0. *Mr. Gunn* / **Charles Hains Gunn**

New Year's Eve [verse], 539. ½ col. £1.11.6. *Miss Minshall* / **Miss Minshall**

Claret, 539–45. 11 cols. £5.15.6. *Dixon* / **Edmund Saul Dixon**

Guzla [legend], 545–50. 9 cols. £4.14.6. *B. St. John* / **Bayle St. John**

Christmas Toys, 550–52. 6 cols. £3.3.0. *Sidney* / **Samuel Sidney**

January 12, 1856. No. 303, pp. 553–72

Nob and Snob [officer's life in the guards vs. in the line], 553–56. 7¾ cols.; should read 7. £4.0.0. *Measom* / **Malcolm Ronald Laing Meason**

Old Blois [hist. associations of], 556–61. 10¾ cols. £5.15.6. *White* / **the Rev. James White**

Chip:
– The Legend of Argis [Balkan legend], 561–63. 3 cols. £1.11.6. *B. St. John* / **Bayle St. John**

Double Life [verse], 563. ½ col. £1.1.0. *Duthie* / **William Duthie**

The Land-Shark [story], 563–70. 14¾ cols. £7.17.6. *W. Howitt* / **William Howitt**

A Zoological Auction, 570–72. 4 cols. £2.2.0. *Buckland* / **Francis Trevelyan Buckland**

VOLUME XIII January 19 – July 12, 1856

January 19, 1856. No. 304, pp. 1–24

Insularities [of the English], 1–4. 6 cols. *C.D.* / **Charles Dickens**

Ben Serraq [Charles Richard, *Algérie. Scènes de mœurs arabes,* 1850], 4–7. 7 cols. £4.4.0. *Dixon* / **Edmund Saul Dixon**

Langthwaite [story], 7–13. 11¾ cols. £6.6.0. *Miss Lynn* / **Eliza Lynn**

Murmurs [verse], 13. ½ col. £1.11.6. *Miss Procter* / **Adelaide Anne Procter**

Our Wicked Mis-statements [Harriet Martineau, *The Factory Controversy,* 1855], 13–19. 11½ cols. *Morley* / **Henry Morley**

Coming South a Century Ago [Margaret Steuart Calderwood, *A Journey in England, Holland, and the Low Countries,* 1842 ed.], 19–22. 6 cols. £3.13.6. *Spellan* / prob. **John Nathaniel Spellen**

The Roving Englishman: The Show Officer [passage from Galati to Sulina], 22–24. 5 cols. £3.0.0. *R. E.* / **Grenville Murray**

January 26, 1856. No. 305, pp. 25–48

A Nightly Scene in London [the shelterless poor], 25–27. 4¼ cols. *C.D.* / **Charles Dickens**

The Scapegrace [story], 27–35. 16½ cols.; should read 15¾. £8.18.6. *Payn* / **James Payn**

Chip:
– Small Change [scarcity of small coins], 35–37. 5 cols. £2.12.6. *Dixon* / **Edmund Saul Dixon**

A Shadow of George Herbert [verse], 37. ½ col. £1.1.0. ——— / ———

A King Who *Could* Do Wrong [James I of England: from Robert Pitcairn, comp., *Criminal Trials in Scotland,* 1833], 37–42. 10 cols. £5.0.0. *White* / **the Rev. James White**

Common Cookery, 42–46. 8½ cols. £4.14.6. *Miss Lynn & W.H.W.* / **Eliza Lynn & W. H. Wills**

Military Fans [Charles C. Tevis, *La Petite Guerre et le service des avant-postes,* 1855], 46–48. 5 cols. £2.12.6. *W. B. Jerrold* / **William Blanchard Jerrold**

February 2, 1856. No. 306, pp. 49–72

Beef, 49–52. 7 cols. £3.13.6. *Sala* / **George A. Sala**

Adventures of a Russian Soldier [Pushkin, *The Captain's Daughter,* 1836], 52–58. 13 cols. £6.6.0. *W. B. Jerrold* / **William Blanchard Jerrold**

P.N.C.C. [a cricket club], 58–61. 5½ cols. £2.12.6. *Payn* / **James Payn**

Lavater's Warning [verse], 61. ½ col. £1.1.0. *Miss Procter* / **Adelaide Anne Procter**

The Friend of the Lions [Sir Edwin Landseer, on lions in Zoological Gardens], 61–63. 3¼ cols. *C.D.* / **Charles Dickens**

The Manchester Strike, 63–66. 6½ cols. *Morley* / **Henry Morley**

The Hall of Wines [in Paris], 66–70. 7½ cols. £4.4.0. *Dixon* / **Edmund Saul Dixon**

Three Wives [story], 70–72. 5½ cols. £2.12.6. *Payn* / **James Payn**

February 9, 1856. No. 307, pp. 73–96

The Sulina Mouth of the Danube, 73–77. 8¼ cols. £4.14.6. *R.E.* / **Grenville Murray**

Day-Workers at Home [lodging-house for working girls], 77–78. 2¾ cols. *Morley* / **Henry Morley**

Two College Friends [story], chaps. i–ii, 78–84. 11¼ cols. £9.9.0 for the 2 instalments ("Cheque £9.9 in all"). *White* / **the Rev. James White**

Sorrow and My Heart [verse], 84. ¾ col. £1.11.6. ——— / ———

French and English Staff Officers, 84–88. 8½ cols. £4.14.6. *Meason* / **Malcolm Ronald Laing Meason**

Chips:
- The Russian Budget, 88–90. 3½ cols. £1.11.6. *Dr. Ruge* / **Arnold Ruge**
- A Small Monkish Relic [300-year-old fish-spine], 90–91. 2½ cols. £1.11.6. ——— / **Francis Trevelyan Buckland**

Little Saint Zita [saint's legend], 91–96. 11¼ cols. £6.0.0. *Sala* / **George A. Sala**

February 16, 1856. No. 308, pp. 97–120

The Great Hotel Question [motivated by Albert Smith, *The English Hotel Nuisance*, 1855], chap. i [French and Swiss hotels], 97–103. 12 cols. £10.0.0 "for the two," i.e., for chaps. i and ii, but sum of payment notations for the 2 chaps. = £10.10.6. *Sala* / **George A. Sala**

Meteors, 103–105. 5 cols.; should read 4. £2.2.0. *Warr* / **Warr**

Two College Friends, chaps. iii-iv, 105–116. 22½ cols. *White* / **the Rev. James White**

Chip:
- English Cookery [excerpt from German newspaper], 116. 1¼ cols. £1.1.0. *Wenckstern* / **Otto von Wenckstern**

Early Days in Dulminster [social life of the 1820s], 116–20. 8½ cols. £4.14.6. *Browne* / **Browne** or **Brown**

February 23, 1856. No. 309, pp. 121–44

Houseless and Hungry [a London refuge for the destitute], 121–26. 10½ cols. £5.15.6. *Sala* / **George A. Sala**

My Country Town [story], 126–36. 22 cols. £11.11.0. *Marston* / **John Westland Marston**

Drip, Drip, O Rain! [verse], 136. ½ col. £1.1.0. *J. Chester* / **J. Chester**

The New Jerusalem [Swedenborg and his influence], 136–40. 8 cols. £4.4.0. *Hogarth* / **George Hogarth**

Chip:
- An Election Bill [a publican's charges], 140–41. ½ col. £0.10.6. *Fitzpatrick* / **Fitzpatrick**

The Great Hotel Question, chap. ii [German hotels], 141–44. 8 cols. Payment record with chap. i. *Sala* / **George A. Sala**

March 1, 1856. No. 310, pp. 145–68

Why? [English absurdities and irrationalities], 145–48. 6½ cols. *C.D.* / **Charles Dickens**

The Great Hotel Question, chap. iii [Italian hotels; a New York hotel], 148–54. 13 cols. £6.16.6. *Sala* / **George A. Sala**

Far East [Paul B. Whittingham, *Notes on the Late Expedition against the Russian Settlements in Eastern Siberia; and of a Visit to Japan and to the Shores of Tartary, and of the Sea of Okhotsk*, 1856], 154–57. 6 cols. *Morley* / **Henry Morley**

A Vision of Old Babylon [verse], 157. 1 col. £2.12.6. *Ollier* / **Edmund Ollier**

A Rogue's Life. Written by Himself [short novel], chap. i, 157–66. 17 cols. £50.0.0 for the 5 instalments. *Wilkie Collins* / **Wilkie Collins**

Looking Out of Window [attitude toward life], 166–68. 5½ cols. *Morley* / **Henry Morley**

March 8, 1856. No. 311, pp. 169–92

The Royal Literary Fund, 169–72. 7½ cols. *Morley* / **Henry Morley**

English Hotels, 172–78. 10½ cols. £5.5.0. *Sala* / **George A. Sala**

Feudal Fetters for Farmers [relationship between land owner and tenant farmer], 178–81. 6½ cols. £3.13.6. *Sidney* / **Samuel Sidney**

A Rogue's Life. Written by Himself, chap. ii, 181–91. 20½ cols. *Wilkie Collins* / **Wilkie Collins**

One Cure More [Mathias Roth, M.D., *Hand-Book of the Movement Cure*, 1856], 191–92. 4 cols. *Morley* / **Henry Morley**

March 15, 1856. No. 312, pp. 193–216

Gibbet Street [a thieves' quarter, London], 193–96. 7¼ cols. £3.13.6. *Sala* / **George A. Sala**

The British Dervish [Richard F. Burton, ... *Pilgrimage to El-Medinah and Meccah*, 1855–56], 196–203. 13 cols. £6.6.0. *Sidney* / **Samuel Sidney**

Chip:
– Gold Mines at Home, 203–204. 2½ cols. £1.11.6. *Miss Jewsbury* / **Geraldine Endsor Jewsbury**

The Holy Well [verse], 204–205. 2 cols. £2.12.6. *Miss Parr* / **Harriet Parr**

A Rogue's Life. Written by Himself, chap. iii, 205–214. 16 cols.; should read 17. *Wilkie Collins* / **Wilkie Collins**

The Roving Englishman: Messina, 214–16. 6 cols. £3.3.0. *R.E.* / **Grenville Murray**

March 22, 1856. No. 313, pp. 217–40

Theatrical Ashes [Covent Garden Theatre fire], 217–20. 6¾ cols. £5.5.0. *Albert Smith* / **Albert Richard Smith**

Poison, 220–24. 9 cols. *Morley* / **Henry Morley**

Chip:
– Burning a Priest [funeral ceremony, Burma], 224–26. 3½ cols.; should read 2½. £2.2.0. ——— / ———

The Seven Victims of Mittelbron [innocent peasants tortured, executed, 18 cent.], 226–28. 4½ cols. £2.12.6. *Miss Jewsbury* / **Geraldine Endsor Jewsbury**

Watch Cry. From a German Patois Song [verse], 228. ¾ col. £1.11.6. *Miss Procter* / **Adelaide Anne Procter**

A Rogue's Life. Written by Himself, chap. iv, 228–37. 18 cols. *Wilkie Collins* / **Wilkie Collins**

Waiter! [waiters], 237–40. 7 cols. £3.13.6. *Sala* / **George A. Sala**

March 29, 1856. No. 314, pp. 241–64

Law and Order [reform of statute law], 241–45. 8 cols. *Morley* / **Henry Morley**

Malines, 245–47. 6 cols. £3.3.0. *Murray* / **Grenville Murray**

Chip:
– A Royal Visitor [eagle in Windsor Forest], 247–48. 1½ cols. £1.1.0. *Buckland* / **Francis Trevelyan Buckland**

Wensleydale, 248–51. 5½ cols. £3.0.0. *Miss Parr* / **Harriet Parr**

A Fable Versified [verse], 251. ¾ col. £1.11.6. *Miss Procter* / **Adelaide Anne Procter**

A Rogue's Life. Written by Himself, chap. v, 251–63. 24 cols. *Wilkie Collins* / **Wilkie Collins**

Turkish Contrasts [paradoxes in character, customs, etc.], 263–64. 3 cols. £1.1.0. *Murray* / **Grenville Murray**

April 5, 1856. No. 315, pp. 265–88

The Dalgetty Race [soldiers of fortune], 265–69. 10 cols. £5.5.0. *Sala* / **George A. Sala**

An Ordeal [story], chaps. i–iii, 269–74. 10½ cols. £5.5.0. *Miss James* / **Marian James**

Chips:
- A Perplexing Parenthesis [legal technicalities], 274–75. 1¾ cols. £1.1.0. *J. O. Head* / **John Oswald Head**
- A London Parish [from William Rogers, *The Educational Prospects of St. Thomas Charterhouse*, 1854], 275–76. 1 col. *W.H.W.* / **W. H. Wills & William Rogers**

Rent Day round Madras [*Report of the Commissioners for the Investigation of Alleged Cases of Torture in the Madras Presidency*, 1855, Parliamentary Paper], 276–79. 6½ cols. £3.15.0. *Dr. Russell* / **Charles William Russell**

Saint Patrick, 279–83. 9½ cols. £5.0.0. *Allingham* / **William Allingham**

Wightmouth [sketch of town and harbour], 283–85. 4½ cols. £2.12.6. *Payn* / **James Payn**

A Golden Ass [Apuleius], 285–88. 7 cols. £3.13.6. *Sala* / **George A. Sala**

April 12, 1856. No. 316, pp. 289–312

A Defence of Owls, 289–93. 10 cols. £5.5.0. *Costello* / **Dudley Costello**

An Ordeal, chaps. iv–vi, 293–300. 13½ cols. £6.0.0. *Miss James* / **Marian James**

A Remembrance of Autumn [verse], 300. ½ col. £1.11.6. *Miss Procter* / **Adelaide Anne Procter**

A Player's Benison [Edward Alleyn and Dulwich college], 300–305. 10 cols.; should read 9. *Morley* / **Henry Morley**

Post to Australia [disrupted steamship service], 305–306. 3 cols. £2.2.0. *Whitty* / prob. **Edward Michael Whitty**

Further Travels in Search of Beef, 306–312. 12 cols. £6.0.0. *Sala* / **George A. Sala**

April 19, 1856. No. 317, pp. 313–36

Horse-Eating, 313–18. 11 cols. £5.15.6. *Dixon* / **Edmund Saul Dixon**

Women at Aldershot, 318–20. 5 cols.; should read 4¼. £2.2.0. *Mrs. Young* / **Marianne Young**

Some German Sundays, 320–25. 9 cols. £4.14.6. *Duthie* / **William Duthie**

Chips:
- Sick Railway Clerks [suggested establishment of fund for], 325. 1 col. £1.1.0. *Thompson* / **Thompson**
- Hornet Architecture, 325–26. 1 col. £1.1.0. *Miss Catherine Hill* / **Miss Catherine Hill**

Too Late! [verse], 326. 1 col. £2.2.0. *Miss Parr* / **Harriet Parr**

Nemesis [story], chaps. i–ii, 326–34. 16 cols. £7.10.0. *Whitehead* / **Charles Whitehead**

Doctor Veron's Time [Louis Désiré Véron, *Mémoires d'un bourgeois de Paris*, 1853–55], 334–36. 5 cols. £2.12.6. *Sala* / **George A. Sala**

April 26, 1856. No. 318, pp. 337–60

All Up with Everything [Eugène Huzar, *La Fin du monde par la science*, 1855], 337–39. 5¾ cols. £3.3.0. *Sala* / **George A. Sala**

Attraction and Repulsion [Charles Richard, *Algérie. Scènes de mœurs arabes*, 1850], 339–44. 9 cols. £4.14.6. *Dixon* / **Edmund Saul Dixon**

Nemesis, chaps. iii–iv, 344–53. 20¼ cols.; should read 18¼. £7.10.0. *Whitehead* / **Charles Whitehead**

Madame Freschon's [young ladies' school, France], 353–59. 11½ cols. £5.5.0. *Miss Parr* / **Harriet Parr**

The Marker [billiard players], 359–60. 4 cols. £2.2.0. *Payn* / **James Payn**

May 3, 1856. No. 319, pp. 361–84

Proposals for a National Jest-Book [absurdities and blunders of statesmen and others], 361–64. 6 cols. *C.D.* / **Charles Dickens**

Bond and Free [story], 364–72. 17 cols. £10.0.0. *Payn* / **James Payn**

The Love Test [verse], 372–74. 4¼ cols. £4.4.0. *Miss Parr* / **Harriet Parr**

Economic Botany, 374–80. 12 cols. £6.6.0. *Dixon* / **Edmund Saul Dixon**

A Summer Night's Dream [story], 380–84. 9 cols. £4.4.0. *White* / **the Rev. James White**

May 10, 1856. No. 320, pp. 385–408

Railway Dreaming [the French; Paris], 385–88. 6¾ cols. *C.D.* / **Charles Dickens**

Black Thursday [story], 388–95. 15 cols. £7.17.6. *W. Howitt* / **William Howitt**

A British Interest Betrayed [civil service examinations], 395–97. 3 cols. *Morley* / **Henry Morley**

Dawn [verse], 397. 1¾ cols.; should read ¾. £2.2.0. ——— / ———

Epidemics [Southwood Smith, *Epidemics Considered with Relation to Their Common Nature*, 1856], 397–400. 6 cols. £3.3.0. *Miss Lynn* / **Eliza Lynn**

More Sundays Abroad [in Austria, Germany, France], 400–404. 9 cols. £4.14.6. *Duthie* / **William Duthie**

Mr. Rowlands [story], 404–408. 8½ cols. £4.4.0. *White* / **The Rev. James White**

May 17, 1856. No. 321, pp. 409–432

Time's Sponge [Andrew Amos, *Ruins of Time Exemplified in Sir Matthew Hale's History of the Pleas of the Crown*, 1856], 409–413. 8 cols. *Morley* / **Henry Morley**

Fallen among Thieves [story], 413–17. 9½ cols. £5.5.0. *Miss Bell* / **Mrs. Bell**

Ragged Robin [girls' industrial school and workshop], 417–20. 5 cols. £3.0.0. *Mrs. Hill* / **Mrs. Hill**

Alice [verse], 420. 1 col. £2.2.0. *Harris* / **Harris**

Strychnine, 420–24. 9½ cols.; should read 8½. £4.14.6. *Harvey* / **Harvey**

A Fearful Night [story], 424–27. 5½ cols. £3.0.0. *Yates* / **Edmund Yates**

Banking, 427–32. 11 cols. £5.15.6. *Dixon* / **Edmund Saul Dixon**

May 24, 1856. No. 322, pp. 433–56

Curacies, 433–37. 8¼ cols. £5.0.0. *Payn* / **James Payn**

Minerals That We Eat, chap. i, 437–42. 12 cols.; should read 11¼. £6.6.0. *Hart* / **Ernest Abraham Hart**

Billeted in Boulogne [account of four French soldiers], 442–45. 5½ cols. £2.12.6. *Miss French* / **Miss French**

The Domestic Mercury [*Mercurius Domesticus*, Dec. 19, 1679], 445–48. 5 cols. £2.12.6. *Delepierre* / **Joseph Octave Delepierre**

Gold-Hunting [story], part i, 448–54. 13½ cols. £7.7.0. *W. Howitt* / **William Howitt**

Number Seven, 454–56. 4½ cols. £2.12.6. *Sidney Gibson* / **William Sidney Gibson**

May 31, 1856. No. 323, pp. 457–80

My Blind Sister [story], 457–61. 8 cols. £4.4.0. *Miss Parr* / **Harriet Parr**

Moneysworth [uniform international currency], 461–64. 7 cols. £3.13.6. *Dixon* / **Edmund Saul Dixon**

Putters Down [story], 464–70. 11¾ cols. £6.0.0. *W. Marston* / **John Westland Marston**

Sowing and Reaping [verse], 470. ¾ col. £1.11.6. *Miss Procter* / **Adelaide Anne Procter**

The Official Black Swan [the Post Office], 470–72. 4 cols. *Morley* / **Henry Morley**

Gold-Hunting, part ii, 472–79. 13½ cols. £7.7.0. *Howitt* / **William Howitt**

The Man on the Iceberg [corpse seen by ship's crew], 479–80. 4 cols. £2.2.0. *Cobbe* / **Cobbe**

June 7, 1856. No. 324, pp. 481–504

Laid Up in Two Lodgings, i: My Paris Lodging, 481–86. 12½ cols.; should read 11¾. £7.7.0. *Wilkie Collins* / **Wilkie Collins**

Minerals That We Eat, chap. ii, 486–90. 7 cols. £3.13.6. *Hart* / **Ernest Abraham Hart**

Flowers of British Legislation [legislation concerning charity trusts: based in part on article vi, *Law Magazine and Law Review*, Vol. I, No. 1, 1856], 490–93. 6 cols. *Morley* / **Henry Morley**

Ocean [verse], 493. 1¼ cols. £2.2.0. *Harris* / **Harris**

The Ninth of June [story], chaps. i–ii. 493–500. 12¼ cols. *W.H.W.* / **W. H. Wills**

A Leaf from the Oldest of Books [fossils on Isle of Sheppey], 500–502. 5 cols. £3.0.0. *Owen* / **Richard Owen**

Unhappiness in the Elysian Fields [murder of Countess de Caumont-Laforce, 1856], 502–504. 5 cols. £2.12.6. *Robertson* / prob. **John Robertson**

June 14, 1856. No. 325, pp. 505–528

The Demeanour of Murderers, 505–507. 5 cols. *C.D.* / **Charles Dickens**

Chip:
- The Salt in the Sea [correction of typographical error in "Minerals That We Eat," May 24], 507. ¼ col. *W.H.W.* / **W. H. Wills**

The Ninth of June, chap. iii, 507–511. 8 cols. *W.H.W.* / **W. H. Wills**

The World of Insects [John W. Douglas, *The World of Insects*, 1856], 511–16. 10½ cols. £5.15.6. *Dixon* / **Edmund Saul Dixon**

The Chain [verse], 516–17. 1 col. £2.2.0. *Miss Procter* / **Adelaide Anne Procter**

Laid Up in Two Lodgings, ii: My London Lodging, 517–23. 12½ cols. £6.6.0. *Wilkie Collins* / **Wilkie Collins**

A Tale of a Pocket Archipelago [story], 523–27. 8 cols. £4.4.0. *Bayle St. John* / **Bayle St. John**

Keeping the Peace [Devon celebration of end of Crimean War], 527–28. 3¾ cols. £2.0.0. *Payn* / **James Payn**

June 21, 1856. No. 326, pp. 529–52

A Criminal Trial [conduct of], 529–34. 10½ cols. *Morley* / **Henry Morley**

Chip:
- Red Rockets [signals at sea], 534–35. 3 cols. £1.11.6. *Postans* / prob. **Robert Baxter Postans**

The Ninth of June, chaps. iv–vi, 535–41. 12 cols. *W.H.W.* / **W. H. Wills**

Gold in Great Britain, 541–43. 4¼ cols. £2.12.6. *Robert Hunt* / **Robert Hunt**

Navvies As They Used to Be, 543–50. 14½ cols. £7.7.0. *H. J. Brown* / **H. J. Brown**

Coast Folk, 550–52. 4¾ cols. £2.12.6. *Robertson* / prob. **John Robertson**

June 28, 1856. No. 327, pp. 553–76

Out of the Season [a watering place], 553–56. 7½ cols. *C.D.* / **Charles Dickens**

The Mofussil [corrupt administration of East India Co.], 556–59. 6¼ cols.; should read 5½. £3.0.0. *Capper* / **John Capper**

Chip:
- The Fairy Puff-Puff [railway in south Devon], 559–61. 3¼ cols. £2.12.6. *Payn* / **James Payn**

The Omnibus Revolution [omnibus service, London], 561–64. 6½ cols. £3.3.0. *Sala* / **George A. Sala**

Neighbour Nelly [verse], 564. ¾ col. £1.11.6. *R. Brough* / **Robert Barnabas Brough**

The Ninth of June, chaps. vii–x, 564–75. 20¾ cols. *W.H.W.* / **W. H. Wills**

Hints for the Self-Educated [admonition vs. pride and anti-social attitude], 575–76. 4 cols. £2.2.0. *Heraud* / **John Abraham Heraud**

July 5, 1856. No. 328, pp. 577–600

Belgian Flower-Growing, 577–83. 13½ cols. £7.17.6. *Dixon* / **Edmund Saul Dixon**

Marriage Gaolers [*Remarks upon the Law of Marriage and Divorce; Suggested by the Hon. Mrs. Norton's Letter to the Queen*, 1855 or 1856 ed.], 583–85. 4 cols. £2.2.0. *Miss Lynn* / **Eliza Lynn**

Scotch Coast Folk, 585–90. 10 cols.; should read 9¼. £4.14.6. *Robertson* / prob. **John Robertson**

The Grave in the Moorland [verse], 590. ¾ col. £1.11.6. *Miss Parr* / **Harriet Parr**

Eric Walderthorn [story], chaps. i–iii, 590–98. 16 cols. £7.10.0. *Mrs. Bateman* / prob. **Mrs. J. C. Bateman**

Chip:
- Pastor Rhadamanthus [clergymen as magistrates], 598–99. 1¼ cols. *Morley* / **Henry Morley**

Intellectual Fleas [training of fleas], 599–600. 3¾ cols. £2.12.6. *Buckland* / **Francis Trevelyan Buckland**

July 12, 1856. No. 329, pp. 601–620

Milverston Worthies [descr. of provincial town; stories about its inhabitants] [i], 601–605. 8 cols. £4.4.0. *Miss Parr* / **Harriet Parr**

The Rhododendron Garden [flower display, Chelsea], 605–606. 3 cols. *Morley* / **Henry Morley**

Eric Walderthorn, chaps. iv–vii, 606–616. 20 cols.; should read 19¼. £7.10.0. *Mrs. Bateman* / prob. **Mrs. J. C. Bateman**

A Way to Remember [understanding astronomical phenomena], 616–18. 4 cols. £2.2.0. *Heraud* / **John Abraham Heraud**

The Sandiman Mystery [story], 618–20. 5 cols. £2.12.6. *Payn* / **James Payn**

VOLUME XIV July 19 – December 27, 1856

July 19, 1856. No. 330, pp. 1–24

The Diary of Anne Rodway [story], chap. i, 1–7. 12¼ cols. £10.0.0. *Wilkie Collins* / **Wilkie Collins**

Bird History [Pierre Belon, *L'Histoire de la natvre des oyseavx*, 1555], 7–12. 11¾ cols.; should read 10½. £6.6.0. *Dudley Costello* / **Dudley Costello**

Rhine-Land [verse], 12–13. 1½ cols. £2.12.6. *Meredith* / **George Meredith**

Milverston Worthies [ii], 13–16. 6 cols. £3.3.0. *Miss Parr* / **Harriet Parr**

Scotch Coast Folk. Footdee in the Last Century, 16–20. 9 cols. £4.10.0. *Robertson* / prob. **John Robertson**

Chip:
– The Congressional Prize-Ring [fight between two U.S. congressmen, 1805], 20. 1 col. £0.10.6. *W.H.W.* / **W. H. Wills**

Charles the Fifth's Glove [Ghent], 20–24. 9 cols. £4.10.0. *Dixon* / **Edmund Saul Dixon**

July 26, 1856. No. 331, pp. 25–48

A Dish of Frogs [natural history; gastronomy], 25–30. 11½ cols. £5.15.6. *Costello* / **Dudley Costello**

The Diary of Anne Rodway, chap. ii, 30–38. 16 cols. £10.0.0. *Wilkie Collins* / **Wilkie Collins**

The Shadow of the Hand [verse], 38–39. 1 col. £2.2.0. *Miss Macready* / **Catherine Frances Macready**

Not Very Common Things [... *Prizes for Common Things Offered and Awarded by Miss Burdett Coutts*, 1856], 39–41. 4 cols. *Morley & W.H.W.* / **Henry Morley & W. H. Wills**

At the Sign of the Silver Horn [story], 41–46. 10 cols. £5.5.0. *Fitzgerald* / **Percy Fitzgerald**

Chip:
– Copy of Court-Roll [copyhold land tenure], 46. 1¼ cols. £1.1.0. *Head* / **John Oswald Head**

Milverston Worthies [iii], 46–48. 4½ cols. £2.12.6. *Miss Parr* / **Harriet Parr**

August 2, 1856. No. 332, pp. 49–72

A Campaign with the French [vs. Arabs in Algeria], 49–56. 14¼ cols. £7.7.0. *Measom* / **Malcolm Ronald Laing Meason**

The Scattering of Seed, 56–59. 6¾ cols. £3.13.6. *Warr* / **Warr**

Milverston Worthies [iv], 59–62. 5½ cols. £2.10.0. *Miss Parr* / **Harriet Parr**

Life and the Bird [verse], 62. 1½ cols. £2.2.0. *Ollier* / **Edmund Ollier**

The Opal Ring [story], 62–69. 13 cols. £7.17.6. *Miss Power* / **Marguerite A. Power**

At Bruges and Ostend, 69–72. 7½ cols. £4.4.0. *Dixon* / **Edmund Saul Dixon**

August 9, 1856. No. 333, pp. 73–96

Ego et Balbus [misinformation, vouched for as fact], 73–75. 4¾ cols. £2.12.6. *Payn* / **James Payn**

The Last Days of a German Revolution [1848–49], 75–81. 12 cols. £6.6.0. *Von Corvin & Morley* / **Otto von Corvin & Henry Morley**

English Coast Folk [British coast folk], 81–85. 8 cols. £4.4.0. *Robertson* / prob. **John Robertson**

Wishes [verse], 85. ½ col. £0.10.6. *Bennett* / **William Cox Bennett**

American Party Names [background of 1856 presidential election], 85–89. 7¼ cols. £3.13.6. *Olmsted & W.H.W.* / **Frederick Law Olmsted & W. H. Wills**

My Little Ward [story], 89–95. 12½ cols. £6.6.0. *Payn* / **James Payn**

Plurality of Mites [provinciality; limits of knowledge], 95–96. 3¼ cols. £2.2.0. *W. Brough* / **William Brough**

August 16, 1856. No. 334, pp. 97–120

Ushers [under-masters], 97–102. 10 cols. £5.5.0. *Payn* / **James Payn**

On 'Change in Paris [story], 102–108. 12¼ cols. £6.6.0. *W. B. Jerrold* / **William Blanchard Jerrold**

Apothecaries, 108–115. 13 cols. *Morley* / **Henry Morley**

The Giglio Festa [trade guilds fête, Italy], 115–18. 6 cols. £3.3.0. *Wreford* / **Henry G. Wreford**

Two Hundred Pounds Reward [story], 118–20. 5¾ cols. £3.3.0. *Payn* / **James Payn**

August 23, 1856. No. 335, pp. 121–44

My Spinsters [marriageable young ladies], 121–26. 12 cols. £6.6.0. *Wilkie Collins* / **Wilkie Collins**

Seaside Eggs [ova of shellfish, sharks, etc.], 126–30. 6 cols. £3.13.6. *Robertson* / prob. **John Robertson**

Chip:
– A Colonial Patriot [personal letter to Dickens], 130. 1½ cols. £1.1.0, payment presumably to correspondent. *Correspondent & Howitt* / **John Pascoe Fawkner**

Hawkswell Place [verse], 130–33. 5 cols. £5.5.0. *Miss Parr* / **Harriet Parr**

Slaves and Their Masters [Frederick Law Olmsted, *A Journey in the Seaboard Slave States*, 1856], 133–38. 10 cols. £5.5.0. *Miss Lynn & W.H.W.* / **Eliza Lynn & W. H. Wills**

Two-Pence an Hour [governesses], 138–40. 3½ cols.; should read 4½. £1.11.6. *Miss Parr* / **Harriet Parr**

Condemned to Death [in German prison], 140–44. 9 cols. £4.14.6. *Von Corvin & Morley* / **Otto von Corvin & Henry Morley**

August 30, 1856. No. 336, pp. 145–68

Nobody, Somebody, and Everybody [Govt. maladministration, evasion of responsibility], 145–47. 4 cols. *C.D.* / **Charles Dickens**

Beating against the Bars [in German prison], 147–54. 15 cols. £8.0.0. *Von Corvin & Morley* / **Otto von Corvin & Henry Morley**

Timber-Bending [new American method of], 154–56. 4 cols. £2.2.0. *Ollier* / **Edmund Ollier**

The Angel of Love [verse], 156–57. 1½ cols. £2.2.0. *Miss Macready* / **Catherine Frances Macready**

Mother Shipton [in large part from *Mother Shiptons Prophesies*, 1663], 157–64. 13¾ cols. £7.0.0. *Costello* / **Dudley Costello**

Chip:
– Pen and Ink Pies [writing for periodicals], 164. 1 col. £0.10.6. *Dixon* / **Edmund Saul Dixon**

Schobry the Bandit [Hungarian bandit], 164–68. 9 cols. £4.4.0. *Fonblanque & Morley* / **Fonblanque & Henry Morley**

September 6, 1856. No. 337, pp. 169–92

My Black Mirror [travel on the Continent], 169–75. 12½ cols. £6.16.6. *Wilkie Collins* / **Wilkie Collins**

The Orsons of East Africa [Richard F. Burton, *First Footsteps in East Africa*, 1856], 175–79. 9 cols. *Morley* / **Henry Morley**

Chip:
– Signals and Engine-Drivers, 179–80. 1¼ cols. £0.10.6. *Head* / **John Oswald Head**

My Journal [verse], 180–81. 1¼ cols. £2.2.0. *Miss Procter* / **Adelaide Anne Procter**

Taxes, 181–85. 8½ cols. £4.14.6. *Dixon* / **Edmund Saul Dixon**

Sir Caribert of the Leaf [story], 185–90. 11¾ cols. £6.6.0. *White* / **the Rev. James White**

The North against the South [nature of northern and southern peoples], 190–92. 4 cols. £2.2.0. *Heraud* / **John Abraham Heraud**

September 13, 1856. No. 338, pp. 193–216

To Think, or Be Thought For? [the cant of Art criticism], 193–98. 10 cols. £5.5.0. *Wilkie Collins* / **Wilkie Collins**

Mr. Speckles on Himself [story], 198–201. 7½ cols. *Morley* / **Henry Morley**

Fly Leaves [houseflies], 201–205. 7½ cols. £3.13.6. *The Revd. C. H. Townshend* / **Chauncy Hare Townshend**

Six Years in a Cell [in German prison], 205–213. 16 cols. £8.8.0. *Von Corvin & Morley* / **Otto von Corvin & Henry Morley**

Perfectly Contented [English life and customs, past and present], 213–16. 7 cols. £3.13.6. *Brown & Morley* / **Browne** or **Brown & Henry Morley**

September 20, 1856. No. 339, pp. 217–40

From Paris to Chelmsford [livestock and agric. exhibitions], 217–23. 12¾ cols. £7.0.0. *Sidney* / **Samuel Sidney**

Down at Red Grange [story], 223–27. 8½ cols. £4.14.6. *Fitzgerald* / **Percy Fitzgerald**

Chip:
– Soden [recommendation of German spa], 227–28. 2½ cols. £1.11.6. *Von Corvin & Morley* / **Otto von Corvin & Henry Morley**

Love of Beauty [verse], 228–29. 1 col. £2.2.0. *Harris* / **Harris**

Royal Treasures [Léon E. S. J. de Laborde, *Notice des émaux, bijoux et objets divers, exposés dans les galeries du Musée du Louvre*, 1853], 229–34. 11¼ cols. £7.17.6. *Costello* / **Dudley Costello**

Our Poisonous Wild Flowers [Charles Johnson, *British Poisonous Plants*, 1856], 234–36. 4 cols. *Morley* / **Henry Morley**

How We Lost Our Minister [story], 236–40. 8 cols. £4.4.0. *Payn* / **James Payn**

September 27, 1856. No. 340, pp. 241–64

Sea-Gardens [marine flora and fauna], 241–45. 8 cols. £4.4.0. *Robertson* / prob. **John Robertson**

Dick Dallington [story], 245–52. 14 cols. £7.7.0. *Sidney* / **Samuel Sidney**

An Autumn Shadow [verse], 252. 1 col. £2.2.0. *Miss Parr* / **Harriet Parr**

Agricultural Machinery, 252–56. 7½ cols. £3.13.6. *Sidney* / **Samuel Sidney**

Quiet People [people without opinions], 256–58. 4¾ cols. £2.12.6. *Heraud* / **John Abraham Heraud**

St. George and the Dragon [from 17-cent. chronicle], 258–61. 6 cols. £3.0.0. *R[?]. Wilson* / **R.? Wilson**

A Flat Walk [from Calais to Guînes], 261–64. 7¼ cols. £3.13.6. *R. Brough* / **Robert Barnabas Brough**

October 4, 1856. No. 341, pp. 265–88

A Journey Due North [Russia: descr. and travel] [i], 265–76. 22 cols. £240 for the 22 instalments, plus some additional payment (so stated in Straus, *Sala*, chap. viii). *Sala* / **George A. Sala**

A Wife's Pardon [verse], 276. ½ col. £0.10.6. *Miss Power* / **Marguerite A. Power**

Black and Blue [account of a half-caste, prob. factual], 276–82. 12½ cols. £6.6.0. *Laing* / **John Lang**

Our Iron Constitution [iron and steel manufacture], 282–87. 9 cols. *Morley* / **Henry Morley**

Mad Dancing [Belgian and French festivities], 287–88. 4 cols. £2.2.0. *Miss Costello* / **Louisa Stuart Costello**

October 11, 1856. No. 342, pp. 289–312

The Murdered Person [i.e., literal and figurative: general unconcern for], 289–91. 5 cols. *C.D.* / **Charles Dickens**

The World Unseen [microscopic organisms], 291–96. 9¾ cols. £5.5.0. *Dixon* / **Edmund Saul Dixon**

Salome and I [story], chaps. i–ii, 296–301. 9½ cols. £16.0.0 for the 3 instalments. *T. Speight* / **Thomas Wilkinson Speight**

The Burthen Lightened [verse], 301. 1½ cols. £3.3.0. *Miss Lynn's friend* / **Eliza Lynn's friend**

A Journey Due North [ii], 301–308. 14 cols. *Sala* / **George A. Sala**

An Indian Court Circular [William Knighton, *The Private Life of an Eastern King*, 1855], 308–312. 8½ cols. £4.4.0. *Dixon* / **Edmund Saul Dixon**

October 18, 1856. No. 343, pp. 313–36

Health and Education [young ladies' schools], 313–17. 9½ cols. £5.5.0. *Carter* / **Robert Brudenell Carter**

Salome and I, chaps. iii–iv, 317–22. 10 cols. *T. Speight* / **Thomas Wilkinson Speight**

The Shingle Movement, 322–24. 4½ cols. £2.2.0. *Postans* / prob. **Robert Baxter Postans**

A Journey Due North [iii], 324–32. 15½ cols. *Sala* / **George A. Sala**

A Dull Day on Exmoor, 332–36. 9 cols. £4.14.6. *Payn* / **James Payn**

October 25, 1856. No. 344, pp. 337–60

Talk-Stoppers [interrupters of conversation], 337–42. 11 cols. £6.16.6. *W. Collins* / **Wilkie Collins**

Under-Water Existence [*Crustacea, Mollusca*, etc.], 342–47. 10½ cols. £5.5.0. *Robertson* / prob. **John Robertson**

Chip:
– The National Gallery and the Old Masters ["restorations" on Velazquez's *Boar Hunt*], 347–48. 2 cols. £1.12.0. *W. Collins* / **Wilkie Collins**

The Faithful Mirror [verse], 348. ¼ col. £1.1.0. *B. Brough* / **Robert Barnabas Brough**

A Journey Due North [iv], 348–55. 13½ cols. *Sala* / **George A. Sala**

Salome and I, chaps. v–vi, 355–60. 11 cols. *T. Speight* / **Thomas Wilkinson Speight**

November 1, 1856. No. 345, 361–84

Lost in the Pit [colliery disaster, Wales, July 1856], 361–66. 10¼ cols. *Morley* / **Henry Morley**

A Day of Reckoning [story], chaps. i–iii, 366–72. 12¾ cols.; should read 11¾. £7.7.0. *Miss Parr* / **Harriet Parr**

Monmouth [verse], 372–73. 2½ cols. £3.3.0. *Meredith* / **George Meredith**

A Journey Due North [v], 373–77. 7¾ cols. *Sala* / **George A. Sala**

Microscopics, 377–81. 9¾ cols.; should read 9. £5.5.0. *Dixon* / **Edmund Saul Dixon**

The Captain of the Boats [recollections of Eton], 381–84. 6½ cols. £3.13.6. *Delaware Lewis* / **John Delaware Lewis**

November 8, 1856. No. 346, pp. 385–408

Two Difficult Cases: The First Case [Spencer Cowper *et al* tried for murder, 1699], 385–91. 12 cols. £5.5.0. *Miss French & Miss Jewsbury's friend* / **Miss French & Geraldine Endsor Jewsbury's friend**

The Purple Shore [marine flora and fauna], 391–95. 9 cols. £4.14.6. *Robertson* / prob. **John Robertson**

Chip:
– A Blank Prize [lottery swindles], 395–96. 2¼ cols. £1.5.0. *Fonblanque* / **Fonblanque**

Springs in the Desert [verse], 396–97. 1½ cols. £2.2.0. *Miss Macready* / **Catherine Frances Macready**

A Journey Due North [vi], 397–402. 10 cols. *Sala* / **George A. Sala**

A Day of Reckoning, chaps. iv–vii, 402–408. 12¾ cols. £7.7.0. *Miss Parr* / **Harriet Parr**

November 15, 1856. No. 347, pp. 409–432

The First Vigilance Committees [in California], 409–416. 14 cols. £7.7.0. *Bergenroth* / **Gustav Adolf Bergenroth**

Kester's Evil Eye [story], 416–21. 12 cols. £6.6.0. *Miss Parr* / **Harriet Parr**

The Life-Shore [verse], 421–22. 1½ cols. £3.3.0. *Miss Parr* / **Harriet Parr**

A Journey Due North [vii], 422–27. 10½ cols. *Sala* / **George A. Sala**

The Poor Man's Fish [pilchard fishing, Cornwall], 427–30. 5½ cols. £3.3.0. *T. Hood* / **Tom Hood**

Where I Found an Owl's Nest [Trebizond], 430–32. 5 cols. £2.12.6. *Carter* / **Robert Brudenell Carter**

November 22, 1856. No. 348, pp. 433–56

American Changes of Names, 433–36. 7¾ cols. £4.0.0. *Colley Grattan* / **Thomas Colley Grattan**

The Forbidden Fruit [story], 436–40. 7¾ cols. £4.4.0. *Miss Power* / **Marguerite A. Power**

Minims [microscopic examination of], 440–45. 10¾ cols. £6.0.0. *Dixon* / **Edmund Saul Dixon**

Word Analogies [verse], 445. ½ col. £1.1.0. *Miss Lynn's friend* / **Eliza Lynn's friend**

A Journey Due North [viii], 445–53. 15 cols. *Sala* / **George A. Sala**

John Houghton's Wisdom [Houghton, *A Collection for Improvement of Husbandry and Trade*, 1681–1703], 453–56. 6¾ cols. £3.13.6. *Dodd* / **George Dodd**

November 29, 1856. No. 349, pp. 457–80

Justice at Naples [treatment of political prisoners], 457–60. 6½ cols. £3.13.6. *D. L. Meadowes* / **D. L. Meadowes**

My Brother Robert [story], 460–64. 9¾ cols. £5.5.0. *Miss Parr* / **Harriet Parr**

Psellism [stammering], 464–69. 8½ cols. £4.14.6. *Dixon* / **Edmund Saul Dixon**

A Journey Due North [ix], 469–73. 8 cols. *Sala* / **George A. Sala**

Two Difficult Cases: Case the Second [Mary Blandy, murderess, hanged 1752], 473–75. 5 cols. *Morley* / **Henry Morley**

Suburban Belgium [residence in], 475–80. 10 cols. £5.5.0. *B. Brough* / **Robert Barnabas Brough**

December 6, 1856. No. 350, pp. 481–504

A Petition to the Novel-Writers [characteristics of contemp. popular fiction], 481–85. 9½ cols. *Wilkie Collins* / **Wilkie Collins**

The Frenchman of Two Wives [criminal case, France, 17 cent.], 485–90. 10¾ cols.; should read 9¾. £5.15.6. *Miss Jewsbury* / **Geraldine Endsor Jewsbury**

John Houghton's Advertisements [in Houghton, *A Collection for Improvement of Husbandry and Trade*, 1692–1703], 490–93. 6 cols. £3.3.0. *Dodd* / **George Dodd**

Patient and Faithful [verse], 493. ¾ col. £2.2.0. *Yates* / **Adelaide Anne Procter**

A Journey Due North [x], 493–98. 9¾ cols. *Sala* / **George A. Sala**

Monsters [mythical], 498–504. 12 cols. £6.16.6. *Dudley Costello* / **Dudley Costello**

December 13, 1856. No. 351, pp. 505–528

Bold Words by a Bachelor [wife's jealousy of husband's friends], 505–507. 5¾ cols. *Wilkie Collins* / **Wilkie Collins**

Aluminium, 507–510. 6 cols. £3.3.0. *Dixon & W.H.W.* / **Edmund Saul Dixon & W. H. Wills**

The Poor Clare [story], chap. i, 510–15. 10 cols. £25.0.0 for the 3 instalments. *Mrs. Gaskell* / **Elizabeth Gaskell**

A Journey Due North [xi], 515–24. 16 cols. *Sala* / **George A. Sala**

Cyrano de Bergerac, 524–28. 10¼ cols. £5.15.6. *Oxenford* / **John Oxenford**

December 20, 1856. No. 352, pp. 529–52

A Petty Protector [Jörgen Jörgensen, Danish adventurer], 529–32. 7 cols. *Morley* / **Henry Morley**

The Poor Clare, chap. ii, 532–44. 23½ cols. *Mrs. Gaskell* / **Elizabeth Gaskell**

The Better [verse], 544. ¾ col. £1.11.6. *Dr. Kennedy* / **Dr. Kennedy**

A Journey Due North [xii], 544–50. 12¼ cols. *Sala* / **George A. Sala**

What Is to Become of Chatham? [dockyard], 550–52. 4 cols. £2.2.0. *Morley & J. C. Gooder* / **Henry Morley & James Chisholm Gooden**

Christmas 1856. Extra Christmas Number: The Wreck of the Golden Mary. Being the Captain's Account of the Loss of the Ship, and the Mate's Account of the Great Deliverance of Her People in an Open Boat at Sea, pp. 1–36. Running date: Dec. 6. Stated on title page of Vol. XIV as included in that vol.; title and section titles of the three parts listed at end of "Contents" of that vol.

The Wreck

[The Captain's Account: no separate title in Office Book or in *H.W.*], 1–10. 20 cols. *C.D.* / **Charles Dickens**

John Steadiman's Account [title thus in Office Book; sentence-title in *H.W.*], 11–13. 5 cols. *Wilkie Collins* / **Wilkie Collins**

The Beguilement in the Boats [story titles as in Office Book; no separate titles in *H.W.*]

The Armourer's Story,* 13–18. 10 cols. £8.8.0. *Fitzgerald* / **Percy Fitzgerald**

Poor Dick's Story,† 18–21. 6¾ cols. £5.5.0. *Miss Parr* / **Harriet Parr**

The Supercargo's Story, 21–25. 7½ cols. £5.5.0. *Fitzgerald* / **Percy Fitzgerald**

The Old Sailor's Story‡ [verse], 25–27. 4¼ cols.; should read 3½. £5.5.0. *Miss Procter* / **Adelaide Anne Procter**

The Scotch Boy's Story, 27–29. 5 cols. £4.4.0. *White* / **the Rev. James White**

The Deliverance, 30–36. 14 cols. *Wilkie Collins* / **Wilkie Collins**

*In this and in the other prose stories of "The Beguilement," passages identifying the narrator and linking him with the framework are not set off typographically from the stories themselves. Dickens and Collins collaborated on the number. For suggestion as to the link passages or parts of the link passages probably written by each, see Stone, ed., *Charles Dickens' Uncollected Writings from Household words*. In reprinting "The Armourer's Story," Fitzgerald deleted from the opening paragraph only the explanatory comment "(It was the Armourer who spun this yarn.)."

†The hymn that concludes "Poor Dick's Story" has been attributed to Dickens (see identification note on Miss Parr). Miss Parr reprinted the entire "Poor Dick" item.

‡Introduced by a 4-line paragraph identifying the narrator and linking him with the framework.

December 27, 1856. No. 353, pp. 553–72

King Missirie [Hôtel d'Angleterre, Constantinople], 553–56. 8 cols. £4.4.0. *Carter* / **Robert Brudenell Carter**

I Promise to Pay [bank-notes], 556–59. 6 cols. £3.3.0. *Dodd & W.H.W.* / **George Dodd & W. H. Wills**

The Poor Clare, chap. iii, 559–65. 10½ cols. *Mrs. Gaskell* / **Elizabeth Gaskell**

A Christmas Carol [verse], 565. 1¼ cols. £2.2.0. ——— / ———

A Journey Due North [xiii], 565–69. 6¾ cols. *Sala* / **George A. Sala**

Left, and Never Called For [the lonely, unsuccessful, unhappy], 569–72. 7 cols. £3.3.0. *Payn* / **James Payn**

VOLUME XV January 3 – June 27, 1857

January 3, 1857. No. 354, pp. 1–24

Murderous Extremes [over-reliance on police; individual responsibility], 1–2. 3¾ cols. *C.D.* / **Charles Dickens**

A Journey Due North [xiv], 2–8. 10 cols. *Sala* / **George A. Sala**

Crédit Mobilier, 8–12. 9½ cols.; should read 8½. £5.5.0. *Dixon* / **Edmund Saul Dixon**

The Dead Secret [novel], chap. i, 12–18. 12 cols. *Wilkie Collins* / **Wilkie Collins**

Two Days at Sinope, 18–23. 9¾ cols. £5.15.6. *Carter* / **Robert Brudenell Carter**

A Few Really Great Men [giants], 23–24. 3¾ cols. *Morley* / **Henry Morley**

January 10, 1857. No. 355, pp. 25–48

The Lambeth-Marsh Mulcibers [steam-engine construction works], 25–27. 5¾ cols. £3.3.0. *W.H.W.* / **W. H. Wills**

Slavery at Surinam [W. R. van Hoëvell, *Slaven en vrijen,* 1855 ed.], 27–32. 8 cols.; should read 8¾. £3.13.6. *C. H. Gunn* / **Charles Hains Gunn**

Chip:
– A Side Wind from Due North [correction of error in "Journey Due North," Nov. 15, 1856], 32. ¼ col. *Sala* / **George A. Sala**

Weeds [based on abstracts of Irish agric. statistics for 1856], 32–35. 6 cols. *Morley* / **Henry Morley**

The Brave Women of Tann [verse], 35–36. 1½ cols. £2.2.0. *Miss Lynn's friend* / **Eliza Lynn's friend**

The Dead Secret, chap. ii, 36–41. 11¼ cols. *Wilkie Collins* / **Wilkie Collins**

The Gift of Tongues [need for study of modern foreign languages], 41–43. 4 cols. £2.2.0. *Jerdan* / **William Jerdan**

Odd Fish [accounts from Pliny and other writers], 43–48. 10 cols. £4.14.6. *Costello* / **Dudley Costello**

January 17, 1857. No. 356, pp. 49–72

Something That Shakespeare Lost [conjectural 17-cent. reviews of *Hamlet*], 49–52. 6 cols. *Morley* / **Henry Morley**

A Journey Due North [xv], 52–55. 7 cols. *Sala* / **George A. Sala**

Calumet Island [story], 55–59. 7 cols. £3.13.6. *E. Yates* / **Edmund Yates**

Hammering It In [current interest in geology], 59–60. 3¾ cols. *Morley* / **Henry Morley**

A Daisy on a Grave [verse], 60–61. 1¼ cols. £1.11.6. *Mrs. Broderip* / **Frances Freeling Broderip**

The Dead Secret, chap. iii, 61–67. 11½ cols. *Wilkie Collins* / **Wilkie Collins**

The Coco-Palm, 67–72. 11¾ cols. £6.6.0. *Robertson* / prob. **John Robertson**

January 24, 1857. No. 357, pp. 73–96

Fiction Crushing [doubtful authenticity of events and persons commonly accepted as historical], 73–76. 8 cols. £4.4.0. *White* / **the Rev. James White**

The Soulages Collection [at Marlborough House], 76–80. 7½ cols. £4.0.0. *Dodd* / **George Dodd**

A Journey Due North [xvi], 80–84. 8½ cols. *Sala* / **George A. Sala**

Gone Before [verse], 84–85. ½ col. £1.1.0. *E. Yates* / **Edmund Yates**

The Dead Secret, chap. iv. 85–90. 10 cols. *Collins* / **Wilkie Collins**

Promotion, French and English [military], 90–92. 6 cols. £3.0.0. *Reeves* / **Reeves**

The Poisoner of Springs [incident in writer's travel in Italy], 92–96. 8 cols. £4.4.0. *George Cayley* / **George John Cayley**

January 31, 1857. No. 358, pp. 97–120

Men Made by Machinery [address of Edwin Chadwick on improvements in machinery as affecting condition of labourers, reported in *Jour. of the Society of Arts*, Nov. 14, Dec. 26, 1856], 97–100. 7 cols. *Morley* / **Henry Morley**

Coco-Eaters [human and animal], 100–107. 14 cols.; should read 13¼. £6.16.6. *Robertson* / prob. **John Robertson**

Memnon and His Mate [verse], 107–108. 2 cols. £3.3.0. *T. M. Holme* / **T. M. Holme**

The Dead Secret, chap. v, 108–114. 12½ cols. *Wilkie Collins* / **Wilkie Collins**

The Stoker's Poetry [poetry implicit in railways], 114–16. 4½ cols. £2.12.6. *Thornbury* / **George Walter Thornbury**

A Journey Due North [xvii], 116–20. 8 cols. *Sala* / **George A. Sala**

February 7, 1857. No. 359, pp. 121–44

A Testimony in Praise of Testimonials [French decorations of merit and their English equivalent], 121–24. 6½ cols. £3.13.6. *White* / **the Rev. James White**

Wolves, 124–28. 9¼ cols. £4.14.6. *Dudley Costello* / **Dudley Costello**

Our Specialities [account of Guînes], 128–33. 10 cols. £5.5.0. *Dixon* / **Edmund Saul Dixon**

The Dead Secret, chap. vi, 133–39. 11¾ cols. *Wilkie Collins* / **Wilkie Collins**

Hovelling [salvaging wrecked vessels and their cargoes and crews], 139–42. 5 cols. £2.12.6. *Laing* / **John Lang**

Crumpled Rose-Leaves at St. Boniface [the college fellow], 142–44. 6 cols. £3.3.0. *Payn* / **James Payn**

February 14, 1857. No. 360, pp. 145–68

The Lost English Sailors [England's duty to make further search for Franklin expedition], 145–47. 5¾ cols. *Morley* / **Henry Morley**

A Journey Due North [xviii], 147–53. 11½ cols. *Sala* / **George A. Sala**

Sketching at a Slave Auction [in Virginia], 153–56. 5 cols. £2.12.6. *E. Crowe, Junr.* / **Eyre Crowe**

The Music of the Winds [verse], 156. ½ col. £1.1.0. *Graham* / **Graham**

The Dead Secret, chaps. vii–viii, 156–62. 12¾ cols. *Wilkie Collins* / **Wilkie Collins**

A Parisian Polite Letter Writer [Paul Persan, *Le Secrétaire universel*], 162–65. 5¾ cols. £3.0.0. *Sidney* / **Samuel Sidney**

My Ghosts [a spectre-haunted childhood], 165–68. 6½ cols. £3.13.6. *Robertson* / prob. **John Robertson**

February 21, 1857. No. 361, pp. 169–92

The Murder of the Archbishop of Paris [Jan. 3, 1857], chaps. i–iii, 169–75. 12 cols. £6.6.0. *Robertson* / prob. **John Robertson**

A Journey Due North [xix], 175–80. 10¼ cols. *Sala* / **George A. Sala**

Winter [verse], 180–81. 1¾ cols. £2.2.0. *Chester* / **J. Chester**

The Dead Secret, chap. ix, 181–90. 18 cols. *Wilkie Collins* / **Wilkie Collins**

A Room near Chancery Lane [work of the Patent Office], 190–92. 6 cols. £3.3.0. *Dodd* / **George Dodd**

February 28, 1857. No. 362, pp. 193–216

They Order This Matter Better in France? [*claque* system in theatre], 193–96. 7 cols. £3.13.6. *Fitzgerald* / **Percy Fitzgerald**

Mummy, 196–98. 3¼ cols. *Morley* / **Henry Morley**

A Journey Due North [xx], 198–203. 9½ cols. *Sala* / **George A. Sala**

Chip:
– Compromising Compromises [lawyers' chicanery], 203. 1½ cols. £1.1.0. *W.H.W.* / **W. H. Wills**

The Sighing Shade [verse], 203–204. 1 col. £2.2.0. *Miss Parr* / **Harriet Parr**

The Dead Secret, chaps. x–xi, 204–210. 11½ cols. *Wilkie Collins* / **Wilkie Collins**

The Murder of the Archbishop of Paris, chaps. iv–v, 210–16. 13¾ cols. £7.7.0. *Robertson* / prob. **John Robertson**

March 7, 1857. No. 363, pp. 217–40

Stores for the First of April [private and public foolishness], 217–22. 10 cols. *C.D.* / **Charles Dickens**

Chip:
– Hovelling [reader's suggestion on derivation of word], 222. ¼ col. *Item not in Office Book* / ———

A Journey Due North [xxi], 222–27. 10¾ cols. *Sala* / **George A. Sala**

Song of an Exile [verse], 227–28. ½ col. £1.1.0. *Anonymous* / ———

The Dead Secret, chap. xii, 228–34. 13 cols. *Wilkie Collins* / **Wilkie Collins**

Many Needles in One Housewife [lodging-house for working girls], 234–36. 4½ cols. *Morley* / **Henry Morley**

Perfumes [George W. S. Piesse, *The Art of Perfumery*, 1855], 236–40. 8 cols. £4.4.0. *Miss Lynn* / **Eliza Lynn**

March 14, 1857. No. 364, pp. 241–64

The Predatory Art [as perfected by James T. Saward, William J. Robson, Leopold Redpath, John D. Paul, and others], 241–46. 10 cols. *Morley* / **Henry Morley**

Little Commissions [impositions of friends], 246–49. 6¼ cols. £3.3.0. ——— *& Morley* / ——— **& Henry Morley**

A Journey Due North [xxii], 249–54. 10 cols. £5.5.0. *Sala* / **George A. Sala**

The Dead Secret, chap. xiii, 254–60. 12¾ cols. *Wilkie Collins* / **Wilkie Collins**

Across Country [S. N. Carvalho, *Incidents of Travel ... in the Far West*, 1857], 260–64. 10 cols.; should read 9¼. *Morley* / **Henry Morley**

March 21, 1857. No. 365, pp. 265–88

The Himalaya Club [social life, India], 265–72. 15¼ cols. £8.8.0. *Lang* / **John Lang**

A Whale in Whitechapel [exhibit of], 272–75. 6¾ cols. £3.13.6. *Frank Buckland* / **Francis Trevelyan Buckland**

The Midnight Boat [verse], 275–76. 1¾ cols. £3.3.0. *Owen O'Ryan* / **Owen O'Ryan**

The Dead Secret, chap. xiv, 276–83. 14¼ cols. *Wilkie Collins* / **Wilkie Collins**

The Humble Confession of a Tenor [story], 283–85. 4 cols. £2.2.0. *H. O. Pearson* / **H. O. Pearson**

Jemima Court-House [social life of a Virginia town], 285–88. 6¼ cols. £3.3.0. *John Samuel* / **John Samuel**

March 28, 1857. No. 366, pp. 289–312

The Collier at Home, 289–92. 7 cols. *Morley* / **Henry Morley**

How the Avalanche Comes Down at Barèges, 292–94. 4 cols. £2.2.0. *Miss Martin* / **Miss Martin**

A Vision of a Studious Man [story], 294–99. 11 cols. £5.15.6. *Fitzgerald* / **Percy Fitzgerald**

Chip:
– A Puzzling Gazetteer [American place-names], 299–300. 2 cols. *Morley* / **Henry Morley**

The Dead Secret, chap. xv, 300–306. 13 cols. *Wilkie Collins* / **Wilkie Collins**

Bashi-Bazouks, 306–312. 12 cols. £6.6.0. *Carter* / **Robert Brudenell Carter**

April 4, 1857. No. 367, pp. 313–36

Shadows of the Golden Image [life in Tasmania in 1851], 313–18. 10 cols. £5.0.0. *Mrs. Meredith* / **Louisa Anne Meredith**

Chip:
– The Lawyer's Best Friends [laws and law reform], 318–19. 2¾ cols. £1.10.0. *J. O. Head* / **John Oswald Head**

Circassia [Julien-François Jeannel, *Excursion en Circassie,* 1856], 319–25. 11 cols. £5.15.6. *Dudley Costello* / **Dudley Costello**

Her Grave [verse], 325. ½ col. £1.1.0. *Owen O'Ryan* / **Owen O'Ryan**

Long Life under Difficulties [life of "Old Parr"], 325–28. 7½ cols. £3.13.6. *White* / **the Rev. James White**

The Art of Unfattening [Jean François Dancel, *Préceptes ... pour diminuer l'embonpoint,* 1850], 328–32. 7 cols. £3.13.6. *Dixon* / **Edmund Saul Dixon**

A Mother [story], 332–36. 9½ cols. £6.6.0. *Miss Lynn* / **Eliza Lynn**

April 11, 1857. No. 368, pp. 337–60

Election Time [electioneering tactics], 337–40. 7¾ cols. £2.12.6. *Mr. Logsden & Morley* / **Logsden & Henry Morley**

Our Ducasse [Flemish fête], 340–44. 8 cols. £4.4.0. *Dixon* / **Edmund Saul Dixon**

My London Ghosts [Newton, Bacon, and others], 344–49. 9 cols. £4.14.6. *Robertson* / prob. **John Robertson**

The Dead Secret, chap. xvi, 349–55. 11¼ cols. *Wilkie Collins* / **Wilkie Collins**

Old Scraps of Science, 355–57. 4¼ cols. £2.2.0. *Jerdan* / **William Jerdan**

A Forgotten Notability [Pierre de la Ramée], 357–60. 7½ cols. £4.0.0. *Miss Lynn* / **Eliza Lynn**

April 18, 1857. No. 369, pp. 361–84

Westminster Elections, 361–66. 11 cols. £3.13.6. *Logsden & Morley* / **Logsden & Henry Morley**

A Few Pleasant French Gentlemen [clever criminals], 366–69. 6 cols. £3.3.0. *Miss Lynn* / **Eliza Lynn**

The Cat, 369–73. 8 cols. £3.3.0. *Morley & Dixon* / **Henry Morley & Edmund Saul Dixon**

The Summer-Land [verse], 373. ½ col. *Item not in Office Book* / **Harris**

The Dead Secret, chaps. xvii–xviii, 373–80. 13 cols. *Wilkie Collins* / **Wilkie Collins**

Chip:
– Coprolite, 380–81. 2 cols. *Correspondent* / ———

An Experience of Austria [writer's imprisonment], 381–84. 8 cols. £4.4.0. *J. Lang* / **John Lang**

April 25, 1857. No. 370, pp. 385–408

Official Patriotism [Lady Franklin's appeals for search for Franklin expedition; Govt. inaction], 385–90. 11 cols. *Morley* / **Henry Morley**

Charnwood [Cistercian monastery], 390–93. 6½ cols. £3.3.0. *Speight* / **Thomas Wilkinson Speight**

Germans in Texas [Frederick Law Olmsted, *A Journey through Texas,* 1857], 393–97. 7 cols. *Morley* / **Henry Morley**

The Dead Secret, chaps. xix–xx, 397–405. 16 cols. *W. Collins* / **Wilkie Collins**

Wehrwolves, 405–408. 6¾ cols. £3.13.6. *Ollier* / **Edmund Ollier**

May 2, 1857. No. 371, pp. 409–32

Mercy in Naples [persecution of Italian officer], 409–411. 4½ cols. £2.10.0. *Wreford* / **Henry G. Wreford**

To My Young Friends [discourse on attitude to elders], 411–14. 7 cols. £3.13.6. *Dixon* / **Edmund Saul Dixon**

Crystals, 414–19. 9 cols. £4.14.6. *Carter* / **Robert Brudenell Carter**

Pan [verse], 419–20. 1¼ cols. £2.2.0. *Ollier* / **Edmund Ollier**

The Dead Secret, chap. xxi, 420–25. 10¾ cols. *Wilkie Collins* / **Wilkie Collins**

Manners Made to Order [Eliza Leslie, *The Behaviour Book*, 1853], 425–27. 4 cols. £2.2.0. *W. B. Jerrold* / **William Blanchard Jerrold**

Dragons, Griffins, and Salamanders, 427–32. 11¾ cols. £5.5.0. *Costello* / **Dudley Costello**

May 9, 1857. No. 372, pp. 433–56

The New Boy at Styles's [story], 433–40. 15 cols. £7.17.6. *H. Spicer* / **Henry Spicer**

An Old Peace Conference [Utrecht, 1713], 440–43. 7 cols. £3.13.6. *Fitzgerald* / **Percy Fitzgerald**

Two Millions of Tons of Silver [silver in sea water], 443–45. 3 cols. £1.11.6. *Harvey* / **Harvey**

The Lattice [verse], 445. ½ col. £1.1.0. *Fanny Hall* / **Fanny Hall**

The Dead Secret, chap. xxii, 445–50. 10¾ cols. *Wilkie Collins* / **Wilkie Collins**

Canton-English, 450–52. 3¾ cols. £2.2.0. *Mylne* / **William Charles Milne**

The Metropolitan Cattle Market [in Copenhagen Fields], 452–56. 8½ cols. £4.4.0. *Sidney* / **Samuel Sidney**

May 16, 1857. No. 373, pp. 457–80

Grand Jury Powers [exemplified in case of Dr. Charles Snape, 1856], 457–63. 12 cols. *Morley* / **Henry Morley**

Royally "Hard Up" [a German spa, after the season], 463–66. 9¼ cols.; should read 6¾. £4.14.6. *Fitzgerald* / **Percy Fitzgerald**

May-Meeting at Westminster [Parliamentary inaction on needed domestic legislation], 466–67. 2½ cols. *Item not in Office Book* / ———

Late in Spring [verse], 467–68. 1½ cols. £2.2.0. *Mrs. MacIntosh* / **Mrs. MacIntosh**

The Dead Secret, chap. xxiii, 468–74. 12 cols. *W. Collins* / **Wilkie Collins**

Chips:
- Revivals [rejuvenescence], 474–75. 2¼ cols. £1.1.0. *Miss Lynn* / **Eliza Lynn**
- The Samaritan Institution [correction of statement in "Predatory Art," March 14], 475. ¼ col. *C.D.* / **Charles Dickens**

Our Boys and Girls [schooling of English children in France, specifically in Guînes], 475–80. 10 cols. £5.5.0. *Dixon* / **Edmund Saul Dixon**

May 23, 1857. No. 374, pp. 481–504

Comets, and Their Tails of Prophets [supposed portents of disaster], 481–84. 6½ cols. £3.13.6. *Ollier* / **Edmund Ollier**

The Painter's Pet [story], 484–90. 12¾ cols. £7.0.0. *Miss Power* / **Marguerite A. Power**

One of Her Majesty's Usual Customs [customs regulations; sale of forfeited imports], 490–93. 6 cols. £3.3.0. *Dodd* / **George Dodd**

Return [verse], 493–94. 1¼ cols. £2.12.6. *Owen O'Ryan* / **Owen O'Ryan**

The Dead Secret, chap. xxiv, 494–500. 12¾ cols. *Wilkie Collins* / **Wilkie Collins**

Chip:
- Monthly Salaries [for Govt. clerks], 500–501. 1 col. *Correspondent* / ———

To My Elderly Friends [advice on conduct of life], 501–504. 8 cols. £4.4.0. *Dixon* / **Edmund Saul Dixon**

May 30, 1857. No. 375, pp. 505–528

Witchcraft and Old Boguey, 505–511. 13 cols. £6.16.6. *Costello* / **Dudley Costello**

Crime's Artificial Flowers [J.B., *Scenes from the Lives of Robson and Redpath*, 1857; and a murder melodrama], 511–15. 9 cols. £4.14.6. *Payn* / **James Payn**

Weariness [verse], 515–16. ½ col. £0.10.6. *Heraud* / **John Abraham Heraud**

The Dead Secret, chap. xxv, 516–22. 13½ cols. *Wilkie Collins* / **Wilkie Collins**

The Nerves, 522–25. 6½ cols. £3.3.0. *C. W. Mann* / **Christopher Wharton Mann**

Family Names [Nathaniel I. Bowditch, *Suffolk Surnames*, 1857], 525–28. 6¾ cols. £3.10.0. *White* / **the Rev. James White**

June 6, 1857. No. 376, pp. 529–52

French and English [Charles Basset, *Contes excentriques*, 1855], 529–34. 11 cols. £5.15.6. *Sidney* / **Samuel Sidney**

Tremendous Bores [teredos], 534–36. 3 cols. £1.11.6. *Roberts per Frank Buckland* / **Roberts**

The Hospital Student [story], 536–42. 12 cols. £6.6.0. *White* / **the Rev. James White**

The Dead Secret, chap xxvi, 542–49. 14½ cols. *Wilkie Collins* / **Wilkie Collins**

Chip:
- The Roll of Cookery [14-cent. cookery-book], 549–50. 4 cols.; should read 3¼. £2.2.0. *Hardman* / **William Hardman**

Talking Ships [signalling code], 550–52. 4½ cols. *Morley* / **Henry Morley**

June 13, 1857. No. 377, pp. 553–76

Tilling the Devil's Acre [a nurseryman's employment and rehabilitation of young criminals], 553–58. 10½ cols. *Morley* / **Henry Morley**

The Patron Saint of Paris, 558–61. 5¾ cols. £3.0.0. *Robertson* / prob. **John Robertson**

The Circulation [Pierre Flourens, *Histoire de la découverte de la circulation du sang*, 1854], 561–65. 8 cols. £4.4.0. *Dixon* / **Edmund Saul Dixon**

Story of a Grave [verse], 565. 1½ cols. £2.12.6. *Mrs. MacIntosh* / **Mrs. MacIntosh**

The Dead Secret, chaps. xxvii–xxviii, 565–70. 9 cols. *W. Collins* / **Wilkie Collins**

Make Your Game, Gentlemen! [Louis Désiré Véron, *Mémoires d'un bourgeois de Paris*, 1853–55], 570–73. 6¾ cols. £3.10.0. *Fitzgerald* / **Percy Fitzgerald**

Chip:
- Dogs before Men [ancient attitudes toward dogs], 573–74. 1¾ cols. £1.5.0. *Miss Lynn* / **Eliza Lynn**

Parish Doctors, 574–76. 4¼ cols. £2.2.0. *Payn* / **James Payn**

June 20, 1857. No. 378, pp. 577–600

The Best Authority [anonymous misinformation], 577–79. 6 cols. *C.D.* / **Charles Dickens**

Grayrigg Grange [story], 579–87. 15¼ cols. £8.8.0. *Speight* / **Thomas Wilkinson Speight**

Chip:
- Why Is the Negro Black? [from John W. Draper, *Human Physiology*, 1856], 587–88. 2 cols. £1.1.0. *Miss Lynn* / **Eliza Lynn**

Handel [Victor Schœlcher, *The Life of Handel*, 1857], 588–93. 9 cols. *Morley* / **Henry Morley**

The Milky and Watery Way [milk adulteration, France], 593–96. 6 cols. £3.3.0. *W. B. Jerrold* / **William Blanchard Jerrold**

Duelling in England, 596–600. 10 cols. £5.5.0. *Miss Lynn & W.H.W.* / **Eliza Lynn & W. H. Wills**

June 27, 1857. No. 379, pp. 601–620

Up and down the Line [responsibilities and duties of railway executives and employees], 601–607. 13 cols. £6.16.6. *Speight* / **Thomas Wilkinson Speight**

How the Old Love Fared [story], 607–612. 10½ cols. £5.5.0. *Richardson* / **Richardson**

Chip:
- The Deodorisation of Crime [Discharged Prisoners' Aid Society], 612–14. 3 cols. £1.11.6. *Payn* / **James Payn**

Duelling in France, 614–20. 13¾ cols. £6.6.0. *Mis[s] Lynn & C.D.* / **Eliza Lynn & Charles Dickens**

VOLUME XVI July 4 – December 12, 1857

July 4, 1857. No. 380, pp. 1–24

Superstitions and Traditions, 1–6. 10½ cols. £5.5.0. *Dudley Costello* / **Dudley Costello**

Meaning Me, Sir? [story], 6–9. 7 cols. £3.13.6. *White* / **the Rev. James White**

Disinfectants [R. Angus Smith, "On Disinfectants," *Jour. of the Society of Arts*, April 24, 1857], 9–12. 6 cols. £3.3.0. *Miss Lynn* / **Eliza Lynn**

The Dismal Pool [verse], 12–13. 1¼ cols. £2.12.6. *Owen O'Ryan* / **Owen O'Ryan**

Helena Mathewson [story], 13–22. 17 cols. £8.18.6. *Miss Meta Gaskell* / **Margaret Emily Gaskell**

At the Coulisses in Paris [backstage at theatre], 22–24. 5½ cols. £2.12.6. *Fitzgerald* / **Percy Fitzgerald**

July 11, 1857. No. 381, pp. 25–48

Doctors' Bills [Parliamentary bills concerning medical profession], 25–28. 7 cols. *Morley* / **Henry Morley**

Gaston, the Little Wolf [Henry de La Madelène, *Le Comte Gaston de Raousset-Boulbon*, 1856], 28–31. 7¼ cols.; should read 6½. £3.13.6. *Miss Lynn* / **Eliza Lynn**

Stickytoes [tree-toads as pets], 31–34. 5 cols.; should read 5¾. £2.12.6. *Dixon & W.H.W.* / **Edmund Saul Dixon & W. H. Wills**

Chip:
– The French War-Office in Seventeen Hundred and Eighty-five, 34–36. 3 cols. £1.11.6. *Fitzgerald* / **Percy Fitzgerald**

Unopened Buds [verse], 36. ¼ col. £0.10.6. *Harris* / **Harris**

Agnes Lee [story], 36–46. 20¼ cols. £10.10.0. *Miss Jewsbury* / **Geraldine Endsor Jewsbury**

Next Week [procrastination], 46–48. 4 cols. £2.2.0. *W. Brough* / **William Brough**

July 18, 1857. No. 382, pp. 49–72

Inch by Inch Upward [Samuel Smiles, *The Life of George Stephenson*, 1857], 49–55. 12½ cols. *Morley* / **Henry Morley**

A Fair Penitent [Marie-Jeanne Gautier (1692–1757), *Récit de la conversion*, in Pierre de La Place, *Pièces intéressantes et peu connues*], 55–59. 9 cols. *Collins* / **Wilkie Collins**

Three Generations [story], 59–65. 11½ cols. £5.15.6. *Payn* / **James Payn**

Cairo, 65–69. 7 cols. £3.13.6. *Capper* / **John Capper**

Extract of Funeral Flowers [17-cent. funeral sermons], 69–72. 7½ cols. £3.13.6. *Fitzgerald* / **Percy Fitzgerald**

July 25, 1857. No. 383, pp. 73–96

Your Life or Your Likeness [the biography and photography mania], 73–75. 5½ cols. £3.0.0. *White* / **the Rev. James White**

The Witches of Scotland, 75–83. 14 cols. £7.7.0. *Miss Lynn* / **Eliza Lynn**

Chip:
– Who Was He? [parentage of Sir Robert Dudley], 83–84. 2 cols. £1.1.0. *Miss Costello* / **Louisa Stuart Costello**

An Encumbered Estate [under Chancery Court administration], 84–89. 11 cols. £5.15.6. *E. Mitchell* / **E. Mitchell**

Boulogne Wood, 89–93. 7 cols. £3.13.6. *Robertson's friend* / **Robertson's friend**

Tracks in the Bush [search for stockman lost in the bush, Australia], 93–96. 7½ cols. £4.0.0. *Lang* / **John Lang**

August 1, 1857. No. 384, pp. 97–120

Curious Misprint in the Edinburgh Review [James F. Stephen, "The License of Modern Novelists," *Edin. Rev.*, July 1857], 97–100. 6¼ cols. *C.D.* / **Charles Dickens**

A Remarkable Revolution [accession of Elizabeth, Empress of Russia, 1741], 100–104. 9½ cols. *W. Collins* / **Wilkie Collins**

Opium, chap. i: India, 104–108. 8 cols. £4.4.0. *G. Dodd* / **George Dodd**

A Dead Past [verse], 108–109. ½ col. £1.1.0. *Miss Procter* / **Adelaide Anne Procter**

Invisible Ghosts [a haunted house], 109–111. 6 cols. £3.3.0. *Laing* / **John Lang**

French Tavern Life, chap. i, 111–18. 13 cols. £6.16.6. *Dudley Costello* / **Dudley Costello**

An Immeasurable Wonder [marine *Annelida* and *Nemertea*], 118–20. 5 cols. £2.12.6. *Robertson* / prob. **John Robertson**

August 8, 1857. No. 385, pp. 121–44

The Yellow Tiger [story], 121–30. 18½ cols. £10.10.0. *Fitzgerald* / **Percy Fitzgerald**

A Companionable Sparrow, 130–32. 3½ cols. £2.12.6. *Robertson & Miss Fitton* / **John Robertson**, prob., **& Sarah Mary Fitton**

Autumn [verse], 132. ½ col. £1.1.0. *O'Ryan* (*Owen O'Ryan* in cancelled Office Book listing) / **Owen O'Ryan**

Microscopic Preparations, 132–38. 11½ cols. £5.15.6. *Dixon* / **Edmund Saul Dixon**

The Witches of England, 138–41. 7½ cols. £3.13.6. *Miss Lynn* / **Eliza Lynn**

Powers of Calculation [Jean Jacques Winkler, mathematical genius], 141–44. 6 cols. £3.3.0. *Dixon* / **Edmund Saul Dixon**

August 15, 1857. No. 386, pp. 145–68

The Star of Bethlehem [Bethlehem Hospital], 145–50. 10½ cols. *Morley* / **Henry Morley**

My Window [story], 150–54. 8½ cols. £4.4.0. *Miss Parr* / **Harriet Parr**

A Mutiny in India [in vicinity of Poona, "years ago"], 154–56. 4¼ cols. £2.10.0. *E. Townsend* / **E. Townsend**

A Queen's Revenge [Pierre le Bel, *Relation de la mort du Marquis de Monaldeschi*, first pub. 1664], 156–62. 11 cols. *W. Collins* / **Wilkie Collins**

Chip:
– A School for Cooks [for girls, London], 162–63. 2 cols. £1.1.0. *W.H.W.* / **W. H. Wills**

The Rinderpest; or, Steppe Murrain, 163–66. 6 cols. £3.3.0. *Sidney* / **Samuel Sidney**

Doctor Garrick [German play based on real or supposed incident in Garrick's life], 166–68. 5½ cols. £2.12.6. *Fitzgerald* / **Percy Fitzgerald**

August 22, 1857. No. 387, pp. 169–92

Prussian Police, 169–73. 8½ cols. £4.4.0. *Von Corvin & Morley* / **Otto von Corvin & Henry Morley**

The Amphlett Love-Match [story], 173–81. 16 cols. £8.8.0. *Miss Lynn* / **Eliza Lynn**

Opium, chap. ii: China, 181–85. 9 cols. £3.13.6. *Dodd* / **George Dodd**

Béranger, 185–91. 11 cols. £5.15.6. *Kent* / **William Charles Mark Kent**

A Voice from the Cloister [celibate restriction of college fellows], 191–92. 3¾ cols. £2.0.0. *Payn* / **James Payn**

August 29, 1857. No. 388, pp. 193–216

A Healthy Year in London [current reports of Medical Officers of Health], 193–97. 9½ cols. *Morley* / **Henry Morley**

Eleanor Clare's Journal for Ten Years [story], chap. i, 197–202. 12½ cols.; should read 10. £26.5.0 for the 4 instalments. *Miss Parr* / **Harriet Parr**

A Hint from Siam [distinguishing lords from commoners], 202–204. 2¾ cols. *Item not in Office Book* / ———

Our P's and Q's [manuals on diction, letter-writing, etiquette], 204–207. 7½ cols. £3.13.6. *Payn* / **James Payn**

French Tavern Life, chap. ii, 207–213. 10½ cols. £5.5.0. *Costello* / **Dudley Costello**

The Datchley Philharmonic [story], 213–16. 8 cols. £4.4.0. *Fitzgerald* / **Percy Fitzgerald**

September 5, 1857. No. 389, pp. 217–40

A Journey in Search of Nothing [enforced idleness], 217–23. 13 cols. *Wilkie Collins* / **Wilkie Collins**

The Self-Made Potter [autobiog. of Georges Pull: from "Le Potier de Vaugirard," *Revue des beaux-arts*, June 1857], 223–26. 5¼ cols. £2.12.6. *Robertson* / prob. **John Robertson**

Burning, and Burying [*Burning the Dead, or Urn Sepulture. By a Member of the Royal College of Surgeons*, 1857], 226–27. 3¾ cols. *Morley* / **Henry Morley**

The Leaf [verse], 227–28. ¾ col. £1.1.0. *Owen O'Ryan* / **Owen O'Ryan**

Sepoy Symbols of Mutiny, 228–32. 8 cols. £4.4.0. *Robertson* / prob. **John Robertson**

Eleanor Clare's Journal for Ten Years, chap. ii, 232–39. 13½ cols. *Miss Parr* / **Harriet Parr**

How the Writer Was Despatch-Boxed [Govt. waste, mismanagement, red tape], 239–40. 4 cols. £2.2.0. *Carter* / **Robert Brudenell Carter**

September 12, 1857. No. 390, pp. 241–64

Londoners over the Border [insalubrity of two London suburbs], 241–44. 6¼ cols. *Morley* / **Henry Morley**

Indian Irregulars, 244–46. 4 cols. £2.2.0. *Townsend* / **E. Townsend**

The Sweetest of Women [Edmund Waller], 246–51. 11½ cols. £6.0.0. *Kent* / **William Charles Mark Kent**

Angela [verse], 251–52. 1 col. £2.2.0. *O'Ryan* / **Owen O'Ryan**

Eleanor Clare's Journal for Ten Years, chap. iii, 252–60. 15½ cols. *Miss Parr* / **Harriet Parr**

Romantic Breach of Promise [of Mme. de Montespedon: from *Mémoires de la vie de François de Scepeaux*], 260–62. 5½ cols. £2.12.6. *Bayle St. John* / **Bayle St. John**

Rogues' Walk [section of Piccadilly and Haymarket, frequented by underworld], 262–64. 4½ cols. £3.0.0. *Albert Smith* / **Albert Richard Smith**

September 19, 1857. No. 391, pp. 265–88

The Brave Coucou Driver [a trip in France], 265–71. 13¾ cols. £6.16.6. *Dudley Costello* / **Dudley Costello**

Eleanor Clare's Journal for Ten Years, chap. iv, 271–76. 10 cols. *Miss Parr* / **Harriet Parr**

The First Sack of Delhi [by Nadir Shah, 1739], 276–79. 5½ cols. £2.12.6. *Markham* / **Clements Robert Markham**

The Debtor's Best Friend [*An Accurate Description of Newgate. ... Written for the Public Good, by B.L., of Twickenham*, 1724], 279–82. 6½ cols. *Wilkie Collins* / **Wilkie Collins**

Thor and the Giants [Prose Edda], 282–85. 5 cols. £2.12.6. *E. Ollier* / **Edmund Ollier**

Wastdale Head [excursion to], 285–88. 7¼ cols. £3.13.6. *Payn* / **James Payn**

September 26, 1857. No. 392, pp. 289–312

Mrs. Badgery [story], 289–93. 9 cols. *Wilkie Collins* / **Wilkie Collins**

A Very Black Act [press censorship, India], 293–94. 2 cols. £1.1.0. *Capper* / **John Capper**

Forebodings of Thomas Raikes, Esquire [*A Portion of the Journal Kept by Thomas Raikes, Esq., from 1831 to 1847*, 1856–57], 294–300. 11½ cols. £6.0.0. *Kent* / **William Charles Mark Kent**

My Sister [verse], 300. ½ col. £1.1.0. *Joseph Harding* / **Joseph Harding**

Bourbon Paris, Photographed [details from contemp. almanacs], 300–303. 5½ cols. £3.0.0. *Fitzgerald* / **Percy Fitzgerald**

Our Family Picture [story], chaps. i–ii, 303–308. 10½ cols. £18.0.0 for the 3 instalments. *Speight* / **Thomas Wilkinson Speight**

Old Hawtrey [an old man's reminiscences], 308–310. 4½ cols. *W. Jerdan* / **William Jerdan**

Her Grace of the Hobnails [Emily Lowe, *Unprotected Females in Norway*, 1857], 310–12. 5 cols. *Morley* / **Henry Morley**

October 3, 1857. No. 393, pp. 313–36

The Lazy Tour of Two Idle Apprentices [excursion to Cumberland and elsewhere; interspersed stories], chap. i, 313–19. 14 cols. *C.D. & Collins* / **Charles Dickens & Wilkie Collins**

Indian Recruits and Indian English, 319–22. 4¾ cols. £2.2.0 to Townsend; £1.1.0 to Hamilton. *Townsend & A. H. A. Hamilton* / **E. Townsend & Alexander Henry Abercromby Hamilton**

Herrick's Julia [Robert Herrick], 322–26. 9 cols. £4.14.6. *Kent* / **William Charles Mark Kent**

Our Family Picture, chaps. iii–iv, 326–33. 14 cols. *Speight* / **Thomas Wilkinson Speight**

Lord W. Tyler [needed legislation on lodgings of the poor], 333–36. 6 cols. *Morley* / **Henry Morley**

October 10, 1857. No. 394, pp. 337–60

The Lazy Tour of Two Idle Apprentices, chap. ii, 337–49. 24½ cols. *C.D. & W. Collins* / **Charles Dickens & Wilkie Collins**

The Manchester School of Art [Exhibition of Art Treasures], 349–52. 5½ cols. *W.H.W.* / **W. H. Wills**

Photographees, 352–54. 5 cols. £2.12.6. *Payn* / **James Payn**

Falling Leaves [botany], 354–55. 4 cols.; should read 3. £2.2.0. *Dr. Brown* / **Dr. Brown**

Our Family Picture, chaps. v–vi, 355–60. 10 cols. *Speight* / **Thomas Wilkinson Speight**

October 17, 1857. No. 395, pp. 361–84

The Lazy Tour of Two Idle Apprentices, chap. iii, 361–67. 13¾ cols. *C.D. & Collins* / **Charles Dickens & Wilkie Collins**

The Snow Express [perilous journey in Canada], 367–72. 8¾ cols. £5.0.0. *A. Mitchell* / **Andrew Mitchell**

Touching the Lord Hamlet [Saxo Grammaticus], 372–76. 8½ cols. £5.0.0. *Oxenford* / **John Oxenford**

Canton City, 376–81. 10½ cols. £5.5.0. *Von Corvin & Morley* / **Otto von Corvin & Henry Morley**

Poor Tom. – A City Weed [clerk in a commercial office], 381–84. 7 cols. £3.13.6. *Hollinshed* / **John Hollingshead**

October 24, 1857. No. 396, pp. 385–408

The Lazy Tour of Two Idle Apprentices, chap. iv, 385–93. 17½ cols. *C.D. & Collins* / **Charles Dickens & Wilkie Collins**

Calcutta, 393–97. 8 cols. £4.4.0. *Capper* / **John Capper**

The Wand of Light [verse], 397–98. 1 col. £2.2.0. *E. H. Osborn* / **Edward Haydon Osborn**

Down among the Dutchmen [Holland: descr. and travel] [i], 398–402. 8 cols. £4.4.0. *Fitzgerald* / **Percy Fitzgerald**

Chip:
– Edmund Waller [signatures of], 402. ½ col. *De Morgan* / **Augustus De Morgan**

Stepping-Stones [episodes in lives of literary and hist. figures], 402–407. 10 cols. £5.5.0. *Kent* / **William Charles Mark Kent**

A Touching (and Touched) Character [a harmless madman, Paris], 407–408. 3½ cols. £2.2.0. *A.R.* [2nd initial unclear] *Scoble* / **Andrew Richard Scoble**

October 31, 1857. No. 397, pp. 409–432

The Lazy Tour of Two Idle Apprentices, chap. v, 409–416. 15¼ cols. *C.D. & Collins* / **Charles Dickens & Wilkie Collins**

Friends of the Patagonian [William P. Snow, *A Two Years' Cruise off Tierra del Fuego*, 1857], 416–21. 10 cols. *Morley* / **Henry Morley**

The Queen's Guest [imprisonment for debt], 421–23. 4 cols. £3.3.0. *Wraxall* / **Frederick Charles Lascelles Wraxall**

Captain Doineau [murders in Algeria, 1856; murder trial of Auguste E. Doineau], 423–30. 13 cols. £6.16.6. *Robertson* / prob. **John Robertson**

Two First-Class Passengers [a customs duty evader; a pickpocket], 430–32. 6 cols. £3.3.0. *Payn* / **James Payn**

November 7, 1857. No. 398, pp. 433–56

Brother Müller and His Orphan-Work [*A Narrative of ... the Lord's Dealings with George Müller*, 1837–56], 433–38. 10¼ cols. *Morley* / **Henry Morley**

The Monkey-King [Léon Gozlan, *Les Emotions de Polydore Marasquin*, 1857], 438–42. 9 cols. £4.14.6. *Miss Lynn* / **Eliza Lynn**

The Two Janes [Lady Jane Grey, Jane Shore], 442–44. 4¼ cols. £2.10.0. *Payn* / **James Payn**

Twenty Shillings in the Pound [unscrupulous business practices], 444–46. 4¼ cols. £2.5.0. *Hollinshed* / **John Hollingshead**

Down among the Dutchmen, ii, 446–50. 7¾ cols. £4.0.0. *Fitzgerald* / **Percy Fitzgerald**

The Lightning Doctor [faradisation], 450–53. 4¾ cols.; should read 5½. £2.5.0. *Von Corvin* / **Otto von Corvin**

Cat's Grease [Gottfried Keller, "Spiegel, das Kätzchen," *Die Leute von Seldwyla*, 1856], 453–56. 7¼ cols. £3.13.6. *Oxenford* / **John Oxenford**

November 14, 1857. No. 399, pp. 457–80

Wanderings in India [i], 457–63. 12¼ cols. £6.10.0. *Lang* / **John Lang**

Polarisation [of light], 463–68. 10¾ cols. £5.10.0. *Dixon* / **Edmund Saul Dixon**

The First Snow on the Fell [verse], 468. ½ col. £1.1.0. *Payn* / **James Payn**

Lyndon Hall [story], chaps. i–iv, 468–76. 14½ cols. £7.10.0. *Miss Lynn* / **Eliza Lynn**

The New Colonists of Norfolk Island [descr. of island: from Wiliam B. Ullathorne, *The Catholic Mission in Australasia*, first pub. 1836], 476–77. 2 cols. *Item not in Office Book* / ———

A Discursive Mind [association of ideas], 477–80. 8 cols. £4.0.0. *Sorrell* / **Sorrell**

November 21, 1857. No. 400, pp. 481–504

At Home in Siam, 481–88. 14½ cols. £7.10.0. *Mrs. Hillier* / **Mrs. Charles B. Hillier**

The Best Man [trial by combat], 488–90. 4½ cols. £2.2.0. *Brough* / **William Brough**

Lutfullah Khan [*Autobiography of Lutfullah, a Mohamedan Gentleman*, 1857], 490–96. 11½ cols. £6.16.6. *Townsend* / **E. Townsend**

Lyndon Hall, chaps. v–vii, 496–501. 12 cols.; should read 11. £6.6.0. *Miss Lynn* / **Eliza Lynn**

Down among the Dutchmen, iii, 501–504. 6½ cols. £3.10.0. *Fitzgerald* / **Percy Fitzgerald**

November 28, 1857. No. 401, pp. 505–528

Wanderings in India [ii], 505–511. 12 cols. £6.6.0. *Lang* / **John Lang**

Nature's Greatness in Small Things [the cell], 511–13. 4¼ cols. £2.10.0. *Hart* / **Ernest Abraham Hart**

The Night Porter [story], 513–18. 9½ cols. *Morley* / **Henry Morley**

Things within Dr. Conolly's Remembrance [treatment of the insane], 518–23. 11 cols. *Morley* / **Henry Morley**

Marie Courtenay [supposed daughter of William Courtenay, Earl of Devon], 523–25. 5 cols. £2.12.6. *Robertson* / prob. **John Robertson**

Debtor and Creditor, 525–28. 6½ cols. £3.10.0. *Hollinshed* / **John Hollingshead**

December 5, 1857. No. 402, pp. 529–52

My Lost Home [story], 529–34. 11 cols. £5.15.6. *Hollingshed* / **John Hollingshead**

Hard Roads [taxes exacted from travellers in Japan: from a French source], 534–36. 3 cols. £1.1.0. *A. H. A. Hamilton & W.H.W.* / **Alexander Henry Abercromby Hamilton & W. H. Wills**

Chip:
- One of Sir Hans Sloane's Patients [case described in letter "To the Proprietors," *Universal Magazine*, Sept. 1757], 536–37. 2 cols. *Morley* / **Henry Morley**

Prattleton's Monday Out [South Kensington Museum], 537–40. 6¼ cols. *Morley* / **Henry Morley**

Paris on London [Francis A. Wey, *Les Anglais chez eux*, 1857 ed.], 540–45. 11 cols. £5.15.6. *Dixon* / **Edmund Saul Dixon**

Re-Touching the Lord Hamlet [*The Hystorie of Hamblet*], 545–48. 5 cols. £2.12.6. *Heraud* / **John Abraham Heraud**

Sand and Roses [story], 548–52. 10 cols. £5.5.0. *Bayle St. John* / **Bayle St. John**

December 12, 1857. No. 403, pp. 553–72

Riding the Whirlwind [ride on train locomotive], 553–56. 7½ cols. £4.0.0. *Hollingshed* / **John Hollingshead**

The Sun-Horse [Slovak fairy tale, from Ján Francisci], 556–60. 7 cols. £3.13.6. *Oxenford* / **John Oxenford**

Fair-Time at Leipsic, 560–62. 5 cols. £2.12.6. *Duthie* / **William Duthie**

George Levison; or, The Schoolfellows [verse], 562–64. 4 cols. £4.4.0. *Allingham* / **William Allingham**

A Piece of Work [recommendations of Mathias Roth, M.D., for gymnastics, baths, etc.], 564–68. 8½ cols. *Morley* / **Henry Morley**

Number Five, Hanbury Terrace [story], 568–72. 8 cols. £4.4.0. *Miss French* / **Miss French**

VOLUME XVII December 19, 1857 – June 12, 1858

December 19, 1857. No. 404, pp. 1–24

The City of Unlimited Paper [over-extension of credit; 1857 financial crisis], 1–4. 7½ cols. £3.13.6. *Hollingshed* / **John Hollingshead**

Something Like an Art Gallery [the Louvre under Napoleon], 4–9. 9 cols. £4.14.6. *Kent* / **William Charles Mark Kent**

Street Memories, 9–12. 7 cols. £3.13.6. *Hollingshed* / **John Hollingshead**

Wanderings in India [iii], 12–20. 15 cols. £7.17.6. *Lang* / **John Lang**

Two in a Legion [story], 20–24. 9½ cols. £4.14.6. *Yates* / **Edmund Yates**

Christmas 1857. Extra Christmas number: The Perils of Certain English Prisoners, and Their Treasure in Women, Children, Silver, and Jewels, pp. 1–36. Running date: Dec. 7. Stated on title page of Vol. XVI as included in that vol. Title and chapter titles listed at end of "Contents" of that vol.

Chap. i. The Island of Silver-Store, 1–14. 26 cols. *C.D.* / **Charles Dickens**

Chap. ii. The Prison in the Woods, 14–30. 33 cols. *W. W. Collins* / **Wilkie Collins**

Chap. iii. The Rafts on the River, 30–36. 12¾ cols. *C.D.* / **Charles Dickens**

December 26, 1857. No. 405, pp. 25–48

Old Saint Ann's Gateway [story], 25–35. 20 cols. £15.15.0. *Miss Parr* / **Harriet Parr**

A Christmas Phantasy [verse], 35–36. 2 cols. £3.0.6. *E. Ollier* / **Edmund Ollier**

Lemonfingers [story], 36–40. 9 cols. £4.4.0. *Speight* / **Thomas Wilkinson Speight**

The Elfin Charm [verse], 40–44. 8 cols. £10.0.0. *Mrs. MacIntosh* / **Mrs. MacIntosh**

Max and His Companions [incident concerning German university student, stated to be fact], 44–48. 9½ cols. *Townsend* / **Townsend**

January 2, 1858. No. 406, pp. 49–72

Deep Design on Society [John Timbs, *Things Not Generally Known*, 1856], 49–53. 8 cols. *Wilkie Collins* / **Wilkie Collins**

The Legend of My Native Town [story], 53–58. 11¼ cols. £6.0.0. *Thomas* / **William Moy Thomas**

Sixty New Years' Days Ago [verse], 58–60. 3¾ cols. £5.5.0. *Miss Procter* / **Adelaide Anne Procter**

A Morning Call on a Great Personage [launching of the *Great Eastern*], 60–64. 7 cols. £3.13.6. *Hollinshed* / **John Hollingshead**

Wanderings in India [iv], 64–70. 13¾ cols. £6.16.6. *Lang* / **John Lang**

Vestiges of Protection [licensing of boot-blacks, street vendors, etc.], 70–72. 4 cols. £2.2.0. *Hollinshed* / **John Hollingshead**

January 9, 1858. No. 407, pp. 73–96

A Lesson Lost upon Us [sanitary measures effected during Crimean War], 73–80. 14¼ cols. *Morley* / **Henry Morley**

The Little Huguenot [Jacques de Caumont La Force], 80–84. 9½ cols. *Collins* / **Wilkie Collins**

A New Idea of an Old Slave-Captain [Hugh Crow, *Memoirs*, 1830], 84–87. 6 cols. £3.3.0. *Hollingshead* / **John Hollingshead**

Wanderings in India [v], 87–94. 13 cols. £6.10.0. *Lang* / **John Lang**

Down among the Dutchmen, iv, 94–96. 4½ cols. £2.12.6. *Fitzgerald* / **Percy Fitzgerald**

January 16, 1858. No. 408, pp. 97–120

Save Me from My Friends [trials of a writer], 97–102. 10½ cols. *Collins* / **Wilkie Collins**

Beyond the Prairies [travel in the U.S.], 102–108. 13 cols. £6.6.0. *Adams S. Hill* / **Adams Sherman Hill**

Famine Aboard! [story], 108–112. 6 cols.; should read 6¾. £3.3.0. *Thomas* / **William Moy Thomas**

Wanderings in India [vi], 112–18. 12¾ cols. £6.6.0. *Lang* / **John Lang**

Down among the Dutchmen, v, 118–20. 4¼ cols. £2.12.6. *Fitzgerald* / **Percy Fitzgerald**

January 23, 1858. No. 409, pp. 121–44

Thanks to Doctor Livingstone [David Livingstone, *Missionary Travels ... in South Africa*, 1857], 121–25. 8½ cols. *Collins* / **Wilkie Collins**

The Vital Point [physiology], 125–26. 4 cols.; should read 3. £2.2.0. *Robertson* / prob. **John Robertson**

The Patagonian Brothers [story], 126–31. 10 cols. £5.5.0. *Miss Amelia Edwards* / **Amelia Ann Blandford Edwards**

Chip:
– A British Nuisance [animal slaughter in London], 131–32. 2 cols. £1.1.0. *Jerdan* / **William Jerdan**

A Tree in the Street [verse], 132–33. ¾ col. £1.1.0. *Kent* / **William Charles Mark Kent**

Running Away [man's inclination to forsake society, responsibilities, etc.], 133–35. 5 cols. £2.12.6. *Thomas* / **William Moy Thomas**

Wanderings in India [vii], 135–44. 18 cols. £9.9.0. *Lang* / **John Lang**

January 30, 1858. No. 410, pp. 145–68

All Night on the Monument [London, the City], 145–48. 7 cols. £3.13.6. *Hollingshed* / **John Hollingshead**

Wanderings in India [viii], 148–56. 15 cols. £7.17.6. *Lang* / **John Lang**

At Rest [verse], 156. ½ col. £0.10.6. *G. Turner* / **G. Turner**

Down among the Dutchmen, vi, 156–60. 8 cols. £4.4.0. *Fitzgerald* / **Percy Fitzgerald**

Chips:
– A Plea for Playgrounds, 160–61. 2¾ cols. £1.1.0. *Mrs. Howitt & Morley* / **Sophia Elizabeth De Morgan & Henry Morley**
– Macaroni-Making, 161–63. 3 cols. £1.11.6. *Wreford* / **Henry G. Wreford**

The Pet of the Law [the professional thief], 163–65. 4¼ cols. £2.10.0. *Hollingshed* / **John Hollingshead**

A Royal Pilot-Balloon [Montgolfier balloon ascent, 1783], 165–68. 7 cols. £3.13.6. *Fitzgerald* / **Percy Fitzgerald**

February 6, 1858. No. 411, pp. 169–92

Strike! [boycotts to effect reforms], 169–72. 7½ cols. *Collins* / **Wilkie Collins**

Unsuspected Neighbours [microscopic organisms], 172–76. 8 cols. £4.4.0. *Dixon* / **Edmund Saul Dixon**

Feats at the Ferry [athletic sports], 176–79. 6 cols.; should read 5. £3.3.0. *Payn* / **James Payn**

A Woman's Question [verse], 179. ¾ col. £1.1.0. *Miss Procter* / **Adelaide Anne Procter**

Wanderings in India [ix], 179–86. 13¼ cols. £6.6.0. *Lang* / **John Lang**

An Autobiographical Jail-Sermon [*The Life of David Haggart. ... Written by Himself, While under Sentence of Death*, 1821], 186–92. 12½ cols. *Morley* / **Henry Morley**

February 13, 1858. No. 412, pp. 193–216

Give Us Room! [parties in private homes], 193–96. 6¾ cols. *Collins* / **Wilkie Collins**

Down among the Dutchmen, vii, 196–201. 10 cols. £5.5.0. *Fitzgerald* / **Percy Fitzgerald**

My First Patron [story], 201–205. 7½ cols. £3.13.6. *C. Collins* / **Charles Allston Collins**

Sleep [verse], 205. ¼ col. £0.10.6. *Harris* / **Harris**

The Shell-Moth, 205–206. 2 cols. £1.1.0. *Robertson* / prob. **John Robertson**

Siamese Embassy in the Seventeenth Century [to court of Louis XIV: from contemp. sources], 206–210. 8 cols. £4.4.0. *W. Lycester* / prob. **William Leycester**

Bankruptcy in Six Easy Lessons, 210–12. 2¾ cols. £1.11.6. *Hollingshed* / **John Hollingshead**

Wanderings in India [x], 212–16. 10 cols. £5.5.0. *Lang* / **John Lang**

February 20, 1858. No. 413, pp. 217–40

Well-Authenticated Rappings [ridicule of spiritualists' phenomena], 217–20. 6½ cols. *C.D.* / **Charles Dickens**

Wanderings in India [xi], 220–24. 8½ cols. £4.4.0. *Lang* / **John Lang**

Wanted, a Secretary [nepotism], 224–27. 6½ cols. £3.3.0. *Hollingshed* / **John Hollingshead**

Words [verse], 227–28, ¾ col. £1.1.0. *Miss Procter* / **Adelaide Anne Procter**

Over, Under, or Through? [English Channel crossing], 228–32. 8½ cols. £4.4.0. *Dixon* / **Edmund Saul Dixon**

Coo-ee! [lost in the bush, Australia], 232–36. 9 cols. £4.14.6. *F. Vincent* / **Frank Vincent**

A Train of Accidents [story], 236–40. 8 cols. £4.4.0. *Payn* / **James Payn**

February 27, 1858. No. 414, pp. 241–64

Nearly Lost on the Alps, 241–44. 7 cols. £3.13.6. *Albert Smith* / **Albert Richard Smith**

A Sermon for Sepoys [decision of a 17-cent. Indian vizier], 244–47. 5¾ cols. *Collins* / **Wilkie Collins**

Down among the Dutchmen, viii, 247–51. 8 cols. £4.4.0. *Fitzgerald* / **Percy Fitzgerald**

Gone Away [verse], 251. ¾ col. £1.10.0. Payment notation reads: "£14 for this No. 420 & 422"; but sum of payment notations for the 3 items = £14.2.0. *Miss M. H. Gibson* / **Miss Mary W. A. Gibson**

Old Times and New Times [the London *Times*], 251–54. 5¾ cols. £3.0.0. *Joseph Ede* / **Joseph Ede**

Wanderings in India [xii], 254–60. 12 cols. £6.6.0. *Lang* / **John Lang**

"A Gude Conceit o' Oursels" [story], 260–64. 8 cols. £4.4.0. *White* / **the Rev. James White**

March 6, 1858. No. 415, pp. 265–88

Dramatic Grub Street. Explored in Two Letters [contemp. English theatre], 265–70. 11 cols. *Wilkie Collins* / **Wilkie Collins**

A Nautch, 270–73. 5 cols. £2.12.6. *Capper* / **John Capper**

Border-Land [microscopic organisms], 273–76. 7½ cols. £3.13.6. *Dixon* / **Edmund Saul Dixon**

Marion's Orchard [verse], 276–77. 1 col. £2.2.0. *Anonymous* / ———

The Apparition of Monsieur Bodry [story], 277–84. 14¼ cols. £7.7.0. *Dudley Costello* / **Dudley Costello**

Chip:
– Slow Conveyancing, 284–85. 2½ cols. £1.1.0. *Head* / **John Oswald Head**

Down among the Dutchmen, ix, 285–88. 6¾ cols. £3.3.0. *Fitzgerald* / **Percy Fitzgerald**

March 13, 1858. No. 416, pp. 289–312

An Idea of Mine [models and properties in contemp. paintings], 289–91. 4½ cols. *C.D.* / **Charles Dickens**

Mr. Pearson [story], 291–94. 6¾ cols. £3.13.6. *A. W. Doubleday, Esquire* / prob. **Augustus William Dubourg**

Shadowless Men [fraudulent financiers], 294–99. 13 cols.; should read 9¾. £6.16.6. *Robertson* / prob. **John Robertson**

How I Fell among Monsters [heraldry], 299–301. 3½ cols. *Item not in Office Book* / **John Hollingshead**

Civilisation in California [Ernest Seyd, *California and Its Resources*, 1858], 301–304. 5¼ cols. £3.0.0. *Miss Lynn* / **Eliza Lynn**

Meat and Drink in Shakespeare's Time [Tobias Venner, *Via Recta ad Vitam Longam*, 1620], 304–309. 11¾ cols. *Morley* / **Henry Morley**

Fine Shaving [George Packwood, *Packwood's Whim. The Goldfinch's Nest*, 1796], 309–312. 6 cols. £3.3.0. *Fitzgerald* / **Percy Fitzgerald**

March 20, 1858. No. 417, pp. 313–36

A Shy Scheme [plight of bashful lover], 313–16. 7¼ cols. *Wilkie Collins* / **Wilkie Collins**

Indian Hill Stations, 316–19. 8½ cols.; should read 6. £4.4.0. *Townsend* / **E. Townsend**

Debt, 319–21. 3 cols. £1.11.6. *Hollinshed* / **John Hollingshead**

Wine, No Mystery [G. J. Mulder, *The Chemistry of Wine*, 1857], 321–25. 7½ cols. £3.13.6. *Miss Lynn* / **Eliza Lynn**

Little Constancy's Birthday [story], 325–34. 18 cols. £9.9.0. *Fitzgerald* / **Percy Fitzgerald**

Aboard the Japan, Whaler [autobiog.], 334–36. 6¾ cols.; should read 5¾. £3.13.6. *Snow* / **George Henry Snow**

March 27, 1858. No. 418, pp. 337–60

Awful Warning to Bachelors [*The Etiquette of Courtship and Matrimony*, 1852], 337–40. 7 cols. *Wilkie Collins* / **Wilkie Collins**

Germination, 340–43. 6 cols. £3.3.0. *Robertson* / prob. **John Robertson**

Surrey's Geraldine [Henry Howard, Earl of Surrey], 343–47. 8 cols. £4.4.0. *Kent* / **William Charles Mark Kent**

Two Dark Days [verse], 347–48. 1½ cols. £2.2.0. *Miss Procter* / **Adelaide Anne Procter**

Blown Away! [execution of Sepoy seditionaries], 348–50. 4¾ cols. £2.10.0. *George Craig* / **George Craig**

A Packet-Ship's Company [story], 350–53. 6 cols. £3.3.0. *Miss Martin* / **Miss Martin**

Finnish Mythology, 353–57. 8 cols. £4.4.0. *Oxenford* / **John Oxenford**

Down among the Dutchmen, x, 357–60. 6¾ cols. £3.10.0. *Fitzgerald* / **Percy Fitzgerald**

April 3, 1858. No. 419, pp. 361–84

Use and Abuse of the Dead [bodies for dissection], 361–65. 8¼ cols. *Morley* / **Henry Morley**

Calmuck [story], 365–70. 11 cols. £5.15.6. *Brough* / **Robert Barnabas Brough**

Chinese Charms [amulets, etc.], 370–72. 3 cols. £1.11.6. *Mylne* / **William Charles Milne**

Among the Tombs [gravestone epitaphs], 372–75. 6 cols. £3.3.0. *Payn* / **James Payn**

Infusoria, 375–79. 8 cols. £4.4.0. *Dixon* / **Edmund Saul Dixon**

Celtic Bards, 379–84. 11¾ cols. *Morley* / **Henry Morley**

April 10, 1858. No. 420, pp. 385–408

A Needle of Sense in a Haystack of Law [Herman L. Prior, *A Complete Manual of Short Conveyancing*, 1857], 385–87. 5 cols. £2.12.6. *Head & W.H.W.* / **John Oswald Head & W. H. Wills**

Down among the Dutchmen, xi, 387–91. 6½ cols. £3.10.0. *Fitzgerald* / **Percy Fitzgerald**

A Tale of an Old Man's Youth [story], 391–96. 10 cols. £5.5.0. *Miss Gibson* / **Miss Mary W. A. Gibson**

A Microscopic Dream [minute organisms], 396–400. 8 cols. £4.4.0. *Dixon* / **Edmund Saul Dixon**

Green-Beard and Slyboots [August Schleicher, collector and translator, *Litauische Märchen*, 1857], 400–405. 10½ cols. £5.5.0. *Oxenford* / **John Oxenford**

The Afflicted Duke of Spindles [ills that flesh is heir to], 405–408. 7¼ cols. £3.13.6. *Hollingshed* / **John Hollingshead**

April 17, 1858. No. 421, pp. 409–432

Mrs. Bullwinkle [a monthly nurse], 409–411. 4½ cols. *Wilkie Collins* / **Wilkie Collins**

Years and Years Ago [story], 411–16. 9½ cols. *Miss Power* / **Marguerite A. Power**

John Chinaman in Australia, 416–20. 8 cols. £4.4.0. *F. Vincent & Morley* / **Frank Vincent & Henry Morley**

Poetry and Philosophy [verse], 420. ½ col. £1.1.0. *Desmond G. Fitzgerald, Esquire* / **Desmond G. Fitz-Gerald**

Two Very Small Clubs [a yacht club, a Freemasons' lodge], 420–23. 5½ cols. £3.0.0. *Payn* / **James Payn**

Portland Island [Dorset peninsula], 423–29. 13 cols. £6.6.0. *Mr. Moule & Morley* / **Henry Moule,** prob., **& Henry Morley**

Mine Oyster [newspaper advertisements], 429–32. 6½ cols. £3.10.0. *Morley* / **Henry Morley**

April 24, 1858. No. 422, pp. 433–56

My Annular Eclipse [story], 433–36. 7¼ cols. £3.13.6. *W.H.W.* / **W. H. Wills**

The Blue Dye Plant, 436–38. 4 cols. £2.2.0. *Robertson* / prob. **John Robertson**

Lost Alice [story], 438–45. 14 cols. £7.7.0. *Miss Gibson* / **Miss Mary W. A. Gibson**

Home and Rest [verse], 445, ½ col. £1.1.0. *Miss Procter* / **Adelaide Anne Procter**

Fetishes at Home, 445–47. 3¾ cols. £2.0.0. *Hollingshed* / **John Hollingshead**

A Pair of Siamese Kings [the reigning sovereigns], 447–51. 7 cols. £3.13.6. *Mrs. Hillier* / **Mrs. Charles B. Hillier**

Everything after Its Kind [in nature], 451–53. 4½ cols. £2.2.0. *Mann* / **Christopher Wharton Mann**

The British Lion in a Weak Aspect [the nuisance of formal dinners], 453–56. 7 cols. £3.13.6. *Fitzgerald (Percy)* / **Percy Fitzgerald**

May 1, 1858. No. 423, pp. 457–80

Please to Leave Your Umbrella [exercising one's own judgment in matters of art, morality, etc.], 457–59. 4½ cols. *C.D.* / **Charles Dickens**

A Primitive Old Epic [*Beowulf*], 459–64. 10 cols.; should read 11. *Morley* / **Henry Morley**

Too Late [imagined consequences of unpunctuality], 464–67. 4 cols. £2.2.0. *Hollingshed* / **John Hollingshead**

The Fourfold Dream [story], 467–69. 4¾ cols. £2.12.6. *Payn* / **James Payn**

Swallows [verse], 469. ¾ col. £1.1.0. *Turner* / **G. Turner**

Character Books, 469–74. 9¾ cols. £4.14.6. *Carter* / **Robert Brudenell Carter**

Good-Will [attitude of tradesmen toward consumer], 474–76. 4 cols. £2.2.0. *Hollingshed* / **John Hollingshead**

By Night Express [story], 476–80. 9 cols. £4.14.6. *Fitzgerald* / **Percy Fitzgerald**

May 8, 1858. No. 424, pp. 481–504

The First Idea of Everything [prototypes in nature], 481–84. 6¾ cols. £3.13.6. *Mrs. Linton* / **Eliza Lynn Linton**

A Phantom Opera [Covent Garden Theatre under construction], 484–86. 4 cols. £2.2.0. *Hollingshed* / **John Hollingshead**

The Balcombe Street Mystery [story], 486–93. 14 cols. £6.6.0. *Fitzgerald* / **Percy Fitzgerald**

Familiar Words [verse], 493. ¾ col. £1.1.0. *Call* / **Wathen Mark Wilks Call**

Turpin's Corner [the poor in Southwark], 493–96. 5 cols. *Morley* / **Henry Morley**

People's Umbrellas [as indices to character], 496–98. 5 cols. £2.12.6. *Hollingshed* / **John Hollingshead**

Anglo-Saxon Bookmen, 498–500. 4¼ cols. *Morley* / **Henry Morley**

Australian Jim Walker [a sheepherder], 500–504. 8 cols. £4.4.0. *Vincent* / **Frank Vincent**

May 15, 1858. No. 425, pp. 505–528

New Wheels within Wheels [Pierre H. Boutigny, *Etudes sur les corps a l'état sphéroïdal*, 1857 ed.], 505–509. 9 cols. £4.14.6. *Dixon* / **Edmund Saul Dixon**

The Six Giants of Lehon [saint's legend], 509–518. 18 cols. £7.7.0. *McCabe* / **William Bernard MacCabe**

My Friend's Friend [perhaps a Mrs. Harris?], 518–20. 4 cols. £2.2.0. *Payn* / **James Payn**

Chips:

- How to Make a Madman [an injustice under criminal law administration], 520–22. 4¼ cols.; should read 3½. £2.2.0. *Hollingshed* / **John Hollingshead**
- The Boiled Beef of Old England, 522–23. 3 cols. £1.11.6. *Hart* / **Ernest Abraham Hart**

Walker [John Walker, *A Critical Pronouncing Dictionary*], 523–26. 6 cols. £3.3.0. *J.R.*; also *Jennett Humphreys* / **Jennett Humphreys**

Down among the Dutchmen, xii, 526–28. 4 cols. £2.2.0. *Fitzgerald* / **Percy Fitzgerald**

May 22, 1858. No. 426, pp. 529–52

All Smoke [inert, irresponsible Govt. leadership], 529–31. 4½ cols. £2.12.6. *Head* / **John Oswald Head**

A Sweep through the Stars [astronomy], 531–35. 8¾ cols. £4.4.0. *Dixon* / **Edmund Saul Dixon**

The Devil's Mark [story], 535–41. 11½ cols. £5.15.6. *Miss Parr* / **Harriet Parr**

Really Dangerous Classes [careless people], 541–43. 3¾ cols. £2.0.0. Hollingshed / **John Hollingshead**

Havelok the Dane, 543–48. 9½ cols. *Morley* / **Henry Morley**

My Long Lost Chee-yld! [sentimental comedy, melodrama], 548–52. 10 cols. £5.5.0. *Fitzgerald* / **Percy Fitzgerald**

May 29, 1858. No. 427, pp. 553–76

Earthquake Experiences [an Englishman's aid to earthquake victims, Italy], 553–58. 10 cols. £5.5.0. *Wreford* / **Henry G. Wreford**

The Ether, 558–60. 5¾ cols. £3.0.0. *Dixon* / **Edmund Saul Dixon**

White Washerton [County Courts' leniency to debtors], 560–62. 4 cols. £2.2.0. *Hollingshed* / **John Hollingshead**

The Galleys [under Louis XIV], 562–66. 6¼ cols. £3.3.0. *Thornbury* / **George Walter Thornbury**

The Pixham Explanation [a political meeting], 566–69. 6½ cols. £3.3.0. *Payn* / **James Payn**

Boscobel [Charles II], 569–75. 12½ cols. £6.16.6. *Kent* / **William Charles Mark Kent**

Passing the Time [waiting in lawyer's office], 575–76. 3¼ cols. £1.11.6. *Hollingshed* / **John Hollingshead**

June 5, 1858. No. 428, pp. 577–600

Parish Poor in London [allocation of funds for support of], 577–78. 3 cols. *Morley* / **Henry Morley**

The Lady on the Mall [story], 578–80. 4½ cols. £2.10.0. *Miss Parr* / **Harriet Parr**

Spirits over the Water [excerpts from Boston *Spiritual Age*], 580–83. 6 cols. £3.3.0. *Payn* / **James Payn**

Journey to the Moon [in part from Charles H. Lecouturier, *Panorama des mondes*, 1858], 583–88. 10 cols. £5.5.0. *Dixon* / **Edmund Saul Dixon**

Dust and Ashes [verse], 588–89. ½ col. £0.10.6. *Miss Gibson* / **Miss Mary W. A. Gibson**

The Eve of a Revolution [French Revolution: from contemp. records, as by John Moore, Arthur Young, and others] [i], 589–95. 12 cols. £6.6.0. *Fitzgerald* / **Percy Fitzgerald**

Chips:
- Workers in Kent Street [correction of certain statements in "Turpin's Corner," May 8], 595. 1¼ cols. *Morley* / **Henry Morley**
- A Human Waif [infant corpse found adrift], 595–97. 2¼ cols. £1.1.0. *Laing* / **John Lang**

The Waters Are Out [flood in New South Wales], 597–600. 8 cols. £4.4.0. *Vincent* / **Frank Vincent**

June 12, 1858. No. 429, pp. 601–620

Personal [the "domestic trouble"], 601. 1 col., but occupies space of 2. *C.D.* / **Charles Dickens**

The Nurse in Leading Strings [in part from Florence Nightingale, *The Institution of Kaiserswerth*, 1851], 602–606. 8¼ cols. *Morley* / **Henry Morley**

Ethics of Broadcloth [symbolism of a boy's first jacket], 606–607. 3¾ cols. £2.0.0. *Mrs. Linton* / **Eliza Lynn Linton**

Chip:
- The Goliath among Bridges [Victoria Bridge, Montreal], 607–608. 1 col. *Morley* / **Henry Morley**

The Blood of the Sundons [story], 608–617. 19 cols. £9.9.0. *Fitzgerald* / **Percy Fitzgerald**

Water Music [verse], 617–18. 1 col. £1.11.6. *Roberts*, Sheffield / **Roberts**

Stephen Girard, the Money Maker, 618–20. 4½ cols. £2.10.0. *Hollingshed* / **John Hollingshead**

VOLUME XVIII June 19 – November 27, 1858

June 19, 1858. No. 430, pp. 1–24

My Lady Ludlow [novel], chap. i, 1–7. 12½ cols. £100 for the 14 instalments. *Mrs. Gaskell* / **Elizabeth Gaskell**

The Eve of a Revolution [ii], 7–11. 10 cols. £5.5.0. *Fitzgerald* / **Percy Fitzgerald**

Chip:
– Fly-Catching [an adroit pickpocket], 11–12. 1½ cols. £1.1.0. Item twice entered in Office Book, assigned in first entry to *Hollingshed*, in second to *Payn* / **John Hollingshead** or **James Payn**

Three Scenes for the Study [verse], 12–13. 1¼ cols. £2.2.0. *Landor* / **Walter Savage Landor**

Vital Heat [Jules Gavarret, ... *De la chaleur produite par les êtres vivants*, 1855], 13–18. 10¾ cols. £5.5.0. *Dixon* / **Edmund Saul Dixon**

A Western Campaign [vs. Indians in Minnesota Territory, 1857], 18–21. 4¼ cols. £2.2.0. *Goëtznitz* / **Von Goetznitz**

The Growth of Our Gardens [native and foreign plants, 21–24. 7 cols. £3.13.6. *Mrs. Linton* / **Eliza Lynn Linton**

June 26, 1858. No. 431, pp. 25–48

The Thistle in Bud [Robert Chambers, *Domestic Annals of Scotland*, 1858], 25–29. 9 cols. *Morley* / **Henry Morley**

My Lady Ludlow, chap. ii, 29–34. 10¾ cols. *Mrs. Gaskell* / **Elizabeth Gaskell**

Shot [manufacture of], 34–37. 4¼ cols. £2.2.0. *Hollingshed* / **John Hollingshead**

History of a Miracle ["Our Lady of La Salette"], 37–42. 11½ cols. £5.15.6. *Miss Robertson* / **Miss Robertson**

Too Weak for the Place [luncheon hour at a City tavern], 42–44. 3 cols. £2.0.0. *Hollingshed* / **John Hollingshead**

Bardana Hill [John Hill, M.D., 18 cent.], 44–48. 9 cols. £4.14.6. *Kent* / **William Charles Mark Kent**

July 3, 1858. No. 432, pp. 49–72

Wanted, a Court-Guide [the Royal Household], 49–51. 4½ cols. £2.2.0. *Hollingshed* / **John Hollingshead**

My Lady Ludlow, chap. iii, 51–56. 9¼ cols. *Mrs. Gaskell* / **Elizabeth Gaskell**

At the Siege of Delhi, 56–60. 8½ cols. £3.13.6. *Edgeworth* / **Edgeworth**

The Lady's Dream [verse], 60. 1 col. £2.2.0. *Call* / **Wathen Mark Wilks Call**

Strawberries, 60–64. 8 cols. £4.4.0. *Dixon* / **Edmund Saul Dixon**

Infamous Mr. Fuller [the imposter William Fuller, 1670–1717?], 64–71. 12¾ cols. £6.6.0. *Thomas* / **William Moy Thomas**

A Counterfeit Presentment [the photography mania], 71–72. 3¾ cols. £2.0.0. *Hollingshed* / **John Hollingshead**

July 10, 1858. No. 433, pp. 73–96

The End of Fordyce, Brothers [story], 73–79. 13½ cols. £6.16.6. *Hollingshed* / **John Hollingshead**

A Way to Clean Rivers [sewage disposal], 79–82. 4¼ cols. *Morley* / **Henry Morley**

Horse-Taming, 82–85. 6 cols. £3.3.0. *Henry Dixon* / **Henry Hall Dixon**

My Lady Ludlow, chap. iv, 85–89. 9½ cols. *Mrs. Gaskell* / **Elizabeth Gaskell**

Saxon-English, 89–92. 6 cols. £3.3.0. *Rushton & Morley* / **William Lowes Rushton & Henry Morley**

My First Summons [story], 92–96. 8 cols. £4.4.0. *Dudley Costello* / **Dudley Costello**

July 17, 1858. No. 434, pp. 97–120

French Duelling Extraordinary [hist. incident, 1794–1813], 97–99. 5¾ cols. £3.0.0. *Dixon* / **Edmund Saul Dixon**

My Lady Ludlow, chap. v, 99–104. 9 cols.; should read 10. *Mrs. Gaskell* / **Elizabeth Gaskell**

Various Kinds of Paper, 104–109. 8½ cols. £4.4.0. *Mrs. Linton* / **Eliza Lynn Linton**

The Last Devil's Walk [verse], 109. 1 col. £2.2.0. *Brough* / prob. **Robert Barnabas Brough**

A Negro-Hunt [in Puerto Rico], 109–113. 6 cols.; should read 6¾. £3.3.0. *Goëtznitz* / **Von Goetznitz**

The Reverend Alfred Hoblush's Statement [story], 113–18. 10 cols. £5.5.0. *Fitzgerald* / **Percy Fitzgerald**

Nine Kings [Hudson's Bay Co.], 118–20. 5½ cols. £2.12.6. *Holingshed* / **John Hollingshead**

July 24, 1858. No. 435, pp. 121–44

Dirty Cleanliness [sewage disposal], 121–23. 5 cols. £2.12.6. *Dixon* / **Edmund Saul Dixon**

My Lady Ludlow, chap. vi, 123–28. 10¼ cols. *Mrs. Gaskell* / **Elizabeth Gaskell**

A Reminiscence of Battle [spectacle of siege of Delhi], 128–30. 2 cols. £1.1.0. *Payn* / **James Payn**

Saráwak [career of Rajah Brooke], 130–36. 12 cols. *Morley* / **Henry Morley**

Truth in Irons [contemp. murder case, France], 136–43. 14¼ cols. £7.7.0. *Miss Robertson* / **Miss Robertson**

An Official Scarecrow [the licenser of stage plays], 143–44. 3½ cols. £1.11.6. *Hollingshed* / **John Hollingshead**

July 31, 1858. No. 436, pp. 145–68

When George the Third Was King [William N. Massey, *A History of England,* Vol. II, 1858], 145–47. 6 cols. *Morley* / **Henry Morley**

Chip:
– A Postscript upon Saráwak [Rajah Brooke], 147–48. ¾ col. *Morley* / **Henry Morley**

My Lady Ludlow, chap. vii, 148–53. 10¾ cols. *Mrs. Gaskell* / **Elizabeth Gaskell**

A Princess Royal [encounter with outlaws in Texas], 153–56. 6 cols. £3.3.0. *Goëssnitz* / **Von Goetznitz**

Human Chrysalis [emergence of curate from undergraduate], 156–59. 4¾ cols. £3.0.0. *Payn* / **James Payn**

The Golden Melon [nonsensical controversies], 159–61. 4¼ cols. £2.12.6. *Gostick* / **Joseph Gostick**

What Mr. Burleigh Could Not See [the demise of the stage-coach], 161–68. 15 cols. £7.7.0. *Hollingshed* / **John Hollingshead**

August 7, 1858. No. 437, pp. 169–92

Ozone [Henri Scoutetten, *L'Ozone,* 1856], 169–73. 9¾ cols. £5.0.0. *E. S. Dixon* / **Edmund Saul Dixon**

How Jones Got the English Verse-Medal [prize poem competition], 173–75. 4 cols. £2.2.0. *Payn* / **James Payn**

My Lady Ludlow, chap. viii, 175–81. 11¾ cols. *Mrs. Gaskell* / **Elizabeth Gaskell**

The Savage Muse [Kinahan Cornwallis, *Yarra Yarra; or, The Wandering Aborigine*, 1858 ed.], 181–84. 5½ cols. £2.10.0. *Payn* / **James Payn**

Old Dog Tray [man's love of dogs], 184–89. 9½ cols. £4.14.6. *Fitzgerald* / **Percy Fitzgerald**

The Blankshire Thicket [encounters with highwaymen], 189–92. 6 cols.; should read 7. £3.3.0. *Payn* / **James Payn**

August 14, 1858. No. 438, pp. 193–216

The Humiliation of Fogmoor [electioneering tactics], 193–204. 22½ cols. £11.11.0. *Hollingshed* / **John Hollingshead**

Patience [verse], 204. ¾ col. £1.11.6. *Mrs. Broderip* / **Frances Freeling Broderip**

Chip:
– The Abors [an Assam tribe], 204–205. 2½ cols. £1.5.0. *Lang* / **John Lang**

My Lady Ludlow, chap. ix, 205–211. 10¾ cols. *Mrs. Gaskell* / **Elizabeth Gaskell**

Rat Tales [rat battue at Montfaucon], 211–16. 11 cols. £5.5.0. *Dixon* / **Edmund Saul Dixon**

August 21, 1858. No. 439, pp. 217–40

The Unknown Public [readership of "penny novel-journals"], 217–22. 11½ cols. *Wilkie Collins* / **Wilkie Collins**

The Last Victim of the Gauntlet [in Austrian army, 1851], 222–24. 4 cols. £2.2.0. *Von Goetznitz* / **Von Goetznitz**

Our Vegetable Friends [useful plants], 224–29. 8½ cols. £4.15.0. *Mrs. Linton* / **Eliza Lynn Linton**

Three Roses [verse], 229. ½ col. £1.1.0. *Miss Procter* / **Adelaide Anne Procter**

The Canon's Clock [story], 229–38. 17½ cols. £8.8.0. *Fitzgerald* / **Percy Fitzgerald**

My Uncle the Dean [story], 238–40. 5¼ cols. £2.12.6. *Payn* / **James Payn**

August 28, 1858. No. 440, pp. 241–64

A Shockingly Rude Article [characters in contemp. popular fiction], 241–45. 8½ cols. *Wilkie Collins* / **Wilkie Collins**

Names [Robert Ferguson, *English Surnames*, 1858], 245–47. 4 cols. £2.2.0. *Ruston* / **William Lowes Rushton**

My Lady Ludlow, chap. x, 247–52. 9¾ cols. *Mrs. Gaskell* / **Elizabeth Gaskell**

An Ideal [verse], 252. ¾ col. £1.11.6. *Miss Procter* / **Adelaide Anne Procter**

British Columbia, 252–56. 8 cols. *Morley* / **Henry Morley**

Buying in the Cheapest Market, 256–58. 4½ cols. £2.2.0. *Hollingshed* / **John Hollingshead**

Her Face [story], 258–64. 13 cols. £6.6.0. *Charles Collins* / **Charles Allston Collins**

September 4, 1858. No. 441, pp. 265–88

Bristles and Flint [railway fiascos], 265–70. 10 cols. £5.5.0. *Hollingshed* / **John Hollingshead**

Thunder and Lightning, 270–74. 8½ cols. £4.10.0. *Mrs. Linton* / **Eliza Lynn Linton**

Sea-Breezes with the London Smack [a seaside resort], 274–77. 6 cols. *Wilkie Collins* / **Wilkie Collins**

Gone Forth [verse], 277. ½ col. £1.1.0. *Wilson Holme* / **James Wilson Holme**

My Lady Ludlow, chap. xi, 277–82. 10½ cols. *Mrs. Gaskell* / **Elizabeth Gaskell**

Gertrude's Wyoming [George Peck, *Wyoming; Its History ... and Romantic Adventures*, 1858], 282–85. 5¼ cols. *Morley* / **Henry Morley**

A Travelling Acquaintance [a garrotter], 285–88. 6½ cols. £3.3.0. *Payn* / **James Payn**

September 11, 1858. No. 442, pp. 289–312

On the Canal [canal travel in England], stage i, 289–93. 9 cols. £4.14.6. *Hollingshed* / **John Hollingshead**

The Harvest Moon [nature and effect of moonlight], 293–96. 6 cols. £3.3.0. *Dixon* / **Edmund Saul Dixon**

A Cornish Hug [story], 296–99. 5¼ cols. £2.12.6. *Ollier* / **Edmund Ollier**

My Lady Ludlow, chap. xii, 299–305. 13 cols. *Mrs. Gaskell* / **Elizabeth Gaskell**

Chip:
– The Tradescants, 305–306. 1 col. £1.1.0. *Correspondent* / **John Hooper**

Training for the Tropics [Melchior J. E. Daumas, *Mœurs et coutumes de l'Algérie*, 1853; Ferdinand Hugonnet, *Souvenirs d'un chef de Bureau Arabe*, 1858], 306–312. 13 cols. £6.10.0. *Dixon* / **Edmund Saul Dixon**

September 18, 1858. No. 443, pp. 313–36

The Poisoned Meal [murder trial and imprisonment of Marie-Françoise-Victoire Salmon, 18 cent.], chaps. i–ii, 313–18. 10 cols. *Wilkie Collins* / **Wilkie Collins**

On the Canal, stage ii, 318–23. 10¼ cols. £5.5.0. *Hollingshed* / **John Hollingshead**

Chip:
– The Man behind My Chair [the footman], 323–24. 2¼ cols. £1.1.0. *Hollingshed* / **John Hollingshead**

The Hero of a Hundred Plays [Chinese drama], 324–27. 5 cols. £2.12.6. *Bourne & Morley* / **Henry Richard Fox Bourne & Henry Morley**

My Lady Ludlow, chap. xiii, 327–32. 11 cols. *Mrs. Gaskell* / **Elizabeth Gaskell**

Calling Bad Names [scientific nomenclature], 332–34. 3½ cols. £1.10.0. *Ruston* / **William Lowes Rushton**

Our Back Garden [attempts at housekeeping economies], 334–36. 4 cols. £2.2.0. *Payn* / **James Payn**

September 25, 1858. No. 444, pp. 337–60

Hindoo Law [Laws of Manu], 337–41. 8 cols. £4.4.0. *Bourne* / **Henry Richard Fox Bourne**

My Lady Ludlow, chap. xiv, 341–46. 11½ cols. *Mrs. Gaskell* / **Elizabeth Gaskell**

Grave Voices [verse], 346–47. 1¼ cols. £2.2.0. *Ollier* / **Edmund Ollier**

The Poisoned Meal, chaps. iii–iv, 347–52. 10½ cols. *Wilkie Collins* / **Wilkie Collins**

Historic Doubt [Joseph Octave Delepierre, *Doute historique*, 1854], 352–54. 3¼ cols. £1.11.6. *Bourne* / **Henry Richard Fox Bourne**

On the Canal, stage iii, 354–60. 13 cols. £6.16.6. *Hollingshed* / **John Hollingshead**

October 2, 1858. No. 445, pp. 361–84

Highly Proper! [social prejudice in private schools], 361–63. 5½ cols. *Wilkie Collins* / **Wilkie Collins**

The Profits of a Holiday [story], 363–69. 11 cols. £5.15.6. *Oxenford* / **John Oxenford**

A Very Old Gentleman [first no. of *Gent. Mag.*], 369–72. 6 cols. £3.3.0. *Ede & W.H.W.* / **Joseph Ede & W. H. Wills**

Beyond [verse], 372. 1 col. £2.2.0. *Miss Procter* / **Adelaide Anne Procter**

Safe Harbour [Edward K. Calver, *On the Construction and Principle of a Wave Screen*, 1858], 372–77. 8½ cols. *Morley* / **Henry Morley**

Segment's Shadow [story], 377–79. 5 cols. £2.12.6. *Payn* / **James Payn**

One Other Hospital for Children [Liverpool], 379–80. 3 cols. *Morley* / **Henry Morley**

The Poisoned Meal, chap. v, 380–84. 8 cols. *Wilkie Collins* / **Wilkie Collins**

October 9, 1858. No. 446, pp. 385–408

A Clause for the New Reform Bill [tasteless municipal displays during Queen's visits], 385–87. 5¼ cols. *Wilkie Collins & C.D.* / **Wilkie Collins & Charles Dickens**

Tried Friendship [story], 387–97. 20 cols. £9.9.0. *Thomas* / **William Moy Thomas**

Two Worlds [verse], 397–98. 1 col. £1.11.6. *Miss Procter* / **Adelaide Anne Procter**

Apprenticeship of Frederick the Great [Carlyle, *History of Friedrich II*, Vols. I–II, 1858], 398–402. 9¼ cols. *Morley* / **Henry Morley**

Frightful; but Fashionable [story], 402–404. 3¾ cols. £2.2.0. *Payn* / **James Payn**

Literary Small Change [cheap French periodicals], 404–408. 8¾ cols. £4.4.0. *Dixon* / **Edmund Saul Dixon**

October 16, 1858. No. 447, pp. 409–432

Five Comets [of 1858], 409–412. 7½ cols. £3.13.6. *Dixon* / **Edmund Saul Dixon**

The Heir of Hardington [story], 412–19. 14¼ cols. £7.7.0. *Miss Parr* / **Harriet Parr**

On the Gold Coast [Gold Coast natives; English law courts], 419–23. 8 cols. £4.4.0. *Miss Martin* / **Miss Martin**

The Smallport Monte-Cristo [story], 423–28. 10 cols. £5.5.0. *Charles Collins* / **Charles Allston Collins**

Amateur Horse-Training [the John S. Rarey system], 428–32. 8 cols. £4.4.0. *Sidney* / **Samuel Sidney**

October 23, 1858. No. 448, pp. 433–56

Water, 433–37. 9 cols. £4.14.6. *Mrs. Linton* / **Eliza Lynn Linton**

Chip:
– Books for the Indian Army, 437–38. 1 col. *Correspondent* / ———

The Fleur de Lys [story], 438–44. 13¼ cols. £6.6.0. *Fitzgerald* / **Percy Fitzgerald**

Amalek Dagon [thimbleriggers, card-sharpers], 444–47. 5¼ cols. £2.12.6. *Payn* / **James Payn**

Coffee and Pipes [travel in Lebanon], 447–54. 12½ cols.; should read 13¼. £6.6.0. *Meesom-Lang* / **Malcolm Ronald Laing Meason**

Mr. W. Shakespeare, Solicitor [William Lowes Rushton, *Shakespeare a Lawyer*, 1858], 454–56. 6 cols. *Morley* / **Henry Morley**

October 30, 1858. No. 449, pp. 457–80

At a Bull-Fight, 457–63. 13¼ cols. £6.16.6. *Thornbury* / **George Walter Thornbury**

Farewell to the Comet [Donati's comet], 463–66. 5 cols. £2.12.6. *Dixon* / **Edmund Saul Dixon**

Domestic Castle-Building [a real-estate swindle], 466–70. 9½ cols. £4.14.6. *Hollingshed* / **John Hollingshead**

A Sabbath Hour [Edinburgh Sundays], 470–72. 4 cols. £2.2.0. *Payn* / **James Payn**

National Contrasts, 472–76. 7 cols. £3.13.6. *Mrs. Linton* / **Eliza Lynn Linton**

The Great Dunkerque Failure [story], 476–80. 9 cols. £4.14.6. *Charles Collins* / **Charles Allston Collins**

November 6, 1858. No. 450, pp. 481–504

A Picture of Merchandise [French tariff system], 481–86. 10½ cols. £5.5.0. *Dixon* / **Edmund Saul Dixon**

Three Masters [cruelty to animals], 486–90. 8½ cols. £4.4.0. *Hollingshed* / **John Hollingshead**

My Model Theatre [theatre management], 490–92. 4 cols. £2.2.0. *Hollingshed* / **John Hollingshead**

Seville, 492–98. 12¾ cols. £6.6.0. *Thornbury* / **George Walter Thornbury**

Black, White, and Whity-Brown [broad, uncritical judgments], 498–500. 3 cols. £1.11.6. *Hollingshed* / **John Hollingshead**

A Backwoods-Preacher [Peter Cartwright, *The Backwoods Preacher*, an 1858 London ed.], 500–504. 9 cols. £4.14.6. *Mrs. Linton* / **Eliza Lynn Linton**

November 13, 1858. No. 451, pp. 505–528

Railway Nightmares [an abandoned railway line; a Govt.-managed railway], 505–508. 7 cols. £3.13.6. *Hollingshed* / **John Hollingshead**

Sherry, 508–514. 11 cols. £5.15.6. *Thornbury* / **George Walter Thornbury**

Monstrous Clever Boys [Adrien Baillet, *Des enfans devenus célèbres par leurs études ou par leurs écrits, 1688*], 514–16. 5 cols. £2.12.6. *Morley* / **Henry Morley**

A Paradoxical Experience [story], 516–22. 12 cols. *Wilkie Collins* / **Wilkie Collins**

Neapolitan Energy [continuation of "Earthquake Experiences," May 29], 522–24. 4 cols. £2.2.0. *Wreford* / **Henry G. Wreford**

Life and Death in Saint Giles's [George Buchanan, M.D., *St. Giles in 1857, 1858*], 524–28. 8 cols. *Morley* / **Henry Morley**

November 20, 1858. No. 452, pp. 529–52

In Search of Don Quixote [decadence of Spanish character], 529–34. 11 cols. £5.15.6. *Thornbury* / **George Walter Thornbury**

Lina Fernie [story], 534–38. 8½ cols. £4.4.0. *Miss Parr* / **Harriet Parr**

Jews in Rome [from Edmond About's articles in *Moniteur*], 538–40. 4 cols. £2.2.0. *Lumley* / prob. **George Lumley**

Long Ago [verse], 540–41. 1 col. £1.1.0. *Elizabeth Addey* / **Elizabeth Addey**

Chips from the Comet [Donati's comet; the stellar universe], 541–44. 5 cols. £2.12.6. *Dixon* / **Edmund Saul Dixon**

A Wonderful Wild Beast [animal that terrified southern France, 18 cent.], 544–47. 7 cols. £3.13.6. *Costello* / **Dudley Costello**

Old Customs [murder of a revenue officer and an informer, 1747], 547–52. 11 cols. £5.15.6. *Thomas* / **William Moy Thomas**

November 27, 1858. No. 453, pp. 553–72

The Sin of a Father [story], 553–61. 16 cols. £8.8.0. *Mrs. Gaskell* / **Elizabeth Gaskell**

A Golden Legend [R. H. Schomburgk's edition, 1848, of Ralegh's *Discovery of ... Guiana*], 561–65. 8½ cols. £4.4.0. *Miss Lynn (Mrs. Linton)* / **Eliza Lynn Linton**

Everybody's Referee [asking advice of uninformed person], 565–66. 4 cols.; should read 3. £2.2.0. *Hollingshed* / **John Hollingshead**

Three Years Older [statistics on public health, educ., etc.], 566–69. 4½ cols. *Morley* / **Henry Morley**

Going for a Song [story], 569–72. 8 cols. £4.4.0. *Fitzgerald* / **Percy Fitzgerald**

VOLUME XIX December 4, 1858 – May 28, 1859

December 4, 1858. No. 454, pp. 1-24

A Ride through the Raisin Country [Spain], 1–7. 13 cols. £6.6.0. *Thornbury* / **George Walter Thornbury**

Saving Little: Wasting Much [story], 7–13. 11 cols. £5.15.6. *Mrs. Linton* / **Eliza Lynn Linton**

Behind the Scenes [verse], 13. 1 col. £1.1.0. *Kent* / **William Charles Mark Kent**

Britannia's Figures [statistics on poverty, crime, emigration], 13–16. 5¾ cols. *Morley* / **Henry Morley**

Irritable Plants, 16–18. 3¾ cols. £1.11.6. *Robertson* / prob. **John Robertson**

The Reverend Alfred Hoblush's Further Statement [story], 18–24. 12¾ cols. £5.15.6. *Fitzgerald* / **Percy Fitzgerald**

December 11, 1858. No. 455, pp. 25–48

Trading in Fetters [French tariff system], 25–29. 9¼ cols. £4.4.0. *Dixon* / **Edmund Saul Dixon**

Her First Appearance [story], 29–33. 8 cols. £3.13.6. *Payn* / **James Payn**

Mosses, 33–35. 4 cols. £2.2.0. *Robertson* / prob. **John Robertson**

Little Bell [verse], 35–38. 5 cols. £3.3.0. *Mrs. Meredith* / **Louisa Anne Meredith**

King Cotton [sources of cotton supply], 38–40. 4¾ cols. £2.15.0. *Miss Martin* / **Miss Martin**

Chip:

– Siamese Women and Children, 40–42. 2½ cols. £1.5.0. *Mrs. Hellier* / **Mrs. Charles B. Hillier**

Gib [Gibraltar], 42–47. 10 cols. £4.14.6. *Thornbury* / **George Walter Thornbury**

Sultry December [climate of Australia], 47–48. 2 cols.; should read 3¼. £1.1.0. *Charles Gill* / **Charles Gill**

December 18, 1858. No. 456, pp. 49–72

Doctor Dulcamara, M.P. [Charlotte M. Yonge, *The Heir of Redclyffe*, 1853], 49–52. 7½ cols. *Wilkie Collins & C.D.* / **Wilkie Collins & Charles Dickens**

The Gringe Family [story], 52–58. 10¾ cols. £5.5.0. *Fitzgerald* / **Percy Fitzgerald**

Minerva by Gaslight [evening classes at King's College, London], 58–62. 7½ cols. *Morley* / **Henry Morley**

Bathilda [verse], 62. 1 col. £1.11.6. *Mrs. T. K. Hervey* / **Eleanora Louisa Hervey**

The Alhambra, 62–68. 11 cols. £5.5.0. *Thornbury* / **George Walter Thornbury**

Cœlebs in Search of a Dinner [a Sunday excursion], 68–72. 9¼ cols. £4.14.6. *Charles Collins* / **Charles Allston Collins**

Christmas 1858. Extra Christmas Number: A House to Let, pp. 1–36. Announced pub. date and running date: Dec. 7. Stated on title page of Vol. XVIII as included in that vol.; title listed at end of "Contents" of that vol.

Over the Way, 1–6. 12 cols.; should read 10½. *Collins* / **Wilkie Collins**

The Manchester Marriage,* 6–17. 25 cols.; should read 22¾. £17.17.0. *Mrs. Gaskell* / **Elizabeth Gaskell**

Going into Society,† 18–23. 10 cols. *C.D.* / **Charles Dickens**

Three Evenings in the House‡ [verse], 23–26. 6½ cols. £7.7.0. *Miss Procter* / **Adelaide Anne Procter**

Trottle's Report,§ 26–32. 12 cols. *Collins* / **Wilkie Collins**

Let at Last, 32–36. 9 cols. *Do. & C.D.* / **Wilkie Collins & Charles Dickens**

*Followed by a transition passage set off typographically from the story. Stone, ed., *Charles Dickens' Uncollected Writings from Household Words*, states that the passage was probably written by Collins – Dickens's collaborator on the number – and revised by Dickens. The 25-col. Office Book length notation ("four" seems to be overwritten to read "five") was obviously intended to include the length (¾ col.) of the transition passage. The story ends on p. 17; the transition passage, on p. 18.

†Followed by a transition passage set off typographically from the story. The passage is included in editions of Dickens's collected works. The 10-col. Office Book length notation includes the length (1½ cols.) of the transition passage. The story ends on p. 22; the transition passage, on p. 23.

‡Followed by a transition passage.

§The 12-col. Office Book length notation includes the length (¾ col.) of the transition passage following "Three Evenings in the House."

December 25, 1858. No. 457, pp. 73–96

Home Again! [story], 73–80. 15 cols. £7.7.0. *Fitzgerald* / **Percy Fitzgerald**

The Innocent Holder Business [fraudulent financial dealings], 80–84. 7 cols. £3.13.6. *Hollingshed* / **John Hollingshead**

The Schoolroom at Christmas Time [verse], 84. 1 col. £1.11.6. *Miss Parr* / **Harriet Parr**

Lisbon, 84–89. 10 cols. £5.5.0. *Thornbury* / **George Walter Thornbury**

A Gipsy King [story], 89–92. 5¼ cols. £2.12.6. *Hollingshed* / **John Hollingshead**

The Almanac-Tree [French almanacs], 92–96. 9½ cols. £4.4.0. *Dixon* / **Edmund Saul Dixon**

January 1, 1859. No. 458, pp. 97–120. Announced in advts. in the 3 preceding nos. as "A New Year's Number."

New Year's Day [recollections of], 97–102. 10¾ cols. *C.D.* / **Charles Dickens**

A New Oddity [Reichenbach's od], 102–105. 6 cols. £3.3.0. *Dixon* / **Edmund Saul Dixon**

A New Mother [verse], 105–107. 4¼ cols. £5.0.0. *Miss Procter* / **Adelaide Anne Procter**

A New Mind [story], 107–114. 14 cols. *Wilkie Collins* / **Wilkie Collins**

New Toys [proper toys for children], 114–16. 4 cols. £2.2.0. *Oxenford* / **John Oxenford**

A New Baby [story], 116–19. 6½ cols. £3.3.0. *Spicer* / **Henry Spicer**

New Year's Eve [verse], 119–20. 1¾ cols. £2.12.6. *Ollier* / **Edmund Ollier**

January 8, 1859. No. 459, pp. 121–44

Ground and Lofty Tumbling [story], 121–32. 22 cols. £9.9.0. *J* [?]. *White* / prob. **the Rev. James White**

Hidden Chords [verse], 132. ¼ col. £1.1.0. *Miss Procter* / **Adelaide Anne Procter**

Spanish Hotels, 132–37. 11¼ cols. £5.15.6. *Thornbury* / **George Walter Thornbury**

Rustic Townsmen [cheap trains for City workers], 137–39. 3½ cols. *Morley* / **Henry Morley**

Chip:
- Character-Murder [facts of the Gaunt case: from "A Disappearance Cleared Up," Feb. 21, 1852, and other sources], 139–40. 2¼ cols. *Morley* / **Henry Morley**

Michelet's Bird [*L'Oiseau*, 1856], 140–44. 8 cols. £4.4.0. *Dixon* / **Edmund Saul Dixon**

January 15, 1859. No. 460, pp. 145–68

Pity a Poor Prince [official attentions to Midshipman Alfred], 145–47. 5½ cols. *Wilkie Collins* / **Wilkie Collins**

A Yorkshire Tragedy [story], 147–51. 7 cols. £3.3.0. *Gunn* / **Charles Hains Gunn**

Dwellers in Tents [Godfrey Rhodes, *Tents and Tent-Life*, 1858], 151–55. 7¾ cols. £3.13.6. *Miss Lynn (Mrs. Linton* / **Eliza Lynn Linton**

The Blooming Rose [verse], 155–58. 6¼ cols. £5.5.0. *Mrs. MacIntosh* / **Mrs. MacIntosh**

A New Way of Making an Old Article [story], 158–63. 9¾ cols. £4.14.6. *Dudley Costello* / **Dudley Costello**

Steward! [on board ship], 163–68. 10½ cols.; should read 11¼. £5.5.0. *Thornbury* / **George Walter Thornbury**

January 22, 1859. No. 461, pp. 169–92

The Clergyman's Wife [the poor in a rural parish] [i]: Poor Cottages, 169–72. 6¾ cols. £3.3.0. *Mrs. Blacker* / **Mrs. Blacker**

My Name [frustrating surnames], 172–74. 3¼ cols. £1.11.6. *Hollingshed* / **John Hollingshead**

Perils in India [William Edwards, *Personal Adventures during the Indian Rebellion*, 1858], 174–79. 11¾ cols. *Morley* / **Henry Morley**

The Smallchange Family [story], 179–86. 12 cols. £5.5.0. *Charles Collins* / **Charles Allston Collins**

Up and down the Giralda [visit to cigar factory; to the Giralda], 186–92. 14 cols. £7.7.0. *Thornbury* / **George Walter Thornbury**

January 29, 1859. No. 462, pp. 193–216

A Journey in Kafirland, 193–97. 9 cols. £4.0.0. *Andrew Mitchell* / **Andrew Mitchell**

The Clergyman's Wife [ii]: Life in Lightlands, 197–201. 7 cols. £3.13.6. *Mrs. Blacker* / **Mrs. Blacker**

Miss Cicely's Portrait [story], 201–204. 8 cols. £4.4.0. *Fitzgerald* / **Percy Fitzgerald**

Calm [verse], 204–205. ½ col. £1.1.0. *Duthie* / **William Duthie**

Idle Hours in Cadiz, 205–210. 14 cols.; should read 11. £7.7.0. *Thornbury* / **George Walter Thornbury**

New Puppets for Old Ones [false stereotype of capitalist, alderman, etc.], 210–12. 4¾ cols. *Hollingshed* / **John Hollingshead**

The Eastern Kingdom [Japan], 212–16. 8 cols. £3.13.6. *Mrs. Linton* / **Eliza Lynn Linton**

February 5, 1859. No. 463, pp. 217–40

Douglas Jerrold [William Blanchard Jerrold, *The Life and Remains of Douglas Jerrold*, 1859], 217–22. 10 cols. *W. Collins* / **Wilkie Collins**

Cast Away [story], 222–27. 11 cols. £5.5.0. *Miss Marryatt* / **Miss Marryat**

Pearls, 227–30. 6 cols. £3.3.0. *Miss Robertson* / **Miss Robertson**

In a Military Prison [autobiog.], 230–37. 13½ cols. £3.3.0. *Private Douglas* / **William Douglas**

Japanese Social Life [Andrew Steinmetz, *Japan and Her People*, 1859], 237–40. 6½ cols. £3.3.0. *Miss Martin* / **Miss Martin**

February 12, 1859. No. 464, pp. 241–64

Burns. Viewed As a Hat-Peg [Burns centennial celebrations], 241–43. 5 cols. *W. Wilkie Collins* / **Wilkie Collins**

The Inquisition's Gala-Day [an auto-da-fé: from book, 1680, by Serafin de Carcel (not identified)], 243–49. 12 cols. £6.6.0. *Thornbury* / **George Walter Thornbury**

Chloroform, 249–52. 7 cols. £3.13.6. *Dr. Priestley* / **William Overend Priestley**

Two Leaves from the Devil's Book [defence of French theatre], 252–58. 10¾ cols. £5.15.6. *Charles Collins* / **Charles Allston Collins**

New Year's Day in China, 258–60. 3¾ cols. £1.11.6. *Mrs. Grumride*[?] / **Mrs. Grumride?**

A Relic of the Middling Ages [story], 260–64. 10 cols. £5.5.0. *Hollingshed* / **John Hollingshead**

February 19, 1859. No. 465, pp. 265–88

Bogie Albion [French stage-version of Englishmen], 265–69. 9½ cols. £4.4.0. *Fitzgerald* / **Percy Fitzgerald**

Rather Low Company [a schoolmistress's village friends], 269–71. 3¾ cols. £1.11.6. *Miss Stone* / **Miss Stone**

Murillo and His Picture Children, 271–75. 9¾ cols.; should read 8¾. £4.14.6. *Thornbury* / **George Walter Thornbury**

My Two Partners [story], 275–80. 8 cols. £4.4.0. *Hollingshed* / **John Hollingshead**

Michelet and Insects [*L'Insecte*, 1858], 280–86. 13 cols. £5.15.6. *Dixon* / **Edmund Saul Dixon**

Fire-Worshippers [Dosabhoy Framjee, *The Parsees*, 1858], 286–88. 5 cols. £2.2.0. *Bourne & Morley* / **Henry Richard Fox Bourne & Henry Morley**

February 26, 1859. No. 466, pp. 289–312

Uncommon Good Eating [Peter L. Simmonds, *The Curiosities of Food*, 1859], 289–93. 9 cols. £4.14.6. *Mrs. Linton* / **Eliza Lynn Linton**

Dishonoured [story], 293–99. 12 cols. £5.15.6. *Costello* / **Dudley Costello**

My Model Director [railway mismanagement], 299–301. 4¼ cols. £2.2.0. *Head* / **John Oswald Head**

Out of Doors in Malaga, 301–306. 8½ cols. £4.4.0. *Thornbury* / **George Walter Thornbury**

Chip:

– A Column to Burns [reader's response to "Burns," Feb. 12], 306. 1 col. *Item not in Office Book* / intro. comment prob. by **Wilkie Collins**

Novelty [attitudes toward change], 306–309. 4½ cols. £2.2.0. *Charles Collins* / **Charles Allston Collins**

Much Too Good Boys [contemp. children's books], 309–312. 6 cols.; should read 8. *Morley* / **Henry Morley**

March 5, 1859. No. 467, pp. 313–36

The Highest Testimonials [untruthful letters of recommendation], 313–15. 5 cols. £2.12.6. *Mrs. Blacker* / **Mrs. Blacker**

Going to Africa [Gibraltar], 315–21. 11 cols. £5.15.6. *Thornbury* / **George Walter Thornbury**

At Work in the Dark [London workshop for the blind], 321–24. 7 cols. *Morley* / **Henry Morley**

A Warning [verse], 324–25. ¾ col. £1.1.0. *Miss Procter* / **Adelaide Anne Procter**

The Lagging Easter [ecclesiastical calendar], 325–30. 10¼ cols. £5.5.0. *Dixon* / **Edmund Saul Dixon**

Third Statement of Reverend Alfred Hoblush [story], 330–36. 13½ cols. £6.6.0. *Fitzgerald* / **Percy Fitzgerald**

March 12, 1859. No. 468, pp. 337–60

The Great (Forgotten) Invasion [French landing on Welsh coast, 1797], 337–41. 8½ cols. *Wilkie Collins* / **Wilkie Collins**

The Chetwyndes [story], 341–46. 14¼ cols.; should read 10½. £7.7.0. *Miss Parr* / **Harriet Parr**

Men in Masks [poseurs], 346–48. 4 cols. £2.2.0. *Hollingshed* / **John Hollingshead**

Envy [verse], 348. ¾ col. £1.1.0. *Miss Procter* / **Adelaide Anne Procter**

In Africa [Gibraltar to Ceuta], 348–54. 11¼ cols. £5.15.6. *Thornbury* / **George Walter Thornbury**

Physical Force [W. R. Grove, *On the Correlation of Physical Forces*, first pub. 1846; Alfred Smee, *The Monogenesis of Physical Forces*, 1857], 354–59. 9½ cols. £4.4.0. *Dixon* / **Edmund Saul Dixon**

Match-Making Majesty [Louis Napoleon at Plombières], 359–60. 4 cols. £2.2.0. *Mrs. Ward* / **Mrs. Ward**

March 19, 1859. No. 469, pp. 361–84

A Breach of British Privilege [new Adelphi Theatre], 361–64. 6 cols. *W. Wilkie Collins* / **Wilkie Collins**

Bush and Beach [British officers' life on Gold Coast], 364–67. 7 cols. £3.13.6. *Miss Martin* / **Miss Martin**

Mineral Springs, 367–73. 12½ cols. £4.4.0. *Sidney Gibson* / **William Sidney Gibson**

Haunted [verse], 373–74. ¾ col. £1.1.0. *Miss Gibson* / **Miss Mary W. A. Gibson**

The Lucky Leg [story], 374–80. 12¼ cols. £5.5.0. *Mrs. Stretton* / **Sarah Smith**

The Real Cook's Oracle [Antoine Gogué, *Les Secrets de la cuisine française*, 1856], 380–84. 9 cols. £4.4.0. *Fitzgerald* / **Percy Fitzgerald**

March 26, 1859. No. 470, pp. 385–408

A Group of Noble Savages [Paul Kane, *Wanderings ... among the Indians of North America*, 1859], 385–90. 10 cols. *Morley* / **Henry Morley**

Spanish Proverbs, 390–93. 5¾ cols. £2.12.6. *Thornbury* / **George Walter Thornbury**

The Parcels-Post, 393–94. 3 cols. £1.11.6. *Dr. Cormack* / **John Rose Cormack**

An Old Story [verse], 394–96. 4¼ cols. £4.4.0. *Call* / **Wathen Mark Wilks Call**

Out of Tune [story], 396–403. 13 cols. £6.6.0. *Fitzgerald* / **Percy Fitzgerald**

The Father of Caoutchouc [Thomas Hancock, ... *Origin and Progress of ... India-Rubber Manufacture in England*, 1857], 403–407. 8 cols. £4.4.0. *Mrs. Linton* / **Eliza Lynn Linton**

A Court without Appeal [Courts of Love], 407–408. 2½ cols. £1.5.0. *Bourne* / **Henry Richard Fox Bourne**

April 2, 1859. No. 471, pp. 409–432

Pictures and Ballads [of Spain], 409–415. 13¾ cols. £6.6.0. *Thornbury* / **George Walter Thornbury**

The Cure of Sick Minds [John C. Bucknill, M.D., "Reports of Lunatic Asylums," *Jour. of Mental Science*, Jan. 1859], 415–19. 6½ cols. *Morley* / **Henry Morley**

My Lady Crump [contentment with one's lot], 419–21. 5 cols. £2.12.6. *Mrs. Broderip* / **Frances Freeling Broderip**

The Reverend Alfred Hoblush Finds a New Broom [story], 421–26. 8¼ cols. £4.4.0. *Fitzgerald* / **Percy Fitzgerald**

Chip:
– Art in Its Chimney-Corner [Robert Rawlinson, *Designs for ... Tall Chimney Shafts*, 1858], 426. 1½ cols. *Morley* / **Henry Morley**

Michelet's Love [*L'Amour*, 1858], 426–32. 12 cols. £5.5.0. *Dixon* / **Edmund Saul Dixon**

April 9, 1859. No. 472, pp. 433–56

Out-Conjuring Conjurors [J. E. Robert-Houdin, *Confidences d'un prestidigitateur*, 1859], 433–39. 12¼ cols. £6.6.0. *Dixon* / **Edmund Saul Dixon**

Navy Dry-Rot [Admiralty mismanagement], 439–43. 7 cols. £3.13.6. *Hollingshed* / **John Hollingshead**

Chip:
– To Let [lodgings in provincial town], 443–44. 2 cols. £1.1.0. *J. A. Hammersley* / **James Astbury Hammersley**

Dreaming [verse], 444. ¼ col. £0.10.6. *Miss Gibson* / **Miss Mary W. A. Gibson**

Spanish Dinners, 444–49. 10 cols. £5.5.0. *Thornbury* / **George Walter Thornbury**

White Ants [Henry Smeathman, ... *The Termites ... in Africa and Other Hot Climates*, 1781], 449–54. 8 cols.; should read 9¼. £3.13.6. *Robertson* / prob. **John Robertson**

An Illustrious British Exile ["George Barrington," pickpocket], 454–56. 6 cols. £3.3.0. *Laing* / **John Lang**

April 16, 1859. No. 473, pp. 457–80

From First to Last [story], chaps. i–ii, 457–61. 9 cols. £12.12.0 for the 3 instalments. *Miss Parr* / **Harriet Parr**

To and from Tunis, 461–67. 11 cols. £5.5.0. *H. Spicer* / **Henry Spicer**

My Brother's Dinner [Peter L. Simmonds, *The Curiosities of Food*, 1859], 467–69. 4 cols. £2.2.0. *Hollingshed* / **John Hollingshead**

Violets [verse], 469. 1½ cols. £2.2.0. *Mrs. MacIntosh* / **Mrs. MacIntosh**

Laughing Philosophers [Aristophanes], 469–74. 8¾ cols. £4.4.0. *Call* / **Wathen Mark Wilks Call**

Fossil Geography [etymology of place-names], 474–77. 7 cols. £3.13.6. *Dixon* / **Edmund Saul Dixon**

A Bad Name [author thought a madman], 477–80. 6½ cols. £3.3.0. *Laing* / **John Lang**

April 23, 1859. No. 474, pp. 481–504

Hospitable Patriarchs [the Maronites, Lebanon], 481–84. 7½ cols. £3.10.0. *Meason* / **Malcolm Ronald Laing Meason**

The Tournament at the Alhambra [a Granada madhouse; the Alhambra], 484–89. 9¾ cols. £4.14.6. *Thornbury* / **George Walter Thornbury**

A Special Convict [Sir Henry Browne Hayes, transported 1802], 489–91. 5¼ cols.; should read 4½. £2.12.6. *Laing* / **John Lang**

My Vision [verse], 491–92. ½ col. £1.1.0. *Fanny Hall* / **Fanny Hall**

From First to Last, chaps. iii–vii, 492–98. 12 cols. *Miss Parr* / **Harriet Parr**

Oyster Seed [oyster culture, France], 498–503. 10¼ cols. £4.14.6. *Dixon* / **Edmund Saul Dixon**

A Duel in Jest [17 cent., in Spain], 503–504. 3¼ cols. *Morley* / **Henry Morley**

April 30, 1859. No. 475, pp. 505–528

Some Wild Ideas [for improvements in streets, housing, police force, children's books], 505–510. 10 cols. £5.5.0. *Charles Collins* / **Charles Allston Collins**

On the West African Coast [inland trip, Gold Coast], 510–14. 8½ cols. £4.4.0. *Miss Martin* / **Miss Martin**

Going A-maying [English poets on May and maying], 514–17. 7 cols. £3.13.6. *Kent & W.H.W.* / **William Charles Mark Kent & W. H. Wills**

My Turkish Master at Seville, 517–22. 9 cols. £4.14.6. *Thornbury* / **George Walter Thornbury**

From First to Last, chaps. viii–x, 522–26. 8½ cols. *Miss Parr* / **Harriet Parr**

British Fire-Worship [purpose of vitrified forts], 526–28. 5 cols. £2.12.16. *Dr. Cormack* / **John Rose Cormack**

May 7, 1859. No. 476, pp. 529–52

The Brookrudder Book-Club [story], 529–32. 7 cols. £3.13.6. *Fitzgerald* / **Percy Fitzgerald**

Ten Italian Women [T. A. Trollope, *A Decade of Italian Women*, 1859], 532–37. 10¼ cols. £5.5.0. *Mrs. Linton* / **Eliza Lynn Linton**

Baron Wald [transported convict], 537–41. 7 cols. £3.13.6. *Laing* / **John Lang**

All the Year Round [verse], 541. 1½ cols. £2.12.6. *Mrs. MacIntosh* / **Mrs. MacIntosh**

Another Laughing Philosopher [Lucian], 541–46. 9½ cols. £4.14.6. *Call* / **Wathen Mark Wilks Call**

Only a Governess [attitude toward governesses], 546–49. 5 cols. £2.12.6. *Miss Wilson* / **Florence Wilson**

A May Day in the Pyrenees [account of a peasant girl], 549–52. 8 cols. £4.4.0. *Miss Martin* / **Miss Martin**

May 14, 1859. No. 477, pp. 553–76

Three Celebrities [transported convicts], 553–57. 9¾ cols. £5.0.0. *Laing* / **John Lang**

Beltane, or May-Day, 557–61. 6½ cols. £3.3.0. *Dr. Cormack* / **John Rose Cormack**

Japan Traits [Andrew Steinmetz, *Japan and Her People*, 1859], 561–65. 8¾ cols. £4.4.0. *Miss Martin* / **Miss Martin**

My Spanish Kaleidoscope [regions of Spain], 565–70. 8½ cols. £4.4.0. *Thornbury* / **George Walter Thornbury**

Rencontres [incidents of travel], 570–72. 4¼ cols. £2.12.6. *Miss Wilson* / **Florence Wilson**

A French Pepys [Saint-Simon, *Memoirs*, 1857 trans.], 572–76. 10¾ cols.; should read 9¾. £5.5.0. *Mrs. Linton* / **Eliza Lynn Linton**

May 21, 1859. No. 478, pp. 577–600

Street Minstrelsy [popular songs], 577–80. 6 cols. £3.3.0. *Mrs. Linton & W.H.W.* / **Eliza Lynn Linton & W. H. Wills**

The Spain of Cervantes and the Spain of Gil Blas, 580–84. 7½ cols. £3.13.6. *W. Thornbury* / **George Walter Thornbury**

Friends in Australia [story], 584–88. 10 cols.; should read 8. £5.5.0. *Miss Marryatt* / **Miss Marryat**

Nicholas the Rope-Dancer [story], 588–94. 12 cols. £6.6.0. *Miss Jewsbury* / **Geraldine Endsor Jewsbury**

Over the Way [dwellers in a Paris lodging-house], 594–96. 4½ cols. £2.2.0. *Bayle St. John* / **Bayle St. John**

Chip:
- Flamborough Head [etymology of place-name], 596. ½ col. *Correspondent* / ———

Kate Crawford [transported convict (fictitious name)], 596–600. 9 cols. £4.14.6. *Laing* / **John Lang**

May 28, 1859. No. 479, pp. 601–620

All the Year Round [announcement of], 601. 2 cols. *C.D.* / **Charles Dickens**

My Farewell Dinner at Gib, 602–605. 7½ cols. £3.13.6. *Thornbury* / **George Walter Thornbury**

Nobody's Philanthropist [slum children], 605–608. 6¼ cols. £3.3.0. *W. B. Jerrold* / **William Blanchard Jerrold**

Chips:
- A Smock-Frock Parliament [an association of labourers], 608–609. 2 cols. *Morley* / **Henry Morley**
- A Dramatic Author [Edward Fitzball, *Thirty-five Years of a Dramatic Author's Life*, 1859], 609–610. 2 cols. *Wilkie Collins* / **Wilkie Collins**

Bad Bargains [civil service career in East India Co.], 610–13. 6 cols. £3.3.0. *Laing* / **John Lang**

Miss Saint Felix [transported convict (fictitious name)], 613–17. 8 cols. £4.4.0. *Laing* / **John Lang**

An Executor [of a will], 617–20. 6½ cols. £3.3.0. *Hollingshed* / **John Hollingshead**

A Last Household Word, 620. ½ col. *C.D.* / **Charles Dickens**

PART TWO
Household Words Contributors

EXPLANATORY NOTE

In the following list of contributors and their contributions, the manner of transcribing contributors' names from the Office Book and of recording titles of *H.W.* items is the same as in Part One, *Household Words* Table of Contents (see Explanatory Note to Part One).

The word "contributor" is here taken to mean a person living at the time that his writing appeared in *H.W.*, whether or not he intended the writing for publication in the periodical. The word is used to mean a staff member as well as a contributor in the usual sense of the term.

Included as entries in the list are contributors' pseudonyms given in the Office Book, and also initials and certain other designations that substitute for a contributor's name. For identified contributors, these are cross-referred to the contributor's name. Not included as separate entries are the variant forms in which a contributor's name appears in the Office Book (as with or without initials, with or without title, etc.) or the variant spellings of a name, except for names so misspelled as to warrant a separate entry with cross-reference. (The variant forms and spellings are listed with the entry for the contributor's name.) Not included as entries are the Office Book designations "Correspondent," "Chance correspondent," "Communicated," and "Anonymous." Identified contributors so designated are listed under their names; unidentified contributors so designated are, together with unidentified contributors of no designation, listed separately, immediately following the alphabetical listing.

Women contributors are listed under the name under which they contributed to *H.W.*, with cross-reference from either maiden or married name for writers who published under both names.

Set off by vertical bars, following a contributor's name, is the designation (or designations) under which the contributor appears in the Office Book. In the instances in which a contributor's address (or the address to which payment for an item was sent) as given in the Office Book is essential, or might be essential, in establishing a contributor's identity, the address is included with the designation. Other addresses are not recorded.

The identification note on a contributor gives basic biographic facts if these facts are available; otherwise, it records whatever biographic information is stated or implied in the writer's contributions. If the information is available, the note on a contributor states his relationship with or attitude toward Dickens, the circumstances under which he became a *H.W.* contributor, and whatever association of interest he may have had with the periodical. References in *H.W.* to the contributor or to his writings or other work are mentioned. If the contributor wrote for *A.Y.R.* as well as for *H.W.*, that fact is stated. The reprinting of a writer's contributions by *Harper's New Monthly Magazine* (occasionally by other periodicals) is mentioned, as indicating the reader-interest that the items were thought to have; also mentioned is the inclusion of a writer's contributions in certain books of *H.W.* selections.

Since the location of all *H.W.* items is given in the Title Index (included in this volume), items mentioned in identification notes usually appear without notation of date. The date of an item mentioned is given only when the date has a specific bearing on the matter under discussion (as when the item mentioned is motivated by an item in a preceding number, when the item mentioned motivates an item in a following number, or when the date of the item has other relevancy), when reference is to a specific instalment of an item, or (in one instance) when reference is to one of two items of the same title.

At the end of the identification note is a reference to a biographical or other compilation in which the contributor's name appears (if it does appear in such compilation). For writers listed in the original volumes of *D.N.B.*, the reference is given as *D.N.B.*; for those listed in supplements, the date of the supplement is given. References to Allibone, Boase, and similar works are either to the original volumes or to the supplements (or to both).

In the list of a writer's contributions, prose items are listed separately from verse. In the absence of a heading, items are understood to be prose. Lead items are marked "lead"; "chips" are marked "chip." For an item that appears in the Office Book with joint names in the author-column, the joint names as there given (with correction indicated, where necessary, only for complete misassignment) are recorded in italics following the title of the item (or following the "lead," "chip" notation). Items are listed chronologically as they appeared in *H.W.* (except as explained below). Contributions to extra Christmas numbers are placed in the Dec. 25 position of the year of publication.

The information on the reprinting of items is recorded in order to confirm the Office Book authorship ascription or, occasionally, to establish authorship. The reprintings accepted as confirming or establishing authorship are those brought out by the contributor himself or, in two instances, by a contributor's widow, and, in another two instances, by a contemporary biographer or editor. The reprinting listed is, with a few exceptions, the first reprinting. Not stated, in general, are title changes or the extent of revision that occurs in the reprinted material.

The reprinting of items for which the Office Book lists joint names is recorded in conjunction with the contributions of the jointly listed writer who was responsible for the reprinting; it is not recorded a second time in conjunction with the contributions of the other jointly listed writer. That is, the reprinting by William Duthie of items for which the Office Book lists Morley's name jointly with his is recorded in conjunction with Duthie's contributions; it is not recorded a second time in conjunction with Morley's.

In the instances in which a writer reprinted more than one volume of his contributions (or included contributions in more than one volume of his writings), the items reprinted in each volume are grouped together. This arrangement departs somewhat from the chronological order in which items appeared in *H.W.*; nevertheless, it is preferable to the awkward alternative of a multiplicity of printers' symbols to designate reprinted items. Because of the large number of items to which Wills's name is attached, this arrangement is followed also in recording his *H.W.* writings, despite the fact that Wills brought out only one volume of reprinted pieces.

A

Addey, Elizabeth |*Elizabeth Addey*, 47 Grafton St., Dublin|. Thom's 1849 Dublin directory lists the resident at the Grafton St. address as George Addey, conducting there a "millinery, lace, stay, shirt, & hosiery establishment," his premises being valued at £85. The 1863 directory lists at the address George Addey & Co., "merchant tailors, hosiers, shirt cutters, and clothiers." Elizabeth Addey was presumably the wife or daughter of George Addey.

VERSE

Long Ago   XVIII, 540–41. Nov. 20, 1858

Addiscott. *Not identified.* The writer's contribution is the story of a sober, honest English labourer, who, through poverty, takes to poaching and is transported; his later conduct redeems his character from its "one black spot." The writer finds the enforcement of the game laws harsh. Payment for the contribution recorded as "Handed by W.H.W."

The One Black Spot
Addiscott & W.H.W.
III, 196–201. May 24, 1851

Allingham, William |*Mr. Allingham, Junr., Allingham, W. Allingham*|, 1824–1889, poet and man of letters. Born in Ireland of an English family long settled there. Received limited schooling, but educated himself by study and wide reading. For some twenty years served intermittently as customs official in Ireland and England. Contributed to *Howitt's Journal, Leigh Hunt's Journal, Athenaeum, Fraser's,* and other periodicals. Appointed subeditor of *Fraser's*, 1870; editor, 1874–79. Published some fifteen volumes of poetry, many containing revised versions of poems earlier published; also edited anthologies of poems. *Varieties in Prose*, a collection of his prose writings prepared by him for publication shortly before his death, published by his widow, 1893. In 1864 granted Civil List pension of £60 a year "In consideration of the literary merit of his poetical works"; also a second pension, 1870 (Colles, *Literature and the Pension List*).

Allingham shared in the general admiration of Dickens. "It seems odd to me now that I never dreamed of the possibility of seeing the great man, much less of making his acquaintance," he wrote in 1870, of an early stay in London. "A glimpse of the author of *Nicholas Nickleby* would have been bliss too much almost for earth" (*Rambles of Patricius Walker*, in *Varieties in Prose*). He later became acquainted with Dickens, recording in *Rambles* some of his association with him. On the publication of his *Laurence Bloomfield in Ireland*, Allingham presented a copy to Dickens with the author's "kind respects" (Stonehouse, *Catalogue*). Allingham held no high opinion of Dickens as a connoisseur of poetry. "No one admires and enjoys Dickens more than I do," he wrote in 1852 to Leigh Hunt, "but I don't believe he cares a rush for Poetry in the stricter sense." Though he became a contributor to *H.W.* with the first number, Allingham had little liking for Dickens's periodical (*Letters to William Allingham*, pp. 14–16).

Allingham held that his "Lady Alice" had been mutilated in the *H.W.* editorial office (Champneys, *Memoirs ... of Coventry Patmore*, II, 174–75), but he recorded that payment for the poem was accompanied by "a compliment from Dickens" (*Diary*, p. 58). Dickens had praise for at least two other of Allingham's contributions: "The Dirty Old Man" he thought was "capital" (to Wills, Dec. 29, 1852); "George Levison" he found "mournfully true," writing to Allingham (Nov. 9, 1857) that it had moved him "very much."

Allingham saw a connection between the two poems and two of Dickens's novels: "The Dirty Old Man" and "The Schoolfellows" (i.e., "George Levison"), he wrote, "I believe had the honour of suggesting to the great novelist something in *Great Expectations* and in *A Tale of Two Cities* respectively" (*Songs, Ballads, and Stories*, p. 334).

Dickens invited Allingham to write for the 1853 Christmas number. Whatever he might contribute, Dickens was sure, would "do something to enrich" the number (Sept. 8 [9], 1853). No contribution by Allingham appeared in the number.

The *H.W.* article "Street Minstrelsy" referred to Allingham as a poet "whose muse has long been recognised by critics of the highest rank, for tenderness, grace, and polish," and quoted four stanzas from his "Lovely Mary Donnelly."

D.N.B. suppl. 1901

PROSE

The Irish "Stationers" II, 29–33. Oct. 5, 1850
Irish Ballad Singers and Irish Street Ballads [lead] IV, 361–68. Jan. 10, 1852
Round the Midsummer Fire V, 426–28. July 17, 1852
Saint Patrick XIII, 279–83. April 5, 1856

The 4 items repr. in *Varieties in Prose, By William Allingham.* 3 vols. London: Longmans, Green and Co., 1893. Pub. in *H.W.* not acknowledged.

VERSE

The Wayside Well I, 19. March 30, 1850
The Lady Alice I, 84. April 20, 1850

The 2 items repr. in *Poems. By William Allingham.* London: Chapman and Hall, 1850. Pub. in *H.W.* not acknowledged.

Wayconnell Tower II, 181 Nov. 16, 1850
The Dirty Old Man. A Lay of Leadenhall VI, 396–97. Jan. 8, 1853
The Lover and Birds VII, 372–73. June 18, 1853
Windlass Song VII, 469. July 16, 1853
The Bright Little Girl. Song to an Irish Tune VIII, 325. Dec. 3, 1853
Sonnet in a Spring Grove IX, 176. April 8, 1854

The 6 items repr. in *Day and Night Songs. By William Allingham.* London: George Routledge and Co., 1854. Pub. in *H.W.* acknowledged.

Choosing a Field-Flower VII, 324. June 4, 1853
Wishing. A Nursery Song VIII, 564. Feb. 11, 1854
The Sailor. A Romaic Ballad IX, 393. June 10, 1854

The 3 items repr. in *The Music Master, a Love Story. And Two Series of Day and Night Songs. By William Allingham.* London: G. Routledge & Co., 1855. Preface states that some of the poems had appeared in periodicals, but gives no specific reference to *H.W.*

Express VII, 396–97. June 25, 1853

Repr. in *Life and Phantasy, By William Allingham.* London: Reeves and Turner, 1889. Pub. in *H.W.* not acknowledged.

The Wondrous Well VII, 445. July 9, 1853

Repr. in *Songs, Ballads, and Stories, By William Allingham.* London: George Bell and Sons, 1877. Pub. in *H.W.* not acknowledged.

George Levison; or, The Schoolfellows XVI, 562–64. Dec. 12, 1857

Repr. in *Fifty Modern Poems. By William Allingham.* London: Bell and Daldy, 1865. Pub. in *H.W.* not acknowledged.

A Cottage Memory I, 588. Sept. 14, 1850
Our Coachman IX, 152. April 1, 1854

Andersen, Hans Christian |*Andersen*|, 1805–1875, Danish author. Poorly educated; according to some of his European contemporaries spoke no language correctly. Achieved first important literary success with his *Improvisatoren*, 1835; in same year appeared earliest instalment of his fairy tales. From the Continent, his reputation spread to England; hailed there in the mid-1840s as an exciting literary discovery.

Andersen was an enthusiastic worshipper of Dickens; Dickens, in his letters to Andersen, expressed admiration of Andersen's writings. Andersen met Dickens on a visit to England in 1847. He dedicated to him *A Christmas Greeting to My English Friends*, 1847; *A Poet's Day Dreams*, 1853; and the English edition (1857) of *To Be, or Not to Be?*. In 1857 he was Dickens's guest at Gad's Hill. In 1860 he published in a Danish periodical an account of the visit; it did not appear in English translation until after Dickens's death. In Aug. 1860, however, *Bentley's Misc.* published a review of Andersen's account of the visit, based, as Bredsdorff (*Hans Andersen and Charles Dickens*, pp. 131–32) makes clear, on a translation of the account included in a German collection of some of Andersen's tales and sketches. Titled "A Visit to Charles Dickens by Hans Christian Andersen," the *Bentley* article recorded Andersen's praise of Mrs. Dickens and his depiction of the happy family life at Gad's Hill. Dickens can hardly have missed seeing the article. It would, as Bredsdorff states, have provided Dickens with what would have been to him a valid reason for breaking off his friendship with Andersen, though, as a matter of fact, he seems not to have written to Andersen after 1857. Andersen wrote to Dickens several times after 1857 (letters of introduction for friends, probably also personal letters) and had a picture of himself and a copy of one of his books sent to him. Receiving no acknowledgment of the letters or the gifts, he finally ceased his attempt to keep in contact with Dickens, though he continued to speak of him with affection and admiration. The death of "my dear Dickens," he wrote to friends, filled him with sorrow.

The Office Book records no payment for "The World's Fairest Rose," nor does it indicate through whose agency the item arrived at the editorial office. It was, of course, not sent by Andersen, for whose stories and sketches *Bentley's Misc.* was the English repository. Moreover, from the summer of 1851 to the summer of 1856, no correspondence is known to have passed between Andersen and Dickens (Bredsdorff, p. 39). The story, titled "Verdens deiligste Rose," was published in Copenhagen, first, apparently, in a *Folkekalender* for 1852 (brought out prob. Dec. 1851), then, in April 1852, in *Historier af H. C. Andersen* by the Copenhagen publisher C. A. Reitzel (information from Universitetsbiblioteket, Copenhagen). Under the title "The World's Most Beautiful Rose," it was included in *A Poet's Day Dreams*, published by Bentley, Feb. 28, 1853. Obviously, neither Andersen nor Bentley was aware that one of the stories in the new English collection had appeared (in a variant translation) in an English periodical some five months before.

In *H.W.*, praise of Andersen's stories for children appeared in "A Witch in the Nursery," and mention of his tales in "The School of the Fairies"; a brief reference to Andersen appeared in "Strings of Proverbs" (Feb. 28, 1852). In *A.Y.R.*, Wilkie Collins's "The Bachelor Bedroom," Aug. 6, 1859, contained a ludicrous depiction of Andersen (see Lohrli, "Andersen, Dickens, and 'Herr von Müffe,'" *Dickensian*, Winter 1966).

In the Office Book, Andersen is recorded as author of "The Cup and the Lip," Sept. 4, 1852; his name is marked out and substituted by that of Leigh Hunt.

Ency. Brit.

The World's Fairest Rose [chip]
v, 610. Sept. 11, 1852

Arbuthnot, Sir Robert |*General Sir Robert Abruthnot*|, 1773–1853, military officer. Entered army in 1797 as cornet, 23rd Light Dragoons; captain, 20th Light Dragoons; major-general, 1830; lieut.-general,

1841; colonel, 76th Foot, 1843. Served in Africa, in South America, on the Continent in Peninsular War, in Ceylon, in India. "Few officers have taken part in so many general actions" (*D.N.B.*). Received numerous military decorations. K.C.B. 1815.

The brief *H.W.* item by Arbuthnot was written, he stated, "at the request of a few friends," to give the correct account of his feat of horsemanship at Land's End in 1804 – an episode recounted in the *H.W.* article "If This Should Meet His Eye," March 13, 1852, with the comment that the performer of the feat was "since dead." Arbuthnot's account was introduced by the editorial statement that General Sir Robert Arbuthnot was still alive and that the "distinguished gentleman" had "been good enough to give us his own version of his performance." The item is the only writing assigned to Arbuthnot in *Biblio. Cornub.*; *D.N.B.* records no writings by him.

D.N.B.

An Equestrian Miracle [chip]
v, 519. Aug. 14, 1852

Arnold, Sir Edwin |*Ed. Arnold, E. Arnold*|, 1832–1904, poet, scholar, journalist. B.A. Oxford, 1854; M.A. 1856. Principal of the Deccan College, Poona, 1856–61. Joined staff of *Daily Telegraph* as leader writer, 1861; editor, 1873–89. Contributed to *Once a Week, Fortnightly, Scribner's*, and other periodicals, many of his articles dealing with his life and travels in Japan, India, and elsewhere. Published collections of his periodical articles. Author of *The Marquis of Dalhousie's Administration of British India*, 1862–65. Published many volumes of poems, original and translated, the most popular being *The Light of Asia*, 1879. C.S.I. 1877; K.C.I.E. 1888.

Twenty-two years after the appearance of Arnold's "Invocation" in *H.W.*, the authorship of the lyric became the subject of a curious controversy. In revising the poem, Arnold had destroyed some of its charm by needless lengthening and by a change of title (to "A Ma Future"). Even in this form, however, the poem found admirers, among them Francis Mahony ("Father Prout"), who copied out the lyric in 1856 on its appearance in Arnold's *Griselda*. Finding the MS poem among Mahony's papers in Mahony's handwriting, William Blanchard Jerrold took it to be by Mahony and reproduced it in facsimile in *The Final Reliques of Father Prout*, 1876. The publication of the *Reliques* led to a series of letters in the *Athenaeum* (June 24, July 15, 22, Aug. 26, 1876) concerning the authorship of the poem. After various statements and misstatements, Arnold's authorship was perforce accepted as established, though without reference to the publication of the poem in *H.W.*, which publication Arnold had not acknowledged in his reprinting.

D.N.B. suppl. 1901–1911

VERSE

*Invocation	IX, 368. June 3, 1854
Mine Host	IX, 608. Aug. 12, 1854

*Repr. in *Griselda, a Tragedy; and Other Poems. By Edwin Arnold.* London: David Bogue, 1856. Pub. in *H.W.* not acknowledged.

Arnold, William Delafield |*Arnold, W. D. Arnold*|, 1828–1859, Govt. official in India, writer; fourth son of Dr. Thomas Arnold of Rugby. Educated at Rugby; student at Oxford, 1846. Lieut., 58th Regt. Bengal Native Infantry. Became assistant commissioner in the Punjab; in 1857 appointed director of public education in the Punjab. Died at Gibraltar on his way to England on sick leave. Commemorated in Matthew Arnold's "Stanzas from Carnac" and "A Southern Night." Author of *Oakfield; or, Fellowship in the East*, 1853, a novel exposing the low moral tone of a certain element in the Indian army; *The Palace at Westminster, and Other Historical Sketches*, 1855. Published, 1854, translation of L. A. Wiese's *German Letters on English Education.*

The first item listed below is assigned in the Office Book merely to "Arnold." Its authorship is established by the comment in the article that the writer "had spent several years in remote districts

on the north-western frontier" of India, and "more recently in the Punjaub."
Rugby School Register; D.N.B.

The Steam Whistle in India
VIII, 440–42. Jan. 7, 1854
Mr. Speaker in the Chair
IX, 89–92. March 11, 1854

Athans, Dr. The contributor has before him broadsheets of Turkish ballads that had sprung up before and during the Crimean War; he quotes from them at length. His ability to read Turkish and his knowledge of the Near East suggest that he may be Giovanni d'Athanasi, a Greek born about 1798 in Lemnos, who was for a time employed by Ernest Missett, British consul-general in Egypt. Before leaving Egypt in 1816, Missett recommended d'Athanasi "as interpreter in Arabic and Turkish" to Henry Salt, Missett's successor (d'Athanasi, *Brief Account of the Researches and Discoveries in Upper Egypt*, p. 4). Until Salt's death in 1827, d'Athanasi served as interpreter to Salt's secretary and as Salt's assistant in the excavation and collection of Egyptian antiquities. Salt's letters mention some of the discoveries made by d'Athanasi, whom Salt refers to as "Yanni" (Halls, *Life and Correspondence of Henry Salt*). Some years later, d'Athanasi went to England to assist Leigh Sotheby in drawing up the sale catalogue of one of Salt's collections. In 1836 he published *A Brief Account of the Researches and Discoveries in Upper Egypt, Made under the Direction of Henry Salt, Esq., by Giovanni d'Athanasi.* He formed also his own collection of Egyptian antiquities and of Etruscan ornaments.

Turkish Poems on the War
XII, 155–58. Sept. 15, 1855

B

Bakewell, Esther |*Miss Bakewell*|, author of *The Book of One Syllable*, 1842; *Glenwood Manor-House. A Novel*, 1857.

"My First Place" is the story of a young girl and of her experiences as servant in an upper-class household where dishonest servants attempt to make her appear guilty of falsehood and theft. The story seems a forestudy to *Glenwood Manor-House*, in which much of the plot concerns the machinations of a housekeeper, likewise in an upper-class household, to make the mistress's young companion appear a thief. Both the story and the novel end with the exculpation of the innocent and the exposure and punishment of the evil-doers.

Harper's reprinted "My First Place," without acknowledgment to *H.W.*
Allibone

My First Place IV, 376–82. Jan. 10, 1852

Ballentine, George |*Ballantine*|. The contributor writes: "I am a Scotchman by birth, but enlisted into the American service." He states that he was some three months in the camp and trenches at Vera Cruz, Mexico, then describes the action of "General Twiggs, with his division, comprising the regiment to which I belonged," against the enemy in the battle of Cerro Gordo.

The Ballentine (not Ballantine) listed in the army documents (National Archives, Washington, D.C.) whose record accords with these details is George Ballentine. Ballentine's enlistment paper gives his birthplace as Renfrewshire, Scotland; his occupation as weaver; his age as thirty-three at the date of enlistment, Aug. 12, 1845, in New York City, for a period of five years. Other documents record Ballentine's serving in Companies I and F of the 1st Regt. U.S. Artillery, both of which participated in the battle of Cerro Gordo, April 1847, in the U.S. war with Mexico. Brig.-General David E. Twiggs commanded one of the divisions in this engagement.

Ballentine was – or became – a well-read man. In his article he compares his reaction under fire with that described by Goethe in *Campaign in France*; he brings in a phrase from Campbell's

"Hohenlinden" and echoes a line from *Macbeth.*

First under Fire XII, 115–17. Sept. 1, 1855

Barrett, Elizabeth: *See* Browning, Elizabeth (Barrett)

Bateman, Mrs. J. C., prob. |*Mrs. Bateman*|, novelist. Author of *The Netherwoods of Otterpool,* 1858; *Forgiveness,* 1860; and three other novels of love and adventure with a generous element of religious sentiment.

"Eric Walderthorn" is a story of coincidence and misunderstanding, of love and noble thoughts – and an encounter with wolves in a German forest. (A wolf hunt is one of the episodes of Mrs. Bateman's historical novel *Ierne of Armorica,* 1873.) Dickens revised and shortened the story (letter to Wills, June 22, 1856, to appear in Pilgrim *Letters*).

Allibone

Eric Walderthorn
XIII, 590–98. July 5, 1856, and the following no.

Bell, Mrs. |*Mrs. Bell, Miss Bell*|. *Not identified.* On April 12, 1854, Dickens wrote to Wills: "Miss – I mean Mrs. – Bell's story very nice. I have sent it to the Printer, and entitled it The Green Ring and the Gold Ring." The Office Book assigns the story to Mrs. Bell, as it does also the first item listed below; the third it assigns to "Miss Bell." The three stories (one is stated to be factual) are clearly by the same contributor. All have an atmosphere of mystery and terror. Payment for the first contribution made by post-office order; for the second, by cheque; for the third, in cash.

Harper's reprinted "The Green Ring and the Gold Ring," without acknowledgment to *H.W.*

The Longest Night in a Life [lead]
IX, 21–25. Feb. 25, 1854

The Green Ring and the Gold Ring
IX, 272–77. May 6, 1854

Fallen among Thieves
XIII, 413–17. May 17, 1856

Bell, Robert |*R. Bell*|, 1800 (or 1803?)–1867, journalist, misc. writer. Educated at Trinity College, Dublin. For many years editor of the *Atlas,* then of *Monthly Chronicle* (which he helped found), later of *Home News.* Contributed to *Ainsworth's, Fraser's, Bentley's Misc., Once a Week;* "Stranger Than Fiction" to *Cornhill.* Collaborated with Horne on *A New Spirit of the Age,* 1844. For Lardner's *Cabinet Cyclopaedia,* wrote *A History of Russia* and biographical material. Wrote life of George Canning; three comedies, two novels, a book of travel sketches. Brought out *The Annotated Edition of the English Poets,* 1854–57, his principal work.

According to Sala (*Things I Have Seen,* I, 93), Bell was "an intimate friend of Dickens's." He was present at the "christening" of *The Haunted Man;* he played a role in one of Dickens's presentations of *Not So Bad As We Seem.* As a member of the General Committee of the Royal Literary Fund, he was Dickens's chief opponent in the controversy concerning the management of the organization (Fielding, ed., *Speeches of Charles Dickens*).

Ley (*Dickens Circle,* p. 253) states that Bell was "a frequent contributor" to *H.W.* and *A.Y.R.* Bell's only connection with *H.W.,* aside from the article listed below, was his handing to the editorial office, for publication, a letter written to him by a friend in Australia ("Life in the Burra Mines," June 7, 1851).

D.N.B.

The Overland Mail Bag
IV, 229–34. Nov. 29, 1851

Bennett, William Cox |*Mr. Bennett, Bennet, Bennett*|, 1820–1895, misc. writer. Born in Greenwich. Attended a school in Greenwich, but forced by death of father to discontinue his schooling at an early age. Despite scanty education, became well-read man. Took active part in educational and social betterment of his native borough, as in formation of a literary institution, reform of a charity school, establishment of public baths and wash houses. Instrumental in securing Gladstone's return to Parliament for the borough, 1868. Honorary auditor of Association for the Repeal of Taxes on Knowledge; member of London council of Education League. Contributed to *People's Journal, Howitt's Journal, Ladies' Companion*, London *Figaro*, and other periodicals. On staff of *Weekly Dispatch*. Privately printed two volumes of verse, 1843, 1845; thereafter published some ten volumes. With one class of readers his verse was "very sorry stuff" (*North Brit. Rev.*, Feb. 1861); with another class it gained immense popularity. Most popular were what Bennett called his "Home Poems" – particularly his poems on infants, which earned him the title "Laureate of the Babies" (Sala, *Breakfast in Bed*, p. 45). "Critics have said," wrote Bennett, "that 'Baby May,' 'Baby's Shoes,' and 'The Worn Wedding-ring,' have been reprinted in almost every newspaper and popular periodical of England, America, and our Colonies" ("Preface," *Poems*, 1862). In 1869 awarded Hon. LL.D. by Tusculum College, Tennessee. Thereafter was "Dr. Bennett" to his contemporaries.

Many years after Bennett's death, Bennett's name became connected with one of the literary forgeries of Thomas J. Wise. Bennett had been a friend of Mary Russell Mitford, Mrs. Browning's favourite correspondent. This fact provided Wise the pretext for naming Bennett as the person from whom he had obtained copies of the "Reading: 1847" edition of Mrs. Browning's *Sonnets*. In 1934, shortly before the exposure of the forgeries, Wise cleared Bennett of complicity in the matter: what he had obtained from Bennett, Wise now remembered, was a copy of Bennett's privately printed *My Sonnets*, 1843 – not copies of Mrs. Browning's sonnets.

Bennett was addicted to sending to eminent contemporaries – acquainted or unacquainted with him – copies of his verses. Dickens, one of the recipients of this attention, wrote Bennett a note of thanks, Aug. 29, 1848, addressing him as "Dear Sir": "I beg to assure you, in reply to your obliging note, that I have felt from the first the liveliest interest in those verses which you have kindly sent me from time to time, and that I have very highly esteemed those marks of your remembrance. Believe me I feel indebted to you for giving me this opportunity of saying, that I have been deeply moved and affected by some of your writings, and that I thank you with all my heart" (*Further Testimonials in Favour of W. C. Bennett, ... Candidate for the Secretaryship of the London School Board*, pp. 7–8). Later, Bennett presented to Dickens a copy of *Our Glory-Roll, and Other National Poems*, inscribed to him "with the profound admiration and respect" of the author, and a copy of *Proposals for ... a Ballad History of England*, similarly inscribed (Stonehouse, *Catalogue*). Bennett also expressed publicly his admiration of Dickens. In an untitled sonnet on Gad's Hill, he gave praise to "England's world-loved Dickens," and, on Dickens's death, he published in the *Penny Illustrated Paper*, June 18, 1870, an "In Memoriam" poem on Dickens.

About three months before the first number of *H.W.* appeared, Bennett inquired of Dickens about the possibility of his becoming a contributor. Dickens wrote to him, Jan. 3, 1850, that he hoped to have the pleasure of being able to accept contributions from Bennett once the periodical was in existence (MS Times Bookshop, London).

The *H.W.* article "Street Minstrelsy" named Bennett as a writer of songs and ballads popular with the people.

D.N.B. suppl. 1901

VERSE

The Seasons I, 65. April 13, 1850
A Village Tale I, 276–77. June 15, 1850

The 2 items repr. in *Poems. By W.C. Bennett*. London: Chapman and Hall, 1850. Pub. in *H.W.* not acknowledged.

The Deeds of Wellington
VI, 229–31. Nov. 20, 1852

Repr. in *War Songs. By W.C. Bennett*. London: Effingham Wilson, 1855. Pub. in *H.W.* not acknowledged.

Wishes xiv, 85. Aug. 9, 1856

Repr. in *Queen Eleanor's Vengeance. And Other Poems. By W.C. Bennett.* London: Chapman and Hall, 1857. Pub. in *H.W.* not acknowledged.

Bergenroth, Gustav Adolf |*Bergenroth*|, 1813–1869, historical scholar. Born in East Prussia. Educated at Univ. of Königsberg. Lost his civil service post during political reaction following the revolutionary outbreak of 1848; helped Gottfried Kinkel escape from Spandau, then left Germany for California; returned to Europe, 1851. In 1857 began study of Tudor history, utilizing first the materials available in England, then proceeding to Spain to examine the archives at Simancas; mastered the intricate ciphers and triumphed over obstacles placed in his way by the Spanish archivists; in 1862 brought out a calendar of the documents relating to English affairs from 1485 to 1509, prefaced by "a brilliant review of the relations between England and Spain during the period" (*D.N.B.*); continued the work in a second volume, 1866; published also a supplemental volume, 1868. Contributed to *Fraser's* and *Athenaeum.*

Bergenroth's *H.W.* article, describing conditions in California in 1850 and 1851 that led to the organization of vigilance committees, was his first published writing in English. Dickens had in his library a copy of Cartwright's memorial sketch of Bergenroth (*Stonehouse,* Catalogue).

D.N.B.

The First Vigilance Committees [lead] xiv, 409–416. Nov. 15, 1856

Repr. in *Gustave Bergenroth: A Memorial Sketch, By W.C. Cartwright.* Edinburgh: Edmondston and Douglas, 1870. Pub. in *H.W.* acknowledged.

Bergh, Francis | *Francis Bergh, Francis Berg*|, *b.* 1777, sailor. Born at sea aboard a brig belonging to Hull, of which his father was master. Learned to read and write. In 1790, as apprentice on a brig, began his fifty years of sea-faring life. Four times pressed between 1798 and 1807; served on British men-of-war that convoyed merchant ships, captured French and Spanish prizes, and gave chase to American vessels. After "the Peace," shipped on a cargo boat sailing to Riga, on a South Seas whaler, on a cargo boat in Mediterranean trade, and on other vessels. Shipwrecked in 1820; lived a solitary castaway on an island for 270 days before being rescued by American schooner. In later life again served in the navy, this time of his own volition. Received honourable discharge, 1844; settled in Gosport. There, related to be written down the story of his life, intended to show the Lord's "wonderful mercies" to him in his providential escapes from death on land and sea, and to admonish readers to have trust in the Almighty.

H.W. prefaced Bergh's life story with the explanation that it was "the real autobiography of an Ancient Mariner still living," given in the old man's own words. "We may sometimes omit a few passages, and may sometimes alter his orthography, but we shall in no other respect interpose between him and the homely truth of his narrative." In book form, the autobiography was brought out for Bergh's benefit "by his friends and employers."

A statement in the autobiography that reflected on the business dealings of a reputable wharfinger led to Wills's insertion of the "chip" "Another Leaf from the Story of a Sailor's Life," July 5, 1851. In it, Wills explained that the statement had been made by mistake; he stated also that Bergh was the author of the autobiography – one of the few instances in which *H.W.* made public the name of a contributor.

At the standard rate, payment for Bergh's contribution would have amounted to about twenty-six pounds; Bergh was paid fifteen. A third of the sum was handed to him by Wills; the remainder was sent to Elizabeth Bergh. Elizabeth was probably Bergh's fourth wife. Bergh had been three times a widower.

Mrs. Gaskell apparently knew Bergh – or at least knew of him. In a letter of May 1851 to her daughter Marianne, she wrote: "I never see the Household Words, do you? Tell me if my dear old sailor's narrative is appearing yet. You'll know it by the old spelling if by nothing else" (*Letters*, No. 97+).

The Story of a Sailor's Life
III, 211–16. May 24, 1851, and the 4 following nos.

Repr. as *The Story of a Sailor's Life As Related by Francis Bergh.* Gosport: To be had of George Legg; Portsmouth: To be had of George Austin Legg, 1852. Pub. in *H.W.* not acknowledged.

Berwick, Miss; Mary Berwick: *See* Procter, Adelaide Anne

Birkbeck, Miss: *See* Mednyánszky, Sándor

Blackborne. *Not identified.* Payment for the contribution made in cash.

A River Picture in Summer [chip]
XI, 379. May 19, 1855

Blacker, Mrs. *Not identified.* According to her *H.W.* articles, the contributor was a lady of good family, wife of a Church of England clergyman (non-Puseyite) who served for some time in an English country parish inhabitated largely by the poor and labouring class. (Several clergymen named Blacker flourished at the time.) Helped her husband in his parish work. Was some fifty years old at the time of contributing to *H.W.*

Sending the first of her articles to Wills, Dickens wrote of the new contributor (Jan. 8, 1859): "She has an excellent knowledge of a poor country parish, some very pretty womanly humour, some very good womanly observation, and a decided faculty for writing." He stated that he had read several of Mrs. Blacker's papers and had "generally advised her how to make them better." He had "rather a strong hope" that she would prove to be "a very useful contributor."

Mrs. Blacker contributed at least one paper to *A.Y.R.* Dickens wrote to Wills, May 3, 1859, that it was "so very good – the Nurse's story so exceedingly well done," that he had at once sent the MS to the printer's. Dickens's comment and the date of his letter make it clear that the story referred to is "Eleven O'clock, among the Fir-Trees," *A.Y.R.*, May 28, 1859.

The Clergyman's Wife:
Poor Cottages [lead]
XIX, 169–72. Jan. 22, 1859
Life in Lightlands
XIX, 197–201. Jan. 29, 1859
The Highest Testimonials [lead]
XIX, 313–15. March 5, 1859

Blackmore. *Not identified.* Perhaps Richard Doddridge Blackmore, 1825–1900, author of *Lorna Doone*, who by the date of the *H.W.* poem had published three volumes of poetry and who throughout his literary career contributed both verse and prose to periodicals. The poem, if it is by him, adds nothing to his reputation as poet.

VERSE
A Poet's Home XI, 609. July 28, 1855

Blackwell. The contributor's article displays a sound knowledge of geology; it discusses the varieties of granite, slate, sandstone, coal, etc., to be seen in London streets, buildings, lapidaries' yards, and elsewhere. Payment for the contribution made by cheque.

The contributor may be John Kenyon Blackwell, F.G.S., cousin of Anna Blackwell (below); mentioned by Elizabeth Blackwell (*Pioneer Work in Opening the Medical Profession to Women*, chap. iv) as a South Staffordshire ironmaster; author of a report to Parliament on the ventilation of mines, 1850, and of the pamphlet *Explosions in Coal Mines*, 1853, dated from 1 Westbourne Place, Hyde Park. Or the contributor may be Samuel H. Blackwell of Dudley, F.G.S., author of

"The Iron-Making Resources of the United Kingdom," published in *Lectures on the Results of the Great Exhibition of 1851*, 2nd ser., 1853.

The *H.W.* article seems more appropriate to the Blackwell of the London address than to the Blackwell of Dudley.

London Stones xii, 228–29. Oct. 6, 1855

Blackwell, Anna |*Miss Blackwell*|, misc. writer, spiritualist; sister of Elizabeth Blackwell, M.D. Born in Bristol; educated by governesses; lived for a time in the U.S., where her father, because of business reverses, took his family in 1832. With two of her sisters, conducted a school for young ladies in Cincinnati, 1838–42. Later lived in Paris. Friend of Bessie Rayner Parkes; one of signers of Barbara Leigh Smith's petition, 1856, for a Married Women's Property Bill (Haight, ed., *George Eliot Letters*, iv, 377n). Contributed to *Once a Week*, *English Woman's Journal*; also to French periodicals. Translated George Sand's *Jacques*, Elie Sauvage's *The Little Gypsy*; published *Poems*, 1853. Had been, she stated, from her cradle "a believer both in the preexistence of the soul and in the fact of spirit-manifestation"; had "the great honour and happiness of being *the earliest pioneer of 'Spiritualism' on the Continent*" as also "the *earliest pioneer of 'Spiritism' in my native England*" (*Spiritualism and Spiritism*). Friend of the spiritualist Allan Kardec (i.e., Léon H. D. Rivail); translated his writings into English, 1875–78.

In her *Philosophy of Existence*, 1871, Miss Blackwell demonstrated the universality of the belief in reincarnation by citing passages in support thereof from ancient and modern writings. From *Oliver Twist* (chap. xxxii), she cited a passage indicating Dickens's awareness of the doctrine: "The memories which peaceful country scenes call up are not of this world, or of its thoughts, or hopes. Their gentle influence may teach us to weave fresh garlands for the graves of those we loved, may purify our thoughts, and bear down before it old enmity and hatred; but, beneath all this, there lingers, in the least reflective mind, a vague and half-formed consciousness of having held such feelings long before, in some remote and distant time. ..."

"Never Despair" was reprinted in *Harper's*, without acknowledgment to *H.W.*; marked anonymous, it was included in *Harper's Cyclopaedia of British and American Poetry*, 1881.

Allibone

VERSE

Never Despair *Miss Blackwell & W.H.W.* iii, 491–92. Aug. 16, 1851

Repr. in *Poems. By Anna Blackwell*. London: John Chapman, 1853. Pub. in *H.W.* not acknowledged.

Blanchard, Sidney Laman |*Blanshard, Sidney Blanchard, Sidney Blanshard, S. Blanshard, S. Blanchard, Blanchard*|, 1827?–1883, journalist; eldest son of Laman Blanchard. After Laman Blanchard's suicide in 1845, friends of the family came to the aid of the widow and children. According to S. M. Ellis (ed., *A Mid-Victorian Pepys*, p. 165n), it was through the efforts of Forster, Bulwer-Lytton, and Harrison Ainsworth that the three sons were placed in situations. Sala recorded: "I think that Sidney began his career as private secretary to Mr. Disraeli; then he drifted away into London journalism" (*Things I Have Seen*, i, 94). Was on reporting staff of *Daily News*. For a time shared chambers with J. A. Crowe, who was keeping terms at Inner Temple (Crowe, *Reminiscences*, p. 91). Spent some time in France. In 1853 went to India, where he was some years newspaper editor; on his return to England, according to Sala, was called to the bar. In the 1860s, served as officer in the militia; described his experiences in "Out with the Militia," *A.Y.R.*, July 25, 1868. Published *The Ganges and the Seine*, 1862, a collection of articles from *H.W.* and *A.Y.R.*, together with some previously unpublished material; and *Yesterday and To-day in India*, 1867, a collection of articles mainly from *A.Y.R.* and *Temple Bar*; also wrote a novel, *Riddles of Love*, 1871.

Dickens had been a friend of Blanchard's father. In a letter of 1838 to the father, he mentioned his being much amused at reading a play that young Blanchard had written as a boy (Pilgrim *Letters*, I, 475). On Sept. 4, 1845, Dickens wrote for Blanchard a letter of introduction to Thomas Beard, stating that the young man was anxious to obtain an engagement "in some reporting capacity" on the *Morning Herald*: "He is not untried, having attended railway committees for the Globe in the course of last session, and having given, as I am assured, every satisfaction." Later in the same year, Dickens engaged Blanchard as reporter for the *Daily News*.

Locker-Lampson (*My Confidences*, pp. 326–27) recorded that Blanchard on one occasion submitted to *H.W.* some verses titled "Orient Pearls at Random Strung," and that Dickens returned them with the comment: "Dear Blanchard, too much string, – Yours, C.D."

Three of Blanchard's *H.W.* contributions were reprinted in *Harper's*, without acknowledgment to *H.W.* "Student Life in Paris" was included in the Putnam volume of selections from *H.W.*: *The World Here and There*, 1852.

Boase

*A Biography of a Bad Shilling
II, 420–26. Jan. 25, 1851
*A Ball at the Barriers
III, 190–92. May 17, 1851
*Painting the Lily
III, 235–38. May 31, 1851
*Student Life in Paris
III, 286–88. June 14, 1851
*A Visit to Robinson Crusoe
III, 397–400. July 19, 1851
*More French Revolutions
S. Blanshard & W.H.W.
III, 585–88. Sept. 13, 1851
*The French Flower Girl
IV, 10–12. Sept. 27, 1851
*Thirty Days of Pleasure for Fifteen Francs IV, 71–72. Oct. 11, 1851
A Musician in California
IV, 94–96. Oct. 18, 1851
*The True Bohemians of Paris
IV, 190–92. Nov. 15, 1851
*French Horse-Racing
IV, 213–16. Nov. 22, 1851
*A Genteel Establishment
Sidney Blanshard & W.H.W.
IV, 559–64. March 6, 1852
*My Aunt in Paris
V, 112–16. April 17, 1852
*Literary Mystifications
V, 374–77. July 3, 1852
*Printed Forgeries
V, 444–50. July 24, 1852
*Dining with the Million
V, 489–93. Aug. 7, 1852
*Munchausen Modernised
VI, 533–38. Feb. 19, 1853
More Modern Munchausens
VII, 402–405. June 25, 1853
*The Santals XII, 347–49. Nov. 10, 1855
*The Road in India
XII, 517–21. Dec. 29, 1855

*Repr. in *The Ganges and the Seine: Scenes on the Banks of Both. By Sidney Laman Blanchard.* 2 vols. London: Chapman and Hall, 1862. Pub. in *H.W.* acknowledged.

Bourne, Henry Richard Fox |*Bourne*|, 1837–1909, author, reformer. Born in Jamaica. Entered London University, 1856; at other London institutions, also attended classes and lectures, among them Henry Morley's lectures on language and literature at King's College; later became Morley's friend and assistant. Clerk in War Office, 1855–70, spending his leisure time in writing. Contributed to *Examiner*, *Reader*, *Athenaeum*, *Gent. Mag.*, and other periodicals. Owner of *Examiner*, 1870–73; editor of *Weekly Dispatch*, 1876–87. Thereafter, devoted his life almost entirely to work of the Aborigines Protection Society; edited Society's journal; wrote articles and books bringing to public attention the cruel treatment of native races, and protesting against slave traffic. Author of *A Memoir of Sir Philip Sidney*, 1862; *English Merchants*, 1866, and other books tracing England's commercial growth and colonial expansion; *The Life of John Locke*, 1876; *English Newspapers*, 1887.

In the Office Book, the first item listed below is recorded as by "Day & Morley"; the "Day" is marked out and substituted by "Bourne." For that and the three following items, Bourne's name is written in ink of different colour from that used in other parts of the entries; the name was apparently recorded after other parts of the entries had been written. *D.N.B.* mentions Bourne as a *H.W.* contributor.

In 1880 Bourne submitted to *A.Y.R.* some papers on Malta; Charles Dickens, Jr., did not find them suited to the periodical (*A.Y.R.* Letter-Book, March 22, 1880).

D.N.B. suppl. 1901–1911

The Hero of a Hundred Plays *Bourne & Morley* XVIII, 324–27. Sept. 18, 1858
Hindoo Law [lead] XVIII, 337–41. Sept. 25, 1858
Historic Doubt XVIII, 352–54. Sept. 25, 1858
Fire-Worshippers *Bourne & Morley* XIX, 286–88. Feb. 19, 1859
A Court without Appeal XIX, 407–408. March 26, 1859

Boyle, Mary Louisa |*The Honble Miss Boyle*|, 1810–1890, writer; daughter of Vice-Admiral the Hon. Sir Courtenay Boyle. For the most part privately educated, but attended a young ladies' school for about four years. Moved in social circle of the titled and the literary. Author of *The State Prisoner* and *The Forester*, novels influenced by those of G. P. R. James; *Tangled Weft*, two stories; *The Bridal of Melcha*, a drama in verse; a privately printed volume of poems dedicated to Landor; biographical notices of the portraits at Longleat and at other estates, privately printed. Her pleasant book of reminiscences, *Mary Boyle, Her Book*, published posthumously.

Miss Boyle met Dickens in 1849; thereafter she was often a guest of the Dickenses. Dickens thought her the best amateur actress that he had ever seen and was delighted to have her take part in his theatricals. Charles Lever, who credited himself with having trained Miss Boyle in the art of acting, called her "Dickens's *prima donna*" (Downey, *Charles Lever*, II, 83–84). Dickens carried on a flirtation with Miss Boyle, and she frequently presented him with little tokens of affection. The two became close friends. Dickens was grateful for her sympathetic and affectionate letters written at the time that "lies" were being circulated about him after his separation from his wife.

Dickens found "many things" in Miss Boyle's *H.W.* contribution *"very pretty."* He was reluctant to say more, he wrote to her, Feb. 21, 1851, because of his "heavy sense ... of the responsibility of encouraging anyone to enter on that thorny track, where the prizes are so few and the blanks so many. ..." The "thorny track" must refer to periodical writing; Miss Boyle, at the date of Dickens's letter, was already author of four books. Dickens devoted "a couple of hours" to revising her tedious story, attempting to lighten it and make it more compact. He had exercised "the pruning-knife," he wrote, "with the utmost delicacy and discretion" and hoped that she would read the revised version "with as loving an eye as I have truly tried to touch it with a loving and gentle hand."

Miss Boyle contributed at least one article to *A.Y.R.* – "Will You Take Madeira?", Sept. 16, 1865.

Allibone

My Mahogany Friend *The Honble Miss Boyle & C.D.* II, 558–62. March 8, 1851

Bradburn, Mrs. Address: Shirley, Southampton. Southampton directories, 1849–59, do not list a Mrs. Bradburn. The address must have been a temporary one. The contributor may be Eliza Weaver Bradburn, daughter of the Rev. Samuel Bradburn (the Office Book at times confounds "Miss" and "Mrs."), editor of her father's *Sermons*, 1817, and writer of booklets for children. Copies of three of the booklets are in the Brit. Mus.: *The Story of Paradise Lost, for Children*, 1830; *The Endless Story, in Rhyme*, 1843, little moral stories taken from F. W. Carové's *Mährchen ohne Ende*; and *Rosa; or, The Two Castles*, 1863, a pious little tale adapted from "a French work." *The End-*

less Story is dated from La Haule, Jersey. Living on one of the Channel Islands, the author may well have become familiar with Channel Island legends and stories, as with the Guernsey tradition related in the *H.W.* poem (the story appears in F. F. Dally, *The Channel Islands*, 1858). The writing is that of an amateur.

VERSE
A Guernsey Tradition
II, 84–85. Oct. 19, 1850

Brockedon, William |*Brockenden*|, 1787–1854, painter, author, inventor. F.R.S. Attended school in Totnes, Devon. For five years after death of his father, carried on father's business of watchmaker, meanwhile devoting free time to drawing. Studied at Royal Academy, 1809–1815; exhibited at Royal Academy and at British Institution; elected member of Academy of Rome and of Florence. His career as author resulted from his interest in determining route taken by Hannibal across the Alps (his conclusion: the pass of the Little St. Bernard); in 1824 made first excursion for this purpose (had previously made excursions to the Alps in 1821 and 1822); during following years crossed the Alps nearly sixty times. Published, 1827–29, *Illustrations of the Passes of the Alps*, both letterpress and drawings by him; *Journals of Excursions in the Alps*, 1833; *Italy, Classical, Historical, and Picturesque*, 1842–44. Also edited or wrote parts of other travel books. Contributed to *Literary Gazette*, *Fraser's*, *Blackwood's*. Throughout his life was interested in mechanical and scientific matters; devoted later years largely to this interest; patented various of his inventions, as for corks, wadding for firearms, use of compressed lead dust in pencil making, application of vulcanized India rubber to manufactures (Brockedon coined the word "vulcanization").

Brockedon and Dickens were acquainted. In a letter to Wills, July 17, 1851, Dickens wrote that he was glad of "Brockedon's note" (apparently the *H.W.* contribution), and added of Brockedon: "He knows a good deal about some curious places – is very ingenious – and may be very useful" – "useful," apparently, as a contributor to *H.W.* Dickens's letter to Wills, July 27, 1851, mentioning his regret that "the Brockedon business" should have arisen does not make clear what that business was. "I have written to the wrathful being," wrote Dickens, "with a view to mollification." In 1853 Brockedon pointed out to Dickens what he thought an error in Dodd's "India-Rubber."

Brockedon's *H.W.* contribution is a protest against the desecration of Chamonix by the establishment there of a gaming casino. The article states that the writer had first visited the Alpine village in 1822 and had "since been there five or six times." Dickens's reprimand to Wills (July 27, 1851) for having deleted from the article "that allusion to the Hôtel de Londres" is not clear. The hotel, as also its proprietors, is several times mentioned in the article with high commendation; perhaps the mentions had originally been more extended.

Several references to Brockedon and his work appeared in *H.W.* The article "Arcadia" contained an oblique reference to his painting of Alpine scenes. "Penny Wisdom" and "Going a Little Farther" explained the process that he had "happily hit upon" for making "most excellent blacklead pencils." "The Father of Caoutchouc" discussed Brockedon's association with Thomas Hancock in devising applications of vulcanized India rubber to manufactures, specifically the bringing to "real perfection" of Brockedon's corks.

D.N.B.

Chamouny [chip]
III, 451–52. Aug. 2, 1851

Broderip, Frances Freeling (Hood) |*Mrs. Broderip*|, 1830–1878, writer; daughter of Thomas Hood the poet. In 1849 married the Rev. John Somerville Broderip. Early began writing verses, some of which she set to music. Her first book, *Way-Side Fancies*, 1857, dedicated to her father. Wrote stories and verse for children, e.g., *Funny Fables for Little Folks*, *Mamma's Morning Gossips*, *Wild Roses*, *Merry*

Songs for Little Voices, The Whispers of a Shell; some of her children's books written jointly with her brother, Tom Hood (below); others illustrated by him. Collaborated with her brother on *Memorials of Thomas Hood*, 1860, and on two editions of Hood's *Works*. Also edited, 1869, a collection of Hood's *Early Poems and Sketches*.

Dickens had been a friend of Hood and had known his children from their childhood. Mrs. S. C. Hall ("Frances Freeling Broderip," *Social Notes*, Dec. 21, 1878) recorded her recollection of Frances Hood at one of the Dickenses' birthday parties for their eldest son, to which the two Hood children had been invited despite the illness of their father. Dickens had told the parents, said the little girl, that "we must come, it would do us good!"

In the Office Book, Mrs. MacIntosh is recorded as author of "A Daisy on a Grave"; the "MacIntosh" is marked out and substituted by "Broderip."

D.N.B.

PROSE

My Lady Crump
XIX, 419–21. April 2, 1859

VERSE

*A Daisy on a Grave
XV, 60–61. Jan. 17, 1857

Patience XVIII, 204. Aug. 14, 1858

*Repr. in *Way-Side Fancies. By Frances Freeling Broderip.* London: Edward Moxon, 1857. Pub. in *H.W.* not acknowledged.

Brooks, Mr. The Office Book records "A Lynch Trial in California" as arriving at the editorial office "per C. Buxton Esq." Payment is recorded as "Enclosed & sent." Editorial comment prefaced to the item states that the writer is "a University Graduate who was an eyewitness" to the lynch trial, and that his communication is dated from Grass Valley, Nevada County, May 23, 1851. The "communication" may be an authentic one; or, like another "Brooks" publication, it may be a hoax.

In 1849 the London publisher David Bogue brought out *Four Months among the Gold-Finders in Alta California: Being the Diary of an Expedition from San Francisco to the Gold Districts. By J. Tyrwhitt Brooks, M.D.* The book was highly successful. It was noticed by all reviewers, brought out in the year of publication in a New York edition, and translated into several foreign languages. For some years it passed current as an authentic description of conditions in the diggings and as the "true account" of the gold discovery told by Captain Sutter to the English doctor and recorded by him (so he wrote), "as near as I can recollect, in the Captain's own words." Finally, the diary came to the attention of Sutter. He indignantly declared it fictitious.

"J. Tyrwhitt Brooks" was Henry Vizetelly (1820–1894), printer, publisher, journalist, contributor to (among other periodicals) *A.Y.R.* He had been inspired to write the fictitious diary by reading Frémont's report on his expedition to Oregon and California. In *Glances Back through Seventy Years*, Vizetelly recounted the procedure gone through by him and his publisher to keep secret the authorship of the book.

If Vizetelly could masquerade so convincingly as the doctor who administers calomel and febrifuge to one of his fellow gold-seekers and dresses the wounds of others, he could equally well have masqueraded as the university graduate who helps start a lyceum in the "rising town" of Grass Valley, is present at the lynch trial, and explains the necessity of retaining lynch law.

The "C. Buxton Esq." through whose agency the item arrived at the editorial office may be Charles Buxton, 1823–1871, M.P., with whom Vizetelly was acquainted. Buxton was among the members of Parliament who agreed to give their support to the London penny daily that Vizetelly, in 1864, planned to establish (*Glances Back through Seventy Years*, II, 118–19).

The *Examiner* reprinted four paragraphs of "A Lynch Trial."

A Lynch Trial in California [chip]
III, 611–12. Sept. 20, 1851

Brough, Robert Barnabas |*Brough, R.*

Brough, B. Brough|, 1828–1860, writer. Attended a school in Newport, Monmouthshire. Had ability in drawing, but received no training in art. Worked as clerk in Manchester. In 1847, in Liverpool, started a satirical weekly, the Liverpool *Lion*. After removal to London, became contributor to the comic press: *Man in the Moon, Diogenes, Comic Times*; then to *Illus. Times*, the *Train*. For a time Brussels correspondent of *Sunday Times*; editor for short time of *Atlas* and of *Welcome Guest*. Author of *Songs of the "Governing Classes,"* 1855; *The Life of Sir John Falstaff*, 1857–58; *Which Is Which? or, Miles Cassidy's Contract*, 1860; and other writings. Published, 1856, translation of Béranger's songs. Wrote many successful pieces for the stage, some of them alone, some in collaboration with his brother William (below).

Brough's extravaganza *William Tell* was one of the pieces acted at Tavistock House as a children's theatrical under Dickens's direction. Brough wrote a short parody of *Hard Times*, published in *Our Miscellany, (Which Ought to Have Come Out, but Didn't)*, 1856, jointly edited by him and Edmund Yates.

The publication in *H.W.* of "Calmuck," stated by Brough to be "thoroughly true," brought upon Dickens the anger of Holman Hunt. The story, as was evident not only to Hunt, but to his friends and to members of his family, was a thinly disguised account of Hunt and of his association with the girl who had posed for the shepherdess in his painting *The Hireling Shepherd* (1852). Hunt, in conversation and correspondence with Dickens, evidently convinced him of this fact. Dickens pointed out to Hunt the impossibility of altering the text of "Calmuck" "in future copies" of *H.W.*, and the inadvisability of inserting in the periodical the explanation that a certain artist had "no more to do with [the story] than I have." He wrote Hunt a letter, for display to friends and family, stating that he had accepted "Calmuck" as fiction, that it *was* fiction, and that he regretted not having struck out "the pretence that it is true." He had never liked the story, he stated; it had been "lying at the office, unused, a long time" (Diana Holman-Hunt, *My Grandfather*, pp. 81–84, 190–94).

Of the prose items listed below, the first two (also the last) are assigned in the Office Book merely to "Brough." "Something Like a Dramatic Author," a discussion of Lope de Vega, is based in part on a French memoir of the dramatist; it refers to one German history of Spanish drama and quotes from another; it cites, in translation, passages from Pérez de Montalván, and, both in Spanish and in translation, a sentence from one of Lope de Vega's works. The article is probably by Robert Brough, who, according to Sala ("Memoir" of Brough, prefaced to his *Marston Lynch*), "taught himself plenty of French, and some German, and a little Spanish"; William Brough is mentioned as having a knowledge of French only. "An Excursion Train" is clearly by Robert Brough: The writer aligns himself with the "extremely common people" who ride in "vulgar" railway carriages, people who "never saw the inside of a London club, and who know nothing of the merits of well-fitting gloves, or patent leather boots – except, perchance, from having made them," people despised by the "gentleman" and probably too by the "highly respectable" reader. The spirit is that of *Songs of the "Governing Classes"*:

> 'Tis a curse to the land – deny it who can?
> That self-same boast, "I'm a gentleman!"

Yates wrote that Brough held a "deep vindictive hatred of wealth and rank and respectability" (*Recollections and Experiences*, p. 215).

Of the verse items listed below, the first two are assigned in the Office Book to Robert Brough. "Neighbour Nelly" is mentioned by Sala as a charming little poem contributed by Brough to one of Dickens's periodicals; it is included among Brough's poems in Miles, *The Poets and the Poetry of the Century* (v, 312–13). "The Last Devil's Walk" – a variation on Coleridge's "The Devil's Thoughts" – is assigned in the Office Book merely to "Brough." It is probably by the Brough who contributed the other two verse items, though both brothers wrote verse.

According to Sala, Brough contributed

to *A.Y.R.* as well as to *H.W.* He probably wrote but little for the second periodical, since it had been in progress only a year at the time of his death.

D.N.B.

PROSE

Something Like a Dramatic Author xii, 93–96. Aug. 25, 1855
An Excursion Train xii, 270–73. Oct. 20, 1855
A Flat Walk xiv, 261–64. Sept. 27, 1856
Suburban Belgium xiv, 475–80. Nov. 29, 1856
*Calmuck xvii, 365–70. April 3, 1858

*Repr. in *Heads and Tales: A Medley. By Robert B. Brough.* London: Richard Bentley, 1859. Pub. in *H.W.* acknowledged.

VERSE

Neighbour Nelly xiii, 564. June 28, 1856
The Faithful Mirror xiv, 348. Oct. 25, 1856
The Last Devil's Walk xviii, 109. July 17, 1858

Brough, William |*W. Brough, Brough*|, 1826–1870, writer. Like his brother Robert (above), attended a school in Newport, Monmouthshire. For a time apprenticed to a printer. His first literary effort, a series of papers titled "Hints upon Heraldry," appeared in his brother's Liverpool *Lion.* Later, wrote for London periodicals. Alone and in collaboration with his brother, also in collaboration with Andrew Halliday, composed extravaganzas, farces, and other stage entertainments. His *Field of the Cloth of Gold,* first produced at Strand Theatre, 1868, played 298 times. Was member of Dramatic Authors' Society.

Brough's literary reputation was overshadowed by that of his younger brother. Yates (*Recollections and Experiences,* p. 213) contrasted the two by the comment that "Robert the brilliant was sallow and sickly" whereas "William the methodical was neat and wholesome." Neither had much in worldly goods. On learning that the actress Anne Romer was to marry William Brough, Dickens wrote to Bulwer-Lytton, Feb. 6, 1851: "... I fear her husband will have to refer the baker to the Haymarket Treasury, oftener than is hopeful."

The first two items listed below are assigned in the Office Book to W. Brough; the third, merely to "Brough." William Brough's authorship of that item is established by the Office Book memorandum that accompanies "Next Week": "2.2 for the other paper 'The best Man.'" For "Something Like a Dramatic Author" and "The Last Devil's Walk," assigned merely to "Brough," see Robert Brough.

D.N.B.

Plurality of Mites xiv, 95–96. Aug. 9, 1856
Next Week xvi, 46–48. July 11, 1857
The Best Man xvi, 488–90. Nov. 21, 1857

Brown, Dr. *Not identified.* The contributor calls his article a "gossip about leaves." It is a botanical discussion for laymen.

Falling Leaves xvi, 354–55. Oct. 10, 1857

Brown, H. J. *Not identified.* "Navvies As They Used to Be" gives the following information about the contributor: Was born in a remote corner of Hertfordshire; attended school for six years in an academy near Harrow, completing his studies there in 1834, at age sixteen. Watching the construction of the London and Birmingham Railway line near Harrow, became interested in engineering; with the aid of Grier's *Mechanic's Calculator* and "Jones on Levelling," taught himself the rudiments of what he resolved was to be his profession. Despite his guardian's opposition, set out in March 1835 for the nearest railway works, determined to follow in the wake of the Smeatons, Stephensons, and Brunels. Worked with tunnel and embankment construction gangs in Hertfordshire, beginning as tip-boy and bucket-steerer, becoming assistant to a subcontractor, then being placed in charge of certain work himself. In his article, describes the navvies of the mid-1830s at work and in their shanty lodgings, and pictures their drunken brawls and brutal fights that made their name "a bye-word and a terror."

Navvies As They Used to Be xiii, 543–50. June 21, 1856

Browne or **Brown.** Address: Paris. *Not identified.* The Office Book records payment for the first item listed below as made to Browne by "Cheque to Paris"; for the second, it gives the writer as "Brown (of Paris)" and records payment as made in cash. In his first contribution, which seems to be factual, the writer tells of living for a time on a farm in the outskirts of Paris, "for the sake of experience"; he takes "a lively interest in ... agricultural affairs." The interest in farming suggests that he may be Browne of the Boulogne address (below).

The second item is a story, told in first person, of a young Englishman who goes to Paris, becomes foreman of a manufactory, and after some slight complications marries the daughter of a retired butcher. Dickens wrote to Wills from Paris, Nov. 15, 1855: "I return the No. – a most alarmingly shy one, and really requiring something better to bring it up at last than that Much Ado About Nothing. Pray overhaul your stock, and see if you can't find something better than *that* at any rate." "Much Ado" appeared not as last item in the number, but as fourth item.

Two French Farmers
xi, 105–108. March 3, 1855
Much Ado about Nothing
xii, 422–27. Dec. 1, 1855

Browne or **Brown.** *Not identified.* The items listed below (with Office Book ascription recorded for each) are of mild historical and antiquarian interest, so similar in content and attitude as to indicate that they are clearly the writing of one contributor. They are based on books, periodicals, documents, and old letters, as well as on the writer's own recollection of conditions of some thirty years ago. The writer's attitude, in general, is that the present is preferable to "the good old times."

Payment for "Plagues of London" and "Weird Wisdom" made by cheque; for "Wigs" in cash; payment for "Early Days in Dulminster" recorded as "Advanced."

Plagues of London *Browne*
xi, 316–19. May 5, 1855
Wigs *Brown* xi, 619–20. July 28, 1855
Weird Wisdom *Brown*
xii, 141–44. Sept. 8, 1955
The Light of Other Days *Brown*
xii, 201–203. Sept. 29, 1855
Barbarous Torture *Browne*
xii, 247–49. Oct. 13, 1855
Scrooby *Brown*
xii, 499–502. Dec. 22, 1855
Early Days in Dulminster *Browne*
xiii, 116–20. Feb. 16, 1856
Perfectly Contented *Brown & Morley*
xiv, 213–16. Sept. 13, 1856

Browne, Miss. *Not identified.* Perhaps the Miss Browne to whom payment was handed for the item assigned to Browne of Boulogne (below). Payment to Miss Browne for her contribution made by post-office order.

VERSE

The Sister's Farewell
Miss Browne & Horne
i, 539–40. Aug. 31, 1850

Browne, Mr. Address: Rue de Ville [? word unclear], Boulogne. *Not identified.* The writer is an Englishman. His article recounts the life of an Irish peasant who, by hard work and perseverance, has risen from "a herd-boy to a country jontleman." The account is given in the Irishman's own words, as told by him to the writer. Instead of the Government's attempt to solve the "Irish Difficulty" by "illigant schames" that look fine on paper but are unworkable in reality, says the Irishman, "Why not tache the boys to do as I have done?" Like the Browne (or Brown) of Paris (above), the writer has an interest in farming. He may be the same person.

Payment for the contribution recorded as "Handed enclosed to Miss Browne."

The "Irish Difficulty" Solved by Con McNale i, 207–210. May 25, 1850

Browning, Elizabeth (Barrett), 1806–1861, poet. Largely self-educated. Early began writing verse. Before her marriage, 1846, contributed to *New Monthly, Literary Gazette, Athenaeum, Graham's Magazine* (Philadelphia), and other periodicals; also to annuals. After her marriage contributed less often and to fewer periodicals, mainly to *Blackwood's* and to New York *Independent*: "... Robert doesn't like my writing for magazines" (*Letters to Her Sister*, p. 98). Reprinted many of her periodical contributions, together with previously unpublished material, in *The Seraphim, and Other Poems*, 1838; in *Poems*, 1844; and in *Poems*, 1850; the last named included "Sonnets from the Portuguese." Published also *Casa Guidi Windows*, 1851; *Aurora Leigh*, 1857 [1856]; *Poems before Congress*, 1860. Proposed by *Athenaeum* as Wordsworth's successor for laureateship.

T. C. Evans, who called on Dickens in 1859, recorded that Dickens spoke of Mrs. Browning "with the affectionate enthusiasm which she seemed to inspire in all hearts"; Dickens thought it unfortunate, stated Evans, that Mrs. Browning's style had been affected by her husband's (*Of Many Men*, p. 34n). Mrs. Browning acknowledged Dickens to be a writer of genius, though she considered him inferior in art and power to Victor Hugo, Balzac, and George Sand. She enjoyed reading some of his books. Dickens's scepticism concerning spiritualism finds occasional mention in her letters.

Some weeks before the first number of *H.W.* appeared, Mrs. Browning, as also her husband, was invited to become a contributor; her immediate reaction was to predict the periodical's non-success. From Florence, March 12, 1850, she wrote to her sister Arabel: "Mr. Forster has written to ask us to contribute to Dickens' new periodical – which wont succeed, I predict, especially as they have adopted the fashion of not printing the names of contributors" (quoted by Philip Kelley, reply to "Greek Slave Mystery," *N. & Q.*, May 1967). Her other reasons for prophesying the failure of *H.W.* Mrs. Browning did not specify. Neither she nor her husband sent any contribution in response to Forster's invitation, but one sonnet by her – "Hiram Power's [*sic*] Greek Slave" – did appear in *H.W.*, Oct. 26, 1850.

The item is listed in the Office Book without author's name and without record of payment. On its misattribution to Dickens, see Introduction, p. 39.

"Hiram Powers's Greek Slave" first appeared in book form in *Poems*, 1850, published Nov. 9 (advertisement, *Athenaeum*). Mrs. Browning, in Florence, had asked Sarianna Browning to correct the proofs of the book, an arrangement, as she wrote, whereby "Mr. Forster will have access to the sheets" (quoted by Kelley). Forster was at the time part-proprietor of *H.W.*, meeting occasionally with Dickens and Wills to discuss editorial matters. In this capacity, and in the capacity of supervisor of the proof-correction of *Poems*, he was the one person who would have had access to the sonnet and at the same time could have arranged for its publication in *H.W.* He would, obviously, have obtained Mrs. Browning's consent for the publication. Motivation for the insertion of the sonnet in *H.W.* was of course its timeliness: Powers's much-admired statue was to be on display in 1851 in the Great Exhibition.

In his *H.W.* article "Ground in the Mill," Morley quoted two lines from Mrs. Browning's "Cry of the Children"; Hannay, in "The Sailors' Home," borrowed a phrase from "Lady Geraldine's Courtship"; and Howitt, in "A Day at Waterloo," quoted from *Casa Guidi Windows* a "simple but sublime truth," as also another passage from the same poem.

D.N.B.

VERSE

Hiram Power's Greek Slave

II, 99. Oct. 26, 1850

Repr. in *Poems. By Elizabeth Barrett Browning*. 2 vols. New ed. London: Chapman & Hall, 1850. Pub. in *H.W.* not acknowledged.

Buckland, Francis Trevelyan |*Buckland, Frank Buckland*|, 1826–1880, naturalist. B.A. Oxford, 1848; M.A. 1851. Studied medicine at St. George's Hospital. M.R.C.S. 1851. Assistant-surgeon, 2nd Life Guards, 1854–63. In 1867 appointed inspector of fisheries; thereafter devoted himself largely to pisciculture. Contributed to *Bentley's Misc.*, *Leisure Hour*, *Daily News*, *Times*, and other periodicals. On staff of the *Field*. With some friends, founded *Land and Water*, 1866; wrote much for the periodical. Author of *Curiosities of Natural History*, 1857–66; *Log-Book of a Fisherman*, 1875; *Natural History of British Fishes* and *Notes and Jottings from Animal Life*, both published posthumously.

Buckland was apparently acquainted with Dickens. Occasional entries in his diary record his taking an article "to Dickens" (Bompas, *Life of Frank Buckland*). In a letter to Percy Fitzgerald, Nov. 11, 1869, Dickens referred to an article on monkeys as having been "exceedingly well done" by Buckland in *Land and Water*.

Buckland was responsible for the appearance in *H.W.* of "Tremendous Bores" by his friend Roberts; in the Office Book, the item is recorded as by "Roberts per Frank Buckland." In the Office Book, "An Immeasurable Wonder" by Robertson is recorded as by "Robertson per F. Buckland"; the Buckland notation is marked out.

D.N.B.

*Old Bones viii, 83–84. Sept. 24, 1853
*Oxford Fossils [chip] viii, 209–210. Oct. 29, 1853
A Dish of Fish ix, 16–17. Feb. 18, 1854
Sensible News of a Sea-Snake [chip] ix, 373–74. June 3, 1854
*Catch-Pennies x, 5–6. Aug. 19, 1854
*A Zoological Auction xii, 570–72. Jan. 12, 1856
*A Small Monkish Relic [chip] xiii, 90–91. Feb. 9, 1856
*A Royal Visitor [chip] xiii, 247–48. March 29, 1856
*Intellectual Fleas xiii, 599–600. July 5, 1856
*A Whale in Whitechapel xv, 272–75. March 21, 1857

*Repr. in whole or part in *Curiosities of Natural History. Second Series. By Francis T. Buckland.* London: Richard Bentley, 1860 (part of one item repr. in appendix to a later ed. of *Second Series*); or in *Curiosities of Natural History. A New Series. By Frank Buckland.* 2 vols. London: Richard Bentley, 1866. For some items, pub. in *H.W.* acknowledged.

Buckley, Theodore Alois William (name thus in *Alumni Oxon.*; Theodore William Alois Buckley in *D.N.B.*) |*Buckley*|, 1825–1856, classical scholar, misc. writer, F.S.A. Self-taught from age twelve. Early began reading in British Museum; collected material for edition of Apuleius's *De deo Socratis*. Became protégé of the Greek scholar George Burges, who brought him to attention of patrons of ancient literature. As a result, cost of publishing *De deo Socratis*, 1844, was defrayed by the Rt. Hon. Thomas Grenville, and Buckley received servitorship to Christ Church, Oxford. Was brilliant Latin student; also had musical ability. B.A. 1849; M.A. 1853. Became one of chaplains of Christ Church. Had recourse to opium (a habit formed in early life) and subsequently to alcohol, supposedly because of disease. Removed to London. Supported himself by writing for periodicals – *Eliza Cook's Journal*, *Sharpe's*, the *Press*, and others; and by working for the booksellers. Translated and edited numerous Greek and Roman classics for Bohn and other publishers; edited *Canterbury Tales*, Milton's *Poetical Works*, and other English classics; also various historical and ecclesiastical works. Translated Guizot's life of Washington. Author of *The Great Cities of the Ancient World* and other serious works; also of such popular writings as *The Boy's First Help to Reading*, *The Diverting ... Adventures of Mr. Sydenham Greenfinch*.

Buckley and Dickens were acquainted. Buckley was mentioned by his friend Burges as a *H.W.* contributor (obit., *Gent. Mag.*, March 1856). His contributions dealt mainly with matters of church and school, usually in story form; his "History of a Certain Grammar-School" was a fictionized account of the Robert Whiston case, much in the news at the time (Collins, "Dickens and the Whiston

Case," *Dickensian*, Winter 1962). Dickens found "The Babbleton Book Club" very weak – "A kind of imbecile thing that seems to want crutches" (to Wills, Oct. 7, 1852); in "St. Vorax's Singing-Birds" he detected "a gleam of Puseyism ... that I don't like" (to Wills, July 10, 1853: MS Huntington Library).

Payment for nine of Buckley's contributions is marked "Advanced."

D.N.B.

The Curates of Tittlebatington
III, 381–84. July 12, 1851

The History of a Certain Grammar-School [lead] III, 457–61. Aug. 9, 1851

The Vicar of St. Carrabas
III, 501–504. Aug. 16, 1851

The Dean of St. Vitus
III, 549–52. Aug. 30, 1851

Hampstead Heath
IV, 15–18. Sept. 27, 1851

Wanted, an Organist!
IV, 142–44. Nov. 1, 1851

Our Parish Poor Box
IV, 204–207. Nov. 22, 1851

A Few Miracles IV, 260–64. Dec. 6, 1851

What Christmas Is If You Outgrow It
Extra No. for Christmas 1851, pp. 20–23

Three and Sixpence
IV, 393–97. Jan. 17, 1852

Gable College IV, 546–50. Feb. 28, 1852

Town and Gown *Buckley & Morley*
V, 101–104. April 17, 1852

Quarter-Day V, 342–45. June 26, 1852

The Schoolmasters of Broad-Bumble
V, 377–80. July 3, 1852

Tom's Salad Days
V, 580–82. Sept. 4, 1852

The Babbleton Book Club
VI, 129–33. Oct. 23, 1852

St. Vorax's Singing-Birds *Buckley & W.H.W.* VII, 454–56. July 9, 1853

What Shall a Railway-Clerk Have for Dinner? [chip]
XII, 186–87. Sept. 22, 1855

Bulwer-Lytton, Edward George Earle Lytton, first Baron Lytton |*Sir Bulwer Lytton*|, 1803–1873, author, M.P. B.A. Cambridge, 1826; M.A. 1835; Hon. LL.D. Oxford, also Cambridge. Created baronet 1838; in 1843, on succeeding to Knebworth estate, added Lytton to his surname; raised to peerage 1866. M.P. for many years at various periods of his life. As editor and as contributor, connected with numerous periodicals, e.g., *New Monthly, Monthly Chronicle, Edin. Rev., Blackwood's, Quart. Rev.* Author of more than twenty-five works of fiction; dramatist; author of poems and miscellaneous works.

Bulwer-Lytton and Dickens were friends, their acquaintance dating from about 1838. They had frequent personal and social contacts. Dickens named his seventh son after Bulwer-Lytton. The two men were closely associated in the founding of the Guild of Literature and Art. Bulwer-Lytton expressed generous admiration of Dickens's novels; Dickens had high praise for Bulwer-Lytton as novelist, dramatist, and poet, and greatly valued his critical advice. It was on that advice that he altered what he had originally written as the ending of *Great Expectations.* At Dickens's urgent request, Bulwer-Lytton contributed his novel *A Strange Story* to *A.Y.R.* Smith, Elder & Co.'s *Monthly Circular* found it a matter for comment that Sir Edward Bulwer-Lytton was "not above writing in a cheap weekly journal under the editorship of Mr. Charles Dickens" (Huxley, *House of Smith Elder*, p. 167).

In his *H.W.* article on the Guild of Literature and Art, May 10, 1851, Dickens wrote of Bulwer-Lytton's part in "the origination of the scheme" and of his donation of land and the copyright of a comedy to the Guild. Other *H.W.* articles referred to Bulwer-Lytton's connection with the drama and to his plays: "Crotchets of a Playgoer," "Shakspeare and Newgate," "Wanderings in India" (Jan. 2, Jan. 16, 1858). Various articles referred to his novels: "The Blue-Jacket Agitation" mentioned *Harold;* "The City of Sudden Death" mentioned *The Last Days of Pompeii;* "House-Tops" quoted a passage from *The Caxtons;* "Mine Inn" referred to the inns so "excellently depicted" in Bulwer-Lytton's novels. "Malines" mentioned the "noble and tender" love story "The Maid of Malines" in *The Pilgrims of the Rhine;* of all that has been written about Malines, stated the article, only Bulwer-Lytton's story comes to the recollection of those who visit the city, "so abiding is the remembrance of the lightest creation of a master."

The Office Book assigns to Bulwer-Lytton only the first imitation from Phaedrus listed below; the second, appearing in the *H.W.* number of the following week, seems obviously to be by him, though the authorship cannot be proved. No payment is recorded for either. The *Examiner* reprinted "The Revenge of Æsop."

D.N.B.

VERSE

The Revenge of Æsop. Imitated from Phædrus I, 288. June 15, 1850

The Two Sacks. Imitated from Phædrus I, 304. June 22, 1850

Byng, Mr. *Not identified.* "The Sailor at Home" gives information on Sailors' Homes established in the U.S.; lists also Homes in the British Isles not mentioned in the *H.W.* article "The Sailors' Home," March 22, 1851. The contributor obviously sent the material to *H.W.* to supplement the information given in "The Sailors' Home."

The Sailor at Home [chip]
W.H.W. & Mr. Byng
III, 160. May 10, 1851

C

Call, Wathen Mark Wilks |*Call*|, 1817–1890, poet and scholar. B.A. Cambridge, 1843; M.A. 1846. Took holy orders, though with hesitation; curate, 1846–56 (*Alumni Cantab.*); then withdrew from Church on conscientious grounds as result of his speculations and his study of Comte. Thereafter devoted himself to literature and philosophy; took much interest in social and political reform. Friend of George Eliot and G. H. Lewes. One of original editors of *Cambridge Magazine.* Contributed to *Leader, Westm. Rev., Cornhill, Theological Review, Fortnightly.* At least one of his poems appeared in *A.Y.R.* Author of *Lyra Hellenica,* 1842, translations from the Greek; *Reverberations* and *Golden Histories,* poems; *Final Causes,* a volume of essays, published posthumously.

Boase

PROSE

Laughing Philosophers
XIX, 469–74. April 16, 1859

Another Laughing Philosopher
XIX, 541–46. May 7, 1859

VERSE

Familiar Words XVII, 493. May 8, 1858

The Lady's Dream XVIII, 60. July 3, 1858

An Old Story
XIX, 394–96. March 26, 1859

The 3 items repr. in *Golden Histories, Etc. By Wathen Mark Wilks Call.* London: Smith, Elder & Co., 1871. Prefatory note states that many poems in the volume had appeared in periodicals; states that "The Lion of Androclus" ("An Old Story" in *H.W.*) had appeared in *H.W.*

Campbell, Robert Calder |*Calder Campbell*|, 1798–1857, military officer, misc. writer. Entered service of East India Co. as cadet, 1817; lieut., 1818; captain, 1826; served in Burmese War, 1826–27; invalided, 1831; subsequently promoted to a majority. Contributed to annuals and to numerous periodicals. "We take it for granted that everybody knows something of Major Campbell," wrote a reviewer in 1851, since everybody "reads *some* magazine or another," and Major Campbell "writes in *all* the magazines" (*People's & Howitt's Journal,* IV, 244). Author of *Lays from the East,* 1831; *Winter Nights,* 1850; *Episodes in the War-Life of a Soldier,* 1857; and other volumes of poems, sketches, and stories. Generally praised by reviewers for the melody of his verse and the interest of his prose pieces. W. M. Rossetti ("Memoir" of D. G. Rossetti, in *Dante Gabriel Rossetti: His Family-Letters,* I, 110) called him "a lively writer in a minor way."

D.N.B.

VERSE
The Summer Sabbath
I, 270. June 15, 1850

Cape. The contributor's verse personifies Miasma, who lurks in a festering drain near a cotter's back door. The cotter, though warned, does nothing about the reeking slime; his children play about it. Miasma, after "biding his time," rises from the "slop, and rot" of the "poisonous pool" and wraps the children in "Cholera's cloak of death."

Cholera had broken out in England in Sept. 1853 (*Ency. Brit.*, 9th ed., Vol. v, "Chronology").

The contributor may be George A. Cape, Jr., secretary to the Lambeth Baths and Wash Houses Co.; author of *Baths and Wash Houses*, 1854; co-author, with W. G. Harrison, of *The Joint Stock Companies Act*, 1856. Cape's pamphlet on baths and wash houses describes the Lambeth establishment and gives suggestions for the erection and management of such establishments. It preaches the virtue of "simple soap and water" in "improving the health and morals of the lowly and indigent" and in combatting disease. It describes the crowded, filthy hovels of the poor as the breeding place of fever and plague, and warns that "the pestilence ... that is bred in a hut, may spread to the palace."

The preface to Cape's pamphlet is dated Dec. 1, 1853; "Miasma" appeared in *H.W.* on Dec. 10. It seems likely that Cape's earnest preaching of sanitary reform overflowed into rhyme.

VERSE
Miasma VIII, 348. Dec. 10, 1853

Capper, John |*Mr. Capper, J. Capper, Capper*|, *b.* 1813 or 1814, *d.* 1898, journalist. F.R.A.S. Resident in Ceylon as early as 1836, sometime manager of coffee plantation. Connected for almost forty years with the press in Ceylon and India. On title page of one of his books, 1852, designated himself "Late Editor of the 'Emigrants' Journal' " (periodical title given on title page of later book as "Emigrant's Journal"); on title page of another book, 1853, designated himself "Late Editor of the Ceylon Examiner." For many years associated with J. O. B. Saunders, proprietor of Calcutta *Englishman*; in the 1870s edited Ceylon *Times*. Also correspondent for London *Times* and representative for that paper of Mincing Lane interests. Occasional contributor to *Chambers's*. Died in London, where, up to the time of his death, was active member of Ceylon Association. Author of books on Australia: *The Emigrants' Guide to Australia*, 1852, and *Australia: As a Field for Capital, Skill, and Labour*, 1854. Recorded himself on title pages of two of his books as author of *Our Gold Colonies*; on title page of another, as author of *The Gold Fields*; the two titles not listed in bibliographies of his writings or in *Brit. Mus. Cat.* Also author of books on India and Ceylon: *The Three Presidencies of India*, 1853; *The Duke of Edinburgh in Ceylon. A Book of Elephant and Elk Sport*, 1871; *A Full Account of the Buddhist Controversy, Held at Pantura*, 1873; and two collections of stories and sketches of Ceylon (see below).

Dickens wrote to Wills, June 27, 1853: "Pull at the Pagoda Tree, very good."

Two of Capper's articles motivated replies from readers, published as "chips": "Lloyd's List," Oct. 2, 1852, corrected a statement made in Capper's "Underwriting"; "Criminal Lunatics," Dec. 23, 1854, recorded a reader's knowledge of certain facts at variance with what Capper had stated in "During Her Majesty's Pleasure."

The authorship of "Electric Light," listed below among items not reprinted, is not entirely clear. For the number in which it appears, the Office Book gives first a partial listing of contents, which is marked out because of error; then a second listing, which is still incorrect. In the cancelled listing the names "Dodd Capper" (no ampersand) stand in the author-column for the item (in the uncancelled listing, Miss Procter's name, through misalignment, stands in that position). The item is appropriate to the interests of both Dodd and Capper, though more particularly to those of Dodd. It may possibly be the joint writing of the two contributors, though joint authorship seems unlikely; the Office Book records no collaboration of Dodd and Capper on other items.

For "India Pickle," also listed below among items not reprinted, two names appear in the Office Book author-column: "Capper Sidney" (no ampersand). "Capper" is in part written over another notation or is itself in part overwritten, but the name is not marked out. Payment in one sum, rather than split payment, implies that the article was not a joint writing of the two contributors. Capper, resident in India and Ceylon, would be the more logical author of the item; but Sidney, who had not been in India, also contributed an article (derivative) on India.

In the Office Book, Capper is recorded as author of "Indian Hill Stations"; his name is marked out and substituted by that of Townsend.

Three of Capper's *H.W.* contributions were reprinted in *Harper's*, without acknowledgment to *H.W.* Three were included in the Putnam volume of selections from *H.W.*: *The World Here and There*, 1852.

Boase

The Cocoa-Nut Palm
II, 585–89. March 15, 1851
Coffee Planting in Ceylon
III, 109–114. April 26, 1851
The Garden of Nutmeg Trees
IV, 147–52. Nov. 8, 1851
The Art of Catching Elephants
IV, 305–310. Dec. 20, 1851
A Dutch Family Picture
IV, 372–76. Jan. 10, 1852
An Indian Wedding [lead]
IV, 505–510. Feb. 21, 1852
The Garden of Flowers
V, 556–61. Aug. 28, 1852

The 7 items repr., with one item from *Chambers's*, as *Pictures from the East. By John Capper*. London: Chapman and Hall, 1854. Pub. in *H.W.* acknowledged.

My Pearl-Fishing Expedition
III, 75–80. April 19, 1851
A Peep at the "Peraharra"
III, 252–56. June 7, 1851
Law in the East V, 347–52. June 26, 1852
Number Forty-two
VIII, 17–20. Sept. 3, 1853

The 4 items repr. (together with *H.W.* items in *Pictures from the East*) in *Old Ceylon, Sketches of Ceylon Life in the Olden Time: By John Capper*. Colombo: Ceylon Times Press, 1877 (prefatory note dated Sept. 1878). Pub. in *H.W.* acknowledged.

A Cinnamon Garden
II, 546–48. March 1, 1851
The Peasants of British India
IV, 389–93. Jan. 17, 1852
British Cotton V, 51–54. April 3, 1852
The Great Chowsempoor Bank [lead]
V, 237–40. May 29, 1852
The Wonders of Mincing Lane
V, 273–76. June 5, 1852
Off to the Diggings! [lead]
V, 405–410. July 17, 1852
Monsters of Faith
V, 506–508. Aug. 14, 1852
Underwriting V, 585–89. Sept. 4, 1852
The Great Yorkshire Llama
VI, 250–53. Nov. 27, 1852
Really a Temperance Question
VI, 296–300. Dec. 11, 1852
The Crusade of the Needle
VI, 306–309. Dec. 11, 1852
A Penny a Week
VI, 538–40. Feb. 19, 1853
Silken Chemistry
VII, 129–31. April 9, 1853
A Reference to Character
VII, 390–94. June 25, 1853
A Pull at the Pagoda Tree [lead]
Capper & W.H.W.
VII, 433–37. July 9, 1853
Honourable John
VII, 516–18. July 30, 1853
First Stage to Australia *Capper & W.H.W.*
VIII, 42–45. Sept. 10, 1853
The Great Indian Bean-Stalk
VIII, 60–64. Sept. 17, 1853
Tribunals of Commerce
VIII, 100–104. Oct. 1, 1853
Air Maps VIII, 128–33. Oct. 8, 1853
A Great Screw
VIII, 181–84. Oct. 22, 1853
The Northern Wizard
VIII, 225–28. Nov. 5, 1853

Iron Incidents
viii, 412–15. Dec. 31, 1853
The Stop the Way Company
viii, 449–54. Jan. 7, 1854
Regular Trappers
viii, 471–76. Jan. 14, 1854
Bulls and Bears
viii, 517–23. Jan. 28, 1854
Lancashire Witchcraft
viii, 549–51. Feb. 4, 1854
Oranges and Lemons
ix, 145–50. April 1, 1854
Waste ix, 390–93. June 10, 1854
Our Sister ix, 471–74. July 1, 1854
Our Russian Relations [chip]
x, 333. Nov. 18, 1854
During Her Majesty's Pleasure [chip]
x, 344. Nov. 25, 1854
A Mail-Packet Town
x, 501–504. Jan. 6, 1855
When London Was Little
x, 558–60. Jan. 27, 1855
Prevention Better Than Cure [chip]
xi, 141–42. March 10, 1855
When the Wind Blows
xi, 188–91. March 24, 1855
Electric Light *Dodd Capper*
xi, 251–54. April 14, 1855
Trade xi, 323–26. May 5, 1855
Important Rubbish
xi, 376–79. May 19, 1855
The Scale of Promotion [chip]
xi, 379–80. May 19, 1855
A Leviathan Indeed
xi, 406–408. May 26, 1855
Strictly Financial
xi, 439–42. June 9, 1855
India Pickle *Capper Sidney*
xi, 446–53. June 9, 1855
Rice xi, 522–26. June 30, 1855
The Mofussil xiii, 556–59. June 28, 1856
Cairo xvi, 65–69. July 18, 1857
A Very Black Act
xvi, 293–94. Sept. 26, 1857
Calcutta xvi, 393–97. Oct. 24, 1857
A Nautch xvii, 270–73. March 6, 1858

Cardale, John Bate |*Cardale*|, 1802–1877, solicitor; member of Irvingite (Catholic Apostolic) Church. Educated at Rugby. Articled to his father, a solicitor; head, 1824–34, of London firm of Cardale, Iliffe, and Russell. From 1832 to his death was Irvingite apostle; also named prophet. Served as legal adviser to Irving; ordained Irving. Was frequently at Albury, Surrey, the centre of Irvingite activity and site of Irvingite church; in July 1835, retired to Albury with other apostles and prophets to spend two and a half years in consultation. Died at Albury. Author of works on doctrinal matters; various of his sermons and discourses privately printed.

In the 1850s, Cardale was Dickens's neighbour in Tavistock Square; Dickens wrote him occasional notes on neighbourhood and business matters. The motivation for Cardale's *H.W.* contribution was the discussion of locusts in "The Roving Englishman," Dec. 30, 1854. Cardale's brief item records his attempt to preserve by application of chemicals "an insect of the locust tribe" which "about twelve years ago ... flew or was blown into the windows of a house on Albury Heath." The Office Book records no payment for the item.

Boase

Long Life of Locusts [chip]
xi, 67. Feb. 17, 1855

Carter, Robert Brudenell |*Carter*|, 1828–1918, surgeon. Studied at London Hospital. M.R.C.S. 1851; L.S.A. 1852; F.R.C.S. 1864. Staff surgeon in Turkey during Crimean War. Became authority on ophthalmology. Ophthalmic surgeon to St. George's and other hospitals. Held also other important professional appointments. Hunterian professor, 1876–77; president of Medical Society of London, 1886. While in Turkey, wrote articles for *Lancet* and *Times;* was later on staff of both publications. As writer for *Times,* placed before the public the views of medical profession on subjects of the day. Wrote for professional journals; also occasionally for general periodicals; two articles in *Contemp. Rev.,* one in *Cornhill.* Author of *On the Pathology and Treatment of Hysteria,* 1853, and works on ophthalmology. His *Students' Manual* on ophthalmology was most widely used text of the time on that subject.

In a letter of Sept. 21, 1856 (MS Huntington Library), Dickens stated that he was sending Wills a paper by R. B. Carter; a following letter (Sept. 28) identified the paper as Carter's "Health and Education." Wills was to delete from it a depreciatory reference to mesmerism, which would hurt the feelings of Dr. John Elliotson. Dickens supplied the title for Carter's "How the Writer Was Despatch-Boxed" (to Wills, Aug. 13, 1857).

Plarr's Lives

Health and Education [lead] XIV, 313–17. Oct. 18, 1856
Where I Found an Owl's Nest XIV, 430–32. Nov. 15, 1856
King Missirie [lead] XIV, 553–56. Dec. 27, 1856
Two Days at Sinope XV, 18–23. Jan. 3, 1857
Bashi-Bazouks XV, 306–312. March 28, 1857
Crystals XV, 414–19. May 2, 1857
How the Writer Was Despatch-Boxed XVI, 239–40. Sept. 5, 1857
Character Books XVII, 469–74. May 1, 1858

Cattermole, Richard |*Cattermole*|, 1795?–1858, divine, misc. writer; brother of George Cattermole, the artist. B.D. Christ's College, Cambridge, 1831. For many years secretary to Royal Society of Literature. In 1825 became connected with Church of St. Matthew, Brixton, Surrey. Vicar of Little Marlow, Bucks., 1848–58. Died in Boulogne. Author of *Becket, an Historical Tragedy ... and Other Poems*, 1832; *The Book of the Cartoons* [of Raphael], 1837; *The Great Civil War of Charles I and the Parliament*, with engravings from drawings by George Cattermole, 1841; *The Literature of the Church of England Indicated in Selections from the Writings of Eminent Divines*, 1844. Also published sermons. Was one of editors of *Sacred Classics, or Select Library of Divinity*, 1834–36.

The first item listed below is a familiar essay recounting, from ancient times to modern, the historical and literary associations of the bed. The allusions to the lives and writings of divines – Lancelot Andrewes, Bishop Jewel, Bishop Hall, the Bishop of Sodor and Man – seem more numerous than they would be if the writer were not himself a divine. The essay on Le Sage begins by quoting the worn inscription chiselled on a dark block of marble over the doorway of the house in Boulogne in which Le Sage died. The specific identification of the house – the second house on the left that one passes in walking from the Cathedral up the Street of the Château – is obviously the writing of someone who had himself walked up the street to read the inscription. Cattermole lived in Boulogne for some years before his death. A census of the city taken in June 1856 lists him and his family as residents (information from Archives du Pas-de-Calais, Arras).

Dickens was a close friend of Cattermole's brother George, who had married a distant relative of Dickens's. Cattermole was a member of the short-lived Society of British Authors, at the second meeting of which Dickens presided (Besant, "The First Society of British Authors," *Contemp. Rev.*, July 1889). He and Dickens may well have been acquainted.

D.N.B.

PROSE

Tucked Up VIII, 424–28. Dec. 31, 1853
The Author of Gil Blas X, 488–93. Jan. 6, 1855

VERSE

The Prisoner IX, 8. Feb. 18, 1854

Cayley, George John |*George Cayley*|, 1826–1878, barrister, writer; son of Edward Stillingfleet Cayley, M.P. Student at Eton; admitted pensioner, Trinity College, Cambridge, 1845; awarded Chancellor's Medal (English), 1848; did not take degree. Admitted at Inner Temple, 1848; called to the bar, 1852. Travelled and lived in foreign countries, often adopting native dress. Newspaper correspondent in the Crimea during the War. Took some part in politics. Friend of Thackeray and his daughters. Contributed occasionally to periodicals. Author of *Las Alforjas*, 1853 (first published as "The Saddlebags; or, The Bridle Roads of Spain" in *Bentley's Misc.*), and some miscellaneous writings in prose and verse.

Dickens was evidently acquainted with Cayley's parents, but not with Cayley. Relating to his wife, in 1853, the gossip that he had heard in Naples – specifically, Brinsley Norton's relationship with a Capri peasant girl and his subsequent marriage to her, Dickens added: "Another Booby of the name of Cayley ... lately disguised himself, without the least necessity, as a Sicilian mariner with legs operatically naked, and rowed away in the dead of night with another young Capri virgin – who would have gone, with the greatest cheerfulness and without any opposition, from her relations and friends, in the blaze of noon" (*Mr. & Mrs. Charles Dickens*, ed. Dexter, pp. 209–210).

In *Las Alforjas* (II, 80–83), Cayley discussed the writing of Dickens and Thackeray, giving his explanation of "why the young men of the present day prefer Thackeray to Dickens." He contrasted Dickens's "exquisite genius" with his "much less exquisite taste." As a result of the popularity that his writings brought him, wrote Cayley, Dickens "fell to imitating himself" instead of "going on improving his taste, and struggling earnestly to produce some perfect work." Cayley looked on *Pickwick* "as a free translation of Don Quixote, into the manners of modern England," with Mr. Pickwick as Quixote, Sam Weller as the Sancho of British low life, and other correspondences of character. Kitton (*Novels of Charles Dickens*, p. 6) credited Lord Jeffrey with noting the resemblance; actually, it was Cayley who suggested it to Jeffrey: "I remember once asking Lord Jeffrey about this likeness between Pickwick and Quixote, and he said it had not struck him before, but he thought there was some truth in it" (*Las Alforjas*, II, 81).

Cayley's *H.W.* contribution relates an incident that occurred while Cayley – "dressed like a Neapolitan lout" – was travelling in the Kingdom of Naples, on his way to the siege of Sebastopol. He mentions his being a barrister of the Inner Temple and his father's being an M.P.

Boase

The Poisoner of Springs
xv, 92–96. Jan. 24, 1857

Chester, J. |*J. Chester, Chester*|. *Not identified.* Payment for the writer's first contribution made in cash. One contemporary Chester with "J" as one of his initials was the Rev. Greville John Chester, who published a volume of poems in 1856 and one in 1883. The *H.W.* poems do not appear in the volumes.

VERSE

Drip, Drip, O Rain!
XIII, 136. Feb. 23, 1856

Winter — XV, 180–81. Feb. 21, 1857

Chesterton, George Laval |*Chesterton, Col. Chesterton*|, *d.* 1868, military officer, prison administrator. Attended an academy in Knightsbridge; thereafter studied classics with clergyman. Served, 1812–17, in Field Train Dept. of Royal Artillery in Peninsular War, in war with the U.S., and with Army of Occupation on the Continent. Late in 1818 enlisted in British Legion recruited in England on behalf of Bolívar; returned to England from South America in 1820. Did some journalistic work; began study for holy orders. In 1829 appointed governor of Middlesex House of Correction, Coldbath Fields; held governorship to 1854; instituted reforms that changed a viciously corrupt prison into a well-managed one. Author of *A Narrative of Proceedings in Venezuela*, 1820; *Peace, War, and Adventure*, 1853; *Revelations of Prison Life*, 1856.

Dickens first visited Coldbath Fields prison in 1835, while collecting material for *Sketches by Boz.* He became acquainted with Chesterton and came to have great admiration for his work as prison administrator, as also for his character. In *American Notes* (I, 121–22n) he praised

Chesterton for the "firmness, zeal, intelligence, and humanity" with which he discharged his administrative duties. In 1847 and for some years thereafter, he had much contact with Chesterton in connection with Miss Burdett-Coutt's Urania Cottage, a home for the rehabilitation of fallen women. Dickens, who had a large part in the establishment and supervision of the Cottage, recommended that Chesterton be made a member of the committee responsible for its administration, and he relied much on Chesterton's help and advice in matters of organization and management. On Oct. 28, 1847, he wrote to Miss Burdett-Coutts: "I cannot tell you how much cause I have seen, and see daily, during the preparation of this place, to admire the goodness and devotion of Mr Chesterton, whose time is always at our command, and whose interest in the design cannot be surpassed" (*Heart of Charles Dickens*, ed. Johnson, p. 96). Until 1850, when Coldbath Fields prison came to be used only for male offenders, Dickens was often at the prison consulting with Chesterton on the selection of prospective inmates for the Cottage. This activity, recorded Chesterton, was objected to by the magistrate Benjamin Rotch, who held that it was not "to be tolerated that Mr. Charles Dickens should walk into the prison whenever he pleased" (*Revelations of Prison Life*, II, 186).

Dickens supplied the title for Chesterton's "Coolness among Thieves." The paper, he wrote, "has not much in it," but "altered by the softening of some of [Chesterton's] hardest words and finest writing, will – do. I can't say more for it" (to Wills, March 28, 1851).

The *H.W.* article "Innocence and Crime" depicted Chesterton conducting a visitor through Coldbath Fields prison and explaining to him the cant term "shaking the doll."

Harper's reprinted "A Prison Anecdote," without acknowledgment to *H.W.*

Allibone

A Prison Anecdote
II, 496–98. Feb. 15, 1851

Coolness among Thieves [chip]
III, 189–90. May 17, 1851

The episodes related in the 2 items retold in *Peace, War, and Adventure; an Autobiographical Memoir of George Laval Chesterton.* 2 vols. London: Longman, Brown, Green, and Longmans, 1853; also in *Revelations of Prison Life; with an Enquiry into Prison Discipline and Secondary Punishments. By George Laval Chesterton.* 2 vols. London: Hurst and Blackett, 1856. Neither book states that the episodes had first been related in *H.W.*

Chisholm, Caroline (Jones) |*Mrs. Chisholm*|, 1808–1877, philanthropist. Born in Northamptonshire. Lived in Madras, 1832–38, where her husband, Capt. Archibald Chisholm, was stationed; there established school for neglected children of soldiers. In Australia, 1838–46; established Female Immigrants' Home in Sydney; conducted groups of immigrants into interior to find them suitable situations; established Registry Office for immigrant families. In England, 1846–54; worked to make possible emigration of wives and children of liberated convicts then in Australia; established Family Colonization Loan Society to enable the poor to emigrate. Wrote pamphlets on emigration; obtained help of influential persons – among them, Lord Ashley, M.P., and Sidney Herbert, M.P. – in forwarding her projects. Supervised the sending out of emigrant ships. Again in Australia, 1854–66; then returned to England. In 1867 granted Civil List pension of £100 a year "In consideration of the valuable and distinguished services rendered by her to emigrants in New South Wales (Colles, *Literature and the Pension List*).

On Feb. 24, 1850, Elizabeth Herbert, wife of Sidney Herbert, who interested herself much in emigration, wrote to Mrs. Chisholm:

"I saw Mr. Dickens to-day and he has commissioned me to say that if you will allow him, and unless he hears to the contrary from you, he will call upon you at *2 o'clock on Tuesday next*, the 26th.

"I told him about your emigrants' letters, and he seemed to think that the giving them publicity would be an important engine towards helping on our work, and he has so completely the confidence of the lower classes (who all read his Books if they can read at all), that I think if you can persuade him to bring them out in his new work it will be an immense step gained.

"He is so singularly clever and agreeable that I hope you will forgive me for having made this appointment without your direct sanction, and for having also told him that I knew you wished to make his acquaintance" (Shepard, "Dickens and His Models," *Month*, April 1902).

Mrs. Chisholm's "emigrants' letters" appeared in the first number of Dickens's "new work," i.e., *H.W.* Writing to Wills, March 6, 1850, Dickens mentioned "A Bundle of Emigrants' Letters" as "a little article of my own ... introducing some five or six originals [i.e., original letters], which are extremely good." (For the two versions of the article, see Introduction, p. 46. The Office Book assigns the article to Dickens and Mrs. Chisholm. Mrs. Chisholm's share in it, in addition to her furnishing the letters to Dickens, was her giving him information on her experience with emigrants and on the Family Colonization Loan Society, and perhaps a copy of her *A.B.C. of Colonization* (from which the article quotes). In the article, Dickens paid tribute to Mrs. Chisholm's work in behalf of emigration; he stated and endorsed the purpose of the Colonization Society, and explained its plan, which he considered essentially sound.

On March 4 – in the week following the appointment arranged by Mrs. Herbert for his calling on Mrs. Chisholm – Dickens wrote to Miss Burdett-Coutts: "I dream of Mrs Chisholm, and her housekeeping. The dirty faces of her children are my continual companions" (*Heart of Charles Dickens*, ed. Johnson, p.166). Mrs. Chisholm's preoccupation with philanthropic works, to the neglect of her home and family, obviously suggested to Dickens the similar characteristics of Mrs. Jellyby in *Bleak House*, though another *H.W.* contributor – Harriet Martineau – was generally credited in contemporary report as being Mrs. Jellyby's original.

In the two years following the publication of "A Bundle of Emigrants' Letters," support of Mrs. Chisholm's Family Colonization Loan Society and commendation of her work for emigration appeared in other *H.W.* articles. Two such articles ("Safety for Female Emigrants" and "Official Emigration") were by Wills; the others were by Samuel Sidney, who had of course often mentioned Mrs. Chisholm and her work in his *Emigrant's Journal*. In his *H.W.* article "Family Colonisation Loan Society," Sidney explained the purpose and advantages of Mrs. Chisholm's organization. In "Two Scenes in the Life of John Bodger," which may be the fictionized life story of an actual emigrant communicated to Sidney by his brother, Sidney pictured "Mrs. C." on one of her expeditions into the interior and recorded her conversation with a prosperous farmer who had left England as a workhouse pauper. (The story as reprinted in *Gallops and Gossips* expands "Mrs. C." to "Mrs. Chisholm.") In "Three Colonial Epochs," Sidney wrote of Mrs. Chisholm as "teaching the Government" of Australia how to solve the problem of the unemployed. In "Better Ties Than Red Tape Ties," he pictured Mrs. Chisholm in her home at Islington interviewing an intending emigrant, and gave a detailed account of the work that had made her name "in very many humble homes a household word." In "What to Take to Australia," Sidney mentioned the commendable washing arrangements on the Colonization Society's emigrant ships.

Mrs. Chisholm's own *H.W.* article was essentially propaganda for emigration. It described settlers in rural districts of New South Wales as enjoying substantial prosperity, with "no rent, no taxes, no rates"; it pictured one family as sitting down to Sunday dinner of a fine round of beef and a large hind-quarter of pork (cf. Mrs. Chisholm's *Comfort for the Poor! Meat Three Times a Day!!*, 1847). The article was written in first person, the writer being addressed by settlers as "Mrs. C———"; persons with emigration in mind can have had no difficulty in reading "Mrs. C———" as "Mrs. Chisholm."

D.N.B.

A Bundle of Emigrants' Letters
Mr. C.D. & Mrs. Chisholm
I, 19–24. March 30, 1850
Pictures of Life in Australia
Mrs. Chisholm & R.H.H.
I, 307–310. June 22, 1850

Chorley, Henry Fothergill |*Mr. Chorley*|, 1808–1872, critic, author. Received some years' schooling in Lancashire, but was early placed as clerk in mercantile office. Took advantage of opportunities for self-culture that offered; had great interest in music. Before he was twenty, began to contribute to annuals and minor periodicals. In 1834 settled in London and became member of *Athenaeum* staff. "Had I sought all the world over, I could not have found a situation more to my mind" (*Autobiography,* I, 98–99). Remained on staff for more than thirty years, becoming – in Espinasse's phrase – "*Athenæum*-Chorley" (*Literary Recollections,* p. 231). Best known as *Athenaeum*'s music critic, but was important as literary critic as well. Contributed also to other periodicals, e.g., *London & Westm. Rev., People's Journal, Howitt's Journal, Edin Rev.* For a time edited *Ladies' Companion.* Author of *The Lion; a Tale of the Coteries,* 1839, and other novels; also dramas and libretti; *Music and Manners in France and Germany,* 1841, and other works on music. Compiled *Memorials* of Mrs. Hemans, 1836; edited selection of Mary Russell Mitford's letters.

During the last fifteen or so years of Dickens's life, Chorley was one of Dickens's close friends. He was a frequent and always welcome guest at Gad's Hill, seldom missing the Christmas festivities there. Mary Dickens wrote: "My father was very fond of him, and had the greatest respect for his honest, straightforward, upright, and generous character." Chorley wrote of Dickens as "one of the noblest and most gifted men I have ever known, whose regard for me was one of those honours which make amends for much failure and disappointment." At the suggestion of Sir Charles Wentworth Dilke, Chorley himself wrote the obituary of Dickens in the *Athenaeum,* "unwilling that it should be entrusted to any less reverent hand" (*Autobiography,* II, 239–40, 320–21).

Chorley reviewed in the *Athenaeum A Christmas Carol* and five of Dickens's novels (*Chuzzlewit, Copperfield, Bleak House, Great Expectations, Our Mutual Friend*), his praise for the novels being not entirely unmixed with blame. In *Bleak House,* for instance, in which he found much to admire, Chorley deprecated the repugnant depiction of physical defects in certain characters, and, in others, the too undisguised portraiture of living persons. His review of *Our Mutual Friend* – the "new novel by the greatest novelist living" – brought Chorley a letter of thanks from Dickens (Oct. 28, 1865) for the generous appreciation and sympathy expressed. Dickens, on his part, had high praise for Chorley's novel *Roccabella;* he found it "a very remarkable book" of "high merits," so moving that he "cried over it heartily"; he pointed out to Chorley, however, what he thought unfair in the presentation of the Italian characters (Feb. 3, 1860).

According to his biographer, Chorley contributed "several sketches and poems" to *H.W.* and *A.Y.R.* (*Autobiography,* II, 176). He obviously wrote more for the second periodical than he did for the first. Dickens's letters to Wills mention as by Chorley a paper (or papers) on music published in *A.Y.R.* Percy Fitzgerald (*Memoirs of an Author,* I, 151–52) mentioned Dickens's good-naturedly yielding to Chorley's insistence that "The Area Sneak" (obviously "An Area Sneak," *A.Y.R.,* April 15, 1865) be accepted for publication, despite Dickens's inability to "'make head or tail of it,' or discover what the author would be at." Dickens considered publishing Chorley's *A Prodigy* in *A.Y.R.,* but decided that the novel would not lend itself well to serialization (to Frederic Chapman, Jan. 28, 1865: typescript Huntington Library).

Commendatory mention of Chorley's *Old Love and New Fortune* appeared in Dickens's *H.W.* article "The Amusements of the People" (April 13, 1850). "We would have [the office of dramatic licenser] exercise a sound supervision over the lower drama," wrote Dickens, "instead of stopping the career of a real work of art, as it did in the case of Mr. Chorley's play ..., for a sickly point of form." *Old Love and New Fortune*, after a successful opening night at the Surrey Theatre, had been withdrawn because the management, through oversight, had not obtained a license for its presentation (*Autobiography*, II, 19–20).

D.N.B.

The Brown Hat I, 133–35. May 4, 1850
Poetry in the Bye-Ways
I, 151–53. May 11, 1850

Clark. Address: Delhi. *Not identified.* According to his article, the contributor lived as a child in coal-mining district of England; at the time of writing had been at least sixteen years in India, apparently engaged in business; writes of his home and family as in Calcutta.

By Dawk to Delhi
VIII, 365–70. Dec. 17, 1853

Clark or **Clarke.** *Not identified.* The first article listed below begins with the statement: "We intend to give, in the way of an occasional sketch, a plain account of the manner in which the government business of this country is transacted." That article and the two that follow thus constitute a series, each discussing a Government office – its history, function, administration, officials, etc. The second article gives footnote reference to the first. The articles are well written and clearly organized. They are obviously by one writer – Clark or Clarke, as indicated below. Payment for the contributions made by cheque.

The Home Office *Clark & Morley*
X, 270–75. Nov. 4, 1854
The Board of Trade *Clarke*
XI, 101–105. March 3, 1855
The Audit Board *Clarke & Morley*
XI, 543–46. July 7, 1855

Clarke, W. H. *Not identified.* The two items assigned to the contributor indicate his interest in British colonial policy. London directories of the 1850s list (aside from tradesmen named W. H. Clarke) the following: William Henry Clarke, Esq., accountant, Clement's Inn; William Henry Clarke, Esq., Eaton Place; William Henry Clarke, Esq. (listed also as Clark), North Brixton; William Henry Clarke, Esq. (listed in 1860 directory as William Hender Clarke), Islington; and William Hislop Clarke, Esq., barrister, with chambers in Lincoln's Inn. Payment for the first contribution made by cheque.

The Gwalior Janissaries
VII, 375–76. June 18, 1853
An Ashantee Palaver [chip]
VIII, 207–209. Oct. 29, 1853

Cobbe. *Not identified.* The contributor seems to have been a member of a ship's crew; he tells of seeing the body of a man on an iceberg in mid-ocean. Payment for the contribution made by cheque.

The Man on the Iceberg
XIII, 479–80. May 31, 1856

Cole, Alfred Whaley |*Mr. Cole, Alfred Cole, A. Cole*|, 1823–1896, judge, Q.C. Born at Highbury, near London. Student at London University. For short time, clerk in office of his uncle, a London solicitor. Undecided as to career, embarked in 1841 on emigrant ship bound for New Zealand; ship wrecked off coast of Cape Town. Stayed five years in Cape Colony, then returned to England. Admitted at Middle Temple, 1847; called to the bar, 1850. While waiting for briefs, turned to writing, but found writing hard to earn a living by. Sailed for Cape Town, 1856. Admitted advocate, Cape Colony bar; successful in private practice; appointed acting judge, later judge; Q.C., 1880; retired, 1891. At various times represented in Parliament four separate divisions of the Colony; was for many years

Colonial Law lecturer. Died at Wynberg, near Cape Town. Best account of Cole is in *South African Law Journal*, Feb. 1935.

In early life contributed to *Bentley's Misc.* and *Sharpe's*. Published *The Cape and the Kafirs*, 1852; *Legends in Verse*, 1855; two novels, and three books of tales and sketches. In Cape Colony was co-founder and for some years editor of *Cape Monthly Magazine*; for shorter time, editor of *South African Magazine*; contributed articles, also verse, to periodicals. His "Three Idylls of a Prince," written on occasion of Prince Alfred's first visit to the Cape, said to have "heartily amused" Queen Victoria and the Princess Royal. Published *Reminiscences*, 1896.

During the time that he kept terms at the Middle Temple, wrote Cole (*Reminiscences*, p. 3), Dickens and Thackeray were "among my fellow 'students.'" (Dickens had entered his name at the Middle Temple in 1839, but did not eat dinners there, stated Forster, until "many years later.") In his *Reminiscences*, Cole recorded some few comments made to him by his friends Richard Bentley and George Cruikshank, concerning Dickens.

Editorial comment prefaced to the first instalment of Cole's "'Cape' Sketches" in *H.W.* identified the writer as a "gentleman ... who has passed five active years in the colony of the Cape of Good Hope," and characterized the sketches as "amusing and instructive."

Cole's "Martyrs of Chancery," dealing with the offence of contempt of Court and citing instances of persons who had been "Chancery prisoners" for ten, twenty, and thirty years, provoked a reply from Sir Edward B. Sugden, framer of the act of 1830 intended to clear prisons of persons so confined. The *H.W.* article, wrote Sugden in a letter to the *Times*, Jan. 7, 1851, contained misstatements; it misinterpreted facts; it was calculated "to prejudice the due administration of justice, and to direct public feeling into a wrong channel." Sugden took the author of "Martyrs of Chancery" to be Dickens. "I grieve," he wrote, "to see a writer of such distinguished reputation ... condescend to write such an article." *H.W.*'s reply to Sugden's letter, assigned in the Office Book to Wills and Cole, pointed out that certain of Sugden's statements were self-contradictory; that his "excellent" act of 1830 was a "curative after mischief done," rather than a preventive of mischief; and that, even as such, its provisions were largely inoperative in the present state of Chancery administration. It cited, with name and dates, a case proving this point.

Harper's reprinted "Good Intentions," without acknowledgment to *H.W.*; "How We Went Whaling," with acknowledgment.

South African Biblio.

*"Cape" Sketches
I, 588–91. Sept. 14, 1850
I, 607–610. Sept. 21, 1850
II, 118–20. Oct. 26, 1850
II, 165–67. Nov. 9, 1850

"Good Intentions." A Story of the African Blockade II, 45–47. Oct. 5, 1850

*How We Went Whaling off the Cape of Good Hope II, 58–59. Oct. 12, 1850

The Treasures of the Deep [chip]
II, 94–95. Oct. 19, 1850

The Martyrs of Chancery
II, 250–52. Dec. 7, 1850

The Martyrs of Chancery. Second Article *W.H.W. & A. Cole*
II, 493–96. Feb. 15, 1851

*Most of the material in "'Cape' Sketches" is embedded, some of it verbatim, in *The Cape and the Kafirs: or, Notes of Five Years' Residence in South Africa. By Alfred W. Cole*. London: Richard Bentley, 1852. "How We Went Whaling" appears with but minor revision in the same book. Pub. in *H.W.* not acknowledged.

Cole, Charles Augustus |*Mr. Charles Cole*|, Public Record Office clerk. Served as assistant commissioner of Great Exhibition, 1851; under his superintendence, in connection with Paris Exhibition, 1867, was issued *The Imperial Paris Guide*. Claimed to have originated "journalistic gossip" (Hatton, *Journalistic London*, p. 89). Author of *Apsley House* (verse), 1853, dated from Garrick Club. Editor of *Memorials of Henry the Fifth*, 1858.

Cole's *H.W.* article describes the hazards of fire, flood, and destruction by vermin to which the documents stored in the Tower of London, in the Rolls House and Chapel in Chancery Lane, in the Chapter House of Westminster Abbey, and in Carlton Ride were exposed. Cole was employed in the Carlton Ride repository at the time that the article appeared (*Brit. Imperial Calendar*, 1850). About a fourth of the text of the article is taken from Henry Cole, "Neglect of the Public Records," *Westm. Rev.*, April 1849.

Nonesuch *Letters* mentions, but does not give the text of, a letter from Dickens to Charles Cole, Sept. 5, 1860 (addressee's name given in index as Charles A. Cole). The letter, to appear in Pilgrim *Letters*, concerns material submitted by Cole to *A.Y.R.* The material referred to is the articles titled "Five Hundred Years Ago," published in *A.Y.R.* Oct. 6, Oct. 27, Dec. 1, 1860. The articles are clearly by Charles Augustus Cole; the first mentions the documents on English history brought out "during the last three years" under the direction of the Master of the Rolls. Cole's edition of *Memorials of Henry the Fifth* was one of the publications thus issued.

Cole and Dickens were acquainted, as indicated by Dickens's letter to Cole, Aug. 7, 1862.

Allibone

The Adventures of the Public Records
Mr. Charles Cole & W.H.W.
I, 396–99. July 20, 1850

Cole, H. The contributor pictures himself attending a session of the Round Catch and Canon Club, a device that provides him the opportunity of telling something of the history of various musical clubs and of naming the famous seventeenth- and eighteenth-century composers of glees, catches, and madrigals. He commends the efforts made during the past few years to popularize music education – John P. Hullah's classes, M. Jullien's cheap concerts, and the teaching of singing in the army and navy. Music, he holds, improves the manners and tastes of a people.

The contributor may be Henry (later Sir Henry) Cole, 1808–1882 (*D.N.B.*), well-known public official, one of whose strong interests was music. As a young man Cole helped Thomas Love Peacock write critiques of musical performances. Later, he was instrumental in founding the National Training School for Music. He advocated an increase in congregational singing in churches and was successful in inducing church officials to institute week-day musical services. He hoped to make England again what she had once been – "a musical nation" where "people had their glees and madrigals, which contributed to the happiness of men and women" (*Fifty Years of Public Work*, I, 365ff; II, 357ff).

Whether or not Henry Cole was a contributor to *H.W.*, he had, in one way or another, a connection with several articles in the periodical. His "Neglect of the Public Records," *Westm. Rev.*, April 1849, served in part as the text of "The Adventures of the Public Records." His enumeration of the thirty-five "official stages, so far as they can be made out, which an inventor must undergo in obtaining letters patent" formed the basis of Dickens's "A Poor Man's Tale of a Patent." (Dickens read Cole's report in proof-sheets; it was shortly thereafter published by the Society of Arts in *Rights of Inventors*, 1850.) Various proposals made by Cole (as "Denarius") in his pamphlet *Shall We Keep the Crystal Palace and Have Riding and Walking in All Weathers among Flowers – Fountains – and Sculpture?*, 1851, were quoted in Morley's article "What Is Not Clear about the Crystal Palace." The 1852 Marlborough House exhibition illustrating household objects and wearing apparel in poor taste, which Cole was mainly instrumental in organizing, was the subject of Morley's "A House Full of Horrors." Sala, referring to the exhibition, in his "Case of Real Distress," mentioned Cole's riding his hobbies "desperately hard." Cole's connection with the purchase and exhibition of the Soulages collection was mentioned in Dodd's "The Soulages Collection."

London Musical Clubs
III, 179–81. May 17, 1851

Collins, Charles Allston |*C. Collins, Charles Collins*|, 1828–1873, painter, writer. Studied at Royal Academy schools; became associated with Pre-Raphaelite painters, but was not a member of the Brotherhood. Exhibited at Royal Academy. After 1857, devoted himself almost entirely to writing. Art critic for the *Echo* (Boase); contributed to *Macmillan's, Cornhill.* Author of *A Cruise upon Wheels,* three works of fiction, and two other books.

Collins married Dickens's daughter Kate in 1860. Dickens liked Collins, but he had misgivings about the marriage; he doubted that Kate really loved Collins, and he was concerned about Collins's ill health. Dickens's apprehensions about Kate's being left a young widow became, after some years, so ill concealed that, according to Charles Fechter, they aroused the resentment of Collins's brother Wilkie and led to an estrangement between Wilkie and Dickens (Adrian, "A Note on the Dickens-Collins Friendship," *Huntington Library Quart.,* Feb. 1953). In 1857 Collins had appeared in one of Dickens's presentations of *The Frozen Deep*; in 1862, when Dickens was thinking of a trip to Australia, on which he would take along as secretary "some man of literary pretensions," he wondered whether Collins would be an appropriate choice (to Forster, Oct. 22, 1862). In 1869 Collins designed the *Edwin Drood* cover illustration, which Dickens liked very much; his ill health made impossible his carrying out his intention of drawing the illustrations for the book itself.

Collins's first *H.W.* contribution is marked in the Office Book as "per W. Collins"; Wilkie Collins was at the time on the editorial staff. Collins's "Smallport Monte-Cristo" Dickens thought "very whimsical and good." He liked to look over Collins's contributions before they were set up in final form: "A very little erasure here and there, makes a considerable difference in his case," he wrote to Wills (Oct. 18, 1858).

Collins contributed both fiction and non-fiction to *A.Y.R.,* some of his stories appearing in the Christmas numbers. Dickens particularly liked the "Our Eye-Witness" sketches, which he urged Collins to continue. In a helpful letter of criticism to Collins, Nov. 19, 1859, Dickens pointed out the lack of coherence and ease in one of Collins's *A.Y.R.* contributions, the over-intrusion of a non-participating narrator, and the "want of touches of relief, and life, and truth"; he mentioned Collins's "correct and delicate observation" and his "excellent humour." (The *Saturday Review,* Oct. 4, 1862, found in Collins's *Cruise upon Wheels* "a humour that forcibly recalls Mr. Dickens, perhaps all the more that it is frequently exaggerated and overdone.") Of Collins's books, *A New Sentimental Journey,* 1859; *The Eye-Witness,* 1860; and *At the Bar,* 1866, originally appeared in *A.Y.R.*

D.N.B.

My First Patron
xvii, 201–205. Feb. 13, 1858

Her Face xviii, 258–64. Aug. 28, 1858

The Smallport Monte-Cristo
xviii, 423–28. Oct. 16, 1858

The Great Dunkerque Failure
xviii, 476–80. Oct. 30, 1858

Cœlebs in Search of a Dinner
xix, 68–72. Dec. 18, 1858

The Smallchange Family
xix, 179–86. Jan. 22, 1859

Two Leaves from the Devil's Book
xix, 252–58. Feb. 12, 1859

Novelty xix, 306–309. Feb. 26, 1859

Some Wild Ideas [lead]
xix, 505–510. April 30, 1859

Collins, William Wilkie |*Wilkie Collins, W. Collins, Collins, W. W. Collins, W. Wilkie Collins*|, 1824–1889, novelist. Attended a private school in Highbury. Admitted at Lincoln's Inn, 1846; called to the bar, 1851; interest lay in writing, rather than in law. First signed story appeared in Douglas Jerrold's *Illuminated Magazine,* 1843; later contributed to *Bentley's Misc., Cornhill, Cassell's, Temple Bar, Belgravia, Canadian Monthly,* and other periodicals. In 1848 published memoir of his father, William Collins the artist; in 1850, *Antonina,* the first of his some thirty works of fiction. Achieved fame as writer of sensation and detective novels; turned to writing propaganda novels; wrote also plays.

Collins met Dickens in 1851 and became, stated Forster, "for all the rest of the life of Dickens, one of his dearest and most valued friends" (*Life*, Book VI, sect. V). Collins came to share in many of Dickens's activities. He took part in the theatricals, which included presentations of his plays *The Lighthouse* (in 1855) and *The Frozen Deep* (in 1857). He was Dickens's companion for convivial evenings, as well as for holiday excursions at home and on the Continent. He was a frequent guest at Dickens's home.

In their literary association, the two writers collaborated on stories and plays; they consulted each other about their writings, Dickens frequently giving Collins helpful advice and criticism. Most critics agree that each influenced the writing of the other, though some contend that Dickens's writing was not influenced by Collins's. Collins held a high opinion of some of Dickens's novels; others he thought badly written. *A Tale of Two Cities* he mentioned in his preface to *The Woman in White* as "the most perfect work of constructive art that has ever proceeded from [Dickens's] pen." Marginalia in his copy of Forster's *Life* record his opinion that *Martin Chuzzlewit* was in some respects Dickens's finest novel, *Barnaby Rudge* his weakest; that *Oliver Twist*, though badly constructed, was admirable for its character of Nancy; and that the latter half of *Dombey* "no intelligent person can have read without astonishment at the badness of it" (Robinson, *Wilkie Collins*, p. 258). Collins dedicated *Hide and Seek*, 1854, to Dickens "as a token of admiration and affection." Dickens thought it "a very remarkable book," "in some respects masterly" (to Georgina Hogarth, July 22, 1854). He had similar high praise for other of Collins's novels. The literary kinship that Dickens felt with Collins, as also his affection for him, appears in a letter of Oct. 14, 1862. Having learned that Collins, while working on *No Name*, had become seriously ill, Dickens offered to take over the writing at any moment that Collins might ask him to: "Absurdly unnecessary to say that it would be a makeshift! But I could do it at a pinch, so like you as that no one should find out the difference." "Call me, and I come." Certain of Dickens's friends found the close friendship and literary association of the two men difficult to explain, seeing in it a kind of degradation of Dickens to the level of a man whom they considered his inferior. (Some commentators on Dickens have held the same attitude.)

Sala, after Dickens's death, expressed the hope that either Forster or Collins would write the authorized biography of Dickens. Both writers, he stated, "had opportunities of studying and of judging the personal character of Charles Dickens – opportunities possessed by none other of his contemporaries" (*Charles Dickens*, p. 95).

Collins began to contribute to *H.W.* the year after he had become acquainted with Dickens. Dickens valued him highly as a writer for that periodical and for its successor; various of his letters mention Collins's industry, his dependability, his capacity for taking pains. And Dickens was eager to retain Collins as a *H.W.* contributor as Collins's reputation, in time, brought him offers from other periodicals. In a letter to Wills, April 1, 1856, Dickens instructed him to pay Collins fifty pounds for "A Rogue's Life," explaining: "I think it [the payment] right, abstractedly, in the case of a careful and good writer on whom we can depend for Xmas Nos. and the like. But further, I know of offers for stories going about – to Collins himself for instance – which make it additionally desirable that we should not shave close in such a case." The letter implies that Dickens considered the amount a generous payment; actually, it was a few shillings less than the standard rate of a guinea a page.

After Collins had been a *H.W.* contributor for four and a half years, Dickens induced him to join the editorial staff. His salary was to be five guineas a week. The offer was not, as Collins saw, a very advantageous one to him; he accepted it only on the agreement that a novel by him be serialized in *H.W.*, with his authorship announced. *The Dead Secret* was so announced, first on Dec. 6,

1856 (in the Christmas number "The Wreck of the Golden Mary"). After Oct. 25 of that year the Office Book records no further payment to Collins for individual items. Toward the end of 1857, Dickens increased Collins's salary by an "extra Fifty" per year. "... I have no doubt of his being devoted to H.W., and doing great service," he wrote to Wills, Oct. 2.

Collins's principal work as staff member was to write original material for the periodical, sometimes – as in "Highly Proper!" – articles on subjects suggested by Dickens. What his other duties were the Dickens-Wills correspondence does not specify. The fact that the Office Book does not list his name jointly with the names of outside contributors implies that revising contributed material was probably not part of his work.

"Highly Proper!", dealing with social prejudice in private schools, is assigned in the Office Book to Collins alone. It was probably revised by Wills, in accordance with Dickens's instructions to him (Sept. 24, 1858) that there be left in it nothing that might be "unnecessarily offensive to the middle class"; Collins, Dickens remarked, always had "a tendency to overdo that." The two articles published in 1858 to which Dickens's initials are attached jointly with Collins's name – "A Clause for the New Reform Bill" and "Doctor Dulcamara" – were not actual collaborations of the two writers; the articles were written by Collins and revised or added to by Dickens (see Stone, ed., *Charles Dickens' Uncollected Writings from Household Words*). "The Lazy Tour of Two Idle Apprentices," however, was an actual collaboration of Dickens and Collins; each narrated a part of their uneventful "tour," and each contributed a story to the account. Certain of the Christmas numbers were also collaborations of Dickens and Collins. The original idea of "The Perils of Certain English Prisoners" was Collins's; Collins wrote the second chapter of the story, Dickens writing the first and third. "Each revised the work of the other" (Robinson, p. 118). For "The Wreck of the Golden Mary" and "A House to Let" Dickens devised the framework. In the working out of his idea, in the actual writing of the framework, and in fitting into it the stories that form a part of the numbers, Collins was his close collaborator, as Dickens's letters make clear. (Of these two Christmas numbers, as also of the 1854 and 1855 Christmas numbers, certain sections that the Office Book assigns to Collins alone are reprinted by Stone, in *Charles Dickens' Uncollected Writings*, as in part by Dickens. The present Table of Contents and the present listing of writers' contributions follow the Office Book ascriptions.)

Among Collins's *H.W.* stories for which Dickens had high praise were "Sister Rose" and "The Diary of Anne Rodway." "The Diary" moved him to tears. Among Collins's non-fiction items that Dickens particularly liked were "The Cruise of the Tomtit," "To Think, or Be Thought For?", "A Petition to the Novel-Writers," and "The Unknown Public."

At least two of Collins's *H.W.* contributions brought a remonstrance to the editorial staff: Harriet Martineau, in her indignant letter to Wills, cited "The Yellow Mask" (which she had not herself read) as an instance of *H.W.*'s vicious anti-Catholic policy that in part motivated her determination no longer to write for *H.W.* (*Autobiography*, II, 94–95); and a son of the theatrical manager Robert William Elliston wrote to Dickens in protest against the epithets that Collins, in his article "Douglas Jerrold," had applied to Elliston (*My Miscellanies*, II, 85–86n). The articles "To Think, or Be Thought For?" and "Dramatic Grub Street," stated Collins, provoked "some remonstrance both of the public and the private sort" (*My Miscellanies*, II, 193n).

A complimentary reference to Collins appeared in *H.W.* the month before he became a contributor. In "If This Should Meet His Eye," Dixon mentioned him and "his pleasant book" on Cornwall – i.e., *Rambles beyond Railways*. Later, in addition to the announcement of Collins's authorship of *The Dead Secret*, there appeared thirteen advertisements for the novel "BY WILKIE COLLINS" as a 2-vol. Bradbury & Evans publication. (*A Child's*

History of England and *Hard Times* were the only other books so advertised in *H.W.*)

On the cessation of *H.W.*, Collins served for a time on the staff of *A.Y.R.* Some years later he assisted Wills for a time in editorial work during Dickens's American reading tour. Collins wrote for *A.Y.R.*, aside from short items, *The Woman in White*, *No Name*, and *The Moonstone*. Dickens had high praise for the first two novels and also, on his reading its opening chapters, for *The Moonstone*. It was undoubtedly an estrangement between him and Collins (see Charles Collins, above) that prompted Dickens's later comment that the construction of *The Moonstone* was "wearisome beyond endurance" and that the "vein of obstinate conceit" in the novel made enemies of its readers (to Wills, July 26, 1868). Actually, according to Tinsley (*Random Recollections*, I, 114–15), both *The Woman in White* and *The Moonstone* did much to increase the circulation of *A.Y.R.* Collins contributed an occasional item to *A.Y.R.* under the editorship of Charles Dickens, Jr.

Of the items listed below as not reprinted, one of those that appeared in *H.W.* after Collins's brother had begun to write for the periodical is assigned in the Office Book merely to "Collins" and is not referred to in Dickens's letters as by Wilkie Collins. This is "A Sermon for Sepoys." The fact that no payment is recorded for the item indicates that it is by Wilkie Collins and not by his brother. *C.B.E.L.* attributes the item to Wilkie Collins. "A Column to Burns," also listed below among items not reprinted, is not included in the Office Book. It consists of a letter from a *H.W.* reader in Glasgow, introduced by a paragraph of editorial comment. The motivation for the letter was Collins's article on Burns in a preceding number. Since Collins was on the staff, it is logical to assume that correspondence concerning his own article should have been referred to him and that he should have written the editorial comment prefaced to the Glasgow letter. *C.B.E.L.* attributes the item to him.

Harper's reprinted "A Terribly Strange Bed," without acknowledgment to *H.W.*; it reprinted "The Fourth Poor Traveller" as "A Lawyer's Story. By Charles Dickens." According to the *Dickensian* (June 1916, pp. 143–44), a Philadelphia publisher reprinted "Sister Rose," probably in the year of its publication in *H.W.*, as a work by Dickens.

D.N.B. suppl. 1901

A Terribly Strange Bed
v, 129–37. April 24, 1852
Gabriel's Marriage
VII, 149–57. April 16, 1853, and the following no.
The Fourth Poor Traveller
Seven Poor Travellers (Christmas 1854), pp. 19–26
Sister Rose [chap. i = lead]
XI, 217–25. April 7, 1855, and the 3 following nos.
The Yellow Mask [1st instalment = lead]
XI, 529–39. July 7, 1855, and the 3 following nos.

The 5 items repr. in *After Dark. By Wilkie Collins.* 2 vols. London: Smith, Elder and Co., 1856. Pub. in *H.W. acknowledged.*

The Cruise of the Tomtit
XII, 490–99. Dec. 22, 1855

Repr. as postscript in *Rambles beyond Railways; or, Notes in Cornwall Taken A-foot. By Wilkie Collins.* New ed. London: Richard Bentley, 1861. Pub. in *H.W.* not acknowledged.

The Ostler Holly-Tree Inn (Christmas 1855), pp. 9–18
The Diary of Anne Rodway [chap. i = lead]
XIV, 1–7. July 19, 1856, and the following no.
Brother Morgan's Story of the Dead Hand [so titled in reprinting; no separate title in "Lazy Tour of Two Idle Apprentices," where item appears as interpolated story] XVI, 340–49. Oct. 10, 1857
A Paradoxical Experience
XVIII, 516–22. Nov. 13, 1858
A New Mind XIX, 107–114. Jan. 1, 1859

The 5 items repr. in *The Queen of Hearts. By Wilkie Collins.* 3 vols. London: Hurst and

Blackett, 1859. Pub. in *H.W.* not acknowledged.

A Rogue's Life. Written by Himself
xiii, 157–66. March 1, 1856, and the 4 following nos.

Repr. as *A Rogue's Life: From His Birth to His Marriage. By Wilkie Collins.* London: Richard Bentley and Son, 1879. Pub. in *H.W.* acknowledged.

Laid Up in Two Lodgings:
My Paris Lodging [lead]
xiii, 481–86. June 7, 1856
My London Lodging
xiii, 517–23. June 14, 1856
My Spinsters [lead]
xiv, 121–26. Aug. 23, 1856
My Black Mirror [lead]
xiv, 169–75. Sept. 6, 1856
To Think, or Be Thought For? [lead]
xiv, 193–98. Sept. 13, 1856
Talk-Stoppers [lead]
xiv, 337–42. Oct. 25, 1856
A Petition to the Novel-Writers [lead]
xiv, 481–85. Dec. 6, 1856
Bold Words by a Bachelor [lead]
xiv, 505–507. Dec. 13, 1856
A Remarkable Revolution
xvi, 100–104. Aug. 1, 1857
A Queen's Revenge
xvi, 156–62. Aug. 15, 1857
A Journey in Search of Nothing [lead]
xvi, 217–23. Sept. 5, 1857
Mrs. Badgery [lead]
xvi, 289–93. Sept. 26, 1857
Save Me from My Friends [lead]
xvii, 97–102. Jan. 16, 1858
Give Us Room! [lead]
xvii, 193–96. Feb. 13, 1858
Dramatic Grub Street. Explored in Two Letters [lead]
xvii, 265–70. March 6, 1858
Mrs. Bullwinkle [lead]
xvii, 409–411. April 17, 1858
The Unknown Public [lead]
xviii, 217–22. Aug. 21, 1858
A Shockingly Rude Article [lead]
xviii, 241–45. Aug. 28, 1858
The Poisoned Meal [1st instalment = lead] xviii, 313–18. Sept. 18, 1858, and the 2 following nos.
Douglas Jerrold [lead]
xix, 217–22. Feb. 5, 1859
The Great (Forgotten) Invasion [lead]
xix, 337–41. March 12, 1859

The 20 items repr., with 5 items from *A.Y.R.*, as *My Miscellanies. By Wilkie Collins.* 2 vols. London: Sampson Low, Son, & Co., 1863. Pub. in *H.W.* and *A.Y.R.* acknowledged.

The Dead Secret
xv, 12–18. Jan. 3, 1857, and (except for no. of April 4) the 22 following nos., ending xv, 565–70. June 13, 1857

Repr. as *The Dead Secret. By Wilkie Collins.* 2 vols. London: Bradbury & Evans, 1857. Pub. in *H.W.* not acknowledged.

The National Gallery and the Old Masters [chip]
xiv, 347–48. Oct. 25, 1856
The Wreck: John Steadiman's Account [title thus in Office Book; sentence-title in *H.W.*] Wreck of the Golden Mary (Christmas 1856), pp. 11–13
The Deliverance
Wreck of the Golden Mary (Christmas 1856), pp. 30–36
A Fair Penitent
xvi, 55–59. July 18, 1857
The Debtor's Best Friend
xvi, 279–82. Sept. 19, 1857
The Lazy Tour of Two Idle Apprentices [all chaps. = lead] *C.D. & Collins*, except for chap. ii, marked *C.D. & W. Collins* xvi, 313–19. Oct. 3, 1857, and the 4 following nos. [In *The Queen of Hearts*, Collins repr. one interpolated story from this joint work. See above.]
The Prison in the Woods
Perils of Certain English Prisoners (Christmas 1857), pp. 14–30
Deep Design on Society [lead]
xvii, 49–53. Jan. 2, 1858
The Little Huguenot
xvii, 80–84. Jan. 9, 1858
Thanks to Doctor Livingstone [lead]
xvii, 121–25. Jan. 23, 1858
Strike! [lead] xvii, 169–72. Feb. 6, 1858
A Sermon for Sepoys
xvii, 244–47. Feb. 27, 1858
A Shy Scheme [lead]
xvii, 313–16. March 20, 1858

Awful Warning to Bachelors [lead]
xvii, 337–40. March 27, 1858
Sea-Breezes with the London Smack
xviii, 274–77. Sept. 4, 1858
Highly Proper! [lead]
xviii, 361–63. Oct. 2, 1858
A Clause for the New Reform Bill [lead]
Wilkie Collins & C.D.
xviii, 385–87. Oct. 9, 1858
Doctor Dulcamara, M.P. [lead]
Wilkie Collins & C.D.
xix, 49–52. Dec. 18, 1858
Over the Way [lead] A House to Let
(Christmas 1858), pp. 1–6
Trottle's Report A House to Let
(Christmas 1858), pp. 26–32
Let at Last *Do.* [i.e., Collins] *& C.D.*
A House to Let
(Christmas 1858), pp. 32–36
Pity a Poor Prince [lead]
xix, 145–47. Jan. 15, 1859
Burns. Viewed As a Hat-Peg [lead]
xix, 241–43. Feb. 12, 1859
A Column to Burns [chip]
xix, 306. Feb. 26, 1859
A Breach of British Privilege [lead]
xix, 361–64. March 19, 1859
A Dramatic Author [chip]
xix, 609–610. May 28, 1859

Cooper, Thomas |*Cooper*|, 1805–1892, author, known as "Cooper the Chartist." Attended Bluecoat school, Gainsborough; thereafter educated himself by reading and study; called himself "the self-educated shoe-maker." For a time a schoolmaster, then newspaper writer. Became leader in Chartist agitation; arrested on charges of conspiracy and sedition; two years in Stafford gaol; released in 1845. Subsequently disassociated himself from Chartist activities. Lectured and wrote; became devout itinerant preacher. As reporter, editor-proprietor, and contributor, connected with various provincial newspapers; contributed, among London periodicals, to *Douglas Jerrold's Weekly Newspaper*, *Howitt's Journal*, the *Reasoner*; edited the *Plain Speaker*; brought out short-lived *Cooper's Journal*. Author of *The Purgatory of Suicides*, 1845; *The Paradise of Martyrs*, 1873; some prose fiction; *The Life of Thomas Cooper*, 1872. Published also sermons and some miscellaneous writings.

Cooper and Dickens were acquainted. In his attempts, in 1845, to find a publisher for his *Purgatory of Suicides*, Cooper left the poem with Douglas Jerrold, and thereafter called on Jerrold to hear his verdict. Jerrold, according to Cooper, was enthusiastic about the poem and stated that he had showed it to Dickens, who "was so taken with [it] that he asked to take it home" (*Life of Thomas Cooper*, p. 276). Dickens "afterwards received me," wrote Cooper, "in the same fraternal spirit" as had Jerrold (Conklin, *Thomas Cooper*, p. 265). In a letter to Cooper, Oct. 7, 1845, Dickens wrote: "... I am not yet prepared to report to you upon your MS," and added: "You can have access to your papers at any time you please for the purpose of taking out the Verses. ..." Which of his MSS Cooper had asked Dickens to read the letter does not state, nor is it clear why Cooper should have wished to take out the verses. The reference seems to be to *The Baron's Yule Feast*; his prefatory comments to that book Cooper dated Dec. 20, 1845; and in his notes (p. 120) he acknowledged Dickens's "kind attention" and his pointing out the similarity of one of the stories in the book to a story in the *Decameron*.

Cooper had some admiration for Dickens's writings. Though he warned young working men against promiscuous novel reading, he allowed them – "when overworn with labour, and unfit for sterner thought or study" – an occasional novel by Fielding, Smollett, Scott, or Dickens (*Eight Letters to the Young Men of the Working-Classes*, p. 17).

In his *Life* (p. 282) Cooper stated: "... for one of [Dickens's] periodicals I wrote a little." "Griper Greg" is assigned in the Office Book merely to "Cooper." Its similarity to various of Cooper's humorous doggerels and its use of alliterative names – a frequent practice of Cooper's (e.g., Tibbald Trudgit, Derrick Double, Crinkum Crankum) – are sufficient justification for taking the "Cooper" to be Thomas Cooper. The non-appearance of "Griper Greg" in Cooper's *Poetical Works*, 1877, does not rule out his authorship. Cooper did not include in the collection all his fugitive verses – with which, he wrote, he "could easily have filled a portly volume."

D.N.B. suppl. 1901

VERSE

Griper Greg. A Capriccio
VII, 301–302. May 28, 1853

Cormack, Sir John Rose|*Dr. Cormack*|, 1815–1882, physician. M.D. Univ. of Edinburgh, 1837. F.R.C.P. Edinburgh, 1841. Physician to Royal Infirmary and to Fever Hospital, Edinburgh, to 1845. Practised in London, 1847–66. Removed to France. M.D. Univ. of France, 1870. During siege of Paris rendered conspicuous service to British residents and to the wounded of both sides. Made Chevalier of Legion of Honour, 1871; knighted 1872. Established Edinburgh *Monthly Jour. of Medical Science*, 1841; editor to 1846. Established London *Jour. of Medicine*, 1849; editor to 1852. Editor of *Association Medical Jour.*, 1853–55. Contributed occasionally to non-professional periodicals, e.g., *Athenaeum*. Published *Clinical Studies*, 1876, a collection of his principal writings. F.R.S.

Cormack's reference to himself in the second item listed below establishes him as the *H.W.* contributor. The article states that the fire-altar theory of vitrified forts "was advocated by Doctor Cormack, in a paper read before the Scottish Society of Antiquaries on the second of May, eighteen hundred and forty-two." *Archaeologica Scotica*, Vol. IV, Appendix, p. 32, records that on May 2, 1841 [*sic*], John R. Cormack, M.D., read before the Society his "Essay on Vitrified Forts: Fire altars of Baal or Belus, in which it was contended that these remains ... were Altars of the God of Fire" (information from Society of Antiquaries of Scotland, Edinburgh). A footnote to the article "Beltane" refers the reader to "British Fire-Worship"; the text of "Beltane" mentions "the vitrified remains" of fire-altars "of which an account was given in Household Words for April sixteenth" (incorrect reference to "Fossil Geography," April 16, instead of to "British Fire-Worship," April 30).

"Christmas in the Frozen Regions," assigned in the Office Book to "Dr. Cormack & C.D.," is by Robert McCormick.

D.N.B.

The Parcels-Post
XIX, 393–94. March 26, 1859
British Fire-Worship
XIX, 526–28. April 30, 1859
Beltane, or May-Day
XIX, 557–61. May 14, 1859

Corning, Dr. Von |*Dr. Von Corning, Dr. Corning*|. *Not identified.* The contributor states that he first visited the sierra and the pampas of Buenos Ayres Province in 1848–49. By that date, had apparently lived for some time in the province; tells of visiting slaughter-house in vicinity of Buenos Ayres; refers to "my residence at Azul." Mentions cultivating the acquaintance of a cacique "with the view of gathering information as to the religion and peculiar customs of the Pampas Indians." Refers to himself as "an old traveller"; is obviously familiar with the Continent. His reference to England as "this country" implies that he was in England at the time of writing the articles; so too does the Office Book notation that the first section of "South American Scraps" was paid for "in advance by W.H.W." and that the sum paid for the second section was "Advanced at various times." (No payment is recorded for "Life in a Saladero.")

Both "Life in a Saladero" and "South American Scraps" underwent revision. The first, revised by Wills, displays few eccentricities of language. But the second, despite the revision, contains unidiomatic constructions, bookish vocabulary, and ponderous sentences, with clause piled on clause, that indicate that the writer is not a native speaker of English. The second section of the "Scraps" Dickens damned in a letter to Wills, July 23, 1851 (MS Huntington Library) for its violations of grammar and its unintelligibility. The last two pages he characterized as an "involved, inextricable damnable whirlwind of words."

This second section of the "Scraps" was included in the Putnam volume of selections from *H.W.*: *The World Here and There*, 1852.

Life in a Saladero *Dr. Von Corning & W.H.W.* II, 417–20. Jan. 25, 1851
South American Scraps:
La Plata *Dr. Von Corning & Keys* III, 378–81. July 12, 1851
The Pampas Indians; An Adventure with a Lizard; the Sierra de St. Catherina *Dr. Corning, Keys & W.H.W.* III, 425–30. July 26, 1851

Corvin-Wiersbitzki, Otto Julius Bernhard von |*Von Corvin*|, 1812–1886, journalist and author. Born in East Prussia; educated in Prussian cadet-schools. Commissioned lieutenant in Prussian army, 1830; resigned from army, 1835, to devote himself to writing. In revolutionary movement of 1848–49, took prominent part in the Baden uprising; as prisoner of war, after surrender of Rastatt, tried by court-martial, sentenced to death; shortly before its execution, sentence commuted to imprisonment; six years in solitary confinement. Went to London, 1856; in time became connected with the press. To the U.S., 1861, as Civil War correspondent for London *Times* and Augsburg *Allgemeine Zeitung*. In 1867, to Berlin as correspondent for New York *Times*. During Franco-Prussian War, correspondent for Vienna *Neue freie Presse* and other journals. Contributed to *Temple Bar*, among English periodicals. Author of *Abriss der Geschichte der Niederlande*, 1841; *Illustrirte Weltgeschichte*, with F. W. Held, 1844–51; *Historische Denkmale des christlichen Fanatismus*, 1845 (later retitled *Pfaffenspiegel*). His autobiography published as *Aus dem Leben eines Volkskämpfers*, 1861; in revised and enlarged edition, including account of his later years, as *Erinnerungen aus meinem Leben*, 1880; abridged English translation, 1871, titled *A Life of Adventure*.

Von Corvin was acquainted with Dickens and admired him. In "Eine Vorlesung von Charles Dickens," *Gartenlaube*, 1861, he gave high praise to Dickens as a reader, although he had, before hearing him read, felt that Dickens was demeaning himself by appearing on the platform. In "Charles Dickens," *Europa*, 1870, published shortly after Dickens's death, Von Corvin paid tribute to Dickens as the literary artist, but stressed particularly his influence as social reformer and as champion of the common people.

H.W. played a dual role for Von Corvin – as his English instructor and as repository of his first English composition. Von Corvin taught himself English during his imprisonment by reading what English works were allowed him, among which were some thirty volumes of the Tauchnitz Edition of *H.W.* His first contribution to the periodical he submitted in German; this the editorial office returned with the request that he write its substance in English as well as he could (*A Life of Adventure*, III, 403). He did so, stating in one of his articles, "This is now the first time, that I try to express my thoughts by writing in the English language; it is to me as if I must walk with a hundred weight attached to my foot." Von Corvin's articles were of course revised to conform to English idiom; but *H.W.* printed also some paragraphs of unedited Von Corvin to let readers see "what English style was compassed by this energetic German gentleman in his solitary cell."

Von Corvin contributed also to *A.Y.R.* His *Life of Adventure* was the subject of an *A.Y.R.* article, March 4, 1871, which described the autobiography as entertaining and exciting, and Von Corvin himself as "a very dashing sort of adventurer."

Harper's reprinted "Six Years in a Cell," without acknowledgment to *H.W.*

Allgemeine deutsche Biog.

*The Last Days of a German Revolution
Von Corvin & Morley
XIV, 75–81. Aug. 9, 1856
*Condemned to Death
Von Corvin & Morley
XIV, 140–44. Aug. 23, 1856
*Beating against the Bars
Von Corvin & Morley
XIV, 147–54. Aug. 30, 1856
*Six Years in a Cell
Von Corvin & Morley
XIV, 205–213. Sept. 13, 1856
Soden [chip] *Von Corvin & Morley*
XIV, 227–28. Sept. 20, 1856
Prussian Police [lead]
Von Corvin & Morley
XVI, 169–73. Aug. 22, 1857
Canton City *Von Corvin & Morley*
XVI, 376–81. Oct. 17, 1857
The Lightning Doctor
XVI, 450–53. Nov. 7, 1857

*Repr. with revision in *A Life of Adventure: An Autobiography, By Colonel Corvin*. 3 vols. London: Richard Bentley, 1871. Preface states that "some passages" of the autobiography, "when published, created some interest in England," but does not state that they had appeared in *H.W.*

Costello, Dudley |*Mr. Dudley Costello, Dudley Costello, D. Costello, Costello*|, 1803–1865, journalist and author. Educated at Royal Military College, Sandhurst; obtained commission, served in army in North America and in West Indies. Retired on half pay, 1828. Thereafter for some time in Paris, copying illuminated MSS in Bibliothèque Royale; later worked with his sister (below) on illuminations of some of her books. Was good linguist; became foreign correspondent for *Morning Herald*, later, foreign editor of *Daily News*. Connected with *Constitutional*; from 1845 to his death with *Examiner*. Contributed to *Bentley's Misc., Ainsworth's, Chambers's, New Monthly*. Author of *A Tour through the Valley of the Meuse*, 1845; *Piedmont and Italy*, 1859–61; three novels. Published two collections of stories and sketches. In 1861 granted Civil List pension of £75 a year "In consideration of the many years devoted by him to the pursuit of literature, and the high character of his works" (Colles, *Literature and the Pension List*).

Costello wrote for *Bentley's Misc.* under Dickens's editorship; Dickens referred to two of his papers as "most pleasant productions" (Oct. 22, 1838). Dickens engaged Costello as foreign editor of the *Daily News*. Costello acted in some of Dickens's theatrical productions. According to Percy Fitzgerald (*Memories of Charles Dickens*, p. 307), he became an "intimate friend" of Dickens; according to Ley (*Dickens Circle*, p. 250), there is "absolutely no record of any intimacy" between the two men.

One of Costello's *H.W.* contributions Dickens mentioned to Wills (Sept. 21, 1854) as "really good"; of another he wrote (June 18, 1853): "Costello good enough as far as it goes, but it don't go to the Camp, and therefore is at present a *coup manqué*." The reference is to "Private Bridoon," which recounts two visits to the military camp at Chobham; obviously, Costello added material to the article as he had originally written it. Dickens supplied the title "Called to the Savage Bar" for another of Costello's articles (to Wills, July 9, 1854: MS Huntington Library).

Costello wrote also for *A.Y.R.*

"Alchemy and Gunpowder" was reprinted in *Harper's*, with acknowledgment to *H.W.* "The Modern 'Officer's' Progress" was included in *Choice Stories from Dickens' Household Words*, pub. Auburn, N.Y., 1854.

D.N.B.

*Alchemy and Gunpowder
I, 135–39. May 4, 1850
The Modern "Officer's" Progress
I, 304–307. June 22, 1850, and the 2 following nos.
The Magic Crystal *T. H. Wilson, D. Costello, & W.H.W.*
II, 284–88. Dec. 14, 1850
The Modern Soldier's Progress
II, 391–95. Jan. 18, 1851, and the 2 following nos.
The Pedigree of Puppets
W.H.W. & Dudley Costello
IV, 438–43. Jan. 31, 1852
Picture Advertising in South America
IV, 494–98. Feb. 14, 1852

Old Household Words
v, 80–83. April 10, 1852
Privileges of the French Nobility [chip]
v, 203–204. May 15, 1852
Private Bridoon vii, 541–45. Aug. 6, 1853
Dead Reckoning at the Morgue
viii, 112–16. Oct. 1, 1853
Blank Babies in Paris
viii, 379–82. Dec. 17, 1853
Our Wine Merchant
viii, 403–406. Dec. 24, 1853
History in Wax ix, 17–20. Feb. 18, 1854
Doing Business in France
ix, 425–28. June 17, 1854
The Incomplete Letter-Writer
ix, 474–76. July 1, 1854
Called to the Savage Bar
ix, 531–33. July 22, 1854
*Lobsters ix, 567–69. July 29, 1854
*The Ghost of Pit Pond
x, 170–76. Oct. 7, 1854
*Crabs x, 176–81. Oct. 7, 1854
Rag Fair in Paris x, 344–48. Nov. 25, 1854
Old Friends with New Faces
x, 429–31. Dec. 16, 1854
Misprints xi, 232–38. April 7, 1855
Boots and Corns xi, 348–54. May 12, 1855
A Defence of Owls [lead]
xiii, 289–93. April 12, 1856
*Bird History xiv, 7–12. July 19, 1856
A Dish of Frogs [lead]
xiv, 25–30. July 26, 1856
*Mother Shipton
xiv, 157–64. Aug. 30, 1856
Royal Treasures
xiv, 229–34. Sept. 20, 1856
*Monsters xiv, 498–504. Dec. 6, 1856
Odd Fish xv, 43–48. Jan. 10, 1857
Wolves xv, 124–28. Feb. 7, 1857
Circassia xv, 319–25. April 4, 1857
*Dragons, Griffins, and Salamanders
xv, 427–32. May 2, 1857
*Witchcraft and Old Boguey [lead]
xv, 505–511. May 30, 1857
*Superstitions and Traditions [lead]
xvi, 1–6. July 4, 1857
French Tavern Life
xvi, 111–18. Aug. 1, 1857
xvi, 207–213. Aug. 29, 1857
The Brave Coucou Driver [lead]
xvi, 265–71. Sept. 19, 1857
*The Apparition of Monsieur Bodry
xvii, 277–84. March 6, 1858
My First Summons
xviii, 92–96. July 10, 1858
A Wonderful Wild Beast
xviii, 544–47. Nov. 20, 1858
A New Way of Making an Old Article
xix, 158–63. Jan. 15, 1859
Dishonoured xix, 293–99. Feb. 26, 1859

*Repr., with 3 additional items, as *Holidays with Hobgoblins: and Talk of Strange Things. By Dudley Costello.* London: John Camden Hotten, 1861. Pub. in *H.W.* not acknowledged.

Costello, Louisa Stuart |*Miss Costello*|, 1799–1870, miniature painter, author. Born in Ireland; in 1814 went with her widowed mother to Paris. By her miniature painting supported her brother (above) while he was at Sandhurst, also later. On her removal to London, continued miniature painting as profession; gained much distinction by her work. In 1835 published *Specimens of the Early Poetry of France*, with illuminations executed by her and her brother. The work brought her the friendship of Sir Walter Scott and first made her generally known as a writer; thereafter devoted herself almost entirely to literature. Contributed to *Literary Gazette, Athenaeum, Bentley's Misc., Ainsworth's, New Monthly, Ladies' Companion,* and other periodicals. Edited *The Rose Garden of Persia*, 1845, translations from Persian poets, with illuminations by her and her brother. Author of *The Maid of the Cyprus Isle*, 1815, and other volumes of poems; *Memoirs of Eminent Englishwomen*, 1844; books of travel, and semi-historical novels. Elizabeth Barrett suggested to Horne in 1843 that his *New Spirit of the Age* should certainly include Miss Costello, "who is a highly accomplished woman, and full of grace and sense of beauty" (*Letters ... to Richard Hengist Horne*, ii, 154–55). In 1852 granted Civil List pension of £75 a year "In consideration of her merits as an authoress, and her inability, from the state of her health, to continue her exertions for a livelihood" (Colles, *Literature and the Pension List*).

Dickens thought "A Literary Lady's Maid" just passable; the juxtaposition of that article with "Corporation Dreams" made him "thrill and shudder with indescribable anguish" (to Wills, July 25, 1853).

The Office Book records payment for five of Miss Costello's contributions as made by "cheque to D.C." or "to Dudley."

Harper's reprinted "My Little French Friend" and "The Ghost of a Love Story," without acknowledgment to *H.W.*

D.N.B.

My Little French Friend
v, 169–71. May 8, 1852
The Widow of Sixteen
v, 322–24. June 19, 1852
Something New [chip]
v, 519–21. Aug. 14, 1852
Blind Sight-Seeing
vi, 85–90. Oct. 9, 1852
Imperial Anecdotes
vi, 270–75. Dec. 4, 1852
Madame Obé's Establishment
vi, 474–78. Jan. 29, 1853
Two Old Saints
vii, 36–41. March 12, 1853
The Ropemaker's Wife
vii, 214–16. April 30, 1853
A Literary Lady's Maid
vii, 513–16. July 30, 1853
The Sack of Chesnuts
viii, 460–66. Jan. 14, 1854
The Ghost of a Love Story
viii, 559–61. Feb. 11, 1854
Modern Ancients
ix, 221–24. April 22, 1854
Primoguet [chip]
ix, 253–54. April 29, 1854
Pastimes and Plays
x, 6–9. Aug. 19, 1854
The Poigné-Bandel Property
x, 106–109. Sept. 16, 1854
The First Mentchikoff
x, 413–20. Dec. 16, 1854
An Old French Town
x, 441–45. Dec. 23, 1854
Mad Dancing xiv, 287–88. Oct. 4, 1856
Who Was He? [chip]
xvi, 83–84. July 25, 1857

Cox, Miss. Address: Kensington. *Not identified.* A Miss Cox (no first name) is listed in Kelly's *Post Office London Directory*, 1850, as living at 3 Bullingham Place, Church St., Kensington.

"Easy Spelling and Hard Reading" reproduces the letter of an illiterate Englishman who had emigrated to Australia. Introductory comment criticizes the "want of national means of education" in England, as a result of which the son of poor parents grows up without the schooling that would make him "a literate and useful citizen." The comment was probably written by Wills. In "The Schoolmaster at Home and Abroad," April 20, 1850, he had called attention to the "lamentable deficiency of the commonest rudiments of education" among the humbler classes in England, and the fact that a man too poor to pay for schooling could "get none of it for himself or his offspring."

Easy Spelling and Hard Reading [chip]
Miss Cox & W.H.W.
i, 561–62. Sept. 7, 1850

Craig, George |*George Craig,* Telegraph & Courier, Bombay|, journalist. The *Bombay Almanac and Book of Direction, for 1855* lists Craig as manager and subeditor of the *Telegraph and Courier* and as editor of the *Oriental News.* The *Bombay Calendar and Almanac for 1858* lists him as editor of the *Telegraph and Courier.* J. A. Crowe, *Reminiscences* (p. 267), mentioned the *Telegraph* as "directed by Mr. Craig, but financed by natives." The *H.W.* contributor Meason had preceded Craig as editor of the *Telegraph.* The periodical at times reprinted items from *H.W.*

Blown Away!
xvii, 348–50. March 27, 1858

Craik, Dinah Maria (Mulock): *See* Mulock, Dinah Maria

Craik, Georgiana Marion |*Miss Craik*|, 1831–1895, novelist; daughter of George Lillie Craik (*D.N.B.*). In 1886 married Allan Walter May, artist. Contributed her first stories to periodicals. Published some twenty-five novels; *Lost and Won*, 1859, the most popular. Wrote also books for children; one of her "So-Fat and Mew-Mew" stories seemed to George Eliot "a little chef-d'oeuvre" (*Letters*, IV, 69).

In an undated letter to Wills, Dickens wrote of Miss Craik and one of her *H.W.* contributions: "Her imitation of me is too glaring – I never saw anything so curious. She takes the very words in which Esther [i.e., Esther Summerson] speaks, without seeming to know it."

A letter from Charles Dickens, Jr., to Miss Craik, June 9, 1879 (*A.Y.R.* Letter-Book), indicates that Miss Craik submitted material to *A.Y.R.*

All three of Miss Craik's *H.W.* contributions were reprinted in *Harper's*, without acknowledgment to *H.W.* "My Fortune" (re-titled "Fortune Wildred, the Foundling") appeared as the first of three stories "By Charles Dickens" in a collection (n.d.) published by the New York firm De Witt & Davenport (the second item in the collection was one of Mrs. Gaskell's *H.W.* stories; the third, one of Howitt's).

Boase

The Three Sisters
v, 359–64. July 3, 1852, and the following no.

My Fortune vi, 223–29. Nov. 20, 1852

Berthalde Reimer's Voice
vi, 507–515. Feb. 12, 1853

Cramer. *Not identified.* The writer's contribution is a somewhat amusing story laid in France and told in first person. It concerns a hoax which the narrator had no part in contriving, but which made him rich. Payment marked "Enclosed & fetched." Item included in the Putnam volume of selections from *H.W.*: *Home and Social Philosophy*, 2nd ser.

The Way I Made My Fortune
iv, 105–107. Oct. 25, 1851

Crowe, Catherine (Stevens) |*Mrs. Crowe*|, 1800?–1876, novelist, writer on the supernatural. Contributed to *Chambers's*, *Ladies' Companion*, *Once a Week*, and other periodicals. Published plays, children's books, novels, and collections of stories. Best known of the novels were *Adventures of Susan Hopley*, 1841, and *The Story of Lilly Dawson*, 1847. Best known of the collections of stories was *The Night Side of Nature; or, Ghosts and Ghost Seers*, 1848, accounts of supernatural happenings, prophetic dreams, presentiments, etc., gathered from many sources and animated in the retelling by Mrs. Crowe's belief in what she related; the book went through several editions; the title, recorded J. A. Crowe mischievously (*Reminiscences*, p. 74), Douglas Jerrold once paraphrased "in a way I cannot repeat." In 1859 published *Spiritualism, and the Age We Live In*. Well known in literary circles of Edinburgh and London; correspondent of Sydney Smith; conjectured to be author of *Vestiges of ... Creation* during the time that the authorship of the book was a matter of speculation. For an amusing instance of her quasi-acceptance of the authorship, see Lehmann, *Ancestors and Friends*, p. 125.

In Feb. 1854, Mrs. Crowe had a serious attack of illness, reported in the newspapers to be madness. Two of Dickens's letters of March of that year record her appearing in the streets of Edinburgh "stark mad" and "stark naked." Mrs. Crowe issued a public statement denying the madness. She lived to a ripe age and died, according to Boase, of "natural decay."

Dickens wrote for the *Examiner* (Feb. 26, 1848) a review of *The Night Side of Nature*, which he termed "one of the most extraordinary collections" of ghost stories ever published. Of Mrs. Crowe he wrote: "She can never be read without pleasure and profit, and can never write otherwise than sensibly and well."

"Loaded Dice" was among the items that Dickens had on hand before the first number of *H.W.* appeared. He found it "horribly dismal"; the "part about the sister's madness," he wrote, "must not on any account remain" (to Wills, Feb. 28, 1850). In the story as published in *H.W.*, the sister does not succumb to madness.

"The Young Advocate" was reprinted in *Harper's*, with acknowledgment to *H.W.*; "Esther Hammond's Wedding-Day," without acknowledgment. "Loaded Dice" was included in *Choice Stories from Dickens' Household Words*, pub. Auburn, N.Y., 1854.

D.N.B.

Loaded Dice I, 77–82. April 20, 1850
*The Young Advocate
I, 292–97. June 22, 1850
Esther Hammond's Wedding-Day
IV, 425–31. Jan. 24, 1852

*Repr. in *Light and Darkness; or, Mysteries of Life. By Mrs. Catherine Crowe.* 3 vols. London: Henry Colburn, 1850. Preface states that "most of the tales" in the collection had appeared "in various periodicals," but does not specify the periodicals.

Crowe, Eyre |*E. Crowe, Junr.*|, 1824–1910, historical and genre painter; eldest son of Eyre Evans Crowe (below). Born in London, but passed his boyhood mainly in France. Education directed largely by his father. Studied painting under Paul Delaroche; thereafter, at Royal Academy schools. Exhibited at the Academy and at British Institution. Several of his works in public galleries. A.R.A. 1875. Author of *With Thackeray in America*, 1893; *Thackeray's Haunts and Homes*, 1897.

Crowe's *H.W.* article recounts his sketching slaves at a Virginia slave auction and his expulsion from the auction rooms by the angry dealers. The incident took place in 1853 while Crowe was accompanying Thackeray on his American lecture tour. Thackeray thought that the foolhardy action might reflect unfavourably on him and "cut short his popularity" (*Letters*, III, 222). An account of the incident appeared in the New York *Daily Tribune*, March 10, 1853.

D.N.B. suppl. 1901–1911

Sketching at a Slave Auction
XV, 153–56. Feb. 14, 1857

Retold in *With Thackeray in America, By Eyre Crowe, A.R.A.* London: Cassell and Company, 1893. Previous recounting of the episode in *H.W.* acknowledged.

Crowe, Eyre Evans |*E. E. Crowe*|, 1799–1868, journalist, historian. Student at Trinity College, Dublin; left at age sixteen, without degree, to work as journalist in London. Paris correspondent, later leader writer, for *Morning Chronicle.* Engaged by Dickens as leader writer for *Daily News*; succeeded Forster as editor, Oct. 1846; made to resign editorship, 1851. Thereafter lived in France. Wrote for *Examiner*, *Athenaeum*; occasionally contributed to *Quart. Rev.*, *Edin. Rev.* Author of several novels, and of *The Greek and the Turk*, 1853; *History of the Reigns of Louis XVIII. and Charles X.*, 1854; *The History of France*, 1858–68 (revised and enlarged from earlier publication in Lardner's *Cabinet Cyclopaedia*).

Of Crowe's second *H.W.* contribution, an account of an Irish peasant feud and of strife between an estate manager and tenant farmers, Dickens wrote to Wills, Dec. 24, 1852 (article-title omitted in Nonesuch *Letters*; reads *the Golden Vale* in MS Huntington Library): "If my mind could have been materialised, and drawn along the tops of all the spikes on the outside of the Queen's Bench prison, it could not have been more agonized than by the Golden Vale; which for imbecility, carelessness, slovenly composition, relatives without antecedents, universal chaos, and one absorbing whirlpool of jolterheadedness, beats anything in print and paper I have ever 'gone at' in my life."

D.N.B.

Swords and Ploughshares
V, 297–302. June 12, 1852
The Golden Vale VI, 377–81. Jan. 1, 1853

Crowe, Sir Joseph Archer |*Mr. Joseph Crowe, J. A. Crowe*|, 1825–1896, journalist, foreign service official, art historian; second son of Eyre Evans Crowe (above). Born in London, but passed his boyhood mainly in France. Education directed largely by his father. Like his brother Eyre (above), wished to become artist; studied for a time under Paul Delaroche, whose atelier he described in the *H.W.* article "Young France at the Easel." For some time kept terms at Inner Temple. Reporter for *Morning Chronicle*; correspondent and reporter, later foreign subeditor, for *Daily News*; correspondent for *Illus. London News* during Crimean War; for the *Times* during Indian Mutiny and Austro-Italian War. Wrote for *Examiner, Athenaeum, Westm. Rev., Edin. Rev.* From 1860 on, held appointments in diplomatic service, first as consul-general at Leipzig, then at Düsseldorf; thereafter as commercial attaché for Berlin and Vienna, then for whole of Europe. Author of *The Early Flemish Painters*, 1856; *A New History of Painting in Italy*, 1864–68; and other histories of art, which held important place in art criticism. As art historian, was aided in his research by G. B. Cavalcaselle. C.B. 1885; K.C.M.G. 1890.

Crowe was a good friend of Wills and his wife. He of course knew Dickens, who had engaged him as assistant Paris correspondent for the *Daily News*. In the account of one of his early Continental tours, Crowe recorded meeting a German student "who vowed eternal friendship to me after he found out that I was acquainted with Charles Dickens" (*Reminiscences*, p. 60). In his *Reminiscences*, Crowe's only reference to his contributing to *H.W.* is his mention of a "pot-boiler" written for the periodical (p. 101).

"A Paris Newspaper" was reprinted in *Harper's*, with acknowledgment to *H.W.*; it was included in the Putnam volume of selections from *H.W.*: *Home and Social Philosophy*, 2nd ser.

D.N.B. suppl. 1901

A Paris Newspaper
i, 164–67. May 11, 1850

A Sentiment in Stone
J. A. Crowe & Morley
v, 127–28. April 24, 1852

The Thirsty Boys of Bonn
J. A. Crowe & Morley
v, 137–38. April 24, 1852

Young France at the Easel
J. A. Crowe & Morley
v, 149–52. May 1, 1852

Crowns in Lead viii, 11–13. Sept. 3, 1853

Crowe, W. *Not identified.* The contributor's article describes the activities in a Continental gaming casino. Dickens thought the paper better than Jerrold's "Paris upon Wheels" (to Wills, Oct. 6, 1854: MS Huntington Library). Office Book memorandum reads: "Cheque to Dr. Stonar."

The Game Season at Spürt
x, 262–64. Oct. 28, 1854

Cunningham, Peter |*Peter Cunningham, Cunningham, P. Cunningham*|, 1816–1869, author and scholar. Educated at Christ's Hospital. Held position in Audit Office, 1834–60. Member of Shakespeare Society. F.S.A. During later years became victim of what Vizetelly called "convivial indulgence" (*Glances Back through Seventy Years*, i, 259), i.e., chronic alcoholism; one of boon companions of the convivial years was Frederick Dickens. Contributed to *Ladies' Companion, Gent. Mag., Builder, Athenaeum, Illus. London News*, and other periodicals. His *Extracts from the Accounts of the Revels at Court* printed for the Shakespeare Society, 1842; later denounced as forgery (see Tannenbaum, *Shakspere Forgeries in the Revels Accounts*). Wrote life of Inigo Jones and of Nell Gwyn. In 1849 published *A Handbook for London* (1850 edition: *Hand-Book of London*). Edited *Works* of Goldsmith, Johnson's *Lives* of the poets, *Letters* of Horace Walpole, and other works.

Dickens had "a hearty regard" for Cunningham, wrote Forster (*Life*, Book vii, sect. ii), and the two men were for some years good friends. They corresponded and saw each other socially. Dickens at times consulted Cunningham concerning theatrical and other matters. Cunningham accompanied Dickens's amateur theatrical tour of 1848; later he played a role in Dickens's presentation of *Not So Bad As We Seem.* In the 1850 edition of his *Hand-Book of London*, Cunningham printed the first of Dickens's two letters to the *Times* concerning public executions. He presented a copy of the book to Dickens, who wrote to thank him for the "valuable book in its new form" (May 12, 1850). Cunningham had the year before presented Dickens with a copy of the first edition. Later he presented a copy of his edition of Johnson's *Lives* and of Walpole's *Letters* to Dickens (Stonehouse, *Catalogue*).

Dickens was angered by the comment in Cunningham's "Town and Table-Talk," *Illus. London News*, March 4, 1854, that his inquiry into the Preston strike was said to have suggested the title of *Hard Times* and in some respects "the turn of the story." The comment, he wrote to Cunningham, March 11, was "altogether wrong"; in the future Cunningham should ascertain from Dickens what the facts were before making statements concerning him. In a later letter to Cunningham, Feb. 11, 1859, Dickens expressed annoyance at Cunningham's having made some remarks about him in the matter of the Garrick Club affair.

Dickens's first reference to Cunningham in connection with *H.W.* appears in his letter of May 12, 1850. Cunningham had obviously suggested various materials that he thought appropriate for the periodical and had made some suggestions concerning the *Household Narrative*. Certain "documents" that Cunningham had mentioned, wrote Dickens, "I am afraid we shall not have room for." But, he continued, "I am delighted with the Christ's Hospital subject. And I think I see my way to a long perspective of good papers on divers subjects, if you should be inclined to walk along it." The Office Book assigns to Cunningham no paper on Christ's Hospital, nor is there an unassigned paper dealing with the subject. Cunningham's first *H.W.* contribution Dickens referred to in a letter to Wills, Sept. 27, 1851, as "a curious chip from Peter Cunningham." Later letters mention as by Cunningham two other of his contributions: "A Bowl of Punch" and "Peter the Great in England" (to Cunningham, June 24, 1853 [undated in Nonesuch *Letters*]; to Wills, Sept. 16, 1855). From Dickens's letter concerning "A Bowl of Punch," it is clear that the article had contained an indirect allusion to Dickens, which Wills had deleted. Dickens was "quite pained," he wrote, at Wills's alteration of Cunningham's "excellent" article.

Among *H.W.* articles that referred to Cunningham as author of the *Handbook for London* or as authority on London were Sala's "A Cup of Coffee," "Curiosities of London," and "Houseless and Hungry"; Wills's "Street-Cab Reform" and Miller's "The Old Boar's Head." Blanchard, in "Printed Forgeries," devoted a paragraph to a discussion of the material contained in Cunningham's "interesting introduction" to his father's *Poems and Songs*. Wills, in "The Manchester School of Art," praised Cunningham's work in connection with the Manchester Art Treasures Exhibition (1857). Cunningham himself, in "Last Moments of an English King," stated that an incident concerning Nell Gwyn related in a newly discovered MS account of the death of Charles II was "unknown to Mr. Cunningham" (i.e., not mentioned in Cunningham's life of Nell Gwyn).

D.N.B.

Superstitious Murder [chip]
IV, 92. Oct. 18, 1851
What We Do with Our Letters
VI, 139–42. Oct. 23, 1852
A Bowl of Punch
VII, 346–49. June 11, 1853
North Country Courtesies
VIII, 191–92. Oct. 22, 1853
Last Moments of an English King
IX, 277–80. May 6, 1854
The Man of Ross
X, 527–28. Jan. 13, 1855
The Fate of a Toast
X, 551–52. Jan. 20, 1855
Vails to Servants XI, 10–12. Feb. 3, 1855
Stealing a Calf's Skin [chip]
XI, 140–41. March 10, 1855
Tom D'Urfey
XI, 186–88. March 24, 1855
The Muse in Livery
XI, 308–312. April 28, 1855
Peter the Great in England
XII, 223–28. Oct. 6, 1855
Pope's Sir John Cutler
XII, 427–29. Dec. 1, 1855

D

D., Mr. C.; C.D.: *See* Dickens, Charles

Dallas, William Sweetland |*Dallas*|, 1824–1890, writer on natural history. Born in London. Clerk in commercial house in the City. Largely self taught in natural history. For some ten years, occupied in preparing lists of insects for British Museum. Thereafter curator of museum of Yorkshire Philosophical Society, 1858–68; from 1868, assistant secretary to Geological Society of London. F.L.S., F.G.S. Contributed to *Philosophical Magazine, Annals and Magazine of Natural History, Westm. Rev.* Edited *Popular Science Review*, 1877–81. Translated scientific and other works from the German and the Swedish. Author of *A Natural History of the Animal Kingdom*, 1856 (first published as part of Orr's *Circle of the Sciences*); *Elements of Entomology*, 1857.

Dallas's *H.W.* article (on sticklebacks) is based in part on Albany Hancock's "Observations on the Nidification of Gasterosteus aculeatus and Gasterosteus spinachia," *Annals and Magazine of Natural History*, Oct. 1852, which describes the activities of the fish as Hancock had observed them in a glass trough. In the discussion of sticklebacks in his *Natural History of the Animal Kingdom*, Dallas again referred to Hancock's article. One of Dallas's additions to Jane Loudon's *Entertaining Naturalist*, of which he brought out a revised and enlarged edition in 1867, was the section "The Stickleback." The same facts, of course, appear in each of Dallas's discussions, though the *H.W.* article describes nidification in greater detail than do the other two.

Boase

Tittlebat Tactics [chip]
vi, 260–61, Nov. 27, 1852

Day. *Not identified.* The writer's contribution briefly recounts the life of Henry Stuart, Cardinal York, and tells of a British officer's meeting the Cardinal in Basilicata during the Napoleonic campaigns in southern Italy. The officer had given the contributor an account of the meeting. Payment for the contribution made by post-office order.

In the Office Book, "The Hero of a Hundred Plays" is recorded as by "Day & Morley"; the "Day" is marked out and substituted by "Bourne."

Henry the Ninth of England! [chip]
x, 275–76. Nov. 4, 1854

Delepierre, Joseph Octave |*Delepierre*|, 1802–1879, antiquary, author. Born in Bruges. LL.D. Univ. of Ghent. Practised as advocate in Brussels; then for some twenty years was archivist in Bruges. In 1849 appointed Belgian secretary of legation in London; held position for many years; also consul-general for Belgium in London. Popular among English men and women of literary, artistic, and social distinction, many of whom were to be seen at his Sunday evening receptions. Member of Philobiblon and other learned societies, to whose publications he contributed. F.S.A. Contributed to *St. James's Magazine.* Author of more than fifty works, most of them in French, some in English, e.g., *Old Flanders*, 1845; *A Sketch of the History of Flemish Literature*, 1860.

Among the clubs to which Delepierre belonged was Our Club, of which Dickens's son Charles was also a member (Masson, *Memories of London in the 'Forties*, p. 222).

Delepierre's *H.W.* article, a description of the contents of the Dec. 19, 1679 *Mercurius Domesticus* (the only number issued), is in line with his antiquarian interests. Occasional constructions and phrases indicate that English is not the writer's native language. Bourne's *H.W.* article "Historic Doubt" was based on "Doute historique," one of Delepierre's contributions to the Philobiblon *Miscellanies.*

D.N.B.

The Domestic Mercury
XIII, 445–48. May 24, 1856

De Mérey, Mme. |*Mad. De Meley*|, *d.* 1855, Hungarian refugee. Well-educated woman; wife of wealthy nobleman, a staff officer in Hungarian army. Both husband and wife were friends of Kossuth. Lost their property during Hungarian revolution; fled Hungary in 1849 under assumed name. By Sept. 1850, M. De Mérey was living in Manchester under name "Marton"; his wife arrived shortly thereafter, with their children. In 1851 the family re-assumed the name De Mérey, "which as far as I recollect," wrote Susanna Winkworth, "was their true one." In Manchester, befriended by the Winkworths, the Gaskells, the Salis Schwabes. Were very poor; made living by giving lessons – M. De Mérey in Hungarian and on violin, Mme. De Mérey in French and German. On death of husband in 1853, Mme. De Mérey set up millinery establishment (Susanna Winkworth, ed., *Letters and Memorials of Catherine Winkworth*, I, 251–52n, 333n, et passim; *Letters of Mrs Gaskell*, passim). According to a letter of Stephen Winkworth (*Letters and Memorials*, I, 259), Mme. de Mérey was the "Caroline Marton" who wrote "Louis Kossuth and His Family," *Bentley's Misc.*, Oct. 1850.

"The Wild-Flower of the Danube" is a legend told to Mme. De Mérey by a peasant girl in Hungary. Mme. de Mérey had entrusted the story to Mrs. Salis Schwabe. Mrs. Gaskell wrote to the latter, ca. May 1852: "... Mme de Mery [*sic*] has just called; and I have persuaded her to let me *try* Her Hungarian Legend at Household Words. I think they will take it." If Mrs. Salis Schwabe had "*not* sent it off anywhere else," Mrs. Gaskell requested that she send it to Wills at the *H.W.* office, "*With Mrs Gaskell's compliments* just that they may know which MS to open, when I write to them about it" (*Letters*, No. 128). In the Office Book the notation "per Mrs. Gaskell" accompanies the contributor's name.

The Wild-Flower of the Danube
V, 266–70. June 5, 1852

De Morgan, Augustus |*De Morgan*|, 1806–1871, mathematician. B.A. Cambridge, 1827. F.R.A.S. For more than thirty years professor of mathematics at University College, London. The list of his books and of his contributions to professional journals, to the *Penny Cyclopaedia*, and to other encyclopaedic works covers fifteen pages in Mrs. De Morgan's *Memoir* of her husband; in addition, made "voluminous contributions" to *Athenaeum* and *N. & Q.* In 1870 granted Civil List pension of £100 a year "In consideration of his distinguished merits as a mathematician" (Colles, *Literature and the Pension List*).

De Morgan and his wife (below) enjoyed Dickens's novels, some of which De Morgan read aloud to her as the monthly parts appeared. On one occasion, when they disagreed about an illustration in *Nickleby*, De Morgan wrote to Dickens to settle the question; Dickens's letter, April 12, 1840, explained the matter to "the gentleman and lady unknown." De Morgan met Dickens in 1851, being introduced to him by Charles Knight (*Memoir*, pp. 93–94; 265–66 and n). Crabb Robinson (*On Books and Their Writers*, II, 815) recorded De Morgan's leaving with him in 1865 a copy of the doggerel that circulated for some years:

> A splendid muse of fiction hath Charles Dickens,
> But now and then just as the interest thickens
> He stilts his pathos, and the reader sickens.

(Variants of the lines appear in Kitton, *Dickensiana*, pp. 467–69.) De Morgan was a reader of both *H.W.* and *A.Y.R.* On one occasion he noted the anachronistic use of the word "reliable" by "one of the tale-writers" in *A.Y.R.* (*Memoir*, p. 322); on another, the absence of certain information relevant to a case related in one of Thornbury's "Old Stories Re-told" (Dickens to De Morgan, Sept. 20, 1867: typescript Huntington Library).

De Morgan's brief *H.W.* item, motivated by an article on the poet Waller, Sept. 12, 1857, concerns the known signatures of Waller. It states that the British Museum has no specimen of Waller's penmanship, or, at least, had none "five years ago," but that "a well-known bibliographer" (i.e., Bolton Corney) possesses one, and that the writer of the *H.W.* article possesses a second, that signature being in a copy of J. A. Borelli's *Euclides Restitutus*, 1658. In the De Morgan Collection in the University of London Library (to which De Morgan's books were presented after his death) is the copy of Borelli referred to. Two notes (one signed by De Morgan) are pasted to the half-title of the book, and two letters are tipped in. The notes and the letters contain De Morgan's proof of the facts stated in the *H.W.* article.

In *H.W.*, incidental references to De Morgan appeared in "National-Debt Doctors," "The Catalogue's Account of Itself," "Play," and "A Ride through the Raisin Country."

D.N.B.

Edmund Waller [chip]
XVI, 402. Oct. 24, 1857

De Morgan, Sophia Elizabeth (Frend), 1809–1892, misc. writer; daughter of William Frend (*D.N.B.*); wife of Augustus De Morgan (above). Educated largely under superintendence of her father, who taught her Hebrew at an early age and encouraged her reading of philosophical and metaphysical works. Took active interest in social betterment and reform movements, as in education for women, improvement of conditions in workhouses, playgrounds for "gutter children," antivivisection crusade. Became a spiritualist. Contributed occasional articles to periodicals. Wrote stories for children, a memoir of her husband, an autobiography, and a book on spirit manifestation – *From Matter to Spirit*, 1863.

Mrs. De Morgan was a member of the committee organized by the Rev. David Laing for the establishment of playgrounds: "We had a dinner at the Freemasons' Tavern," she wrote, "at which Mr. Charles Dickens presided, and spoke as warmly as he was known to feel for the little vagrants, who, like the dweller in *Tom All-alone's*, were always being 'chivied' away" (*Memoir of Augustus De Morgan*, p. 265). In a footnote she added, "I wrote in *Household Words* 'A Plea for Playgrounds,' and a longer article in *Good Words* some time after for Miss Octavia Hill's playground." In *Threescore Years and Ten*, p. 246, she again mentioned the article on playgrounds "which I sent to *Household Words*." The Office Book assigns the article to Mrs. Howitt and Morley.

Allibone

A Plea for Playgrounds [chip]
Mrs. Howitt & Morley
XVII, 160–61. Jan. 30, 1858

Dickens, Charles |*Mr. C.D., C.D., Charles Dickens, C. Dickens*|, 1812–1870, novelist. Received little schooling. Worked as office boy in attorneys' office; learned shorthand. Became Parliamentary and general reporter; on reporting staff of *Mirror of Parliament, True Sun, Morning Chronicle.* Contributed sketches to *Monthly Magazine* (first published sketch, 1833), *Morning Chronicle, Evening Chronicle, Bell's Life in London*; contributed occasionally to other periodicals. Edited *Bentley's Misc.*, 1837–39. Established *Daily News*; edited the paper, Jan.-Feb. 1846. Established *H.W.*; edited *H.W.*, 1850–59; and its successor, *A.Y.R.*, 1859 to his death. Published *Pickwick*, 1836–37; thirteen other novels and the incomplete *Edwin Drood*; also Christmas books, some volumes of sketches, two travel books, some dramatic pieces. Organized theatricals; gave readings based on his works.

In the partnership agreement under which *H.W.* was set up, Dickens was, with the publishers Bradbury & Evans, with Forster and with Wills, one of the joint proprietors; he held an interest of one-half share. On Forster's relinquishing his one-eighth share in 1856, Dickens divided that one-eighth between himself and Wills. Dickens's salary as editor was £500 a year; he was to receive payment also for what he wrote in the periodical (Lehmann, ed., *Charles Dickens As Editor*, pp. 19, 195–97). (In the Office Book, Wills did not record the payments made or credited to Dickens for his *H.W.* writings.)

Dickens set the editorial policy of *H.W.* and supervised its being carried out. He had, in Wills, a capable and efficient subeditor on whose judgment he came more and more to rely; yet, especially in the early years of *H.W.*, he concerned himself with every detail of its production. Before the first number appeared, he wrote to friends and acquaintances asking them to become contributors. He read – especially during the early years of *H.W.* – hundreds of MSS, some submitted directly to him, others referred to him by Wills for final acceptance or rejection. When possible, he conferred weekly, sometimes more often, with Wills on editorial matters. When personal conference was not possible, he sent his instructions and suggestions by letter – instructions and suggestions ranging from matters of editorial policy to matters of typography and punctuation. He revised – sometimes almost entirely rewrote – contributed papers; he read proofs – sometimes revises of proofs that he had in the first place altered or emended. He suggested subjects for articles; he sent to the office materials to serve as the basis for articles. On occasion, he made excursions in company with a staff member to gather material for articles. He wrote much for the early volumes of *H.W.*, comparatively little for the later volumes. Morley's writings in the periodical exceeded his by some 300 pages. Nevertheless, as he stated when he brought *H.W.* to a close ("A Last Household Word"), his name had been, "as his pen and himself" had been, "inseparable from the Publication" throughout its entire existence.

Most of Dickens's writings in *H.W.*, like almost all contributions of other writers, appeared anonymously. Only *Hard Times*, the one of his novels that he serialized in the periodical, carried with the title of the work in each instalment the ascription "BY CHARLES DICKENS." Four weeks before the serialization of that book began, it was announced: ☞ "NEW TALE *by Mr.* CHARLES DICKENS"; thereafter, each week's *H.W.* number announced the portion of *Hard Times* by Charles Dickens that was to appear the following week; before the appearance of the final chapters, as also after the completion of the serialization, *H.W.* published advertisements for the novel in book form as a Bradbury & Evans publication. *A Child's History of England*, Dickens's only other extended work in *H.W.*, appeared in the various instalments without Dickens's name after the title, but, during the serialization, advertisements in *H.W.* for the *History* in book form as a Bradbury & Evans publication stated Dickens's authorship.

Of various other of his *H.W.* writings Dickens also made his authorship known. "Personal," his statement concerning the "domestic trouble," bore his name as signature. "Curious Misprint in the Edinburgh Review," his reply to J. F. Stephen's article "The License of Modern Novelists," announced: "the hand of Mr. Dickens writes this paper." In "A Nightly Scene in London," it was "I, the Conductor of this journal," who told of coming upon the poor souls crouched before a Whitechapel workhouse. The footnote that Dickens added to "Three Graces of Christian Science" he signed "C.D." Writing in first or third person, Dickens also made clear that he was author of the introductory and closing comments in *H.W.* ("A Preliminary Word," "All the Year Round," "A Last Household Word"), as of "Pet Prisoners," the detective police articles, "The Guild of Literature and Art," "The Late Mr. Justice Talfourd," and "To Working Men."

In bold type, the words "CONDUCTED BY CHARLES DICKENS" appeared on the *H.W.* masthead; in small type they spanned the verso and recto of facing pages. In the first five years of *H.W.*'s publication, Dickens's name appeared in more than seventy-five *H.W.* advertisements and announcements in connection with the periodical and one of its supplementary publications, and in connection with *A Child's History* and *Hard Times* (in some advertisements and announcements his name appeared as many as three times). In the last year of *H.W.*'s publication, readings by Mr. Charles Dickens were announced in forty-one *H.W.* numbers. Dickens was omnipresent in his periodical.

In view of this fact, as also for other

obvious considerations, Dickens naturally wanted in *H.W.* stories and articles no laudatory references to himself – or references that might be so construed. Thus, in "Our Society at Cranford," he substituted mentions of Hood and Hood's writings for Mrs. Gaskell's mentions of Boz and Boz's *Pickwick* and *Christmas Carol*: "... with my name on every page of Household Words," he wrote to Mrs. Gaskell (Dec. 5 [4], 1851), "there would be – or at least I should feel – an impropriety in so mentioning myself." In a letter to Cunningham, June 24, 1853, he referred to his "usual precaution" in deleting from articles references that "unmistakably" applied to himself. An exception to this policy was the publication in *H.W.* of a personal letter from John Pascoe Fawkner, in which Fawkner stated that Dickens's writings had "beguiled many an hour of my life," and wished Dickens "many years of healthful employment in the highly useful manner" in which he had been so long engaged ("A Colonial Patriot").

But the observation of a reader (a reader of "a quick wit and a happy comprehension," as Dickens characterized him) that Dickens's writings had the tendency "to hold up to derision those of the higher classes" also found a place in *H.W.* pages ("Ready Wit").

Impersonal references to himself and to his books Dickens had no objection to. Mention of "Mr. Dickens" appeared of necessity in Morley's "Our Wicked Misstatements"; in occasional articles by non-staff writers mention of Dickens was appropriate and unobtrusive. References to his novels – *Pickwick, Oliver Twist, Nickleby, Chuzzlewit, Dombey, Copperfield, Bleak House, Hard Times, Little Dorrit* – their characters, place-names, distinctive phraseology – appeared in one or more items by Stone, Dodd, Capper, Oxenford, Miss Lawrance, Payn, Morley, Costello, the Rev. James White, Samuel Sidney, Kent, Percy Fitzgerald, Wilkie Collins, Mrs. Linton, and Thornbury. (The reference to Mrs. Gamp in "Railway Waifs and Strays" could be by either of the joint authors – Wills or Hill.) Of these references, the most extended was Fitzgerald's recital, in "My Long Lost Cheeyld!", of the plot of a melodrama based on *Dombey*; the most amusing was White's depiction, in "Fiction Crushing," of a Dora-like wife who comes to despise her *Copperfield* prototype. In at least seven of his own articles, and in one by him and Wills, Dickens referred to characters in his novels. In a footnote to "Pet Prisoners" he mentioned *American Notes*, and in "That Other Public" he quoted from the book.

Various of Dickens's *H.W.* writings elicited praise from contemporaries. Among his articles in the early volumes, for example, "A Child's Dream of a Star" seemed to Percy Fitzgerald written with Dickens's "most delicate touch"; and nothing, thought Fitzgerald, could be "more witty or sarcastic" than "Red Tape" (*Memories of Charles Dickens*, pp. 137, 155). Crabb Robinson found one of the "Raven" articles "a witty paper," "a capital satire" (*On Books and Their Writers*, II, 704). The *Quart. Rev.* (June 1856) mentioned Dickens's "excellent papers" on the London detective police. Mrs. Cowden Clarke wrote to a friend: "The 'Christmas Tree' paper is charming, is it not?" (*Letters to an Enthusiast*, p. 32). Among Dickens's articles that antagonized certain readers were "Frauds on the Fairies," "Pet Prisoners," and "Whole Hogs." Dickens's remonstrance, in "Frauds on the Fairies," against George Cruikshank's rewriting "Hop-o'-My-Thumb" to serve propaganda purposes provoked a reply from Cruikshank, in which he justified his treatment of fairy tales and set Dickens right "upon one or two points" (*George Cruikshank's Magazine*, Feb. 1854). Dickens's comments on prison chaplains, in "Pet Prisoners," resulted in his being "severely mauled at the hands of certain Reverend Ordinaries" ("Small-Beer Chronicles," *A.Y.R.*, Dec. 6, 1862). "Whole Hogs" aroused the indignation of temperance advocates (Kitton, "Introduction" to *Old Lamps for New Ones and Other Sketches and Essays*, by Dickens; also, Dickens's *H.W.* article "Sucking Pigs"). Dickens's statement, in *H.W.*, concerning his domestic affairs was generally condemned as in poor taste.

Dickens's relationship with most of his

contributors was amicable. To some who were newcomers in the field of writing he at times wrote detailed criticisms of their submitted MSS, with words of advice and encouragement. Among *H.W.* writers who, at one time or another, showed their regard for him by dedicating to him a book were Marston, the Rev. James White, Wickenden, Forster, Prince, Landor, Charles Knight, Samuel Sidney, Wilkie Collins, Marguerite Power, Duthie, Spicer, Wills, Yates, Lever, Kent, Percy Fitzgerald, Payn, and Thornbury. Hans Christian Andersen, who was technically not a contributor, but one of whose stories appeared in *H.W.*, dedicated three books to Dickens.

Of the items included by Dickens in *Reprinted Pieces*, "A Plated Article," recorded in the Office Book as by Dickens and Wills, was reprinted by Wills in his *Old Leaves: Gathered from Household Words*, 1860, there indicated as written in part by Dickens. Wills's Office Book ascription of the item to Dickens and to himself is more authoritative as to its authorship than is Dickens's reprinting.

As Dickens's letters and as occasional comments by contributors indicate, Dickens made changes – deletions, additions, emendations – in more items than those for which the initials "C.D." appear in the Office Book jointly with the name of a contributor. Thus, it is not inconceivable that he might have written the hymn, sometimes attributed to him, that concludes "Poor Dick's Story" in the 1856 Christmas number (see identification note on Harriet Parr). The attribution, however, seems to be in error.

Harper's reprinted, in whole or part, seventeen of Dickens's *H.W.* articles and stories (including "A Plated Article," claimed by both Dickens and Wills), three acknowledged to *H.W.*, nine to Dickens personally, and five unacknowledged to any source. *Harper's* reprinted as by Dickens eight items not by him (see Elizabeth Gaskell, Horne, Sala, Morley, the Rev. James White, Harriet Martineau, Wilkie Collins, Eliza Lynn Linton). Two of Dickens's items were included in the Putnam volumes of selections from *H.W.*: *Home and Social Philosophy*, 1st and 2nd ser. The collection of Dickens's *H.W.* items published in 1859 by the Philadelphia publishing firm T. B. Peterson, *Dickens' Short Stories. Containing Thirty-one Stories Never Before Published in This Country*, contained no items that Dickens had not included in *Reprinted Pieces*.

D.N.B.

PROSE

A Child's Dream of a Star [lead]
I, 25–26. April 6, 1850

The Begging-Letter Writer [lead]
I, 169–72. May 18, 1850

A Walk in a Workhouse
I, 204–207. May 25, 1850

The Ghost of Art [lead]
I, 385–87. July 20, 1850

A Detective Police Party [both instalments = lead]
I, 409–414. July 27, 1850
I, 457–60. Aug. 10, 1850

Three "Detective" Anecdotes [lead]
I, 577–80. Sept. 14, 1850

A Poor Man's Tale of a Patent [lead]
II, 73–75. Oct. 19, 1850

A Christmas Tree [lead]
II, 289–95. Dec. 21, 1850

"Births. Mrs. Meek, of a Son" [lead]
I, 505–507. Feb. 22, 1851

A Monument of French Folly [lead]
II, 553–58. March 8, 1851

Bill-Sticking [lead]
II, 601–606. March 22, 1851

On Duty with Inspector Field [lead]
III, 265–70. June 14, 1851

Our Watering Place [lead]
III, 433–36. Aug. 2, 1851

A Flight [lead] III 529–33. Aug. 30, 1851

Our School [lead] IV, 49–52. Oct. 11, 1851

A Plated Article [lead] *C.D. & W.H.W.*
V, 117–21. April 24, 1852

Our Honorable Friend [lead]
V, 453–55. July 31, 1852

Our Vestry [lead]
V, 549–52. Aug. 28, 1852

Our Bore [lead] VI, 73–76. Oct. 9, 1852

Lying Awake [lead]
VI, 145–48. Oct. 30, 1852

The Poor Relation's Story [lead]
A Round of Stories
(Christmas 1852), pp. 1–5

The Child's Story A Round of Stories (Christmas 1852), pp. 5–7
Down with the Tide [lead] VI, 481–85. Feb. 5, 1853
The Noble Savage [lead] VII, 337–39. June 11, 1853
The Schoolboy's Story [lead] Another Round of Stories (Christmas 1853), pp. 1–5
Nobody's Story Another Round of Stories (Christmas 1853), pp. 34–36
The Long Voyage [lead] VIII, 409–412. Dec. 31, 1853
Our French Watering-Place [lead] X, 265–70. Nov. 4, 1854
Prince Bull. A Fairy Tale [lead] XI, 49–51. Feb. 17, 1855
Out of Town [lead] XII, 193–96. Sept. 29, 1855
Out of the Season [lead] XIII, 553–56. June 28, 1856

The 31 items repr. as *Reprinted Pieces* in *The Old Curiosity Shop; and Reprinted Pieces. By Charles Dickens*, 1858, Vol. VIII of *Works of Charles Dickens*, Library Edition. London: Chapman and Hall, and Bradbury and Evans.

A Child's History of England [chap. i = lead] II, 409–412. Jan. 25, 1851, and 38 following nos. (not consecutive), ending VIII, 360. Dec. 10, 1853

Repr. as *A Child's History of England. By Charles Dickens.* 3 vols. London: Bradbury & Evans, 1852–54. Pub. in *H.W.* not stated.

Hard Times [all instalments = lead] IX, 141–45. April 1, 1854, and the 19 following nos., ending IX, 597–606. Aug. 12, 1854

Repr. as *Hard Times. For These Times. By Charles Dickens.* London: Bradbury & Evans, 1854. Pub. in *H.W.* not stated.

The First [Poor Traveller] [lead] Seven Poor Travellers (Christmas 1854), pp. 1–10
The Road Seven Poor Travellers (Christmas 1854), pp. 35–36
The Guest [lead] Holly-Tree Inn (Christmas 1855), pp. 1–9
The Boots Holly-Tree Inn (Christmas 1855), pp. 18–22
The Bill Holly-Tree Inn (Christmas 1855), pp. 35–36

The 5 items repr. in "Additional Christmas Stories," *The Uncommercial Traveller, and Additional Christmas Stories. By Charles Dickens*, 1867, in *Dickens' Works*, Diamond Edition. Boston: Ticknor and Fields. Pub. in *H.W.* stated.

A Preliminary Word [lead] I, 1–2. March 30, 1850
Valentine's Day at the Post-Office *C.D. & W.H.W.* I, 6–12. March 30, 1850
The Amusements of the People I, 13–15. March 30, 1850; I, 57–60. April 13, 1850
A Bundle of Emigrants' Letters *Mr. C.D. & Mrs. Chisholm* I, 19–24. March 30, 1850
Perfect Felicity. In a Bird's-Eye View I, 36–38. April 6, 1850
The Household Narrative [lead] I, 49. April 13, 1850
Some Account of an Extraordinary Traveller [lead] I, 73–77. April 20, 1850
Supposing! I, 96. April 20, 1850
Pet Prisoners [lead] I, 97–103. April 27, 1850
The Heart of Mid-London [lead] *Mr. C.D. & W.H.W.* I, 121–25. May 4, 1850
From the Raven in the Happy Family I, 156–58. May 11, 1850
A Card from Mr. Booley I, 175–76. May 18, 1850
A Popular Delusion [lead] *Mr. C.D. & W.H.W.* I, 217–21. June 1, 1850
From the Raven in the Happy Family [lead] I, 241–42. June 8, 1850
Old Lamps for New Ones [lead] I, 265–67. June 15, 1850
The Sunday Screw [lead] I, 289–92. June 22, 1850
The Old Lady in Threadneedle Street [lead] *C.D. & W.H.W.* I, 337–42. July 6, 1850
Chips [chip] I, 350–51. July 6, 1850
Supposing I, 480. Aug. 10, 1850

From the Raven in the Happy Family [lead] I, 505–507. Aug. 24, 1850
A Paper-Mill [lead] *Mr. C.D. & Mark Lemon* I, 529–31. Aug. 31, 1850
Foreigners' Portraits of Englishmen [lead] *C.D., W.H.W., & Eustace Murray* I, 601–604. Sept. 21, 1850
The Individuality of Locomotives [chip] I, 614. Sept. 21, 1850
Two Chapters on Bank Note Forgeries, chap. ii *W.H.W. & C.D.* I, 615–20. Sept. 21, 1850
The Doom of English Wills [Cathedral Number One] [lead] *C.D. & W.H.W.* II, 1–4. Sept. 28, 1850
The Doom of English Wills: Cathedral Number Two [lead] *C.D. & W.H.W.* II, 25–29. Oct. 5, 1850
The "Good" Hippopotamus [lead] II, 49–51. Oct. 12, 1850
Lively Turtle [lead] II, 97–99. Oct. 26, 1850
A Crisis in the Affairs of Mr. John Bull. As Related by Mrs. Bull to the Children [lead] II, 193–96. Nov. 23, 1850
Mr. Booley's View of the Last Lord Mayor's Show [lead] II, 217–19. Nov. 30, 1850
A December Vision [lead] II, 265–67. Dec. 14, 1850
Christmas in the Frozen Regions *Dr. Cormack* [should read *Dr. McCormick*] *& C.D.* II, 306–309. Dec. 21, 1850
Mr. Bendigo Buster on Our National Defences against Education [lead] *Mr. C.D. & Mr. Morley* II, 313–19. Dec. 28, 1850
The Last Words of the Old Year [lead] II, 337–39. Jan. 4, 1851
Railway Strikes [lead] II, 361–64. Jan. 11, 1851
Plate Glass [lead] *C.D. & W.H.W.* II, 433–37. Feb. 1, 1851
Red Tape [lead] II, 481–84. Feb. 15, 1851
My Mahogany Friend *The Honble Miss Boyle & C.D.* II, 558–62. March 8, 1851
Spitalfields [lead] *C.D. & W.H.W.* III, 25–30. April 5, 1851
Small Beginnings [chip] *W.H.W. & C.D.* III, 41–42. April 5, 1851
Common-Sense on Wheels *C.D., W.H.W., & Murray* III, 61–66. April 12, 1851
The Metropolitan Protectives [lead] *C.D. & W.H.W.* III, 97–105. April 26, 1851
The Guild of Literature and Art [lead] III, 145–47. May 10, 1851
Cain in the Fields *R.H.H. & C.D.* III, 147–51. May 10, 1851
The Finishing Schoolmaster [lead] III, 169–71. May 17, 1851
The Wind and the Rain [lead] *C.D. & Morley* III, 217–22. May 31, 1851
Epsom [lead] *W.H.W. & C.D.* III, 241–46. June 7, 1851
Supposing III, 264. June 7, 1851
The Tresses of the Day Star [lead] *Charles Knight & C.D.* III, 289–91. June 21, 1851
A Few Conventionalities [lead] III, 313–15. June 28, 1851
The Great Exhibition and the Little One *Horne & C.D.* III, 356–60. July 5, 1851
A Narrative of Extraordinary Suffering [lead] III, 361–63. July 12, 1851
Whole Hogs [lead] III, 505–507. Aug. 23, 1851
One Man in a Dockyard [lead] *C.D. & Horne* III, 553–57. Sept. 6, 1851
Supposing III, 576. Sept. 6, 1851
Shakspeare and Newgate [lead] *C.D. & Horne* IV, 25–27. Oct. 4, 1851
Sucking Pigs [lead] IV, 145–47. Nov. 8, 1851
A Free (and Easy) School [lead] *Morley & C.D.* IV, 169–73. Nov. 15, 1851
Homœopathy [chip] IV, 189–90. Nov. 15, 1851
A Black Eagle in a Bad Way [lead] *Murray, Morley, & C.D.* IV, 193–95. Nov. 22, 1851
My Uncle [lead] *W.H.W. & C.D.* IV, 241–46. Dec. 6, 1851
A Free (and Easy) School [chip] IV, 260. Dec. 6, 1851
What Christmas Is, As We Grow Older [lead] Extra No. for Christmas 1851, pp. 1–3

A Curious Dance round a Curious Tree [lead] *C.D. & W.H.W.*
IV, 385–89. Jan. 17, 1852

A Sleep to Startle Us [lead]
IV, 577–80. March 13, 1852

The Fine Arts in Australia [chip]
IV, 597. March 13, 1852

Post-Office Money-Orders [lead] *C.D. & W.H.W.*
V, 1–5. March 20, 1852

Drooping Buds [lead] *C.D. & Morley*
V, 45–48. April 3, 1852

First Fruits [lead] *Sala & C.D.*
V, 189–92. May 15, 1852

Betting-Shops [lead]
V, 333–36. June 26, 1852

Boys to Mend [lead] *Morley & C.D.*
V, 597–602. Sept. 11, 1852

North American Slavery [lead] *Morley & C.D.* VI, 1–6. Sept. 18, 1852

Discovery of a Treasure near Cheapside [lead] *C.D. & Morley*
VI, 193–97. Nov. 13, 1852

Trading in Death [lead]
VI, 241–45. Nov. 27, 1852

Where We Stopped Growing [lead]
VI, 361–63. Jan. 1, 1853

The Ghost of the Cock Lane Ghost Wrong Again [chip]
VI, 420. Jan. 15, 1853

Proposals for Amusing Posterity [lead]
VI, 505–507. Feb. 12, 1853

Received, a Blank Child [lead] *C.D. & W.H.W.*
VII, 49–53. March 19, 1853

H.W. [lead] *C.D. & Morley*
VII, 145–49. April 16, 1853

Home for Homeless Women [lead]
VII, 169–75. April 23, 1853

The Spirit Business [lead]
VII, 217–20. May 7, 1853

In and Out of Jail [lead] *C.D., Morley, & W.H.W.*
VII, 241–45. May 14, 1853

Idiots [lead] *C.D. & W.H.W.*
VII, 313–17. June 4, 1853

A Haunted House [lead]
VII, 481–83. July 23, 1853

Gone Astray [lead]
VII, 553–57. Aug. 13, 1853

Frauds on the Fairies [lead]
VIII, 97–100. Oct. 1, 1853

Things That Cannot Be Done [lead]
VIII, 121–23. Oct. 8, 1853

On Her Majesty's Service [lead] *C.D. & Murray*
VIII, 433–37. Jan. 7, 1854

Fire and Snow [lead]
VIII, 481–83. Jan. 21, 1854

Ready Wit [chip]
VIII, 532–33. Feb. 4, 1854

On Strike [lead]
VIII, 553–59. Feb. 11, 1854

The Late Mr. Justice Talfourd [lead]
IX, 117–18. March 25, 1854

It Is Not Generally Known [lead]
X, 49–52. Sept. 2, 1854

Legal and Equitable Jokes [lead]
X, 121–24. Sept. 23, 1854

To Working Men [lead]
X, 169–70. Oct. 7, 1854

An Unsettled Neighbourhood [lead]
X, 289–92. Nov. 11, 1854

Reflections of a Lord Mayor [lead]
X, 313–15. Nov. 18, 1854

Mr. Bull's Somnambulist [lead]
X, 337–39. Nov. 25, 1854

The Lost Arctic Voyagers [both instalments = lead]
X, 361–65. Dec. 2, 1854, and the following no.

The Lost Arctic Voyagers [lead] *Dr. Rae & C.D.*
X, 433–37. Dec. 23, 1854

That Other Public [lead]
XI, 1–4. Feb. 3, 1855

Gaslight Fairies [lead]
XI, 25–28. Feb. 10, 1855

Supposing XI, 48. Feb. 10, 1855

Gone to the Dogs [lead]
XI, 121–24. March 10, 1855

Fast and Loose [lead]
XI, 169–70. March 24, 1855

The Thousand and One Humbugs [all instalments = lead]
XI, 265–67. April 21, 1855, and the 2 following nos.

The Toady Tree [lead]
XI, 385–87. May 26, 1855

Cheap Patriotism [lead]
XI, 433–35. June 9, 1855

Smuggled Relations [lead]
XI, 481–83. June 23, 1855

The Great Baby [lead]
XII, 1–4. Aug. 4, 1855

Our Commission [lead]
XII, 25–27. Aug. 11, 1855

The Worthy Magistrate [lead]
XII, 73. Aug. 25, 1855

A Slight Depreciation of the Currency
[lead] xii, 313–15. Nov. 3, 1855
Our Almanac [lead]
xii, 385. Nov. 24, 1855
Insularities [lead] xiii, 1–4. Jan. 19, 1856
A Nightly Scene in London [lead]
xiii, 25–27. Jan. 26, 1856
The Friend of the Lions
xiii, 61–63. Feb. 2, 1856
Why? [lead] xiii, 145–48. March 1, 1856
Proposals for a National Jest-Book [lead]
xiii, 361–64. May 3, 1856
Railway Dreaming [lead]
xiii, 385–88. May 10, 1856
The Demeanour of Murderers [lead]
xiii, 505–507. June 14, 1856
Nobody, Somebody, and Everybody [lead]
xiv, 145–47. Aug. 30, 1856
The Murdered Person [lead]
xiv, 289–91. Oct. 11, 1856
The Wreck [The Captain's Account: no separate title in Office Book or in *H.W.*] [lead]
Wreck of the Golden Mary (Christmas 1856), pp. 1–10
Murderous Extremes [lead]
xv, 1–2. Jan. 3, 1857
Stores for the First of April [lead]
xv, 217–22. March 7, 1857
The Samaritan Institution [chip]
xv, 475. May 16, 1857
The Best Authority [lead]
xv, 577–79. June 20, 1857
Duelling in France *Mis[s] Lynn & C.D.*
xv, 614–20. June 27, 1857
Curious Misprint in the Edinburgh Review [lead] xvi, 97–100. Aug. 1, 1857
The Lazy Tour of Two Idle Apprentices [all chaps. = lead] *C.D. & Collins*, except for chap. ii, marked *C.D. & W. Collins* xvi, 313–19. Oct. 3, 1857, and the 4 following nos.
The Island of Silver-Store [lead]
Perils of Certain English Prisoners (Christmas 1857), pp. 1–14
The Rafts on the River
Perils of Certain English Prisoners (Christmas 1857), pp. 30–36
Well-Authenticated Rappings [lead]
xvii, 217–20. Feb. 20, 1858
An Idea of Mine [lead]
xvii, 289–91. March 13, 1858
Please to Leave Your Umbrella [lead]
xvii, 457–59. May 1, 1858
Personal [lead] xvii, 601. June 12, 1858
A Clause for the New Reform Bill [lead] *Wilkie Collins & C.D.*
xviii, 385–87. Oct. 9, 1858
Doctor Dulcamara, M.P. [lead] *Wilkie Collins & C.D.*
xix, 49–52. Dec. 18, 1858
Going into Society A House to Let (Christmas 1858), pp. 18–23
Let at Last *Do.* [i.e., Wilkie Collins] *& C.D.* A House to Let (Christmas 1858), pp. 32–36
New Year's Day [lead]
xix, 97–102. Jan. 1, 1859
All the Year Round [lead]
xix, 601. May 28, 1859
A Last Household Word
xix, 620. May 28, 1859

VERSE

Hidden Light *Miss Berwick & C.D.*
x, 37. Aug. 26, 1854

Dixon, Edmund Saul |*The Revd. J. Dixon, Dixon, E. S. Dixon*|, 1809–1893, divine, misc. writer. Born in Norwich. B.A. Cambridge, 1831; M.A. 1834. Ordained deacon, 1832; priest, 1833 (*Alumni Cantab.*). Rector of Intwood with Keswick, Norfolk, 1842 to his death; resided some time at Guînes, Pas-de-Calais, where he died. Contributed to *Gardeners' Chronicle*, *Bell's Weekly Messenger*, *Quart. Rev.*, *Titan*, *Cornhill*, and other periodicals. Author of *Ornamental and Domestic Poultry*, 1848; *The Dovecote and the Aviary*, 1851; *Pigeons and Rabbits*, 1854; *Flax and Hemp*, 1854; *The Kitchen Garden*, 1855; *The Flower Garden*, 1856; the first two books under his own name, the others under pseudonym "E. Sebastian Delamer" or "Eugene Sebastian Delamer"; joint author, with his wife, of *Wholesome Fare, or The Doctor and the Cook* "By Edmund S. and Ellen J. Delamere," 1868.

In 1836 Dickens wrote a letter to the publisher John Macrone introducing "my friend the Reverend Mr. Dixon, who after contributing to the New Monthly, and Metropolitan, has just come up to town with a Novel which he wishes to publish"

(Pilgrim *Letters*, I, 186). In the volumes of the *New Monthly* and *Metropolitan* of the early 1830s, many items are unsigned (or signed by a pseudonym); of the signed items, none is signed Dixon; thus, it is not possible to establish "the Reverend Mr. Dixon" of Dickens's letter as Edmund Saul Dixon, but the identification seems probable. At all events, Edmund Saul Dixon and Dickens seem to have been acquainted. In June 1849, Dixon presented to Dickens a copy of *Ornamental and Domestic Poultry* inscribed to him with the author's "sincere and kind respect" (Stonehouse, *Catalogue*).

Of the 145 items listed below, only three are assigned in the Office Book to a "Dixon" with the name accompanied by initial or initials: "The Great Convocation of Poultry" to "The Revd. J. Dixon"; "Cognac" and "Ozone" to "E. S. Dixon." All the items are by Edmund Saul Dixon.

B. W. Matz, supplying for the 1906 Chapman & Hall edition of the *H.W.* Christmas numbers the names of the contributors to the numbers, identified the *H.W.* "Dixon" as William Hepworth Dixon (advt., *Dickensian*, Dec. 1906). R. C. Lehmann, in *Charles Dickens As Editor*, 1912, made the same identification, stating (p. 101n) that Hepworth Dixon was "a fairly regular contributor" to *H.W.* Since later commentators have followed Matz and Lehmann in this misidentification, it is necessary to state here the facts that establish Edmund Saul Dixon as the *H.W.* contributor. They are as follows:

(1) Boase states that Edmund Saul Dixon wrote "many articles" for *H.W.* (*Alumni Cantab.* makes the same statement, obviously obtaining the information from Boase). *Biblio Cornub.* lists the three *H.W.* "Dixon" articles on Cornwall and the search for Cornish choughs ("If This Should Meet His Eye," "Not Found Yet," "Still on the Wing") as by Edmund Saul Dixon.

(2) Edmund Saul Dixon was one of the poultry judges at the Birmingham and Midland Counties Cattle and Poultry Exhibition, Dec. 1851 (Birmingham *Journal*, Dec. 13, 1851). The *H.W.* "Dixon" article "Great Convocation of Poultry" is an account of the poultry judging by one of the judges.

(3) Under his pseudonym "E. Sebastian Delamer," Edmund Saul Dixon contributed to the *Titan*, in 1857, "The Hare and Her Hunters" and "The Fox and His Analogies," both "From the French of Toussenel." Five *H.W.* "Dixon" articles are from the French of Toussenel.

(4) The Office Book ascription to E. S. Dixon of "Cognac" affords reasonable proof that Edmund Saul Dixon was author of all the "Dixon" articles on the related subject of wines and vineyards; the ascription to E. S. Dixon of "Ozone" affords reasonable proof that Edmund Saul Dixon was author of all the "Dixon" items (based (as is "Ozone") on contemporary scientific treatises.

(5) Though not so indicated by title, various of the "Dixon" items actually constitute a series, as, for instance, the five from Toussenel, the four from Turgenev, the three from Richard's *Algérie*, the three on comets, etc. Each individual series is clearly by one writer. Further, the various series articles, as also the non-series articles, are by one writer, as indicated by the relationships that exist between an article dealing with one subject and an article dealing with quite another. Among the numerous instances that might be cited of such interrelationship, the following serve as illustration: Richard's *Algérie* is not only the source of three articles, but also a subject of conversation in the story "My Folly." The admonition against killing harmless moths appears not only in "The World of Insects," but also in "To My Young Friends." An article on under-water exploration suggests that the diving bell be called a "Payerne"; in a later article the diving bell is so called. An article on bottle manufacture refers to "Prince Rupert's drops," very like "the painted tears which you saw on the gravestones in the cemetery"; the painted tears that the reader saw "on the gravestones in the cemetery" were described to him in a preceding article, "Last Homes."

(6) What seem clearly to be autobiographical comments in the "Dixon" articles accord with Edmund Saul Dixon's

interest in ornithology and horticulture: "When a boy, I was a great pigeon-keeper" ("The Cat"); "I happened, many years ago, to be making an ornithological trip in East-Anglia" ("When the Mill Goes"); "... sketch any sort of caricature you please, put 'Very fond of gardening' under it, and I'll not deny that it may apply to me" ("My Garden Walks"). More significant are the numerous comments that concern Norfolk, where Edmund Saul Dixon was born and where he was rector, and Guînes, where he lived for some time. "What Is to Become of Us?" refers to the Norfolk cliffs as the scene of "my boyhood" walks. Three articles ("Our Specialities," "Our Ducasse," "Our Boys and Girls") describe the life of the French town in which the writer lives, identified in the last of the articles as Guînes. Another article ("The Rights of French Women") pictures faggot-laden peasant women "wending their way to Guînes, perhaps to cook my very own dinner."

Certain payment notations in the Office Book could be cited as indicating various of the "Dixon" / "E. S. Dixon" items to be by the same writer; but the above data suffice to establish the identity of the *H.W.* contributor.

The *A.Y.R.* Letter-Book indicates that Edmund Saul Dixon contributed also to *A.Y.R.*

Two of Dixon's *H.W.* papers Dickens thought very poor: "Hermit Island" seemed to him "a wretched translation from a wretched original"; of "Literal Claims" he wrote from Paris: "It is as weak as the Paris flies are in this post" (to Wills, March 10, 1853; Nov. 15, 1855). "Brother Bruin," based on Toussenel's *L'Esprit des bêtes*, Dickens asked Wills to revise so as to make clear throughout "that it is M. Toussenel who is speaking, and not H.W. conducted by C.D." (Aug. 5, 1853). The opening paragraph of the article Dickens wrote himself – or adapted from what Dixon had written. In "Equine Analogies," Wills was likewise to make clear that the ideas expounded were Toussenel's.

In a letter to Wills, July 25, 1853, Dickens wrote of one of Dixon's contributions: "Dixon's paper admirably told, though nothing new in it"; in a letter of Sept. 23, 1855, he stated that Dixon's "Sportsmanship in Earnest" should "most decidedly" stand as lead item. The fact that twenty of Dixon's items appeared in lead position indicates that the contributions as a whole met with Dickens's approval.

In a letter to Wills, Jan. 10, 1856, Dickens suggested a comparison of foreign and British railways as the subject for a *H.W.* article. "I suppose Dixon could do it directly," he wrote. No article by Dixon on that subject appeared in *H.W.*

Dixon's articles on Cornwall and his search for choughs brought to the editorial office responses from three readers, published as "chips": "A Great Catch," April 17, 1852, recorded a Cornish reader's correction of a statement about pilchard fishing made in Dixon's "If This Should Meet His Eye." "An Equestrian Miracle," Aug. 14, 1852, gave Sir Robert Arbuthnot's account of his feat of horsemanship at Land's End, an episode recounted in "If This Should Meet His Eye." "Cornish Choughs Found at Last," Sept. 4, 1852, printed a Cornish coastguardsman's letter giving information on the whereabouts of choughs. In addition, Wills, in "The 'Logging' Stone," Nov. 20, 1852, attempted to set right the matter of Lieut. Hugh C. Goldsmith's capsizing of the celebrated Logan Rock, which capsizing Dixon, in "Still on the Wing," had asserted was a deliberate act of vandalism. Dixon's article, wrote Wills, had "been thought" to leave an undeserved "slur on the character of a meritorious naval officer." In his "chip" "Millionnaires and Measures," Dixon himself answered the queries raised by "a learned and valued correspondent" concerning certain comments in "Decimal Money" and "Decimal Measures," and corrected, also, a mis-reading that had appeared in the latter article.

For a variant version of Dixon's "To Hang or Not to Hang" in the article "Truth in Irons," see Miss Robertson (below).

The *H.W.* article "A Flight with the Birds" was based on Dixon's *The Dovecote and the Aviary.*

In the Office Book, Oxenford is recorded as author of "A Last Emotion"; his name is marked out and substituted by that of Dixon. Dixon is recorded as author of "The Golden Mean"; his name is marked out and substituted by that of Marston.

Harper's reprinted, in whole or part, four of Dixon's *H.W.* contributions, without acknowledgement to *H.W.*

Boase

The Great Convocation of Poultry
iv, 382–84. Jan. 10, 1852
If This Should Meet His Eye –
iv, 598–600. March 13, 1852
Not Found Yet! v, 186–88. May 8, 1852
Still on the Wing
v, 204–207. May 15, 1852
The Rights of French Women
v, 218–21. May 22, 1852
Last Homes v, 258–60. May 29, 1852
What Is to Become of Us?
v, 352–56. June 26, 1852
French Provincial News
v, 440–44. July 24, 1852
The Flying Bridge
v, 466–71. July 31, 1852
More Work for the Ladies
vi, 18–22. Sept. 18, 1852
Wholesale Diving vi, 76–81. Oct. 9, 1852
Tricks upon Travellers
vi, 161–65. Oct. 30, 1852
When the Mill Goes –
vi, 317–24. Dec. 18, 1852
The Charwoman's Story
A Round of Stories
(Christmas 1852), pp. 25–27
French National Defences
vi, 363–68. Jan. 1, 1853
Municipal Lights [chip]
vi, 381. Jan. 1, 1853
Tit for Tat vi, 397–99. Jan. 8, 1853
What Sand Is vi, 422–27. Jan. 15, 1853
The Field of the Cloth of Flax
vi, 466–69. Jan. 29, 1853
Beet-Root Sugar vi, 563–69. Feb. 26, 1853
Hermit Island vii, 88–94. March 26, 1853
Colza Oil vii, 115–18. April 2, 1853
The Norfolk Gridiron
vii, 163–65. April 16, 1853
Red-Hot Bubble-Blowing
vii, 175–79. April 23, 1853
Abd-el-Kader on Horseback
vii, 190–92. April 23, 1853
Domestic Pets vii, 248–53. May 14, 1853
The First of Streams
vii, 293–97. May 28, 1853
Holiday Times vii, 329–32. June 4, 1853
Dunkerque Tower
vii, 357–60. June 11, 1853
Cats' Mount [lead]
vii, 385–90. June 25, 1853
Mahuot Cocquiel
vii, 466–69. July 16, 1853
Over the Water
vii, 483–88. July 23, 1853
A Last Emotion
vii, 498–99. July 23, 1853
A Midsummer Night's Lodging
vii, 548–52. Aug. 6, 1853
The Mind of Brutes
vii, 564–69. Aug. 13, 1853
Brother Bruin [lead]
vii, 577–82. Aug. 20, 1853
What Mushrooms Cost
vii, 594–97. Aug. 20, 1853
Equine Analogies
vii, 611–15. Aug. 27, 1853
The Phalansterian Menagerie
viii, 64–69. Sept. 17, 1853
A Norman Story
viii, 78–83. Sept. 24, 1853
African Zephyrs [lead]
viii, 145–50. Oct. 15, 1853
The Camp at Helfaut
viii, 272–76. Nov. 19, 1853
A Sensible Town
viii, 302–305. Nov. 26, 1853
Uncle George's Story *Dixon & W.H.W.*
Another Round of Stories
(Christmas 1853), pp. 25–29
Founded on Fact ix, 4–8. Feb. 18, 1854
My Folly ix, 106–114. March 18, 1854
Wings and Toes x, 31–37. Aug. 26, 1854
Jean Raisin x, 307–312. Nov. 11, 1854
Wheel within Wheel [lead]
x, 481–83. Jan. 6, 1855
The Hill of Gold xi, 28–36. Feb. 10, 1855
A Bottle of Champagne
xi, 51–57. Feb. 17, 1855
The Children of the Czar
xi, 108–114. March 3, 1855
The Royal Balloon
xi, 149–53. March 17, 1855
More Children of the Czar
xi, 227–32. April 7, 1855
Nothing Like Russia-Leather
xi, 286–88. April 21, 1855
Cognac [lead] xi, 361–67. May 19, 1855

Poultry Abroad
xi, 399–402. May 26, 1855
Quite Revolutionary
xi, 474–77. June 16, 1855
French Soldiers in Camp *Sala & Dixon*
xi, 483–88. June 23, 1855
A Dear Cup of Coffee [lead]
xi, 505–509. June 30, 1855
My Garden Walks [lead]
xi, 601–605. July 28, 1855
To Hang or Not to Hang
xii, 22–24. Aug. 4, 1855
Wet Garden Walks
xii, 53–58. Aug. 18, 1855
A Very Tight Little Island [lead]
Dixon & Mrs. Lehmann
xii, 145–49. Sept. 15, 1855
Roses xii, 158–64. Sept. 15, 1855
Model Officials
xii, 204–209. Sept. 29, 1855
Sportsmanship in Earnest [lead]
xii, 217–23. Oct. 6, 1855
A Dash through the Vines [lead]
xii, 241–47. Oct. 13, 1855
Truffles xii, 284–88. Oct. 20, 1855
The Porcupine Club
xii, 328–33. Nov. 3, 1855
Decimal Money
xii, 349–56. Nov. 10, 1855
Decimal Measures
xii, 365–70. Nov. 17, 1855
My Garden Library [chip]
xii, 370–71. Nov. 17, 1855
Mind Your Manners
xii, 385–90. Nov. 24, 1855
A Russian Singing-Match
xii, 402–405. Nov. 24, 1855
Literal Claims xii, 420–22. Dec. 1, 1855
Millionnaires and Measures [chip]
xii, 487–89. Dec. 22, 1855
Claret xii, 539–45. Jan. 5, 1856
Ben Serraq xiii, 4–7. Jan. 19, 1856
Small Change [chip]
xiii, 35–37. Jan. 26, 1856
The Hall of Wines
xiii, 66–70. Feb. 2, 1856
Horse-Eating [lead]
xiii, 313–18. April 19, 1856
Attraction and Repulsion
xiii, 339–44. April 26, 1856
Economic Botany
xiii, 374–80. May 3, 1856
Banking xiii, 427–32. May 17, 1856
Moneysworth xiii, 461–64. May 31, 1856

The World of Insects
xiii, 511–16. June 14, 1856
Belgian Flower-Growing [lead]
xiii, 577–83. July 5, 1856
Charles the Fifth's Glove
xiv, 20–24. July 19, 1856
At Bruges and Ostend
xiv, 69–72. Aug. 2, 1856
Pen and Ink Pies [chip]
xiv, 164. Aug. 30, 1856
Taxes xiv, 181–85. Sept. 6, 1856
The World Unseen
xiv, 291–96. Oct. 11, 1856
An Indian Court Circular
xiv, 308–312. Oct. 11, 1856
Microscopics xiv, 377–81. Nov. 1, 1856
Minims xiv, 440–45. Nov. 22, 1856
Psellism xiv, 464–69. Nov. 29, 1856
Aluminium *Dixon & W.H.W.*
xiv, 507–510. Dec. 13, 1856
Crédit Mobilier xv, 8–12. Jan. 3, 1857
Our Specialities xv, 128–33. Feb. 7, 1857
The Art of Unfattening
xv, 328–32. April 4, 1857
Our Ducasse xv, 340–44. April 11, 1857
The Cat *Morley & Dixon*
xv, 369–73. April 18, 1857
To My Young Friends
xv, 411–14. May 2, 1857
Our Boys and Girls
xv, 475–80. May 16, 1857
To My Elderly Friends
xv, 501–504. May 23, 1857
The Circulation
xv, 561–65. June 13, 1857
Stickytoes *Dixon & W.H.W.*
xvi, 31–34. July 11, 1857
Microscopic Preparations
xvi, 132–38. Aug. 8, 1857
Powers of Calculation
xvi, 141–44. Aug. 8, 1857
Polarisation xvi, 463–68. Nov. 14, 1857
Paris on London
xvi, 540–45. Dec. 5, 1857
Unsuspected Neighbours
xvii, 172–76. Feb. 6, 1858
Over, Under, or Through?
xvii, 228–32. Feb. 20, 1858
Border-Land xvii, 273–76. March 6, 1858
Infusoria xvii, 375–79. April 3, 1858
A Microscopic Dream
xvii, 396–400. April 10, 1858
New Wheels within Wheels [lead]
xvii, 505–509. May 15, 1858

A Sweep through the Stars
xvii, 531–35. May 22, 1858
The Ether xvii, 558–60. May 29, 1858
Journey to the Moon
xvii, 583–88. June 5, 1858
Vital Heat xviii, 13–18. June 19, 1858
Strawberries xviii, 60–64. July 3, 1858
French Duelling Extraordinary [lead]
xviii, 97–99. July 17, 1858
Dirty Cleanliness [lead]
xviii, 121–23. July 24, 1858
Ozone [lead] xviii, 169–73. Aug. 7, 1858
Rat Tales xviii, 211–16. Aug. 14, 1858
The Harvest Moon
xviii, 293–96. Sept. 11, 1858
Training for the Tropics
xviii, 306–312. Sept. 11, 1858
Literary Small Change
xviii, 404–408. Oct. 9, 1858
Five Comets [lead]
xviii, 409–412. Oct. 16, 1858
Farewell to the Comet
xviii, 463–66. Oct. 30, 1858
A Picture of Merchandise [lead]
xviii, 481–86. Nov. 6, 1858
Chips from the Comet
xviii, 541–44. Nov. 20, 1858
Trading in Fetters [lead]
xix, 25–29. Dec. 11, 1858
The Almanac-Tree
xix, 92–96. Dec. 25, 1858
A New Oddity xix, 102–105. Jan. 1, 1859
Michelet's Bird xix, 140–44. Jan. 8, 1859
Michelet and Insects
xix, 280–86. Feb. 19, 1859
The Lagging Easter
xix, 325–30. March 5, 1859
Physical Force
xix, 354–59. March 12, 1859
Michelet's Love
xix, 426–32. April 2, 1859
Out-Conjuring Conjurors [lead]
xix, 433–39. April 9, 1859
Fossil Geography
xix, 474–77. April 16, 1859
Oyster Seed xix, 498–503. April 23, 1859

Dixon, Henry Hall |*Henry Dixon*|, 1822–1870, sporting writer. Educated under Dr. Arnold at Rugby. B.A. Cambridge, 1846. Articled to firm of solicitors, Doncaster; there became intimate friend of the sporting writer James White (below), through whom he made the acquaintance of sporting worthies and was influenced to become writer on the turf. Admitted at Middle Temple, 1848; called to the bar, 1852 (*Notable Middle Templars*); for a time went the Midland Circuit. Turned to writing for a livelihood. Wrote for *Bell's Life in London* (the editorship of which was offered him in 1852), Doncaster *Gazette, Sporting Review, Sporting Magazine, Illus. London News, Mark Lane Express, Gent. Mag., Daily News,* and other periodicals. Some of his books first appeared in part in periodicals. Author, as "The Druid," of *The Post and the Paddock*, 1856; *Silk and Scarlet*, 1859; *Scott and Sebright*, 1862; *Saddle and Sirloin*, 1870. Also author of *A Treatise on the Law of the Farm*, 1858; *Field and Fern*, 1865.

Dixon's *H.W.* article devotes a paragraph to the celebrated jockey and horse-breaker Dick Christian, whom Dixon quotes at length in some of his books. Dixon was a reader of *H.W.*: two chapters in *Saddle and Sirloin* he prefaced with a quotation from the periodical.

D.N.B. suppl. 1901

Horse-Taming xviii, 82–85. July 10, 1858

Dodd, George |*Dodd, G. Dodd*|, 1808–1881, misc. writer. Wrote numerous articles for the various cyclopaedias and other publications brought out by Charles Knight; edited for him the *Cyclopaedia of the Industry of All Nations*, 1851. Dodd's "careful observation and his punctual industry," wrote Knight, made him "one of the most useful contributors to serial works" (*Passages of a Working Life*, ii, 222). Collected various of his articles in book form. Wrote for serial publications of the publishers Chambers and compiled various works for them. His writings include *Days at the Factories*, 1843; *The Curiosities of Industry*, 1852; *The Food of London*, 1856; *Where Do We Get It, and How Is It Made?*, 1862; *Railways, Steamers, and Telegraphs*, 1867; also two historical works.

Dickens evidently regarded Dodd as a useful but rather pedestrian writer. One of Dodd's *H.W. articles* – "Penny Wisdom" – he found "very interesting and good," but another he dismissed with the remark, "Dodd as bad as need be. Nothing in it" (to Wills, Oct. 7, 1852; Oct. 14, 1854). "An Artificial Ocean," apparently by Dodd, in *A.Y.R.* (Sept. 8, 1866), prompted Dickens's comment: "O Lord! O Lord!! Its efforts at humour. Make Dodd a fine comic writer" (to Wills, Aug. 26, 1866: MS Huntington Library).

Dickens discovered – or was informed of – certain inaccuracies in Dodd's "Diets of Gold and Silver"; likewise, certain supposed misstatements in "India-Rubber" were called to his attention. Dickens asked Wills (March 18, 1853) to have Dodd report whatever he might have to say on the various statements alleged to be incorrect. "... if it should turn out – which it may not – that he has again committed and misled us ... , it is quite clear it won't do. Nothing can be so damaging to Household Words as carelessness about facts. It is as hideous as dullness."

In his *H.W.* articles Dodd dealt with many of the subjects that he dealt with in his books; thus, some of the same material appears in both, often in very similar phraseology. Dodd obviously had before him his *H.W.* article "All about Pigs" while writing chap. vii of *The Food of London*; he made use of material in various sections of his *Curiosities of Industry* in writing some of his *H.W.* articles, e.g., "Wood, and How to Cut It," "Pot and Kettle Philosophy," "Several Heads of Hair."

The authorship of "Electric Light," listed below, is not entirely clear. For the number in which it appears, the Office Book gives first a partial listing of contents, which is marked out because of error; then a second listing, which is still incorrect. In the cancelled listing the names "Dodd Capper" (no ampersand) stand in the author-column for the item (in the uncancelled listing, Miss Procter's name, through misalignment, stands in that position). The item is appropriate to the interests of both Dodd and Capper, though more particularly to those of Dodd. It may possibly be the joint writing of the two contributors, though joint authorship seems unlikely; the Office Book records no collaboration of Dodd and Capper on other items.

D.N.B.

All about Pigs v, 471–74. July 31, 1852
The Present Hollow Time v, 589–93. Sept. 4, 1852
Walking-Sticks v, 610–13. Sept. 11, 1852
Penny Wisdom [lead] vi, 97–101. Oct. 16, 1852
Umbrellas vi, 201–204. Nov. 13, 1852
A Pack of Cards vi, 328–33. Dec. 18, 1852
Overland Tour to Bermondsey vi, 462–66. Jan. 29, 1853
Wallotty Trot vi, 499–503. Feb. 5, 1853
A Pill-Box vi, 517–21. Feb. 12, 1853
Wood, and How to Cut It vi, 541–45. Feb. 19, 1853
Diets of Gold and Silver vii, 17–20. March 5, 1853
India-Rubber vii, 29–33. March 12, 1853
Saint Crispin vii, 76–80. March 26, 1853
Exploring Expedition to the Isle of Dogs vii, 273–77. May 21, 1853
Music Measure vii, 297–301. May 28, 1853
House-Tops vii, 324–29. June 4, 1853
Dolls vii, 352–56. June 11, 1853
A Century of Inventions vii, 367–70. June 18, 1853
Books for the Blind vii, 421–25. July 2, 1853
Whip and Spur *Dodd & W.H.W.* vii, 545–48. Aug. 6, 1853
Little Bits vii, 586–89. Aug. 20, 1853
A Brilliant Display of Fireworks viii, 45–48. Sept. 10, 1853
Nothing Like Leather viii, 57–60. Sept. 17, 1853
Accommodation for Quidnuncs *Dodd & Morley* viii, 88–91. Sept. 24, 1853
A Russian Stranger viii, 91–94. Sept. 24, 1853
Bouquets viii, 230–33. Nov. 5, 1853
The House That Jack Built viii, 286–88. Nov. 19, 1853
Pot and Kettle Philosophy viii, 333–36. Dec. 3, 1853
The Harmonious Blacksmith viii, 400–403. Dec. 24, 1853
Slates viii, 466–69. Jan. 14, 1854

Half-a-Dozen Leeches
viii, 492–95. Jan. 21, 1854
Bottled Information [lead]
viii, 529–32. Feb. 4, 1854
Moiré Antique ix, 37–38. Feb. 25, 1854
Several Heads of Hair *Dodd & W.H.W.*
ix, 61–65. March 4, 1854
Splitting Straws
ix, 85–89. March 11, 1854
Oil upon the Waves
ix, 98–100. March 18, 1854
Amber Witchery
ix, 123–26. March 25, 1854
Patchwork ix, 178–81. April 8, 1854
Wire-Drawing ix, 217–21. April 22, 1854
Busy with the Photograph
ix, 242–45. April 29, 1854
The Art of Boreing
ix, 295–97. May 13, 1854
Done to a Jelly ix, 438–40. June 24, 1854
A Good Brushing ix, 492–95. July 8, 1854
A Bundle of Crotchets
ix, 533–36. July 22, 1854
Herb Gardens ix, 558–60. July 29, 1854
Imitation ix, 580–83. Aug. 5, 1854
Going a Little Farther
x, 43–46. Aug. 26, 1854
Cornish Stone x, 92–96. Sept. 9, 1854
Pilchards x, 129–32. Sept. 23, 1854
Cornwall's Gift to Staffordshire
x, 187–90. Oct. 7, 1854
Be Assured x, 365–69. Dec. 2, 1854
Potichomania xi, 129–32. March 10, 1855
A Few More Leeches [chip]
xi, 141. March 10, 1855
Electric Light *Dodd Capper*
xi, 251–54. April 14, 1855
A Dip in the Brine
xi, 561–65. July 14, 1855
Flags xii, 105–107. Sept. 1, 1855
Music in Poor Neighbourhoods
xii, 137–41. Sept. 8, 1855
John Houghton's Wisdom
xiv, 453–56. Nov. 22, 1856
John Houghton's Advertisements
xiv, 490–93. Dec. 6, 1856
I Promise to Pay *Dodd & W.H.W.*
xiv, 556–59. Dec. 27, 1856
The Soulages Collection
xv, 76–80. Jan. 24, 1857
A Room near Chancery Lane
xv, 190–92. Feb. 21, 1857
One of Her Majesty's Usual Customs
xv, 490–93. May 23, 1857
Opium:
India xvi, 104–108. Aug. 1, 1857
China xvi, 181–85. Aug. 22, 1857

Doubleday, A. W., Esquire: *See* Dubourg, Augustus William

Douglas, William |*Private Douglas*|, soldier. Born in Lanarkshire; by trade a joiner. In 1845, at age eighteen, enlisted, in Dublin, in 1st Dragoons, transferring the following year to 10th Royal Hussars; served with that regiment in Ireland, England, India, the Crimea, and thereafter again in England. Twice promoted to corporal; on each occasion reduced to the ranks. On several occasions, from 1857 to 1861, forfeited regular pay by reason of absence; also forfeited good conduct pay. In 1858, at Aldershot, recorded as among "Soldiers in Confinement for Military and Civil Offences"; recorded confined in guard room and in military prison. In 1865, after twenty years' service, discharged at own request, in Cahir, Ireland, with rank of private (Muster Rolls, Public Record Office, London. Court-martial records not seen).

Author of *Soldiering in Sunshine and Storm*, 1865, an account of his regiment in India and in the Crimea and its return to England; *Horse-Shoeing As It Is and As It Should Be*, 1873; *Duelling Days in the Army*, 1887. On title page of *Duelling Days*, recorded himself as author of three *Historical Records* – one of the Household Cavalry, one of the 10th Royal Hussars, and one of H.M. 27th Foot. His "Historical Records" of the 10th Royal Hussars appeared (unsigned) in *United Service Magazine*, Feb. 1874–Jan. 1876; in last instalment, stated that he hoped to publish the "Records" in book form in spring of 1876; apparently did not do so. The other two "Records" probably published also in a periodical.

The *H.W.* article assigned to Douglas is a detailed account of life in a military prison (not named, but indicated to be in southern England) to which the writer was sentenced (no date given) for forty-two days for "a breach of one of the many Articles of War." It is a criticism of courts-martial, which are "only a matter of form," of over severity of punishment, of prison discipline with its "harassing" labour and its "torture" of solitary confinement. Editorial comment prefaced to the article stated that it was written by a "Private Soldier" and explained: "We do not adopt his opinions, but we give him the opportunity of expressing them"; the comment did concede that "Dietary and Labour" in military prisons were "too severe." Payment for the 13½-col. article recorded as £3.3.0 – a fraction of the standard payment for an article of that length.

In 1861 Douglas contributed to *A.Y.R.* the article "Lost in the Jungle" (Oct. 19), reprinted, with Dickens's permission, in *Soldiering in Sunshine and Storm.* Dickens had a copy of the book in his library (Stonehouse, *Catalogue*).

In 1876 Douglas again submitted an article to *A.Y.R.* (he may have submitted others in the meantime). Charles Dickens, Jr., wrote to him, Sept. 13, that the "interesting paper on military law" was too long for acceptance as Douglas had written it; he suggested Douglas's shortening it and at the same time arranging the material so as to admit of the paper's being published in two parts (*A.Y.R.* Letter-Book). "Military Law. From the Point of View of a Private Soldier" appeared in *A.Y.R.* Nov. 18. It is a criticism of the "system" that makes impossible a soldier's having justice done him; it recounts instances of courts-martial weighted against the soldier, unfairly conducted, and marked by overseverity of sentence and punishment. Editorially, "Military Law" fared much as had Douglas's *H.W.* article. It was published in *A.Y.R.*, stated the prefatory comment, "as a genuine contribution to the discussion of a question of national interest and importance," but "the Conductor of this Journal" wished it understood that he did "not bind himself to an agreement, in all particulars, with the views and opinions expressed."

Allibone

In a Military Prison
XIX, 230–37. Feb. 5, 1859

Dowdall, P. Address: Monivea, Ireland. *Not identified.* The parish records of Monivea contain no record of the contributor. Payment for the contribution made by post-office order.

An Anecdote of the Irish Poor Law [chip]
II, 94. Oct. 19, 1850

Dubourg, Augustus William, prob. |*A. W. Doubleday, Esquire,* 91 Stanley St., Pimlico|, playwright. The *Post Office London Directory* for 1858, also for 1857, lists the Stanley St. address as that of Augustus William Dubourg, Esq. "A. W. Doubleday" would seem to be a pseudonym for A. W. Dubourg. Dubourg was author of *Bitter Fruit, Vittoria Contarini, Angelica,* and other plays; co-author, with Tom Taylor, of *A Sister's Penance* and *New Men and Old Acres*; with Edmund Yates, of *Without Love.* He contributed to periodicals, e.g., *Once a Week, Temple Bar.* He published two novels and two novelettes under the title *Four Studies of Love,* 3 vols., 1877.

The *H.W.* story assigned to Doubleday relates the obstacles – monetary and other – that threatened to bar the marriage of a young man and woman. The story is told in a letter written by the young woman after her marriage. "We are so happy," she writes from Switzerland. "Ernest generally paints in the open air, and I sit near him working. ..." "... papa made us an allowance, and with what Ernest gets by painting, it is quite as much as we require." She then describes an alpine scene, finding in the sunshine, the rainbow, and the rain "a solemn but gentle admonition from Heaven on the transitoriness of earthly things."

One of Dubourg's novels has a somewhat similar ending. *Saved by Love,* the story of a young woman's marrying a rich man whom she does not love, for the sake of providing for her parents and her sister, ends with a letter announcing the woman's marriage, after the death of the rich husband, to the man whom she has always loved. "... we are so happy," she writes from Switzerland. "Frank is making fair though slow progress in his profession, he works so hard, dear boy. That cruel will took away every penny I derived ... from the property, but if need be, I can return for awhile to my old teaching. ..." She then describes an alpine sunset – "it seems as if one can see more of the wonderful ways of the Almighty in this mountain-land than in England." The dying of the crimson flush on the mountain tops "into the cold dead desolation of twilight" fills her with apprehension, until she remembers that the crimson will in the morning again light the peaks, spreading downwards like a rich mantle and then fading into "the bright light of the perfect day."

Allibone

Mr. Pearson xvii, 291–94. March 13, 1858

Duff-Gordon, Lady Lucie (Austin) |*Lady Duff Gordon*|, 1821–1869, translator and author. Received little regular schooling; from a childhood stay in Germany spoke German like her native language; was taught Latin by her mother; showed interest in learning Greek; for a time attended a young ladies' school. In 1840 married Sir Alexander Duff-Gordon. Their home in Westminster was centre of brilliant circle of friends and acquaintances, English and foreign. Noted for her beauty and charm, her independence of mind and keen intellect. Because of her health, obliged to spend last years of her life in Egypt. Contributed to *Bentley's Misc.*, *Macmillan's*, and other periodicals. Translated various works from the German and the French. Author of *Letters from the Cape*, 1864 (in Francis Galton, ed., *Vacation Tourists*); *Letters from Egypt*, 1865; *Last Letters from Egypt*, published posthumously.

Dickens was acquainted with the Duff-Gordons. In a letter to Mark Lemon, Jan. 26, 1858, he referred to Lady Duff-Gordon as "a literary woman of real ability." An unpublished letter to her from Dickens, Oct. 6, 1855 (to appear in Pilgrim *Letters*), is in answer to her query about submitting to *H.W.* an article based on a foreign book. Her one contribution to *H.W.* is based on a German source.

The *H.W.* article "Amber Witchery" mentioned Lady Duff-Gordon's "admirable translation" of Meinhold's *Maria Schweidler*.

Harper's reprinted "Darling Dorel," without acknowledgment to *H.W.*

D.N.B.

Darling Dorel *Lady Duff Gordon & W.H.W.* ii, 581–85. March 15, 1851

Dulton. *Not identified.* The contributor recounts his ascent of Vesuvius; he states that he had previously done some climbing in Switzerland.

Up Vesuvius v, 235–36. May 22, 1852

Duthie, William |*Duthie, Mr. Duthie*|, goldsmith, writer. Born in London of decent working-class parents. Learned trade of goldsmith and became model workman – industrious, sober, eager to improve himself. Studied at a Mechanics' Institution, later dedicating *The Pearl of the Rhone* to his Latin teacher, John Robson, in gratitude for Robson's efforts "to help poor youths, myself among the number, along the rugged path of knowledge." During a period of depression among London goldsmiths, went to Hamburg, where he worked for some months; then, as journeyman, knapsack on back, tramped through Europe, working at his trade. After three and a half years, returned to England; utilized his experiences and travels for his *H.W.* articles and thereafter for his *Tramp's Wallet*. Contributed verse and prose to *Welcome Guest*; also contributed verse, he stated, to *Cornhill*, *A.Y.R.*, and "other popular serials." His sonnet in memory of Douglas Jerrold was included in *The Life and Remains of Douglas Jerrold*. Published, in addition to *A Tramp's Wallet* and *The Pearl of the Rhone*, two novels: *Counting the Cost*, 1867, and

Proved in the Fire. A Story of the Burning of Hamburg, 1867.

Duthie was apparently acquainted with both Dickens and Wills. *A Tramp's Wallet* he dedicated "by permission" to Dickens, "in grateful acknowledgment of his sympathy and encouragement during the publication of the greater portion of its contents; and as a slight tribute of admiration for his unwearying labours as a public writer, to the advancement of the whole people." *Counting the Cost* he dedicated to Wills "in sincere acknowledgment of much kindly help in the literary life of the author."

Dickens suggested a change of title for one of Duthie's articles and asked Wills to "Look to the slang talk" of "Licensed to Juggle." "More Sundays Abroad" he found "washy in the last degree," feeble in its treatment of a potentially good subject. "I would as soon dine off an old glove," he wrote to Wills, "as read such pale literary boiled veal" (June 27, Aug. 5, 1853; April 27, 1856).

Duthie was one *H.W.* writer who did not rebel against editorial alteration in his contributions. On the contrary, he expressed his "sincere thanks" for the "careful and valuable revision" accorded his articles in the *H.W.* office and acknowledged, in particular, his obligation to the "unknown collaborator" (it was Morley) who added to one of the articles "some valuable information."

Harper's reprinted "A Taste of Austrian Jails" and "Down in a Silver Mine," without acknowledgment to *H.W.*

Allibone

PROSE

A Taste of Austrian Jails
iv, 368–72. Jan. 10, 1852

The German Workman
v, 410–15. July 17, 1852

Down in a Silver Mine
v, 593–96. Sept. 4, 1852

Travel on Tramp in Germany:
Hamburgh to Lubeck *Duthie & Morley*
vi, 420–22. Jan. 15, 1853
Lübeck to Berlin
vi, 492–96. Feb. 5, 1853

A Walk through a Mountain *Duthie & Morley* vii, 9–13. March 5, 1853

Cause and Effect vii, 437–40. July 9, 1853

Licensed to Juggle
vii, 593–94. Aug. 20, 1853

The French Workman *Duthie & Morley* viii, 199–204. Oct. 29, 1853

A Lift in a Cart ix, 34–37. Feb. 25, 1854

The Turks' Cellar
x, 188–20. Sept. 16, 1854

Père Panpan xi, 68–72. Feb. 17, 1855

What My Landlord Believed
xi, 418–20. June 2, 1855

Some German Sundays
xiii, 320–25. April 19, 1856

More Sundays Abroad
xiii, 400–404. May 10, 1856

Fair-Time at Leipsic
xvi, 560–62. Dec. 12, 1857

The 15 items repr. in *A Tramp's Wallet; Stored by an English Goldsmith during His Wanderings in Germany and France. By William Duthie.* London: Darton and Co., 1858. Pub. in *H.W.* acknowledged.

VERSE

*The Flowers' Petition
xi, 278. April 21, 1855

*A City Weed xii, 301. Oct. 27, 1855

*Double Life xii, 563. Jan. 12, 1856

Calm xix, 204–205. Jan. 29, 1859

*Repr. in *The Pearl of the Rhone and Other Poems. By William Duthie.* London: Robert Hardwicke, 1864. Pub. in *H.W.* acknowledged.

Dutton, Miss. *Not identified.* Payment for the contribution made by post-office order.

VERSE

The Legend of the Ladye's Cross
iii, 181–82. May 17, 1851

E

Earle, Miss. *Not identified.* In the Office Book, "The Orphan's Voyage Home" is accompanied by a memorandum that makes it clear that Horne was merely the reviser of the item despite the fact that his name stands first. The authorship ascription for "The Power of Mercy" is recorded below. It is reasonable to assume the two items, published in the same month, to be by one contributor. Payment for each was made by post-office order, the order for the prose item being on Croyden. Directories afford no help in identifying the contributor. She may be Miss Erle (below).

Harper's reprinted the writer's two contributions, with acknowledgment to *H.W.*

PROSE

The Power of Mercy *Earle* [preceded by indecipherable word, overwritten by capital letter: perh. "H"?] *& W.H.W.* I, 323–25. June 29, 1850

VERSE

The Orphan's Voyage Home *Mr. Horne & Miss Earle* I, 253. June 8, 1850

Ede, Joseph |*Joseph Ede*, 17 Lansdowne Terrace, Caledonian Road; *Ede*|. The Street Directory section of Kelly's *Post Office London Directory*, 1858, does not record a No. 17 at Lansdowne Terrace; the Court Directory sections of Kelly's directories, 1857–59, record no Joseph Ede. The only work by a Joseph Ede listed in the *Brit. Mus. Cat.* is *The Economy of Prayer*, London, 1851, with preface dated from Highgate. The author of that work may be the *H.W.* contributor. The two items that the Office Book assigns to the contributor are, like *The Economy of Prayer*, the writing of an educated man: "Old Times and New Times" discusses the first number of the London *Times*; "A Very Old Gentleman" discusses the first number of the *Gent. Mag.*

Old Times and New Times XVII, 251–54. Feb. 27, 1858

A Very Old Gentleman *Ede & W.H.W.* XVIII, 369–72. Oct. 2, 1858

Edgeworth. *Not identified.* "At the Siege of Delhi" is an account of the siege, Sept. 1857, told by a participant who served "as a volunteer in the batteries" for some twenty days previous to the assault as well as during the assault itself, and thereafter accompanied the "pursuing force" marched on Sept. 23 "in the direction of Bolundshuhur." He describes the work of the battery unit in breaching the wall near the Cashmere Gate, Sept. 12 and 13, and his execution of the charge assigned to him on Sept. 14 – the taking of certain pieces of ordnance into the city through the Cashmere Gate after the gate had been opened. He speaks of himself as an officer ("dinner [was] none the less welcome to us officers"). There seems no reason to question the authenticity of the account or to take it as other than the writer's actual report of his work during the assault.

The only Edgeworth listed in the *East-India Register* of appropriate dates is Michael Pakenham Edgeworth, 1812–1881 (*D.N.B.*), son of Richard Lovell Edgeworth. Michael Pakenham Edgeworth was a student at the East-India College, Haileybury; entered civil service of East India Co., Bengal Establishment, 1831. Held various administrative posts; in 1850 appointed one of the five commissioners for settlement of the Punjab, being stationed first at Multan, then at Jullundur. Served in India until 1858 or 1859. Contributed papers on botany to *Transactions* and *Journal* of Linnean Society; and "Grammar and Vocabulary of the Cashmiri Language" to *Journal* of the Asiatic Society of Bengal, 1841. No mention of him, in biographical accounts, in connection with the Mutiny.

The India Office Records division, Commonwealth Relations Office, London, reports that the name Edgeworth does not appear in the Muster Rolls of East India Co. troops or Army lists or in the lists of Mutiny Medal Awards to officers and men of the various artillery regiments of the Royal and Bengal Armies.

At the Siege of Delhi XVIII, 56–60. July 3, 1858

Edwards, Amelia Ann Blandford |*Miss Amelia Edwards*|, 1831–1892, journalist, novelist, Egyptologist. Educated at home, mainly by her mother. Was talented as musician and artist; for some years studied under a music teacher; gave lessons in music; served as church organist. Turned to writing to earn a livelihood. Contributed to *Chambers's*, *Sharpe's*, *English Woman's Journal*, the *Graphic*, the *Academy*, and other periodicals. According to *D.N.B.*, was on staff of *Saturday Review* and *Morning Post*. Author of *Barbara's History*, 1864; *Lord Brackenbury*, 1880; and six other novels; some went through many editions. Also wrote verse, stories, children's books, histories, travel narratives. Edited two anthologies of poetry. On visit to Egypt in winter of 1873–74, became interested in Egyptology; devoted remainder of her life largely to that interest. Instrumental in founding Egypt Exploration Fund; contributed articles on Egyptological subjects to English and foreign journals. In 1889–90, in the U.S., delivered series of lectures on Egypt. Awarded three honorary degrees by American colleges. A few months before her death, granted Civil List pension of £75 a year "in consideration of her services to literature and archaeology."

Women Novelists of Queen Victoria's Reign, 1897, mentioned "The Patagonian Brothers," Miss Edwards's one contribution to *H.W.*, as one of her "exciting" and "extremely popular" stories. Miss Edwards contributed to the *A.Y.R.* Christmas number "Mugby Junction," and, according to *D.N.B.*, also to other of the Christmas numbers. Her novel *Half a Million of Money* was serialized in *A.Y.R.*, 1865, as "By the Author of 'Barbara's History.'" Miss Edwards wrote for *A.Y.R.* also under the editorship of Charles Dickens, Jr.

D.N.B. suppl. 1901

The Patagonian Brothers
xvii, 126–31. Jan. 23, 1858

Repr. in *Miss Carew. By Amelia B. Edwards.* 3 vols. London: Hurst and Blackett, 1865. Pub. in *H.W.* not acknowledged.

Elliot, Hugh Hislop, military officer, India. Entered military service as cornet, 1849, 1st Regt. Light Cavalry Lancers; lieut., 1853 (or 1852); aide-de-camp, 1854–56, to Lord Elphinstone, governor of Bombay; captain, 1860.

In March 1852, Elliot joined Lieut. William Rice of the 25th Regt. Bombay Native Infantry, on Rice's third tiger-shooting expedition in Rajpootana. While stooping to look for tiger prints, Elliot was seized by a wounded tigress and dragged some ten or twenty yards; he was saved by Rice's well-placed shot through the top of the animal's skull. Rice related the incident in detail in his *Tiger-Shooting in India*, 1857 (pp. 104–109), in which he included a full-page plate with the legend "ELLIOT BEING SEIZED." The brief account of the incident that appeared in *H.W.* seems to be an excerpt from a letter written by Elliot. Either by intent or through typographical error, the *H.W.* account gives Rice's name as "Grice" and his regiment as the 26th. The Office Book records the item without notation of author or payment.

Harper's reprinted the item, without acknowledgment to *H.W.*

East-India Register

A Tiger's Jaws [chip] vi, 69. Oct. 2, 1852

Ellis, Miss. *Not identified.* "A Confident Prediction" is the story of a French officer of Napoleonic times who for three years lives in the belief that his death will occur on the day predicted by a mad monk. Payment made by post-office order.

Some five English women writers named Ellis published books in the mid-century.

A Confident Prediction
ii, 465–68. Feb. 8, 1851

Erle, Miss. *Not identified.* Perhaps Miss Earle (above). In the Office Book, "Miss Berwick" is recorded as author of "And He Took a Child"; the "Berwick" is marked out and substituted by "Erle." Payment for "Dirge" made by cheque.

VERSE

Dirge vii, 157. April 16, 1853

"And He Took a Child"
vii, 229. May 7, 1853

Evans. *Not identified.* "The Caitiff Postman" is an ironic little tale exposing the heinousness of persons who thwart a baronet's attempt to ruin a lowly postman. Office Book payment notation reads: "pd to Evans."

The Caitiff Postman *Morley & Evans*
XII, 237–38. Oct. 6, 1855

Evelyn. *Not identified.* "A Christian Paynim" relates the chivalrous deed of a Moslem warrior fighting against the Christians in Spain. The contributor may be Alexander John Evelyn, author of *English Alice, a Poem in Five Cantos,* London, 1851, which recounts the machinations of Spanish Inquisitors and the rescue of Alice by English intervention. Payment for the contribution marked "Enclosed."

VERSE
A Christian Paynim. A Legend
II, 516. Feb. 22, 1851

F

F., Mr. J.; J.F.: *See* Forster, John

Farmer, Miss Fanny. Apparently a verse writer. "The Sky-Lark's Song" by Fanny Farmer appeared in *Chambers's,* March 20, 1852. Payment for the *H.W.* contribution made by post-office order.

VERSE
What May Be Ours
X, 156–57. Sept. 30, 1854

Fawkner, John Pascoe [*Correspondent*], 1792–1869, pioneer settler in Australia. Born in London; received a few years' schooling. His father, sentenced to transportation, permitted to take his family with him in convict expedition dispatched from England in April 1803. Until 1835, young Fawkner followed numerous and varied callings, mainly in Van Diemen's Land. In 1835, arranged expedition to Port Phillip from Van Diemen's Land for purpose of settlement; the settlement ultimately became Melbourne. Brought out Melbourne *Advertiser,* 1838, first newspaper in Victoria; then Port Phillip *Patriot.* Took active part in matters relating to governing of Victoria, both before and after separation of the colony from New South Wales. Held various official posts; for eighteen years member of Legislative Council of Victoria. Achieved prominent and respected position.

Fawkner's pioneering work in Port Phillip received mention in *H.W.* in the first instalment of Howitt's "The Old and New Squatter," Dec. 8, 1855. Howitt called Fawkner the "Romulus" – "the undoubted founder" – of Melbourne, and stated that he was "to this day, a conspicuous member of the legislative council."

It was this mention that prompted Fawkner's writing to Dickens the letter that appeared in *H.W.* under the title "A Colonial Patriot," referred to in the editorial comment as an "interesting scrap from Melbourne." The letter was actually a personal letter to Dickens, not a communication meant for insertion in the periodical. "I pray you to pardon this liberty," wrote Fawkner, "but I could not refrain from thanking you for the very favourable manner in which my conduct has been reported in your journal" – in "your or your contributor's article." Fawkner had, he stated, almost all of Dickens's works, as well as "your Household Words and Narratives from the very first." "... I have often wished I dared write to you; your tales and essays have beguiled many an hour of my life, and I am thus in your debt."

In *Tallangetta,* 1857, Howitt reprinted "The Old and New Squatter" with other of his *H.W.* Australian items. Referring to these items, he wrote in the preface of the book: "... Mr. Dickens has sent me a letter from Mr. John Fawkner ..., expressing his unqualified pleasure in their perusal." The letter sent by Dickens to Howitt was obviously that published in *H.W.* under the title "A Colonial Patriot."

The Office Book assigns the item to "Correspondent & Howitt"; actually Howitt had no connection with it aside from the fact that his "Old and New Squatter" motivated Fawkner's writing to Dickens. It was probably because of that motivation that Wills attached Howitt's name to the item. The Office Book records payment, presumably to Fawkner (though the payee is not named), of £1.1.0 for the 1½-col. item.

D.N.B.

A Colonial Patriot [chip]
Correspondent & Howitt
XIV, 130. Aug. 23, 1856

Fitton, Sarah Mary (name thus in *Brit. Mus. Cat.*; Sarah Margaret Fitton in Allibone) |*Miss Fitton*|, writer of children's stories and lesson books. An Englishwoman, long resident in Paris; dated several of her booklets from her Paris address: 15, Rue de la Ville l'Evêque. Described by Mrs. Browning in two letters written from Paris, Dec. 1851, as "an elderly woman, shrewd and kind" and rich; "there seems to be a good deal in her"; numbered among her acquaintances or friends John Kenyon, the Carmichael-Smyths, and Eugène Sue (*Letters of Elizabeth Barrett Browning*, ed. Kenyon, II, 41; *Letters of the Brownings to George Barrett*, ed. Landis and Freeman, p. 158). Author of two books on botany: *Conversations on Botany*, 1817, a dialogue between Mother and her little son Edward; written, according to the *Brit. Mus. Cat.*, with the assistance of Elizabeth Fitton; went through eight editions; and *The Four Seasons*, 1865, lectures written for the Working Men's Institute in Paris, dedicated by Miss Fitton to her "excellent old friend" Sir William Jackson Hooker. (Some paragraphs of *Conversations* appear practically verbatim in *The Four Seasons.*) Also wrote books on music: *Conversations on Harmony*, 1855, so well received that Miss Fitton brought out a French translation, 1857; and *Little by Little*, lessons in the art of reading music (no copy in Brit. Mus.). In addition, published in booklet form three stories for children: *The Grateful Sparrow*, *Dicky Birds*, and *My Pretty Puss*; and one story for adults, *How I Became a Governess* (reprinted from *Good Words*).

The Office Book record for the one item assigned to Miss Fitton is confused. The contents of the number in which it appears are twice recorded; the first listing is placed in the wrong position chronologically and is marked out. In that listing "A Companionable Sparrow" is assigned to Robertson. In the second listing, rightly recorded for Aug. 8, the item is again assigned to Robertson; his name is marked out and substituted by that of Miss Fitton; then, above the marked-out "Robertson" is written "Robertson &." Miss Fitton's authorship is established by her reprinting of the story (see below) and by her designating herself on the title pages of three of her later booklets as "Author of 'The Grateful Sparrow.'" Robertson may have done no more than send the item to *H.W.* from Paris; Miss Fitton was quite capable of writing it herself.

The *H.W.* article "Mosses," Dec. 11, 1858, assigned in the Office Book to Robertson alone, transcribes practically verbatim from Miss Fitton's *Conversations on Botany* or from her *Four Seasons* (the transcribed passages are among those that appear in both books) what amounts to some fifty lines of the article. There is no acknowledgment to Miss Fitton as author.

Miss Fitton may be author of "Boulogne Wood," July 25, 1857, assigned in the Office Book to "Robertson's friend." The ascription indicates that Robertson sent the item to *H.W.*

Brit. Mus. Cat.

A Companionable Sparrow
Robertson & Miss Fitton
XVI, 130–32. Aug. 8, 1857

Repr. as *The Grateful Sparrow. A True Story* [anon.]. London: Griffith and Farran, 1859. Pub. in *H.W.* acknowledged.

Fitz-Gerald, Desmond G. |*Desmond G. Fitzgerald, Esquire,* 27 Upper Berkeley St.|, analytical chemist. Kelly's *Post Office London Directory,* 1858, lists 27 Upper Berkeley St. (W) as the address of a baker; 27 Upper Berkeley St. West (W) as that of a lodging-house. Fitz-Gerald was presumably staying at the lodging-house. Contributed the article "Natural Science. – Its Adaptation to the Youthful Mind" to *The School and the Teacher,* June 1, 1858; reprinted the article as addendum to his pamphlet *Education. A Lecture,* 1858. On one occasion "quitted the laboratory" to teach the "general principles of chemical science, especially in its application to Physiology," in a village school in Middlesex. In his article described his teaching experience and his philosophy of teaching; in his lecture stated his concept of education, as combining study of the humanities with study of natural science. The concept underlies his *H.W.* poem, which states that the writer loves both poetry and natural philosophy, that love of one does not rule out love of the other, and that the "sisters twain" constitute the true guide in life.

In the Office Book, "D. G. Fitzgerald," with the Berkeley St. address, is recorded as author of the poem "Home and Rest," April 24, 1858. The name and address are marked out, and the author correctly written above the marked-out name as Miss Procter.

Brit. Mus. Cat.

VERSE

Poetry and Philosophy
XVII, 420. April 17, 1858

Fitzgerald, Percy Hetherington |*Fitzgerald, Fitzgerald (Percy)*|, 1834-1925, novelist, misc. writer. B.A. Trinity College, Dublin, 1855; M.A. 1863. Called to Irish bar; was for several years Crown prosecutor; turned to writing. Stated in 1882 (*Recreations of a Literary Man,* p. 6) that he had written "for almost every magazine that has been born, died, or exists"; e.g., *Belgravia, Gent. Mag., Once a Week, Tinsleys', Cassell's,* and, later, *Cornhill.* Published novels and collections of stories (*C.B.E.L.* lists 25 titles); books on the stage and biographies of theatrical personages, also biographies of literary and historical figures; books on Roman Catholicism. A prolific writer – and a hasty, slipshod one. Reviews in the *Athenaeum, Saturday Review,* and other periodicals pointed out the confusion, the padding, the lack of critical judgment, and the inaccuracy in various of his specimens of "book-making"; Crabb Robinson counted as wasted the day that he spent reading Fitzgerald's "paltry compilation" on Lamb and his friends (*On Books and Their Writers,* II, 819).

Fitzgerald took the occasion of Dickens's being in Dublin in 1858, on a reading tour, to introduce himself to him. In the friendship that followed, wrote Fitzgerald, he became "a favourite" with Dickens, a friend with whom Dickens's relationship was most "close and familiar" and "confidential" – a relationship of "precious intimacy, lasting on nigh fifteen [*sic*] years" ("Preface," *Life of Charles Dickens; Memories of Charles Dickens,* p. 5). Dickens's letters do not support the extravagant claim, though they show Dickens to have had a kindly regard for the young man. Dickens welcomed Fitzgerald to Gad's Hill; he wrote him many letters; he expressed admiration of some of his writings and gave him advice and encouragement in his literary work. He thought Fitzgerald "a very clever fellow." When his daughter Mary was approaching thirty with no prospects of marriage, Dickens hoped that she might become interested in Fitzgerald; Mary showed no interest.

Fitzgerald dedicated to Dickens his novel *Never Forgotten;* he delivered a lecture on Lamb and Dickens as essayists (published 1864). After Dickens's death, he published *The History of Pickwick, Bozland, Pickwickian Manners and Customs,* and other volumes of Dickensiana, including an anthology, *Pickwickian Wit and Humour.* He wrote a laudatory life of "the Master" and also *Memories of Charles Dickens.* He used Dickens as literary capital for more than twenty periodical articles; one gave offence to Georgina Hogarth; another brought a public reprimand from Dickens's son Henry (Adrian, *Georgina Hogarth and the Dickens Circle*, pp. 235–36). He executed busts of Dickens, founded the Boz Club, and was first president of the Dickens Fellowship.

Fitzgerald became a *H.W.* contributor through the intervention of Forster, to whose notice Fitzgerald had contrived to bring himself. Forster (as Fitzgerald several times related) took one of Fitzgerald's papers to the *H.W.* office and demanded that it be read and duly considered. The published paper was (according to Fitzgerald) "a striking success." Wills informed Fitzgerald that Dickens would be glad to receive further contributions, especially one for the 1856 Christmas number. Two of Fitzgerald's stories appeared in that number. Fitzgerald contributed only one long item to *H.W.* – "Down among the Dutchmen." According to his own statement (in last instalment), his depiction of the Dutch was much resented by them, as being written in "an unfair and partial spirit."

To *A.Y.R.* Fitzgerald contributed many long items, including several novels, among them *Never Forgotten, The Second Mrs. Tillotson, The Dear Girl*, and *Fatal Zero*. Of *Never Forgotten* Fitzgerald recorded with pride that Dickens revised "every line," added "little points" and "scraps of dialogue," and struck out what he himself had considered some of "the best bits"; the story "Howard's Son," he stated, Dickens also "corrected throughout," writing in "whole passages," deleting others, and altering and improving the punctuation (*Life of Charles Dickens*, II, 320n; I, 261–62). This alteration of his MSS – extending even to the improvement of punctuation – Fitzgerald construed as a mark of Dickens's great interest in him, not as a mark of the inadequacy of the original writing. Other of Fitzgerald's papers – "School-Days at Saxonhurst," for example – also cost Dickens hours of editorial work to get into passable shape for publication. As an established contributor, Fitzgerald had the privilege of sending his MSS directly to the printer's; his slipshod writing made this an awkward arrangement. On Nov. 18, 1869, Dickens wrote to him: "For my sake – if not for Heaven's – do, I *entreat you*, look over your manuscript before sending it to the printer. Its condition involves us all in hopeless confusion. ..." In a later letter, March 9, 1870, Dickens again reprimanded Fitzgerald for his carelessness and for his undertaking more writing than he could reasonably do well – specifically, his writing three works of fiction, each for a different periodical, at the same time.

In various of his books, Fitzgerald recorded the praise that Dickens had given one or another of his writings. An article based on Fitzgerald's life of Sterne appeared July 2, 1864, in *A.Y.R.*; the book was there described as a "lively biography, bright, liberal, and very interesting." An article based on his biography of Garrick appeared in *A.Y.R.* March 21, 1868.

The Woman with the Yellow Hair (see below) was published anonymously; Fitzgerald's authorship is established by his listing the book in the bibliography of his writings in *Memoirs of an Author*. Also listed in that bibliography is "Down among the Dutchmen," a *H.W.* contribution apparently not reprinted. The subject of Fitzgerald's *H.W.* article "Doctor Garrick" is referred to in the text of his *Life of David Garrick*, with footnote reference to the article.

In the Office Book, Fitzgerald is recorded as author of "Pictures and Ballads"; his name is marked out and substituted by that of Thornbury.

Allibone

At the Sign of the Silver Horn
XIV, 41–46. July 26, 1856

The Armourer's Story [title thus in Office Book; no separate title in *H.W.*]
Wreck of the Golden Mary (Christmas 1856), pp. 13–18

A Vision of a Studious Man
XV, 294–99. March 28, 1857

The Yellow Tiger [lead]
XVI, 121–30. Aug. 8, 1857

The Balcombe Street Mystery
XVII, 486–93. May 8, 1858

The Blood of the Sundons
XVII, 608–617. June 12, 1858

The Canon's Clock
XVIII, 229–38. Aug. 21, 1858

The 7 items repr. in *The Woman with the Yellow Hair and Other Modern Mysteries*

Chiefly from "Household Words" [anon.]. London: Saunders, Otley, and Co., 1862.

Down at Red Grange
xiv, 223–27. Sept. 20, 1856
The Supercargo's Story [title thus in Office Book; no separate title in *H.W.*] Wreck of the Golden Mary (Christmas 1856), pp. 21–25
Little Constancy's Birthday
xvii, 325–34. March 20, 1858
The British Lion in a Weak Aspect
xvii, 453–56. April 24, 1858
By Night Express
xvii, 476–80. May 1, 1858
The Fleur de Lys
xviii, 438–44. Oct. 23, 1858
Home Again! [lead]
xix, 73–80. Dec. 25, 1858
Out of Tune
xix, 396–403. March 26, 1859

The 8 items repr. in *The Night Mail, Its Passengers, and How They Fared at Christmas, By Percy Fitzgerald.* London: Ward and Lock, 1862. Pub. in *H.W.* not acknowledged.

They Order This Matter Better in France? [lead]
xv, 193–96. Feb. 28, 1857
At the Coulisses in Paris
xvi, 22–24. July 4, 1857
My Long Lost Chee-yld!
xvii, 548–52. May 22, 1858

The 3 items repr. in *The World behind the Scenes, By Percy Fitzgerald.* London: Chatto and Windus, 1881. Pub. in *H.W.* not acknowledged.

The Datchley Philharmonic
xvi, 213–16. Aug. 29, 1857
The Reverend Alfred Hoblush's Statement xviii, 113–18. July 17, 1858
The Reverend Alfred Hoblush's Further Statement
xix, 18–24. Dec. 4, 1858
Third Statement of Reverend Alfred Hoblush xix, 330–36. March 5, 1859
The Reverend Alfred Hoblush Finds a New Broom
xix, 421–26. April 2, 1859
The Brookrudder Book-Club [lead]
xix, 529–32. May 7, 1859

The 6 items repr. in *The Rev. Alfred Hoblush and His Curacies: A Memoir, By the Author of "Roman Candles," "The Night Mail," etc.* ["Preface" signed P.F.]. London: John Maxwell and Company, 1864. Pub. in *H.W.* acknowledged.

An Old Peace Conference
xv, 440–43. May 9, 1857
Royally "Hard Up"
xv, 463–66. May 16, 1857
Make Your Game, Gentlemen!
xv, 570–73. June 13, 1857
The French War-Office in Seventeen Hundred and Eighty-five [chip]
xvi, 34–36. July 11, 1857
Extract of Funeral Flowers
xvi, 69–72. July 18, 1857
Doctor Garrick
xvi, 166–68. Aug. 15, 1857
Bourbon Paris, Photographed
xvi, 300–303. Sept. 26, 1857
Down among the Dutchmen
xvi, 398–402. Oct. 24, 1857, and 11 following nos.(not consecutive), ending
xvii, 526–28. May 15, 1858
A Royal Pilot-Balloon
xvii, 165–68. Jan. 30, 1858
Fine Shaving
xvii, 309–312. March 13, 1858
The Eve of a Revolution
xvii, 589–95. June 5, 1858
xviii, 7–11. June 19, 1858
Old Dog Tray
xviii, 184–89. Aug. 7, 1858
Going for a Song
xviii, 569–72. Nov. 27, 1858
The Gringe Family
xix, 52–58. Dec. 18, 1858
Miss Cicely's Portrait
xix, 201–204. Jan. 29, 1859
Bogie Albion [lead]
xix, 265–69. Feb. 19, 1859
The Real Cook's Oracle
xix, 380–84. March 19, 1859

Fitzpatrick. *Not identified.* "An Election Bill" reproduces the bill of a publican for providing food, drink, bed, and other services to the freeholders supporting the candidacy of Sir Marcus S———. The item contains no writing by the contributor; his only connection with it was his sending it to the *H.W.* office.

An Election Bill [chip]
XIII, 140–41. Feb. 23, 1856

Fonblanque. *Not identified.* The first item listed below recounts a hoax played on the Austrian police by the Hungarian bandit Schobry (i.e., Jóska Sobri or Zsobri, *d.* 1837) and his being captured and shot while attempting to carry out a "Robin Hoodish" act of generosity; contributor seems to be familiar with the parts of Hungary and Serbia where Schobry's exploits took place; is familiar with Austrian military regulations, one of which he explains. The second item deals with fraudulent lottery practices of German Jews and mentions the difficulties of an honest German landlord in getting a lottery ticket redeemed for the writer.

Various members of the Fonblanque family flourished in the 1850s. The two most likely to have had an interest in the Hungarian bandit are (1) Thomas de Grenier de Fonblanque, *d.* 1860, for twenty years British consul-general for Serbia, stationed at Belgrade; no record, however, of his having written books or periodical articles; and (2) Edward Barrington de Fonblanque, 1821–1895, son of the consul-general; published his first book in 1857; "wrote much anonymously in periodicals" (Boase).

Schobry the Bandit
Fonblanque & Morley
XIV, 164–68. Aug. 30, 1856
A Blank Prize [chip]
XIV, 395–96. Nov. 8, 1856

Forster, John |*Mr. J.F., J.F.*|, 1812–1876, editor, historian, biographer. Studied at University College, London. Admitted at Inner Temple, 1828; called to the bar, 1843, but did not practise law. Secretary to commissioners of lunacy, 1855–61; appointed one of commissioners, 1861. Contributed at various times to *Athenaeum*, *Edin. Rev.*, *Quart. Rev.*, and other periodicals. In 1830s, dramatic critic of *True Sun*; literary and dramatic critic of *Examiner*. Editor of *Foreign Quart. Rev.*, 1842–43; of *Daily News* (on Dickens's relinquishing the editorship), Feb.–Oct. 1846; of *Examiner*, 1847–55. Author of *The Statesmen of the Commonwealth of England*, 1840 (first published in Lardner's *Cabinet Cyclopaedia*); *Arrest of the Five Members by Charles the First*, 1860; and other historical works; biography of Goldsmith, 1848; of Landor, 1869; of Dickens, 1872–74.

Forster met Dickens in 1836; he became and remained Dickens's staunch and loyal friend. Dickens appointed Forster co-executor of his will and bequeathed to him – "to my dear and trusty friend" – the MSS of works in Dickens's possession at the time of his death. Forster was frequently in Dickens's company during the earlier years of their friendship, less frequently during the later years. He took part in many of the activities in which Dickens engaged, as in the theatrical presentations. He was Dickens's adviser and counsellor in personal matters, representing him in the working out of the separation arrangement between him and his wife. He came to Dickens's aid in Dickens's bargaining with publishers. He was Dickens's adviser and counsellor in literary matters. After the fourteenth number of *Pickwick*, stated Forster, there was nothing that Dickens wrote "which I did not see before the world did, either in manuscript or proofs" (*Life*, Book II, sect. i). In his life of Dickens, Forster recorded his high opinion of Dickens's writings. He dedicated to him his biography of Goldsmith. Dickens expressed great admiration for the biography as he did for *Arrest of the Five Members* and for the biography of Landor. He dedicated to Forster in 1858 the Library Edition of his works, in "grateful remembrance of the many patient hours" that Forster had devoted to the correction of proof-sheets of the original editions and "in affectionate acknowledgment" of Forster's "counsel, sympathy, and faithful friendship, during my whole literary life." The long and intimate association of the two writers was not unmarked by clashes of temperament. In his letters Dickens made disparaging remarks about Forster; he caricatured his mannerisms in Podsnap of *Our Mutual Friend*.

In the partnership agreement under which *H.W.* was set up, Forster was, with Dickens, with the publishers Bradbury & Evans, and with Wills, one of the joint proprietors; he held an interest of one-eighth share, in consideration of which he was "from time to time" to contribute literary articles, without payment. According to an unsigned copy of a memorandum among Wills's papers, Forster, in 1854, informed his co-proprietors of his inability to continue his contributions; he did not exercise his option of retaining his share on condition of making a payment of £1100; in 1856, he relinquished his share (Lehmann, ed., *Charles Dickens As Editor*, pp. 19, 195–97).

In connection with *H.W.*, Forster was important as consultant and adviser, rather than as contributor. He presided, as it were, at the conception and birth of *H.W.*, as he did at its dissolution. It was to Forster that Dickens first mentioned his plan for the periodical: "I have not breathed the idea to any one" (Oct. 7, 1849). It was Forster's finding the original plan impracticable that led to a change of design. It was in letters to Forster that Dickens recorded his various ideas for a title and his choice of the final one. It was Forster who suggested the selection of Wills as assistant editor. Once the periodical was established, Dickens referred to Forster various matters concerning items on which he wanted a final opinion – which title was best for an item, for instance, whether Dickens's comments in an article were too severe, whether certain submitted poems were original or plagiarized. Forster corrected the proof of various of Dickens's articles. He attended some of the staff meetings. Finally, he acted for Dickens in 1858 in Dickens's attempt to dislodge Bradbury & Evans as printers and publishers of *H.W.* – the first step in the proceedings that led to the discontinuance of the periodical.

Forster's severance of direct ties with *H.W.* – that is, his reporting, in 1854, that he was unable to continue his contributions and his relinquishing, in 1856, his one-eighth share – may have been due in part to the animosity that had grown up during the years between him and Wills, and to his conviction that Wills did not defer sufficiently to him in the management of the periodical. In a letter of 1853, from Florence, Dickens wrote to his wife that he had twice heard from Forster: "He complains of Wills as not consulting him enough, and is evidently very sore in that connexion" (*Mr. & Mrs. Charles Dickens*, ed. Dexter, p. 219).

While still active in *H.W.* matters, however, Forster had various connections with the periodical aside from his serving as consultant and adviser. One of these was his connection with the *Household Narrative of Current Events*, a supplementary publication brought out from 1850 to 1855. According to Percy Fitzgerald (*Memories of Charles Dickens*, p. 124), "this department," i.e., the *Narrative*, "was allotted to Forster"; according to Morley, Forster wrote the lead article in the various numbers of the *Narrative* (Solly, *Life of Henry Morley*, p. 200). (The actual compiling of the news summaries for the *Narrative* was the work of George Hogarth. See Hogarth, below.) Forster had, moreover, a connection with an occasional *H.W.* item not of his writing. He invited both Browning and his wife to become contributors to *H.W.*, and he was obviously the intermediary through whom a sonnet of Mrs. Browning's made its appearance in *H.W.* pages (see Elizabeth Browning, above). He also furnished to the editorial office the letters of the emigrants Harrold and his sister (in the Office Book, only the second of the Harrold items is marked "per Forster," but obviously the letters that constitute the first item must have arrived at the editorial office through the same agency. See Harrold, below). An important auxiliary service that Forster rendered to *H.W.* was the publicity that he gave the periodical in the *Examiner* during the years of his editorship that coincided with the publication of *H.W.* (to end of 1855). In addition to various mentions of the periodical – "the delightful *Household Words* of Mr. Dickens" – there appeared in the *Examiner* during these years selections (all duly acknowledged) from some forty *H.W.* items, extravagant praise of the Christmas numbers, and high commendation of the *H.W. Almanac.*

Dickens had no commendatory comments on Forster's *H.W.* articles. In a letter to Wills, Nov. 3, 1852, concerning "The Reason Why," he referred sarcastically to Forster's "blunder" in having taken Robert Stephen Hawker's Trelawny ballad to be in entirety an ancient ballad (see Hawker, below): "Of course [Forster] makes out that there is a positive merit in having made the blunder, and that if it really had been the old ballad, his intention would have rather failed upon the whole. I have taken the liberty of assaulting this conclusion between the eyes, and knocking it over heads and heels." In a letter to Wills, Feb. 17, 1853, concerning the proofs of a forthcoming number, Dickens wrote: "I don't like Forster's paper to lead off with, but don't think Sala's better." The number was that of March 5, in which the first instalment of Forster's "Seventy-eight Years Ago" appeared as lead item, and Sala's "The Last Crusader" as fifth item. To Forster's article on Edmund Cartwright, Dickens gave the title "The Power-Loom" (to Wills, June 18, 1853).

In *H.W.*, reference to Forster's biography of Goldsmith appeared in Whitehead's "Off! Off!" and reference to "our friend, THE EXAMINER newspaper," in Dickens's "That Other Public." In *A.Y.R.*, the article on Forster's *Arrest of the Five Members* (May 26, 1860) gave high praise to that book – "this splendid piece of history"; the article on his biography of Sir John Eliot (April 23, 1864) praised that work for its scholarship and its fine perceptiveness and judgment. The article on Forster's biography of Landor (July 24, 1869) Dickens wrote himself. "It rarely befals an author," he stated, "to have such a commentator: to become the subject of so much artistic skill and knowledge, combined with such infinite and loving pains."

Harper's reprinted "Francis Jeffrey," with acknowledgment to *H.W.*

D.N.B.

Francis Jeffrey I, 113–18. April 27, 1850
New Life and Old Learning
I, 130–32. May 4, 1850
The Reason Why
VI, 155–56. Oct. 30, 1852
The Reason Why [chip]
VI, 233–34. Nov. 20, 1852
Seventy-eight Years Ago [lead]
VII, 1–6. March 5, 1853
VII, 157–63. April 16, 1853
The Power-Loom
VII, 440–45. July 9, 1853

Fox, Franklin |*Mr. Franklyn Fox, Franklyn Fox*|, *b.* ca. 1824, sea captain, writer. Youngest of the three children born to William Johnson Fox (1786–1864) and his wife, Eliza Florance Fox. Remained for the most part with his mother after his father separated from his wife and established ménage in 1835 with Miss Eliza Flower. Was not, however, at odds with his father. Saw him at various times; was with him during the Oldham election of 1840 (Garnett, *Life of W. J. Fox*, passim). Made his first voyage in 1841 as midshipman aboard an East Indiaman; later shipped on American vessels. Became surveyor to Lloyd's Agency at Karachi and captain in Peninsular and Oriental Steam Navigation service. In the late 1880s was living at St. Albans, having given up the sea. To *People's Journal*, *Howitt's Journal*, and *H.W.* contributed sketches based on his experiences at sea and in foreign parts. Edited, 1869, a *Memoir* of his mother. Wrote *China: Chinese Colonisation, the French, the Opium Question*, 1884; *How to Send a Boy to Sea*, 1886; *Frank Allreddy's Fortune*, 1891, a boys' adventure story. Recorded himself on title page of *How to Send a Boy to Sea* as author of two additional titles; titles not listed in *Brit. Mus. Cat.* or in *Eng. Cat.*

Fox's father was a friend of Dickens and a leader-writer on the *Daily News* under Dickens's and Forster's editorship.

Allibone

A Cape Coast Cargo *Mr. Franklyn Fox & W.H.W.* II, 252–57. Dec. 7, 1850
A Dark Suspicion
II, 532–35. March 1, 1851

The 2 items repr. in *Glimpses of the Life of a Sailor. By Franklin Fox.* London: Charles Fox, 1862. Pub. in *H.W.* acknowledged.

French, Miss. *Not identified.* Two of the items listed below are related by a masculine narrator: "Billeted in Boulogne" by an Englishman staying with an English family in Boulogne; "Number Five, Hanbury Terrace," by a solicitor's clerk of Irish background who had been a pupil at Christ's Hospital. Dickens found the Boulogne item "weak" (to Wills, April 27, 1856). The second item listed below is an account of the trial of Spencer Cowper and three other barristers for the alleged murder, 1699, of the Quakeress Sarah Stout. (The second of "Two Difficult Cases" is by Morley and has no connection with the first case.) Payment for first and third contribution made by cheque.

Billeted in Boulogne
xiii, 442–45. May 24, 1856
Two Difficult Cases: The First Case [lead] *Miss French & Miss Jewsbury's friend* xiv, 385–91. Nov. 8, 1856
Number Five, Hanbury Terrace
xvi, 568–72. Dec. 12, 1857

Fusco, Edoardo Nicolà |*Fusco*|, *b.* 1824, *d.* 1872 or 1873, educator. Born in Trani, Apulia, in southern Italy; studied in Naples. Took prominent part in 1848 revolutionary movement in Kingdom of Naples; on its failure, fled to Corfu; lived there for some time; also for some years in Athens and Constantinople. In 1854 went to England; taught Italian and modern Greek in London and at Eton; lectured on Italian literature. His lecture "Italian Art and Literature before Giotto and Dante," delivered at Queen's College, in English, published in *Macmillan's*, Jan. and July 1876, with prefatory note on Fusco by his friend Matthew Arnold. Knew many prominent families in England. (The copy of his *Dell'associazione commerciale artigiana di pietà in Costantinopoli*, 1852, in the Brit. Mus. bears Fusco's inscription to Lady Stratford de Redcliffe.) In 1859 or 1860, returned to Italy. There laboured unceasingly in cause of education; became inspector-in-chief of schools in the provinces of the former Kingdom of Naples; held chair of anthropology and pedagogy at Univ. of Naples. Founded and edited the periodical *Progresso educativo*. Some of his writings published posthumously, among them *L'incivilimento in Turchia* and a collection of lectures on anthropology and pedagogy.

Fusco's *H.W.* article describes a review of Turkish troops in Constantinople, Oct. 1853, at which he was a spectator.

Enciclopedia "Italiana"

Turks under Arms *Fusco & Morley*
ix, 414–17. June 17, 1854

G

Garrow, Theodosia: *See* Trollope, Theodosia (Garrow)

Gaskell, Elizabeth Cleghorn (Stevenson) |*Mrs. Gaskell*|, 1810–1865, novelist. Attended the Misses Byerley's school in Stratford-on-Avon. In 1832 married William Gaskell (below). Her first published writing, verse written in collaboration with her husband, appeared in *Blackwood's*, 1837. Thereafter contributed to *Howitt's Journal, Sunday School Penny Magazine*, both of Dickens's periodicals, *Cornhill*; occasionally to other periodicals. Published in book form *Mary Barton*, 1848; *Ruth*, 1853; and *Sylvia's Lovers*, 1863; published her other novels first as serials in periodicals; *Wives and Daughters* was appearing in *Cornhill* at time of her death. Author also of *The Life of Charlotte Brontë*, 1857.

Mrs. Gaskell sent Dickens a copy of *Mary Barton* soon after the book was published; she seems to have first met him in 1849. In that year she was among the guests at the *David Copperfield* celebration dinner. Later, Dickens at times visited the Gaskells when he was in Manchester. On occasion, in the early years of their acquaintance, Mrs. Gaskell asked him for information or assistance in helping people in whom she was interested – an unfortunate girl to be helped to emigrate to Australia, the Manchester prison philanthropist Thomas Wright to be championed in *H.W.* as worthy recipient of a Government pension. Otherwise, their association was entirely that of contrbutor and editor, and, in that relationship – until their dissension concerning the serialization of *North and South* – she held him in friendly regard. In a letter of 1852 (addressee unknown), she stated that she was not in the habit of writing for periodicals and wrote occasionally for *H.W.* only "as a personal mark of respect & regard to Mr Dickens" (*Letters,* No. 519, misdated 1862). Mrs. Gaskell, naturally, shared "the well-grounded feeling of dislike to the publicity" that Dickens gave to his domestic affairs in 1858. It had, she wrote, made him "extremely unpopular," and she did not wish to be announced as a contributor to his new periodical that was to appear in April of the following year (*Letters,* No. 418).

Mrs. Gaskell was among the first writers whom Dickens asked to contribute to *H.W.*: "... I do honestly know," he wrote to her, Jan. 31, 1850, "that there is no living English writer whose aid I would desire to enlist in preference to the authoress of Mary Barton (a book that most profoundly affected and impressed me). ..." If Mrs. Gaskell preferred to speak with him about the matter of contribution, he would be glad to call on her in Manchester to explain whatever she might wish to know.

In response to the request, Mrs. Gaskell sent Dickens "Lizzie Leigh," the first chapter of which appeared in the opening number immediately following Dickens's "Preliminary Word." Thereafter, at Dickens's repeated urging, she sent him from time to time additional stories, as also articles, for some of which he had exceedingly high praise, and for their author pretty compliments. The "Cranford" stories were delightful; "The Old Nurse's Story" was "Nobly told, and wonderfully managed." Mrs. Gaskell was his "Scheherazade"; she could not write too much for *H.W.* and had "never yet written half enough"; anything that she might write would please Dickens; "it only needs be done by you to be well done" (Dec. 5 [4], Dec. 21, 1851; Nov. 6, 1852; Nov. 25, 1851; April 13, Sept. 19, 1853). When he felt it advisable to make more than slight changes in her stories he did so in consultation with her and did not insist on changes that she did not approve. (The letter in which Mrs. Gaskell objected to Dickens's alteration in "Our Society at Cranford" – his substituting mention of Hood and Hood's writings for her mention of Boz and Boz's writings – reached Dickens only after the number in which the story was to appear was already in print. He hoped that she would not blame him for what he had done "in perfect good faith." "I would do anything rather than cause you a minute's vexation arising out of what has given me so much pleasure ...," Dec. 5 [4], 1851).

On Aug. 19, 1854, *H.W.* announced the forthcoming publication in its pages of "NORTH AND SOUTH. By the AUTHOR OF MARY BARTON." The same authorship ascription appeared with the title of the novel in each instalment – this being the only instance, except for *Hard Times,* in which statement of authorship accompanied a title. *North and South* was unsuited to Dickens's serialization formula, and its publication disrupted the amicable relationship that had existed between author and editor. Points of dispute centred on the condensing of material, the quantity to be included in each *H.W.* number, and the fitting of chapters into weekly instalments. Divided as Mrs. Gaskell insisted, wrote Dickens, the novel was "wearisome in the last degree," and the resultant decrease in *H.W.* sales was not to be wondered at. The whole matter was "a dreary business" (to Wills, Oct. 14, 1854). His version of the vexatious author-editor relationship during the months of the novel's serialization Dickens gave in a letter to Wilkie Collins, March 24, 1855: "You have guessed right! The best of it was that she [Mrs. Gaskell] wrote to Wills, saying she must particularly stipulate not to have her proofs touched, 'even by Mr. Dickens.' That immortal creature had gone over the proofs with great pains – had of course taken out the stiflings – hard-plungings, lungeings, and other convulsions – and had also taken out her weakenings and damagings of her own effects. 'Very well,' said the gifted Man, 'she shall have her own way. But after it's published show her this Proof, and ask her to consider whether her story would have been the better or the worse for it.' " Mrs. Gaskell admitted, to Anna Jameson, that toward the end of the novel she had infringed "all the bounds & limits they set me as to quantity," but that every page had been "grudged" her (*Letters*, No. 225). She was acutely distressed by the unsatisfactory state in which the novel had appeared. In bringing it out in book form, she explained that the serial publication had made impossible the development of the story as she had originally planned and that she had, toward the close, been compelled "to hurry on events with an improbable rapidity." To remedy these matters in some degree, she made various alterations and additions in the book publication.

Despite the altercation, Mrs. Gaskell continued to contribute to *H.W.* (the instalment division of one of her stories – "Half a Life-Time Ago" – again caused contention). To *A.Y.R.* Mrs. Gaskell did not wish to become a contributor. Concerning a story for which she hoped to find an American publisher, she wrote to C. E. Norton, March 9, 1859; "I *know* it is fated to go to this new Dickensy periodical, & I did so hope to escape it" (*Letters*, No. 418). Mrs. Gaskell did not comply with Dickens's request that she write a novel for *A.Y.R.*, though she did contribute shorter items. After she became a contributor to *Cornhill*, she reserved for that periodical what she considered her best writing; Dickens got the second best. She made the distinction clear in a letter to George Smith: a story *"not good enough"* for *Cornhill* "might be good enough" for Dickens's periodical (*Letters*, No. 451a).

Some of the material that Mrs. Gaskell contributed to *H.W.* she had used before in an essay and a story published in *Sartain's Union Magazine*. The social background of the country town described in "The Last Generation in England," and some of the incidents related in that essay, appeared in the "Cranford" stories; "Martha Preston," in revised and expanded form, became "Half a Life-Time Ago" (see Hopkins, *Elizabeth Gaskell*, and Sharps, *Mrs. Gaskell's Observation and Invention*). Mrs. Gaskell obviously contributed the material to *H.W.* as previously unpublished, and Dickens so accepted it.

Mrs. Gaskell was generously paid for most of her *H.W.* contributions, though for some she was paid at the standard rate. In a letter written after she had been almost three years a contributor, she stated that she did not know the rate at which she was paid (*Letters*, No. 519, misdated 1862). The overgenerous twenty pounds that she received for her first contribution, however, so startled her that she wondered whether she were "swindling" the proprietors (*Letters*, No. 70).

Mrs. Gaskell was "extremely annoyed & hurt" by the way in which an incident related in her "Disappearances" was handled in Morley's "Character-Murder," Jan. 8, 1859. In her article Mrs. Gaskell had told of the disappearance of an apprentice, with unmistakable implication that "the poor lad" had been murdered – a suspicion that had been disproved more than fifteen years before. Morley, quoting part of her account, cited it as an instance of the public's unwillingness to let rumours and scandals die even "after all the truth had been most publicly and perfectly explained." He did not, of course, mention the author of "Disappearances"; but since Mrs. Gaskell had reprinted the article in *Lizzie Leigh; and Other Tales*, her authorship was not a secret. Mrs. Gaskell wrote to Wills, protesting that Morley's article made her "say by implication" more than she had actually said; Wills's reply gave her no satisfaction (Gaskell, *Letters*, No. 418). Before the appearance of "Character-Murder," two short *H.W.* items ("A Disappearance" and "A Disappearance Cleared Up") had printed letters from readers stating facts that disproved the murder-rumour (see John and William Gaunt, below). The first of the items was appended to "Disappearances" in the Tauchnitz Edition of the *Lizzie Leigh* collection.

In addition to contributing to *H.W.*, Mrs. Gaskell at times sent to the editorial office writings of her friends and acquaintances. Not all were accepted for publication. Those that did appear in *H.W.* were the poem "The Outcast Lady," a story by Mme. De Mérey, and two papers by Mrs. Jenkin.

A commendatory reference to Mrs. Gaskell's novels appeared in the *H.W.* article "Doctor Dulcamara, M.P.," written by Wilkie Collins and to some extent revised by Dickens: to recover from the effect produced by reading *The Heir of Redclyffe*, stated the article, the writer had had recourse to the "restoratives" provided by better women novelists than Charlotte Yonge, among them Mrs. Gaskell.

H.W. readers probably liked Mrs. Gaskell's "Cranford" stories best of her contributions to the periodical; among the many admirers of the stories were Forster, Ruskin, Charlotte Brontë, Monckton Milnes, and Charles Eliot Norton. Landor stated that a story related in Mrs. Gaskell's "Modern Greek Songs" had provided him with "the rudiments of a story" on which he based his poem "A Modern Greek Idyl."

Of the items listed below as not reprinted by Mrs. Gaskell, "Cumberland Sheep-Shearers" is established as her writing by Forster's letter to her, Jan. 20, 1853 (typescript in Brotherton Collection, University of Leeds Library); "Modern Greek Songs" is so established by a letter from Dickens to her, Feb. 18, 1854. Mrs. Gaskell's being a guest, in the spring of 1852, at Lord Hatherton's seat, Teddesley Park, where John Burton was head gardener from 1851 to 1853 (Sharps, *Mrs. Gaskell's Observation and Invention*, p. 145n), authenticates her authorship of "The Schah's English Gardener."

Bibliographers and biographers have attributed to Mrs. Gaskell three verse items published in *H.W.*: "Bran," "The Scholar's Story," and "A Christmas Carol." The first two are by William Gaskell, with the brief prose introduction to "The Scholar's Story" being written, according to J. A. Green, by Mrs. Gaskell (see Gaskell, below). The authorship of the third has not been ascertained. Its attribution to Mrs. Gaskell rests on a misunderstanding of the Office Book system of recording. See Introduction, pp. 39–40.

Harper's reprinted seven of Mrs. Gaskell's *H.W.* contributions (one, only in part), two of them acknowledged to *H.W.*; of the two, one was "Lizzie Leigh," listed in the table of contents as "By Charles Dickens." The New York publishers De Witt & Davenport brought out a pirated edition, 1850, of "Lizzie Leigh" as "By Charles Dickens." They included "Lizzie Leigh" in a collection (n.d.) of three stories "By Charles Dickens" (the first item in the collection was one of Georgiana Craik's *H.W.* stories; the third, one of Howitt's). "Lizzie Leigh" "By Charles Dickens" appeared as the first of the "spirit-stirring sketches of imagined or of real life" that constituted the *Irving Offering*, 1851, the picture that served as frontispiece bearing the legend "Lizzie Leigh." "Lizzie Leigh" was included in *Choice Stories from Dickens' Household Words*, pub. Auburn, N.Y., 1854. "Disappearances" was included in the Putnam volume of selections from *H.W.*: *Home and Social Philosophy*, 2nd ser.

D.N.B.

Lizzie Leigh I, 2–6. March 30, 1850, and the 2 following nos.

The Well of Pen-Morfa II, 182–86. Nov. 16, 1850, and the following no.

The Heart of John Middleton II, 325–34. Dec. 28, 1850

Disappearances III, 246–50. June 7, 1851

The Old Nurse's Story A Round of Stories (Christmas 1852), pp. 11–20

Morton Hall [chap. i = lead] VIII, 265–72. Nov. 19, 1853, and the following no.

Traits and Stories of the Huguenots VIII, 348–54. Dec. 10, 1853

My French Master [chap. i = lead] VIII, 361–65. Dec. 17, 1853, and the following no.

The Squire's Story Another Round of Stories (Christmas 1853), pp. 19–25

Company Manners IX, 323–31. May 20, 1854

The 10 items repr. in *Lizzie Leigh; and Other Tales. By the Author of "Mary Barton," "Ruth," &c.* Cheap edition. London: Chapman and Hall, n.d.; also in identical "Cheap edition" dated 1855. Pub. in *H.W.* acknowledged in both editions.

Our Society at Cranford [lead]
IV, 265–74. Dec. 13, 1851
A Love Affair at Cranford
IV, 349–57. Jan. 3, 1852
Memory at Cranford
IV, 588–97. March 13, 1852
Visiting at Cranford
V, 55–64. April 3, 1852
The Great Cranford Panic
VI, 390–96. Jan. 8, 1853, and the following no.
Stopped Payment, at Cranford
VII, 108–115. April 2, 1853
Friends in Need, at Cranford
VII, 220–27. May 7, 1853
A Happy Return to Cranford
VII, 277–85. May 21, 1853

The 8 items repr. as *Cranford. By the Author of "Mary Barton," "Ruth," &c.* London: Chapman & Hall, 1853. Pub. in *H.W.* acknowledged.

North and South
X, 61–68. Sept. 2, 1854, and the 21 following nos., ending X, 561–70. Jan. 27, 1855

Repr. as *North and South. By the Author of "Mary Barton," "Ruth," "Cranford," &c.* 2 vols. London: Chapman and Hall, 1855. Pub. in *H.W.* acknowledged.

An Accursed Race
XII, 73–80. Aug. 25, 1855
Half a Life-Time Ago
XII, 229–37. Oct. 6, 1855, and the 2 following nos.
The Poor Clare
XIV, 510–15. Dec. 13, 1856, and the 2 following nos.
My Lady Ludlow [chap. i = lead]
XVIII, 1–7. June 19, 1858, and (except for no. of Aug. 21) the 13 following nos., ending XVIII, 341–46. Sept. 25, 1858

The 4 items repr., with introductory and linking material and with 2 stories not from *H.W.*, as *Round the Sofa. By the Author of "Mary Barton," "Life of Charlotte Bronte," &c. &c.* 2 vols. London: Sampson Low, Son & Co., 1859. Pub. in *H.W.* acknowledged. Before being included in *Round the Sofa,* "My Lady Ludlow" had been repr. separately as *My Lady Ludlow. A Novel. By Mrs. Gaskell.* New York: Harper & Brothers, 1858.

The Sin of a Father [lead]
XVIII, 553–61. Nov. 27, 1858
The Manchester Marriage
A House to Let (Christmas 1858), pp. 6–17

The 2 items repr. in *Right at Last, and Other Tales. By the Author of "Mary Barton," "Life of Charlotte Bronte," "Round the Sofa," &c. &c.* London: Sampson Low, Son & Co., 1860. Pub. in *H.W.* acknowledged.

The Schah's English Gardener
V, 317–21. June 19, 1852
Cumberland Sheep-Shearers
VI, 445–51. Jan. 22, 1853
Modern Greek Songs
IX, 25–32. Feb. 25, 1854

Mrs. Gaskell's friend: *See* Jenkin, Henrietta Camilla (Jackson)

Gaskell, Margaret Emily |*Miss Meta Gaskell*|, 1837–1913, second daughter of the Rev. William Gaskell (below) and his wife Elizabeth (above). Mrs. Gaskell wrote of her daughter to George Smith: "Please always call her Meta – she never was called 'Margaret' from her birth. ..." (*Letters,* No. 451). Attended a school conducted by Miss Rachel Martineau in Liverpool. Travelled much with her mother on the Continent. Worked with her mother in relieving distress of the poor in Manchester; taught in Ragged School; once thought of nursing as a career, but did not actively pursue the plan. Was the most talented and intellectual of the Gaskell daughters. Had ability in music and art; received drawing lessons from Ruskin; at one time thought of becoming professional artist. After parents' death, continued to live in Manchester; was active in support of charitable and civic institutions. Her writing confined almost entirely to letter writing, in which she showed much ability. A letter written by her after a visit to Haworth with her mother contains "one of the best extant accounts of life at the parsonage in Mr. Brontë's later years" (Hopkins, *Elizabeth Gaskell*, p. 310).

Helena Mathewson

xvi, 13–22. July 4, 1857

Gaskell, William |*Mr.Gaskell*|, 1805–1884, Unitarian minister. M.A. Univ. of Glasgow, 1825 (*Graduates of the Univ. of Glasgow*); thereafter divinity student at Manchester College, York. From 1828 to his death, minister of Cross Street Chapel, Manchester. Professor of English history and literature at Manchester New College; lecturer at Owens College. For many years one of editors of *Unitarian Herald.* Published sermons and controversial tracts, and *Two Lectures on the Lancashire Dialect*, 1854. Also wrote verse: "Sketches among the Poor," *Blackwood's*, 1837, written in collaboration with his wife (above); *Temperance Rhymes*, 1839; *Cottonopolis*, 1882. Composed and translated hymns.

Through Mrs. Gaskell's connection with Dickens, Gaskell and Dickens were acquainted. Gaskell, on at least two occasions, asked Dickens's assistance in support of sanitation projects; Dickens was unable to comply with the requests. Dickens read with pleasure a copy of Gaskell's lectures that Mrs. Gaskell sent him in 1854; he found them "sagacious and unaffected" (to Mrs. Gaskell, June 16 [15]–17, 1854). During the altercation between Dickens and Mrs. Gaskell concerning the *H.W.* serialization of *North and South*, Gaskell intervened in his wife's behalf.

Both items listed below are translations from Hersart de la Villemarqué's collection of Breton ballads, *Barzaz-Breiz*, 3rd ed., 1845. To the ballad "Bran" in *H.W.* is attached a footnote reproducing in part (largely in direct translation) the editorial material that accompanies the ballad in *Barzaz-Breiz*; the source of the ballad and of the explanatory footnote is not acknowledged. The source of "The Scholar's Story," in the *H.W.* Christmas number, is vaguely acknowledged: the prefatory comment states that the ballad "was taken down ... seventy-one years ago, by the mother of the person who communicated it to M. Villemarqué when he was making his collection of Breton Ballads" (see "Argument" to "Le Clerc de Rohan," *Barzaz-Breiz*).

Both translations are by William Gaskell. Both have been reprinted as by Mrs. Gaskell.

The Office Book notation for "Bran" reads "per Mrs. Gaskell" with "Mr. Gaskell" inserted very lightly before that notation. The word "Mr." is not clearly written; it might possibly be read as "Mrs." If Mrs. Gaskell had sent in the item as her own writing, however, there would have been no occasion for the "per" notation. C. K. Shorter, in his World's Classics Edition of Mrs. Gaskell's writings (Vol. x, 1915), first attributed the item to Mrs. Gaskell and reprinted it in that edition; the basis of his ascription was the Office Book, which he either consulted himself or had consulted for him. On the basis of Shorter's ascription, "Bran" appears in *C.B.E.L.* and other bibliographies as by Mrs. Gaskell.

The Office Book ascription of "The Scholar's Story" reads "Mrs. Gaskell." The ballad is prefaced, as stated above, by some introductory remarks, supposedly spoken by the scholar-narrator to his fireside listeners. In *A Bibliographical Guide to the Gaskell Collection in the Moss Side Library*, 1911, J. A. Green wrote concerning this item: "This story was translated by Mr. Gaskell from a Breton ballad by the Vicomte de la Villemarqué, and the introductory remarks were written by Mrs. Gaskell." Green did not state the source of his information. Since he was a Manchester librarian and was acquainted with members of the Gaskell family, it seems likely, however, that he obtained the information from a trustworthy source. Why Mrs. Gaskell, rather than her husband, should have written the two brief introductory paragraphs, and why Green should have thought that fact worthy of remark, is not clear. One of

Mrs. Gaskell's stories appeared in the same Christmas number; presumably she was thought or thought herself able to introduce the scholar-narrator in a way that would place him appropriately among the other story tellers around the Christmas fire.

On the basis of the Office Book ascription, Shorter reprinted "The Scholar's Story" as by Mrs. Gaskell in his World's Classics Edition of her writings (Vol. x); he made no mention of Green's statement. *C.B.E.L.* includes the poem among Mrs. Gaskell's writings; the title is there followed by the notation (for which no authority is given) that the poem is a translation made not by Mrs. Gaskell but by her husband, and that only the "introduction" is her writing. Other bibliographies record the same (or part of the same) information.

D.N.B.

VERSE

Bran viii, 179–81. Oct. 22, 1853

The Scholar's Story
Another Round of Stories (Christmas 1853), pp. 32–34

Gaunt, John and **William Gaunt** |*Communicated*|, sons of John Gaunt, confectioner of North Shields. In 1827, after the disappearance of a doctor's apprentice from North Shields, John Gaunt the elder became suspected of having murdered the apprentice for the purpose of selling the body for dissection. The utterly unfounded suspicion led to ostracism and persecution of the entire Gaunt family. Their confectionery trade was ruined, and the sons John and William, who had obtained work in a glass manufactory, were obliged to support their parents. Townspeople insulted members of the family and solicited the sons' employers to dismiss them. On discovery of the Burke and Hare murders, the Gaunt house was nightly surrounded by a threatening mob, and the family were in danger of being murdered. Seven years after the disappearance of the apprentice, a meeting in North Shields, May 9, 1834, cleared Gaunt of the suspicion by bringing to light the fact that the apprentice had enlisted in the service of the East India Co. and had died of cholera in 1832.

Mrs. Gaskell, without taking the precaution of ascertaining whether the facts of the case had been determined, related the disappearance of the apprentice in her *H.W.* article "Disappearances," June 7, 1851, unmistakably implying that "the poor lad" had been murdered. John and William Gaunt, then old bachelors living in Coatham, Yorks., read Mrs. Gaskell's article and thereupon wrote to *H.W.*, enclosing in their letter an account of the North Shields meeting. *H.W.* published their letter, with a brief statement of the facts of the case, under the title listed below. Before the publication of their communication, *H.W.* had already published, in "A Disappearance," June 21, 1851, the letter of a reader which showed the murder-rumour to be without foundation.

Despite repeated public announcement of John Gaunt's innocence, the murder-rumour was again revived, apparently late in 1858. Thereupon Morley, in his article "Character-Murder," Jan. 8, 1859, rehearsed the entire case and took opportunity to denounce the public's "morbid thirst for mystery," indulged in at the expense of truth. Too "interesting and familiar to be put aside," the discredited Gaunt murder-rumour had lived and spread, wrote Morley, and had found its way even "into our pages." But he managed, in part, to turn that fact to *H.W.*'s advantage: the publication of "Disappearances" had motivated the Gaunt brothers' writing to *H.W.*, and the resultant statement of the case in the periodical had provided "a second public refutation of the slander." Morley expressed deep sympathy with the Gaunt family. The two brothers, he wrote, had "borne with Christian patience a heavy cross, and lived without spot to their honour."

A Disappearance Cleared Up [chip]
iv, 513–14. Feb. 21, 1852

George, Frances (Southwell) |*Mrs. Shale St. George, Mrs. St. George*|. The Office

Book records payment for "Where Dwell the Dead?" as made by post-office order (i.e., presumably to an address in England, though the contributor cannot have been in England on Sept. 9, 1850, the recorded payment date); for "From a Settler's Wife" as "Remitted to New Zealand"; for "An Emigrant's Glance Homeward" as "Remitted to Auckland." In "From a Settler's Wife" the contributor states that she was brought up as "an idle English lady," dividing her time between "books and amusements, but giving much more of it to pleasure than to study." With her husband, an attorney, she emigrated to New Zealand. After a voyage "of four months and fourteen days," she writes, "we reached Auckland, our destined home ... on the 18th December."

Information from the Alexander Turnbull Library, Wellington: The *New Zealander*, Dec. 21, 1850, records that the *Sir Edward Paget* arrived in Auckland on Dec. 18, and that the vessel had left England on Aug. 5. The voyage, thus, lasted four months and fourteen days. Included in the passenger list published by the newspaper are Mr. T. George and wife. Thomas Shayle George, solicitor, appears in the Auckland electoral rolls and in Auckland directories of the 1850s and 1860s, the latest listing being for 1869. *Chapman's Auckland Almanac* for 1873–74 lists a school on Alten Road, Auckland, managed by Mrs. Shayle George; the school is also listed (under Mrs. T. George) in *Wise's New Zealand Post Office Directory* for 1875–76. The Registrar-General's Office, Wellington, appears not to have the death certificate for either Thomas Shayle George or his wife. The birth registration for one of the George children, in the Registrar-General's Office, supplies the Christian and maiden name of Mrs. George.

PROSE

From a Settler's Wife
Mrs. St. George & Morley
IV, 585–88. March 13, 1852

VERSE

Where Dwell the Dead?
I, 596. Sept. 14, 1850

An Emigrant's Glance Homeward
V, 80. April 10, 1852

Gibson, Miss Mary W. A. |*Miss M. H. Gibson*, 6 Cottage Place, Brompton; *Miss Gibson*|. *Not identified.* Directories do not list a Miss Gibson at the address given.

The second initial recorded for Miss Gibson in the Office Book entry for her first contribution cannot be read as other than "H"; it may be intended for "A," or it may be a mis-recording. The contributor is clearly the Miss Gibson to whom Dickens wrote on Dec. 17, 1857. Sotheby's 1938 sales catalogue of a portion of Count de Suzannet's library lists Dickens's letter of that date, addressed to Miss Mary W. A. Gibson, and quotes some lines from it; Nonesuch *Letters* gives the entire letter, with the addressee recorded as "Miss Mary A. W. Gilson." Dickens's letter indicates that Miss Gibson had written to ask for help or advice in getting her writings published. Dickens wrote that no touch of his pen would do for the writings what they could not do for themselves, and then suggested: "If you should desire to offer anything to Household Words, I will promptly read it myself." He proposed, also, two days on which Miss Gibson might call to see him; he would see her, he wrote, with "the greatest readiness." The first contribution that the Office Book assigns to Miss Gibson appeared a little more than two months after Dickens's invitation to her to become a contributor.

Dickens's letter of Oct. 20, 1858, to "Miss Gibson," thanking her for her "warm-hearted and earnest letter" at the time of the scandal concerning his domestic affairs, is probably to the same Miss Gibson.

Alice and Phoebe Cary included "Lost Alice" in their *Josephine Gallery*, 1859.

PROSE

A Tale of an Old Man's Youth
XVII, 391–96. April 10, 1858

Lost Alice XVII, 438–45. April 24, 1858

VERSE

Gone Away XVII, 251. Feb. 27, 1858

Dust and Ashes
XVII, 588–89. June 5, 1858

Haunted XIX, 373–74. March 19, 1859

Dreaming XIX, 444. April 9, 1859

Gibson, William Sidney |*Sidney Gibson*|, 1814–1871, barrister, misc. writer. Privately educated. Admitted at Lincoln's Inn, 1839; called to the bar, 1845. Registrar of Newcastle-upon-Tyne district court of bankruptcy, 1843–69. Hon. M. A. Univ. of Durham. F.S.A., F.G.S., and member of other learned societies in England and on the Continent. Lectured on antiquarian and other subjects. Contributed to *N. & Q.*, *Bentley's Misc.*, *New Monthly*, and other periodicals. Published works on literary and antiquarian matters, e.g., *The History of the Monastery Founded at Tynemouth*, 1846–47; *Remarks on the Mediaeval Writers of English History*, 1848; *A Memoir of Northumberland*, 1860.

D.N.B.

Number Seven XIII, 454–56. May 24, 1856
Repr., with revision, in *Lectures and Essays on Various Subjects, Historical, Topographical, and Artistic. By Wm. Sidney Gibson, Esq.* London: Longmans and Co., 1858. Pub. in *H.W.* acknowledged.

Mineral Springs
XIX, 367–73. March 19, 1859
Repr., with additions, in *Miscellanies Historical and Biographical; Being a Second Series of Essays, Lectures, and Reviews: By William Sidney Gibson, Esq.* London: Longman, Green, Longman, Roberts, and Green, 1863. Pub. in *H.W.* acknowledged.

Gill, Charles. *Not identified.* The contributor is an Englishman, resident for six years in Victoria, Australia. His article discusses the climate of Victoria; it contains a reference to the bush fire of 1851, "already described in this Journal" – i.e., in Howitt's "Black Thursday," May 10, 1856. The "already described in this Journal" is probably an editorial insertion.

Sultry December
XIX, 47–48. Dec. 11, 1858

Godfrey, Miss. *Not identified.* "A Cousin in Need" tells of a young clergyman's being given a ride to Berlin by a man in uniform who turns out to be Frederick William I. A parallel incident is related by Augustus J. C. Hare, *The Story of My Life* (II, 373–74), the persons in that account being an acquaintance of Hare's and the Crown Prince of Prussia.

Payment for the contribution made by cheque.

Jessie Bedford, who wrote under the pseudonym "Elizabeth Godfrey," published, among other writings, a book on Germany – *Heidelberg: Its Princes and Its Palaces.* Since her first book did not appear until 1892, however, she seems unlikely to be the *H.W.* contributor.

Dickens, in 1839, wrote two letters to a Mrs. Godfrey, apparently a schoolmistress, concerning a book of children's stories that she planned to publish. That Mrs. Godfrey might conceivably be the *H.W.* contributor.

The best known contemporary woman writer of the name was of course the novelist Mrs. G. W. Godfrey (Mary Rose Godfrey).

A Cousin in Need
XII, 381–84. Nov. 17, 1855

Goetznitz, Von |*Goëtznitz, Goëssnitz, Von Goetznitz*|. *Not identified.* Of the variant forms in which the contributor's name appears in the Office Book, the third form is probably the correct one. (Wills had trouble with umlauts.) The four items listed below give the following information about the contributor: Was a German officer; took a proper pride in his nationality and his profession; had served in the army in Saxony in 1848 and had been in Bohemia in autumn of 1851. Had apparently visited Puerto Rico and had lived for some time in the U.S. In his wandering life there, had been at Fort Snelling in the Minnesota Territory, also in Arkansas and Texas; only date given in connection with his stay in the U.S. is April 1857. Was familiar with London.

The incidents that the contributor relates are dramatically told. There was "good stuff" in "The Last Victim of the Gauntlet," wrote Dickens to Wills, Aug. 21, 1858, after reading the published article, but it had not been carefully looked over before being set in type: " 'That' is constantly put for 'who,' which is a great vulgarity. Such an expression too as 'vowed him revenge' is extremely bad."

A Western Campaign
xviii, 18–21. June 19, 1858
A Negro-Hunt
xviii, 109–113. July 17, 1858
A Princess Royal
xviii, 153–56. July 31, 1858
The Last Victim of the Gauntlet
xviii, 222–24. Aug. 21, 1858

Gooden, James Chisholm |*J. C. Gooder*|, author of the pamphlet *Thames and Medway Admiralty Surveys. A Letter to the Members of the Select Committee of the House of Commons Appointed to Inquire into and Report upon the Basin and Dock Accommodation of the Royal Dockyards*, 1864. The brief pamphlet consists of "Observations on a Comparison of Various Maps and Charts of the River Medway, below Rochester," drawn up by a civil engineer at Gooden's request, and a prefatory letter by Gooden. In the letter Gooden states, on the basis of the observations, that until a new survey of the Medway has been completed, no true estimate can be formed of the deplorable condition of the Medway embankments. He stresses the importance of prompt investigation of the matter. The *H.W.* article listed below deals with the same subject – "the state of the Medway, and the desperate prospects of the dockyard of Chatham."

Gooden was a member of the Athenaeum Club. He lived during the 1850s at 33 Tavistock Square, and was thus a neighbour of Dickens.

What Is to Become of Chatham?
Morley & J. C. Gooder
xiv, 550–52. Dec. 20, 1856

Gore, Augustus Frederick |*Gore*|, 1826–1887, colonial Govt. official; son of Capt. Edward Gore, R.N. Served as private secretary to chief justice, then to second puisne judge, Ceylon, 1850–51; during next fifteen years served in various Govt. capacities in British Honduras and in British Guiana; then colonial secretary, Barbados, 1867–74; lieut.-governor of Tobago, 1877–80; of St. Vincent, 1880–86. F.R.G.S. C.M.G. (*Colonial Office List*, 1868 and later dates).

Gore's *H.W.* article recounts a shooting excursion in Ceylon stated to have been "in the month of June, 1840." The date 1840 is obviously a typographical error: Gore began his work in Ceylon in 1850; in 1840 he was a boy of fourteen, not (as is the writer of the article) a cheroot-smoking sportsman. The article itself also proves the date wrong: Gore states that in one village "our appearance was not ... hailed by the natives with cordiality – perhaps a ripple of the severities of August, 1848, had reached their quiet spot. ..."

Concerning the very ordinary article, Dickens wrote to Gore, July 4, 1851: "I am happy to retain your sporting adventure for insertion in Household Words. It is very graphic and agreeable and I have read it with pleasure" (Dawson's Book Shop *Catalogue 323*, where, however, Gore's first name is transcribed as "Augustis" and the date of the letter as "Fourth July, 1857").

Harper's reprinted Gore's article, without acknowledgment to *H.W.*

Boase

Shots in the Jungle
iii, 402–404. July 19, 1851

Gostick, Joseph, afterwards **Gostwick** |*Gostick*|, 1814–1887, translator, journalist, misc. writer. Contributed to *Douglas Jerrold's Shilling Magazine*, *People's Journal*, *Chambers's*; his "Trade-Unions, and the Relations of Capital and Labour" included in *Cobden Club Essays*, 2nd ser., 1872. Reviewed books on German literature and philosophy for *Athenaeum*.

Connected with *Daily News*, where his work consisted in part of translating items from German periodicals (J. A. Crowe, *Reminiscences*, p. 72). In 1848 published three numbers of *Gostick's Magazine for Life and Literature* (written, except for one item, entirely by Gostick). Published translations from and discussions of German literature, e.g., *The Spirit of German Poetry*, dedicated to Bulwer-Lytton; *Outlines of German Literature* (with Robert Harrison), dedicated to Carlyle; also *German Culture and Christianity*, 1882. Among his other writings were *Manual of Music; English Poets; English Grammar, Historical and Analytical*; and a handbook of American literature.

Dickens had in his library a copy of Gostick's *Spirit of German Poetry* (Stonehouse, *Catalogue*, p. 94).

Allibone

Routine xi, 550–52. July 7, 1855
The Golden Melon
xviii, 159–61. July 31, 1858

Graham. *Not identified.* At least five English writers named Graham were publishing verse in the mid-century.

VERSE
The Music of the Winds
xv, 156. Feb. 14, 1857

Grattan, Thomas Colley |*Colley Grattan*|, 1792–1864, misc. writer. Born in Dublin; studied law, served for a time in regiment of militia, then went to the Continent and turned to writing. British consul to the U.S., at Boston, 1839–46. Contributed to *New Monthly, Westm. Rev.*, and other periodicals. Author of *Highways and Byways*, 1823 (and later series), and other volumes of tales; also of historical novels, histories, a tragedy, books dealing with the U.S.

Grattan was several times in Dickens's company when Dickens was in Boston on his visit to America in 1842; he was a speaker at the banquet held in Feb. in Dickens's honour. In his *Civilized America*, Grattan referred briefly to Dickens's visit and to his *American Notes*. The two writers corresponded occasionally.

D.N.B.

American Changes of Names [lead]
xiv, 433–36. Nov. 22, 1856

Repr. in Vol. ii, chap. xi, of *Civilized America. By Thomas Colley Grattan.* 2 vols. London: Bradbury and Evans, 1859. Acknowledgment reads: "Portions of this chapter have already appeared in a London weekly periodical."

Greenwell, Dora, christened **Dorothy** |*Miss Dora Greenwell, Miss Greenwell, Dora Greenwell*|, 1821–1882, poet and essayist. Dedicated throughout her life to benevolent and humanitarian works – the welfare of the poor, the care of the afflicted, the prevention of cruelty to animals. Worked actively in support of Royal Albert Asylum for idiots and imbeciles. Contributed to *Ladies' Companion, North Brit. Rev., Good Words*, and other periodicals. Several of her poems included in *Home Thoughts and Home Scenes*, 1865, a collection of poems for children. From 1848 to 1876 published seven volumes of poems, e.g., *Carmina Crucis*, 1869; *The Soul's Legend*, 1873; was as true a poet, wrote Dr. John Brown, as George Herbert, Henry Vaughan, or Cowper (*North Brit. Rev.*, Feb. 1861). Published several books on the religious and spiritual life; the best known of these, *The Patience of Hope*, praised by Whittier for its earnest Christian spirit and its beauty of style. Wrote biography of Jean Lacordaire, 1867, and brief memoir of John Woolman, 1871.

In a letter of June 14, 1871, Charles Dickens, Jr., wrote to Miss Greenwell that a poem that she had submitted to *A.Y.R.* was too long for his present arrangements, but that he would be happy if at a future time he could use material that she might send (*A.Y.R.* Letter-Book).

Harper's reprinted two of Miss Greenwell's *H.W.* contributions: "The Railway

Station," with acknowledgment to *H.W.*; "Work Away!", without acknowledgment. *Good Words* in 1860 reprinted, with Miss Greenwell's initials, the slightly revised version of "The Railway Station" that had appeared in *Stories That Might Be True.*

D.N.B.

PROSE

The Eve of a Journey
VIII, 173–77. Oct. 22, 1853

VERSE

The Railway Station
I, 132–33. May 4, 1850

The Singer I, 574–75. Sept. 7, 1850

The 2 items repr. in *Stories That Might Be True with Other Poems. By Dora Greenwell.* London: William Pickering, 1850. Pub. in *H.W.* not acknowledged.

The Broken Chain II, 484. Feb. 15, 1851

Repr. in *Poems, By the Author of "The Patience of Hope."* Edinburgh: Alexander Strahan and Co., 1861. Pub. in *H.W.* not acknowledged.

Likeness in Difference
II, 524. Feb. 22, 1851

Work Away! III, 155–56. May 10, 1851

The Heart of England. (Suggested by Seeing a Venerable Oak in Warwickshire, Which Is Supposed to Occupy the Exact Centre of England)
IV, 156. Nov. 8, 1851

Friendship's Valentine
IV, 492–93. Feb. 14, 1852

Gretton, A. L. V. (Mrs. G.) |*Mrs. George Gretton,* Genoa|, contributor to periodicals; author of two books: *The Vicissitudes of Italy, since the Congress of Vienna,* 1859; and *The Englishwoman in Italy: Impressions of Life in the Roman States and Sardinia, during a Ten Years' Residence,* 1860. On the title page of her first book (preface dated from Genoa), the writer gave her name as A. L. V. Gretton; on the title page of the second, as Mrs. G. Gretton. The two books are by the same writer, as the following facts indicate: First, a review of *The Vicissitudes of Italy* in the *English Woman's Journal,* Aug. 1859, refers to the author of that book as "Mrs. Gretton" and states that she was "Resident in Italy, intimately acquainted with the history of the country and the people"; as the title of the second book records, Mrs. Gretton was resident in Italy for ten years. Second, in *The Vicissitudes of Italy,* the author tells of an Ancona woman "of abandoned character" who in Aug. 1849 brought about the execution of her aged husband by hiding a dagger in the palliasse of his bed and denouncing him to the Austrian occupation authorities for having a concealed weapon in his possession – "an incident that came under my own observation"; in *The Englishwoman in Italy,* the author relates the same incident (the wife is "a reckless, abandoned woman") as happening in Ancona in 1849 (though the weapon is here spoken of as a sword rather than a dagger, and the execution is stated to have taken place on the morning following the denunciation, rather than within two hours of the denunciation).

In *The Vicissitudes of Italy,* Mrs. Gretton incorporated three of her articles that had appeared in the *British and Foreign Evangelical Review,* 1857; in *The Englishwoman in Italy,* she included several of her articles that had appeared in *Chambers's* in 1853, and two of her articles that had appeared in the *English Woman's Journal,* 1859.

An unpublished letter from Dickens to Mrs. Gretton (to appear in Pilgrim *Letters*) indicates that Dickens returned to her an earlier *H.W.* contribution than the one that he accepted; an unpublished letter of March 1859 to Emile De la Rue (to appear in Pilgrim *Letters*) indicates that Dickens attempted to help Mrs. Gretton find a publisher for her first book (published May 1859, preface dated Jan. 27).

Harper's reprinted "The Blind Man's Wreath," without acknowledgment to *H.W.*

Brit. Mus. Cat.

The Blind Man's Wreath
IX, 51–56. March 4, 1854

Grey, Lady Anna Sophia (Ryder), *d.* 1893, wife of Sir George Grey, who was Home Secretary, 1846–52 (also later). In the Office Book, Wills assigned "Ballinglen" to himself alone. More than half of the item consists of a letter written, according to Wills's editorial comment, "to a friend" by "a lady who is nearly related to a Minister of State." Sending the letter, with other materials, to Wills, Dickens wrote, July 16, 1851: "The enclosed note and *its* enclosed papers are from Lady Grey (Lord Grey's wife). I have written to her. Can you make a chip out of them, and correct our orthography of the place?"

Lady Grey's letter tells of her trip to the Ballinglen experimental farm in Ireland and gives details concerning the farm. An account of the establishment and progress of the farm had appeared in Sidney Smith's "The Spade in Ireland," April 26, 1851. Such was the interest that the farm had aroused, wrote Smith, "that ladies of rank and quality ... have travelled alone and in mid-winter to the spot, to verify, with their own eyes, the reports of the overseer." The publication in *H.W.* of Lady Grey's letter was thus appropriate in that it gave readers an account of the farm by one of the "ladies of rank and quality"; the publication afforded also a means of correcting the misspelling (obviously a printer's mistranscription) that had appeared in Smith's article – "Ballinglew" for "Ballinglen."

Ballinglen [chip] III, 450–51. Aug. 2, 1851

Griffiths, Miss Eliza |*Eliza Griffiths,* Kinsale; *Miss Griffiths, Miss Griffith*|. *Not identified.* There seem to be no records that list a Griffiths living in Kinsale in the early 1850s; a George Griffith, 5 Brass Cock Hill, is listed in Valuation Papers of Ireland, compiled for Kinsale about 1852 (information from Cork City Library and from National Library of Ireland, Dublin).

"The Dumb Child" appears to have been Miss Griffiths's most popular *H.W.* contribution. It was reprinted in the Manchester *Courier*, Jan. 4, 1851, with acknowledgment to *H.W.*, and in *Harper's*, without acknowledgment; it was included in Henry T. Coates's *Fireside Encyclopaedia of Poetry. Comprising the Best Poems of the Most Famous Writers,* there marked "Author unknown." *Harper's* reprinted also, without acknowledgment to *H.W.*, "The Orphan's Dream of Christmas" and "From Gold to Gray."

VERSE

The Dumb Child II, 205. Nov. 23, 1850
The Orphan's Dream of Christmas Extra No. for Christmas 1851, pp. 16–17
Fragment of a Poet's Life IV, 444–45. Jan. 31, 1852
From Gold to Gray V, 104. April 17, 1852
The Tale Unfinished V, 152. May 1, 1852
The Fiery Trial. A Legend V, 248–50. May 29, 1852
The Lady and the Child V, 345–46. June 26, 1852
The Tower of the Seine VI, 60–61. Oct. 2, 1852
School Friendship VI, 181. Nov. 6, 1852
A Child's First Letter VI, 204. Nov. 13, 1852
The Mother's Story A Round of Stories (Christmas 1852), pp. 33–36
School and Summer VII, 421. July 2, 1853

Grumride[?], Mrs. *Not identified.* The contributor is an Englishwoman. Her article does not make clear whether she is a visitor in China or a resident.

New Year's Day in China XIX, 258–60. Feb. 12, 1859

Gunn, Charles Hains |*Mr. Gunn; C. H. Gunn,* 242 Noord Blaak, Rotterdam; *Gunn*|, *b.* 1823, in Norwich; language instructor, misc. writer. The *Adresboek van Rotterdam,* 1856, lists the resident at the above address as C. H. Gunn; *Wijkregister volkstelling,* 1849, gives Gunn's first name as Charles (information from Bibliotheek en Leeszalen der Gemeente, Rotterdam).

In his first book, *Desultory Hours*, 1844, Gunn included the poem "On Being Invited to Reside Abroad"; in it, he protested that no "proffered gold" could ever tempt him "in foreign lands to dwell." In 1848, nevertheless, became resident of Rotterdam; worked there as tutor and teacher of English. Latest Rotterdam directory in which his name appears is that for 1859; presumably left Rotterdam in that or the following year. In the 1860s was lecturer on English language and literature at Municipal Gymnasium, Amsterdam. Edited, in Amsterdam, the *English and American Monthly Reviewer*, 1864. Published works on English composition and phraseology, also readers and manuals for the use of students learning English. His "Rules for the Use of Will and Shall" reprinted, with Gunn's permission, in 2nd ed. (1858) of Sir Edmund W. Head's *"Shall" and "Will,"* as useful for "the guidance of foreigners." Compiled *The Golden Treasury of English Poetry*, Amsterdam, 1862, in which he included some of his own verses.

In his *Manual of Modern English Prose Literature*, 1862, Gunn included, in the section on Dickens, selections from *Pickwick*, *Copperfield*, *Old Curiosity Shop*, and *A Child's History of England*. He gave a brief sketch of Dickens's career, and commented on the vigour and naturalness of his character-drawing and the interest of his novels. "Of all our English writers," wrote Gunn, "perhaps none has succeeded in impressing his own characteristics on popular contemporaneous literature so effectually as this pleasing and successful writer."

Allibone

Smuggling Notes [chip]
XII, 538–39. Jan. 5, 1856

Slavery at Surinam
XV, 27–32. Jan. 10, 1857

A Yorkshire Tragedy
XIX, 147–51. Jan. 15, 1859

Gwynne, Francis |*Mr. Gywnne*|, squatter and land owner, New South Wales. Attended school in England, a nephew of Lord Brougham's being one of his schoolfellows. Emigrated to Australia. In partnership with his brothers Richard and Henry, took up Crown Lands outside the "Limits of Location." The Gwynne brothers are recorded, in 1848, as holding the Barratta cattle station, north of the Edward River, and the Werai, south of the Edward, in the Murrumbidgee squatting district. Barratta they held until 1853. When they dissolved their partnership, Henry Gwynne took over the Werai, holding it until 1876. In 1855 Francis Gwynne bought the Murgah station, adjoining the Barratta to the west (see map, end-paper, Ronald, *The Riverina*), with 750 head of cattle, for £6750. He sold the property in 1872. In the 1860s he was justice of the peace in the Moulamein district. His brother Henry had earlier served as justice of the peace (Ronald, *The Riverina*, pp. 55, 110, 112–13, et passim).

The two letters that constitute the *H.W.* item were addressed by the writer, according to the editorial comment, "to a relative in Cheshire" – apparently a brother named William. In the first letter the writer states: "When we separated from our partner, Mr. W., it became necessary to look for stations outside the limits of the colony. ... R. and I first took the stock up to the station on the Murray ..."; then "R. very kindly gave me the option" of remaining with the stock on the Murray or of forming new stations on the Edward. "R." is clearly the writer's brother Richard. In the second letter, telling of an attack by the blacks, the writer states: "... there were only four of us at Barratta, viz., H., (who had just arrived), myself and two men. ..." "H." seems clearly to be the writer's brother Henry. The writer, therefore, is the third of the Gwynne brothers in Australia, i.e., Francis.

Gwynne's letters record the raids of the blacks on the Gwynnes' cattle and their attacks on the Gwynnes' two stations. *H.W.* published the letters to "furnish some idea of how new localities are colonised, by such enterprising pioneers" as the writer.

In his *Reminiscences of Australian Early Life*, 1893 (pp. 66–70), John Phillips gives an account of an attack on one of the Gwynnes' stations and of one of the cattle raids.

Two Letters from Australia
Mr. Gywnne & W.H.W.
I, 475–80. Aug. 10, 1850

H

Hale. *Not identified.* The contributor recounts a shooting excursion that he made in Albania in 1851 in company with two other English sportsmen. The three went by yacht from the Isle of Wight to Malta, to Corfu, then to the Albanian coast.

Three Guns in Albania
V, 16–19. March 20, 1852

Hall, Fanny. *Not identified.*

VERSE
The Lattice XV, 445. May 9, 1857
My Vision XIX, 491–92. April 23, 1859

Haly, William Taylor |*Mr. W. T. Haly, Mr. Haly*|, Parliamentary reporter, politician. Published *Report of the Proceedings at the Bread Street Ward Scrutiny*, 1843, to make available to Londoners information affecting their franchise; and *The Opinions of Sir Robert Peel, Expressed in Parliament and in Public*, 1843, a compilation found valuable by many M.P.'s. In 1857 and in 1859 unsuccessfully contested the Parliamentary election in Poole. In *Poole Election*, 1865, a pamphlet published by the committee for promoting the return to Parliament of H. D. Seymour and Charles Waring, was accused of having traduced the character of the two candidates.

Haly was a member of the reporting staff engaged for the *Daily News* on the establishment of that journal (McCarthy and Robinson, *The "Daily News" Jubilee*, p. 9, citing Thomas Britton). He was probably acquainted with Dickens.

Brit. Mus. Cat.

Law at a Low Price
Mr. W. T. Haly & W.H.W.
I, 176–80. May 18, 1850
Savings' Bank Defalcations
Mr. Haly & W.H.W.
I, 267–70. June 15, 1850
The Royal Rotten Row Commission
Mr. Haly & W.H.W.
I, 274–76. June 15, 1850

Hamilton, Alexander Henry Abercromby |*A. H. A. Hamilton.* Address for 1st entry: Millbrook House [? word unclear], Exeter|, 1829–1911, public official. Student at Eton. B.A. Oxford, 1850. Justice of the peace for Devonshire; also deputy lieutenant. Shareholder in East India Co. (*East-India Register*, 1850 and other dates). Delivered lectures and addresses, some of which he published: *Paris*, 1868; *Rome, Ancient and Modern* (two lectures), 1868; both items published for benefit of Albert Memorial Museum, Exeter (Macmillan, *Bibliographical Catalogue*); *William Pitt and William Gladstone*, 1887. Contributed to *Fraser's*. Edited *Note Book of Sir John Northcote*, 1877. Author of *Ballads from Hebrew History*, 1873; and *Quarter Sessions from Queen Elizabeth to Queen Anne*, 1878.

The first item listed below is not a joint writing of the two contributors whose names are attached to it; it consists of two separate sections (unrelated except by the fact that both are motivated by the Indian Mutiny), placed under the joint heading obviously by the editorial office. The first section – the longer – has no subtitle; the second has the subtitle "Indian English." The order of names attached to the item indicates that the first section is by Townsend, the second by Hamilton. The payment allotment – two guineas to Townsend, one guinea to Hamilton – confirms this ascription. "Indian English" protests against the "barbaric words" appearing in news accounts from India. "Am I to sit down to my Times," asks the writer, "with a Tamil lexicon on one side and a Teloogoo on the other?" "Hard Roads," based on a French source, deals with taxes exacted from travellers in Japan. The item was paid for by post-office order.

Allibone

Indian Recruits and Indian English *Townsend & A. H. A. Hamilton* XVI, 319–22. Oct. 3, 1857

Hard Roads *A. H. A. Hamilton & W.H.W.* XVI, 534–36. Dec. 5, 1857

Hammersley, James Astbury |*J. A. Hammersley*, School of Art, Manchester|, 1815–1869, painter. Received art education under James Baker Pyne. Head master of Manchester School of Design, 1849–62; president of Manchester Academy of Fine Arts, 1857–61. Commissioned by Prince Albert to paint two scenes in Germany. Exhibited at Royal Academy and elsewhere. Published an address on Continental schools of art and an occasional article. Did lithotint drawings of sketches for G. R. Dartnell's *Brief Narrative of the Shipwreck of the Transport "Premier,"* 1845.

"Children of All Work," *A.Y.R.*, June 8, 1861, quoted Hammersley on the schooling of working children in and about Manchester.

D.N.B.

To Let [chip] XIX, 443–44. April 9, 1859

Hannay, James |*J. Hannay, Mr. Hannay, Hannay*|, 1827–1873, journalist and author. After his early school years, educated himself largely by study and wide reading. From age thirteen to eighteen served in Royal Navy; dismissed, 1845, on charges of insubordination. Turned to journalism; lectured on literary subjects. From 1868 was British consul in Barcelona. Friend of Thackeray and Carlyle. Early in his journalistic career, founded a penny comic weekly, *Pasquin*, with Sutherland Edwards. Also worked with Edwards on the *Puppet-Show*. Thereafter contributed to *Punch, United Service Magazine, Leader, Athenaeum, Quart. Rev., Illus. Times, Welcome Guest, Cornhill,* and other periodicals. Also contributed various series of articles to newspapers, e.g., "From Our Own Correspondent," to New York *Tribune*; "From an Englishman in Spain," to *Pall Mall Gazette*. Editor, 1860–64, of Edinburgh *Courant*. Reprinted from periodicals various of his sketches, stories, and critical articles. Author of two 3-vol. novels: *Singleton Fontenoy, R.N.*, 1850, and *Eustace Conyers*, 1855; also *Studies on Thackeray*, 1869.

Hannay had little admiration for Dickens or for Dickens's writings. In one of his letters to the Dumfries *Courier*, at the time of Dickens's separation from his wife, he remarked on Dickens's lack of judgment in communicating to "the whole world" his "private domesticities"; in another, commenting on the Garrick Club affair, he wrote of Thackeray's superiority over his "assailants and their backers-up" (Worth, *James Hannay*, pp. 80–81). As a novelist, wrote Hannay, Dickens displayed "the faults belonging to a too zealous and narrow worship of modern social ideas, and a too great neglect of established, classical, and ancient literature" (*A Course of English Literture*, p. 321).

Dickens had few comments on Hannay's *H.W.* contributions. He supplied the title – "In the Name of the Prophet – Smith!" – for Hannay's article on Joseph Smith and Mormonism. Concerning it he wrote to Wills (July 1851): "I wish Hannay would not imitate Carlyle. Pray take some of the innumerable dashes out of his article – and for God's sake don't leave in anything about such a man [i.e., Smith] believing in himself – which he has no right to do and which would by inference justify almost anything." Smith's belief in himself is mentioned in the article, but not stressed. Dickens also supplied the title for Hannay's "Graves and Epitaphs" – and again he instructed Wills (Oct. 7, 1852): "See to the dashes. ... They are at present innumerable." This was an article that Miss Burdett-Coutts liked (*Heart of Charles Dickens*, ed. Johnson, p. 209).

In his preface to *Sand and Shells*, 1854, Hannay stated that the sketches that comprise the book were reprinted from the *United Service Magazine* and from *H.W.* None of the sketches are from *H.W.*, though H.M.S. *Bustard* and Captain Jigger of *Sand and Shells* find occasional mention in the *H.W.* articles.

Hannay contributed to the early numbers of *A.Y.R.* Twenty years after his death, the *A.Y.R.* article "Some Forgotten Novelists" (July 22, 1893) mentioned him as a writer who had "hardly received due justice" and was no longer read by the general public; but there would always be a few readers, maintained the *A.Y.R.* writer, who would regard *Singleton Fontenoy* as a "cherished" possession.

Hannay's "English Songs" was included in the Putnam volume of selections from *H.W.*: *Home and Social Philosophy*, 2nd ser.

D.N.B.

Christmas in the Navy
II, 298–300. Dec. 21, 1850
A Metaphysical Mystery
II, 359–60. Jan. 4, 1851
Pleb-Biddlecumb Education
II, 479–80. Feb. 8, 1851
A Salt Growl II, 502–504. Feb. 15, 1851
The Sailors' Home
II, 612–15. March 22, 1851
The Blue-Jacket Agitation
III, 36–41. April 5, 1851
The Great Coffee Question [lead]
III, 49–53. April 12, 1851
The Palace of Flowers
III, 117–20. April 26, 1851
Our Phantom Ship in Dock
III, 277–80. June 14, 1851
In the Name of the Prophet – Smith! [lead] *Hannay & W.H.W.*
III, 385–89. July 19, 1851
Edward Baines *Hannay & W.H.W.*
III, 414–19. July 26, 1851
The "Dreadnought"
III, 516–19. Aug. 23, 1851
Lambs to Be Fed
III, 544–49. Aug. 30, 1851
The London Tavern [lead]
Hannay & W.H.W.
IV, 73–77. Oct. 18, 1851
English Songs IV, 173–78. Nov. 15, 1851
The "Merchant Seaman's Fund"
IV, 274–77. Dec. 13, 1851
The Queen's Head *Hannay & W.H.W.*
IV, 510–13. Feb. 21, 1852
The Sister-Ship V, 138–40. April 24, 1852
Bold Admiral Blake
V, 326–31. June 19, 1852
London Bridge in the Afternoon
V, 570–72. Aug. 28, 1852
Graves and Epitaphs
VI, 105–109. Oct. 16, 1852
Joseph Train VII, 475–77. July 16, 1853
An Old Scholar XI, 76–82. Feb. 24, 1855

Harding, Joseph. Address: Amersham Park Cottage, New Cross. Joseph Harding, Esq., is first listed at the above address in Kelly's *Post Office London Directory*, 1860.

The contributor seems clearly to be the Joseph Harding who in the 1850s was "Travelling Secretary of the Associate Institution for the Protection of Women," a zealous worker for "the suppression of female vice, and the promotion of virtuous principles among the young" (note by editor of *Christian Family Record* in Harding, *The River of Death*). In his crusade against sexual immorality, Harding delivered to young men, as also to their parents and guardians, earnest, plain-spoken lectures on the subject; commended by clergymen and laymen on judicious manner in which he handled the delicate matter. On this evil, as also on contributing evils of drunkenness and desecration of the Sabbath, wrote articles and letters in *Christian Family Record* and published various tracts (some being reprints of items from the periodical); edited also two tracts by Henry Ward Beecher.

The *H.W.* poem assigned to Harding is a plea for sympathy and help for "our sister" – the woman once young, blooming, and fair, now fallen to want and despair and misery; the poem assigns no specific reason for the woman's fall from her former happy state. The lines "Weep for our sister, / Pray for our sister, Succour our sister" are similar in phraseology and spirit to the admonition in Harding's

River of Death that Christians "*pity the drunkard, weep for the fallen,* watch over the young. ..."

Brit. Mus. Cat.

VERSE

My Sister xvi, 300. Sept. 26, 1857

Hardman, Sir William |*Hardman*|, 1828–1890, public official, newspaper editor. B.A. Cambridge, 1851; M.A. 1854. Admitted at Inner Temple, 1848; called to the bar, 1852. Practised for some years as equity draftsman and conveyancer. Stood as Conservative candidate for East Surrey, 1868. Chairman (unpaid) of Surrey Quarter Sessions, 1865–90 ("Preface," *A Mid-Victorian Pepys*, ed. Ellis); recorder of Kingston-on-Thames, 1875–90. Served as alderman of Surrey County Council; mayor of Kingston-on-Thames, 1870. Knighted, 1885, for his long public service. Contributed an occasional article to periodicals. Editor, 1872–90, of *Morning Post*. Edited and published John McDouall Stuart's *Explorations in Australia*, 1864. F.R.G.S.

Hardman had a wide circle of friends – among them, in particular, Shirley Brooks and George Meredith. He was no friend of Dickens. On the occasion of one of Dickens's resignations from the Garrick Club, Hardman noted that the Garrick would undoubtedly "survive the terrible blow" (*A Mid-Victorian Pepys*, p. 81). Dickens's wife was a friend of the Hardmans, at times a guest at their London home. Dickens's treatment of her seemed to them shameful. Particularly Dickens's failure to communicate with Mrs. Dickens at the time of the death of the son Walter seemed to Hardman shabby and unforgiveable conduct: "If anything were wanting to sink Charles Dickens to the lowest depth of my esteem, *this* fills up the measure of his iniquity. As a writer, I admire him; as a man, I despise him" (*Letters and Memoirs*, ed. Ellis, p. 148).

The article that the Office Book assigns to Hardman is a discussion of a fourteenth-century cookery-book – a subject in line with Hardman's connoisseurship in matters of food and drink. *A Mid-Victorian Pepys*, p. 190n, credits the article to William Hardman.

Boase

The Roll of Cookery [chip]

xv, 549–50. June 6, 1857

Harper, Mr. |*Mr. Harper, Harper, Mr. Harpur, Harpur*|. *Not identified.* Contributed more verses to *H.W.* than did any other writer except Miss Procter and Ollier. No clue in Office Book as to his identity. Payment for some of his items marked "Enclosed & fetched"; payment for others made by cheque; two of cheque payments marked as by "C.D." The contributor cannot be the Manchester poet William Harper (1806–1857), author of *The Genius and Other Poems* and *Cain and Abel*, since that writer, aside from contributing to the Manchester *Keepsake*, 1844, published all his shorter poems in the Manchester *Courier* (obit., Manchester *Courier*, Jan. 31, 1857). Moreover, William Harper's poems, as *D.N.B.* states, contain "good and even lofty lines." The statement cannot be made of the prosaic verses of the *H. W.* contributor.

In June 1851, Harper was paid "10£ for six poems." The poems include "Knowledge and Ignorance," June 21, and the four poems assigned to Harper in the three following numbers, but not "Change and the Changeless" (for which payment is specifically recorded as £1.1.0 "Enclosed"). The sixth poem included in the £10.0.0 is probably "Smiles," July 19, recorded in the Office Book without authorship or payment notation. The poem is included in the listing below.

"Human Brotherhood," the first item assigned to Harper (and included in the listing below), is probably by Prince. See Prince (below).

Harper's reprinted "The Warnings of the Past" and "The Mighty Magician," without acknowledgment to *H.W.*

VERSE

Human Brotherhood

ii, 229. Nov. 30, 1850

The Chords of Love

ii, 334–35. Dec. 28, 1850

A Winter Sermon
II, 372–73. Jan. 11, 1851
A World at Peace
II, 565–66. March 8, 1851
A Vagrant's Deathbed
III, 13. March 29, 1851
The Grave of Faction
III, 60–61. April 12, 1851
The Blast of War III, 132. May 3, 1851
Knowledge and Ignorance
III, 301. June 21, 1851
The Warnings of the Past
III, 331–32. June 28, 1851
The Song of the Sabre
III, 348. July 5, 1851
The Claims of Labour III, 356. July 5, 1851
The Use of Wealth III, 372. July 12, 1851
Smiles III, 396–97. July 19, 1851
Change and the Changeless
III, 539. Aug. 30, 1851
The Last Words of Summer
III, 612. Sept. 20, 1851
Uncultured Gifts IV, 12–13. Sept. 27, 1851
The Law of Mercy IV, 60. Oct. 11, 1851
Room in the World
IV, 228–29. Nov. 29, 1851
A Lesson of Hope IV, 305. Dec. 20, 1851
The Voice of Cheer IV, 324. Dec. 27, 1851
The Source of Joy IV, 397. Jan. 17, 1852
Forgive! IV, 420. Jan. 24, 1852
Roll On! IV, 469. Feb. 7, 1852
The Mighty Magician
IV, 564. March 6, 1852
The Use of Flowers
IV, 588. March 13, 1852
The Thinker and the Doer
V, 464. July 31, 1852
The Path of Faith
V, 561–62. Aug. 28, 1852
The Feast of Life VII, 108. April 2, 1853
The Casket VIII, 228. Nov. 5, 1853

Harris. *Not identified.* Author of two volumes of poems, both published anonymously: *Wandering Cries* (titled from "In Memoriam"), 1860, and *Songs from Fairyland and Other Poems*, 1863. In the first volume included three of his *H.W.* poems, stating that he reserved the others "for a future collection"; in the second volume included all his *H.W.* poems, as well as three from *A.Y.R.* Obviously attached some importance to the fact that his poems had appeared in Dickens's periodicals; in *Songs from Fairyland* gave them a separate half-title ("Contributions to 'Household Words' and 'All the Year Round' ") and stated the month and year in which each had appeared in one or the other of the two periodicals. In both volumes acknowledged Dickens's permission to reprint.

Payment for the first, second, and fifth item made by post-office order; for the third, by cheque.

VERSE
Exiled IX, 440–41. June 24, 1854
Mary IX, 560–61. July 29, 1854
Alice XIII, 420. May 17, 1856
Ocean XIII, 493. June 7, 1856
Love of Beauty XIV, 228–29. Sept. 20, 1856
The Summer-Land XV, 373. April 18, 1857
Unopened Buds XVI, 36. July 11, 1857
Sleep XVII, 205. Feb. 13, 1858

The last 3 items listed above repr. in *Wandering Cries* [anon.]. London: Partridge and Co., 1860. All 8 items repr. in *Songs from Fairyland and Other Poems* [anon.]. London: Whittaker & Co., 1863. Pub. in *H.W.* acknowledged in both books.

Harrold, C. B., 1816–1883; and **his sister** |*Harrold*|. In the Great Register of Voters, 1869–71, Alpine Co., Calif., Harrold is listed as Christian Bayfield Harrold; so also in the Great Register, 1871–78, San Joaquin Co.; the records of Linden Cemetery, San Joaquin Co., give his first name as "Christopher," as do the *H.W.* items. Information concerning the sister may appear under her married name (not known) in California records; "A Woman's Experience in California" refers to her as "L."

The Harrolds were working-class people of Leicestershire. Late in 1848, Harrold, his wife Charlotte, and their children, also Henry Thornlac ("Mr. T." in *H.W.*), and, according to *H.W.*, Harrold's married sister "L." and her husband, emigrated to New Zealand; remained there about nine months. On confirmation of the news of the California gold discovery, sailed for San Francisco. Lived some months in Stockton, where Harrold worked as carpenter, and his sister earned money by dress-making, washing, and cooking (*H.W.*). Then Harrold and Thornlac purchased Oak Ranch on the Calaveras River, some twenty miles from Stockton; farmed the land and kept a "road-side house" (*H.W.*), where they sold provisions and provided lodging for persons on their way to the diggings. About 1855, Harrold bought out Thornlac's interest in Oak Ranch; became successful farmer and later sheep-raiser.

The first item listed below consists, with some editorial comment, of extracts from letters written, from California, by Harrold and his sister to relatives in England. Wills assigned the item to himself, obviously on the basis that he wrote the editorial comment. No payment is recorded. The second item consists of a letter from the sister, introduced by a paragraph of editorial comment. The Office Book assigns it to "Harrold (per Forster) & W.H.W." and records £1.1.0 payment. *H.W.* published the letters as they were obviously written, with various lapses in grammar.

Hist. of San Joaquin County (entry: Christopher Henry Harrold)

A Woman's Experience in California [chip] II, 450–51. Feb. 1, 1851
A "Ranch" in California [chip] *Harrold & W.H.W.* III, 471–72. Aug. 9, 1851

Hart, Ernest Abraham |*E. A. Hart, Hart*|, 1835–1898, medical journalist, sanitary reformer. Educated at City of London School; his prize school essay printed in *Three Essays on ... King Lear. By Pupils of the City of London School,* 1851. Studied medicine at St. George's Hospital. M.R.C.S. 1856. Ophthalmic surgeon at St. Mary's Hospital, 1863–68; held also other important professional appointments. President of Harveian Society, 1868. Hon. D.C.L. Univ. of Durham, 1893. Individually, and as chairman of various organizations, worked for improvement of working conditions of naval and military medical officers, for enactment of measures to prevent spread of disease, for medical care of the sick poor, for protection of infants subjected to baby farming, and other reforms. Adviser to George Smith of Smith, Elder & Co. on the firm's publication of medical works. On staff of *Lancet;* edited *British Medical Jour.,* 1867–97 (except for one year). Wrote for medical journals; also occasionally for general periodicals, e.g., *Fortnightly, Nineteenth Century.* Published addresses on matters of health and sanitation; books on medical subjects.

Hart began contributing to *H.W.* at age eighteen. Dickens later became acquainted with him, apparently, through their common interest in the welfare of the poor. In a letter to Hart, Feb. 1866, concerning a meeting of the Association for the Improvement of the Infirmaries of the London Workhouses, of which Hart was secretary, Dickens referred to Hart's having "manfully" called attention to the deplorable conditions in workhouse infirmaries.

Harper's reprinted "Lives of Plants," without acknowledgment to *H.W.*

D.N.B. suppl. 1901

The History of a Coal Cell [chip] VIII, 354–55. Dec. 10, 1853
Lives of Plants VIII, 483–86. Jan. 21, 1854
Birth of Plants [lead] IX, 1–4. Feb. 18, 1854
Plant Architecture IX, 129–32. March 25, 1854
Nature's Changes of Dress IX, 304–306. May 13, 1854
Minerals That We Eat XIII, 437–42. May 24, 1856
XIII, 486–90. June 7, 1856
Nature's Greatness in Small Things XVI, 511–13. Nov. 28, 1857
The Boiled Beef of Old England [chip] XVII, 522–23. May 15, 1858

Harvey, Mr. Cattle rancher in the Argentine. Editorial comment prefaced to the first instalment of "Life in an Estancia" identifies the contributor as a Northumbrian "many years settled in South

America" and working for the past four years as manager of a ranch in the pampas of Buenos Ayres. The comment states that the article consists of passages selected from letters written by the rancher to relatives in England. The Office Book records the three instalments as arriving at the editorial office through the agency of Charles Knight, and records payment as handed to Knight. Ten years after the publication of the article in *H.W.*, there appeared in *A.Y.R.* (May 11, 1861) "Cattle Farmers in the Pampas." It began with the announcement: "Some time ago I sent you a general description of an estancia, or cattle farm, in La Plata." A footnote attached to the announcement referred the reader to the *H.W.* "Life in an Estancia." In his *A.Y.R.* article, the writer described himself as "an old La Plata cattle farmer" who had lived in the pampas for fifteen years and was "well contented with his lot."

The contributor was a man of some education. Occasional literary references appear in his *H.W.* article. He mentions *Don Quixote*, one of Peter Nicholson's works on mathematics, and Adam Smith's *Wealth of Nations* as among the books in his pampas library.

He would seem to be the C. S. Harvey, Esq., Buenos Ayres, listed in John Timbs, *Curiosities of London*, 1855, as a subscriber to that work.

Life in an Estancia
II, 190–92. Nov. 16, 1850, and the 2 following nos.

Harvey. The two items listed below deal with various scientific experiments; they seem clearly to be by one contributor. The first article describes the effect of nux vomica and strychnine on animals and human beings; it discusses the substances as articles of the pharmacopoeia, names possible antidotes, and describes tests for detection of the poisons. The writer's knowledge of physiology, medicine, and materia medica suggests that he may be Alexander Harvey, M.D., physician to the Aberdeen Royal Infirmary, professor of materia medica in the Univ. of Aberdeen, and co-author of *Syllabus of Materia Medica*, 1873. The second article discusses experiments to detect silver in sea water; among the experiments referred to is that mentioned in "Metal in Sea-Water," the *H.W.* "filler" taken from the *Athenaeum*.

Strychnine XIII, 420–24. May 17, 1856
Two Millions of Tons of Silver
XV, 443–45. May 9, 1857

Hawker, Charlotte Elizabeth (I'Ans) [*Mrs. Hawker*], *b.* ca. 1782, *d.* 1863, first wife of Robert Stephen Hawker (below). Well educated; a good German scholar. According to her husband's biographers, was a charming woman with sound judgment, discretion, and a sense of humour. Was more than twenty years older than Hawker, whom she married in 1823. Her husband's *Records of the Western Shore* dedicated to her. Published translation, from the German, of A. G. Öhlenschläger's ballad "Earl Sinclair," *Sharpe's*, Dec. 6, 1845; and, also from the German, two religious tales for children: *Follow Me*, 1844; and *The Manger of the Holy Night*, 1847 (from Guido Gorres); her husband had a part in both little books. The translations from the German included in editions of Hawker's poems were the joint work of husband and wife. "The Wreck," an original poem by Mrs. Hawker (except for the last three stanzas, which are by Hawker), appeared in her husband's *Ecclesia*, 1840, without indication that it was her writing (Byles, ed., *Cornish Ballads & Other Poems*, by R. S. Hawker, p. 291).

The story that Mrs. Hawker contributed to *H.W.* her husband referred to as a "Translation from Toni." For it, he stated, she received £1.10.0, "which she gave at once to a Fund ... to feed our Starving Poor" (Byles, *Life and Letters of R. S. Hawker*, p. 252). The Office Book records payment of £1.11.6.

Biblio. Cornub.

Too Late VIII, 546–49. Feb. 4, 1854

Hawker, Robert Stephen |*Hawker, Mr. Hawker*|, 1803–1875, divine, poet. B.A. Oxford, 1828; M.A. 1836. In Dec. 1834, instituted to vicarage of Morwenstow, a village on Cornish coast with which his name has ever since been associated. In last hours of his life received into Roman Catholic church, a proceeding that aroused a bitter periodical controversy. Distributed some of his verses first as fugitive leaflets; contributed to *N. & Q.*, *Willis's Current Notes*, the *Lamp*, and other periodicals. Published *Tendrils*, 1821; *Records of the Western Shore*, 1832; *Ecclesia*, 1840; *Echoes from Old Cornwall*, 1846; *The Quest of the Sangraal*, 1864; and other works.

Hawker came into correspondence with Dickens in 1852, as a result of the appearance in *H.W.*, Oct. 30, of Forster's article "The Reason Why," which quoted, as in entirety an ancient ballad, a version of Hawker's Trelawny ballad. In a "chip" in a following number, Forster corrected "our mistake," and gave praise to Hawker's *Ecclesia* (in which the ballad had appeared) as a volume of poems "remarkable for their feeling and grace of expression," deserving more recognition than they had received.

The incident led to Hawker's being asked to contribute to *H.W.* "I am in cordial correspondence with Dickens," wrote Hawker, Nov. 30, to his brother, "and I am to contribute to *Household Words*, and 'cannot send MSS. too often.'" Hawker sent only three contributions, but he noted with satisfaction that Dickens "*does* pay" (Byles, *Life and Letters of R. S. Hawker*, pp. 249, 252). It was not until Hawker began contributing to *A.Y.R.* some ten years later that he found occasion to complain of Dickens's editorial arrangements: the remuneration was "Scrivener's pay" – no more than a solicitor paid his copying clerk; expected cheques failed to arrive; Wills neglected to acknowledge contributions; he gave absurd or irrelevant reasons for rejecting papers; and he mutilated Hawker's articles. From one paper he cut out the "best parts" and put in "some trash of his own"; from another he cut out a paragraph and inserted it in a paper not by Hawker. "... it is most debasing to have one's MSS. at the mercy of such a Man as Wills." Nor did Dickens escape unscathed: mentioning "The Uncommercial Traveller" and one of his rejected papers, Hawker commented: "It does not really annoy me that I cannot write down to the Cockney slipslop of modern serial literature" (*Life and Letters*, chap. xxiii, passim).

D.N.B.

PROSE

The Gauger's Pocket
VI, 515–17. Feb. 12, 1853

The Light of Other Days [chip]
VIII, 305–306. Nov. 26, 1853

The 2 items repr. in *Footprints of Former Men in Far Cornwall. By R. S. Hawker, Vicar of Morwenstow*. London: John Russell Smith, 1870. Pub. in *H.W.* not acknowledged. "The Gauger's Pocket" contains the poem titled "The Smuggler's Song" in Alfred Wallis's edition of Hawker's *Poetical Works*.

VERSE

The Bush with the Bleeding Breast
VI, 324–25. Dec. 18, 1852

Repr. as "Modryb Marya" in *The Cornish Ballads and Other Poems of the Rev. R. S. Hawker, Vicar of Morwenstow*. Oxford and London: James Parker and Co., 1869. Pub. in *H.W.* not acknowledged. In his edition of Hawker's *Poetical Works*, Wallis dates the poem 1838; so do other editors.

Head, John Oswald |*J. O. Head*, Hexham; *Head*|, solicitor. *History, Topography, and Directory of Northumberland*, 1855, lists John Oswald Head, Hexham, as solicitor, member of the firm of Charles Head and Son. The firm were commissioners in chancery, common pleas, and exchequer courts. Head's articles criticize antiquated statutes, cumbersome and costly legal procedures, the malpractices of joint stock companies, etc. Content and style make it evident that all the articles are by the same writer.

A Perplexing Parenthesis [chip]
XIII, 274–75. April 5, 1856

Copy of Court-Roll [chip]
xiv, 46. July 26, 1856
Signals and Engine-Drivers [chip]
xiv, 179–80. Sept. 6, 1856
The Lawyer's Best Friends [chip]
xv, 318–19. April 4, 1857
Slow Conveyancing [chip]
xvii, 284–85. March 6, 1858
A Needle of Sense in a Haystack of Law [lead] *Head & W.H.W.*
xvii, 385–87. April 10, 1858
All Smoke [lead]
xvii, 529–31. May 22, 1858
My Model Director
xix, 299–301. Feb. 26, 1859

Heraud, John Abraham |*H. Heraud, Heraud*|, 1799–1887, poet and dramatist. The initial recorded for Heraud in the Office Book entry for his first contribution cannot be read as other than "H"; it may be intended for "A," or it may be a misrecording. Various contemporaries recorded Heraud's name incorrectly: Howitt, in *Homes and Haunts of the Most Eminent British Poets*, wrote it as "Herraud"; Percy Fitzgerald, in *Memories of Charles Dickens*, as "S. A. Heraud"; E. L. Blanchard, in a diary entry (*Life and Reminiscences of E. L. Blanchard*, ed. Scott and Howard), as "James Abraham Héraud"; Morley, in *Early Papers and Some Memories*, as "John Anthony Heraud"; the *Illus. London News*, obit., April 30, 1887, as "John H. Heraud."

Heraud was privately educated; for some time engaged in business as law stationer, but found the duties distasteful. Early began writing verse. By long and patient study, became a man of wide and varied erudition. Was excellent German scholar; attempted to popularize in England the philosophy of Schelling. Friend of Southey, who gave him encouragement and advice on literary career, and helpful criticism on his poems; friend of Wordsworth, Coleridge, Lockhart, Carlyle; much influenced by Coleridge and Carlyle. Was never very successful financially; at one time became bankrupt through no fault of his own; admitted a brother of the Charterhouse, 1873. Contributed to *Quart. Rev., Howitt's Journal, Chambers's, Temple Bar, Belgravia,* and other periodicals. Assisted in editorship of *Fraser's*, 1830–33; editor of *Sunbeam*, 1838–39; subsequently of *Monthly Magazine* and of *Christian Monthly Magazine.* Dramatic critic for *Athenaeum*, 1843–68; for *Illus. London News*, 1849–80. As poet, best known for his two epics, *The Descent into Hell*, 1830 (dedicated to Southey), and *The Judgement of the Flood*, 1834. His dramas *Videna* and *Wife or No Wife* both successfully produced; wrote also other dramatic works. Published an oration on Coleridge, 1834; a life of Savonarola, 1843; *Shakspere, His Inner Life As Intimated in His Works*, 1865; and other writings.

Heraud and Dickens were evidently acquainted. Dickens addressed at least one letter to him. Dickens subscribed to the fund raised for Heraud in 1848 (letter to G. H. Lewes, Sept. 11); in 1865 he mentioned in a letter to Bulwer-Lytton (Oct. 28) the possibility of Heraud's presenting himself as a candidate to receive assistance from the Guild of Literature and Art. Heraud reviewed, in the *Athenaeum*, Dec. 20, 1845, *The Cricket on the Hearth.* He found the story equal in "style and careful execution" to the best of Dickens's other writings; in many parts, he wrote, it "rises to a tone of sentiment that, in its elevation, must command the sympathy of the wisest and the best."

Heraud's first *H.W.* contribution contained the suggestion that theatres pay into a public fund a fee for performing the plays of Shakespeare and other early dramatists, the fund to be used for the maintenance of a National Theatre and for the encouragement and support of contemporary poetic drama. To this suggestion was attached the editorial footnote, probably by Dickens: "This is the individual Play-goer's 'Crotchet.' We doubt its efficacy, and do not adopt it." Heraud's last *H.W.* contribution was obviously motivated by Oxenford's "Touching the Lord Hamlet," Oct. 17, 1857.

Men of the Time, 1868, states that Heraud was a contributor to *A.Y.R.*

Harper's reprinted "A Way to Remember," without acknowledgment to *H.W.*

D.N.B.

PROSE

Crotchets of a Playgoer II, 188–90. Nov. 16, 1850

Hints for the Self-Educated XIII, 575–76. June 28, 1856

A Way to Remember XIII, 616–18. July 12, 1856

The North against the South XIV, 190–92. Sept. 6, 1856

Quiet People XIV, 256–58. Sept. 27, 1856

Re-Touching the Lord Hamlet XVI, 545–48. Dec. 5, 1857

VERSE

Weariness XV, 515–16. May 30, 1857

Hervey, Eleanora Louisa (Montagu) |*Mrs. T. K. Hervey*|, 1811–1903, author. Early began contributing to annuals and publishing poems in book form, e.g., *The Bard of the Sea-Kings*, 1833; *Edith of Graystock*, 1833. Accorded a compliment by Leigh Hunt in "Blue-Stocking Revels," 1837. In 1843 married Thomas Kibble Hervey (below). Contributed to *Churchman's Family Magazine*, *Chambers's*, *Athenaeum*, *Once a Week*, *Ladies' Companion*, *Illus. London News*, *A.Y.R.*, and other periodicals. Her contributions to the *Illus. London News*, stated the *Cyclopaedia of Female Biography*, 1857, had made her name "familiar to hundreds of thousands of readers, both at home and abroad." Published stories for children, gift books, tales; *Snooded Jessaline*, 1865, a 3-vol. novel.

Allibone

VERSE

Bathilda XIX, 62. Dec. 18, 1858

Repr. in *Our Legends and Lives. A Gift for All Seasons. By Eleanora Louisa Hervey.* London: Trübner and Co., 1869. Book contains also items repr. from *A.Y.R.*: permission to reprint acknowledged to proprietor of *A.Y.R.*

Hervey, Thomas Kibble |*T. K. Hervey*|, 1799–1859, poet, critic, editor. Educated at Manchester grammar school. Articled to solicitor; began study for the bar; for two years a student at Cambridge. Both his legal studies and his university career ended by his sudden prominence as poet on the appearance of "Australia." Contributed to annuals; edited the annuals *Friendship's Offering* and *Amaranth*. In 1831 began writing for *Athenaeum*; editor of *Athenaeum*, 1846–53. Later contributed to *Art Journal*. Published *The Poetical Sketch-Book*, 1829; *Illustrations of Modern Sculpture*, 1832 (some parts not by him); *The Book of Christmas*, 1837. Compiled anthology of nineteenth-century poetry, *The English Helicon*, 1841, in which he included several of his own poems and some by Eleanora Louisa Montagu (above, under Hervey), who later became his wife.

Hervey's *Athenaeum* reviews of Dickens's novels consisted largely of extracts. In his review of *Bleak House* (March 6, 1852), he stated that *David Copperfield* was "in our opinion [the] finest of all Mr. Dickens's works."

D.N.B.

VERSE

The Wreck of 'The Arctic' X, 420–21. Dec. 16, 1854

Repr. in *The Poems of Thomas Kibble Hervey. Edited by Mrs. T. K. Hervey.* Boston: Ticknor and Fields, 1866. Pub. in *H.W.* not acknowledged.

Hill, Mrs. The item listed below gives an account of a small industrial school in London in which girls from Ragged Schools were taught to make dolls' house furniture for sale; in charge of the girls and their work was Octavia Hill (*Life of Octavia Hill*, pp. 16–19) – "Miss O.P.Q." in the article.

The Mrs. Hill recorded as contributor may be Octavia Hill's mother – Caroline Southwood Smith Hill, 1809?–1902, daughter of Dr. Southwood Smith; author of *Memoranda of Observations and Experiments in Education* and of books for children. Before her marriage, Mrs. Hill had contributed to the *Monthly Repository*; at the time that the *H.W.* article appeared, she was engaged in writing articles. In a letter of Feb. 27, 1856, her daughter Miranda remarked: "It is indeed delightful that Mama has found some one to take her articles. I long to read them" (*Life of Octavia Hill*, p. 75).

Ragged Robin xiii, 417–20. May 17, 1856

Hill, Adams Sherman |*Adams S. Hill*|, 1833–1910, journalist, university professor. Born in Boston, Mass. B.A. Harvard, 1853; LL.B. 1855. Admitted to New York bar, 1855. From 1856 to 1870 (except for extended stays in Europe for sake of his health) was law reporter, editorial writer, and correspondent for N.Y. *Tribune*, N.Y. *Evening Post*, Chicago *Tribune*. Assistant professor of rhetoric, Harvard, 1872–76; Boylston Professor of Rhetoric and Oratory, 1876–1904. Hon. LL.D. Harvard, 1903. Contributed to *Atlantic Monthly*, *Putnam's Monthly Magazine*, *North American Review*, *Harper's*, *Scribner's*, and other periodicals. Author of *Our English*, 1889, and of textbooks on rhetoric and composition that went through numerous editions.

The *Report of the Harvard Class of 1853* (ed. Rantoul), referring to Hill's periodical writing during 1856–58, states that one of his articles, "sent to 'All the Year Round,' then edited by Dickens, brought [Hill] an autograph letter, expressive of approbation, from the illustrious novelist" (*A.Y.R.* should of course read *H.W.*). Dickens's approbation of Hill's article, which records a trip from St. Louis to St. Paul, is understandable. The proper Bostonian – quite in the spirit of *American Notes* – finds Westerners a crude people, unschooled in "the fine arts of civilisation," unpolished in manners, "picking their teeth with their forks," "squirting tobacco-juice" – and bolting their food, while he consumes his in leisurely manner "as I was brought up to do." He concedes, however, that it is unreasonable as yet to expect "parlour graces" from Westerners, and assures his readers that sooner or later "the noble elements of the Western character will unfold themselves. ... All Americans have faith in the West. Give it time."

Who Was Who in America

Beyond the Prairies
xvii, 102–108. Jan. 16, 1858

Hill, Miss Catherine. *Not identified.* Referred to in editorial comment as "a correspondent in Adelaide, Australia."

Hornet Architecture [chip]
xiii, 325–26. April 19, 1856

Hill, Christopher |*Chris^{er} Hill*|. *Not identified.* "Railway Waifs and Strays" enumerates articles left on trains by travellers and describes the efforts made by railway companies to restore articles to their owners. For his share in the item, the contributor was paid £1.1.0. In *Old Leaves: Gathered from Household Words*, Wills reprinted the item as his writing, without acknowledgment of the joint authorship that he had recorded in the Office Book.

Railway Waifs and Strays
W.H.W. & Chris^{er} Hill
ii, 319–22. Dec. 28, 1850

Hill, Louisa. *Not identified.*

VERSE
Angel Eyes v, 224. May 22, 1852

Hill, Matthew Davenport |*D. M. Hill, M. D. Hill*|, 1792–1872, K.C. (Q.C.), reformer of criminal law. Attended a school conducted by his father. Admitted at Lincoln's Inn, 1814; called to the bar, 1819. Because of his ability and his known sympathies with radical party, was retained for the defence in many important political trials. Elected M.P. for Hull, 1832. K.C., 1834. Appointed recorder of Birmingham, 1839; held the office for twenty-six years; as Charles Knight said, made "'Recorder of Birmingham' a household word" (Hill and Hill, *Recorder of Birmingham*, p. 457); his charges delivered to grand jury greatly helped effect reform in criminal law. Commissioner in bankruptcy for Bristol district, 1851–69. Was ardent advocate of liberal and humanitarian causes – political, civil, social, religious. Took part in founding of Society for the Diffusion of Useful Knowledge. Early began writing for newspapers; contributed to *Monthly Repository*, *Knight's Quarterly Magazine*, and other periodicals; wrote also for professional journals. Author of *Suggestions for the Repression of Crime*, 1857; *Papers on the Penal Servitude Acts*, 1864; and other works.

Dickens was well acquainted with Hill and at various times consulted him concerning "cases" in which Miss Burdett-Coutts had an interest in connection with Urania Cottage (to Miss Burdett-Coutts, March 3, 1848 [1849]; May 16, 1849; April 25, 1850, in *Heart of Charles Dickens*, ed. Johnson). In one letter Dickens stated that he knew Hill "to be a man of good experience and discernment, and much kind feeling, in all these matters"; he placed great reliance on Hill's investigations and judgment.

In a letter to Lord Brougham concerning the exaggerations and misrepresentations charged against Dickens and Reade in "The License of Modern Novelists," *Edin. Rev.*, July 1857, Hill wrote: "Dickens is open to censure for rarely, if ever, introducing a member of the upper classes into his works except to hold him up to reproach or contempt; but to inveigh against him for his attack on what he calls the 'Circumlocution Office' is childish. He may have exaggerated; but exaggeration directed against an institution, and exaggeration against an individual, are very different things. ... Indeed if Dickens had known the facts he might have made more of the Circumlocution Office" (*Recorder of Birmingham*, p. 333).

In *H.W.*, a commendatory reference to Hill appeared in "In and Out of Jail," an article based on the book *Crime: Its Amount, Causes, and Remedies* by Hill's brother Frederic. The article referred to Frederic Hill as a man who had served the public well, "like others of his name and lineage." "Down among the Dutchmen" (March 6, 1858) mentioned "Mr. Recorder Hill" in connection with the contemporary interest in the reformation of criminals.

The memoir of Hill written by two of his daughters mentions both of Hill's *H.W.* articles by title and date of publication and quotes a paragraph from the second.

Harper's reprinted "The Duties of Witnesses and Jurymen" in part, with acknowledgment to *H.W.*

D.N.B.

The Duties of Witnesses and Jurymen
II, 100–104. Oct. 26, 1850
Bringing Out the Truth
IV, 38–40. Oct. 4, 1851

Hillier, Mrs. Charles B. |*Mrs. Hillier, Mrs. Hellier*|, wife of British consul to Siam. In her first *H.W.* article, Mrs. Hillier wrote of an audience that she, her husband, and their party, *en route* from Singapore to Bangkok, had with a Malay sultan, and of her informing the sultan "that a treaty of commerce had been concluded between England and Siam, that a consul had been nominated, and that C. was on his way ... to commence, in that character, his duties at Bangkok." "C." was Charles B. Hillier, appointed July 4, 1856, as British consul to Siam, with residence in Bangkok (*Foreign Office List*, 1856).

At Home in Siam [lead]
XVI, 481–88. Nov. 21, 1857
A Pair of Siamese Kings
XVII, 447–51. April 24, 1858
Siamese Women and Children [chip]
XIX, 40–42. Dec. 11, 1858

Hoare, Mrs. |*Miss Hoare, Mrs. Hoare*|, Irish author. Listed in *Publishers' Circular*, March 1, 1851, as "Hoare (W.)." Lived, at least during early 1850s, in Monkstown, Co. Cork. Contributed to *Sharpe's* (verse and prose), to *Howitt's Journal* (at least one sketch), to *H.W.*, and to other periodicals. In 1851 published

Shamrock Leaves, her one book, a collection of some of her tales and sketches that had appeared in periodicals.

Mrs. Hoare "had from childhood been an ardent admirer" of Mary Russell Mitford's writings; in 1852 she began a correspondence with Miss Mitford that continued "till within a short period of Miss Mitford's death." In the second year of their correspondence, Miss Mitford wrote: "I do, indeed, adopt you, dearest Mrs. Hoare, as 'a friend upon paper' – a true and dear friend!" *Shamrock Leaves,* of which Mrs. Hoare sent Miss Mitford a copy, Miss Mitford thought a "painful book" for its depiction of the famine years in Ireland; but she found in it "unmistakable truth, a quality rare among ... the works of living Irish writers" (*Life of Mary Russell Mitford,* III, 229n, 264, 238–39; *Friendships of Mary Russell Mitford,* p. 357).

Mrs. Hoare was apparently acquainted with Wills. In the Office Book, Wills recorded "A Suburban Romance" (Dec. 14, 1850) as by "W.H.W. (suggested by Mrs. Hoare)," with payment of £0.10.6 to Mrs. Hoare for the suggestion. In reprinting the story in his collection of his *H.W.* contributions, *Old Leaves: Gathered from Household Words,* Wills did not acknowledge Mrs. Hoare's suggestion (though in reprinting "To Clergymen in Difficulties," suggested to him by "facts derived from a correspondent," he did make such acknowledgment).

Mrs. Hoare's *H.W.* contributions were evidently much liked. Of the eighteen items, eleven were reprinted in *Harper's,* two of them acknowledged to *H.W.* One of her contributions, "Father and Son," was included in *Choice Stories from Dickens' Household Words,* pub. Auburn, N.Y., 1854.

*Father and Son I, 213–16. May 25, 1850
*Little Mary. A Tale of the Black Year
I, 392–96. July 20, 1850
An Irish Peculiarity
I, 594–96. Sept. 14, 1850
"Give Wisely!" An Anecdote
II, 117–18. Oct. 26, 1850
The Story of Fine-Ear
II, 383–84. Jan. 11, 1851
"Judge Not!" II, 431–32. Jan. 25, 1851
How to Be Idolised
II, 455–56. Feb. 1, 1851
The Story of Giovanni Belzoni
W.H.W. & Mrs. Hoare
II, 548–52. March 1, 1851
The Modern Haroun-al-Raschid
II, 617–20. March 22, 1851
The Two Roads III, 72. April 12, 1851
The History of a Rose
III, 334–36. June 28, 1851
The Ghost-Raiser
V, 83–84. April 10, 1852
A Tale of Mid-Air
V, 197–98. May 15, 1852
Too Much Blue V, 291–93. June 12, 1852
Mechanics by Instinct
VI, 278–81. Dec. 4, 1852
Barryhooraghan Post-Office
VI, 503–504. Feb. 5, 1853
Flower-Bells *Morley & Mrs. Hoare*
VIII, 196–99. Oct. 29, 1853
The Irish Letter-Writer
X, 190–92. Oct. 7, 1854

*Repr. in *Shamrock Leaves; or, Tales and Sketches of Ireland. By Mrs. Hoare.* Dublin: J. M'Glashan; London: Partridge & Oakey, 1851. Preface states that the tales and sketches "originally appeared in various periodicals" but does not specify the periodicals.

Hogarth, Jr. |*Hogarth, Hogarth, Junr.*|, son of George Hogarth (below). There is some uncertainty about the number of children that George Hogarth had; Christie, *The Ancestry of Catherine Thomson Hogarth,* lists five daughters and five sons. The second of the sons, *d.* 1841, does not enter into consideration here. Record of other sons: Robert Hogarth, first son, *b.* 1816, still living in the 1870s (see Adrian, *Georgina Hogarth and the Dickens Circle,* p. 208); William Thomson Hogarth ("William Thomas" in *D.N.B.*), third son, *b.* 1823, no death date recorded; James Ballantyne Hogarth, fourth son, *d.* 1876 (*D.N.B.*); Edward Hogarth, fifth son, *d.* 1879 at age forty-five (*Life and Reminiscences of E. L. Blanchard,* ed. Scott and Howard, II, 485, where name is given as "Edward Norris Hogarth").

The two items listed below give the following information about the contributor: Had emigrated to Australia before the gold-rush days; at "the beginning of the Winter of 1850 ... was working quietly in Sydney, by no means dissatisfied with [his] position," when rumours of the Bathurst gold discovery reached the city; resigned his position, advertised in the Sydney *Morning Herald* for "a gentleman, willing to join him in and to share the expenses of" going to Turon diggings; chose as partner one of men who answered the advertisement; proceeded with him to the diggings; worked there about four months ("The Cradle and the Grave"); obviously found the venture unsuccessful; was in Melbourne in Nov. 1852, having been there apparently for some time ("Look Before You Leap").

The Office Book assigns "Look Before You Leap" to Horne and Hogarth. Horne had arrived in Melbourne in Sept. 1852; about a fortnight after his arrival he obtained a position as commander of a Bendigo-Melbourne gold-escort; he resigned after a short time and thereafter stayed some weeks in Melbourne. It must have been shortly after his arrival from England that he collaborated with Hogarth on the article. He was, during about his first ten months in Australia, also sending his own articles to *H.W.* For "Look Before You Leap" the Office Book records split payment to Horne and Hogarth. For "The Cradle and the Grave" it records payment made "To Hogarth senr."

The Mitchell Library, Sydney, reports that Hogarth's advertisement for a partner seems not to appear in the Sydney *Morning Herald*, that no Hogarth is listed in the 1850 Sydney directories, but that a William Hogarth is listed in *Sands, Kenney & Co.'s Melbourne Directory*, 1861.*

*See "Plorn's Australian Uncles," *Dickensian*, Autumn 1972: two of George Hogarth's sons – William and James – went to Australia.

Look Before You Leap [chip]
Horne & Hogarth
VI, 497–99. Feb. 5, 1853

The Cradle and the Grave
Hogarth, Junr., & Morley
VIII, 317–25. Dec. 3, 1853

Hogarth, George |*Mr. Hogarth, Hogarth*|, 1783–1870, lawyer, music critic, journalist. Studied law; Writer to the Signet, Edinburgh. In 1830 gave up law for journalism. Removed to London, 1834. Joined staff of *Morning Chronicle*; appointed editor of *Evening Chronicle*; music critic for *Daily News*, 1846–66. Wrote also for *Illus. London News* and other periodicals. Author of *Musical History, Biography, and Criticism*, 1835; *Memoirs of the Musical Drama*, 1838; and other works.

Hogarth became acquainted with Dickens in 1834, when Dickens began writing for the *Morning Chronicle*. He took a kindly interest in the young man, gave him introductions that were of value to him, and, in a *Morning Chronicle* review, praised *Sketches by Boz*. Dickens liked and respected Hogarth; he became a friend of the Hogarth family; in 1836 he married Hogarth's daughter Catherine. During the years immediately preceding Dickens's separation from his wife, Hogarth came in for a share of Dickens's increasing dislike of the Hogarths. Hogarth himself, however, "apparently never acted upon, or even shared, the acrimony of his wife and his daughter Helen toward Dickens," and Dickens seems to have retained no permanent rancour toward him (Adrian, *Georgina Hogarth and the Dickens Circle*, pp. 61–62, 130).

In his first journalistic association with Dickens, Hogarth was Dickens's superior on the two papers for which they both worked. Thereafter, the roles shifted. Dickens, as editor of *Bentley's Misc.*, accepted contributions from Hogarth for that periodical; and, as editor of the *Daily News*, he engaged Hogarth for the staff.

Hogarth's duties in connection with *H.W.* are not entirely clear. Three weeks before the first number appeared, Dickens wrote to Wills concerning an article (subject not stated): "I should wish Hogarth to see that article before it is used. Will you see him, and set him to work on something else? He has nothing in hand now" (March 6, 1850). Later, Dickens asked Wills to have Hogarth look over an article on the Erards – a subject, of course, specifically within Hogarth's province – to see that it contained nothing "against his positive knowledge" (Sept. 18, 1855). Hogarth was paid for the articles that he wrote for *H.W.*; that fact indicates that he was not a salaried member of the editorial staff. His main work seems to have been the compiling of news summaries for the *Household Narrative of Current Events*, a supplementary publication brought out from 1850 to 1855, at first under the direction of Forster (see Forster, above), later under that of Wills. Morley referred to "Poor nice old Hogarth," "the good old simple-minded man who ... compounds the news of household narrative out of the papers" (Solly, *Life of Henry Morley*, p. 200). Sala mentioned the "monthly compendium of news" (which he miscalled the *Household Budget*) as "edited by Mr. George Hogarth, Dickens's father-in-law" (*Life and Adventures*, p. 314).

Harper's reprinted Hogarth's first *H.W.* contribution, with acknowledgment to *H.W.*

D.N.B.

An Incident in the Life of Mad^lle^ Clairon
I, 15–19. March 30, 1850

Heathen and Christian Burial
Mr. Hogarth & W.H.W.
I, 43–48. April 6, 1850

Music in Humble Life
Mr. Hogarth & W.H.W.
I, 161–64. May 11, 1850

The New Jerusalem
XIII, 136–40. Feb. 23, 1856

Holland, Elizabeth (Gaskell) |*Mrs. Holland*|, 1812–1892, sister of William Gaskell (above). In 1838 married Charles Holland, a Liverpool merchant. Described by Catherine Winkworth (*Letters and Memorials*, I, 146) as "a very striking-looking woman. In her manners she is something like Mrs. Gaskell, as well as in her appearance (she is not a bit like her brother), is very clever, energetic, and animated." Appears in Mrs. Gaskell's letters to the Gaskell daughters as "Aunt Lizzie" and "Aunt Lizzy."

To a letter written by Mrs. Gaskell to her daughter Marianne (*Letters*, No. 134, dated [25 September 1852]), Mrs. Gaskell's daughter Margaret Emily added a note containing the comment: "I won't tell you any more amusing things but about the Growth of goodness (voilà the 'Magic of an Alliteration') wch Aunt Lizzie has written in the HWords –" In the word "goodness" (which might conceivably read "goodings"), the letter "d" is written over what may have been another letter in that position; the letters following the "d" are not marked out (MS Yale University Library. The note is not given in *Letters*).

The Office Book lists "The Growth of Good" without author's name, but with the notation "per Horne," and records payment as made to Horne. Horne was no longer a staff member at the time that the item appeared in *H.W.*, but he was still a regular contributor. He must have numbered the Hollands among his numerous friends and acquaintances.

"On the Yorkshire Moors" is assigned in the Office Book to Mrs. Holland, with payment recorded as made by post-office order. The article recounts an excursion to the moors and records various little incidents that occurred. Since Elizabeth Holland had contributed one item to *H.W.*, she is the likely Mrs. Holland to have contributed a second.

PROSE

On the Yorkshire Moors
X, 284–87. Nov. 4, 1854

VERSE

The Growth of Good
V, 54–55. April 3, 1852

Hollingshead, John |*Hollinshed, Hollingshed, Hollingshead, Holingshed*|, 1827–1904, journalist, theatre manager. Attended "a so-called 'Pestalozzian Academy'" at Homerton. Worked as warehouse clerk, commercial traveller, and cloth merchant. Did much reading; developed ambition to write for the press.

Contributed to the *Train, Cornhill* (at Thackeray's invitation), *Good Words, Punch, Leader, Morning Post,* and some twenty other periodicals; dramatic critic for *Daily News.* Published some ten collections of his periodical contributions; also a selected 3-vol. edition. After some fifteen years as journalist, turned his attention to the theatre; manager of Gaiety Theatre, 1868–86; instituted various improvements and innovations in theatres and theatre management; was first English producer to stage a play by Ibsen. Worked for removal of paper duty, for reform of copyright law, for abolition of licensing regulations and other restrictions on stage performances.

It was as contributor to *H.W.* that Hollingshead became acquainted with Dickens. He admired Dickens and his writings; copies of books that he presented to Dickens he inscribed as from "his affectionate friend" (Stonehouse, *Catalogue*); but he was not a Dickens idolater. He saw in Dickens various limitations, as parochiality of sympathies, and characterized him as "an inspired Cockney," using the term, as he explained, "in no depreciating spirit, but as a brand of character" (*My Lifetime,* I, 188). In addition to their association as contributor and editor, the two men had in common their interest in the theatre. Dickens on one occasion suggested various alterations in a farce that Hollingshead had written; later he wrote to congratulate Hollingshead on its success on the stage. Hollingshead invited Dickens to performances at the Gaiety; Dickens attended one performance. Hollingshead arranged for the stage the trial scene from *Pickwick*; he edited Dickens's *Readings* and published some articles on Dickens.

Hollingshead's rise from a "penny-a-liner" to a professional journalist owed much to the example of his friend William Moy Thomas. Thomas was a regular contributor to *H.W.*, and Hollingshead, following his friend's lead, sent to the periodical a sketch titled "Poor Tom." Dickens found it "a pretty little paper of a good deal of merit" and felt that the writer might become "very serviceable" to *H.W.* (to Wills, Sept. 26, 1857). Hollingshead proved very serviceable not only to *H.W.*, but also to *A.Y.R.* Dickens (according to Hollingshead) liked his new contributor's "readiness and versatility," and Hollingshead became the periodical's "champion out-door young man." Hollingshead had the ability to write the kind of "readable" though at times superficial papers that Dickens liked; occasionally, when a subject for a paper was suggested, stated Hollingshead, Dickens would say: "Let Hollingshead do it. ... He's the most ignorant man on the staff, but he'll cram up the facts, and won't give us an encyclopaedical article" (*My Lifetime,* I, 96–97, 190). Hollingshead called himself "a Dickens young man" and wrote of Dickens as "my master"; he took pains, however, to make it clear that he was not a Dickens imitator and that his *H.W.* and *A.Y.R.* contributions were not subjected to Dickensian touches: "My subjects were not very much *à la Dickens,* and, bad or good, I had a blunt plain style of my own. Of the many articles I wrote for Dickens ..., I can honestly say that Dickens's editorship did not alter six lines in as many years" (*My Lifetime,* I, 96).

Of Hollingshead's *H.W.* articles, "The City of Unlimited Paper" was the most publicized. It was quoted in the *Times* and other newspapers, and thought by the *Daily Telegraph* to display "the powerful hand of Dickens"; it was admired by Thackeray (*My Lifetime,* I, 95; Thackeray, *Letters,* IV, 157). Lord Rosebery liked "The Humiliation of Fogmoor"; and Carlyle – so Hollingshead was informed – "approved of my actuality papers in *Household Words* in preference to many of what he called 'Dickens's Word-Spinnings' " (*My Lifetime,* I, 116, 158). William Bodham Donne naturally resented "An Official Scarecrow," which satirized as obsolescent and ridiculous the office of dramatic licenser (C. B. Johnson, ed., *William Bodham Donne,* p. 227).

D.N.B. suppl. 1901–1911

Poor Tom. – A City Weed
XVI, 381–84. Oct. 17, 1857

Twenty Shillings in the Pound
XVI, 444–46. Nov. 7, 1857

Debtor and Creditor
xvi, 525–28. Nov. 28, 1857
My Lost Home [lead]
xvi, 529–34. Dec. 5, 1857
The City of Unlimited Paper [lead]
xvii, 1–4. Dec. 19, 1857
Vestiges of Protection
xvii, 70–72. Jan. 2, 1858
All Night on the Monument [lead]
xvii, 145–48. Jan. 30, 1858
Bankruptcy in Six Easy Lessons
xvii, 210–12. Feb. 13, 1858
Wanted, a Secretary
xvii, 224–27. Feb. 20, 1858
How I Fell among Monsters
xvii, 299–301. March 13, 1858
Debt xvii, 319–21. March 20, 1858
The Afflicted Duke of Spindles
xvii, 405–408. April 10, 1858
Good-Will xvii, 474–76. May 1, 1858
White Washerton
xvii, 560–62. May 29, 1858
Passing the Time
xvii, 575–76. May 29, 1858
Too Weak for the Place
xviii, 42–44. June 26, 1858
The End of Fordyce, Brothers [lead]
xviii, 73–79. July 10, 1858
Buying in the Cheapest Market
xviii, 256–58. Aug. 28, 1858
Bristles and Flint [lead]
xviii, 265–70. Sept. 4, 1858
Domestic Castle-Building
xviii, 466–70. Oct. 30, 1858
Railway Nightmares [lead]
xviii, 505–508. Nov. 13, 1858
The Innocent Holder Business
xix, 80–84. Dec. 25, 1858
New Puppets for Old Ones
xix, 210–12. Jan. 29, 1859
My Two Partners
xix, 275–80. Feb. 19, 1859
An Executor xix, 617–20. May 28, 1859

The 25 items repr. as *Under Bow Bells: A City Book for All Readers. By John Hollingshead.* London: Groombridge and Sons, 1860. Pub. in *H.W.* acknowledged.

Riding the Whirlwind [lead]
xvi, 553–56. Dec. 12, 1857
A Morning Call on a Great Personage
xvii, 60–64. Jan. 2, 1858
A Phantom Opera
xvii, 484–86. May 8, 1858
Shot xviii, 34–37. June 26, 1858
What Mr. Burleigh Could Not See
xviii, 161–68. July 31, 1858
On the Canal [1st instalment = lead]
xviii, 289–93. Sept. 11, 1858,
and the 2 following nos.

The 6 items repr. in *Odd Journeys In and Out of London. By John Hollingshead.* London: Groombridge and Sons, 1860. Pub. in *H.W.* acknowledged.

Street Memories
xvii, 9–12. Dec. 19, 1857
Fetishes at Home
xvii, 445–47. April 24, 1858
Too Late xvii, 464–67. May 1, 1858
People's Umbrellas
xvii, 496–98. May 8, 1858
Really Dangerous Classes
xvii, 541–43. May 22, 1858
A Counterfeit Presentment
xviii, 71–72. July 3, 1858
Three Masters xviii, 486–90. Nov. 6, 1858
Black, White, and Whity-Brown
xviii, 498–500. Nov. 6, 1858
A Gipsy King xix, 89–92. Dec. 25, 1858
My Name xix, 172–74. Jan. 22, 1859
A Relic of the Middling Ages
xix, 260–64. Feb. 12, 1859
Men in Masks
xix, 346–48. March 12, 1859

The 12 items repr. in *Ways of Life, By John Hollingshead.* London: Groombridge and Sons, 1861. Pub. in *H.W.* acknowledged.

A New Idea of an Old Slave-Captain
xvii, 84–87. Jan. 9, 1858

Repr. in *Footlights, By John Hollingshead.* London: Chapman and Hall, 1883. Pub. in *H.W.* acknowledged.

The Pet of the Law
xvii, 163–65. Jan. 30, 1858
How to Make a Madman [chip]
xvii, 520–22. May 15, 1858
Wanted, a Court-Guide [lead]
xviii, 49–51. July 3, 1858
Nine Kings xviii, 118–20. July 17, 1858
An Official Scarecrow
xviii, 143–44. July 24, 1858
The Humiliation of Fogmoor [lead]
xviii, 193–204. Aug. 14, 1858

The Man behind My Chair [chip]
xviii, 323–24. Sept. 18, 1858
My Model Theatre
xviii, 490–92. Nov. 6, 1858
Navy Dry-Rot xix, 439–43. April 9, 1859
The 9 items repr. in *Rubbing the Gilt Off. A West End Book for All Readers. By John Hollingshead.* London: John Camden Hotten, 1860. Pub. in *H.W.* acknowledged.

Stephen Girard, the Money Maker
xvii, 618–20. June 12, 1858
*Fly-Catching [chip]
xviii, 11–12. June 19, 1858
Everybody's Referee
xviii, 565–66. Nov. 27, 1858
My Brother's Dinner
xix, 467–69. April 16, 1859
*Item twice entered in Office Book, assigned in first entry to *Hollingshed,* in second to *Payn.*

Holme, James Wilson |*Wilson Holme,* 34 Old Jewry|, solicitor. The *Post Office London Directory,* 1859, lists the firm of Tilleard, Son, Godden & Holme, solicitors, at the above address, with cross-reference from James Wilson Holme to the firm name. Holme had only recently become a partner in the firm; the 1858 directory does not include his name in the firm name.

See also T. M. Holme (below).

VERSE
Gone Forth xviii, 277. Sept. 4, 1858

Holme, T. M. Address: 1 Tanfield Court. *Not identified.* London directories, 1856–58, list no Holme at the above address, nor do they list a T. M. Holme at another address. The address indicates that the contributor was probably in the legal profession; he may be the solicitor James Wilson Holme (above). The initials recorded in the Office Book seem clearly to read "T.M."; they may, however, be intended for "J.W."

In *Bentley's Misc.,* 1838, appeared a poem by M. Torre Holme. The Office Book occasionally records a contributor's initials in reverse order.

VERSE
Memnon and His Mate
xv, 107–108. Jan. 31, 1857

Hood, Tom |*T. Hood, Junr., T. Hood*|, 1835–1874, humorist, misc. writer; son of Thomas Hood the poet. Studied for a time at University College, London, then at Pembroke College, Oxford, with intent of entering the church; abandoned the idea, did not take degree. Early began contributing verse and prose to periodicals. From about 1856 to 1860 lived in Cornwall (his *H.W.* article deals with Cornish fishing and fishermen); there edited a newspaper for about two years. Clerk in War Office, 1860–65. Editor of *Fun,* 1865 until his death; wrote much for the periodical; also drew and engraved many of illustrations. In 1867 first issued *Tom Hood's Comic Annual.* Wrote book on versification; several novels; also books for children, some alone, others jointly with his sister, Frances Broderip (above); illustrated some of her stories. Collaborated with her on *Memorials of Thomas Hood,* 1860, and on two editions of Hood's *Works;* wrote preface to two collections of Hood's poems.

Dickens had known Tom Hood and his sister from their childhood.

The Office Book memorandum for "The Poor Man's Fish" reads: "Taken out of a paper of treble the length."

D.N.B.

PROSE
The Poor Man's Fish
xiv, 427–30. Nov. 15, 1856

VERSE
The Secret of the Stream
vii, 181. April 23, 1853
Grains of Gold *T. Hood, Junr., & W.H.W.* vii, 589. Aug. 20, 1853

Hooper, John |*Correspondent*|, *d.* 1878, divine. B. A. Cambridge, 1823; M.A.

1824 (according to Crockford; 1828, according to *Alumni Cantab.*); vicar of Meopham, Kent, 1854–75. The contributor identifies himself as incumbent of the parish of Meopham. His article gives, from Ashmole's diary and from a document in his possession, information concerning the Tradescants. It was motivated by the reference to Tradescant the elder in "The Growth of Our Gardens," June 19, 1858. *H.W.* printed the item without comment except that it had been sent by "a correspondent." Payment of £1.1.0 for the 1-col. item was twice the standard rate.

Alumni Cantab.

The Tradescants [chip]
XVIII, 305–306. Sept. 11, 1858

Horne, Richard Henry or **Hengist** [*Mr. R. H. Horne, Mr. Horne, R. H. Horne, R. H. H., Horne, H. Horne*], 1802–1884, author. Student at Royal Military College, Sandhurst; withdrawn at end of probationary year for having, according to official record, "failed to pass probation" (Blainey, *The Farthing Poet*, p. 9). Thereafter served some months in Mexican navy. Began literary career as periodical contributor and journalist; contributed to more than fifty periodicals – British, Australian, and American. Editor, 1836–37, of *Monthly Repository*. In 1833 published his first book, *Exposition of the False Medium and Barriers Excluding Men of Genius from the Public*; later prose writings included *The Poor Artist*, 1850; *The Dreamer and the Worker*, 1851; some books for children. Wrote poetic dramas: *Cosmo de' Medici*, 1837; *The Death of Marlowe*, 1837; and others. Best known to his contemporaries as author of *Orion*, "the farthing epic," 1843. With assistance of Elizabeth Barrett and Robert Bell, wrote *A New Spirit of the Age*, 1844. Thought his genius unappreciated in England; went to Australia, 1852. There obtained some Government employment; wrote *Australian Facts and Prospects* and a lyrical drama, *Prometheus, the Fire-Bringer*. Returned to England, 1869. In 1874 granted Civil List pension of £50 a year "In recognition of his contributions to literature"; pension later augmented to £100 (Colles, *Literature and the Pension List*).

Horne became acquainted with Dickens in the late 1830s; the two men were for some years good friends. Horne played a role in Dickens's presentation of *Not So Bad As We Seem*; he and his wife were at times Dickens's guests at Devonshire Terrace and at Broadstairs. Horne presented to Dickens a copy of his plays *The Death of Marlowe* and *Judas Iscariot*, and also of his *Ballad Romances* (Stonehouse, *Catalogue*). Dickens expressed generous admiration of some of Horne's prose writings and poems, gave Horne helpful advice on proposed publications, and attempted to interest publishers in bringing out some of his books. Horne contributed to *Bentley's Misc.* under Dickens's editorship and was engaged by Dickens as reporter for the *Daily News*. In 1862 Dickens wrote a letter in strong support of Horne's application for aid from the Royal Literary Fund (Fielding, "Charles Dickens and R. H. Horne," *English*, Spring 1952). When Horne returned from Australia, however, Dickens refused to see him or to correspond with him, indignant at Horne's having contributed little to the support of his wife during his Australian years. Horne, commenting later on the talk about him and his "self-divorced wife," stated that he had refrained from making a public pronouncement on the matter: "... I have never followed the bad example of Dickens in parading my private grievances" (draft of letter to Meredith, Aug. 1, 1875, *Letters from George Meredith*, pp. 10–11).

In *A New Spirit of the Age*, Horne devoted a long chapter to Dickens, analysing his strengths and weaknesses as a novelist. In later years, he wrote of Dickens in various periodical articles that recounted his recollections of famous contemporaries. His mentions of Dickens and his reference to Georgina Hogarth in "John Forster; His Early Life and Friendships," *Temple Bar*, April 1876, incensed Miss Hogarth (Adrian, *Georgina Hogarth and the Dickens Circle*, pp. 231–33).

Horne was at work on articles for *H.W.* some weeks before the first number of the periodical appeared. On May 18, 1850, he was engaged for a three-month period as assistant to Wills. His duties were the writing of original material and the revising of contributed items. In mid-Aug., when this engagement was about to terminate, a sharp disagreement arose between Dickens and Wills concerning Horne's work. Wills stated that Horne was not giving five guineas' worth of service for his five-guinea weekly salary (Lehmann, ed., *Charles Dickens As Editor*, pp. 35–36). Dickens took the attitude that the criticism emanated from Wills's dislike of Horne, and, after conferring with Horne by letter, assured Wills that Horne was "willing and anxious" to render him assistance "in any way in which you will allow yourself to be assisted" (Aug. 27, 1850). In March of the following year, Wills returned to the charge. Dickens's letter to Horne, March 18, 1851, is in reply to a letter in which Horne, obviously, had discussed the matter. Dickens's suggestion was that Horne "continue on the old terms, for at least another month." To mid-May of that year, the Office Book records no payment to Horne for individual items, indicating that to that date he continued a member of the staff.

Between that date and the date of his leaving for Australia (June 1852), Horne contributed to *H.W.* about as many items as he had written for the periodical during the year that he was a staff member; he continued his connection with *H.W.* also in other ways. It was through his agency that an occasional item not of his writing arrived at the editorial office, and it was to him that payment was made for several contributions not of his writing – among them, some poems by Meredith and by Ollier. In addition, the record of his name in the Office Book jointly with that of Miss Tomkins for one poem, and jointly with that of Meredith for another, indicates that he revised the two poems. In what capacity he served as reviser – whether as the friend of the two contributors or, at the request of Wills, as a former staff member – is not clear.

Before Horne left for Australia, Dickens entered on an engagement with him whereby Horne was to write for *H.W.* articles connected with his voyage and his gold mining experiences. The arrangement proved unsatisfactory.

Dickens valued Horne as a writer for *H.W.* He hoped that Horne, on ceasing to be a staff member, would continue as contributor, promising him that "the rate of remuneration shall be higher in your case" (March 18, 1851). (It was not.) Of the four articles assigned in the Office Book jointly to Horne and Dickens, three Dickens merely revised or added material to. "One Man in a Dockyard," however, was an actual collaboration; the two writers made an excursion to Chatham to gather material for the article, and each wrote part of the article. Among Horne's articles that Dickens particularly liked was "The Hippopotamus" (to Wills, July 12, 1850); Horne's suggestion of snails as the subject for a paper Dickens thought admirable (to Horne, April 6, 1852). "Household Christmas Carols," "The Great Peace-Maker," and "The Camera-Obscura" he called to F. M. Evans's attention (April 10, 1852) as "remarkable poems."

Some of Horne's contributions Dickens did not care for, among them, apparently, "The New Zealand Zauberflöte," which seems to be the "New Zealand sketch" that he mentioned to Wills (Aug. 10, 1850) as weighing "frightfully" on his mind. In a letter to Wills, Dec. 29, 1852, Dickens dismissed one of Horne's poems as "very indifferent"; no poem assigned to Horne appeared in *H.W.* after the date of the letter. The tedious "Digger's Diary," which Horne sent from Australia, Dickens was obliged to cut "to shreds" to make usable to the periodical (to Horne, March 2, 1853).

One of Horne's articles Dickens asked Wills to have checked for accuracy, since Horne might "unintentionally commit us to some mistake" (March 27, 1851). In his article on Waghorn, Horne did commit *H.W.* to mistakes, which Wills was obliged to correct in a "chip" ("Lieutenant Waghorn and His Widow," Nov. 16, 1850); a misstatement in another of Horne's articles ("The Pen and the Pickaxe") was called to the attention of the editorial office by a reader ("Gas Perfumery," June 28, 1851). Horne was a careless writer. In "A Melancholy Place," he stated casually that "we were so unfortunate as to omit" mention of a certain matter from a preceding article, "A Tower of Strength"; the omission he supplied in "A Melancholy Place" (which gives, for "A Tower of Strength," the incorrect *H.W.* number and page reference).

Mention, in *H.W.*, of Horne and his writings appeared in Horne's own contributions. "A Witch in the Nursery" told of the proposal made to a publisher by "the author of 'The Good-natured Bear.'" "More Dumb Friends" referred to the senses of animals as having "been discussed ... by Mr. R. H. Horne, in his charming book entitled 'The Poor Artist; or Seven Eyesights and One Object,'" and quoted a long paragraph from the book. (The complimentary reference was probably the insertion of Dickens, carrying out his suggestion to Horne, April 6, 1852, that he would be "delighted to have an opportunity of referring to so excellent a book.") "The Hunter and the Student" quoted two stories "found in 'The Poor Artist.'" "Shakspeare and Newgate" (revised by Dickens) mentioned the production at Sadler's Wells of "MR. HORNE's reconstruction" of *The Duchess of Malfi.*

Dickens's reference, by title or otherwise, to some twelve *H.W.* items as by Horne confirms the Office Book ascription of those items; Horne's comment (*Australian Facts and Prospects*, p. 89n) that he had undertaken for *H.W.* "to go through the Dust-heaps, the Dead-meat Markets and Horse-slaughterers' Yard of Smithfield, and the Gunpowder Mills at Hounslow" confirms his authorship of another four: "Dust," "The Cattle-Road to Ruin" – by implication also "The Smithfield Bull" – and "Gunpowder." A diary entry recorded in *The Life of Richard Owen*, I, 361, mentions Horne as author of "the 'Zoological Meeting,'" – i.e., "Zoological Sessions."

Ten of Horne's *H.W.* contributions were reprinted in whole or part in *Harper's*, five of them acknowledged to *H.W.*, and one – "London Sparrows" – credited to Dickens. Three of his contributions were included in the Putnam volumes of selections from *H.W.*: *Home and Social Philosophy*, 1st and 2nd ser. H. B. Forman, in 1871, printed for private distribution "The Great Peace-Maker," stating that it had not been publicly claimed by Horne, but that at the time of its appearance "there was no doubt in literary circles as to the authorship."

See also Mr. Loader (below) and Thomas Oldcastle (below).

D.N.B.

PROSE

The True Story of a Coal Fire
I, 26–31. April 6, 1850, and the 2 following nos.

Work! An Anecdote
I, 35–36. April 6, 1850

The Fire Brigade of London [lead]
I, 145–51. May 11, 1850

The Black Diamonds of England
I, 246–50. June 8, 1850

The Fire Annihilator
I, 277–82. June 15, 1850

Pictures of Life in Australia
Mrs. Chisholm & R.H.H.
I, 307–310. June 22, 1850

The Cattle-Road to Ruin
I, 325–30. June 29, 1850

The Old Churchyard Tree. A Prose Poem [chip] ——— *& Mr. Horne*
I, 377–78. July 13, 1850

Dust; or Ugliness Redeemed
I, 379–84. July 13, 1850

The Wonders of 1851
I, 388–92. July 20, 1850

Innocence and Crime. An Anecdote
Mr. Horne & ———
I, 431–32. July 27, 1850

The Hippopotamus
I, 445–49. Aug. 3, 1850

The Life and Labours of Lieutenant Waghorn I, 494–501. Aug. 17, 1850

The Steam Plough
I, 604–607. Sept. 21, 1850

The Oldest Inhabitant of the Place de Grêve [chip] I, 614–15. Sept. 21, 1850

Zoological Sessions. (Exclusive)
II, 4–10. Sept. 28, 1850

Mr. Van Ploos on Penmanship
II, 38–42. Oct. 5, 1850

Gunpowder and Chalk
II, 60–65. Oct. 12, 1850

The New Zealand Zauberflöte
II, 75–81. Oct. 19, 1850, and the 2 following nos.

Gottfried Kinkel; a Life in Three Pictures [lead] II, 121–25. Nov. 2, 1850

The Cow with the Iron Tail [lead]
II, 145–51. Nov. 9, 1850
The Jolly Burglars
II, 196–203. Nov. 23, 1850
A Coal Miner's Evidence
II, 245–50. Dec. 7, 1850
The Baron of Beef and the Marquis of Wellington [chip]
II, 322–23. Dec. 28, 1850
Lighthouses and Light-Boats
II, 373–79. Jan. 11, 1851
Father Thames II, 445–50. Feb. 1, 1851
The Builder's House, and the Bricklayer's Garden. By an Eye-Witness and Sufferer II, 513–16. Feb. 22, 1851
The Female School of Design in the Capital of the World [lead]
II, 577–81. March 15, 1851
A Time for All Things
II, 615–17. March 22, 1851
Lives and Cargoes [chip]
III, 18–19. March 29, 1851
London Sparrows
III, 85–88. April 19, 1851
Cain in the Fields *R.H.H. & C.D.*
III, 147–51. May 10, 1851
The Successful Candidate. Committee-Room, with Closed Doors
III, 171–79. May 17, 1851
The Pen and the Pickaxe [lead]
III, 193–96. May 24, 1851
Elephants. Wholesale and Retail
III, 229–35. May 31, 1851
Complaint and Reply [chip]
III, 306. June 21, 1851
The Great Exhibition and the Little One *Horne & C.D.* III, 356–60. July 5, 1851
A Penitent Confession
III, 436–45. Aug. 2, 1851
One Man in a Dockyard [lead] *C.D. & Horne*
III, 553–57. Sept. 6, 1851
A Witch in the Nursery [lead]
III, 601–609. Sept. 20, 1851
Shakspeare and Newgate [lead] *C.D. & Horne* IV, 25–27. Oct. 4, 1851
Ballooning [lead] IV, 97–105. Oct. 25, 1851
Life and Luggage IV, 152–56. Nov. 8, 1851
A Zoological Problem [chip]
IV, 156–57. Nov. 8, 1851
The Pasha's New Boat
IV, 209–213. Nov. 22, 1851
Wonderful Swallows [chip]
IV, 234–35. Nov. 29, 1851

Household Crime
IV, 277–81. Dec. 13, 1851
What Christmas Is to a Bunch of People
Extra No. for Christmas 1851, pp. 3–7
Gunpowder [lead]
IV, 457–65. Feb. 7, 1852
Lord Peter the Wild Woodsman; or, The Progress of Tape
IV, 465–67. Feb. 7, 1852
Strings of Proverbs
IV, 469–72. Feb. 7, 1852
IV, 524–26. Feb. 21, 1852
IV, 538–40. Feb. 28, 1852
Floating Sentinels [lead]
V, 21–25. March 27, 1852
A Tower of Strength
V, 66–68. April 3, 1852
More Dumb Friends
V, 124–27. April 24, 1852
A Melancholy Place [chip]
V, 156–57. May 1, 1852
The Hunter and the Student
V, 157–62. May 1, 1852
Snails V, 240–44. May 29, 1852
A Digger's Diary [1st instalment = lead]
VI, 457–62. Jan. 29, 1853
VI, 545–51. Feb. 19, 1853
VII, 125–29. April 9, 1853
VIII, 6–11. Sept. 3, 1853
Look Before You Leap [chip] *Horne & Hogarth*
VI, 497–99. Feb. 5, 1853
Gentlemen and Bullocks
VII, 105–107. April 2, 1853
Canvass Town [lead]
VII, 361–67. June 18, 1853
Digging Sailors [chip]
VII, 425–26. July 2, 1853
A Digger's Wedding [chip]
VII, 511–12. July 30, 1853
Convicts in the Gold Regions [lead]
VIII, 49–54. Sept. 17, 1853

VERSE

*Arctic Heroes. A Fragment of Naval History I, 108–109. April 27, 1850
A Wish I, 245. June 8, 1850
The Orphan's Voyage Home *Mr. Horne & Miss Earle*
I, 253. June 8, 1850
"Press On." A Rivulet's Song *Mr. ——— & Mr. Horne*
I, 301. June 22, 1850

A Stroll by Starlight
Mr. Morley & R.H.H.
I, 350. July 6, 1850
A Great Man Departed
I, 396. July 20, 1850
Sorrows and Joys *Meredith & Horne*
I, 517–18. Aug. 24, 1850
The Sister's Farewell
Miss Browne & Horne
I, 539–40. Aug. 31, 1850
Lines to a Dead Linnet. By a Solitary Student I, 547. Aug. 31, 1850
A Sacred Grove I, 607. Sept. 21, 1850
The Two Blackbirds
Mr. Meredith & R.H.H.
II, 157. Nov. 9, 1850
The Youth and the Sage
II, 262. Dec. 7, 1850
Household Christmas Carols
II, 310–12. Dec. 21, 1850
*The Church Poor-Box
II, 420. Jan. 25, 1851
The Smithfield Bull to His Cousin of Nineveh II, 589–90. March 15, 1851
Two Sonnets [with brief prose comment]: The Good Great Man [by Coleridge]; Answer III, 252. June 7, 1851
The Great Peace-Maker. A Sub-Marine Dialogue III, 275–77. June 14, 1851
A Word to Young Poets
III, 430. July 26, 1851
Arcadia III, 445–46. Aug. 2, 1851
Winter Violets *Miss Tomkins & Horne*
III, 468. Aug. 9, 1851
The Round Game of the Christmas Bowl [instructions in prose]
Extra No. for Christmas 1851, pp. 23–24
War *Meredith & Horne*
IV, 517. Feb. 21, 1852
The Camera-Obscura. A Sunday Morning Lecture
V, 11–12. March 20, 1852
The Cities of Time V, 489. Aug. 7, 1852

*Repr. in *Cosmo de' Medici, an Historical Tragedy; and Other Poems, By Richard Hengist Horne.* London: George Rivers, 1875. Pub. in *H.W.* not acknowledged.

Hough, Lewis |*Hough*|, *b.* ca. 1829, writer, military man. Student at Eton. B.A. Cambridge, 1852; M.A. 1857. Captain, 3rd Middlesex Militia; major, 1872; hon.-colonel, 3rd Battalion, Royal Fusiliers. Contributed stories to *Chambers's, Once a Week,* and other periodicals. Published a collection of his stories; also a 3-vol. novel, *William Bathurst,* 1865; and two books for boys – *Dr. Jolliffe's Boys: A Tale of Weston School,* 1884, and *For Fortune and Glory: A Story of the Soudan War,* 1885. Recorded himself on title pages of two of his books as author of two additional titles; titles not listed in *Brit. Mus. Cat.* or in *Eng. Cat.*

Alumni Cantab.; Allibone

A Shepherd's Autobiography
VII, 309–312. May 28, 1853

Repr. in *Hits. By Lewis Hough, M.A.* London: F. Pitman [1865]. Pub. in *H.W.* acknowledged.

Howitt, Anna Mary |*Miss Howitt*|, 1824–1884, writer, art student; elder daughter of William and Mary Howitt (below). Received part of her education in Germany, where the Howitts resided for some years to give their children the advantage of German training; studied painting in London; then, in Munich, under Wilhelm von Kaulbach. Earned some praise for her work as an artist. D. G. Rossetti thought her *Gretchen at the Fountain* a very good picture – "much better than I fancied she could paint" (*Letters,* I, 162). A criticism by Ruskin, however, so crushed her spirit that she gave up art, except for the drawings that she produced as a medium after she became a convert to spiritualism. "If only the spirits had let her alone," wrote W. M. Rossetti, "she would have drawn and painted very much better than she ever did under their inspiration" (*Some Reminiscences,* I, 171). Mrs. Newton Crosland recorded that Miss Howitt "was, I believe, generally acknowledged to be of a higher order of intellect than either of her parents" (*Landmarks of a Literary Life,* pp. 195–96). Barbara Leigh Smith, who referred to herself as "one of the cracked people of the world," considered her friend Anna Mary also one of "the cracked" (Burton, *Barbara Bodichon*, p. 92). In 1859 Miss Howitt married Alaric Alfred Watts (below).

Contributed to *Athenaeum*, *Illus. Mag. of Art*, and other periodicals. Author of *An Art-Student in Munich*, 1853; *A School of Life*, 1855; and an account of her father's work in spiritualism; co-author, with her husband, of *Aurora*, 1875, a volume of verse, published anonymously.

Through her parents, Miss Howitt was probably acquainted with Dickens. In a letter to her father, March 4, 1857, Dickens wrote that he hoped to find time to call on the Howitts and to see Miss Howitt's pictures.

H.W. introduced "Bits of Life in Munich" with the explanation that the fair young contributor was studying painting in Munich "in company with a female friend" (Jane Benham), and that the sketches illustrated the independent life that two young ladies could lead there "with perfect propriety and security." Miss Howitt's story "The Right One" Dickens found "poor – but I think just passable"; her "May Festival" he thought "very good" (to Wills, July 27, Aug. 10, 1851). For all but one of her contributions Miss Howitt was paid less than the standard rate – for some items substantially less, £3.10.0, for instance, for a 9-col. article.

Harper's reprinted the first section of one of Miss Howitt's "Bits of Life in Munich," the whole of another, and also "The Right One," without acknowledgment to *H.W.*

Allibone

*Bits of Life in Munich
II, 133–37. Nov. 2, 1850
II, 358–59. Jan. 4, 1851
II, 395–97. Jan. 18, 1851
II, 535–40. March 1, 1851
III, 9–13. March 29, 1851
III, 43–46. April 5, 1851
III, 209–211. May 24, 1851
III, 261–64. June 7, 1851

*A Chapter of Models
III, 298–301. June 21, 1851

The Right One III, 473–77. Aug. 9, 1851

*The May Festival at Starnberg
III, 511–16. Aug. 23, 1851

*A Beginning and an End
IV, 286–88. Dec. 13, 1851

*Sledging V, 64–66. April 3, 1852

*Repr. in whole or part, with revision, in *An Art-Student in Munich. By Anna Mary Howitt*. 2 vols. London: Longman, Brown, Green, and Longmans, 1853. Pub. in *H.W.* not acknowledged.

Howitt, Mary (Botham) |*Mrs. W. Howitt, Mrs. Howitt*|, 1799–1888, misc. writer, translator. Attended Friends' schools. In 1821 married William Howitt (below). Like her husband, took deep interest in social reform and in humanitarian and philanthropic matters. Contributed to *Chambers's*, *Monthly Repository*, *People's Journal*, *Ladies' Companion*, *Leisure Hour*, *Good Words*, and other periodicals; contributed to annuals; for three years edited *Fisher's Drawing Room Scrap-Book*. Collaborated with her husband on several works, including a history of Scandinavian literature. Wrote popular accounts of natural history, children's stories, fiction for adults; also verse, which was very popular both in England and in the U.S. Translated some of Hans Christian Andersen's books and the novels of Fredrika Bremer. According to *D.N.B.*, wrote, edited, or translated some 110 works. In 1879 granted Civil List pension of £100 a year "In consideration of her literary services" (Colles, *Literature and the Pension List*).

The Howitts had become acquainted with Dickens by the mid-1840s and occasionally met him at social gatherings. Despite her husband's later altercation with Dickens, Mrs. Howitt remained on friendly terms with him. She and Dickens occasionally corresponded; his letter to her, Sept. 7, 1859, concerns a memoir of him that she had written.

The Howitts became *H.W.* contributors at Dickens's invitation, conveyed in a pleasant letter of Feb. 1850, intended for both husband and wife: "... if you would ever write for [*Household Words*], you would delight me, and I should consider myself very fortunate indeed in enlisting your assistance." Both she and her husband, stated Mrs. Howitt, agreed "most willingly" to Dickens's request (*Autobiography*, II, 58–59). What Dickens particularly wanted from the Howitts, he explained in a following letter, were stories "with such a general purpose in them as we all three have in all we do," though he added: "Whatever you may write earnestly and to your own pleasure, will be most welcome to me" (Woodring, *Victorian Samplers*, p. 152).

Mrs. Howitt's first prose contribution was the translation of a story by Meïr A. Goldschmidt. In their *Literature and Romance of Northern Europe*, published in the same year as the contribution, the Howitts mentioned Goldschmidt as author of "a collection of highly interesting short stories"; Mrs. Howitt published a translation, or adaptation, of his novel *Jacob Bendixen, the Jew*. Her second *H.W.* article she extracted, in part, from *Literature and Romance of Northern Europe*, the three introductory paragraphs of the article, as also the lines from the *Kalevala* and three of the selections from Johan Ludvig Runeberg, being transcribed practically verbatim; she did not indicate, in the article, that the material was taken from *Literature and Romance*. Two of her verse contributions – "The Ballad of Richard Burnell" and "Thomas Harlowe" – Mrs. Howitt mentioned by title in her *Autobiography* (II, 63). "A Plea for Playgrounds," assigned to her in the Office Book, is by Sophia De Morgan.

The *H.W.* article "A Witch in the Nursery" mentioned Mrs. Howitt as among English authors who had written "excellent stories and songs for children." "Fairyland in 'Fifty-four" referred to "The Spider and the Fly" (without mention of author or title) as a "popular ballad."

"Thomas Harlowe" was reprinted in *Harper's*, with acknowledgment to *H.W.* "Birth Song" and "Song of Death," marked anonymous, were included in *Harper's Cyclopaedia of British and American Poetry*, 1881.

D.N.B.

PROSE

Johan Falsen; from the Danish of Mr. Goldschmidt VI, 148–55. Oct. 30, 1852
The Poetry of Finland IX, 583–88. Aug. 5, 1854
Old Scandinavian Heroes XII, 112–15. Sept. 1, 1855

VERSE

Swedish Folk-Songs:
Fair Carin I, 180. May 18, 1850
The Dove on the Lily I, 204. May 25, 1850
Birth Song. Song of Death I, 229–30. June 1, 1850
The Ballad of Richard Burnell I, 372–74. July 13, 1850
An Every-Day Hero I, 492–94. Aug. 17, 1850
Thomas Harlowe II, 397–400. Jan. 18, 1851

Howitt, William [*Mr. William Howitt, Mr. W. Howitt, W. Howitt, Mr. Howitt, Howitt*], 1792–1879, misc. writer. Attended Friends' schools; extended his education by reading and by study of foreign languages. Early began writing verse and contributing sketches to obscure periodicals; later wrote for *Chambers's, Tait's, Monthly Repository, People's Journal*, and other periodicals, including spiritualist magazines. Brought out *Howitt's Journal of Literature and Popular Progress*, 1847–48. In the *Journal*, as in his writing in other periodicals and in his books, supported humanitarian causes and social reform. In 1823 published *The Forest Minstrel, and Other Poems*, written jointly with his wife (above); also collaborated with her on other works. Author of books on rural English life, books based on his stay in Germany and in Australia, historical works, works on religion, books for boys, adult fiction. Published some translations from the German; also aided his wife in translations from the Swedish. In 1865 granted Civil List pension of £140 a year "In consideration of the long and useful career of literary labour in which both he and his wife have been engaged" (Colles, *Literature and the Pension List*).

Howitt admired Dickens's writings particularly for their social awareness (*People's Journal*, Jan. 3, 1846). He was acquainted with Dickens, who asked both him and his wife to contribute to *H.W.* (see Mary Howitt, above). The amicable relationship between the two men was broken late in 1859 by a quarrel resulting from Dickens's skepticism concerning supernatural phenomena and Howitt's conviction in spiritualism. It was carried on in person, by letter, and, by Howitt, in the pages of the *Spiritual Magazine* (Woodring, *Victorian Samplers*, pp. 202–204). The article "Rather a Strong Dose," *A.Y.R.*, March 21, 1863, ridiculed the ideas advanced by Howitt in his *History of the Supernatural.*

Dickens obviously valued Howitt as a *H.W.* contributor. When he was obliged to refuse one of Howitt's papers because its subject had already been dealt with, he took pains to explain the situation to Howitt and to assure him that he liked his paper "very much" (Nov. 11, Nov. 12, 1850). When Howitt on one occasion was displeased with Wills's handling of his contributions, Dickens suggested Howitt's sending them in the future directly to him. It would give him pain, he assured Howitt, if anything disagreeable arose out of their association (May 18, 1852: typescript Huntington Library). According to Anna Mary Howitt, the Australian sketches and tales that Howitt contributed to *H.W.* "received warm encomium from Dickens" (*Pioneers of the Spiritual Reformation*, p. 237).

In his preface to *Tallangetta,* Howitt took occasion to refute the statement of an Australian critic that those sketches were "evidently the work of two hands" and that it was "probably Dickens himself" who had "breathed into them the breath of genius." No hand but his own, wrote Howitt, had "touched a syllable of those papers."

At the time of its appearance in *H.W.*, "The Miner's Daughters" was thought by some readers to be the writing of Mrs. Gaskell or of "Currer Bell." The Office Book ascription to Howitt of that story, as also of the article "Epping Forest," is confirmed by mention of the two items in Mrs. Howitt's *Autobiography* (II, 59, 166–67). So too is the Office Book ascription of "Mrs. Ranford's New Year's Dinner": the item is obviously the "beautiful story" that Mrs. Howitt mentioned her husband as writing in Nov. 1850 for the Christmas number of that year (*Autobiography*, II, 63). Dickens had written to Howitt, Nov. 12, that he would let him know about the space in the Christmas number. There had evidently been no room for the story; it appeared in the number of Jan. 4. Howitt's "religious credulity paper," the subject of Dickens's letter of May 18, 1852, is "Volunteer Apostles." Dickens's reference to one of Howitt's papers as "all right" is a reference to "The Land-Shark"; Dickens wanted the German poetry deleted or given also in English (to Wills, Jan. 1, 1856); the poetry was deleted. Howitt had no connection with the writing of "A Colonial Patriot," to which his name is attached in the Office Book. See Fawkner (above).

Occasional references to Howitt appeared in *H.W.* The article "Ebenezer Elliott" recorded from Howitt's *Homes and Haunts of the Most Eminent British Poets* the description of Elliott's Sheffield warehouse; Ollier's "Faces" mentioned Howitt; and Payn's "The Two Janes" referred to "Mr. Howitt's pleasant breezy volumes." In his own article "Epping Forest," Howitt quoted at length the evidence given by "Mr. Howitt" in his *Year-Book of the Country* (1850) that people of all classes enjoyed excursions to Epping.

Five of Howitt's *H.W.* contributions were reprinted in whole or part in *Harper's*, two of them – "The Miner's Daughters" and "The Warilows of Welland" – acknowledged to *H.W.* "The Miner's Daughters" was included in a collection (n.d.) of three stories "By Charles Dickens" published by the New York firm De Witt & Davenport (the first item in the collection was one of Georgiana Craik's *H.W.* stories; the second, one of Mrs. Gaskell's). "The Miner's Daughters" was also included in *Choice*

Stories from Dickens' Household Words, pub. Auburn, N.Y., 1854.

D.N.B.

The Miner's Daughters. – A Tale of the Peak I, 125–30. May 4, 1850, and the 2 following nos.
The Last of a Long Line [chap. i = lead] I, 433–39. Aug. 3, 1850, and the following no.
The Warilows of Welland; or, The Modern Prodigal II, 12–19. Sept. 28, 1850
The Sea-Side Churchyard II, 257–62. Dec. 7, 1850
Mrs. Ranford's New Year's Dinner II, 339–48. Jan. 4, 1851
The Queen's Tobacco-Pipe II, 355–58. Jan. 4, 1851
Epping Forest III, 156–60. May 10, 1851
A Pilgrimage to the Great Exhibition from Abroad III, 321–24. June 28, 1851
A Day at Waterloo III, 539–44. Aug. 30, 1851
Two Aspects of Ireland IV, 6–10. Sept. 27, 1851, and the following no.
The Duke's Agent IV, 498–502. Feb. 14, 1852
Volunteer Apostles [lead] V, 261–66. June 5, 1852
Two Days in Rio Janeiro XII, 4–11. Aug. 4, 1855
The Ursinus XII, 176–80. Sept. 22, 1855
*The Old and New Squatter / Squatters: The Old Squatter [lead] XII, 433–41. Dec. 8, 1855
The New Squatter XII, 471–78. Dec. 15, 1855
*The Landlord Holly-Tree Inn (Christmas 1855), pp. 22–30
*The Land-Shark XII, 563–70. Jan. 12, 1856
*Black Thursday XIII, 388–95. May 10, 1856
*Gold-Hunting XIII, 448–54. May 24, 1856, and the following no.

*Repr. as interpolated stories in *Tallangetta, the Squatter's Home. A Story of Australian Life. By William Howitt.* 2 vols. London: Longman, Brown, Green, Longmans, & Roberts, 1857. Pub. in *H.W.* acknowledged.

Hudson, Charles Thomas |*C. T. Hudson, Hudson*|, 1828–1903, schoolmaster, naturalist. B.A. Cambridge, 1852; M.A. 1855; LL.D. 1866. Before becoming student at Cambridge, had been schoolmaster in Glasgow and Liverpool. Thereafter, second master, then head master, Bristol grammar school, 1852–60. Established and conducted private school in Clifton, 1861–81. Devoted his leisure to microscopic research; discovered several genera and species of *Rotifera*; became in this branch of science "the chief authority of his time" (*Jour. of the Royal Microscopical Society*, Feb. 1904). F.R.M.S. 1872; F.R.S. 1889. Contributed numerous articles to scientific journals. Author of *The Rotifera*, 1886, written with assistance of Philip Henry Gosse.

Hudson's *H.W.* articles show the methods and devices of the schoolmaster. In the first, "Mr. Bubs" makes repeated observations of Mars, finally arriving at a correct understanding of the planet's orbit. In the second, by question and answer, by reference to tangible objects, and by computation of distances in terms of the speed of railway travel, Hudson leads the reader, step by step, to a concept of astronomical distances.

The Office Book authorship ascription for Hudson's first article reads "C. T. Hughes," the "Hughes" being in part blotted and overwritten; the name "Hudson" is written, clearly, above the overwritten name. Hughes's article "Mr. Bubb's Visit to the Moon," May 17, was motivated by Hudson's article.

D.N.B. suppl. 1901–1911

Mr. Bubs on Planetary Disturbances III, 58–60. April 12, 1851
Very Long Chalks [chip] III, 472–73. Aug. 9, 1851

Hughes, Mr. *Not identified.* The writer's contribution begins with a reference to Hudson's article "Mr. Bubs on Planetary Disturbances," April 12, 1851: "Mr. Bubbs after his visit to the Sun (as described in a former number) ... thought ... that he would take a nice quiet ride in the moon. ..." The Office Book indicates some preliminary confusion as to the authorship of the two items. "Mr. Bubs on Planetary Disturbances" is recorded as by C. T. Hughes, the "Hughes" being in part blotted and overwritten; the name "Hudson" is written, clearly, above the overwritten name. For "Mr. Bubb's Visit to the Moon" the name "Hughes" is preceded by an overwritten name, the first letter of which is "R." Payment is marked "Handed by W.H.W."

In a "chip," "Mr. Bubbs and the Moon," May 31, Wills stated that "Mr. Bubbs" had written to *H.W.* "in a state of alarm" concerning an erroneous reading in his article, which he took to be a printer's error. Wills gave the corrected reading, but stated that the reading that had appeared in *H.W.* was not a misprint, but one that had appeared in the contributor's own MS.

Mr. Bubb's Visit to the Moon [chip]
III, 187–88. May 17, 1851

Humphreys, Jennett |*J.R.*; also *Jennett Humphreys*|, periodical contributor, writer of stories and verse for children. Contributed to *New Monthly, Little Folks, Newbery House Magazine,* and other periodicals. Nine of her poems included in *Home Thoughts and Home Scenes,* 1865, a collection of poems for children. In 1864 submitted to Chapman & Hall a novel that was rejected by Meredith as the publishers' reader; also a second novel so rejected (Stevenson, *Ordeal of George Meredith,* pp. 153–54). Author of *Tales Easy and Small for the Youngest of All, Maud's Doll and Her Walk in Picture and Talk, Insect Ways on Summer Days,* and other children's books, some of them several times reprinted. Her *Old Welsh Knee Songs, Lullabies, Frolic Rhymes, and Other Pastime Verse. Now First Collected and Issued in English Form* published in Caernarvon by Welsh National Press Co., 1894; 2nd ed. same year.

In the Office Book, the item listed below is assigned to "J.R.," the "R" being written over what seems to have been a "B." Written after the initials, in another hand than Wills's, appears the name "Jennett Humphreys." The "J.R." is obviously in error, and the "Jennett Humphreys" correct.

The *H.W.* article cites and discusses various of the comments on pronunciation, also some on word-coinages and borrowings, given in one of the early editions of John Walker's *Critical Pronouncing Dictionary.* Miss Humphreys's interest in lexicography is evidenced by her article "Among the Dictionaries," *Cornhill,* June 1881. The *Cornhill* article, which traces the history of dictionary-making from the early glosses to the work in progress on the *Oxford English Dictionary,* does no more than refer to Walker: "There was Walker, saying (on Sheridan's report), how Swift used to jeer the people who called the wind winn'd ..."; but the article quotes, in connection with Walker and Sheridan, the same two remarks that appear in the *H.W.* article.

To *A.Y.R.*, under the editorship of Charles Dickens, Jr., Miss Humphreys contributed a series of some fifteen articles titled "Learning to Cook" and a series titled "Early Workers" (i.e., child workers), as well as articles on other subjects (*A.Y.R.* Letter-Book; see also Ellis, *William Harrison Ainsworth and His Friends,* II, 271).

Allibone

Walker XVII, 523–26. May 15, 1858

Hunt, Frederick Knight |*Mr. F. K. Hunt, F. K. Hunt, Mr. Hunt (F.K.)*|, 1814–1854, journalist. Educated himself largely by wide reading. Worked as printer's boy, also as clerk to a barrister, through whom he obtained a connection with a newspaper. Meanwhile studied medicine at Middlesex Hospital. M.R.C.S. 1840. Established *Medical Times,* 1839; forced by financial or other difficulties to relinquish the periodical. Was for a year medical officer to a poor-law union in Norfolk; thereafter returned to London. Subeditor, then editor, of *Pictorial Times.* Brought out *Hunt's London Journal,* 1844. On establishment of *Daily News*, was engaged as provincial editor of the periodical; editor, 1851 to his death. Author of *The Rhine: Its Scenery and Historical & Legendary Associations*, 1845, dedicated by special permission to Queen Victoria; *The Fourth Estate: Contributions towards a History of Newspapers*, 1850, his only important writing.

Vizetelly (*Glances Back through Seventy Years*, I, 247) stated that his recommendation of Hunt to Wills led to Dickens's appointment of Hunt to the *Daily News* staff. Hunt, in *The Fourth Estate* (II, 189), mentioned the *Daily News* as starting "with the prestige of a highly popular literary name, and with a staff of writers such as no previous Paper had ever mustered to prepare a first number" – the latter comment implying a compliment to Hunt himself. Occasional other references to Dickens also appear in *The Fourth Estate*.

Hunt wrote for *H.W.* during the first two years of its publication. In addition to contributing himself, he secured from his friend Robert McCormick an article for the 1850 Christmas number (see McCormick, below). Dickens thought highly of Hunt's work for *H.W.* In a letter to Horne, March 18, 1851, he wrote that what Hunt and Morley "have done for us (especially Mr Hunt) has unquestionably done us *very good service indeed*." Hunt's "Swinging the Ship" Dickens thought a very good article (to Wills, July 12, 1850). Curiously, payment for most of Hunt's contributions was less than the standard payment. For a 6-col. article, for instance, Hunt was paid £2.10.0, instead of the standard £3.3.0; for a 16-col. article, £7.0.0, instead of the standard £8.8.0.

Wills's *H.W.* article "Newspaper Antecedents" was based in part on Hunt's *Fourth Estate*; "The Appetite for News," also by Wills, quoted a paragraph from the same book.

"Greenwich Weather-Wisdom," included in the list below, is unassigned in the Office Book, the title of the article being repeated in the author-column. The article is by Hunt, as proved by comments in it and in a preceding and a following article by Hunt. "The Planet-Watchers of Greenwich," an account of the Greenwich Observatory, states that the meteorological branch of the Observatory is "to be spoken of hereafter." The meteorological branch is the subject of "Greenwich Weather-Wisdom" in the following *H.W.* number. That article, in turn, contains a reference to the preceding article: "as was said when speaking of the Astronomical Observatory." "The Registrar-General on 'Life' in London" again refers to "Greenwich Weather-Wisdom": it mentions certain diagrams recording weather changes and states that "we have already" spoken of them "in some words about weather wisdom."

Harper's reprinted, in whole or part, five of Hunt's *H.W.* contributions, three of them acknowledged to *H.W.*

D.N.B.

A Visit to the Arctic Discovery Ships
I, 180–82. May 18, 1850

The Planet-Watchers of Greenwich
I, 200–204. May 25, 1850

Greenwich Weather-Wisdom
I, 222–25. June 1, 1850

The Registrar-General on "Life" in London I, 330–33. June 29, 1850

How to Spend a Summer Holiday
I, 356–58. July 6, 1850

A Few Facts about Matrimony
I, 374–77. July 13, 1850

"Swinging the Ship." A Visit to the Compass Observatory
I, 414–18. July 27, 1850

What There Is in the Roof of the College of Surgeons
I, 464–67. Aug. 10, 1850

The Late American President
I, 525–28. Aug. 24, 1850

London Pauper Children
I, 549–52. Aug. 31, 1850

The Modern Robbers of the Rhine
II, 90–93. Oct. 19, 1850

A Great Day for the Doctors
II, 137–39. Nov. 2, 1850

What a London Curate Can Do If He Tries II, 172–76. Nov. 16, 1850

Rats! II, 214–16. Nov. 23, 1850

A Visit to the Registrar-General
II, 235–40. Nov. 30, 1850

Wings of Wire [lead]
II, 241–45. Dec. 7, 1850

The Hunterian Museum
II, 277–82. Dec. 14, 1850

Christmas among the London Poor and Sick II, 304–305. Dec. 21, 1850
Twenty-four Hours in a London Hospital [lead] II, 457–65. Feb. 8, 1851
Man Magnified IV, 13–15. Sept. 27, 1851

Hunt, James Henry Leigh |*Mr. Leigh Hunt, Leigh Hunt*|, 1784–1859, poet and essayist. Educated at Christ's Hospital. Contributed to *Atlas, True Sun, Morning Chronicle, New Monthly,* and other periodicals. Editor of *Examiner,* 1808–1821; *Reflector,* 1810–11; *Indicator,* 1819–21; *Tatler,* 1830–32; *Leigh Hunt's London Journal,* 1834–35; and other periodicals. Author of *The Story of Rimini,* 1816, and other volumes of verse; *Lord Byron and Some of His Contemporaries,* 1828; *Autobiography,* 1850. Published collections of his critical and familiar essays; various anthologies; translations from Italian authors. In 1847 granted Civil List pension of £200 a year "In consideration of his distinguished literary talents" (Colles, *Literature and the Pension List*).

Hunt was more than fifty years old when he met Dickens and became his friend and admirer. Dickens invited Hunt to his home, addressed friendly letters to him, sent him copies of his books, and organized a theatrical performance in his benefit. After these pleasant associations, came his depiction of Hunt as Skimpole. It gave Hunt deep pain. Dickens's attempts, in conversation with Hunt, to exonerate himself from his ungentlemanly conduct could amount, as Forster wrote, to nothing more than "a friendly evasion of the points really at issue" (*Life,* Book VI, sect. vii). Hunt made no public pronouncement on the matter. On June 16, 1855, Dickens published in *H.W.* an appreciative article on Hunt's *Stories in Verse* ("By Rail to Parnassus" by Morley). This commendatory notice in his journal, wrote Dickens to Hunt (June 28, 1855) seemed to him the best means of expressing himself publicly on the "painful subject," which he hoped Hunt would not think it necessary to renew with him. In that "unmistakable association with you by name," he wrote, "let all end." Dickens dealt with the Skimpole incident in an article that he published in *A.Y.R.,* Dec. 24, 1859, based on Thornton Hunt's edition of Hunt's *Autobiography;* his self-righteous attitude is evident in the title: "Leigh Hunt. A Remonstrance." A second article on Hunt in *A.Y.R.* (April 12, 1862), "A Literary Life," was written by Hunt's friend Edmund Ollier.

Hunt welcomed the advent of *H.W.* with a sonnet to Dickens, in which he made bold

> to join in summoning men's ears
> To this thy new-found music of our spheres,
> In hopes that by thy Household Words and thee
> The world may haste to days of harmony.

His contributions, only eleven in all, began with the first number and continued after the Skimpole incident. "Kilspindie" was the one of Hunt's *H.W.* poems that Dickens mentioned liking (*Correspondence of Leigh Hunt,* II, 160); that poem, and two others from the periodical, appeared in *Stories in Verse,* which Dickens referred to as a "delightful volume" (to Hunt, May 4, 1855). But for Hunt's prose contributions Dickens had little enthusiasm. "Gore House," he wrote to Wills (Aug. 5, 1853), was "very poor." Wills was to strike out part of a paragraph: "It is Skimpole, you know – the whole passage. I couldn't write it more like him." In reprinting "Gore House" Hunt restored the deleted passage or substituted another (see *H.W.,* VII, 591, and *Old Court Suburb,* I, 75). Hunt's article "Kensington," which had been preceded by "Lounging through Kensington," moved Dickens to the derisive exclamation to Wills (Aug. 7, 1853): "O Heaven, Hunt's not lounging, and being in earnest!!!" (punctuation supplied from MS Huntington Library).

Edmund Blunden (*Leigh Hunt and His Circle,* p. 317) states that Hunt "received 'the highest rate of payment' for his [*H.W.*] articles." For the six articles for which the Office Book records payment, Hunt was paid the standard rate. Three of the payments are marked "Advanced." Of the poems, "Dream within Dream" is not listed in the Office Book. Payment for "The Trumpets of Doolkarnein" is marked "Advanced," but no sum is recorded. The payment for "Abraham and the Fire-Worshipper," however, is twice the customary rate of payment for verse; for "Kilspindie" the payment is more than twice the customary rate, but that payment may have been augmented to include payment for "The Cup and the Lip" in the same number (for which no payment is recorded).

In addition to the article devoted to *Stories in Verse*, several *H.W.* articles contained references to Hunt's writings. Kent's "Going A-maying" quoted some lines from "the English poet of the Italian Rimini"; Stone's "Sleep" cited a passage from one of Hunt's papers in the *Indicator*; Robertson's "Coast Folk" referred to a paper by Hunt in the *Liberal*; and Ollier's "Faces" mentioned a remark in the *Autobiography*. Other references appeared in "Bed," "The Doom of English Wills" (Nov. 2, 1850), "All about Pigs," "Left Behind," and "Beef, Mutton and Bread."

In the Office Book, Andersen is recorded as author of "The Cup and the Lip"; his name is marked out and substituted by that of Hunt. Andersen is properly credited with the "chip" in the immediately following number.

Harper's reprinted "Holland House" in part, without acknowledgment to *H.W.*

D.N.B.

PROSE

The Cup and the Lip [chip]
v, 582. Sept. 4, 1852

*Lounging through Kensington
VII, 533–38. Aug. 6, 1853

*Gore House VII, 589–93. Aug. 20, 1853

*Kensington VIII, 13–17. Sept. 3, 1853

*Kensington Church
VIII, 276–81. Nov. 19, 1853

*Kensington Worthies
VIII, 325–30. Dec. 3, 1853

*Holland House IX, 8–15. Feb. 18, 1854, and the following no.

*Repr., with additions and some revision, in *The Old Court Suburb; or Memorials of Kensington, Regal, Critical, and Anecdotical. By Leigh Hunt.* 2 vols. London: Hurst and Blackett, 1855. Pub. in *H.W.* acknowledged in "Preface" (but "Preface" does not appear in all copies of 1st ed.; see Brewer, *My Leigh Hunt Library ... The First Editions*, p. 260).

VERSE

Abraham and the Fire-Worshipper. A Dramatic Parable
I, 12–13. March 30, 1850

Dream within Dream; or, Evil Minimised
I, 82. April 20, 1850

Kilspindie v, 585. Sept. 4, 1852

The Trumpets of Doolkarnein
VI, 12–13. Sept. 18, 1852

"Abraham and the Fire-Worshipper," "Kilspindie," and "The Trumpets of Doolkarnein" repr. in *Stories in Verse. By Leigh Hunt. Now First Collected.* London: Geo. Routledge & Co., 1855. All 4 items repr. in *The Poetical Works of Leigh Hunt. Now First Entirely Collected, Revised by Himself, and Edited with an Introduction by S. Adams Lee.* 2 vols. Boston: Ticknor and Fields, 1857. Pub. in *H.W.* not acknowledged in either collection.

Hunt, Robert |*Robert Hunt*|, 1807–1887, scientist, writer on science. F.R.S. Attended school in Plymouth and in Penzance; studied medicine in London; acquired some knowledge of practical chemistry. Devoted himself to scientific research, particularly on chemical influence of solar rays and on electrical phenomena in mineral veins. Keeper of Mining Records, 1845–83; during greater part of that time compiled *Mineral Statistics of the United Kingdom*, issued annually as a Blue Book. For some years lecturer on mechanical science and experimental physics, Royal School of Mines. Contributed largely to scientific journals; for many years wrote scientific columns in *Athenaeum*; contributed to *Art Journal*, also to general periodicals. Brought out three revised and enlarged editions of Andrew Ure's *Dictionary of Arts, Manufactures, and Mines*. Author of *A Popular Treatise on the Art of Photography*, 1841; *Researches on Light*, 1844; *Elementary Phy-*

sics, 1851; *British Mining*, 1884; and many other works.

D.N.B.

Gold in Great Britain
XIII, 541–43. June 21, 1856

I

Inman, Thomas |*Dr. Inman*|, 1820–1876, physician, writer. M.B. King's College, London, 1842; M.D. University of London, 1844. M.R.C.S. 1842. On completion of his medical training, settled in Liverpool; there, was lecturer to Royal Infirmary School of Medicine; house surgeon, then physician, to Royal Infirmary; attached also to Fever Hospital and Workhouse Infirmary. Retired from practice, 1871. Published works on medicine and hygiene. Contributed to *Proceedings* of Liverpool Literary and Philosophical Society. Read widely. Came to hold idea that phallic worship was key to all mythology. Propounded the idea in various papers and in *Ancient Faiths Embodied in Ancient Names*, 1868–69; *Ancient Pagan and Modern Christian Symbolism*, 1869; *Ancient Faiths and Modern*, 1876.

"Six Years among Cannibals" is an account of Marquesan customs, related – in response to his physician's questioning – by a hospital patient who had been shipwrecked on one of the Marquesas Islands. The writer begins his article with the statement: "I am physician to a hospital in a large seaport town." Of the three Inmans listed in medical directories of the 1850s, only Thomas Inman was hospital physician in a seaport town. The article shows the writer's knowledge of and interest in taboo, initiation rites, language, names, etc., among savage peoples – knowledge and interests that accord with those of Thomas Inman.

Of the *H.W.* staff, it was Morley who was acquainted with Inman. The two had been fellow students at King's College; Inman had contributed to the *King's College Magazine*, of which Morley was one of the founders. In *Early Papers and Some Memories* (p. 16), Morley mentioned Inman's later becoming known "as a writer upon matters of curious learning."

D.N.B.

Six Years among Cannibals
VII, 134–38. April 9, 1853

Irwin. *Not identified.* In the second item listed below, the contributor describes a stormy passage from Macao to Singapore. In other of his contributions, all of which deal with Australasia, he mentions having been in the Auckland Islands and in Norfolk Island. Of the latter he writes: "I know the place well and the people living there, convicts and all. How I came by my knowledge is a question which I am not obliged to answer; but, for the comfort of the clean-fingered, I may state that I am not legally pitch."

In 1880, W. Irwin, Esq., submitted to *A.Y.R.* some papers that Charles Dickens, Jr., did not find suited to the requirements of the periodical. In his letter of rejection, Aug. 23, Dickens stated that he was returning the papers (subject not mentioned) "together with Mr. Wills's letters" (*A.Y.R.* Letter-Book). The reference to Wills may indicate that W. Irwin had had some association with Wills during Wills's subeditorship of *H.W.* or *A.Y.R.*

Norfolk Island *Irwin & Morley*
V, 73–77. April 10, 1852
Caught in a Typhoon
VIII, 177–79. Oct. 22, 1853
Sentimental Geography [chip]
VIII, 306–307. Nov. 26, 1853
The Antecedents of Australia [chip]
VIII, 476–77. Jan. 14, 1854
The Albatross at Home [chip]
IX, 15–16. Feb. 18, 1854

J

Jackowski, Ignacy |*J. Jackowski*|, *d.* 1873, Polish advocate, author, politician. Born in Nowogrodek. Took part in Polish uprising of 1830–31; on defeat of the insurrection went into exile in England; remained there until 1857. In London, associated with Prince Adam Czartoryski's circle. Member of the London Literary Association of the Friends of Poland (of which Dickens was for a time a member). Served for more than twenty years as deputy paymaster to Polish refugees receiving relief from British Government; in 1855 appointed chief paymaster of Polish division of the Cossacks of the Sultan in the British service. Died in Nowogrodek. Privately printed, London, 1853, a collection of his political articles contributed to a London Polish newspaper. Author of *Panorama*, 1852, a poem; *Powieść czasu mojego czyli przygody litewskie* [The story of my time, or Lithuanian adventures], priv. printed (anon.), London, 1854 (Jackowski's authorship at first disputed, thereafter established).

During his exile Jackowski wrote not only for Polish newspapers published in London, but also for English periodicals. The 1852 *Report* (May) of the London Literary Association mentions his having contributed, during the year covered by the report, "many interesting articles of a literary or political character to various magazines and periodical works"; the 1853 *Report* mentions him as one of the members who "have during the year contributed many articles to the periodical literature of this country." The *H.W.* contributor is clearly Ignacy Jackowski. Wills, in recording Jackowski's name, may have misread the initial; or Jackowski may have written the lengthened "I" as initial.

Harper's reprinted "A Specimen of Russian Justice," without acknowledgment to *H.W.*

Polski słownik biog.

A Specimen of Russian Justice
J. Jackowski & W.H.W.
II, 598–600. March 15, 1851

James, Marian |*Miss James*|, novelist. Contributed fiction to *Hogg's Instructor*, *Titan*, *Chambers's*, *Fraser's*; a poem to *A Welcome*, 1863. Published *Ethel: or, The Double Error*, 1854; *Not an Angel*, 1863; *A Girl's Romance*, 1867; and four other works of fiction (some had originally appeared in periodicals).

In a letter to Miss James, Aug 8, 1859 (*A.Y.R.* Letter-Book), Wills stated that he was returning to her an article on Rome that she had submitted to *A.Y.R.* In suggesting certain changes that would make the article acceptable, he mentioned Miss James's "sharp and observant faculty for accurate description." The letter implies that Miss James was acquainted with Wills.

Allibone

An Ordeal XIII, 269–74. April 5, 1856, and the following no.

Repr. in *Types of Womanhood. In Four Stories. By the Author of "Ethel," "Sister Anne," Etc.* London: Sampson Low, Son, and Co., 1858. Pub. in *H.W.* acknowledged.

Jenkin, Henrietta Camilla (Jackson) |*Mrs. Gaskell's friend, Mrs. Jenkyn*|, 1807?–1885, novelist. Born in Jamaica, of Scottish parentage. Was talented in drawing and singing. In 1832 married Charles Jenkin, midshipman, afterwards captain R.N. The Jenkins lived at various times in England – where their son Fleeming was born; in Scotland, and on the Continent. Mrs. Jenkin became friend of Agostino and Giovanni Ruffini; was the original of the English girl Lucy in the latter's *Doctor Antonio* (Corrigan, "Giovanni Ruffini's Letters to Vernon Lee," *English Miscellany*, 1962, p. 231). During a residence in Manchester, became acquainted with the Gaskells; though Mrs. Gaskell regarded Mrs. Jenkin merely as an "acquaintance," she later wrote that she "had quite a reflected lustre" from the fact that she could say to admirers of *Cousin Stella* "that I knew & could tell them all about the authoress" (*Letters of Mrs Gaskell*, No. 455).

Author of twelve works of fiction, the first published probably about 1840, the last in 1874. According to R. L. Stevenson, had no natural taste for literature and wrote novels only to earn money (*Memoir of Fleeming Jenkin*, pp. 21–22); some of her novels, however, highly praised by reviewers. *Cousin Stella*, 1859, and all six of her following novels, published by Smith, Elder & Co., to which firm Mrs. Gaskell gave her an introduction (*Letters*, No. 412).

Her appearance in *H.W.*, like her introduction to Smith, Elder, Mrs. Jenkin owed to the good offices of Mrs. Gaskell. Mrs. Jenkin, living in Paris in 1855, evidently sent to Mrs. Gaskell in that year various papers to be placed in periodicals – a commission that Mrs. Gaskell carried out. The first item listed below is assigned in the Office Book to "Mrs. Gaskell's friend"; payment is recorded as sent to Mrs. Gaskell. The second is assigned to "Mrs. Jenkyn." The two papers appeared in consecutive numbers. Mrs. Gaskell had obviously sent both to *H.W.* at the same time, and with them, apparently, as Dickens's letters seem to indicate, also other material by Mrs. Jenkin. Shortly after the publication of the two items, Dickens wrote to Wills, Sept. 4 (MS Huntington Library), about a paper "by a Mrs Jenkyn – Mrs Gaskell's friend –" concerning which the author had written to him from Paris and which he had promised to read. In a following letter to Wills, Sept. 20 (MS Huntington Library), Dickens again mentioned a paper by "Mrs Gaskell's friend Mrs Jenkyn" (perhaps the same paper referred to in the earlier letter), which Wills was to return to the writer; if he did not have her Paris street number, he was to send her the paper in care of Mrs. Gaskell.

Harper's reprinted "Coralie," without acknowledgment to *H.W.*

D.N.B.

Coralie	XII, 60–66. Aug. 18, 1855
The Child-Seer	XII, 80–85. Aug. 25, 1855

Jerdan, William |*Jerdan, W. Jerdan*|, 1782–1869, journalist. Received what he described as "a common Scottish provincial education" (*Autobiography*, IV, 377); early had literary ambitions. About 1805, began his long and industrious journalistic career, during which, as reporter, contributor, editor, and proprietor, was connected with numerous publications. Longest service was as editor, 1817–50, of *Literary Gazette* – the periodical that stood during the 1820s as critical arbiter in British literary world. Forced by financial and other difficulties to terminate connection with *Gazette*; thereafter continued to contribute to periodicals, e.g., *Fraser's*, *Gent. Mag.*, *Leisure Hour*, *N. & Q.* Edited and wrote nearly whole of *National Portrait Gallery of Illustrious and Eminent Personages of the Nineteenth Century*, 1830–34; author of *Men I Have Known*, 1866, and other works. Member of many societies and clubs; one of founders of Royal Society of Literature. In 1853 granted Civil List pension of £100 a year "In consideration of his services to literature for many years, and his distressed circumstances at an advanced period of life" (Colles, *Literature and the Pension List*).

"With Dickens," wrote Jerdan in his *Autobiography*, "I can claim long friendly relations." Jerdan contributed to *Bentley's Misc.* under Dickens's editorship. As a friend of both Bentley and Dickens, he represented Bentley in the final negotiations that terminated Dickens's association with the publisher. Jerdan contributed an item to *The Pic Nic Papers*, 1841, the volume that Dickens brought out for the benefit of John Macrone's widow. Dickens was one of the young writers for whom Jerdan prophesied literary fame and whose books he noticed favourably in the *Literary Gazette*. On the appearance of Sam Weller in the pages of *Pickwick*, Jerdan was "so charmed," he stated, "that I could not resist the impulse to write to the author, express my admiration, and counsel him to develop the novel character largely – to the utmost." Jerdan was much gratified at being invited to the *Pickwick* celebration dinner; he was present, also, at other Dickens celebrations. Dickens, in turn, accepted an invitation to a *Literary Gazette* anniversary celebration and sent Jerdan cordial congratulations on the occasion. Dickens was a member of the committee that organized a testimonial in Jerdan's honour on the cessation of Jerdan's editorship of the *Gazette*; he contributed also to the subscription raised for Jerdan (*Autobiography*, IV, 364–66, 370–75).

Jerdan's connection with *H.W.* came toward the end of his long journalistic career; he was almost seventy-five when he sent the first of his four contributions to the periodical; thereafter, according to Ley (*Dickens Circle*, p. 122), he contributed also to *A.Y.R.* In a friendly letter to Jerdan, July 21, 1857, Dickens wrote, obviously in answer to Jerdan's query, that he was sure that both of Jerdan's "brief contributions" to *H.W.* had been published, though he did not have at hand the means of verification. According to the Office Book, Jerdan had contributed only two items by the date of Dickens's letter. The Office Book records payment for both, as also for Jerdan's fourth contribution, but not for the third. Wills's cheque (amount not stated) in payment for that contribution Dickens sent to Jerdan in a letter of Aug. 19, 1857 (cited in Grubb, "Dickens the Paymaster Once More," *Dickensian*, Spring 1955).

D.N.B.

The Gift of Tongues
xv, 41–43. Jan. 10, 1857
Old Scraps of Science
xv, 355–57. April 11, 1857
Old Hawtrey
xvi, 308–310. Sept. 26, 1857
A British Nuisance [chip]
xvii, 131–32. Jan. 23, 1858

Jerrold, William Blanchard |*W. B. Jerrold, B. Jerrold, Jerrold (W. B.), Jerrold*|, 1826–1884, journalist and author; eldest son of Douglas Jerrold (1803–1857). Attended school in England and in France; studied to become an artist; turned to journalism. After 1855, spent much time in France; knew Gustave Doré and Napoleon III. Wrote for his father's *Weekly Newspaper*. Contributed to *Illus. London News, Athenaeum, Welcome Guest, Once a Week, Gent. Mag.*, and other periodicals. From 1857 to time of his death was editor of *Lloyd's Weekly*. Author of comedies, novels, books on gastronomy; books on French society, institutions, politics; a life of his father, one of Napoleon III, and one of George Cruikshank. Wrote letterpress to Doré's *London. A Pilgrimage*, 1872; at time of his death, engaged on life of Doré. Edited works of his father, *The Final Reliques of Father Prout*, poetical works of Laman Blanchard.

Dickens was a friend of Jerrold's father (who declined to write for *H.W.* because of Dickens's policy of anonymous publication); he took an interest in the son. Jerrold played a role in one of Dickens's presentations of *Every Man in His Humour*; he was engaged by Dickens as reporter for the *Daily News*. Marked bitterness between Jerrold and Dickens resulted when, on the death of Jerrold's father, Dickens set about organizing benefits for the Jerrold family. Jerrold naturally resented Dickens's officiousness; Dickens was indignant at Jerrold's lack of proper gratitude. Amicable relations were later re-established between the two. Jerrold's life of his father contains some of his father's letters to Dickens, which Dickens had placed at Jerrold's disposal. His presentation copy of the book to Dickens Jerrold inscribed: "To Charles Dickens, Esquire, the first 'perfect' copy of the Life of his dear friend" (Stonehouse, *Catalogue*). Jerrold wrote a memorial tribute to Dickens, *Gent. Mag.*, July 1870; he devoted to Dickens the first number (June 1871) of his series titled *The Best of All Good Company*. He contributed to *A.Y.R.*, reprinting various of his contributions in *The Cupboard Papers*, 1881, and in other books.

Dickens found Jerrold's "Broken Language" and "The French Waiter" very poor (to Wills, May 4, July 9, 1854: MSS Huntington Library).

Wilkie Collins's *H.W.* article "Douglas Jerrold," based on Jerrold's life of his father, gave high praise to that work: "It is good as the record of a literary life: it is still better as a tribute to the memory of a father, offered by the love and duty of a son."

Ten of Jerrold's *H.W.* contributions were reprinted in *Harper's*, four of them acknowledged to *H.W.* Three were included in the Putnam volumes of selections from *H.W.*: *Home and Social Philosophy*, 1st and 2nd ser.

D.N.B.

PROSE

Fate Days I, 596–98. Sept. 14, 1850
The Subscription List *W. B. Jerrold & W.H.W.* II, 10–12. Sept. 28, 1850
Atlantic Waves II, 22–24. Sept. 28, 1850
The Methusaleh Pill II, 36–38. Oct. 5, 1850
Spiders' Silk II, 65–67. Oct. 12, 1850
Protected Cradles II, 108–112. Oct. 26, 1850
Why People Let Lodgings II, 167–68. Nov. 9, 1850
Christmas in Lodgings *W. B. Jerrold & W.H.W.* II, 295–98. Dec. 21, 1850
Efforts of a Gentleman in Search of Despair II, 369–72. Jan. 11, 1851
The Queen's Bazaar II, 522–24. Feb. 22, 1851
The British Museum a Century Ago [chip] III, 130–31. May 3, 1851
Science at Sea III, 468–71. Aug. 9, 1851
Ruins with Silver Keys [chip] III, 592–94. Sept. 13, 1851
The Constant Reader III, 599–600. Sept. 13, 1851
Budding Chathams IV, 22–24. Sept. 27, 1851
Eyes Made to Order [chip] IV, 64–66. Oct. 11, 1851
Pipe-Clay and Clay Pipes IV, 526–28. Feb. 21, 1852
Smithfield Races V, 162–64. May 1, 1852
The Harmonious Blacksmith V, 198–202. May 15, 1852
Provisionally Registered *W. B. Jerrold & W.H.W.* VII, 445–48. July 9, 1853
Completely Registered VIII, 469–71. Jan. 14, 1854
The Iron Seamstress VIII, 575–76. Feb. 11, 1854
An Old Portrait from The Hague IX, 569–72. July 29, 1854
The Milky and Watery Way XV, 593–96. June 20, 1857

The 24 items repr. in *The Chronicles of the Crutch. By Blanchard Jerrold.* London: William Tinsley, 1860. Pub. in *H.W.* acknowledged.

Pork Insurance [chip] IV, 285–86. Dec. 13, 1851

Repr. in *The Threads of a Storm-Sail, A Little Book on the Benefits of Assurance, By W. Blanchard Jerrold.* London: The Birkbeck Life Assurance Company, 1853. Pub. in *H.W.* not acknowledged.

King Charles's Post-Bag V, 293–95. June 12, 1852
I Give and Bequeath VII, 22–24. March 5, 1853
Gentlemen in History VII, 394–96. June 25, 1853

The 3 items repr. in *A Book for the Beach. By Blanchard Jerrold.* 2 vols. London: Charles J. Skeet, 1863. Pub. in *H.W.* not acknowledged.

For the Benefit of the Cooks IX, 42–44. Feb. 25, 1854
Deadly Lively IX, 138–40. March 25, 1854
Behind the Louvre IX, 185–88. April 8, 1854
Paris with a Mask On IX, 245–48. April 29, 1854
Broken Language IX, 331–32. May 20, 1854
Rabbit-Skins IX, 519–21. July 15, 1854
The French Waiter IX, 546–48. July 22, 1854
Near the Pantheon IX, 613–16. Aug. 12, 1854
Paris upon Wheels X, 382–84. Dec. 2, 1854

The 9 items repr. in *Imperial Paris; Including New Scenes for Old Visitors, By W. Blanchard Jerrold.* London: Bradbury & Evans, 1855. Pub. in *H.W.* acknowledged.

Food for the Factory II, 225–29. Nov. 30, 1850
The Wealth of the Woods II, 282–84. Dec. 14, 1850
Acorn-Coffee [chip] III, 203–204. May 24, 1851
What Godfathers Have Done for Omnibuses [chip] V, 438–39. July 24, 1852
Our Ruins [chip] V, 521–22. Aug. 14, 1852
"Moving" *W. B. Jerrold & W.H.W.* VI, 61–63. Oct. 2, 1852
Hobson's Choice VI, 451–53. Jan. 22, 1853
Anybody's Child VIII, 551–52. Feb. 4, 1854
The Turk at Home IX, 56–61. March 4, 1854
Turks at Sea IX, 444–47. June 24, 1854

Military Fans xiii, 46–48. Jan. 26, 1856
Adventures of a Russian Soldier xiii, 52–58. Feb. 2, 1856
On 'Change in Paris xiv, 102–108. Aug. 16, 1856
Manners Made to Order xv, 425–27. May 2, 1857
Nobody's Philanthropist xix, 605–608. May 28, 1859

VERSE
Peace and War ii, 455. Feb. 1, 1851

Jewsbury, Geraldine Endsor |*Miss Jewsbury*|, 1812–1880, novelist. Educated at a young ladies' boarding school; then received some instruction in languages and drawing. Lived for many years in Manchester. Contributed to Manchester papers, to *Douglas Jerrold's Shilling Magazine*; at least one article to *Westm. Rev.* One of her novels serialized in Manchester *Examiner and Times*, one in *Ladies' Companion*; contributed "Mediaeval Sketches" to *Victoria Regia.* For almost thirty years, reviewer for *Athenaeum*; publisher's reader for Hurst and Blackett, and, for some fifteen years, for Bentley's. Gettmann, *A Victorian Publisher*, quotes many of her incisive, outspoken judgments on MSS submitted to Bentley's. Author of *Zoe*, 1845, which shocked many readers but was very popular in the circulating libraries; *The Half-Sisters*, 1848; *The Sorrows of Gentility*, 1856, dedicated to John Forster; and three other novels; also two children's books. In 1874 granted Civil List pension of £40 a year "In consideration of her services to literature" (Colles, *Literature and the Pension List*). Remembered chiefly for her friendship with the Carlyles; Mrs. Carlyle, writing in 1854, called her "the most intimate friend I have in the world" (*Letters and Memorials of Jane Welsh Carlyle*, ed. Froude, ii, 246).

By the time that *H.W.* began, in 1850, Miss Jewsbury had published her first two novels. In Feb. of that year, Dickens wrote to her: "Dear Miss Jewsbury, – I make no apology for addressing you thus, for I am a reader of yours, and I hope I have that knowledge of you which may justify a frank approach." His letter was an urgent request that Miss Jewsbury contribute to his forthcoming journal: "... if I could induce you to write any papers or short stories for it I should, I sincerely assure you, set great store by your help, and be much gratified in having it." Payment, wrote Dickens, was to be "prompt and good," and he would "be truly earnest" in his desire to make Miss Jewsbury's connection with the journal most agreeable to her. "If I were to write a whole book on the subject I hardly know that I could do more than impress you with a sense of my being in want of your aid, because I estimate its value highly" (*Selections from the Letters of Geraldine Endsor Jewsbury*, ed. Mrs. A. Ireland, p. xi).

Miss Jewsbury hardly seemed eager to become a contributor. To Mrs. Carlyle, in a letter postmarked March 9, 1850, she wrote: "... I had to answer the letter Dickens sent me, and I told him I would write him something suitable as soon as I had time; that, though I never kept my MS. on hand, yet I had written out a little tale which I believed was true; that it was in your hands, and, if he liked, he might have it; and that I would ask you to send it on to him. ..." Mrs. Carlyle had obviously raised some objections to the story, and Miss Jewsbury, on reconsidering them, added a postscript to her letter: "... I think you are right about the story. So put it into the fire, and tell Dickens you did so by my directions. Just write him a line that he may not be expecting anything from me. ..." (*Selections*, pp. 363–64). Perhaps Miss Jewsbury again changed her mind about the "little tale" that she believed to be true, for in a *H.W.* number of the following month appeared her "Young Jew of Tunis," which she informed readers was a true account. About a year later Miss Jewsbury sent Dickens a packet of material, partly by herself, partly by another writer, which Dickens did not find suited to *H.W.* "I must confess," he wrote, June 25, 1851, "to a little disappointment when I found that your packet was not all your own." Miss Jewsbury may have been on a visit to London at the time; Dickens, to avoid disruption of his days by visitors to the Great Exhibition who arrived with letters of introduction to him, had "taken refuge" at Broadstairs. "I fear I may not have the pleasure, consequently, of seeing you," he wrote. "But it would give me great pleasure to improve our personal acquaintance, and to tell you how very glad I should be, if you *could* find time to write something for *Household Words*" (Howe, *Geraldine Jewsbury*, pp. 207–208). Some months later Miss Jewsbury did send in a contribution, and Dickens wrote to Wills, Sept. 27: "*I want Miss Jewsbury's paper.* I must read it myself, and write to her." The paper referred to was probably rejected; the date of Dickens's letter makes it unlikely that his reference should be to "A Curious Page of Family History," published Dec. 6.

Harper's reprinted "A Curious Page of Family History" and "A Forgotten Celebrity," without acknowledgment to *H.W.*

D.N.B.

The Young Jew of Tunis
I, 118–20. April 27, 1850
A Curious Page of Family History
IV, 246–49. Dec. 6, 1851
A Forgotten Celebrity
IV, 534–38. Feb. 28, 1852
A Page from a Sad Book
V, 474–76. July 31, 1852
The Black Lad
VII, 206–208. April 30, 1853
The Great Saddleworth Exhibition
VIII, 109–112. Oct. 1, 1853
My Dream IX, 65–68. March 4, 1854
Specimens of the Alchemists
[chap. i = lead]
XI, 457–65. June 16, 1855, and the following no.
More Alchemy XI, 540–43. July 7, 1855
Instructive Comparisons
Morley & Miss Jewsbury
XII, 211–14. Sept. 29, 1855
Tardy Justice XII, 298–301. Oct. 27, 1855
Disputed Identity [lead]
XII, 481–87. Dec. 22, 1855
Gold Mines at Home [chip]
XIII, 203–204. March 15, 1856
The Seven Victims of Mittelbron
XIII, 226–28. March 22, 1856
The Frenchman of Two Wives
XIV, 485–90. Dec. 6, 1856
Agnes Lee XVI, 36–46. July 11, 1857
Nicholas the Rope-Dancer
XIX, 588–94. May 21, 1859

Miss Jewsbury's friend. *Not identified.* The contributor may be the same person as the writer of the papers which Miss Jewsbury sent to Dickens in 1851 and which Dickens found unsuited to the requirements of *H.W.* (Howe, *Geraldine Jewsbury*, pp. 95, 207–208). The item listed below recounts the trial of Spencer Cowper and three other barristers for the alleged murder, 1699, of the Quakeress Sarah Stout. (The second of "Two Difficult Cases" is by Morley and has no connection with the first case.)

Two Difficult Cases: The First Case
[lead] *Miss French & Miss Jewsbury's friend* XIV, 385–91. Nov. 8, 1856

Jolly, Emily |*Miss Jolley, Miss Jolly, Miss Emily Jolly*|, novelist; daughter of a justice of the peace, Bath. Contributed to *Hogg's Instructor, Chambers's, Blackwood's, Cornhill,* and other periodicals. Author of fourteen works of fiction, e.g., *Mr. Arle,* 1856; *Caste,* 1857; *Bond and Free,* 1860; *Safely Married,* 1874. Edited *The Life and Letters of Sydney Dobell,* 1878.

Miss Jolly had not yet published a book when she sent her "Wife's Story" to *H.W.* Dickens wrote to her, July 17, 1855: "... I have never been so much surprised and struck by any manuscript I have read, as I have been by yours." In the story, he wrote, "I recognise ... such great merit and unusual promise, and I think it displays so much power and knowledge of the human heart, that I feel a strong interest in you as its writer." "... I believe you have a great fame before you if you do justice to the remarkable ability you possess. ..." Dickens thought the catastrophe of the story "unnecessarily painful," however, and suggested an ending that would, instead of hardening readers' hearts, "bring tears from many eyes." The story appeared in

H.W. with the ending that Dickens had suggested.

At least three stories that Miss Jolly submitted to *H.W.* Dickens rejected. But "An Experience" he accepted for *A.Y.R.* with much enthusiasm. It was, he wrote to her, "a very special thing," a story that would "always stand apart in my mind from any other story I ever read" (July 22, 1869). Dickens repeated the praise in a letter to Forster and in one to Percy Fitzgerald. Kitton's statement, however, that the story "suggested an alteration of plot" in *Edwin Drood* (*Novels of Charles Dickens*, p. 217) is a misconstruction of the passage in Forster's *Life* (Book XI, sect. ii) that quotes Dickens's comment on the story and on the novel.

Miss Jolly was evidently despondent about the reception accorded her first book, *Mr. Arle.* In a letter to her, April 10, 1857, Dickens gave the book what praise he felt justified in giving and assured her that he had always heard *Mr. Arle* well spoken of. He felt that she had no reason for despondency and counselled her, in her writing, "to look into the life about you, and to strive for what is noblest and true." In the prefatory note to *A Wife's Story, and Other Tales,* Miss Jolly published three of Dickens's letters to her, to show "the great novelist's generous and helpful sympathy with younger writers."

Miss Jolly's novel *Safely Married* appeared in *A.Y.R.* under the editorship of Charles Dickens, Jr.

Allibone

*A Wife's Story [chap. i = lead]
XII, 97–105. Sept. 1, 1855,
and the 3 following nos.
The Sisters [lead] XII, 529–38. Jan. 5, 1856

*Repr. in *A Wife's Story, and Other Tales. By the Author of "Caste," "Safely Married," &c., &c.* 3 vols. London: Hurst and Blackett, 1875. Pub. in *H.W.* acknowledged.

Jones. *Not identified.* According to his article, the contributor was an Englishman "for some time domesticated in the village of Betela on the Lebanon"; resided, with his wife, "in that portion of the village belonging to the younger branch of sheiks"; in his article tells of the customs and beliefs of the Druses inhabiting the village. Payment recorded as "Advanced by W.H.W."

The contributor may perhaps be the "English gentleman, long resident in Lebanon, ... in whose word the most implicit reliance can be placed," mentioned by M. R. L. Meason in "The Druses of Lebanon," *Once a Week*, July 28, 1860. The Englishman had related to Meason an instance of a sheik's display of magical power.

Allibone lists E. J. Jones as author of *Assyria and Palestine Recollections*, 1857; the *Eng. Cat.*, 1835–63, gives the author of that book as E. J. Jonas. The book is not listed in the *Brit. Mus. Cat.*

The Gossip of Lebanon [chip] *Jones & Morley* V, 439–40. July 24, 1852

K

Kavanagh, Julia [*Miss Julia Kavannah*], 1824–1877, novelist and biographer. Born in Ireland, but lived when young mainly in France. Despite "her continental education," stated the *Cyclopaedia of Female Biography*, had "sound and healthy" tone in her writings. Contributed stories and sketches to *People's Journal, Eliza Cook's Journal, Ladies' Companion,* and other periodicals; reviewed books on French literature and history for *Athenaeum.* Was one of contributors to *Victoria Regia.* Author of *Madeleine*, 1848; *Nathalie*, 1850; *Adèle*, 1858; and other works of fiction. Had the reputation, according to Percy Fitzgerald, of being "a very 'respectable' writer." "I well recall," he wrote, "when it was correct to send to the libraries for her last novel, whose merits were discussed at dinner parties" (*Memories of Charles Dickens*, p. 276). Author of *Woman in France during the Eighteenth Century, English Women of Letters,* and other biographical compilations; also *A Summer and Winter in the Two Sicilies.*

Dickens was acquainted with Miss Kavanagh (letter to Alfred Hachette, June 9, 1856).

Forget-Me-Nots, a posthumously published collection of stories by Miss Kavanagh, includes some of her *A.Y.R.* contributions.

D.N.B.

An Excellent Opportunity *Miss Julia Kavannah & W.H.W.*
I, 421–26. July 27, 1850

Repr. in *Seven Years, and other Tales. By Julia Kavanagh.* 3 vols. London: Hurst and Blackett, 1860 [1859]. Pub. in *H.W.* not acknowledged.

Kay, Miss. *Not identified.* The writer's contribution is the account of a girl's school days – now long past – spent at a small and very genteel establishment in Russell Square. Various of the details recorded suggest that the account may be autobiographical. Payment for the contribution made by cheque.

Fifty-two, Wriothesley Place
XI, 36–39. Feb. 10, 1855

Keene, Mr. *Not identified.* Perhaps one of the Keenes listed below. In the Office Book, "Miss Berwick" is recorded as author of "The Leaf"; the name is marked out and substituted by "Mr. Keene." Payment for the contribution marked "Enclosed."

VERSE
The Leaf VI, 469. Jan. 29, 1853

Keene, J. R. *Not identified.* "An Ancient Tariff" is based on a 1642 book of rates setting forth import and export duties on various commodities; writer is opposed to protective tariffs. His article alludes to *The Taming of the Shrew* and echoes a line from *Hamlet*. Payment made by post-office order.

An Ancient Tariff [chip]
VIII, 283–84. Nov. 19, 1853

Keene, John, or **James Keene** |*Mr. Keene*, 7 Kingsmead St., Bath|. At the Kingsmead St. address, John and James Keene printed and published *Keenes' Bath Journal* (founded 1744), of which they were the proprietors. The Keenes also did commercial printing and sold patent medicines.

Payment for "A Golden Newspaper" made in cash "to Mr. Keene."

A Golden Newspaper [chip] *Mr. Keene & W.H.W.* IV, 207–208. Nov. 22, 1851

Kelly. *Not identified.* Various comments in "Animal Mechanics" seem to imply that the contributor was or had been a member of a mechanics' institution. He refers, for instance, to experiments that can be made with simple apparatus; science lectures in mechanics' institutions were frequently accompanied by experiments and demonstrations. He explains certain principles of physics as stated in Charles Bell's *Animal Mechanics*; *Animal Mechanics* was among the books published under the superintendence of the Society for the Diffusion of Useful Knowledge – an organization that brought out books with the needs of mechanics' institutions in mind.

The contributor may be Thomas W. Kelly, a London schoolmaster; member, 1831–37, of the London Mechanics' Institution (Kelly, *George Birkbeck*, p. 293n); author of *Rosemary Leaves*, 1854, and other books of verse.

Harper's reprinted "Animal Mechanics," without acknowledgment to *H.W.*

Animal Mechanics
V, 398–400. July 10, 1852

Kennedy, Dr. Various Kennedys who wrote verse flourished in the mid-century.

At least two held the title "Dr.": Benjamin Hall Kennedy, D.D. (1804–1889), and Richard Hartley Kennedy, M.D. (*d.* 1865). Benjamin Hall Kennedy (*D.N.B.*), classical scholar, contributed some verses to the charity publication *Christmas Comfits;* no record of his contributing verse to general periodicals. Richard Hartley Kennedy (Boase), medical officer with British army in India, 1811–43; alderman, City of London, 1853–58; contributed verse to the *Bijou*, 1829, designating himself "R. H. Kennedy, M.D."; designated himself "M.D." on title pages of two of his poetical works, *Visconti*, 1829, and *The Relicquary* [*sic*], 1835. Contributed to a London periodical the material that he later published in book form as *The Sutti*, 1855. Seems the most likely Kennedy to have been the *H.W.* contributor.

VERSE

The Better xiv, 544. Dec. 20, 1856

Kent, William Charles Mark |*Kent*|, 1823–1902, journalist and author. Educated at St. Mary's College, Oscott. Admitted at Middle Temple; called to the bar, 1859, but did not practise law. Editor of the *Sun*, 1845–71; of *Weekly Register and Catholic Standard*, 1874–81. Contributed to *New Monthly*, *Westm. Rev.*, *Blackwood's*, and other periodicals. Published collections of his political sketches written for the *Sun;* two volumes of poems and a collected edition; also other works. Edited a volume of selections from Leigh Hunt, the miscellaneous writings of Bulwer-Lytton, and the works of Burns, Moore, and other authors. In 1887 granted Civil List pension of £100 a year "In recognition of the value of his contributions to biographical and other literature" (Colles, *Literature and the Pension List*).

Kent was, as Percy Fitzgerald said, a "faithful follower and worshipper" of Dickens (*Memories of Charles Dickens*, p. 319). The acquaintance of the two men came about through Dickens's writing to Kent as editor of the *Sun*, asking him to express "Mr. Dickens' warmest acknowledgments and thanks" to the writer of a review of *Dombey* that had appeared in the paper. Kent himself had written the review. The friendship that followed continued unbroken to the end of Dickens's life. One of the last letters that Dickens wrote on the day before his death was a letter to Kent, arranging to see him the following day. Kent dedicated his *Footprints on the Road* to Dickens "with earnest regard and grateful admiration." The dedication, wrote Dickens, "heartily, most heartily, gratifies me, as the sincere tribute of a true and generous heart." He was charmed with the book (to Kent, Nov. 6, 1865). In the *Athenaeum*, June 3, 1871, Kent published a verse tribute to Dickens:

> O Friend! O Brother! dearer to my heart
> Than ev'n thy loving friendship could discern ... .

In 1872 he published *Charles Dickens As a Reader*, a book which he had begun some time before Dickens's death and for which Dickens had placed various materials at his disposal. Kent edited two books of selections from Dickens's writings and published some miscellaneous Dickensiana.

D.N.B. states that Kent "wrote largely" for *H.W.* and *A.Y.R.*

D.N.B. suppl. 1901–1911

PROSE

Béranger xvi, 185–91. Aug. 22, 1857
The Sweetest of Women
xvi, 246–51. Sept. 12, 1857
Forebodings of Thomas Raikes, Esquire
xvi, 294–300. Sept. 26, 1857
Herrick's Julia xvi, 322–26. Oct. 3, 1857
Stepping-Stones
xvi, 402–407. Oct. 24, 1857
Something Like an Art Gallery
xvii, 4–9. Dec. 19, 1857
Surrey's Geraldine
xvii, 343–47. March 27, 1858
Boscobel xvii, 569–75. May 29, 1858
Bardana Hill xviii, 44–48. June 26, 1858
Going A-maying *Kent & W.H.W.*
xix, 514–17. April 30, 1859

The 10 items, some considerably enlarged, repr. in *Footprints on the Road. By Charles Kent.* London: Chapman and Hall, 1864. Pub. in *H.W.* acknowledged.

VERSE

A Tree in the Street xvii, 132–33. Jan. 23, 1858

Behind the Scenes xix, 13. Dec. 4, 1858

The 2 items repr. in *Poems. By Charles Kent.* New ed. London: Charlton Tucker, 1870. Pub. in *H.W.* not acknowledged.

Keys. *Not identified.* Keys's name appears three times in the Office Book, in each instance as the second among the writers' names attached to an article. The position suggests that Keys worked as reviser of the articles.

The second section of "South American Scraps," to which Keys's name (but also Wills's) is attached, Dickens damned for its violations of grammar and its unintelligibility (to Wills, July 23, 1851: MS Huntington Library); Wills should not have let such disgraceful slovenliness appear in *H.W.*

Writing to Wills from Broadstairs on July 27, a few days after the appearance of that second section,* Dickens stated concerning Keys (name omitted in Nonesuch *Letters;* reads *Keys* in MS Huntington Library):

"It is impossible to go on with that unfortunate Mr. Keys. I met him in the street the last time I was in town, and told him that if I could ever give him anything to do, I would. But that I saw no means or opening.

"Pray explain to him that his condition can have nothing to do with him in the character of a contributor as between us and the public – that whatever goes into the Journal goes in for its own sake, and not through any interest of any sort – otherwise I should make contributors of a legion of clients, including all my poor relations."

**H.W.* numbers bore a Saturday date but appeared on the preceding Wednesday.

South American Scraps:

La Plata *Dr. Von Corning & Keys* III, 378–81. July 12, 1851

The Pampas Indians; An Adventure with a Lizard; The Sierra de St. Catherina *Dr. Corning, Keys, & W.H.W.* III, 425–30. July 26, 1851

The Jews in China *Soutar, Keys, & Morley* III, 452–56. Aug. 2, 1851

King, John William |*King,* Sheffield|, misc. writer. Among writers named King who published verse in the mid-century, the writer resident in Sheffield was John William King. King began life as an artisan, composing his first printed verses after "the busy labours of the toilsome day" ("Preface," *The Emigrant*). Listed in Sheffield directories as type caster, 1849; news-agent and stationer, 1852; bookseller and stationer, 1856. Does not appear in later Sheffield directories. In 1848, brought out by subscription *The Emigrant, and Other Poems,* printed in Sheffield "for the author" (2nd ed., London, 1850, re-titled *Lays of a Struggling Heart*); also had printed or published in Sheffield *Tales for the Christmas Hearth,* 1851; a sketch of Ebenezer Elliott, and a brief life of Gavazzi. His *Memoir,* 1858, of his friend James Montgomery of Sheffield records on title page both London and Sheffield publication. His other writings had London publishers: *The Patriot: A Poem,* dedicated to Mazzini; *Ernest, The Pilgrim: A Dramatic Poem,* dedicated to "my valued friend and instructor, Alessandro Gavazzi"; *Characters and Incidents,* an account of travels in England and Wales; *Continental Europe from 1792–1859,* and a continuation of the same in *The War in Italy.*

In his *Memoir* of Montgomery, King referred to Dickens's books as teaching and elevating their readers. Dickens, he stated, was "not the less a poet for writing prose" (p. 389).

Harper's reprinted "Lighten the Boat!", without acknowledgment to *H.W.*

Allibone

VERSE

Lighten the Boat! *King & W.H.W.* VII, 563–64. Aug. 13, 1853

King, Miss Louisa |*Miss Louisa King, Miss King*|. *Not identified.* The contributor is a well-educated woman; various literary and classical allusions appear in her two *H.W.* stories, as also a quotation in Latin and one in Greek. Payment for each of the contributions made by cheque.

Dickens wrote Miss King two letters (Feb. 9, Feb. 24, 1855) concerning her "Mother and Step-Mother." He found *"very great merit"* in the story – "good touches of character, passion, and natural emotion," but stated that it was too long for *H.W.* and needed great compression if he were to accept it. He pointed out also the expository, rather than dramatic, treatment of the material, and objected to some of the dialogue. The talk of one of the boys was "a little too 'slangy' "; the conversation of the Italian maid with her mistress was unnatural. As the story appeared in *H.W.*, it had evidently been revised in accordance with Dickens's criticism.

At the close of his first letter to Miss King, Dickens wrote concerning the story: "I repeat ... that I am much impressed by its merits, and that if I had read it as the production of an entire stranger, I think it would have made exactly this effect upon me." The comment may imply that Dickens was acquainted with Miss King, or it may refer merely to the fact that she had already appeared in *H.W.* In a letter to Wills, Sept. 4, 1855 (MS Huntington Library), Dickens stated that he found a later contribution by Miss King unsuited to *H.W.*

Harper's reprinted the first of Miss King's contributions without acknowledgment to *H.W.*

Why My Uncle Was a Bachelor
viii, 564–70. Feb. 11, 1854
Mother and Step-Mother
xi, 341–48. May 12, 1855, and the 2 following nos.

Kingston: *See* Knighton, William

Knight. *Not identified.* The contributor listed jointly with Murray as author of "The Crown of Ionia" – an article on Smyrna – cannot be Charles Knight (below). Neither the subject nor the association with Murray is appropriate to Charles Knight. Nor is the appearance of the article in *H.W.* Vol. xii appropriate. Charles Knight stated (*Passages of a Working Life*, iii, 113) that his contributions were "to the two first volumes" of the periodical (actually, they were to the first five).

The Crown of Ionia *Murray & Knight*
xii, 451–55. Dec. 8, 1855

Knight, Charles |*Mr. Charles Knight, Mr. Chas. Knight, Mr. C. Knight, Charles Knight, C. Knight*|, 1791–1873, author and publisher. Received few years' schooling, but gained knowledge of books through apprenticeship to his father, a bookseller and printer. As publisher on his own behalf and as superintendent of the publications of the Society for the Diffusion of Useful Knowledge, brought out numerous serials and compilations of information, instruction, and diversion, designed to make good reading cheaply available to the masses, e.g., *Knight's Quarterly Magazine*, the *British Almanac*, the *Library of Entertaining Knowledge*, the *Penny Magazine*, the *Penny Cyclopaedia*, *Knight's Store of Knowledge for All Readers*, the series titled *Knight's Weekly Volume*, and *Half-Hours with the Best Authors*. Wrote much in these publications. His separately published writings included verse, books on labour and industry, a history of England, a biography of Shakespeare. Brought out an edition of Shakespeare's works. Contributed occasionally to periodicals with which he was connected neither as editor nor as publisher, e.g., *Once a Week*.

Knight had known Dickens from the late 1830s; the two men became well acquainted about 1850. They shared in common their interest in extending education and in making good reading material available in cheap publication. It was to Dickens as "one of the most earnest labourers in that popular literature which elevates a people" that Knight, in 1854, dedicated his *Old Printer and the Modern Press.* Both Knight and Dickens were members of the Shakespeare Society. Knight accompanied one of Dickens's amateur theatrical tours and played a role in Dickens's production of *Not So Bad As We Seem.* Dickens praised Knight's biography of Shakespeare as "a charming piece of honest enthusiasm and perseverance" (to Knight, April 13, 1846). Knight included a selection from *Nickleby* in various editions of his *Half-Hours with the Best Authors;* in the comment prefaced to the selection, he mentioned Dickens's ability to delineate manners, his command of the comic and the pathetic, and his creation of characters as "familiar in our mouths as household words"; some of Dickens's works published serially or in parts he found wanting in proportion.

Knight became a contributor to *H.W.* at Dickens's invitation. A week or two before the first number appeared, Dickens wrote to him: "If you will write in my paper you will give me the utmost gratification, and be more welcome than the flowers in May." Much less engrossed in his publishing activities at the time than he had been before, Knight willingly lent his aid, he stated, to a cheap publication that was to disseminate wholesome reading (*Passages of a Working Life,* III, 112).

Dickens liked Knight's contributions. His "Illustrations of Cheapness" he thought "most desirable"; the first of these, he wrote to Knight (March 26, 1850), came out "gloriously" in the number in which it was to appear; "The Steel Pen" he thought "very good" (to Wills, Aug. 21, 1850). Another of Knight's ideas for a series of papers Dickens found "a most delightful one"; he would be more than pleased to have the papers, he wrote to Knight on March 7, 1851, and was eager for them to begin. The date indicates that Knight's suggestion concerned the three "May Day" papers. Of Knight's "Shadows," the one on Margery Paston Dickens found "most excellent" and a later one "charming" (to Knight, July 27, 1851; June 29, 1852).

"The Tresses of the Day Star," assigned in the Office Book jointly to Knight and Dickens, was revised by Dickens; it was not an actual collaboration of the two writers. In general, Dickens apparently did not take editorial liberties with Knight's contributions. His contention that an alteration of tense was desirable in the Margery Paston "Shadow" Dickens explained to Knight in painstaking detail, ending with the suggestion that – "If I am right" – Knight make the changes himself (July 27, 1851).

It was through Knight that the letters of the cattle rancher Harvey, published in *H.W.* as "Life in an Estancia," arrived at the editorial office (see Mr. Harvey, above).

As Dickens's friend and as a *H.W.* contributor, Knight was often invited, during the early years of the periodical's publication, to the dinners held for staff members, contributors, and guests.

Occasional references to Knight's compilations appeared in *H.W.*, as in "The Fire Brigade of London," "Father Thames," and "Dragons, Griffins, and Salamanders."

Five of Knight's *H.W.* contributions were reprinted in *Harper's,* three of them acknowledged to *H.W.* One of the "Illustrations of Cheapness" – that on tea – was included in the Putnam volume of selections from *H.W.*: *Home and Social Philosophy,* 2nd ser.

D.N.B.

PROSE

Illustrations of Cheapness:
*The Lucifer Match
I, 54–57. April 13, 1850
A Globe I, 84–87. April 20, 1850
*Eggs I, 158–61. May 11, 1850
*Tea I, 253–56. June 8, 1850
*The Steel Pen [lead]
I, 553–55. Sept. 7, 1850
A Christmas Pudding
II, 300–304. Dec. 21, 1850
The Law II, 407–408. Jan. 18, 1851
Three May-Days in London:
*The May-Pole in Cornhill. (1517)
[lead] III, 73–75. April 19, 1851
*May Fair. (1701)
III, 105–109. April 26, 1851
The May Palace. (1851) [lead]
III, 121–24. May 3, 1851
The Tresses of the Day Star [lead]
Charles Knight & C.D.
III, 289–91. June 21, 1851

*Shadows:
The Shadow of Lucy Hutchinson
III, 430–32. July 26, 1851
The Shadow of Margery Paston
III, 464–68. Aug. 9, 1851
The Shadow of Peter Carewe
III, 527–28. Aug. 23, 1851
The Shadow of Ben Jonson's Mother
III, 609–611. Sept. 20, 1851
The Shadows of Philip Sidney and Fulke Greville
V, 346–47. June 26, 1852
The Shadow of Fanny Burney at Court
V, 392–96. July 10, 1852
The Shadow of the Island of Madeira
V, 542–46. Aug. 21, 1852
*The Popular Poets of Fifty Years Ago [lead] V, 357–59. July 3, 1852

*Repr. in whole or part, with some items much revised, in *Once upon a Time. By Charles Knight.* 2 vols. London: John Murray, 1854. Pub. in *H.W.* acknowledged.

VERSE

Shadows: The Shadows of Ellen and Mary III, 564–65. Sept. 6, 1851

Repr. in *Once upon a Time* (as above).

Knighton, William |*Knighton, Kingston*|, 1824–1900, writer, Govt. official in India. Born in Dublin. According to Boase, was educated at Univ. of Glasgow; may have been, but details of education (also certain other details) inaccurate in Boase. Obtained Ph.D. from Giessen Univ., 1851 (information from Justus Liebig-Universität), but did not style himself "Ph.D." on title pages of his books. (On Englishmen's obtaining Ph.D.'s from Giessen and other German universities, see the *H.W.* articles "Doctor of Philosophy" and "Twenty Guinea Diplomas.") Styled himself "M.A." for the first time on title page of *Forest Life in Ceylon*, 1854; on title pages of books published in the 1860s and thereafter, styled himself "LL.D."

Stated: "I had but just completed my nineteenth year, when I first landed in Ceylon," in 1843; stayed there for four years, first as manager of coffee-estate, then as editor of Ceylon *Herald*. Went to Calcutta; was lecturer on history and logic at the Hindu College; also editor of a newspaper (*Tropical Sketches; Forest Life in Ceylon*); "lived in Ceylon and Calcutta for seven years and a half" (*The Policy of the Future in India*, p. 5). At various times in the 1850s lived in London "attempting literary essays" and lecturing on education; became acquainted with the Carlyles; spent many evenings with them ("Conversations with Carlyle," *Contemp. Rev.*, June 1881). In 1859 or 1860, appointed assistant commissioner in Oudh; held commissionership to (apparently) 1868. After his retirement lived in England. M.R.A.S., M.R.S.L.

Contributed occasional articles to *Illus. Mag. of Art, Fraser's, Contemp. Rev., Nineteenth Century*; some of his papers read before the Royal Society of Literature were published in Society's *Transactions*. His books included, in addition to those mentioned above, *The History of Ceylon*, 1845; *The Private Life of an Eastern King*, 1855; *Edgar Bardon: An Autobiographical Novel*, 1856; *Elihu Jan's Story*, 1865; *Struggles for Life*, 1886.

Knighton's best known book, *The Private Life of an Eastern King*, was the subject of the *H.W.* article "An Indian Court Circular." The article quoted extracts from the book and referred readers to its "strange but truthful pages."

In "Conversations with Carlyle," Knighton mentioned his talking with Mrs. Carlyle "about a paper of mine that had recently appeared in *Household Words*, on 'The Buried City of Ceylon.'" The Offce Book assigns the article to "Kingston."

Boase

An Ascent of Adam's Peak
IV, 420–24. Jan. 24, 1852
The Buried City of Ceylon *Kingston & Morley* V, 25–27. March 27, 1852

Content of the 2 items re-used, some lines appearing verbatim, in *Forest Life in Ceylon. By W. Knighton, M.A.* 2 vols. London: Hurst and Blackett, 1854. Previous use of the material in *H.W.* not acknowledged.

Knox, James |*J. Knox, Knox*|, 1807–1869, Edinburgh publisher of the firm Sutherland & Knox. Contributed to *Tait's*; was for three years Scottish editor of *Daily News*; founded and edited the *Torch* (Edinburgh), 1846 (Jan.-May).

The *H.W.* contributor cannot be proved to be the Edinburgh publisher, but available evidence seems sufficient for the identification. Of the six items listed below, only one ("The Tyrant of Minnigissengen," adapted from a novelette by Alphonse Karr) furnishes nothing that can be interpreted as connecting the contributor with the Edinburgh publisher. In "What *I* Call Sensible Legislation," the writer states that he is "a Scotchman"; various comments in "Seals and Whales" and in "Fishing for Herrings" imply his residence in Scotland; in "Who Murdered Downie?" he relates a disastrous prank played by Marischal College students toward the close of the eighteenth century. Pointing more specifically to the identification is the fact that "Colour-Blindness" is based on an article ("On the Prevalence of Chromato-Pseudopsis" by the Edinburgh professor George Wilson) that appeared in the *Monthly Jour. of Medical Science* – a publication of Sutherland & Knox. (The periodical source of "Colour-Blindness" is not stated in that article; the source is vaguely acknowledged in a later article by Morley, "Colours and Eyes," Dec. 29, 1855, which is based on the book – also a Sutherland & Knox publication – in which Wilson reprinted "On the Prevalence of Chromato-Pseudopsis.")

Payment for five of Knox's contributions recorded as made by post-office order.

Harper's reprinted "Seals and Whales" and "Who Murdered Downie?", without acknowledgment to *H.W.* Wills, in *Old Leaves: Gathered from Household Words*, included "The Tyrant of Minnigissengen" as his writing, without acknowledgment of the joint authorship that he had recorded in the Office Book.

Boase

The Tyrant of Minnigissengen *W.H.W. & J. Knox* II, 507–513. Feb. 22, 1851
Seals and Whales [chip] III, 562–64. Sept. 6, 1851
Fishing for Herrings III, 595–99. Sept. 13, 1851
What *I* Call Sensible Legislation *Knox & Morley* IV, 341–44. Jan. 3, 1852
"Who Murdered Downie?" V, 436–38. July 24, 1852
Colour-Blindness *Knox & W.H.W.* VIII, 255–57. Nov. 12, 1853

L

Landor, Walter Savage |*Landor*|, 1775–1864, author. Educated at Rugby and at Oxford; did not take degree. Published his first volume of poems in 1795 and his last, *Heroic Idyls*, in year before his death; two volumes of *Imaginary Conversations*, 1824, followed by additional volumes in later years. Contributed to the annuals *Book of Beauty* and *Keepsake*, and to many periodicals, e.g., *Athenaeum*, *Monthly Repository*, *Examiner*, *Foreign Quart. Rev.*, *Blackwood's*, *Leigh Hunt's Journal.*

Landor and Dickens first met, apparently, in Jan. 1840 (Super, *Walter Savage Landor*, p. 563). Their friendship remained unbroken to the end of Landor's life. Landor, in his letters and in conversation with friends, extravagantly praised Dickens and his writings; he published verse tributes to him; in 1853 he dedicated to him, in laudatory language, *Imaginary Conversations of Greeks and Romans.* Dickens named his second son Walter Landor Dickens. His article in *A.Y.R.*, July 24, 1869, on Forster's biography of Landor, gave him occasion to pay tribute to Landor's fine qualities and to express his admiration for his old friend. According to Dickens, Landor took "in hearty good-humor" Dickens's depiction of him as Boythorn in *Bleak House* and "seemed rather proud of the picture" (Fields, *Yesterdays with Authors*, p. 371); according to Eliza Lynn Linton (*My Literary Life*, p. 73), Landor did not relish the picture.

Landor was a reader of *H.W.* from the first year of its publication to within a year of the termination of the periodical, when a niece cancelled his subscription on his leaving England in July 1858 (Super, p. 602). The year before, he had written to a friend that his reading at the time consisted chiefly of *Punch* and *H.W.*: "I want amusing ideas, not serious ones" (*Letters and Other Unpublished Writings*, ed. Wheeler, pp. 118–19). Landor's admiration for *H.W.* was one of his typically extravagant admirations. It was a publication, he wrote in 1854, "which I think will have imparted more of pure pleasure and of useful knowledge than any since the invention of letters" (note accompanying "A Modern Greek Idyl"). One of Landor's letters published in the *Examiner* and two of his poems (one in the *Examiner*, the other in the *Athenaeum*) owed their motivation to *H.W.* articles: "Professor Kinkel" was motivated by the *H.W.* article "Gottfried Kinkel" and "On the Death of M. D'Ossoli and His Wife Margaret Fuller" by the article "Margaret Fuller"; "A Modern Greek Idyl" was suggested by a story related in "Modern Greek Songs."

In their bibliography of Landor, Wise and Wheeler gave Forster's *Works and Life* of Landor as the place of publication of Landor's *H.W.* poem, stating (p. 401): "This may have been printed previously in some periodical, but no trace of it has so far been discovered." Wheeler, in his edition of Landor's *Poems*, recorded the publication of the poem by Forster, but printed a MS version.

D.N.B.

VERSE

Three Scenes for the Study

XVIII, 12–13. June 19, 1858

Repr. as "Three Scenes, Not for the Stage" in Vol. VII of *The Works and Life of Walter Savage Landor*, ed. John Forster. 8 vols. London: Chapman and Hall, 1876. Pub. in *H.W.* not stated.

Lang, John |*Lang, J. Lang, Laing*|, date of birth variously given as 1816, 1817, 1818; *d.* 1864; barrister, journalist, novelist. Born in Parramatta, New South Wales. Student at Sydney College; matriculated at Cambridge, 1838. Admitted at Middle Temple, 1838; called to the bar, 1841. Returned to Sydney. In 1842 went to India, where for the most part he lived thereafter, though he spent some time on the Continent (*The Forger's Wife* is dated from Vienna) and in England. Practised as barrister; according to Vizetelly (*Glances Back through Seventy Years*, II, 8–9), his success in pleading the suit of "some millionaire begum" against East India Co. brought him munificent recompense and spread his fame among native princes. In 1845 established the *Mofussilite* at Meerut; later, for a short time edited the *Optimist* in Calcutta. Died in Mussoorie, having ruined his health (according to Vizetelly) by yielding to "insatiable craving for champagne." Contributed to *Fraser's* and *Welcome Guest*. Author of *Wanderings in India*, 1859, and ten works of fiction (or semi-fiction). His Anglo-Indian novels include *The Wetherbys* and *Too Clever by Half*, both published 1853. His writings connected with Australia were based on actual persons and incidents, usually with names disguised: *The Forger's Wife*, 1855; *Botany Bay*, 1859. Among his books with neither India nor Australia as setting was *The Secret Police; or, Plot and Passion*, 1859. Stated that he was joint author with Tom Taylor of the play *Plot and Passion* and that that play was dramatized from *The Secret Police*; Taylor denied both statements (*Athenaeum*, May 13, May 27, 1871). Some of Lang's books were very popular. *Too Clever by Half* went through twelve editions by 1878. *Botany Bay* (below) was frequently reprinted; one London edition was titled *Clever Criminals*; others were titled *Remarkable Convicts*; a Melbourne edition (reprinting only ten of the thirteen stories that constitute the book) was titled *Fisher's Ghost and Other Stories of the Early Days of Australia*.

Lang's "Starting a Paper in India," wrote Dickens to Wills, March 10, 1853, "is very droll – to us," but he objected to the many printers' terms in the article – terms "that the public don't understand, and don't in the least care for." Wills was to revise the article and strengthen it if he could. As it appeared in *H.W.*, the article contained few technical terms; those that were used were paraphrased to make their meaning clear.

Harper's reprinted "Fisher's Ghost," without acknowledgment to *H.W.*

Miller, *Australian Lit.*

Fisher's Ghost vii, 6–9. March 5, 1853
Tracks in the Bush
xvi, 93–96. July 25, 1857
An Illustrious British Exile
xix, 454–56. April 9, 1859
A Special Convict
xix, 489–91. April 23, 1859
Baron Wald xix, 537–41. May 7, 1859
Three Celebrities [lead]
xix, 553–57. May 14, 1859
Kate Crawford
xix, 596–600. May 21, 1859
Miss Saint Felix
xix, 613–17. May 28, 1859

The 8 items repr., with 5 additional stories, as *Botany Bay. By John Lang, Esq., Barrister-at-Law.* London: William Tegg, 1859. Pub. in *H.W.* acknowledged.

The Mahommedan Mother
vii, 339–46. June 11, 1853
Black and Blue xiv, 276–82. Oct. 4, 1856
The Himalaya Club [lead]
xv, 265–72. March 21, 1857
Wanderings in India [1st 2 instalments = lead] xvi, 457–63. Nov. 14, 1857, and 11 following nos. (not consecutive), ending
xvii, 254–60. Feb. 27, 1858

The 4 items repr., with 2 chaps. of additional material, as *Wanderings in India: and Other Sketches of Life in Hindostan. By John Lang.* London: Routledge, Warne, and Routledge, 1859. Pub. in *H.W.* acknowledged.

Wedding Bells vi, 551–52. Feb. 19, 1853
Wolf Nurses vi, 562–63. Feb. 26, 1853
An Inundation in Bengal
vii, 53–54. March 19, 1853
Starting a Paper in India
vii, 94–96. March 26, 1853
Hovelling xv, 139–42. Feb. 7, 1857
An Experience of Austria
xv, 381–84. April 18, 1857
Invisible Ghosts
xvi, 109–111. Aug. 1, 1857
A Human Waif [chip]
xvii, 595–97. June 5, 1858
The Abors [chip]
xviii, 204–205. Aug. 14, 1858
A Bad Name xix, 477–80. April 16, 1859
Bad Bargains xix, 610–13. May 28, 1859

Lawrance, Hannah |*Miss Laurence*|, 1795–1875, author. Reviewed historical works for *Athenaeum.* Listed in *Wellesley Index* as prob. author of "The Anglo-Norman Trouvères," *Blackwood's,* 1836. Was obviously the "Miss Lawrence" whose name was announced in an advertisement as one of contributors to *Hood's Magazine* (*Memorials of Thomas Hood,* ii, 185). Author of *Historical Memoirs of the Queens of England, from the Commencement of the Twelfth Century,* 1838–40, and of *The History of Woman in England, and Her Influence on Society and Literature,* 1843. Would seem to be author also of *London in the Olden Time; or, Tales Intended to Illustrate the Manners and Superstitions of Its Inhabitants, from the Twelfth to the Sixteenth Century,* 1825–27, anon. (attributed in Halkett and Laing to "Miss H. Laurence"). Surmised by Elizabeth Barrett to be a "deeper-minded woman" than Agnes Strickland "and qualified to take, in literature, the higher place" (*Letters ... to Richard Hengist Horne,* i, 210).

In a letter of April 19, 1854, Dickens wrote: "Mr Charles Dickens presents his compliments to Miss Lawrence, and begs to say he will be happy to read the papers Miss Lawrence has by her, if she will have the kindness to forward them for his perusal. He thinks the idea Miss Lawrence describes, a very suitable one for Household Words; but of course the manner of its execution is important" (typescript Huntington Library).

In the month following the date of Dickens's letter, appeared in *H.W.* the first item that the Office Book assigns to "Miss Laurence," the other four items appearing within the course of the following year. Based on seventeenth- and eighteenth-century books, newspapers, pamphlets, and mss, the articles depict English social and literary life of the time. References to such comparatively obscure writers as Thomas Coryate and Elkanah Settle indicate the author's thorough familiarity with the writing of the time.

Hannah Lawrance's scholarly *Historical Memoirs of the Queens of England* and *History of Woman in England* depict much of English social history to the end of the Middle Ages; the two books are based largely on contemporary sources – "those voluminous and often rare works, which, although well known to the historian and the antiquary, are for the most part inaccessible to the general reader" ("Preface," *Historical Memoirs*). Her prose contributions to *Hood's Magazine* (signed "H.L.") are historical tales set in various periods of English history; in some, the story element is little more than a framework providing the author the opportunity to picture manners and customs of the past.

The similarity of detail and phraseology in Miss Lawrance's tale "Old Mr. Fleming's Journey," *Hood's Magazine*, Oct. 1844, and in the *H.W.* article "An Excursion Train" (from a 1748 MS diary) makes it evident that the contributor to the two periodicals is the same writer. "Old Mr. Fleming's Journey," for instance, states that "a journey, one hundred years ago, was something to be talked of, to be thought about, to be deliberated upon"; "An Excursion Train" states that with "our great grandfathers" a journey "was an event to be talked about for the rest of the year." Both mention the stage-coaches "Wonder" and "Dispatch," and the gentleman traveller's taking along his scarlet rocquelaure. Both refer to Senex's road guide: In "Old Mr. Fleming's Journey," Mr. Fleming pulls out "his road-book, 'Ogilby's Survey, reduced to a size portable for the pocket, by John Senex,' which he had purchased at the Black Horse, in Cornhill, for this very journey"; in "An Excursion Train," two of the travellers consult *en route* "'The Roads through England Delineated, revised, improved, and reduced to a size portable for the pocket, by John Senex,' ... purchased for this very journey at the Black Horse in Cornhill."

Boase

John Dunton Was a Citizen
IX, 338–44. May 27, 1854
Flying Coaches
IX, 608–613. Aug. 12, 1854
Old Domestic Intelligence
X, 79–83. Sept. 9, 1854
An Excursion Train, before Steam
X, 151–56. Sept. 30, 1854
Mistress Hannah Woolley
XII, 18–22. Aug. 4, 1855

Lawson, E. |*Mr. Lawson, Mr. E. Lawson*|. *Not identified.* Payment for the first contribution marked "Enclosed & fetched"; for the second, "Enclosed."

VERSE
An Old Haunt I, 444–45. Aug. 3, 1850
The Forest Temple II, 479. Feb. 8, 1851

Lee, Miss: *See* Parr, Harriet

Le France, Miss. *Not identified.* The contributor relates an incident recorded in Jacob von Stählin-Storcksburg, *Originalanekdoten von Peter dem Grossen*, 1785. Her source is the French translation of the book.

New Shoes [chip] I, 352. July 6, 1850

Lehmann, Nina (Chambers), prob. |*Mrs. Lehmann*|, *b.* 1830, eldest daughter of the Edinburgh author and publisher Robert Chambers. In 1852 married Frederick Lehmann. Mrs. Lehmann's connection with *H.W.* would have been through the Willses, her aunt Janet being Wills's wife. The Lehmanns did not become close friends of Dickens until about 1860.

"A Very Tight Little Island," assigned to Dixon and Mrs. Lehmann, deals with Heligoland. The article begins with mention of the strategic importance of the island and gives some account of its history, then turns to the suggestion that English vacationers spend their holidays there "for a change in the beaten routine of watering-places," and sketches the social life of "the Heligoland season." A possible reconstruction of the joint authorship may be that the *H.W.* office assigned

Dixon to write the political and historical section of the article to serve as introduction to Mrs. Lehmann's account of the social life. Mrs. Lehmann was acquainted with Heligoland, as she was with various other Continental and English watering places. Her letters contain sprightly descriptions of life on the Isle of Wight, at Biarritz, and elsewhere. About the seaside town of St. Jean de Luz she had the same attitude as that implied about Heligoland in the *H.W.* article – that it deserved to be better known to seasonal visitors than it was. To make the town better known, she wrote in a letter to her husband, Feb. 28, 1867, "I have had a try at an article." Her letter writing, however, exhausted Mrs. Lehmann's time and energy; as a result, she confessed, "I am a mute inglorious authoress. Amen!" (Lehmann, comp. and ed., *Memories of Half a Century*, p. 194).

A Very Tight Little Island [lead]
Dixon & Mrs. Lehmann
XII, 145–49. Sept. 15, 1855

Leigh, Percival |*Mr. Percival Leigh, Mr. P. Leigh, P. Leigh, Percival Leigh, Leigh*|, 1813–1889, comic writer. Studied medicine at St. Bartholomew's Hospital. L.S.A. 1834; M.R.C.S. 1835. For some years practised medicine; then abandoned that profession for writing. Joined staff of *Punch* shortly after periodical was founded; remained contributor to time of his death, though what he wrote in his later years was unusable. Among his *Punch* contributions was the text accompanying Richard Doyle's illustrations for *Manners and Customs of ye Englyshe.* Contributed to *George Cruikshank's Table-Book;* occasionally to *Bentley's Misc.* and other periodicals. Author of *The Comic Latin Grammar, The Comic English Grammar,* both published 1840; and other similar books.

Leigh was not a close friend of Dickens, but he was at various times one of Dickens's guests; he played a role in Dickens's presentation, 1845, of *Every Man in His Humour.* Among references to Dickens in Leigh's writings is the comment that "the talented author of the Pickwick Papers" was one of the main figures responsible for making the "Victorian Age" the "Age of Comicality": Dickens's genius, wrote Leigh, "has revolutionized the republic of letters ... and has become, as it were, a mirror, which will reflect to all posterity the laughter-loving spirit of his age" ("Introduction," *Comic Latin Grammar*).

Leigh became a contributor to *H.W.* at Dickens's invitation. Some weeks before the first number appeared, Dickens wrote to say that he would be "sincerely pleased" to have Leigh as one of the contributors. Dickens was enthusiastic about Leigh's "Tale of the Good Old Times," which expressed ideas on social progress similar to Dickens's own; he suggested some slight changes that would "adapt [the tale] perfectly to my purpose." The subject of "A Sample of the Old School" Dickens thought excellent, and the purpose commendable. He suggested that the article be written in first person; as it appeared in *H.W.*, it was so written (to Leigh, Feb. 23, March 10, April 8, 1850: typescripts Huntington Library). With his scientific and medical training, Leigh was useful to Dickens also in writing papers on science for the layman. When Dickens obtained from Faraday the lecture notes of certain of Faraday's lectures, he entrusted them to Leigh to serve as the basis of *H.W.* articles.

Four of Leigh's *H.W.* contributions were reprinted in *Harper's*, with acknowledgment to H.W. Five were included in the Putnam volumes of selections from *H.W.*: *Home and Social Philosophy*, 1st and 2nd ser. One was included in *Choice Stories from Dickens' Household Words*, pub. Auburn, N.Y., 1854.

D.N.B.

A Tale of the Good Old Times
I, 103–106. April 27, 1850
A Sample of the Old School. By an Old Boy I, 187–92. May 18, 1850
Address from an Undertaker to the Trade. (Strictly Private and Confidential) I, 301–304. June 22, 1850
The Chemistry of a Candle
I, 439–44. Aug. 3, 1850
The Laboratory in the Chest
I, 565–69. Sept. 7, 1850

The Mysteries of a Tea-Kettle
II, 176–81. Nov. 16, 1850
The Irish California
II, 348–53. Jan. 4, 1851
The Chemistry of a Pint of Beer
II, 498–502. Feb. 15, 1851
The Rational Doctor
III, 13–18. March 29, 1851
Some Account of Chloroform
III, 151–55. May 10, 1851
The Latest Intelligence from the Irish California [chip] III, 595. Sept. 13, 1851

Lemon, Mark |*Mr. Mark Lemon, Mark Lemon*|, 1809–1870, playwright and journalist. Attended a school in Cheam, Surrey. Learned hop business from his uncle; for a time manager of a brewery, Kentish Town. Early began sending verses and tales to periodicals. In 1836 began career as playwright. Author of some seventy dramas, farces, operettas, extravaganzas, and other pieces for the stage; also of songs, fairy tales, novels, and a jest book; but remembered almost solely as "Mark Lemon of *Punch*." One of the cofounders of the periodical, 1841; at first joint editor, thereafter sole editor until his death. Connected as editor and contributor also with other periodicals, e.g., *London Journal, Once a Week, Illus. London News.*

Lemon was much disliked by some of his contemporaries and much liked by others. Among the latter was Dickens, who thought him a "most affectionate and truehearted fellow" (to A. H. Layard, April 3, 1855). The two men – and also their families – were often together. Lemon dedicated *The Enchanted Doll* to Dickens's daughters Mary and Kate. He took part in many of the children's theatricals staged by Dickens and also in the plays staged for private and public presentation. Among these was Lemon's *Mr. Nightingale's Diary*, to the text of which Dickens added so much that the farce became in effect a joint work. Lemon dramatized *The Haunted Man* and collaborated with Gilbert à Beckett in dramatizing *The Chimes*. In his poem " 'The Cricket on the Hearth.' A Fairy Tale of Home," he paid tribute to another of Dickens's Christmas books. Lemon was among the first writers who agreed to serve on the *Daily News* under Dickens's editorship (McCarthy and Robinson, *The "Daily News" Jubilee*, p. 4).

In a letter to Lemon, April 26, 1855, Dickens wrote of Lemon's kindness to him on the death of the child Dora: "... I have not forgotten (and never shall forget) who sat up with me one night when a little place in my house was left empty." The remembered kindness did not prevent Dickens's bitter quarrel with his friend – a quarrel occasioned by the refusal of Lemon and the publishers of *Punch* to insert in that periodical Dickens's statement concerning his separation from his wife. Dickens's nine-year estrangement with Lemon was ended only by the deathbed plea of Clarkson Stanfield.

In *H.W.*, reference to "Mr. Mark Lemon's ingenious Adelphi drama, Sea and Land," appeared in Fitzgerald's "Down among the Dutchmen" (April 10, 1858).

The title of the book in which Lemon reprinted two of his *H.W.* contributions was a misnomer, said Douglas Jerrold; it should have read not *Prose and Verse*, but *Prose and Worse* (Mackay, *Forty Years' Recollections*, II, 305–306).

D.N.B.

PROSE

A Paper-Mill [lead] *Mr. C.D. & Mark Lemon* I, 529–31. Aug. 31, 1850

VERSE

*Spring-Time in the Court
I, 199. May 25, 1850
*"I Would Not Have Thee Young Again"
I, 392. July 20, 1850
"All Things in the World Must Change"
I, 468. Aug. 10, 1850
Gentle Words II, 4. Sept. 28, 1850
The Emigrant's Bird
II, 12. Sept. 28, 1850

*Repr. in *Prose and Verse. By Mark Lemon.* London: Bradbury and Evans, 1852. Pub. in *H.W.* not acknowledged.

Lever, Charles James |*Lever*|, 1806–1872, novelist. B.A. Trinity College, Dublin,

1827; M.B. 1831. Practised medicine. After 1845 lived on the Continent. Vice-consul at Spezia, 1858–67; consul at Trieste, 1867 until his death. Contributed *The Confessions of Harry Lorrequer* (1837–40) and many of his following novels to *Dublin Univ. Magazine*; edited *Dublin Univ. Magazine*, 1842–45. Contributed to *Blackwood's, Cornhill, St. Paul's Magazine,* and other periodicals. Author of some thirty books. Hon. LL.D. Trinity College, 1871.

Dickens was annoyed by advertisements for *Harry Lorrequer* that quoted a reviewer as emphatically preferring that novel to *Pickwick* and *Nickleby*. Lever wrote to Dickens to repudiate the advertising tactics and to express his admiration of Dickens's writing (Stevenson, *Dr. Quicksilver*, pp. 95–96). The two men later became friends. Their association as periodical contributor and editor was entirely in connection with *A.Y.R.*, except for the one item that Lever wrote for *H.W.*

During an early residence in Brussels, Lever had contributed to the *Dublin Univ. Magazine* (1839) a series of sketches titled "Continental Gossipings." He had, at the time, written to the manager about continuing the series, bringing in "hints upon the Continent that only a residence suggests" (Stevenson, p. 66). The *H.W.* "Continental Ways and Means" is an article of that order. It discusses some of the advantages and disadvantages of residence on the Continent, the information being based on the writer's "actual domestication" there, as distinguished from mere travel.

Lever contributed some short papers to *A.Y.R.*, then entered into correspondence with Dickens concerning further contributions. Dickens wrote him a cordial letter, Oct. 16, 1859, welcoming whatever he might send: anything in the way of fiction, observation, reflection – "anything grave or gay about anything in the wide world" – would suit him. Dickens was enthusiastic about the first portion of *A Day's Ride: A Life's Romance* that Lever sent in response to the invitation. The novel had run less than two months, however, when Dickens decided that it was responsible for the declining circulation of *A.Y.R.* (to Lever, Oct. 6, 1860); to offset this, he began the serialization (on Dec. 1) of *Great Expectations*, which displaced *A Day's Ride* from lead position during the remaining months that Lever's novel continued. In his letters to Lever, Dickens took pains to state that he thought highly of *A Day's Ride* despite its lack of appeal to *A.Y.R.* readers and its unsuitability to serial publication; he would be greatly distressed, he wrote, if Lever discontinued writing for the periodical. Lever continued his contributions.

The novel *A Rent in a Cloud*, which appeared in *A.Y.R.* in 1864, is stated in the *A.Y.R.* "General Index," Vol. XX, to be by Lever. According to *N. & Q.*, 7th ser., VI (Aug. 11, 1888), it "is understood to have been the work of [Lever's] daughter."

Dickens acted as Lever's mediator with Chapman & Hall in negotiations for the book publication of *A Day's Ride*, as also in other of Lever's dealings with the publishers. Lever, obviously in gratitude for the kindness, dedicated *Barrington* to Dickens, stating in the dedication his admiration of Dickens's genius. Later, in *Cornelius O'Dowd upon Men and Women*, 2nd ser. (p. 21), he wrote of Dickens as the "greatest imaginative writer, unquestionably, since Shakespeare." Comments in Lever's letters indicate, however, that his admiration of Dickens was by no means uncritical.

D.N.B.

Continental Ways and Means
IV, 490–92. Feb. 14, 1852

Lewis, John Delaware |*Mr. Delaware Lewis, Delaware Lewis, Lewis*|, 1828–1884, misc. writer. Born in St. Petersburg; son of a Russia merchant. Student at Eton; B.A. Cambridge, 1850; M.A. 1853. Admitted at Lincoln's Inn; called to the bar, 1858; went the South-eastern Circuit. M.P. for Devonport, 1868–74. Among his contributions to periodicals was an article on Eton in *Macmillan's*. Author of *Sketches of Cantabs*, 1849; *Across the Atlantic*, 1850; *Our College*, 1857; *Science and Revelation*, 1871; *Hints for the "Evidences of Spiritualism,"* 1872. Also wrote works in French; published edition of Juvenal's satires and a translation of Pliny's letters. At time of his death, engaged on edition of Seneca and an English-French dictionary.

James Payn thought *Sketches of Cantabs* "the liveliest little book ever written by an undergraduate" (*Some Literary Recollections*, p. 53). Its "keenness of observation," he wrote, "greatly impressed Dickens, who told me that he had applied to [Lewis] in consequence to write for 'Household Words,' and added that it was the only case in which he had ever done so."

His first *H.W.* contribution, in the form of a letter to the editor, Lewis signed "John Smith" – the pseudonym under which he had published *Sketches of Cantabs.*

D.N.B.

PROSE

A Voice from a "Quiet" Street [chip] II, 143–44. Nov. 2, 1850
The "Freshman's" Progress II, 157–63. Nov. 9, 1850
University Omission and Commission II, 219–25. Nov. 30, 1850
The Momentous Question III, 167–68. May 10, 1851
The City of Sudden Death V, 171–76. May 8, 1852
Preservation in Destruction V, 280–84. June 5, 1852
The Captain of the Boats XIV, 381–84. Nov. 1, 1856

VERSE

City Graves II, 277. Dec. 14, 1850

Leycester, William, prob. |*W. Lycester*|, 1826–1893, barrister, reporter. Student at Cambridge. Admitted at Middle Temple, 1863; called to the bar, 1866. Parliamentary reporter for *Morning Post*; from 1886, official reporter in Court of Probate and Divorce; chief of *Times* Parliamentary staff.

The item listed below describes, from contemporary sources, the visit of a Siamese embassy to the court of Louis XIV. With the pomp and ceremony of that visit, it contrasts the scant official attention accorded the Siamese ambassadors who visited England in the autumn of 1857, the scant attention being due, says the writer, to the ambassadors' having arrived "in the middle of the dead season and the parliamentary recess." The reference to the Siamese custom of displaying gifts on the day of audience with royalty, "as was the case at Windsor, the other day," implies that the writer was perhaps present at the audience given to the ambassadors by the Queen. (Henry Vizetelly, who was present, gives an account of the audience and of other circumstances connected with the ambassadors' visit, *Glances Back through Seventy Years*, I, 427–31.)

Alumni Cantab.

Siamese Embassy in the Seventeenth Century XVII, 206–210. Feb. 13, 1858

Linton, Eliza or **Elizabeth (Lynn)** |*Miss Lynn, Mrs. Linton, Miss Lynn (Mrs. Linton)*|, 1822–1898, journalist and novelist; daughter of a Cumberland clergyman. No schooling; "did lessons" with eldest sister; read books in her father's library; taught herself languages. Early began writing verses and stories. In 1845, with grudging consent of her father, went to London to read at British Museum and complete a novel that she had begun. Published *Azeth, the Egyptian*, 1846, at her own expense; the book favourably reviewed in the *Times*. Sold her second novel, *Amymone*, 1848, to Bentley. In the *Examiner*, July 22, 1848, appeared the laudatory verses: "Walter Savage Landor to Eliza Lynn, on her *Amymone*." Had met Landor shortly before; became his close friend – his "dear daughter." Turned to journalism for a livelihood. In 1848 obtained position on staff of *Morning Chronicle* at twenty guineas a month; was thus first English woman newspaper writer to draw fixed salary. From that time to end of her life wrote for more than thirty-five periodicals; much of her writing in *Literary Gazette, Saturday Review, Cornhill, Pall Mall Gazette.* Author of some twenty-five novels and collections of stories, her two best novels being *The*

True History of Joshua Davidson and *The Autobiography of Christopher Kirkland.* Also brought out in book form some of her periodical articles. Was throughout her life an independent thinker in matters of religion and social relationships; in middle life abandoned the "advanced" ideas that she had formerly held on position of women. In 1858 married William James Linton, the wood engraver; the marriage an unsatisfactory one.

Through Landor, in her early days of friendship with him, Miss Lynn made the acquaintance of Dickens. She thereafter saw Dickens socially at various times, but was never a close friend of his. She shrewdly appraised him as having "a strain of hardness in his nature," despite his writing "so tenderly, so sentimentally, so gushingly." "... if I had wanted a tender and sympathetic father confessor, I would have gone to the creator of Becky Sharp rather than to him who wrote 'The Chimes' and 'The Christmas Carol' " (*My Literary Life*, pp. 64, 70). Miss Lynn's business transactions with *H.W.* and *A.Y.R.* were not through Dickens, but through Wills, later a close personal friend. She first met Wills in Paris, where in the early 1850s she was working for a periodical, and from Paris she sent her first contributions to *H.W.* Often in straitened circumstances at the time, she was grateful for the advance payments forwarded to her from Wellington Street.

Dickens came to value Miss Lynn highly as a writer for his journals. "Good for anything, and thoroughly reliable" he wrote against her name when at one time making out a list of contributors (Layard, *Mrs. Lynn Linton*, p. 81). Some of her early *H.W.* contributions, however, he was critical of for one reason or another. "Marie's Fever," in which he altered some of the wording, was "twaddly"; "French Love," a "Balzac-imitation in poking a little knife into the social peculiarities of France," was inopportune at the time that Miss Lynn submitted it; Wills was to let it stand over. "Sentiment and Action," though very clever, was less "wholesome" than Emily Jolly's "A Wife's Story" and appeared to disadvantage beside Harriet Parr's *Gilbert Massenger* (to Wills, July 17, 1853; Oct. 14, 1854; July 22, 1855). Other of Miss Lynn's contributions (or supposed contributions) he saw as verging too close to impropriety for his family journal. One of her items motivated his comment: "I don't know how it is that she gets so near the sexual side of things as to be a little dangerous to us at times" (to Wills, Oct. 6, 1854: MS Huntington Library). An item that he characterized as "bawdy" was "By Miss Lynn, I suppose"; and "Langthwaite" was to be scrutinized for the possible "court Bawdry" that it might contain (to Wills, Nov. 24, 1855; Jan. 9, 1856: MSS Huntington Library). Among Miss Lynn's contributions that Dickens liked was "Winifred's Vow" – "a very pretty story indeed"; "Epidemics" was commendable for having "a purpose in it" (to Wills, Sept. 5, 1855; April 27, 1856). "Duelling in France," assigned in the Office Book jointly to Miss Lynn and Dickens, was revised by Dickens; it was not an actual collaboration of the two writers.

When Bradbury & Evans in 1859 established *Once a Week* as a rival to Dickens's *A.Y.R.*, Mrs. Linton was asked to contribute to their periodical. Reluctant to refuse the advantageous offer and equally reluctant to seem disloyal to Dickens, she wrote to ask whether he objected to her writing for both journals. Dickens "replied that she could not write too much" for *A.Y.R.*, that whatever she wrote would be warmly welcomed and would have precedence in the periodical. "He said that he looked upon himself as her editor of right, and made it perfectly clear that any commerce with the opposition would be regarded as a personal injury" (Layard, p. 126). Mrs. Linton refused *Once a Week*'s tempting offer. Dickens's letters during the years of Mrs. Linton's *A.Y.R.* contributorship indicate that he treated her with something of the consideration due her as a well-known professional journalist whose writings were in demand. When he thought an adjective should be deleted from a comment in one of her articles, he suggested that Wills make the deletion "and let her know"; when he took out certain comments from her "John Wilson" (Nov. 29, 1862), he asked Wills to explain the reason – a personal one – for the deletion. The article itself he found "admirable" – "most admirable" (to Wills, July 12, 1860; Nov. 11, 1862). Some of her contributions, however, he did not like; and one article that he had asked her to write – a review of Forster's *Life* of Landor – he did not publish. Dickens admired Forster's book; Mrs. Linton thought it "a cold and carping and unsympathetic biography, which I for one did my best to show in its true colours" (*My Literary Life*, p. 57).

The *A.Y.R.* article "Worse Witches Than Macbeth's," March 15, 1862, based on Mrs. Linton's *Witch Stories*, recommended that no reader interested in witchcraft "should be without Mrs. Linton's admirable book."

Harper's reprinted fifteen of Mrs. Linton's *H.W.* contributions (the text of "Duelling in England" and "Duelling in France," somewhat shortened, rearranged as one article), none acknowledged to *H.W.*, but "The Sixth Poor Traveller" credited to Dickens.

D.N.B. suppl. 1901

Marie's Fever VII, 518–26. July 30, 1853
Two Cousins VIII, 246–52. Nov. 12, 1853
Wild and Tame [lead]
X, 25–31. Aug. 26, 1854
Mildred's Lovers
X, 296–300. Nov. 11, 1854
Langthwaite XIII, 7–13. Jan. 19, 1856

The 5 items repr. in *With a Silken Thread and Other Stories, By E. Lynn Linton.* 3 vols. London: Chatto and Windus 1880. Book contains also material repr. from *A.Y.R.*: permission to reprint acknowledged to editor of *A.Y.R.*

The Witches of Scotland
XVI, 75–83. July 25, 1857
The Witches of England
XVI, 138–41. Aug. 8, 1857

The first item repr., with additions and some alteration, in *Witch Stories, Collected by E. Lynn Linton.* London: Chapman and Hall, 1861. Pub. in *H.W.* not acknowledged. The second item mentions or relates briefly various of the witchcraft accounts dealt with in detail in the same book; some lines of the article appear verbatim in the book.

Miss Harrington's Prediction
VI, 437–45. Jan. 22, 1853
The Sensitive Mother
VII, 414–19. July 2, 1853
A Splendid Match
VIII, 150–56. Oct. 15, 1853
The Old Lady's Story
Another Round of Stories (Christmas 1853), pp. 5–9
Pharisees and Sinners
VIII, 486–91. Jan. 21, 1854
Rights and Wrongs of Women
IX, 158–61. April 1, 1854
One of Our Legal Fictions
IX, 257–60. April 29, 1854
The True Story of the Nuns of Minsk
IX, 290–95. May 13, 1854
Under Canvas IX, 368–73. June 3, 1854
French Domesticity
IX, 434–38. June 24, 1854
Faithful Margaret X, 12–18. Aug. 19, 1854
Devil Worshippers X, 57–61. Sept 2, 1854
The Sixth Poor Traveller
Seven Poor Travellers (Christmas 1854), pp. 29–34
Obsolete Cookery XI, 21–24. Feb. 3, 1855
My Confession XI, 93–96. Feb. 24, 1855
Ralph the Naturalist
XI, 157–62. March 17, 1855
Passing Faces XI, 261–64. April 14, 1855
French Love XI, 442–46. June 9, 1855
Winifred's Vow
XII, 196–201. Sept. 29, 1855
Sentiment and Action
XII, 315–21. Nov. 3, 1855, and the 3 following nos.
The Workmen of Europe
XII, 390–94. Nov. 24, 1855
The Community of Gault [chip]
XII, 450–51. Dec. 8, 1855
Common Cookery *Miss Lynn & W.H.W.* XIII, 42–46. Jan. 26, 1856
Epidemics XIII, 397–400. May 10, 1856
Marriage Gaolers
XIII, 583–85. July 5, 1856
Slaves and Their Masters *Miss Lynn & W.H.W.* XIV, 133–38. Aug. 23, 1856
Perfumes XV, 236–40. March 7, 1857
A Mother XV, 332–36. April 4, 1857
A Forgotten Notability
XV, 357–60. April 11, 1857
A Few Pleasant French Gentlemen
XV, 366–69. April 18, 1857
Revivals [chip] XV, 474–75. May 16, 1857

Dogs before Men [chip]
xv, 573–74. June 13, 1857
Why Is the Negro Black? [chip]
xv, 587–88. June 20, 1857
Duelling in England *Miss Lynn & W.H.W.*
xv, 596–600. June 20, 1857
Duelling in France *Mis[s] Lynn & C.D.*
xv, 614–20. June 27, 1857
Disinfectants xvi, 9–12. July 4, 1857
Gaston, the Little Wolf
xvi, 28–31. July 11, 1857
The Amphlett Love-Match
xvi, 173–81. Aug. 22, 1857
The Monkey-King
xvi, 438–42. Nov. 7, 1857
Lyndon Hall xvi, 468–76. Nov. 14, 1857, and the following no.
Civilisation in California
xvii, 301–304. March 13, 1858
Wine, No Mystery
xvii, 321–25. March 20, 1858
The First Idea of Everything [lead]
xvii, 481–84. May 8, 1858
Ethics of Broadcloth
xvii, 606–607. June 12, 1858
The Growth of Our Gardens
xviii, 21–24. June 19, 1858
Various Kinds of Paper
xviii, 104–109. July 17, 1858
Our Vegetable Friends
xviii, 224–29. Aug. 21, 1858
Thunder and Lightning
xviii, 270–74. Sept. 4, 1858
Water [lead] xviii, 433–37. Oct. 23, 1858
National Contrasts
xviii, 472–76. Oct. 30, 1858
A Backwoods-Preacher
xviii, 500–504. Nov. 6, 1858
A Golden Legend
xviii, 561–65. Nov. 27, 1858
Saving Little: Wasting Much
xix, 7–13. Dec. 4, 1858
Dwellers in Tents
xix, 151–55. Jan. 15, 1859
The Eastern Kingdom
xix, 212–16. Jan. 29, 1859
Uncommon Good Eating [lead]
xix, 289–93. Feb. 26, 1859
The Father of Caoutchouc
xix, 403–407. March 26, 1859
Ten Italian Women
xix, 532–37. May 7, 1859
A French Pepys
xix, 572–76. May 14, 1859
Street Minstrelsy [lead] *Mrs. Linton & W.H.W.* xix, 577–80. May 21, 1859

Loader, Mr. |*Loader, Mr. Loader*|. The first item listed below is assigned in the Office Book to "Loader," with payment marked as "Enclosed & fetched"; the second is assigned to "Mr. Loader per Horne," with the notation "Cheque called for."

Shumaker, in his bibliography of R. H. Horne's writings, includes "Pearls from the East" as one of Horne's contributions to *H.W.* He states that "Mr. Loader" was among the pseudonyms that Horne used, which pseudonyms "have been verified." He does not explain the nature of the verification, nor does he give any instance of Horne's using the Loader pseudonym except for "Pearls from the East." "The Tub School" he does not list.

Horne was no longer a staff member at the time that the two items appeared in *H.W.*, but he was still a regular contributor. Dickens valued him as a contributor and for the most part liked his contributions. Obviously, the best recommendation to *H.W.* that an article by Horne could have had was his name on the MS. There was no reason for his submitting copy under a pseudonym – one that, at all events, would go no further than the Office Book record and would never meet the public eye (as other of his pseudonyms did).

But Horne acted at times on motives fathomable to Horne alone. The two "Loader" items may be by him.

Harper's reprinted "The Tub School," without acknowledgment to *H.W.*

The Tub School iv, 46–48. Oct. 4, 1851
Pearls from the East [lead]
iv, 337–41. Jan. 3, 1852

Logsden, Mr. |*Mr. Logsden, Logsden*|. *Not identified.* The two articles assigned to the contributor recount instances of bribery, intimidation, exertion of Government influence, and other tactics resorted to in Parliamentary elections. Though the results of present day elections are not much to be proud of, he states, at least the elections themselves "present no such scenes of national disgrace and iniquity" as did elections of former times.

Election Time [lead] *Mr. Logsden & Morley* xv, 337–40. April 11, 1857
Westminster Elections [lead] *Logsden & Morley* xv, 361–66. April 18, 1857

Loudon, Agnes |*Agnes Loudon*|, *b.* 1832 (according to Mrs. Crosland) or 1834 (according to Allibone), *d.* 1864, writer of children's stories; only child of John Claudius Loudon, writer on botany, and his wife Jane (Webb) Loudon, known for her popular manuals on gardening. Mrs. Newton Crosland, *Landmarks of a Literary Life* (pp. 185–89), Lady Priestley, *The Story of a Lifetime* (pp. 115–16), and Mrs. Cowden Clarke, *My Long Life* (pp. 128–29, 133–34), recorded their recollections of Miss Loudon:

Was a pretty, clever girl; sometimes visited, in Edinburgh, the daughters of Robert Chambers, one of whom became Lady Priestley. In London, was early allowed by her widowed mother to take part in the receptions, *conversazioni*, and parties held at the Loudon home – social events attended by "all the celebrities of the day"; mentioned among the celebrities are Douglas Jerrold, the Milner Gibsons, John Tenniel, Charles and Edwin Landseer, Clara Novello, Louis Blanc. As a result of her "precocious mixing so much in animated society," according to Mrs. Crosland, was at seventeen already "what is called *blasée*. A mere evening party, or carpet-dance ... was too tame for her taste; she already required private theatricals or a fancy ball." Married Markham Spofforth, a barrister.

Miss Loudon's "The Lost Gloves, or We Shall See. A Story for Little Girls" appeared in *Chambers's* on Jan. 11, 1845, when, according to Allibone, the young lady had not yet "numbered eleven years." Contributed also "a number of papers to the English periodicals" (Allibone). Wrote six of the eleven stories in *Tales for Young People*, 1846 (published under her name), the book being dedicated, by permission of Her Majesty, to the Princess Royal; also *Tales of School Life*, 1850.

The Loudons were friends of the Willses.

Harper's reprinted "The Little Chorister," without acknowledgment to *H.W.*

Allibone

The Little Chorister
xii, 27–36. Aug. 11, 1855

Lowe, James |*James Lowe, Lowe*|, *d.* 1865, journalist, translator. Began journalistic career as editor of a Preston newspaper. Thereafter, 1843–63, edited the *Critic*, a London literary journal. Contributed to the *Field*, the *Queen*, and other periodicals. Projected *Selected Series of French Literature*, of which he brought out one title: *Madame de Sévigné*, 1853. Translated, 1857, Victor Schœlcher's *Life of Handel.*

Two of Lowe's *H.W.* articles have a connection with Preston, where Lowe began his journalistic work. "The Deseret News" details the contents of a copy of the Mormon newspaper that had come to his hands through the agency of a Mormon convert, formerly a Preston weaver; "Locked Out" describes the Preston factory workers idled by the managers' lock-out.

D.N.B.

The Deseret News
viii, 252–55. Nov. 12, 1853
Locked Out viii, 345–48. Dec. 10, 1853
A Manchester Warehouse
ix, 268–72. May 6, 1854

Lumley, George, prob. |*G. Lumlay, Lumley*|. The contributor is prob. the George Lumley who contributed the signed article "La Lanterne" to the *Contemp. Rev.*, Jan. 1869. "La Lanterne" is a discussion of

Henri Rochefort's periodical of that title; it gives extensive quotations from the periodical. The source of the *H.W.* article "Jews in Rome" is likewise a French periodical. Motivated by public interest in the sensational Mortara case, the article describes the Jewish ghetto in Rome and the conditions under which the Jews live, the information being taken from a series of articles by Edmond About in the *Moniteur.*

"Fatalism," like "Jews in Rome," is also derivative. It relates a Serbian folk tale from the collection compiled by Vuk Stefanović Karadžić. The contributor's source is obviously the German translation *Volksmärchen der Serben,* 1854, where the story appears as "Das Schicksal." (The contributor seems not to have been overfamiliar with German – or he occasionally read his text carelessly: "versetzte ihr ... einen Schlag über den Rücken" he translates "put a snake down her back.") The contributor's only comment on the story is that it illustrates the curse that a fatalistic belief can be to a people. The same story is related in the *A.Y.R.* article "Servian Story-Telling," Sept. 20, 1862.

Fatalism xi, 167–68. March 17, 1855
Jews in Rome xviii, 538–40. Nov. 20, 1858

Lunn, William Arthur Brown, prob. |*Lunn*|, *d.* 1879, inventor of a system of musical notation, misc. writer, under pseudonyms "Arthur Wallbridge" and "Wallbridge Lunn." Contributed to *People's Journal.* Published *The Sequential System of Musical Notation,* 1843. Author of the booklets *Jest and Earnest,* 1840; *Bizarre Fables,* 1842; *Torrington Hall* (account of visit to lunatic asylum), 1845; *The Council of Four: A Game at "Definitions"* (calls himself editor), 1847. Reprinted the four last-mentioned items in *Miscellanies* "By Wallbridge Lunn; ('Arthur Wallbridge.')," 1851; and, in whole or part and with some additions, in *The Wallbridge Miscellanies,* 1874, and later dates.

On Nov. 15, 1841, Dickens wrote a letter to J. Lunn, Esquire, identified in Pilgrim *Letters* as the playwright Joseph Lunn (1784–1863, *D.N.B.*). Dickens's letter was in reply to the request made by Lunn that Dickens introduce Lunn's son to Chapman & Hall as possible publishers of a book that the son had written. In the letter Dickens explained his understanding with the publishers that his introduction of a writer was in no way to influence their decision concerning "the acceptance or rejection" of a work. "I cannot therefore," he wrote, "introduce the author of Jest and Earnest to them, 'in a manner which will induce them to purchase and publish his second work'. But I will introduce him and his desire, gladly. And I will add (which is perfectly true) that I think very highly of his little book. Beyond this, I cannot go. ... If you will let me know ... that your son has no objection to this mode of introduction, I will *say* all I can to them, – which is better than writing it.

"Let me assure you, and your son, most unfeignedly that I write this with a real interest in the author of Jest and Earnest, and a real desire for his success."

On Nov. 22, Dickens wrote again to Lunn, stating that he would see Chapman & Hall the following day; on Nov. 24, he informed Lunn that he had spoken with the publishers and left them *Jest and Earnest* to look at. "All I can do," he wrote, "I have done." (*Bizarre Fables,* the "second work" of "the author of Jest and Earnest," was published not by Chapman & Hall, but by W. S. Orr & Co.)

Dickens's interest in young Lunn makes it probable that whatever Lunn might have submitted to *H.W.* would have been favourably considered. The obviousness of "Two Nephews" suggests that it is the writing of an amateur; some of the stories and sketches published by Lunn as his writing give the same impression.

Boase

Two Nephews xi, 526–28. June 30, 1855

Lycester, W.: *See* Leycester, William

Lynn. *Not identified.* Evidently the "correspondent" whose description of a public reading-room in Paris Morley quotes in the item listed below.

Free Public Libraries *Morley & Lynn*
III, 80–83. April 19, 1851

Lynn, Miss: *See* Linton, Eliza (Lynn)

Miss Lynn's friend. *Not identified.* Payment for the writer's first two contributions made in cash.

VERSE
The Burthen Lightened
XIV, 301. Oct. 11, 1856
Word Analogies XIV, 445. Nov. 22, 1856
The Brave Women of Tann
XV, 35–36. Jan. 10, 1857

Lytton, Edward George Earle Lytton Bulwer: *See* Bulwer-Lytton, Edward George Earle Lytton

M

MacAdam. *Not identified.* The contributor quotes from, and briefly comments on, some of the remedies contained in *A Rich Storehouse or Treasurie for the Diseased,* a sixteenth-century treatise variously attributed to A.T., to George Wateson (or Watson), and to George Whetstone. He refers to Ralph Blower as "author of the Treasurie"; Blower was not the author, but the co-printer of the 1596 edition and the printer of several seventeenth-century editions. Payment for the contribution made by post-office order.

Physic A-field XI, 304–307. April 28, 1855

MacCabe, William Bernard |*McCabe*|, 1801–1891, journalist, historian. Born in Dublin of Roman Catholic parents. From about 1823 was connected with Dublin press and with provincial Irish newspapers. About 1833 settled in London; was Parliamentary reporter, also writer of critical reviews, for *Morning Chronicle;* later for *Morning Herald.* During Parliamentary recesses spent most of his time on the Continent, where his knowledge of languages made him valuable as foreign correspondent. About 1852 renewed his connection for a time with Dublin press, as editor of *Telegraph.* Then retired from journalistic work and lived for many years in Brittany. Contributed to *Dublin Review, Once a Week, N. & Q.,* and other periodicals. Author of *A Catholic History of England,* 1847–54; and of historical romances, e.g., *Florine, Princess of Burgundy,* 1855; *Adelaide, Queen of Italy,* 1856.

MacCabe and Dickens must have become acquainted when both were reporters for the *Morning Chronicle,* though Dickens evidently did not, some years after, remember MacCabe clearly. In a letter to Thomas Beard, Feb. 14, 1844, in reply to Beard's request that Dickens provide MacCabe an introduction to Chapman & Hall, Dickens wrote of "Mr. McCabe": "... I entertain (I think I do, at least?) a very pleasant recollection of him as an especially cheerful and good natured old colleague." Nonesuch *Letters* identifies "Mr. McCabe" as the Irish historian.

"The Six Giants of Lehon" is a Celtic saint's legend told to the writer in Brittany by an Irishman resident there. The writer indicates that he himself is from Ireland. His explanation that Breton and Irish are to some extent mutually intelligible shows his interest in, and knowledge of, languages.

D.N.B.

The Six Giants of Lehon
XVII, 509–518. May 15, 1858

McCormick, Robert |*Dr. Cormack*|, 1800–1890, naval surgeon, naturalist. Student at Guy's Hospital and at St. Thomas's. M.R.C.S. 1822. Entered navy in 1823 as assistant surgeon. Found various of his appointments disagreeable, but "had the good fortune," he wrote, "to be engaged in three of the most memorable expeditions of the present century" – that under Capt. William Edward Parry to the Arctic in 1827, that under Capt. James Clark Ross to the Antarctic in 1839–43, and that in search of Franklin in 1852–53. Published two books, based mainly on diaries that he kept during his voyages.

McCormick's antarctic diary, which constitutes the first part of his *Voyages of Discovery in the Arctic and Antarctic Seas, and round the World*, 1884, contains a description of the Christmas 1841 and New Year 1842 festivities of the crews of the *Erebus* and the *Terror* (*Voyages*, I, 251–55). This diary material (then unpublished) McCormick used, some lines of it verbatim, for his *H.W.* article. His ponderous account of the origin of the article appears in his diary entry for Dec. 4, 1850, given in his "Autobiography" (which is appended to *Voyages*): "Having written an article on 'Christmas Day at the South Pole,' which my friend Hunt, the editor of the *Daily News*, had asked me for, as a contribution to the Christmas number of *Household Words*, for Charles Dickens, I took it to him, when it was at once sent to press, and appeared in that number" (*Voyages*, II, 314–15). (McCormick's friend Hunt was at the time one of the subeditors of the *Daily News*; he did not become editor until late in 1851.)

The Office Book assigns "Christmas in the Frozen Regions" to "Dr. Cormack & C.D." and records payment as "Handed to F. K. Hunt." Since McCormick had no contact with the *H.W.* office either in submitting the article or in receiving payment, Wills's error in recording his name is understandable.

D.N.B.; Plarr's Lives

Christmas in the Frozen Regions
Dr. Cormack & C.D.
II, 306–309. Dec. 21, 1850

MacIntosh, Mrs. *Not identified.* The writer's last *H.W.* contribution, which appeared during the weeks when *H.W.* and *A.Y.R.* were both being issued, was obviously inspired by the title of the second periodical: the words "All the year round" introduce each of its ten stanzas. The *A.Y.R.* Letter-Book indicates that Mrs. MacIntosh was invited to contribute to the 1859 *A.Y.R.* Christmas number. In the Letter-Book is a copy of a form letter, dated Sept. 26, 1859, written by Wills in Dickens's behalf, requesting contributions to that number. In the list of names written below the letter – obviously the names of writers to whom a copy of the letter was or was to be sent – is the name of Mrs. MacIntosh.

Payment for the writer's first *H.W.* contribution made by post-office order; for the third, by cheque and post-office order; for the sixth, by cheque.

In the Office Book, Mrs. MacIntosh is recorded as author of "A Daisy on a Grave"; the "MacIntosh" is marked out and substituted by "Broderip."

VERSE

Gone! VIII, 133. Oct. 8, 1853
The Bells VIII, 445–46. Jan. 7, 1854
The Robins IX, 128–29. March 25, 1854
Late in Spring XV, 467–68. May 16, 1857
Story of a Grave XV, 565. June 13, 1857
The Elfin Charm
XVII, 40–44. Dec. 26, 1857
The Blooming Rose
XIX, 155–58. Jan. 15, 1859
Violets XIX, 469. April 16, 1859
All the Year Round XIX, 541. May 7, 1859

Mackay, Alexander |*Mr. Alex Mackay, Mr. Alexander Mackay, Mr. Alex^r Mackay, Mr. Alex Mackie*|, date of birth given as 1806, also as 1808; *d.* 1852; journalist. Born in Scotland. Began journalistic career as "conductor of a newspaper in Toronto, Canada" (*D.N.B.*). Went to London. Admitted at Middle Temple, 1843; called to the bar, 1847. Meanwhile, had obtained position on staff of *Morning Chronicle*;

in 1846 sent by the *Chronicle* to the U.S. to report Congressional debates on Oregon boundary dispute and ascertain public opinion on the matter. Thereafter, in connection with Henry Mayhew's project to publish in the *Chronicle* a survey of the English poor and labouring classes, wrote articles on the poor in rural districts (Bourne, *English Newspapers*, II, 154–55). Also turned his attention to politics; delivered speeches on political reform. In 1851 sent to India on behalf of the Manchester and other chambers of commerce to investigate cultivation of cotton. Died at sea on return voyage. Author of *The Western World; or, Travels in the United States in 1846–47*, 1849, pronounced by Charles Mackay (*Forty Years' Recollections*, II, 153) as "equal in many respects" to Tocqueville's *Democracy in America*; *The Crisis in Canada*, 1849; *Western India*, published posthumously. Wrote also a book on electoral districts and one on the Australian Colonies' Government Bill.

Mackay's "The Devil's Acre" deals with a dormitory and industrial schools established in a squalid London district and with the effectiveness of the institutions in reforming young criminals. Dickens's letter to Wills, July 12, 1850, and Wills's reply of the same date (in Lehmann, ed., *Charles Dickens As Editor*, pp. 30–31) concern a statement in the article that Dickens apparently wished to modify in a subsequent number of *H.W.* The prison chaplain John Clay, writing on July 26, 1850, called Mackay's article "the best account" of the industrial schools established in "The Devil's Acre" (W. L. Clay, *The Prison Chaplain*, p. 450).

The fourth item listed below is assigned in the Office Book not to Mackay, but to "Mackie"; it is clearly Mackay's account of his passage to Canada as a young immigrant: The writer of the article is a Scotsman of some education who relates his voyage, steerage class, on the *Seagull*, sailing from Greenock to Quebec. Details are recorded much in the way in which Mackay, in *The Western World*, recorded details of his 1846 voyage on the *Hibernia* to Boston. Some of the phraseology, even, is similar. "An Emigrant Afloat," for instance, states: "It is difficult for an emigrant to reconcile himself to less than eight or nine knots an hour. ... We, one day, made but about twenty miles, and I apprehended a mutiny. On another we made two hundred, and nothing could exceed the hilarity and good-humour of those on board. At one time, the Seagull was the merest tub. ... At another, she was one of the best vessels afloat. ..." In *The Western World*, Mackay writes: "No passenger can reconcile himself at sea to anything short of two hundred miles a day; and on our reckoning, one day, showing a run of only eighty miles, a state of feeling pervaded the saloon, which ... might have ripened into mutiny. ... Next day we had a splendid run – 250 miles – and what ship was ever in such favour as the Hibernia then?"

Concerning the article, Dickens wrote to Wills, Aug. 14, 1850, that he had shorn Mackay (name omitted in Nonesuch *Letters*; reads *Mckay* in MS Huntington Library) "of his humour in the emetical line, and also of his account of a calm – which is less correct than I hope his other facts are."

The *H.W.* article "Food for the Factory" referred to the plan of the Manchester Chamber of Commerce to send Mackay to investigate cotton cultivation in India; the article "India Pickle" recorded some of Mackay's comments from his *Western India*.

D.N.B.; Notable Middle Templars

How We Went Fishing in Canada
I, 243–45. June 8, 1850
"The Devil's Acre"
I, 297–301. June 22, 1850
How We Went Hunting in Canada
I, 364–68. July 13, 1850
An Emigrant Afloat
I, 534–39. Aug. 31, 1850

Mackenzie, Dr. Ord. [? or **O.W.**?]. *Not identified.* The contributor describes the sites and buildings on St. Helena associated with Napoleon. His four-day visit to the island took place after "a long residence in the tropics." Payment for the contribution made by post-office order.

Twenty Shillings for a Napoleon [chip]
v, 295–97. June 12, 1852

Macpherson, Ossian |*Ossian Macpherson, Macpherson*|. *Not identified.* The first three items listed below indicate the contributor's interest in the eradication of abuses and in the betterment of social conditions. "The Smithfield Model" concerns the removal of the Smithfield cattle market from the heart of London to an outlying district; it states one of the specious arguments raised by a man who opposes the removal. "A Few Facts about Salt" denounces the Government tax laid on salt in India and takes the part of the natives who suffer under the "odious" imposition. "Excursion Trains" tells of the initial reluctance of railway companies to institute cheap excursion trains, which, when once under way, yielded a profit to the companies and proved a boon to the people; the writer suggests that fares on such trains be still further reduced. A reader's qualification of one of the statements in the article appeared two weeks later ("The Tax on Excursion Trains").

No specific social purpose underlies "The Harvest of Gold," but there is no reason to assume that the Macpherson recorded as one of the joint authors is other than the Macpherson who contributed the three preceding items. The article relates the history of the discovery of gold in Australia, describes (among other matters) conditions in the gold fields as recorded in newspapers and in letters from the emigrant Mulock (below), and comments on the probable decrease in the value of gold as a result of the Australian discovery. The discussion of the decrease in the value of gold is probably the writing of Morley, who dealt with that matter in an article of the following month ("Change for a Sovereign"). What share Macpherson had in "The Harvest of Gold" it is not possible to state.

The Office Book affords no clue as to the identity of Macpherson and no indication as to whether the name under which he submitted his articles was a real or an assumed one. The fact that the initials "O.M." appear as signature to his first contribution (in the form of a letter to the editor) seems to indicate that Ossian Macpherson was his real name.

It seems positive, however, that he was not the Ossian Macpherson who in 1848 brought out by subscription *The Dreamer, a Poem, in Three Cantos, with Other Poems* – a book to which Dickens was a subscriber ("List of Subscribers" at end of volume.) The author of *The Dreamer* was so fascinated by his own "blighted" prospects and by his "declining existence," with the "light of vitality" trembling to extinction, that he could not possibly have had a thought for any one besides his own hypochondriac self.

The Smithfield Model of the Model Smithfield [chip]
II, 572–73. March 8, 1851

A Few Facts about Salt [chip]
III, 354–55. July 5, 1851

Excursion Trains [chip]
III, 355–56. July 5, 1851

The Harvest of Gold [lead]
Morley, Macpherson, & Mulock
v, 213–18. May 22, 1852

Macready, Catherine Frances Birch |*Miss Macready*|, 1834–1869, verse writer; daughter of William Charles Macready. Did charitable work among the poor. Died at sea on voyage from Madeira to England. Author of *Leaves from the Olive Mount*, 1860, dedicated to her father; *Cowl and Cap; or, The Rival Churches*, 1865; *Devotional Lays*, 1868.

As an intimate friend of Macready's, Dickens was on friendly terms with the members of the Macready family. His letters contain affectionate mentions of Catherine Macready – "little Kate," "Katey," "Katie."

Miss Macready's *H.W.* contributions were apparently sent to Dickens by her father. Concerning the first, Dickens wrote to him that he would be "truly delighted" to publish it in *H.W.*; the second, which he liked "very much indeed," he agreed with Macready in holding "a great advance upon the first" (July 8, Aug. 8, 1856). Miss Macready or her father had evidently intended the poems to be gratuitous contributions. Dickens insisted on paying for them. "Katey's case," he wrote, was to be no "different from Adelaide Procter's."

In the Office Book, Miss Procter is recorded as author of "The Shadow of the Hand"; the "Procter" is marked out and substituted by "Macready."

Boase

VERSE

The Shadow of the Hand
xiv, 38–39. July 26, 1856

The Angel of Love
xiv, 156–57. Aug. 30, 1856

Springs in the Desert
xiv, 396–97. Nov. 8, 1856

The 3 items repr. in *Leaves from the Olive Mount. Poems, By Catherine Frances B. Macready.* London: Chapman and Hall, 1860. Pub. in *H.W.* not acknowledged.

Mann, Christopher Wharton |*C. W. Mann, Mann*|, surgeon. Medical student at King's College, London. L.S.A. 1842; M.R.C.S. 1842. In early 1850s was medical officer to Northern District of Clerkenwell. Contributed some letters to medical journals.

Of the *H.W.* staff, it was Morley who was a friend of Mann's. As fellow students at King's College, Mann and Morley, together with Charles H. Hitchings, a medical student at St. Bartholomew's, had formed a literary club which brought out the *King's College Magazine*, 1841–42. Mann's contributions to the magazine included, in addition to many original poems, a translation of "Prometheus Bound" and a translation of Schiller's "The Robbers" (Morley, *Early Papers and Some Memories*, pp. 14–15). In 1843 Morley lodged for a time with Mann; later he occasionally visited Mann in London (Solly, *Life of Henry Morley*, pp. 43–44, 56, 144, et passim). In 1844 Mann and Hitchings published *Echoes of Mind*, which they "affectionately dedicated" to Morley as "their friend and fellow author." The book contains six poems by Mann. In the following year Morley "affectionately dedicated" *The Dream of the Lilybell* to Mann, "the Author's friend and fellow rhymer." The translation of "The Robbers" that appears in Morley's edition of *Schiller's Poems and Plays*, 1889, is Mann's translation.

London and Prov. Med. Directory, 1851

The Nerves xv, 522–25. May 30, 1857

Everything after Its Kind
xvii, 451–53. April 24, 1858

Markham, Sir Clements Robert |*Markham*|, 1830–1916, geographer, historical writer. F.R.S. Educated at Westminster School. Served in Royal Navy, 1844–51, taking part in Capt. Horatio Austin's expedition in search of Sir John Franklin. In 1852–53 travelled in Peru. Went again to South America in 1860, charged with collecting cinchona plants for cultivation in India. In charge of geographical work of India Office, 1867–77. Geographer to Abyssinian expedition, 1868. Took active part in promoting revival of Arctic exploration. Recognized during latter part of his life as foremost authority on geography. C.B. 1871; K.C.B. 1896. Hon. LL.D., Cambridge, 1907. Recipient of foreign orders of honour. President of Hakluyt Society for twenty years; edited some twenty works for the Society. President of Royal Geographical Society for twelve years; editor, 1872–78, of Society's *Geographical Magazine.* Contributed numerous articles to Society's publications. Contributed occasionally to general periodicals, e.g., *Quart. Rev.*, *Macmillan's.* Author of more than fifty books: biographies, histories, records of travel and exploration, historical romances.

Markham's first *H.W.* article recounts his crossing the Isthmus of Panama, Oct. 1852, on his trip from New York to Peru; the details given accord with those given in A. H. Markham, *Life of Sir Clements R. Markham*, pp. 133–35. "Leaves from Lima" is unassigned in the Office Book. It records the writer's arriving in Lima, Oct. 1852; it recounts his excursion to Coca-Chacra and to Pachacamac, and his being attacked by Negro assailants on his return from both excursions. Markham arrived in Lima in Oct. 1852. The *Life*, pp. 136–37, records his making the excursion to Pachacamac and his being attacked by Negroes on his return journey, but it confounds into one attack the two attacks related in the *H.W.* article.

D.N.B. suppl. 1912–21

Crossing the Isthmus of Panama
vi, 521–24. Feb. 12, 1853

Leaves from Lima
vii, 202–205. April 30, 1853

*The First Sack of Delhi
xvi, 276–79. Sept. 19, 1857

*Repr. as part of chap. xii in *A General Sketch of the History of Persia. By Clements R. Markham.* London: Longmans, Green, and Co., 1874. Pub. in *H.W.* not acknowledged.

Marryat, Miss |*Miss Marryatt*|. The first item listed below is the story of a young English lady who, with her fellow passengers, is shipwrecked on a voyage to Australia. The second, narrated by an Englishman who takes a voyage to Australia for the sake of his health, records a horseback trip in New South Wales and some incidents, "for the most part true," related by the Englishman's friend concerning his experiences in Australia "twenty years ago, less or more." The item does not imply the writer's personal acquaintance with Australia.

Among Frederick Marryat's daughters who wrote books, two – Augusta and Emilia – each wrote a book with Australia as setting. Augusta wrote *Left to Themselves. A Boy's Adventures in Australia,* 1878. Emilia, writing in the 1850s as Emilia Marryat, later as Emilia Marryat Norris, wrote a boys' book laid in Australia – *The Early Start in Life,* 1867, and also a boys' book with a New Zealand setting – *Amongst the Maoris,* 1874. Augusta or Emilia seems the most likely "Miss Marryatt" to have written the two *H.W.* items.

Percy Fitzgerald, discussing the contributors to Dickens's two periodicals, stated that Florence Marryat was a "contributor of an occasional kind," writing "stories which were much read, besides a few light articles for the journal" (*Memories of Charles Dickens,* p. 297). Fitzgerald does not make clear which "journal" he is referring to. His comment cannot be taken as establishing Florence Marryat as the *H.W.* contributor, though she may have been.

Frederick Marryat and Dickens were friends, seeing each other socially and at times corresponding. Dickens wrote one or two letters to Florence Marryat, as also a letter of introduction for her to the publisher Frederic Chapman; occasional mention of her appears in his letters; one letter mentions her as author of *Véronique,* a novel that she dedicated to Dickens. A book by Marryat's brother Joseph, *Collections towards a History of Pottery and Porcelain,* was the subject of the *H.W.* article "Pottery and Porcelain"; a book by Marryat's son Frank (Francis Samuel), *Mountains and Molehills,* was the subject of the article "Tinder from a Californian Fire."

Cast Away xix, 222–27. Feb. 5, 1859

Friends in Australia
xix, 584–88. May 21, 1859

Marsh, Anne (Caldwell), prob. |*Mrs. Marsh*|, 1791–1874, novelist, known after 1858 as Mrs. Marsh-Caldwell. Born in Staffordshire; daughter of recorder of Newcastle-under Lyme. Received a "careful education" (*Cyclopaedia of Female Biography*). In 1817 married Arthur Cuthbert Marsh (*d.* 1849), junior partner in London banking firm. On death of her brother, 1858, assumed by Royal license additional surname of Caldwell. Author of some twenty-five works of fiction; most of them published anonymously, in deference to her husband's wish that the mother of his daughters not be known "as the author of what the world might consider second-rate novels" (Martineau, *Autobiography,* I, 284). Among her most praised writings were *Two Old Men's Tales,* 1834; *Mount Sorel,* 1845; *Emilia Wyndham,* 1846. At least one of her tales serialized in a periodical before appearing in book form: *Lettice Arnold,* in *Ladies' Companion,* 1850. Published *The Protest-*

ant Reformation in France, 1847, and some translations from the French.

Mrs. Marsh and Dickens were acquainted (Dickens to Alfred Hachette, June 9, 1856).

Dickens took great pains in revising "The Spendthrift's Daughter." In a letter to Wills, Oct. 8, 1851, he wrote that he had undertaken to correct the story so as to show Mrs. Marsh what he considered "its faults of detail"; he instructed Wills to be particularly careful that the corrections were printed with scrupulous accuracy, repeating the admonition in a following letter of the same date (MSS Huntington Library). On Oct. 9, he wrote to Wills: "Mrs. Marsh's story [name omitted in Nonesuch *Letters*; reads *Marsh* in MS Huntington Library] will be very good now, I think. It would be as easy (almost) to write one, as I found it to get point and terseness out of such an infernal hash." Dickens himself sent the author payment for the story (Office Book: "£20 per C.D.").

A commendatory reference to Mrs. Marsh's novels appeared in the *H.W.* article "Doctor Dulcamara, M.P.," written by Wilkie Collins and to some extent revised by Dickens: to recover from the effect produced by reading *The Heir of Redclyffe*, stated the article, the writer had had recourse to the "restoratives" provided by better women novelists than Charlotte Yonge, among them Mrs. Marsh.

D.N.B.

The Spendthrift's Daughter
IV, 52–56. Oct. 11, 1851, and the 3 following nos.

Marston, John Westland |*Marston, W. Marston*|, 1819–1890, dramatic poet. At fifteen came to London from Lincolnshire, to be articled to solicitor; interested in literature and the stage rather than in law. Contributed to Heraud's *Sunbeam* and other periodicals; some of his verses and reviews appeared in *Athenaeum*. Editor of *Psyche*, 1840; co-editor for some years of *National Magazine*. As dramatist, attempted to revive poetic drama. Author of three verse tragedies: *The Patrician's Daughter*, 1841; *Strathmore*, 1849; *Philip of France and Marie de Méranie*, 1850; also of romantic and comic pieces and domestic dramas. Published a volume of poems, a novel, two collections of stories, and *Our Recent Actors*, 1888. Hon. LL.D., Univ. of Glasgow, 1863.

Marston and Dickens were friends. Forster stated that *The Patrician's Daughter*, Marston's first play, attracted Dickens less "by the beauty of its composition ... than by the courage with which its subject had been chosen from the actual life of the time" (*Life*, Book IV, sect. i). Dickens wrote to Macready (Nov. 12, 1842) that he felt a prologue would help assure the success of the play on opening night – would "Get the curtain up with a dash, and begin the play with a sledge-hammer blow." The play was produced at Drury Lane, Dec. 10, 1842, Dickens's verse prologue being spoken by Macready. "How shall I thank Mr. Dickens for the spontaneous kindness which has furnished me with so excellent a letter of introduction to the audience?" wrote Marston in his preface to the second edition of the play. Dickens was present at Marston's rehearsal presentation of *Strathmore* as a public reading – an ineffectual, monotonous performance, at the end of which Dickens himself read aloud some scenes from the play to show Marston "how you ought to do it" (Wright, *Life of Charles Dickens*, p. 257). In 1851 Marston played a role in Dickens's production of *Not So Bad As We Seem*. In 1858 Dickens attended a performance of Marston's prose play *A Hard Struggle*. It moved him to tears. "I am at a loss to let you know how much I admired it ... or how heartily I cried over it," he wrote in a letter to Marston, Feb. 3. The letter was included in the first published collection of Dickens's letters; in *Our Recent Actors*, II, 185, Marston referred to it as containing Dickens's "emphatic praise" of the play. Dickens praised the play also in his letters to friends and sent a copy to F. J. Régnier in an attempt to interest him in presenting it at the Théâtre Français.

Marston dedicated to Dickens *Gerald; a Dramatic Poem*, 1842, "as a very humble acknowledgment of many delightful hours" for which he was indebted to Dickens's writings; in addition to the enjoyment that the books had given him, he wrote, "I would hope ... that I have been in some degree susceptible of their tendencies to foster generous feelings and benevolent sentiments." In his *Athenaeum* review of *The Battle of Life* and his review of *The Haunted Man* (Dec. 26, 1846; Dec. 23, 1848), he again dwelt on the value of Dickens's books in awakening and fostering altruistic feelings. "To few living writers are we more indebted than to Mr. Dickens for lessons in the Philosophy of the Heart," he wrote in his review of the first; in his review of the second, he commended the "moral suggestiveness" of the "touching chronicle" – its depicting the power of suffering "to educate human sympathy."

In the Office Book, Dixon is recorded as author of "The Golden Mean"; his name is marked out and substituted by that of Marston.

D.N.B.

Dreamers xii, 45–48. Aug. 11, 1855
Out and Home Again
xii, 405–408. Nov. 24, 1855
The Golden Mean
xii, 469–71. Dec. 15, 1855
My Country Town
xiii, 126–36. Feb. 23, 1856
Putters Down xiii, 464–70. May 31, 1856
The 5 items repr. in *The Family Credit and Other Tales, By Westland Marston.* London: Ward and Lock, 1862. Pub. in *H.W.* acknowledged. *The Family Credit* is recorded as first pub. 1861. Copy of 1861 edition not seen.

Martin, Miss. *Not identified.* The Office Book record of payment made on the same date (May 7) for the last four items assigned to Miss Martin indicates that they are by one contributor. The four items deal with Africa, the Pyrenees, and Japan – as do the first five items so assigned. All nine items, therefore, are the writing of one contributor.

The two articles on Japan are based on Andrew Steinmetz, *Japan and Her People*, 1859; they do not indicate that the writer has visited Japan. The two sketches laid in the Pyrenees do indicate that the writer has been there. "King Cotton," which urges that England import cotton from west Africa, cites various comments of the British consul at Lagos and of other persons acquainted with Africa; it could have been written by someone who had not been in Africa; so, too, could "A Packet-Ship's Company," though the voyage that that story relates originates on the west African coast.

The remaining three articles, however, seem clearly to be the writing of someone who has lived on the west African coast. The west coast – its flora and fauna, its natives and its European inhabitants – is not incidental to the articles; it is the subject of the articles. The narrator of "Bush and Beach" and "On the West African Coast" is an Englishman stationed at a British garrison. In the first article he tells of his fifty-mile trip from Oke Amolo to Ogbomoshaw (Ogbomosho) to aid an English officer in trouble; in the second, he tells of an inland trip with his friend Brown, up the Ogbomoshaw River and down the Saccoom; on both trips he is accompanied by his native servant Quobna. It is difficult to conceive of the articles as a woman's writing.

In "On the Gold Coast" the writer discusses, among other matters, the motives of Europeans in going to west Africa and the effect of west Africa on them: "The fact is, that we Europeans who go to the Gold Coast do not go to work. ... We do not go to colonise. ... We do not encumber ourselves with philanthropic motives or aims. We go because we expect to make money fast. ... The first half-dozen attacks of fever demoralise us; and, like the natives, we live to eat, to drink, and to sleep." Much of the article deals with the British law courts of the west coast and the cases tried there. The account given is authentic, as is proved by its correspondence with facts recorded in – for example – Brodie Cruickshank's *Eighteen Years on the Gold Coast of Africa*, 1853. The *H.W.* writer explains, for instance, that natives, before they appear in court, have a letter-writer put down, "in what English he can, the facts communicated to him, and thus a preliminary statement, from both plaintiff and defendant, reaches the presiding officer"; Cruickshank (II, 264) states that natives who are parties to a suit have representations of their cases drawn out by native scribes and handed in on court days. The *H.W.* writer gives an example of one of these letters to the court – "an exact copy of one now lying before me" – and remarks that the handwriting in such letters is always "remarkably clear and good"; Cruickshank comments on the ease with which natives acquire the art of penmanship. The *H.W.* writer states: "When addressing the judge or any superior, the native lowers the cloth or blanket, worn on state occasions, from the left shoulder, baring his breast"; Cruickshank (II, 282) describes the same custom: natives salute Europeans, he says, "by slightly removing their robe from their left shoulder. ... When they wish to be very respectful, they uncover their shoulder altogether, ... the whole of the person from the breast upwards being left exposed."

The only Miss Martin whom it seems possible to associate with west Africa is Anna Martin, 1827–1870, who in 1852 married the missionary David Hinderer and in the same year accompanied him to the mission in Ibadan, where the two zealously laboured for many years. The account of her life (*Seventeen Years in the Yoruba Country. Memorials of Anna Hinderer*, 1872), however, shows that neither she nor her husband – who might conceivably have used his wife's maiden name as a pseudonym – can have been the *H.W.* contributor.

How the Avalanche Comes Down at Barèges XV, 292–94. March 28, 1857
A Packet-Ship's Company XVII, 350–53. March 27, 1858
On the Gold Coast XVIII, 419–23. Oct. 16, 1858
King Cotton XIX, 38–40. Dec. 11, 1858
Japanese Social Life XIX, 237–40. Feb. 5, 1859
Bush and Beach XIX, 364–67. March 19, 1859
On the West African Coast XIX, 510–14. April 30, 1859
A May Day in the Pyrenees XIX, 549–52. May 7, 1859
Japan Traits XIX, 561–65. May 14, 1859

Martin, Mrs. *Not identified.* The contributor's account of Breton wedding customs is obviously based on her own observation. The opening paragraph of the article refers to the account as a "companion picture" to "A Welsh Wedding" in a preceding number (Feb. 15, 1851). *Harper's*, June 1851, reprinted "A Breton Wedding," without acknowledgement to *H.W.* The description of Breton wedding customs in "Social Customs of Brittany," *Harper's*, Jan. 1854, contains many of the same phrases and lines that appear in the *H.W.* article; the description seems to be an expanded and revised version of the *H.W.* article.

A Breton Wedding [chip] III, 115–17. April 26, 1851

Martineau, Harriet |*Miss Martineau*|, 1802–1876, misc. writer. By her own account, received "an education of a very high order, including sound classical instruction and training" (*Autobiography*, II, 405). Made her first appearance in print in *Monthly Repository*, at age nineteen; for some years continued writing for that periodical; wrote for *Westm. Rev.*, *People's Journal*, *Leader*, *Daily News* (more than 1600 articles), *Edin. Rev.*, *Once a Week*, and other British periodicals; for *National Anti-Slavery Standard* and other American periodicals. Reprinted in book form some of periodical contributions. Her writings included verse, children's books; didactic tales exemplifying principles of political economy, sanitation, etc.; *Deerbrook*, a novel; books on the U.S., a book on mesmerism, historical works. Translated Comte's *Positive Philosophy* (condensed version). Obtained international reputation; was quite aware of her celebrity.

Miss Martineau's personal association with Dickens was slight, though in that association, as in his correspondence with her, she wrote, he exhibited always a "frank kindness and consideration" that won her "cordial regard." In her *Autobiography* – written in 1854–55 – she described him as "a virtuous and happy family man" whose generous heart was "kept steady by the best domestic influences." She admired some of Dickens's novels, though with reservation (*Autobiography*, II, 60–63). Dickens thought her *Society in America* the best book written on the U.S. (Webb, *Harriet Martineau*, p. 157).

Before *H.W.* made its appearance, Dickens invited Miss Martineau to write for the periodical. She condescended to do so only because of its "wide circulation" (*Autobiography*, II, 25) – though how this consideration could have influenced her decision before that circulation was established is not clear. Her first contributions were in narrative form, so written, she said, "at the express and earnest request of Mr. Dickens," but with "little satisfaction to herself," since she felt that she had then "passed out of that stage of mind in which I could write stories well" (*Autobiography*, II, 565, 67). Instead of contributing stories, therefore, she proposed that she write for *H.W.* a series of articles on manufacturing processes; the proposal, she stated, was "eagerly accepted," and the articles were at the time designed, "at the suggestion of the Proprietors [i.e., Dickens and Wills], for ultimate republication" (*Autobiography*, II, 68; "Preface," *Health, Husbandry, and Handicraft*).

Dickens found Miss Martineau's first contribution "heavy" (to Wills, March 29, 1850), but he liked her article "The Irish Union" and was enthusiastic about her "Deaf Playmate's Story" (to Miss Burdett-Coutts, Nov. 3, 1852, in *Heart of Charles Dickens*, ed. Johnson; to Wills, 1852). He instructed Wills (Aug. 19, 1854) to "Look to the punctuation" of one of her contributions. "Woodruffe the Gardener" he cut, but so "scientifically" that he thought Miss Martineau would not "exactly know where." From "How to Get Paper" he deleted what he thought too positively stated an assumption, noting, in that article, Miss Martineau's grim determination on "the enlightenment of mankind" (to Wills, Aug. 21, 1850; Oct. 14, 1854). To "Three Graces of Christian Science" he added a footnote mentioning his acquaintance with a young deaf, blind, and dumb man discussed at length in the article.

About 1853 Miss Martineau began to feel "uneasy" about her connection with *H.W.*, her misgivings originating in her "disapproval of the principles, or want of principles" on which the periodical was conducted. Dickens and Wills, she in time became convinced, were "grievously inadequate to their function, philosophically and morally." This inadequacy she found manifest in the attitude toward women expressed in *H.W.*, in the periodical's treatment of factory disputes, and in its anti-Catholic policy. Her conclusion that *H.W.* not only suppressed the truth about Catholicism, but maligned that religion by publishing dishonourable slanders, led to her "plain-spoken" letter to Wills and to her "secession from the corps of Mr. Dickens's contributors" (*Autobiography*, II, 91–95). (Miss Martineau's account of the dispute is much confused in dates. Charles Dickens, Jr., in a footnote to an article on Miss Martineau in *A.Y.R.*, April 7, 1877, stated that information in his possession showed her account to be in error in "almost every statement." Her dispute with *H.W.*, he wrote, "arose about a trifle" and involved "a far from formidable difference of opinion.") According to Wills, Miss Martineau was the only contributor who ever deserted the *H.W.* ranks (to R. H. Patterson, Nov. 3, 1859: *A.Y.R.* Letter-Book).

Late in 1855, in her pamphlet *The Factory Controversy*, Miss Martineau launched a vehement attack on Dickens, as also on his periodical, as the sentimental advocate of "meddling and mischievous" factory legislation. Her quarrel with *H.W.* centred on a series of articles (by Morley) on accidents in textile mills; she found the articles inaccurate and dishonest. Her quarrel with Dickens, in his joint capacity of editor and novelist, was his putting himself forward as social reformer without a sound knowledge of political philosophy. His doing so demonstrated his "conceit, insolence, and wilful one-sidedness." Like Mrs. Jellyby, he was a "humanity-monger" – though, unlike that lady, not a harmless one. (According to contemporary report, Miss Martineau herself had served Dickens as the model for Mrs. Jellyby.)

Dickens's first reaction to "Miss Martineau's vomit of conceit" (thus in MS Huntington Library; *outpouring of conceit* in Nonesuch *Letters*) was to give it no notice in *H.W.*, "if only for the mortification" that the ignoring of the pamphlet would cause her. "I do suppose," he wrote, "that there never was such a wrong-headed woman born – such a vain one – or such a Humbug." Morley, however, had written a reply to the attack, and Dickens, after carefully going over it, decided on its publication (to Wills, Jan. 3, Jan. 6, 1856). "Our Wicked Mis-statements" appeared Jan. 19, 1856. It was a temperate, well-written article, replying to Miss Martineau's accusations, pointing out her errors of fact and the speciousness of some of her arguments.

Morley's article referred to the "many good works" that Miss Martineau had written and the "many good deeds" that she had done. Earlier *H.W.* articles also contained references to her writings and her reputation. Dickens, in "Pet Prisoners," supported his contention that prisoners' piously mouthed repentances were manifestly insincere by quoting Miss Martineau's observations on Philadelphia prisoners. Wills, in "A Little Place in Norfolk," quoted Miss Martineau as an authority on the proper management of small farms; and Horne, in "The Steam Plough," on the importance of land cultivation in improving social conditions. In "A Witch in the Nursery," Horne referred to Miss Martineau as among English authors who had written "excellent stories" for children; and, in "Traits and Stories of the Huguenots," Mrs. Gaskell mentioned her as among the Huguenot descendants who "bear honoured names among us." In *A.Y.R.*, April 7, 1877, appeared an appreciative review of Miss Martineau's *Autobiography* – "this record of a famous woman's life." It was written by her friend James Payn.

Of Miss Martineau's *H.W.* contributions, "The Sickness and Health of the People of Bleaburn" is established as her writing by mention in her *Autobiography*. (Crabb Robinson, reading the "very wise and valuable" tale a few months after its publication, decided on the basis of its subject that it was "evidently by H. Martineau" [*On Books and Their Writers*, II, 704].) Of the items listed below as not reprinted, nine are mentioned by title in the *Autobiography* (II, 31, 33, 69–70); others are there referred to as papers on "the treatment of Blindness, Deafness, Idiotcy, &c." (II, 91).

These papers on "Personal Infirmities," stated Miss Martineau, "were the last I sent to 'Household Words,' except two or three which filled up previous schemes." The paper on blindness appeared June 17, 1854. Four papers after that date are assigned to Miss Martineau in the Office Book: "Freedom, or Slavery?", "Cheshire Cheese," "How to Get Paper," and "The Rampshire Militia." Concerning the first three there is no question of authorship: "Freedom, or Slavery?" dealt with slavery in the U.S., one of Miss Martineau's major interests; "Cheshire Cheese" (reprinted) and "How to Get Paper" (referred to by title in the *Autobiography*) "filled up previous schemes." But "The Rampshire Militia," Jan. 13, 1855, is a questionable ascription: the item is, first of all, written in narrative, rather than expository form; it has, next, a definite link with two of Payn's *H.W.* contributions.

In contrast with the didactic heaviness of Miss Martineau's stories of confirmed authorship, "The Rampshire Militia" is lively writing. It recounts, in a series of letters, the formation and training of a volunteer military unit of country "bumpkins," who at the end of their several periods of drill acquire soldierly bearing and efficiency. Ned Barry, a farm labourer, is one of the Rampshire militiamen selected "for the regulars" from the hundreds who volunteer for that service in the autumn of 1853; six months later he embarks for the East from "Rampling Harbour." What is to become of "the Rampshire as a regiment" Ned does not know; perhaps there "may be drafts from it, from time to time, for the line"; or perhaps some of the men will be sent to garrison duty abroad to relieve the regulars. "Some think that if the war lasts long, the Rampshire may even see fighting."

The "Rampshire" military unit appears in two of Payn's *H.W.* papers: "Back from the Crimea," March 3, 1855, and "Embarkation," May 12, 1855. "Embarkation" describes the embarking of "R.R.R." – the Royal Rampshire Regiment – on H.M.S. *Obstinate*; the regiment – the first that "volunteered in England for foreign service" – is made up of labourers and artisans who had not intended to enter the army, but had enlisted merely to pass "six weeks' holiday in playing at soldiers"; it is "a regiment of very young men (for the flower of the corps volunteered long since from the Royal Rampshire into the line)." "Back from the Crimea" mentions the Royal Rampshire militiamen assembled at the dockyard to help bear sick and wounded Crimean soldiers from the transport; it mentions the Royal Rampshire officers as writing letters for the soldiers in the hospital.

It is unlikely that two contributors should each have devised a "Rampshire" military unit. "The Rampshire Militia" seems to be by Payn.

Six of Miss Martineau's *H.W.* contributions (one, only in part) were reprinted in *Harper's*, one of them acknowledged to *H.W.*, and one – "The Deaf Playmate's Story" – credited to Dickens. "The Wonders of Nails and Screws" was included in the Putnam volume of selections from *H.W.*: *Home and Social Philosophy*, 2nd ser.

D.N.B.

The Sickness and Health of the People of Bleaburn [1st instalment = lead]
I, 193–99. May 25, 1850, and the 3 following nos.

Repr. as *The Sickness and Health of the People of Bleaburn* [anon.]. Boston: Crosby, Nichols, and Company; New York: Charles S. Francis and Company, 1853. Pub. in *H.W.* acknowledged.

Flower Shows in a Birmingham Hot-House IV, 82–85. Oct. 18, 1851

The Magic Troughs at Birmingham
IV, 113–17. Oct. 25, 1851

The Wonders of Nails and Screws
IV, 138–42. Nov. 1, 1851

Kendal Weavers and Weaving
IV, 183–89. Nov. 15, 1851

The Bobbin-Mill at Ambleside
IV, 224–28. Nov. 29, 1851

An Account of Some Treatment of Gold and Gems
IV, 449–55. Jan. 31, 1852

Rainbow Making
IV, 485–90. Feb. 14, 1852

Needles IV, 540–46. Feb. 28, 1852

Time and the Hour
IV, 555–59. March 6, 1852

Guns and Pistols
IV, 580–85. March 13, 1852

Birmingham Glass Works
V, 32–38. March 27, 1852

What There Is in a Button
V, 106–112. April 17, 1852

Tubal-Cain V, 192–97. May 15, 1852

Household Scenery
V, 513–19. Aug. 14, 1852

Shawls V, 552–56. Aug. 28, 1852

The Life of a Salmon
V, 606–610. Sept. 11, 1852

Peatal Aggression
VI, 13–18. Sept. 18, 1852

Triumphant Carriages [lead]
VI, 121–25. Oct. 23, 1852

Hope with a Slate Anchor
VI, 156–61. Oct. 30, 1852

Butter VI, 344–50. Dec. 25, 1852

Cheshire Cheese X, 52–56. Sept. 2, 1854

The 21 items repr. in *Health, Husbandry, and Handicraft. By Harriet Martineau.* London: Bradbury and Evans, 1861. Pub. in *H.W.* acknowledged.

The Home of Woodruffe the Gardener
I, 518–24. Aug. 24, 1850, and the 2 following nos.

The Ghost That Appeared to Mrs. Wharton II, 139–43. Nov. 2, 1850

The Marsh Fog and the Sea Breeze
III, 53–58. April 12, 1851, and the following no.

A New Plea for a New Food
III, 138–40. May 3, 1851

A Real Sister of Charity
III, 291–98. June 21, 1851

The Highest House in Wathendale
III, 389–96. July 19, 1851

The Fortunes of the Reverend Caleb Ellison III, 533–39. Aug. 30, 1851

Malvern Water iv, 67–71. Oct. 11, 1851
What Christmas Is in Country Places
Extra No. for Christmas 1851, pp. 8–11
The Miller and His Men
iv, 415–20. Jan. 24, 1852
The New School for Wives
v, 84–89. April 10, 1852
The Forbidden Land
v, 431–36. July 24, 1852
News of an Old Place
v, 537–42. Aug. 21, 1852
The English Passport System
vi, 31–34. Sept. 25, 1852
The Irish Union [lead]
vi, 169–75. Nov. 6, 1852
The Famine Time
vi, 214–16. Nov. 13, 1852
The Deaf Playmate's Story
A Round of Stories (Christmas 1852), pp. 27–30
Mr. Wiseman in Print
viii, 339–43. Dec. 10, 1853
Deaf Mutes ix, 134–38. March 25, 1854
Idiots Again ix, 197–200. April 15, 1854
Three Graces of Christian Science
ix, 317–20. May 20, 1854
Blindness ix, 421–25. June 17, 1854
Freedom, or Slavery?
ix, 537–42. July 22, 1854
How to Get Paper [lead]
x, 241–45. Oct. 28, 1854
The Rampshire Militia [lead]
x, 505–511. Jan. 13, 1855

Marton, Caroline: *See* De Mérey, Mme.

Mass, Charles |*Correspondent*|, coastguardsman. In the item listed below, the writer states that he was mate of the revenue cruiser *Nimble* under command of Lieut. Hugh C. Goldsmith, at the time that Goldsmith and members of his crew capsized the Logan Rock, April 1824; he explains that he himself, however, had no part in Goldsmith's "act of Vandalism." Documents in the Library of H.M. Customs and Excise, King's Beam House, London, record that the mate of the *Nimble* at the above date was Charles Mass.

Mass was a native Cornishman. During his service in the Coast Guard, he stated, he had been "all round the coast of Cornwall ... and into almost every creek and cove on it." His writing to *H.W.* was motivated by Dixon's articles concerning the search for Cornish choughs (see Dixon, above). "I am a constant reader of Household Words," wrote Mass. The Office Book records no payment for his brief "communication."

Cornish Choughs Found at Last [chip]
v, 582–83. Sept. 4, 1852

Maxwell, H. H. Initials not clearly written in Office Book, but seem to read "H.H." The two items assigned to the contributor describe, respectively, a visit to an opium factory in India and to a lac factory; they indicate that the writer knows England – at least London – and Ireland. His comment about having "only two days' leave" for one of the excursions indicates that he was probably in military service; his visiting a factory at Ghazipur indicates that he was in the Bengal Presidency. The Office Book records payment for both items as made, by cheque, Dec. 11, 1854, long after their publication.

The contributor may be Henry Hamilton Maxwell, 1824–1892 (Boase). Henry Hamilton Maxwell was of Irish background; entered service of East India Co. in 1842 as lieutenant in Bengal Artillery; served in Gwalior and Sutlej campaigns and during the Mutiny; became lieut.-colonel in Royal Artillery; promoted to colonel, then general. C.B. 1873. Published a translation, from the German, of Taubert's *On the Use of Field Artillery on Service,* and, from the French, of G. S. Marey Monge's *Memoir on Swords.* Author of pamphlet on providing maimed poor with artificial limbs, *Arms and Legs in Rome,* 1882.

Henry Hamilton Maxwell may be the Maxwell – "a captain in the Bengal artillery" – whom J. A. Crowe mentioned meeting in the Danubian Principalities in the winter of 1853–54; Crowe stated that Maxwell was correspondent for the *Morn-*

ing Chronicle (*Reminiscences*, pp. 117–18).

An Opium Factory
VI, 118–20. Oct. 16, 1852

Good Lac *H. H. Maxwell & Morley*
VII, 463–66. July 16, 1853

Mayhew, Horace |*Horace Mayhew*|, 1816–1872, author. Wrote for *Punch*; was for some years subeditor of the periodical. Contributed to *George Cruikshank's Table-Book*; also to *Bentley's Misc.*, *Ladies' Companion*, *Lloyd's Weekly*, *Illus. London News*, and other periodicals. Edited Cruikshank's *Comic Almanack*, 1848, 1849. Published *Change for a Shilling*, 1848; *Letters Left at the Pastry-cook's*, 1853; and other books. His pantomime *Plum Pudding* produced at Olympic Theatre, 1847. During about last fifteen years of his life was in easy circumstances and wrote comparatively little. Was a *bon vivant* of Bohemian London, well known and very popular in society; a friend of Dickens.

Mayhew's *H.W.* contribution touches the subject dealt with in his brother Henry's *London Labour and the London Poor*. It pictures the poverty-pinched tradesmen and costermongers whose pennies of City tax and toll go toward providing the turtle and venison with which the Lord Mayor regales his guests at the Mansion House. The item appeared in *H.W.* immediately preceding Miss Costello's "A Literary Lady's Maid." The juxtaposition of the two pieces made Dickens "thrill and shudder with indescribable anguish" (to Wills, July 25, 1853).

D.N.B.

Corporation Dreams [chip]
VII, 512–13. July 30, 1853

Meadowes, D. L. *Not identified.* The contributor is an Englishman who writes, apparently from personal knowledge, of the treatment of political prisoners in the Kingdom of Naples; he states that the atrocities described five years before in Gladstone's letters to Lord Aberdeen still continue.

Justice at Naples [lead]
XIV, 457–60. Nov. 29, 1856

Meason, Malcolm Ronald Laing |*Meason, Laing Meason, Measom, Meesom-Lang*|, *b.* 1824, in Edinburgh; military man, journalist. Educated in France and, in England, at St. Gregory's College. In the army, 1839–51, serving during that time in second Afghan and Gwalior campaigns. After selling out, turned to journalism. Editor of Bombay *Telegraph and Courier*, 1851–54; of *Weekly Register*, 1866–70. Paris correspondent for *Daily News*, 1855; later contributor; special correspondent for New York *Herald* during Franco-Prussian War; correspondent for *Daily Telegraph*. Contributed also to *Once a Week*, *Macmillan's*, the *Month*, and other periodicals. Published books on fraudulent financial practices, particularly those of joint stock companies: *The Bubbles of Finance*, 1865, sketches reprinted from *A.Y.R.*; *The Profits of Panics*, 1866 (reprinted, 1875, together with *Bubbles of Finance*, as *Three Months after Date and Other Tales*); *Sir William's Speculations*, 1886. Also, *Turf Frauds and Turf Practices*, 1868, two chapters of which had appeared in *A.Y.R.* Dickens had in his library a copy of *Profits of Panics* (Stonehouse, *Catalogue*).

Dickens gave the title "Nob and Snob" to the article that Meason had titled "The Guards and the Line." The article, wrote Dickens to Wills, Jan. 1, 1856, "has a distinct and appropriate purpose"; Wills was to see to the punctuation and the "slovenly composition here and there." In "Military Mismanagement," *A.Y.R.*, Dec. 5, 1863, Meason referred to his having published in *H.W.* "A Campaign with the French."

Allibone

Regulars and Irregulars
XII, 58–60. Aug. 18, 1855

The Regimental Market
XII, 325–28. Nov. 3, 1855

Nob and Snob [lead]
XII, 553–56. Jan. 12, 1856

French and English Staff Officers
xiii, 84–88. Feb. 9, 1856
A Campaign with the French [lead]
xiv, 49–56. Aug. 2, 1856
Coffee and Pipes
xviii, 447–54. Oct. 23, 1858
Hospitable Patriarchs [lead]
xix, 481–84. April 23, 1859

Mednyánszky, Sándor, 1816–1875, Hungarian military officer. Born in Eger, Heves; son of govt. official. Began military career in 1832. Took active part in revolution of 1848, serving for a time as aide to Gen. Georg Klapka. On defeat of Hungarian army, went into exile in England. Lived in London for eighteen years, earning his living first by writing, then by working as bank clerk. Married, as his first wife, Anna Margaret Birkbeck (1818–1867), daughter of George Birkbeck, the pioneer in adult education; date of marriage given by Godard (*George Birkbeck*, p. 196) as 1857. Was for some time with Kossuth in Italy. Returned to Hungary, 1869. Elected to Parliament. Contributed to Hungarian periodicals. In London, his name commemorated in the Alexander Mednyanszky Prize established at the London Mechanics' Institution (now Birkbeck College) by his wife in her will.

The Office Book assigns "The Golden Age of Hungary" to Miss Birkbeck. *Rural and Historical Gleanings from Eastern Europe*, in which the article was reprinted, likewise bears her name as author. The book is by Mednyánszky. He dictated it to Miss Birkbeck and had it published under her name, probably not wishing, as a political refugee, to reveal his authorship. Other sections of the book, "By Miss A. M. Birkbeck," first appeared in *Sharpe's*, 1853–54.

Miss Birkbeck dedicated *Rural and Historical Gleanings*, by permission, to Lady Langdale, in admiration of Lady Langdale's generous conduct toward Hungarian refugees. In her dedication Miss Birkbeck wrote, concerning the book itself: "... I am indebted for the materials of which it is composed partly to the kindness of a friend, who, during a long sojourn in Hungary, acquired an accurate knowledge of that land, as well as of its inhabitants; and partly to the living chronicles of their own and their country's misfortunes, the exiles, whom the force of the political earthquake of 1848 cast upon our shores." The book was brought out in a second edition in the same year in which the first edition appeared. It was praised by the *Atlas*, the *Examiner*, and other periodicals.

Magyar Írók Élete és Munkái

The Golden Age of Hungary
vi, 342–44. Dec. 25, 1852
Repr. with some revision as chap. xvi of *Rural and Historical Gleanings from Eastern Europe. By Miss A. M. Birkbeck.* London: Published for the author by Darton and Co., 1854. Pub. in *H.W.* not acknowledged.

Meredith, George |*Meredith, Mr. Meredith*|, 1828–1909, poet and novelist. Attended two schools in England, thereafter a Moravian school in Neuwied, Germany. Articled to London solicitor; abandoned study of law to turn to writing. Contributed poem to *Chambers's*, 1849, apparently his first published piece. Later contributed verse, stories, novels, and essays to *Once a Week, Fortnightly, Cornhill, New Quarterly Magazine, Macmillan's, Pall Mall Magazine, Scribner's*, and other periodicals. For some years, journalist for Ipswich *Journal, Pall Mall Gazette, Morning Post.* For more than thirty years, reader for Chapman & Hall. Published his first book, *Poems*, in 1851; his novels from 1856 to 1895.

Meredith and Dickens were acquainted. Meredith, who was still an occasional contributor to *H.W.* at the time that *The Shaving of Shagpat* was published, left a copy of the book, inscribed with Dickens's name, at the *H.W.* office. Dickens sent him a note of thanks (May 10, 1856) before he had read the book.

Meredith disliked Dickens's novels and deprecated the exaggerated praise heaped on them. Though he amicably owned himself convinced by Alice Meynell's article in the *Pall Mall Gazette* that the "popular favourite" had claim to being "a lord outside cockaigne" (to Alice May-nell, Jan. 20, 1899, *Letters*, II, 500–501), Meredith obviously held Cockaigne to be Dickens's realm. To Edward Clodd he remarked: "Not much of Dickens will live, because it has so little correspondence to life. He was the incarnation of cockneydom, a caricaturist who aped the moralist. ... If his novels are read at all in the future, people will wonder what we saw in them, save some possible element of fun meaningless to them. The world will never let Mr. Pickwick, who to me is full of the lumber of imbecility, share honours with Don Quixote" (Clodd, "George Meredith," *Fortnightly*, July 1909). Meredith's criticism of a passage that he considered one of the "blots" in *An Inland Voyage* was that "It is in the style of Dickens" (to R. L. Stevenson, June 4, 1878, *Letters*, I, 290). On reading the *Spectator*'s obituary of Dickens, Meredith wrote to his friend Hardman (June 15, 1870, *Letters*, I, 206): "The 'Spectator' says he beat Shakespeare at his best, and instances Mrs. Gamp as superior to Juliet's nurse. This is a critical newspaper!"

Meredith's connection with *H.W.* began at the very outset of his literary career, obviously through the agency of his friend Horne, who was then on the *H.W.* staff. (The Office Book records payment for Meredith's first poem, as also for some later ones, as made to Horne.) Meredith's confining his *H.W.* contributions almost entirely to verse is explained by his remark to Tom Taylor that he could not "properly do facts on the broad grin, and the tricky style Dickens encouraged" (Stevenson, *Ordeal of George Meredith*, p. 68). Meredith ceased to write for *H.W.* at the end of 1856. In 1859, when Bradbury & Evans launched *Once a Week* in opposition to Dickens's newly established *A.Y.R.*, he at once became a contributor. He identified himself with *Once a Week* and its interests, and was eager that it have an individuality of its own, as distinct as possible from that of Dickens's periodical. "... we must be careful not to seem to be copying the enemy ...," he wrote to Samuel Lucas, the editor (Stevenson, p. 87).

Of Meredith's *H.W.* poem "Monmouth," Dickens wrote to Wills, Sept. 29, 1856 (MS Huntington Library): "Monmouth would be well enough, but for its breaking down so direfully at the end. Still I think there is sufficient merit in it to justify its acceptance."

The joint names accompanying the titles of four of Meredith's poems, as listed in the Office Book, indicate that those poems underwent revision, one being revised by Wills, three by Horne. At the time of revising "Sorrows and Joys" and "The Two Blackbirds," Horne was on the *H.W.* staff. In Feb. 1852, however, when "War" appeared in *H.W.*, he was no longer on the staff, his engagement having terminated in mid-May 1851. In what capacity he is listed as reviser is, thus, not clear. As Meredith's friend and as his mentor in the art of poetry, he may have worked on the poem personally with Meredith; or, as former staff member, he may have been asked to revise the poem for its appearance in *H.W.*

Meredith, in later life, hoped that his early immature verses would be allowed to escape into obscurity. When B. W. Matz, in 1906, identified those in *H.W.*, by means of the Office Book, he was informed by Meredith's publishers "that Mr. Meredith was annoyed at their being discovered, that he did not wish them published, and, indeed, was not sure that he wrote all of them" (letter to the Editor, *Times*, Feb. 23, 1911). Matz, nevertheless, privately printed twenty-five copies of the hitherto unreprinted poems: *Twenty Poems by George Meredith*, 1909. In 1911, in "Some Unknown Poems of George Meredith," *T.P.'s Weekly*, Feb. 17, he made public announcement of his discovery of the poems, as also of the prose item assigned in the Office Book to Meredith. The article led to an exchange of letters between him and Meredith's son William Maxse Meredith, published in the columns of the *Times* (Feb. 21, 23, 25, 28, March 2, 1911). Meredith's son repudiated the evidence of the Office Book for all the items except the two poems that Meredith had reprinted and "Monmouth" (later, through the *T.L.S.*, May 23, 1912, he acknowledged Meredith's authorship of an additional poem – "Infancy and Age"). Poems assigned in the Office Book to Meredith with payment recorded as sent to the address at which the Merediths lived, he contended, must have been in whole or part the writing of Meredith's wife, Mary Ellen Meredith (see also his comment in *Letters of George Meredith*, I, 8n). Meredith's son had not seen the Office Book; he did not understand its system of recording; his repudiation of its evidence has no weight.

Matz, in his letters to the *Times*, correctly interpreted the Office Book entries, except in one matter: he took the contributor "Mrs. Meredith" (i.e., Mrs. Charles Meredith, see below), to whom two items are assigned, to be Mrs. George Meredith. (Matz had no occasion, in the *Times* letters, to mention the payment notation accompanying "A Child's Prayer," to which notation, in "Some Unknown Poems of George Meredith," he had accorded undue weight. See "A Child's Prayer," p. 480). As far as can be determined, the only connection of Meredith's wife with *H.W.* is that Meredith, in "The Two Blackbirds," retold an episode that she had made the subject of a poem in the MS *Monthly Observer* in 1849 (Forman, *George Meredith and the Monthly Observer*, pp. 18–19).

Of the poems listed below as not reprinted, four are authenticated by evidence outside the Office Book as Meredith's writing. In a letter of Dec. 12, 1850, to John W. Parker, concerning the poems to be included in the volume brought out in the following year, Meredith wrote: " 'Sorrows and Joys,' 'The Two Blackbirds,' 'Infancy and Age' are a selection from those published in 'Household Words' " (*Letters*, I, 8). (Actually, the three poems mentioned were not "a selection from" Meredith's poems "published in 'Household Words' ": the first two were the only poems of his that had been published in the periodical. "Infancy and Age" did not appear until April 19, 1851 – four months after the date of Meredith's letter.) Versions of "Queen Zuleima," "Rhine-Land," and "Monmouth," in Meredith's handwriting, appear in an interleaved copy of Meredith's *Poems* [1851] in the Berg Collection, New York Public Library.

A note by Meredith's son in the Memorial Edition of *The Works of George Meredith* (XXVII, 299) states that Meredith did not wish "Monmouth" reprinted among his collected poems.

In the Office Book, Meredith is recorded as author of "The Burial of the Old Year"; his name is marked out and substituted by that of Miss Siddons. Meredith is recorded as author of "A Child's Prayer"; his name is marked out but not substituted by another. See "A Child's Prayer," p. 480.

See also "An Arabian Night-mare," p. 477, and "A Cry from the Dust!", p. 480.

Harper's reprinted "Sorrows and Joys," with acknowledgment to *H.W.*

D.N.B. suppl. 1901–1911

PROSE

A New Way of Manufacturing Glory IV, 472–76. Feb. 7, 1852

VERSE

*Sorrows and Joys *Meredith & Horne* I, 517–18. Aug. 24, 1850

*The Two Blackbirds *Mr. Meredith & R.H.H.* II, 157. Nov. 9, 1850

New Year's Eve II, 325. Dec. 28, 1850

The Congress of Nations II, 572. March 8, 1851

Infancy and Age III, 85. April 19, 1851

Time *Meredith & W.H.W.* III, 204. May 24, 1851

Force and His Master III, 588–89. Sept. 13, 1851

The Gentleness of Death IV, 37–38. Oct. 4, 1851

A Word from the Cannon's Mouth IV, 109. Oct. 25, 1851

Queen Zuleima IV, 131–32. Nov. 1, 1851

Britain IV, 204. Nov. 22, 1851

Familiar Things IV, 254. Dec. 6, 1851

The Glastonbury Thorn IV, 301–302. Dec. 20, 1851

A Wassail for the New Year IV, 348–49. Jan. 3, 1852

The Linnet-Hawker IV, 372. Jan. 10, 1852

War *Meredith & Horne* IV, 517. Feb. 21, 1852

The First-Born V, 392. July 10, 1852

Holidays VIII, 397. Dec. 24, 1853

Motley VIII, 539–40. Feb. 4, 1854

Rhine-Land XIV, 12–13. July 19, 1856

Monmouth XIV, 372–73. Nov. 1, 1856
*Repr. in *Poems: By George Meredith.* London: John W. Parker and Son [1851]. Pub. in *H.W.* not acknowledged.

Meredith, Louisa Anne (Twamley) |*Mrs. Meredith*|, 1812–1895, misc. writer. Born near Birmingham. Taught chiefly by her mother, but also attended school; schoolmate of Mrs. Gaskell. In 1835 published *Poems;* in 1836, *The Romance of Nature,* dedicated to Wordsworth; both books illustrated by her own drawings; published also other volumes. Mentioned by Leigh Hunt, "Blue-Stocking Revels," 1837, as "young Twalmley" [*sic*] "Whose pen and whose pencil give promise like spring." In 1839 married her cousin Charles Meredith (no relation, said George Meredith, to his branch of the family), who had been a squatter in New South Wales. In same year accompanied her husband to Sydney. Later the Merediths removed to Tasmania, which thereafter remained their home. Mrs. Meredith, much interested in politics, wrote unsigned articles for Tasmanian newspapers; contributed to *Australian Ladies' Annual;* sent an occasional item to British periodicals, e.g., *Chambers's, Once a Week.* Became a "prominent personality in the literary history of Tasmania" (Miller, *Australian Lit.,* I, 215). Published *Notes and Sketches of New South Wales,* 1844; *My Home in Tasmania,* 1852, "still one of the best authorities on Tasmanian life and society" of the time (Miller, I, 216); George Eliot found the book "charming" and "delightful" (*Westm. Rev.,* Oct. 1853). Wrote two books describing Tasmanian flowers, insects, etc., the descriptions being interspersed with verses and illustrated by colour plates from her drawings: *Some of My Bush Friends in Tasmania,* 1860, dedicated "by the Royal Command" to Her Majesty the Queen; and a second series of *Bush Friends,* 1891, the proof-sheets of which Sir Joseph Hooker checked "to prevent botanical errors." Wrote also *Tasmanian Friends and Foes: Feathered, Furred, and Finned* (in story form), *Grandmamma's Verse Book for Young Australia, Waratah Rhymes for Young Australia,* and other books. After her husband's death, 1880, was granted pension of £100 a year by Tasmanian Government.

On Jan. 15, 1859, Mrs. Meredith wrote to Leigh Hunt: "If certain papers by 'A Settler's Wife' appear in H. W. perchance you will see them" (Brewer, *My Leigh Hunt Library: The Holograph Letters,* p. 384). The reference may be to papers of Mrs. Meredith's submitted to but not accepted by *H.W.,* though this supposition is very unlikely; or the reference may be to "Shadows of the Golden Image," though that article had appeared in *H.W.* more than a year and a half before. (No articles in the early volumes of *A.Y.R.* seem to be Mrs. Meredith's writing, though her poem "A Friend in a Flower" appeared in the number of July 23, 1859.) There was some delay, and evidently some confusion, about payment for "Shadows of the Golden Image." Dickens's letter to Wills, Oct. 22, 1858, indicates that Mrs. Meredith had written to W. C. Macready about the matter. The payment date recorded in the Office Book is April (or Aug.?) 5, 1858.

The *H.W.* article "A Brazilian in Bloomsbury" referred to the account of an opossum given in Mrs. Meredith's *My Home in Tasmania.*

Miller, *Australian Lit.*

PROSE

Shadows of the Golden Image [lead] XV, 313–18. April 4, 1857

VERSE

Little Bell XIX, 35–38. Dec. 11, 1858
Repr. in *Some of My Bush Friends in Tasmania: Native Flowers, Berries, and Insects Drawn from Life, Illustrated in Verse and Briefly Described by Louisa Anne Meredith.* London: Day & Son, 1860. Pub. in *H.W.* not acknowledged.

Michelsen, Edward Henry |*Dr. Michelsen*|, 1795–1870, writer. Born in Dresden; son of Lutheran minister named Michaelowitz (Boase). His name given in "General List of Articles," *Dublin Review,* April 1896, as "Dr. Michelowicz" and as "Michelsen (Michelowicz)." According to Boase, received M.D. degree from Univ. of Heidelberg, 1827; on title pages of various of his works designated himself

Ph.D. According to Boase, went to England in 1832, then lived in the U.S. for some years, thereafter in England. His *H.W.* articles indicate that he lived or travelled some time in Italy and in the East. Occasional contributor to *Dublin Review* and *Once a Week*. Author of *The Ottoman Empire and Its Resources*, 1853; *The Life of Nicholas I*, 1854; *England: Since the Accession of Queen Victoria*, 1854; *Modern Jesuitism*, 1855. Compiled *The Merchant's Polyglot Manual*, 1860; on title page designated himself member of Board of Trade.

A memorandum in the Office Book concerns what was, apparently, a confusion in the matter of payment for Michelsen's article of Nov. 19, 1853, and Irwin's article of Nov. 26.

Boase

Fishing for Tunny *Dr. Michelsen & Morley* VII, 499–503. July 23, 1853
Chinese Players [chip] VIII, 281–83. Nov. 19, 1853

Michie, Sir Archibald |*Mitchie*|, date of birth given as 1810, also as 1813; *d.* 1899; jurist and statesman. Educated at Westminster School. Admitted at Middle Temple, 1834; called to the bar, 1838. Went to Sydney in 1838 or 1839; practised law; also did journalistic work; connected with *Atlas* newspaper. About 1848 returned to England, going back to Australia some time in 1852. Settled in Melbourne; practised law; Q.C. For about two years, proprietor of Melbourne *Herald*. Member of Victoria Legislative Council, 1852; member for Melbourne of first Legislative Assembly of Victoria; was twice attorney-general; was minister of justice. For six years agent-general for Victoria in London. K.C.M.G. On his retirement returned to Melbourne, where he died. Distinguished as speaker and lecturer; published several of his speeches and lectures in pamphlet form, e.g., *Colonists: Socially, and in Their Relations with the Mother Country*, 1859; *Victoria: Retrospective & Prospective*, 1866; *Great Britain and New Guinea*, 1875. Some of lectures reprinted in *Readings in Melbourne*, 1879.

Michie and Dickens were probably acquainted. In a letter of Dec. 1865 to Horne (then in Australia), Dickens mentioned his appreciation of Michie's kindness to young Alfred Dickens, who had emigrated to Australia in May of that year (in Nonesuch *Letters*, the name appears not as *Michie*, but as *Michael*; but see Dickens, *Notes and Comments on Certain Writings ... by Richard Henry Horne*, priv. printed for Thomas J. Wise). One of Michie's lectures mentions Dickens as "the master of our laughter and our tears"; others contain other references to him and to his writings.

In the first item listed below, the writer identifies himself as one of the "London barristers" in Sydney and states that his "own 'diggins' were in the Supreme Court"; he records a trip to Maitland in connection with the assize held there. He describes Sydney as he saw the city on his first arrival and as he came to know it in "a subsequent nine years' experience." Michie had resided in Sydney about nine years (ca. 1839–48).

Notable Middle Templars;
Miller, *Australian Lit.*

Going Circuit at the Antipodes *Mitchie & Morley* IV, 344–48. Jan. 3, 1852
A Visit to the Burra Burra Mines [chip] IV, 567–68. March 6, 1852

Miller, Thomas |*Miller*|, 1807–1874, author. Born in Lincolnshire; reared in poverty; received little schooling. Apprenticed to basket-maker. Brought out volume of poems, 1832. About 1835 went to London; brought himself to notice of Lady Blessington, who became for a time his patroness. Thomas Moore, Samuel Rogers, William Jerdan, and others also interested themselves in the "basket-maker poet." Set up as bookseller and publisher; unsuccessful. Some of his poems published in *Friendship's Offering*; contributed verse and prose to periodicals – *Literary Gazette*, *Illus. London News*, *Athenaeum*, *Chambers's*. Author of some forty-five works – volumes of poems, novels, children's books, and "country books," e.g., *A Day in the Woods*, 1836; *Rural Sketches*, 1839. His miscellaneous writing included *History of the Anglo-Saxons*, 1848; *Picturesque Sketches of London*, 1852.

Miller was at times in great poverty. In 1851 he addressed to Dickens a plea for assistance. Dickens, writing to Bulwer-Lytton (Aug. 14, 1851), enclosed Miller's letter and said of Miller and his plight: "I am afraid it is a case in which no permanent good can be done – I have several times sat upon it when at the Literary Fund, and I fear he has mistaken his vocation, and is a little impracticable besides – but he seems in great affliction now." According to Vizetelly (*Glances Back through Seventy Years*, I, 309), the Literary Fund made Miller "frequent timely gifts."

Men of the Time, 1868, mentions Miller as a *H.W.* contributor.

D.N.B.

PROSE

The Old Boar's Head
xi, 546–50. July 7, 1855

VERSE

Spring Lights and Shadows
xi, 181–82. March 24, 1855

Milne, William Charles |*Mylne, Milne*|, 1815–1863, missionary; son of William Milne (1785–1822), missionary. On title page of *Life in China*, 1857, designated himself "M.A." Went to China in 1839; "with the exception of an absence of two years, continued to labour there till near the beginning of 1854, under the auspices of the London Missionary Society" ("Preface," *Life in China*). Stationed at various times in Macao, Ningpo, Hong Kong, Shanghai; disguised as Chinese, made 1300-mile journey into interior. Served on Bible translation committee. After terminating connection with Missionary Society, served as interpreter for British Government, 1858–62, first at Hong Kong, then at Foochowfoo; thereafter, assistant Chinese secretary to Legation at Peking, 1862–63 (*Foreign Office List*, 1859 and later dates). Died in Peking. Contributed an occasional article to *Chinese Repository, Transactions* of China branch of Royal Asiatic Society, *Chambers's, Edin. Rev.* Published *Critical Remarks on Dr. Medhurst's Version of the First Chapter of St. John* and *Life in China*. The *Life* exposes the falsity of many concepts held about the Chinese; denounces the loose generalizations of ill-informed writers, as, for instance, the comments of that "shallow observer of human nature" Bayard Taylor.

D.N.B. (entry: William Milne)

*Francis Moore in China
x, 203–204. Oct. 14, 1854

The Chinese Adam
xi, 67–68. Feb. 17, 1855

The Chinaman's Parson
xi, 202–204. March 31, 1855

The Chinese Postman
xi, 259–61. April 14, 1855

Canton-English xv, 450–52. May 9, 1857

Chinese Charms
xvii, 370–72. April 3, 1858

*Repr. in *Life in China. By Rev. William C. Milne, M.A.* London: G. Routledge & Co., 1857. Pub. in *H.W.* acknowledged.

Minshall, Miss. *Not identified.*

VERSE

New Year's Eve xii, 539. Jan. 5, 1856

Mitchell, Andrew |*A. Mitchell*, 23 Tonbridge Place; *Andrew Mitchell*, 8 Timmans Gardens|, English military officer, some time stationed in Canada. London directories, 1857–59, do not list an A. Mitchell or an Andrew Mitchell at either of the above addresses; they do list a Miss Mitchell at 29 Tonbridge Place.

Mitchell contributed to *Once a Week*, Feb. 4, 1860, the signed article "A Night on the Ice," recounting a dangerous adventure that befell him in Canada soon after he had arrived there from England; he stated that no experience had left a deeper impression on his mind, though since that time "the chances of a soldier's life have brought me through many adventures." The *H.W.* articles relate two of the adventures: "The Snow Express" recounts a hazardous trip that Mitchell undertook "many years ago," when as a young subaltern he was stationed at Blockhouse Point, at the mouth of the Green Snake River, on the north side of Lake Huron; "A Journey in Kafirland" recounts a trek that he made to escort his sister and her child from Cape Colony to Natal, where the sister's husband was Kaffir agent. "... Fortune," writes Mitchell, "has sent me wandering to and fro upon the earth."

The Snow Express
xvi, 367–72. Oct. 17, 1857
A Journey in Kafirland [lead]
xix, 193–97. Jan. 29, 1859

Mitchell, E. Address: 1 Charleville Road, Rathgar, Dublin. *Not identified.* Thom's Dublin directory for 1857 lists the resident at the above address as Mrs. Mitchell, no first name or initial. The contributor relates his experience in acting as receiver for an encumbered Tipperary property under administration of the Court of Chancery.

An Encumbered Estate
xvi, 84–89. July 25, 1857

Mitchie: *See* Michie, Sir Archibald

Moncrieff, William Thomas |*Moncrieff*|, 1794–1857, dramatist. Real name (*Brit. Mus. Cat.*): William Thomas Thomas. Son of a tradesman; worked in London solicitor's office; was for some time law stationer, music shop proprietor. Early became theatre manager; connected throughout his life with numerous theatres; for a time manager of Astley's and of Vauxhall Gardens. Composed for the stage some one hundred pieces, original and adapted – extravaganzas, burlettas, farces, comedies, and dramas, many of them highly successful. Most popular of the adaptations was *Tom and Jerry,* based on Pierce Egan's *Life in London.* Member of Dramatic Authors' Society. Wrote theatrical criticisms for *Satirist* and *Scourge;* contributed to *New Monthly, Sunday Times,* and other periodicals. Published some books of verse; also some miscellaneous non-dramatic prose writings. Became totally blind in 1843; admitted a brother of the Charterhouse, 1844 (*D.N.B.*).

Among Moncrieff's stage adaptations were pieces based on *Pickwick* and *Nicholas Nickleby.* His version of "the very original, graphic, and clever" *Pickwick,* wrote Moncrieff, had increased the popularity and sale of that book, and he was at a loss to understand the indignation of Dickens's "injudicious friends" at his making the successful stage version (advertisement to *Sam Weller,* cited in FitzGerald, *Dickens and the Drama,* pp. 83–87). The adaptation of *Nickleby,* which (like that of *Pickwick*) appeared on the stage before Dickens had completed publication of the novel in monthly parts, led to an ugly quarrel between the two writers. Dickens introduced into *Nickleby* (chap. xlviii) a caricature of Moncrieff in the person of the "literary gentleman" who in his time had dramatized "two hundred and forty-seven novels as fast as they had come out – some of them faster than they had come out." Moncrieff replied in a long address "To the Public" (cited in Fitz-Gerald, pp. 121–26), in which he admitted the unfairness of novelists' having no control over the adaptation of their works, but defended his right to make adaptations; he termed the caricature "intemperate and vulgar" and regretted that Dickens, forgetful of the manners of a gentleman, had resorted to "scurrility and abuse."

Dickens was convinced (in part by information given to Bulwer-Lytton by Moncrieff) that the conditions under which the brothers of the Charterhouse lived were deplorable, and, as he wrote to Bulwer-Lytton, Feb. 4, 1852, had for some time wished to publish in *H.W.* an article on the subject. The article, assigned in the Office Book to Morley and Moncrieff, appeared four months later. It related the history of the Charterhouse and, on the basis of "a few visits" that "we have lately been paying" to the institution, described the indignities to which the brothers were subjected and the meagre provision for their needs, in contrast with the luxurious living that the master of the foundation (William H. Hale) secured to himself. *Lives of the Illustrious*, 1852 (II, 295), enumerating some of the "public wrongs, nuisances, and abuses" dealt with in *H.W.*, stated: "The Charter-House received a castigation in an article the data of which were furnished by Moncreiff [*sic*], the old dramatist who spoiled 'Nickleby,' that injury being remembered, be it said to Dickens's honour, only to be forgiven." Wills, who was a friend of Moncrieff, made him the generous payment of five guineas for his share in the article.

A second article on "the public scandal of the Charterhouse," also by Morley, appeared in *H.W.* Dec. 1, 1855.

D.N.B.

The Poor Brothers of the Charterhouse
[lead] *Morley & Moncrieff*
v, 285–91. June 12, 1852

Montagu, Eleanora Louisa: *See* Hervey, Eleanora Louisa (Montagu)

Morley, Henry |*Mr. H. Morley, Mr. Morley, Mr. Henry Morley, H. Morley, Morley*|, 1822–1894, man of letters. Attended boarding schools in England, then for two years a Moravian school in Neuwied, Germany. Student at King's College, London, in faculties of arts and medicine. With two fellow students, brought out *King's College Magazine*, 1841–42. L.S.A. 1843. Practised medicine, 1844–48; then for two years conducted own school. On staff of *H.W.* and *A.Y.R.*, 1851–65; subeditor, then editor (1861–67) of *Examiner*. Lecturer in English language and literature, King's College, 1857–65; professor of English language and literature, University College, 1865–89; held also other academic appointments. Hon. LL.D. Univ. of Edinburgh, 1880. Contributed to *Fraser's*, *Athenaeum*, *Inquirer* (Unitarian journal), *Quart. Rev.*, *Edin. Rev.*, and other periodicals. Author of books of poems, fairy tales; biography of Bernard Palissy, of Jerome Cardan, of Cornelius Agrippa; *Memoirs of Bartholomew Fair*, 1858; *Clement Marot, and Other Studies*, 1871; *English Writers*, 10 vols. completed at time of his death. In latter part of his life, edited some 300 vols. of English and foreign classics, constituting Morley's Universal Library, Cassell's National Library, and other series.

Morley's acquaintance with Dickens came about through his connection with *H.W.* During the years that he knew Dickens, wrote Morley many years after Dickens's death, he acquired for him "a strong and well-grounded affection." "A thousand evidences of his worth have made his memory most dear to me" ("Introduction" to *A Christmas Carol*). Copies of his books that he presented to Dickens during the 1850s, however, Morley formally inscribed to the older writer with his "respect" – "hearty," "sincere," or "true" (Stonehouse, *Catalogue*) – rather than in more personal or familiar terms.

In a letter of 1850, Morley expressed high admiration of Dickens's writing, but stated at the same time that Dickens lacked "sound literary taste": "his own genius, brilliant as it is, appears often in a dress which shows that he has more heart and wit than critical refinement." In a later letter of the same year he remarked: "Dickens has great genius, but not a trained and cultivated reason" (Solly, *Life of Henry Morley*, pp. 149, 163). Thirty years later, those judgments remained essentially unchanged. In his history of Victorian literature, Morley wrote of Dickens as a writer who "spent the gifts of a rare genius in strenuous service to humanity." Dickens's works, he stated, inevitably showed, "at times, some traces of the want of early culture"; to fastidious readers, his "generous emotions" appeared occasionally to "outrun his judgment," and his writings seemed "at times, often perhaps," to be vulgar. The charge of vulgarity Morley countered by the general statement that in "a writer who deliberately gives his labour to the highest aims in life" there could be "no essential vulgarity." The complaint that Dickens based his novels on "accidental questions of the day and not upon essential truths" Morley held unjust, pointing out in *Bleak House* a deeper purpose than a mere attack on contemporary abuses. Morley mentioned also *A Child's History of England*; though commendable in intent, he wrote, the book required for its execution "much knowledge in which Dickens was deficient" (*Of English Literature in the Reign of Victoria*, chap. xii).

Morley's connection with *H.W.* resulted from Dickens's interest in certain papers on sanitation and health that Morley had written. Two of the papers, published in the *Journal of Public Health*, had been widely reprinted in newspapers, and Forster had agreed to publish the series in the *Examiner*. Dickens's request that Morley write for *H.W.* on matters of sanitation was enclosed in a letter from Forster that reached Morley on April 5, 1850. Morley was not eager to become a contributor. "I don't care very much for *Household Words*," he wrote, having seen the first (and possibly the second) number; but for the sake of making Dickens's acquaintance and having "a second pulpit from which to preach 'health,'" he set to work to write some papers on the subject. He found the task uncongenial: "... in the *Journal of Public Health* I had a sanitary assembly to speak to, in the *Examiner* I speak to people who are clever, liberal-minded, and love wit. *Household Words* has an audience which I cannot write for naturally." Finally he lighted on a device and style for an article that he thought would be "just what Dickens wants of me": written in the person of a garrulous old lady and stringing together "odds and ends ... bearing on sanitary discipline," the article required "no polished composition" – "only a quizzical slip-slop." It was Morley's first article published in *H.W.* During the following thirteen months, some thirty of Morley's contributions appeared in *H.W.*, a few on sanitation, most of them on other subjects. Some of his papers were rejected, some returned for revision or rewriting; some were "mangled" at the editorial office. Particularly distressing to Morley was the mangling of his verses (Horne was the "mangler"). Many of his papers were much liked, wrote Morley, and requests for his contributions continued (*Life of Henry Morley*, pp. 149–51, et passim).

In June 1851, Morley was offered a position on the *H.W.* staff at a salary of five guineas a week. Reluctant to abandon his school and uncertain about trusting his livelihood to his pen, he sought the advice of Forster. Then, after much earnest thought, he accepted the position. It was thus, as Morley later wrote, Dickens's offer that brought about his giving up "all I was then working for" ("Introduction" to *A Christmas Carol*) to enter on the career of a journalist – forerunner to his career as author and university professor.

Morley was the one university-educated man on the *H.W.* staff. He was twelve and a half years younger than Wills, for whom he acted, he said, "as a sort of deputy-lieutenant" (*Early Papers and Some Memories*, p. 30). His main work was to write for the periodical on subjects of his own choosing and on matters that Dickens wanted discussed – the Charterhouse, for instance, the administration of the Royal Literary Fund, regulations concerning the sale of poisons. In addition, he manufactured articles from books, reports, and other materials that Dickens forwarded for the purpose; he contrived "chips" out of readers' letters to the editor; he revised or rewrote contributed papers to make them "suitable for the journal" (his "careful and valuable revision" was publicly acknowledged by the contributor Duthie); he helped in the planning of some of the Christmas numbers, and, as he said, made himself "generally useful." It was at his suggestion that the *Household Words Almanac* was brought out. Morley wrote more than 300 items for *H.W.* – more than did any other writer. The items constitute some 300 more pages than do Dickens's writings in the periodical.

Dickens valued Morley as a staff member and had high praise for some of his articles. That based on Edward R. Sullivan's *Rambles and Scrambles in North and South America* he thought "Quite a model" of what such a paper should be (to Wills, Oct. 7, 1852). "The Quiet Poor" and "Frost-Bitten Homes" affected him deeply; of the first he wrote to Morley: "I think it is absolutely impossible that it should have been better done" (*Life of Henry Morley*, p. 224). "A Home Question" Dickens thought "exceedingly well done" (to Macready, Nov. 1, 1854). Occasional articles of Morley's Dickens disliked: "The Stereoscope" was "dreadfully literal" and "Back Ways to Fame" "dreadfully heavy" (to Wills, Aug. 5, 1853; July 30, 1854). Some of Morley's articles, like some of his narrative items, Dickens found unclear and confusing. Of Morley's writing in general he remarked in a letter to Wills, Jan. 10, 1856: "Morley always wants a little screwing up and tightening. It is his habit to write in a loose way."

The articles assigned in the Office Book jointly to Morley and Dickens were revised or added to by Dickens; they were not actual collaborations of the two writers. One of these – "The Wind and the Rain" – bears the additional Office Book notation "Rewritten by W.H.W."

Four of Morley's articles motivated Dickens's writing a "chip" for the purpose of correction, disclaimer, or denial. In "Homœopathy," Nov. 15, 1851, Dickens quoted from John Epps, *Homœopathy and Its Principles Explained*, to correct what had been called to his attention as an unfair description of homeopathic principles in "The Work of the World"; in "A Free (and Easy) School," Dec. 6, 1851, he stated that the prospectus of the school from which Morley had quoted (in the article of the same title) was not the prospectus of the school described in the article (although it was); in "The Ghost of the Cock Lane Ghost Wrong Again," Jan. 15, 1853, he denied the report that he had attended the séance described in Morley's article of similar title; in "The Samaritan Institution," May 16, 1857, he explained that "The Predatory Art" had wrongly included the secretary of the Samaritan Institution among the notorious swindlers dealt with in the article.

Morley's articles on preventible factory accidents were denounced by millowners and ridiculed by newspapers favourable to millowner interests; they were abusively attacked by Harriet Martineau in *The Factory Controversy*. But they also brought to the *H.W.* office letters from readers in agreement with Morley's stand. Morley's paper on needy women sent to Australia under Sidney Herbert's Emigration Fund ("A Rainy Day on 'The Euphrates' ") was greatly liked by persons connected with the Fund. "They have bought up lots of the number containing it," wrote Morley, "to be sent with the girls to Sydney" (*Life of Henry Morley*, p. 214). Among other of Morley's contributions that called forth praise from readers was "Brother Mieth and His Brothers," an account of Morley's school days at Neuwied. At the insistence of a friend "who is just crazy about 'Brother Mieth,' " Mrs. Gaskell wrote to find out who had written the "charming" paper (*Letters*, No. 205a).

Occasional references to Morley's books appeared in *H.W.* Dodd, in "The Soulages Collection," mentioned Morley's "admirable memoir" of Palissy; Costello, in "Witchcraft and Old Boguey," referred to Morley's biography of Cornelius Agrippa. Morley himself, in "A Piece of Work," mentioned two tracts on health and sanitation that he had published in 1847, though without stating that they were his writing.

Of the items listed below as not reprinted, some forty are mentioned (by title or subject) as Morley's writing, in Solly's life of Morley.

Eighteen of Morley's *H.W.* contributions were reprinted in whole or part in *Harper's*, three of them acknowledged to *H.W.*, and one – "Drooping Buds" – credited to Dickens. Seven of his contributions were included in the Putnam volumes of selections from *H.W.*: *Home and Social Philosophy*, 1st and 2nd ser., and *The World Here and There*. "My Wonderful Adventures in Skitzland" was included in *Choice Stories from Dickens' Household Words*, pub. Auburn, N.Y., 1854. "Drooping Buds," acknowledged to *H.W.*, was issued in 1852 as a promotional pamphlet by the Hospital for Sick Children, Great Ormond St. (Eckel, *First Editions of the Writings of Charles Dickens*). Morley reprinted various of his *H.W.* contributions in more than one collection of his writings.

D.N.B.

PROSE

My Wonderful Adventures in Skitzland
I, 225–29. June 1, 1850

The Golden Fagots. A Child's Tale
I, 288. June 15, 1850

Class Opinions. A Fable
I, 330. June 29, 1850

The King of the Hearth
II, 229–33. Nov. 30, 1850

The Death of a Goblin
II, 335–36. Dec. 28, 1850

A Free (and Easy) School [lead]
Morley & C.D.
IV, 169–73. Nov. 15, 1851

A Christmas Piece
IV, 310–12. Dec. 20, 1851

A Rainy Day on "The Euphrates" [lead]
IV, 409–415. Jan. 24, 1852

A Great Idea V, 546–48. Aug. 21, 1852

The Enemy V, 577–80. Sept. 4, 1852

The Gardens of Rye
VI, 55–60. Oct. 2, 1852

The Ghost of the Cock Lane Ghost [lead]
VI, 217–23. Nov. 20, 1852

A House Full of Horrors [lead]
VI, 265–70. Dec. 4, 1852

A Foe under Foot [lead]
VI, 289–92. Dec. 11, 1852

Scholastic [lead]
VI, 409–413. Jan. 15, 1853

Playthings VI, 430–32. Jan. 15, 1853

The Club Surgeon [lead]
VI, 433–37. Jan. 22, 1853

Black Monday VI, 569–72. Feb. 26, 1853

How to Kill Labourers [lead]
VII, 97–102. April 2, 1853

Ten Years Old VII, 245–48. May 14, 1853

Country News VII, 426–30. July 2, 1853

Apartments, Furnished [lead]
VII, 457–63. July 16, 1853

Why Shave? *Morley & W.H.W.*
VII, 560–63. Aug. 13, 1853

Out for a Walk [lead]
VIII, 25–27. Sept. 10, 1853

Trust and No Trust
VIII, 94–96. Sept. 24, 1853

Lanna Tixel VIII, 123–28. Oct. 8, 1853

The Modern Practice of Physic [lead]
VIII, 169–73. Oct. 22, 1853

Near Christmas [lead]
VIII, 337–39. Dec. 10, 1853

Seasonable Gains
VIII, 454–56. Jan. 7, 1854

School-Keeping
VIII, 499–504. Jan. 21, 1854

Shadows of Dark Days [lead]
IX, 93–98. March 18, 1854

Preventible Accidents
IX, 105–106. March 18, 1854

The Quiet Poor
IX, 201–206. April 15, 1854

The Cankered Rose of Tivoli
IX, 314–17. May 20, 1854

Brother Mieth and His Brothers
IX, 344–49. May 27, 1854

British Phenomena
IX, 386–90. June 10, 1854

Medical Practice among the Poor [lead]
X, 217–21. Oct. 21, 1854

Conversion of a Heathen Court [lead]
X, 409–413. Dec. 16, 1854

Infant Gardens [lead]
XI, 577–82. July 21, 1855

Hobbies [lead] XII, 337–39. Nov. 10, 1855

Hospitals [lead] XII, 457–61. Dec. 15, 1855

Looking Out of Window
XIII, 166–68. March 1, 1856

Apothecaries XIV, 108–115. Aug. 16, 1856

Mr. Speckles on Himself
XIV, 198–201. Sept. 13, 1856

Something That Shakespeare Lost [lead]
XV, 49–52. Jan. 17, 1857

The Predatory Art [lead]
XV, 241–46. March 14, 1857

The 46 items, together with some poems, repr. as *Gossip. By Henry Morley ... Reprinted from "Household Words."* London: Chapman & Hall, 1857.

The Two Guides of the Child
I, 560–61. Sept. 7, 1850

The Night Porter
XVI, 513–18. Nov. 28, 1857

Much Too Good Boys
XIX, 309–312. Feb. 26, 1859

The 3 items repr. in *Fables and Fairy Tales. By Henry Morley.* London: Chapman and Hall, 1860. Pub. in *H.W.* acknowledged.

Letter from a Highly Respectable Old Lady I, 186–87. May 18, 1850

Improving a Bull [chip] *W.H.W. & Mr. Morley* I, 450–51. Aug. 3, 1850

The Water-Drops. A Fairy Tale
I, 482–89. Aug. 17, 1850

The Irish Use of the Globe, in One Lesson II, 51–56. Oct. 12, 1850

The Penny Saved; a Blue-Book Catechism
II, 81–84. Oct. 19, 1850

Views of the Country [lead]
II, 169–72. Nov. 16, 1850
Mr. Bendigo Buster on Our National Defences against Education [lead] *Mr. C.D. & Mr. Morley*
II, 313–19. Dec. 28, 1850
Our Phantom Ship: Negro Land
II, 400–407. Jan. 18, 1851
Our Phantom Ship: Central America
II, 516–22. Feb. 22, 1851
A Plea for British Reptiles
II, 573–76. March 8, 1851
The Short Cut to California [chip] *H. Morley & W.H.W.*
II, 597–98. March 15, 1851
The Cape and the Kaffirs. A History
III, 30–35. April 5, 1851
Our Phantom Ship among the Ice
III, 66–72. April 12, 1851
Free Public Libraries *Morley & Lynn*
III, 80–83. April 19, 1851
The Last of the Sea-Kings
III, 124–30. May 3, 1851
The Great Southern Reflector [chip]
III, 131–32. May 3, 1851
Our Phantom Ship: Japan
III, 160–67. May 10, 1851
The World of Water
III, 204–209. May 24, 1851
The Wind and the Rain [lead] *C.D. & Morley* III, 217–22. May 31, 1851
Madagascar: A History
III, 270–75. June 14, 1851
Our Phantom Ship: China
III, 325–31. June 28, 1851
Mr. Bendigo Buster on the Model Cottages [lead] III, 337–41. July 5, 1851
The Globe in a Square
III, 370–72. July 12, 1851
The Lighting of Eastern Seas [chip]
III, 396. July 19, 1851
What Is Not Clear about the Crystal Palace III, 400–402. July 19, 1851
A Hint to Hatters [chip]
III, 419–21. July 26, 1851
Fish Dinners III, 421–25. July 26, 1851
Foreign Airs and Native Places
III, 446–50. Aug. 2, 1851
The Jews in China *Soutar, Keys, & Morley* III, 452–56. Aug. 2, 1851
A Tale of the Forest of Dean *Wickenden & Morley*
III, 461–64. Aug. 9, 1851
Ice [lead] *Morley & W.H.W.*
III, 481–84. Aug. 16, 1851
The Story of Reineke the Fox
III, 484–91. Aug. 16, 1851, and the following no.
Our Phantom Ship on an Antediluvian Cruise III, 492–96. Aug. 16, 1851
The Catalogue's Account of Itself
III, 519–23. Aug. 23, 1851
Soldiers' Wives [chip] *W.H.W. & Morley*
III, 561–62. Sept. 6, 1851
The Labourer's Reading-Room
III, 581–85. Sept. 13, 1851
The Work of the World
III, 589–92. Sept. 13, 1851
Light and Air III, 612–16. Sept. 20, 1851
The Birth and Parentage of Letters [lead]
IV, 1–6. Sept. 27, 1851
Pottery and Porcelain
IV, 32–37. Oct. 4, 1851
The Good Side of Combination
IV, 56–60. Oct. 11, 1851
Gold IV, 77–82. Oct. 18, 1851
Indian Furlough Regulations
IV, 107–109. Oct. 25, 1851
Mr. Bull at Home in the Middle Ages [lead] IV, 121–26. Nov. 1, 1851
Tribunals of Commerce [chip]
IV, 157–58. Nov. 8, 1851
Building and Freehold Land Societies
IV, 158–64. Nov. 8, 1851
The First Time, and the Last Way, of Asking IV, 164–66. Nov. 8, 1851
A Black Eagle in a Bad Way [lead] *Murray, Morley, & C.D.*
IV, 193–95. Nov. 22, 1851
Wisdom in Words [chip]
IV, 208–209. Nov. 22, 1851
Need Railway Travellers Be Smashed? [lead] IV, 217–21. Nov. 29, 1851
A Roving Englishman: Benighted; Out Shooting *Murray & Morley*
IV, 221–24. Nov. 29, 1851
Neapolitan State Prisoners [chip] *Wreford & Morley*
IV, 235–37. Nov. 29, 1851
The Story of a Nation
IV, 249–54. Dec. 6, 1851, and the following no.
A Roving Englishman: The Apple-Green Spencer; Gastein Baths *Murray & Morley* IV, 299–301. Dec. 20, 1851
Little Red Working-Coat
IV, 324–25. Dec. 27, 1851
The True Tom Tiddler's Ground
IV, 329–32. Dec. 27, 1851

Discovery of a Treasure near Cheapside [lead] *C.D. & Morley* vi, 193–97. Nov. 13, 1852
Francis Moore, Physician vi, 197–201. Nov. 13, 1852
Justice to Chicory vi, 208–210. Nov. 13, 1852
A Dip in the Nile vi, 235–39. Nov. 20, 1852
Funerals in Paris [chip] *Morley & W.H.W.* vi, 257–60. Nov. 27, 1852
Another Lung for London [chip] vi, 275–77. Dec. 4, 1852
Forty Famous Arm-Chairs vi, 300–306. Dec. 11, 1852
Rational Schools [lead] *Morley & W.H.W.* vi, 337–42. Dec. 25, 1852
Frozen Up in Siberia vi, 350–56. Dec. 25, 1852
Silk from the Punjaub vi, 388–90. Jan. 8, 1853
Travel on Tramp in Germany: Hamburgh to Lubeck *Duthie & Morley* vi, 420–22. Jan. 15, 1853
Information against a Poisoner vi, 427–30. Jan. 15, 1853
Sailors' Homes Afloat [lead] *Rinder & Morley* vi, 529–33. Feb. 19, 1853
We Mariners of England [lead] *Rinder & Morley* vi, 553–57. Feb. 26, 1853
A Walk through a Mountain *Duthie & Morley* vii, 9–13. March 5, 1853
Self-Acting Railway Signals vii, 43–45. March 12, 1853
Photography *Morley & W.H.W.* vii, 54–61. March 19, 1853
Fresh Air in Finsbury [chip] vii, 107–108. April 2, 1853
Gentleman Cadet [lead] *J. Payne & Morley* vii, 121–25. April 9, 1853
H.W. [lead] *C. D. & Morley* vii, 145–49. April 16, 1853
Chloroform vii, 179–81. April 23, 1853
Bavarian Poachers vii, 227–29. May 7, 1853
Patent Wrongs vii, 229–34. May 7, 1853
A Puff of Smoke vii, 234–35. May 7, 1853
In and Out of Jail [lead] *C.D., Morley, & W.H.W.* vii, 241–45. May 14, 1853
Our Last Parochial War [lead] vii, 265–70. May 21, 1853
Diffusion of Knowledge among Cattle [chip] vii, 285–86. May 21, 1853
The Life of Poor Jack vii, 286–88. May 21, 1853
Magazines of Meat [chip] vii, 356–57. June 11, 1853
Ben Close, of Baggenham *White & Morley* vii, 370–72. June 18, 1853
Quails ——— & *Morley* vii, 448–50. July 9, 1853
The River of Yesterday vii, 450–54. July 9, 1853
Good Lac *H. H. Maxwell & Morley* vii, 463–66. July 16, 1853
In Presence of the Sword vii, 492–98. July 23, 1853
Fishing for Tunny *Dr. Michelsen & Morley* vii, 499–503. July 23, 1853
Lilliput in London *Morley & W.H.W.* vii, 573–76. Aug. 13, 1853
Lodged in Newgate [lead] *T. H. Wilson & Morley* viii, 1–6. Sept. 3, 1853
The Stereoscope *Morley & W.H.W.* viii, 37–42. Sept. 10, 1853
Accommodation for Quidnuncs *Dodd & Morley* viii, 88–91. Sept. 24, 1853
Bad Luck at Bendigo *Morley's brother & Morley* viii, 133–39. Oct. 8, 1853
Mr. Gulliver's Entertainment viii, 142–44. Oct. 8, 1853
A Brazilian in Bloomsbury viii, 162–65. Oct. 15, 1853
Old Settlers of Tennessee viii, 188–91. Oct. 22, 1853
Flower-Bells *Morley & Mrs. Hoare* viii, 196–99. Oct. 29, 1853
The French Workman *Duthie & Morley* viii, 199–204. Oct. 29, 1853
Adeliza Castle [lead] viii, 217–20. Nov. 5, 1853
Among the Shallows *Payne & Morley* viii, 233–35. Nov. 5, 1853
Only an Earthquake *W. L. Reynolds & Morley* viii, 235–38. Nov. 5, 1853
Unspotted Snow [lead] viii, 241–46. Nov. 12, 1853
The Cradle and the Grave *Hogarth, Junr., & Morley* viii, 317–25. Dec. 3, 1853
Manchester Men at Their Books viii, 377–79. Dec. 17, 1853
Beef [lead] viii, 385–88. Dec. 24, 1853
An Ugly Nursling viii, 406–408. Dec. 24, 1853
Voices from the Deep [chip] viii, 424. Dec. 31, 1853
The Horse Guards Rampant viii, 428–31. Dec. 31, 1853
Science and Sophy [lead] viii, 505–508. Jan. 28, 1854

The Styrian Mecca
viii, 512–16. Jan. 28, 1854
Your Very Good Health
viii, 524–26. Jan. 28, 1854
Frozen and Thawed
viii, 533–39. Feb. 4, 1854
Modern Human Sacrifices
viii, 561–64. Feb. 11, 1854
Change of Air viii, 570–72. Feb. 11, 1854
Jack and the Union Jack
ix, 32–33. Feb. 25, 1854
Breakfast with the Black Prince *Smith & Morley* ix, 48–51. March 4, 1854
A Russian Cauldron in Full Boil
ix, 118–23. March 25, 1854
Goblin Life ix, 170–74. April 8, 1854
A Call upon Sophy
ix, 174–76. April 8, 1854
Ground in the Mill
ix, 224–27. April 22, 1854
Doctor Pablo ix, 280–84. May 6, 1854
A Lesson in Multiplication [chip]
ix, 398. June 10, 1854
Death's Doors ix, 398–402. June 10, 1854
Man As a Monster
ix, 409–414. June 17, 1854
Turks under Arms *Fusco & Morley*
ix, 414–17. June 17, 1854
The War with Fever
ix, 447–49. June 24, 1854
The Learned Sailor
ix, 458–62. July 1, 1854
Sea Views ix, 506–510. July 15, 1854
Back Ways to Fame
x, 20–24. Aug. 19, 1854
Brute Sense [chip] x, 56–57. Sept. 2, 1854
Colouring [chip] x, 138–40. Sept. 23, 1854
Madame Grondet's *Miss Lee & Morley*
x, 140–44. Sept. 23, 1854
Sick Body, Sick Brain
x, 148–51. Sept. 30, 1854
Piping Days x, 196–99. Oct. 14, 1854
Out in the Wilds
x, 209–213. Oct. 14, 1854
Shot through the Heart
x, 245–48. Oct. 28, 1854
The Home Office *Clark & Morley*
x, 270–75. Nov. 4, 1854
Mr. Whittlestick x, 287–88. Nov. 4, 1854
A Home Question
x, 292–96. Nov. 11, 1854
Wild Legends x, 315–19. Nov. 18, 1854
Commission and Omission
x, 319–24. Nov. 18, 1854
At Home with the Russians
x, 533–38. Jan. 20, 1855
Robertson, Artist in Ghosts [lead]
x, 553–58. Jan. 27, 1855
Tinder from a Californian Fire
xi, 88–93. Feb. 24, 1855
Houses in Flats
xi, 182–86. March 24, 1855
Frost-Bitten Homes [lead]
xi, 193–96. March 31, 1855
Starvation of an Alderman
xi, 213–16. March 31, 1855
Fencing with Humanity [lead]
xi, 241–44. April 14, 1855
The Soldier's Wife *Morley & W.H.W.*
xi, 278–80. April 21, 1855
Death's Cyphering-Book [lead]
xi, 337–41. May 12, 1855
An Old Picture of Justice
xi, 356–60. May 12, 1855
Mechanics in Uniform [lead]
xi, 409–414. June 2, 1855
By Rail to Parnassus
xi, 477–80. June 16, 1855
Deadly Shafts [chip]
xi, 494–95. June 23, 1855
The School of the Fairies
xi, 509–513. June 30, 1855
Latest Intelligence from Spirits
xi, 513–15. June 30, 1855
The Audit Board *Clarke & Morley*
xi, 543–46. July 7, 1855
More Grist to the Mill
xi, 605–606. July 28, 1855
Robertson in Russia
xii, 14–18. Aug. 4, 1855
Wrecks at Sea xii, 36–39. Aug. 11, 1855
Wild Court Tamed
xii, 85–87. Aug. 25, 1855
Two Shillings per Horse-Power
xii, 130–31. Sept. 8, 1855
Supernatural Zoology
xii, 187–90. Sept. 22, 1855
Instructive Comparisons *Morley & Miss Jewsbury* xii, 211–14. Sept. 29, 1855
The Caitiff Postman *Morley & Evans*
xii, 237–38. Oct. 6, 1855
An Enemy's Charge [lead]
xii, 265–70. Oct. 20, 1855
Charter-House Charity [lead]
xii, 409–414. Dec. 1, 1855
Colours and Eyes
xii, 521–24. Dec. 29, 1855
Our Wicked Mis-statements
xiii, 13–19. Jan. 19, 1856

Her Grace of the Hobnails
xvi, 310–12. Sept. 26, 1857
Lord W. Tyler xvi, 333–36. Oct. 3, 1857
Canton City *Von Corvin & Morley*
xvi, 376–81. Oct. 17, 1857
Friends of the Patagonian
xvi, 416–21. Oct. 31, 1857
Brother Müller and His Orphan-Work [lead] xvi, 433–38. Nov. 7, 1857
Things within Dr. Conolly's Remembrance
xvi, 518–23. Nov. 28, 1857
One of Sir Hans Sloane's Patients [chip]
xvi, 536–37. Dec. 5, 1857
Prattleton's Monday Out
xvi, 537–40. Dec. 5, 1857
A Piece of Work
xvi, 564–68. Dec. 12, 1857
A Lesson Lost upon Us [lead]
xvii, 73–80. Jan. 9, 1858
A Plea for Playgrounds [chip] *Mrs. Howitt* [should read *Mrs. De Morgan*] *& Morley*
xvii, 160–61. Jan. 30, 1858
An Autobiographical Jail-Sermon
xvii, 186–92. Feb. 6, 1858
Meat and Drink in Shakespeare's Time
xvii, 304–309. March 13, 1858
Use and Abuse of the Dead [lead]
xvii, 361–65. April 3, 1858
Celtic Bards xvii, 379–84. April 3, 1858
John Chinaman in Australia *F. Vincent & Morley*
xvii, 416–20. April 17, 1858
Portland Island *Mr. Moule & Morley*
xvii, 423–29. April 17, 1858
Mine Oyster xvii, 429–32. April 17, 1858
A Primitive Old Epic
xvii, 459–64. May 1, 1858
Turpin's Corner
xvii, 493–96. May 8, 1858
Anglo-Saxon Bookmen
xvii, 498–500. May 8, 1858
Havelok the Dane
xvii, 543–48. May 22, 1858
Parish Poor in London [lead]
xvii, 577–78. June 5, 1858
Workers in Kent Street [chip]
xvii, 595. June 5, 1858
The Nurse in Leading Strings
xvii, 602–606. June 12, 1858
The Goliath among Bridges [chip]
xvii, 607–608. June 12, 1858
The Thistle in Bud [lead]
xviii, 25–29. June 26, 1858
A Way to Clean Rivers
xviii, 79–82. July 10, 1858
Saxon-English *Rushton & Morley*
xviii, 89–92. July 10, 1858
Saráwak xviii, 130–36. July 24, 1858
When George the Third was King [lead]
xviii, 145–47. July 31, 1858
A Postscript upon Saráwak [chip]
xviii, 147–48. July 31, 1858
British Columbia
xviii, 252–56. Aug. 28, 1858
Gertrude's Wyoming
xviii, 282–85. Sept. 4, 1858
The Hero of a Hundred Plays *Bourne & Morley* xviii, 324–27. Sept. 18, 1858
Safe Harbour xviii, 372–77. Oct. 2, 1858
One Other Hospital for Children
xviii, 379–80. Oct. 2, 1858
Apprenticeship of Frederick the Great
xviii, 398–402. Oct. 9, 1858
Mr. W. Shakespeare, Solicitor
xviii, 454–56. Oct. 23, 1858
Monstrous Clever Boys
xviii, 514–16. Nov. 13, 1858
Life and Death in Saint Giles's
xviii, 524–28. Nov. 13, 1858
Three Years Older
xviii, 566–69. Nov. 27, 1858
Britannia's Figures
xix, 13–16. Dec. 4, 1858
Minerva by Gaslight
xix, 58–62. Dec. 18, 1858
Rustic Townsmen
xix, 137–39. Jan. 8, 1859
Character-Murder [chip]
xix, 139–40. Jan. 8, 1859
Perils in India xix, 174–79. Jan. 22, 1859
Fire-Worshippers *Bourne & Morley*
xix, 286–88. Feb. 19, 1859
At Work in the Dark
xix, 321–24. March 5, 1859
A Group of Noble Savages [lead]
xix, 385–90. March 26, 1859
The Cure of Sick Minds
xix, 415–19. April 2, 1859
Art in Its Chimney-Corner [chip]
xix, 426. April 2, 1859
A Duel in Jest
xix, 503–504. April 23, 1859
A Smock-Frock Parliament [chip]
xix, 608–609. May 28, 1859

VERSE

*A Stroll by Starlight *Mr. Morley & R.H.H.* i, 350. July 6, 1850

The Birth of Morning I, 420. July 27, 1850
*The Love of Nature I, 452. Aug. 3, 1850
*The Sower II, 128. Nov. 2, 1850
*Wealthy and Wise
II, 469–70. Feb. 8, 1851

*Repr. in *Gossip* (as above). Two stanzas of "A Stroll by Starlight" appear in *Gossip* as "A Stroll by Starlight"; two appear as "At Night by the Furnace."

Morley, Joseph |*Morley's brother*|, *b.* 1816, elder brother of Henry Morley (above). Attended a boarding school in Stony Stratford and one in Chichester; then student at Charterhouse at the time that Thackeray was there (Henry Morley, *Early Papers and Some Memories*, p. 26). In contrast with his idealistically minded, sometimes impractical younger brother, was apparently a conventional, matter-of-fact man. Considered Henry's becoming a Unitarian a "going to the devil"; sent him long letters of theological argument. On one occasion suggested Henry's joining him in "the wholesale pickle trade." Married in 1843; outlived by his wife (Solly, *Life of Henry Morley*, pp. 92, 138, 141, et passim).

According to his *H.W.* article, went to Australia without intent to dig gold (Morley *père*, in 1849, had recommended Henry's getting "a tutorship in Australia"); took with him numerous letters of introduction from influential persons in England to influential persons in Melbourne; found the letters "altogether valueless," since people in Melbourne "received a great many more drafts upon their courtesy than it was possible for them to honour"; therefore went with some of his shipmates to Bendigo to try his luck at the diggings; unsuccessful in the venture; soon returned to England.

Bad Luck at Bendigo *Morley's brother & Morley* VIII, 133–39. Oct. 8, 1853

Moule, Henry, prob. |*Mr. Moule*|, 1801–1880, divine, inventor. B.A. Cambridge, 1821; M.A. 1826. Curate of Gillingham, Dorset, 1825–29; vicar of Fordington, Dorset, 1829 to his death. For some years chaplain to troops in Dorchester barracks. As inventor, important for his discovery of "dry earth system" for disposal of sewage and excreta; patented the process. Also proposed plan for extracting gas from Kimmeridge shale (letters to the *Times*). Published verse, sermons and theological works, several accounts of the dry earth system, books concerning the welfare of the poor and the working class.

The *H.W.* article assigned to Moule discusses the Dorset peninsula known as Portland Island – its inhabitants, its historical associations, its geological formation, and its quarries, and gives an account of the work going on at the time in the construction of the breakwater. The reference to the peninsula as "our island" seems to imply that the writer is a resident of Dorset, as Henry Moule was for more than fifty years. The writer's detailed account of the geological formation of Portland Island accords with Henry Moule's knowledge of earth structure. The Office Book payment record for the article reads "Cheque to Evans." Evans is probably Frederick Mullett Evans of the firm Bradbury & Evans, publishers of some of Moule's books and pamphlets. Moule, in 1824, had married Mary Mullett Evans.

D.N.B.

Portland Island *Mr. Moule & Morley*
XVII, 423–29. April 17, 1858

Mulock. *Not identified.* The first and third items listed below are letters (or extracts from letters) written by the contributor in 1851, from Geelong, to a friend in England; extracts from other of his letters occupy 4 cols. (pp. 215–16) of the second item. According to the letters and the few editorial remarks accompanying them, the contributor was "a recent settler" in Australia, a young man. In partnership with a Mr. Rumble, he had bought a farm at Mount Swardle in the Geelong district and had become a successful farmer. His reference to "the restoration of my health" during his Australian residence suggests that he may have emigrated with the hope of regaining his health.

Payment for the third item is marked "Handed by W.H.W.," July 10. The contributor was presumably in Australia in July 1852; payment may have been handed to the friend to whom he addressed his letters or to the person who placed them at the disposal of the editorial office (perhaps the same person).

The Mitchell Library, Sydney, reports that Mulock's name does not appear in the relevant Victoria directories in the Library holdings, but that William Rumble, labourer, New Town, is listed in the "Geelong and vicinity" section of an 1851 directory. William Rumble may be Mulock's partner, or he may be one of the partner's four brothers, who were also in Victoria.

A Bush Fire in Australia [chip]
III, 523–24. Aug. 23, 1851

The Harvest of Gold [lead]
Morley, Macpherson, & Mulock
V, 213–18. May 22, 1852

We, and Our Man Tom
V, 396–98. July 10, 1852

Mulock, Dinah Maria |*Miss Mulock*|, 1826–1887, novelist. According to *D.N.B.*, received a good education; according to other accounts, a very defective one. In 1865 married George Lillie Craik, partner in publishing firm of Macmillan. Contributed to *Sharpe's, Macmillan's, Good Words, Once a Week, Cornhill, Good Words for the Young, Contemp. Rev.*, and other periodicals. Was one of contributors to *Victoria Regia*. Published more than fifty works – novels, collections of stories, books for the young, essays, poems. Best known as author of *John Halifax, Gentleman*, 1856. Allibone suppl., 1891, stated: "Her books are said to be more widely read than those of any other novelist except Dickens." According to George Eliot, was "read only by novel readers, pure and simple, never by people of high culture" (*Letters*, III, 302). In 1864 granted Civil List pension of £60 a year as "Authoress of 'John Halifax, Gentleman,' and other well-known works of fiction" (Colles, *Literature and the Pension List*).

On March 8, 1855, Dickens wrote to Miss Burdett-Coutts: "I think I have just got the best Ghost story (sent by a lady for Household Words) that ever was written, and with an idea in it remarkably new. My hand is stayed for the moment, however, by an apprehension that the lady cannot have written it. It is so very clever, that I think (though I never saw or heard of it) it must have been written by some wild Frenchman – and I am trying to find out." During the following week, Dickens must have satisfied himself that the author of the story was really Miss Mulock and not "some wild Frenchman." On March 17, he sent Miss Burdett-Coutts the proofs, saying that she might perhaps "like to read the great ghost story before it comes out" (*Heart of Charles Dickens*, ed. Johnson, p. 293).

D.N.B.

A Ghost Story XI, 170–81. March 24, 1855
Repr. as "M. Anastasius" in *Nothing New. Tales. By the Author of "John Halifax, Gentleman," &c. &c.* 2 vols. London: Hurst and Blackett, 1857. Pub. in *H.W.* acknowledged.

Murray, Eustace Clare Grenville |*Mr. Murray, E. Murray, Eustace Murray, E. C. Murray, Murray; R.E.* (i.e., *Roving Englishman*)|, 1824–1881, journalist, member of diplomatic corps. Said to have been natural son of Richard Grenville, second Duke of Buckingham and Chandos. Matriculated at Oxford, 1848; did not take degree. Admitted at Inner Temple, 1850. In his early twenties began contributing to periodicals. Entered diplomatic service under patronage of Palmerston; from 1851 to 1868, held posts successively in Vienna, Hanover, Constantinople, Mytilene, and Odessa, in a career marked by bitter friction with officials under whom he served. Returned to England, 1868, and engaged in journalism. An article in an abusive society paper with which he was connected resulted in his being horsewhipped by Lord Carington; in legal proceedings that followed, was charged with perjury;

left for France, 1869, while on bail; did not again return to England. In Paris, served as correspondent for *Daily News*; contributed to *Pall Mall Gazette*, *Cornhill*, *Illus. London News*, and other English periodicals; also to French and American publications. According to Yates (*Recollections and Experiences*, p. 451), was rumoured to have conducted a kind of "literary manufactory," it being thought impossible that all the writing credited to him simultaneously should have sprung from one man. Co-founder, with Yates, of the *World*, 1874. Author of some thirty works, fiction and nonfiction, some of them reprintings of his periodical contributions. Among his well-known books were the "Roving Englishman" series; *The Member for Paris*, 1871; *Young Brown*, 1874; *French Pictures in English Chalk*, 1876, 1878.

Murray admired Dickens; in his *Embassies and Foreign Courts* (p. 356) he referred to him as "one of the greatest and kindliest public teachers England has ever known." Yates stated that before he made Murray's acquaintance in the 1860s, he "had often heard much [of Murray] from Dickens and others" (*Recollections*, p. 447). The "others" must have included Wills, who was a good friend of both Yates and Murray. It was to Wills that Murray dedicated *The Roving Englishman*.

Murray became a *H.W.* contributor at Wills's suggestion. The collapse of certain "great expectations" having left him at his "wits' end," he went to the Continent, apparently about 1850; it was in that year that Wills mentioned to him that Dickens "would have no objection" to publishing in *H.W.* "any useful, practical hints or sketches of foreign manners" that Murray might pick up. Murray acted on the suggestion, and with some pride saw his early contributions in print. The sketches soon began to appear under the collective title "The Roving Englishman" – which became one of Murray's pseudonyms. Having, meanwhile, been appointed to a diplomatic post, Murray wrote the sketches in his "moments of idleness" ("Preface," *The Roving Englishman*). His connection with *H.W.*, stated Murray, "opened to me a new life." It launched him on the journalistic career that was to win him exaggerated acclaim as "one of the most brilliant journalists of the day" (J. C. Francis, comp., *John Francis*, II, 492) – "the ablest journalist of the century" ("Anecdotal Photographs," *Truth*, Dec. 29, 1881).

According to Yates (*Recollections*, p. 448), Dickens greatly liked Murray's "Roving Englishman" series. In Dickens's letters, however, the few comments on Murray's contributions are for the most part critical of their content and style. One of Murray's articles ("Common-Sense on Wheels") Dickens mistrusted in the matter of accuracy of information. Another contained statements "much too strong for me to commit myself to without a positive knowledge of the facts"; it was not to be used. The same article was reprehensible also for its slovenly writing (to Wills, March 29, 1851; July 4, 1853). Another was "conceited"; and one for *A.Y.R.* was objectionable in phraseology; Wills was to delete "anything 'swell' – such as the word 'shindy,' or any similar yaw-yawdom" and to strike the entire paragraph touching the "gallant steed" (Aug. 7, 1854; Nov. 25, 1862). One of Murray's contributions to *A.Y.R.*, however, Dickens did refer to as "very good" (to Wills, Dec. 6, 1867). The articles assigned in the Office Book jointly to Murray and Dickens were revised by Dickens; they were not actual collaborations of the two writers. (For versions of the revision of "Foreigners' Portraits of Englishmen," see Stone, ed., *Charles Dickens' Uncollected Writings from Household Words*, Appendix A.)

It was the *H.W.* lead article "On Her Majesty's Service" that brought to public attention the most notorious of Murray's feuds with officialdom – that with Sir Stratford Canning, then ambassador to Turkey. Dickens, who worked on the article himself, was unaware that the "Sir Hector Stubble" of the satirical sketch was Canning, but Canning's friends and enemies immediately recognized the original and sent Canning copies of the *H.W.* number; thus, on arrival of the English mail at Constantinople, "the usual bags of the Foreign Office were found supplemented by an enormous number of newspaper sacks, all filled with copies of *Household Words*" (Yates, *Recollections*, pp. 448–49). Canning was furious and attempted, unsuccessfully, to wreck Murray's diplomatic career. The incident did not disrupt Murray's contributorship to *H.W.* Murray continued writing for the periodical to 1856, and wrote thereafter for *A.Y.R.*

An oblique reference to Murray appeared in Dixon's *H.W.* article "Quite Revolutionary," which mentioned the diversity of terrestrial landscape as more startling than what "the most roving Englishman" might create in his imagination.

Harper's reprinted, in whole or part, ten of Murray's *H.W.* contributions, one of them acknowledged to *H.W.*

D.N.B.

A German Picture of the Scotch
II, 71–72. Oct. 12, 1850

A Roving Englishman: Benighted; Out Shooting *Murray & Morley*
IV, 221–24. Nov. 29, 1851

A Roving Englishman: The Apple-Green Spencer; Gastein Baths *Murray & Morley* IV, 299–301. Dec. 20, 1851

The Roving Englishman: A Masked Ball; Advertisements *Murray & Morley*
IV, 358–60. Jan. 3, 1852

The Roving Englishman: In Praise of Salad *Murray & Morley*
IV, 406–408. Jan. 17, 1852

The Roving Englishman: A Brace of Blunders *Murray & Morley*
IV, 431–32. Jan. 24, 1852

The Roving Englishman: Concerning a Pair of Demons
IV, 514–17. Feb. 21, 1852

The Roving Englishman: A Ramble to Rehburg V, 522–24. Aug. 14, 1852

A Cheap Dinner [chip]
VI, 35–36. Sept. 25, 1852

The Roving Englishman: A Golden Wedding VI, 46–48. Sept. 25, 1852

The Roving Englishman: A German Joe Miller VI, 142–44. Oct. 23, 1852

The Roving Englishman: His Hints to Travellers VI, 211–14. Nov. 13, 1852

The Roving Englishman: His Philosophy of Dining VI, 231–33. Nov. 20, 1852

The Roving Englishman: On Horseback
VI, 309–312. Dec. 11, 1852

The Roving Englishman: With a Baron Much Interested in Him
VI, 333–36. Dec. 18, 1852

The Roving Englishman: A Few More Hints VI, 358–60. Dec. 25, 1852

The Roving Englishman: Travelling Servants; Yachting
VI, 453–56. Jan. 22, 1853

The Roving Englishman: Cares of State
VI, 478–80. Jan. 29, 1853

The Roving Englishman at Constantinople
VIII, 204–207. Oct. 29, 1853

The 19 items repr., with some revision, in *The Roving Englishman. Reprinted from "Household Words"* [anon.]. London: G. Routledge & Co., 1854.

The Roving Englishman; and the Prince de Vendome VIII, 355–60. Dec. 10, 1853

The Roving Englishman: A Greek Feast
VIII, 393–97. Dec. 24, 1853

The Roving Englishman: Greek Easter at Constantinople; A Defence of Fleas
VIII, 415–18. Dec. 31, 1853

On Her Majesty's Service [lead] *C.D. & Murray* VIII, 433–37. Jan. 7, 1854

Her Majesty's Service Again [chip]
VIII, 523–24. Jan. 28, 1854

The Roving Englishman: Education in Turkey IX, 79–80. March 11, 1854

The Roving Englishman: Captain Jorgey
IX, 102–104. March 18, 1854

The Roving Englishman: Greek Fire
IX, 132–34. March 25, 1854

The Roving Englishman: Free Quarters; A Saint's Brother
IX, 206–209. April 15, 1854

The Roving Englishman: The Cadi
IX, 254–56. April 29, 1854

My Cavass and I
IX, 306–308. May 13, 1854

The Roving Englishman: A Greek Girl
IX, 321–23. May 20, 1854

The Roving Englishman: Regular Turks
IX, 349–52. May 27, 1854

The Roving Englishman: A Turkish Auctioneer IX, 362–64. June 3, 1854

The Roving Englishman: Greek Waters
IX, 402–404. June 10, 1854

The Roving Englishman: The Pasha
IX, 462–64. July 1, 1854

Her Majesty's Consular Service
IX, 482–87. July 8, 1854

The Roving Englishman: Village Diplomatists; The Schoolmaster and His Lesson IX, 510–13. July 15, 1854
The Roving Englishman: The Bin-Bashee IX, 542–43. July 22, 1854
The Roving Englishman: Hadji Hassan IX, 556–58. July 29, 1854
The Roving Englishman: The Sea Captain and His Ship *Murray & Sala* IX, 606–608. Aug. 12, 1854
The Roving Englishman: A Greek Carnival X, 77–79. Sept. 9, 1854
The Roving Englishman: Dolma Bakjah; A Turkish Bath X, 369–73. Dec. 2, 1854
The Saucy Arethusa X, 396–97. Dec. 9, 1854
Army Interpreters X, 431–32. Dec. 16, 1854
The Roving Englishman: A Roadside Picture X, 477–78. Dec. 30, 1854

The 26 items repr., with some revision, in *The Roving Englishman in Turkey. Sketches from Life. Reprinted in Part from "Household Words"* [anon.]. London: G. Routledge & Co., 1855.

The Roving Englishman: Locusts X, 478–80. Dec. 30, 1854
The Roving Englishman at the Pera Theatre X, 570–72. Jan. 27, 1855
The Roving Englishman: From Constantinople to Varna XI, 142–44. March 10, 1855
The Roving Englishman: From Varna to Balaklava XI, 153–57. March 17, 1855
The Roving Englishman: A Dinner in Camp XI, 191–92. March 24, 1855

The 5 items repr., with some revision, in *Pictures from the Battle Fields. By "The Roving Englishman," Author of "Turkey," Etc.* London: G. Routledge & Co., 1855. Pub. in *H.W.* not acknowledged. The book relates an incident told in the *H.W.* article "From Giurgevo to Bucharest," but does not reprint the article.

The Roving Englishman: Down the Danube XII, 502–504. Dec. 22, 1855

Repr. in *Turkey: Being Sketches from Life by The Roving Englishman, Reprinted in Part from "Household Words," with Numerous Additions.* London: George Routledge and Sons, 1877. The book, called "a new edition" of *The Roving Englishman in Turkey*, contains all but one of the *H.W.* items repr. in *The Roving Englishman in Turkey* (above).

Railway Comfort [chip] *W.H.W. & Mr. Murray* I, 449–50. Aug. 3, 1850
The Strangers' Leaf for 1851 [chip] *E. Murray & W.H.W.* I, 515–17. Aug. 24, 1850
Foreigners' Portraits of Englishmen [lead] *C.D., W.H.W., & Eustace Murray* I, 601–604. Sept. 21, 1850
German Advertisements *W.H.W., E. C. Murray, & Mr. Walker* II, 33–35. Oct. 5, 1850
Domestic Servants in Austria [chip] III, 42–43. April 5, 1851
Common-Sense on Wheels *C.D., W.H.W., & Murray* III, 61–66. April 12, 1851
Cheap Pleasures. – A Gossip *Murray & W.H.W.* III, 201–203. May 24, 1851
A Black Eagle in a Bad Way [lead] *Murray, Morley, & C.D.* IV, 193–95. Nov. 22, 1851
Nobility in Spain [chip] V, 38–41. March 27, 1852
A Primitive People [chip] V, 104–106. April 17, 1852
Hoary Abuses [chip] VI, 10–11. Sept. 18, 1852
The Roving Englishman: Monsieur le Curé; Ma Sœur, the Governess VII, 20–22. March 5, 1853
The Roving Englishman: The Great Do VII, 67–72. March 19, 1853
The Roving Englishman: After the Boars VII, 118–20. April 2, 1853
The Roving Englishman: Beautiful Naples VII, 302–305. May 28, 1853
The Roving Englishman: Diplomacy VII, 373–75. June 18, 1853
The Roving Englishman: A Canter with Polychronopulos VII, 472–75. July 16, 1853
The Roving Englishman: Britons in Turkey IX, 256–57. April 29, 1854
The Roving Englishman: Very Cold at Bucharest; The Theatre; The Terrible Officer XI, 82–85. Feb. 24, 1855
The Roving Englishman: From Varna to Rustchuk XI, 307–308. April 28, 1855
The Roving Englishman: A Bulgarian Post-House XI, 335–36. May 5, 1855

The Roving Englishman: Rustchuk
xi, 427–29. June 2, 1855
The Roving Englishman: The Passage of the Danube xi, 465–68. June 16, 1855
The Roving Englishman: From Giurgevo to Bucharest
xi, 558–61. July 14, 1855
The Roving Englishman: From Bucharest to Kraiova xii, 109–112. Sept. 1, 1855
Holiday Quarters
xii, 214–16. Sept. 29, 1855
The Roving Englishman: From Kraiova to London xii, 282–84. Oct. 20, 1855
The Roving Englishman in Belgium
xii, 309–312. Oct. 27, 1855
The Crown of Ionia *Murray & Knight*
xii, 451–55. Dec. 8, 1855
The Roving Englishman: The Show Officer xiii, 22–24. Jan. 19, 1856
The Sulina Mouth of the Danube [lead]
xiii, 73–77. Feb. 9, 1856
The Roving Englishman: Messina
xiii, 73–77. Feb. 9, 1856
Malines xiii, 245–47. March 29, 1856
Turkish Contrasts
xiii, 263–64. March 29, 1856

Murray, Mrs. Eustace Clare Grenville |*Mrs. Grenville Murray, Mrs. Murray*|. According to the *Biograph*, Dec. 1881, Grenville Murray (above) "married Clara, the only daughter and heiress of Count Reickhart Usedom; and Anne, daughter of Colonel Sholto Douglas d'Archambault." Other references mention only one marriage of Murray's – that to a "French lady" (F. M. Thomas, comp. and ed., *Fifty Years of Fleet Street*, p. 212) or to a "Spanish lady" (*D.N.B.*) or to a "lady with a Spanish title" ("Anecdotal Photographs," *Truth*, Dec. 29, 1881), whose title – de Rethel d'Aragon – Murray assumed on his marrying her, apparently some time after his taking up residence in Paris in 1869. It is "Clara Comitissa de Rethel d'Aragon" whose name appears as Murray's widow on his tomb in the Passy cemetery (Richard Bentley and Son, *List of the Principal Publications Issued ... during the Year 1853*). Obviously, the order in which the two ladies are named in the *Biograph* should be reversed; and, if the *Biograph* article is correct in the matter of names (it is incorrect in some other matters), Murray's first wife – the Mrs. Grenville Murray (Mrs. Murray) of the Office Book entries – was Anne d'Archambault. The date of the first marriage was apparently 1843. In Sept. 1853, from Prince's Island (Sea of Marmara), Murray dedicated *Doïne; or, The National Songs and Legends of Roumania* "to her who has been for ten years the companion of my studies; ... who has been the light of my hearth and the pride of my heart – the bride of my youth, the friend of my manhood. ..." Children born of the marriage of whom there is record were Reginald (*b.* ca. 1846) and Douglas (*b.* 1848) (*Alumni Oxon.*, *Men-at-the-Bar*).

During 1852–54, payment for some fifteen of Murray's *H.W.* contributions is recorded in the Office Book as made to "Mrs. M." or to "Mrs. Murray."

The first item listed below describes a visit that "we" (identified as English) made to Tangier in 1847, a visit motivated by our desire to see whether the Moors "had black or copper-coloured faces; ... whether they resembled our play-going recollections of Othello." The second item relates a legend that the writer heard in Tangier. The third, told in the person of the Londoner Mr. Croxpound, recounts a shooting excursion in Scotland. The play on the word "Moors" / "moors" in that article – "not the Moors where Othello was, but the moors where Glenfern is" – is the writer's cryptic reference to her first *H.W.* contribution.

Among Mrs. Murray's other writings were "Durkhein: A Tale of the Haardt," *Ladies' Companion*, Dec. 1852; and "The Flower of Liege," *Keepsake*, 1854.

Among the Moors v, 276–79. June 5, 1852
Among the Moors. The Legend of the Castle v, 567–70. Aug. 28, 1852
A Gun among the Grouse
vi, 115–18. Oct. 16, 1852

Mylne: *See* Milne, William Charles

N

Napier. *Not identified.* The contributor recounts his voyage from Aden to Bombay in the summer of 1851; has friends in Bombay and seems to be visiting the city for pleasure, not in connection with military or other service. Discusses numerous matters of interest concerning Bombay – its trade and commerce, its lack of adequate coastal defence, its neglect of the fine arts, its natives and their characteristics, the social life of its British residents. Looks at the city with an artist's eye: "Were another Paul Veronese to arise ... , what a field would Bombay present to his pencil!" Writes of his own taste as delighting in "the rich Venetian tone of colour, in preference to the cold tints of Rome or Florence." Has travelled on the Continent, has seen Rio de Janeiro.

Various members, titled and untitled, of the Napier families had connections with India, were interested in art, travelled extensively, and wrote periodical articles and books. The Office Book ascription indicates that the contributor was probably an untitled Napier. His article arrived at the editorial office "per Bradbury."

Bombay v, 181–86. May 8, 1852

Norris, Miss. *Not identified.* The Office Book assigns "The Uses of Sorrow" to "Sophy Traddles," the name being written in quotation marks. The memorandum attached to the entry records a post-office order sent to Miss Norris, Camden House, Peckham. "The Son of Sorrow" is also assigned to "Sophy Traddles," with memorandum of post-office order to Miss Norris, Camden Lodge, Peckham. For this entry both the name and the notation are marked out; by the marked-out name is written the direction "(See No. 7)" – i.e., the number in which "The Uses of Sorrow" appeared.

The *Post Office London Directory*, 1850, gives no Camden House or Camden Lodge at Peckham, but does give Camden Place. No Norris is listed at Camden Place, but two schools are there listed: Robert Sugden's boarding school, and the "ladies' school" of the Misses Louisa and Emily Grove. The contributor who sent her verses to *H.W.* under the Dickensian pseudonym may have been a young lady attending or teaching at the Misses Grove's school.

The name of Tommy Traddles's "dearest girl" first appears in *David Copperfield* in chap. xxxiv ("My Aunt Astonishes Me"), one of the three chapters that formed the eleventh monthly instalment, published March 1850. Traddles's marriage to Sophy is reported in chap. lix ("Return"), which formed part of the nineteenth monthly instalment, published (with the twentieth) in Nov. 1850. In her pseudonym, the contributor thus anticipated by more than five months Dickens's announcement of the happy conclusion of Traddles's love story.

Harper's reprinted "The Uses of Sorrow," with acknowledgment to *H.W.*

VERSE

The Uses of Sorrow I, 156. May 11, 1850
The Son of Sorrow. A Fable from the Swedish I, 238. June 1, 1850

Norton, Caroline Elizabeth Sarah (Sheridan), later **Lady Stirling-Maxwell** |*Hon. Mrs. Norton, The Honble Mrs. Norton*|, 1808–1877, poet and novelist. Reasonably well educated. Began writing as young girl; during much of her life forced to earn her living by her pen. Industriously edited annuals, contributed to periodicals – *New Monthly, Morning Chronicle, Macmillan's,* and others. Published *The Undying One, The Dream, The Lady of La Garaye,* and other poems. Had high contemporary reputation as poet; called by the *Quart. Rev.*, Sept. 1840 "the Byron of our modern poetesses"; in Horne's *New Spirit of the Age*, 1844, shared chapter with Elizabeth Barrett. Among her works of fiction, *Stuart of Dunleath*, 1851, praised by the *Examiner*, May 3, as shining "pre-eminent and peerless" among the new novels of the year. Was prominently before the public not only as writer, but as figure in the court proceedings and related scandals in which her unfortunate marriage involved her. Most notorious was her husband's *crim. con.* action, 1836, brought against Lord Melbourne; Melbourne triumphantly acquitted. Separated from her husband; custody of children a matter of dispute. In 1853 brought suit against her husband for his failure to pay her allowance and for his claiming proceeds of her literary work. Her unhappy marital experience motivated her pamphlets urging reform in infant custody, marriage, and divorce laws. Meanwhile had become subject of unpleasant publicity on the rumour that she had, in 1845, revealed a cabinet secret to the *Times*; the unfounded slander revived by Meredith, seven years after her death, in his using her as model for heroine of *Diana of the Crossways*. In 1877, two years after death of her first husband, married Sir William Stirling-Maxwell.

Dickens reported for the *Morning Chronicle* the Norton-Melbourne trial; he obviously had it in mind in writing the Bardell-Pickwick trial scene. He was not at the time acquainted with Mrs. Norton; he later met her and became her friend; like his contemporaries, he admired her striking beauty. Mrs. Norton, in the *English Bijou Almanac* for 1842, published a verse tribute to Dickens, praising him for the influence for good in his writings. In *The Child of the Islands*, 1845, she singled out *A Christmas Carol* for praise. However little it resembled a solemn discourse on the duties of rich and poor, she wrote, the *Carol* would "stand its ground as one of the best sermons on charity."

Two *H.W.* articles dealt with Mrs. Norton and her efforts to bring about reform in infant custody, marriage, and divorce laws. In "One of Our Legal Fictions," Miss Lynn, without mentioning Mrs. Norton by name, related the history of Mrs. Norton's marriage to illustrate the gross injustices to which women were subject under laws that deprived a wife of a legal existence, made her the husband's chattel, and denied her, if separated from her husband, access to her children. The infant custody law had been in one respect changed, wrote Miss Lynn, "mainly, because this sufferer [i.e., Mrs. Norton] laboured hard to show its cruelty." Miss Lynn's article was based on Mrs. Norton's pamphlet *English Laws for Women in the Nineteenth Century*, 1854. An article by Wills, "A Legal Fiction," was based on Mrs. Norton's *Letter to the Queen on Lord Chancellor Cranworth's Marriage and Divorce Bill*, 1855. Wills praised Mrs. Norton's energy in working for reform and remarked on the eloquence of her protests. Her "spirited" *Letter to the Queen*, he wrote, "ought to give such a stimulus to public opinion and sense of right, as will hasten the slow operations of law-making." The pamphlet *Remarks upon the Law of Marriage and Divorce; Suggested by the Hon. Mrs. Norton's Letter to the Queen* formed the subject of a third *H.W.* article – Miss Lynn's "Marriage Gaolers." Merely citing from the pamphlet various instances of gross injustice to wives, Miss Lynn had no occasion to mention Mrs. Norton or the hardships inflicted on her by her "marriage gaoler."

Flourishing at the same time as Caroline Norton was another "Hon. Mrs. Norton" – the Hon. Mrs. Erskine Norton, likewise a writer of verse and prose, a contributor to periodicals (*Metropolitan*, *Bentley's Misc.*), and author of books (*The Martyr: A Tragedy*, 1848; *The Gossip*, 1852). The *H.W.* contributor, however, is clearly the famous, rather than the obscure, Hon. Mrs. Norton. It is reasonable to assume that Wills, in his Office Book entries, would have indicated the Christian name of the contributor had she been another than *the* Hon. Mrs. Norton. What seems clearly to be the autobiographical nature of "The Invalid's Mother" also points to Caroline Norton as the *H.W.* contributor. The poem presents a mother praying "To the Sun, at Lisbon," for the restoration of her child's health. Caroline Norton had spent some weeks in Lisbon in 1848–49, nursing back to health her son Fletcher.

See "An English Wife," p. 481.

D.N.B.

VERSE

A Household Word to My Cousin Helen
v, 440. July 24, 1852

The Invalid's Mother. To the Sun,
at Lisbon xii, 108–109. Sept. 1, 1855

O

Old, Mr. Thomas. Address: Salisbury. *Not identified.* In the Office Book, the name "Thomas," lightly written, is inserted between "Mr." and "Old." Available Salisbury directories do not list a Thomas Old.

Harper's reprinted "Ebenezer Elliott," with acknowledgment to *H.W.*

Ebenezer Elliott I, 310–12. June 22, 1850

Oldcastle, Thomas, prob. The Office Book assigns to Horne the item listed below; it records no payment. Horne was at the time on the *H.W.* staff. The item may be the actual writing of a Thomas Oldcastle, or it may be a hoax.

The motivation for the item was Horne's account, in "The Black Diamonds of England," June 8, 1850, of his meeting at the London Coal Exchange "Thomas Oldcastle, of Durham, captain of the collier brig 'Shiner,' of South Shields." Horne unflatteringly described the captain's appearance, recorded some of his conversation, ridiculed his quoting twenty-year-old statistics as though they were current, and remarked – of the captain's liking for the brightly coloured wall decorations of the Exchange – that "our honest friend had no good taste in pictures."

"From Mr. T. Oldcastle" is in the form of a letter to the editor, written from the Blue Dragon Arms, South Shields, and signed "Thomas Oldcastle." The writer states that the information given by him to the author "of these coal-papers" is true, and stoutly defends his own taste in pictures. He is somewhat dubious about the honour of being mentioned by name in *H.W.*: "I suppose I ought – and therefore I do – consider it a great honour; and what Captain of a collier-brig would not?"

Available directories do not list an Oldcastle or a Blue Dragon Arms in South Shields or in North Shields. North Shields was the port of registry of the *Shiner*; no crew lists for the vessel have been preserved (information from Public Record Office, London).

From Mr. T. Oldcastle concerning the Coal Exchange [chip]
I, 352. July 6, 1850

Oliver, Richard, prob. |*Dr. Oliver*|, medical officer. The first "Treatment of the Insane" listed below is recorded in the Office Book as "per C.D." The initials "C.D." are in alignment with the names in the author-column, indicating that the item was originally assigned to Dickens as author; then, before the initials, projecting into the number-column, is inserted the word "per." The article is, thus, unassigned in the Office Book. The second "Treatment of the Insane" is assigned to "Morley & Dr. Oliver." Payment for each item recorded as £2.12.6.

The *Brit. Med. Directory*, 1853, as also the *London and Prov. Med. Directory*, 1850 and later years, lists only one Oliver as connected with an institution for the insane: Richard Oliver, L.R.C.S. Edinburgh; L.R.C.P. London; resident medical officer and superintendent of Salop and Montgomery Counties Lunatic Asylum; contributor of the paper "On the Transfusion of Blood" to the Edinburgh *Medical and Surgical Jour.*, 1840. This Oliver is probably the Dr. Oliver listed, with Morley, as author of the second item, and, consequently, the probable author also of the first. The first "Treatment of the Insane" quotes a letter on official business written to the steward of a county lunatic asylum and one written to the superintendent of a county lunatic asylum, as also the superintendent's observations on the case dealt with in the second letter – documents to which, presumably, only an officer of such an institution would have access.

The first "Treatment of the Insane" is the subject of Dickens's letter, Aug. 9, 1851, to John Hills. Hills had submitted the paper to Dickens on behalf of the writer (not named in the letter). Dickens found it – "the paper on the Treatment of Lunatics" – "a little too dry and didactic" and also "a little too long." "Nor am

I quite sure," he stated, "if it would be well to give such a Government as ours, a monopoly, in a question of such magnitude or that I could make that proposal mine. But [the paper] suggests, and very well puts, considerations of importance, and I am unwilling to reject it if the author will give me leave to take some editorial liberties with it.

"As I think you told Miss Hogarth that he had some idea of making a pamphlet of the article, and as he might therefore object to it being altered, I shall not consider it as subject to my discretion unless you should be empowered to give me the assurance that it is so."

Obviously, permission for Dickens to take "some editorial liberties" was granted. The article appeared in *H.W.* the following month.

The second "Treatment of the Insane" is the subject of Dickens's letter, Feb. 28, 1852, to John Hills. Hills had submitted the paper to Dickens on behalf of the writer (not named in the letter). Dickens found it – "the paper on the treatment of the insane" – "too didactic," "far too long," and in several passages circumlocutory. However, he stated: "I should be happy to accept it and to reduce it without compromising any principle maintained in it, if I were sure of the author's sanction. But as I am not, and as I remember that he was not perfectly satisfied on a former occasion I prefer not to touch it, and to leave him to withdraw it intact if he should desire so to do."

The author decided, obviously, not to withdraw the paper. It appeared in *H.W.* a little more than three months after the date of Dickens's letter. Dickens may have made some revision in the paper; but whatever major revision was undertaken was the work of Morley, the medical man on the staff, whose name is listed jointly with Oliver's.

The two articles have much in common. The first deals mainly with indigent insane accommodated in county lunatic asylums and with non-indigent insane accommodated in "licensed houses." It states that when certain provisions enacted by law shall have been carried out, "we may, perhaps, indulge a hope that little will be left to wish for respecting the domiciliation" of the indigent. Concerning the non-indigent, it states that the system of licensed houses is "vicious and unsound" in principle and is subject to no legislative control. The protection and care of the non-indigent, as of the indigent, should be the duty of the State.

The second article, though it deals mainly with the non-indigent insane, mentions also the indigent. Like the first article, it states that after certain provisions enacted by law are put into effect, "the care of the insane poor will be placed on a safe footing." The three institutions discussed in the article are county lunatic asylums, lunatic hospitals, and licensed houses. The article disapproves of the placing of non-indigent insane in county lunatic asylums; it criticizes the arrangements of certain lunatic hospitals; it condemns the system of licensed houses as a "bad system" that should be abolished. It quotes John Conolly – "the highest living authority upon these matters" – to the effect that all insane "should become the care of the state" and that every institution for the insane "should be the property of the state."

Dickens's uncertainty as to whether or not he approved of the Government's having "a monopoly" in the matter of custody of the insane – his doubt as to whether or not "I could make that proposal mine" – had evidently been resolved.

Brit. Med. Directory

The Treatment of the Insane III, 572–76. Sept. 6, 1851
The Treatment of the Insane *Morley & Dr. Oliver* V, 270–73. June 5, 1852

Ollier, Edmund |*E. Ollier, Ollier, Edmund Ollier, Ed. Ollier*|, 1827–1886, misc. writer; son of Charles Ollier, the publisher of Leigh Hunt, Keats, and Shelley. Privately educated. Contributed to *Athenaeum, Examiner, Daily News,* and other periodicals. Connected in editorial capacity with *Leader, Atlas, London Review* (Boase). Published a volume of poems.

Compiled various works for the firm of Cassell, Petter, and Galpin, e.g., *The Doré Gallery, History of the United States, History of the Russo-Turkish War*. Edited first series of *Essays of Elia* and Leigh Hunt's *Tale for a Chimney Corner, and Other Essays*.

Dickens had in his library a copy of Ollier's *Poems from the Greek Mythology* (Stonehouse, *Catalogue*).

A letter from Dickens to Ollier, Jan. 12, 1850, indicates that, some ten weeks before the first number of *H.W.* appeared, Ollier had written to ask about a possible connection with the periodical. Dickens stated that he could not "pledge himself, beforehand, to the acceptance of any article" or offer Ollier "any regular engagement," but that plans for the "projected Miscellany" called for the use of good occasional contributions.

Dickens's published letters contain no references to Ollier's *H.W.* prose writings. An unpublished letter to Wills, Aug. 24, 1854 (MS Huntington Library), refers to "Faces," assigned in the Office Book to Ollier, as by Morley. A letter of 1864 to Ollier concerns the points that Dickens wanted made in an *A.Y.R.* article.

Leigh Hunt, in the *Spectator*, 1859, stated that Ollier's verse contributions to *H.W.* (as also his prose writings) were "well appreciated by its illustrious conductor" (cited in *Leigh Hunt's Literary Criticism*, ed. Houtchens and Houtchens, p. 623). Dickens, in a letter to Mrs. Cowden Clarke, Dec. 28, 1852, referred to Ollier as "an excellent and true young poet, as I think"; but his letters to Wills hardly indicate great admiration for the writings of the "excellent and true" poet. Of "Sir Graelent" Dickens wrote: "Ollier's ballad will do"; in "Starlight in the Garden" Ollier was to alter a line that contradicted a preceding one; a poem "full of strange conceits and strange metre" which Dickens took to be by Ollier prompted his comment: "Tennyson is ruining all these writers"; and a poem that Ollier submitted to *A.Y.R.* Dickens termed "maudlin" (Aug. 7, Sept. 18, 1853; Nov. 24, 1855; Nov. 25, 1862).

Leigh Hunt thought "Starlight in the Garden" "the most beautiful among the many beautiful things" that Ollier had written: "the whole poem, every word, is lovely, and dainty, and fanciful, and imaginative, and full of subtlest truth and feeling." Hunt planned to read the poem to Robert Bell and to talk to Bell about it, "and I am sure he will talk of it elsewhere, and make people aware of the poet they have got in *Household Words*" (*Correspondence*, II, 189–90).

Another admirer of Ollier's *H.W.* poems was Mrs. Cowden Clarke, who owned herself "quite smitten with this young poet's verse." In contrast with the "crabbed obscurity and far-fetched, incomprehensible mysticism" of other poets, Ollier's writing she found to be "smooth, clear, understandable, true poetry" – "quite in the genuine taste and sweet versification of Leigh Hunt's school." "The Host's Story" Mrs. Cowden Clarke thought to be "by dear Leigh Hunt" himself, until informed by Dickens that it was by Ollier (*Letters to an Enthusiast*, pp. 166–67).

Of the prose items listed below, "Timber-Bending" seems unrelated to Ollier's interests; the contributor's name is not clearly written in the Office Book, but seems to read "Ollier."

Harper's reprinted "Speed the Plough" and "Vampyres," without acknowledgment to *H.W.*

D.N.B.

PROSE

Eternal Lamps VIII, 185–88. Oct. 22, 1853
Ghostly Pantomimes VIII, 397–400. Dec. 24, 1853
An Old Book of Geography IX, 75–79. March 11, 1854
A Marvellous Journey with the Old Geographer IX, 228–33. April 22, 1854
Left Behind IX, 543–46. July 22, 1854
Faces [lead] X, 97–101. Sept. 16, 1854
A Scientific Figment X, 453–56. Dec. 23, 1854
Mark Hansel's Visitor X, 483–88. Jan. 6, 1855
Vampyres XI, 39–43. Feb. 10, 1855
A Set of Odd Fellows XI, 196–202. March 31, 1855
Timber-Bending XIV, 154–56. Aug. 30, 1856
Wehrwolves XV, 405–408. April 25, 1857
Comets, and Their Tails of Prophets [lead] XV, 481–84. May 23, 1857

Thor and the Giants
xvi, 282–85. Sept. 19, 1857
A Cornish Hug
xviii, 296–99. Sept. 11, 1858

VERSE
A Lay of London Streets
ii, 36. Oct. 5, 1850
*The Brothers. A Tale of "Araby the Blest" iii, 324–25. June 28, 1851
The Water-Elf iii, 516. Aug. 23, 1851
A Sultan's Warning
iv, 85–87. Oct. 18, 1851
An Idyl for Christmas In-Doors
Extra No. for Christmas 1851, pp. 7–8
*The Legend of the Miraculous Rose-Trees v, 128–29. April 24, 1852
The Rhyme of the Caliph
v, 512–13. Aug. 14, 1852
*Speed the Plough vi, 84–85. Oct. 9, 1852
The Ghosts' Banquet
vi, 277–78. Dec. 4, 1852
The Host's Story A Round of Stories (Christmas 1852), pp. 20–21
*The Masque of the New Year
vi, 371–73. Jan. 1, 1853
The Flowing of the Waters
vi, 562. Feb. 26, 1853
The Ballad of the Gold-Digger
vii, 61–63. March 19, 1853
*The Test of Time
vii, 205–206. April 30, 1853
*Eleusinia: Lines Suggested by the Bas-reliefs on the Portland Vase; the Figures of Which are Supposed to Be Illustrative of the Eleusinian Mysteries
vii, 349. June 11, 1853
*The Boy Mahomet vii, 492. July 23, 1853
Sir Graelent. A Breton Legend
vii, 609–611. Aug. 27, 1853
*Starlight in the Garden
viii, 108–109. Oct. 1, 1853
*Song for November
viii, 276. Nov. 19, 1853
The Lady of the Fen
viii, 370–73. Dec. 17, 1853
New Year's Eve viii, 418. Dec. 31, 1853
The Goblins of the Marsh. A Masque
viii, 491–92. Jan. 21, 1854
*Proserpina in the Shades
ix, 56. March 4, 1854
The Withered King x, 12. Aug. 19, 1854
Walter Hurst x, 466–69. Dec. 30, 1854
*The First Death xi, 468–70. June 16, 1855
The Masque of Life
xii, 13–14. Aug. 4, 1855
*Ghost-Music xii, 203–204. Sept. 29, 1855
A Vision of Old Babylon
xiii, 157. March 1, 1856
*Life and the Bird xiv, 62. Aug. 2, 1856
*Pan xv, 419–20. May 2, 1857
A Christmas Phantasy
xvii, 35–36. Dec. 26, 1857
*Grave Voices
xviii, 346–47. Sept. 25, 1858
*New Year's Eve xix, 119–20. Jan. 1, 1859

*Repr. in *Poems from the Greek Mythology: and Miscellaneous Poems. By Edmund Ollier.* London: John Camden Hotten, 1867. Pub. in *H.W.* acknowledged.

Olmsted, Frederick Law |*Olmsted*|, 1822–1903, writer, landscape architect, conservationist. Born in Hartford, Conn. Desultory schooling; for a year attended lectures at Yale. In early life, interested in engineering and agriculture; for some time occupied in farming as a career. Published *Walks and Talks of an American Farmer in England*, 1852. In 1853–54, contributed to N.Y. *Times* two series of letters depicting social and economic conditions of the South; the letters later brought out in book form. As landscape architect, designed numerous public grounds, including Central Park in New York City and the capitol grounds in Washington, D.C. Published articles and books on landscape architecture. As conservationist, was instrumental in making public reservations of Yosemite and Niagara Falls. Hon. M.A. Harvard, also Amherst. Hon. LL.D. Harvard, also Yale.

Of Dickens's works, *A Christmas Carol* was one that Olmsted particularly admired. "I never read anything I liked better," he wrote as a young man. "It affected me wonderfully" (Mitchell, *Frederick Law Olmsted*, p. 30n). Olmsted was a reader of *H.W.*: in *A Journey in the Seaboard Slave States* (1856), he quoted a passage from the *H.W.* article "Rice"; in *A Journey through Texas* (1857), the first paragraph of "The Noble Savage."

Olmsted made a trip to the Continent

and England in 1856. Bayard Taylor (*Life and Letters*, I, 321) mentioned him as a guest at a dinner given by Thackeray on Aug. 1 of that year. Olmsted must, therefore, have been in London during the latter part of July – the date by which an article would have had to be submitted to *H.W.* to appear (as did his) by the second week in August. The Office Book records payment for Olmsted's article as to be made "to Mr. Joyce." "Mr. Joyce" was probably the Joyce in the employ of the publishers Bradbury & Evans (Dickens's letters contain several references to him). Olmsted was in contact with publishing houses, the purpose of his trip being mainly to conduct business for the New York publishing firm Dix & Edwards, of which he was at the time a partner (Mitchell, pp. 51–52). (Dix & Edwards reissued or reprinted some part of *H.W.*)

Two *H.W.* articles were based on Olmsted's writings. "Slaves and Their Masters" was based in large part on *A Journey in the Seaboard Slave States*; it referred to Olmsted as "a careful and temperate pathologist of the disease" of slavery, a "thoughtful and thorough abolitionist." "Germans in Texas" was based on *A Journey through Texas*, termed in the article "a very profitable book."

D.A.B.

American Party Names *Olmsted & W.H.W.* XIV, 85–89. Aug. 9, 1856

O'Ryan, Owen |*Owen O'Ryan*, Queen's College, Cork; *O'Ryan*|, *d.* 1895, university professor, librarian. B.A. Royal Univ. of Ireland, 1858; Hon. M.A. 1880; Hon. D.Lit. 1882 (*Calendar for the Year 1896*, p. 298). Appointed professor of modern languages, Queen's College, Cork, 1879; librarian, 1887; held both positions to time of his death. From 1886, Fellow of Royal Univ. of Ireland.

Boase

VERSE

The Midnight Boat XV, 275–76. March 21, 1857
Her Grave XV, 325. April 4, 1857
Return XV, 493–94. May 23, 1857
The Dismal Pool XVI, 12–13. July 4, 1857
Autumn XVI, 132. Aug. 8, 1857
The Leaf XVI, 227–28. Sept. 5, 1857
Angela XVI, 251–52. Sept. 12, 1857

Osborn, Edward Haydon |*E. H. Osborn*, 30 Upper Gower St.|, *b.* 1832. Kelly's *Post Office London Directory*, 1857, lists the resident at the Gower St. address as the Rev. Edward Osborn. The Rev. Edward Osborn, *d.* 1859, was the father of Edward Haydon Osborn. Edward Haydon Osborn matriculated at St. John's College, Oxford, 1852; Bible clerk, 1852–55; demy, Magdalen College, 1855–57. Gained Newdigate Prize, 1855, for his "Mosque Rising in the Place of the Temple of Solomon." B.A. 1856. Became inspector of factories, Rochdale.

See also Osborne (below).

Alumni Oxon.

VERSE

The Wand of Light XVI, 397–98. Oct. 24, 1857

Osborne. *Not identified.* Perhaps Edward Haydon Osborn (above). Payment for the contribution made in cash.

VERSE

Two Sonnets X, 348–49. Nov. 25, 1854

Owen, Sir Richard |*Professor Owen*, *Owen*|, 1804–1892, naturalist. F.R.S. Studied medicine at Univ. of Edinburgh and at St. Bartholomew's Hospital. M.R.C.S. 1826. Hunterian professor of comparative anatomy and physiology at Royal College of Surgeons; conservator of Hunterian Museum; superintendent of natural history departments of British Museum; instrumental in establishment of Museum of Natural History, South Kensington. Lecturer on scientific subjects. Contributor for more than sixty years to scientific journals; occasional contributor to general periodicals, e.g., *Athenaeum, Quart. Rev., Blackwood's, Edin. Rev.* Author of numerous scientific monographs, treatises, books. K.C.B. 1884, and recipient of many other honours.

Owen met Dickens in 1843; the two men became friends. Dickens at times visited the Owens and corresponded with them; on at least one occasion he invited them to one of his readings. One of Dickens's novels that Owen enjoyed was *Martin Chuzzlewit.* Dickens read with much interest Owen's *On the Extent and Aims of a National Museum of Natural History* and his *Memoir on the Gorilla.* Owen had presented to Dickens a copy of the *Memoir.* Dickens had high regard and respect for Owen.

According to Owen's biographer, it was Forster who "in the first instance" suggested Owen's writing for *H.W.* (R. S. Owen, *Life of Richard Owen,* I, 389). Owen expressed interest in writing for Dickens's periodical, though he found little time for such writing. In a letter of May 7, 1851 (misdated 1857, in Nonesuch *Letters*), Dickens wrote to him: "Both your proposals are most delightful to me, especially the zoological one." Though not stated to be so, the "proposals" would seem to have been suggestions for *H.W.* articles. In the following year, Dickens wrote to Owen: "[Forster] perfectly overwhelmed me with delight by telling me you had intimated to him that you might sometimes find leisure to write some familiar papers on Natural History" for *H.W.* "It would be in vain for me to attempt to tell you with what pride and pleasure I should receive such assistance, or what high store I should set by it." Soon after the publication of Owen's first *H.W.* paper (which Owen specifically mentioned in a letter to his sister Catherine), Dickens suggested that Owen write for the periodical a series of papers "describing the peculiarities and points of interest" of animals in the Zoological Gardens, the papers to appear under "some such title as 'Private Lives of Public Friends'" (*Life of Richard Owen,* I, 389–92). Owen contributed only one paper of the suggested series, that on the hyena.

Many references to Owen appeared in *H.W.* Among Dickens's references was that in "A Monument of French Folly," which mentioned Owen as "one of the most distinguished physiologists in the world." Horne, in "Zoological Sessions," wrote of Owen's activities in connection with the animals in the Zoological Gardens; and Hart, in "Nature's Greatness in Small Things," explained the significance of Owen's work on the vertebrates. Other references to Owen appeared in articles by Morley, Rinder, Sala, Dodd, Dixon, and Costello. Owen referred to himself in two of his own articles. "Justice to the Hyæna," written in the person of a non-zoologist, recorded the writer's visiting the Hunterian Museum and finding "the Hunterian Professor himself engaged with the osteological collection"; "A Leaf from the Oldest of Books" referred to a quadruped "which Owen has called the Hyrcotherium" and to a fossil terrapene which "will be the subject of two beautiful plates in the forthcoming number of Owen's History of British Fossil Reptiles."

The *A.Y.R.* article "Owen's Museum," Sept. 27, 1862, pictured a British museum of natural history as Owen envisioned it. The writer of the article hoped that the museum, when it came into existence, would be named after Owen – "our greatest living naturalist."

D.N.B.

Poisonous Serpents
VI, 186–88. Nov. 6, 1852

Justice to the Hyæna
VI, 373–77. Jan. 1, 1853

A Leaf from the Oldest of Books
XIII, 500–502. June 7, 1856

Owen, William |*Owen (Junr.)*|, 1837–1886, Foreign Office clerk; only son of Sir Richard Owen (above). Attended Westminster School, thereafter studied in Germany. In 1869 appointed to Foreign Office clerkship; held the position to time of his death. Died by drowning, in Kingston, Surrey.

As a visitor at the home of Owen's parents, Dickens was acquainted with William Owen. In various of his letters to the parents, Dickens included regards to the son; on the occasion of the young man's marriage in 1867, Dickens sent his congratulations to the father (R. S. Owen, *Life of Richard Owen*, II, 174–75).

While a student in Germany, Owen on one occasion wrote a short descriptive sketch of his fellow-diners at the table d'hôte where he took his mid-day meal. He sent the sketch to his father, who showed it to Dickens. "Dickens was so struck by it," wrote the father to F. G. Kitton, "that he requested to have it for a Number of the *Household Words*. ... My son was rather angry with me for parting with the MS., and positively declined to accept the fee to 'Contributors.' Mr. Dickens presented him with a complete series of the Volumes of the *Household Words* up to the date of the Number including ... 'A German Table d'Hôte' " (Kitton, *Charles Dickens by Pen and Pencil*, suppl., p. 37). The Office Book records payment of £2.2.0 cash.

Record of Old Westminsters; Foreign Office List, 1870 and later dates

A German Table d'Hôte
XII, 478–80. Dec. 15, 1855

Oxenford, John |*Oxenford*|, 1812–1877, dramatist, translator, critic. Almost entirely self-educated; articled to solicitor; turned to writing. Contributed to *Punch*, *Ainsworth's*, *Illus. London News*, *Westm. Rev.*, *Cornhill*, *Macmillan's*, and other periodicals; also to Knight's *Penny Cyclopaedia* and *George Cruikshank's Table-Book*. Reviewer of German works for *Athenaeum*; dramatic critic for almost thirty years for the *Times*. Wrote some ninety pieces for the stage – farces, comedies, serio-comic dramas, libretti – some of them original pieces, others translations or adaptations. Noted for his scholarly translations from Spanish, Italian, French, and German literature, as from Calderón, Boiardo, Molière, Goethe.

Oxenford was acquainted with Dickens. One of his pieces for the stage was an adaptation (1868) of *Oliver Twist* (Fitz-Gerald, *Dickens and the Drama*, p. 108).

Dickens supplied the title for Oxenford's "Receipt of Fern-Seed," which had originally been titled "Vegetable Miracles"; he liked Oxenford's "Touching the Lord Hamlet" (to Wills, March 10, 1853; Sept. 26, 1857). The latter contribution obviously motivated Heraud's article "Re-Touching the Lord Hamlet," Dec. 5, 1857. Oxenford wrote also for *A.Y.R.*

In the Office Book, Oxenford is recorded as author of "A Last Emotion"; his name is marked out and substituted by that of Dixon.

D.N.B.

PROSE

Snakes Magical and Mythological
VII, 41–43. March 12, 1853

Receipt of Fern-Seed
VII, 138–39. April 9, 1853

A French Audience
VII, 349–52. June 11, 1853

Garden-Games VII, 538–41. Aug. 6, 1853

More Splendid Than a Badger
X, 18–20. Aug. 19, 1854

An Imaginary Voyage
X, 259–62. Oct. 28, 1854

Fiend-Fancy XI, 492–94. June 23, 1855

Whittington in Servia
XI, 539–40. July 7, 1855

The Papyrus XII, 66–68. Aug. 18, 1855

Cyrano de Bergerac
XIV, 524–28. Dec. 13, 1856

Touching the Lord Hamlet
XVI, 372–76. Oct. 17, 1857

Cat's Grease XVI, 453–56. Nov. 7, 1857

The Sun-Horse XVI, 556–60. Dec. 12, 1857

Finnish Mythology
XVII, 353–57. March 27, 1858

Green-Beard and Slyboots
XVII, 400–405. April 10, 1858

The Profits of a Holiday
XVIII, 363–69. Oct. 2, 1858

New Toys XIX, 114–16. Jan. 1, 1859

VERSE

The Lady Hertha
VIII, 516–17. Jan. 28, 1854

P

Parr, Harriet |*Miss Lee, Miss Parr*|, 1828–1900, novelist. Born and educated in York. Contributed to *Titan, National Magazine, People's Magazine,* and other periodicals. One of her stories in *Victoria Regia.* Under pseudonym "Holme Lee" published between 1854 and 1883 some thirty novels and collections of stories, e.g., *Maude Talbot, Gilbert Massenger, Kathie Brande, Sylvan Holt's Daughter, Legends from Fairy Land;* some of novels very popular in lending libraries. Under her own name, published three historical and biographical works. Described by Allingham, who met her at a social gathering in 1868, as looking "like a quiet little old-maidish governess" (*Diary,* p. 178).

In 1855 Miss Parr submitted *Gilbert Massenger* to *H.W.* Dickens found the novel "masterly." He read it, he wrote to the author, "with the strongest emotion – and with a very exalted admiration of the great power displayed in it"; it moved him deeply and, indeed, "completely unsettled" him for the day. Two considerations, however, prevented his accepting the novel for *H.W.* – its length and its subject. The length, stated Dickens, was the basic obstacle. By 1855, however, he had already published two novels in *H.W.* and was later to publish others. Clearly, it was the subject – hereditary insanity – that determined his rejection. The story, he wrote, would awaken fear and despair in readers who were in some way linked "to a similar terrible possibility – or even probability" (to Miss Parr, Aug. 14; to Wills, July 22, 1855). Hereditary insanity was the subject of two of Miss Parr's contributions that were accepted for *H.W.* – one of the stories in "Milverston Worthies" and the poem "Hawkswell Place"; these presentations, however, were probably considered not personal or powerful enough to awaken great fear or despair.

In his letter to Miss Parr concerning *Gilbert Massenger,* Dickens expressed the hope that she would become a *H.W.* contributor. It seems, however, that she had already become a contributor, under her pseudonym.

The first four prose items listed below as not reprinted are assigned in the Office Book to "Miss Lee." Various women writers named Lee flourished at the time; nevertheless, the "Miss Lee" of the Office Book seems clearly to be "Holme Lee." There is similarity between the items assigned to "Miss Lee" and some of those assigned to Miss Parr: "Madame Grondet's" and "Madame Freschon's" both describe, in first person, a young English girl's stay in a French boarding school; "A Very Little Town" and "A Very Little House" have some similarity in content, attitude, and manner of treatment with "The Post-Mistress" and some parts of "Milverston Worthies." After Dickens's correspondence with Miss Parr concerning *Gilbert Massenger,* "Miss Lee" does not again appear in the Office Book. Nonesuch *Letters,* II, 587n, identifies the author of the "Madame Grondet" sketches as "Holme Lee," but does not substantiate the identification.

Dickens made occasional minor alterations in some of Miss Parr's contributions. "Holidays at Madame Grondet's" he referred to as being "good and true" (to Wills, Oct. 6, 1854: MS Huntington Library).

On the basis of a passage in Forster's *Life* (Book XI, sect. iii), the hymn that concludes Miss Parr's "Poor Dick's Story," in "The Wreck of the Golden Mary," has been attributed to Dickens. Forster states that Dickens received a letter from a clergyman who "had been struck by the hymn" and that Dickens acknowledged the letter thus: "I beg to thank you for your very acceptable letter – not the less gratifying to me because I am myself the writer you refer to. ..." (For B. W. Matz's interpretation of the passage in Forster, see "A Child's Hymn," *Dickensian,* May 1916.) Offsetting that statement is the fact that the *H.W.* hymn attracted the attention of Dr. Henry Allon when he was editing the *New Congregational Hymn Book* in 1856–57, that Allon applied to Dickens for permission to include the hymn in the collection, and that Dickens referred him to Miss Parr as author (see S. W. Duffield,

English Hymns: Their Authors and History, 1886; *Dickensian*, July 1916, pp. 192–93). The hymn was duly included in the *Hymn Book*, 1859, credited to Miss Parr. In the following year, Miss Parr reprinted, with but minor changes, the story in which the hymn appears. The hymn seems to be Miss Parr's writing.

Miss Parr contributed also to *A.Y.R.*

D.N.B. suppl. 1901

PROSE

The Poor Pensioner
Holly-Tree Inn (Christmas 1855), pp. 31–35

Madame Freschon's
XIII, 353–59. April 26, 1856

My Blind Sister [lead]
XIII, 457–61. May 31, 1856

Milverston Worthies
XIV, 13–16. July 19, 1856
XIV, 59–62. Aug. 2, 1856

A Day of Reckoning
XIV, 366–72. Nov. 1, 1856, and the following no.

Kester's Evil Eye
XIV, 416–21. Nov. 15, 1856

My Brother Robert
XIV, 460–64. Nov. 29, 1856

Poor Dick's Story [title thus in Office Book; no separate title in *H.W.*]
Wreck of the Golden Mary (Christmas 1856), pp. 18–21

My Window XVI, 150–54. Aug. 15, 1857

Old Saint Ann's Gateway [lead]
XVII, 25–35. Dec. 26, 1857

The Devil's Mark
XVII, 535–41. May 22, 1858

The Lady on the Mall
XVII, 578–80. June 5, 1858

The Heir of Hardington
XVIII, 412–19. Oct. 16, 1858

From First to Last [1st instalment = lead]
XIX, 457–61. April 16, 1859 and the 2 following nos.

The 14 items repr. in *The Wortlebank Diary, and Some Old Stories from Kathie Brande's Portfolio. By Holme Lee.* 3 vols. London: Smith, Elder and Co., 1860. Pub. in *H.W.* acknowledged.

Lina Fernie XVIII, 534–38. Nov. 20, 1858

The Chetwyndes
XIX, 341–46. March 12, 1859

The 2 items repr. in *Country Stories, Old and New. In Prose and Verse. By Holme Lee.* 2 vols. London: Smith, Elder & Co., 1872. Note states that stories are "chiefly reprinted from various Periodicals"; no specific acknowledgment to *H.W.*

Madame Grondet's *Miss Lee & Morley*
X, 140–44. Sept. 23, 1854

Holidays at Madame Grondet's
X, 237–40. Oct. 21, 1854

A Very Little Town
XI, 209–213. March 31, 1855

A Very Little House
XI, 470–74. June 16, 1855

The Post-Mistress
XII, 305–309. Oct. 27, 1855

Wensleydale XIII, 248–51. March 29, 1856

Milverston Worthies [lead]
XIIII, 601–605. July 12, 1856
XIV, 46–48. July 26, 1856

Two-Pence an Hour
XIV, 138–40. Aug. 23, 1856

Eleanor Clare's Journal for Ten Years
XVI, 197–202. Aug. 29, 1857, and the 3 following nos.

VERSE

*The Holy Well
XIII, 204–205. March 15, 1856

*Too Late! XIII, 326. April 19, 1856

*The Love Test XIII, 372–74. May 3, 1856

*The Grave in the Moorland
XIII, 590. July 5, 1856

*Hawkswell Place
XIV, 130–33. Aug. 23, 1856

*An Autumn Shadow
XIV, 252. Sept. 27, 1856

*The Life-Shore
XIV, 421–22. Nov. 15, 1856

*The Sighing Shade
XV, 203–204. Feb. 28, 1857

The Schoolroom at Christmas Time
XIX, 84. Dec. 25, 1858

*Repr. in *Country Stories, Old and New* (as above).

Parry, John Docwra |*J. D. Parry*, substituted for original entry *Unknown correspondent*|, *b.* ca. 1799; prob. date of death (1833) given in *D.N.B.* is incorrect. Divine, misc. writer; native of Bedfordshire. B.A. Cambridge, 1824; M.A. 1827. Curate of Aspley Guise, Beds., 1827; of Brighton, 1833. In preface to one of his works, wrote of the discouragement under which he laboured; a passage in one of his letters to Sir Robert Peel, cited in *Alumni Cantab.*, mentions his poverty and distress and his lack of success in the church; *Alumni Cantab.* suggests that he had perhaps been unfrocked. Contributed articles, and at least one poem, to *Gent. Mag.*; contributed to *Builder*, furnishing to the periodical "perhaps, the greatest amount of statistics in connection with the city churchyards that has yet appeared" (*Builder*, Sept. 19, 1846). Sometime editor of Portsmouth *Herald.* Compiled anthology of ballads, *The Legendary Cabinet*, 1829; and *The Anthology: ... Selections Adapted to the Amusement and Instruction of Youth*, 1830; in both, included his ballad "Ella"; in the second, also his "Grecian Epitaph." Author of *Select Illustrations, Historical and Topographical, of Bedfordshire*, 1827; *History and Description of Woburn and Its Abbey*, 1831 (2nd part reissued in same year as *A Guide to Woburn Abbey*); *An Historical and Descriptive Account of the Coast of Sussex*, 1833, dedicated by permission to Their Majesties King William and Queen Adelaide. In *Urban Burial. An Account of the London Churchyards, with Suggestions for Joint Parochial Cemeteries*, 1847, reprinted some of items he had contributed to *Builder*. Dickens had a copy of the pamphlet in his library (Stonehouse, *Catalogue*, p. 89).

The *H.W.* article to which Parry's name is jointly attached denounces the cruelties practised in animal slaughter. Further remarks on the same subject, "drawn forth" (according to the editorial comment) from "a clergyman in Bedfordshire" on his reading the article, were cited in Wills's "Torture in the Way of Business," Sept. 14. The "clergyman in Bedfordshire" may have been Parry himself, though it is not possible to establish from directories that Parry was resident in Bedfordshire in 1850.

D.N.B.

Nice White Veal [chip] *W.H.W. & J. D. Parry* I, 467–68. Aug. 10, 1850

Patmore, Coventry Kersey Dighton |*Coventry Patmore, Patmore*|, 1823–1896, poet, critic. Privately educated. Assistant in printed books department, British Museum, 1846–65. Contributed to *North Brit. Rev.*, the *Germ*, *Edin. Rev.*, *Macmillan's*, *Pall Mall Gazette*, *St. James's Gazette*, and other periodicals. Published *Poems*, 1844; *Tamerton Church-Tower*, 1853; the four parts of *The Angel in the House*, 1854–62 in book form; *The Unknown Eros*, 1877; *Amelia*, 1878; collections of some of his periodical articles, e.g., *Principle in Art*, 1889, and *Religio Poetae*, 1893.

In his article "Popular Serial Literature," *North Brit. Rev.*, May 1847, Patmore pointed out various excellencies and various shortcomings in Dickens's writing. Passages that showed "a master's touch" he found offset by passages of mawkishness and of wearisome description, by passages characterized by exaggeration and mannerism. Scott, wrote Patmore, was "a greater than he" – i.e., than Dickens.

Patmore's prose contribution to *H.W.* is a childish story titled by a line from Thomas Hood. Dickens "touched" the ending, he wrote to Wills, Aug. 14, 1850, to make less disagreeable the feeling towards each other of the two sisters who appear as characters.

Certain verses that Patmore submitted to *H.W.* in 1854 Dickens did not accept for publication (unpublished letter to Patmore, to appear in Pilgrim *Letters*). The two poems that were accepted have interest in the fact that Patmore salvaged parts of them, as he did of some of his other early poetry, for inclusion in the final version of the *Angel.* Approximately half of the lines of "The Golden Age" appear, with some revision, in Letter vii of Book III of *Faithful for Ever*, 1860 (Letter xviii in Oxford Edition of *Poems*); twelve lines of "Honour" appear, with but minor revision, as part of a Prelude ("The Joyful Wisdom") first added to Canto x of "The Betrothal" in the second edition of the *Angel*, 1858.

Harper's reprinted "The Golden Age," without acknowledgment to *H.W.*

D.N.B. suppl. 1901

PROSE

"Evil Is Wrought by Want of Thought" I, 580–87. Sept. 14, 1850

VERSE

The Golden Age II, 132–33. Nov. 2, 1850
Honour XI, 204. March 31, 1855

The 2 items repr. in part (as stated above), the first in *Faithful for Ever. By Coventry Patmore.* London: John W. Parker and Son, 1860; the second in *The Angel in the House ... By Coventry Patmore.* 2nd ed. London: John W. Parker and Son, 1858. Pub. in *H.W.* not acknowledged.

Patterson, Robert Hogarth |*Mr. R. H. Patterson, Mr. Paterson, H. Pattison*|, 1821–1886, journalist, misc. writer. Born in Edinburgh; educated as civil engineer, but turned to newspaper work. Contributed to *Blackwood's* (more than eighty articles), *Bentley's Misc., Dublin Univ. Magazine, North Brit. Rev., Edin. Rev.,* and other periodicals. Edited Edinburgh *Advertiser,* 1852–58. In 1858 became editor of the *Press,* London; thereafter proprietor. Later, editor of the *Globe* and the Glasgow *News.* Was long a conspicuous figure in Conservative journalism. Gained reputation as financial expert. Author of *The New Revolution; or, The Napoleonic Policy in Europe,* 1860; books on capital and finance, and other subjects; also a lyrical drama, *Robespierre,* 1877. Espinasse (*Literary Recollections,* p. 403) stated that some of Patterson's books "made even the currency question interesting."

At the time that he contributed to *H.W.,* Patterson was not acquainted with Dickens; he was later in correspondence with him. A letter from Wills to Patterson, Nov. 3, 1859 (*A.Y.R.* Letter-Book), concerns a "review of All the Year Round" (i.e., of the first volume), which Patterson had sent to Wills before its publication. Wills pointed out two inaccurate statements in the review. As it appeared in Patterson's *Press,* Nov. 12, 1859, the review had obviously been corrected in accordance with the information given in Wills's letter.

D.N.B.

Bed I, 333–36. June 29, 1850
*Youth and Summer I, 404–407. July 20, 1850
*Genius and Liberty II, 19–22. Sept. 28, 1850

*Repr. in *Essays in History and Art, By R. H. Patterson.* Edinburgh and London: William Blackwood and Sons, 1862. Pub. in *H.W.* not acknowledged.

Payn, James |*J. Payne, Payne, Payn*|, 1830–1898, novelist. Student at Eton and at Royal Military Academy, Woolwich. B.A. Cambridge, 1853. While undergraduate, brought out two volumes of poems; also began sending verse and prose to periodicals, e.g., *Bentley's Misc., Chambers's, H.W.* Decided to make writing his career. Co-editor, thereafter editor, of *Chambers's,* 1858–74, first in Edinburgh, then in London; editor of *Cornhill,* 1883–96. Reader for Smith, Elder & Co.; literary adviser to the firm. Author of almost fifty novels, among the best known being *Lost Sir Massingberd* and *By Proxy.* Many of his novels serialized in *Chambers's;* others in *Once a Week, Belgravia, Canadian Monthly, Longman's Magazine, Cornhill, Good Words. At Her Mercy, Halves,* and *What He Cost Her* serialized in *A.Y.R.* under editorship of Charles Dickens, Jr. Published collections of the stories that he had contributed to periodicals; also several volumes of essays collected from *Nineteenth Century,* the *Times, Cornhill, Illus. London News,* and other periodicals.

Miss Mitford found Payn in 1852 a young coxcomb with a condescending attitude toward "the Jerrolds, and Dickenses, and Robert Brownings" (*Friendships of Mary Russell Mitford,* p. 373). Payn himself wrote that Dickens was "the chief figure" in his "literary Pantheon" of early years, and that his meeting him in 1856 was "an epoch in my existence." Some thirty years later, he wrote that he still felt for Dickens "the same love and admiration" that he had on his early association with him (*Some Literary Recollections,* pp. 179, 184). Payn was at various times in Dickens's company, and Dickens, he stated, wrote many letters to him. Payn's writings contain frequent references to Dickens – among them, the comment that Dickens "wrote letters as good as any of his books" (*Gleams of Memory*, p. 120). Payn presented to Dickens a copy of at least two of his books (Stonehouse, *Catalogue*), and dedicated to him his novel *Mirk Abbey. Lost Sir Massingberd* was one of Payn's novels for which Dickens had praise.

The "sad blot" on Dickens's character, Payn sorrowfully had to admit, was Dickens's "putting away" his wife – "a public outrage, a blazoned defiance of all ordinary rules of conduct," which Dickens "ostentatiously, and even offensively obtruded on public notice" and for which no apology could be offered. "How a man with so many good qualities should have so conducted himself" appeared to Payn almost inexplicable. Perhaps, he wrote, Dickens "was in a degree intoxicated with universal applause, as well as spoiled by the sycophants who hung about him, and sanctioned his vagaries" ("Dickens' Life: Conclusion," *Chambers's*, March 21, 1874).

The first of Payn's articles to appear in *H.W.* was "Gentleman Cadet," an account of the brutal treatment of boys at the Royal Military Academy. It brought Dickens a sharp protest from the governor of the Academy, who was certain that it had been written by "an outsider" – not by a cadet. Dickens replied to the governor and wrote also to Payn concerning the matter – his first letter to him. The acceptance of "Gentleman Cadet" was followed by the rejection of many papers that Payn thereafter submitted to *H.W.*; not until seven months later did his second contribution appear. Meanwhile, however, he received encouragement from Dickens, and became, during the next five years, a frequent contributor. He wrote for *H.W.* even during the first year of his editorship of *Chambers's*, but then acceded to Robert Chambers's request that he confine his writing to that periodical. Payn's announcement of this request brought Dickens's reply: "I am heartily sorry to have lost you as a fellow-workman, but heartily glad to have gained you as a friend" (*Some Literary Recollections*, pp. 42–43, 61, 72, 195–96).

Of Payn's *H.W.* contributions, "P.N.C.C." Dickens thought "desperately poor"; "The Two Janes" he thought "as bad as need be," but just passable (to Wills, Jan. 19–20, 1856; Sept. 28, 1857: MS Huntington Library).

Of the items listed below as not reprinted, "Sharpening the Scythe" is a prose variant of Payn's "The Scythe-Stone Cutter" in *Stories from Boccaccio and Other Poems*; "A Sabbath Hour" is mentioned by Payn (as "A Sabbath Morn") in *Some Literary Recollections* as one of his *H.W.* contributions. In two chapters of his autobiographical writing, Payn mentioned his delight in "the first snow on the fell" – the title of his *H.W.* poem.

"The Rampshire Militia," Jan. 13, 1855, assigned in the Office Book to Miss Martineau, seems to be by Payn. See Harriet Martineau (above).

Harper's reprinted "Sharpening the Scythe," without acknowledgment to *H.W.*

D.N.B. suppl. 1901

PROSE

Under the Sea XI, 502–504. June 23, 1855
Back at Trinity XI, 519–22. June 30, 1855
On the Downs XII, 11–13. Aug. 4, 1855
Another Tight Little Island XII, 273–76. Oct. 20, 1855
Lodgings XII, 356–60. Nov. 10, 1855
The Railway Companion XII, 441–44. Dec. 8, 1855
Blobbs of Wadham XII, 513–15. Dec. 29, 1855
P.N.C.C. XIII, 58–61. Feb. 2, 1856
Bond and Free XIII, 364–72. May 3, 1856
The Sandiman Mystery XIII, 618–20. July 12, 1856
Ego et Balbus [lead] XIV, 73–75. Aug. 9, 1856
My Little Ward XIV, 89–95. Aug. 9, 1856
Ushers [lead] XIV, 97–102. Aug. 16, 1856
How We Lost Our Minister XIV, 236–40. Sept. 20, 1856

The 14 items repr. in *Stories and Sketches. By James Payn*. London: Smith, Elder, & Co., 1857. Pub. in *H.W.* acknowledged.

The Marker XIII, 359–60. April 26, 1856
A Dull Day on Exmoor XIV, 332–36. Oct. 18, 1856

Two First-Class Passengers
xvi, 430–32. Oct. 31, 1857
My Friend's Friend
xvii, 518–20. May 15, 1858
How Jones Got the English Verse-Medal
xviii, 173–75. Aug. 7, 1858
The Blankshire Thicket
xviii, 189–92. Aug. 7, 1858
Our Back Garden
xviii, 334–36. Sept. 18, 1858
Amalek Dagon
xviii, 444–47. Oct. 23, 1858

The 8 items repr. in *People, Places, and Things. By the Author of "Lost Sir Massingberd," & "Married beneath Him."* London: S. O. Beeton, 1865. Pub. in a Dickens periodical acknowledged.

Two Hundred Pounds Reward
xiv, 118–20. Aug. 16, 1856
The Fourfold Dream
xvii, 467–69. May 1, 1858
A Travelling Acquaintance
xviii, 285–88. Sept. 4, 1858
Her First Appearance
xix, 29–33. Dec. 11, 1858

The 4 items repr. in *Two Hundred Pounds Reward and Other Tales, By James Payn.* New ed. London: Chatto & Windus, 1887. In this edition, pub. in *H.W.* not acknowledged. Copy of 1st ed. not seen.

Wastdale Head xvi, 285–88. Sept. 19, 1857
Feats at the Ferry
xvii, 176–79. Feb. 6, 1858

The 2 items repr. in *Leaves from Lakeland. By James Payn.* London: Hamilton, Adams & Co. [1858]. Pub. in *H.W.* acknowledged.

Gentleman Cadet [lead] *J. Payne & Morley* vii, 121–25. April 9, 1853
Among the Shallows *Payne & Morley*
viii, 233–35. Nov. 5, 1853
Sharpening the Scythe
ix, 150–52. April 1, 1854
Back from the Crimea
xi, 119–20. March 3, 1855
The Camel-Troop Contingent
xi, 225–26. April 7, 1855
Embarkation xi, 354–56. May 12, 1855
School-Girls xii, 39–41. Aug. 11, 1855
Wanted, Some General Information [chip]
xii, 394–96. Nov. 24, 1855
Miss Davies xii, 429–32. Dec. 1, 1855
Our Shakespeare xii, 455–56. Dec. 8, 1855
The Scapegrace xiii, 27–35. Jan. 26, 1856
Three Wives xiii, 70–72. Feb. 2, 1856
Wightmouth xiii, 283–85. April 5, 1856
Curacies [lead] xiii, 433–37. May 24, 1856
Keeping the Peace
xiii, 527–28. June 14, 1856
The Fairy Puff-Puff [chip]
xiii, 559–61. June 28, 1856
Left, and Never Called For
xiv, 569–72. Dec. 27, 1856
Crumpled Rose-Leaves at St. Boniface
xv, 142–44. Feb. 7, 1857
Crime's Artificial Flowers
xv, 511–15. May 30, 1857
Parish Doctors xv, 574–76. June 13, 1857
The Deodorisation of Crime [chip]
xv, 612–14. June 27, 1857
Three Generations
xvi, 59–65. July 18, 1857
A Voice from the Cloister
xvi, 191–92. Aug. 22, 1857
Our P's and Q's
xvi, 204–207. Aug. 29, 1857
Photographees xvi, 352–54. Oct. 10, 1857
The Two Janes xvi, 442–44. Nov. 7, 1857
A Train of Accidents
xvii, 236–40. Feb. 20, 1858
Among the Tombs
xvii, 372–75. April 3, 1858
Two Very Small Clubs
xvii, 420–23. April 17, 1858
The Pixham Explanation
xvii, 566–69. May 29, 1858
Spirits over the Water
xvii, 580–83. June 5, 1858
*Fly-Catching [chip]
xviii, 11–12. June 19, 1858
A Reminiscence of Battle
xviii, 128–30. July 24, 1858
Human Chrysalis
xviii, 156–59. July 31, 1858
The Savage Muse
xviii, 181–84. Aug. 7, 1858
My Uncle the Dean
xviii, 238–40. Aug. 21, 1858
Segment's Shadow
xviii, 377–79. Oct. 2, 1858
Frightful; but Fashionable
xviii, 402–404. Oct. 9, 1858
A Sabbath Hour
xviii, 470–72. Oct. 30, 1858

*Item twice entered in Office Book, assigned in first entry to *Hollingshed,* in second to *Payn.*

VERSE

The First Snow on the Fell
xvi, 468. Nov. 14, 1857

Pearson, H. O. *Not identified.* The contributor writes in the person of a shy bachelor who in 1855 joins a Hullah singing class (conducted by one of Hullah's deputies) through which he meets the lady who later becomes his wife. "What can I recommend better to the inhabitants of small towns and villages in general," he writes, "than a Hullah singing class." Payment for the contribution made by cheque.

John Pyke Hullah's work in improving instruction in music and in establishing singing classes was the subject of the *H.W.* article "Music in Humble Life." In *A.Y.R.*, Jan. 5, 1861, appeared the article "Mr. Hullah's Classes."

The Humble Confession of a Tenor
xv, 283–85. March 21, 1857

Peppé, Mr. |*Mr. Peppé, Pepé*|. *Not identified.* Of the two forms of the contributor's name recorded in the Office Book, the correct one is evidently "Peppé": in the entry for the first item listed below, the name is written "Pepé," then overwritten to read "Peppé"; for the second item, the name stands as "Pepé." According to his articles, the contributor had been some time in England, then lived in India with his brother in an English settlement; mentions specifically having lived in a northwest province in the summer of 1846. Was in England at the time of writing for *H.W.*, as indicated by the Office Book notation that payment for the second article was "Handed by W.H.W." Was interested in electric apparatuses; both articles deal with his exploits with galvanic batteries. Had some education; refers to books of travel that he has read and quotes two lines from *Paradise Lost.* (His ignorance of the distinction between "lie" and "lay" cannot stamp him as more illiterate than certain supposedly educated *H.W.* contributors.) His use of the Americanism "snag" (the meaning of which he explains) may indicate that he had been in the U.S. Is a repulsive person who finds satisfaction in blowing crocodiles to bits and in horsewhipping a fakir.

Harper's reprinted both contributions, without acknowledgment to *H.W.*

The Crocodile Battery
ii, 540–43. March 1, 1851

A Fuqueer's Curse
iii, 310–12. June 21, 1851

Perrott, Miss. *Not identified.* "Died in India" is addressed to the friends and family of a young woman who died in "a strange alien land"; it offers them the consolation that she found death more welcome than life and that she is now with the angels, watching over her loved ones on earth. In the event that her name was misspelled in the Office Book, the contributor may be Marianne Parrott, writer of scripture stories and moral tales in verse and prose for children, and occasional contributor to periodicals.

VERSE

Died in India ix, 33–34. Feb. 25, 1854

Phipps, Edmund |*Phipps (Ed.)*|, 1808–1857, barrister-at-law, writer; younger brother of Lord Normanby. B.A. Oxford, 1828; M.A. 1831. Admitted at Inner Temple; called to the bar, 1832. Went the Northern Circuit. Recorder of Scarborough, later of Doncaster. Contributed to *New Monthly.* Wrote two pamphlets on monetary crisis, 1847, 1848; and one on trusts, 1854. Translated Henrik Hertz's *King René's Daughter.* Wrote *Memoirs of the Political and Literary Life of Robert Plumer Ward,* 1850.

Dickens was a good friend of Lord Normanby; he was acquainted with Phipps. Phipps sent his *H.W.* contribution to Dickens from Florence. It recounts his visits to an Italian man and wife, Protestants, imprisoned for alleged violations of Tuscany's laws regarding religious practices. Concerning the article Dickens wrote to Wills, Nov. 1852: "There is not much in it, but the subject ... attracts so much attention just now, that I think it worth a push to get it into this Number" (i.e., No. 139).

D.N.B. (entry: Henry Phipps)

An Interview with the Madiai
vi, 239–40. Nov. 20, 1852

Postans, Marianne: *See* Young, Marianne

Postans, Robert Baxter, prob. |*Postans*|, 1787–1892, naval man, journalist. In naval service of East India Co. to 1840. Associated with the founding of *Punch*; contributed prose and verse to the periodical; also pen and ink sketches. Contributed to *Bentley's Misc.* Was close friend of George Hodder and Henry Mayhew.

The first item listed below urges improvement of the rocket-signal system to help prevent casualties at sea; the second states the various theories accounting for shingle movement and discusses shingle beaches. The interest in ships and the sea indicates that the contributor is probably a naval man.

Boase

Red Rockets [chip]
xiii, 534–35. June 21, 1856
The Shingle Movement
xiv, 322–24. Oct. 18, 1856

Power, Marguerite A. |*Miss Power*|, 1815?–1867, writer. Contributed to *Book of Beauty* and *Keepsake* during years that the two annuals were edited by her aunt Lady Blessington; edited *Keepsake*, 1851–57. Contributed to *Illus. London News*, *Once a Week*, and other periodicals. Wrote memoir of Lady Blessington; five novels; a narrative poem in blank verse; *Arabian Days and Nights*, 1863, an account of a winter's residence in Egypt.

Dickens came to know Miss Power during the years that she was living with Lady Blessington at Gore House – then the brilliant resort of the literary and the titled. His letters show his affection for her and his solicitude for her when, in later years, she was living in comparative poverty and earning her living by writing. He had high admiration for her self-reliance and perseverance and did all he could to help her. In Oct. 1857, he wrote to Lord Brougham to ask financial aid for her (Johnson, *Charles Dickens*, ii, 912); later in the same year he joined with Thackeray and Forster in raising for her a purse of £200 by private subscription from the friends of Gore House days (to Thackeray, Dec. 4, 1857; Thackeray, *Letters*, iv, 61). During her editorship of the *Keepsake*, Dickens contributed a story ("To Be Read at Dusk") to the annual (1852); he aided her in securing a publisher for *Arabian Days and Nights*, for which book he suggested the title. In the introductory chapter to the book, Miss Power referred to the many obligations she owed to Dickens. Earlier, she had dedicated to him her novel *The Forsters* "as a humble tribute of profound admiration and most sincere regard."

In a letter to Miss Power, Dec. 15, 1856, Dickens referred to a story that she had submitted to *H.W.* as "exceedingly pretty"; later letters contain commendatory references to some of her *A.Y.R.* contributions.

D.N.B.

PROSE
The Opal Ring xiv, 62–69. Aug. 2, 1856
The Forbidden Fruit
xiv, 436–40. Nov. 22, 1856
The Painter's Pet
xv, 484–90. May 23, 1857
Years and Years Ago
xvii, 411–16. April 17, 1858

VERSE
A Wife's Pardon xiv, 276. Oct. 4, 1856

Priestley, Sir William Overend |*Dr. Priestley*|, 1829–1900, physician. Studied at King's College, London; also at other institutions. M.R.C.S. England, 1852; M.D. Univ. of Edinburgh, 1853; F.R.C.P. Edinburgh, 1858; F.R.C.P. London, 1864. Held appointments at various hospitals and universities as lecturer on midwifery, professor of obstetric medicine, consulting physician on obstetrics. Private practice included persons of Royalty. Hon. LL.D. Univ. of Edinburgh, 1884; knighted 1893. Elected M.P. for Universities of Edinburgh and St. Andrews, 1896. Published medical works.

Priestley's wife (Eliza Chambers) was the niece of Mrs. Wills. It was probably through the Willses that the Priestleys met Dickens, evidently soon after they settled in London in 1856. In Jan. 1857, they were guests at a performance of *The Frozen Deep* at Tavistock House. Dickens stated that he had "a great personal liking" for Priestley – "the great ladies' doctor," as he called him. Priestley was among those invited to hear Dickens's trial reading of the Sikes-Nancy murder scene; it was he who took Dickens aside before the reading to warn him that "if only one woman cries out when you murder the girl, there will be a contagion of hysteria all over this place" (Dickens to F. C. Beard, Feb. 16, 1866; to Mrs. James T. Fields, Dec. 16, 1868).

Lady Priestley stated that when her husband began medical practice in London and had as yet but few patients, "there was abundance of time for the young M.D. to write articles for *All the Year Round*" (*Story of a Lifetime*, p. 98). Priestley may have written for *A.Y.R.*, but during his first years of medical practice in London, it was of course *H.W.*, not *A.Y.R.*, that was being published (elsewhere in her book, Lady Priestley also confounds the two periodicals). Priestley's *H.W.* article mentions Dr. James Young Simpson's experiments with chloroform and Simpson's introduction of chloroform as an anaesthetic. Priestley had been Simpson's private assistant in Edinburgh; he was co-editor of two volumes of Simpson's writings, 1855–56.

D.N.B. suppl. 1901

Chloroform XIX, 249–52. Feb. 12, 1859

Prince, John Critchley [*Mr. Prince, Prince*], 1808–1866, poet, known as the "Bard of Hyde," the "poet of the people," the "factory bard." Born in Lancashire, son of a reed-maker for weavers; brought up to his father's uncertain trade. Had scanty schooling; read avidly whatever books he could get. Made precarious living as factory hand and shopkeeper, and by sale of his books and proceeds from begging-letters. According to Axon, was "a thorough Bohemian of the shabbiest type" (*Cheshire Gleanings*, p. 22); died in extreme poverty. Contributed verses to fugitive publications; to Manchester and Preston newspapers, *People's Journal*, *Eliza Cook's Journal*. Editor, 1845–51, of *Loyal Ancient Shepherds' Quarterly Magazine*. Author of *Hours with the Muses*, 1841; 6th ed., 1857; and four other volumes of verse.

Dickens subscribed to two copies of Prince's *Hours with the Muses*; he corresponded with Prince. In a letter of 1843, he praised one of Prince's poems; in another letter of the same year, he expressed the hope that he might meet Prince in Manchester; in a third letter, obviously in reply to an inquiry from Prince, he wrote favourably of the possibility of Prince's connecting himself "with a London Magazine"; he suggested his submitting verses to *Blackwood's*, *Ainsworth's*, and *Tait's*. By permission, Prince dedicated his *Poetic Rosary*, 1851, to Dickens "as a sincere testimony of the high esteem in which his humanizing writings, with their wide and generous sympathies, are held by his obedient servant, the author."

One of Prince's contributions submitted to *H.W.* (apparently not accepted for publication) called forth Dickens's comment to Wills, Oct. 12, 1852: "The fault of Prince's poem, besides its intrinsic meanness as a composition, is, that it goes too glibly with the comfortable idea ... that a man is to sit down and make himself domestic and meek, no matter what is done to him. It wants a stronger appeal to rulers in general to let men do this, fairly, by governing them thoroughly well. As it stands, it is about the Tract Mark (Dairyman's daughter, &c.) of political morality."

Of the items listed below, at least two had been published elsewhere before they appeared in *H.W.*: "The Household Jewels" in the *Loyal Ancient Shepherds' Quarterly Magazine*, Oct. 1848 (Lithgow, ed., *Poetical Works of ... Prince*, II, 10n); "The Price of Time" as the first of four "Autumn Sonnets" in *Eliza Cook's Journal*, Nov. 30, 1850.

The Office Book ascription to Prince of "The Two Interpreters" is in error; the poem is by Miss Procter. The ascription to Prince of "The Two Trees" seems to be in error (though payment is recorded as "Forwarded by Mr. C.D."). According to Axon (*Cheshire Gleanings*, p. 22), Prince collected for reprinting "as far as possible every scrap of his own composition." It is very unlikely that he would have neglected to include in one of his collections a poem that had achieved the distinction of publication in Dickens's journal.

The Office Book ascription to Harper, rather than to Prince, of "Human Brotherhood," Nov. 30, 1850, also seems in error. In *Autumn Leaves*, Prince included a poem of that title (first published, according to Lithgow, in *Oddfellows' Magazine*); its central idea, as also the development of the idea, is identical with that of the *H.W.* "Human Brotherhood."

Harper's reprinted "The Household Jewels," with acknowledgment to *H.W.*; "The Waste of War," without acknowledgment.

D.N.B.

VERSE

*The Household Jewels I, 564–65. Sept. 7, 1850
The Two Trees II, 108. Oct. 26, 1850
*Mercy II, 444–45. Feb. 1, 1851
*The Waste of War II, 540. March 1, 1851
*A Voice from the Factory III, 35–36. April 5, 1851
*Geraldine III, 109. April 26, 1851
*The Price of Time III, 421. July 26, 1851
*Bread of Life V, 321–22. June 19, 1852
*Last Christmas Eve VI, 445. Jan. 22, 1853
*Dew XII, 444. Dec. 8, 1855

*Repr. in *Autumn Leaves: Original Poems. By John Critchley Prince.* Hyde: Printed by G. Booth, and sold by the author [1856]. "The Household Jewels" previously repr. in *The Poetic Rosary. By John Critchley Prince.* London: Partridge & Oakey, 1851. Pub. in *H.W.* acknowledged in neither book.

Procter, Adelaide Anne [*Miss Berwick, Miss Adelaide Procter (Mary Berwick), Miss Procter (Mary Berwick), Miss Procter, Procter (Miss)*], 1825–1864, poet; daughter of Bryan Waller Procter (below). Grew up in literary atmosphere of home where eminent writers were frequent guests. Early began writing verses, some of which circulated in MS among her friends. Contributed verse to *Book of Beauty*, to both of Dickens's periodicals, *Cornhill, Good Words*; both verse and prose to *English Woman's Journal*. Published two collections of *Legends and Lyrics*, 1858, 1861; and, on behalf of a charity, *A Chaplet of Verses*, 1862. Edited the *Victoria Regia*, 1861, in which she included one of her poems.

Miss Procter's poems had great popular appeal. Patmore, writing in 1877 (B. W. Procter, *An Autobiographical Fragment*, ed. Patmore), stated that they then outsold those of any living writer except Tennyson. It was to these two poets that Queen Victoria turned in writing a letter of consolation to a friend in 1872. She quoted a phrase from "In Memoriam" and a line from "The Angel of Death" ("The Angel" in *H.W.*) – "a most beautiful poem by Ad. Procter" (*Letters of Queen Victoria*, ed. Bolitho, p. 189). Miss Procter was very modest about her poetic talent and, according to Mrs. Belloc (*In a Walled Garden*, p. 170), was somewhat pained that her popularity exceeded that of her father. "Papa is a poet," she said. "I only write verses."

Miss Procter became a *H.W.* contributor under a pseudonym, preferring, as she told her parents, to take her chance "fairly with the unknown volunteers" rather than as the daughter of Dickens's friend; if her verses did not please Dickens, he would thus be spared the pain of returning them, as likewise the unhappy alternative of printing them "for papa's sake, and not for their own" ("Introduction," *Legends and Lyrics*, 1866).

Dickens published her verses for almost two years before discovering that "Miss Berwick" was the Adelaide Procter whom he had known from her girlhood. The discovery is commemorated in the Office Book by the record for the 1854 Christmas number, where Miss Procter's name appears for the first time, followed by the pseudonym in parentheses. One of Dickens's most delightful letters is that to Miss Procter, Dec. 17, 1854, in which he pictures himself and Wills sagely speculating on the life and personality of the imaginary Miss Berwick. "... you have given me so much pleasure, and have made me shed so many tears," he concluded, "that I can only think of you now in association with the sentiment and grace of your verses."

An occasional contribution of Miss Procter's Dickens did not like, and one he singled out in particular as the epitome of bad verse: Her "Knight-Errant" ("A True Knight" in *H.W.*) he admitted to the periodical only half-heartedly (to Wills, April 12, 1854); her "Beyond" occasioned his plea to Wills (Oct. 2, 1858): "Pray, pray, *pray,* don't have Poems unless they are good. We are immeasurably better without them: Beyond, is really Beyond anything I ever saw, in utter badness."

Miss Procter's contributions account for about a sixth of the total number of poems published in *H.W.* They were undoubtedly the most popular. When they appeared in book form, wrote Mrs. Belloc (*In a Walled Garden*, p. 170), Miss Procter received "a pathetic appeal from a young lady, who asked her *could* it be true that these lovely verses were all hers, for her lover had been in the habit of assuring her, as each poem successively appeared, that it was his own!"

In 1866 Bell & Daldy published a collected edition of *Legends and Lyrics,* originating, wrote Dickens, "in the great favour" with which the poems had been received by the public. For this edition, at the request of Miss Procter's parents, he wrote a brief introduction, relating the few incidents of Miss Procter's life and writing of her dedication to works of charity. He made no critical comment on her poems, stating merely that one among her first *H.W.* contributions showed "much more merit" than the "shoal of verses" constantly pouring in to the editorial offce, and that one of her contributions to "The Seven Poor Travellers" was "a very pretty poem." Miss Procter, he wrote, "would far rather have died without seeing a line of her composition in print, than that I should have maundered about her, here, as 'the Poet,' or 'the Poetess.' "

Of the items listed below as reprinted, two are incorrectly assigned in the Office Book: "The Two Interpreters" to Prince, "Patient and Faithful" to Yates. For "Home and Rest," D. G. Fitzgerald is recorded as author; his name is marked out and substituted by that of Miss Procter. Of the items listed below as not reprinted, some may be incorrectly assigned. For "Hidden Chords," see B. W. Procter (below).

In the Office Book, "The Leaf" (Jan. 29, 1853) and "And He Took a Child" are recorded as by "Miss Berwick"; "The Shadow of the Hand," as by Miss Procter. In each entry the "Berwick" or "Procter" is marked out; it is substituted, for the first item, by "Mr. Keene"; for the second, by "Miss Erle"; for the third, by "Miss Macready."

D.N.B.

VERSE

Old Echoes vi, 492. Feb. 5, 1853
Friend Sorrow vii, 13. March 5, 1853
Hush! vii, 253. May 14, 1853
The Settlers vii, 277. May 21, 1853
Echoes viii, 13. Sept. 3, 1853
Pictures in the Fire
viii, 36–37. Sept. 10, 1853
Life and Death viii, 60. Sept. 17, 1853
A Lament for the Summer
viii, 156. Oct. 15, 1853
Now viii, 302. Nov. 26, 1853
The Angel's Story
Another Round of Stories
(Christmas 1853), pp. 17–19
The Voice of the Wind
ix, 80–81. March 11, 1854
Home-Sickness
ix, 104–105. March 18, 1854
Treasures ix, 297. May 13, 1854
A True Knight ix, 320–21. May 20, 1854
Illusion ix, 487–88. July 8, 1854

Recollections ix, 513. July 15, 1854
Shining Stars ix, 536–37. July 22, 1854
Waiting x, 204–205. Oct. 14, 1854
My Picture x, 228–29. Oct. 21, 1854
A Vision x, 300–301. Nov. 11, 1854
Give x, 324–25. Nov. 18, 1854
The Third Poor Traveller Seven Poor Travellers (Christmas 1854), pp. 16–19
The Seventh Poor Traveller Seven Poor Travellers (Christmas 1854), pp. 34–35
The Two Spirits x, 516–17. Jan. 13, 1855
The Cradle Song of the Poor x, 560–61. Jan. 27, 1855
The Lesson of the War xi, 12. Feb. 3, 1855
Passing Clouds xi, 132. March 10, 1855
One by One xi, 157. March 17, 1855
The Unknown Grave xi, 226–27. April 7, 1855
A False Genius xi, 254. April 14, 1855
God's Gifts xi, 319. May 5, 1855
A First Sorrow xi, 376. May 19, 1855
Strive, Wait, and Pray xi, 446. June 9, 1855
A Vision of Hours xi, 515–16. June 30, 1855
The Angel xi, 540. July 7, 1855
Time's Cure xi, 565. July 14, 1855
Judge Not xii, 36. Aug. 11, 1855
Comfort xii, 60. Aug. 18, 1855
Wishes xii, 180. Sept. 22, 1855
A Dream xii, 229. Oct. 6, 1855
The Present xii, 252–53. Oct. 13, 1855
The Dark Side xii, 371–72. Nov. 17, 1855
The Two Interpreters xii, 469. Dec. 15, 1855
The Barmaid Holly-Tree Inn (Christmas 1855), pp. 30–31
The Tomb in Ghent xii, 515–17. Dec. 29, 1855
Murmurs xiii, 13. Jan. 19, 1856
Sowing and Reaping xiii, 470. May 31, 1856
The Chain xiii, 516–17. June 14, 1856
My Journal xiv, 180–81. Sept. 6, 1856
Patient and Faithful xiv, 493. Dec. 6, 1856
The Old Sailor's Story [title thus in Office Book; no separate title in *H.W.*] Wreck of the Golden Mary (Christmas 1856), pp. 25–27
A Dead Past xvi, 108–109. Aug. 1, 1857
Sixty New Years' Days Ago xvii, 58–60. Jan. 2, 1858
A Woman's Question xvii, 179. Feb. 6, 1858
Words xvii, 227–28. Feb. 20, 1858
Two Dark Days xvii, 347–48. March 27, 1858
Home and Rest xvii, 445. April 24, 1858

The 57 items repr. in *Legends and Lyrics. A Book of Verses, By Adelaide Anne Procter.* London: Bell and Daldy, 1858. Pub. in *H.W.* acknowledged.

Listening Angels vii, 516. July 30, 1853
The Wind xi, 420. June 2, 1855
Lavater's Warning xiii, 61. Feb. 2, 1856
A Remembrance of Autumn xiii, 300. April 12, 1856
Three Roses xviii, 229. Aug. 21, 1858
An Ideal xviii, 252. Aug. 28, 1858
Beyond xviii, 372. Oct. 2, 1858
Two Worlds xviii, 397–98. Oct. 9, 1858
Three Evenings in the House A House to Let (Christmas 1858), pp. 23–26
A New Mother xix, 105–107. Jan. 1, 1859
A Warning xix, 324–25. March 5, 1859
Envy xix, 348. March 12, 1859

The 12 items repr. in *Legends and Lyrics. A Book of Verses, By Adelaide Anne Procter. Second Volume.* London: Bell and Daldy, 1861. Book contains also items repr. from *A.Y.R.*: pub. in *A.Y.R.* acknowledged.

Moonrise viii, 84. Sept. 24, 1853
Words upon the Waters ix, 272. May 6, 1854
Hidden Light *Miss Berwick & C.D.* x, 37. Aug. 26, 1854
Watch Cry. From a German Patois Song xiii, 228. March 22, 1856
A Fable Versified xiii, 251. March 29, 1856
Hidden Chords xix, 132. Jan. 8, 1859

Procter, Bryan Waller |*Mr. Procter, W. B. Procter, Procter*|, 1787–1874, poet. Educated at Harrow. Studied law. Practised as solicitor in London; served as commissioner of lunacy, 1832–61. Contributed to *Literary Gazette, London Magazine, Athenaeum, Fraser's, Edin. Rev.,* and other periodicals; also to annuals. Published, under pseudonym "Barry Cornwall," *Dramatic Scenes and Other*

Poems, 1819; and, in next four years, three additional volumes of dramatic, narrative, and lyric verse; *Mirandola*, 1821, a tragedy, performed at Covent Garden; *English Songs*, 1832. Wrote *Life* of Edmund Kean, *Memoir* of Lamb; prefatory memoir to works of Ben Jonson and of Shakespeare. With Forster, edited *Selections from the Poetical Works of Robert Browning*, 1863. Knew almost all his literary contemporaries – from William Lisle Bowles, whom he met in 1805, to Swinburne, who in 1868 sent him a tribute in verse; much loved for his kindliness, his generosity, his unassuming good nature.

Dickens was yet "a young aspirant" in the literary world, he wrote, when he was honoured with Procter's friendship ("Introduction" to A. A. Procter, *Legends and Lyrics*). The two men remained friends throughout Dickens's life. In his letters to Procter, Dickens conveyed his thanks for copies of Procter's books and expressed his admiration of them. In a letter to Forster and in one to Thomas Mitton, he quoted from Procter's poem "The Sea." Procter, in his old age, reread Dickens's novels. "Tell Dickens – ," he wrote to Forster, "I have been improving my mind by reading Pickwick again. ... It is cheerful healthy reading." While Forster was working on his biography of Dickens, Procter wrote to him: "To me, [Dickens] was always a kind, good genial fellow, and I liked him much" (Armour, *Barry Cornwall*, pp. 281, 285, 338).

Procter obviously intended his contributions to *H.W.* to be gratuitous. The Office Book entry for the first of his poems is accompanied by the notation "Mr. P. would not be paid"; the words are marked out and substituted by the notation "Cheque C.D." The Office Book records payment of £1.1.0 for each of the poems assigned to Procter, though they range in length from less than ½ col. to 1¾ cols.

In a letter to Forster, Aug. 1, 1850, Procter wrote, obviously with reference to *H.W.*: "If you think the verses on the other side will suit Dickens, they are at his service" (Armour, p. 230). The Office Book records no poem by Procter for the months of 1850 following the date of the letter. If the poem was published in *H.W.* (and it probably was), it may be a poem wrongly assigned in the Office Book; or it may be "Battle with Life!", Sept. 21, recorded without author or payment notation (see p. 479). It cannot be either of the two unassigned poems ("A Lesson for Future Life," "A Memory") with payment recorded as £0.10.6 – that being but half the honorarium regularly made to Procter (Procter, moreover, could never have been guilty of the bathos of "A Lesson for Future Life"); and it is of course not the unassigned "Outcast Lady" (payment also £0.10.6), which arrived at the editorial office "per Mrs. Gaskell."

On Dec. 19, 1858, Dickens wrote to Procter: "A thousand thanks for the little song. I am charmed with it, and shall be delighted to brighten Household Words with such a wise and genial light." The Office Book assigns no poem to Procter in the *H.W.* numbers that follow the date of the letter, nor are there in those numbers any poems listed in the Office Book without author's name. It seems likely that Procter's "little song" is "Hidden Chords," ¼ col., £1.1.0 payment, published Jan. 8, 1859, less than three weeks after the date of Dickens's letter. The Office Book assigns "Hidden Chords" to Miss Procter. Since she did not reprint it among her collected poems, it is probably not her writing; it is unlikely that in 1858 she would have contributed to a periodical a poem that she did not think worthy of collecting.

His "One Spot of Green," published in *H.W.* in 1854, Procter reprinted in a collection of 1857 (see below) among "Miscellaneous Poems," which he stated in his preface had "never been before printed." In Feb. 1853, he had sent a copy of the poem, titled "A Song with a Moral," to his friend James T. Fields (Fields, *Yesterdays with Authors*, p. 406).

For the early numbers of *A.Y.R.* Procter wrote a series of "Trade Songs," which Dickens found "simply ADMIRABLE" (to Procter, March 19, 1859). Procter must have discussed the songs with Dickens some months before he submitted them to him for publication, for Dickens, in his letter of Dec. 19, 1858, reminded him: "... I still hope to hear more of the trade-songs, and to learn that the blacksmith has hammered out no end of iron into good fashion of verse, like a cunning workman, as I know him of old to be." The reference is obviously to the second of the "Trade Songs," titled "The Blacksmith," *A.Y.R.*, April 30, 1859. Dickens's reciting two lines of that poem in conversation with John Bennet Lawes (Forster, *Life*, Book VIII, sect. v) has been taken to mean that the poem was composed by Dickens. In view of Dickens's letter to Procter, it is clear that Dickens was reciting lines that he remembered from Procter's poem, not lines that he himself had composed.

Procter's high contemporary reputation as a song writer is reflected in Mrs. Linton's *H.W.* article "Street Minstrelsy": Barry Cornwall's songs, wrote Mrs. Linton, are loved and sung by "the million," while at the same time they are esteemed by the cultivated – charming "the most critical taste" and delighting "the finest ear." Mackay, in "An Emigrant Afloat," recorded that he had, before experiencing "the disagreeables" of shipboard life, listened with "a sort of enthusiasm" to such songs as Procter's "The Sea." Morley, in "Constitutional Trials," quoted Procter's lines in praise of beer.

D.N.B.

VERSE

Flowers I, 325. June 29, 1850

Repr. in *English Songs, and Other Small Poems. By Barry Cornwall.* Cover-title includes notation: "A New Edition, with Additions." London: Chapman and Hall, 1851. Pub. in *H.W.* not acknowledged, though "Preface" states that some of "additions" had "already appeared in print."

One Spot of Green VIII, 469. Jan. 14, 1854

Repr. in *Dramatic Scenes. With Other Poems, Now First Printed. By Barry Cornwall.* London: Chapman and Hall, 1857.

A Dialogue of Shadows I, 38. April 6, 1850

Precepts of Flowers III, 229. May 31, 1851

An Old Offender IX, 344. May 27, 1854

R

R., J.: *See* Humphreys, Jennett

R., S. *Not identified.* The initials appear in the Office Book and also as signature to the writer's contribution, which is in the form of a letter to the editor. The writer states that the method of preventing colliery explosions proposed in "A Remedy for Colliery Explosions," Dec. 28, 1850, is but a partial and uncertain method; he endorses the system of Government inspection urged in the editorial comment at the end of the article "A Coal Miner's Evidence," Dec. 7, 1850. No payment recorded for the contribution.

The True Remedy for Colliery Explosions [chip] II, 427. Jan. 25, 1851

R.E.: *See* Murray, Eustace Clare Grenville

Rae, John |*Dr. Rae*|, 1813–1893, arctic explorer. Studied medicine in Edinburgh. L.R.C.S. Edinburgh, 1833. In 1833 entered service of Hudson's Bay Co. as ship-surgeon. Remained in service of Company to end of 1854, serving for about ten years as clerk, surgeon, and trapper at Company's post at Moose Factory; then as chief trader and chief factor of Mackenzie River district and as explorer engaged in surveying and mapping unexplored land and coastline. During this time, under Admiralty orders, took part in 1848–49 and 1851 expeditions in search of Sir John Franklin and his crews. In 1854, while on surveying expedition, obtained from Eskimos first decisive information concerning fate of Franklin expedition. In the 1860s conducted land surveys for telegraph lines. Contributed to *Nature*, to *Journal* of Royal Geographical Society, and to other periodicals. Author of *Narrative of an Expedition to the Shores of* *the Arctic Sea, in 1846 and 1847*, 1850. Hon. M.D. McGill College, Montreal, 1853; Hon. LL.D. Univ. of Edinburgh, 1856. F.R.G.S., F.R.S.

Rae's appearance in *H.W.* occurred in connection with his defence of his conclusion that the survivors of the Franklin expedition had resorted to cannibalism before dying of starvation. Rae had stated this conclusion in his report (letter dated July 29, 1854) to the Admiralty, which report the Admiralty had released for publication. It had appeared in the *Times*, Oct. 23, 1854. Dickens was among those who held that Rae's statement was based on unreliable and inconclusive evidence and that, moreover, the admirable discipline and the moral character of Franklin's men rendered the alleged conduct in the highest degree improbable. These convictions Dickens stated emphatically in his *H.W.* article "The Lost Arctic Voyagers," Dec. 2, Dec. 9, 1854. The article cast no aspersions on Rae himself. A man of conscientious and modest character, of "high reputation as a skilful and intrepid" arctic traveller, Rae had carried out his duty in giving the Admiralty a faithful report of his information and his conclusions, stated Dickens. It was the Admiralty's release of the report, with its "painful" aspect of alleged cannibalism, that was ill advised.

Rae's reply to Dickens's article, obviously sent to the periodical rather than to Dickens personally, was published in two instalments, individually titled: "The Lost Arctic Voyagers," Dec. 23, and "Dr. Rae's Report," Dec. 30. In his article Rae replied to the points that Dickens had raised and reasserted his conviction that the survivors had resorted to cannibalism. He acknowledged the difficulty of countering opinions expressed in so "very ably-written" an article as "The Lost Arctic Voyagers" of Dec. 2 and 9, particularly since that article expressed "the popular view" of the matter under discussion. Rae's comments indicate that he was not aware that Dickens was the author of the article to which he was writing a reply. Before Rae's article appeared in *H.W.*, however, Dickens had written Rae a letter; in it, presumably, he made his authorship known (Dickens to Wills, Dec. 16, 1854: MS Huntington Library).

The Office Book assigns the first instalment of Rae's article to Rae and Dickens, the second instalment to Rae alone. The first instalment is not, of course, jointly written; Dickens's share in it consists (aside from four lines of introductory comment) merely of a long passage cited from Sir John Barrow's *Voyages of Discovery and Research within the Arctic Regions* (1846), intended to cast doubt on the opinions expressed by "our esteemed friend, DR. RAE," in Rae's portion of the article.

The second item by Rae to appear in *H.W.* – "Sir John Franklin and His Crews" – is not an article written by him for the periodical (though the Office Book records for it payment of £5.5.0). It is a copy of Rae's official report of his 1853–54 expedition, addressed to the Secretary of the Hudson's Bay Co., in London, dated Sept. 1, 1854 (but written in part after Sept. 1); the report contains substantially the same information in regard to Franklin's crews as that given in Rae's letter to the Admiralty. Dickens printed the report in *H.W.* as a historical document recording what he believed to be unwarranted conclusions concerning the cannibalism – conclusions that future investigation might well prove to be untrue. Prefatory editorial comment stated: "In order that our readers, at a future time, when the Esquimaux stories shall have been further tested, may be in possession of them as originally brought home, we have procured from DR. RAE a faithful copy of his Report for publication. We do not feel justified in omitting or condensing any part of it; believing, as we do, that it is a very unsatisfactory document on which to found such strong conclusions as it takes for granted."

The copy of the report as printed in *H.W.* differs in more than 800 instances from the copy (in a clerk's handwriting, but signed by Rae) in the archives of the Hudson's Bay Co. published in *John Rae's Correspondence with the Hudson's Bay Company*, 1953. Most of the differences are in punctuation and capitalization, though many result from the *H.W.* practice of spelling out numbers. Some occur in spelling and paragraphing. But there are also variants in text. The copy in *Correspondence*, for instance, states that a certain river was named "in honor of Sir Roderick Murchison"; *H.W.* erroneously reads "in honour of Sir Frederick Murchison." Again, in stating what was found near the bodies of Franklin's men, the copy in *Correspondence* reads: "... fresh bones and feathers of geese were noticed near the scene of the sad event"; for "fresh bones," *H.W.* reads "fishbones."

Two *H.W.* articles of 1857 – "The Lost English Sailors" and "Official Patriotism" – mentioned Rae and the information contained in his reports and letters concerning Franklin's crews. The first article dismissed as "assuredly" without foundation the dark "hints of cannibalism"; the second contained a commendatory reference to Rae, in a letter from Lady Franklin. An earlier article, "Regular Trappers," mentioned Rae's heading the Hudson's Bay Co. exploration expedition of 1846–47.

D.N.B.

The Lost Arctic Voyagers [lead] *Dr. Rae & C.D.* x, 433–37. Dec. 23, 1854
Dr. Rae's Report [lead] x, 457–59. Dec. 30, 1854
Sir John Franklin and His Crews xi, 12–20. Feb. 3, 1855

Rankin, Miss. *Not identified.* "Not very long ago," writes the contributor, "the course of duty carried me abroad, and I spent some time in a little continental town. ..." The name and location of the town she takes pains to conceal, for, she says, "I am about to tell the true tale of a person living in that town, and wish so to do without directing anybody's eyes towards him." The tale that she tells is the life of the town executioner, as the account was told her by the priest whose services she was in the habit of attending.

One Miss Rankin flourishing at the time was Jessica Rankin, an occasional contributor to *Once a Week.* Another Miss Rankin, a cousin of Harriet Martineau, was governess in the family of Sir Isaac and Lady Goldsmid; she accompanied Miss Martineau and a friend to the Continent in 1839 (Webb, *Harriet Martineau*, p. 247). Miss Martineau was a *H.W.* contributor at the time that Miss Rankin's contribution appeared.

The Hermit of Damburgville ix, 126–28. March 25, 1854

Reeves. *Not identified.* The contributor explains the French military system, in which a recruit advances in the ranks on the basis of merit and length of time in service, and is eligible for further promotion on the same basis. With the French system, the contributor contrasts the English system, in which promotion from the ranks is the exception and in which commissions are obtained by purchase. The evils of "our military system," he writes, are "of so crying a nature" that common sense prompts the adoption, perhaps in modified form, of the French system.

Promotion, French and English xv, 90–92. Jan. 24, 1857

Reynolds, W. L. *Not identified.* The contributor is an English office clerk – "a man who throughout life has been engaged, mostly, in climbing up and down an office stool"; has lived for many years in Corfu. He recounts a brief holiday trip in Albania that he made twenty years before in company with three young officers from the British garrison stationed in Corfu.

Only an Earthquake *W. L. Reynolds & Morley* viii, 235–38. Nov. 5, 1853

Richardson. *Not identified.* The writer's contribution is an amateurish story; contains some literary references: "Mariana" (Tennyson), "The Ancient Mariner," *As You Like It*; a tobacco-spitting American gratuitously brought in.

How the Old Love Fared xv, 607–612. June 27, 1857

Rinder, Samuel |*Render*, 22 Rockingham St., Leeds; *Rinder*|, 1825?–1907, businessman and public official of Victoria, Australia. Born near Leeds; son of Methodist preacher. Attended school at Garforth, Yorks. Early had love of the sea and of adventure. Shipped as cabin boy on sailing vessel plying between Liverpool and New York. In early 1840s, as apprentice on the *Hope* of Plymouth, made voyage to Melbourne; stayed some years in Tasmania, where his uncle was Wesleyan minister. On news of California gold discovery, determined to go to California; found no vessel bound for California; shipped, instead, on vessel bound for Callao, Peru. From Callao, shipped on the *Abbots Reading* bound for Liverpool. After about three years in England, again made voyage to Melbourne; lived in Victoria remainder of his life. Started butcher's business in Melbourne suburb; worked for two years carting goods between Melbourne and the Castlemaine diggings; operated general merchandise stores; became one of leading businessmen, graziers, and farmers of Korong district. For forty years, secretary and treasurer of Korong shire; also justice of the peace, coroner. Was able speaker and writer; contributed to Victoria newspapers. Mentioned in obit., Wedderburn *Express*, Dec. 13, 1907, as writer of a *H.W.* article.

The biographical data in the Wedderburn *Express* obituary were obtained from "relatives and friends"; certain dates there given of events in Rinder's early life seem to be incorrect. The obituary gives Rinder's date of birth as Nov. 12, 1823; the Crew List of the *Abbots Reading*, Public Record Office, London, gives his age as twenty-four at the time of his joining the vessel in Callao, Dec. 7, 1849. The obituary states that Rinder made the voyage from Liverpool to New York at age twelve, i.e. (according to the birth date given), in 1835; in "Sailors' Homes Afloat" Rinder mentions the voyage as made in 1837. The obituary states that on his second voyage to Australia, Rinder arrived in Melbourne in 1852; as "Four-Legged Australians" makes clear, Rinder was still living in Leeds at the time of writing that article, i.e., during the early months of 1853). (The Rockingham St. address given for Rinder in the Office Book was the address of Benjamin Rinder, butcher [Slade and Roebuck's Leeds directory, 1851] – obviously a relative.) The only article that Rinder wrote for *H.W.* while living in Australia was "Australian Carriers."

Rinder's two lead articles are sharp criticisms of regulations concerning British merchant seamen and of conditions under which seamen live and work on shipboard. Morley's "The Life of Poor Jack," written as the supposed contribution of a retired seaman, strongly endorsed the criticisms made in "We Mariners of England" – "the remarks made by a tar in your honoured journal" – and cited instances from various sources to substantiate the criticism. A letter from "a master mariner at the Antipodes" (in "Voices from the Deep") confirmed the criticisms made in Rinder's "Sailors' Homes Afloat."

The Guano Diggings
VI, 42–46. Sept. 25, 1852

The Topmost City of the Earth *Render & Morley* VI, 125–29. Oct. 23, 1852

South American Christmas
VI, 325–28. Dec. 18, 1852

Black-Skin A-head!
VI, 399–404. Jan. 8, 1853

Sailors' Homes Afloat [lead] *Rinder & Morley* VI, 529–33. Feb. 19, 1853

We Mariners of England [lead] *Rinder & Morley* VI, 553–57. Feb. 26, 1853

Four-Legged Australians
VII, 208–214. April 30, 1853

Australian Carriers
XI, 420–27. June 2, 1855

Roberts. Naturalist. Roberts's *H.W.* article, which deals with teredos, arrived at the editorial office "per Frank Buckland." Buckland reprinted it in his *Curiosities of Natural History*, 2nd ser. (1860), stating that Roberts had published it in *H.W.* and that it was the result "of much patient investigation." Various observations on sea creatures that Buckland recorded in the first two series of *Curiosities* had come to him, he stated, from Roberts. Roberts had also furnished some information on *Pholas* to Buckland's father, Dr. William Buckland. Buckland referred to Roberts as "my learned informant and friend" and as "a great observer" of natural phenomena. He mentioned Roberts's having lived at Lyme Regis, then at Worthing and at Dover.

Roberts may be the George Roberts who published *Topography and Natural History of Lofthouse and Its Neighbourhood; with the Diary of a Naturalist and Rural Notes,* 2 vols., 1882–85. In the "Natural History" section of the book, Roberts cites a comment from Buckland's *Curiosities of Natural History,* 1st ser.

Tremendous Bores
xv, 534–36. June 6, 1857

Roberts. Address: Sheffield. *Not identified.* Sheffield directories of the 1850s list some thirty or forty male residents of the name Roberts.

VERSE
Water Music xvii, 617–18. June 12, 1858

Robertson, Miss. *Not identified.* The contributor's interests, as indicated by the three items assigned to her, are contemporary happenings in France and natural history – the same interests as those of Robertson – prob. John Robertson (below). Of the items, only one – "Truth in Irons" – calls for comment.

Three years before the publication of that article, appeared Dixon's article "To Hang or Not to Hang" (Aug. 4, 1855). Dixon's article is a brief account of a *cause célèbre* of miscarriage of justice in the French courts: the conviction and seven-year imprisonment of the young schoolmaster Lesnier (i.e., Jean-François Lesnier, 1833–1858) for the murder, on the night of Nov. 15–16, 1847, in the Dept. Gironde, of the old man Claude Gay; the discovery of the real murderer and his accomplices, their sentence, and the establishment in 1855 of Lesnier's innocence.

Miss Robertson's "Truth in Irons" is a long account of the conviction and imprisonment of the young schoolmaster Jules Delorme for the murder, July 23, 1846, in the Dept. Gironde, of the old man Eugène Gay; the discovery of the real murderer and his accomplice, their sentence, and the establishment of Delorme's innocence.

Dixon's account accords in the main with the facts of the case given in *Grand Dictionnaire Universel* (entry: Lesnier).

History of a Miracle
xviii, 37–42. June 26, 1858
Truth in Irons xviii, 136–43. July 24, 1858
Pearls xix, 227–30. Feb. 5, 1859

Robertson, John, prob. |*Robinson, Robertson*|. The Office Book gives no clue as to the identity of the contributor, but he is clearly the Robertson mentioned in Dickens's letters to Wills, Sept. 18 and Nov. 10, 1855. The first letter indicates that in Sept. Robertson sent to Dickens the article "Pierre Erard," accompanying it by a letter in which he addressed Dickens familiarly. Dickens sent Robertson's letter to Wills, remarking: "I don't know that I have the least knowledge of Mr. Robertson, though he addresses me as 'Dear Dickens.'" Dickens accepted the article for *H.W.*; Wills recorded it in the Office Book as by "Robinson." There was obviously some confusion about the writer's address, for in Nov. Dickens wrote from Paris: "There has called on me in my absence, a Mr. John Robertson, 15, Rue de Monceau, Faubourg St. Roule. I believe this to be the writer of the Erard paper." Wills was to ascertain whether Dickens's supposition was correct and, if so, to send the writer payment for the contribution. Wills recorded payment as made by cheque, Nov. 16. His recording of "Robinson" as the contributor's name is clearly in error. Dickens's first letter establishes the writer as Robertson; his second letter almost as definitely establishes him as John Robertson. The writer, at all events, was the Robertson who contributed to *H.W.* during the following three and a half years. Like the writer of various of the articles assigned to Robertson, the writer of "Pierre Erard" is in

Paris and is interested in contemporary happenings in France.

The articles assigned to Robertson give the following information concerning him: He was a Scotsman, a Protestant, born in Aberdeen; attended school in Aberdeen. Was a student at a university. From his boyhood years came his interest in fisher folk, in the sea, and in marine flora and fauna. Had a devout attitude toward "the vegetal and animal world," seeing it as "the work of a Divine Intelligence." Was impatient with the bookishness of "the savans" and had little use for antiquaries. Made various visits to Brighton. Lived for a time in London, but writes of that residence as in the past. Was familiar with London clubs and greatly interested in London's historical associations. In his walks, peopled the city with the ghosts of the great men who had once been there – Bacon, Shakespeare, and Cromwell being among his "principal London ghosts." During the 1850s lived in France, apparently in Paris; acquainted with some of English residents in Paris.

"Notes on the Fishers of the Scotch East Coast," *Blackwood's*, March 1842, assigned in the *Wellesley Index* to "Mr. Robertson," is by the *H.W.* contributor. Various observations and comments in the article correspond with the material given in Robertson's *H.W.* articles on Scottish and English coast folk.

Among the numerous Robertsons writing in the mid-century, at least three were born in Aberdeen: Joseph Robertson, record scholar, journalist, antiquary; James Craigie Robertson, historian, canon of Canterbury; and John Robertson, journalist. It is John Robertson, remembered for his association with John Stuart Mill and with the Carlyles, who seems to have been the *H.W.* contributor.

Accounts of Robertson appear in Bain, *John Stuart Mill*, p. 59n; Espinasse, *Literary Recollections*, chap. vii; Masson, *Memories of London in the 'Forties*, chap. i; references to him appear in Bain's *Autobiography*, in Mill's *Autobiography*, in the letters of the Carlyles, and occasionally in the writings of other contemporaries; Mill's letters to him appear in *Earlier Letters of John Stuart Mill*, ed. Mineka; the record of his admission at Lincoln's Inn and his call to the bar appears in *Records of ... Lincoln's Inn*; a brief notice of him is given in Boase.

According to these sources, the facts of Robertson's life are as follows: *b.* ca. 1811, *d.* 1875. Educated at Univ. of Aberdeen and Univ. of Glasgow, intended for the ministry. Went to London "as a literary adventurer" (Masson). Admitted at Lincoln's Inn, 1834; called to the bar, 1839. Meanwhile, had become connected with *Morning Chronicle* – as a reporter, according to Boase, as "a prominent political contributor," according to Espinasse. Contributed article on Bacon to *London Review*, 1836; one on Shakespeare to *London & Westm. Rev.*, 1836; both articles elicited praise. Was acting editor of *London & Westm. Rev.* during Mill's proprietorship of the periodical, 1837–40; aroused anger of Carlyle by cancelling his engagement to write article on Cromwell, which Robertson decided to write himself. On Mill's relinquishment of the *Review*, was "once more adrift in the London world" (Masson). Wrote for London newspapers and was correspondent for several provincial papers. In the early 1840s had some hope of being returned M.P. for a Scottish constituency; hope did not materialize. Was member of Reform Club. Was active in organizing the short-lived Society of British Authors, 1843 (Besant, "The First Society of British Authors," *Contemp. Rev.*, July 1889). According to Bain (*John Stuart Mill*), "disappeared from London" about 1844 "and was afterwards rarely heard of"; according to Espinasse, "little or nothing was seen or heard" of him in public after 1848; appears to have visited the Carlyles last in 1849. Espinasse states that Robertson "made, I believe, a good marriage" later in life, after having had at least one matrimonial hope demolished by his too evident indication that he wanted a wife "chiefly to make her of use to him in his literary labours." Masson remarks, without explanation, on "what a strange romance, tragic on the whole," Robertson's life would seem "if it could be all told." What that life was after the 1840s no one seems to have recorded. Boase states that Robertson died at Old Gore, Hereford, and was buried in Brighton.

Robertson's brief prominence as "a stirring man" in the London journalistic world made him acquainted with numerous contemporaries besides those mentioned above. He was introduced to Lord Melbourne and Lord Normanby; he was acquainted with Crabb Robinson; he was a friend of Louis Blanc and of Bulwer-Lytton. Forster knew him at least by repute (Garnett, *Life of W. J. Fox*, p. 195). Geraldine Jewsbury and Harriet Martineau, who later became contributors to *H.W.*, were acquainted with him.

No contemporary seems to have recorded that Dickens and Robertson were acquainted; there were opportunities for such acquaintance. Dickens was reporter for the *Morning Chronicle*, 1834–36; Robertson was connected with the same periodical. Dickens presided at the second meeting of the Society of British Authors; Robertson was a prime mover of the organization. From Thackeray, in conversation, and from Mrs. Carlyle, in a letter, Dickens heard of Robertson, and to Mrs. Carlyle's letter he sent a reply (Jane Welsh Carlyle, *Letters to Her Family*, pp. 188–89).

This Robertson seems the most likely writer to be the "Mr. John Robertson" of Paris who addressed the conductor of *H.W.* as "Dear Dickens" and became a contributor to his periodical.

Dickens liked "Pierre Erard"; the opening section of "Captain Doineau" he found overlong and confused; Wills was to alter it (to Wills, Sept. 18, 1855; Sept. 28, 1857: MS Huntington Library).

In the Office Book, "An Immeasurable Wonder" is recorded as by Robertson "per F. Buckland"; the Buckland notation is marked out.

For Robertson's connection with "A Companionable Sparrow" and with Miss Fitton, and for his appropriation of some of her writing, see Sarah Mary Fitton (above). See, also, "Robertson's friend" (below).

Boase

Pierre Erard xii, 238–40. Oct. 6, 1855
Unhappiness in the Elysian Fields xiii, 502–504. June 7, 1856
Coast Folk xiii, 550–52. June 21, 1856
Scotch Coast Folk xiii, 585–90. July 5, 1856
Scotch Coast Folk. Footdee in the Last Century xiv, 16–20. July 19, 1856
English Coast Folk xiv, 81–85. Aug. 9, 1856
Seaside Eggs xiv, 126–30. Aug. 23, 1856
Sea-Gardens [lead] xiv, 241–45. Sept. 27, 1856
Under-Water Existence xiv, 342–47. Oct. 25, 1856
The Purple Shore xiv, 391–95. Nov. 8, 1856
The Coco-Palm xv, 67–72. Jan. 17, 1857
Coco-Eaters xv, 100–107. Jan. 31, 1857
My Ghosts xv, 165–68. Feb. 14, 1857
The Murder of the Archbishop of Paris [1st instalment = lead] xv, 169–75. Feb. 21, 1857, and the following no.
My London Ghosts xv, 344–49. April 11, 1857
The Patron Saint of Paris xv, 558–61. June 13, 1857
An Immeasurable Wonder xvi, 118–20. Aug. 1, 1857
A Companionable Sparrow *Robertson & Miss Fitton* xvi, 130–32. Aug. 8, 1857
The Self-Made Potter xvi, 223–26. Sept. 5, 1857
Sepoy Symbols of Mutiny xvi, 228–32. Sept. 5, 1857
Captain Doineau xvi, 423–30. Oct. 31, 1857
Marie Courtenay xvi, 523–25. Nov. 28, 1857
The Vital Point xvii, 125–26. Jan. 23, 1858
The Shell-Moth xvii, 205–206. Feb. 13, 1858
Shadowless Men xvii, 294–99. March 13, 1858
Germination xvii, 340–43. March 27, 1858
The Blue Dye Plant xvii, 436–38. April 24, 1858
Irritable Plants xix, 16–18. Dec. 4, 1858
Mosses xix, 33–35. Dec. 11, 1858
White Ants xix, 449–54. April 9, 1859

Robertson's friend. *Not identified.* The contributor seems to be a resident of Paris; may be Sarah Mary Fitton (above).

Boulogne Wood xvi, 89–93. July 25, 1857

Rogers, Mary Eliza |*Miss Rogers*|, *b.* 1827, writer; daughter of William Gibbs Rogers, wood carver (*D.N.B.*). Contributed to *Art Journal* (Allibone); contributed occasional verses to *Sharpe's, Once a Week*; and "The Moslem Lover's Complaint" to *A Welcome*, 1863. Author of *Domestic Life in Palestine*, 1862 [1861], the pleasant account of her residence in the East (1855–59) with her brother Edward Thomas Rogers, then vice-consul in Haifa; and *My Vis-à-Vis*, 1865, verses "written during intervals of rest from work of a more serious nature." Among the verses is "Esther Summerson's Sorrow," based on Esther's words in *Bleak House*, "O, too late to know it now, too late, too late." Wrote "'Saint Valentine" expressly for *H.W.*, weaving into the lines (with a poet's licence of variation) the quotation from Dickens's masthead: "Familiar in our mouths ... / As Household Words."

Allibone

VERSE

Saint Valentine II, 493. Feb. 15, 1851

Repr. in *My Vis-à-Vis; or, Harry's Account of His Courtship, and Other Poems. By Mary Eliza Rogers.* London: Bell and Daldy, 1865. Pub. in *H.W.* acknowledged.

Rogers, William, 1819–1896, divine, educational reformer. Student at Eton. B.A. Oxford, 1842; M.A. 1844. Curate of St. Thomas's, Charterhouse, 1845–63; thereafter rector of St. Botolph's, Bishopsgate. Worked for improvement of social condition of his parishioners; established numerous schools for the poor and the middle class. Published reports of the schools; also sermons.

On Feb. 23, 1856, appeared in *H.W.* the article "Houseless and Hungry," describing a London refuge for the destitute. "As a pendant to that description," stated the prefatory editorial comment in "A London Parish," April 5, "we now present our readers with a brief notice of the parish in which [the refuge] stands: – St. Thomas Charterhouse. We are indebted for it to the Reverend William Rogers, its incumbent." The body of "A London Parish" consists of three paragraphs reprinted (without acknowledgment of the published source) from Rogers's *Educational Prospects of St. Thomas Charterhouse*, 1854.

Rogers was, thus, not a contributor to *H.W.* in the sense of writing for the periodical. The editorial comment implies that he called his account of the parish to the attention of the editorial office and perhaps furnished the office a copy of his *Educational Prospects*. The Office Book assigns the item to Wills; it records no payment.

D.N.B.

A London Parish [chip]
XIII, 275–76. April 5, 1856

Ross, Thomasina |*Miss Ross*|, *b.* ca. 1796, *d.* 1875, translator; daughter of William Ross, reporter and translator for the *Times*. On staff of *Literary Gazette* when Jerdan became editor of that periodical in 1817; was, according to him, a "ready and excellent translator," a writer "whose talents were of a sound order, especially for a youthful female" (*Autobiography*, II, 178, 236–37). Contributed to *Polytechnic Journal* and *Bentley's Misc.* Published, 1823, translation of Bouterwek's *History of Spanish Literature*; 1847, Tschudi's *Travels in Peru*; 1849, *El Buscapié*; 1852, Humboldt's *Personal Narrative of Travels to the Equinoctial Regions*. Commended by Ticknor, *History of Spanish Literature* (1849, I, 33n), for "taste and skill" of her translation of Bouterwek; by *Quart. Rev.* (Sept. 1847) for "ease and fluency" of her translation of Tschudi. In 1856 granted Civil List pension of £50 a year "In consideration of her literary merits" (Colles, *Literature and the Pension List*).

Dickens was acquainted with the Ross family, his uncle Edward Barrow being the husband of Miss Ross's sister Janet. Dickens took an interest in Miss Ross's literary career and admired her work as translator. He brought her to the attention of Chapman & Hall and, Oct. 20, 1842, gave her a letter of introduction to the publishers. In a letter of April 1, 1847, thanking her for a copy of her translation of Tschudi, he gave her work high praise: "It is as if the book were not a translation, but had been written originally in English, and in thorough good English too" (Rolfe, "Additions to the Nonesuch Edition of Dickens' Letters," *Huntington Library Quart.*, Oct. 1941).

A letter from Dickens to Miss Ross, Jan. 21, 1850, indicates that she had written to him suggesting that she contribute to his forthcoming periodical. "I think I may often avail myself of your offer, to our mutual advantage," wrote Dickens, asking her to suggest a Spanish or German book or subject of which she might write "a popular account." Some days later he wrote that he had asked Wills to communicate with her for the purpose of arranging a subject (Jan. 29: MS Stark Library, University of Texas).

All of Miss Ross's *H.W.* contributions were translations. For all except the last, she was paid less than the standard rate. For the 10-col. article "The 'Mouth' of China," for instance, she received £4.0.0, as against the standard payment of £5.5.0 for an article of that length.

Miss Ross's "A Lunatic Asylum in Palermo" was reprinted in *Harper's*, with acknowledgment to *H.W.* Three of her contributions were included in the Putnam volumes of selections from *H.W.*: "Winged Telegraphs" in *Home and Social Philosophy*, 2nd ser.; "Tahiti" and "The 'Mouth' of China" in *The World Here and There.*

Boase

The Belgian Lace-Makers *Miss Ross & W.H.W.* I, 320–23. June 29, 1850
Winged Telegraphs *W.H.W. & Miss Ross* I, 454–56. Aug. 3, 1850
A Very Old Soldier [chip] *Miss Ross & W.H.W.* I, 562–64. Sept. 7, 1850
Gossip about Brussels II, 42–45. Oct. 5, 1850
A Lunatic Asylum in Palermo II, 151–55. Nov. 9, 1850
Tahiti III, 301–305. June 21, 1851
The "Mouth" of China III, 348–53. July 5, 1851
Adventures of a Diamond [chip] IV, 66–67. Oct. 11, 1851

Rowan, Frederica Maclean |*Miss F. Rowan*|, 1814–1882, author and translator. Born in West Indies; as very young child, taken by her widowed mother to Copenhagen; later lived in Weimar and Paris, thereafter in London; became proficient in Scandinavian languages as well as in German and French. For many years was private secretary to Sir Francis Henry Goldsmid, M.P.; assisted him in his philanthropic work. During later years of her life was a Swedenborgian. Published *History of the French Revolution*, 1844; wrote, for Chambers's Library for Young People, a history of England and one of Scotland. Edited *Morceaux choisis des auteurs modernes*, 1847. Translated a novel from the Swedish of C. A. Wetterbergh and, from the German, the life of Friedrich Schleiermacher. Commissioned by Queen Victoria to translate selections from *Stunden der Andacht*, a devotional work generally attributed to J. H. D. Zschokke; the selections published in 2 vols., 1862, 1863. Contributed "A Norwegian Legend. From the Danish" to *A Welcome*, 1863. Translated various reports and pamphlets for the Foreign Office. Described by George Eliot, who met her in 1852, as "a learned lady in spectacles" (*Letters*, II, 9).

D.N.B.

Little Mari's Betrothal. From the Danish VI, 22–24. Sept. 18, 1852

Ruge, Arnold |*Dr. Ruge*|, 1802–1880, philosopher, political writer. Born in Bergen on island of Rügen. Studied at Halle, Jena, and Heidelberg. Became adherent of party that sought to create free, united Germany. Imprisoned, 1824–30, for his views and activities. Was for some years university professor. Co-founder, 1838, of *Hallische Jahrbücher für deutsche Wissenschaft und Kunst*, in which he discussed questions of the time from point of view of Hegelian philosophy; the periodical suppressed in 1843. In revolutionary movement of 1848, organized Extreme Left in Frankfurt Parliament. Forced to flee Germany; took refuge in London. There helped form European Democratic Committee, but soon withdrew from its activities. Settled in Brighton; resided there for remainder of his life, having become naturalized British citizen; supported himself by teaching and writing; at times lectured in London. In 1866 strongly supported Prussia against Austria, and in 1870 Germany against France. In last years of his life received pension from German government. Was important not only for philosophical and political writings, but for literary and aesthetic criticism; was also dramatist, poet, narrative writer. His *Gesammelte Schriften*, 10 vols., published 1846–48; his memoirs, *Aus früherer Zeit*, 1862–67. Mention of him in English writings appears in memoirs and letters, as in those of William James Linton, Gustave Strauss, George Eliot, and others.

Ruge's *H.W.* article gives statistics on Russian finances and military manpower, summarized from a report by "Mr. Donai," a "German gentleman in the United States, long resident in Russia." "Donai" is obviously a mistranscription of "Douai." The German gentleman is probably "the German editor, Dr. Douai," mentioned by Olmsted, *A Journey through Texas*, p. 187.

Allgemeine deutsche Biog.

The Russian Budget [chip]
XIII, 88–90. Feb. 9, 1856

Rushton, William Lowes |*Rushton, Ruston*|, barrister; son of Edward Rushton, stipendiary magistrate of Liverpool. Admitted at Gray's Inn, 1861; called to the bar, 1865; resided in Liverpool; member of Northern Circuit (*Men-at-the-Bar*). In 1858 published his first book, *Shakespeare a Lawyer*; its contents appropriated by Chief Justice Lord Campbell in *Shakespeare's Legal Acquirements*, 1859, without acknowledgment to Rushton. Continued the subject of Shakespeare and law in later writings: *Shakespeare's Legal Maxims, Shakespeare's Testamentary Language, Shakespeare Illustrated by the Lex Scripta.* His other books on Shakespeare were *Shakespeare Illustrated by Old Authors, Shakespeare's Euphuism, Shakespeare Hymn Tune Book, Shakespeare an Archer, Shakespeare and "The Arte of English Poesie."* Some of material in his books first appeared in *Archiv für das Studium der neueren Sprachen und Literaturen*; some in *N. & Q.* His books show extensive knowledge of early English law and wide reading in early English authors; commended by reviewers. Rushton's "valuable pamphlets on Shakespearean subjects" referred to by the Cowden Clarkes (*Recollections of Writers*, p. 112). Picture of him in Jaggard's *Shakespeare Bibliography.* Published *Rules and Cautions in English Grammar*, 1869; edited letters of his father: *Letters of a Templar*, 1903. Was corresponding member of Society for the Study of Modern Languages, Berlin; of State Historical Society of Wisconsin; and of Manchester Shakespeare Society.

The first item listed below deals with Old and Middle English; the second is based on Robert Ferguson's *English Surnames and Their Place in the Teutonic Family*, 1858; the third, using "honorificabilitudinitatibus" as starting point, protests against the imposition of scientific terminology on common things. The knowledge of language and philology displayed in the articles, as also the many references to early English writings, establishes the contributor as W. L. Rushton.

In his *H.W.* article "Mr. W. Shakespeare, Solicitor," Morley good-naturedly ridiculed the attempts of commentators to prove Shakespeare a member of one or another profession. Much of the article is based on Rushton's *Shakespeare a Lawyer.*

Allibone

Saxon-English *Rushton & Morley*
XVIII, 89–92. July 10, 1858
Names XVIII, 245–47. Aug. 28, 1858

Calling Bad Names
xviii, 332–34. Sept. 18, 1858

Russell, Charles William |*Dr. Russell, Maynooth*|, 1812–1880, theologian, president of St. Patrick's College, Maynooth. Educated at St. Patrick's College; ordained 1835. Professor of ecclesiastical history, St. Patrick's College; appointed president, 1857. Exercised considerable influence on Tractarian movement in England. Noted for his antiquarian research. Closely associated with Wiseman in editorship of *Dublin Review* from time of its founding to 1863; wrote numerous articles for the periodical. Contributed also to *Edin. Rev., North Brit. Rev.*, the *Month*, and other periodicals. Author of *The Life of Cardinal Mezzofanti*, 1858; co-editor of *A Report on the Carte Manuscripts in the Bodleian Library*, 1871; editor of *Calendar of Irish State Papers*, 1872–77.

Among Russell's contributions to the *Dublin Review* for 1843 was a highly complimentary review of Dickens's *Christmas Carol*: "... it is long since we read prose or poetry which pleased us more." Russell praised the *Carol* particularly for its "beautiful moral"; the only defect that he pointed out – and this a "negative" rather than a "positive" one – was that the spirits in the story centred their attention exclusively on the "creature comforts" of Christmas – "the beef, and poultry, and pudding," and made no reference to the Christian nature of the festival. The *Carol*, wrote Russell, "exhibits in a small scale almost all the beauties and all the defects" of Dickens's writings.

Russell's *H.W.* contribution is based on the Parliamentary Paper *Report of the Commissioners for the Investigation of Alleged Cases of Torture in the Madras Presidency*, 1855. His long and detailed article "The Use of Torture in India," written jointly with Major Smith (perh. Richard Baird Smith), *Edin. Rev.*, Jan. 1856, is based on the same *Report*.

D.N.B.

Rent Day round Madras
xiii, 276–79. April 5, 1856

Russell, Sir William Howard |*Russell*|, 1820–1907, war correspondent. Attended Trinity College, Dublin; took no degree. Admitted at Middle Temple, 1846; called to the bar, 1850; did not long pursue legal career. Became periodical contributor and newspaper reporter. For some time on staff of *Morning Chronicle*. In July 1850, sent by the *Times* to report Schleswig-Holstein War and later in same year to report a French naval review at Cherbourg. In 1854 sent to the Crimea; his Crimean letters in the *Times* established his fame as war correspondent. Served thereafter as correspondent during Indian Mutiny, American Civil War, Austro-Prussian War, Franco-Prussian War, South African War. In 1860 founded *Army and Navy Gazette*; edited it to time of his death. Contributed to *Cornhill* and other periodicals. Published some fifteen books, most of them reprintings or recastings of his journalistic work (*D.N.B.*). Hon. LL.D. Trinity College, 1856; knighted 1895; recipient of many medals and orders.

Russell did not join the staff of the *Daily News* at the time of its founding by Dickens, though apparently he had the opportunity to do so. Dickens "was not a good editor," wrote Russell; "he was the best reporter in London, and as a journalist he was nothing more. He had no political instincts or knowledge, and was ignorant of and indifferent to what are called 'Foreign Affairs' " (Atkins, *Life of Sir William Howard Russell*, i, 58). Russell and Dickens became good friends. Dickens was present at the farewell supper given for Russell on his leaving England as a foreign correspondent in 1854. He was among the friends who gave Russell advice and encouragement on the Crimean lectures that Russell delivered in 1857. Dickens attended one of Russell's rehearsals and was a guest at the dinner that Russell gave to mark his advent as a lecturer. In 1858, when Russell was in India, Dickens wrote to thank him for his kindness to Walter Dickens, then in the army in India. It was with "unspeakable pleasure," wrote Dickens, that he would see Russell at home in England again. As for Russell's writings as war correspondent, "Everybody talks about your letters and everybody praises them," wrote Dickens. "No one says, or can say, more of them than they deserve."

Men of the Time, 1856, states that Russel was "a contributor to 'Household Words.'" (Later editions omit the statement.) Allibone also records Russell as a *H.W.* contributor. The two articles that the Office Book assigns to Russell are based on his stay in Belgium and in Italy; they are appropriate as his writing, since Russell had been several times on the Continent by 1852, the date at which the articles appeared. In the first article Russell stated that his stay in Belgium was in connection with "a mission" that required his sending "frequent despatches to London the instant they were written."

Russell was mentioned in several *H.W.* articles. In one of the instalments (Nov. 15, 1856) of his "Journey Due North," Sala referred to an account of the Moscow coronation illuminations as written "by the Man who fought the Battle of England in the Crimea, better and more bravely than the whole brilliant staff who have been decorated with the order of the bath." In "A Side Wind from Due North" (Jan. 10, 1857), he corrected the statement, explaining that the account had been written by Mr. John Murphy of the *Daily News*, not by "Mr. William Russell, the distinguished correspondent of the Times newspaper." Dickens, in "The Best Authority," ridiculing the misinformed informant who always had access to secret documents and to private information on all matters of national and international concern, mentioned this "Best Authority" as having been in the Russian lines in the Crimea and in the English camp and as "always coming home to put MR. RUSSELL right." John Capper, in "A Very Black Act," stated that in exposing in his Indian newspaper the true state of affairs in India – the maladministration of the East India Co., the wavering irresolution of the British governor-general, the official truckling to incipient mutineers among the natives, "the cruel neglect of our own British soldiery" – he had had "some faint hope of emulating in a humble sphere and in a limited manner, the usefulness of William Russell, of the Times."

D.N.B. suppl. 1901–1911

Belgian Briskness VI, 70–72. Oct. 2, 1852
Yourself at Turin VI, 189–92. Nov. 6, 1852

S

St. George, Mrs. Shale; Mrs. St. George: *See* George, Frances (Southwell)

St. John, Bayle |*Bayle St. John, St. John, B. St. John*|, 1822–1859, author; second son of James Augustus St. John (below). Until 1839, studied to become artist. For several years assisted his father in research for *The History of the Manners and Customs of Ancient Greece*, 1842. Contributed to *Sunday Times, Penny Magazine, Fraser's* (his "De Re Vehiculari" in *Fraser's*, 1842, has been misattributed to William Maginn), *Foreign Quart. Rev., Chambers's*, and other periodicals. For a time, Paris correspondent for *Daily Telegraph.* Travelled in Egypt and studied Arabic; lived at various times in France and in Italy. His books based on his travel and residence abroad included *Adventures in the Libyan Desert*, 1849; *Two Years' Residence in a Levantine Family*, 1850; *The Turks in Europe*, 1853; *Purple Tints of Paris*, 1854; *The Subalpine Kingdom*, 1856. Wrote also works of fiction, a biography of Montaigne. Helped found Ethnological Society and Syro-Egyptian Society.

In a letter to Wills, Aug. 24, 1854, from Boulogne (MS Huntington Library), Dickens wrote that he was returning the proof of "the nice little Eastern story"; the date of the letter indicates that the reference is probably to St. John's "The Betrothed Children." Dickens did not see the proof of "The Flying Artist" before the paper was in print; it was objectionable, he wrote to Wills, for reasons that he would later explain; "Notes from the Lebanon" Dickens dismissed as trivial (to Wills, Aug. 31, 1851; Aug. 28, 1854: MSS Huntington Library); "A Tale of a Pocket Archipelago," "as a story," he thought "almost too blear-eyed to fall into the ranks" (to Wills, April 27, 1856).

Morley's *H.W.* article "A Dip in the Nile" was based on St. John's *Village Life in Egypt;* Mrs. Linton's "A French Pepys," on his abridged translation of the *Memoirs* of Saint-Simon. In his article "Doctor Veron's Time," Sala suggested French social life of the First Empire as the subject for a book by "the ingenious author of 'Purple Tints of Paris.' "

Of the items listed below as reprinted, "A Syrian Legend" is assigned in the Office Book merely to "St. John"; two of the items not reprinted – "A Border of the Black Sea" and "Love and Self-Love," both published in 1854 – are also so assigned. Both items are obviously by Bayle St. John, who by 1854 had become a fairly regular *H.W.* contributor, rather than by his father, whose name is specifically recorded for only one item (in 1852). "A Border of the Black Sea" continues the discussion of Bulgaria begun in "Varna," which item is assigned to Bayle St. John. Bayle St. John may also be the author of "Old Cairo and Its Mosque," assigned in the Office Book merely to "St. John." See J. A. St. John (below).

Harper's reprinted eight of St. John's *H.W.* contributions, without acknowledgment to *H.W.*

D.N.B.

The Dealer in Wisdom
III, 507–511. Aug. 23, 1851
The Flying Artist III, 557–61. Sept. 6, 1851
*The Legend of the Weeping Chamber
IV, 296–99. Dec. 20, 1851
Paradise Lost IV, 455–56. Jan. 31, 1852
The Man from the West
V, 145–49. May 1, 1852
The Merry Men of Cairo
V, 602–606. Sept. 11, 1852
The Whispering Tree
VII, 33–36. March 12, 1853
*The Legend of Bucharest
VII, 503–504. July 23, 1853
Something Divine
VII, 557–60. Aug. 13, 1853
*The Merchant's Heart
VIII, 54–57. Sept. 17, 1853
Moldo-Wallachia
VIII, 84–88. Sept. 24, 1853
Bucharest VIII, 104–108. Oct. 1, 1853
The Gipsy Slaves of Wallachia
VIII, 139–42. Oct. 8, 1853
A Wallachian Squire
VIII, 228–30. Nov. 5, 1853
Turks in Bulgaria
VIII, 257–59. Nov. 12, 1853
A Little Republic
VIII, 284–86. Nov. 19, 1853
Protégés of the Czar
VIII, 343–45. Dec. 10, 1853
Varna *Bayle St. John & W.H.W.*
VIII, 373–77. Dec. 17, 1853
A Border of the Black Sea
VIII, 495–99. Jan. 21, 1854
*Miriam the Shadow
IX, 81–85. March 11, 1854
Love and Self-Love
IX, 181–85. April 8, 1854
Out in the Desert
IX, 194–97. April 15, 1854
*A Syrian Legend
IX, 233–36. April 22, 1854
*The Little Flower
IX, 393–98. June 10, 1854
The Oriental Merchant
X, 46–48. Aug. 26, 1854
*The Betrothed Children
X, 124–29. Sept. 23, 1854
Notes from the Lebanon
X, 162–65. Sept. 30, 1854
Conscript Sons X, 213–16. Oct. 14, 1854
*The Secret of the Well
XI, 4–10. Feb. 3, 1855
The Black Sea Five Centuries Ago
XI, 62–67. Feb. 17, 1855
*The Sister of the Spirits
XI, 124–29. March 10, 1855
*The Story of a King
XI, 402–406. May 26, 1855
Doctor Dubois XI, 429–32. June 2, 1855
Brides for Sale XII, 41–45. Aug. 11, 1855
*Guzla XII, 545–50. Jan. 5, 1856
*The Legend of Argis [chip]
XII, 561–63. Jan. 12, 1856
A Tale of a Pocket Archipelago
XIII, 523–27. June 14, 1856
Romantic Breach of Promise
XVI, 260–62. Sept. 12, 1857
Sand and Roses XVI, 548–52. Dec. 5, 1857
Over the Way XIX, 594–96. May 21, 1859

*Repr. as *Legends of the Christian East. By Bayle St. John.* London: Addey and Co., 1856. Pub. in *H.W.* acknowledged.

St. John, James Augustus | *St. John, J. A. St. John*|, 1801–1875, author and traveller. Educated at village school in Carmarthenshire; with help of a clergyman, became good classical scholar and linguist. In 1824, named assistant editor of *Oriental Herald,* London; co-founder, 1827, of London *Weekly Review.* Later wrote letters on politics in *Sunday Times* and leaders in *Daily Telegraph.* Contributed to annuals, and to *Athenaeum, Bentley's Misc., Sharpe's,* and other periodicals. Lived at various times on the Continent; travelled extensively in north Africa and in the East. His books based on this residence and travel included *Journal of a Residence in Normandy,* 1831; *Egypt, and Mohammed Ali,* 1834; *Isis: an Egyptian Pilgrimage, 1853; There and Back Again in Search of Beauty,* 1853. Wrote biography of Louis Napoleon and of Sir Walter Ralegh; also historical and other works; five works of fiction. Edited *Religio Medici, Pilgrim's Progress,* Milton's prose works, and other English classics.

"Old Cairo and Its Mosque," listed below, is assigned in the Office Book merely to "St. John." It may be by either J. A. St. John or Bayle St. John (above). The payment notation – "Sent by W.H.W. to J. A. St. John" – may mean that J. A. St. John was author of the article. Usually, however, for items of single authorship, the Office Book states the name of the person to whom payment was made only when that person is other than the author. Wills may have sent to J. A. St. John, who was then presumably in England, payment for an article by his son, who (according to *D.N.B.*) was living in Paris at the time that he began writing for *H.W.* Other items assigned merely to "St. John" are by Bayle St. John.

"Old Cairo and Its Mosque" was included in the Putnam volume of selections from *H.W.*: *The World Here and There,* 1852.

D.N.B.

Old Cairo and Its Mosque
III, 332–34. June 28, 1851
A Chinaman's Ball
V, 331–32. June 19, 1852

Sala, George Augustus Henry |*Sala*|, 1828–1895, journalist. Attended school in Paris and in London; thereafter received some instruction in drawing. Earned living for a time as scene-painter, illustrator, engraver. For some months edited a halfpenny weekly. With intent of becoming a journalist, studied back numbers of *Quart. Rev.* and *Examiner.* In 1851 became contributor to *H.W.* In 1857 began his long connection with *Daily Telegraph*; sent by the paper as "special correspondent" to the U.S., the Continent, and elsewhere. Contributed to *Illus. Times, Cornhill, Illus. London News, Belgravia,* and other periodicals. For a short time editor of *Welcome Guest*; of *Temple Bar,* 1860–66. Brought out *Sala's Journal,* 1892–94. Published some forty works, fiction and non-fiction, almost all of them reprinted from his periodical writings; also various ephemeral pieces. In 1895 granted Civil List pension of £100 a year. Regarded by some of his contemporaries as the "great" Sala, the "brilliant" Sala, the man of "commanding talent"; by Matthew Arnold (*Friendship's Garland*), as the "rowdy Philistine."

In submitting his first contribution to *H.W.*, Sala wrote Dickens a letter, reminding him that "he had known me when I was a boy, and that he had been very kind to me and mine" (*Things I Have Seen,* I, 67). The allusion is to Dickens's acquaintance with Sala's mother, a singer and actress, who had played a role in two of Dickens's plays; through her, young Sala had met Dickens. Of all the writers who first became known through their connection with *H.W.*, it was Sala, wrote Forster, in whom Dickens had "the strongest personal interest" (*Life,* Book VI, sect. iv). Sala wrote of Dickens: "I revered the writer and I loved the man"; but for Dickens's friendship and encouragement, he stated, "I should never have been a journalist or a writer of books" (*Life and Adventures,* p. 305; *Charles Dickens,* p. vi). The two men were not intimate friends, though Sala was frequently invited to the dinners held at the *H.W.* office, and, during his residences in Paris, he was often in the company of Dickens there. On Dickens's death, Sala wrote for the *Telegraph* a memorial sketch of Dickens, later enlarged and published in booklet form. In it, he gave lavish praise to Dickens's writings and predicted for Dickens "perpetuity of renown" among the greatest literary masters. In other of his books that touched on Dickens and his writings, Sala's comments were not uncritical. *Pictures from Italy,* for instance, he mentioned as illustrating Dickens's contempt for foreigners and his ignorance of art, and *A Tale of Two Cities* as "a dramatic but very superficial picture of French life and manners" at the time of the Revolution (*Things I Have Seen,* I, 104–105, 108). Sala was among those who knew of Dickens's relationship with Ellen Ternan. He held that the matter was no concern of the public. According to Thomas Wright (*Life of Charles Dickens,* p. 283), he was "furious" when he learned in 1893 that Wright was collecting material for a life of Dickens that would reveal certain circumstances of Dickens's later years that Forster had not revealed.

Sala's connection with *H.W.* began with Dickens's enthusiastic acceptance in 1851 of "The Key of the Street." Dickens found it "a very remarkable piece of description"; he instructed Wills to ask for additional articles and himself suggested topics for Sala to write on. "There is nobody about us whom we can use, in his way, more advantageously than this young man" (to Wills, Aug. 13, Sept. 27, 1851). For the following five years Sala contributed regularly to *H.W.* Dickens found some of his papers "capital," "very good," "excellent"; in others he found subjects inadequately treated and tastelessly handled. The Office Book records Dickens's initials jointly with Sala's name for but one item (for another – "How I Went to Sea" – Dickens's initials are entered, then marked out); actually, Dickens made changes in many of Sala's contributions. He cut passages and compressed material; sometimes he added material; he corrected misstatements; he altered comments that might shock readers; he changed phraseology. The "Dickensian touches," admitted Sala, were "always for the better," but they gave him, he wrote, the undeserved reputation of being a slavish Dickens imitator (*Things I Have Seen,* I, 78–79).

Dickens on one occasion instructed Wills to be generous to Sala in the matter of payment: "Don't run him too close in the money way. I can't bear the thought of making anything like a hard bargain with him" (Aug. 7, 1854). The Office Book record, for items for which payment is recorded, is that for about forty items in the regular numbers Sala was paid somewhat more than the standard rate and for about forty items somewhat less; for items in the Christmas numbers he was paid, as was the custom, more than the standard rate. No payment to Sala is recorded for items contributed during about six months of 1854; during those months, payment was evidently on another basis than that of payment for individual items.

Of the items that Sala wrote for *H.W.* during his first two and a half years as contributor (during which time his contributions were paid for on an individual basis), more than half are marked as paid for in advance. On one occasion, when such payments amounted to twenty guineas, Dickens "told Wills delicately to make [Sala] a present" of the amount; on another occasion he wiped from the slate arrears of some seventy pounds (Forster, *Life,* Book VI, sect. iv; Sala, *Things I Have Seen,* I, 120). From August 1854, the Office Book records no further payments as made to Sala in advance, though Dickens made him at least one such payment in Jan. 1856. Dickens was much concerned at that time about Sala's dilatoriness in sending in copy (to Wills, Jan. 10, Jan. 14, 1856).

Later in the same year, Sala proposed that Dickens send him to Russia to gather material for a series of papers on Russian life and manners (*A Journey Due North*); Dickens agreed to the proposal. Sala's dispute, on his return, about travelling expenses and his delay in completing the stipulated number of papers led to a bitter quarrel with Dickens. Sala was informed that his services were dispensed with and that permission to publish the Russian papers in book form was refused.

In 1858 Dickens and Sala again became

friends, and Sala later contributed to *A.Y.R.* For that periodical Dickens accepted from him the novel *Quite Alone*; when Sala delayed overlong in sending in the final chapters, Dickens had the serial completed by Andrew Halliday.

Some of Sala's *H.W.* contributions were much overpraised by his contemporaries. Thackeray thought "The Key of the Street" "almost the best magazine paper that ever was written" (*Letters*, III, 470–71). Vizetelly called "Colonel Quagg's Conversion" "one of the most amusing short stories in the language" (*Glances Back through Seventy Years*, II, 111–12); the Marquis of Stafford and some of his friends, according to Yates (*Recollections and Experiences*, p. 213), "were loud in praise" of the same tedious story; and Swinburne found it highly amusing (*Letters*, I, 64).

Six of Sala's *H.W.* contributions were reprinted in whole or part in *Harper's*, one of them acknowledged to *H.W.*, and one – "What Christmas Is in the Company of John Doe" – credited to Dickens. "Liberty, Equality, Fraternity, and Musketry" was included in the Putnam volume of selections from *H.W.*: *Home and Social Philosophy*, 2nd ser. "The Key of the Street" Sala found included in a volume titled *Nouveaux contes de Charles Dickens*.

D.N.B.

The Key of the Street
III, 565–72. Sept. 6, 1851
Down Whitechapel Way
IV, 126–31. Nov. 1, 1851
Jack Alive in London
IV, 254–60. Dec. 6, 1851
Getting Up a Pantomime [lead]
IV, 289–96. Dec. 20, 1851
Things Departed
IV, 397–401. Jan. 17, 1852
City Spectres [lead]
IV, 481–85. Feb. 14, 1852
Travels in Cawdor Street
IV, 517–21. Feb. 21, 1852
Houses to Let V, 5–11. March 20, 1852
Phases of "Public" Life
V, 224–30. May 22, 1852
V, 250–55. May 29, 1852
VI, 101–105. Oct. 16, 1852
Cheerily, Cheerily! [lead]
VI, 25–31. Sept. 25, 1852
How I Went to Sea [lead]
VI, 49–55. Oct. 2, 1852
The Sporting World
VI, 133–39. Oct. 23, 1852
Day-Break VI, 204–208. Nov. 13, 1852
Perfidious Patmos [lead]
VII, 25–29. March 12, 1853
Leicester Square
VII, 63–67. March 19, 1853
My Swan [lead]
VII, 73–76. March 26, 1853
Powder Dick and His Train
VII, 235–40. May 7, 1853
Arcadia VII, 376–82. June 18, 1853
Down Whitechapel, Far Away
VII, 569–73. Aug. 13, 1853
Fashion [lead] VIII, 193–96. Oct. 29, 1853
The Secrets of the Gas [lead]
IX, 45–48. March 4, 1854
The Bottle of Hay [lead]
IX, 69–75. March 11, 1854
Where Are They?
IX, 152–58. April 1, 1854
Tattyboys Rents
IX, 297–304. May 13, 1854
Strollers at Dumbledowndeary
IX, 374–80. June 3, 1854
Tattyboys Renters IX 466–71. July 1, 1854
The Musical World
IX, 561–67. July 29, 1854
A Little More Harmony [lead]
X, 1–5. Aug. 19, 1854
Music in Paving Stones
X, 37–43. Aug. 26, 1854
Yellowknights XII, 249–52. Oct. 13, 1855
Houseless and Hungry [lead]
XIII, 121–26. Feb. 23, 1856
Gibbet Street [lead]
XIII, 193–96. March 15, 1856

The 32 items repr. as *Gaslight and Daylight, with Some London Scenes They Shine Upon. By George Augustus Sala.* London: Chapman & Hall, 1859. Pub. in *H.W.* not acknowledged.

Liberty, Equality, Fraternity, and Musketry [lead] IV, 313–18. Dec. 27, 1851
Monsieur Gogo's IV, 445–49. Jan. 31, 1852
The Great Invasion [lead]
V, 69–73. April 10, 1852
Open-Air Entertainments [lead]
V, 165–69. May 8, 1852

Four Stories v, 336–42. June 26, 1852
Cities in Plain Clothes
v, 417–22. July 17, 1852
Little Blue Mantle [lead]
v, 429–31. July 24, 1852
Ten Minutes "Cross Country"
v, 464–66. July 31, 1852
A Handful of Foreign Money [lead]
v, 573–77. Sept. 4, 1852
Sunday Morning vi, 81–84. Oct. 9, 1852
Time and the Hour
vi, 356–58. Dec. 25, 1852
My Man. A Sum [lead]
vi, 385–88. Jan. 8, 1853
Roger the Monk
vii, 305–309. May 28, 1853
Shops vii, 405–408. June 25, 1853
The Length of the Quays
vii, 582–86. Aug. 20, 1853
An Irish Stew vii, 617–20. Aug. 27, 1853
A Dead Secret viii, 27–36. Sept. 10, 1853
Slang [lead] viii, 73–78. Sept. 24, 1853
Always United viii, 220–25. Nov. 5, 1853
Mine Inn viii, 238–40. Nov. 5, 1853
Case of Real Distress [lead]
viii, 457–60. Jan. 14, 1854
The Complaint of the Old Magician
viii, 540–46. Feb. 4, 1854
The Present Moment
ix, 100–102. March 18, 1854
The Faculty ix, 588–93. Aug. 5, 1854
The Dodderham Worthy
x, 9–12. Aug. 19, 1854
Sunday Out [lead] x, 73–77. Sept. 9, 1854
Sunday Tea-Gardens [lead]
x, 145–48. Sept. 30, 1854
Mars a la Mode [lead]
x, 193–96. Oct. 14, 1854
The Compassionate Broker
x, 199–203. Oct. 14, 1854
Numbers of People
x, 221–28. Oct. 21, 1854
Bullfrog x, 333–36. Nov. 18, 1854
Second-Hand Sovereigns
x, 511–16. Jan. 13, 1855
Doors [lead] x, 529–33. Jan. 20, 1855
Yadacé xi, 319–23. May 5, 1855
Mr. Philip Stubbes [lead]
xi, 553–58. July 14, 1855
County Guy xi, 599–600. July 21, 1855
Poor Angelica xii, 87–93. Aug. 25, 1855
Last Words with Philip Stubbes
xii, 117–20. Sept. 1, 1855
Sunday Music xii, 261–64. Oct. 13, 1855
The Great Hotel Question [chap. i = lead]
xiii, 97–103. Feb. 16, 1856,
and the 2 following nos.
English Hotels xiii, 172–78. March 8, 1856
The Dalgetty Race [lead]
xiii, 265–69. April 5, 1856

The 42 items repr. as *Looking at Life; or, Thoughts and Things. By George Augustus Sala.* London: Routledge, Warne, and Routledge, 1860. Pub. in *H.W.* acknowledged.

Old Clothes! [lead]
v, 93–98. April 17, 1852
First Fruits [lead] *Sala & C.D.*
v, 189–92. May 15, 1852
Our Doubles v, 388–91. July 10, 1852
Shadows:
Day and Night v, 450–52. July 24, 1852
The Shadow of a Dutch Painter
vi, 6–10. Sept. 18, 1852
The Captain's Prisoner
vi, 469–74. Jan. 29, 1853
The Kingdom of Reconciled Impossibilities
vii, 102–105. April 2, 1853
Want Places [lead]
vii, 601–608. Aug. 27, 1853
More Places Wanted
viii, 156–62. Oct. 15, 1853
Little Children [lead]
viii, 289–93. Nov. 26, 1853
Twenty Miles x, 68–72. Sept. 2, 1854
Doctor Pantologos
x, 101–106. Sept. 16, 1854
Demetrius the Diver
x, 165–68. Sept. 30, 1854
The Golden Calf x, 437–41. Dec. 23, 1854
Colonel Quagg's Conversion
x, 459–65. Dec. 30, 1854
Old Ladies [lead]
xi, 97–101. March 3, 1855
Poetry on the Railway
xi, 414–18. June 2, 1855
The Metamorphosed Pagoda
xii, 444–50. Dec. 8, 1855
Beef [lead] xiii, 49–52. Feb. 2, 1856
Little Saint Zita xiii, 91–96. Feb. 9, 1856
Further Travels in Search of Beef
xiii, 306–312. April 12, 1856

The 21 items repr. as *Dutch Pictures; with Some Sketches in the Flemish Manner. By George Augustus Sala.* London: Tinsley Brothers, 1861. Preface states that "the majority" of the sketches appeared originally in *H.W.* All of them appeared there.

Stone Pictures v, 176–81. May 8, 1852
Dumbledowndeary
v, 312–17. June 19, 1852
Up a Court v, 508–512. Aug. 14, 1852
English Milords vii, 270–73. May 21, 1853
Sir John Barleycorn at Home
vii, 488–92. July 23, 1853
Flags to Furl [lead]
vii, 529–33. Aug. 6, 1853
Legs ix, 209–212. April 15, 1854
A Tour in Bohemia
ix, 495–500. July 8, 1854
Madame Busque's x, 393–96. Dec. 9, 1854
The Great Red Book
x, 404–408. Dec. 9, 1854
Chambers in the Temple
xi, 132–40. March 10, 1855
Bright Chanticleer
xi, 204–209. March 31, 1855
Birthdays xi, 238–40. April 7, 1855
Unfortunate James Daley
xi, 582–84. July 21, 1855
Waiter! xiii, 237–40. March 22, 1856

The 15 items repr. in *After Breakfast; or, Pictures Done with a Quill. By George Augustus Sala.* 2 vols. London: Tinsley Brothers, 1864. Pub. in *H.W.* acknowledged.

The Last Crusader
vii, 13–17. March 5, 1853
An Exploded Magazine
viii, 20–24. Sept. 3, 1853

The 2 items repr. in *Accepted Addresses, By George Augustus Sala.* London: Tinsley Brothers, 1862. Pub. in *H.W.* not acknowledged.

A Journey Due North [1st instalment = lead] xiv, 265–76. Oct. 4, 1856, and 21 following nos., ending xv, 249–54. March 14, 1857. No. of Jan. 10 contains only a "chip," not repr.; no. of Feb. 7 contains no instalment.

Repr. as *A Journey Due North; Being Notes of a Residence in Russia, in the Summer of 1856. By George Augustus Sala.* London: Richard Bentley, 1858. Pub. in *H.W.* not acknowledged.

The Foreign Invasion
iv, 60–64. Oct. 11, 1851
What Christmas Is in the Company of John Doe Extra No. for Christmas 1851, pp. 11–16
A Cup of Coffee
v, 562–66. Aug. 28, 1852
Some Compliments of the Season [lead] *Thomas & Sala*
vi, 313–17. Dec. 18, 1852
Legal Houses of Call
vii, 253–57. May 14, 1853
Something to Drink
vii, 430–32. July 2, 1853
A Day after Battle Fair
vii, 469–72. July 16, 1853
Fairyland in 'Fifty-four [lead] *W.H.W. & Sala* viii, 313–17. Dec. 3, 1853
Over the Way's Story
Another Round of Stories (Christmas 1853), pp. 9–17
The Girl I Left behind Me
ix, 161–64. April 1, 1854
A Canny Book ix, 249–53. April 29, 1854
Some Amenities of War
ix, 521–24. July 15, 1854
The Roving Englishman: The Sea Captain and His Ship *Murray & Sala*
ix, 606–608. Aug. 12, 1854
Justice Is Satisfied [chip]
x, 83–84. Sept. 9, 1854
Play x, 357–60. Nov. 25, 1854
The Second Poor Traveller
Seven Poor Travellers (Christmas 1854), pp. 10–16
The Fifth Poor Traveller
Seven Poor Travellers (Christmas 1854), pp. 26–29
Mr. Pope's Friend xi, 43–48. Feb. 10, 1855
Convicts, English and French
xi, 85–88. Feb. 24, 1855
Colonel Grunpeck and Mr. Parkinson
xi, 254–59. April 14, 1855
Gambling xi, 280–86. April 21, 1855
French Soldiers in Camp *Sala & Dixon*
xi, 483–88. June 23, 1855
Curiosities of London
xi, 495–502. June 23, 1855
Cats and Dogs xi, 516–19. June 30, 1855
Cries from the Past
xi, 606–609. July 28, 1855
Doctoring Begins at Home
xii, 68–72. Aug. 18, 1855
Two Dinner Failures
xii, 164–68. Sept. 15, 1855
A Golden Ass xiii, 285–88. April 5, 1856
Doctor Veron's Time
xiii, 334–36. April 19, 1856
All Up with Everything [lead]
xiii, 337–39. April 26, 1856

The Omnibus Revolution
XIII, 561–64. June 28, 1856
A Side Wind from Due North [chip]
XV, 32. Jan. 10, 1857

Samuel, John |*John Samuel*, Philadelphia|, 1829–1913, lawyer. Born in Philadelphia. Attended Wesleyan Univ. in Connecticut, and Univ. of Pennsylvania. Admitted to Philadelphia bar, 1850; had distinguished legal career of more than sixty years. Contributed to periodicals articles on legal and literary subjects; during Civil War, wrote editorials for the *Age* on matters of national concern; as a Democrat, was opposed to Lincoln's policies (Barratt, *Memorial of John Samuel*).

The Office Book records payment for Samuel's article as sent to B. Samuel, Esq., 31 Throgmorton St.; Kelly's *Post Office London Directory*, 1857, lists at that address Bunford Samuel and Isaac Bunford Samuel, stockbrokers. They were relatives of the American Samuel, whose father was of English Jewish ancestry and one of whose sons was named Bunford.

Samuel's *H.W.* article describes the life of a small Virginia town as he saw it during the three days that he spent there – a life so "new and curious to him" that he thinks it will be of interest also to "our cousins across the ocean."

Martin's Bench and Bar

Jemima Court-House
XV, 285–88. March 21, 1857

Satchell, Thomas |*Mr. Tom Satchell, Satchell*|, *d.* 1887, naturalist. For some years edited *Angler's Note-Book and Naturalist's Record.* Compiled *Provisional Index to a Glossary of Fish Names*, pamphlet priv. printed, 1879. Edited, from a MS of about 1450, a work attributed to Dame Juliana Berners (or Bernes or Barnes), the *Treatyse of Fysshynge with an Angle*, priv. printed, 1883, for presentation to members of English Dialect Society; in 1884 brought out edition of a sixteenth-century work by Leonard Mascall, *A Booke of Fishing with Hooke and Line*; in both books acknowledged linguistic help of Prof. W. W. Skeat. Collaborated with Thomas Westwood on *Bibliotheca Piscatoria*, 1883, an enlarged version of Westwood's original 1861–69 bibliography; contributed notes and additions to Westwood's 1883 edition of *The Chronicle of the "Compleat Angler."*

According to his *H.W.* articles, Satchell spent three years in British Guiana; he mentions specifically being there in 1848. The object of his expedition was evidently the study of flora and fauna and the collection of specimens.

Harper's reprinted three of Satchell's *H.W.* contributions, without acknowledgment to *H.W.*

Brit. Mus. Cat.

A New Phase of Bee-Life
II, 353–55. Jan. 4, 1851
A Spider in Disguise
III, 46–48. April 5, 1851
A Bird-Hunting Spider [chip]
IV, 45–46. Oct. 4, 1851
Animal and Vegetable Disguises [chip]
IV, 92–94. Oct. 18, 1851
Anecdotes of Monkeys [chip]
IV, 357–58. Jan. 3, 1852

Scoble, Sir Andrew Richard |*A. R.* [2nd initial unclear] *Scoble*, 1 Brick Court|, 1831–1916, Q.C.; advocate-general, Bombay. Kelly's *Post Office London Directory*, 1858, lists 1 Brick Court as the address of Andrew Richard Scoble, barrister. Scoble was admitted at Lincoln's Inn, 1852; called to the bar, 1856. Q.C., 1876; advocate-general and member of Legislative Council of Bombay, 1870–77; bencher, 1879. K.C.S.I. During 1850s published translation of various of Guizot's historical works, and of various writings of Lamartine, Mignet, and Mérimée; also translation of *Mémoires* of Philippe de Comines, prefaced by life of the historian. Edited *Poetical Works* of James Russell Lowell, 1853.

Scoble's *H.W.* contribution is the kindly told life story of a harmless Italian madman who spent much time in the reading room of the Bibliothèque Royale in Paris, becoming "well known to the habitués" of the library. Scoble, obviously, was among the readers at the Bibilothèque.

Allibone; *Men-at-the-Bar*

A Touching (and Touched) Character
XVI, 407–408. Oct. 24, 1857

Sharp. *Not identified.* The contributor's article is motivated by "the great events of the last few weeks" in the Crimea, i.e., the siege of Sebastopol, the battles of Balaklava and Inkerman. It gives detailed information on military units, their equipment, munition, position in line of battle, etc., and explains occasional military terms that might not be familiar to the general reader. The writer draws his information from various sources: a "practical work" compiled by "several experienced Artillery officers," John Henry Lefroy's *Handbook for Field Service*, certain instructions issued by the French Minister of War, and, as seems probable, his own military experience. The article contains two quotations from Shakespeare.

Field Service X, 339–44. Nov. 25, 1854

Shiel. *Not identified.* The writer gives an account of the quicksilver mine at Almadén, Spain, which he has visited. Payment for the contribution made in cash.

Quicksilver VII, 615–17. Aug. 27, 1853

Shillinglaw, John Joseph, prob. |*Mr. Shillinglaw*|, 1830–1905, public official, historian. F.R.G.S. Born in London; studied, 1844–52, under assistant hydrographer to the Navy; abandoned studies in 1852 to accompany his father to Australia. Held various official posts in Melbourne; longest service as registrar of seamen and shipping master for the Port of Melbourne, 1856–69; in that capacity published *The Australian Shipmaster's Guide*, 1858. Was important for his research in early Australian history. In 1870 acquired the *Colonial Monthly Magazine* to serve as repository for information on this subject. Discovered various important historical documents, which were published, under his editorship, by the Victorian Government, as *Historical Records of Port Phillip*, 1879. Earlier had published *A Narrative of Arctic Discovery*, 1850; had edited from Capt. Thomas Musgrave's journals the account of the wreck of the *Grafton*, published as *Castaway on the Auckland Isles*, 1865.

The item listed below discusses the need for better life-saving equipment on vessels and a better system of beacons; it urges Government attention to these matters. The subject is appropriate to the interests of John Joseph Shillinglaw. According to the *Australian Ency.*, Shillinglaw wrote "a good deal" for the British as well as for the Australian press.

Australian Ency.

The Preservation of Life from Shipwreck
W.H.W. & Mr. Shillinglaw
I, 452–54. Aug. 3, 1850

Siddons, Miss. *Not identified.* In the Office Book, Meredith is recorded as author of "The Burial of the Old Year"; his name is marked out and substituted by that of Miss Siddons.

VERSE
The Burial of the Old Year
II, 348. Jan. 4, 1851

Siddons, Joachim Heyward |*J. Stoqueler, Stocqueler*|, 1801?–1885, journalist and compiler under his own name and under pseudonym "J. H. Stocqueler"; appears in biographical compilations under pseudonym.

In answer to an inquiry from the Library of Congress, Siddons's son, Frederick Lincoln Siddons (1864–1931), associate justice of the Supreme Court of the District of Columbia, wrote to the librarian, Feb. 19, 1917: "... my father's full name was Joachim Heyward Siddons, and as I remember the date of his birth, it was July 21, 1801. I think in his earlier life he frequently used as a pseudonym an anglicized form of his mother's name, and in that form as you have it 'J. H. Stocqueler'; but he did not always use the pseudonym in writing.

"My impression is, although I have no personal knowledge, that his father and mother had separated, she returning with her children to England, my father and a brother and sister having been born in India, and it may be, although I do not know it, of course, that she may have gone back to her maiden name in the anglicized form that I have mentioned."

According to his *Memoirs*, Siddons attended an academy in Camden Town; enlisted, as "Stocqueler," in military service of East India Co.; stationed six months at Chatham barracks; sent with his detachment to Bombay, 1819; served as army office clerk; at about age twenty-four purchased discharge from army, having become interested in journalism; was proprietor and editor of various newspapers and sporting magazines in Bombay and Calcutta, among them the Calcutta *Englishman*; made two visits to England before his final departure from India in 1843. In England, had some connection with theatre as writer of farces and as actor and manager; lectured on India and on the Crimean War; became connected with various periodicals, e.g., *Atlas*, *Court Journal*, *United Service Gazette*. Sent to the U.S. in 1860 to spread favourable publicity for the vessel *Great Eastern*; gave lectures and readings; wrote for New York *Evening Post* during Civil War; returned to England in 1864. Author or compiler of some thirty works: books of travel, military and historical handbooks, works on India, a life of Wellington, a history of the U.S., a Shakespeare cyclopaedia. His *Memoirs of a Journalist*, first published in the *Times of India*, then in book form, 1873, was suppressed (*D.N.B.*).

His association with Dickens Siddons recounted in his *Memoirs* and in "Souvenirs of Charles Dickens," *Wood's Illustrated Household Magazine* (Newburgh, N.Y.), 1875; the "Souvenirs" is reprinted by J. A. Carter in "Memories of 'Charley Wag,'" *Dickensian*, Autumn 1966. In the two accounts, Siddons recorded that while stationed at Chatham he had become acquainted with Dickens when Dickens was a young boy; that while he was in India, Dickens sent him a copy of *Pickwick*, accompanied by a letter recalling their early association; and that, on his furloughs from India, he visited Dickens. Late in 1845, Siddons must have written to Dickens concerning the *Daily News*. Carter's article mentions an undated letter from Dickens to him, explaining the editorial policy of the forthcoming newspaper. Among the public readings that Siddons delivered in New York was one of Dickens's readings – the Bardell-Pickwick trial scene; that, combined with his reading of scenes from Shakespeare, resulted in his being asked to become "Professor of Elocution and English Literature" at Columbia College (*Memoirs*, p. 247).

Writing about the sources of information on the East and on the Crimean War available to Englishmen, Sala, in his *H.W.* article "Some Amenities of War," mentioned Siddons's diorama lectures: "A shilling, and half-an-hour's walk, and Messrs. Grieve and Telbin, or Mr. Beverley, will transport us to the seat of war, and show us water as blue, and minarets as white ... as the actual things of three thousand years ago; while the urbane Mr. Stocqueler, or the voluble Mr. Kenney, will talk like agreeable books, and save us the trouble of reading and travelling, and yet teach us more than we might gain by either."

D.N.B.

Christmas in India
II, 305–306. Dec. 21, 1850

Justice for "Natives"
VII, 397–402. June 25, 1853

Sidney, John, *b.* 1821, son of Abraham Solomon, M.D. Like his brother Samuel (below), changed his name to "Sidney." According to *A Voice from the Far Interior of Australia. By a Bushman,* "arrived in New South Wales at seventeen years of age, fresh from school, with ...

the best sort of English and French education that a lad up to that age gets, when he prefers hunting, shooting, and fishing, to prizes and schoolmasters' praise." Stayed in New South Wales for six years, working "in the wildest parts of the colony" at sheep, cattle, and horse raising. Returned to England, 1844. In 1847 Smith, Elder & Co. published *A Voice from the Far Interior of Australia. By a Bushman*, with prefatory note reading: "To the magistrates and country gentlemen of England, Scotland, and Ireland, these observations are respectfully addressed, by their obedient humble servant, John Sidney." Samuel Sidney stated, concerning the book: "... I wrote [it] for my brother, who was a close observer but no writer" ("Preface," *The Three Colonies of Australia*, 2nd ed.). Co-author with his brother of *Sidney's Australian Hand-book*, 1848; co-editor with his brother of first numbers of *Sidney's Emigrant's Journal*. Returned to Australia "in 1848, before the fifth number [of the *Journal*] was published" (Samuel Sidney, "Preface," *The Three Colonies of Australia*, 2nd ed.). Mentioned – as "my brother the bushman" – by Samuel Sidney in *The Three Colonies of Australia*, 1st ed., as one of the "experienced authorities" on whose information Sidney based his directions for emigrants, and cited by Sidney – as "the bushman, brother of the author" – as source of information on conditions and life in New South Wales.

In his letter to Miss Burdett-Coutts, Feb. 4, 1850 (see Samuel Sidney, below), Dickens stated that the Sidneys (unnamed) had written him "a very earnest letter, expressive of their desires" to become contributors to *H.W.* on the subject of emigration; by the date of his writing, however, he remarked, "I fancy the Bushman brother has gone back again" – i.e., to Australia. Since John Sidney had returned to Australia more than a year before the date of Dickens's letter, Samuel Sidney must have written the "very earnest letter" in his and his brother's name.

"Milking in Australia" (not listed in the Office Book) appeared, as a "filler," in the original issue only of *H.W.* No. 1 (see Introduction, p. 46). It was there stated to be "*From 'Scenes in the Life of a Bushman.' (Unpublished.).*" In *Sidney's Emigrant's Journal*, the unpublished "Scenes" is attributed to the Sidneys jointly and, also, to Samuel Sidney alone: In the *Journal*, Aug. 1849, appeared a chapter from "Scenes from [*sic*] the Life of a Bushman," stated to be "an unpublished Australian Tale, 'Raphael Armorer, the Bushman,' by the Authors of 'The Australian Hand-book.'" Chapters that appeared in later numbers were stated to be from "Scenes in the Life of Raphael Armorer, the Bushman"; one of these later chapters was indicated as "By the Editor" – i.e., Samuel Sidney, who was then sole editor of the *Journal*. The "Scenes" was evidently a joint composition of the two brothers in the same sense as was *A Voice from the Far Interior of Australia*.

Aside from his share in "Milking in Australia," John Sidney appears in *H.W.* indirectly, as the source of the personal observations, experiences, and stories related in various of Samuel Sidney's Australian contributions. In addition, Samuel Sidney's "Rio de Janeiro and Its Feather-Flowers," stated to be an excerpt from "the manuscript journal of a traveller," may be based on or taken from John Sidney's record of his second voyage to Australia.

Harper's reprinted "Milking in Australia," without acknowledgment to *H.W.*

Miller, *Australian Lit.*

Milking in Australia I, 24. March 30, 1850

Sidney, Samuel |*Mr. Sidney, Mr. Samuel Sidney, Mr. S. Sidney, S. Sidney, Sidney*|, 1813–1883, writer on railways, emigration, agriculture and livestock; son of Abraham Solomon, M.D. Educated for the law; worked for a time as solicitor in Liverpool; turned to journalism, assuming, in lieu of "Solomon," the name "Sidney"; used it thereafter for all purposes. From 1846 to 1848 published several books on railways and the gauge question. With his brother John (above), who had been six years in New South

Wales, wrote *Sidney's Australian Handbook*, 1848; book was immediate popular success; sold thousands of copies. Brought out *Sidney's Emigrant's Journal*, 1848–50 (for first few numbers, John Sidney was co-editor). Made speeches on emigration, wrote pamphlets on the subject. In 1852 published *The Three Colonies of Australia.* Was for many years hunting correspondent and writer on agricultural exhibitions for *Illus. London News*; for *Live Stock Journal* wrote series of articles titled "Horse Chat." Was one of assistant commissioners for Great Exhibition. In 1860 appointed secretary of Agricultural Hall Co.; organized and managed horse shows at the Hall. Brought out, 1858, enlarged edition of John S. Rarey's manual on horse taming; edited and in large part rewrote W. C. L. Martin's *The Pig*; also William Youatt's treatise on the pig. His most important writing was *The Book of the Horse*, 1873.

Sidney's acquaintance with Dickens and his connection with *H.W.* resulted from the prominence that Sidney and his brother had attained as authorities on Australian emigration. In a letter to Miss Burdett-Coutts, Feb. 4, 1850 (*Heart of Charles Dickens*, ed. Johnson, p. 164), in which he referred to Samuel Sidney merely as "the brother," to John Sidney as "the Bushman brother," and to the brothers jointly as "the writers of those pamphlets," Dickens stated that he had some time before directed a gentleman to "confer with them on the practicability of our doing something useful, in the Periodical, on the subject of emigration." He continued: "In sending me those books, they wrote me a very earnest letter, expressive of their desires to become contributors on that subject." The books, stated Dickens, gave him knowledge of the state of society in New South Wales "of which one could have no previous understanding, and which would seem to be quite misunderstood, or very little known, even in the cities of New South Wales itself." (The Sidneys' *Voice from the Far Interior of Australia. By a Bushman*, 1847, contains such information.) As a result of this, and probably other, consultations and arrangements, there appeared in the first number of *H.W.* an excerpt from the Sidneys' "Scenes in the Life of a Bushman" (discussed under John Sidney, above, and included in the listing below), and Sidney became a regular *H.W.* contributor, writing first on Australian matters, later on other subjects of his interest. Never in Australia himself, he based his *H.W.* writings on Australia (as he did his other writings on Australia) on histories and other works, statistical and other reports, information from persons – such as Caroline Chisholm – connected with emigration, letters sent to him by emigrants, and information furnished him by his brother.

Occasional references to Sidney appear in Dickens's MS "Emigration" (*A Dickens Library*, p. 12), as also in Dickens's letters. Sidney dedicated his *Gallops and Gossips in the Bush of Australia* to Dickens with the author's "warm feelings of admiration and esteem." In *The Book of the Horse*, he quoted Dickens's description of the travelling carriage bought for the first trip to Italy, and mentioned a curricle and a cabriolet that appear in Dickens's novels.

Dickens's letters contain comparatively few comments on Sidney's *H.W.* contributions. "A Gallop for Life" Dickens found "surprisingly good" (to Wills, Aug. 31, 1851: MS Huntington Library). "Lost and Found in the Gold Fields" he thought "very poor"; another of Sidney's articles was "such careless slip-slop as to be almost unintelligible, and quite unsuitable unless the second part be much better" (to Wills, March 10, 1853; Aug. 7, 1854). An article on Robert Stephenson that Sidney submitted to *A.Y.R.* Dickens did not publish, holding that enough had already been written on the recently deceased engineer; Wills was to "*Pay well for the article nevertheless*" (to Wills, Oct. 30; to Sidney, Nov. 3, 1859). One of Sidney's later articles Dickens printed despite its "disgusting snobbery," revising it so as to make the snobbery as little offensive as it could be made (to Wills, Aug. 26, 1866: MS Huntington Library).

Wills's "chip" "Official Emigration," May 1, 1852, indicates that one of Sidney's statements in "Three Colonial Epochs" had been called into question.

Sidney had quoted Earl Grey as saying that after the cessation of the distress caused by the railroad failures, persons who emigrated under Government auspices were chiefly "the refuse of workhouses." Wills explained that the statement resulted from "the misconstruction (for which we are in no degree responsible) of a sentence in the minutes" recording a conversation of Earl Grey.

Of the items listed below as not reprinted, "Better Ties Than Red Tape Ties" is mentioned by Sidney in the preface to *The Three Colonies of Australia*, 2nd ed., as one of his *H.W.* contributions. For "India Pickle," also listed below among items not reprinted, two names appear in the Office Book author-column: "Capper Sidney" (no ampersand). "Capper" is in part written over another notation or is itself in part overwritten, but the name is not marked out. Payment in one sum, rather than split payment, implies that the article was not a joint writing of the two contributors. Capper, resident in India and Ceylon, would be the more logical author of the item; but Sidney, who had not been in India, also contributed an article (derivative) on India.

In *H.W.* Sidney's name was mentioned in the editorial comment introducing the emigrant's letter that constitutes the article "News of Natal": "Mr. Samuel Sidney, the author of the 'Emigrant's Guide.' " Sidney wrote no work of that specific title.

Twenty-three years after the publication in *H.W.* of Sidney's "Two-Handed Dick," the story appeared on the editorial desk of Charles Dickens, Jr., as a contribution to *A.Y.R.* submitted by H. Clifford. Dickens wrote to Clifford, Oct. 20, 1873: "Before publicly exposing this bare-faced attempt at imposition, which I shall most certainly do, I shall be glad to hear if you have any sort of explanation to offer on the subject" (*A.Y.R.* Letter-Book). Receiving no reply to his letter, Dickens carried out his threat: "Editorial Note," *A.Y.R.*, Nov. 8, 1873.

Harper's reprinted, in whole or part, six of Sidney's *H.W.* contributions, two of them acknowledged to *H.W.* It reprinted also "Milking in Australia," evidently the joint composition of Sidney and his brother (see John Sidney, above).

D.N.B.

An Australia Ploughman's Story
I, 39–43. April 6, 1850

Two-Handed Dick the Stockman. An Adventure in the Bush
I, 141–44. May 4, 1850

The Gentleman Beggar. An Attorney's Story I, 510–14. Aug. 24, 1850

Father Gabriel; or, The Fortunes of a Farmer II, 67–71. Oct. 12, 1850

Father Gabriel's Story
II, 85–90. Oct. 19, 1850

Two Adventures at Sea
II, 104–108. Oct. 26, 1850

Rio de Janeiro and Its Feather-Flowers [chip] II, 164–65. Nov. 9, 1850

Letters of Introduction to Sydney [chip]
II, 187–88. Nov. 16, 1850

Land Ho! – Port Jackson [chip]
II, 276–77. Dec. 14, 1850

Christmas Day in the Bush
II, 309–310. Dec. 21, 1850

Two Scenes in the Life of John Bodger
II, 484–91. Feb. 15, 1851

A Gallop for Life [lead]
III, 577–81. Sept. 13, 1851

A Fashionable Forger
IV, 178–82. Nov. 15, 1851

What Christmas Is after a Long Absence
Extra No. for Christmas 1851, pp. 17–20

Fox-Hunting [chip]
IV, 443–44. Jan. 31, 1852

Going to the Dogs [lead]
V, 309–312. June 19, 1852

The 16 items repr., with a framework and some additional material, as *Gallops and Gossips in the Bush of Australia; or, Passages in the Life of Alfred Barnard. By Samuel Sidney.* London: Longman, Brown, Green, and Longmans, 1854. Pub. in *H.W.* acknowledged.

What to Take to Australia [chip]
V, 364–66. July 3, 1852

Repr. in *The Three Colonies of Australia: New South Wales, Victoria, South Australia; Their Pastures, Copper Mines, & Gold Fields. By Samuel Sidney.* London: Ingram, Cooke, & Co., 1852. Pub in *H.W.* acknowledged.

Milking in Australia I, 24. March 30, 1850

An Exploring Adventure
I, 418–20. July 27, 1850
Family Colonisation Loan Society [chip]
I, 514–15. Aug. 24, 1850
The Good Governor
I, 547–49. Aug. 31, 1850
Indian Railroads and British Commerce
II, 590–95. March 15, 1851
News of Natal III, 83–85. April 19, 1851
Profitable Investment of Toil – New Zealand [chip]
III, 228–29. May 31, 1851
The Five Travellers
IV, 318–21. Dec. 27, 1851
Three Colonial Epochs [lead]
IV, 433–38. Jan. 31, 1852
Better Ties Than Red Tape Ties [lead]
IV, 529–34. Feb. 28, 1852
Climate of Australia [chip]
V, 391–92. July 10, 1852
The Guest's Story A Round of Stories (Christmas 1852), pp. 30–33
My Friend Spanner
VI, 368–71. Jan. 1, 1853
Lost and Found in the Gold Fields
VII, 84–88. March 26, 1853
"The Corner" VIII, 382–84. Dec. 17, 1853
The Colonel's Story
Another Round of Stories (Christmas 1853), pp. 29–32
Mighty Hunters VIII, 446–49. Jan. 7, 1854
The Blankshire Hounds
VIII, 508–512. Jan. 28, 1854
Beef, Mutton, and Bread *Sidney & W.H.W.* X, 113–18. Sept. 16, 1854
Old Clothes and New Clothes
X, 248–53. Oct. 28, 1854
The Christmas Cattle Show [chip]
X, 465–66. Dec. 30, 1854
Ruined by Railways
XI, 114–19. March 3, 1855
Our Bedfordshire Farmer
XI, 162–67. March 17, 1855
India Pickle *Capper Sidney*
XI, 446–53. June 9, 1855
Sardinian Forests and Fisheries
XI, 584–87. July 21, 1855
The Sardinians XII, 131–37. Sept. 8, 1855
Coal Mining on the Ohio [chip]
XII, 141. Sept. 8, 1855
The Buckler Squires [lead]
XII, 169–76. Sept. 22, 1855
Bound for Brazil XII, 257–61. Oct. 13, 1855
The Beechgrove Family [lead]
XII, 289–96. Oct. 27, 1855
A Ladies' Warehouse
XII, 301–305. Oct. 27, 1855
Coats and Trousers
XII, 321–25. Nov. 3, 1855
Travellers' Contrivances [lead]
XII, 505–511. Dec. 29, 1855
Christmas Toys XII, 550–52. Jan. 5, 1856
Feudal Fetters for Farmers
XIII, 178–81. March 8, 1856
The British Dervish
XIII, 196–203. March 15, 1856
From Paris to Chelmsford [lead]
XIV, 217–23. Sept. 20, 1856
Dick Dallington
XIV, 245–52. Sept. 27, 1856
Agricultural Machinery
XIV, 252–56. Sept. 27, 1856
A Parisian Polite Letter Writer
XV, 162–65. Feb. 14, 1857
The Metropolitan Cattle Market
XV, 452–56. May 9, 1857
French and English [lead]
XV, 529–34. June 6, 1857
The Rinderpest; or, Steppe Murrain
XVI, 163–66. Aug. 15, 1857
Amateur Horse-Training
XVIII, 428–32. Oct. 16, 1858

Sketchley, R[?]. Initial not clearly written in Office Book; could be intended for "R" or "F" or "K." The contributor may be Richard Forster Sketchley, assistant keeper of South Kensington Museum, 1864–94; in charge of Dyce and Forster Collections from time of their arrival. Contributed an occasional verse to *Once a Week*. Became contributor to *Punch* in 1864; served as staff member, 1868–80 (Spielmann, *History of "Punch,"* pp. 368–69).

Payment for the contribution made in cash.

VERSE
Asleep XII, 349. Nov. 10, 1855

Smale, Miss. *Not identified.* Perhaps related to the Mr. Smale who in 1853 presented himself at Dickens's hotel in Paris "with an article for Household Words." "Smale's paper was impracticable," wrote

Dickens, "but (strange to say) not at all bad" (*Mr. & Mrs. Charles Dickens*, ed. Dexter, pp. 178, 193).

"Princess Ilse" is the translation of a German legend. A translation of the same legend by Lady Grace Wallace was published as a 63-page booklet by Bell & Daldy, 1855 or 1856, with the same title: *Princess Ilse*. That translation and the *H.W.* translation contain many identical phrases, e.g., "turned the head of many a foolish child," "lead you to the good old Weser and your young companions." But the identical phrases are such as any two translators would probably use in translating from an identical source (not identified). The marked differences in significant phraseology indicate that the two versions are not by the same translator, e.g.: *H.W.*: "Was it for me to demean myself in the plains, carrying drink to sheep and oxen, and washing their muddy feet?"; Lady Wallace: "Was I to descend into the valley, and traverse the plain like a common brook for menial service to slake the thirst of cows and sheep, and to wash their plebeian feet?"; *H.W.*: "... how then was he to entrap the child again?" Lady Wallace: "How should he contrive again to clutch the ethereal child?"

Payment for the contribution made by cheque.

Princess Ilse XII, 414–20. Dec. 1, 1855

Smales. "The Moral of This Year" concerns the epidemics that swept through England in 1854 killing thousands of people. It pictures the "Giant-King" pestilence reaping his harvest of death in squalid slum dwellings; it urges that class barriers be forgotten in "this day of death" and that the rich concern themselves with the lot of the poor:

> Scant right to call on God to move this evil from our door,
> If man cares naught for brother man, and the rich forget the poor!

The contributor may be Edwin C. Smales, author of *Echoes of the City*, 1883, which has similar sociological interest. One poem in the book pictures little Tim, the "Child of the street," cold and ill-clad; another, the betrayed woman who casts herself into the river. Another urges that the rich ease the burden of their "sad helpless brothers":

> ... have we not our humble 'poor'
> Crying hard for food and raiment even at our very door?

Dickens called the poem to the attention of Miss Burdett-Coutts: "I wish you would read, in next week's No. of Household Words ... a Poem called The Moral of this Year" (Oct. 26, 1854).

VERSE

The Moral of This Year X, 276–77. Nov. 4, 1854

Smith. *Not identified.* The Office Book records "Breakfast with the Black Prince" as arriving at the editorial office "per Ollier." Payment was made by cheque. The article describes the military parade and the reception and other festivities held on the occasion of a ceremonial visit of Admiral Sir Home Riggs Popham to Henri Christophe in Cape Henry (Cap-Haïtien) in 1820. The contributor refers to himself as an officer ("I stepped [into a carriage] with a brother officer"); he was attached to one of the sloops accompanying Popham's flag-ship the *Sybille*. Among the various Smiths listed in the muster rolls of the seven sloops, the *H.W.* contributor does not seem possible of identification.

The contributor states, also, that he saw Napoleon on board the *Bellerophon* at Plymouth. His comment does not make clear whether he was one of the Smiths attached to the *Bellerophon* in 1815, or whether he was one of the hundreds of people who went out in boats in Plymouth harbour to see the Emperor.

Breakfast with the Black Prince *Smith & Morley* IX, 48–51. March 4, 1854

Smith, Albert Richard |*Albert Smith*|, 1816–1860, author, entertainer. Educated at Merchant Taylors' school; studied medicine at Middlesex Hospital. L.S.A. 1838; M.R.C.S. 1838. Practised for a time as surgeon-dentist. Was early contributor to *Punch*; later, with Angus B. Reach, brought out comic sixpenny monthly, the *Man in the Moon*, 1847–49, as rival to *Punch*. Contributed to *Bentley's Misc.*; was for some time dramatic critic of *Illus. London News*. Composed plays, burlesques, extravaganzas; wrote satirical sketches that were extremely popular, and novels that Hollingshead called "admirable mixtures of Bulwer and Dickens" (*My Lifetime*, I, 142). Achieved fame as "one of the lions of the day" by his "entertainments" – lectures, interspersed with songs, jokes, and impersonations, which he delivered in front of large dioramas and for which he provided various properties. The most famous was "The Ascent of Mont Blanc." An element of the vulgar and the ridiculous in the entertainments did not hinder their popularity. Smith himself was thought by some of his contemporaries to be eminently vulgar and obnoxious.

Smith was a good friend of Dickens, seeing much of him particularly in the Tavistock House days. But even Dickens found something of impertinence in Smith's self-advertisement and was amused at Smith's assumption of importance (to Douglas Jerrold, Oct. 24, 1846; Speilmann, *History of "Punch,"* p. 304). If he ever glanced at the *Man in the Moon*, Dickens must have been angered by that periodical's ridicule of his writing. At Dickens's request, Smith dramatized *The Cricket on the Hearth* and, with Dickens's consent, *The Battle of Life*. Smith wrote a short verse prologue to Edward Stirling's stage adaptation of *Martin Chuzzlewit*, praising Dickens as the "household friend" who called up laughter and tears and who "never penn'd / One line that might his guileless pages spot" (Fitz-Gerald, *Dickens and the Drama*, p. 183). Smith's burletta *Guy Fawkes* was one of the pieces acted at Tavistock House as a children's theatrical under Dickens's direction.

For the first of his three *H.W.* contributions – an article on the Covent Garden Theatre fire – Smith was paid much more than the standard rate – £5.5.0 for the 6¾-col. article.

Various references to Smith appeared in *H.W.* Dickens, in "The Lost Arctic Voyagers" (Dec. 9, 1854), mentioned Smith's account of his Mont Blanc ascent as "an excellent little book" and related from it some of Smith's remarks. Sala, in "The Great Hotel Question" and "English Hotels," for which Smith's *English Hotel Nuisance* (1855) provided the motivation, acknowledged "the honest Mont Blanc chronicler," "the lively explorer of the Bernese Oberland," to be an authority on travel and hotels, though he did not acquiesce in Smith's entire condemnation of "English hostelries." Sala referred to Smith also in two other of his articles. Payn, in "A Dull Day on Exmoor," cited a line from one of Smith's entertainments, and Mrs. Linton, in "Uncommon Good Eating," quoted him on Chinese fare.

In addition, Smith seems clearly to be the man "well-known to the public" who appears in "A Nightly Scene in London," Jan. 26, 1856, as Dickens's companion on a chance walk to Whitechapel. In a letter to Wills, Jan. 9, 1856 (MS Huntington Library), Dickens instructed him to ask Smith to call at the *H.W.* office to read proof of the article: "I should like him to see it." If Smith had had no connection with the article, there would obviously have been no occasion for his being shown the proof.

D.N.B.

Theatrical Ashes [lead]
XIII, 217–20. March 22, 1856
Rogues' Walk XVI, 262–64. Sept. 12, 1857
Nearly Lost on the Alps [lead]
XVII, 241–44. Feb. 27, 1858

Smith, Catharine Amelia (Pybus) |*Mrs. Sidney Smith*|, *d.* 1852, wife of the Rev. Sydney Smith. From the time of her marriage in 1800, was her husband's helpmate, counsellor, and admirer, ambitious for his advancement. Saved from destruction some of the lectures that he would have flung into the fire; often, at his request, looked over his MSS, to "put in dots to the *i*'s and strokes to the *t*'s." After his death in 1845, her one desire was to leave to the world a "memorial of my noble-hearted husband"; for that purpose collected, transcribed, and arranged his letters and papers, but felt herself incapable of writing a memoir or editing the letters. "Her pride in her husband was only equalled by her humility about herself," wrote Sarah Austin; "and nothing could persuade her that she was competent to do what she so intensely longed to see done" (*Memoir of the Reverend Sydney Smith*, I, 113, et passim; II, xx–xxi). The *Memoir*, written by her daughter, Lady Holland, together with a selection of Smith's letters edited by Mrs. Austin, was published in 1855. James White's *H.W.* article "Sydney Smith" was based on the book.

"Mrs. Sydney" – as she appears in Smith's familiar letters – shared the friendship of the famous contemporaries who were her husband's friends. Among them was Dickens, who named his fifth son after Smith.

The Office Book assigns "True Anecdote of the Last Century" to Mrs. Smith and Wills, but the identification of Mrs. Smith in the opening paragraph is clearly Dickens's writing. The paragraph begins: " 'More than sixty years ago,' said my friend – a lady, whom I am proud to call by that name, in memory of my deceased friend, her husband, the Master of English Wit and Sense – 'my mother and sister were robbed by two highwaymen. ...' " The identification made the authorship of the item clear to the contemporary reader. Dickens sent to Mrs. Smith, Green St., Grosvenor Square, a proof of the article, accompanied by a brief note (May 5, 1851: typescript Huntington Library) asking her to strike from the copy whatever she did not like. The Office Book records no payment for the item.

True Anecdote of the Last Century [chip]
Mrs. Sidney Smith & W.H.W.
III, 188–89. May 17, 1851

Smith, Mrs. Prince, prob. |*Miss Prince Smith*|. John Prince Smith, 1774?–1822, law reporter (*D.N.B.*), was survived by a son and a daughter. If the Office Book designation "Miss" is correct, the contributor was the daughter of John Prince Smith.

It is probable, however, that the "Miss" should read "Mrs." In that event, the contributor was the wife of John Prince Smith the younger, 1809–1874, political economist (*D.N.B.*). Smith the younger was born and educated in England; went to Germany as a young man; there became leader of the Free Trade party and member of the Reichstag. Wrote, in German, various works on economic policy, international trade, monetary practices; translated into English a German treatise on political economy. In 1846 married Auguste Sommerbrod, daughter of a Berlin banker.

"Adventures of a Translation" deals with Elisabeth von Arnim's *Goethes Briefwechsel mit einem Kinde*. The contributor's strictures on high import duties and on the customs regulations that kept the book from the English reading public indicate that, like Smith the younger, she favoured free trade. Occasional instances of incorrect tense sequence and unidiomatic word order give the impression that the contributor was not a native speaker of English. She does refer to English as "our language" and to London docks as "our London docks"; she may have assumed English nationality in writing for an English periodical in which her article would appear anonymously.

Payment for the article, which consists largely of quotation, was little more than half the standard rate. The Office Book memorandum reads: "paid to Mr. Davenport Francis" (not identified).

Adventures of a Translation
II, 56–58. Oct. 12, 1850

Smith, Sarah |*Mrs. Stretton*|, 1832–1911, novelist and writer of children's stories under pseudonym "Hesba Stretton." Born in Shropshire. Attended girls' day school, but gained much of her education by reading books in shop of her father, a bookseller and publisher. Early began writing stories. Her "Jessica's First Prayer" in *Sunday at Home*, July 1866, thereafter published in book form, won wide popularity; thousands of copies sold; was translated into every European language and into many Asiatic and African tongues. Published some fifty titles, many of them short tales issued by Religious Tract Society; also novels: *The Clives of Burcot*, 1866; *The Doctor's Dilemma*, 1872; and others. Earned her living by her pen. Took active part in philanthropic and humanitarian movements; assisted Miss Burdett-Coutts in her works of charity.

Miss Smith's connection with *H.W.* came about through her sister Elizabeth's sending "The Lucky Leg" to Dickens, without the author's knowledge. In accepting it, Dickens suggested that he would welcome further contributions, and a friendship sprang up between him and Miss Smith (*D.N.B.*). Among her contributions to *A.Y.R.* was "The Travelling Post-Office" in the 1866 Christmas number, "Mugby Junction." Dickens's letters to Wills occasionally mention Miss Smith's *A.Y.R.* contributions and suggest what she should do to improve certain papers that she intended to collect and publish in book form.

Miss Smith's *H.W.* contribution is the story of a widower who proposes to a lady who has a wooden leg, each of his two former wives having had a wooden leg. Augustus J. C. Hare, in *The Story of My Life* (v, 33–38), related practically the identical account as an actual happening.

D.N.B. suppl. 1901–1911

The Lucky Leg

XIX, 374–80. March 19, 1859

Smith, Sidney |*Sidney Smith*|, misc. writer. The *Athenaeum*, Dec. 22, 1849, reviewing one of Smith's books, more than hinted that "Sidney Smith" was a pseudonym, most impertinently and indiscreetly assumed by the author "on the strength of some supposed affinity" between the thought and language of his book and that of "the writings of Peter Plymley." If the author's name was really Sidney Smith, he had, to be sure, a right to use it, admitted the reviewer grudgingly, and "we have of course no more to say." Sidney Smith was Smith's real name. Author of *The Principles of Phrenology*, 1838, assigned in some catalogues to Sidney Smith "Phrenologist," but proved by announcement on verso of title page of *Whether to Go, and Whither?* to be by the writer here discussed. As secretary to National Anti-Corn-Law League, delivered in 1840 three lectures in Devizes, reported in Wiltshire *Independent* and reprinted as pamphlet, *Anti-Corn-Law Lectures*. Author of two guide books for emigrants, *The Settler's New Home: or The Emigrant's Location* and *Whether to Go, and Whither?*, both published 1849, and brought out in following year under a joint title. In 1849 published also *The Mother Country: or, The Spade, the Wastes, and the Eldest Son*, an analysis of the agricultural, economic, and social condition of England; dedicated the book to Baron Lionel Rothschild, "In return for much considerate kindness and many useful acts of effective service," and in tribute to Rothschild's character and his management of wealth to the benefit of mankind. The dedication suggests that *Falkland. An Historical Play*, 1876, dedicated to Alfred de Rothschild "by his obliged servant, Sidney Smith," is probably by the same Sidney Smith. Smith had much interest in seventeenth-century English history.

In *The Settler's New Home* (p. 21), recounting some of the pleasures of life that even the poorest settler could enjoy, Smith included books – among them, in very respectable company, those of Dickens. Would the settler have society, he wrote, "Plato, Shakespeare, the dear old vicar of Wakefield, Burns, Fielding, Scott, or Dickens, will join the fire-side with small importunity."

Smith's *H.W.* articles deal with the use of waste land and with agriculture. His contention, in "The Ace of Spades," that a man could make a good living by spade cultivation of a few acres was disputed by several *H.W.* readers from agricultural districts. Replying to them in his following article, "The Spade," Smith cited evidence in support of his contention. Toward the end of the article appeared the statement: "Those of our readers who desire to pursue this subject ... will find a mass of information gathered from all available sources in the small work entitled 'The Mother Country; or, the Spade, the Wastes, and the Eldest Sow [*sic*],' by Sidney Smith.'

The *H.W.* article "Ballinglen" referred to Smith's "The Spade in Ireland" and corrected a typographical error in that article.

Allibone

The Devonshire Dorado *Sidney Smith & W.H.W.* II, 262–64. Dec. 7, 1850
The Ace of Spades [chip] II, 477–78. Feb. 8, 1851
The Spade [chip] *Sidney Smith & W.H.W.* II, 595–97. March 15, 1851
The Spade in Ireland [chip] III, 114–15. April 26, 1851

Snow, George Henry |*Snow*|. The contributor recounts some of his experiences as "a youngster" aboard the whaler *Japan* in "the Eastern seas." The Crew List of the *Japan*, Public Record Office, London, lists George Henry Snow as apprentice on a voyage to the southern whale fisheries, between June 25, 1838, and Aug. 11, 1841. Snow, born in Wiltshire, was fourteen at the date of signing on. His previous ship had been the *London Packet.*

Aboard the Japan, Whaler XVII, 334–36. March 20, 1858

Sommerville. "The Great British Gum Secret" relates the discovery of the process of making adhesive paste and the subsequent commercial manufacture of such paste. The introductory paragraphs of the article, referring to the adhesive on postage stamps and connecting the article with "The Queen's Head" (Feb. 21, 1852), are evidently an editorial addition. Payment for the contribution recorded as "Advanced by W.H.W."

The contributor may perhaps be Alexander Somerville, 1811-1885, social reformer (*D.N.B.*). Somerville wrote for periodicals; in the 1840s he was correspondent for the Manchester *Examiner;* he was author of *The Autobiography of a Working Man*, 1848, with which Dickens was familiar; of *The Whistler at the Plough*, 1852; and of other works.

On Sept. 20, 1855, Dickens wrote Wills a letter (MS Huntington Library) to accompany certain papers that were to receive Wills's attention. The paper that he marked No. 1 (apparently a letter), Dickens stated, "relates to the Whistler at the Plough. I have no objection to making him any small advance you think right, if your knowledge of what has taken place between you interposes no bar." In context, Dickens's comment seems clearly to indicate that the "small advance" had no connection with a *H.W.* article. (Grubb, "Dickens the Paymaster Once More," *Dickensian*, Spring 1955, assumes that the "small advance" was for a *H.W.* article. But no article published in *H.W.* during the last four months of 1855 can have been Somerville's writing; no articles published during these months are unassigned in the Office Book, and none seems misassigned.) However, in view of Somerville's correspondence with Dickens and in view of his having at some time had some conference with Wills, it is possible that the 1852 article assigned to "Sommerville" may be by Alexander Somerville.

Harper's reprinted the article, without acknowledgment to *H.W.*

The Great British Gum Secret V, 202–203. May 15, 1852

"Sophy Traddles": *See* Norris, Miss

Sorrell. The contributor pictures himself in his book-lined library sitting down to compose an article for *H.W.* – an intention that is thwarted by his love of idleness (Thomas Idle of "The Lazy Tour of Two Idle Apprentices" is "a fellow completely after my own heart") and by the stream-of-consciousness working of his "discursive mind." An example of the latter process is his recollection of a sunset viewed from the Drachenfels, of Weimar, and of "the mighty" Goethe, called forth by his lighting a German tobacco pipe. The recollection leads to his taking from the shelf Eckermann's *Conversations with Goethe* – "an especially delightful book." Among other matters referred to in the article are Punch and Judy shows and their French and Italian counterparts.

The writer's interests indicate that he may be William J. Sorrell, member of the Dramatic Authors' Society, joint author of various dramatic pieces, and author of "Drawing Room Theatricals," which forms the first part of T. H. Lacy's *Amateur's Hand-Book and Guide to Home Drawing Room Theatricals* [1866]. In his portion of this work, Sorrell refers to "the great master" Goethe and quotes from Eckermann's *Conversations*. Lacy, in his preface to the book, speaks of Sorrell as an experienced amateur actor and "a literary gentleman and dramatist."

A Discursive Mind
xvi, 477–80. Nov. 14, 1857

Soutar. The item listed below relates the early history of the ancient Jewish colony in K'ai-Fung-Foo and gives also the information obtained by the Jewish Society of London, early in 1851, concerning the survivors of the colony. The order of names attached to the item in the Office Book suggests that Soutar wrote the article, that it was first revised by Keys, then further revised by Morley.

The contributor may be Robert Soutar, actor and stage manager. Soutar was brought up as a journalist; was connected with *Morning Advertiser*, of which his father was for many years working editor. Began his connection with the stage in 1852 as amateur actor. Was for some ten years Hollingshead's stage manager at Gaiety Theatre (Hollingshead, *Gaiety Chronicles*, p. 39, et passim; *Life and Reminiscences of E. L. Blanchard*, ed. Scott and Howard, ii, 443, et passim). Composed pantomimes and other pieces for the stage; edited Joseph A. Cave's reminiscences, *A Jubilee of Dramatic Life and Incident*, 1892.

"The Jews in China" was included in the Putnam volume of selections from *H.W.*: *The World Here and There*, 1852.

The Jews in China *Soutar, Keys, & Morley* iii, 452–56. Aug. 2, 1851

Speight, Thomas Wilkinson |*T. Speight, Speight*|, 1830–1915, novelist. Born in Liverpool; educated at a foundation-school in north of England. For many years held a position with a railway company (his *H.W.* article "Up and down the Line" records in detail the responsibilities and duties of railway executives and employees). Mentioned in Allibone as contributor to *H.W.*, *A.Y.R.*, and *Belgravia*. Some of his shorter novels appeared in the *Gentleman's Annual*. From 1867 to 1912, published some fifty works of fiction, long and short, e.g., *Under Lock and Key* (which he assured readers he had written before reading *The Moonstone*), *A Secret of the Sea*, *The Mysteries of Heron Dyke*, *A Bootless Crime*. Reviewers found his mystery novels "fascinating," "thrilling," "sensational."
Allibone

Salome and I xiv, 296–301. Oct. 11, 1856, and the 2 following nos.
Charnwood xv, 390–93. April 25, 1857
Grayrigg Grange
xv, 579–87. June 20, 1857
Up and down the Line [lead]
xv, 601–607. June 27, 1857
Our Family Picture
xvi, 303–308. Sept. 26, 1857, and the 2 following nos.
Lemonfingers xvii, 36–40. Dec. 26, 1857

Spellen, John Nathaniel, prob. |*Spellan*|, barrister. Admitted at Gray's Inn, 1833; called to the bar, 1838 (*Men-at-the-Bar*). Is evidently the J. N. Spellen recorded in

Brit. Mus. Cat. as author of *The Inner Life of the House of Commons*, 1854, and of five pamphlets constituting part of the Parish Officers' Library, e.g., *The Constables' Guide and Director*, *The Overseers' Assistant*, *The Vestry Clerk and Parish Lawyer*.

"Mr. J. N. Spellan" is listed as a member of the reporting staff engaged for the *Daily News* on the establishment of that journal (McCarthy and Robinson, *The "Daily News" Jubilee*, p. 9, citing Thomas Britton).

"Coming South a Century Ago" is based on the Maitland Club edition, 1842, of Margaret Steuart Calderwood's *Journey in England, Holland, and the Low Countries*. Payment for the contribution made by cheque.

Coming South a Century Ago
xiii, 19–22. Jan. 19, 1856

Spicer, Henry |*H. Spicer, Spicer*|, *d.* 1891, dramatist, misc. writer. Brought out theatrical periodical, the *Curtain*, 1847; co-lessee of Olympic Theatre, 1847–49; some of his plays produced there. Author of *The Lords of Ellingham*, 1839; *Honesty*, 1842; both in five acts, in verse; and other plays; also of a volume of poems, some volumes of prose fiction, and books on spirit-manifestation. As writer on spiritualism, was to Mrs. Browning "the famous Mr. Spicer" (*Letters to Her Sister*, p. 193).

Spicer was, according to Boase, an "intimate friend" of Dickens. He dedicated his *Old Styles's* to Dickens, "with the regard and gratitude of the author." He presented to Dickens a copy of his *Strange Things among Us* (Stonehouse, *Catalogue*). In *Some Experiences of a Barrister's Life* (i, 140), William Ballantine, writing of Dickens, recorded: "I and Mr. Spicer, a friend of his and mine, had put him up at the Union Club, and, to our great grief, the news of his death reached us upon the day on which he would have been elected."

Spicer's "A White Hand and a Black Thumb" and various other items appeared in *A.Y.R.* In a letter to Wills, Nov. 25, 1862, Dickens suggested a subject for a possible "droll paper" by Spicer; in a letter of Dec. 20, 1863, he mentioned his having deleted and then restored an incident in one of Spicer's stories, stating that he had himself written to Spicer concerning the matter.

Boase

*The New Boy at Styles's [lead]
xv, 433–40. May 9, 1857
*A New Baby xix, 116–19. Jan. 1, 1859
To and from Tunis
xix, 461–67. April 16, 1859

*Repr. in *Old Styles's. By Henry Spicer, Esq.* London: Bosworth & Harrison, 1859. Pub. in *H.W.* acknowledged.

Starr. *Not identified.* The contributor discusses, as a subject of general interest probably unfamiliar to many readers, the cultivation of teasel; he briefly describes the use of teasel-heads in broadcloth manufacture. Payment for the contribution marked "Enclosed & fetched."

Teasle [chip] x, 538–40. Jan. 20, 1855

Stocqueler: *See* Siddons, Joachim Heyward

Stone, Miss. *Not identified.* "Rather Low Company" is an amusing, kindly sketch of the villagers whom the narrator knew when she was a schoolmistress.

At least six English women writers named Stone published books between 1840 and 1890.

Rather Low Company
xix, 269–71. Feb. 19, 1859

Stone, Thomas |*Dr. T. Stone, Dr. Stone*|, M.D. Apprenticed to surgeon in London. Studied medicine in Edinburgh. There published *The Evidences against the Sys-*

tem of Phrenology, 1828, and in following year two other pamphlets countering the claims of phrenologists. President, 1829, of Royal Medical Society, Edinburgh. Graduate in medicine, Univ. of Edinburgh, 1831; thesis: "De Cranio Humano." Entered on private practice in London, where, according to Horne, who at one time had been a close friend of his, he "mingled science, general literature, and Bond Street lounging in about equal proportions" ("By-Gone Celebrities of Bond Street," *Harper's*, Oct. 1871). Fellow of London Medico-Chirurgical Society. Editor, Jan.–June 1844, of *London Polytechnic Magazine, and Journal of Science, Literature, and the Fine Arts* (title varies); co-editor, July–Dec. 1844. During his editorship, wrote two articles for the periodical. According to Horne, contributed numerous articles to *Medico-Chirurgical Review, Jour. of Psychological Medicine*, and "many other magazines."

Of medical men named Stone with initial "T" who flourished in the mid-century, Thomas Stone, graduate in medicine, Univ. of Edinburgh, is the only one recorded as having written either periodical articles or books. Evidence that he was the *H.W.* contributor is furnished by a statement in the article "Dreams," assigned in the Office Book to "Dr. Stone." The writer of the article refers to the Burke-Hare murders, which took place in Edinburgh, 1827–28, and for which Burke was hanged in Jan. 1829. The writer states: "We had ourselves an interview with Burke, after his condemnation. ..." Thomas Stone was studying medicine in Edinburgh in 1828–31 (prob. also before); in 1829 he published in Edinburgh *Observations on the Phrenological Development of Burke, Hare, and Other Atrocious Murderers ..., Presenting an Extensive Series of Facts Subversive of Phrenology*. He had, before publishing his observations, presented them in a paper read before the Royal Medical Society, Edinburgh.

Stone may have been acquainted with Dickens. He was a member of the short-lived Society of British Authors, 1843, at the second meeting of which Dickens presided as chairman (Besant, "The First Society of British Authors," *Contemp. Rev.*, July 1889). He seems obviously to be the "Dr. Stone" mentioned in Dickens's letter to Horne, April 18, 1852, as having proposed to Horne a subject for a *H.W.* article.

On Sept. 17, 1850, Dickens wrote to Wills: "I will look over Hints on Emergencies, with the view you suggest, *if* it comes." Stone's article so titled appeared in *H.W.* in the following month. Based on John Flint South's very popular *Household Surgery; or, Hints on Emergencies*, it warns that South's suggestions for the layman's practising on himself and his family with lancet and scalpel are unwise. Whatever changes were made in the article must have been made by Wills, as indicated by his assigning it to himself and Stone. On Feb. 2, 1851, Dickens wrote a long letter to Stone concerning the article "Dreams," which he thought might be made "a little more original, and a little less recapitulative of the usual stories in the books." To this end, Dickens suggested some of his own ideas on the subject; he would "be happy to appoint a time for discussing the subject still further" if Stone thought the ideas worth considering; otherwise, he would publish Stone's paper as written and then present his own ideas in a separate paper. The article as published in *H.W.* incorporates some of Dickens's suggestions; Dickens did not carry out his alternative plan of writing a paper on the subject himself.

Four of Stone's *H.W.* contributions were reprinted in *Harper's*, two of them acknowledged to *H.W.* Four were included in the Putnam volume of selections from *H.W.*: *Home and Social Philosophy*, 1st ser.

Graduates in Medicine, Univ. of Edinburgh; Allibone

A Shilling's Worth of Science
I, 507–510. Aug. 24, 1850
Chemical Contradictions
I, 591–94. Sept. 14, 1850
Hints on Emergencies *W.H.W. & Dr. Stone*
II, 47–48. Oct. 5, 1850
Physiology of Intemperance
II, 413–17. Jan. 25, 1851
Sleep II, 470–75. Feb. 8, 1851
Dreams II, 566–72. March 8, 1851
Somnambulism III, 132–38. May 3, 1851

Stone, W. H. *Not identified.* "The Nineveh Bull" is a soliloquy in which the bull, one of the Assyrian statues excavated by Austen Henry Layard and sent to England in 1850, tells of his birth, of the civilizations that he has seen rise and fall, and of his being transported to a strange land, far from his native realm. The writer is thoroughly familiar with ancient history.

More than one W. H. Stone flourished in the mid-century:

William Henry Stone, 1799–1863: Admitted at Trinity College, Cambridge, 1817. Admitted at Middle Temple, 1820; called to bar, 1825. Commissioner in bankruptcy (*Alumni Cantab.*).

William Henry Stone, 1830–1891: As a boy took to classics with avidity; was brilliant student. B.A. Oxford 1852; M.A. 1855. Studied at St. Thomas's Hospital; M.R.C.S., F.R.C.S., M.R.C.P., F.R.C.P. Lectured and wrote papers and books on medicine, physics, music (*Plarr's Lives*).

William Henry Stone, *d.* 1896: Admitted at Trinity College, Cambridge, 1853, age nineteen; B.A. (30th Wrangler, 8th Classic) 1857; M.A. 1860. Director of London and County Banking Co.; M.P. for Portsmouth, 1865–74 (*Alumni Cantab.*).

William Henry Stone, 1838–1863: Admitted at Trinity College, Cambridge, 1858; Browne Scholar; B.A. (6th Classic) 1862. In 1862–63 compiled notes to Martial's epigrams, which appeared in F. A. Paley's edition of the *Epigrams*, 1868 (*Alumni Cantab.*).

"The Nineveh Bull" was included in the Putnam volume of selections from *H.W.*: *Home and Social Philosophy*, 2nd ser.

The Nineveh Bull II, 468–69. Feb. 8, 1851

Stoqueler, J. *See* Siddons, Joachim Heyward

Strange, Charles |*C. Strange, Strange*|, chemist and druggist. Listed in Slater's 1850 directory of Manchester and vicinity as chemist and druggist. Contributed an occasional article to *Once a Week*, e.g., "Nest-Building Fish," "The Confession of a Tea-Kettle; or a Hint to Housewives." Author of two booklets dealing with his hobby – indoor aquaria: *Ponds in the Parlour* and *Neptune's Garden*, both published in Manchester (London publisher also given on title pages), 1861.

The second and third items listed below indicate the contributor's knowledge of chemical and other substances and their effect on the human body. The references to Manchester in the first and second items imply that the contributor was a resident of that city. In the first, he tells of seeing a sign in the window of a house while he "was passing through a bye-street in Manchester," of his later returning to ask the meaning of the sign, and of his discovering how some of "our Manchester friends" earn a livelihood. In the second item he describes an experiment conducted by a friend of his, "a chemist in Manchester."

The Office Book assigns "The Knocking-up Business" to Strange alone, but with the notation "rewritten by W.H.W."

The Knocking-up Business [chip]
I, 501–502. Aug. 17, 1850
Death in the Teapot [chip] *Strange & W.H.W.* II, 277. Dec. 14, 1850
Death in the Bread-Basket [chip]
W.H.W. & Strange II, 323. Dec. 28, 1850

Stretton, Mrs.: *See* Smith, Sarah

Szczepanowska, Mme. |*Mad. Sczszpanowska, Madm. Schszepanowska*|. *Not identified.* The Office Book recordings of the contributor's name are obviously mistranscriptions of "Szczepanowska." According to the annual reports of the London Literary Association of the Friends of Poland, the number of Polish refugees in England during various years of the 1840s and 1850s ranged from 460 to about 1000. Mme. Szczepanowska was obviously one of these refugees. In her first *H.W.* contribution she mentioned having travelled in Poland "last year"; she was apparently in England at the time of contributing the item, as indicated by the Office Book notation that cash was "handed over" by Wills; she was probably in England also at the time of contributing her second item, which was paid for by post-office order. Her name does not appear in reference works on Polish writers.

One refugee of the writer's name was Lieut. Ignatius Szczepanowski, a well-educated man who in 1839 served as resident secretary to the London Literary Association of the Friends of Poland and in the 1840s worked as a teacher in Ipswich (*Report of the Proceedings*, 1839, 1843). Dickens was for a time a member of the Literary Association.

The first item listed below, assigned in the Office Book jointly to the contributor and Wills, is marked in addition "Re-written by W.H.W." It is the story of a Polish peasant girl who became a prima donna. It was reprinted in the *International Magazine* and included in *Choice Stories from Dickens' Household Words*, pub. Auburn, N.Y., 1854. The second item is an account of the betrothal and wedding, in 1759, of the daughter of an ancient Polish family, Barbara Krasinska, recorded from the diary of Barbara's sister. In his *Life of Adventure* (I, 6), Otto von Corvin (above), a descendant of the Corvin-Krasinskis, mentioned the publication in *H.W.* of the "very interesting extract" from the sister's diary.

The Serf of Pobereze
Mad. Sczszpanowska & W.H.W.
I, 342–50. July 6, 1850
Barbara's Nuptials IX, 488–92. July 8, 1854

T

Talfourd, Sir Thomas Noon |*Mr. Justice Talfourd, Justice Talfourd*|, 1795–1854, judge, author. Attended a dissenters' school, then Reading grammar school. Admitted at Middle Temple, 1813; called to the bar, 1821; serjeant-at-law, 1833; judge of the Common Pleas, 1849; knighted 1849. Three times returned M.P. for Reading; introduced Custody of Infants Bill and Copyright Bill. Universally respected for his high moral character, his integrity. Died suddenly on the Bench while delivering to jury a charge in which he deplored the lack of understanding and sympathy between the rich and the poor. Contributed to *Pamphleteer, Monthly Repository, New Monthly, Retrospective Review, London Magazine, Edin. Rev.*, and other periodicals, including professional journals. Author of *Poems on Various Subjects*, 1811; *Ion*, a classical tragedy famous in its day, produced by Macready in 1836; and other plays: *The Athenian Captive, Glencoe, The Castilian.* As literary executor of his friend Charles Lamb, brought out edition of Lamb's *Letters*, 1837; also *Final Memorials* of Lamb, 1848.

Talfourd held a place of some prominence in the legal, political, and literary world when Dickens became acquainted with him and, in 1837, dedicated to him the book publication of *Pickwick*. The dedication, wrote Dickens, was in tribute to Talfourd's important work in the matter of copyright legislation; it was also a token of Dickens's "fervent admiration" of Talfourd's fine qualities of head and heart, and "a memorial of the most gratifying friendship I have ever contracted." Dickens had no friend, wrote Forster, to whom he was more attached than he was to Talfourd. The association of the two men was frequent. Talfourd was vice-chairman at the *Pickwick* celebration dinner and took part also in celebrations commemorating the publication of other of Dickens's books. The two writers presented each other copies of their works, and each expressed high admiration of the other's writing. Talfourd, in presenting Dickens a copy of the privately printed *Ion*, wrote of him as "the subtlest and the most genial delineator of human manners and affections who has arisen among us since the days of Fielding"; his friendship with Dickens was to him "one of the greatest blessings and honors" of his life (in Pilgrim *Letters*, I, 685). Talfourd also addressed a eulogistic sonnet to Dickens on his *Oliver Twist.* At Dickens's request, he contributed a sonnet to *The Pic Nic Papers*, 1841, the volume brought out for the benefit of John Macrone's widow. Talfourd served as Dickens's counsel in the suit that Dickens brought in 1844 against publishers who plagiarized his books. Various commentators have suggested that Dickens modelled Traddles of *Copperfield* in part on Talfourd.

On Talfourd's death, Dickens published in *H.W.*, March 25, 1854, his tribute to "this upright judge and good man." Crabb Robinson, on reading the article – Dickens's "deeply feeling lines" – recorded in his diary: "A little overdoing is to be expected, but it is not excessive here" (*On Books and Their Writers*, II, 739). Mention of Talfourd appeared in occasional other *H.W.* articles. Whitehead, in "Off! Off!", referred to Talfourd as "Lamb's excellent biographer." Morley, in "The Manchester Strike," quoted Talfourd's last words: "If I were asked what is the greatest want in English society to mingle class with class, I would say in one word, the want of sympathy"; striking workers, wrote Morley, had headed one of their manifestos with Talfourd's words, and certain millowners had chosen them as a motto. Dixon, in "Quite Revolutionary," recalled to readers' memories "good Justice Talfourd's dying words."

The Office Book records payment for none of Talfourd's contributions, the first of which is marked "Not to be paid." Evidently Dickens accorded Talfourd the privilege of writing for the periodical as his personal friend, rather than as paid contributor.

Browning, on being assured that the *H.W.* sonnet "To Robert Browning" was by Talfourd, sent the author, from Paris, his thanks for "this public appreciation" of his writing (*Letters of Robert Browning*, ed. Hood, p. 37).

D.N.B.

PROSE

A Glimpse of the Cairngorm Mountains
IV, 40–45. Oct. 4, 1851

VERSE

Sonnet to Lord Denman. Retiring from the Chief Justiceship of England
I, 60. April 13, 1850

Sonnet. To Robert Browning; Suggested by a Sunset of Unusual Beauty
IV, 213. Nov. 22, 1851

Sonnet. On Mr. Lough's Statue of "Lady Macbeth" IV, 237. Nov. 29, 1851

A Recollection of Sir Martin Shee. On the Last Occasion of His Presiding at the Festival of the Royal Academy of Art
V, 176. May 8, 1852

The 4 items repr. in *The Dramatic Works of Sir Thomas Noon Talfourd, D.C.L. Eleventh Edition; to Which Are Added, A Few Sonnets and Verses.* London: Edward Moxon, 1852. Pub. in *H.W.* not acknowledged.

Taylor, Mr. Address: Manchester. *Not identified.* Several hundred Taylors lived in Manchester and its suburbs in the 1850s. The article to which Taylor's name is attached describes an institution for pauper children in Swinton, near Manchester. Editorial comment states that "we solicited a gentleman qualified for the task" to visit the institution and that "we have drawn up the following account" on the basis of his information. The Office Book records the article as "Rewritten almost entirely by W.H.W. & abridged one half."

The actual account of the visit to the institution, i.e., the part of the article based on Taylor's information, expresses, in general, approval of the care, schooling, and moral training that children there receive. Prefaced to this account is a long introductory comment by Wills: Pauper children, he states, are of course not responsible for the shiftlessness of their parents, and common sense dictates that they be given training so that they not become "pests to Society." Institutions that can give them such training "at not too great a cost" are therefore commendable. However, the Swinton establishment, with its appearance of "a wealthy nobleman's residence" and with its "sumptuous arrangements," provides for pauper children better schooling, food, and clothing than the industrious poor can provide for their children and thus, in effect, sets a premium on parental shiftlessness and neglect. In Manchester, "the high road to fortune is to be born a pauper."

A paragraph at the end of the article again mentions the fact that Swinton places "the child-pauper above the child of the industrious." The attitude may be that of Taylor as well as that of Wills. The article does not advocate lessening the care given to pauper children, but expresses the hope that in addition to "Pauper Palaces," there be established also "Educational Palaces for all classes and denominations."

In a following article, "London Pauper Children," F. K. Hunt referred to the "architectural display" of the Swinton institution that had won for it "the title of a Pauper Palace."

A Day in a Pauper Palace [lead]
Mr. Taylor & W.H.W.
I, 361–64. July 13, 1850

Taylor, Philip Meadows |*Mr. Meadows Taylor*|, 1808–1876, officer and administrator in India, novelist. Born in Liverpool. Received a few years' schooling – "no education so to speak" (*Story of My Life*, chap. xviii). In 1824 sent to Bombay to enter employ of mercantile house. In same year obtained service with Nizam of Hyderabad; as military officer and civil administrator, remained in service of Nizams for more than thirty years. Administered state of Shorapur during Rajah's minority; had charge of certain ceded districts of the Deccan; kept peace in North Berar during the Mutiny; thereafter administrator of Shorapur and Raichur district. Was trusted and loved by natives. C.S.I. 1869. Wrote for Indian periodicals; was *Times* correspondent in India, 1841–53; sent occasional contributions to *Athenaeum*. After his retirement, contributed articles to *Edin. Rev.* and a novel to *Indian Mail*. As author of *Confessions of a Thug*, 1839, and five historical novels, stands as first important Anglo-Indian novelist. Wrote also letterpress for various volumes of sketches and photographs of Indian scenes, temples, etc.; a history of India, 1870; *The Story of My Life*, published posthumously.

Weld Taylor, who lithographed a portrait of Dickens, recorded: "Mr. Dickens one day was pleased to desire me to say to my brother ... that he had read his work, *Confessions of a Thug*, with great interest, at which my brother was very much gratified. My brother was then in India, but, I think, afterwards made Mr. Dickens's acquaintance" (Kitton, *Charles Dickens by Pen and Pencil*, suppl., p. 6). In his autobiography, Taylor does not mention Dickens; Edgar Johnson (*Charles Dickens*, II, 1121) states that the two writers were acquainted.

Dickens wrote to Taylor, May 1, 1850, thanking him for his "obliging note" and stating that he would be happy to retain his *H.W.* contribution, for which payment would be made on the usual terms, by post. Dickens's letter was sent, presumably, to the address recorded for Taylor in the Office Book – "Harold X Dublin," i.e., Old Court, Harold's Cross, the Taylor family home. According to his autobiography, Taylor was not in Dublin in 1850, but in Shorapur. Taylor had titled his contribution "The Mischief Maker"; in its *H.W.* publication it appeared as "The Great Cat and Dog Question."

D.N.B.

The Great Cat and Dog Question
I, 172–75. May 18, 1850

Thomas, T. M. The two items listed below are the only items that the Office Book assigns to a "Thomas" with the name accompanied by initials. "A Suburban Connemara" is the third item assigned to a Thomas; payment is recorded as "Handed by W.H.W." "Margaret Fuller" is the eleventh item assigned to a Thomas; payment is recorded as "Advanced by W.H.W." The same payment notations appear for various of the items proved by reprinting to be by William Moy Thomas (below). Both items deal with subjects in which William Moy Thomas had an interest. "A Suburban Connemara" describes a squalid district of London; William Moy Thomas's "Milton's Golden Lane" does the same. "Margaret Fuller" discusses the American writer; William Moy Thomas, though he confessed that he had little acquaintance with American literature, did write an article on Poe (*Pictures in a Mirror*). The initials "T.M." seem to be a mis-recording for "W.M."

The article "Margaret Fuller" motivated Landor's poem "On the Death of M. D'Ossoli and His Wife Margaret Fuller," *Examiner*, May 8, 1852.

A Suburban Connemara
II, 562–65. March 8, 1851
Margaret Fuller v, 121–24. April 24, 1852

Thomas, William Moy |*Mr. Thomas, Thomas*|, 1828–1910, journalist, scholar. Began study for the law, but soon turned his attention to writing; became private secretary to Charles Wentworth Dilke of the *Athenaeum*. Contributed to *Athenaeum, Chambers's, Economist, N. & Q.*, and other periodicals. London correspondent for New York *Round Table*; on staff of *Daily News*; dramatic critic for *Graphic* and for *Academy*. First editor of *Cassell's*, in which his novel *A Fight for Life* appeared. Edited scholarly edition of William Collins's poems, 1858, and of Lord Wharncliffe's *Letters and Works* of Mary Wortley Montagu, 1861. Established certain biographical facts concerning Chatterton and Richard Savage. Mentioned by Hatton, *Journalistic London* (p. 62), as "a writer of rare acumen and large knowledge of books, plays and actors."

Thomas was introduced to Dickens in 1850 by Talfourd. Dickens came to think highly of Thomas's ability and judgment. In a letter of June 28, 1858, concerning an article on the Royal Literary Fund that Thomas was about to send to the *North Brit. Rev.*, Dickens expressed himself as thoroughly confident that the article would be "manly and right." Thomas wrote for *Social Notes*, Oct. 25, 1879, an article on the social purpose in Dickens's novels. He served as one of the vice-presidents of the Dickens Fellowship.

Some seven months after Thomas had begun contributing to *H.W.*, Dickens wrote to ask Wills what had become of "the Alice-and-the-Angel man, whose name I always forget" (Aug. 31, 1851: MS Huntington Library). In later letters to Wills he suggested subjects that he thought Thomas would handle well. Thomas's paper on hops Dickens thought "*extremely well done*"; another (apparently "Market Gardens") he liked very much but would have wished to be "a little more picturesque" (to Wills, Oct. 12, 1852; June 18, 1853). "Miss Furbey" Dickens found "very good indeed. Close, original, vigorous, and graphic." He suggested a slight alteration to give the story greater interest and "quiet pathos" (to Wills, May 30, 1854); as it appeared in *H.W.*, the story incorporated Dickens's suggestion. In his preface to *When the Snow Falls*, Thomas stated that he was indebted to Wills for "the idea of the principal incident" in "The Two Rivers" (titled "Somebody's Story" in *H.W.*), and to Dickens for "the outline" of "The Last Howley of Killowen"; Thomas thought that Dickens had received the outline "from a correspondent," as a suggestion for a *H.W.* story. Thomas did not contribute to *H.W.* during the last half year of its publication, but he did contribute to *A.Y.R.* A humorous article in the *Queen*, Dec. 21, 1861, depicted him in company with Dickens, Wills, Sala, Wilkie Collins, and Hollingshead, concocting the Christmas number of that year.

"Market Gardens," listed below among items not reprinted, ends with the announcement: "... we intend to arouse [*H.W.* readers] at daybreak one fine morning, with a summons to accompany us to Covent Garden Market" ("Covent Garden Market" appeared four weeks later). The comment confirms the Office Book ascription to Thomas of "Market Gardens."

Of the items not reprinted, only one calls for comment – "Transported for Life." This is an account of the transportation to Norfolk Island, then to Van Diemen's Land, of William Henry Barber (not named in the article). Barber, a solicitor convicted of complicity in a case of fraud and forgery, had been transported in 1844; he had received a final unconditional pardon in 1848. (Dickens had in his library a copy of *The Case of Mr. W. H. Barber* [Stonehouse, *Catalogue*, p. 89]; at least six editions of *The Case* were issued in London in 1849.) The *H.W.*

account, told in first person, is stated to have "been taken down from the lips of the narrator, whose sufferings are described; with the object of shewing what Transportation, at the present time, really is." Why Barber should have had his narrative "taken down," in place of writing it himself, is not clear; there seems no reason to assume the "Thomas" who took it down to be other than William Moy Thomas. W. L. Clay (*The Prison Chaplain*, p. 215n) referred to the article as a "painfully interesting narrative" giving "a good account of Norfolk Island" under the administration of Major Joseph Childs. Certain regulations as recorded in the article were no longer in force at the time that the article appeared in *H.W.*; this fact had apparently been called to the attention of Dickens or of Wills. In the "chip" "Transportation for Life," Aug. 28, 1852, Wills recorded certain of the regulations that had superseded earlier ones.

Harper's reprinted "A Guild Clerk's Tale," with acknowledgment to *H.W.*; "A Leaf from the Parish Register," without acknowledgment.

See also T. M. Thomas (above).

D.N.B. suppl. 1901–1911

The Other Garret II, 364–69. Jan. 11, 1851
A Guild Clerk's Tale
II, 437–44. Feb. 1, 1851
Alice and the Angel [lead]
III, 1–9. March 29, 1851
The Island in the River
III, 315–21. June 28, 1851, and the 2 following nos.
The Home of the Hundred Blind Men
IV, 195–204. Nov. 22, 1851
A True Account of an Apparition
V, 27–31. March 27, 1852
A Guest for the Night
VI, 175–81. Nov. 6, 1852
Cogswell's VI, 253–57. Nov. 27, 1852
Doctor Chillingworth's Prescription
VI, 292–96. Dec. 11, 1852
Somebody's Story A Round of Stories (Christmas 1852), pp. 7–11
My Shadowy Passion
VI, 485–92. Feb. 5, 1853
Myself and My Family [lead]
VII, 193–202. April 30, 1853
The Borrowed Book
VII, 317–24. June 4, 1853
A Leaf from the Parish Register
VIII, 437–40. Jan. 7, 1854
Miss Furbey IX, 417–21. June 17, 1854
The Last Howley of Killowen
IX, 513–19. July 15, 1854
Dr. Graves of Warwick Street
XII, 524–28. Dec. 29, 1855
The Legend of My Native Town
XVII, 53–58. Jan. 2, 1858
Famine Aboard!
XVII, 108–112. Jan. 16, 1858
Running Away XVII, 133–35. Jan. 23, 1858
Tried Friendship
XVIII, 387–97. Oct. 9, 1858

The 21 items repr. in *When the Snow Falls. By W. Moy Thomas.* 2 vols. London: Sampson Low, Son, & Co., 1859. Pub. in *H.W.* acknowledged.

An Englishman's Castle
IV, 321–24. Dec. 27, 1851
How to Be an Evergreen
V, 42–44. March 27, 1852
Hops VI, 109–115. Oct. 16, 1852
Milton's Golden Lane
VI, 181–86. Nov. 6, 1852
Bookstalls [lead]
VII, 289–93. May 28, 1853
Covent Garden Market [lead]
VII, 505–511. July 30, 1853
Twelve Miles from the Royal Exchange
XII, 333–36. Nov. 3, 1855
Infamous Mr. Fuller
XVIII, 64–71. July 3, 1858
Old Customs XVIII, 547–52. Nov. 20, 1858

The 9 items repr. (with other periodical items) in *Pictures in a Mirror. By W. Moy Thomas.* London: Groombridge and Sons, 1861. Pub. in "various magazines" acknowledged.

Sentimental Journalism
IV, 550–52. Feb. 28, 1852
Transported for Life
V, 455–64. July 31, 1852, and the following no.
Some Compliments of the Season [lead]
Thomas & Sala
VI, 313–17. Dec. 18, 1852
Market Gardens [lead]
VII, 409–414. July 2, 1853

Missing, a Married Gentleman
IX, 227–28. April 22, 1854
Revolvers IX, 352–56. May 27, 1854

Thompson. *Not identified.* The contributor suggests that railway clerks, poorly paid as they are, should unite to establish a fund to provide them assistance in time of sickness or disability. The £1.1.0 payment for the 1-col. item is twice the standard rate of payment.

Some sixty writers named Thompson flourished at the time.

Sick Railway Clerks [chip]
XIII, 325. April 19, 1856

Thornbury, George Walter |*Thornbury, W. Thornbury*|, 1828–1876, misc. writer. Privately educated. Studied to become artist, then turned his attention to writing. His first articles appeared in Bristol *Journal*, 1845. Became art critic for *Athenaeum*. For thirty years was industrious contributor of prose and verse to periodicals – *Ainsworth's*, *Bentley's Misc.*, *Welcome Guest*, *Once a Week*, *Art Journal*, *Chambers's*, and many others. Published some twenty-five books, several of them being collections of his periodical contributions. They include works on social history of England, a life of the artist Turner, sketches of travel and life in foreign countries; also some novels, translations, and volumes of verse. Gained some contemporary reputation as poet.

Thornbury and Dickens were on friendly terms. Copies of three of his books that he presented to Dickens Thornbury inscribed with his "kind regards" or his "very kind regards" (Stonehouse, *Catalogue*). His *Tour round England* he dedicated to Dickens.

Dickens in general liked Thornbury's *H.W.* and *A.Y.R.* contributions. For some years, he wrote to Thornbury in 1866, he had found pleasure in reading his articles. Dickens's letters to Thornbury concern mainly Thornbury's proposals for a series of *A.Y.R.* articles titled "Old Stories Retold." Various of the proposals Dickens rejected as being "mere Newgate Calendar" material without significant bearing on social history. Too much material of that kind, he wrote, would be not only unwholesome for readers, but also distasteful to them. "We must not have too many murders" (April 1, July 10, 1867). Thornbury reprinted a selection of the articles (*Old Stories Re-told*, 1870).

One of Thornbury's early *A.Y.R.* contributions – "Her Majesty's Irish Mail" (July 16, 1859) – angered Irish readers, resulting, wrote Dickens, in "coarse and unreasonable attacks" on himself; he saw nothing in the "innocently meant article" that could have given such "desperate offence" (to Percy Fitzgerald, Aug. 2, 1859; Fitzgerald, *Memoirs of an Author*, I, 113–14). Dickens suggested to Thornbury the writing for *A.Y.R.* of "a tour through England," bringing in historical, biographical, and legendary material that would interest the general reader. Thornbury carried out the suggestion, reprinting the articles in 1870, with some revision, as *A Tour round England.* In *Turkish Life and Character*, 1860; *Tales for the Marines*, 1865; and *Criss-Cross Journeys*, 1873, Thornbury reprinted various other of his *A.Y.R.* contributions.

In the Office Book, Fitzgerald is recorded as author of "Pictures and Ballads"; his name is marked out and substituted by that of Thornbury.

D.N.B.

The Stoker's Poetry
XV, 114–16. Jan. 31, 1857
The Galleys XVII, 562–66. May 29, 1858
*At a Bull-Fight [lead]
XVIII, 457–63. Oct. 30, 1858
*Seville XVIII, 492–98. Nov. 6, 1858
*Sherry XVIII, 508–514. Nov. 13, 1858
*In Search of Don Quixote [lead]
XVIII, 529–34. Nov. 20, 1858
*A Ride through the Raisin Country [lead]
XIX, 1–7. Dec. 4, 1858
*Gib XIX, 42–47. Dec. 11, 1858
*The Alhambra XIX, 62–68. Dec. 18, 1858
*Lisbon XIX, 84–89. Dec. 25, 1858
*Spanish Hotels XIX, 132–37. Jan. 8, 1859

*Steward! xix, 163–68. Jan. 15, 1859
*Up and down the Giralda
xix, 186–92. Jan. 22, 1859
*Idle Hours in Cadiz
xix, 205–210. Jan. 29, 1859
*The Inquisition's Gala-Day
xix, 243–49. Feb. 12, 1859
*Murillo and His Picture Children
xix, 271–75. Feb. 19, 1859
*Out of Doors in Malaga
xix, 301–306. Feb. 26, 1859
*Going to Africa
xix, 315–21. March 5, 1859
*In Africa xix, 348–54. March 12, 1859
*Spanish Proverbs
xix, 390–93. March 26, 1859
*Pictures and Ballads [lead]
xix, 409–415. April 2, 1859
*Spanish Dinners
xix, 444–49. April 9, 1859
*The Tournament at the Alhambra
xix, 484–89. April 23, 1859
*My Turkish Master at Seville
xix, 517–22. April 30, 1859
*My Spanish Kaleidoscope
xix, 565–70. May 14, 1859
*The Spain of Cervantes and the Spain of Gil Blas xix, 580–84. May 21, 1859
*My Farewell Dinner at Gib
xix, 602–605. May 28, 1859

*Repr., with two additional chaps., as *Life in Spain: Past and Present. By Walter Thornbury.* 2 vols. London: Smith, Elder and Co., 1859. Pub. in *H.W.* acknowledged.

Tiffin. *Not identified.* Payment for the contribution made by post-office order.

VERSE

King Dirt. A Song Adapted to a Slow Sanitary Movement
v, 31–32. March 27, 1852

Tomkins, Mary Jane |*Miss Tomkins*|. The Office Book notation accompanying payment record for the first item listed below reads: "Enclosed & left in Russell Place." The Tomkins residing in Russell Place in the 1850s was John Newton Tomkins (1812–1876), resident surgeon at the National Vaccine Establishment, 8 Russell Place. (Address correctly given as Russell Place, *Plarr's Lives*, i, xxiii; incorrectly given as Russell Square, ii, 423.) Tomkins's work was the examination of specimens of vaccine to be sent to various vaccination stations throughout the country. "In these examinations he was assisted by a favourite sister" – Mary Jane. Mary Jane Tomkins "had some reputation as a writer of poems." She became the wife of Dr. Gustavus Plarr, an Alsatian; she and her husband lived some time on the Continent; when their house was burned down during the Franco-Prussian War, they removed to Scotland. They were the parents of Victor Gustave Plarr, librarian to the Royal College of Surgeons of England (*Plarr's Lives*, ii, 422–23; i, vii).

The Office Book record of Horne's name jointly with Miss Tomkins's for "Winter Violets" indicates that Horne revised the poem. At the date that the poem appeared, however, Horne was no longer on the *H.W.* staff, his engagement having terminated in mid-May 1851. In what capacity he is listed as reviser is, thus, not clear. He may have known Miss Tomkins and worked on the poem with her personally; or, as former staff member, he may have been asked to revise the poem for its appearance in *H.W.* It is possible, though unlikely, that he revised the poem before the termination of his engagement; items once accepted for publication did not usually remain for more than two months unpublished.

VERSE

The Mother's Test ii, 612. March 22, 1851
Winter Violets *Miss Tomkins & Horne*
iii, 468. Aug. 9, 1851
Alice's Posies vi, 36–37. Sept. 25, 1852
The Two Statues vi, 540–41. Feb. 19, 1853
Old London Bridge *Miss Tomkins & W.H.W.* viii, 204. Oct. 29, 1853
At Thy Peril ix, 248–49. April 29, 1854
Before Sebastopol xi, 85. Feb. 24, 1855

Townsend. *Not identified.* The contributor is obviously an Englishman who has spent some time in Germany. States that he found "Amy, the Child" in "an old

German pocket-book"; that he was well acquainted with the German university student Max of whom he tells in "Max and His Companions" and that the incident that he relates is true. No payment recorded for either contribution. The first reprinted in *Harper's*, without acknowledgment to *H.W.*

Amy, the Child VIII, 431–32. Dec. 31, 1853
Max and His Companions
XVII, 44–48. Dec. 26, 1857

Townsend, E. |*E. Townsend, Townsend*|. *Not identified.* The third item listed below is not a joint writing of the two contributors whose names are attached to it; it consists of two separate sections (unrelated except by the fact that both are motivated by the Indian Mutiny), placed under the joint heading obviously by the editorial office. The first section – the longer – has no subtitle; the second has the subtitle "Indian English." The order of names attached to the item indicates that the first section is by Townsend, the second by Hamilton. The payment allotment – two guineas to Townsend, one guinea to Hamilton – confirms this ascription.

The first section of that article and the four other articles listed below are clearly by one writer (prob. not the Townsend, above, who contributed the two German items). The articles indicate the writer to be an educated man, an English officer of long service in India, thoroughly familiar with the country and its people, critical of British military regulations and policy there. In his first contribution the writer states that "years ago" he was brigade-major in a unit of irregular cavalry stationed in the vicinity of Poona, under command of a brigadier whom he names as "Daintry." Daintry's order that the men shave off their beards resulted in the mutiny of the troops and their killing of Daintry. The matter was "hushed up," states the writer, the mutinous regiment being disbanded and its name "blotted out of the Company's books." The writer's vague reference to the date of the mutiny makes it impossible to identify it with any mutiny recorded in military histories; but there is no reason to regard the account as other than factual (cf. the Vellore mutiny, 1806). The writer's reference (in "Indian Irregulars") to his seeing a Sikh cut down "not far from where Lord Gough was standing" in an engagement during "one of the Sutlej affairs" indicates that he was in India during the first Sikh War, 1845–46, or during the second Sikh War, 1848–49. His reference to news that "may be wafted to us from India" indicates that he was not in India at the time of writing for *H.W.*

Payment for two of the contributions made by cheque.

The Townsends with initial "E" listed in the *East-India Register* from the 1820s to and including the 1850s are the following, each of whom served in the Military Division, Bengal Presidency, beginning his service in the 1820s: Edward Townsend, conductor, Dept. of Public Works, 2nd Division, thereafter warrant officer; Edward Nelson Townsend, captain, 31st Regt. Native Infantry; Edward Richard Townsend, assistant surgeon.

In the Office Book, Capper is recorded as author of "Indian Hill Stations"; his name is marked out and substituted by that of Townsend.

A Mutiny in India
XVI, 154–56. Aug. 15, 1857
Indian Irregulars
XVI, 244–46. Sept. 12, 1857
Indian Recruits and Indian English
Townsend & A. H. A. Hamilton
XVI, 319–22. Oct. 3, 1857
Lutfullah Khan
XVI, 490–96. Nov. 21, 1857
Indian Hill Stations
XVII, 316–19. March 20, 1858

Townshend, Chauncy Hare |*Townshend, The Revd. C. H. Townshend*|, 1798–1868, poet. Student at Eton. B.A. Cambridge, 1821; M.A. 1824. Took holy orders but was not long active in the ministry. Had means and could devote himself to various aesthetic pursuits; was amateur painter, musician; collected pictures, coins, gems. Became interested in clairvoyance and mesmerism. Spent much time in travel; passed greater part of his later years at his villa in Lausanne. Contributed to *Knight's Quarterly Magazine, Blackwood's.* Author of *A Descriptive Tour in Scotland,* 1840; *Sermons in Sonnets,* 1851, and other volumes of poems; two books on mesmerism.

Townshend met Dickens in 1840, through Dr. John Elliotson, and became his devoted friend. "I never, never, never was better loved by man than I was by him, I am sure. Poor dear fellow, good affectionate gentle creature," wrote Dickens to Georgina Hogarth, March 12, 1868, on learning of Townshend's death. "It is not a light thing to lose such a friend, and I truly loved him." Among the miscellaneous sonnets in *Sermons in Sonnets ... and Other Poems,* Townshend included the sonnet "To the Author of Oliver Twist, Nicholas Nickleby, &c.," in which he praised Dickens for his "portraitures of life" wherein evil was redeemed by good; he included in the volume also "Song of Emily," based on the character in *David Copperfield.* Townshend dedicated to Dickens *The Three Gates;* in his dedicatory poem he expressed his love for Dickens and paid tribute to Dickens's "wielding the pen" against social wrongs. Dickens dedicated *Great Expectations* to Townshend and presented to him the MS. In his will, Townshend appointed Dickens his literary executor, charged with publishing a selection of Townshend's notes, to make known his religious views. Out of the disorganized mass of papers left by Townshend, Dickens contrived a book, *Religious Opinions of the Late Reverend Chauncy Hare Townshend,* 1869, which he doubted that anyone would ever read. Percy Fitzgerald thought that he recognized a sketch of Townshend in Cousin Feenix of *Dombey and Son,* as well as in Twemlow of *Our Mutual Friend* (*Memories of Charles Dickens,* p. 317; *Life of Charles Dickens,* I, 259; II, 135).

On Aug. 19, 1854, Dickens sent Wills a poem by Townshend to be inserted in *H.W.*; it was better, he wrote, than one that Wills had used. Dickens stated that he had in hand two other of Townshend's poems. On Nov. 10, 1855, he mentioned to Wills "some Xmas Verses of Townshend's," asking Wills to send them to him: "... I will try to put them into shape for the ordinary No." The date of the letter indicates that the poem referred to is "Work for Heaven," though it is difficult to see how "Work for Heaven" could originally have been a Christmas verse. In reprinting the poem, Townshend made no change in its wording. In a letter to Wills, Aug. 10, 1856 (to appear in Pilgrim *Letters*), Dickens asked Wills to insert in *H.W.* a paper of Townshend's of which he did not think highly, but which he wished to have used because he had rejected numerous articles that Townshend had submitted. "Fly Leaves," the only prose item that the Office Book assigns to Townshend, appeared the following month. The Office Book records payment for that item, but not for the three poems by Townshend.

D.N.B.

PROSE

Fly Leaves XIV, 201–205. Sept. 13, 1856

VERSE

The True Voice X, 84–85. Sept. 9, 1854
Remedy X, 132–33. Sept. 23, 1854
Work for Heaven XII, 396. Nov. 24, 1855

The 3 items repr. in *The Three Gates. In Verse. By Chauncy Hare Townshend.* London: Chapman and Hall, 1859. Pub. in *H.W.* acknowledged.

Trollope, Theodosia (Garrow) |*Mrs. Trollope*|, 1825–1865, author; first wife of Thomas Adolphus Trollope. Was talented as musician, artist, linguist, verse writer. In her writing, was encouraged by Landor, who expressed extravagant admiration of her verses; through his introduction became contributor in 1839 to Lady Blessington's *Book of Beauty;* contributed also to *Keepsake.* Published, 1846, translation of Niccolini's *Arnaldo da Brescia,* dedicated to Landor. Married in 1848. At Villino Trollope, a centre of social and literary life in Florence, was a celebrated hostess; to her husband, was "the angel in the house" (*What I Remember,* p. 515). After her marriage, continued her literary work, both in translation and in original writing. Set some of her verses to music. One of her poems appeared in *English Woman's Journal*, 1858; a prose contribution in *Victoria Regia*. Contributed to *Athenaeum* a series of letters in cause of Italian freedom; reprinted, 1861, as *Social Aspects of the Italian Revolution*. Contributed to *Cornhill* articles on three contemporary Italian poets.

The baby Beatrice of the *H.W.* poem was the daughter born to Mrs. Trollope in March 1853. In "English Authors in Florence," *Atlantic Monthly*, Dec. 1864, Kate Field mentioned the poem by title as an "exceedingly charming" example of Mrs. Trollope's poetry, stating that it had "appeared several years ago in 'Household Words.' "

According to the *Reader*, April 22, 1865, Mrs. Trollope wrote "papers on home topics for *All the Year Round*."

D.N.B.

VERSE

Baby Beatrice xi, 303–304. April 28, 1855

Turner, G. |*G. Turner*, followed by what is apparently address: Mr. Grey, Edgeley, Stockport; *Turner* (overwritten), Adswood|. Directories afford no help in identifying the contributor. He seems most likely to be the journalist Godfrey Wordsworth Turner, 1825–1891 (Allibone, Boase), usually mentioned by his contemporaries as "Godfrey Turner." Godfrey Wordsworth Turner studied art, then turned to journalism. As contributor and staff member was connected with numerous periodicals, e.g., *Spectator, Morning Chronicle, Leader, John Bull, Comic Times, Train, Daily News*; longest connection was with *Daily Telegraph*. Mentioned by Hatton, *Journalistic London* (p. 138), as writer of "graceful verse and literary sketches." Author of *Jest and Earnest*, 1861, a medley of prose and verse; two works on paintings, a guide to International Fisheries Exhibition, a handbook titled *Picturesque Wales*. Was friend of the young *H.W.* writers Sala, Yates, Hollingshead, the Broughs. Recorded that he met Dickens "at various times in my very young days, when in fact I was but a schoolboy and he a young and successful author"; later saw Dickens in a performance of *Not So Bad As We Seem* (Kitton, *Charles Dickens by Pen and Pencil*, pp. 182–83). Wrote " 'Boz' and the Play," *Theatre*, April 1885.

Another G. Turner – George Gladstone Turner – published, between 1881 and 1887, three volumes of narrative and lyric poems.

VERSE

At Rest xvii, 156. Jan. 30, 1858
Swallows xvii, 469. May 1, 1858

Twamley, Louisa Anne: *See* Meredith, Louisa Anne (Twamley)

Tyas. *Not identified*. The contributor relates a story of Basque passion and vengeance, told to him while he was travelling in the Pyrenees. Payment made by cheque. Item reprinted in *Harper's*, without acknowledgment to *H.W.*

Among writers named Tyas who flourished at the time were Robert Tyas (1811–1879), author of *Flowers and Heraldry, Flowers from Foreign Lands*, and other works; and George Tyas, author of *The Battles of Wakefield*, 1854.

Basque Blood ix, 364–68. June 3, 1854

V

Vincent, Frank or perh. **Francis** |*F. Vincent*, 4 St. James's Barton, Bristol; *Vincent*|. Bristol directories of the late 1850s list various tradesmen named Vincent, none recorded as resident at the St. James's Barton address. The only Vincent with initial "F" is Francis Vincent, listed in 1856 (also later) as owner or manager of a lodging-house, 48 College St.

The contributor is a well-educated Englishman. According to his *H.W.* articles, he went to the Port Phillip district of Australia "many years ago, when Australia was little more than a vast sheep-walk"; "unwilling to settle prematurely," he took a tour from one station to another in what later became Victoria, having letters of introduction to several squatters. Later he settled at Gundagai, on the Murrumbidgee River, New South Wales, and brought his wife "up from Sydney." During one of his years of residence at Gundagai – in the late evening and the night of the last day of March – occurred a flood that inundated the entire Gundagai valley and resulted in the loss of "several lives." There is record, from 1844 to 1852 (after which date the Gundagai settlement was moved to a higher site) of several floods in that district. The flood that the writer tells of was not the flood of 1852 – the "great flood," which occurred in June and resulted in the loss of more than a hundred lives (Gormly, *Exploration and Settlement in Australia,* pp. 196–98, et passim); but it could have been any one of the intervening floods that may have occurred at the end of March. Thus, the writer's account does not serve to establish the exact date of his Gundagai residence. The latest date that the writer mentions in connection with his residence in Australia is 1853, when he visited the gold fields of Victoria. He must have left Australia not later than the latter months of 1857. The Office Book records (with the Bristol address) payment for his first contribution as made Feb. 8, 1858.

In conversation that the writer records in "The Waters Are Out," his wife addresses him as "Frank"; another person asks "if that was the residence of Mr. Frank," i.e., of the writer. His Christian name would thus appear to be Frank (or perh. Francis).

Sands' Country Directory and Gazetteer of New South Wales for 1881–82, compiled by James Tingle, lists a Frank Vincent, newspaper proprietor of Uralla in the Gundagai district (information from Mitchell Library, Sydney). This may be the *H.W.* contributor.

The similarity of name and the connection with Bristol seem to indicate some relationship between the *H.W.* contributor and Francis Vincent, 1822–1884, born in Bristol, who emigrated to the U.S. by 1839 and became a Delaware newspaper proprietor (*Appleton*).

Coo-ee! XVII, 232–36. Feb. 20, 1858
John Chinaman in Australia *F. Vincent & Morley* XVII, 416–20. April 17, 1858
Australian Jim Walker XVII, 500–504. May 8, 1858
The Waters Are Out XVII, 597–600. June 5, 1858

Vizetelly, Henry, perh.: *See* Brooks, Mr.

W

Walker, Thomas, prob. |*Mr. Walker*|, 1822–1898, journalist. Attended school from age six to ten; apprenticed to carpenter. Determined to become journalist. Learned shorthand; educated himself by reading and study; received some instruction in languages from Gustave Strauss (*Reminiscences of an Old Bohemian,* pp. 277–78); learned German in order to read Kant in the original. Reporter for *Medical Times;* contributed to *Eliza Cook's Journal* and *Daily News.* Obtained subordinate post on staff of *Daily News;* in 1851 became foreign and general subeditor; editor, 1858–69. Thereafter editor of London *Gazette.* Devoted his later years to philanthropic work.

A memorandum in the Office Book states that "German Advertisements" was written by Wills, with Murray furnishing the "idea & some ads" and Walker furnishing "the other ads." Thomas Walker, at the time that the item appeared in *H.W.*, was working for the *Daily News* under the foreign subeditor J. A. Crowe. His work, stated Walker, was to translate and condense news from European and South American journals. Crowe (*Reminiscences,* p. 72) specifically mentioned Walker's work as translating material from German periodicals.

D.N.B.

German Advertisements *W.H.W., E. C. Murray, & Mr. Walker*
II, 33–35. Oct. 5, 1850

Ward, Mrs. *Not identified.* The contributor describes the Emperor Louis Napoleon as she chanced to see him in 1858 in the château garden at Plombières. She has some interest in and some knowledge of international politics; she refers to the political implication of certain of the Emperor's moves.

The Mrs. Ward most likely to be the *H.W.* contributor is Mrs. Harriet Ward (Allibone). Mrs. Harriet Ward was wife of an English officer; lived at various times on the Continent and had much interest in France and the French. Contributed to *Bentley's Misc.* and *Sharpe's.* Author of *Helen Charteris,* 1848, and other novels; *Five Years in Kaffirland,* 1848; and a few other books.

Another Mrs. Ward – Emma Georgina Elizabeth Ward – lived for many years in France. Author of *Outside Paris during the Two Sieges. By an Englishwoman,* 1871, originally intended for private circulation only. No record, however, of her writing other books or contributing to periodicals.

Match-Making Majesty
XIX, 359–60. March 12, 1859

Ward, Nathaniel Bagshaw |*Mr. Ward*|, 1791–1868, botanist. Studied at London Hospital. M.R.C.S. Succeeded to his father's medical practice in Whitechapel. From boyhood had ardent interest in botany; by chance discovered principle of growing plants in glazed cases; later demonstrated value of Wardian cases in transporting living plants for great distances over long periods of time. Examiner in botany to Society of Apothecaries, 1836–54. Original member of Edinburgh Botanical Society; co-founder of Microscopical (later Royal Microscopical) Society. F.L.S. 1817; F.R.S. 1852. His name commemorated by his friends W. H. Harvey and W. J. Hooker in *Wardia,* a genus of South African mosses. Author of *On the Growth of Plants in Closely Glazed Cases,* 1842.

"Back Street Conservatories" relates Ward's discovery of the principle of growing plants in glazed cases, gives brief directions for constructing such cases, and advocates the practice of window-gardening especially among city-dwellers of "the humbler orders." The article quotes from Ward's *On the Growth of Plants,* which it ascribes in a footnote to "H. B. Ward." The "inventor of the 'miniature conservatory,'" states the article, "has, we believe, received no testimonial whatever of the services he has rendered to horticulture from those who have been most benefited by the invention. He reaps his reward, however, in the consciousness of the good he has done 'in his generation,' and in the feeling that, in the homes of many, his name, associated with ferns and flowers, has become a 'Household Word.'"

D.N.B.

Back Street Conservatories *Mr. Ward & W.H.W.* II, 271–75. Dec. 14, 1850

Warr. *Not identified.* The writer's contributions contain many references to the observations of naturalists and travellers, as also occasional literary references. Payment for the first contribution made in cash.

Meteors XIII, 103–105. Feb. 16, 1856
The Scattering of Seed
XIV, 56–59. Aug. 2, 1856

Watts, Anna Mary (Howitt): *See* Howitt, Anna Mary

Watts, Alaric Alexander |*A. A. Watts*|, 1797–1864, poet, journalist. Attended a grammar school and an academy in Kent. Worked as tutor and as clerk. About 1818 became connected in editorial capacity with *New Monthly*. Became contributor to *Literary Gazette*; for some years continued his connection with the periodical. Editor, 1822–25, of Leeds *Intelligencer*; then of Manchester *Courier*. In 1827 took part in establishing the *Standard*. Founder and for some years editor of *United Service Gazette*; connected also with other periodicals, many of them minor provincial journals. Edited the *Literary Souvenir*, one of earliest and most popular of the annuals, for which he secured contributions from distinguished writers, also fine engravings. Published collections of fugitive verse; initiated the series *Men of the Time*. Published some volumes of poems; also some prose works. Personally, as also in his capacity of author and editor, was butt of ridicule and abuse in *Fraser's*, which re-christened him "Alaric Attila Watts." In 1854 granted Civil List pension of £100 a year "In consideration of his services to literature and to art" (Colles, *Literature and the Pension List*).

Watts's poems, particularly those on the domestic affections, were very popular and earned some high tributes. His "Death of the First-Born," wrote the *Athenaeum* in 1850, had "passed into so many collections that it must be 'familiar as household words' to the reader of the present day." To be the author of that poem and of "My Own Fireside," wrote Sir Robert Peel to Watts, was "an honourable distinction to any one" ("Preface," *Lyrics of the Heart*).

His "Lament for the Fairies" Watts contributed to *H.W.* at the time that the collection in which the poem was to appear was already in the hands of the printers. In the *Examiner*, Longman's first announcement of *Lyrics of the Heart* as "preparing for immediate publication" appeared on Oct. 5 – a week before the poem was published in *H.W.* Three weeks later the book was advertised as "Just ready," but following advertisements announced postponements of the publication date. On Dec. 7 came the explanation that "In consequence of an accident at the Printing-office" publication was further "postponed for a week or ten days." Finally, on Dec. 21, the book was announced as "Now ready." The title page, however, bears the date 1851.

In its book publication "A Lament for the Fairies" contains three stanzas that do not appear in the poem in *H.W.* In the book publication, the line "Yet these fair fictions of our earlier day" (same in *H.W.* and in book publication) is supplied with the erratum notation: for "earlier" read "youthful."

D.N.B.

VERSE

A Lament for the Fairies
II, 59–60. Oct. 12, 1850

Repr. in *Lyrics of the Heart: with Other Poems. By Alaric A. Watts.* London: Longman, Brown, Green, and Longmans, 1851 [1850]. Pub in *H.W.* not acknowledged.

Watts, Alaric Alfred |*A. Watts (Junr.), A. Watts, Junior*|, 1825–1901, clerk in Inland Revenue Office; son of Alaric Alexander Watts (above). In his preface to *Lyrics of the Heart*, Alaric Alexander Watts stated that in 1844 Sir Robert Peel, in recollection of Watts's early poems which Peel so much admired, placed at Watts's disposal a Treasury appointment for his son. Alaric Alfred Watts held the clerkship from that year (*Brit. Imperial Calendar*, 1844). In 1859 married Anna Mary Howitt (above); like his wife, was for a time a believer in spiritualism. Author of a life of his father, 1884; co-author, with his wife, of *Aurora*, 1875, a volume of verse, published anonymously.

Brit. Mus. Cat.

A Premier's Correspondents
IV, 302–305. Dec. 20, 1851

The Carver's College
XII, 107–108. Sept. 1, 1855

Webb, Jonathan. *Not identified.* According to his article, the contributor was an Englishman, some time in the employ of the East India Co. as navigation engineer, stationed in Calcutta. Describes his supervising the launching of the steamer *Megna,* which, on one of its runs from Calcutta to Allahabad in 1838, had grounded at Damadapore. Refers to his having left Calcutta "some years ago"; was apparently in England at the time of writing the article. Payment made by post-office order.

Bengal registers of the late 1830s list the *Megna* and also the *Jumna* (another vessel mentioned in Webb's article); they list some residents named Webb, but not Jonathan Webb.

Aground up the Ganges
VII, 165–68. April 16, 1853

Weir, William |*Mr. Weir, Weir*|, 1802–1858, journalist. Born in Ayrshire. Attended Ayr Academy; studied at Univ. of Göttingen. Called to Scottish bar, 1827. First editor of Glasgow *Argus.* Removed to London; contributed to *Spectator* and to various of Charles Knight's compilations. Engaged by Dickens on staff of *Daily News;* served as the paper's "chief authority on railway and commercial affairs" (Bourne, *English Newspapers,* II, 224–25); in 1854 succeeded F. K. Hunt (above) as editor; held editorship to time of his death. Had extensive and thorough knowledge of literature.

The subjects dealt with in the items that the Office Book assigns to "Mr. Weir" and "Weir" – commerce, transportation, literature, law – accord with the interests of William Weir.

"Comic Leaves from the Statute Book" motivated Knox's article "What *I* Call Sensible Legislation," Jan. 3, 1852.

The first "Short Cuts across the Globe" was reprinted in *Harper's,* with acknowledgment to *H.W.* Both the first and second were included in the Putnam volume of selections from *H.W.*: *The World Here and There,* 1852.

D.N.B.

Short Cuts across the Globe *Mr. Weir & W.H.W.* I, 65–68. April 13, 1850

Short Cuts across the Globe: The Isthmus of Suez *Mr. Weir & W.H.W.*
I, 167–68. May 11, 1850

William Wordsworth
I, 210–13. May 25, 1850

Comic Leaves from the Statute Book *W.H.W. & Weir*
I, 502–504. Aug. 17, 1850

Wells, Sir Thomas Spencer |*Wells*|, 1818–1897, surgeon. Studied at Trinity College, Dublin, and at St. Thomas's Hospital, London. M.R.C.S. 1841; F.R.C.S. (by election) 1844. Assistant surgeon for six years in naval hospital, Malta; left Navy in 1848, but later again entered naval service. Meanwhile, had settled in practice in London. For twenty years surgeon at Samaritan Free Hospital, London; then consulting surgeon. In perfecting technique of ovariotomy, became originator of modern abdominal surgery. Filled all principal offices of the Royal College of Surgeons of England. Recipient of honorary degrees and distinctions, British and foreign. Created baronet 1883. Surgeon to Queen's Household, 1863–96. For some years editor of *Medical Times and Gazette.* Published works on medicine and surgery.

The writer of "In the Dardanelles" tells of his exploring "the classic ground of Troy," minutely familiar to him from his schoolboy studies of Homer. His exploration, he states, took place during the five days in Aug. (no year given) during which H.M. sloop *Modeste,* to which he was attached, was forced to lie at anchor off the town of the Dardanelles while her captain obtained from Constantinople permission to ascend the Strait.

Admiralty Records in the Public Record Office, London, record that the *Modeste* was in the Mediterranean, at sea and at various ports, from the latter part of 1851 through 1853 (as well as later); that on Aug. 25, 1852, a Turkish pilot was taken on at the Dardanelles to pilot the ship to Constantinople; that Thomas Spencer Wells was assigned to the *Modeste* as surgeon Sept. 4, 1851, and discharged from the ship (not from the service) April 7, 1853, at Malta, at own request. The only other Wells listed for the *Modeste* for these years is William Wells, captain's cook, serving Sept.-Nov. 1851.

D.N.B.

In the Dardanelles
VIII, 330–33. Dec. 3, 1853

Wenckstern, Otto von |*Dr. Wenckstern, Dr. Wencstern, Dr. Wenckestern, Wenckstern, Dr. Wenkstern*|, 1819–1869, journalist, author, translator. Born in Rawitsch, Duchy of Posen; son of a German officer. Educated in Bonn. For a time edited *Bonner Zeitung*. Published *Polenlieder*, 1843; *Gedichte*, 1845. Married an Englishwoman. In 1846 went to London, where, in time, he became connected with the *Daily News* and the *Times*. In 1854 served as war correspondent in the Crimea (his *H.W.* article "Heroes Afloat" recounts his voyage to the seat of war). Contributed to *Saturday Review* and to *Fraser's*. Published, in London, translations from the Hungarian and the German: Eötvös's *Village Notary* and Klapka's *Memoirs of the War of Independence in Hungary*; an anthology of Goethe's *Opinions*, compiled from the correspondence and conversations; Max Schlesinger's *Saunterings in and about London*. Also published original works, e.g., *History of the War in Hungary in 1848 and 1849*, 1859, dedicated to the Hon. Mrs. Norton; *Prussia and the Poles*, 1862; *Ten Years of the Schleswig-Holstein Question*, 1863. Died in Port of Spain, Trinidad, where he was newspaper editor in his later years.

Wenckstern had some liking for Dickens's writings. During his apprentice days in a newspaper office, he stated in "The German Exile's New Year's Eve," he translated *A Christmas Carol* into German as a "labour of love."

In his second *H.W.* article, Wenckstern told of his poverty and misery during his first weeks in London and of his fruitless attempts to find employment. The article appeared with the editorial explanation that the writer was "a German gentleman of education, who fled from hopeless poverty, occasioned by political persecution at home, to endure poverty, with hope of better days, in London. ... His hope was that he might earn bread by translating German works, and he had a fancy that he would begin with Hegel; he was prepared also to labour in original composition as an English writer. That he can write English well, our extracts from his autobiographical sketch testify." An editorial comment appended to the article stated that the writer did finally procure employment, as his abilities became known, and that he "is now connected with the Foreign department of an eminent journal, and prospers." The only Office Book notation on revision of Wenckstern's contributions is that "Troops and Jobs in Malta" was "The result of a great pile of MS."

Wenckstern's first two contributions were included in the Putnam volume of selections from *H.W.*: *The World Here and There*, 1852.

Literatur-Lexikon

A Short Trip into Bosnia
III, 182–87. May 17, 1851
Lost in London III, 372–78. July 12, 1851
The Bohemian Schoolmaster
III, 496–501. Aug. 16, 1851
An Austrian State Trial
IV, 18–22. Sept. 27, 1851
The German Exile's New Year's Eve
IV, 325–29. Dec. 27, 1851
When I Served in the Militia
VI, 245–50. Nov. 27, 1852
Pass-Words through All the Russias
VI, 381–84. Jan. 1, 1853
Troops and Jobs in Malta
IX, 266–68. May 6, 1854
Heroes Afloat IX, 593–96. Aug. 5, 1854
English Cookery [chip]
XIII, 116. Feb. 16, 1856

White, James |*White*, Doncaster|, 1794–1861, sporting writer. For many years turf editor of Doncaster *Gazette*. Author, under pseudonym "Martingale," of *Sporting Scenes, and Country Characters*, 1840; *English Country Life*, 1843; *Turf Characters*, 1851.

White was intimately acquainted with the countryside about Doncaster, wrote his friend Henry Hall Dixon (above), and in his wanderings in the woods loved to weave an old legend into shape: "The deserted hut, where a poacher had lived and died, a very lord of the soil to the last, seemed to conjure up in his mind a network of dark romance" (*Saddle and Sirloin*, p. 335). "Ben Close, of Baggenham" is the amusingly told account of a poacher. White says, "I knew him well."

Boase

Ben Close, of Baggenham *White & Morley* VII, 370–72. June 18, 1853

White, James |*Rev. J. White, White, Rev. James White, The Revd. J. White, J [?]. White*|, 1803–1862, divine, author. Studied at Univ. of Glasgow, then at Oxford; B.A. 1827. Curate in Suffolk, then vicar of Loxley, War. Resigned the living on his wife's inheriting a considerable property. Retired to Bonchurch, Isle of Wight; there devoted himself to writing. From 1828 to within a year of his death, contributed to *Blackwood's* more than a hundred essays, reviews, tales, poems. Author of some fifteen works: books of verse; *The Earl of Gowrie*, 1845; *The King of the Commons*, 1846; and other historical plays; various historical accounts of a popular nature, e.g., *Landmarks of the History of England*, 1855; *The Eighteen Christian Centuries*, 1858.

White was a friend of Dickens, a welcome guest at Dickens's home, and the recipient of friendly letters from him. "I knew him many years, and had a great affection for him," wrote Dickens to Alexander Duff-Gordon on White's death (Rolfe, "Additions to the Nonesuch Edition of Dickens' Letters," *Huntington Library Quart.*, Oct. 1941). White was very popular with Dickens, stated Forster, "for his eager good fellowship" (*Life*, Book VI, sect. iii); to enjoy that fellowship, Dickens took a house in Bonchurch for his summer holiday of 1849. Dickens admired White's writings. *The Earl of Gowrie*, of which White presented him a copy, Dickens praised to its author as "a work of most remarkable genius" (Feb. 24, 1846). He expressed high admiration, too, for certain of White's *Blackwood's* articles (to White, Sept. 23, 1849). White dedicated to Dickens *John Savile of Haysted*, 1847, with "the highest admiration and affection of his friend the author."

On Feb. 5, 1850, seven weeks before the first number of *H.W.* appeared, Dickens invited White to become a contributor to the periodical: "... if you would ever write anything for it, you would please me better than I can tell you." "... our money," he added, "is as good as Blackwood's any day in the week." During 1850–51, White did not write for *Blackwood's* – at least, he contributed no prose items (*Wellesley Index*); in Jan. 1852, he again began writing for that periodical, and in the summer of that year sent his first contribution to Dickens. Thereafter, he wrote more frequently for *H.W.* than he did for *Blackwood's*.

In a letter to White, Oct. 19, 1852, Dickens outlined the plan for the Christmas number of that year and asked whether White would write one of the stories. White sent him "The Grandfather's Story." It was, Dickens wrote to him (Nov. 22, 1852), "a very good story indeed," but he was at first doubtful about its suiting "the spirit of the Christmas number"; he did nevertheless use it for that number. Dickens asked White to contribute to the 1853 Christmas number and apparently expected him to write for that of 1858 (to White, Sept. 30, 1853; to Wills, Oct. 2, 1858); White contributed to neither. "The Scotch Boy's Story," White's contribution to the 1856 Christmas number, had been "greatly liked," Dickens wrote to White (Feb. 8, 1857). "When are you going to send something more to H.W.?" he added. One of Dickens's letters (March 7, 1854) mentioned his liking "Club Law": "It is most capitally done. ..." On Jan. 4, 1856, Dickens sent to Wills a paper of White's that he had not read; but, he wrote, "I know the design and it is a good subject." Later in the same month he wrote to Wills that a certain paper by White was bad as lead item. No paper by White appeared as lead item in 1856.

White's amusing "Ignoble Conduct of a Nobleman" brought Dickens a reprimand from a reader who took the story to be by Dickens and saw in it Dickens's tendency "to hold up to derision those of the higher classes." Dickens printed the letter ("Ready Wit," Feb. 4, 1854), remarking that the reader "thoroughly understands a joke, and possesses a quick wit and a happy comprehension."

As far as can be determined, all the items listed below are by the Rev. James White, whether or not specifically so assigned in the Office Book. All are, in one way or another, appropriate as his writing. Three – "A Play in a Great Many Acts," "Tapping the Butts," and "The Little Oak Wardrobe" – are specifically assigned to the Rev. James White. "Ground and Lofty Tumbling" is assigned to "White" with an initial that could be read as "J" or "T"; it is probably by the Rev. James White. The remaining items are assigned merely to "White." Of these, four – the two stories in the Christmas numbers, "Club Law," and "Old Blois" – are established by Dickens's letters as by the Rev. James White. For certain others, the date of payment provides some confirmation of their being by the Rev. James White: payment for "The Deluge at Blissford" and "Jane Markland" was made on the same date as for "The Little Oak Wardrobe"; payment for "General and Mrs. Delormo," on the same date as for "Club Law."

According to Ley (*Dickens Circle*, p. 260), White wrote often for the regular numbers of *A.Y.R.*

Harper's reprinted two of White's *H.W.* contributions, "The Grandfather's Story" and "Two College Friends," neither acknowledged to *H.W.*, but the first credited to Dickens.

D.N.B.

PROSE

A Play in a Great Many Acts v, 366–68. July 3, 1852
Spanish Romance v, 415–17. July 17, 1852
Tapping the Butts [chap. i = lead] v, 501–506. Aug. 14, 1852, and the following no.
Dead, or Alive? vi, 37–42. Sept. 25, 1852
Stop Thief! vi, 281–84. Dec. 4, 1852
The Grandfather's Story A Round of Stories (Christmas 1852), pp. 21–25
The Little Oak Wardrobe vi, 557–62. Feb. 26, 1853
The Deluge at Blissford vii, 80–84. March 26, 1853
Down among the Dead Men viii, 418–24. Dec. 31, 1853
Ignoble Conduct of a Nobleman viii, 477–80. Jan. 14, 1854
Standing on Ceremony viii, 526–28. Jan. 28, 1854
Club Law ix, 114–16. March 18, 1854
General and Mrs. Delormo ix, 449–52. June 24, 1854
Very Advisable [lead] xi, 73–76. Feb. 24, 1855
A Yarn about Young Lions [lead] xi, 145–49. March 17, 1855
Bread Cast on the Waters xi, 326–35. May 5, 1855
What It Is to Have Forefathers xi, 380–84. May 19, 1855
Petition Extraordinary xi, 453–56. June 9, 1855
Alexander the First xi, 573–76. July 14, 1855
Parish Broils [lead] xii, 49–53. Aug. 18, 1855
Sydney Smith [lead] xii, 121–23. Sept. 8, 1855
War and Washing xii, 190–92. Sept. 22, 1855
Nostradamus xii, 296–98. Oct. 27, 1855
Daisy Hope xii, 461–69. Dec. 15, 1855
Old Blois xii, 556–61. Jan. 12, 1856
A King Who *Could* Do Wrong xiii, 37–42. Jan. 26, 1856
Two College Friends xiii, 78–84. Feb. 9, 1856, and the following no.
A Summer Night's Dream xiii, 380–84. May 3, 1856
Mr. Rowlands xiii, 404–408, May 10, 1856
Sir Caribert of the Leaf xiv, 185–90. Sept. 6, 1856
The Scotch Boy's Story [title thus in Office Book; no separate title in *H.W.*] Wreck of the Golden Mary (Christmas 1856), pp. 27–29
Fiction Crushing [lead] xv, 73–76. Jan. 24, 1857

A Testimony in Praise of Testimonials [lead] XV, 121–24. Feb. 7, 1857
Long Life under Difficulties XV, 325–28. April 4, 1857
Family Names XV, 525–28. May 30, 1857
The Hospital Student XV, 536–42. June 6, 1857
Meaning Me, Sir? XVI, 6–9. July 4, 1857
Your Life or Your Likeness [lead] XVI, 73–75. July 25, 1857
"A Gude Conceit o' Oursels" XVII, 260–64. Feb. 27, 1858
Ground and Lofty Tumbling [lead] XIX, 121–32. Jan. 8, 1859

VERSE

Jane Markland. A Tale VII, 131–34. April 9, 1853
Banoolah XI, 57–62. Feb. 17, 1855

Whitehead, Charles |*Whitehead*|, 1804–1862, author. Received good schooling. Was for a time clerk to a London commercial firm; turned to writing. Contributed to annuals – *Friendship's Offering, Amaranth*; wrote for *Monthly Magazine, Court Magazine, Bentley's Misc.*, and other periodicals. For some time editor of Chapman & Hall's *Library of Fiction*; for about eight years, publisher's reader and reviser for Bentley. Unsuccessful in making a living by writing; five times, from 1836 to 1854, found himself forced to ask for financial assistance from Royal Literary Fund; assistance granted in each instance. Stated in his last appeal that he intended to go to New Zealand to set up as schoolmaster. Emigrated to Australia, 1857; no more successful there than he had been in England. Died destitute in Melbourne hospital. Author of *The Solitary*, 1831 (reprinted in *The Solitary, and Other Poems*, 1849); *The Autobiography of Jack Ketch*, 1834; *Richard Savage. A Romance of Real Life*, 1842; also *The Cavalier*, a play produced at the Haymarket, 1836; a life of Sir Walter Ralegh, and other works. Brought out revised edition, 1846, of Dickens's *Memoirs of Joseph Grimaldi.*

The literary association of Whitehead and Dickens resulted from their both being periodical editors and contributors. In 1836, when Chapman & Hall wished to obtain as contributor to their *Library of Fiction* the author of certain sketches in the *Monthly Magazine*, whose name they did not know, Whitehead informed them that the writer was Dickens; Dickens contributed two sketches to the *Library of Fiction* under Whitehead's editorship. Whitehead was, thus, responsible for Dickens's initial connection with Chapman & Hall. There is, however, no substantiation for the story that Whitehead, having declined to write for Chapman & Hall the letterpress for Robert Seymour's sporting sketches, suggested Dickens in his stead – thus leading to the writing of *Pickwick* (Fielding, "Charles Whitehead and Charles Dickens," *Review of English Studies*, April 1952). Whitehead wrote for *Bentley's Misc.* under Dickens's editorship (as also later); Dickens had highly recommended him to Bentley (Dec. 5, 1836) as a contributor – a writer "equally admirable" in "humourous and grave sketches."

Dickens took an earnest concern in Whitehead's struggle with poverty, with the details of which he was acquainted. Whitehead's third and fourth appeals for assistance from the Literary Fund were each supported by a letter from Dickens. In his first letter, Nov. 6, 1843, Dickens stated that he was writing at Whitehead's request. Of Whitehead he wrote: "I know him to be a gentleman of very great accomplishments, and of very high original power as a writer of Fiction. I have always considered him to be an author of remarkable ability; have read his productions with strong interest; and have borne my testimony to their merit on many occasions, when I little thought he would ever need such a service as this at my hands" (Fielding, "Charles Whitehead and Charles Dickens"). In 1845 Dickens agreed to become a subscriber to a book that Whitehead was planning to bring out. This may have been *The Solitary, and Other Poems*, for which Dickens was engaged four years later in obtaining subscribers (letter to Miss Burdett-Coutts, May 7, 1849, in *Heart of Charles Dickens*, ed. Johnson; to Bulwer-Lytton, May 11, 1849).

Dickens's interest in Whitehead further appears in connection with him as a contributor to *H.W.* On Dec. 30, 1855, Dickens wrote to Wills: "If an article comes to the office from Charles Whitehead, will you immediately read it, and – unless it be out of the question: which I hope it won't be – immediately get it cast off, and immediately pay for it: with a turn of the scale in his favour? He is going to New Zealand." The only item by Whitehead to appear in *H.W.* after the date of Dickens's letter was "Nemesis" – a story, not an article (mentioned by title and author in a later letter from Dickens to Wills, April 7, 1856: MS Huntington Library). If it was this item that Dickens wished to have paid for generously, his wishes were ignored. For the 34¼-col. story (marked in the Office Book 36¼ cols.) Whitehead was paid only £15.

D.N.B.

Off! Off! VIII, 442–45. Jan. 7, 1854
Nemesis XIII, 326–34. April 19, 1856, and the following no.

Whitelock. *Not identified.* The contributor could be either English or American. He relates an incident that took place in a gaming-house in Arkansas, illustrating the Americanism "sloped for Texas." Payment marked "Enclosed." Item reprinted in *Harper's*, without acknowledgment to *H.W.*

"Sloped for Texas" [chip] II, 163–64. Nov. 9, 1850

Whitty, Edward Michael, prob. |*Whitty*|, 1827–1860, journalist. Educated at Liverpool Institute and in Hanover. Became reporter on provincial press; from 1846 to 1849 wrote the Parliamentary summary of the *Times*; London correspondent of Liverpool *Journal*; for some years on staff of *Leader*, to which he contributed satirical sketches of Parliamentary proceedings and debates, also sketches of members. Collected some of his *Leader* articles in *History of the Session 1852–3. A Parliamentary Retrospect* and in *The Governing Classes of Great Britain. Political Portraits*, both published 1854. Editor, 1857–58, of *Northern Whig*. Emigrated to Australia to work on Melbourne *Argus*. Died in Melbourne. Author of satirical novel, *Friends of Bohemia*, 1857.

"Post to Australia" is a criticism of Government lack of interest in commerce and trade and of Government dilatoriness in re-establishing the Indian Ocean steamship service that had been discontinued during the Crimean War. "... for mercy's sake," says the writer, "get the circumnavigating discussion out of the Circumlocution Office as fast as possible." The subject is appropriate to the interests of Edward Michael Whitty.

The journalist Michael James Whitty, 1795–1873, Edward Michael Whitty's father, began his career in London, but after 1829 was connected with Liverpool as newspaper editor, borough constable, and newspaper proprietor.

D.N.B.

Post to Australia XIII, 305–306. April 12, 1856

Wickenden, William S. |*Wickenden*|, date of birth and death variously given; *Alumni Cantab.* gives 1797–1864; author. Born in Forest of Dean; son of a farmer. Attended a village day school. Encouraged in his early writing by Dr. Edward Jenner, "who subsequently conferred on me the name of the 'Bard of the Forest,' by which appelation I was afterwards so well known" ("A Sketch of the Early Life of the Author," in Wickenden, *Poems and Tales*). While still a farm labourer, published three books of verse and prose. Learning from Southey's memoir of Henry Kirke White that expenses of a sizar at Cambridge were not so great as he had thought, determined to enter St. John's College; matriculated 1821; his university life made difficult by his poverty and inadequate preparation. B.A. 1825. Ordained; held, in succession, three curacies, but his days plagued by illness and poverty. For many years received assistance from clerical funds. Author of some twenty books, e.g., *The Rustic's Lay, and Other Poems*, 1817; *Adventures in Circassia*, 1847; *A Queer Book*, 1850; *Adventures before Sebastopol*, 1855; *Revelations of a Poor Curate*, 1855.

Dickens subscribed to two copies of Wickenden's *Some Remarkable Passages in the Life of William Wickenden*, 1847 (list of subscribers in *Passages*). Wickenden dedicated to Dickens *Adventures in Circassia*. "I am sprung from the masses," he wrote, "and as you are the Friend of the People, I beg leave to inscribe to you the following pages, and I only regret that the offering is not more worthy of your acceptance."

The narrator of Wickenden's *H.W.* contribution is a young man living in the Forest of Dean.

Boase

A Tale of the Forest of Dean *Wickenden & Morley* III, 461–64. Aug. 9, 1851

Williamson, Miss. Address: Kempston Manor, Bedford. Living at Kempston Manor in the 1850s were the four unmarried daughters of the Rev. Edmond Williamson (*d.* 1839): Frances, Catherine, Elizabeth, and Ann. The eldest was somewhat more than fifty when the items listed below appeared in *H.W.*; the youngest, somewhat more than forty (information from the County Record Office, Bedford). The visit to Norway told of in "Notes from Norway" extended from the summer of 1851 to the winter of that year, lasting perhaps into the early months of 1852. The County Record Office, Bedford, reports that there are at the Office no letters or papers that establish which of the Miss Williamsons made the trip.

The second item listed below is recorded in the Office Book without author or payment notation. It is probably by Miss Williamson. "Notes from Norway" ends with a section titled "Frosty Weather." It seems probable that "Christmas Customs" was originally a section following "Frosty Weather" and that Wills reserved that section for insertion in *H.W.* at a more appropriate time of the year than May.

Notes from Norway
V, 230–35. May 22, 1852, and the following no.

Christmas Customs in Norway [chip]
VI, 356. Dec. 25, 1852

Wills, William Henry |*W.H.W.*|, 1810–1880, journalist. Received limited education; must have acquired knowledge of books by wide reading. J. A. Crowe (*Reminiscences*, p. 71) wrote of him as "well read in Shakespeare and the poets of the last two centuries." According to Vizetelly (*Glances Back through Seventy Years*, I, 247), was "brought up as a wood-engraver" in office of Vizetelly's father, then "drifted into literature." Contributed to *Penny Magazine*, *Saturday Magazine*, and other periodicals. Was on original staff of *Punch*; sometime dramatic critic for the periodical. In Edinburgh, 1842–45, was assistant editor of *Chambers's*. Married Janet Chambers, sister of the Edinburgh publishers. Was on original staff of *Daily News*. From 1850 to 1869, connected with *H.W.* and *A.Y.R.* Author of *The Law of the Land*, produced at Surrey Theatre, 1837. Brought out an edition of the Sir Roger de Coverley papers, 1850; a selection of his *H.W.* contributions and a selection of his contributions to *Chambers's*; an anthology, *Poets' Wit and Humour*, 1861, in which he included two of his own pieces. According to Tinsley (*Random Recollections*, II, 290), was one "of the best known men of his time in the London literary world."

Wills sent at least two items to *Bentley's Misc.* at the time that Dickens was editor of the periodical; Dickens accepted one, returned the other, and invited further contributions. In the latter months of 1845, Wills served as Dickens's secretary during Dickens's establishment of the *Daily News*; he was engaged by Dickens as a member of the staff and remained on the staff under Forster's editorship, after Dickens's resignation as editor. It was Forster who suggested to

Dickens the engagement of Wills as assistant editor of *H.W.*

In the partnership agreement under which *H.W.* was set up, Wills was, with Dickens, with the publishers Bradbury & Evans, and with Forster, one of the joint proprietors; he held an interest of one-eighth share. He was to serve as sub-editor at a salary of eight pounds a week. On Forster's relinquishing his one-eighth share in 1856, Dickens allotted half of that one-eighth to Wills. In the partnership agreement under which *A.Y.R.* was set up, Wills was, with Dickens, joint proprietor; he held an interest of one-fourth share. At a salary of £420 a year, he was to serve as subeditor and also as general manager of "the Commercial Department" (Lehmann, ed., *Charles Dickens As Editor*, pp. 19, 195–97, 212, 261).

H.W. and *A.Y.R.* were Dickens's periodicals. Dickens wanted no brother near the editorial throne. Throughout the nineteen years during which Wills was his co-worker, Dickens accorded him no higher title than "subeditor."* But in the public mind, Wills was as much a part of the two periodicals as was Dickens. Of *H.W.* (or at times of *H.W.* and *A.Y.R.* jointly), he was variously referred to as "acting editor" (*Athenaeum*, Sept. 4, 1880), "working editor" (Hollingshead, *My Lifetime*, I, 98), "assistant editor" (Lady Priestley, *Story of a Lifetime*, p. 95), "co-editor" (*Athenaeum*, Oct. 29, 1892), "editor" (W. J. Linton, *Memories*, p. 161). Patmore, writing of one of Allingham's poems that had been published at the time that Wills was Dickens's only editorial assistant, expressed his disgust at the way in which it had been treated "by the Editor (not Dickens) of 'Household Words' " (Champneys, *Memoirs ... of Coventry Patmore*, II, 175). Harriet Martineau, levelling her attack at "the editors" – "the proprietors" – of *H.W.* as philosophically and morally inadequate to their function, held Wills equally as responsible for editorial policy as she did Dickens (*Autobiography*, II, 91–95). Samuel Smiles (*Autobiography*, p. 261) called Wills "editor of *All the Year Round*." Commenting on the fact that Dickens's periodicals bore Dickens's name alone as editor, Tinsley wrote (*Random Recollections*, II, 290–91): "... I take the liberty to think that, when 'Household Words' and Charles Dickens's name is mentioned, the name and good work of William Henry Wills should not be forgotten."

It is, of course, only for his connection with Dickens that Wills is remembered. Whatever literary career he might at one time have contemplated was put an end to by his acceptance of the sub-editorship. The book that he was writing in the later years of his life remained unfinished at his death. The subeditorship, in Dickens's understanding, was to engross all of Wills's time and energy. When Wills, in 1855, in order to increase his income, contemplated accepting the editorship of the *Civil Service Gazette* and carrying on the work concurrently with his work on *H.W.*, Dickens flatly informed him that such an arrangement was out of the question. Wills immediately acquiesced in Dickens's decision. In a somewhat pathetic protestation he wrote to Dickens that his "whole life" was bound up in *H.W.* "and in the connexion into which it brings me with you" (Lehmann, p. 166). Wills was two years Dickens's senior.

Wills's position as *H.W.* subeditor was a responsible one. He handled the business transactions of the periodical. He had entire charge of the day-to-day management of the editorial office, carrying on correspondence, conferring with the printers and with contributors, delegating some of the assignments. He accepted and rejected contributions, referring to Dickens those that required Dickens's final decision. He kept, in the Office Book, a record of items published in *H.W.* numbers, with the amounts paid for contributed items – himself determining (roughly within the set payment

*Cf. James Payn on Leitch Ritchie (*Some Literary Recollections*, p. 73): Asking Payn to assist him in the editorship of *Chambers's*, Ritchie wrote: "... will you come and be my *co*-editor?" "I suppose," commented Payn, "five men out of six would have written *sub*-editor; but the natural graciousness of [Ritchie's] disposition caused him to italicise the *co*."

scale) what the payment for any contribution should be. He set up – sometimes in consultation with Dickens, as frequently by himself – the numbers of the periodical, deciding on the contents and the order of items, then carried out Dickens's instructions for whatever changes Dickens wanted made – or, at least, carried out such instructions as well as any man but Dickens himself could have carried them out. Dickens's "Conductorial Injunction" (Nov. 17, 1853) – "KEEP HOUSEHOLD WORDS IMAGINATIVE!" – was a long-range direction that could hardly be executed with literal exactitude from one week to the next – and certainly not by Wills alone. On his own initiative, as also at the direction of Dickens, Wills revised contributed items. (As Dickens's letters and as occasional memoranda in the Office Book indicate, Wills revised or made changes in more items than those of which he listed himself in the Office Book as reviser.) He read and corrected proof. From the letters sent in by readers, he contrived "chips"; he did much of the hackwork of writing "chips" to correct typographical errors and misstatements in items that had appeared. Occasionally he accompanied Dickens to places or institutions and collaborated with him on articles based on the excursions. He wrote original material for the periodical (his original material was, until 1855, considered as paid for in his weekly salary). In addition, probably in 1854 on Forster's discontinuing his active participation in *H.W.* matters, Wills assumed "the labouring oar" in the *Household Narrative of Current Events* (Lehmann, p. 165).

Wills carried out his duties capably and conscientiously. Dickens could have had no better co-worker. "If there were only another Wills," said Thackeray on undertaking the editorship of *Cornhill*, "my fortune would be made!" (Lady Priestley, *Story of a Lifetime*, p. 143).

Dickens realized Wills's value to him. He mentioned Wills at times as his "fellow-workman," even as his "colleague" – but also as his "factotum." In the business management of the periodical and its journalistic routine he relied on Wills completely; the responsibility that he gave him in editorial matters indicates that he thought Wills's literary ability at least competent; his letters indicate that he thought it little more. To Cunningham, he wrote (May 12, 1850): "Wills is a capital fellow for his work, but decidedly of the Nutmeg-Grater, or Fancy-Bread-Rasper School you mention"; and to Bulwer-Lytton (May 15, 1861): "Wills has no genius, and is, in literary matters, sufficiently commonplace to represent a very large proportion of our readers." Representation of "a very large proportion of our readers" may not have seemed to Dickens a quality to be in all ways deplored.

Sending New Year's greetings to Wills on Jan. 2, 1862, Dickens mentioned their many years of association. "And I think," he wrote, "we can say that we doubt whether any two men can have gone on more happily and smoothly, or with greater trust and confidence in one another." The statement was true; yet Dickens was not an easy editor to work for, and, but for Wills's good nature, their association would not have been, for the most part, free from misunderstandings and arguments. Wills was obviously expected to exercise his own judgment in editorial matters; yet, when his judgment failed to coincide with Dickens's, it was Wills's judgment that was at fault. Dickens's criticisms were at times, particularly during the early years of *H.W.*, so offensively phrased as to be humiliating to their recipient. Wills's setting up a certain item as a separate article, rather than as a "chip," Dickens termed "ridiculous." Of an article-title that Wills had suggested, Dickens wrote: "I don't think there could be a worse one within the range of the human understanding" (July 30, 1854; July 12, 1850). On this occasion Wills rose to his defence. He had given, he replied "a 'mild suggestion'" for a title, "for I think it useless to hint what may strike me as a defect without indicating a remedy"; the title might not be the best possible one, "but I am *sure* it is not the worst one within the range of human understanding." Replying to an objection concerning the manner in which he had handled a passage in another item, Wills sensibly explained his point, adding: "I did not suppose you would wish me to consult you upon so simple a matter of mechanical convenience" (Lehmann, pp. 30–32). In a letter to Dickens, Oct. 17, 1851, Wills wrote: "I have my own notions of what such a publication as *Household Words* should be; and, although I have good reason to suppose from the latitude of confidence you give me, that my notions square with your own generally, yet I cannot (less perhaps than many other men) be *always* right; and it would lift a great weight of responsibility from me if everything which passes into the columns of *Household Words* had the systematic benefit of another judgment before publication" (Lehmann, pp. 74–75). During Dickens's absences from London, much that appeared in *H.W.* did not have the benefit of Dickens's surveillance. The editorial work was Wills's.

Begun as a business relationship, the association of Wills and Dickens developed into friendship. Dickens in his later years, wrote Forster (*Life*, Book VI, sect. iv), "had no more intimate friend" than Wills. Dickens's letters – with their frank comments on friends, on family and personal matters – indicate this intimacy. Wills knew, of course, of the Ellen Ternan affair; he was acquainted with Miss Ternan. During his 1867–68 reading tour in America, Dickens enclosed, in letters to Wills, some of his letters to "my dear girl"; Miss Ternan was to go to Wills if she needed help during Dickens's absence (Nisbet, *Dickens & Ellen Ternan*). Wills was at various times in Dickens's company on social occasions, as was also Mrs. Wills. He was a members of Dickens's amateur company that staged a benefit performance for the actress Frances Kelly, Jan. 3, 1846 (playbill, *Dickensian*, XXXV, 241). He accompanied Dickens during a part of the theatrical tour undertaken in 1851 for the benefit of the Guild of Literature and Art; he served as secretary to the Guild. Dickens was instrumental in procuring for Wills the appointment as confidential secretary to, and as almoner for, Miss Burdett-Coutts. He proposed Wills for membership in the Garrick Club, and resigned from the Garrick on Wills's being blackballed. In 1864 Wills gave Dickens the present of a brougham. "It will always be dear to me ...," wrote Dickens (Nov. 30), "as a proof of your ever generous friendship and appreciation, and a memorial of a happy intercourse and a perfect confidence that have never had a break, and that surely never can have any break now (after all these years) but one."

The *Athenaeum* obituary on Wills (Sept. 4, 1880) stated that no man "left behind him fewer enemies and more friends" than did he. With his editorial assistants, Wills's personal relationship was friendly. The friction that developed between him and Horne resulted from Wills's conviction that Horne was not doing sufficient writing for *H.W.* to justify his salary; but personally, wrote Wills, he had "a liking for Horne" (Lehmann, p. 36). Morley called Wills "my dear friend" (*Early Papers and Some Memories*, p. 30); Collins showed his partisanship of Wills by resigning from the Garrick in protest against the Club's blackballing of Wills. Of persons associated with *H.W.*, only Forster disliked Wills – or, rather, came to dislike him, for he must have had a reasonably amicable attitude toward him and some appreciation of his abilities when he suggested him to Dickens as assistant editor of *H.W.* With contributors, Wills's personal relationship was also friendly, though some writers resented his editorial alteration of their contributions. *H.W.* contributors who expressed their regard for him by dedicating to him a book were Murray, Payn (joint dedication to Ritchie and Wills), Percy Fitzgerald, Duthie, and Eliza Lynn Linton (joint dedication to Wills and his wife).

Wills wrote twenty-eight full-length items for the first volume of *H.W.*, but increasingly fewer for the following volumes; for some of the later volumes he wrote none. As he explained in 1855, at the time that his accepting the editorship of the *Civil Service Gazette* was under discussion, he left the writing mainly to others, once a corps of contributors had been established. Since Wills had contemplated the *Gazette* editorship as a means of increasing his earnings, Dickens, in ruling it out of the question, suggested, instead, that Wills be paid for *H.W.* articles in the writing of which he had a substantial share. Wills interpreted this to mean articles that he wrote by himself; in the Office Book he recorded payment for seven such articles and one story.

Of the eighteen articles or sections of articles that Wills recorded in the Office Book as jointly by him and Dickens, some were actual collaborations of the two writers. One – the first section of "The Doom of English Wills" – Dickens mentioned in a letter to Wills (Sept. 8, 1850) as "our joint article." Other of the articles Dickens merely revised or added material to. (For suggestion as to the revision and additions, see Stone, ed., *Charles Dickens' Uncollected Writings from Household Words.*) Reprinting certain of the articles in *Old Leaves: Gathered from Household Words* – which he dedicated to Dickens – Wills wrote that they owed "their brightest tints" to Dickens's "masterly touches." Included in *Old Leaves* was "A Plated Article," which Dickens had reprinted as his writing. Wills's Office Book ascription of the item to Dickens and to himself is more authoritative as to its authorship than is Dickens's reprinting.

Dickens suggested the title for Wills's "The Great Bar in the Harbour of London." He thought Wills's "Review of a Popular Publication" and "To Clergymen in Difficulties" very good, as he did Wills's autobiographical article in *A.Y.R.* (April 8, 1865), "Forty Years in London" (to Wills, July 17, 1851; July 12, 1850; March 9, 1851: MS Huntington Library; March 26, 1865). In a long letter to Wills, April 13, 1855, Dickens analysed one of Wills's stories (not published in *H.W.*), pointing out what he saw as its defects, but mentioning also its merits.

Of the items listed below as reprinted, "Railway Waifs and Strays" and "The Tyrant of Minnigissengen" appeared in *Old Leaves* without acknowledgment of the joint authorship that Wills had recorded for them in the Office Book. "A Suburban Romance," recorded in the Office Book as by "W.H.W. (suggested by Mrs. Hoare)," with payment to Mrs. Hoare for the suggestion, appeared without acknowledgment of Mrs. Hoare's suggestion. "To Clergymen in Difficulties," recorded in the Office Book as by Wills, with payment to the man (name unclear) "who furnished the idea," appeared with acknowledgment that the facts on which the account was based were "derived from a correspondent."

Nine of Wills's *H.W.* articles (including "A Plated Article," claimed by both Wills and Dickens) were reprinted in whole or part in *Harper's,* four of them acknowledged to *H.W.* (In addition, one of Wills's articles – "The Private History of the Palace of Glass" – may have served in part as the basis of "The Crystal Palace," *Harper's,* April 1851.) Three of Wills's articles were included in the Putnam volumes of selections from *H.W.*: *Home and Social Philosophy,* 1st and 2nd ser., and *The World Here and There.* "The Ghost of the Late Mr. James Barber" was included in *Choice Stories from Dickens' Household Words,* pub. Auburn, N.Y., 1854. "A Suburban Romance," credited to Dickens, was included by Alice and Phoebe Cary in their *Josephine Gallery,* 1859. "A Curious Dance round a Curious Tree," credited to Dickens, was twice issued in 1860 as a promotional pamphlet by St. Luke's Hospital for Lunatics (Eckel, *First Editions of the Writings of Charles Dickens*). Three paragraphs from "Post-Office Money-Orders," acknowledged to *H.W.*, were quoted in an anonymous pamphlet, *Methods of Employment,* 1852 (Stone, ed., *Charles Dickens' Uncollected Writings from Household Words*).

D.N.B.

PROSE

*Valentine's Day at the Post-Office *C.D. & W.H.W.* I, 6–12. March 30, 1850

The Troubled Water Question I, 49–54. April 13, 1850

The Ghost of the Late Mr. James Barber. A Yarn Ashore I, 87–90. April 20, 1850

A Coroner's Inquest I, 109–113. April 27, 1850

*The Heart of Mid-London [lead] *Mr. C.D. & W.H.W.* I, 121–25. May 4, 1850

*A Popular Delusion [lead] *Mr. C.D. & W.H.W.* I, 217–21. June 1, 1850

The Golden City [lead] I, 313–17. June 29, 1850

*The Old Lady in Threadneedle Street [lead] *C.D. & W.H.W.* I, 337–42. July 6, 1850

The Modern Science of Thief-Taking
I, 368–72. July 13, 1850
Review of a Popular Publication. In the Searching Style I, 426–31. July 27, 1850
The Railway Wonders of Last Year [lead]
I, 481–82. Aug. 17, 1850
Two Chapters on Bank Note Forgeries:
Chap. i I, 555–60. Sept. 7, 1850
*Chap. ii *W.H.W. & C.D.*
I, 615–20. Sept. 21, 1850
A Suburban Romance
II, 267–71. Dec. 14, 1850
Railway Waifs and Strays *W.H.W. & Chris^er Hill* II, 319–22. Dec. 28, 1850
The Private History of the Palace of Glass [lead] II, 385–91. Jan. 18, 1851
*Plate Glass [lead] *C.D. & W.H.W.*
II, 433–37. Feb. 1, 1851
The Invited Invasion [chip]
II, 475–77. Feb. 8, 1851
The Tyrant of Minnigissengen *W.H.W. & J. Knox* II, 507–513. Feb. 22, 1851
Ten Minutes with Her Majesty [lead]
II, 529–32. March 1, 1851
"To Clergymen in Difficulties"
II, 606–612. March 22, 1851
*Spitalfields [lead] *C.D. & W.H.W.*
III, 25–30. April 5, 1851
*The Metropolitan Protectives [lead] *C.D. & W.H.W.* III, 97–105. April 26, 1851
*Epsom [lead] *W.H.W. & C.D.*
III, 241–46. June 7, 1851
The Great Bar in the Harbour of London [lead] III, 409–414. July 26, 1851
*My Uncle [lead] *W.H.W. & C.D.*
IV, 241–46. Dec. 6, 1851
*A Curious Dance round a Curious Tree [lead] *C.D. & W.H.W.*
IV, 385–89. Jan. 17, 1852
*Post-Office Money-Orders [lead] *C.D. & W.H.W.* V, 1–5. March 20, 1852
*A Plated Article [lead] *C.D. & W.H.W.*
V, 117–21. April 24, 1852
For India Direct [lead]
V, 141–45. May 1, 1852
*Received, a Blank Child [lead] *C.D. & W.H.W.* VII, 49–53. March 19, 1853
*Idiots [lead] *C.D. & W.H.W.*
VII, 313–17. June 4, 1853
A Legal Fiction XI, 598–99. July 21, 1855
Paris Improved [lead]
XII, 361–65. Nov. 17, 1855
The Ninth of June
XIII, 493–500. June 7, 1856, and the 3 following nos.
The Lambeth-Marsh Mulcibers [lead]
XV, 25–27. Jan. 10, 1857
The Manchester School of Art
XVI, 349–52. Oct. 10, 1857
My Annular Eclipse [lead]
XVII, 433–36. April 24, 1858

The 37 items repr. as *Old Leaves: Gathered from Household Words. By W. Henry Wills.* London: Chapman and Hall, 1860. *Indicated in *Old Leaves* as the 15 items written in part by Dickens. Of these, "A Plated Article" was included by Dickens in his *Reprinted Pieces*, 1858.

Heathen and Christian Burial *Mr. Hogarth & W.H.W.* I, 43–48. April 6, 1850
Short Cuts across the Globe *Mr. Weir & W.H.W.* I, 65–68. April 13, 1850
The Schoolmaster at Home and Abroad
I, 82–84. April 20, 1850
Baptismal Rituals
I, 106–108. April 27, 1850
"A Good Plain Cook"
I, 139–41. May 4, 1850
Music in Humble Life *Mr. Hogarth & W.H.W.* I, 161–64. May 11, 1850
Short Cuts across the Globe: The Isthmus of Suez *Mr. Weir & W.H.W.*
I, 167–68. May 11, 1850
Law at a Low Price *Mr. W. T. Haly & W.H.W.* I, 176–80. May 18, 1850
The Appetite for News
I, 238–40. June 1, 1850
The Great Penal Experiments
I, 250–53. June 8, 1850
Young Russia I, 261–64. June 8, 1850
Savings' Bank Defalcations *Mr. Haly & W.H.W.* I, 267–70. June 15, 1850
Newspaper Antecedents
I, 270–74. June 15, 1850
The Royal Rotten Row Commission *Mr. Haly & W.H.W.*
I, 274–76. June 15, 1850
The Belgian Lace-Makers *Miss Ross & W.H.W.* I, 320–23. June 29, 1850
The Power of Mercy *Earle* [preceded by indecipherable word, overwritten by capital letter: perh. "H"?] *& W.H.W.*
I, 323–25. June 29, 1850
The Serf of Pobereze
Mad. Sczszpanowska & W.H.W.
I, 342–50. July 6, 1850
Destruction of Parish Registers [chip]
I, 351. July 6, 1850

Christopher Shrimble on the "Decline of England" I, 358–60. July 6, 1850
A Day in a Pauper Palace [lead] *Mr. Taylor & W.H.W.* I, 361–64. July 13, 1850
From Mr. Thomas Bovington [chip] I, 377. July 13, 1850
Sabbath Pariahs [chip] I, 378–79. July 13, 1850
The Adventures of the Public Records *Mr. Charles Cole & W.H.W.* I, 396–99. July 20, 1850
A Mightier Hunter Than Nimrod I, 399–402. July 20, 1850
A New Joint-Stock Pandemonium Company [chip] I, 403–404. July 20, 1850
The Power of Small Beginnings I, 407–408. July 20, 1850
An Excellent Opportunity *Miss Julia Kavannah & W.H.W.* I, 421–26. July 27, 1850
Railway Comfort [chip] *W.H.W. & Mr. Murray* I, 449–50. Aug. 3, 1850
Improving a Bull [chip] *W.H.W. & Mr. Morley* I, 450–51. Aug. 3, 1850
Lungs for London [chip] I, 451–52. Aug. 3, 1850
The Preservation of Life from Shipwreck *W.H.W. & Mr. Shillinglaw* I, 452–54. Aug. 3, 1850
Winged Telegraphs *W.H.W. & Miss Ross* I, 454–56. Aug. 3, 1850
Health by Act of Parliament I, 460–63. Aug. 10, 1850
Nice White Veal [chip] *W.H.W. & J. D. Parry* I, 467–68. Aug. 10, 1850
Two Letters from Australia *Mr. Gywnne & W.H.W.* I, 475–80. Aug. 10, 1850
A Christian Brotherhood I, 489–92. Aug. 17, 1850
Statistics of Factory Supervision [chip] I, 502. Aug. 17, 1850
Comic Leaves from the Statute Book *W.H.W. & Weir* I, 502–504. Aug. 17, 1850
The Strangers' Leaf for 1851 [chip] *E. Murray & W.H.W.* I, 515–17. Aug. 24, 1850
No Hospital for Incurables [chip] I, 517. Aug. 24, 1850
Topography and Temperance. From Mr. Christopher Shrimble I, 524–25. Aug. 24, 1850
Cheerful Arithmetic I, 531–34. Aug. 31, 1850
Easy Spelling and Hard Reading [chip] *Miss Cox & W.H.W.* I, 561–62. Sept. 7, 1850
A Very Old Soldier [chip] *Miss Ross & W.H.W.* I, 562–64. Sept. 7, 1850
A Little Place in Norfolk I, 575–76. Sept. 7, 1850
Torture in the Way of Business [chip] I, 587–88. Sept. 14, 1850
A Letter about Small Beginnings I, 598–600. Sept. 14, 1850
Foreigners' Portraits of Englishmen [lead] *C.D., W.H.W., & Eustace Murray* I, 601–604. Sept. 21, 1850
The Doom of English Wills [Cathedral Number One] [lead] *C.D. & W.H.W.* II, 1–4. Sept. 28, 1850
The Subscription List *W. B. Jerrold & W.H.W.* II, 10–12. Sept. 28, 1850
The Doom of English Wills: Cathedral Number Two [lead] *C.D. & W.H.W.* II, 25–29. Oct. 5, 1850
German Advertisements *W.H.W., E. C. Murray, & Mr. Walker* II, 33–35. Oct. 5, 1850
Hints on Emergencies *W.H.W. & Dr. Stone* II, 47–48. Oct. 5, 1850
The Monster Promenade Concerts II, 95–96. Oct. 19, 1850
The Doom of English Wills: Cathedral Number Three II, 125–28. Nov. 2, 1850
Poison Sold Here! II, 155–57. Nov. 9, 1850
Lieutenant Waghorn and His Widow [chip] II, 186–87. Nov. 16, 1850
"Household Words" and English Wills [chip] II, 187. Nov. 16, 1850
The Doom of English Wills: Cathedral Number Four II, 203–205. Nov. 23, 1850
The Sunday Question in the Last Century [chip] II, 210. Nov. 23, 1850
A Cape Coast Cargo *Mr. Franklyn Fox & W.H.W.* II, 252–57. Dec. 7, 1850
The Devonshire Dorado *Sidney Smith & W.H.W.* II, 262–64. Dec. 7, 1850
Back Street Conservatories *Mr. Ward & W.H.W.* II, 271–75. Dec. 14, 1850
"Streetography" [chip] II, 275–76. Dec. 14, 1850
Death in the Teapot [chip] *Strange & W.H.W.* II, 277. Dec. 14, 1850

The Magic Crystal *T. H. Wilson, D. Costello, & W.H.W.*
II, 284–88. Dec. 14, 1850
Christmas in Lodgings *W. B. Jerrold & W.H.W.* II, 295–98. Dec. 21, 1850
Death in the Bread-Basket [chip] *W.H.W. & Strange* II, 323. Dec. 28, 1850
Life in a Saladero *Dr. Von Corning & W.H.W.* II, 417–20. Jan. 25, 1851
Death in the Sugar Plum [chip]
II, 426–27. Jan. 25, 1851
A Woman's Experience in California [chip] (*see* Harrold)
II, 450–51. Feb. 1, 1851
The Martyrs of Chancery. Second Article *W.H.W. & A. Cole*
II, 493–96. Feb. 15, 1851
A Royal Speech by James the First [chip]
II, 543–45. March 1, 1851
National-Debt Doctors [chip]
II, 545–46. March 1, 1851
The Story of Giovanni Belzoni *W.H.W. & Mrs. Hoare* II, 548–52. March 1, 1851
Darling Dorel *Lady Duff Gordon & W.H.W.* II, 581–85. March 15, 1851
The Spade [chip] *Sidney Smith & W.H.W.* II, 595–97. March 15, 1851
The Short Cut to California [chip] *H. Morley & W.H.W.*
II, 597–98. March 15, 1851
A Specimen of Russian Justice *J. Jackowski & W.H.W.*
II, 598–600. March 15, 1851
Small Beginnings [chip] *W.H.W. & C.D.*
III, 41–42. April 5, 1851
Common-Sense on Wheels *C.D., W.H.W., & Murray* III, 61–66. April 12, 1851
A Mysterious City
III, 94–96. April 19, 1851
The Sailor at Home [chip] *W.H.W. & Mr. Byng* III, 160. May 10, 1851
A Card [chip] III, 187. May 17, 1851
True Anecdote of the Last Century [chip] *Mrs. Sidney Smith & W.H.W.*
III, 188–89. May 17, 1851
The One Black Spot *Addiscott & W.H.W.*
III, 196–201. May 24, 1851
Cheap Pleasures. – A Gossip *Murray & W.H.W.* III, 201–203. May 24, 1851
Safety for Female Emigrants [chip]
III, 228. May 31, 1851
Mr. Bubbs and the Moon [chip]
III, 228. May 31, 1851
A Disappearance [chip]
III, 305–306. June 21, 1851
Gas Perfumery [chip]
III, 334. June 28, 1851
Another Leaf from the Story of a Sailor's Life [chip] III, 353–54. July 5, 1851
In the Name of the Prophet – Smith! [lead] *Hannay & W.H.W.*
III, 385–89. July 19, 1851
The Tax on Excursion Trains [chip]
III, 396. July 19, 1851
Edward Baines *Hannay & W.H.W.*
III, 414–19. July 26, 1851
South American Scraps: The Pampas Indians; An Adventure with a Lizard; The Sierra de St. Catherina *Dr. Corning, Keys, & W.H.W.*
III, 425–30. July 26, 1851
Ballinglen [chip] (*see* Lady Grey)
III, 450–51. Aug. 2, 1851
A "Ranch" in California [chip] *Harrold* [should read *Harrold's sister*] & *W.H.W.*
III, 471–72. Aug. 9, 1851
Ice [lead] *Morley & W.H.W.*
III, 481–84. Aug. 16, 1851
Soldiers' Wives [chip] *W.H.W. & Morley*
III, 561–62. Sept. 6, 1851
More French Revolutions *S. Blanshard & W.H.W.* III, 585–88. Sept. 13, 1851
The Bush-Fire Extinguisher [chip] *W.H.W. & correspondent*
III, 594–95. Sept. 13, 1851
The London Tavern [lead] *Hannay & W.H.W.* IV, 73–77. Oct. 18, 1851
A Golden Newspaper [chip] *Mr. Keene & W.H.W.* IV, 207–208. Nov. 22, 1851
Street-Cab Reform [chip]
IV, 376. Jan. 10, 1852
The Pedigree of Puppets *W.H.W. & Dudley Costello*
IV, 438–43. Jan. 31, 1852
Wonderful Toys
IV, 502–504. Feb. 14, 1852
The Queen's Head *Hannay & W.H.W.*
IV, 510–13. Feb. 21, 1852
A Genteel Establishment *Sidney Blanshard & W.H.W.*
IV, 559–64. March 6, 1852
A Sea-Coroner [chip]
IV, 597–98. March 13, 1852
Locking Up the Tower of London [chip] *Correspondent & W.H.W.*
V, 15–16. March 20, 1852
A Great Catch [chip]
V, 104. April 17, 1852
Official Emigration [chip]
V, 155–56. May 1, 1852

A Flight with the Birds [lead] *Morley & W.H.W.* v, 381–84. July 10, 1852
Mr. Bovington on the New Cattle-Market [chip] v, 422–23. July 17, 1852
Transportation for Life [chip] v, 566–67. Aug. 28, 1852
"Moving" *W. B. Jerrold & W.H.W.* vi, 61–63. Oct. 2, 1852
The Crimes of Cotton [chip] vi, 188–89. Nov. 6, 1852
An Oriental Firman [chip] vi, 210–11. Nov. 13, 1852
The "Logging" Stone [chip] vi, 234–35. Nov. 20, 1852
Funerals in Paris [chip] *Morley & W.H.W.* vi, 257–60. Nov. 27, 1852
Rational Schools [lead] *Morley & W.H.W.* vi, 337–42. Dec. 25, 1852
Clean Water and Dirty Water [chip] vi, 496–97. Feb. 5, 1853
Doctor of Philosophy [chip] vi, 515. Feb. 12, 1853
Photography *Morley & W.H.W.* vii, 54–61. March 19, 1853
In and Out of Jail [lead] *C.D., Morley, & W.H.W.* vii, 241–45. May 14, 1853
Twenty Guinea Diplomas [chip] vii, 285. May 21, 1853
A Pull at the Pagoda Tree [lead] *Capper & W.H.W.* vii, 433–37. July 9, 1853
Provisionally Registered *W. B. Jerrold & W.H.W.* vii, 445–48. July 9, 1853
St. Vorax's Singing-Birds *Buckley & W.H.W.* vii, 454–56. July 9, 1853
Whip and Spur *Dodd & W.H.W.* vii, 545–48. Aug. 6, 1853
Why Shave? *Morley & W.H.W.* vii, 560–63. Aug. 13, 1853
Lilliput in London *Morley & W.H.W.* vii, 573–76. Aug. 13, 1853
The Stereoscope *Morley & W.H.W.* viii, 37–42. Sept. 10, 1853
First Stage to Australia *Capper & W.H.W.* viii, 42–45. Sept. 10, 1853
Colour-Blindness *Knox & W.H.W.* viii, 255–57. Nov. 12, 1853
Fairyland in 'Fifty-four [lead] *W.H.W. & Sala* viii, 313–17. Dec. 3, 1853
Varna *Bayle St. John & W.H.W.* viii, 373–77. Dec. 17, 1853
Uncle George's Story *Dixon & W.H.W.* Another Round of Stories (Christmas 1853), pp. 25–29
Several Heads of Hair *Dodd & W.H.W.* ix, 61–65. March 4, 1854
The Bottle at Sea [chip] ix, 161. April 1, 1854
Beef, Mutton, and Bread *Sidney & W.H.W.* x, 113–18. Sept. 16, 1854
Criminal Lunatics [chip] x, 453. Dec. 23, 1854
The Soldier's Wife *Morley & W.H.W.* xi, 278–80. April 21, 1855
Brimstone [chip] xi, 398–99. May 26, 1855
Pensioners [chip] xi, 573. July 14, 1855
Common Cookery *Miss Lynn & W.H.W.* xiii, 42–46. Jan. 26, 1856
A London Parish [chip] (*see* W. Rogers) xiii, 275–76. April 5, 1856
The Salt in the Sea [chip] xiii, 507. June 14, 1856
The Congressional Prize-Ring [chip] xiv, 20. July 19, 1856
Not Very Common Things *Morley & W.H.W.* xiv, 39–41. July 26, 1856
American Party Names *Olmsted & W.H.W.* xiv, 85–89. Aug. 9, 1856
Slaves and Their Masters *Miss Lynn & W.H.W.* xiv, 133–38. Aug. 23, 1856
Aluminium *Dixon & W.H.W.* xiv, 507–510. Dec. 13, 1856
I Promise to Pay *Dodd & W.H.W.* xiv, 556–59. Dec. 27, 1856
Compromising Compromises [chip] xv, 203. Feb. 28, 1857
Duelling in England *Miss Lynn & W.H.W.* xv, 596–600. June 20, 1857
Stickytoes *Dixon & W.H.W.* xvi, 31–34. July 11, 1857
A School for Cooks [chip] xvi, 162–63. Aug. 15, 1857
Hard Roads *A.H.A. Hamilton & W.H.W.* xvi, 534–36. Dec. 5, 1857
A Needle of Sense in a Haystack of Law [lead] *Head & W.H.W.* xvii, 385–87. April 10, 1858
A Very Old Gentleman *Ede & W.H.W.* xviii, 369–72. Oct. 2, 1858
Going A-maying *Kent & W.H.W.* xix, 514–17. April 30, 1859
Street Minstrelsy [lead] *Mrs. Linton & W.H.W.* xix, 577–80. May 21, 1859

VERSE

Time *Meredith & W.H.W.* iii, 204. May 24, 1851
Never Despair *Miss Blackwell & W.H.W.* iii, 491–92. Aug. 16, 1851

Lighten the Boat! *King & W.H.W.*
VII, 563–64. Aug. 13, 1853
Grains of Gold *T. Hood, Junr., & W.H.W.*
VII, 589. Aug. 20, 1853
Old London Bridge *Miss Tomkins & W.H.W.* VIII, 204. Oct. 29, 1853

Wilson, Florence |*Miss Florence Wilson, Florence Wilson, Miss Wilson*|, *b.* ca. 1823, daughter of Mrs. Cornwell Baron-Wilson. Miss Wilson's mother was known to both Dickens and Wills – to Dickens, as a contributor to *Bentley's Misc.*; to Wills, in some way darkly hinted at by Vizetelly. Vizetelly (*Glances Back through Seventy Years*, I, 247) wrote that Wills had "drifted into literature" under the wing of Mrs. Wilson, "whose patronage he ill-requited in a fashion that imperilled his liberty," and that as a result "something like a cloud hung over him for several years afterwards."

Florence Wilson, according to her mother ("Stanzas to My Daughter, on Her Birth-day," *A Volume of Lyrics*), early showed her poetic temperament:

> The Poet's numbers graced thy lisping tongue,
> And girlhood promises thou wilt retain
> The Gift of Song. ...

Mrs. Wilson sent to Dickens some of her daughter's verses for publication in *Bentley's Misc.* Dickens was unable to use them for lack of space: "We are so very crowded that I cannot possibly avail myself of your daughter's lines" (Pilgrim *Letters*, I, 354). Miss Wilson contributed an occasional poem to *Friendship's Offering* and the *Ladies' Companion*; was author of *Lyrics for Leisure Hours*, 1842; *Boudoir Lyrics*, 1844. The beautifully printed and bound *Boudoir Lyrics*, with a picture of the elegant young authoress as frontispiece, was published by Smith, Elder & Co., Mrs. Wilson paying for the publication. "I want my daughter to marry," Mrs. Wilson confided to George Smith, "and it is a good thing for a girl to have a literary reputation" (Huxley, *House of Smith Elder*, p. 34).

The first of Miss Wilson's *H.W.* contributions is prefaced by the editorial comment that the "fair Correspondent" had sent it from St. Petersburg. (The Office Book records payment as "Handed to Mrs. Wills to send to Miss F.W.") According to Sala (*Life and Adventures*, pp. 286–87), Miss Wilson was employed as "a governess in a noble family at St. Petersburg during the Crimean War" and was in Russia at the time that news of the first bombardment of Sebastopol reached the capital. Miss Wilson herself, in "Rencontres," stated that she left Russia in the summer of 1854 because of the War. In 1858 she made another trip to Russia. Later she resided in England; about 1865, stated Sala, she worked for a time as his amanuensis.

Allibone

A Marriage in St. Petersburg [chip]
I, 402–403. July 20, 1850
A Golden Coppersmith
VII, 419–21. July 2, 1853
Only a Governess
XIX, 546–49. May 7, 1859
Rencontres XIX, 570–72. May 14, 1859

Wilson, R [?]. *Not identified.* Initial not clearly written in Office Book; seems to read "R"; may perhaps be "K." The contributor relates the life of the patron saint of England as recorded in a seventeenth-century chronicle. Payment for the contribution made by cheque.

St. George and the Dragon
XIV, 258–61. Sept. 27, 1856

Wilson, T. H. *Not identified.* The first item listed below deals with divining crystals and with the "balderdash" put forth in Richard J. Morrison's *Zadkiel's Almanac.* The article affords no specific clue as to the identity of the contributor Wilson. The record of Costello (not a staff member) as joint author obviously implies that Wilson and Dudley Costello were acquainted. In the second item, which is clearly the account of an actual experience, the writer tells of being arrested and gaoled on a false charge. The account indicates that he is a young married man and that he has had some experience of military life. He relates the incident, he states, "simply as so much experience" and has "no desire or talent for constructing any theories upon it."

One T. H. Wilson who flourished at the time was Thomas Harries Wilson, 35th Regt., brother of Florence Wilson (above). He is not listed in biographical compilations.

"The Magic Crystal" was included in the Putnam volume of selections from *H.W.*: *Home and Social Philosophy*, 1st ser.

The Magic Crystal *T. H. Wilson, D. Costello, & W.H.W.* II, 284–88. Dec. 14, 1850
Lodged in Newgate [lead] *T. H. Wilson & Morley* VIII, 1–6. Sept. 3, 1853

Winter: *See* Wynter, Andrew

Wood. *Not identified.* "The Ruined Potter" tells of the poverty and misery of a working-class family and of the good curate who helps them and brings the dying father to peace with God; the author comments on the neglect of the poor by the governing class. Payment for the contribution made by cheque. Item reprinted in *Harper's* with the title "The Kind of Preaching That Does Good to the Poor"; not acknowledged to *H.W.*

"Progress" is a moral reflection on life as a time of toil, self-denial, and sacrifice, ultimately resulting in accomplishment. Item, marked anonymous, included in *Harper's Cyclopaedia of British and American Poetry*, 1881.

PROSE
The Ruined Potter IX, 441–44. June 24, 1854

VERSE
Progress IX, 464. July 1, 1854

Woods. *Not identified.* The contributor's article laments the passing of the picturesque London beggars of former days. Payment marked "Enclosed."

Departed Beggars V, 244–46. May 29, 1852

Wraxall, Sir Frederick Charles Lascelles (name thus in *Burke's Peerage*; Sir C. F. Lascelles Wraxall on title pages of some of Wraxall's books) |*Wraxall*|, 1828–1865, misc. writer. Student at Oxford; did not take degree. Went to the Continent in 1846 for purpose of studying languages; lived there for some years. In 1855 appointed assistant commissary, with rank of captain, in Turkish contingent; served in the Crimea to end of the War. Contributed to *Once a Week*, *St. James's Magazine*, *Boy's Own Magazine*, and other periodicals. Edited *Welcome Guest*, 1860–61. Translated various works from the German and the French. Author of *The Armies of the Great Powers*, 1859, and other books on military matters; *Life and Times of Her Majesty Caroline Matilda, Queen of Denmark and Norway*, 1864; also novels, boys' adventure books. Brought out in book form various collections of his periodical contributions.

The author of the item listed below states that he is writing his article in a county gaol where he is "a guest of her Majesty" as prisoner for debt. He states that he served in "one of the foreign legions" in the Crimea; that on his return to England he had "sixty pounds of debt" hanging over him – money due to the tailor and the bootmaker who had furnished his outfit for the Crimea, and that he was arrested on the writ of the bootmaker.

In the account of his Crimean service, *Camp Life: or Passages from the Story of a Contingent*, 1860, Wraxall does not mention imprisonment for debt. He merely states that on his discharge "... I still owed a ponderous balance to my outfitter – who would be sure to have a heavy bill to make up directly I landed in England." Whether or not the imprisonment was a fact, the correspondence of various passages in the *H.W.* article and in *Camp Life* suffices to establish Lascelles Wraxall as the *H.W.* contributor. Among the correspondences are the following:

The *H.W.* article states that the writer, to receive his military discharge pay, "had to await the Paymaster's good pleasure for three weeks at the Hotel de l'Europe" in Pera; Wraxall, in *Camp Life*, states that he stayed three weeks in Pera, at the Hotel de l'Europe, "awaiting the good pleasure of the Chief Paymaster." The *H.W.* article states that the writer on his arrival in England applied to the War Office for money but that his appeals met with no success; Wraxall, in *Camp Life*, says the same. The *H.W.* article states: "I know that government, to exist, must be unjust, and that individual hardships weigh but little against the common weal"; Wraxall, in *Camp Life*, writes: "I see daily more clearly, that no government can prosper which is not individually unjust: private considerations must be thrown aside on behalf of the *salus publica*."

One detail in the *H.W.* article that does not accord with the facts of Wraxall's life is the statement there that the writer had "a wife and child to support." Wraxall and his wife had no children. The child is a literary embellishment, obviously not out of place in an article published anonymously.

The Office Book records payment of £3.3.0, instead of the standard £2.2.0, for the 4-col. article. Perhaps Wills was acquainted with Wraxall and sympathized with him in his financial straits. Wraxall later had some correspondence with Dickens.

D.N.B.

The Queen's Guest

xvi, 421–23. Oct. 31, 1857

Wreford, Henry G. |*H. Wreford, Wreford*|, 1806–1892, journalist. Born in Bristol. Sent to Italy, when a young man, for sake of his health; remained there for rest of his life; died in Capri. For more than fifty years, from Rome and from Naples, was correspondent for the *Times*, a connection in which he took much pride (obit., *Times*, March 29, 1892). Also correspondent for *Illus. London News* and for *Daily News*. His detailed and vivid *Daily News* articles written during time of Italy's struggle for freedom and unity were praised by Jessie White Mario; Wreford was, according to her, "the correspondent who kept England up anent the rights and wrongs of Italy." Met the Marios in 1860 and was presented by them to Garibaldi as "Italy's best English friend in Naples" (McCarthy and Robinson, *The "Daily News" Jubilee*, pp. 64, 66). Contributed to *Athenaeum*, occasionally to *Macmillan's*. Author of *Rome, Pagan and Papal; by an English Resident in That City*, 1846.

Wreford and Dickens were not acquainted, but Dickens was aware that Wreford was a *H.W.* contributor. Relating to his wife in 1853 the gossip that he had heard in Naples, Dickens mentioned that "one Mr. Reeford who has written some Italian papers in Household Words" was living on the island of Capri and that idle young Englishmen of Naples were accustomed to going there to see him and the Capri girls (*Mr. & Mrs. Charles Dickens*, ed. Dexter, pp. 208–209).

H.W. introduced Wreford's first contribution with the statement that the writer was "a resident in Naples" who could furnish "authentic information" on conditions there. The Office Book assigns the article to Wreford alone, but contains the notation "Cut down from three times the quantity by W.H.W." Only one of the items assigned to Wreford is listed as revised by Morley, but Morley's letters indicate that he revised also others. One letter refers to "material of value" sent in by the contributor from Naples, which had to be recast "before it was suitable for the journal"; another mentions a mass of material from Naples "in a most unreadable hand," on which Morley was required to report (Solly, *Life of Henry Morley*, pp. 196, 204). Morley's reference to his having a "bothering Christmas paper from Naples to dress up" for the 1851 Christmas number (Solly, p. 200) is not clear; no paper by Wreford and no paper on Italy appeared in the 1851 Christmas number.

Included in the list below are two items of 1853 – "Quails" and "A Locust Hunt" – which are not assigned to Wreford, but which seem clearly to be by him. For "Quails" the Office Book gives only the partial authorship ascription "& Morley"; for "A Locust Hunt" it gives no ascription. The fact that Morley is recorded as reviser of "Quails" is one indication that the item is probably by Wreford; revising Wreford's contributions, as stated above, was one of Morley's assignments. Both articles deal with Capri – the first, with netting and shooting quail on the island; the second, with the destruction of locusts there. The two articles are obviously by one writer, as indicated by the parallel phraseology in which he states his being asked to be a spectator of these activities and his acceptance of the invitation. In the first article he writes: "'Will you come and see the quail-netting?' Of course I would"; in the second: "Would I go out and see them [the locusts]? Certainly I would." The invitation to see the locusts is brought to the writer while "I was quietly at work at Capri ... in my study." Wreford, as indicated by the articles assigned to him, made frequent excursions and visits to Capri from Naples. One article mentions his "ascending the heights of the Island of Capri"; others, his talking with fishermen on the island, his attending there a rustic festival and a wedding. Dickens was told in 1853 that Wreford was living on the island. "Quails" and "A Locust Hunt" show the writer's friendly association with Italian villagers and his interest in their beliefs, customs, and activities; Wreford, as indicated by the articles assigned to him, had the same association and interests.

Payment for two of Wreford's contributions was sent to Stuckey's Banking Co., Bristol. Payment for six was sent to "Dr. Wreford." The Dr. Wreford resident in Wreford's native town of Bristol was John Reynell Wreford, D.D., F.S.A., dissenting minister (*Mathews's Annual Bristol Directory*, 1854), presumably Wreford's father.

Boase

Spy Police I, 611–14. Sept. 21, 1850
The Coral Fishery in the Mediterranean
II, 379–83. Jan. 11, 1851
Neapolitan State Prisoners [chip]
Wreford & Morley
IV, 235–37. Nov. 29, 1851
Lazzaroni Literature
IV, 467–69. Feb. 7, 1852
Village Funerals in Naples
V, 19–20. March 20, 1852
Wreck and Ruin V, 494–95. Aug. 7, 1852
A Wedding in the Clouds
VI, 261–64. Nov. 27, 1852
Quails ——— *& Morley*
VII, 448–50. July 9, 1853
Sick Grapes VII, 608–609. Aug. 27, 1853
A Locust Hunt [chip]
VIII, 184–85. Oct. 22, 1853
Neapolitan Purity
VIII, 572–75. Feb. 11, 1854
Vesuvius in Eruption
XI, 435–39. June 9, 1855
Italian Village Doctors
XII, 209–211. Sept. 29, 1855
What a Man May Not Do in the Kingdom of Naples XII, 379–81. Nov. 17, 1855
Christmas in Southern Italy
XII, 511–13. Dec. 29, 1855
The Giglio Festa
XIV, 115–18. Aug. 16, 1856
Mercy in Naples [lead]
XV, 409–411. May 2, 1857
Macaroni-Making [chip]
XVII, 161–63. Jan. 30, 1858
Earthquake Experiences [lead]
XVII, 553–58. May 29, 1858
Neapolitan Energy
XVIII, 522–24. Nov. 13, 1858

Wyley, Mrs. *Not identified.* Payment for the contribution made by post-office order. "A Breton Wedding," April 26, 1851, is referred to as a "companion picture" to "A Welsh Wedding."

A Welsh Wedding [chip]
II, 492–93. Feb. 15, 1851

Wynter, Andrew |*Winter, Wynter*|, 1819–1876, physician, writer. Studied medicine at St. George's Hospital, London. M.D. Univ. of St. Andrews, 1853. M.R.C.P. 1861. Devoted special attention to treatment of the insane. Editor, 1855–60, of *Association Medical Jour.* (later *British Medical Jour.*). Contributed numerous articles to periodicals, as to *Hood's Magazine, Quart. Rev., New Monthly, Ainsworth's, Fraser's, Once a Week, Edin. Rev., Good Words.* Published several collections of his periodical articles, some volumes appearing under the pseudonym "Werdna Retnyw." Collections included *Curiosities of Civilization, Subtle Brains and Lissom Fingers, Peeps into the Human Hive, The Borderlands of Insanity.* In *Odds and Ends from an Old Drawer*, 1855, expressed surprise that "any literary dishes of his preparation would ever be thought worthy of being warmed up afresh." Some of the collections went through several editions.

In his *H.W.* article "Several Heads of Hair," Dodd referred to Wynter's *Quart. Rev.* article "Human Hair" (anon.) and used some of the material from that article.

Wynter's account, in his first *H.W.* contribution, of an operation in the operating theatre of St. George's Hospital – the surgeon's breaking "into the house of life" – Sala remembered forty years later as "a terribly powerful description" (*Life and Adventures*, p. 315).

D.N.B.

Saint George and the Dragon v, 77–80. April 10, 1852
Hyde Park v, 302–304. June 12, 1852

The 2 items repr. in *Pictures of Town and Country Life. By Werdna Retnyw, M.D.* London: George Routledge & Co., 1855. Pub. in *H.W.* acknowledged.

Y

Yates, Edmund Hodgson |*Yates, E. Yates*|, 1831–1894, journalist and novelist. Attended school in Highgate; spent a year in Düsseldorf learning German. Held position in General Post Office, 1847–72. Early "longed for a literary life" and began writing for *Court Journal;* thereafter contributed to *Illus. London News, Bentley's Misc., Chambers's, Welcome Guest,* and other periodicals; wrote gossip column for *Illus. Times* and for *Morning Star;* served as dramatic critic of *Daily News;* correspondent for New York *Herald.* Editor of the *Train*, 1856–58; thereafter of *Town Talk, Temple Bar, Tinsleys', Time.* Co-founder (with Grenville Murray, above) of the *World*, 1874. Author of several farces and some fifteen novels. Privately printed *Mr. Thackeray, Mr. Yates, and the Garrick Club*, 1859, his account of the notorious affair that led to the estrangement between Dickens and Thackeray. Contemporary opinion concerning Yates ranged from that of Renton, who thought Yates "that prince of journalists" (*John Forster and His Friendships*, p. 256), to that of Swineburne, who regarded him as a blackguard and "*cochon sublime*" (*Letters*, I, 304).

Yates, in 1854, took upon himself his introduction to Dickens. Dickens gave him a kindly welcome as the son of the well-known actors Frederick and Elizabeth Yates, whose acting Dickens admired. The two men soon became close friends. An early mark of Dickens's friendship was his standing as godfather to the infant Charles Dickens Theodore Yates. Yates was often in Dickens's company; the two men frequently corresponded; they presented each other copies of their books. Yates dedicated his *After Office-Hours* to Dickens in "slight acknowledgment" of Dickens's "unvarying kindness" to him. In his *Recollections and Experiences* (chap. xi), Yates wrote of the similarity of views and sympathies that existed between him and Dickens, of his devotion to Dickens, of Dickens's great regard for him, of the pleasure that Dickens found in his society, and of the "exceptional insight into his inner life" that Dickens permitted him. Certain circumstances that thus came to his knowledge, wrote Yates, his delicacy prevented his revealing. The circumstances obviously concerned the Ellen Ternan affair. In the matter of Dickens's "domestic trouble" Yates warmly defended Dickens against what he termed the "lies" being circulated about him (*Town Talk*, June 19, 1858). Dickens, in turn, served as Yates's adviser and public backer in the Garrick Club affair.

In addition to the chapter on Dickens in his *Recollections*, Yates published in *Tinsleys'*, Feb. 1869, an article on Dickens's readings; he included reminiscences of Dickens in the lectures that he delivered in his U.S. lecture tour of 1872–73.

Yates held so high an opinion of *H.W.* that he considered his early writing clearly "not up to the *Household Words* standard," and he introduced himself to Dickens with no intention of asking to become a contributor (*Recollections*, p. 174). He did, somewhat later, contribute four items to the periodical. (A fifth item – "Patient and Faithful" – assigned to Yates in the Office Book is not by him but by Adelaide Procter.) "Two in a Legion" Dickens accepted for *H.W.* "with pleasure"; he thought the framework opening of the story "excellent," but the story itself inadequately linked to the framework (to Yates, Nov. 16, 1857).

Though Yates was not – as he called himself – "a frequent contributor" to *H.W.*, he was to its successor. The first novel published in *A.Y.R.* as Yates's writing was *Black Sheep!*. That novel, stated the publisher Tinsley, was "written quite two-thirds" by Mrs. Cashel Hoey; Tinsley was surprised that Dickens had been unaware of the dual authorship and of the deception practised on him (*Random Recollections*, I, 140–41). Yates's novels *Wrecked in Port*, *Castaway*, *The Yellow Flag*, and *A Silent Witness* appeared in *A.Y.R.* in following years.

In his kind attempts to further Yates's literary career, Dickens supplied him with letters of introduction to publishers. Dickens's letter to Fields, Osgood, & Co., June 5, 1870, stressed particularly Yates's reliability and his punctuality in executing his work. The comment contrasts with the account of Charles Dickens, Jr., of his difficulty in getting out an *A.Y.R.* Christmas number in consequence of Yates's lateness in sending in copy. "Seriously," wrote young Dickens, "I have not had so harrassing and troublesome a time in my editorial experience" (*A.Y.R.* Letter-Book, Nov. 28, 1872).

D.N.B.

PROSE

A Fearful Night XIII, 424–27. May 17, 1856

Calumet Island XV, 55–59. Jan. 17, 1857

Two in a Legion XVII, 20–24. Dec. 19, 1857

The 3 items repr. in *After Office-Hours, By Edmund Yates*. London: W. Kent and Co. [1861]. Pub. in *H.W.* acknowledged.

VERSE

Gone Before XV, 84–85. Jan. 24, 1857

Repr. in *After Office-Hours* (as above).

Young, Marianne, formerly **Postans** |*Mrs. Young*|, writer. As wife of Capt. Thomas Postans of Bombay Army, lived some years in India. Contributed to *Sharpe's* articles on India and stories laid in India; published three books: *Cutch; or, Random Sketches, Taken during a Residence in One of the Northern Provinces of Western India*, *Western India in 1838*, and *Facts and Fictions, Illustrative of Oriental Character*. As Mrs. Young, published *Our Camp in Turkey*, 1854; *Aldershot, and All about It*, 1857; *The Moslem Noble: His Land and People*, 1857.

In 1854 Mrs. Young submitted two articles to *H.W.*, one on the maladministration of justice in India, one on Malta; Dickens declined them on the ground that the subjects had already been dealt with in *H.W.* The article that was accepted describes, on the basis of Mrs. Young's own observations, the deplorable conditions under which wives and children of soldiers lived in Aldershot barracks; some of the same details appear in chap. ii of her *Aldershot, and All about It*. Dickens made some changes in the paper; he found it "Execrably written" (to Wills, April 7, 1856: MS Huntington Library).

Allibone

Women at Aldershot XIII, 318–20. April 19, 1856

Unidentified contributors of non-specific designation or of no designation: Below are listed unidentified contributors that appear in the Office Book as "Correspondent," "Chance correspondent," and "Anonymous," and also – indicated by a rule – unidentified contributors lacking all designation in the Office Book and unidentified contributors of items not listed in the Office Book. For the two prose "fillers" that appear in Vol. I (the first two items listed below), as also for the lines from Blackmore and from Southey in the same volume, the rule actually means that the name of the person who inserted the items is not known. Contributors are listed in the order in which the item contributed (or inserted) by each appeared in *H.W.* Contributors of prose items are listed separately from contributors of verse.

Since, for certain of the contributors, the fact that they were or were not paid for their contribution is the only fact known about them, the Office Book payment notation is recorded with each item; the length is also recorded.

CONTRIBUTORS OF PROSE

———. Metal in Sea-Water
I, 24. March 30, 1850
½ col. Item not in Office Book. A "filler" from "Scientific Gossip," *Athenaeum*, Jan. 19, 1850. Appears in original issue only of *H.W.* No. 1 (see Introduction, p. 46). Repr. in *Harper's*, from *H.W.*, with acknowledgment (as in *H.W.*) to *Athenaeum*.

———. Curious Epitaph
I, 168. May 11, 1850
¼ col. Item not in Office Book. Quotes, from "the Churchyard, Pewsey, Dorsetshire" (Wiltshire?), the epitaph of Lady O'Looney, great-niece of Edmund Burke.

——— **& Mr. Horne.** The Old Churchyard Tree. A Prose Poem [chip]
I, 377–78. July 13, 1850
1½ cols. £0.10.0. Relates scenes, associated with a churchyard tree, in the life of a husband and wife, and in the life of their son who took to evil ways. Marked "Partly re-written by Mr. Horne." Repr. in *Harper's*, with acknowledgment to *H.W.*; included in *Choice Stories from Dickens' Household Words*, pub. Auburn, N.Y., 1854.

Mr. Horne & ———. Innocence and Crime. An Anecdote
I, 431–32. July 27, 1850
2¼ cols. No payment recorded. Relates an instance of pocket-picking and explains the term "shaking the doll" – thieves' argot for an apprentice pickpocket's clumsiness. The explanation is recorded as given by the governor of Coldbath Fields prison, i.e., George Laval Chesterton, contributor of two items to *H.W.*

———. A Remedy for Colliery Explosions [chip]
II, 323–25. Dec. 28, 1850
3 cols. Item not in Office Book. The writer is familiar with the working of Northumberland and Durham collieries; he states that he has attended two or three inquests on miners killed in explosions. His contribution, in the form of a letter to the editor, motivated by the article "A Coal Miner's Evidence," Dec. 7, proposes a method of conducting gas from collieries. A following article, "The True Remedy for Colliery Explosions," Jan. 25, 1851, stated the proposed method to be only "partial and very uncertain."

———. Degree Day at Cambridge [chip]
II, 491–92. Feb. 15, 1851
1¼ cols. No payment recorded. The contributor is obviously a Cambridge man. "None but those who have been educated at Cambridge," he writes, "can wholly understand the excitement which pervades that old university town on 'Degree Day.' "

——— *per R. Bell.* Life in the Burra Mines of South Australia
III, 250–52. June 7, 1851
3 cols. £1.1.0. Payment "sent to Mr. R. Bell by W.H.W." The item is in the form of a letter dated from North Kapunda, South Australia, Dec. 25, 1850. It was written, states the editorial comment, to "a gentleman in London," by whom it was "confided to us for publication." The gentleman in London was Robert Bell, contributor of one item to *H.W.*

The writer of the letter had arrived in Australia on Oct. 30, 1850. At the time of writing he was employed in a copper mine, working hard, saving his money, and pleased with his prospects in "the country I have adopted."

W.H.W. & correspondent. The Bush-Fire Extinguisher [chip]
III, 594–95. Sept. 13, 1851
½ col. No payment recorded. The contributor explains how two persons, fighting fire with fire, can "with perfect ease" contain and control a fire such as that described in "A Bush Fire in Australia," Aug. 23, 1851. Obviously, he knew nothing of Australian bush fires.

———. An Arabian Night-mare
IV, 166–68. Nov. 8, 1851
5¾ cols. £2.12.6. Tells of the Moslem merchant Hamet, who abides for a winter with a Muscovite; his nightmare is that of being transported by a bull-faced jin and various hawk-faced jan to the ice palace of Eblis. The story is told in the manner of the *Arabian Nights* tales, but contains phraseology that is distinctively the writer's, e.g., "I ... was even as a peeled wand for thinness"; "And their words struck against the rocks, and ran along the frozen ground. ... " It could be read as a forestudy to *The Shaving of Shagpat*, which Meredith began (at Weybridge) at about the time that the story appeared in *H.W.*

In thanking Meredith for a copy of *Shagpat*, Dickens wrote, May 10, 1856: "A new Arabian Tale is charming to me in the promise it holds out, and I hope I may say that I know already that you are not the man to disappoint me." If Meredith contributed "An Arabian Night-mare" to *H.W.*, Dickens's comment that he knew "already" that he would not be disappointed in the "new Arabian Tale" has a specific reference.

Chance correspondent. "My Uncle" and "My Aunt" [chip] IV, 357. Jan. 3, 1852
¼ col. No payment recorded. The item is in the form of a letter to the editor. The writer states that in France a pawnbroker's establishment is known as "My Aunt" – a fact that he does not find mentioned in the article on pawnbrokers ("My Uncle") by Dickens and Wills, Dec. 6, 1851. He signs himself "Un des Neveux de ma Tante et de Mon Oncle."

Correspondent & W.H.W. Locking Up the Tower of London [chip]
V, 15–16. March 20, 1852
¾ col. No payment recorded. The contributor describes in detail the ceremony of locking up the Tower, still conducted today as in ancient times. He finds the ceremony "pleasantly absurd."

——— **& Morley.** Darkness in Devonshire [chip] V, 325–26. June 19, 1852
1¼ cols. No payment recorded. The contributor has been for twenty years a magistrate in Devonshire, intimately acquainted with Devonshire people and their lives. The "darkness" of which he gives instances is the darkness of ignorance and superstition among the poor.

Correspondent. Lloyd's List [chip]
VI, 69–70. Oct. 2, 1852
¼ col. No payment recorded. The contributor has in his possession copies of Lloyd's List earlier than those stated in Capper's "Underwriting," Sept. 4, 1852, to be the earliest copies extant. He writes to correct the statement in "Underwriting."

———. Summer in Rome
VII, 257–61. May 14, 1853
8 cols. £3.3.0. "Cheque to J. Kenyon Esq. 39 Devonshire Place." The Devonshire Place address is that of John Curteis, brother-in-law of John Kenyon (1784–1856), the wealthy philanthropist, traveller, and amateur of letters, friend of many of the most eminent literary figures of his time. When in London, Kenyon shared Curteis's residence. The author of "Summer in Rome," an Englishwoman, was evidently a friend of Kenyon's. She states that she was compelled by various circumstances to remain in Rome from Nov. 1851 to Oct. 1852, during which residence she lived in the Casa Tarpeia. She had lived in Rome also before that time.

———. From California
IX, 176–78. April 8, 1854
3 cols. £1.10.0. The contributor writes: "I have the honour to be an inhabitant of the village of Salmon Falls, Eldorado,

California." His article describes the little mining community, its activities, and its residents.

———. Smoke or No Smoke
IX, 464–66. July 1, 1854
3¾ cols. No payment recorded. Title repeated in author-column. Discusses the "smoke nuisance" of London and explains various methods of destroying smoke from factory furnaces and from domestic grates.

———. Pulp [chip] XI, 20–21. Feb. 3, 1855
1¼ cols. Item not in Office Book. The writer advocates the manufacture of paper from coarse flax straw – a project that would involve setting up a company with vast capital paid in by large and small investors. This useful enterprise, however, is paralysed, he states, by "the present absurd and crippling state of the law of partnership" which makes every investor subject to unlimited liability. He hopes that Edward Cardwell, M.P., will keep his word to alter, in the present Parliamentary session, this "irrational and unjust law."

Correspondent. The Right Man in the Right Place [chip] XI, 495. June 23, 1855
½ col. No payment recorded. Quotes a letter written to a member of the Board of Guardians of a workhouse by an illiterate man who asks for himself and his wife the position of master and matron of the institution. Editorial comment states that the letter is exactly copied.

———. Burning a Priest [chip]
XIII, 224–26. March 22, 1856
3½ cols.; should read 2½. £2.2.0. The contributor had lived some time in Moulmein, Burma; he mentions having been acquainted with the commissioner of Moulmein. His article gives some account of the Burmese Buddhist priests and describes the funeral ceremony of one.

———. Hovelling [chip]
XV, 222. March 7, 1857
¼ col. Item not in Office Book. States that "a student in the Northern languages" has suggested the Danish word "Overlever" (deliverer) as the origin of "hoveller" – a word for which Lang, in his article "Hovelling," Feb. 7, 1857, could give no derivation.

——— **& Morley.** Little Commissions
XV, 246–49. March 14, 1857
6¼ cols. £3.3.0. The contributor, writing in the person of an amiable old bachelor, complains of the innumerable commissions that his friends expect him to carry out for them during his travels. He asks Mr. Conductor's advice on how to extricate himself from this nuisance without giving his friends cause to think him a "disobliging curmudgeon."

Correspondent. Coprolite [chip]
XV, 380–81. April 18, 1857
2 cols. No payment recorded. The contributor, a resident of south-east Suffolk, gives an account of the coprolite found in that district. Editorial comment prefaced to his account states some of the ancient beliefs concerning the origin of coprolites.

———. May-Meeting at Westminster
XV, 466–67. May 16, 1857
2½ cols. Item not in Office Book. Playing on the grammatical moods, as "May potential" and "May problematical," the contributor predicts that the May Parliament will fail to concern itself with needed domestic legislation, as on education, farm labour, the franchise.

Correspondent. Monthly Salaries [chip]
XV, 500–501. May 23, 1857
1 col. No payment recorded. The contributor, a Government clerk, explains the financial hardship caused such clerks by quarterly, rather than monthly, payment of their salaries; in certain Government offices, he states, clerks dare not memorialize the Treasury for monthly payment. "Will you allow me earnestly to ask your interference," he writes to *H.W.*, to procure this "great good for that numerous and well abused" class of employees. *H.W.* did not editorially endorse the monthly payment arrangement, but publication of the item implied editorial approval.

———. A Hint from Siam
XVI, 202–204. Aug. 29, 1857
2¾ cols. Item not in Office Book. In his witty, satirical essay, the contributor points out the distressing fact that in

England "it is often next to impossible to tell lords from commoners." He suggests a way in which this distinction could always be visibly demonstrated, taking his cue from a colour-plate picturing a Siamese aristocrat, reproduced in Sir John Bowring's *The Kingdom and People of Siam*, 1857.

———. The New Colonists of Norfolk Island xvi, 476–77. Nov. 14, 1857
2 cols. Item not in Office Book. Quotes William B. Ullathorne's description of Norfolk Island from his *Catholic Mission in Australasia*, first published 1836. The occasion for reprinting the description was the Government's removal, in 1856, of the inhabitants of Pitcairn Island to Norfolk Island.

Correspondent. Books for the Indian Army [chip] xviii, 437–38. Oct. 23, 1858
1 col. No payment recorded. The item consists of a letter from a non-commissioned officer serving in India, who, states the editorial comment, "modestly desires us to withhold his name." The officer writes that soldiers are eager for reading material, but that little is available to those serving in India. If the British public were aware of this fact, he feels confident that they would subscribe for books for the soldiers' use. "... may I most respectfully solicit the advocacy of our cause by a few words in your renowned Journal?"

Correspondent. Flamborough Head [chip] xix, 596. May 21, 1859
½ col. No payment recorded. The contributor suggests for the place-name "Flamborough" a derivation that seems to him "more probable and correct" than that given in "Fossil Geography," April 16, 1859. His reference to neighbourhood tradition concerning Flamborough Head and to the local pronunciation of the name may indicate that he lived in the vicinity of the place or perhaps elsewhere in Yorkshire.

CONTRIBUTORS OF VERSE

———. Good Verses of a Bad Poet
i, 36. April 6, 1850
⅛ col. Item not in Office Book. Consists of four lines from Sir Richard Blackmore, prefaced by the comment: "Few things in Dryden or Pope are finer than these lines by a man whom they both continually laughed at; – Sir Richard Blackmore."

———. Lines by Robert Southey
i, 167. May 11, 1850
¼ col. Item not in Office Book. Consists of fifteen lines, beginning "The days of Infancy are all a dream," stated to be "From an Unpublished Autograph" (no further identification). Repr. in Manchester *Courier*, June 15, 1850, with acknowledgment to *H.W.*; in *Harper's*, without acknowledgment.

———. Earth's Harvests
i, 297. June 22, 1850
½ col. No payment recorded. Has as motto Milton's line "Peace hath her victories, no less renowned than War." Repr. in *Harper's*, with acknowledgment to *H.W.*

Mr. ——— & Mr. Horne. "Press On." A Rivulet's Song i, 301. June 22, 1850
¾ col. No payment recorded. Marked "Altered by Horne."

———. "Battle with Life!"
i, 611. Sept. 21, 1850
½ col. No payment recorded. Perhaps by B. W. Procter (see Procter, above). Repr. in *Harper's*, without acknowledgment to *H.W.*

———. A Lesson for Future Life
ii, 65. Oct. 12, 1850
½ col. £0.10.6.

———. A Memory ii, 112. Oct. 26, 1850
½ col. £0.10.6.

——— *per Mrs. Gaskell.* The Outcast Lady ii, 252. Dec. 7, 1850
½ col. £0.10.6. Payment "Enclosed to Mrs. Gaskell."

———. Aspire! ii, 412–13. Jan. 25, 1851
½ col. No payment recorded. On the misattribution of this item to Dickens, see Introduction, p. 39.

———. An Abiding Dream
iv, 182–83. Nov. 15, 1851
1¾ cols. £2.2.0.

———. A Child's Prayer
IV, 277. Dec. 13, 1851

½ col. £0.10.6. Payment "Handed to Horne." Meredith is recorded in the Office Book as author, but his name is marked out. In "Some Unknown Poems of George Meredith," *T.P.'s Weekly*, Feb. 17, 1911, B. W. Matz listed "A Child's Prayer" as one of the twenty-three items (verse and prose) contributed by Meredith to *H.W.*, as recorded in the Office Book. He explained that for the poem Meredith's name was marked out and that payment was recorded as handed to Horne, stating: "Whether it is right to assume that the poem is Mr. Meredith's is a difficult question, but it is included in the list for the reason that in other cases payment was made in this way." Payment for "Sorrows and Joys" (reprinted by Meredith) and for "Infancy and Age" (stated by Meredith to be his writing) is recorded in the Office Book as made to Horne; so also is payment for "Time" and for "War," for Meredith's authorship of which the Office Book is the only evidence. The payment notation "Handed to Horne" may point to Meredith's authorship of "A Child's Prayer," but of itself it is not an indication of his authorship. Payment for three of Ollier's poems was also made to Horne, as was payment for Mrs. Holland's "The Growth of Good." In his privately printed *Twenty Poems by George Meredith*, 1909 (i.e., Meredith's verse contributions to *H.W.* as "disclosed by the entries in the office record," omitting the two poems reprinted by Meredith), Matz had included "A Child's Prayer" without indication that in the Office Book Meredith's name as author was marked out.

It is not outside the range of possibility that Meredith should have written "A Child's Prayer," since he held verse prayer to be appropriate for children and experimented in the writing of it. In a letter, Jan. 8, 1866, to Frederick Maxse, he wrote: "A child should pray in verse – don't you think so? I have thought of trying to write a morning and evening song for Freddy [Maxse's son]. Say if you care to have them." His own son Arthur, added Meredith, "used to repeat some lines," i.e., of verse prayer. Later, discussing the subject again with Maxse, Meredith wrote, Jan. 17, 1867: "The prayer you sketch is not objectionable; but it is not enough to my mind. I will in a few days send you a version." Because of the superstitious ideas that a child associates with the word "God," Meredith held (in 1867) that in a child's prayer that word should be replaced by the designation "Father of all Good" (*Letters*, I, 176, 187–88). The word "God" appears twice in the *H.W.* verse.

——— *per R.H.H.* A Cry from the Dust!
IV, 540. Feb. 28, 1852

½ col. £1.1.0. Marked "Paid to R. H. Horne." The poem is the monologue of a woman, once virtuous and modest, whose plea for work and for bread was spurned by man and whom God himself seemed to have forgotten – "God, too, seemed silent up on high":

> ... 'twas then I fell,
> And bade Hope, Virtue, Heaven, farewell.

The echo of "A Blot in the 'Scutcheon" in the above lines suggests that the poem may perhaps be by Meredith – one of the few *H.W.* poets influenced by Browning. Another indication to the same effect is Meredith's statement to John W. Parker, Dec. 12, 1850 (*Letters*, I, 8), that he had written or was planning to write "two or more numbers" on the theme of "London by Lamplight," "but shorter" than that poem. "London by Lamplight" deals with the ugliness of vice; it pictures women, once innocent country girls, the pride of their parents, now sunk to infamy of body and soul. "A Cry from the Dust!" is shorter than "London by Lamplight" (one-fifth the length); like that poem, it is in octosyllabic couplets. "A Cry from the Dust!" arrived at the editorial office through the agency of Horne; payment for the poem was made to Horne, as was payment for four poems that the Office Book assigns to Meredith (see "A Child's Prayer," above).

———. Hope. An Epigram
v, 297. June 12, 1852
¼ col. No payment recorded. After reading proof of the number in which the item appeared, Dickens wrote to Wills, June 3, 1852: "I could not conceive what 'Hope, An Epigram,' meant, and I declare to you I have not the least idea now! Having nothing to put in its place, I could not disturb the Make-up by taking it out."

———. Gradation
IX, 200–201. April 15, 1854
¾ col. £1.11.6.

———. Aspiration and Duty
XI, 108. March 3, 1855
¼ col. No payment recorded.

Mrs. ———. An English Wife
XII, 489–90. Dec. 22, 1855
3 cols. £3.13.6. Tells of an English wife whose husband had deserted her and her unborn infant, then, later, vowed to take the child from its mother and place it in "a wicked wanton's power." This he could do, the wife was aware, for "Such was merry England's law." She fled with the baby, who soon thereafter died.

The subject is appropriate to the interests and writing of Caroline Norton, whose husband's refusal to permit her access to their children motivated her agitation for change in legislation concerning custody of infants. In her pamphlets on the subject, Mrs. Norton recorded cases involving the same situation as that told of in the poem. In a letter to Mrs. Shelley, Jan. 5, 1837, she wrote: "Conceive, in one of the cases I had from the Law Reports, the mother being obliged to leave her child in the hands of the husband's mistress, and the Court saying it had no power to interfere. Was there ever such a perversion of natural rights?" (Perkins, *Life of Mrs. Norton*, p. 134). For the two items assigned in the Office Book to Mrs. Norton, however, her name appears with its title: "Hon. Mrs. Norton," "The Honble Mrs. Norton." The absence of "Hon." from the incomplete ascription for "An English Wife" makes it impossible to record the item as a probable contribution of Caroline Norton.

———. A Shadow of George Herbert
XIII, 37. Jan. 26, 1856
½ col. £1.1.0.

———. Sorrow and My Heart
XIII, 84. Feb. 9, 1856
¾ col. £1.11.6.

———. Dawn XIII, 397. May 10, 1856
1¾ cols.; should read ¾. £2.2.0. In the Office Book length notation, the "1" is written as a figure, not (as in the non-fraction part of the length notation of other items) as a word; the "1" is written in ink and appears to be intended as part of the length notation. Payment was obviously based on that notation.

———. A Christmas Carol
XIV, 565. Dec. 27, 1856
1¼ cols. £2.2.0. On the misattribution of this item to Mrs. Gaskell, see Introduction, pp. 39–40.

Anonymous. Song of an Exile
XV, 227–28. March 7, 1857
½ col. £1.1.0.

Anonymous. Marion's Orchard
XVII, 276–77. March 6, 1858
1 col. £2.2.0.

Household Words Title Index

EXPLANATORY NOTE

The index is arranged so as to make notations as brief as possible. Titles that admit of abbreviation are abbreviated. The "A" ("An") or "The" at the beginning of a title is omitted. End punctuation of titles is omitted.

The location given for an item in a regular number is the volume in which it appears and the page on which it begins. For items of two instalments (chapters, sections, parts, etc.), the page on which each instalment begins is given. This arrangement is followed also for items in which the instalments, numbering from three to eight, appear at irregular intervals. For all other multi-instalment items, the page on which the first instalment begins is given and the number of instalments is stated. The location given for items in the extra Christmas numbers is the title of the number and the page on which an item begins. Untitled items in the 1856 Christmas number are listed by the titles given in the present Table of Contents for that number.

Two prose items having the same title and dealing with the same subject are given one listing, irrespective of authorship. Two unrelated prose items having the same title are listed separately. Individual verse items having the same title are listed separately.

HOUSEHOLD WORDS: TABLE OF VOLUMES, NUMBERS, DATES

REGULAR NUMBERS

Volume	Numbers (inclusive)	Dates (inclusive)
I	1– 26	March 30, 1850–Sept. 21, 1850
II	27– 52	Sept. 28, 1850–March 22, 1851
III	53– 78	March 29, 1851–Sept. 20, 1851
IV	79–103	Sept. 27, 1851–March 13, 1852
V	104–129	March 20, 1852–Sept. 11, 1852
VI	130–153	Sept. 18, 1852–Feb. 26, 1853
VII	154–179	March 5, 1853–Aug. 27, 1853
VIII	180–203	Sept. 3, 1853–Feb. 11, 1854
IX	204–229	Feb. 18, 1854–Aug. 12, 1854
X	230–253	Aug. 19, 1854–Jan. 27, 1855
XI	254–279	Feb. 3, 1855–July 28, 1855
XII	280–303	Aug. 4, 1855–Jan. 12, 1856
XIII	304–329	Jan. 19, 1856–July 12, 1856
XIV	330–353	July 19, 1856–Dec. 27, 1856
XV	354–379	Jan. 3, 1857–June 27, 1857
XVI	380–403	July 4, 1857–Dec. 12, 1857
XVII	404–429	Dec. 19, 1857–June 12, 1858
XVIII	430–453	June 19, 1858–Nov. 27, 1858
XIX	454–479	Dec. 4, 1858–May 28, 1859

EXTRA CHRISTMAS NUMBERS

1851	Extra number for Christmas (announced in advertisements as "Showing What Christmas Is to Everybody")
1852	A Round of Stories by the Christmas Fire
1853	Another Round of Stories by the Christmas Fire
1854	The Seven Poor Travellers
1855	The Holly-Tree Inn
1856	The Wreck of the Golden Mary. Being the Captain's Account of the Loss of the Ship, and the Mate's Account of the Great Deliverance of Her People in an Open Boat at Sea
1857	The Perils of Certain English Prisoners, and Their Treasure in Women, Children, Silver, and Jewels
1858	A House to Let

ABBREVIATIONS USED

including abbreviated titles of periodicals frequently referred to

The following abbreviations are used in footnotes and in Part One and Part Two, except where an abbreviation would be unclear or inappropriate. Not included in the list are the abbreviations in general use (Lieut., B.A., M.D., etc.) and those commonly used in literary works (chap., col., ser., etc.). Not included among abbreviated periodical titles are those of periodicals commonly referred to by only the first words of the title (as the *Universal Magazine* for *The Universal Magazine of Knowledge and Pleasure*).

advt.
advertisement

agric.
agriculture, agricultural

Ainsworth's
Ainsworth's Magazine

A.R.A.
Associate of the Royal Academy

autobiog.
autobiography

A.Y.R.
All the Year Round

b.
born

B.D.
Bachelor of Divinity

Beds.
Bedfordshire

Bentley's Misc.
Bentley's Miscellany

Blackwood's
Blackwood's Edinburgh Magazine

Brit. Mus.
British Museum

Bucks.
Buckinghamshire

Cassell's
Cassell's Illustrated Family Paper
(title varies)

C.B.
Companion of (the Order of) the Bath

cent.
century

Chambers's
Chambers's Edinburgh Journal
(title varies)

C.M.G.
Companion of (the Order of) St. Michael and St. George

Conn.
Connecticut

contemp.
contemporary

Contemp. Rev.
The Contemporary Review

Cornhill
The Cornhill Magazine

C.S.I.
Companion of (the Order of) the Star of India

d.
died

D.C.
District of Columbia

D.C.L.
Doctor of Civil Law

descr.
description

D. Lit.
Doctor of Literature

do.
ditto

Edin. Rev.
The Edinburgh Review

educ.
education

F.G.S.
Fellow of the Geological Society

F.L.S.
Fellow of the Linnean Society

Foreign Quart. Rev.
The Foreign Quarterly Review

Fortnightly
The Fortnightly Review

F.R.A.S.
Fellow of the Royal Asiatic Society (in Capper identification note)

F.R.A.S.
Fellow of the Royal Astronomical Society (in De Morgan identification note)

Fraser's
Fraser's Magazine for Town and Country

F.R.C.P.
Fellow of the Royal College of Physicians

F.R.C.S.
Fellow of the Royal College of Surgeons

F.R.G.S.
Fellow of the Royal Geographical Society

F.R.M.S.
Fellow of the Royal Microscopical Society

F.R.S.
Fellow of the Royal Society

F.S.A.
Fellow of the Society of Antiquaries

Gent. Mag.
The Gentleman's Magazine

geog.
geographical

govt.
government

Govt.
Government (pertaining to Great Britain)

Harper's
Harper's New Monthly Magazine

hist.
historical

H.W.
Household Words

Illus. London News
The Illustrated London News

Illus. Mag. of Art
The Illustrated Magazine of Art

Illus. Times
The Illustrated Times

Jour.
Journal (in certain periodical titles)

K.C.
King's Counsel

K.C.B.
Knight Commander of (the Order of) the Bath

K.C.I.E.
Knight Commander of (the Order of) the Indian Empire

K.C.M.G.
Knight Commander of (the Order of) St. Michael and St. George

K.C.S.I.
Knight Commander of (the Order of) the Star of India

LL.B.
Bachelor of Laws

LL.D.
Doctor of Laws

Lloyd's Weekly
Lloyd's Weekly London Newspaper (title varies)

London & Westm. Rev.
The London and Westminster Review

L.R.C.P.
Licentiate of the Royal College of Physicians

L.R.C.S.
Licentiate of the Royal College of Surgeons

L.S.A.
Licentiate of the Society of Apothecaries

Macmillan's
Macmillan's Magazine

Mass.
Massachusetts

M.B.
Bachelor of Medicine

misc.
miscellaneous

M.P.
Member of Parliament

M.R.A.S.
Member of the Royal Asiatic Society

M.R.C.S.
Member of the Royal College of Surgeons

M.R.S.L.
Member of the Royal Society of Literature

N. & Q.
Notes and Queries

New Monthly
The New Monthly Magazine (title varies)

North Brit. Rev.
The North British Review

perh.
perhaps

prob.
probable, probably

pub.
publication, published

Q.C.
Queen's Counsel

Quart. Rev.
The Quarterly Review

repr.
reprint, reprinted

R.N.
Royal Navy

Scribner's
Scribner's Magazine

Sharpe's
Sharpe's London Magazine (title varies)

suppl.
supplement

Tait's
Tait's Edinburgh Magazine

Tinsleys'
Tinsleys' Magazine

T.L.S.
The Times Literary Supplement

War.
Warwickshire

Westm. Rev.
The Westminster Review

Yorks.
Yorkshire

Bibliography

BIOGRAPHICAL, BIBLIOGRAPHICAL, AND OTHER COMPILATIONS CITED BY ABBREVIATED TITLE OR OTHER DESIGNATION

Allgemeine deutsche Biog.: *Allgemeine deutsche Biographie.* 56 vols. Leipzig, 1875–1912.

Allibone: Samuel Austin Allibone. *A Critical Dictionary of English Literature and British and American Authors, Living and Deceased, from the Earliest Accounts to the Latter Half of the Nineteenth Century.* 3 vols. Philadelphia, 1858–71 (title pages vary somewhat). With suppl. by John Foster Kirk. 2 vols. Philadelphia, 1891.

Alumni Cantab.: J. A. Venn, comp. *Alumni Cantabrigienses: A Biographical List of All Known Students, Graduates and Holders of Office at the University of Cambridge, from the Earliest Times to 1900.* Part II: from 1752 to 1900. 6 vols. Cambridge, 1940–54.

Alumni Oxon.: Joseph Foster, ed. *Alumni Oxonienses: The Members of the University of Oxford, 1715–1886: Their Parentage, Birthplace, and Year of Birth, with a Record of Their Degrees.* 4 vols. Oxford and London, 1888.

Appleton: James Grant Wilson and John Fiske, eds. *Appletons' Cyclopaedia of American Biography.* 6 vols. New York, 1887–89.

Australian Ency.: A. H. Chisholm, ed. *The Australian Encyclopaedia.* 10 vols. Sydney, 1958.

Biblio. Cornub.: George Clement Boase and William Prideaux Courtney. *Bibliotheca Cornubiensis. A Catalogue of the Writings ... of Cornishmen, and of Works Relating to the County of Cornwall, with Biographical Memoranda and Copious Literary References.* 2 vols. London, 1874, 1878. With 1-vol. suppl., marked Vol. III, 1882.

Boase: Frederic Boase. *Modern English Biography, Containing Many Thousand Concise Memoirs of Persons Who Have Died since the Year 1850, with an Index of the Most Interesting Matter.* 6 vols. Truro, 1892–1921. Vols. IV–VI (title varies slightly from title of other vols.) are marked suppl.

Brit. Imperial Calendar: *The British Imperial Calendar ... or, General Register of the United Kingdom of Great Britain and Ireland, and Its Colonies. ...* An annual. London, 1810–.

Brit. Med. Directory: *The British Medical Directory for England, Scotland, and Wales.* London, 1853, 1854.

Brit. Mus. Cat.: British Museum. *General Catalogue of Printed Books.* London, 1931–65.

C.B.E.L.: *The Cambridge Bibliography of English Literature*, ed. F. W. Bateson. 4 vols. Cambridge, 1941. With 1-vol. suppl., 1957.

Colonial Office List: *The Colonial Office List ... or, General Register of the Colonial Dependencies of Great Britain.* An annual. London, 1862–1925.

Crockford: *The Clerical Directory, a Biographical and Statistical Book of Reference for Facts Relating to the Clergy and the Church.* London, 1858–59; continued as *Crockford's Clerical Directory*, 1860–.

D.A.B.: *Dictionary of American Biography.*

20 vols. New York, 1928–36.

D.N.B.: *Dictionary of National Biography.* 63 vols. London, 1885–1900. With 3-vol. suppl., 1901; 3-vol. 2nd suppl., 1912; and later single-vol. supplements.

East-India Register: *The East-India Register and Directory.* London, 1803–1844; continued as *The East-India Register and Army List.* London, 1845–60.

Enciclopedia "Italiana": *Enciclopedia biografica e bibligrafica "Italiana."* Ser. 38: *Pedagogisti ed educatori.* Milan [1939].

Ency. Brit.: *Encyclopaedia Britannica.*

Eng. Cat.: *The English Catalogue of Books* (also *The London Catalogue* and *The British Catalogue*). London. (See Besterman, *World Bibliography of Bibliographies* for bibliographical data.)

Foreign Office List: *The Foreign Office List for 1852,* and for later dates. An annual. London.

Graduates in Medicine, Univ. of Edinburgh: *List of the Graduates in Medicine in the University of Edinburgh, from MDCCV. to MDCCCLXVI.* Edinburgh, 1867.

Graduates of the Univ. of Glasgow: *A Roll of the Graduates of the University of Glasgow from 31st December, 1827, to 31st December, 1897, with Short Biographical Notes,* compiled by W. Innes Addison. Glasgow, 1898.

Halkett and Laing: Samuel Halkett and John Laing. *Dictionary of Anonymous and Pseudonymous English Literature.* New and enlarged ed., by James Kennedy, W. A. Smith, and A. F. Johnson. 7 vols. Edinburgh and London, 1926–34; continued, by D. E. Rhodes and A. E. C. Simoni, in 2 additional vols., 1956, 1962.

Hist. of San Joaquin County: *An Illustrated History of San Joaquin County, California. Containing a History of San Joaquin County from the Earliest Period of Its Occupancy to the Present Time, Together with Glimpses of Its Future Prospects; with Full-Page Portraits of Some of Its Most Eminent Men, and Biographical Mention of Many of Its Pioneers and Also of Prominent Citizens of To-day.* Chicago: Lewis Publishing Company, 1890.

Literatur-Lexikon: Wilhelm Kosch. *Deutsches Literatur-Lexikon: biographisches und bibliographisches Handbuch.* 4 vols. 2nd ed. Bern, 1949–58.

London and Prov. Med. Directory: *The London and Provincial Medical Directory.* An annual. London, 1848–60.

Magyar Írók Élete és Munkái: József Szinnyei. *Magyar Írók Élete és Munkái* [Lives and works of Hungarian writers], Vol. VIII. Budapest, 1902.

Martin's Bench and Bar: John Hill Martin. *Martin's Bench and Bar of Philadelphia; Together with Other Lists of Persons Appointed to Administer the Laws in the City and County of Philadelphia, and the Province and Commonwealth of Pennsylvania.* Philadelphia, 1883.

Men-at-the-Bar: Joseph Foster. *Men-at-the-Bar: A Biographical Hand-List of the Members of the Various Inns of Court, Including Her Majesty's Judges, etc.* London, 1885.

Men of the Time: *The Men of the Time ..., or Sketches of Living Notables.* London, 1852, and later editions (subtitles vary).

Miller, *Australian Lit.*: Edmund Morris Miller, assisted by F. J. Broomfield. *Australian Literature from Its Beginnings to 1935: A Descriptive and Bibliographical Survey.* ... 2 vols. Melbourne, 1940.

Notable Middle Templars: John Hutchinson. *A Catalogue of Notable Middle Templars, with Brief Biographical Notices.* London, 1902.

Plarr's Lives: *Plarr's Lives of the Fellows of the Royal College of Surgeons of England,* revised by Sir D'Arcy Power with the assistance of W. G. Spencer and G. E. Gask. 2 vols. London, 1930.

Polski słownik biog.: *Polski słownik biograficzny* [Polish biographical dictionary], Vol. x. Breslau, Warsaw, Cracow, 1962–64.

Records of ... Lincoln's Inn: *The Records of the Honorable Society of Lincoln's Inn.* Vol. II: Admissions from A.D. 1800 to A.D. 1893, and Chapel Registers. London, 1896. *The Records of the Honorable Society of Lincoln's Inn. The Black Books.* Vol. IV: from A.D. 1776 to A.D. 1845. London, 1902.

South African Biblio.: Sidney Mendelssohn. *Mendelssohn's South African Bibliography, Being the Catalogue Raisonné of the Mendelssohn Library of Works Relating to South Africa.* ... 2 vols. London, 1910.

Wellesley Index: Walter E. Houghton, ed. *The Wellesley Index to Victorian Periodicals, 1824–1900: Tables of Contents and Identification of Contributors with Bibliographies of Their Articles and Stories*, Vol. I. Toronto, 1966.

Who Was Who in America: *Who Was Who in America*, Library Edition, Vol. I: 1897–1942. Chicago, 1943.

GENERAL BIBLIOGRAPHY

This list does not include *H.W.* contributors' reprintings of their *H.W.* writings, except for books that are quoted from in the text; the list does not include books mentioned, in Part Two, as illustrative of a contributor's writing.

Adrian, Arthur A. *Georgina Hogarth and the Dickens Circle*. London: Oxford University Press, 1957.

– "A Note on the Dickens-Collins Friendship," *Huntington Library Quart.*, XVI (Feb. 1953), 211–13.

Allingham, H., and E. Baumer Williams, eds. *Letters to William Allingham*. London: Longmans, Green and Co., 1911.

Allingham, William. *A Diary*, ed. H. Allingham and D. Radford. London: Macmillan and Co., 1907.

– *Songs, Ballads, and Stories*. London: George Bell and Sons, 1877.

– *Varieties in Prose*. 3 vols. London: Longmans, Green and Co., 1893.

All the Year Round Letter-Book. Press copies of letters by Charles Dickens, William Henry Wills, and Charles Culliford Dickens, 1859–80. Henry E. Huntington Library, HM 17507. Cited as *A.Y.R.* Letter-Book.

"Anecdotal Photographs. Grenville Murray," *Truth*, XI (Dec. 29, 1881), 24–25.

Armour, Richard Willard. *Barry Cornwall: A Biography of Bryan Waller Procter with a Selected Collection of Hitherto Unpublished Letters*. Boston: Meador Publishing Company, 1935.

Arnold, Matthew. *Friendship's Garland: Being the Conservations, Letters, and Opinions of the Late Arminius, Baron von Thunder-Ten-Tronckh*. London: Smith, Elder and Co., 1871.

Athanasi, Giovanni d'. *A Brief Account of the Researches and Discoveries in Upper Egypt, Made under the Direction of Henry Salt, Esq., by Giovanni d'Athanasi. To Which Is Added a Detailed Catalogue of Mr. Salt's Collection of Egyptian Antiquities*. London: John Hearne, 1836.

Atkins, John Black. *The Life of Sir William Howard Russell, C.V.O., LL.D., the First Special Correspondent*. 2 vols. London: John Murray, 1911.

Axon, William E. A. *Cheshire Gleanings*. Manchester: Tubbs, Brook, & Chrystal; London: Simpkin, Marshall, & Co., 1884.

Bain, Alexander. *John Stuart Mill. A Criticism: with Personal Recollections*. London: Longmans, Green, and Co., 1882.

Ballantine, William. *Some Experiences of a Barrister's Life*. 2 vols. 3rd ed. London: Richard Bentley & Son, 1882.

Barratt, Norris S. *A Memorial of John Samuel, Esq.* Pamphlet, repr. from Philadelphia *Legal Intelligencer*, Sept 5, 1913.

Belloc, Bessie Rayner. *In a Walled Garden*. 3rd ed. London: Ward and Downey, 1896.

Bennett, William Cox. *Poems*. New ed., in 1 vol. London: Routledge, Warne, and Routledge, 1862.

Bentley, Richard and Son, publishers. *A List of the Principal Publications Issued from New Burlington Street during the Year 1853*. London: Richard Bentley and Son. Priv. printed, 1919.

Besant, Walter. "The First Society of British Authors (1843)," *Contemp. Rev.*, LVI (July 1889), 10–27.

The Biograph and Review. 6 vols. London: E. W. Allen, 1879–81.

Blackwell, Anna. *The Philosophy of Existence*. Repr. from *Human Nature*. London: Sold by J. Burns, 1871.

– *Spiritualism and Spiritism*. Repr. of letters from *Human Nature*; and unpub. letter to the *Times*. N.p. [1873].

Blackwell, Elizabeth. *Pioneer Work in Opening the Medical Profession to Women*. Everyman's Library. London: J. M. Dent & Sons; New York: E. P. Dutton & Co., n.d.

Blainey, Ann. *The Farthing Poet: A Biography of Richard Hengist Horne, 1802–84, a Lesser Literary Lion.* London: Longmans, Green and Co., 1968.

Blunden, Edmund. *Leigh Hunt and His Circle.* New York: Harper & Brothers, 1930.

Bompas, George C. *Life of Frank Buckland.* London: Smith, Elder, & Co., 1885.

Bourne, H. R. Fox. *English Newspapers: Chapters in the History of Journalism.* 2 vols. London: Chatto & Windus, 1887.

Bredsdorff, Elias. *Hans Andersen and Charles Dickens: A Friendship and Its Dissolution. Anglistica,* VII, 1956.

Brewer, Luther A. *My Leigh Hunt Library ... The First Editions.* Cedar Rapids, Iowa: Priv. printed, 1932.

– *My Leigh Hunt Library. The Holograph Letters.* Iowa City, Iowa: University of Iowa Press, 1938.

Brough, Robert B. *Songs of the "Governing Classes," and Other Lyrics Written in a Seasonable Spirit of "Vulgar Declamation."* London: Henry Vizetelly, 1855.

Browning, Elizabeth Barrett. *Elizabeth Barrett Browning: Letters to Her Sister, 1846–1859,* ed. Leonard Huxley. London: John Murray, 1929; repr. 1931.

– *The Letters of Elizabeth Barrett Browning,* edited with Biographical Additions by Frederic G. Kenyon. 2 vols. New York: Macmillan Company, 1897.

– *Letters of Elizabeth Barrett Browning Addressed to Richard Hengist Horne ... with Comments on Contemporaries,* ed. S. R. Townshend Mayer. 2 vols. London: Richard Bentley and Son, 1877.

– and Robert Browning. *Letters of the Brownings to George Barrett,* ed. Paul Landis with the assistance of Ronald E. Freeman. Urbana: University of Illinois Press, 1958.

Browning, Robert. *Letters of Robert Browning,* collected by Thomas J. Wise, edited with an Introduction and Notes by Thurman L. Hood. New Haven: Yale University Press, 1933.

Bruce, William Downing. *An Account of the Present Deplorable State of the Ecclesiastical Courts of Record; with Proposals for Their Complete Reformation.* London: Henry Adams; W. Arpthorp, 1854.

Buckland, Francis Trevelyan. *Curiosities of Natural History.* 4 vols. London: Richard Bentley, 1857–66.

Buckler, William E. "'Household Words' in America," *Papers of the Bibliographical Society of America,* XLV (Second Quarter, 1951), 160–66.

Burton, Hester. *Barbara Bodichon, 1827–1891.* London: John Murray, 1949.

Byles, C. E. *The Life and Letters of R. S. Hawker (Sometime Vicar of Morwenstow).* London and New York: John Lane, 1905.

Cape, George A., Jr. *Baths and Wash Houses; the History of Their Rise and Progress: Showing Their Utility and Their Effect upon the Moral and Physical Condition of the People. ...* London: Simpkin, Marshall and Co., 1854.

Carlyle, Jane Welsh. *Jane Welsh Carlyle: Letters to Her Famliy, 1839–1863,* ed. Leonard Huxley. London: John Murray, 1924.

– *Letters and Memorials of Jane Welsh Carlyle,* prepared for publication by Thomas Carlyle, edited by James Anthony Froude. 3 vols. London: Longmans, Green, and Co., 1883.

Carter, John Archer, Jr. "Memories of 'Charley Wag,'" *Dickensian,* LXII (Autumn 1966), 147–51.

Cary, Alice, and Phoebe Cary, eds. *The Josephine Gallery.* New York: Derby & Jackson, 1859.

Cayley, George John. *Las Alforjas.* 2 vols. London: Richard Bentley, 1853.

Champneys, Basil. *Memoirs and Correspondence of Coventry Patmore.* 2 vols. London: George Bell and Sons, 1900.

Chesterton, George Laval. *Revelations of Prison Life; with an Enquiry into Prison Discipline and Secondary Punishments.* 2 vols. London: Hurst and Blackett, 1856.

Chorley, Henry Fothergill. *Henry Fothergill Chorley: Autobiography, Memoir, and Letters,* compiled by Henry G. Hewlett. 2 vols. London: Richard Bentley and Son, 1873.

Christie, John. *The Ancestry of Catherine Thomson Hogarth, the Wife of Charles Dickens, Novelist.* Edinburgh: William J. Hay, 1912.

Clarke, Charles Cowden, and Mary Cowden Clarke. *Recollections of Writers.* New York: Charles Scribner's Sons, n.d.

Clarke, Mary Cowden. *Letters to an Enthusiast ... Being a Series of Letters Addressed to Robert Balmanno, Esq., of New York, 1850–1861*, ed. Anne Upton Nettleton. Chicago: A. C. McClurg & Co., 1902.
– *My Long Life: An Autobiographic Sketch.* New York: Dodd, Mead and Company, 1896.
Clay, Walter Lowe. *The Prison Chaplain: A Memoir of the Rev. John Clay, ... with Selections from His Reports and Correspondence, and a Sketch of Prison Discipline in England.* Cambridge and London: Macmillan and Co., 1861.
Clodd, Edward. "George Meredith: Some Recollections," *Fortnightly*, n.s. LXXXVI (July 1909), 19–31.
Coates, Henry T., comp. and ed. *The Fireside Encyclopaedia of Poetry. Comprising the Best Poems of the Most Famous Writers, English and American.* 7th ed. Philadelphia: Porter & Coates [1879].
Cole, Alfred Whaley. *Reminiscences of My Life and of the Cape Bench and Bar.* Cape Town: J. C. Juta and Co., 1896.
Cole, Henry. *Fifty Years of Public Work of Sir Henry Cole, K.C.B., Accounted for in His Deeds, Speeches and Writings.* 2 vols. London: George Bell and Sons, 1884.
Colles, William Morris. *Literature and the Pension List. An Investigation Conducted for the Committee of the Incorporated Society of Authors.* London: Henry Glaisher, 1889.
Collins, Philip. "Dickens and the Whiston Case," *Dickensian*, LVIII (Winter 1962), 47–49.
– "W. H. Wills' Plans for *Household Words*," *Victorian Periodicals Newsletter*, No. 8 (April 1970), pp. 33–46.
Collins, William Wilkie. *My Miscellanies.* 2 vols. London: Sampson Low, Son, & Co., 1863.
Conklin, Robert J. *Thomas Cooper, the Chartist (1805–1892).* Manila: University of the Philippines Press, 1935.
Cooper, Thomas. *The Baron's Yule Feast: A Christmas-Rhyme.* London: Jeremiah How, 1846.
– *Eight Letters to the Young Men of the Working-Classes. (Collected from the 'Plain Speaker.')*. London: J. Watson, 1851.
– *The Life of Thomas Cooper: Written by Himself.* London: Hodder and Stoughton, 1872.
– *The Poetical Works of Thomas Cooper.* London: Hodder and Stoughton, 1877.
Corrigan, Beatrice, "Giovanni Ruffini's Letters to Vernon Lee, 1875–1879," *English Miscellany, A Symposium of History, Literature, and the Arts*, 1962. No. 13, pp. 179–240.
Corvin-Wiersbitzki, Otto Julius Bernhard von. "Charles Dickens," *Europa*, 1870. No. 33, cols. 1045–1056.
– *A Life of Adventure: An Autobiography.* 3 vols. London: Richard Bentley, 1871.
– "Eine Vorlesung von Charles Dickens," *Gartenlaube*, 1861. No. 39, pp. 612–14.
Crosland, Mrs. Newton (Camilla Toulmin). *Landmarks of a Literary Life, 1820–1892.* New York: Charles Scribner's Sons, 1893.
Crowe, Sir Joseph Archer. *Reminiscences of Thirty-five Years of My Life.* London: John Murray, 1895.
Cruikshank, George. "A Letter from Hop-o'-My-Thumb to Charles Dickens, Esq. upon 'Frauds on the Fairies,' 'Whole Hogs,' etc.," *George Cruikshank's Magazine*, Feb. 1854, pp. 74–80.
A Cyclopaedia of Female Biography; Consisting of Sketches of All Women Who Have Been Distinguished by Great Talents, Strength of Character, Piety, Benevolence, or Moral Virtue of Any Kind. ..., ed. H. G. Adams. London: Groombridge and Sons, 1857.
Dawson's Book Shop. *Catalogue 323: Books from the Library of Charles Dickens, Together with Autograph Letters, Books, and Pamphlets by Charles Dickens and Other Books of the Dickens Period from the Langstroth Collections.* Los Angeles, n.d.
De Morgan, Sophia Elizabeth. *Memoir of Augustus De Morgan ... with Selections from His Letters.* London: Longmans, Green and Co., 1882.
– *Threescore Years and Ten: Reminiscences of the Late Sophia Elizabeth De Morgan, to Which Are Added Letters to and from Her Husband, the Late Augustus De Morgan, and Others*, ed.

Mary A. De Morgan. London: Richard Bentley and Son, 1895.

Dexter, Walter, ed. *The Letters of Charles Dickens* and *Mr. & Mrs. Charles Dickens. See* Dickens, Charles.

Dickens, Charles. *American Notes for General Circulation.* 2 vols. London: Chapman and Hall, 1842.

– *The Heart of Charles Dickens As Revealed in His Letters to Angela Burdett-Coutts,* selected and edited by Edgar Johnson. New York: Duell, Sloan and Pearce, 1952.

– Introduction to *Legends and Lyrics,* by Adelaide Anne Procter. New ed., with additions. London: Bell and Daldy, 1866.

– *The Letters of Charles Dickens,* ed. Walter Dexter. 3 vols. Bloomsbury: Nonesuch Press, 1938. Cited as Nonesuch *Letters.*
See also Rolfe, Franklin P. "Additions to the Nonesuch Edition of Dickens' Letters," *Huntington Library Quart.,* v (Oct. 1941), 115–40.

– *The Letters of Charles Dickens,* Pilgrim Edition, ed. Madeline House and Graham Storey, Vols. I–II. Oxford: Clarendon Press, 1965–69. Cited as Pilgrim *Letters.*

– *Mr. & Mrs. Charles Dickens: His Letters to Her,* ed. Walter Dexter. London: Constable & Co., 1935.

– *Notes and Comments on Certain Writings in Prose and Verse by Richard Henry Horne, Author of "Orion."* London: Priv. printed for Thomas J. Wise, 1920.

– *The Speeches of Charles Dickens,* ed. K. J. Fielding. Oxford: Clarendon Press, 1960.

– Volume of transcripts of 118 Dickens letters to various persons, typewritten. Henry E. Huntington Library, HM 27634.

A Dickens Library: Exhibition Catalogue of the Sawyer Collection of the Works of Charles Dickens, Comprising Manuscripts, Autograph Letters, Presentation Copies, the Issues in Original Parts, Dickensiana, Etc. Priv. printed, 1936.

Directories, listed by place-name for which directory is consulted:
Bombay: *Bombay Almanac and Book of Direction, for 1855. Bombay Calendar and Almanac for 1858.*
Bristol: *Mathews's Annual Bristol Directory, and Almanack,* 1854. Kelly's *Post Office Directory of Gloucestershire, with Bath, Bristol, Herefordshire, and Shropshire ...,* 1856.
Dublin: Thom's *Post Office Dublin Directory and Calendar, for 1849;* also for later dates.
Hexham: William Whellan & Co.'s *History, Topography, and Directory of Northumberland ...,* 1855.
Leeds: *Slade and Roebuck's Directory of the Borough of Leeds,* 1851.
London: Kelly's *Post Office London Directory.* An annual.
Manchester: *Slater's General and Classified Directory and Street Register of Manchester and Salford, and Their Vicinities ...,* 1850.
Sheffield: William White's *General Directory of the Town and Borough of Sheffield ...,* 1849. William White's *Gazetteer and General Directory of Sheffield ...,* 1852, 1856.

[Dixon, Henry Hall.] *Saddle and Sirloin, or English Farm and Sporting Worthies, by the Druid.* London: Rogerson & Tuxford, 1870.

Downey, Edmund. *Charles Lever: His Life in His Letters.* 2 vols. Edinburgh and London: William Blackwood and Sons, 1906.

Eckel, John C. *The First Editions of the Writings of Charles Dickens, Their Points and Values: A Bibliography.* Rev. and enlarged ed. New York: Maurice Inman, 1932.

Eliot, George. *The George Eliot Letters,* ed. Gordon S. Haight. 7 vols. New Haven: Yale University Press, 1954–55.

Ellis, S. M., ed. *The Letters and Memoirs of Sir William Hardman* and *A Mid-Victorian Pepys. See* Hardman, Sir William.

– *William Harrison Ainsworth and His Friends.* 2 vols. London: John Lane, 1911.

Espinasse, Francis. *Literary Recollections and Sketches.* London: Hodder and Stoughton, 1893.

Evans, T. C. *Of Many Men.* New York: American News Company, 1888.

Field, Kate. "English Authors in Florence," *Atlantic Monthly*, XIV (Dec. 1864), 660–71.

Fielding, K. J. "Charles Dickens and R. H. Horne," *English*, IX (Spring 1952), 17–19.

– "Charles Whitehead and Charles Dickens," *Review of English Studies*, n.s. III (April 1952), 141–54.

Fields, James T. *Yesterdays with Authors*. Boston and New York: Houghton, Mifflin and Company, 1900.

Fitz-Gerald, Desmond G. *Education. A Lecture*. London: Wyand, Son, and Co., 1858.

– "Natural Science. – Its Adaptation to the Youthful Mind," *The School and the Teacher*, V (June 1, 1858), 216–18.

Fitzgerald, Percy Hetherington. *The Life of Charles Dickens As Revealed in His Writings*. 2 vols. London: Chatto & Windus, 1905.

– *Memoirs of an Author*. 2 vols. London: Richard Bentley and Son, 1894.

– *Memories of Charles Dickens with an Account of "Household Words" and "All the Year Round" and of the Contributors Thereto*. Bristol: J. W. Arrowsmith, 1913.

– *Recreations of a Literary Man, or Does Writing Pay?* New ed. London: Chatto and Windus, 1883.

– "Two English Essayists: Charles Lamb and Charles Dickens," *The Afternoon Lectures on Literature and Art*, 2nd ser. London: Bell and Daldy, 1864.

Fitz-Gerald, S. J. Adair. *Dickens and the Drama, Being an Account of Charles Dickens's Connection with the Stage and the Stage's Connection with Him*. London: Chapman & Hall, 1910.

Forman, Maurice Buxton. *George Meredith and the Monthly Observer*. London: Priv. printed, 1911.

Forster, John. *The Life of Charles Dickens*, edited and annotated with an Introduction by J. W. T. Ley. London: Cecil Palmer, 1928. Cited as *Life*.

Francis, John C., comp. *John Francis, Publisher of the Athenaeum: A Literary Chronicle of Half a Century*. 2 vols. London: Richard Bentley & Son, 1888.

Further Testimonials in Favour of W. C. Bennett, LL.D., ... Candidate for the Secretaryship of the London School Board. Letters from Distinguished Men of the Time. 1838–1868. N.p., n.d.

Garnett, Richard. *The Life of W. J. Fox, Public Teacher & Social Reformer, 1786–1864*. London: John Lane, 1910.

Gaskell, Elizabeth. *The Letters of Mrs Gaskell*, ed. J. A. V. Chapple and Arthur Pollard. Cambridge: Harvard University Press, 1967.

Gettmann, Royal A. *A Victorian Publisher: A Study of the Bentley Papers*. Cambridge: University Press, 1960.

Godard, John George. *George Birkbeck, the Pioneer of Popular Education. A Memoir and a Review*. London: Bemrose & Sons, 1884.

Gomme, G. J. L. "T. B. Aldrich and 'Household Words,' " *Papers of the Bibliographical Society of America*, XLII (First Quarter, 1948), 70–72.

Gormly, James. *Exploration and Settlement in Australia*. Sydney: D. S. Ford, printer, 1921.

Green, John Albert. *A Bibliographical Guide to the Gaskell Collection in the Moss Side Library*. Manchester: Manchester Public Libraries, 1911.

Grubb, Gerald G. "Dickens the Paymaster Once More," *Dickensian*, LI (Spring 1955), 72–78.

Gunn, Charles Hains. *Manual of Modern English Prose Literature*. Haarlem: Erven F. Bohn, 1862.

Hall, Anna Maria (Mrs. S. C.). "Frances Freeling Broderip. A Memory," *Social Notes*, II (Dec. 21, 1878), 663–65.

Halls, J. J. *The Life and Correspondence of Henry Salt, Esq., F.R.S., &c., His Britannic Majesty's Late Consul General in Egypt*. 2 vols. London: Richard Bentley, 1834.

Hannay, James. *A Course of English Literature*. London: Tinsley Brothers, 1866.

Harding, Joseph. *The River of Death and the Upas Tree of Misery and Woe*. Social Reform Tract, No. 1. Repr. from *Christian Family Record*, Jan. 1856. N.p., n.d.

Hardman, Sir William. *The Letters and Memoirs of Sir William Hardman, M.A., F.R.G.S.*, 2nd ser.: 1863–65, ed. S. M. Ellis. London: Cecil Palmer, 1925.

– *A Mid-Victorian Pepys: The Letters and Memoirs of Sir William Hardman, M.A., F.R.G.S.*, ed. S. M. Ellis. London: Cecil Palmer, 1923.

Hare, Augustus J. C. *The Story of My Life.* 6 vols. London: George Allen, 1896–1900.

Harper's Cyclopaedia of British and American Poetry, ed. Epes Sargent. New York: Harper & Brothers, 1881.

Hatton, Joseph. *Journalistic London. Being a Series of Sketches of Famous Pens and Papers of the Day.* London: Sampson Low, Marston, Searle, & Rivington, 1882.

Hawker, Robert Stephen. *Cornish Ballads & Other Poems*, ed. C. E. Byles. London and New York: John Lane, 1904.

Hill, Octavia. *Life of Octavia Hill As Told in Her Letters*, ed. C. Edmund Maurice. London: Macmillan and Co., 1913.

Hill, Rosamond Davenport-, and Florence Davenport-Hill. *The Recorder of Birmingham. A Memoir of Matthew Davenport Hill; with Selections from His Correspondence.* London: Macmillan and Co., 1878.

Holland, Lady Saba. *A Memoir of the Reverend Sydney Smith. ... With a Selection from His Letters, Edited by Mrs. Austin.* 2 vols. 2nd ed. London: Longman, Brown, Green, and Longmans, 1855.

Hollingshead, John. *Gaiety Chronicles.* Westminster: Archibald Constable & Co., 1898.

– *My Lifetime.* 2 vols. London: Sampson Low, Marston & Company, 1895.

– *Under Bow Bells: A City Book for All Readers.* London: Groombridge and Sons, 1860.

Holman-Hunt, Diana. *My Grandfather, His Wives and Loves.* New York: W. W. Norton & Company, 1969.

Hood, Thomas. *Memorials of Thomas Hood*, collected, arranged, and edited by Frances Hood Broderip, with Preface and Notes by Tom Hood. 2 vols. London: Edward Moxon & Co., 1860.

Hopkins, A. B. *Elizabeth Gaskell: Her Life and Work.* London: John Lehmann, 1952.

Horne, Richard H. *Australian Facts and Prospects: To Which Is Prefixed the Author's Australian Autobiography.* London: Smith, Elder and Co., 1859.

– "By-Gone Celebrities of Bond Street, London," *Harper's*, XLIII (Oct. 1871), 755–62.

– *The Great Peace-Maker: A Sub-Marine Dialogue*, with Preface by H. Buxton Forman. London: Printed for private distribution, 1871.

Household Words, selections from:

Choice Stories from Dickens' Household Words. Auburn and Buffalo, New York: John E. Beardsley [1854].

Dickens' Short Stories. Containing Thirty-one Stories Never Before Published in This Country. By Charles Dickens. ("Boz."). Complete in One Volume. Philadelphia: T. B. Peterson and Brothers [1859].

Fortune Wildred, the Foundling. Also, Lizzie Leigh, and The Miner's Daughters. By Charles Dickens. New York: De Witt & Davenport, n.d. (The three stories are, respectively, by Georgiana Craik, Elizabeth Gaskell, and William Howitt.)

Home and Social Philosophy: or, Chapters on Every-Day Topics. From "Household Words," Edited by Charles Dickens, 1st ser.; 2nd ser. Putnam's Library for the People. New York: G. P. Putnam, 1852.

Home Narratives; or, Stories from "Household Words." Edited by Charles Dickens. New York: G. P. Putnam, 1852 (copy not seen).

Household Words. Conducted by Charles Dickens in *Collection of British Authors*, Tauchnitz Edition. 36 vols. Leipzig: Bernhard Tauchnitz, 1851–56.

Novels and Tales Reprinted from Household Words in *Collection of British Authors*, Tauchnitz Edition. 11 vols. Leipzig: Bernhard Tauchnitz, 1856–59.

Pearl-Fishing. Choice Stories, from Dickens' Household Words, 1st ser. Auburn, New York: Alden, Beardsley & Co., 1854.

The World Here and There: or, Notes of Travellers. From "Household Words," Edited by Charles Dickens. Putnam's Library for the People. New York: G. P. Putnam, 1852.

Howe, Susanne. *Geraldine Jewsbury: Her*

Life and Errors. London: George Allen & Unwin, 1935.
Howitt, Mary. *Mary Howitt: An Autobiography,* ed. Margaret Howitt. 2 vols. Boston and New York: Houghton, Mifflin and Co., 1889.
Howitt, William, and Mary Howitt. *The Literature and Romance of Northern Europe: Constituting a Complete History of the Literature of Sweden, Denmark, Norway and Iceland. ...* 2 vols. London: Colburn and Co., 1852.
Howitt, William. *Tallangetta, the Squatter's Home. A Story of Australian Life.* 2 vols. London: Longman, Brown, Green, Longmans, & Roberts, 1857.
Hunt, Frederick Knight. *The Fourth Estate: Contributions towards a History of Newspapers, and of the Liberty of the Press.* 2 vols. London: David Bogue, 1850.
Hunt, James Henry Leigh. *The Correspondence of Leigh Hunt,* ed. Thornton Hunt. 2 vols. London: Smith, Elder and Co., 1862.
– *Leigh Hunt's Literary Criticism,* ed. Lawrence Huston Houtchens and Carolyn Washburn Houtchens. New York: Columbia University Press, 1956.
– *The Poetical Works of Leigh Hunt,* ed. H. S. Milford. London: Oxford University Press, 1923.
[Huxley, Leonard.] *The House of Smith Elder.* London: Printed for private circulation, 1923.
The Irving Offering: A Token of Affection, for 1851. New York: Leavitt and Company, 1851.
Jerdan, William. *The Autobiography of William Jerdan ... with His Literary, Political, and Social Reminiscences and Correspondence during the Last Fifty Years.* 4 vols. London: Arthur Hall, Virtue, & Co., 1852–53.
Jewsbury, Geraldine Endsor. *Selections from the Letters of Geraldine Endsor Jewsbury to Jane Welsh Carlyle,* ed. Mrs. Alexander Ireland. London: Longmans, Green, and Co., 1892.
Johnson, Catharine, B., ed. *William Bodham Donne and His Friends.* London: Methuen & Co., 1905.
Johnson, Edgar. *Charles Dickens: His Tragedy and Triumph.* 2 vols. New York: Simon and Schuster, 1952.
– ed. *The Heart of Charles Dickens. See* Dickens, Charles.
Kelley, Philip. Reply to "Greek Slave Mystery," *N. & Q.,* n.s. XIV (May 1967), 194.
Kelly, Thomas. *George Birkbeck, Pioneer of Adult Education.* Liverpool: Liverpool University Press, 1957.
King, J. W. *The Emigrant, and Other Poems.* Sheffield: Printed for the author by T. Scott, 1848.
– *James Montgomery: A Memoir, Political and Poetical.* London: Partridge and Co.; Sheffield: H. Pawson, 1858.
Kitton, Frederic G. *Charles Dickens by Pen and Pencil, Including Anecdotes and Reminiscences Collected from His Friends and Contemporaries.* 1 vol. and suppl. London: Frank T. Sabin; John F. Dexter, 1890.
– *Dickensiana: A Bibliography of the Literature Relating to Charles Dickens and His Writings.* London: George Redway, 1886.
– *The Novels of Charles Dickens: A Bibliography and Sketch.* London: Elliot Stock, 1897.
– ed. *Old Lamps for New Ones and Other Sketches and Essays Hitherto Uncollected,* by Charles Dickens. New York: New Amsterdam Book Company, 1897.
Knight, Charles. *Passages of a Working Life during Half a Century: with a Prelude of Early Reminiscences.* 3 vols. London: Bradbury & Evans, 1864–65.
Knighton, William. "Conversations with Carlyle," *Contemp. Rev.,* XXXIX (June 1881), 904–920.
– *Forest Life in Ceylon.* 2 vols. London: Hurst and Blackett, 1854.
– *The Policy of the Future in India. A Letter to the Right Hon. Lord Cranborne, Secretary of State for India, &c. &c.* London: Longmans, Green, and Co., 1867.
– *Tropical Sketches; or Reminiscences of an Indian Journalist.* 2 vols. London: Hurst and Blackett, 1855.
Landor, Walter Savage. *Letters and Other Unpublished Writings of Walter Savage Landor,* ed. Stephen Wheeler. London: Richard Bentley and Son, 1897.
Lawrance, Hannah. *Historical Memoirs of the Queens of England, from the*

Commencement of the Twelfth Century. 2 vols. London: Edward Moxon, 1838–40.

Layard, George Somes. *Mrs. Lynn Linton: Her Life, Letters, and Opinions.* London: Methuen & Co., 1901.

Lehmann, John. *Ancestors and Friends.* London: Eyre & Spottiswoode, 1962.

Lehmann, R. C., ed. *Charles Dickens As Editor: Being Letters Written by Him to William Henry Wills, His Subeditor.* New York: Sturgis & Walton Company, 1912.

– comp. and ed. *Memories of Half a Century: A Record of Friendships.* London: Smith, Elder & Co., 1908.

[Leigh, Percival.] *The Comic Latin Grammar; a New and Facetious Introduction to the Latin Tongue.* London: Charles Tilt, 1840.

Lever, Charles James. *Cornelius O'Dowd upon Men and Women and Other Things in General,* 2nd ser. Edinburgh and London: William Blackwood and Sons, 1865.

Ley, J. W. T. *The Dickens Circle: A Narrative of the Novelist's Friendships.* London: Chapman & Hall, 1918.

Linton, Eliza Lynn. *My Literary Life.* London: Hodder and Stoughton, 1899.

Linton, W. J. *Memories.* London: Lawrence and Bullen, 1895.

Lithgow, R. A. Douglas. *The Life of John Critchley Prince.* Manchester: Abel Heywood & Son; London: Simpkin, Marshall, & Co., 1880.

Lives of the Illustrious. (The Biographical Magazine), Vol. II. London: J. Passmore Edwards, 1852.

Locker-Lampson, Frederick. *My Confidences. An Autobiographical Sketch Addressed to My Descendants.* London: Smith, Elder, & Co., 1896.

Lohrli, Anne. "Andersen, Dickens, and 'Herr von Müffe,'" *Dickensian,* LXII (Winter 1966), 5–13.

– "*Household Words* and Its 'Office Book,'" *Princeton University Library Chronicle,* XXVI (Autumn 1964), 27–47.

London Literary Association of the Friends of Poland. *Report of the Proceedings* [of annual meetings, 1834–61]. London.

McCarthy, Justin, and Sir John R. Robinson. *The "Daily News" Jubilee: A Political and Social Retrospect of Fifty Years of the Queen's Reign.* London: Sampson Low, Marston and Company, 1896.

McCormick, Robert. *Voyages of Discovery in the Arctic and Antarctic Seas, and round the World. ... To Which Are Added an Autobiography, Appendix, Portraits, Maps, and Numerous Illustrations.* 2 vols. London: Sampson Low, Marston, Searle, and Rivington, 1884.

Mackay, Alexander. *The Western World; or, Travels in the United States in 1846–47: Exhibiting Them in Their Latest Development, Social, Political, and Industrial; Including a Chapter on California.* 3 vols. London: Richard Bentley, 1849.

Mackay, Charles. *Forty Years' Recollections of Life, Literature, and Public Affairs. From 1830 to 1870.* 2 vols. London: Chapman & Hall, 1877.

Macmillan and Co., publishers. *A Bibliographical Catalogue of Macmillan and Co.'s Publications from 1843 to 1889.* London and New York: Macmillan and Co., 1891.

Markham, Sir Albert H. *The Life of Sir Clements R. Markham, K.C.B., F.R.S.* ... London: John Murray, 1917.

Marston, John Westland. *Gerald; a Dramatic Poem: and Other Poems.* London: C. Mitchell, 1842.

– *Our Recent Actors: Being Recollections Critical, and, in Many Cases, Personal, of Late Distinguished Performers of Both Sexes.* ... 2 vols. London: Sampson Low, Marston, Searle & Rivington, 1888.

– *The Patrician's Daughter. A Tragedy in Five Acts.* 2nd ed. London: C. Mitchell, 1842.

Martineau, Harriet. *The Factory Controversy; a Warning against Meddling Legislation.* Issued by the National Association of Factory Occupiers. Manchester: Printed by A. Ireland and Co., 1855.

– *Harriet Martineau's Autobiography,* ed. Maria Weston Chapman, and *Memorials of Harriet Martineau* by Maria Weston Chapman. 2 vols. Boston: James R. Osgood and Company, 1877.

– *Health, Husbandry, and Handicraft.* London: Bradbury and Evans, 1861.

Masson, David. *Memories of London in*

the 'Forties, arranged and annotated by Flora Masson. Edinburgh and London: William Blackwood & Sons, 1908.
Matz, B. W. "A Child's Hymn in 'The Wreck of the Golden Mary,'" *Dickensian*, XII (May 1916), 128–30.
– "Some Unknown Poems of George Meredith," *T.P.'s Weekly*, XVII (Feb. 17, 1911), 209–10.
Mayhew, Henry, and John Binny. *The Criminal Prisons of London and Scenes of Prison Life*. London: Griffin, Bohn, and Company, 1862.
Meredith, George. *Letters from George Meredith to Richard Henry Horne*. Cape Town: Printed for M. Buxton Forman for private circulation, 1919.
– *Letters of George Meredith*, ed. W. M. Meredith. 2 vols. New York: Charles Scribner's Sons, 1912.
– *Twenty Poems by George Meredith*. London: Priv. printed [for B. W. Matz], 1909.
Miles, Alfred H., ed. *The Poets and the Poetry of the Century*. 10 vols. London: Hutchinson & Co. [1891–97].
Mill, John Stuart. *The Earlier Letters of John Stuart Mill, 1812–1846*, ed. Francis E. Mineka. 2 vols. Toronto: University of Toronto Press, 1963.
Milne, William Charles. *Life in China*. London: G. Routledge & Co., 1857.
Mitchell, Broadus. *Frederick Law Olmsted, a Critic of the Old South*. Johns Hopkins University Studies in Historical and Political Science. Baltimore: Johns Hopkins Press, 1924.
Mitford, Mary Russell. *The Friendships of Mary Russell Mitford As Recorded in Letters from Her Literary Correspondents*, ed. A. G. L'Estrange. New York: Harper & Brothers, 1882.
– *The Life of Mary Russell Mitford ... Related in a Selection from Her Letters to Her Friends*, ed. A. G. L'Estrange. 3 vols. 2nd and rev. ed. London: Richard Bentley, 1870.
Morley, Henry. *Early Papers and Some Memories*. London: George Routledge and Sons, 1891.
– Introduction to *A Christmas Carol and The Chimes*, by Charles Dickens. London: Cassell and Company, 1903.
– *Of English Literature in the Reign of Victoria. With a Glance at the Past*. Leipzig: Bernhard Tauchnitz, 1881.
Murray, Eustace Clare Grenville. *Doïne; or, The National Songs and Legends of Roumania*. London: Smith, Elder, and Co., 1854.
– *Embassies and Foreign Courts. A History of Diplomacy. By "The Roving Englishman."* London: G. Routledge & Co., 1855.
Nisbet, Ada. *Dickens & Ellen Ternan*. Berkeley and Los Angeles: University of California Press, 1952.
Norton, Caroline Elizabeth Sarah. *The Child of the Islands. A Poem*. London: Chapman and Hall, 1845.
Olmsted, Frederick Law. *A Journey through Texas; or, A Saddle-Trip on the Southwestern Frontier; with a Statistical Appendix*. New York: Dix, Edwards & Co., 1857.
Owen, Richard Startin. *The Life of Richard Owen*. 2 vols. London: John Murray, 1894.
Payn, James. "Dickens' Life: Conclusion," *Chambers's*, 4th ser. XI (March 21, 1874), 177–80.
– *Gleams of Memory with Some Reflections*. London: Smith, Elder & Co., 1894.
– "Harriet Martineau," *A.Y.R.*, XXXVIII (April 7, 1877), 126–32.
– *Some Literary Recollections*. 2nd ed. London: Smith, Elder & Co., 1884.
Perkins, Jane Gray. *The Life of Mrs. Norton*. London: John Murray, 1909.
[Phillips, John.] *Reminiscences of Australian Early Life by a Pioneer*. London: A. P. Marsden, 1893.
Priestley, Lady Eliza. *The Story of a Lifetime*. London: Kegan Paul, Trench, Trübner & Co., 1908.
Prince, John Critchley. *The Poetical Works of John Critchley Prince*, ed. R. A. Douglas Lithgow. 2 vols. Manchester: Abel Heywood & Son; London: Simpkin, Marshall, & Co., 1880.
Procter, Adelaide Anne. *Legends and Lyrics*, with an Introduction by Charles Dickens. New ed., with Additions. London: Bell and Daldy, 1866.
– ed. *The Victoria Regia: A Volume of Original Contributions in Poetry and Prose*. London: Emily Faithfull and Co., 1861.
Procter, Bryan Waller. *An Autobiographical Fragment and Biographical Notes, with Personal Sketches of Contem-*

poraries, Unpublished Lyrics, and Letters of Literary Friends, ed. Coventry Patmore. London: George Bell and Sons, 1877.

Rae, John. *John Rae's Correspondence with the Hudson's Bay Company on Arctic Exploration, 1844–1855*, ed. E. E. Rich, assisted by A. M. Johnson. London: The Hudson's Bay Record Society, 1953.

Rantoul, Robert S., ed. *Report of the Harvard Class of 1853, 1849–1913. Issued on the Sixtieth Anniversary for the Use of the Class and Its Friends.* Cambridge: Harvard University Press, 1913.

The Record of Old Westminsters: A Biographical List of All Those Who Are Known to Have Been Educated at Westminster School from the Earliest Times to 1927, compiled by G. F. Russell Barker and Alan H. Stenning. 2 vols. London: Chiswick Press, 1928.

Renton, Richard. *John Forster and His Friendships.* London: Chapman and Hall, 1912.

Rice, William. *Tiger-Shooting in India; Being an Account of Hunting Experiences on Foot in Rajpootana, during the Hot Seasons, from 1850 to 1854.* London: Smith, Elder and Co., 1857.

Robinson, Henry Crabb. *Henry Crabb Robinson on Books and Their Writers*, ed. Edith J. Morley. 3 vols. London: J. M. Dent and Sons, 1938.

Robinson, Kenneth. *Wilkie Collins: A Biography.* London: The Bodley Head, 1951.

Rolfe, Franklin P. "Additions to the Nonesuch Edition of Dickens' Letters," *Huntington Library Quart.*, v (Oct. 1941), 115–40.

Ronald, Robert Bruce. *The Riverina: People and Properties.* Melbourne: F. W. Cheshire, 1960.

Rossetti, Dante Gabriel. *Dante Gabriel Rossetti: His Family-Letters*, with a Memoir by William Michael Rossetti. 2 vols. London: Ellis and Elvey, 1895.

– *Letters of Dante Gabriel Rossetti*, ed. Oswald Doughty and John Robert Wahl. 4 vols. Oxford: Clarendon Press, 1965–67.

Rossetti, William Michael. *Some Reminiscences of William Michael Rossetti.* 2 vols. London: Brown Langham & Co., 1906.

Royal University of Ireland. The Calendar for the Year 1896. Dublin: Printed for the Royal University by Alex. Thom & Co., 1896.

Rugby School Register, revised and annotated by A. T. Michell. Vol. I. Rugby: A. J. Lawrence, 1901.

[Russell, Charles William.] [Review of] "*A Christmas Carol, in Prose; Being a Ghost-Story of Christmas.* By Charles Dickens," *Dublin Review*, xv (Dec. 1843), 510–29.

Sala, George Augustus. *Breakfast in Bed; or, Philosophy between the Sheets. A Series of Indigestible Discourses.* New York: John Bradburn, 1863.

– *Charles Dickens.* London: George Routledge and Sons [1870].

– *The Life and Adventures of George Augustus Sala Written by Himself.* One-vol. ed. London: Cassell and Company, 1896.

– "Memoir of the Author," prefaced to Robert B. Brough, *Marston Lynch; His Life and Times, His Friends and Enemies, His Victories and Defeats, His Kicks and Halfpence: A Personal Biography.* London: Ward and Lock, 1860.

– *Things I Have Seen and People I Have Known.* 2 vols. London: Cassell and Company, 1894.

Scott, Clement, and Cecil Howard, eds. *The Life and Reminiscences of E. L. Blanchard, with Notes from the Diary of Wm. Blanchard.* 2 vols. London: Hutchinson & Co., 1891.

Sharps, John Geoffrey. *Mrs. Gaskell's Observation and Invention: A Study of Her Non-Biographic Works.* Fontwell, Sussex: Linden Press, 1970.

Shepard, I. S. "Dickens and His Models," *Month*, xcix (April 1902), 369–77.

Shumaker, Eri J. *A Concise Bibliography of the Complete Works of Richard Henry (Hengist) Horne (1802–1884).* Granville, Ohio, 1943.

Siddons, Joachim Heyward ["J. H. Stocqueler"]. *The Memoirs of a Journalist.* Bombay: Offices of the *Times of India*; also London, 1873.

Sidney, Samuel. *The Three Colonies of*

Australia: New South Wales, Victoria, South Australia; Their Pastures, Copper Mines, & Gold Fields. London: Ingram, Cooke, & Co., 1852. 2nd ed., rev. London: Ingram, Cooke, and Co., 1853.

– *A Voice from the Far Interior of Australia. By a Bushman.* London: Smith, Elder and Co., 1847.

Smales, Edwin C. *Echoes of the City.* Manchester: Joseph John Alley, 1883.

Smiles, Samuel. *The Autobiography of Samuel Smiles, LL.D.*, ed. Thomas Mackay. New York: E. P. Dutton and Company, 1905.

Smith, Sidney. *The Settler's New Home: or The Emigrant's Location, Being a Guide to Emigrants in the Selection of a Settlement, and the Preliminary Details of the Voyage.* London: John Kendrick, 1849.

Solly, Henry Shaen. *The Life of Henry Morley, LL.D., Professor of the English Language and Literature at University College, London.* London: Edward Arnold, 1898.

Sotheby & Co. *Catalogue of a Further Portion of the Well-Known Library the Property of the Comte de Suzannet ... Comprising the Celebrated Collection of Material Concerning Charles Dickens. ...* London, 1938.

Spielmann, M. H. *The History of "Punch."* London: Cassell and Company, 1895.

Stevenson, Lionel. *Dr. Quicksilver: The Life of Charles Lever.* London: Chapman & Hall, 1939.

– *The Ordeal of George Meredith: A Biography.* New York: Charles Scribner's Sons, 1953.

Stevenson, Robert Louis. *Memoir of Fleeming Jenkin.* London: Longmans, Green, and Co., 1912.

Stone, Harry, ed. *Charles Dickens' Uncollected Writings from Household Words, 1850–1859.* 2 vols. Bloomington: Indiana University Press, 1968.

Stonehouse, John Harrison, ed. *Catalogue of the Library of Charles Dickens from Gadshill. ... Catalogue of the Library of W. M. Thackeray. ...* London: Piccadilly Fountain Press, 1935. Cited as Stonehouse, *Catalogue.*

Straus, Ralph. *Sala: The Portrait of an Eminent Victorian.* London: Constable and Company, 1942.

[Strauss, Gustave Louis Maurice.] *Reminiscences of an Old Bohemian.* New ed. London: Tinsley Brothers, 1883.

Super, R. H. *Walter Savage Landor: A Biography.* New York: New York University Press, 1954.

Swinburne, Algernon Charles. *The Swinburne Letters*, ed. Cecil Y. Lang. 6 vols. New Haven: Yale University Press, 1959–62.

Tannenbaum, Samuel A. *Shakspere Forgeries in the Revels Accounts.* New York: Columbia University Press, 1928.

Taylor, Bayard. *Life and Letters of Bayard Taylor*, ed. Marie Hansen-Taylor and Horace E. Scudder. 2 vols. Boston: Houghton, Mifflin and Company, 1884.

Taylor, Philip Meadows. *The Story of My Life.* New ed., with Introduction and Notes by Henry Bruce. London: Oxford University Press, 1920.

Thackeray, William Makepeace. *The Letters and Private Papers of William Makepeace Thackeray*, ed. Gordon N. Ray. 4 vols. Cambridge: Harvard University Press, 1945–46.

Thomas, Frederick Moy, comp. and ed. *Fifty Years of Fleet Street, Being the Life and Recollections of Sir John R. Robinson.* London: Macmillan and Co., 1904.

Thomas, William Moy. *When the Snow Falls.* 2 vols. London: Sampson Low, Son, & Co., 1859.

Tinsley, William. *Random Recollections of an Old Publisher.* 2 vols. London: Simpkin, Marshall, Hamilton, Kent & Co., 1900.

Trollope, Thomas Adolphus. *What I Remember.* New York: Harper & Brothers, 1888.

Victoria. *Letters of Queen Victoria from the Archives of the House of Brandenburg-Prussia*, translated by Mrs. J. Pudney and Lord Sudley, edited by Hector Bolitho. New Haven: Yale University Press, 1938.

The Victoria Regia. See Procter, Adelaide Anne, ed.

Vizetelly, Henry. *Glances Back through Seventy Years: Autobiographical and Other Reminiscences.* 2 vols. London: Kegan Paul, Trench, Trübner & Co.,

1893.

Waller, Ross D., ed. "Letters Addressed to Mrs. Gaskell by Celebrated Contemporaries," *Bulletin of the John Rylands Library*, XIX (Jan. 1935), 102–169.

Watts, Anna Mary Howitt. *The Pioneers of the Spiritual Reformation. Life and Works of Dr. Justinus Kerner (Adapted from the German.). William Howitt and His Work for Spiritualism. Biographical Sketches.* London: Psychological Press Association, 1883.

Webb, R. K. *Harriet Martineau, a Radical Victorian.* New York: Columbia University Press, 1960.

A Welcome [i.e., to Princess Alexandra]: *Original Contributions in Poetry and Prose.* London: Emily Faithfull, 1863.

Wickenden, William S. *Adventures in Circassia.* London: Printed by W. F. Slee, n.d.

– *Poems and Tales, with an Autobiographical Sketch of His Early Life,* with Preface by Henry Stebbing. London: Arthur Hall, Virtue, and Co., 1851.

Wilson, Mrs. Cornwell Baron-. *A Volume of Lyrics.* London: Hugh Cunningham, 1840.

Winkworth, Susanna, ed. *Letters and Memorials of Catherine Winkworth,* Vol. I. Clifton: E. Austin and Son, printers, 1883.

Wise, Thomas James, and Stephen Wheeler. *A Bibliography of the Writings in Prose and Verse of Walter Savage Landor.* London: Bibliographical Society, 1919.

Women Novelists of Queen Victoria's Reign: A Book of Appreciations, by Margaret Oliphant and others. London: Hurst & Blackett, 1897.

Woodring, Carl Ray. *Victorian Samplers: William and Mary Howitt.* Lawrence: University of Kansas Press, 1952.

Worth, George J. *James Hannay: His Life and Works.* Lawrence: University of Kansas Press, 1964.

Wraxall, Lascelles. *Camp Life: or Passages from the Story of a Contingent.* London: Charles J. Skeet, 1860.

Wright, Thomas. *The Life of Charles Dickens.* New York: Charles Scribner's Sons, 1936.

Yates, Edmund Hodgson. *Edmund Yates: His Recollections and Experiences.* 4th ed. London: Richard Bentley and Son, 1885.